A 'celebration

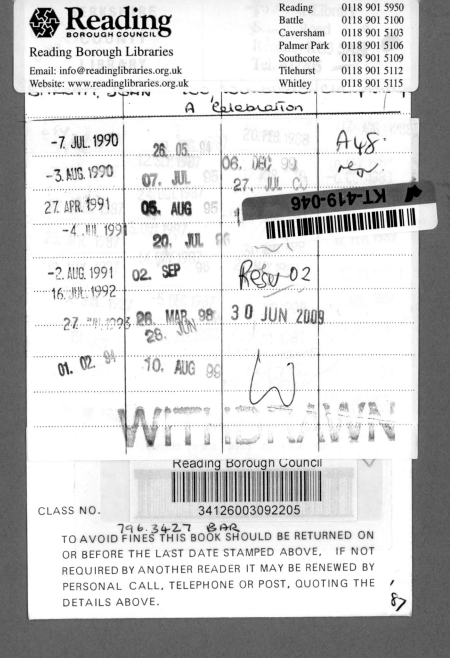

KT-419-046

-7. JUL. 1990   26. 05. 94   20. FEB. 1998   Ay5.

-3. AUG. 1990   07. JUL 95   06. DEC 99   reg

27. APR. 1991   05. AUG 95   27. JUL 0

-4. JUL 1991   20. JUL 98

-2. AUG. 1991   02. SEP   Resv 02

16. JUL 1992

27. ... 1993   26. MAR 98   30 JUN 2009

28. JUN

01. 02. 94   10. AUG 99

WITHDRAWN

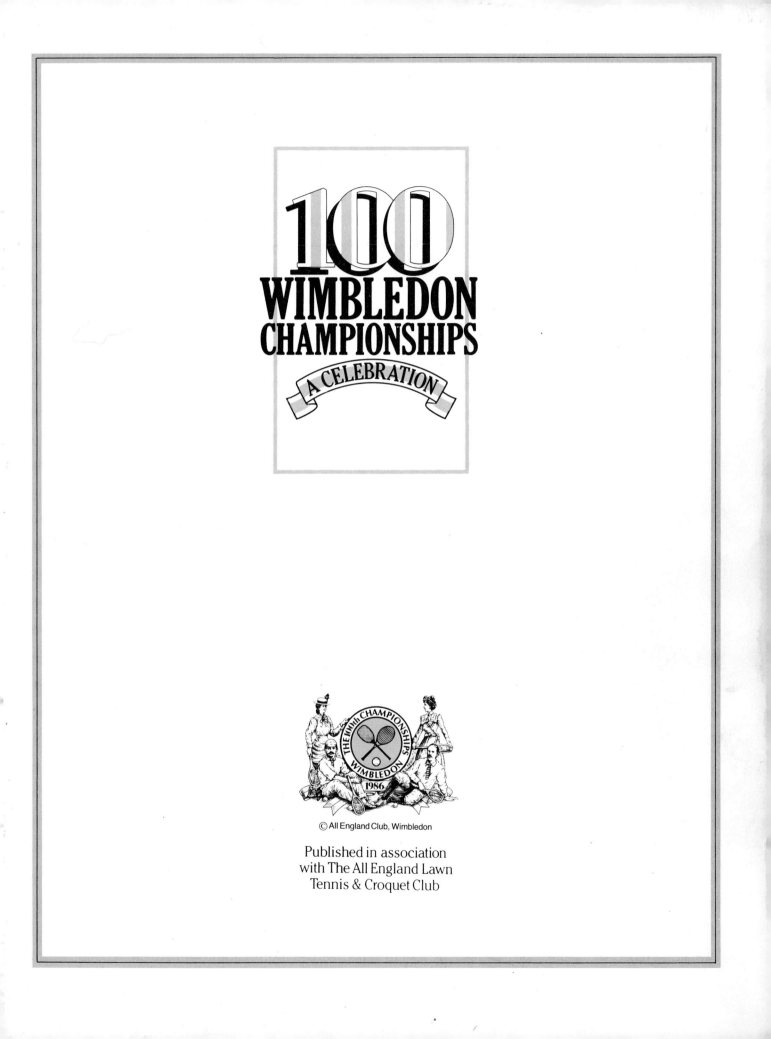

100
WIMBLEDON
CHAMPIONSHIPS
A CELEBRATION

Published in association
with The All England Lawn
Tennis & Croquet Club

TOP: Spectators arrive in style at Worple Road in 1912

ABOVE: Crowds congregate around the main entrance to the Centre Court at the Church Road ground in 1933

OPPOSITE: Fred Perry, triple champion 1934–36.

100 WIMBLEDON CHAMPIONSHIPS

A CELEBRATION

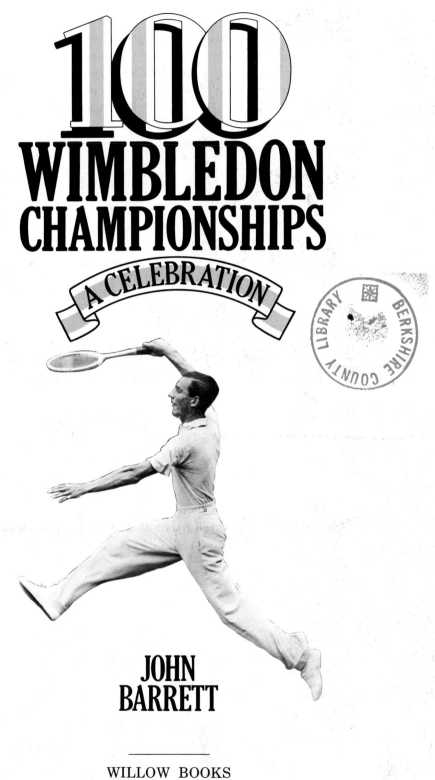

JOHN BARRETT

WILLOW BOOKS
COLLINS
8 GRAFTON STREET, LONDON

1986

DEDICATION

With gratitude to A, M and S-J
who generously gave me the time.

By the same author:
World of Tennis (annually 1969–86)
Play Tennis with Rosewall (with Ken Rosewall)
Tennis and Racket Games

Willow Books
William Collins Sons & Co Ltd
London · Glasgow · Sydney
Auckland · Toronto · Johannesburg

First published in Great Britain 1986

British Library Cataloguing in Publication Data

Barrett, John
100 Wimbledon Championships
1. Lawn Tennis Championships – History
I. Title
796.342'09421'93   GV99
ISBN 0 00 218220 3

Typeset by Ace Filmsetting Ltd, Frome, Somerset
Printed in Great Britain by
Butler & Tanner Ltd, Frome

Designed by Janet James

CONTENTS

ACKNOWLEDGEMENTS

The collection and compilation of material for this book has been a gigantic task. It would have been an impossible one without the help and advice of many friends and colleagues whose encouragement and counsel I have much appreciated.

Chief among them must be my two principal collaborators Lance Tingay and Christine Forrest. For the past 17 years Lance has provided material for *World of Tennis*, our annual contribution to the history of the game. For this work he has written the delightful portraits of the 87 champions which are found at the end of each chapter. In the results section Lance has also painstakingly unearthed the missing nationalities of the players in the days when the Wimbledon programme did not carry them.

My picture researcher, Christine Forrest, another *World of Tennis* colleague, has sorted through literally thousands of prints and slides to produce the final list for selection. The success of her efforts is self-evident. She has been helped immensely by Michael Cole of Le-Roye Productions who is carrying on the tradition established by his father, Arthur, of recording for posterity all the important events of the tennis year. Arthur's immense library of historical photographs has been the main source of our selections though the files of award-winning sports photographer Tommy Hindley have provided some of our coverage of more recent years.

It is no exaggeration to say that without the generous help of Alan Little, the librarian of the Wimbledon Lawn Tennis Museum, and of the curator Valerie Warren and her staff, this book could never have been written. Many of the photographs come from the Museum's comprehensive collection, while Alan, himself an authority on the history of The Championships, has unfailingly produced the answers to my endless stream of questions or has told me where the answers can be found. He has also produced the results from the early years of The Championships so that we

have been able to print for the first time every singles' result that has ever taken place at Wimbledon, together with the results of the final of every men's, ladies' and mixed doubles' event and the finals of the other non-Championship events. This alone places every professional commentator and every keen student of the game for ever in Alan Little's debt. They are also indebted to my former secretary, Gerie Knights, who cheerfully undertook the mammoth job of typing all the results except the singles.

Another whose help has proved invaluable is Richard Milward, a retired Wimbledon schoolmaster, who is Vice-President of The Wimbledon Society and a prolific writer on the history of Wimbledon. He has generously put at my disposal his immense knowledge of the district as well as the manuscript of his fascinating and as yet unpublished work on the streets of Wimbledon. Richard has also kindly read the text and made many helpful comments.

Further local assistance was provided by Arthur Whitehead who has allowed me to quote extensively from his mother's beautiful and evocative account of her Wimbledon childhood. Mr Whitehead still lives on the edge of Wimbledon Common in Lauriston Cottage, which used to be the stable block of Lauriston House before their magnificent mansion was pulled down.

The curious link with King's College School, three of whose pupils became Secretarys of the All England Club, was kindly provided by Frank Miles, a former KCS master who now fills the role of School Archivist.

At the club itself, the Chairman 'Buzzer' Hadingham has made some shrewd and constructive suggestions and Christopher Gorringe, the Chief Executive, has always been ready to help solve the inevitable problems that crop up in a work of this sort. Basil Hutchins, who is responsible for the Museum and was the chairman of the sub-committee that co-ordinated the celebrations for the hundredth Championship meeting, has constantly supported my efforts to achieve both depth and accuracy in the accounts of the development of The Championships. The delightful description by Edwin Fuller of the original site of the Church Road ground was unearthed by former committee member Ted Frith. It was the club's Financial Director, Tony Hughes, who sought out details of the land purchases that preceded the move to Church Road in 1922. They are published here for the first time.

In seeking to capture the atmosphere of days past there is no substitute for personal recollection. That is why the help of three individuals whose own careers have been inextricably bound up with the history of Wimbledon has been so greatly appreciated. During his days as the coach to the All England Club my old friend and BBC television colleague Dan Maskell practised with many of the champions from the 1930s onwards. His memories of those days are recalled with the same enthusiasm he brings to his television commentaries.

Another irrepressible enthusiast with the priceless gift of total recall is Ted Tinling whose life for the past 60 years has revolved around tennis and its personalities. Ted has enjoyed each of the many roles he has filled as umpire, player, Wimbledon 'call-boy', couturier, writer and broadcaster. I once played doubles against Ted shortly after the War when he was partnering George Godsell. He was a shrewd tactician and a great psychologist. It was easy to understand how he had been selected to work in intelligence during the War! Ted has been a close friend ever since and was a great source of information for this book.

Kitty Godfree is a quite remarkable lady. Her own Championship wins were in the 1920s and her memory of her contemporaries remains crystal clear. She has been a tremendous help in bringing to life for me the giants of that era: Suzanne Lenglen, Bill Til-den and Helen Wills. In October 1985, while I was researching this book, I took Kitty back to the Worple Road ground (now the playing fields of Wimbledon High School For Girls), which she had not visited since she last played there in 1921. As we went through the main gate and looked across the hockey pitch to where the giant stands of the old Centre Court had once stood, Kitty gave a little gasp of astonishment and said 'Oh! It's gone!'.

There is someone else who has been a great source of inspiration, despite the fact that he has long since departed this life – doubtless to report on The Championships of the Elysian fields. Even though he died on the eve of Wimbledon in 1939 I feel that I know A. Wallis Myers, the former lawn tennis correspondent of the *Daily Telegraph* who made a significant contribution to the development of our sport as player, reporter, author, visionary and enthusiast. In 1926 he was instrumental in founding the International Lawn Tennis Club of Great Britain, an historic organisation of which currently I have the privilege to be Chairman. In a sense Wallis Myers was a soul-mate. How proud he would be to discover that there are now 26 International Clubs in tennis-playing countries around the world. It is one of my regrets that I never met him. With the insight of a former player, his many writings have the ring of truth about them and have helped to illuminate those early years whose participants have passed for ever beyond questioning.

Finally I must acknowledge my own debt to Louise Haines, the Commissioning Editor at Collins, whose advice I came to respect and whose sense of balance and eagle-eyed identification of repetitions and inconsistencies has helped to eliminate most of the errors. Any that remain belong entirely to me.

These, then, and many others too numerous to mention who have helped to shape my love of tennis in the course of a full and interesting life, are the ones I wish to thank.

PHOTOGRAPHIC
ACKNOWLEDGEMENTS

The author and publishers wish to thank the many
individuals and organisations who have supplied
photographs for this book.

In particular we are indebted to Michael Cole of
Michael Cole Camerawork (and to his father,
Arthur Cole, of Le-Roye Productions), who have
supplied the majority of the black and white and
colour photographs for the years 1946 to 1985, as
well as some of the historical prints. A large number
of the early photographs come from the collection at
the Wimbledon Lawn Tennis Museum.

Tommy Hindley supplied all the photographs for
Chapter Nine as well as many for Chapter Eight
and the colour section.

Other contributors include: Associated Press; Mary
Evans Picture Library; *Illustrated London News*;
Alan Little (page 20, bottom); Photosource; Popper-
foto; Radio Times Hulton Picture Library; Sport and
General; *Tennis World*; and the Wimbledon Society
Museum. We would also like to thank Terry Boxall
for the hand-tinted photographs at the beginning of
the colour section.

Full details of individual photographs can be
supplied by the publishers on request.

PREFACE

This is a celebration, in words and pictures, of a British sporting institution which, after 100 meetings, is equally famous internationally. It is not simply another history of Wimbledon, though inevitably it has been necessary to trace the steps by which a croquet club in Surrey became the home of the world's greatest tennis Championships. In doing so I have tried always to set the developments in historical perspective, to paint the backdrop of world and local events against which the characters who have contributed to the evolution of the All England Croquet Club and The Championships have worked. I hope this will add a new perspective to the story, even for those afficionados who are already familiar with the outline. For those who seek a fuller historical narrative I cannot do better than refer them to Lance Tingay's excellent official history, *100 Years of Wimbledon*, published in 1977 to mark the centenary of The Championships, and Max Robertson's *Wimbledon, Centre Court of the Game*, which appeared the same year. From 1983 onwards there is also the excellent Wimbledon Annual.

At first sight it must seem curious that the centenary year did not coincide with the hundredth Championship meeting that was celebrated in 1986. That, of course, is due entirely to the ten years of armed conflict – those two desperate stanzas, 1914 to 1918 and 1939 to 1945 – when tennis was forgotten while Britain and her allies fought to preserve those very freedoms of spirit and expression which, from the start in 1877, have been embodied in the heroic deeds of Wimbledon's sporting warriors.

It is a romantic story because, quite early on, the players who became champions also became stars in their own right. Before the turn of the century the game had spread to every civilised country and the Wimbledon champions were travelling to compete in overseas Championships. Indeed before long the Wimbledon champions themselves were from overseas. When May Sutton took the ladies' singles title to the United States in 1905 and Norman Brookes captured the men's singles for Australia in 1907 they started a trend that was to increase the international popularity of Wimbledon and add to its prestige.

From the earliest days The Championships have been run with military precision. Latterly there has been a strong ex-services element in the team that runs both the tournament and the club itself. The whole machine operates with clockwork efficiency. The old ground at Worple Road was a wonderfully intimate place for spectators where the marquees and open tea lawn created the friendly atmosphere of a garden party. There were nine courts around the Centre Court where people could stand to watch the play and hear every word that was uttered, that is until a train came roaring past along the railway line that formed the southern boundary of the site. The Centre Court itself was a marvellous amphitheatre where the spectators were still close enough to read every expression on the players' faces and, as it were, to experience their emotions with them. Yet, with almost 7,000 spectators, the arena was big enough to create an electrifying atmosphere. The last great match played there in 1919 between the defending champion Dorothea Lambert Chambers and the brilliant young Frenchwoman Suzanne Lenglen, with its dramatic match points saved, roused the packed gallery to a frenzy of excitement.

With the move to Church Road in 1922, where the new Centre Court had twice the spectator accommodation of the old one, the feeling of drama was intensified. The advent of radio broadcasts of the latter stages in 1927, the rapid growth of newsreel coverage of the finals for the booming cinema industry in the 1930s, and the coming of television in 1937, further increased the world-wide interest in Wimbledon and its champions. Nor let us forget the immense interest created in Britain by the joint Wimbledon successes of Fred Perry and Dorothy Round in the mid-1930s and the equally important British Davis Cup successes of the same period. Already before the Second World War the annual tennis garden party at Wimbledon had become an international sporting occasion as big as any other sport could boast.

Within a few years of the restart in 1946, tickets for the Centre Court at Wimbledon became so sought-after that a public ballot was begun. The next great boost to Wimbledon's already growing popularity came with the arrival of open tennis in 1968. The reappearance of the 'forgotten men' of the professional world added to the star appeal of the leading performers. Within a few years increased media attention and the huge growth in world-wide prize money turned them into millionaire superstars. It was fortunate that the Joint Championships Committee had anticipated the boom and embarked on a programme of building and expansion that has dramatically improved conditions for spectators, players, officials and the media. Today some 400,000 spectators throng the enlarged grounds at Church Road each year in relative comfort during the 13 days of The Championships. However, an exciting match on one of the outside courts still results in the jostling crush that has always been part of Wimbledon's unique appeal. The true fans would not have it any other way.

It has been a fascinating experience delving into the origins of this great and glorious game. The more one discovers the more apparent it becomes that the pioneers – Wingfield, Gem and Perera – and the architects of the first Championship at Wimbledon in 1877 – Jones and Walsh, Marshall and Heathcote – are the ones we should all salute. These visionaries set the course of events for others to follow. Their successors are also to be congratulated for keeping the image of Wimbledon bright and building it into a major multi-million-pound industry that finances the whole of British tennis. Long may it flourish.

FOREWORD

by HRH The Duke of Kent, President
of the All England Club

The All England Lawn Tennis and Croquet Club is to be congratulated for commissioning this excellent book by John Barrett. As President of the club for the past 17 years, carrying on a proud family tradition which began in 1929, it gives me great pleasure to write this foreword.

1986 is a landmark in that it is the 100th time that The Championships have been staged at Wimbledon, for 41 years at the old Worple Road ground and for 59 years, starting in 1922, at its present location in Church Road. Whilst the size and reputation of Wimbledon have steadily grown, it is good that the beautiful grass courts of the All England Club remain the surface upon which Major Wingfield first developed the great game, now played in every country in the world.

One unique feature of this book is that it records the complete scores of every men's and women's singles match of all the hundred Championship Meetings. This will be an invaluable source of reference for journalists, researchers and keen followers of lawn tennis.

In celebrating this 100th Meeting, it is right that we should look back upon the great players of the past, as well as remembering those who, by their foresight and enterprise, have established Wimbledon as the undisputed No. 1 Championships.

One reason why it retains its pre-eminent position is because of the way in which long tradition, dating back to 1877, has not prevented the Committee of Management from keeping pace with the necessary improvement of all the essential aspects of a great championship meeting. Whether it be improved facilities for the public, the players or the media, Wimbledon continues to lead the way.

I wish this book every success.

HRH THE DUKE OF KENT
President

WIMBLEDON LANDMARKS

1868

The All England Croquet Club was founded at a meeting on 23 July in the offices of *The Field*, which was chaired by its editor, J. H. Walsh.

1869

On 24 September the committee agreed to lease a 4-acre site in Worple Road, Wimbledon for three years at £50, £75 and £100 per year.

1870

A gardener was appointed at 4 shillings per day.

The first Croquet Championships were held in July.

1875

The Committee agreed to set apart one croquet 'ground' for tennis and badminton at a cost of £25 on 25 February.

On 24 June MCC laws adopted (which had been issued on 29 May) for the game with hourglass court and rackets scoring.

1876

Four more tennis courts were added and on 29 June George Nicol became the committee member exclusively concerned with lawn tennis.

1877

The club's name was changed to that of 'All England Croquet and Lawn Tennis' on 14 April.

On 2 June it was agreed to hold Championships for lawn tennis on 10 July and following days. The sub-committee consisted of: Henry Jones (Referee), Julian Marshall and C. G. Heathcote. Tennis scoring adopted with advantage sets only in the final. Rectangular court 78×27 feet. Net 5 feet high at posts, 3 feet 3 inches at centre. Service line 26 feet from net.

Tournament began on 9 July. Break in play on Friday and Saturday, 13 and 14 July, because of Eton v Harrow cricket match.

Final won by Spencer Gore on 19 July who beat William Marshall. He held a Challenge Cup worth 25 guineas presented by *The Field*. A crowd of about 200 paid 1 shilling each.

1878

Service line shortened to 22 feet. Net reduced to 4 feet 9 inches at posts and 3 feet at centre.

Decided that holder should not play through but would meet winner of All-Comers' singles in a Challenge Round. This lasted until 1922.

1880

Service line shortened to 21 feet. Net reduced to 4 feet at posts.

1882

Net reduced to 3 feet 6 inches at posts. All court dimensions remain unaltered to this day.

1884

The ladies' singles was introduced and was won by Maud Watson who beat her sister, Lilian, in the final. The first prize was worth 20 guineas.

Men's doubles was introduced using the Cup donated by Oxford University for a doubles' event they had held for five years (1879–83) but abandoned.

1886

Challenge Round introduced for ladies' singles. It was abolished in 1922.

1887

Charlotte 'Lottie' Dod won the ladies' singles aged 15 – she is still the youngest champion of either sex.

1889

William Renshaw won his seventh singles' title, which is still a record for men.

1896

Plate event started for men.

1905

May Sutton (USA) became the first overseas champion.

1907

The Prince of Wales (later George V) visited The Championships and accepted the first Presidency of the club.

Norman Brookes (Australia) became first overseas men's champion.

1909

New club colours of purple and dark green introduced.

1913

Ladies' doubles and mixed doubles introduced as Championship events.

1915–18

No Championships held during the First World War.

1915

Four times champion Anthony Wilding (New Zealand) was killed on active service.

1919

All five titles were won by overseas players for the first time.

1920

Suzanne Lenglen (France) became the first player to win all three titles in same year.

The All England Ground Company Ltd was incorporated.

1922

The club moved to new Church Road ground, which was opened by George V. Rain every day caused the tournament to finish on the third Wednesday.

Challenge Round abolished.

1924

Seeding by nations introduced.

1926

The Jubilee Championships. All surviving men's and ladies' singles champions, plus men's doubles champions, received commemorative medals on the Centre Court from King George V and Queen Mary.

Duke of York (later George VI) competed in the men's doubles with Wing Commander Louis Greig.

1927

Full seeding introduced.

Billie Tapscott (South Africa) caused a sensation by appearing on an outside court without wearing stockings.

First radio broadcasts of the latter stages began.

1930

British Professional Championships held at club for first and only time.

1932

More than 200,000 spectators attended for the first time.

1933

Ladies' Plate event introduced.

1934

Fred Perry and Dorothy Round won their first singles' titles, becoming the first British double since Arthur Gore and Dora Boothby in 1909.

The All England Lawn Tennis Club and the Lawn Tennis Association signed the Agreement which decreed that a Joint Championship Committee should run the tournament and the surplus takings each year should go to the Lawn Tennis Association.

1937

Don Budge (USA) became the first man to win all three titles in the same year.

First television transmissions of the latter stages began.

1938

Don Budge, already the Australian and French champion, won a second singles' title and went on to complete the first Grand Slam.

Helen Wills won the ladies' singles for a record eighth time.

1940–45

No Championships held during the Second World War.

1946

Yvon Petra (France) became the last champion to wear long trousers as The Championships resumed after the six blank years of war.

1948

Boys' and Girls' invitation singles introduced.

1949

Louise Brough (USA) played a record 117 games on finals day.

1957

Queen Elizabeth attended the meeting for the first time.

Althea Gibson (USA) became the first black champion.

1961

The seventy-fifth Anniversary meeting. Princess Marina, the club's President, gave a luncheon party for past champions.

Angela Mortimer became the first British ladies' champion since Dorothy Round in 1937.

1962

Queen Elizabeth attended the meeting for the second time.

1964

Esplanade widened between Courts 2 and 3.

Invitation Men's Veterans event introduced.

1967

Purchase of Barkers' Sports Ground.

A record 301,896 spectators attended The Championships.

First major professional tournament held in August to inaugurate BBC TV's introduction of colour transmissions.

1968

First 'Open' Championships were won by Rod Laver and Billie Jean King.

Total Prize Money totalled £26,150.

1969

Richard 'Pancho' Gonzales and Charlie Pasarell played Wimbledon's longest match – a first-round battle that spanned two days, lasted 5 hours 12 minutes and contained 112 games.

Ann Jones became the second British post-war ladies' champion.

1971

Tie-break introduced at eight-games all in every set except the last.

1973

Seventy-nine members of the ATP withdrew on the eve of The Championships following Nikki Pilic's suspension by his Yugoslav Association for failing to play in a Davis Cup tie.

1975

Arthur Ashe became the first black men's champion.

Total Prize Money (with Bonus Pools) passed £100,000 (£114,875).

1977

The Centenary Championships were attended by Queen Elizabeth in her Jubilee year. Past singles' champions were presented with commemorative medals on Centre Court by the club President, the Duke of Kent, accompanied by the Duchess.

Virginia Wade became the third British post-war ladies' champion.

Total Prize Money (with Bonus Pools) passed £200,000 (£218,385).

Wimbledon Lawn Tennis Museum and Kenneth Ritchie Library opened.

1979

Roof of the Centre Court was raised 1 metre to provide 1,088 more seats on north side.

The tie-break rule was amended to operate from six-games all.

Billie Jean King (USA) won a record twentieth title.

1980

Four new grass courts opened on the north side of the Centre Court.

Bjorn Borg (Sweden) won his fifth consecutive title, which was a record since the abolition of the Challenge Round.

On the Centre and No. 1 Courts the 'Magic Eye' was introduced on the service lines only.

1981

The old No. 1 Court south stand was replaced by a new building to provide accommodation for players, referee, umpires, linesmen and ball boys.

Decided that linesmen should work in teams that are changed every 1½ hours.

Total Prize Money (with Bonus Pools) passed £300,000 (£322,136).

1982

4 July. The first finals, the men's singles and the men's doubles (reduced to the best of three sets), scheduled for a Sunday.

Total Prize Money (with Bonus Pools) passed £½ million (£593,366).

On the north side, Aorangi Park was opened to provide extra public amenities and corporate entertaining facilities.

1983

Ladies' singles draw increased from 96 to 128.

John Lloyd won the mixed doubles with Wendy Turnbull to become the first British man to win a Wimbledon title since Fred Perry in 1936.

1984

The Centenary year of the Ladies' Singles Championship. Seventeen of the surviving twenty champions attended to receive a commemorative gift of engraved crystal from the Duke and Duchess of Kent on the Centre Court.

Total Prize Money (with Bonus Pools) passed £1 million (£1,458,280).

1985

A new building on the east side of Centre Court was opened to provide 800 extra seats, more broadcasting boxes, greatly enlarged media accommodation, enlarged museum and offices for administrative staff.

Record attendances of 397,983.

Boris Becker (West Germany) became the first unseeded winner, the first German men's winner and the youngest Grand Slam winner at 17 years 7 months.

Total Prize Money (with Bonus Pools) passed £1.9 million (£1,934,760).

1986

For the first time yellow Slazenger tennis balls were used. They were in new blue tins with the Flying 'W' emblem.

Record attendances of 400,032.

For the first time since the Challenge Round was abolished in 1922 the four semi-finalists in the men's singles were all Europeans. The last year before that when the four semi-finalists in the All-Comers' singles and the defending champion were all Europeans was 1909.

Never before had all four of the singles' finalists been born in Eastern Bloc countries — three of them in Czechoslovakia (Lendl, Navratilova, Mandlikova).

The attendance of President Weizsacker on the final day was the first visit to The Championships by the Head of State of the Federal Republic of Germany.

Total Prize Money (with Bonus Pools) passed £2 million (£2,119,780).

A new, large, brick-built pavilion was opened in Aorangi Park to accommodate the players and their families during practice and to serve as a changing area for the stewards.

For the first time players and officials were asked to undergo drug tests.

The ancient game of real tennis, which was sometimes called royal or court tennis, had been played in the cloisters of medieval religious houses and in the royal palaces of Europe. It was played on stone indoor courts using heavy wooden rackets which had curved heads. Scoring followed the face of a clock – 15, 30, 45 (later reduced to 40). At 40 points all 'Deuce' was called, which is believed to be a corruption of the French *à deux*. 'Love' is thought to be a corruption of *l'oeuf*, the egg or a circle, signifying zero.

INTRODUCTION

Hardly a ripple disturbed the calm, well-ordered surface of the traditional sporting scene that English summer's day in 1877, when the following announcement appeared in *The Field* magazine of 9 June:

'The All England Croquet and Lawn Tennis Club, Wimbledon, propose to hold a lawn tennis meeting, open to all amateurs, on Monday, July 9th and following days. Entrance fee, £1 1s 0d. Two prizes will be given – one gold champion prize to the winner, one silver to the second player.'

During another busy season the cricketers at Lord's hardly noticed this intrusion and the golfers at the Royal and Ancient Golf Club in far-off St Andrews scarcely even bothered to glance southwards, though the members of the London Scottish – the second oldest golf club in the London area with its course on Wimbledon Common – were probably aware of the development. Yet within a few years the game had taken a firm hold and had spread to distant lands. Ultimately tennis, shorn of its 'lawn', streamlined in its presentation and aggressively marketed, was to overtake cricket and golf and even to rival soccer as the most widely-played ball game in the world.

From the distance of more than a century that simple announcement in *The Field* conceals a great deal of diverse activity. Those of us who take for granted the universal appeal of The Championships at Wimbledon with their 13 days of unparalleled skill and excitement each year, witnessed by some 400,000 spectators at the famous ground in Church Road and by more than 750 million television viewers in 76 countries around the world, sometimes find it hard to believe that things were not always like this.

In 1877 the game was still a novelty. Already it was proving popular at the weekend garden parties of the well-to-do as a more adventurous and energetic form of social relaxation for the young men and women of Victorian England than croquet. Yet lawn tennis was, at the most, 18 years old. It was a game derived from the ancient sport of real tennis or royal tennis which itself had evolved from the earlier *Jeu de Paume* where a ball had been struck first with the bare palm of the hand and later with a gloved one. It had been made possible only because of the discovery by Charles Goodyear, in 1839, of the way to vulcanise raw rubber by heating it with sulphur to make it resilient. It was the

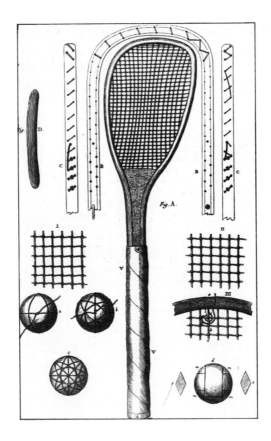

The rackets for real tennis were one-piece bends of ash strung with heavy-gauge sheep's gut. The handles were either plain wood or, like this one, covered with a leather grip. The rackets were heavier than the Sphairistiké and lawn tennis ones because the balls for real tennis, made of compressed rags and covered with a hand-stitched melton cloth, were solid and much heavier than the hollow rubber balls of lawn tennis.

advent of the rubber ball that allowed the indoor game to move outside on to the lawns of Victorian country houses and vicarages. Another invention about this time that contributed to the successful move outdoors, which is recognised by Tom Todd in his excellent publication *The Tennis Players*, was the garden lawn-mower that was being manufactured by Alexander Shanks of Arbroath and Thomas Green of Leeds. The smooth, flat surface essential for a regular bounce would have been well nigh impossible to achieve with sickle and scythe.

From about 1869 in Warwickshire, Harry Gem and his Spanish friend Augurio Perera, both keen rackets players, had been experimenting with a version of the new game which they first called pelota (the Spanish word for 'ball'), to acknowledge Perera's contribution, and later lawn rackets. The croquet lawn behind Perera's house in Edgbaston was the test-bed. The equipment was adapted from real tennis's curved-headed rackets and sagging net suspended on high poles. The scoring was borrowed from rackets; 15 points up completed a game. The dimensions of the playing area were a matter for experiment for the idea was to provide both men and women with a challenging form of exercise.

By 1872 the game had become sufficiently established for Gem and Perera, with two young doctors, Frederic Haynes and Arthur Tomkins, to form a club in Leamington, to which town both men had decided to move. So it was that the world's first lawn tennis club was founded, in the grounds of the Manor House Hotel. According to a sketch by Harry Gem the net no longer sagged but was taut, being supported on five waist-high poles with the cord passing over the end poles and being anchored to the turf with pegs.

During this same period, in remotest North Wales, someone else had been thinking along the same lines. Captain Walter Clopton Wingfield, who had

In 1874 Major Walter Clopton Wingfield, a former officer in the Dragoon Guards, patented a new game he called Sphairistiké after the Greek word for a ball game. Two Midlanders, Harry Gem and Augurio Perera, had been experimenting with a similar game in Edgbaston since 1869 and had founded the world's first tennis club at Leamington Spa in 1872. However, it was Wingfield's vigorous marketing activities (his boxed sets of Sphairistiké sold for 5 guineas) that led to the rapid spread of the game at weekend garden parties in country houses all over England.

retired from the 1st Dragoon Guards in 1861 while still under the age of 30, after serving in India and China, returned to the family home, Rhysnant Hall, in Llandysilio, Montgomeryshire, with no visible means of support. He soon joined the Montgomeryshire Yeomanry Cavalry and remained with them until 1873 when he retired with the rank of Major.

Always of an inventive nature, he turned his mind to the creation of an outdoor game that would be more energetic than croquet, less complicated than real tennis and, crucially important to the impecunious Major, commercially viable. On the lawn beside his house Wingfield began experimenting with the height of the net, the size, weight and colour of the ball, the size of the racket and the dimensions of the court. By 1874, having already done his market research by taking his boxed set of paraphernalia to several country houses for weekend trials, with encouraging results, he was ready to apply for a patent for Sphairistiké, as he called his invention, after the Greek word for a ball game. Applied for on 23 February 1874, the patent, No. 685, was ultimately filed on 22 August, for a total cost of £25.

Thanks to an energetic campaign of publicity and promotion, Wingfield's new game with its hourglass-shaped court, high, sagging net and red India rubber balls imported from Germany, was an immediate success. At 5 guineas per boxed set of net, posts, four rackets and six balls it was not cheap. But since his list of clients included many titled families in London and the Royal Family (as we know by studying the day-book of his first suppliers, Messrs French &

LEFT: A drawing of Wingfield's Sphairistiké court shows that it was shaped like an hourglass and was 10 yards wide at the baseline and 7 yards at the net. The net stood 5 feet high at the posts and sagged towards the centre. The service was delivered from the far end only with the server standing in the small diamond area and projecting the ball alternately into each of the service squares opposite.

BELOW: The first known photograph of lawn tennis on a Sphairistiké court. The exact date and location are not clear but it was probably taken in about 1875 in the Midlands area of England. Attire is the normal day dress of the age. We are some years away from special tennis clothing.

Company, which can still be seen in the Lawn Tennis Museum at the All England Club), as well as many vicarages, cost was not a limiting factor. Yes, 'Sticky', as it became known, had certainly caught the fancy of the Royals and the Reverends of mid-Victorian England and had many imitators. One was the former Cambridge cricket blue and Sussex county captain John Hales (a member of the All England Croquet Club's original committee) with his Germains Lawn Tennis, so named after his house in Chesham, Buckinghamshire. That boded well for the game's future.

But what sort of a world was it that so eagerly embraced the new pastime? The England of 1850 had been a land brimming with the confidence of material prosperity and commercial success. The manufacturers and traders of the post-Industrial Revolution era had become wealthy barons, though lower down the social order life was hard. British products and technology had been exported to all corners of the world. Those were the days of a mighty British Empire when world-wide standards of diplomatic procedure and social deportment were set in London. However, from the early 1870s confidence began to wane. During the next 20 years Britain lost her place as the leading industrial power to the United States and, later, to the newly-united Germany. At home a serious agricultural crisis contributed to a period of depression.

In 1876 Queen Victoria, a widow of 15 years and in the fortieth year of her reign, had been proclaimed Empress of India during Benjamin Disraeli's second Tory administration. Always her favourite Prime Minister because of his chivalrous attitude and the way he had of explaining complicated affairs of state in simple terms, 'Dizzy' was rewarded the following year with the Earldom of Beaconsfield. His great political rival, William Gladstone, out of office since 1874, had given up his Greenwich seat and had embarked on his Midlothian campaign, bent on leading the Liberals once more in the Commons while representing a Scottish constituency.

The annexation of the Transvaal in 1877 was one of Disraeli's less inspired moves. It exacerbated an already delicate situation between Boers and Britons that was to cause continuing strife for the remainder of the century. There were signs of friction in many parts of the world. In the United States the nation experienced its first major industrial dispute, which was the great American railway strike. In Germany the resignation of Bismarck was refused by Wilhelm I and the Chancellor continued to build the foundations of a German Empire that was to cause such grief to future generations. In Bucharest the Romanians proclaimed independence from Turkey even as the Russians invaded that unhappy country. In Japan the Satsuma rebellion heralded the end of the feudal concept as the Samurai forces were defeated by a conscript army.

In Europe the Romantic Movement had flourished between the late eighteenth century and the first half of the nineteenth. It had led to a flowering of free expression in the arts where nationalism, the love of nature and a worship of heroic individuals replaced the narrow orthodoxy of the classical school. There followed some major works from the post-Romantic composers, the Impressionist artists, and daring young sculptors and writers. In 1877 Tchaikovsky's *Swan*

Lake had its first performance and established the Russian as a ballet composer of the highest class. In France, Renoir's *In a Café* and *The Dancing Class* by Degas set art in a new direction while the unveiling of Rodin's sculpture *L'Age d'Airain* caused something of a sensation. Victor Hugo published a collection of poems under the title *L'Art d'être Grand-père* while the American novelist, Henry James, who later became a British citizen, gave note of his worth with *The American*, the first serious attempt to link in fiction the social orders of the Old World and the New.

James was living in London when his novel appeared and was probably unaware of the unique sporting event which took place during July 1877 on a 4-acre site that lay between the South Western Railway and Worple Road in Wimbledon. Now a busy commuter suburb, Wimbledon was then a fast expanding Surrey village whose character would be preserved thanks to the Common being saved from enclosure in 1871 and to the policy of the council of the day to develop recreation grounds in the area.

What was life in Wimbledon like in those days? With land relatively cheap (a building plot in Pelham Road, just off the Broadway near the station, cost £48 in 1850), the lending institutions were eager to advance money to builders as the exodus from inner London gathered pace. The early development had occurred south of the railway. Streets bearing the names of distinguished Prime Ministers – Palmerston, Russell and Gladstone – sprang up with rows of small terraced houses that were typical of the age. The area north of the railway, including Alexandra Road and Worple Road, was developed in the 1880s and 1890s and the land around Wimbledon Park soon became a target for the builders after the opening of the District Railway in 1889, which was a great improvement on the original 1838 rail links with Nine Elms in London and Southampton on the south coast.

Winifred Whitehead was a small child in 1885. Her family lived less than a quarter of a mile from the All England Croquet and Lawn Tennis Club in a comfortable house in Worple Road near the foot of The Downs, a road that still connects Worple Road with The Ridgway. She remembers the day, in 1891, when Worple Road, which until then had ended in open fields at the foot of Arterberry Road, was extended to Raynes Park:

'... the charming fields full of oxeye daisies and pink convolvuluses disappeared for ever. But the opening ceremony was magnificent; every cart, cab and hansom turned out, all decorated with flags and streamers and everyone blowing or beating whistles, trumpets and drums, people shouting and singing and waving, and three local bands accompanying the Mayor and Corporation. Carts were gay with their ponies – much more alive than cars – butchers' carts, and fish-cart boys in their bright, high two-wheeled gigs sitting on a ridiculously small round seat on the lid, swaying with every jolt and turn so that one was amazed that they did not fly off at the corners.'

As Richard Milward points out in his *Short History of Wimbledon* the small houses south of the railway: 'were generally the homes of manual workers

The railway bridge at Wimbledon Station, which was first built in 1838 and was modernised in 1869, as it was when The Championships began in 1877. Across the bridge lay the start of Wimbledon Hill and at its foot, on the left, Worple Road. The railway to the left led towards Kingston and Woking and ran parallel to Worple Road. A dusty footpath ran from the station alongside the railway to the ground about half a mile away and access could be gained through a wicket gate.

whose jobs were local – on the railway, on building sites, in shops or in the houses of the wealthy. . . . Their average earnings were only £1 per week and many suffered from periods of unemployment, from overcrowding or from epidemics of scarlet fever, typhoid and diphtheria.' Life at the bottom of the hill was hard.

Society in Wimbledon, as in the whole of Victorian England, was highly stratified. The churches dispensed soup and solace from their food kitchens among the often bleak lives below and comfortable clichés of reassurance to the 'carriage folk' above.

Some of the large houses around the Common, on Parkside, off The Ridgway and along Arthur Road were impressive piles by any standard. As Mrs Whitehead remembers: 'Wimbledon Park House, Lord Spencer's and one time Lady Sarah, Duchess of Marlborough's, with its vast park and vineyards and a tunnel [an underground tunnel connecting the main house with the servants' quarters] down which a couple of horsemen could ride abreast; Wimbledon House belonging in our day to Sir Henry Peek with its large interesting lake, island, bridges and deer park; Belvedere House and Oakfield; Mount Ararat with its country fields, hedges and cows; Wimbledon Lodge with its meadows and sheep; Westside House with its woods and valleys and excellent pheasant and partridge shooting; Lauriston House [later her home] with its wonderful lawn and huge trees; and Draxmont with its lovely orchards filling the steep

Lauriston House, the home of Winifred Whitehead (second from left) whose father, Sir Arthur Fell, was the MP for Great Yarmouth for 16 years. William Wilberforce had lived there in the early years of the nineteenth century at the time he was campaigning to get his Slave Emancipation Bill passed through the House of Commons. The gardens were famous and were opened to the public in the summer. The house was pulled down soon after the Second World War and 21 small houses built on the site.

little valley on the east side of Sunnyside, which was our happy walk to school; then down the slips and across two fields to the High School in Mansel Road.'

Numerous servants – housemaids, parlourmaids, nurses, cooks, gardeners and coachmen – ministered to the needs of the occupants of these gracious homes, the stockbrokers and diplomats, the new captains of industry and the old aristocratic families. On the summer lawns of these residences the carefree evening hours were passed striking croquet balls or playing the new Sphairis-tiké, the ladies resplendent in long cotton dresses concealing their ankles and wide-brimmed hats adorned with coloured silk ribbons, the gentlemen in knick-erbockers and long coloured socks, long-sleeved shirts that were often striped and black shoes, which had short spikes when the grass was damp and slippery. Doubtless, in an age that was obsessed with decorum and manners, the styles of local dress would have been influenced by the fashions being worn at the annual Championship in Worple Road, for assuredly the well-to-do Wimbledonians would have been regular visitors.

For the residents the only means of transport was the horse-drawn carriage or the bicycle. Despite the patenting of a single cylinder engine in Germany by

It was Henry Jones, a keen croquet player and a committee member of the All England Croquet Club, who had first proposed in 1875 that lawn tennis should be introduced. This was duly agreed and the annual subscription was set at 2 guineas to include both games. In 1877 the name was changed to the All England Croquet and Lawn Tennis Club. The same year Jones was one of three sub-committee men who organised the first lawn tennis tournament in the world and Jones himself acted as Referee.

Gottlieb Daimler in 1885 and the lifting of all road restrictions in Britain ten years later, the motor car did not become a significant means of transport until after the First World War. In the United States Henry Ford, who was a close friend of the inventor Thomas Edison, had started to produce his Model-T in 1908, but in Britain the motor car was still a luxury item until the mass production methods of Morris Motors, founded by William Morris (later Lord Nuffield) in 1912, brought prices down. Nor was there a tram service until 1907. In that year Raynes Park became a satellite suburb of both Wimbledon and Kingston when a new service linked the three districts. At last there was cheap transport for the masses.

The tennis tournament staged in 1877 by the All England Croquet and Lawn Tennis Club (renamed to include the new game only in April that year), had been organised to raise funds for the repair of the broken pony roller that was essential to the upkeep of the croquet lawns – some of which had been turned over to lawn tennis in 1875 in response to the interest among members in the new game. The Croquet Club itself had been founded on 23 July 1868 at a meeting in the offices of *The Field* magazine. However, it had nowhere to play

From a Block by]   [*Maull and Fox*, London.

S. H. C. Maddock.   Rev. A. C. Pearson. Major Lane.   E. C. Haines.   A. Lillie. G. A. Muntz.
J. H. Walsh.   H. Jones ("Cavendish").   Rev. J. I. Heath.   G. Nicol.   Rev. A. Law. Rev. J. B. Riky.   J. D. Heath. G. R. Elsmie
J. H. Hale.   W. J. Whitmore.   C. C. Joad.
W. H. Peel.   W. R. D. Maycock.

GROUP TAKEN AT WIMBLEDON (1870).

A group of keen croquet members photo-graphed outside the new pavilion, which was completed in 1870 at a cost of £160. They include Henry 'Cavendish' Jones (third from left) who was Secretary from 1869 to 1871, and John Walsh (far left) the editor of *The Field* in whose offices the All England Croquet Club had been founded in 1868. Also in 1870 a gardener was engaged at 4 shillings per day. He may have been Mr Coote who was the head gardener in 1881 when his wife was engaged as the attendant in the ladies' changing room for 2/6d per week.

until the following year when the site in Worple Road, which had been discovered by committee member J. H. Clarke Maddock, was leased from an Alfred Dixon for a period of three years at rentals of £50, £75 and £100.

Worple Road was still a muddy lane in those days. The railway ran to the south of the road with its prominent embankment dominating the view in that direction. The new croquet club quickly approved the spending of £1 for the right to have a wicket gate erected giving access to the footpath that ran alongside the railway line to Wimbledon station. What few houses there were had been built at the Hill Road end near the station. Otherwise it was mostly open fields until the 1880s and 1890s when Worple Road itself, and the side roads north and south, became lined with houses as Wimbledon expanded.

The man who had originally donated the pony roller to the club, in return for the election of his daughter to membership, was J. H. Walsh. As editor of *The Field*, Walsh had played a significant part in the formation of the original All England Croquet Club as he had been the Chairman at the inaugural meeting at his office in the Strand. Walsh was also to play a prominent part in promoting the first lawn tennis tournament nine years later through the dona-tion of a silver challenge cup by the magazine, worth 25 guineas.

However, the most important link with *The Field* was that provided by 'Cavendish', one of its regular contributors. The pseudonym concealed the identity of Henry Jones, a 46-year-old doctor who had attended King's College

26

School when it was still in the Strand in the 1840s, before enrolling at St Bartholomew's Hospital to study medicine. A committee member of the All England Croquet Club, Jones had been the moving force behind the introduction of lawn tennis in 1875 and was the chief architect of the inaugural tournament. Besides being the Referee he was responsible, with fellow sub-committee members Julian Marshall, who had been the rackets champion at Harrow, and C. G. Heathcote, a barrister, for framing the rules of the competition.

To their lasting credit this trio decided that the real tennis form of scoring, 15, 30, 40, deuce and advantage should prevail over the more commonly-used rackets scoring of 15 points up which the Marylebone Cricket Club (the governing body of cricket), as guardians of the rules of the new game, had recommended from the start. The latter system, where only the server, the player 'in hand', could advance his score, was part of the code that had originally been adopted by the club on 24 June 1875 for the newly-introduced game.

Moreover, the trio decided that at this first tournament the server should have two chances on each point to deliver a fair serve. Thus was established from the first the inherently exciting method of scoring with its succession of minor climaxes – first within each game where a player on advantage could, in theory at least, be brought back to deuce for ever; then within each advantage set where, from five games all, the same fluctuation could occur; and finally within each five-set match, the opportunity to recover from a two sets' deficit. And, at each moment, there was opportunity to take the calculated gamble of attempting an explosive ace on first serve to extricate oneself from an apparently hopeless position. These were inspired decisions.

The sub-committee also broke with the MCC code in deciding that the shape of the playing area should be rectangular, 78 by 27 feet, instead of the customary hourglass shape. It was another momentous decision that was to have lasting impact, for those very dimensions still represent the outside measurements of every singles' tennis court in the world today.

The one rule that was left unclear concerned the change of ends. It was customary for the players to change ends at the conclusion of each set. However, if there was a particularly strong wind blowing so that there was a distinct advantage from one end the umpire was empowered to decree a change of ends after each game. This, of course, meant that the serve would always be delivered from the same end which hardly seems a true test of ability. Not until 1890 was the present rule introduced whereby a change takes place after every odd game.

Thus it was that the All England Club assumed the leadership and management of the new game, a position happily conceded by the MCC and one which continued until the formation of the Lawn Tennis Association in 1888. But this was by no means the first national governing body for, seven years earlier at a meeting in New York's Fifth Avenue Hotel on 21 May 1881, the United States National Lawn Tennis Association had been formed and had adopted the All England Club rules as laid down for the first Championship. By the early years of the twentieth century the game had spread far and wide with regular tournaments all over Europe, in the United States, in South Africa, in Australia and New Zealand, in India and the Far East, in South America and the Caribbean – in fact wherever sport and recreation were a part of everyday life.

Every leading nation created a national Lawn Tennis Association and on 1 March 1913 representatives from 13 of them met at the headquarters of the Union des Sociétés Française des Sports Athlétiques in Paris to form the International Lawn Tennis Federation, the body that to this day is responsible for the laws of the game. Significantly the US LTA did not join the new Federation. After all they had been the first nation to create an Association and they had founded the Davis Cup in 1900. Furthermore, they objected to the title of World Championships which had been bestowed on Wimbledon in 1913. Only when this title was dropped in 1923 in favour of 'ILTF Official Championships', which was intended to include their own Championships, were the Americans prepared to consider joining, which they did in 1924.

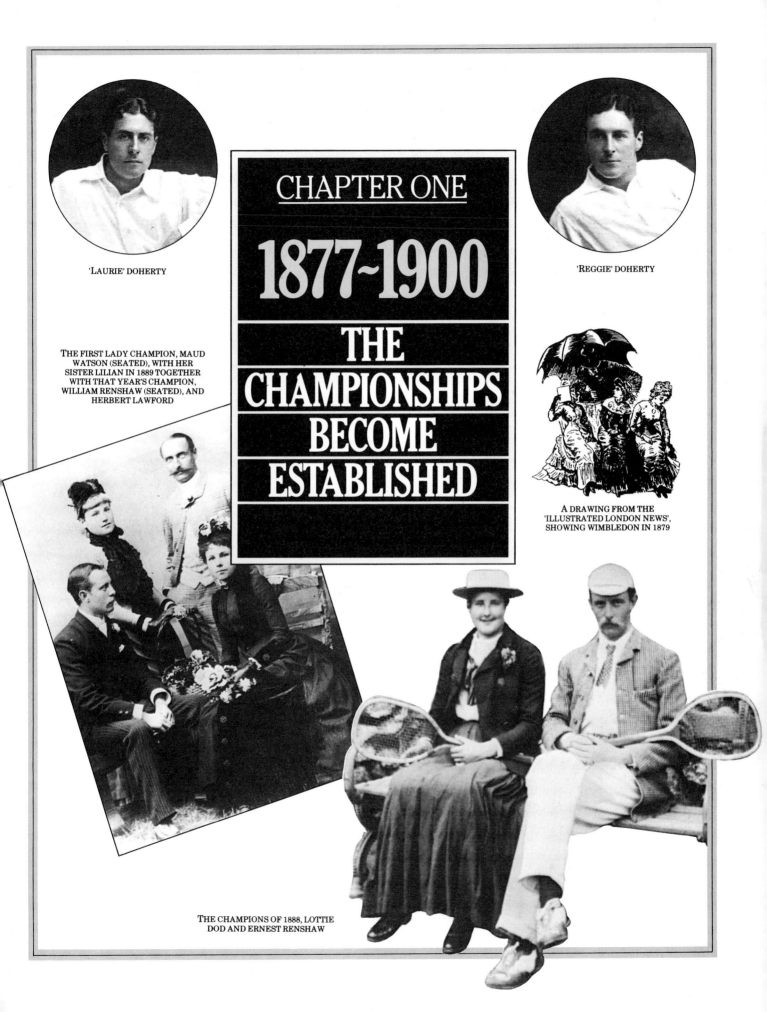

'LAURIE' DOHERTY

'REGGIE' DOHERTY

CHAPTER ONE
1877~1900
THE CHAMPIONSHIPS BECOME ESTABLISHED

THE FIRST LADY CHAMPION, MAUD WATSON (SEATED), WITH HER SISTER LILIAN IN 1889 TOGETHER WITH THAT YEAR'S CHAMPION, WILLIAM RENSHAW (SEATED), AND HERBERT LAWFORD

A DRAWING FROM THE 'ILLUSTRATED LONDON NEWS', SHOWING WIMBLEDON IN 1879

THE CHAMPIONS OF 1888, LOTTIE DOD AND ERNEST RENSHAW

THE 24 Championships between that first historic meeting at Worple Road in 1877 and the turn of the century transformed lawn tennis from a social pastime of the leisured classes into a fully-fledged international sport. That is not to say, however, that many overseas players made the journey to England in those early years – the trickle did not become a flood until the years immediately following the First World War.

In fact, the 13 overseas men who made 15 challenges altogether in this first period were all Americans, for lawn tennis had taken a strong hold across the Atlantic since the first game ever played on that continent at Nahant, near Boston, in August 1874 by James Dwight (who was to serve as President of the US Lawn Tennis Association 21 times) and F. R. Sears, elder brother of the first US National Champion Richard Sears who won seven years running from 1881. The only overseas woman player to challenge at Wimbledon up to the turn of the century was also American. Although Marion Jones, the reigning US Champion, may not have made much of an impression when she appeared at The Championships in 1900 (she lost to Mrs G. Evered in the second round 7-5 6-2), she was certainly a true pioneer and the first of a mighty army of American women players who, over the next 86 years, would come to dominate the game as no other nation has ever done.

Inevitably the first to excel at the new game were the public schoolboys and university men who had achieved some skill in rackets and real tennis, which were the only comparable sports. The first few champions were those who could adapt their techniques to the open air game where there was no friendly wall to return high, fast shots. Control and a sense of length were essential requirements when the very nature of the equipment – loosely-strung rackets that were one-piece bends of ash and soft India rubber balls covered with hand-stitched melton – would have made it impossible to play the sort of power game we are accustomed to seeing today. In any case no one thought it worth trying with a net that was 5 feet high at the posts and which was still 4 feet high five years later.

The service was delivered underarm or from shoulder level, often with heavy cut or slice as in real tennis, and the ground-strokes, too, were sometimes recognisable as wristy cousins of the older games. By today's standards the early game was merely pat-ball but it was no less testing in concentration, nerve, athletic ability and skill with the racket for that.

The Championships went through four distinct periods up to the turn of the century: the early rackets and real tennis-influenced era; the Renshaw-led era of expansion; the slump of the early 1890s; and finally the revival as the Dohertys arrived.

The first four years saw successes for three Englishmen, all old Harrovians, who had excelled in other fields. The first champion, Spencer Gore, had been captain of cricket and a rackets player at school. Appropriately, he had been born at Westside House on Wimbledon Common. However, in 1877 he was living in Wandsworth and according to his grandson, the artist Frederick Gore, he cycled each day to the ground. Spencer was a 27-year-old surveyor at the time of his win against William Marshall, a Cambridge real tennis blue, and was not much impressed by the new game which, he said later, a rackets or real tennis player could hardly be expected to take seriously because: 'the monotony of the game as compared with others would choke him off before he had time to excel in it.' However, Gore did at least have a natural instinct for volleying that set him apart from his fellows and greatly contributed to his win – though some thought his tactics unsporting. Frank Hadow, a 23-year-old tea planter on leave from Ceylon, won in 1878 by beating Gore in the Challenge Round, for until 1922 the defending champion stood out awaiting the winner of the All-Comers' singles. He, too, had played cricket for Harrow and had also won the Public Schools Rackets Championship. Neither Gore nor Hadow ever competed at Wimbledon again though Hadow did attend the 1926 Jubilee celebrations.

The third champion, the Revd John Hartley, was 30 when he won the first of his two consecutive titles in 1879. After Harrow he went up to Oxford and won the University Rackets and Real Tennis Championships and became famous for the hectic journey he undertook to Yorkshire and back in the course of the 1879 tournament. Hartley was the vicar of Burneston in Bedale and, not expecting to proceed very far at Wimbledon, had made no provision for anyone to replace him for the Sunday service: 'So I had to come home on Saturday, breakfast very early on Monday morning, drive ten miles to a station, get to London at two, and to Wimbledon just in time to play – rather tired by my journey and in want of a meal. I nearly lost that game, the semi-final against Parr, but fortunately it came on to rain. We stopped, I got some tea, felt much refreshed and finished off all right.' The following day in the final Hartley accounted for the Irishman 'St Leger', otherwise the notorious Vere Thomas St Leger Goold, who in 1907 was convicted, with his wife Violet, of the murder of a Danish widow, Emma Levin, in Monte Carlo. They both died in prison – Goold on Devil's Island in 1909 and Violet at Montpellier in 1914.

For his second title in 1880 Hartley had to overcome a difficult opponent in Herbert Lawford, a 29-year-old Middlesex man who had been to school at Repton. His fearsome topspin forehand became a shot much discussed on the tea lawn at Worple Road that year. Would it, people asked, be good enough to repel the challenge of the 19-year-old twins from Cheltenham, William and Ernest Renshaw, who, though both victims of O. E. Woodhouse in this, their first Wimbledon, were clearly young men with tremendous talent for the game?

Although they had entered The Championships in 1879 the twins had not competed. However, their reputations were already growing as a result of William's win elsewhere that year against Goold, the first Irish champion, and their success together the following year in the second Oxford University doubles' championship. When William captured the second Irish Championship in 1880 he made everyone aware of his potential.

The impact that these two naturally-gifted players had on the game was immense. Not only did their prodigious deeds on the court excite a huge following throughout the expanding tennis-playing world, but their method of play broke free from the rackets and real tennis mould to create an original lawn tennis style. William, just 15 minutes older than Ernest, was the greater singles player; his seven titles, six of them in succession (1881–86 and 1889), is still a record for men. In 1888 when William, having not defended in 1887 due to a severe case of tennis elbow, lost to Willoughby Hamilton in the last eight of the

ABOVE: The first Championship meeting in 1877 on the 4-acre site off Worple Road in Wimbledon when the net was 5 feet high at the posts (though it doesn't look it in this engraving). The clubhouse is in the distance on the left and the railway embankment is to the right. The tennis balls were supplied by Jefferies of Woolwich and were kept by the ball boys in the canvas 'wells' supplied by a firm in the Strand. The umpire, in top hat, sat on a chair placed on a low platform.

BELOW: The Renshaw twins, William and Ernest, came from Cheltenham and captivated the Wimbledon crowds with their skill and attractive personalities. Their lengthy dominance of the singles' and doubles' events during the 1880s led to the first major boom in interest for the relatively new game. This 1882 final was the first of three between them, all won by William who was older than his brother by 15 minutes. The strokes they used were not derived from the older games of rackets and real tennis and through the Renshaws an individual lawn tennis style evolved.

ABOVE: At the age of 20 William Renshaw (right) defeated Herbert Lawford in five sets in the fifth round of the All-Comers' tournament in 1881 before beating the Revd John Hartley in the Challenge Round to take the first of his seven singles' titles. Like many of his contemporaries, Lawford usually played in knickerbockers with long black socks and he often wore a cap. The scoreboard behind the umpire, with balls that move along the arms, is of the type still used at the US Open at Flushing Meadow on the outside courts. This was the first year that the overarm serve came into use. One year later it was general. It was also in 1881 that the club purchased the freehold of the site for £3,000.

RIGHT: The first of two international matches held at the All England Club following The Championships in 1883, between the Renshaws (near court) and the Clark brothers from Philadelphia, Clarence and Joseph, who had secured the agreement of the US doubles' champions, James Dwight and Richard Sears, to represent their country. By now there were permanent stands at either end of the Centre Court but only a handful of spectators were present to see the Renshaws win both matches without difficulty. These were the first overseas' players to visit the Worple Road ground. The following year Dwight and Sears, together with compatriot A. L. Rives, became the first overseas players to compete in The Championships.

LEFT AND BELOW: At last in 1884 the ladies' singles and the men's doubles were added to the programme and played after the completion of the men's singles. The artist's impression on the left shows Maud Watson beating her sister Lilian from a field of 13 to become the first lady champion. As expected, the Renshaw twins won the

LEFT: Ernest Lewis of Middlesex was an enterprising volleyer who competed at Wimbledon for a decade and reached the All-Comers' final three times, in 1888, 1892 and 1894, and the semi-final once, in 1890, but always found someone too good for him. Ernest Renshaw beat him twice, Wilfred Baddeley once and Joshua Pim once, all of whom became Wimbledon champions. However, Lewis did win the Irish Championships in 1891 and 1892.

doubles. They had twice won 'The Oxford University Challenge Cup for Pairs' organised by the university tennis club between 1879 and 1883 which in its first two years had been contested over the best of seven sets (influenced by rackets). However, even this was not the first doubles' tournament. That distinction belongs to Scotland where a doubles' event had been part of the 1878 Scottish Championships.

All-Comers, Ernest was there to exact vicarious revenge in the next round. Ernest also enjoyed the satisfaction of personal revenge in the Challenge Round when he won his only singles' success by beating Lawford, the man who had beaten him in the previous year's All-Comers' final. The Championships were now attracting a healthy following and crowds of up to 3,500 packed in to watch the Challenge Rounds each year.

Spectators in these early years were drawn from a surprisingly wide catchment area, thanks to the inclusion of Wimbledon on the London and Southampton Railway (later South Western) which had been completed on 21 May 1838. This fast form of communication, first with Nine Elms and from 1846 with Waterloo (at 1s 6d for a first-class ticket) over the next 20 years transformed a village of some 2,000 inhabitants into a fast-growing suburb of London. In 1855 the Wimbledon to Croydon line was opened and four years later the link to Epsom was completed. With the addition of a Kingston connection in 1863 and the vital links to the city at London Bridge (1868) and Ludgate Hill (1869) there was now a network of services which ensured the development of Wimbledon as a desirable area of residence for the successful professional and business people of the capital. The rapid increase in population vividly illustrates the trend, to 4,600 in 1861, 16,000 in 1881 and 41,000 by 1901. Contributing to the latter part of that growth was the construction in 1889 of Putney railway bridge which brought the District Line to Wimbledon and now provided a direct connection with the West End as well as with the city. Accordingly, by 1911 the population of Wimbledon had risen to 55,000.

For the future success of The Championships this ease of communication can hardly be over-emphasised. The large embankment parallel with Worple Road meant that access to the ground could be immediate, which it was from 1883 when, for a few years, the trains would stop opposite the ground during the days of The Championships to disgorge eager tennis fans. Later, when the line became too busy for that, the railway was persuaded to allow passengers to proceed along the dusty footpath from Wimbledon station alongside the embankment as far as the wicket gate that led into the All England Club. Even during the last three Championships held at Worple Road between 1919 and 1921 Kitty Godfree, now the oldest living champion who was competing then for the first time, remembers making that dusty journey.

When the ladies' singles was introduced as a Championship event at Wimbledon in 1884, along with the men's doubles on the demise after five years of the Oxford doubles which the Renshaws had won twice, the game at last recognised one of its essential advantages – the fact that it could be played with skill and enjoyment by both sexes. Although it was to be 29 years before the climate was right to introduce the mixed doubles and ladies' doubles as Championship events, at least there was the exciting spectacle of men's doubles to enjoy and the Renshaws set off on a remarkable chain of victories – five in six years – that strengthened the aura of invincibility that was growing around them.

Since 1885 there had been an All England ladies' doubles title associated with the Buxton Tournament and this remained as a quaint anachronism until the ending of that tournament in 1953. Similarly the All England mixed doubles' title began in Liverpool in 1888 and was shared with Manchester on alternate years until 1938. However, these two popular events did not become part of the Wimbledon programme. From 1899 to 1907 there was a ladies' doubles and from 1900 to 1912 there was a mixed doubles at Worple Road but neither had Championship status until 1913.

Several times before 1884 attempts had been made to include a ladies' singles event but each offer of a trophy had been politely refused. Even the establishment of an Irish Ladies' Championship in 1879, won by May Langrishe, who was thus immortalised as the world's first Lady Champion, failed to prompt any action at Worple Road.

Only when it became clear that the London Athletic Club were serious in their announced intention of holding a Ladies' Championship in 1884 were the committee men goaded into action. On a proposal made by the ubiquitous Henry Jones it was agreed, late in the day, that the ladies' singles would start, like the men's doubles, after the completion of the men's singles championship. A prize worth 20 guineas was offered for the eventual winner and a second prize worth 10 guineas was also announced.

Henry Jones, who had refereed The Championships every year since the beginning, saw the first two years of ladies' tennis safely established before handing over to Julian Marshall, his fellow sub-committee member and one of the founding fathers, who had actually competed in the very first tournament. But Marshall, since 1880, had been the Secretary of the club; he had succeeded Walsh whose enthusiasm remained undimmed but whose responsibilities at *The Field* made it increasingly difficult to devote sufficient time to club affairs. Accordingly, Marshall merely filled in as Referee for one year until Alfred Hickson took on that role in 1887 for a three-year stint.

Marshall himself relinquished the Secretary's seat in 1888 in favour of Herbert Wilberforce, the great-grandson of the celebrated emancipator William Wilberforce (1759–1833) who had lived in Wimbledon at Lauriston House. This was the very house to which Mrs Whitehead's father, Sir Arthur Fell (who became the MP for Great Yarmouth in 1906), had brought the family in the early years of the twentieth century. There had been some celebrated guests 100 years earlier: 'On the lawn was a maple tree known as Pitt's tree, because William Pitt had been a great friend of Wilberforce and frequently visited him at Wimbledon. He used to ride down on horseback from London to stay the weekend at Lauriston House, compose his speeches under the maple tree and enjoy the peaches, peas and strawberries.'

Sir Herbert, as he later became, contributed greatly to the club's development, serving as Secretary for three years until 1891, as President from 1921 to 1929 and as the first Chairman from 1929 to 1936. He described Henry Jones as a dedicated referee, writing: 'He was a familiar figure on the ground, clad in white flannel, a white helmet on his head, bearing a white umbrella with a green lining, and retailing his generally improving reflections to an admiring audience.'

Marshall he recalled as: 'dignified in appearance and varied in culture . . . an agreeable companion, not indifferent to the pleasures of the table, possessed of polished literary style which occasionally led him into controversy, industrious and methodical he maintained the affairs of the club on a businesslike footing although, as his critics averred, failing to render it universally popular.'

The winner of that inaugural Ladies'

Attitude of the present Champion

Miss Bingley's Service

Miss Dod's Service No. 1

Miss Dod's Service No. 2

Play

After the Set

MISS BINGLEY | GAMES
| SETS
MISS DODD | GAMES
| SETS

Just to show there is no Ill Feeling

The Effect of a " Demon " Service

TOP: A match in 1885 with only the singles' court marked because the doubles' event was not begun until the singles had been completed. There is still no 'purpose-built' umpire's chair and the score is displayed by moving balls along protruding arms to represent games and sets. The server here will have to withdraw behind the baseline before his delivery if he is to avoid a foot-fault.

ABOVE: A Wimbledon montage from 1887 when Charlotte 'Lottie' Dod, a Cheshire school-girl, won the All-Comers' singles at the age of 15 years 10 months from a field of only five entries and then astonished everyone by beating the holder, Blanche Bingley, 6-2 6-0 in the Challenge Round. With a strong forehand, underarm serve and powerful smash she had the advantage of playing in shorter skirts than her rivals because of her age. It greatly aided her mobility. The magazines were full of her exploits as she went on to win four times more before retiring undefeated in 1893.

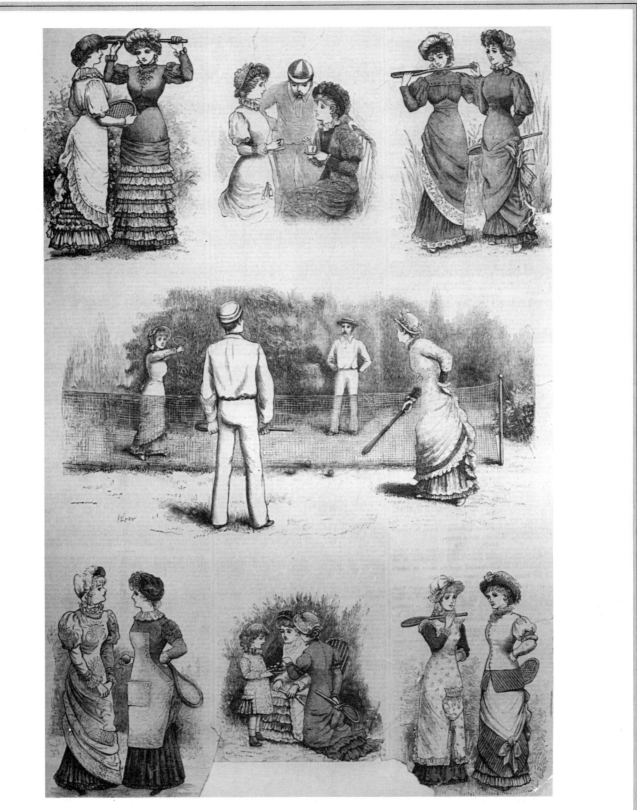

ABOVE: Fashion in the 1880s. In this illustration from *The Queen* in 1881, the ladies display a wide range of styles suitable for tennis, which were all basically normal day wear with ankles, arms and even heads covered. Whalebone corsets, even for the young, were considered essential to maintain the figure; the great American doubles' player Elizabeth Ryan remembered wearing them as late as the years immediately before the First World War.

Championship in 1884, from a field of 13, was Maud Watson, the 19-year-old daughter of the vicar of Berkswell, a parish near Coventry in Warwickshire. In the final she beat her older sister Lilian in three sets having beaten, in the semifinal, 20-year-old Blanche Bingley, a girl who was destined to have a considerable part to play in Wimbledon's history. As a singles' finalist on no less than 13 occasions and a 6-time winner of the title in 24 appearances at The Championships between 1884 and 1913, she became greatly respected for her immense contribution to the game's evolution. According to contemporaries she was a fine mover, the possessor of a lethal forehand and a match player of great determination and coolness. Following her marriage in 1877 to Commander George Hillyard, who was to become the Secretary of the All England Club in 1907, she played an important supportive role in the club's affairs. Blanche won her first title in 1886 and her last in 1900 and in between witnessed, as an unsuccessful challenger, the emergence of one of the sporting world's most remarkable phenomena.

The ladies' champion in 1887 was truly an infant prodigy. Charlotte 'Lottie' Dod was only 15 years and 10 months old when she won the first of her five singles' titles and though it is true that the women's event was not yet attracting a large entry (only once between 1886 and 1897 were there more than nine players and that was in 1894 when Mrs Hillyard won for the third time from a field of eleven), nevertheless the racket skill and sheer athletic ability of the Cheshire youngster was immediately apparent. Never beaten at Wimbledon, Lottie decided to turn her considerable talents to other sports after her fifth win in 1893 and became a hockey international

earning two caps in 1899 and 1900, and a golf champion winning the British Women's Championship at Troon in 1904. Furthermore, she was an accomplished singer, a member of the London Oriana Madrigal Society, a fine pianist, a first-class archer and skater and a marvellous bridge player. Arguably Lottie Dod is still the greatest sporting all-rounder Britain has ever produced.

In 1890 from a field of four, the smallest entry ever for any event at Wimbledon, an Irish girl from Tipperary came across the seas and conquered. The previous year Helena Rice had lost narrowly to Mrs Hillyard in the final of the All-Comers' singles but in 1890 neither Mrs Hillyard, the defending champion, nor Miss Dod had entered. Accordingly, with her two All-Comers' victories, Helena Rice became Wimbledon's least tested champion.

In that same year Bonham Evelegh took over from Hickson as Referee, a post he was to occupy with great dignity for 16 years. Evelegh had been a former croquet champion and the committee member who had seconded Jones's original proposal in 1877 to hold a lawn tennis tournament. Now aged 47 and of some repute as a writer on the game in *The Field*, he became an expert and popular referee at many British tournaments.

The other great character in ladies' tennis during this first period was Charlotte Cooper, who in 1901 became Mrs Alfred Sterry. In the absence of Mrs Hillyard in 1895, 1896 and 1898 she won the first three of her five singles' titles, but lost her crown to that same lady in a fierce three-set final in 1897, and again both in 1899 as the defeated holder in the Challenge Round and in 1900 as the unsuccessful challenger. Even the capture of two Olympic gold medals the same year did not compensate for that

Wimbledon disappointment. However, in 1901 the persistent Middlesex girl did at last bring down Mrs Hillyard and it is a tribute to her determination that, eight years later at the age of 37, she won for a fifth time.

The meagre entries for the women's event coincided with a slump in men's tennis following the departure of the Renshaws. When the defeat of William in the Challenge Round of 1890 by Willoughby Hamilton of Monasterevin, County Kildare, was followed by Ernest's two failures – in the semi-final stage of the All-Comers the following year at the hands of Wilfred Baddeley (the elder of another pair of remarkable tennis twins) and in the second round in 1893 – public support began to wane.

The Championships were not yet the established part of the annual English sporting and social scene that they were to become after the First World War. Nor had the Royal Family so far shown any real interest in the new game. There were other, longer standing attractions in Wimbledon, as Mrs Whitehead remembers: 'The Rifle Meeting, which is now held at Bisley, was held on the Common and was quite as important as the Wimbledon tennis is today. It attracted great crowds and Queen Victoria and other members of the Royal Family came more than once to watch. A special light railway was built for visitors, running past the gravel-pits pond to the Windmill where the great flagstaff stood which was said to be the highest in the world and to have come from Canada.'

The most impressive Royal visit, a Review attended by Queen Victoria's grandson, Kaiser Wilhelm II, in 1891, must have put both the tennis and the rifle shooting in the shade. Mrs Whitehead continues: 'He led the procession on a white horse from Wimbledon station, clad in silver, pale blue and white plumes; on each side of him rode the Prince of Wales and the Duke of Connaught followed by Queen Victoria in an open carriage with the Household Cavalry escorting her . . . it was a perfect summer's day and a brave sight indeed . . . it is easy to see why we children took the Kaiser for a fairy prince. Some say this occasion was called "The modern Field of the Cloth of Gold" because, like Henry VIII and Francis I, the Prince of Wales and the German Emperor, each at the head of his staff, rode out to meet each other in the middle of the Common.' Small wonder that the victories of Wilfred Baddeley and Lottie Dod that year were hardly noticed.

Three of the four men who won the seven titles between 1890 and 1896 were from Ireland, which indicates perhaps that the game's early success in that country had been better sustained than in the land of its birth. That conclusion was certainly a fair one in 1890 for, along with the victory of Miss Rice, her countryman Hamilton won the singles and two more Irishmen, Joshua Pim and Frank Stoker, took the doubles. Hamilton was a fine natural sportsman who had been the Irish champion in 1889 as well as being a soccer international.

Pim, a doctor from Bray, was 24 when he won the first of his two consecutive titles in 1893 and he maintained his standard so well over the next decade that he was selected to represent the British Isles in their second challenge against the United States in 1902 in the newly-created Davis Cup competition. Harold Mahony, who returned the title to Irish keeping for the last time in 1896 following the third success of Wilfred Baddeley the previous year, had been born in Scotland but lived in Ireland. He

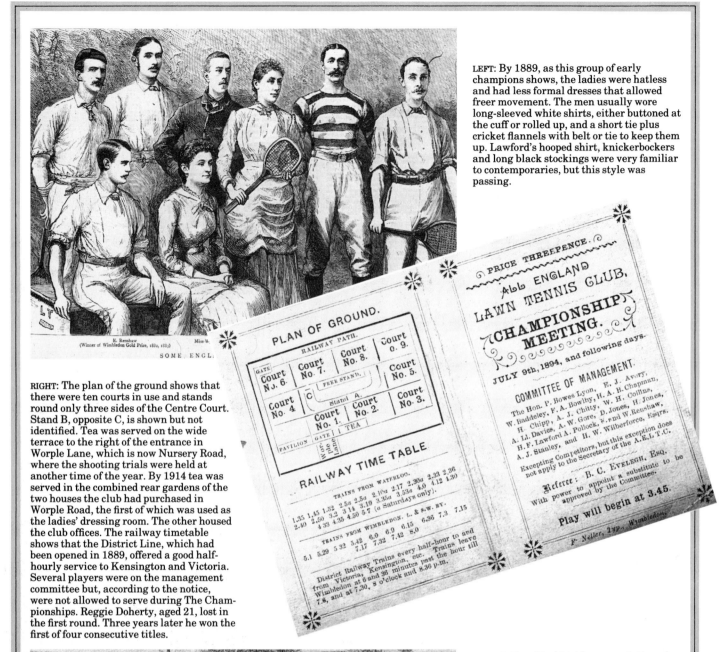

LEFT: By 1889, as this group of early champions shows, the ladies were hatless and had less formal dresses that allowed freer movement. The men usually wore long-sleeved white shirts, either buttoned at the cuff or rolled up, and a short tie plus cricket flannels with belt or tie to keep them up. Lawford's hooped shirt, knickerbockers and long black stockings were very familiar to contemporaries, but this style was passing.

E. Renshaw
(Winner of Wimbledon Gold Prize, 1880, 1881)

Miss W.

SOME ENGL.

PLAN OF GROUND.

RAILWAY PATH.

GATE Court No. 6.	Court No. 7.	Court No. 8.	Court No. 9.
	FREE STAND.		Court No. 5.
Court No. 4.	C Stand A.		
	Court No. 1.	Court No. 2.	Court No. 3.
PAVILION GATE Work ing Ladies	TEA		

RAILWAY TIME TABLE

TRAINS FROM WATERLOO.

1.35 1.45 1.52 2.5a 2.5a 2.10a 2.17 2.30a 2.33 2.36
2.40 2.50 3.2 3.14 3.19 3.35a 4.0 4.12 4.30
4.33 4.35 4.50 5.7 (a Saturdays only).

TRAINS FROM WIMBLEDON. L. & S.W. RY.

5.1 5.29 5.32 5.42 6.0 6.9 6.15 6.36 7.3 7.15
7.17 7.32 7.42 8.0

District Railway Trains every half-hour to and from Victoria, Kensington, etc. Trains leave Wimbledon at 6 and 36 minutes past the hour till 7.8, and at 7.30, 8 o'clock and 8.36 p.m.

PRICE THREEPENCE.

ALL ENGLAND
LAWN TENNIS CLUB,
CHAMPIONSHIP
MEETING.

JULY 9th, 1894, and following days.

COMMITTEE OF MANAGEMENT.

The Hon. P. Bowes Lyon, E. J. Avory,
W. Baddeley, F. A. Bowlby, H. A. B. Chapman,
H. Chipp, A. J. Chitty, W. H. Collins,
A. Ll. Davies, A. W. Gore, D. Jones, H. Jones,
H. F. Lawford A. Pollock, F. and W. Renshaw,
A. J. Stanley, and H. W. Wilberforce, Esqrs.

Excepting Competitors, but this exception does not apply to the Secretary of the A.E.L.T.C.

Referee: B. C. EVELEGH, Esq.
With power to appoint a substitute to be approved by the Committee.

Play will begin at 3.45.

F. Neller, Typ., Wimbledon.

RIGHT: The plan of the ground shows that there were ten courts in use and stands round only three sides of the Centre Court. Stand B, opposite C, is shown but not identified. Tea was served on the wide terrace to the right of the entrance in Worple Lane, which is now Nursery Road, where the shooting trials were held at another time of the year. By 1914 tea was served in the combined rear gardens of the two houses the club had purchased in Worple Road, the first of which was used as the ladies' dressing room. The other housed the club offices. The railway timetable shows that the District Line, which had been opened in 1889, offered a good half-hourly service to Kensington and Victoria. Several players were on the management committee but, according to the notice, were not allowed to serve during The Championships. Reggie Doherty, aged 21, lost in the first round. Three years later he won the first of four consecutive titles.

LEFT: Arthur Hopkins' famous painting of the 1888 Challenge Round in which Ernest Renshaw (near end) scored his only singles' win by beating the holder Herbert Lawford, whose powerful topspin forehand was much respected, in straight sets. This reversed the previous year's result when Lawford, after losing in the final three years running to Ernest's brother William, had taken advantage of the holder's absence due to a painful case of tennis elbow, to beat Ernest 6-4 in the fifth set of the All-Comers' final for his only win. For the first time since 1879 there had been no Challenge Round. In 1889 William won for the seventh time after surviving six match points in the All-Comers' final against H. S. Barlow and then beating his brother in the Challenge Round. Together they won their fifth doubles' title and then retired.

RIGHT: Joshua Pim beating Ernest Lewis in 1892 to win the All-Comers' final. Unfortunately, in the Challenge Round Wilfred Baddeley again defeated him. However, for the next two years Pim turned the tables. In 1893 he won the All-Comers and brought down Baddeley in the Challenge Round and the following year he defended successfully against Baddeley.

BELOW: Lottie Dod with her two brothers William (right) and Anthony with whom she often played mixed doubles. Lottie also had a sister, Ann, and had won the Northern Doubles Tournament with her when she was only 11. There was both a grass and a shale court at Edgworth, the family home in Bebington, Cheshire and so ample opportunity to practise. Lottie and Anthony won the All England Mixed together in 1892 when it was played at Manchester.

RIGHT: The contribution made to Wimbledon's development by the Baddeley twins, Wilfred and Herbert who came from Bromley in Kent, has often been overlooked. Although not as talented as the Renshaw twins who came before, or the Doherty brothers who came after, they were nevertheless a great crowd attraction. Wilfred won the title three times but Herbert, a London solicitor, was never as good a singles' player. They were both good doubles' players with an uncanny sense of anticipation, an attribute that helped them to win the doubles' title four times between 1891 and 1896.

ABOVE: An all-too-familiar sight at Wimbledon over the years. In the 1890s they used four tarpaulins but the die-hards remained in their seats beneath umbrellas just as they do today.

RIGHT: The Dohertys, on the left Laurence who was always 'Laurie' or 'Little Do' and on the right Reginald who was three years older and inevitably 'Reggie' or 'Big Do'. Like the first champion Spencer Gore they were both born in Wimbledon. Unlike him they went to Westminster, not Harrow, and then on to Cambridge where they sharpened their tennis teeth on the excellent courts at Fenner's while earning their blues. At Wimbledon they monopolised the singles and doubles between 1897 and 1906. They became equally famous overseas and expanded the game's horizons. In Ireland they dominated between 1898 and 1902; at the 1900 Olympic Games in Paris they won two gold medals each; in the United States Laurie became the first foreign winner of the singles in 1903. Together, the previous year, they had become the first overseas pair to take the US doubles' title out of the country and they repeated the feat in 1903. Shortly afterwards they beat the Americans in the Davis Cup final in Boston to bring that famous trophy for the first time to Britain where it stayed until the Dohertys retired in 1908. The elegance, charm and athletic ability of the Dohertys made them the game's first superstars.

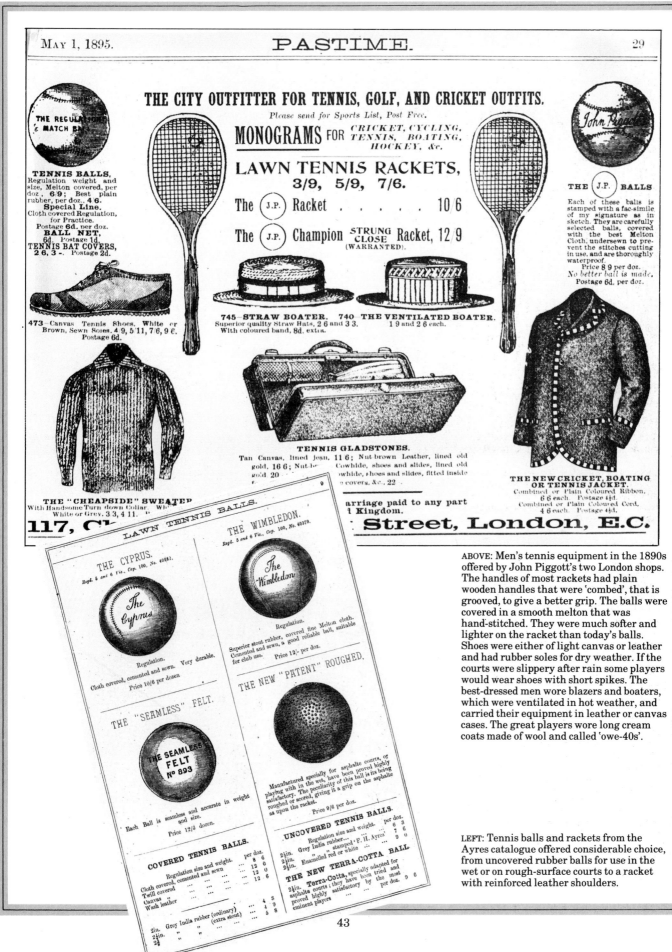

ABOVE: Men's tennis equipment in the 1890s offered by John Piggott's two London shops. The handles of most rackets had plain wooden handles that were 'combed', that is grooved, to give a better grip. The balls were covered in a smooth melton that was hand-stitched. They were much softer and lighter on the racket than today's balls. Shoes were either of light canvas or leather and had rubber soles for dry weather. If the courts were slippery after rain some players would wear shoes with short spikes. The best-dressed men wore blazers and boaters, which were ventilated in hot weather, and carried their equipment in leather or canvas cases. The great players wore long cream coats made of wool and called 'owe-40s'.

LEFT: Tennis balls and rackets from the Ayres catalogue offered considerable choice, from uncovered rubber balls for use in the wet or on rough-surface courts to a racket with reinforced leather shoulders.

had been Pim's victim in the All-Comers' final of 1893 after causing a minor sensation by eliminating Ernest Renshaw in the second round in five sets, but did not reach the quarter-finals again until, three years later, he fought through to the Challenge Round and brought down the holder, Baddeley, in five sets.

The contribution made by the Baddeley twins is often overlooked and it was hardly their fault that they excelled at a time when public interest had waned. When Wilfred won the first of his three titles in 1891 he was only 19 years 5 months and 23 days old, the youngest male champion at Wimbledon until 1985 when the precocious West German, Boris Becker, astonished the entire tennis world by taking the title aged 17 years and 7 months on the seventh day of the seventh month

Wilfred and his younger twin Herbert were expert doubles' players and took the title four times between 1891 and 1896. So alike were they it was almost impossible to tell them apart. It was even rumoured that if one of them was having a bad day on service his brother would serve at both ends! Wilfred's three singles' wins in 1891, 1892 and 1895 were much respected by his contemporaries who believed him to be as astute a tactician and as technically competent a striker of the ball as any of the previous champions.

The last four years of the century heralded a revival in the fortunes of The Championships as another pair of

Court No. 4 backed onto the stand of the Centre Court. To the right are the trees in the gardens of houses in Worple Road. As at Wimbledon today, it was first come first seated around the outside courts. But, at last, the umpire is comfortably installed in one of Slazengers' famous green umpires' chairs that are still in use.

brothers, not twins this time, established an aura of invincibility as powerful as that created by the Renshaws. Reginald Doherty and his younger brother Laurence, 'Reggie' and 'Laurie' as they became popularly known or 'Big Do' and 'Little Do', were to become ambassadors not only for Britain but for the expanding game itself as their successes over the next decade at Cambridge, at Wimbledon, in the United States, in Ireland, at the Olympics of 1900 and especially in the Davis Cup, brought them fame and recognition on a scale previously unknown. They were the game's first superstars, a handsome and cultured pair whose dress, deportment and modest manner, allied to an elegance of style, created a new following for lawn tennis among a public that was becoming increasingly interested in playing the game at the many new tennis clubs that were springing up all over the country.

Reginald defeated Mahony in the Challenge Round of 1897. Then, to close the century on a high note, he successfully defended his title for the next three years against brother Laurie, Arthur Gore and Sydney Smith, who despite, or perhaps because of, a leg brace, covered the court remarkably fast and wielded a forehand that was regarded as the fiercest in the game. At the time few believed that Reggie's younger brother would surpass those achievements in the early years of the next century. But, as we shall see, that is just what Laurie did as, together, they built on their four years of success as a doubles' pair to dominate the game in a quite remarkable way.

BIOGRAPHIES

GENTLEMEN

S. W. Gore

P. F. Hadow

W. Renshaw

H. F. Lawford

1877

SPENCER GORE

Born: 10 March 1850; died: 19 April 1906

The first of the immortals, Spencer Gore was a Wimbledon-born surveyor who had learned rackets at Harrow. He was 27 when on a damp Thursday, 19 July 1877, he beat William Marshall 6-1 6-2 6-4. His volleying was novel and the more controversial because he often stretched across the net.

He preferred cricket and maintained that tennis would not appeal to the good games player, writing that 'the monotony of the game as compared with others would choke him off'. Even so he sportingly defended his title a year later but Wimbledon did not see him again.

1878

FRANK HADOW

Born: 24 January 1855; died: 29 June 1946

Another rackets player from Harrow, he was on leave from tea planting in Ceylon. On reaching the Challenge Round against Gore he was inspired to invent the lob, which proved a winning ploy since no one had learned to smash.

Hadow went back to tea planting – and to hunting big game round the world – and did not see a first-class tennis match again until he attended the Jubilee celebrations in 1926.

His record in being the only man never to lose a set at Wimbledon is unique.

1879, 1880

REVD JOHN HARTLEY

Born: 9 January 1849; died: 21 August 1935

Another Harrovian, John Hartley played rackets and real tennis at Oxford and excelled at long, patient rallying. His first final caught him unprepared and he had to return to Burneston, North Yorkshire, to conduct the Sunday services.

On Monday he rose at dawn to get back in time for the final against V. St Leger Goold who was later convicted of murder, by which time Hartley had become a canon. He was the first champion to defend successfully.

1881, 1882, 1883, 1884, 1885, 1886, 1889

WILLIAM RENSHAW

Born: 3 January 1861; died: 12 August 1904

With his twin, Ernest, William Renshaw created the modern game, perfecting the smash, the hard service and aggressive volleying. He was virtually unbeatable for a decade.

William Renshaw transformed tennis from a pastime into a sport. Crowds came to watch the wealthy twins from Cheltenham and special trains were run to a halt put up by the London and South Western Railway by the side of the All England Club. He was *the* founding father of tennis.

1887

HERBERT LAWFORD

Born: 15 May 1851; died: 20 April 1925

A zealous competitor, he competed first in 1878 at the age of 27 and was overshadowed by the might of the Renshaw twins until he beat Ernest in the All-Comers' final of 1887 and walked over against William.

The 'Lawford Stroke' became famous. It was a wristy whipped forehand of speed and accuracy.

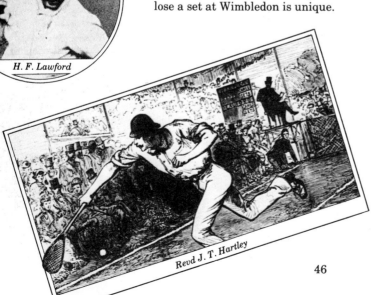

Revd J. T. Hartley

1888

ERNEST RENSHAW

Born: 3 January 1861; died: 2 September 1899
He was almost as good a player as his twin William and was thrice beaten by him in the Challenge Round. Both brothers were equally popular and they rarely lost in doubles. An American challenge against them in 1884 was utterly crushed; by then they had pioneered the technique of 'two up' at the net instead of the standard 'one up, one back'.

1890

WILLOUGHBY HAMILTON

*Born: 9 December 1864;
died: 27 September 1943*

He played soccer for Ireland but his frail appearance brought him the nickname 'The Ghost'. A guileful retriever he was 25 when he had his tennis break-through. In the Challenge Round he came back from a deficit of one set to two to beat William Renshaw, a rare happening.

He never competed again because of ill-health, though he lived until the age of 78.

1891, 1892, 1895

WILFRED BADDELEY

*Born: 11 January 1872;
died: 24 January 1929*

After the Renshaws Wilfred Baddeley was, with his brother Herbert, the most famous of the twins who proliferated in the early days. A sound rather than a spectacular player, he was 19 years 175 days old when he won his first singles. There was no younger men's champion until the West German Boris Becker in 1985.

He flourished after the Renshaw 'boom'. When he won in 1895 Wimbledon made its only loss in history, £33.

1893, 1894

JOSHUA PIM

Born: 20 May 1869; died: 15 April 1942
An Irish doctor, he won at his fourth attempt, and the following year successfully defended his title but did not compete again. His reputation as a former master brought his selection as leader of the British Isles Davis Cup side against the United States in 1902.

Because of his medical commitments his choice was kept secret and he travelled to New York as 'Mr X'. He had no success.

1896

HAROLD MAHONY

Born: 13 February 1867; died: 27 June 1905

The third of the Irish champions, he was playing for the sixth time when he dethroned the patient Wilfred Baddeley after 57 games. It was the longest title match until Drobny v Rosewall in 1954. He went on to play eight further championships without success.

He was described as, 'the most generous hearted, casual, irresponsible 75 inches of Irish bone and muscle that ever walked on court'. He died by falling from his bicycle at the foot of a hill in County Kerry.

1897, 1898, 1899, 1900

REGINALD DOHERTY

*Born: 14 October 1872;
died: 29 December 1910*

His four times success lowered the curtain on the nineteenth century but in the development of the game and in its prosperity he initiated a new era. Never strong, he was tall and thin and declared he had never felt really well for a whole day; he died aged 38.

He played the classic English game, his all-round expertise based on secure control of groundstrokes. He and his younger brother, the stronger Laurie, were a charismatic pair, almost invincible and legendary with their sportsmanship.

Both were born in Hartfield Road, Wimbledon, a stone's throw from the old All England Club in Worple Road, where their presence brought record crowds.

E. Renshaw

W. J. Hamilton

W. Baddeley

J. Pim

H. S. Mahony

R. F. Doherty

47

LADIES

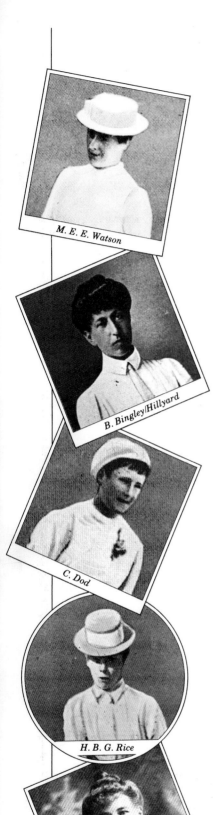

M. E. E. Watson

B. Bingley/Hillyard

C. Dod

H. B. G. Rice

C. Cooper/Sterry

1884, 1885

MAUD WATSON

Born: 9 October 1864; died: 5 June 1946

The inaugural women's champion was 19 when she assured herself of tennis immortality as Wimbledon shed its male exclusivity after seven years. She was the daughter of the vicar of Berkswell, Warwickshire, and beat her elder sister, Lilian, in the final from a field of 13.

She played through to win a second time. The next year the Challenge Round had been instituted and she yielded to Blanche Bingley, losing finalist the year before.

1886, 1889, 1894, 1897, 1899, 1900

BLANCHE BINGLEY/HILLYARD

Born: 3 November 1863; married: 13 July 1887 (to G. W. Hillyard); died: 6 August 1946

An indefatigable champion, she competed in the very first meeting and for the twenty-fourth time 29 years later in 1913. She was 36 when she won for the last time, which was 14 years after the first win.

She had an even longer span of triumph in the South of England Championships at Eastbourne, then a major event, winning first in 1885 and for the eleventh time two decades later in 1905.

Her husband, Commander George Hillyard, became Secretary of the All England Club and was also a tireless competitor.

1887, 1888, 1891, 1892, 1893

CHARLOTTE 'LOTTIE' DOD

Born: 24 September 1871; died: 27 June 1960

She was invincible, unbeaten in all her five years when, moreover, she lost only one set. She was also the youngest champion of all time, 15 years 285 days, when a bright bundle of energetic expertise in short skirts showed how efficiently she had trained with her brothers in Cheshire.

By the standards of her day she became a 'pin up'. As an all-rounder she was almost without equal. She was British Women's Golf Champion, played hockey for England and was an Olympic silver medallist at archery. She performed every winter sport to a high standard. She rowed. She was a talented pianist and had an above average contralto singing voice.

1890

HELENA RICE

Born: 21 June 1866; died: 21 June 1907

She was the most obscure champion and came from Newinn, Tipperary in Ireland. Having won the mixed doubles in her own championship meeting at Dublin in 1889 she came to Wimbledon and was three times at match point against Blanche Bingley. The next year she came back to win – but she was one of just four competitors!

She died, aged 41, on the same day of the year and in the same place where she was born.

1895, 1896, 1898, 1901, 1908

CHARLOTTE COOPER/STERRY

Born: 22 September 1870; married: 12 January 1901 (to A. Sterry); died: 10 October 1966

One of the great women pioneers, she was nearly 25 in 1895 when she won for the first time. In 1908 she won for the fifth time at the age of 37 years 282 days, the oldest woman champion in Wimbledon's history.

Her loss in 1902 to Muriel Robb was unique in coming after 53 games in all. She stood at 6-4 11-13 when play was abandoned due to rain and on the restart the next day she lost 5-7 1-6.

She was 48 when she competed in the singles for the last time in 1919. In 1961, in her ninetieth year, she flew unaccompanied from Edinburgh to London to attend the seventy-fifth anniversary celebrations.

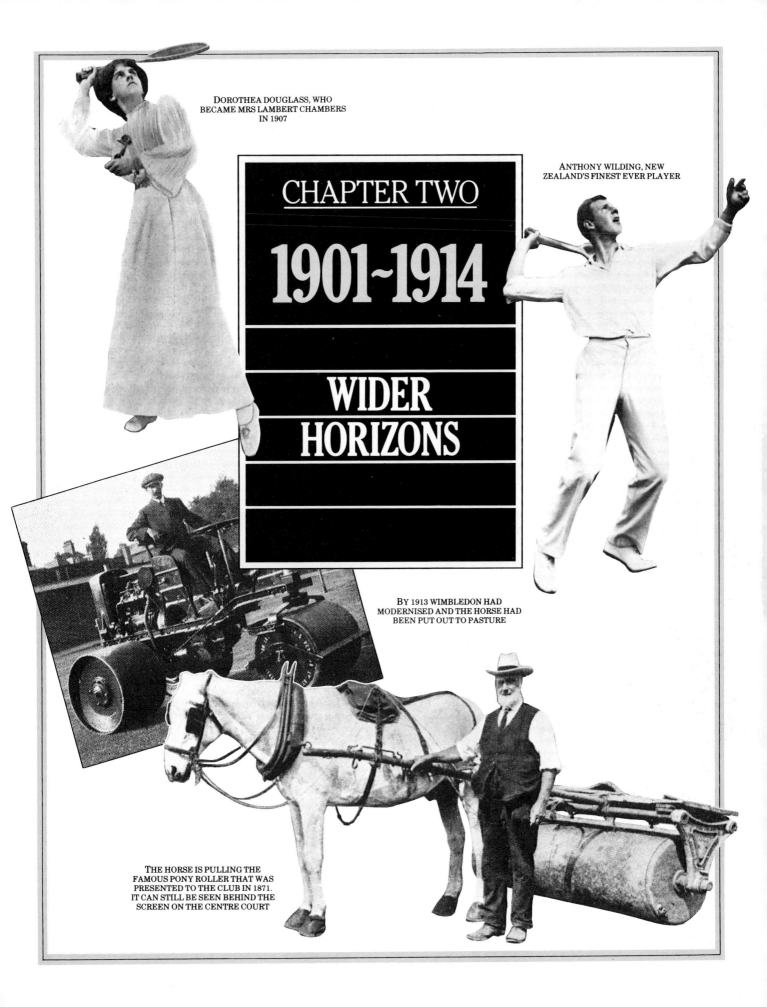

DOROTHEA DOUGLASS, WHO
BECAME MRS LAMBERT CHAMBERS
IN 1907

CHAPTER TWO

1901~1914

WIDER
HORIZONS

ANTHONY WILDING, NEW
ZEALAND'S FINEST EVER PLAYER

BY 1913 WIMBLEDON HAD
MODERNISED AND THE HORSE HAD
BEEN PUT OUT TO PASTURE

THE HORSE IS PULLING THE
FAMOUS PONY ROLLER THAT WAS
PRESENTED TO THE CLUB IN 1871.
IT CAN STILL BE SEEN BEHIND THE
SCREEN ON THE CENTRE COURT

IN Britain the death of Queen Victoria on 22 January 1901 had a profound effect on all aspects of national life. She had reigned for almost 64 years so that hardly anyone under the age of 70 could remember any other monarch. The Prince of Wales, who was 59 when he became Edward VII, had enjoyed a life style rather different from the strict one his father Prince Albert had tried to impose on him and it certainly was not one of which his mother ever approved. His short nine-year reign witnessed a liberalising of attitudes that led to the start of the welfare state with the introduction of old age pensions and of national insurance. Labour was also becoming better organised since the formation of the General Federation of Trade Unions in 1899. It was a time of adaptation and change.

There were changes, too, abroad. The Constitution Act of 1900 established a Commonwealth in Australia, a federation with powers divided between the individual states and central government. In South Africa the position in the Boer War was at last looking more promising for Britain with the relief of Kimberley, Ladysmith and Mafeking in 1900 and the annexation of the Transvaal the following year. After the surrender of the Boers in 1902 the realities of the situation were recognised with the promise of self-government for the Transvaal and the Orange Free State, granted in 1907. The process had begun that would lead to the Act of Union in 1909 which created the Dominion of South Africa.

The changes were not all for the general good. In Germany Admiral Tirpitz persuaded the Reichstag to pass the Navy Act by which the size of the country's navy would be doubled by 1920. In China 45,000 lives were lost as the Russians occupied Manchuria, and the Boxer rebellion, a violent protest against foreign intervention, was crushed by allied European forces aided by the United States and Japan. In the United States President McKinley was assassinated to be succeeded by Theodore Roosevelt.

The year 1901 was also a time of cultural development and scientific advance. Elgar's *Cockaigne* overture and Dvořák's opera *Russalka* were performed for the first time; Edward German completed Sullivan's light opera *The Emerald Isle*; Picasso produced *Bal Tabarin* and Kipling's masterpiece *Kim* was published. When Marconi transmitted morse signals across the Atlantic from Poldhu in Cornwall to St John's, Newfoundland in 1901, little did anyone realise that his act heralded the start of a communications' revolution that would totally transform our way of life. Appropriately, in view of the importance to The Championships of radio and, later, television coverage, those first experiments by Marconi had been tried out in the garden of Gothic Lodge, Wimbledon.

Wimbledon itself was experiencing a transformation. Worple Road, paved now and widened in 1907 to allow the installation of tram tracks, was lined with houses. In the side roads to the north, which cut through open fields to connect with The Ridgway, were built a number of larger, comfortable family homes. These were most desirable residences. Among them a large Roman Catholic church on the hill dominated the view from Worple Road where horse buses vied with the trams for public custom. It was a particularly busy scene during the two weeks of tennis at the All England Club as the growing crowds flocked to see the new stars.

The Championships were being transformed from a largely domestic tournament to a truly international one. The first 14 years of the new century at Worple Road lived up to everyone's expectations. Just four men and six ladies divided the singles' titles; the first overseas champions emerged at last to end for ever Britain's dominance of its own national Championships. Even as the storm clouds were gathering over Europe the ladies' doubles and the mixed doubles were added to the list of Championship events almost as a statement of faith in the future of lawn tennis in a free world.

Already in 1901 a New Zealander was making his own personal statement of faith in the future of Wimbledon by being the first challenger from his country and the first from any country except the United States to enter The Championships. Although Harry Parker, the New Zealand champion, lost early to the eventual winner he paved the way for his famous countryman Anthony Wilding, who was to be champion from 1910 to 1913. The winners in 1901 were Arthur Gore, the last old Harrovian to take the title, and Charlotte Sterry who, as 'Chattie' Cooper, had already won three times the previous century and was to gain a last title in 1908. Gore had won the All-Comers two years earlier and had lost in the final in 1900. The 1901 win was the first of three singles' victories he achieved, the others being in 1908 and 1909, in a remarkable Wimbledon career that stretched over 39 years between 1888 and 1927. He was 41 years and 6 months old when he took that last title in 1909, making him still the oldest singles' winner there has ever been.

Mrs Sterry dethroned the reigning champion Blanche Hillyard but was herself beaten in the Challenge Round the following year by the 23-year-old Newcastle girl Muriel Robb. This last match created a curious Wimbledon record

because it was played twice. At least, it was replayed the next day when rain ended play with the score at 4-6 13-11 from Miss Robb's point of view. When the match was restarted from scratch (there was no continuation from the point where the match had been interrupted as there is now), Miss Robb completed a 7-5 6-1 win.

Then came the run of five successive wins by Laurie Doherty (1902–06), the last such string by a man until Bjorn Borg achieved as much in the 1970s. In the doubles the Wimbledon-born brothers completed a total of eight wins by adding the 1901, 1903, 1904 and 1905 titles to those already won the previous century. It was largely their successes in The Championships, plus their contribution to Britain's capture of the Davis Cup in 1903 and its retention until 1906 (after which they retired), that restored the popularity of Wimbledon as the crowds started to flock back.

Another who must be given credit for the renewed popularity is Dorothea Douglass, one of five children of an Ealing vicar. The public's attitude to women's tennis, and to the position of women in society generally, had not yet made it possible for their exploits to have much impact – we had to wait for the inter-war euphoria surrounding Suzanne Lenglen for that. Yet without the publicity that the men received through the Davis Cup, Mrs Lambert Chambers, as she became, achieved much more than any other lady champion had done before her. She first appeared in 1900 when she lost in the first round to Louise Martin of Ireland; the following year she lost in two sets to the past champion Charlotte Sterry. In 1902 she gave notice of what a formidable player she would become by pressing the eventual winner, Miss Robb, to a

LEFT: The fearsome forehand of the nimble Hampshire player Arthur Wentworth Gore (no relation of Spencer Gore), who won three Wimbledon singles' titles and one in doubles (1909) as well as two Olympic gold medals in 1908. He had learnt the game as a ten-year-old on the sands of Dinard in 1878 and was still competing when he was 59, one year before his death. As well as winning many minor titles in singles and doubles he was the President of the All England Club in 1911 and also Vice-President of the Lawn Tennis Association.

RIGHT: The US doubles' champions of 1899, 1900 and 1901, Holcombe Ward (left) and Dwight Davis, were also finalists at Wimbledon in 1901 when the Doherty brothers beat them in four sets. Davis was the donor of the famous Cup that bears his name and had captained the first American team in 1900 that had won easily against the British Isles. The visiting team lacked the Dohertys and, with magnificent disregard for proper preparation, had travelled to Boston on a sightseeing trip via Niagara Falls. Ward and Davis had won the doubles in the 3-0 US win (one rubber was unfinished and one unplayed). The British captain had been Arthur Gore.

ABOVE: The site of the public tea area at Worple Road changed over the years. In 1906 the unused outside courts were em-ployed. This created a marvellous garden party atmosphere which was consciously preserved at the Church Road ground.

RIGHT: The American champion May Sutton (left) had been born in Plymouth, the daughter of a British naval captain who emigrated with his wife and four daughters to California. Here in the 1907 Wimbledon final she beat Dorothea Lambert Chambers, which was a repeat of the victory she had achieved two years earlier when she had become the first overseas winner at The Championships. Norman Brookes of Australia won the singles in 1907 and when he teamed with Wilding to win the doubles all three titles went overseas – the first time, but by no means the last!

BELOW: The great Charlotte Sterry in the course of beating Agnes 'Agatha' Morton in 1908 for her fifth and last singles' title. It is said that when she cycled home to Surbiton with her racket in a clip on the front fork after winning for the first time in 1895 at the age of 24, she found her father clipping the hedge. 'Where have you been, dear?,' he asked.

'To Wimbledon, of course, father,' she replied.

'Ah, yes, I remember – you were playing the final weren't you? Did you win?'

'Yes, I did actually.'

'Well done, I'm so glad,' replied her father.

This down-to-earth upbringing explains why 'Chattie', as she was known, remained so level-headed despite countless successes that included two gold medals at the 1900 Olympics, plus two Irish singles' titles and one Scottish. Her daughter Gwen became a Wightman Cup player and her son Rex became Vice-Chairman of the All England Club.

LEFT: In 1907 Wimbledon enjoyed its first visit from the Royal Family when the Prince and Princess of Wales came to watch the play. Thus began a long and happy Royal connection. For the next two years Prince George consented to serve as President and, when he became George V, as Patron from 1910 to 1935. Ever since, the reigning monarch has graciously served as Patron. For many years after the Second World War Queen Mary was a frequent visitor and would unwittingly cause consternation in the Royal Box late in the afternoon by moving back row by row to avoid the setting sun. Of course, everyone behind her had to move back too! The role of President has been energetically filled by the Kent family since 1929.

ABOVE: Norman Brookes (far end, left) and Anthony Wilding beating the American pair Karl Behr and Beals Wright (at net) in the 1907 Wimbledon final. Although the Americans reversed the result in the Inter-Zone final of the Davis Cup later that year at Wimbledon, they could not prevent the Australians from winning 3-2, a success that inspired them to beat the British Isles 3-2 in the Challenge Round. This was the first of six Australian victories between 1907 and 1920, which ended with a 5-0 defeat against the USA in Auckland, New Zealand.

close three sets in the semi-final of the All-Comers.

In 1903 Dorothea embarked on a run of seven singles' successes in 11 years that were unparalleled until the redoubtable Helen Wills Moody, in the 1930s, claimed 8 victories, also in 11 years, which is more than any other man or woman has since achieved. It is almost easier to record those years from 1903 until the last pre-war Championship when Mrs Lambert Chambers did not win the singles – namely 1905, 1907–09 and 1912; and these years contained two away from tennis when her sons, Douglas in 1909 and Graham in 1912, were being born. Otherwise she was virtually unbeatable, an altogether intimidating opponent with her tall figure, intense concentration and utter reliability in keeping the ball to a good length on the vital points. She was to figure in one of the most dramatic of all Wimbledon's finals, which was the Challenge Round of 1919 against the French wonder-girl Suzanne Lenglen.

The only player to beat Dorothea Douglass in a Challenge Round before the First World War – and she did it twice – was the American champion May Sutton. In 1905 Dorothea had suffered a wrist injury while playing in the South of France and went into her Challenge Round woefully short of practice. A comprehensive straight sets' victory for Miss Sutton thus brought the first success at Wimbledon by an overseas player if you discount the victories of the Irish men in the 1890s. Although Dorothea regained the title from the American the following year she was beaten again in 1907, three months after her marriage to Robert Lambert Chambers. In 1908 Mrs Sterry won the last of her five titles after a rare victory over Dorothea in the All-Comers and did not defend when Dora Boothby

won the All-Comers the following year. The only other lady champion of the period was Ethel Larcombe, the wife of a future Secretary of the club, Dudley Larcombe. Ethel, who won in 1912, was to turn professional in 1922, the year of the move to the new ground in Church Road.

The year 1905 had a significance beyond the initial success of May Sutton. No fewer than 16 overseas men challenged, five of them Americans who were part of a concerted but unavailing effort by that country to win back the Davis Cup that year, which was actually to remain in British or Australasian hands until 1913. One of the visitors was Norman Brookes, a left-hander from Australia; another was Anthony Wilding from New Zealand. These two were to dominate the post-Doherty era, both at Wimbledon and in the Davis Cup, save for the two years 1908 and 1909 when the remarkable Arthur Gore achieved his second and third Wimbledon titles as already described.

On his second visit in 1907, and a much improved player with a devilish, swerving serve, Brookes became the first man from outside the British Isles to win the singles' crown. He repeated his success on his only other pre-war visit in 1914 to become the last champion before the hostilities broke out. In between, the majestic Wilding reigned – his first victory in 1910 coinciding with the accession of George V. While a new monarch was being crowned at Westminster a new king was being hailed at Wimbledon. There was certainly a regal quality about the athletic Wilding who won four years in a row; his last victory in 1913 being against the hard-hitting Maurice McLoughlin. The American, known popularly as the 'Californian Comet', had the same year helped his country at last to win back the Davis Cup.

A Cambridge blue of exceptional charm, good looks and ability, loved by the ladies and admired by the men, Wilding was the nearest thing to a sporting matinee idol the game had so far produced. He was also a keen motor-cyclist who won a gold medal in a race from Land's End to John O'Groats in 1908 and, two years later, motor-cycled from London to Constantinople via Rheims where he flew in one of the new aeroplanes, which were touches of daredevil eccentricity that greatly increased his appeal. It was tragic that so fine an example of New Zealand manhood, so graceful an exponent of lawn tennis skills, should have joined the hundreds of thousands of wasted young lives who were sacrificed in the stupidity that history refers to as The Great War. Wilding, a captain in the Royal Marines, was killed in action at Neuve Chapelle in France on 9 May 1915.

There were other notable events during this period as The Championships expanded. In 1902, at the behest of a group of leading players, the Slazenger ball replaced the Ayres as the official ball of The Championships. It is a remarkable tribute to the quality of the product and the friendly and efficient working relationship that developed between the many representatives of firm and club over the years that the supply of Slazenger balls, equipment and tournament personnel, voted on annually by the club's committee until the recent contracts of the post 'open' era, has continued until this day.

In 1906 Harry Scrivener, a former Oxford blue and one of the founders of the Lawn Tennis Association in 1888, replaced Bonham Evelegh as Referee and held the office until the War. The same year Archdale Palmer, who had been a most successful club Secretary since 1899, was persuaded by Slazengers to join them as joint Managing Director. He was replaced at the All England Club by Commander George Hillyard who, besides having played cricket for Middlesex and Leicester and for the Gentlemen versus the Players, had also won many singles' and doubles' titles, several of the latter with the Dohertys. Hillyard's appointment did not end his playing days. In fact, in 1907 he won three important tournaments, the South of England, East of England and Sussex Championships and the following year, playing with Reggie Doherty, won the Olympic doubles' title at Wimbledon. During the First World War he rejoined the navy as a Lieutenant-Commander and afterwards picked up where he had left off.

Another important piece of Wimbledon history was made in 1907 through the presence of the Prince of Wales, accompanied by Princess Mary, at the finals of the singles when, for the first time, both titles went overseas. For two years, Prince George consented to become the club's first President. It was the start of a long and happy relationship between the Royal Family and the All England Club that is still as strong as ever today thanks to the frequent attendance at Wimbledon of the club's President, the Duke of Kent, usually acccompanied by the Duchess. This link with the Royal Family sprang from the fact that Commander Hillyard had served on *Britannia*. It was an extremely fortuitous connection for the regular presence of King George and Queen Mary and, later, the Kents, has done so much to add status to The Championships.

By 1913 the proceeds from The Championships were considerable – the accrued profits stood at more than £14,000. Accordingly, in that year the

LEFT: After losing to Brookes in 1914, Wilding lounges with Lord Balfour, a keen tennis fan who had been Prime Minister from 1902 to 1905. Many years later Balfour suggested to Wallis Myers, the lawn tennis correspondent of the *Daily Telegraph*, that he should follow up his wish to foster the comradeship that existed between the young players of so many nations by founding a club. Thus was sown the idea that, in 1924, became the International Lawn Tennis Club of Great Britain. There are now 26 ICs dotted around the world.

RIGHT: Mrs Lambert Chambers receiving her Olympic gold medal from Queen Alexandra in July 1908. The LTA managed the tennis events for the Olympic Committee and staged them in collaboration with the All England Club at Wimbledon. Tennis had become part of the modern Olympics in Athens in 1896 and was included in those at: Paris (1900), St Louis (1904), London (1908), Stockholm (1912), Antwerp (1920) and Paris (1924). Because of the inadequacy of the IOC's management of the tennis events in 1924, a row developed between the ILTF and the IOC that led to a withdrawal of lawn tennis from future games. However, tennis returned as one of the two demonstration events in Los Angeles in 1984 and will become a full medal sport once more in Seoul in 1988.

BELOW: The four outside courts, Nos 6, 7, 8 and 9 (behind the camera), that ran alongside the railway line were the least popular because of the noise from passing trains. So loud were they that, early in Wimbledon's history, scoreboards, operated by the ball boys, were erected on the side opposite the umpire to keep spectators informed of the score.

LEFT: Anthony Wilding's opening match in 1910 was against the British Davis Cup player Herbert Roper Barrett (far end), whom he beat in four sets. Seven matches later he won the first of his four Championships by beating the holder, Arthur Gore (known to his friends as 'Baby'), 6-4 7-5 4-6 6-2 in the Challenge Round. Neither the reserved seats on the Centre Court nor the unreserved seats on Stand D nor the open Railway Stand, which had been rebuilt in 1904 to accommodate 600 spectators, were yet filled on the opening days.

RIGHT: Reginald Doherty (right) came out of retirement in 1912 to win an Olympic gold medal with George Hillyard, who had married Wimbledon champion Blanche Bingley in 1887 and had become Secretary of the All England Club in 1907. Hillyard was an outstanding all-rounder who had played cricket for Middlesex in 1886 and later played for Lancashire. He won the scratch gold medal at the Cannes Golf Club in 1899 and 1903 and won many prizes for swimming and pigeon-shooting. A fine billiards player, a good runner with beagles and a keen motorcyclist, Hillyard was in the finest tradition of the Edwardian amateur sportsman and he had a distinguished war record.

ABOVE: The first Frenchmen to win a Wimbledon title were André Gobert (left) and Max Decugis who took the men's doubles in 1911 with a five sets' victory against Major Ritchie (Major was his christian name – he had never been in the army!) and Tony Wilding. The Frenchmen lost in the following year's Challenge Round to Charles Dixon and Herbert Roper Barrett, but they had paved the way for Suzanne Lenglen to follow after the First World War and the famous Musketeers in the 1920s.

LEFT: Arthur Gore hitting his famous forehand during the 1912 Challenge Round against Anthony Wilding. This was a repeat of their match in 1910. So was the outcome, which was a win in four sets for Wilding. In the far right-hand corner can be seen the famous pony roller.

BELOW: What every well-dressed horse used to wear 75 years ago if he was working on sports grounds.

BELOW: The ladies' tennis wear of the pre-war days was very like the day wear of fashionable spectators as this comparison shows.

The "TYLO"
COMPLETE DIVIDED COSTUME SKIRT.

PATENT 5365.

The device of this Skirt is its unique character, the division not being apparent in any way whatever.

A BOON TO LADIES INDULGING IN ATHLETIC EXERCISES,

viz.:

GOLFING, CYCLING, MOUNTAIN CLIMBING, ASTRIDE RIDING.

Especially Comfortable for MOTORISTS AND STEAMER TRAVELLERS.

PATTERNS & MEASUREMENT FORMS sent on Application.

Price from 2 Gns.

ROLLS & TYLER, CARDIFF.

Costumiers,

SOLID LAWN MOWING HORSE BOOTS
PATENT
EFFECTING A SAVING OF 50 PER CENT.

The Boots being blocked Sole and Upper in one piece, fit better, are more compact, and **much more durable** than any in use. They retain their shape, cannot cut up or mark the Lawn, having no sharp edges, and are superior in every way to the ordinary boot. The top is lined Felt to prevent chafing. **No screws to cramp the hoof.**

New Style
Price per Set of Four—HORSE 36 6, COB 31 6, PONY 26/-
The Best for Unshod Animals. Van and Cart Horse size, extra

Old Style

Of all Saddlers, and of the Inventors

M. JENKINSON
Saddlers, Harness
LONDON
ON HALL,

RIGHT: Already in 1913 the popularity of Wimbledon was causing serious problems of congestion and crowd control in Nursery Road (the greenhouses can be seen over the wall) and in Worple Road in the distance. This was the year when suffragettes tried to burn down the Centre Court. Fortunately, the plot was discovered in time.

LEFT: The pony roller that was presented to the club in 1871 by John Walsh on condition that his daughter would become a life member of the club. The offer was gratefully accepted. It was to raise money for the repair of the then broken roller that the first lawn tennis tournament had been staged in 1877. The pony roller is still used, pushed by hand, and can be seen behind the screens of the Centre Court today.

ABOVE: The last pre-war men's singles was a tragic prelude to the hostilities. The holder for the previous four years, Anthony Wilding, was beaten by his doubles' partner, Norman Brookes (left), and would never return. Within a year the popular New Zealander died in action in France, mourned by the entire tennis world. Brookes did return in 1919 but lost the Challenge Round match to fellow Australian Gerald Patterson.

LEFT: The handsome New Zealander Anthony Wilding at the 1914 meeting, always a target for autograph hunters.

SOME SCENES FROM THE 1912–14 CHAMPIONSHIPS AT WORPLE ROAD

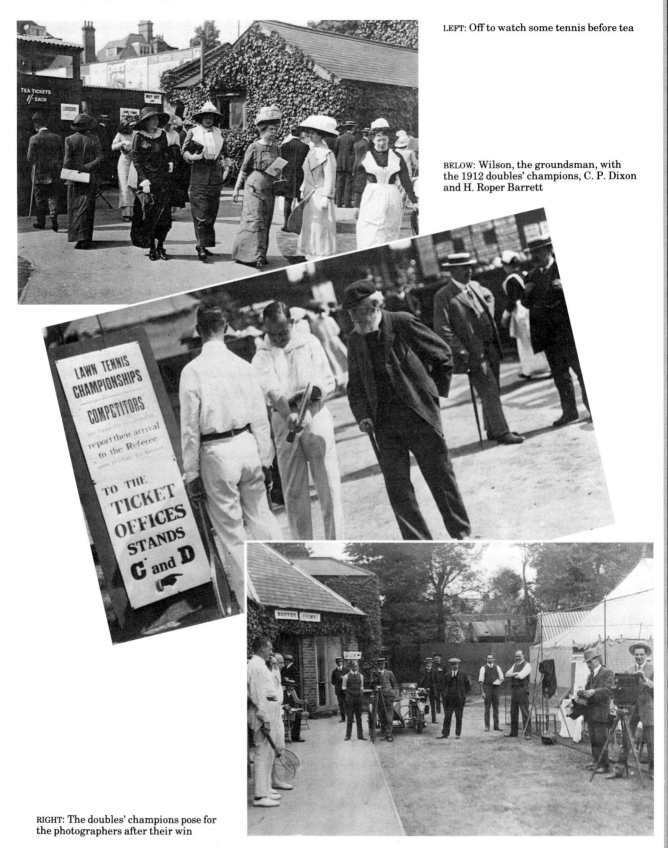

LEFT: Off to watch some tennis before tea

BELOW: Wilson, the groundsman, with the 1912 doubles' champions, C. P. Dixon and H. Roper Barrett

RIGHT: The doubles' champions pose for the photographers after their win

RIGHT: Tea-time on Court No. 1

BELOW: The refreshment tent

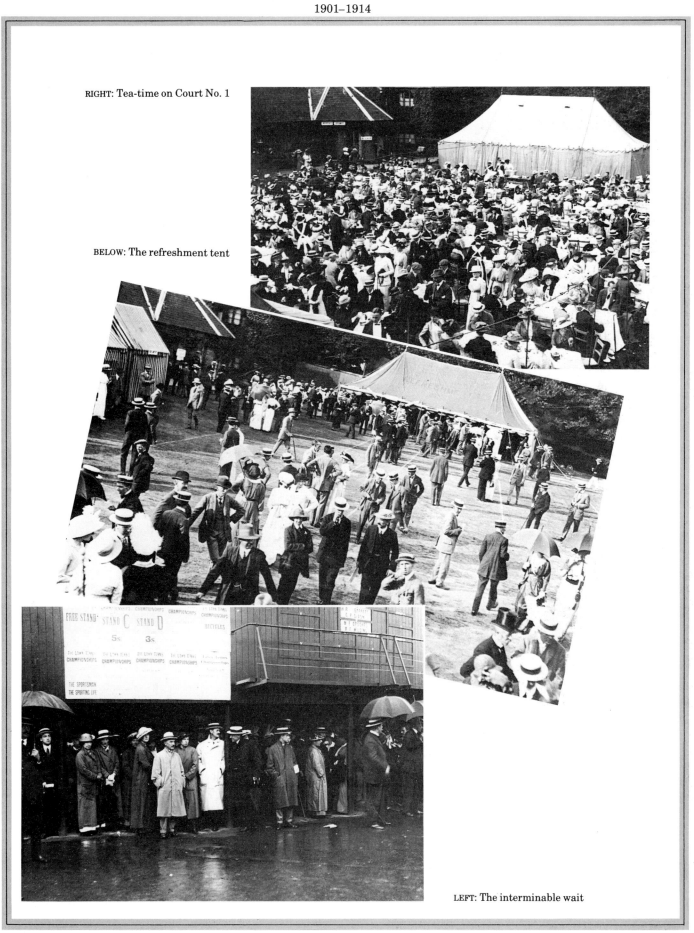

LEFT: The interminable wait

LTA were allocated a share in the surplus for the first time. The same year the title 'World Championship on Grass' was bestowed on Wimbledon by the newly-created International Lawn Tennis Federation, a happening that encouraged the committee to raise the level of the ladies' doubles and mixed doubles to Championship status (since 1899 there had been a ladies' doubles and since 1900 a mixed doubles as extra, non-Championship competitions). Curiously both events had unusual outcomes. In the ladies' doubles Mrs Sterry had to retire with a torn tendon in her leg and in the mixed doubles' final, played before the singles' Challenge Rounds, Mrs Larcombe was hit in the eye by a ball from her partner. He was the former Irish rugby captain, Australian tennis champion and scratch golfer, James Cecil Parke, who was always called J.C. Consequently, Mrs Larcombe could not challenge Mrs Lambert Chambers in the singles.

The huge crowds that year, and the next, were already making it obvious that a new home would soon have to be found if the goodwill of police and local residents, who were experiencing intolerable interruption to their normal lives through the volume of traffic and the huge queues, was to be preserved. Despite the new, larger stands the accommodation was clearly inadequate for the numbers wishing to attend the matches. However, the competitors at least were more comfortable as a result of the purchase by the club of two adjacent houses on Worple Road which were used as dressing rooms for the lady competitors and as club offices. The gardens, which backed onto the club, were used as an outdoor tented dining room for the players and, later, for the public.

Suddenly all thoughts of how these problems should be solved were dwarfed by the gruesome chain of events that unfolded throughout Europe following the assassination of Archduke Franz-Ferdinand in Sarajevo on 28 June 1914, which took place even as the concluding rounds of that year's tournament were being played. Not that the competitors were aware of the significance of that happening or of the succeeding events that threatened to end the very way of life that, despite the domestic unrest and wave of strikes in Britain, still seemed so secure as Brookes and Mrs Lambert Chambers won their titles.

But less than two months later, as the Foreign Secretary, Sir Edward Grey, watched the gas lamps in Whitehall being dimmed on the evening of 4 August, following the declaration of war on Germany, he summed up the feelings of so many when he said, 'The lights are going out all over Europe'. For Wimbledon that garden party world would never be the same again.

BIOGRAPHIES

GENTLEMEN

1901, 1908, 1909

ARTHUR GORE

Born: 2 January 1868; died: 1 December 1928

He was the most zealous competitor of all time, challenging first in 1888 and continuously until 1927, the year before he died at the age of 59.

He was not a pace maker. In taking his third singles in 1909 he was the oldest champion at 41 years 141 days old (and also the last Harrovian in that role). He played the inaugural rubber of the Davis Cup in 1900 against the American Malcolm Whitman. He served as President of the All England Club in 1911.

1902, 1903, 1904, 1905, 1906

LAURENCE DOHERTY

Born: 8 October 1875; died: 21 August 1919

Until Fred Perry he was the greatest British player and he stood out not only as a hero but as a perfect English gentleman. He had immaculate skill, never lost a Davis Cup rubber and won the US Championship in 1903.

With his elder brother Reginald (who was 'Big Do' to his 'Little Do') he won the Wimbledon doubles eight times from 1897 to 1905 and the US doubles in 1902 and 1903.

Laurence Doherty was idolised. When he died in 1919, more than a decade after he had stopped playing, *The Times* honoured him with a laudatory leader.

He and his brother went to Westminster and Cambridge. Their joint careers made for a high watermark in the British game.

1907, 1914

(SIR) NORMAN BROOKES

*Born: 14 November 1877;
died: 28 September 1968*

The father of Australian tennis and the first overseas man to win Wimbledon. His left-handed skills on the volley, where his acuteness of angle was unsurpassed, revealed new facets of the game.

He was 43 when he played his last Davis Cup match and he had six winning Challenge Rounds behind him. He was also a first-class cricketer and golfer and a rich and successful businessman. He was knighted in 1939.

1910, 1911, 1912, 1913

ANTHONY WILDING

Born: 31 October 1883; died: 9 May 1915

A Cambridge-educated New Zealander, he typified the British sporting ideal of his age. He was suave, handsome and the unbeatable amateur in all he did. He replaced the Doherty brothers as Wimbledon's idol and his popularity caused congestion at The Championships. He played side by side with Norman Brookes for what was then Australasia.

He was also a pioneer motor-cyclist and aviator. He was killed on the Western Front, having been awarded the MC.

A. W. Gore

N. E. Brookes

H. L. Doherty

A. F. Wilding

LADIES

M. E. Robb

D. K. Douglass/Lambert Chambers

M. G. Sutton

D. P. Boothby

E. Thomson/Larcombe

1902

MURIEL ROBB

Born: 13 May 1878; died: 12 February 1907

She was from Newcastle and her career was brief. Before her replayed Challenge Round victory over Charlotte Sterry on her fourth appearance at Wimbledon, this plucky competitor had completed a home countries' treble. In 1899 she had won the Welsh singles and the following year she became the Scottish and Irish champion. Her Wimbledon win was her crowning achievement and, for good measure, she also won the non-Championship doubles in 1902.

She never played again and died at the age of 28.

1903, 1904, 1906, 1910, 1911, 1913, 1914

DOROTHEA DOUGLASS/ LAMBERT CHAMBERS

Born: 3 September 1878; married: 6 April 1907 (to R. Lambert Chambers); died: 7 January 1960

Probably the greatest woman player before the First World War. A vicar's daughter from Ealing, she built an overwhelming dominance and, with luck, might have won her eighth title in 1919 when she had two match points against Suzanne Lenglen.

No woman won more singles until Helen Wills Moody. In 1926, when 48, she played in the Wightman Cup against the United States. Like others of her generation she was an all-rounder. She was All England Champion at badminton and played hockey for Middlesex.

1905, 1907

MAY SUTTON

Born: 25 September 1886; married: 11 December 1912 (to T. C. Bundy); died: 4 October 1975

A stocky Californian with a thumping forehand, she set the Edwardian tennis world agog by beating everyone on her first trip to Britain at the age of 18. She was the first overseas player to win a Wimbledon title.

She yielded the singles in 1906 to Dorothea Douglass and won it back the following year. The next time she returned was in 1929 when, at the age of 42, she reached the singles' quarter-final. She was then Mrs Bundy, her husband an American Davis Cup player.

She was born in Plymouth, Devon, the daughter of a British naval captain who later emigrated to the United States and fathered three other girls, all of whom were top-class players. She was US Champion in 1904, a Wightman Cup player in 1925.

1909

DORA BOOTHBY

Born: 2 August 1881; married: 14 Apri' 1914 (to A. C. Green); died: 22 February 1970

From Finchley, she was 27 and competing for the sixth time when she came through in the absence of the giants of her time, Charlotte Sterry and Dorothea Lambert Chambers.

She entered the record books not only by winning but by the manner of her losing. In the 1911 Challenge Round she was beaten by Mrs Lambert Chambers 6-0 6-0, the only whitewash in a Wimbledon singles' final.

1912

ETHEL THOMSON/LARCOMBE

Born: 8 June 1879; married: 15 October 1906 (to D. R. Larcombe); died: 10 August 1965

A doctor's daughter from Islington, she won ten years after her first challenge. This was after getting married and staying away for five years. She was 33.

Mrs Larcombe was a fluent stroke maker and had a round arm smash distinctive enough to be known as 'The Sledge Hammer'. Her husband became the All England Club Secretary.

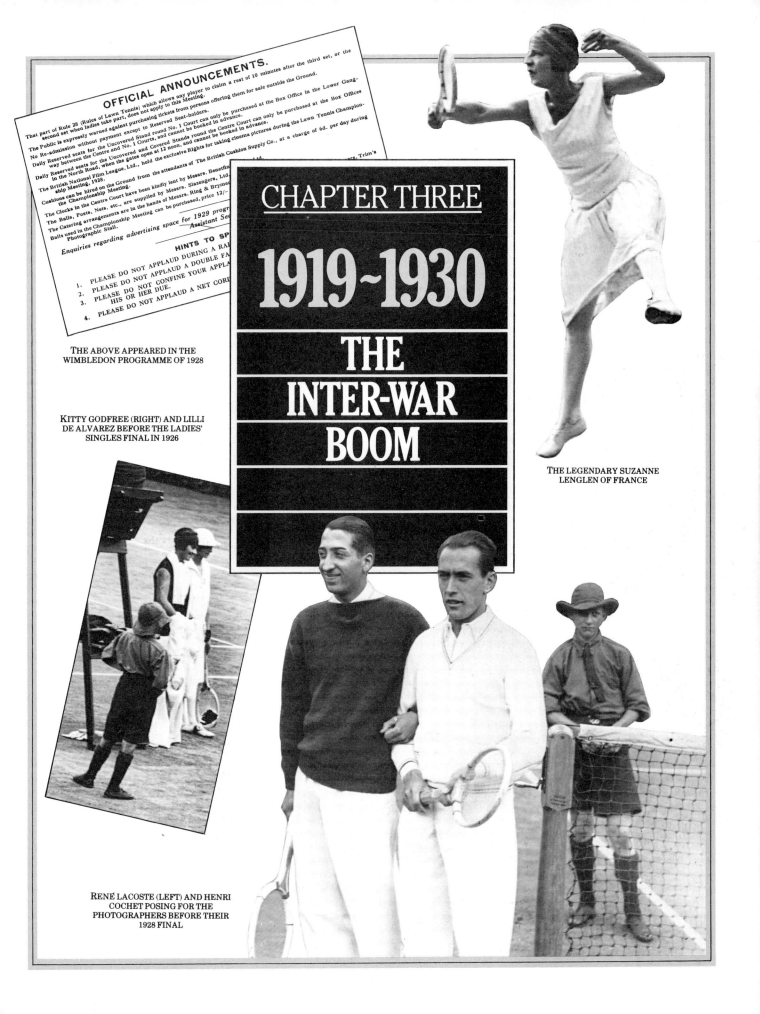

THE ABOVE APPEARED IN THE
WIMBLEDON PROGRAMME OF 1928

KITTY GODFREE (RIGHT) AND LILLI
DE ALVAREZ BEFORE THE LADIES'
SINGLES FINAL IN 1926

CHAPTER THREE

1919~1930

THE INTER-WAR BOOM

THE LEGENDARY SUZANNE
LENGLEN OF FRANCE

RENÉ LACOSTE (LEFT) AND HENRI
COCHET POSING FOR THE
PHOTOGRAPHERS BEFORE THEIR
1928 FINAL

IT was a very different world in which the first Championships after the War were held. A whole generation of European and Commonwealth manhood had been slaughtered; in Britain alone three-quarters of a million young lives had been lost and a further one and a half million were left incapacitated, either wounded or gassed. At home there was a housing shortage and food rationing had been imposed in February 1918. However, at least the War had created full employment with only 300,000 out of work by the end of 1919 as the post-war boom gathered pace, and wages had almost caught up with the cost of living. Everyone felt that they had made some sort of contribution to winning the War so that the promise of Prime Minister Lloyd George to provide a land fit for heroes created some expectations among the civilian population as well as among the servicemen – many of whom experienced the acute frustration of delay in the demobilisation process. The riots in Glasgow and Belfast, the burning down of the town hall in Luton, and the mutiny in Calais gave notice of the popular mood.

After the turmoil and tension, the suffering and sacrifice of five years of war, it was hardly surprising that attitudes had changed. Women, who had played such an important supportive role during the War, began at last to get some recognition. Emmeline Pankhurst, who had been sentenced to three years' penal servitude in 1913 for blowing up Lloyd George's house in Walton, had brought into sharp focus the gross inequalities that existed. In 1918 opinion had softened sufficiently for the Franchise Act to succeed in Parliament. It gave women over the age of 35 and all adult males the vote. Momentously, in 1919, Nancy Astor became the first woman to be elected to a seat in the House of Commons. However, in the eyes of Emmeline's daughter, Sylvia, this was only the signal for her suffragettes to intensify the battle for voting equality which was not finally won until 1928. The greater liberalisation led to a more prominent role for women at Wimbledon and a more casual attitude towards the question of what it was appropriate for women to wear on a tennis court.

Everyday women's wear, too, became much more informal with the slim, boyish lines of the 'flapper' being accentuated in simple, straight dresses and adorned with chiffon scarves and exceptionally long rows of beads while the cloche hats they wore were a reminder of the steel helmets of wartime. Social habits, too, were more relaxed as all classes took up the cigarette habit in preference to pipes and cigars.

Elsewhere there was turmoil and unrest, much of it far enough away from a war-weary Britain for the full import of the events to be immediately recognised. In Russia the Bolshevik revolution of 1917 and the murder of Czar Nicholas and his family the following year was seen only by the prophets of the political scene as of significance. For the rest – the revolt in Egypt in 1919 against British rule which had started in 1914, the riots in the Punjab where a prohibited demonstration by Sikhs near the Holy Temple was quelled by Brigadier-General Dyer in the Amritsar massacre, the suppression of a royalist rising in Portugal – all these events made only a fleeting impression. Nor did many foresee the consequences of the founding, in 1919, of the National Socialist German Workers Party by a certain Adolf Hitler.

Greater impact was caused by the decision of the Irish MPs of the Sinn Fein party in 1919 to break away and form a separate parliament, the Dail. Eamon de Valéra was elected President of the Irish Republic by the Dail in January. Immediately the extremists of the Irish Republican Army, supported by funds collected from sympathisers in the United States, began a guerilla campaign to drive the British out and to unite all Ireland. Despite the attention of some of the best brains in Britain and Eire the same apparently insoluble problem has continued to divide families and communities in that unhappy country for the last 65 years.

In 1920 the Marconi company announced they would be starting public broadcasts the following year and two years later the BBC made the first radio transmissions for entertainment in the world. The cinema was still silent with Charlie Chaplin already in his seventh year of film-making. Buchan, Conrad, Maugham and Shaw were the lions of the literary world. Eliot, Lawrence, Joyce and Huxley were the cubs, though more popular than any of them was thriller writer Edgar Wallace.

There was a feeling of optimism in the air, a belief that with the war to end all wars behind them, the ordinary people of Europe would get back to a normal life and begin to enjoy the prosperity that had always been just out of reach. One who was convinced he knew how to set the world's economies on the road to growth and prosperity was John Maynard Keynes. In 1919 *The Economic Consequences of the Peace* was published; ironically a decade later many nations' economies were heading for the biggest slump the world had ever known.

Certainly the first 12 Championships after the War represented a period of exciting growth. It had already become apparent by 1914 that the facilities at Worple Road were inadequate to cope with the demand for tickets – even with the enlarged Centre Court stands which now seated some 3,200 spectators. The events of 1919, when the police found it difficult to control the swelling crowds whose presence was making life impossible for the local residents, confirmed the view which had already been expressed before the War that a new, larger site must be found. The following year the committee, guided by the President, Wilson Fox MP, who had largely been responsible for keeping the club going during the war years, and boldly led by Hillyard, took the sensible decision to move as soon as a suitable site could be found and an architect commissioned.

A search of the nearby area was undertaken. Edwin Fuller, who was to become the head groundsman in later years, had joined the Worple Road staff as a 13-year-old in 1916 and remained there during the War with Bowyer, a senior groundsman. Together they had kept the courts in order but when hostilities had ceased Thomas Coleman, the head groundsman, returned with some of the other men and the old routines were resumed. They had all heard about the intention to move to a larger site. As Fuller remembers:

'In 1920 the Secretary asked me if I knew a piece of ground which was level, with a lake or a stream nearby. [The water was essential for watering the courts.] I did, but not in Wimbledon, and it was too far from the station. The next thing I heard of about a new ground was when the Secretary asked me to take a note to the surveyor in a field off Wimbledon Park Road, which is now known as Church Road. When I found the place it was a farm. Somewhere among the cows, horses, chickens and pigs was the man I

ABOVE: For the first time all five events went overseas in 1919. In the All-Comers' final Gerald Patterson (left) won in straight sets against Lieutenant Colonel Algy Kingscote and went on to beat the holder Norman Brookes in three sets in the first all-Australian Challenge Round. Patterson had been in dominant mood and had lost only one set throughout the tournament – that to Major Ritchie in the semi-finals. Brookes was clearly short of match practice and this defeat intensified the debate about the advisability of retaining the Challenge Round. As early as 1912 they had talked of eliminating it but the change did not come until 1922.

RIGHT: 'Big Bill' Tilden, a native of Phil-adelphia, was 27 when he won the singles in 1920, the first American to do so. Tilden was a superb analyst of the game whose books on technique, tactics and the psychology of match play were masterpieces of insight. He was also a keen, but poor, amateur actor and playwright whose every match became a dramatic event full of theatrical gestures which alienated his supporters. His 'grizzly bear' sweater became so famous that Dame Nellie Melba, who was an aunt of the Australian player Gerald Patterson, recognised him by it at a London party. In an age when the dangers were not properly understood, he was a chain smoker who would puff away cheerfully at his cigarette over a game of bridge. He drank very little. In 1922 he lost the top of a finger on his racket hand so he simply altered his grip and continued to improve. He turned professional in 1931 and died in Los Angeles 22 years later, penniless and forgotten, after spending two short periods in jail for moral offences.

ABOVE: The Challenge Round in 1919 between the holder Dorothea Lambert Chambers (above) and Suzanne Lenglen was one of Wimbledon's greatest matches. Suzanne, who was on her first visit to Wimbledon, lost only 17 games in 6 matches before the Challenge Round and then saved two match points before claiming a famous victory. The performance, too, of Mrs Lambert Chambers was heroic. Here was the first lady of British tennis at the age of 40 giving away 20 years to the greatest young player the game had ever seen and almost beating her, despite the restrictions of the obligatory stays and voluminous skirts that her trend-setting opponent was young enough to ignore.

RIGHT: Suzanne Lenglen was more than just a supreme champion who was never beaten at Wimbledon in winning six singles', six doubles' and three mixed doubles' titles between 1919 and 1926. Her liberalising impact on the role of women in society through her dress and her fame was immense. She became a model for the girls of the flapper generation. Trained from youth by her father Charles to become the greatest player in the world, she was blessed with a temperament which perfectly fitted the role.

BELOW: The Championships in 1921 were held for the last time at Worple Road where, despite improvements that enabled some 7,000 spectators to view Centre Court matches and several thousands more to sit on the new stands round Courts No. 4 and 6, the facilities had become inadequate to cope with the demand to see the new post-war stars. Already in 1920 the ground in Church Road had been purchased for the move that was planned for 1922.

LEFT: Despite the worst weather in living memory, which extended the tournament to the Wednesday of the third week, the 1922 Championships, opened by King George V, attracted record crowds to the new 13½-acre Church Road ground. The Centre Court, not yet covered in the familiar Virginia creeper, could accommodate 14,000 spectators and thousands more could circulate among the 12 outside courts that came into use that first year. Court No. 1 was not finished until 1924.

was looking for. Eventually I found him in a ditch, sitting in the shade making his plans for drainage. Those of you who know the ground as it is now may be able to visualise what it was like when Church Road was only a cart track along-side the golf course. The other side was the farm, which stretched right across to Dairymaid's Walk [he meant Dairy Walk], with a footpath where Somerset Road now is.'

Fuller was describing the last remnants of a once magnificent park. Local historian Richard Milward has traced the development of this part of Wimbledon with painstaking care. In 1744 the manor house at Wimbledon had passed from Sarah, Duchess of Marlborough, to Lord John Spencer, an ancestor of the present Princess of Wales. (In fact Princess Diana's father, the eighth Earl, is the present Lord of the Manor.) The Spencers lost the house in a fire which burnt it to the ground in 1785; it was rebuilt as Wimbledon Park House in 1799. But already the Spencers had transformed the park. Writes Milward: 'First they increased the size fourfold to over 1,200 acres with its northern wall now on the Portsmouth Road and the circumference about seven miles long. Then they employed Capability Brown, the famous landscape gardener, to lay out new drives, less formal clumps of trees and a large 30-acre lake to drain the boggy ground.'

The new drive through the park down which Fuller strode looking for the surveyor later became Church Road and Victoria Drive and swept in a gentle curve past the lake, up the rise and on over towards what is now Tibbets' Corner where there was a gatehouse. It must have been an idyllic setting. Indeed, as a resident of one of the park lodges in the 1880s remembers: 'it was very lovely; its woods, meadows and glorious trees were magnificent. One could roam about all day and never meet a single person.' The new Wimbledon Park House had been built by Earl Spencer, who was William Pitt's First Lord of the Admiralty. It was an imposing building: 'with peacocks strutting about on the lawns and the grounds beautifully kept.'

Lavinia, the second Earl's wife, was a prominent Whig hostess and famous for her breakfast parties that went on all day. In 1839, the young Queen Victoria stayed at the house when it had been leased to the Duke of Somerset by the impecunious Spencers. In 1846 the entire estate, house and park, was sold to John Beaumont, who had made his money in insurance. Inevitably, with the pressure on building land increasing as Wimbledon became a desirable residential suburb, the gradual break-up of the property was begun. Wimbledon Park House itself fell into disrepair during the Second World War and was demolished in 1949; it is now part of the playing fields of Park House Middle School. As Milward ruefully reflects: 'leaving Wimbledon without a manor house for the first time since the days of the Armada.'

In 1914, long after all the modern roads had been constructed, the council stepped in and bought the area round the lake and built the golf course, the running track and the tennis courts. Across the road lay the farm. The land which interested the club committee was in three parcels. Two of them, totalling $5\frac{3}{4}$ acres, were owned by Mrs Helen Weldon, whose father-in-law Jeremiah Weldon had purchased the land from John Beaumont in 1872 and 1875. The third, a $7\frac{1}{2}$-acre plot, belonged to Lady Lane.

To purchase these plots the club and the LTA had jointly established the All

England Lawn Tennis Ground Ltd in June 1920. Two trustees, Thomas Henderson and Thomas Hope, were empowered to pay a total of £7,870 for the two plots in March and June 1920. They were transferred to the Ground Company in September. When the formalities of purchase had been agreed the well-known architect Captain Stanley Peach was instructed to produce the designs. The venture, a joint undertaking between the All England Club and the Lawn Tennis Association costing some £140,000, was financed by the issue of £50 debenture shares, redeemable every five years, the dividend for which would be tickets for each day of The Championships. It was a brilliant idea which, as the tournament grew in popularity, became a regular source of funds for the many capital improvements which inevitably became necessary to keep the facilities up to the highest standards. The original 1920 Agreement by which the land and buildings were jointly owned by the club and the LTA was revised in 1934 and amended in 1966. Six years later it was extended to 1999. The Agreement gives the LTA the surplus from each year's tournament to run the game in Britain. The Championships themselves are run by a Joint Committee of Management comprising 12 club representatives and 6 from the LTA. It is an arrangement that has worked very well, for the continuing success of Wimbledon has resulted in increased income for the British game. With the recent dramatic increase in revenue (largely as a result of higher overseas television rights fees), the LTA in 1985–86 had a sum of £5,373,444, before tax, to spend on British tennis.

With great hopes that the vast new Centre Court structure, with accommodation for 13,500 spectators, would not become the white elephant that the Jeremiahs forecast for it, the new ground was opened by King George V on 26 June 1922. There followed the wettest two weeks in the tournament's history; it rained every day and the final shots were not struck until the third Wednesday. There were other changes in 1922, notably the abolition of the Challenge Round in singles and men's doubles, the ladies' and mixed doubles not having included a Challenge Round when they had gained Championship status in 1913. The idea had been mooted before the War but a ballot among the players had not been sufficiently in favour for the committee to make the change then. With the more democratic post-war attitude it was no surprise that by a vote of 91 to 27 the players agreed that a change was necessary. Curiously, the Davis Cup Nations' committee of the ITF did not make the same change in that competition until 1972, though partly because of the difficulty in organising a final at short notice.

Six men and three women shared the 12 singles' titles between 1919 and 1930. In that first year after the War there had been talk of restricting the men's entry to 128 because even in the last pre-war Championships there had been players in the draw whose poor standard had been an embarrassment to opponents and public alike. As it happened there were just 128 entries in 1919 so that it was not until 1920 that a method for restricting the number of entrants was imposed. The first winner after the War was Australia's mighty hitter Gerald Patterson. His compatriot, Norman Brookes, had returned to defend his five-year-old title but he was not the same man who had cut down Tony Wilding in 1914. Patterson's heavy serving and powerful backcourt hitting won the day and was to succeed again in 1922, the

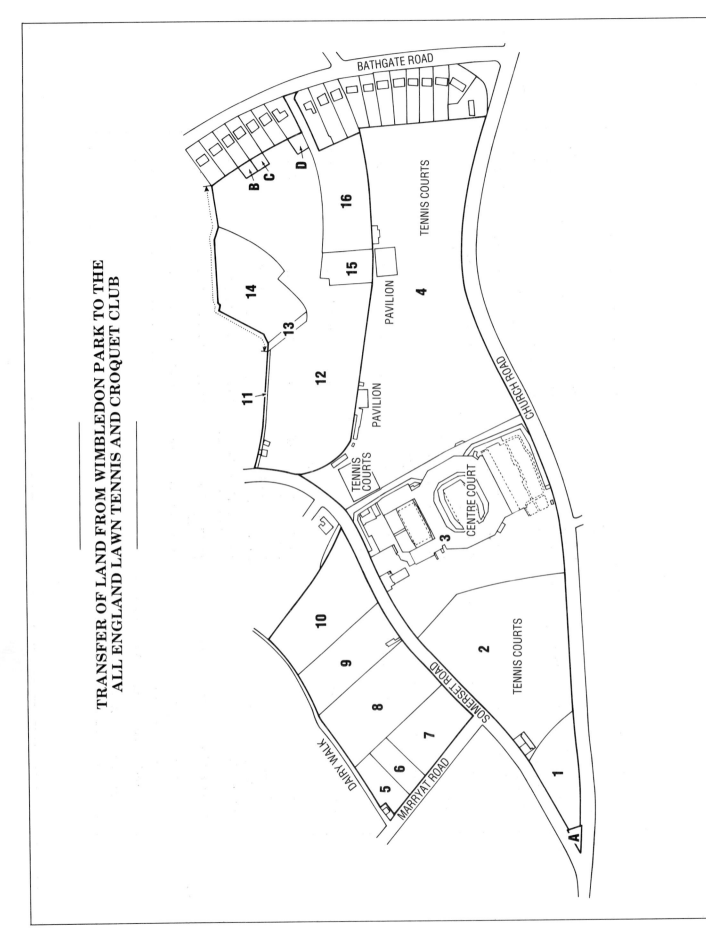

TRANSFER OF LAND FROM WIMBLEDON PARK TO THE ALL ENGLAND LAWN TENNIS AND CROQUET CLUB

Transfer of Land from Wimbledon Park to the All England Lawn Tennis and Croquet Club

DATE	AREA	FROM	TO	PRICE £
12 February 1846	Whole of Wimbledon Park	Lord Spencer	Mr Beaumont	46,000
18 December 1872	Area 1	John Augustus Beaumont	Jeremiah Weldon	750
19 November 1875	Area 2	John Augustus Beaumont	Jeremiah Weldon	2,764
23 March 1920	Area 3 (7½ acres)	Dame Augusta Sara Lane, Carlton Hall, Saxmundham	Thomas Henderson and Thomas O. Hope	4,500
21 June 1920	Areas 1 and 2 (5¾ acres)	Mrs Helen Maria Weldon (Widow of Frederick Weldon)	Thomas Henderson and Thomas O. Hope	3,370
23 June 1920		All England Lawn Tennis Ground Ltd is incorporated		
6 September 1920	Areas 1, 2, 3	Transferred to All England Lawn Tennis Ground Ltd		
8 March 1928	Areas 6, 7, 8, 9 and 10	Leo Victor Kenward of Kenmore and Arthur H. Riseley of Brackley, Weybridge, Surrey	All England Motor Park Ltd	8,100
20 March 1929	Area 5	Mrs Bessie Matilda Patterson of Oak Cottage, Burghley Road	All England Motor Park Ltd	540
2 June 1930	Area 12	Robert Dashwood, through Dashwood Partners Ltd	All England Motor Park Ltd	10,500
11 November 1930	Area 15	Robert Dashwood	All England Motor Park Ltd	—
5 May 1932	Area 16	Robert Dashwood	All England Motor Park Ltd	2,826
25 May 1937	Area 11	Mrs Amelia Wilson Cawthra of Oakfield, Somerset Road	All England Motor Park Ltd	100
11 January 1951	Areas 13 and 14	Mrs Amelia Cawthra (Deceased)	All England Motor Park Ltd	4,000
February 1967	Area 4	John Barker and Company Ltd	All England Lawn Tennis Ground Ltd	150,000

Land Sold by the All England Lawn Tennis and Croquet Club

20 September 1950	Areas A, B, C, D	

73

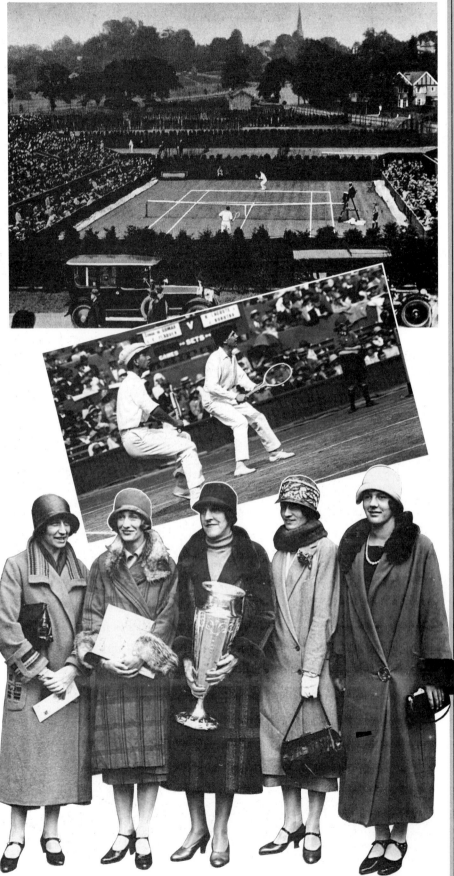

TOP LEFT: James O. Anderson, known popularly as 'Jo', came to Europe in 1922 with the Australian Davis Cup team and won the doubles at Wimbledon with Randolph Lycett after falling in the singles' semi-finals to his fellow countryman Gerald Patterson, the eventual winner. He also became the Australian champion that same year when he beat Patterson in the final.

TOP RIGHT: Looking south over Court No. 2, which was brought into play in 1923, and has been the scene of many dramatic upsets over the years. At this stage there was only one row of courts beyond. VIPs were driven into the ground in style but there was not yet a car service for all competitors. Somerset Road forms the boundary of the club on the right and, to the left, Church Road sweeps past the club and up to Wimbledon village, ending opposite the Dog and Fox Hotel. The spire of St Mary's church sits atop the hill with its crowning weather vane. It is said that if you can see the cockerel it will be fine, if you can't, it will rain.

CENTRE: René Lacoste (left), christened 'Monsieur Le Crocodile', was still 18 when he played in the 1923 doubles with Jean Borotra, the 'Bounding Basque'.

RIGHT: A victorious return home for the British Wightman Cup girls in 1925 who had just retained the trophy by beating the Americans 4-3 at Forest Hills. In the first meeting two years earlier the USA had won 7-0 at Forest Hills and in 1924 at Wimbledon the British girls had won 6-1. From left to right: Kitty McKane, Evelyn Colyer, Dorothea Lambert Chambers (Captain), Ermyntrude Harvey and Joan Fry.

RIGHT: Spectators on Court No. 2 for a first-round ladies' singles in 1925 included Elizabeth Ryan (second row, hatless) as Madame Billout defeated Mrs Lycett 4-6 6-3 11-9. The woodwork for the stands was taken from the old Centre Court at Worple Road.

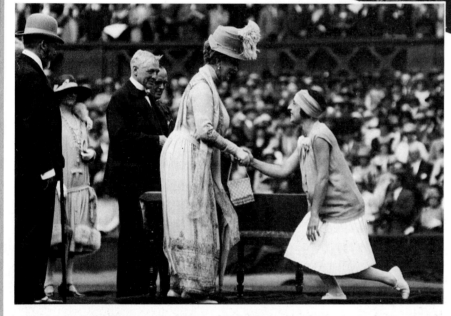

LEFT AND BELOW: The Championships of 1926 were celebrated as the Jubilee meeting. To mark the occasion King George and Queen Mary presented commemorative medals to 34 of the surviving champions on the Centre Court on the opening day. When Suzanne curtsied to the Queen, watched by the club's President Sir Herbert Wilberforce, little did anyone realise that Wimbledon's favourite champion would depart from Wimbledon for ever at the end of the week.

first year when the champions had to play through; however, Bill Tilden, the winner in 1920 and 1921, had not returned to attempt that feat.

Of all the men, the American Tilden created the most impact. It was entirely appropriate that in 1920, the year after Alcock and Brown had blazed an American trans-Atlantic trail by making the first non-stop flight from Newfoundland to Ireland, Tilden should have become the first American to win the title. In 1921 he defended narrowly, but successfully, in Wimbledon's last Challenge Round. It was a curious match, full of psychological overtones, against the young good-looking South African, Brian 'Babe' Norton, who had become his protégé. Not match tight after waiting for two weeks while the All-Comers produced a winner, Tilden lost the first two sets and was booed as he opened the third with a campaign of drop shots. Embarrassed by this treatment of the man he most admired, Norton threw the next two sets amid further unrest in the stands. Many thought the young man could not bring himself to beat Tilden. But, leading 5-4 in the final set, he held two consecutive match points. On the first Tilden hit a drive that he thought would be out and advanced to the net to shake hands. The ball landed on the line and Norton's attempted pass failed. An ace brought deuce and a few points later Tilden had claimed an improbable 4-6 2-6 6-1 6-0 7-5 victory.

For the next five years Tilden remained in the United States where he was building a formidable reputation. During this period 'Big Bill' was virtually unbeatable with a total of seven US National titles from ten finals in twelve years, five of them against his great rival from California, 'Little Bill' Johnston. In 1930 the king of tennis at last overcame

the French 'hoodoo' that had brought him Wimbledon defeats at the hands of Cochet twice and Lacoste once at the semi-final stage in 1927, 1928 and 1929. By claiming singles' titles nine years apart Tilden was setting a record that has not been equalled to this day.

But he did more than that. Tilden introduced a new element of majestic technical authority in every department of the game, together with a commanding presence on the court, that ushered in a new era. Here was the complete player – tall, athletic, capable of every shot in the game, a master of spin, a match player of unsurpassed skill and judgement, with a power of concentration that imposed his personality on an opponent to an intimidating degree – in short, a tennis superman. Every match he played brought a touch of theatre to the court for he was also an amateur actor of modest skill; albeit quietly, the game was experiencing its first taste of 'showbiz'.

In 1931 Tilden turned professional and for a time played exhibition tennis before becoming a teaching pro in California giving lessons to his friends and acquaintances of the film colony. It was infinitely sad that this superb sportsman should have ended his days as a social outcast. A sickly child, he had been brought up in Philadelphia in a claustrophobic female environment that affected his entire personality. A homosexual in an age when such matters could not be discussed, let alone tolerated, he spent two short periods in jail towards the end of his life for offences against teenage boys and finished his days ignored by the public, shunned by all except one or two close friends, and virtually penniless.

In 1923 William Johnston, for so much of his life in the shadow of 'Big Bill' Tilden (after beating him in the final of the US National Championships in 1919 he lost in five subsequent finals), at last had another hour of glory. In the first of eight all-American finals at Wimbledon he beat Frank Hunter in straight sets.

The following year, 1924, marked the beginning of an extraordinary run of French ascendancy that coincided with the introduction of a modified form of seeding. It was decided that nations could nominate up to four players who would be drawn in separate quarters. This was of singular benefit to René Lacoste, Henri Cochet, Jean Borotra and Jacques 'Toto' Brugnon, the doubles' expert among the 'Four Musketeers', as this talented quartet inevitably became known. For the next six years there was a French champion at Wimbledon: Borotra in 1924 and 1926, Lacoste in 1925 and 1928, Cochet in 1927 and 1929. In Paris there was also a Musketeer's name on the honours board for the first eight years of international competition in the French Championship from 1925 to 1932. Even before that, when the tournament had been a national competition, Cochet in 1922 and Borotra in 1924 had won the title. In the United States, however, Lacoste was successful only twice (1926 and 1927), Cochet only once (1928) and Borotra not at all.

The intense national pride and close camaraderie that existed among these four champions, echoing the cry of Alexandre Dumas' famous heroes 'All for one, one for all', brought a new dimension both to The Championships and to the Davis Cup, which competition they won for France six years in a row, from 1927 to 1932. Lacoste's rock-like consistency from the baseline (it is said he wore out a practice wall at home), Borotra's energetic leaps around the court (and into the lap of any pretty girl in the front row) and Cochet's gossamer touch on the half-volley and his effortless grace delighted an ever more discerning gallery in the 1920s and intensified interest in the game.

Of them all Borotra created the most impact at Wimbledon. His fellow Frenchmen became tired of hearing the often-repeated question, 'When is Borotra playing?' But his charm, his liveliness, his sense of fun and his great respect for the traditions of the game made him the most charismatic player of the decade, and the most popular. Dedicated to the amateur ideals of work and play, he was instrumental in launching the International Club of France in 1929 at the invitation of the International Lawn Tennis Club of Great Britain. The founding club had been created in 1924 by A. Wallis Myers, the lawn tennis correspondent of the *Daily Telegraph* and a useful player himself, following a conversation he had had with Lord Balfour about fostering good fellowship among the young tennis players of the world.

Jean played in the inaugural match between the two clubs at London's Queen's Club in 1929 and beat Tilden who was a guest for the British club. Every year since, apart from the wartime break, the two clubs have met twice, in Paris in May and in London in the autumn. Remarkably, in 1985 at the age of 78, Jean played for the hundredth time in this friendly but keen encounter. It was a marvellously nostalgic event which was staged both at Queen's Club and the All England Club and involved over 100 old friends and their wives. The fact that the home club was victorious hardly mattered for it was the spirit of camaraderie engendered by the occasion that will be remembered. That same spirit is now shared by 26 clubs around the world, each with their familiar grey ties containing pink stripes of varying number and width.

ABOVE LEFT AND RIGHT: 1926 was also a Royal occasion in another sense for the Duke of York (later George VI) competed in the doubles with his equerry, Wing Commander Louis Greig (later Sir Louis) who, in 1937, took over from Sir Herbert Wilberforce as Chairman of the club. This is the only time that a member of the Royal Family has competed at Wimbledon. The Duchess of York (now the Queen Mother) was there to watch the match on Court No. 2 as hopes of Royal progress were dashed by the veteran pair Arthur Gore and Herbert Roper Barrett who were both in their fifties and had last won the title 19 years earlier. They won straightforwardly, 6-1 6-3 6-2.

ABOVE LEFT: Suzanne Lenglen leaving her London hotel with her doubles' partner, Diddie Vlasto, who broke the news to Suzanne late on Wednesday morning that the Referee, Frank Burrow, had scheduled her to play a singles' match before their vital doubles against Suzanne's usual partner, Elizabeth Ryan and Mary K. Browne – a programme that Suzanne had particularly asked to be avoided. She attempted, in vain, to telephone the Referee and asked team-mate 'Toto' Brugnon to pass on the message on her behalf.

RIGHT: When Suzanne arrived at the club at 3.30 p.m. to find that she had indeed been scheduled to play a singles before the doubles, she refused to listen to all entreaties to play. Accordingly, she left again with her unopened tennis case on the roof of the car.

ABOVE: Instead of scratching Suzanne as they were entitled to do, the Committee rescheduled the doubles' match for Thursday. After a tremendous battle Miss Browne and Miss Ryan saved two match points and finally won 3-6 9-7 6-2. Following an unfriendly welcome in a first-round mixed doubles on the Saturday, Suzanne, tired and emotionally drained, withdrew from the singles and mixed and returned to Paris. She never hit another ball at Wimbledon.

RIGHT: By 1927 the club had made far-sighted provision for parking in the fields to the west of Somerset Road (bottom of picture). But, already, the golf club on the other side of Church Road was co-operating by making overflow space available.

LEFT: The oldest of the Four Musketeers of France was Jacques 'Toto' Brugnon (left), the doubles expert, who is playing here with the gifted Henri Cochet. When he retired Brugnon worked briefly for MGM in Hollywood and delighted in showing visiting players over the studios. Cochet was born in Lyons and learned to play indoors where the even bounce helped him to perfect his half-volleys that became a feature of his effortless game. He turned professional in 1933 but was reinstated as an amateur after the Second World War.

BELOW: In 1930 Slazengers introduced a temperature-controlled box on the Centre and No. 1 Courts to keep the balls at a constant 68 degrees Fahrenheit – the temperature at which all tennis balls must be tested for compression and rebound according to the International Tennis Federation's Rules of Tennis. Many people, including the cartoonist apparently, mistakenly believed that it was a refrigerator.

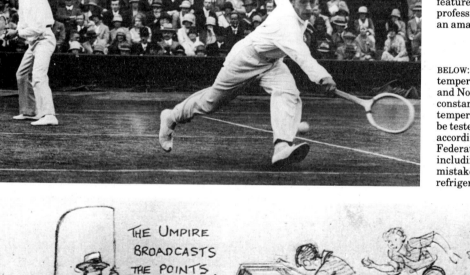

THE UMPIRE BROADCASTS THE POINTS.

VINES v. AOKI GALVANIZED BY THE FAST PLAY, THE BALL-BOYS DASH TO THE ICE-BOX FOR NEW BALLS AND DRINKS BETWEEN SETS –

Cochet's win in 1927 was remarkable for he lost the first two sets in his last three matches. In the semi-final against Tilden, who had not appeared at Wimbledon since his victory in 1921, the Frenchman somehow escaped from 2-6 4-6 1-5 to win the third set 7-5 and the last two 6-4 6-3. It was a complete mystery how so great a player as Tilden could have let his man escape. He had no satisfactory explanation himself afterwards. Then, in the final against Borotra, the casual Cochet saved six match points in the last set before winning it 7-5. This was surely Wimbledon's most perilous success.

Only when Tilden triumphed again at Wimbledon in 1930 was the French reign there brought to an end. For the American, who by now was 37 and had won 7 US Championships and 13 consecutive Challenge Round singles in the Davis Cup, this last Wimbledon victory was a triumphant statement of his ability. No man or woman has achieved what he did that year in winning his last title ten years after his first. Yet, in another era, the ageless Ken Rosewall came within two matches of doubling that record. Had the little Australian won the first and last of his four finals in 1954 and 1974 he would have had titles 20 years apart – an awesome thought.

Even more important than the skill of these fine men players to the development not just of Wimbledon but of the game at large, was the extraordinary impact of Suzanne Lenglen. Even before the War her prodigious achievements in France at a tender age, accompanied and directed always by 'Papa' who had trained her from the beginning, had led to speculation that she might challenge in 1914. This was not to be. When she did arrive in 1919 at the age of 20 it was with the sort of reputation that many players would have found a burden. Everyone, it seemed, knew that she had won the title of World Champion on hard courts at the age of 15 at St Cloud and the other players at least knew that in this year's early Riviera tournaments Suzanne had not even dropped a set. However, fame never intimidated Suzanne; she had been brought up to believe she could become the best player the world had ever seen and her temperament perfectly fitted the role.

She caused a sensation not only for her outstanding brand of free-flowing, graceful tennis but also for her daring decision to discard the stays that were *de rigueur* among the women players of the day. Everybody loved the elegant, shorter-than-normal, diaphanous dresses and the colourful bandeaux that immediately became the fashion. The leading couturiers would make day dresses following the style of the garments that Suzanne had made so popular on the court.

This was Suzanne's first experience of grass courts, which was a surface well suited to her beautifully complete game with its fluid, easy court coverage that reminded everyone who saw her play of the movements of a ballet dancer. As a child she had been sent to ballet classes, which was all part of Papa Lenglen's meticulous attention to detail. The same attention was paid to ball control. For hours she would aim at the pocket handkerchiefs that Papa would place in the corners as targets during her practice sessions with the local young men. The exquisite timing that transmitted pace without effort was entirely natural but the disciplined self control, instilled from her youth by her mesmeric father, Charles, had been acquired.

Suzanne's dramatic victory in the Challenge Round that first year against the 40-year-old defending champion Dorothea Lambert Chambers, who had won the title a record seven times and was giving away a full 20 years to her agile opponent, was the stuff of legend. Twice Suzanne was match point down and twice she survived – encouraged as always by Papa who, as the match boiled towards its climax, threw her sugar lumps soaked in brandy to boost her dwindling reserves of energy. Her ultimate departure from Wimbledon in 1926 under a cloud of misunderstanding after she had won the singles' title six times in seven years (illness had forced her retirement at the semi-final stage in 1924) was disastrous for the game, for there has never been a more dominating champion or a better loved personality at Wimbledon than Suzanne.

The new Secretary at Wimbledon, Major Dudley Larcombe who had taken up office in 1925, had not followed the practice of his predecessor, Commander George Hillyard, of informing Suzanne of the times of her matches on the morrow before she left the club each day. Accordingly, she was unaware that, after asking the Referee, Frank Burrow, to schedule only her doubles on the Wednesday, he had added her second round singles' match against Mrs Evelyn Dewhurst to the programme. The doubles was a potentially difficult and sensitive match with her French partner, Diddie Vlasto, against her former partner Elizabeth Ryan and Mary K. Brown whom Suzanne had struggled to beat in the first round of the singles. It was sensitive because the French Federation had used their control of the expense money available virtually to force the two French girls to play together, thus depriving Suzanne and Elizabeth, who had never lost a tournament match, of the opportunity to add to their already formidable tally of six Wimbledon doubles' titles.

Suzanne, who never read the papers during Wimbledon, was not aware of the change until Diddie Vlasto told her late in the morning and Suzanne's efforts to contact the Referee failed. Her non-appearance is supposed to have offended Queen Mary who had arrived at 3.00 p.m. to see Suzanne play Mrs Dewhurst – a supposition later denied by Buckingham Palace.

At all events Suzanne could not be persuaded to play when she did arrive late at the club, distraught and besieged by newsmen – despite the personal intervention of Jean Borotra, the French team captain, who went into the Lady Champions' dressing room with a towel over his head. Although she was not scratched from either singles or doubles, Suzanne, having lost the postponed doubles and having beaten Mrs Dewhurst, was booed on the Centre Court for the only time in her life when she went to play a mixed doubles with Borotra on the Saturday. The following Monday she scratched from both the singles and the mixed and returned to Paris without visiting Buckingham Palace. The honour of being presented at Court, for which Suzanne had had a dress specially made, was maliciously prevented by the wife of the French Ambassador. She had informed Suzanne that, as a result of her behaviour at Wimbledon, she would not be welcomed at Court, which was a total fabrication. Years later Queen Mary denied that she had ever been offended.

Shortly afterwards Suzanne turned professional and was lost to Wimbledon for ever. She was lost to the world on 4 July 1938 when, after a period of failing health, she died of leukaemia in Paris, mourned by the entire tennis world.

Suzanne's astonishing Wimbledon

record would surely have been enhanced had she continued to compete; as it was she won 91 of the 94 matches she contested in winning 15 titles (six singles, six doubles, all with Elizabeth Ryan, and three mixed); the only matches she lost were two mixed doubles and one ladies' doubles. Furthermore, apart from the notorious retirement against Molla Mallory, the American number one, in 1921 on her only visit to Forest Hills, Suzanne was never beaten in singles again after losing to Marguerite Broquedis in April 1914 when she was still just 14. She won her only meeting with the other great star of the period, Helen Wills, in a challenge match played at the Carlton Hotel in Cannes in 1926.

Amid all the ballyhoo of a heavyweight championship fight, Suzanne beat Helen Wills 6-3 8-6 after surviving a nerve-wracking misunderstanding in the closing stages. The umpire, Commander George Hillyard the former Wimbledon Secretary, having called out 'Game, set and match to Mademoiselle Lenglen' proceeded to summon the players back to action because, he discovered, Helen's final shot had been called out by someone in the crowd and not by the British linesman, Lord Charles Hope, who knew the ball had been in. In the circumstances Suzanne's eventual victory ten minutes later after losing her serve on the resumption was one of the most courageous of her entire career. Never before or since, has there been a record like it.

It was particularly sad that the year of Suzanne's controversial departure was also the year of the Jubilee celebrations to mark 50 years of tennis at Wimbledon. With a military band playing and all the competitors assembled on the Centre Court, men at one end and ladies at the other, King George and Queen Mary presented commemorative gold medals to the 34 past champions, lined up down the sides of the court, who had accepted the club's invitation to attend. Those present included 71-year-old Frank Hadow, the second champion in 1878, and Maud Watson, now 63, the first ladies' champion in 1884, plus eight more of the twelve lady champions. The irrepressible Frenchman Jean Borotra, flying over from Paris via Croydon Airport, nearly missed the parade. Changing into his tennis flannels in the taxi he made a typically dramatic entrance at the very last moment – just in time to be described by Commander Hillyard, now the Director of The Championships, as he stood in front of the Royal Box announcing each of the champions in turn.

To mark the occasion the British champion Kitty Godfree, formerly McKane, and the Dutch champion, Kia Bouman, who was deputising for Lilli de Alvarez of Spain, played an exhibition set against the ever-popular Suzanne and the great American doubles' expert Elizabeth Ryan, who had won their sixth Wimbledon title together the previous year. When the champions were beaten 8-6 (their only loss at Wimbledon and, incidentally, the last time they ever played together), to tumultuous applause for a British win, a friend of Kitty's husband Leslie Godfree (they had married secretly in Kimberley on 18 January during an LTA team tour of South Africa) turned to him in the members' stand and said, 'That could spell trouble ... you know she hates to lose'. How sad that this innocent remark should have proved to be so prophetically accurate.

As a result of the Lenglen tragedy Dudley Larcombe decided to invite 17-year-old Teddy Tinling, who for two years had been associated with the

Riviera tournaments as an umpire for Suzanne's matches and as George Simond's Assistant Referee, to join The Championship staff as the players' call-boy. It was a role he filled with distinction until the storm raised in 1949 over the lace-edged panties he designed for Gussie Moran to wear beneath a stunning Tinling dress. By then Teddy had become the game's foremost fashion designer. Two years earlier there had also been a mistaken belief that he had deliberately encouraged the ladies' finalists, Louise Brough and Margaret du Pont, to carry their bouquets on to court against the wishes of the Chairman, Sir Louis Greig. Before the War, the flowers had traditionally been left in the dressing room, but in 1947 the girls had decided themselves to do what Louise and Pauline Betz had done the previous year, which added a colourful touch that most people had seemed to enjoy. After much soul-searching Teddy decided to resign from the job. Ironically, a deteriorating situation with the players in 1982 would persuade the Committee to invite Ted back to do the same job at the age of 72.

The two other great champions of this period were an athletic Englishwoman and an American lady of statuesque beauty and incomparable match-winning skills. Kitty McKane and Helen Wills met in the final of 1924, the year Suzanne was forced through illness to scratch to Kitty in the semi-finals. It was the American girl's first visit. She was 18, came from San Francisco and was the US National Champion; her reputation for relentless accuracy was already legendary and most experts expected her to beat once more a girl whom she had defeated twice in the United States the previous season. Leading by a set and 4-1, and with a point for 5-1, Helen seemed certain to capture her first Wimbledon title. However, Kitty, keeping the pressure on her opponent and attacking for all she was worth, staged one of her now famous recoveries. Amid mounting excitement from a packed gallery that included Queen Mary, Kitty came back to win the second set 6-4 and then outlasted a tiring opponent to win the decider by the same margin. This first British success since Mrs Lambert Chambers' win in 1914 was immensely popular with the home crowd. Most of them stayed on to see Kitty win the mixed title as well with Brian Gilbert after losing in the doubles' final with Mrs Covell against Helen and Mrs Wightman, the donor of the cup for annual competition between the ladies of the United States and Britain.

Kitty had been a member of the British team that had travelled to the States on the SS *Franconia* the previous year to compete in the inaugural Wightman Cup match. It was the first event to be played at the new Forest Hills stadium in New York and the start had been delayed by one day for the funeral of President Harding. Kitty had had the honour of playing in the first rubber against Helen Wills and had fought well before losing this first encounter against the American teenager 6-2 7-5. She had lost to Helen again in the US Championships but did have the distinction of becoming, with Phyllis Covell, the first overseas winners of the US doubles' title.

Kitty had already established a reputation as a fine athlete in another field. In the winter of 1919–20 she had won the All England badminton championships after only a short acquaintance with the game. It was a title she won on three more occasions, the last being during the winter of 1923–24 when she won the two doubles' events as well for good measure.

Long before her first Wimbledon win, at the Olympic Games of 1920 in Antwerp, Kitty had scored the first of only two successes she ever achieved against Suzanne – both in doubles. In the semifinal, playing with Mrs Geraldine Beamish, she had beaten Suzanne and Mademoiselle d'Ayen and had gone on to win a gold medal. Later she had won a silver in the mixed playing with the famous sporting all-rounder Max Woosnam, and a bronze in the singles by winning the play-off for third and fourth places. Her other win against Suzanne, in partnership with Geraldine Beamish, was scored in Paris in the finals of the 1923 World Hard Court Championships when the French star was playing with Germaine Golding.

Although tennis had been part of the Olympic Games since they were revived in 1896 in Athens, the 1924 Olympics in Paris were the last in which it was included and resulted in a clean sweep for the United States. Vincent Richards and Helen Wills Moody won the singles against Henri Cochet and Diddie Vlasto respectively, Richards and Frank Hunter beat Cochet and 'Toto' Brugnon in the men's doubles, Hazel Wightman and Helen Wills took the ladies' doubles against Kitty Godfree and Phyllis Covell, and in the mixed R. N. Williams and Hazel Wightman beat fellow Americans Richards and Marion Jessup. Kitty Godfree took the bronze medal in the singles as well as the silver in the ladies' doubles.

The ILTF, dissatisfied about the organisation of the tennis events, sought to impose conditions on the IOC for future Games. Following a row between the Belgian spokesman of the ILTF, Paul de Borman, and fellow-Belgian Count Baillet-Latour, President of the IOC, the ILTF withdrew. Sixty years later the way was clear for a return. After six years of negotiations tennis was finally reinstated as a demonstration event at the Los Angeles Olympics of 1984 and would become a full sport at the Seoul Games of 1988.

In 1926 Mrs Godfree was the beneficiary of Suzanne's retirement; she won a second title that year against the pretty Spanish champion Lilli de Alvarez. Kitty also set a Wimbledon record that same year by winning the mixed doubles' title with her husband to become the only married pair to have achieved the feat.

Helen Wills, with two more US titles to her name, returned in 1927 a much more complete player. For four years she was invincible as she swept majestically to four successive titles for the loss of only a single set, that in her very first match in 1927 against Miss Gwen Sterry, the daughter of the former champion Charlotte Sterry. In due course she would add four more singles' titles, the last in 1938, to remain unbeaten since that first defeat in 1924 and the holder of Wimbledon's most exclusive record – eight singles' wins in nine challenges spanning eighteen years.

Thanks to Suzanne, Kitty and Helen, and to 'Big Bill' and the Frenchmen, the Centre Court at Wimbledon had been transformed into the world's most famous sporting arena. Since 1927 the BBC radio broadcasts had been beamed around the world. The world's press were printing millions of words about the heroic deeds of the new star players. The newsreels were projecting millions of feet of film in cinemas around the globe to an awakening audience, many of whom were encouraged to take up the game for the first time. In Britain, as the 1930s dawned, there was a yearning to produce a new male champion. He was not long in coming.

BIOGRAPHIES
GENTLEMEN

1919, 1922

GERALD PATTERSON

Born: 17 December 1895; died: 13 June 1967

An Australian with a 'big game', he dominated in the immediate post-First World War period. He beat his fellow Australian Norman Brookes to win the 1919 Challenge Round at Worple Road but three years later won the first of the Church Road meetings when events were 'played through' for the first time.

Like Brookes he was wealthy and later prominent in the administration of the Australian game.

1920, 1921, 1930

WILLIAM TILDEN

Born: 10 February 1893; died: 5 June 1953

A son of Philadelphia, he is often claimed as the greatest of all time, the master of every shot, with a cannonball service and great intelligence. 'Big Bill' was the first American to win Wimbledon men's singles and it was his first major triumph.

He won his own title seven times and for seven years brought US success in the Davis Cup. His 1930 Wimbledon victory was attained when he was a striking 37 years old.

His flair and personality made the professional game famous after he left the amateur ranks in 1930. In the strict moral climate of his time he suffered as a homosexual. He was far from affluent when he died, but he is remembered as one of the immortals.

1923

WILLIAM JOHNSTON

Born: 2 November 1894; died: 1 May 1946

A Californian, this Davis Cup colleague of Tilden was nicknamed 'Little Bill' and was destined to stand number two behind the master. His singles' triumph was against Frank Hunter, in the first all-American final. He was losing finalist to Tilden in the US Championship five times in six years.

1924, 1926

JEAN BOROTRA

Born: 13 August 1898

'The Bounding Basque' stands as the keenest and most enduring competitor of all time. He was still an active player at the age of 88. His first Wimbledon challenge was in 1922 and he played his 221st match in 1964, continuing in the veteran's events until his 238th in 1977.

Borotra's bubbling charisma captivated Centre Court crowds. His acrobatic volleying was spectacular; he was six times within a point of winning for the third time in 1927. Because he had been French Minister of Sport under the Vichy Government he was asked not to enter The Championships in the immediate post-war meeting, though he had finished the War as a prisoner of the Gestapo.

He was one of the 'Four Musketeers' from France who epitomised the Golden Age of the game.

1925, 1928

RENÉ LACOSTE

Born: 2 July 1904

The quiet intellectual of the 'Four Musketeers', he was a baseliner who viewed the game as one of chess. He maintained a notebook in which the strengths and weaknesses of players were recorded.

He was Tilden's *bête noire* and his defeat of the maestro was the key that unlocked the French success in the Davis Cup in 1927.

Lacoste retired because of ill health in 1929, having won Wimbledon twice, the US title twice and the French title three times, and established the highly successful sports clothing business. His daughter, Catharine, became a world-class golfer.

G. L. Patterson

W. T. Tilden

W. M. Johnston

J. Borotra

J. R. Lacoste

H. J. Cochet

1927, 1929

HENRI COCHET

Born: 14 December 1901

Probably the finest half-volleyer of all time and a touch genius who seemed never to be trying.

His first Wimbledon victory is unlikely to be surpassed in its brinkmanship. He lost the first two sets in the quarter-final against Frank Hunter, the first two sets in the semi-final against Tilden and also the first two sets in the final against Borotra who had six match points. Cochet was the third of the 'Musketeers'.

He became a professional in 1933 but was reinstated nine years later.

LADIES

S. Lenglen

K. McKane/Godfree

H. Wills/Moody

1919, 1920, 1921, 1922, 1923, 1925

SUZANNE LENGLEN

Born: 24 May 1899; died: 4 July 1938

Arguably the greatest woman player of all time, she was from Compiègne in France and taught by her father, a professional cyclist. She won the World Hard Court Championship in 1914 at the age of only 15.

Playing at Wimbledon for the first time in 1919 she won after a memorable Challenge Round against Dorothea Lambert Chambers in which she saved two match points. She was never subsequently beaten save for a controversial trip to the United States in 1921 when, sick, she retired after losing the first set to Molla Mallory.

Her last Wimbledon success in 1925 was after dropping only five games in ten matches, this after winning her French title for the total loss of only four games. She won love sets galore and eight tournaments without yielding any games at all.

She leaped about the court like a ballerina. Though not pretty she had charisma and an imperious personality. She walked out of Wimbledon in 1926 after a quarrel with the organisers and turned professional. She never married and died an early death from leukaemia in 1938.

1924, 1926

KATHLEEN McKANE/GODFREE

Born: 7 May 1896; married: 18 January 1926 (to L. A. Godfree)

She was the only player to beat Helen Wills Moody in singles at Wimbledon. Having received a walk-over from a sick Suzanne Lenglen, Kitty McKane beat the then young American in the final after trailing by a set and 1-4 in the second.

She had her second triumph two years later when, again, Mlle Lenglen had retired. She was then married and won the mixed with her husband, Leslie, the only married couple to do so.

A sparkling 88-year-old Mrs Godfree stole the limelight when the women champions celebrated their centenary at Wimbledon in 1984. At the hundredth Championship she presented Miss Navratilova with the trophy.

1927, 1928, 1929, 1930, 1932, 1933, 1935, 1938

HELEN WILLS/MOODY

Born: 6 October 1905; married: (1) 23 December 1929, to F. S. Moody, (2) 28 October 1939, to A. Roark

'Little Miss Poker Face', as Helen was aptly known, was without equal at Wimbledon with her eight victories. They came after she had dissipated a winning lead at her first visit in 1924. Her groundstrokes were trenchantly powerful and perfectly controlled, despite her slow footwork. She showed no emotion.

She had the grace and beauty of a marble statue. She won the French singles four times, the US seven. She never played again in the United States meeting after withdrawing, injured, from the 1933 final. In the course of her Wimbledon successes she lost a total of only four sets in all.

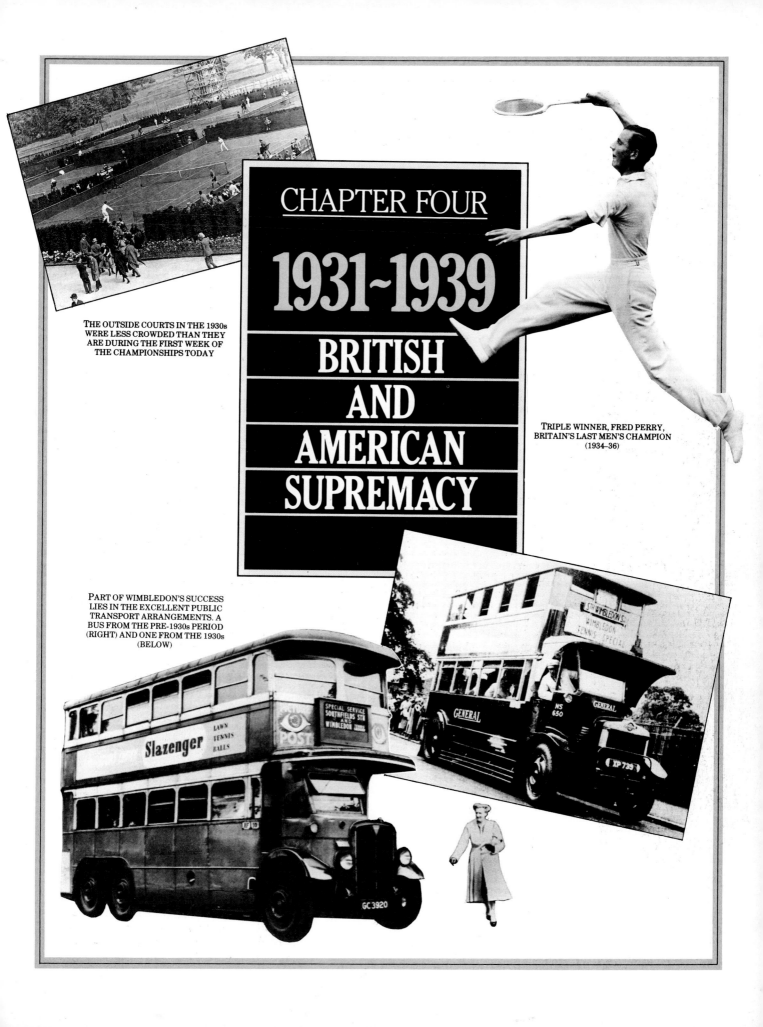

THE OUTSIDE COURTS IN THE 1930s
WERE LESS CROWDED THAN THEY
ARE DURING THE FIRST WEEK OF
THE CHAMPIONSHIPS TODAY

CHAPTER FOUR

1931~1939

BRITISH
AND
AMERICAN
SUPREMACY

TRIPLE WINNER, FRED PERRY,
BRITAIN'S LAST MEN'S CHAMPION
(1934–36)

PART OF WIMBLEDON'S SUCCESS
LIES IN THE EXCELLENT PUBLIC
TRANSPORT ARRANGEMENTS. A
BUS FROM THE PRE-1930s PERIOD
(RIGHT) AND ONE FROM THE 1930s
(BELOW)

IT had been a bleak and depressed Britain to which the United States' Bill Tilden had returned in 1930 to claim a third singles' crown at the age of 37 before joining the ranks of the professionals. The collapse of credit in his own country in 1929 had precipitated a world recession on a scale previously unknown. In Britain that year, a Britain absorbed in the conflicts of the inter-war years – class warfare, Free Trade versus Protectionism and industrial conflict – Ramsay MacDonald had formed his second Labour administration following a general election that for the first time included the 'flapper' vote, women between the ages of 21 and 35. A hunger march from Glasgow to Trafalgar Square revealed the depth of discontent, but there were no swift answers to the misery of rising unemployment. By December 1930 there were 2.5 million out of work and a year later the figure had risen to almost 3 million. Dole queues became a depressingly regular part of the social scene. A run on sterling in 1931 precipitated the resignation of Ramsay MacDonald who then lost favour with his own Labour supporters when he became leader of a national government which secured a loan of £80 million from foreign banks, suspended the gold standard and devalued the pound by 25 per cent.

The evolution of the British Commonwealth took a further confident step forward in 1931 with the creation of Dominion status for the major countries who became self-governing nations under the British crown. However, elsewhere these were uneasy times. In Kroonstadt in 1929 the term 'apartheid' had first been used to describe the separation of black and white cultures, which was an ominous portent for the future. The same year Josef Stalin had banished Leon Trotsky from the Soviet Union as that country had introduced food rationing as part of the first Five Year Plan that was intended to stimulate productivity. Two years later the music of Rachmaninov was banned there as being too bourgeois; more acceptable was Shostakovich whose third symphony, *May the First*, was totally in accord with official taste.

Happily the arts flourished elsewhere. In Britain one of Gustav Holst's last works, his *Chorale Fantasia* (1930), was followed by William Walton's mould-breaking *Belshazzar's Feast* (1931). In that same year, when the Museum of Modern Art was opened in New York, Pablo Picasso, having passed through his cubist period and his flirtation with surrealism, had bought a château in Normandy and was preoccupied with creating sculptures in new materials.

In 1930 no fewer than 107 Nazis were elected to seats in the Reichstag as the allied troops were finally withdrawn from Germany and the Hoover moratorium of 1931 at last proposed a settlement of the long drawn-out arguments over Allied war debts. This was the year when *The Deutschland*, the first of the pocket battleships, was launched; Tirpitz, who had departed this life in retirement the year before, must have been smiling quietly somewhere. By 1932 the Nazis, led by Adolf Hitler, had become the largest political party and the following year Hitler became Chancellor. Antagonism between France and Germany had never really ended and the suspicions of German motives had caused France to begin construction in 1929 of the Maginot Line, a fortified zone between the two countries. When, in 1933, the disarmament conference refused to allow Germany parity with France in the size of their armed forces, Hitler promptly withdrew Germany from the League of Nations. Few realised at the time where this road would lead and those who did express concern over German rearmament were largely ignored or condemned as sensationalists.

In other areas these were times of experiment, expansion and moments of tragic bravery. The BBC began experimental television broadcasts in 1929 and started a regular service seven years later. In 1930, in New York, the Chrysler Building was completed to be the world's tallest building at 1,046 feet; the title was held for less than a year for in 1931 the skyline of the same city was pierced by the towering Empire State Building, all 1,250 feet of it. At Daytona Beach, Florida in March 1929 Henry Seagrave, an American-born racing motorist who had served in the Royal Air Force, broke the land world speed record by reaching 231.44 mph. He was knighted the same year; 12 months later he died when his speedboat overturned on Lake Windermere as he attempted the water speed record.

In 1930 another whose life revolved around speed, Sir Frank Whittle, started to experiment with gas turbines for use in jet engines which, he thought, might one day power aircraft. Little does the present generation of tennis players realise what a debt they owe him as they chase the sun and the dollars round the world's circuits.

By now Wimbledon was a bustling London suburb, a dormitory community of busy commuters. The Stadium, in South Wimbledon, was built in 1928 and offered dog racing and the thrills of speedway. In 1933 the Regal cinema in the Broadway opened its doors to enthusiastic audiences eager for the glittering world of make-believe that Hollywood was providing for the entire English-speaking world.

On Wimbledon Hill in 1930 Jack, the famous old trace horse, was still assisting heavily-laden vehicles to make the difficult journey up the steep incline that defeated all but the most powerful motors. In 1931 the trolley buses arrived to replace the trams. Impressive in their size and comfort these new monsters of the road were dangerous in their silence. They were christened 'whispering deaths' as innocent pedestrians, hearing nothing, stepped into their paths. In 1933 the formation of the London Passenger Transport Board coordinated the services of buses and trolley buses.

The underground link to Morden via South Wimbledon station had opened in 1926 – the same year that Wimbledon's famous department store Elys was celebrating 50 years of trade with a splendid banquet in a newly-constructed building. It was not until 1930 that the overground line to Sutton opened. It was operated by the Southern Railway which, in 1921, had become one of the four railway groups in Britain at which time it had absorbed the London, Brighton South Coast Railway and the London South Western Railway. Now Wimbledon's rail links were complete.

The importance of the excellent rail communications enjoyed by the All England Club since its formation cannot be over emphasised. At Worple Road the railway had made it easy for the crowds to descend on the 4-acre site from Wimbledon station on foot, and at Church Road the addition of the underground station at Southfields made the walk even easier. As road traffic increased it became all the more important to have adequate parking arrangements so that the purchase of the adjacent fields to the west across Somerset Road in 1928, the land to the north between 1930 and 1951 in six parcels and,

RIGHT: For the only time in Wimbledon's history there was an all-German ladies' final in 1931 which resulted in a win for Cilly Aussem (left), who had earlier won the French Championships, against Hilde Krahwinkel. In 1936 Miss Aussem became the Contessa F. M. della Corta Brae. Miss Krahwinkel became Mrs Sperling in 1933 and two years later won the first of her three consecutive French Championships.

ABOVE: Mrs Kitty Godfree (left) congratulating Helen Jacobs of the United States who beat her in the fourth round in 1931 on Court No. 1. The umpire was now in direct touch with the Referee's office by telephone and the water urn sat at the base of the umpire's chair. It was not yet refrigerated.

BELOW LEFT: It was ironic that in 1932 the American No. 3 seed Frank Shields, who the previous year had defaulted to Sidney Wood before the final because of an ankle injury, should have benefited from an ankle injury sustained by 'Buster' Andrews when the New Zealander was leading by two sets to one. Shields went on to win in five sets but was beaten by Britain's Bunny Austin in the quarter-finals. This was the first year that more than 200,000 spectators attended The Championships.

BELOW RIGHT: Ellsworth Vines of the USA (left) had just beaten E. du Plaix of France in an opening-round match in 1932 en route to the title. The ball boys are wearing their new uniforms – including hats.

RIGHT: The famous 1933 final between Jack Crawford of Australia (left) and Ellsworth Vines of the United States, who was the holder, was considered by contemporaries to have been the greatest played at the new Wimbledon. Crawford finally won the gruelling battle, which was played mostly from the baseline, 6-4 in the final set.

BELOW: Fred Perry's three victories from 1934 to 1936 were the first consecutive ones since the four wins of Anthony Wilding (1910 to 1913) in the days of the Challenge Round. As reported in the *Illustrated London News*, this was the peak of British achievement with the Davis Cup in British hands (1933 to 1936), Dorothy Round the Wimbledon ladies' champion in 1934 and 1937, and the mixed champion three years in a row – with R. Miki in 1934 and with Perry in 1935 and 1936, Pat Hughes and Raymond Tuckey winning the men's doubles in 1936, Kay Stammers and Freda James winning the ladies' doubles twice (1935 and 1936), and Bunny Austin reaching two singles' finals in 1932 and 1938.

MISS FREDA JAMES (LEFT) AND MISS K. E. STAMMERS: THE WINNERS OF THE WOMEN'S DOUBLES AT WIMBLEDON.

F. J. PERRY AND MISS DOROTHY ROUND: THE WINNERS OF THE MIXED DOUBLES.

J. H. CRAWFORD (LEFT) AND A. K. QUIST, OF AUSTRALIA: THE WINNERS OF THE MEN'S DOUBLES AFTER A BRILLIANT FINAL.

A GREAT CHAMPION AND A GREAT RUNNER-UP: MRS. F. S. MOODY (LEFT) AND MISS HELEN JACOBS.

F. J. PERRY (RIGHT) RETAINS THE CHAMPIONSHIP AFTER BEATING G. VON CRAMM, OF GERMANY; THE FIRST PLAYER TO WIN IN TWO SUCCESSIVE YEARS AT WIMBLEDON SINCE THE HOLDER WAS MADE TO PLAY THROUGH.

finally, the 11½ acres of playing fields owned by Barkers, the Kensington department store, early in 1967 became essential. As time passed the wisdom of the committee in making these purchases became ever more apparent. Equally important were the special bus services provided by London Transport from both Wimbledon and Southfields stations which had begun before the War in the 1930s.

The preferred method of crossing the Atlantic in the 1930s was still the luxury liner and this is how Frank Shields and his 19-year-old US Davis Cup teammate, Sidney Wood, arrived for the 1931 Championships where they were the third and eighth seeds respectively. Their appearance in the singles' final, following the success of their countryman Tilden the previous year, suggested that the famous French Musketeers were at last losing the tight grip that they had held on affairs since 1924. Shields beat Borotra in a four-set semi-final but, in doing so, injured a knee that forced him to withdraw from further action. Accordingly, Wood became the only Wimbledon champion who has been crowned by default.

With record crowds on every day but one and the largest-ever entry, thanks to the 16 extra pairs allowed into the mixed doubles, the stature of Wimbledon continued to grow. British interest was heightened by the fact that, for the first time since seeding had begun in 1927, there were two British men among the select eight: Fred Perry at 5 and Bunny Austin at 6. Although Perry lost to Wood in the semi-final and Austin went out to Shields in five sets one round earlier, they were both young enough at 22 and 24 respectively to have their best years ahead. The following year Austin confirmed that impression by reaching

the first of two singles' finals he would contest at Wimbledon. In 1932 he was unlucky to run into Ellsworth Vines, a tremendous server and fine match player. In 1938 he was unluckier still for his opponent was one of the greatest champions of all time, Don Budge.

In 1933 Vines himself was unseated by the elegant Australian Jack Crawford in a five-set final that those who witnessed it described as the best match they had ever seen at Wimbledon. This first Australian success since Patterson's wins in 1919 and 1922 was short-lived for the next year Crawford was the victim of an inspired Perry. At last British prayers had been answered – and in a refreshingly unexpected way for Fred was not from the same social background as the members of the tennis Establishment. The son of a Labour MP and born in Stockport, Fred recalls the hidden barriers that were raised by many of the officials with whom he came into contact as he climbed determinedly from relative obscurity to international fame via the world table tennis championships where he first developed his match-winning skills. He tells how in 1934 the member's tie, awarded by tradition to the champion each year ('the easy way to achieve membership of the All England Club'), was not presented to him in the usual way but left draped over the bench in the changing room near his clothes.

The Englishman's three victories between 1934 and 1936 were the first such consecutive successes of the post-Challenge Round era and the feat was not to be repeated for another 42 years when the remarkable young Swede, Bjorn Borg, won for a third time in 1978 and then extended his run to five wins in a row.

Perry's initial victory at Wimbledon in 1933, the first by a Briton since Arthur

Gore's double success in 1908 and 1909, had been presaged by the recapture of the Davis Cup the previous year in a magnificently exciting 3-2 win against the French in Paris in which Perry's two wins, against Cochet and the young André Merlin, and Austin's victory over Merlin, were just enough to end a French reign of six years. For three more glorious years the British men ruled the team world until, following Perry's decision to turn professional before the 1937 campaign, the Americans finally ended a ten-year drought with an emphatic 4-1 win in the Challenge Round, led by a majestic Budge on the same Centre Court where, a few weeks earlier, he had replaced the departed Perry as champion.

Budge's feats in winning all three titles at both the 1937 and 1938 meetings, particularly when he did not drop a set in singles in 1938 and dropped only one in 1937, were thought at the time to be almost superhuman efforts. The fact that the achievement has been repeated only twice by a man, namely Bobby Riggs in 1939 and Frank Sedgman in 1952, suggests that contemporary observers were right. Curiously, it has always seemed easier for the ladies to achieve this level of success, perhaps because the great lady champions have been further ahead of their contemporaries than the men have been ahead of theirs. It is certainly true that there has been greater depth of talent among the men than among the women. Altogether five women have won the triple crown on nine occasions: Lenglen three times (1920, 1922 and 1925); Brough twice (1948, 1950); King twice (1967, 1973); Marble once (1939); and Hart once (1951).

When in 1938 Budge, who had arrived at Wimbledon as the French Champion, went on to add the American and Australian titles to his tally so that he held all four major titles in the same year, the distinguished American writer Alison Danzig suggested that, like a successful bridge player, he had scored a 'Grand Slam' of victories. Subsequently the term has been devalued by those who claim that a player who holds all four titles at the same time, regardless of the year or season in which they fall, though in itself a thoroughly praiseworthy but much less arduous feat, has achieved a Grand Slam. The International Tennis Federation even instituted a Grand Slam award of $1 million in 1983 for any player who held the four titles at the same time, which was a regrettable piece of commercialism that came to an abrupt end when Martina Navratilova promptly claimed the prize on winning the French Open in 1984. It was always quite clear that Danzig had been referring to four wins in the same year or season.

The last pre-war winner was another American who took advantage of Budge's departure to the professional ranks to impose his tactical skills and shrewd match-playing judgement on his opponents in all three events. That Bobby Riggs was a worthy champion no one doubted, but the absence of those who had turned professional and the Australians added to the feeling that this was a sub-standard field. Also absent was von Cramm, surely one of the greatest players never to have won The Championship despite three successive appearances in the final (he was not allowed back at Wimbledon until 1951 by which time he was almost 42). There was nothing sub-standard, though, about Riggs. He was a hustler, on and off the court. A wonderfully agile counter-hitter, he had a gambler's instinct for when to apply the pressure and was a great tactician. Riggs was in three

LEFT: Germany's elegant stylist Baron Gottfried von Cramm, was arguably the greatest pre-war player never to win The Championships. Like Fred Stolle in the 1960s, he reached the final three years in a row. In 1935 and 1936 Fred Perry beat him and the following year he ran into the American Don Budge who was just emerging as the greatest pre-war champion. Von Cramm twice won in Paris, in 1934 and 1936, and had a wonderful Davis Cup record: 82 wins from 102 matches over a span of 22 years, the last being in 1953 when he was 44. After losing the deciding rubber in the 1937 Inter-Zone final against Budge and subsequently criticising Hitler and the Nazi party which he refused to join, von Cramm was jailed for a year and did not play at Wimbledon again until 1951 when, at the age of 41, he lost a close three-set match to Jaroslav Drobny, the No. 2 seed.

BELOW: Chauffeurs, and others without means of access, demonstrate the irresistible appeal of Wimbledon.

RIGHT: When play was cancelled for the day following rain on Court No. 1 during the Inter-Zone final of the Davis Cup in 1937, the angry fans demonstrated their feelings. Since 1904 there have been 28 Davis Cup ties staged at Wimbledon, mostly on Court No. 1, the most recent being against Australia in July 1986. In the four years when Britain held the trophy the Challenge Rounds were played on the Centre Court, the last of these being in 1937 when the USA defeated Britain 4-1 after Fred Perry had turned professional.

BELOW LEFT: The British Davis Cup captain Herbert Roper Barrett, became familiar with his role in this Centre Court scene that was enacted three years in a row in the 1930s. Having won the famous men's team trophy in Paris in 1933, Britain retained it in 1934 with a 4-1 win against the United States. It was successfully defended the following year when the Americans were humbled 5-0, and was retained for the last time in 1936 when the Australians were defeated 3-2.

BELOW RIGHT: In 1938 Don Budge (left) beat Bunny Austin of Britain in a one-sided final. With the help of fellow Americans Gene Mako and Alice Marble, Budge won all three titles for the second year running. No man had achieved that feat before though Suzanne Lenglen had done so in 1920. The red-headed Budge, born in Oakland, was the son of a Scot who had emigrated to California. He had an elder brother, Lloyd, who became a tennis coach. After winning all four major Championships in 1938, the world's first Grand Slam, and helping the United States retain the Davis Cup against the Australians, Budge turned professional.

LEFT: A contrast in heights as Germany's Helga Sperling, the finalist in 1931 and 1936, accompanies the diminutive Gem Hoahing onto Court No. 1 for their first-round match in 1939. Miss Hoahing is a member of the All England Club and still enjoys her regular weekly games of ladies' doubles.

CENTRE: There was much debate whether 16-year-old Jean Nicoll, who had precociously won all three events at the British Junior Championships in 1938, was too young to compete at Wimbledon in 1939. However, she did play and took a set in losing to Miss D. A. Huntbach in the first round. After the War, as Mrs Bostock, she won the singles, doubles and mixed at the British Hard Court Championships at Bournemouth in 1946 and played for Britain with distinction in the Wightman Cup teams of 1946, 1947 and 1948.

BELOW RIGHT: In 1939, for the first time, there were two triple champions. Bobby Riggs beat fellow American Elwood Cooke in the singles' final and then teamed with him in doubles to beat the British pair Charles Hare and Frank Wilde. Alice Marble, who had been a semi-finalist in 1937 and 1938, served and volleyed her way to victory over Britain's Kay Stammers and then partnered Sara Palfrey Fabyan to win the doubles for the second year in a row with a victory over Helen Jacobs and Billie Yorke. Then Bobby and Alice established their unique record when they beat Frank Wilde and Nina Brown to win the mixed.

Small wonder that the pair looked happy when, by tradition, they opened the dancing at the Wimbledon Ball which, until 1976, was held at the Grosvenor House Hotel on the final Saturday of The Championships.

ABOVE: Each year the Wimbledon draw is conducted in public and watched with eagerness by many of the players and by an army of media correspondents from all over the world. In keeping with tradition, the LTA Secretary Anthony Sabelli holds the bag while Hamilton Price, the Referee from 1937 to 1939, draws the numbers that are recorded by the secretaries.

TOP: The affluent used to send messenger boys to queue on their behalf and would arrive shortly before the gates opened to take their place and purchase seats for the day's play.

ABOVE: The patient fans with time to spare bring their own stools and wait for the gates to open at midday before the start of play at 2.00 p.m. Even before the Second World War there were all-night queues for the final two days.

RIGHT: Herbert Wilberforce, later Sir Herbert, served the club in many ways. A great-grandson of the emancipator, William Wilberforce, he represented Cambridge against Oxford from 1883 to 1886 and won the men's doubles at Wimbledon in 1897 with the Hon. Patrick Bowes-Lyon. From 1921 to 1929 he served as President of the All England Club and became Chairman when that post was created in 1929. In 1937 he decided it was time to retire as he was also the Deputy Chairman of the County of London Sessions, an office he filled from 1926 to 1938.

successive US finals, winning in 1939 and 1941 against Welby van Horn and Frank Kovacs and losing in the intervening year to Don McNeill. Like so many, his best years coincided with the War.

This period of women's tennis was dominated by Helen Wills Moody who added four more titles in 1932, 1933, 1935 and 1938 to bring her tally to a record-breaking eight. Four of the last five were gained against her fellow Californian Helen Jacobs who, by the oddest of coincidences, lived just a few streets away from her great rival in San Francisco. Even her contemporaries felt they had never come to know 'Little Miss Poker Face', as the Press dubbed Helen Wills. Her aloof manner contributed to the impression of superiority that the champion gave. On those rare occasions when opponents came close to winning a set against her they felt the pressure of her personality bearing down on them. Her game was built on iron concentration, wonderful control of pace and length on her groundstrokes and the fearless confidence that all great champions possess. After losing to Kitty Mc-Kane on her first visit at the age of 18 in 1924 she was never again beaten in 55 singles' matches. Furthermore, she won the French title four times and her own US Championships seven times, failing in only one final, in 1933, when she retired to Helen Jacobs while trailing 0-3 in the final set – thus depriving the other Helen of her first complete victory. However, in 1936 Miss Jacobs took full advantage of her rival's absence to score a long overdue singles' victory.

The decade had begun unexpectedly. In Mrs Moody's absence in 1931 the women's final was fought out between two German girls, Cilly Aussem and Hilde Krahwinkel, with the former beating her countrywoman in straight sets to

confirm the form she had shown in Paris, where she had won her first major title. Neither before nor since has there been an all-German final.

With the two wins in 1934 and 1937 of the Worcestershire Sunday School teacher, Dorothy Round, coming during and immediately after the time of Perry's ascendancy, British morale was lifted to new heights. Tennis flourished throughout the country as never before. The tennis club became the centre of much social activity and many a marriage had its origins in the mixed doubles and the club dances of the period. It was the golden age of John Betjeman's Miss J. Hunter Dunn, 'Furnish'd and burnish'd by Aldershot sun', an age when at last it seemed that home players would stand alongside the best that the United States, Australia and Europe could produce. Alas, it was a short but wonderful dream. Since then there have been only three singles' titles won at Wimbledon by British players – all of them women – Angela Mortimer in 1961, Ann Jones in 1968 and Virginia Wade in 1977.

As the clouds of war gathered in 1939, an American girl swept imperiously to three titles with a brand of powerful, attacking serve-and-volley tennis that amazed all who saw it. Yes, California's Alice Marble, the winner of that last pre-war singles' final against Britain's Kay Stammers, introduced a new dimension to women's tennis that pointed to the way ahead. She had already won her US National title in 1936 and 1938 and was to win it again in 1939 and 1940. If it had not been for the War her record at Wimbledon might have become as impressive as Helen Wills's had been, except that Alice did not enjoy robust health. However, thanks to her, the days when women played largely from the baseline were numbered.

BIOGRAPHIES

GENTLEMEN

S. B. Wood

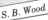

H. E. Vines

J. H. Crawford

F. J. Perry

J. D. Budge

1931

SIDNEY WOOD

Born: 1 November 1911

A precocious player, he first competed at Wimbledon at the age of 15. He is the only champion to have won on a walk-over; his fellow American, Frank Shields, scratched lest he aggravate an injury and mar his subsequent Davis Cup effort.

Wood was only 19 years 256 days old, making him the third youngest victor.

1932

ELLSWORTH VINES

Born: 28 September 1911

This tall Californian won spectacularly at his first attempt. The speed of his service and forehand was extraordinary. His title-winning stroke in the final against the British Bunny Austin was a service of such pace that Austin did not know if the ball had passed him on the forehand or backhand.

Vines lost a wonderful five-set final to the Australian Jack Crawford the following year, which is a match often claimed as the finest ever played. He turned professional the same year. Later he became a top-class golf pro.

1933

JACK CRAWFORD

Born: 22 March 1908

Crawford favoured long-sleeved shirts and a square-headed racket, which evoked the past. Classic driving control marked his play. His groundstrokes notably quelled the pace-making of Vines in a memorable final but one year later he could not cope with the bustling aggression of Fred Perry in the title match. He was perhaps the best loved of the pre-1939 Australians.

1934, 1935, 1936

FRED PERRY

Born: 18 May 1909

The last great British man, he had a running forehand that punished the opposition but which was suicidal to imitate. He was poor in practice, overwhelming in matches.

His bustling skill gave Great Britain victory in the Davis Cup from 1933 to 1936. He was the first man to win the four major titles of Wimbledon, the United States, France and Australia.

The son of a Labour MP, Perry paid scant respect to the snobbish elements in the game. He became a professional in 1936 and later acquired American citizenship.

In 1984 the 'Perry Gates' on Somerset Road were named at the All England Club and his statue was erected near the 'Doherty Gates' on Church Road.

1937, 1938

DON BUDGE

Born: 13 June 1915

A red-headed Californian (whose father had played soccer for Glasgow Rangers), his domination was complete and he was triple Wimbledon champion in his last two years as an amateur. In 1938 he was the first to win the 'Grand Slam'. He was the first to play through and win the men's singles without losing a set.

He wielded a fine serve and a heavy, rolled backhand whose effectiveness changed the tactics of tennis. Many claim that he was the greatest player of all time.

R. L. Riggs

C. Aussem

D. E. Round

H. H. Jacobs

A. Marble

1939

BOBBY RIGGS

Born: 25 February 1918

This Californian holds the unique record of being a triple champion who never lost a match at Wimbledon. His confident and adroit play took over the meeting just before the Second World War. He won his own title the same year.

He turned professional in 1942 but did not dominate the pro-circuit matches of post-war years as he had the amateur game. As a veteran he was involved in two notable man v woman matches. He beat Margaret Court but contrived to lose to Billie Jean King on 20 September 1973 at the Houston Astrodome before 30,492 paying customers, which is the largest crowd ever to attend a tennis match.

LADIES

1931

CILLY AUSSEM

Born: 4 January 1909; married: 11 March 1936 (to Count F. M. della Corta Brae); died: 22 March 1963

She was the only German singles' winner until Boris Becker in 1985. A graceful player, she looked a certainty to be in the 1930 final but hurt her ankle when leading. The next year she won the title in the absence of Helen Wills Moody and after an all-German final against Hilde Krahwinkel, who was a long-legged retriever.

Ill health plagued her and she did not play after 1934.

1934, 1937

DOROTHY ROUND

Born: 13 July 1909; married: 2 September 1937 (to D. L. Little); died: 12 November 1982

The outstanding British woman of the 1930s, she was a sound all-rounder with weighty groundstrokes. She was described in the popular press as the 'Midlands' Sunday School Mistress' after achieving notoriety by refusing to play on a Sunday during the French Championships.

In 1933 she was the first player to take a set from Helen Wills Moody since 1927. She won the title the year following at her seventh attempt. Her 1934 triumph was shared with Fred Perry in the men's singles. It was the last great year for Britain at Wimbledon.

1936

HELEN JACOBS

Born: 6 August 1908

A great American also-ran whose career was in the shadow of Helen Wills Moody near whom she lived in Berkeley, California. She suffered a dramatic setback when in the Wimbledon final of 1935 she fluffed a match point against her great rival.

Her compensation came a year later when, competing for the ninth time and after four previous final defeats, she won. She was a persistent volleyer, an advocate of the chopped approach shot – and a pioneer of shorts for women.

1939

ALICE MARBLE

Born: 28 September 1913

The Californian who changed the face of the women's game by adopting the serve-volley technique. She did so despite ill health and a threat of never being able to play again after collapsing at the Stade Roland Garros in 1934.

She came to an awesome peak at Wimbledon by becoming triple champion just before the Second World War. During that War she became a professional; had history been different she would have been a sporting certainty to win Wimbledon in other years.

Many say she would be the ultimate champion among all great players at their peak.

WIMBLEDON AT WAR

CHAPTER FIVE

1946~1955

POST-WAR AMERICAN DOMINANCE

THE ACROBATIC FREDDIE HUBER OF AUSTRIA

THE ERA WHEN FLANNELS GAVE WAY TO SHORTS

THE 1949 LADIES' DOUBLES FINALISTS. FROM LEFT TO RIGHT: PAT TODD AND GUSSIE MORAN WHO PLAYED LOUISE BROUGH AND MARGARET OSBORNE DU PONT, ONE OF THE GREATEST DOUBLES PAIRS EVER, WHO WON THE TITLE FOR THE THIRD TIME

DESPITE the German bomb which fell on 11 October 1940 and flattened a corner of the Centre Court where the competitors always sit, one of 16 bombs that fell on club property altogether, the All England Club had a useful part to play in the war effort. All but four of the club's staff had been called to active service but, under the watchful eye of Nora Cleather, who carried on as acting Secretary during the war period following Dudley Larcombe's retirement due to failing health, a great deal was accomplished. One of the car parks was ploughed up to grow vegetables, another housed pigs, chickens, ducks, geese and rabbits in temporary wooden homes while the main concourse echoed to the marching feet of detachments of the London Welsh and London Irish regiments who used it as a parade ground, as did the slightly more mature men of 'F' Company, the 54th East Surrey Regiment, Wimbledon's Home Guard. Many of the buildings were occupied by branches of the Civil Defence services, the Red Cross and St John's Ambulance Brigade, the ARP and the Fire Service.

In 1940 they even considered holding a two-day tournament but the difficulties of travel, supplies, food and personnel convinced everyone that the effort was not worth while. During the war years the courts themselves were lovingly cared for by the same Edwin Fuller who had been employed as a groundsman at Worple Road in 1916 when he was 13 and had been appointed head groundsman in 1937. Accordingly, as early as June 1945 a series of Inter-Dominions Services matches, involving teams from Britain, Australia, New Zealand, South Africa and Canada could be staged at the club culminating in two matches played on No. 1 Court. The first, between the Brit- ish Empire Forces and the United States Forces in England at the end of June, was attended by Queen Mary. The second, one month later, between the servicemen of Great Britain and Other Allies attracted over 5,000 spectators who remained to enjoy the tennis until after 8 p.m. along with the distinguished guests, the Regent of Iraq, the Belgian and French Ambassadors and Mrs Winston Churchill.

These matches gave the hungry home tennis fans a unique opportunity to enjoy the playing skills of Squadron Leader Dan Maskell, the All England Club's resident professional who played in both. Dan had spent a rewarding war helping to rehabilitate wounded airmen. First he was stationed at the RAF Hospital for officer air crew at the requisitioned Palace Hotel, Torquay, where he had played many times on the indoor wooden courts, and then following the bombing there on 25 October 1942, he went to the RAF Rehabilitation Unit at Lough- borough. In January 1945 Dan was awarded the OBE for his work and, 37 years later, he received an honorary MA from Loughborough for the many ser- vices he has performed for the place dur- ing a long and devoted professional life. It was marvellous for the public that the man who had played such a crucial behind-the-scenes' role in the pre-war successes of Fred Perry and the Davis Cup team, as the first national coach to be sent overseas, should have been able to play in front of them in those two festi- val matches for as the world returned to peacetime practice he, as a professional, would be barred from competing at Wimbledon. It was also appropriate that the Queen should have seen fit to honour Dan with the CBE in 1982 for his services to tennis. His daily television commen- taries for the BBC since 1951 have made him the voice of Wimbledon for so many fans.

Others who took part included the home players Flight Lieutenant Donald McPhail, who had been the Scottish number one before the War, Flight Lieutenant C. M. 'Jimmy' Jones and Squadron Leader John Olliff. The British pre-war Davis Cup player Staff Sergeant Charles Hare, now a US citizen and serving in the US Army, competed in the American team. Others who took part included several players who would make their marks in post-war tennis including Captain Eric Sturgess of South Africa, Flight Sergeant Bill Sidwell of Australia, Lieutenant Eddie Moylan and Major Frank Guernsey of the USA, Private Philippe Washer and Lieutenant Pierre Geelhand of Belgium and the two Frenchmen Lieutenant Bobby Abdesselam and Lieutenant Bernard Destremau.

It was a wonderful way to celebrate the end of hostilities in Europe after the formal German surrender on 8 May, following the fall of Berlin to the Russian troops six days earlier. But until the Japanese surrender on 14 August there remained a feeling of suspended reality as air raid wardens still reported for duty out of habit and householders still pulled the blinds tight at night, subconsciously observing the black-out. Britain was weary after almost six draining years of privation and hardship. Food and petrol were still rationed, clothing was drab and available only with coupons, war damage was everywhere to be seen in many large cities. The nation was bankrupt, with a huge overseas debt and, in the course of a few short years, left with only the tattered remains of a once mighty Empire. In 1947 the King ceased to be Emperor of India. The following year Ceylon became a dominion, the

independence of Burma was declared and Malaya became a Federation of States with dominion status. Within ten years Egypt would secede, the Gold Coast would become independent and the ill-fated Federation of Rhodesia and Nyasaland would be declared. Life for Great Britain Ltd would never be quite the same again.

The General Election of 26 July 1945 confirmed the fact. In the biggest landslide since 1906 the British people shunned the man who had led them to victory and turned to Labour to create a new promised land. Winston Churchill never got over that act of fickleness; Clement Attlee could hardly believe his good fortune. With this fundamental shift, the British people rapidly came to take for granted the beneficence of the welfare state. It was an irreversible process.

Then, on 6 August, an atomic bomb was dropped on Hiroshima, followed by another on Nagasaki three days later. The stark horror of these events was not then fully comprehended. For the Allies, suddenly the prospect of a final peace, a lasting peace, became a reality. Now the painful process of recovery could be tackled.

But, everywhere, peace meant adapting to new conditions. In the USA President Roosevelt, who had been in office since 1932, had died suddenly in April, just two months after his meeting with Winston Churchill and Joseph Stalin at Yalta; thus Harry S. Truman was thrust into the role of peacemaker at the Potsdam Conference with Stalin and Attlee. The two principal villains were dead – Mussolini had been executed by partisans and Hitler had committed suicide – but, with the Soviet Union, in Churchill's words (spoken the following year in Fulton, Missouri), lowering 'an iron curtain' across Europe, the immense and delicate

ABOVE: Wimbledon at War. The car parks were ploughed up to grow crops and animals were housed in temporary quarters watched by the acting Secretary Nora Cleather and Marie Bompas, who later became assistant to the first post-war Secretary. Red Cross and Civil Defence services took up residence alongside active troops and Home Guard units who used the main concourse as a parade ground. A bomb destroyed part of the Centre Court roof which meant the loss of 1,200 seats at the first post-war meeting in 1946.

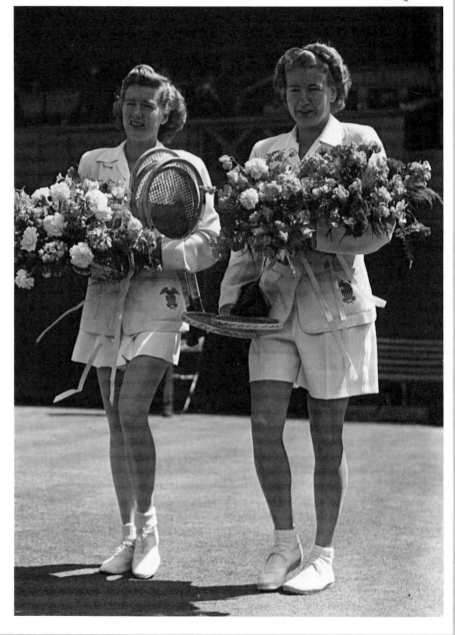

RIGHT: A break with tradition as the three-time US champion, Pauline Betz (left) and Louise Brough, the girl she had beaten in two of those wartime finals (1942 and 1943), carry their bouquets on court before the 1946 final. Traditionally, the Secretary sends flowers to the two lady finalists wishing them both good luck but until this year the flowers had always been left in the dressing room. Miss Betz won again, 6-2 6-4, and was declared a professional soon after winning a fourth US title merely for stating that ultimately she intended to become one.

LEFT: The net has to be changed because the fierce service power of the tall 30-year-old Frenchman, Yvon Petra, has fired a hole in it. Petra confounded the prophets by winning the first post-war Championships from the dynamic little double-handed Australian Geoff Brown. However, Petra was no stranger to Wimbledon for in 1937 he had reached the final of the mixed with Madame Mathieu, with whom he had also won the French mixed title that year. In 1938 he had won the French doubles' title with Bernard Destremau. Always an amiable giant, Petra was the last champion to wear long trousers (though not in the final). He turned professional in 1948 and died in September 1984.

LEFT: Sweden's Lennart Bergelin, who had been a quarter-finalist in 1946, caused the biggest sensation in 1948 when he put out the top seed, Frank Parker of the United States. In a thrilling fourth-round match Parker failed to exploit a severe case of cramp that caused Bergelin to surrender the fourth set 0-6. As the effects wore off Bergelin came back to life and won the decider 10-8. Falkenburg then beat him in the quarter-finals.

BELOW: Service personnel, recruited by Duncan Macaulay, played an important role in these early post-war Championships – not least the Royal Navy who cheerfully sailed out to brush off the water that was lying on the court covers.

problem of redefining the boundaries had to be tackled. So, too, the criminals had to be brought to justice; this gruesome and laborious process was begun at Nuremberg.

In France the Third Republic, inaugurated in 1871, was ended by referendum in 1945 and the following year another referendum ushered in the Fourth Republic. The former Japanese-held territory of Korea was occupied by US and Russian troops, which was to have explosive repercussions five years later. Japan itself was occupied by American troops who were to remain until 1952. In Vietnam a Communist Government was established, again with immense implications for a future American generation. Poland lost Galicia to the Soviet Union but was given the North German city of Danzig which was renamed Gdansk; the 90 per cent German population was expelled. Forty years later a brave attempt to develop a democratic Polish trade union would be crushed in this same city. The Chinese Nationalists under Chiang Kai-shek took Formosa from Japan, supported by the Russians who were allowed concessions in Manchuria.

In 1946 Italy and Hungary became Republics, though the latter would be tragically crushed by the Russian invasion of 1956. In Romania they were more realistic from the start – a Communist People's Republic was proclaimed in 1948 and the same year a communist coup in Czechoslovakia established a People's Republic there. With one gigantic gulp the Soviet Union had swallowed Eastern Europe whole, except for the city of Berlin which, like Austria, was divided into four zones administered by the USA, Britain, France and the Soviet Union. Without risking the start of a third world war there was nothing the impotent West could do about Russian expansion – certainly not through the United Nations Organisation whose General Assembly had met for the first time in London in 1946.

In Cairo the Arab League was launched in 1945; the state of Jordan came into being and three years later agreed to the partition of Jerusalem with the new-born state of Israel, formed in 1948 by Zionist Jews who took over practically the whole of Palestine. Thus were sown the seeds of discontent which produced a bitter harvest of strife that, for years to come, would engulf the entire Middle East in terrorism and bloodshed.

Neither Adolf Hitler nor the tangled skein of events that followed his downfall could dim the creative process. In fact, the experience of war helped inspire some of the century's greatest artistic and philosophic works from men like Ernest Hemingway, Herman Wouk, James Jones and Nicholas Montserrat while Jean-Paul Sartre in middle age was expounding his existentialist ideas. The prolific Picasso, now 63, had joined the Communist Party for humanitarian reasons in 1944 and his immediate post-war paintings had themes of political protest. His lithograph *The Dove* was adopted as the symbol of the World Peace Congress in 1949.

Wimbledon itself had not escaped the horrors of war. One hundred and fifty people were killed in air raids and more than a thousand were injured. Although the borough was not as heavily bombed as some of the inner areas, there was nevertheless considerable damage to property as the Luftwaffe made a target of nearby Bushey Park where General Eisenhower had his headquarters. They also knew that Lord Dowding, the Chief of Fighter Command was living in St Mary's Road and that the Secretary of

State for War, the Rt Hon Hore Belisha, was occupying Warren Farm on the Common. Furthermore, there was the KLG sparking plugs factory on the Portsmouth Road and numerous other factory targets in the neighbouring area. Altogether more than 1,000 bombs of all types fell within the borough and nearly 14,000 Wimbledon homes were destroyed or severely damaged, a large loss for any small community. On the Common there were sited several anti-aircraft batteries and, near the Windmill, a large naval gun. In the same vicinity there was an army camp while on nearby Southside huts were erected to house prisoners of war. In the 1945 General Election, to everyone's astonishment, a Labour MP was elected to represent the parliamentary borough of Merton, Morden and Wimbledon. Thus A. M. F. Palmer was the first, and so far only, Labour MP to represent Wimbledon at Westminster.

For those players who had competed at Wimbledon in the pre-war days it was a very different world and a different Britain to which they returned in 1946 for the first post-war Championship meeting. For some years many overseas players imported steaks and piled them in hotel refrigerators to supplement meals that were inadequate for serious sportsmen.

Four old friends of tennis had not survived the War: Hamilton Price, who had refereed the last three Championships from 1937–39, Sir Herbert Wilberforce, a former President and Chairman, and two former Secretaries of the club, Commander Hillyard and the man who had succeeded him in 1925, Dudley Larcombe, had all died. Also the former player and successful Davis Cup captain, Herbert Roper Barrett, had passed away in 1943 four months short of his seventieth

birthday. It is a curious fact that both Hillyard and Larcombe, like the second Secretary, Henry 'Cavendish' Jones, were all old boys of King's College School which moved from the Strand to Wimbledon Common in 1897. Furthermore, 12 other KCS boys have also competed at Wimbledon, including the Davis Cup men Harry Lee and Buster Mottram. In 1923 W. H. Latchford beat Bunny Austin in the junior championships and went on to play at Wimbledon while he was still at school and in 1919 three members of the teaching staff, H. J. Pullein-Thompson, G. T. C. Watt and B. Wood-Hill, all competed in The Championships.

Inevitably there were changes at the All England Club. The Duchess of Kent had graciously assumed the Presidency in 1943 following the wartime death of the Duke and the committee had appointed a new Secretary, Lieutenant Colonel A. D. C. Macaulay who had taken up his duties as recently as mid-December 1945. Having spent every year since 1922 working at The Championships in some capacity – first as an umpire and in the last years before the War as Assistant Referee – Duncan, as he became universally known, was fully conversant with the way things were done.

The decision whether to hold a tournament at all in 1946 was a difficult one. Not only would it be impossible to repair the damaged section of the Centre Court in the time, which meant a loss of some 1,200 seats, but also the shortages of food, clothing and petrol as rationing was still in force, as well as equipment and personnel, would put a tremendous strain on the management committee. But Duncan, aided by his assistant, the indispensible Marie Bompas, by Dan Maskell, reinstalled as the club's

LEFT: The smallest man in the 1948 draw was Felicissimo Ampon of the Philippines who stood 4 feet 11 inches tall and claimed that his strength came from his diet of raw egg yolks that were being supplied to him by the Philippine Embassy at the rate of two per day, which was no easy task during food rationing.

LEFT AND BELOW: The Secretary, Duncan Macaulay, standing with Gardnar Mulloy and Colonel John Legg, who began his 14-year reign as Referee in 1949, taking over from Captain A. K. Trower who had died after refereeing the first three post-war Championships. This year Mulloy, who had jokingly suggested that Wimbledon draws were 'fixed', had been invited to draw the names out of the hat himself. By an extraordinary quirk of fate the last name out of the hat was his own and the last vacant spot was at the foot of the draw against the No. 1 seed Ted Schroeder (left) who was also his doubles partner. Schroeder won in five sets and went on to win the title in another five-set match against Jaroslav Drobny (below). Schroeder was the first champion to have his trophies presented on the Centre Court.

LEFT AND CENTRE: 1949 will always be remembered as the year of Gussie Moran and her lace-edged panties that had been created by the game's leading designer Teddy Tinling to go with an attractive kilt-length, all-white Tinling dress made of soft knitted rayon trimmed with white satin. Sitting in the Dorchester Hotel, Gussie posed for photographers who had caught a glimpse of the new outfit at the Hurlingham Garden Party on the eve of Wimbledon. Its first appearance had caused a sensation. Fleet Street photographers had camped round her court taking dozens of shots that were wired all over the world. *Life* magazine ran a special feature. When Gussie wore the outfit again in her second-round match at Wimbledon the public and the Press went wild. But the Wimbledon committee was not quite ready for this sort of exposure and in the awkward atmosphere that was created Tinling decided to resign his post as Wimbledon's 'call-boy'.

ABOVE LEFT: In 1950 Budge Patty found time for a welcome moment of rest during the longest doubles' match ever played at Wimbledon at that stage – a 4-hour 14-minute marathon with his partner Tony Trabert against the Australians Frank Sedgman and Ken McGregor. The service-dominated encounter ended in an American victory by 6-4 31-29 7-9 6-2. At one stage the electric scoreboard, unable to go beyond 19, showed 19-0!

ABOVE RIGHT: The US Junior Champion of 1950 was Hamilton Richardson who, like another famous American of an earlier era, Billy Talbert, was a diabetic and had to take insulin. When, in 1951, the 17-year-old Richardson beat Budge Patty, the defending champion, in five tough sets he celebrated with a bowl of strawberries and cream and needed to drink a lot of milk to maintain the balance.

resident professional, by the newly-appointed Referee, Captain A. K. Trower, and by the Royal Navy who provided the stewards at that first meeting, somehow pulled together all the strands of organisation to produce a Championship that, with 23 nations represented, re-established Wimbledon as the world's premier tennis tournament.

The Americans were expected to and indeed did dominate the post-war scene for, though some of their leading men players had experienced war service, tennis tournaments had continued across the Atlantic throughout the five years. In the first decade after the War seven American men won once each and five American women won all ten singles' titles. The admirable professionalism, the keen competitiveness and the technical competence of this new breed of aggressive player set the standard for the rest of the world to follow.

Even though he was seeded No. 2 behind Australia's Dinny Pails, the American Jack Kramer was the popular favourite to win the men's singles in 1946 from an original entry of over 200. The US junior champion of 1936, Jack had won the US National doubles in 1940 and 1941 with Ted Schroeder and again in 1943 with Frank Parker. That same year, as an ensign in the US Navy now, he was also a singles' finalist to Joe Hunt who later lost his life in an air crash. However, at Wimbledon in 1946, severe blisters and an inspired Jaroslav Drobny defeated Kramer in the fourth round after five sets. The tournament was won, rather surprisingly, by the giant Frenchman Yvon Petra, whose thunderous serves (which once actually broke a net) and audacious volleys helped him to survive three furious five-set matches against the top seed Pails in the quarter-finals, the tall Californian Tom

Brown in the semis and the small but powerful double-handed Australian Geoff Brown in the final. In 1947, the year when flying saucers were first sighted in the United States, Kramer returned as if from another planet. With his powerful all-court game working as smoothly as John Cobb's *Railton Special*, which was about to smash the world's land speed record at 394 mph, he was so well prepared that he swept all opposition aside to win like a thoroughbred with the loss of only one set – that to Pails in the semi-finals.

Four superb Americans won in the next four years, each in his own way contributing to the advance of the game. Bob Falkenburg, the 1948 champion who had won the doubles the previous year with Kramer, demonstrated the value of cannonball serving and a cool nerve as he saved two match points to defeat Australia's John Bromwich. Ted Schroeder, with the rolling gait of a sailor and rarely without his beloved pipe, except of course when he was on court, had already won the 1942 US title and at Wimbledon underlined the value of a crowding net attack allied to astute application of pressure at the right moments. When footfaulted at match point down against Frank Sedgman in the quarter-finals, he followed in his second serve and punched a winning volley. Budge Patty, who had fallen in love with Europe during his military service and eventually settled there, emphasised the value of fitness and the devastating effect of forceful forehand volleying. He actually gave up smoking and trained hard for three months before his European trip and then won both in Paris and at Wimbledon. There was surely a moral there for the whole post-war generation. Dick Savitt, who had won the Australian Championship in January, reminded everyone that even on grass heavy, accurate groundstrokes have always been the basic requirement of all tennis players.

Frank Sedgman's win for Australia in 1952 against the Czechoslovak left-hander Jaroslav Drobny was a breath-taking performance from start to finish. His ability to volley from any part of the court and his electrifying court coverage added a new dimension to the game which revealed the effect that Harry Hopman would have on tennis's development over the next 15 years. Hopman, the Australian Davis Cup captain in 1938, had taken over again in 1950 when he had converted the promising Australian Rules footballer Ken McGregor into an able second string to Sedgman. Together these two recaptured the cup for Australia. With 16 successes from 21 Challenge Rounds between 1938 and 1968 Harry built a record that is unlikely ever to be equalled. More significantly, he demonstrated the value of strict discipline and high work-rate allied to a deep knowledge of the individual needs of his charges that presaged the work of later coaches like Ion Tiriac, whose similar methods aided the careers of Guillermo Vilas and Boris Becker, and Lennart Bergelin who helped train Bjorn Borg. Between 1952 and 1971 six of the players Hopman had helped to develop won Wimbledon 14 times and between 1948 and 1974 there were an astonishing 19 Australian doubles' successes, which was a remarkable tribute to the effectiveness of 'The Old Fox's' methods.

The decade ended with two more American wins, separated by one of the most popular victories even Wimbledon has ever seen. By a strange coincidence, in 1953 and 1955 the US Davis Cup team-mates Vic Seixas and Tony Trabert, who took the famous team trophy to the States in 1954, both beat the same unseeded opponent in the Wimbledon final. The strong Dane, Kurt Nielsen, thus established a record of being the only unseeded player to reach the final twice. Seixas, slightly unorthodox for his time with a heavily topspun forehand, was a tremendous athlete and an agile volleyer. Trabert, one of only four men to have won the title without losing a set, had a beautifully rounded game of weighty serves, heavy groundstrokes and penetrating volleys. Two years earlier, and again in 1955, Trabert won his own US Championship and in 1954 he had won the French title in a one-sided final against fellow-American Arthur Larsen. It is amazing to think that, despite some fine American champions who have appeared since, men like Olmedo and McKinley, Smith and Ashe, Connors and McEnroe, no one from that mighty tennis nation has won in Paris since.

In 1954, the year between the two American successes, the Wimbledon victory of the Czech-born left-hander Jaroslav Drobny, at the age of 33, over the brilliant young 19-year-old Australian Ken Rosewall, filled the crowded Centre Court with emotion. 'Old Drob' had been a favourite ever since the first post-war Wimbledon when he had surprisingly eliminated the favourite, Jack Kramer. He was technically Egyptian in 1954 having taken that nationality after leaving his homeland to pursue his tennis career. In 1959 he was to become a British subject and he still lives in England.

After two previous final round losses, to Schroeder in 1949 and Sedgman in 1952, it seemed that Drobny's chance of adding to his two French titles (from five appearances in the Paris final) was gone but his swerving left-handed serves and beautiful touch on the volley finally

LEFT: Billy Knight (left) aged 17 and Tony Pickard, 19, in 1953 – the year Knight won the Invitation Junior event at Wimbledon that had started in 1948. Together they were sent for the winter to Australia where Knight won the Australian Junior Championships. The previous year 16-year-old Knight had sat his final School Certificate exam in English on 24 June in Northampton and had consumed sandwiches and milk while being driven straight to Wimbledon for a first-round match against the No. 2 seed Jaroslav Drobny who was then playing for Egypt. Drobny had won 6-0 6-1 6-3, the identical score by which he beat the other young British hope, Bobby Wilson, in the second round. Wilson had won Wimbledon's Invitation Singles in 1952.

ABOVE: The traditional champions' dance in 1952 brought together the 17-year-old American prodigy Maureen Connolly and the athletic Australian Frank Sedgman. Maureen had sacked her coach, Eleanor 'Teach' Tennant, on the eve of the tournament when she had tried to dissuade her from playing Wimbledon with an injured shoulder. For Frank, who moved with such fluid grace and volleyed from anywhere on the court with tremendous power, the four-set win over Jaroslav Drobny was ample compensation for the loss to Budge Patty in the 1950 final.

LEFT: In 1953, Coronation Year, the crowds flocked to Wimbledon in record numbers. Sadly, Queen Mary was not among them. Early in the year she had passed away having visited Wimbledon for the last time the previous year. Every competitor received a commemorative Coronation ashtray, the exterior of the Centre Court was decorated with the crests of the All England Club and the LTA and was floodlit every evening. Each year there were improvements to the grounds and amenities. In 1951 the seating around Court No. 2 (top left) had been rebuilt and extended and in 1952 a television interview room was constructed within the Centre Court.

LEFT: Jaroslav Drobny (left) and Budge Patty after their marathon third-round singles in 1953 which lasted four and a quarter hours and ended in gathering darkness at 9.17 p.m. with both men exhausted and Drobny the winner by 8-6 16-18 3-6 8-6 12-10 after saving three match points in the fourth set and another three in the fifth. This match will always be remembered for the spirit in which it was played and for the clinging courage and matchless skill of both men. Fittingly, the Committee presented each man with an engraved gold cigarette case to commemorate a precious moment of Wimbledon history.

RIGHT: Imagine the embarrassment when Mexico's petite Melita Ramirez and Australia's beautiful Beth Ruffin arrived on court for their first-round match in 1954 to find that they were both wearing identical Tinling creations – the only two that were the same of the 107 he had provided for 44 players. Melita's sister, Yola, was also a fine player and married the leading French player Pierre Darmon.

LEFT: Both Lord Montgomery and Clement Attlee were regular visitors to Wimbledon where the former Field Marshal enjoyed the man-to-man combat and the former Prime Minister enjoyed a break from the cares of political office.

RIGHT: Beverley Fleitz was one of the wave of great American ladies who dominated post-war women's tennis. She was unusual in that she was totally ambidextrous, hitting forehands on both sides.

prevailed. Young Rosewell, it seemed, would surely win one day; but it was one of fate's most perverse tricks that, despite three more appearances in the final – the last in 1974 at the age of 39 – the most durable of all champions never did add Wimbledon to his impressive list of titles.

Unquestionably the golden age of women's tennis occurred during the post-war decade when eight outstanding American ladies dominated the world game. Of them all Maureen Connolly and Louise Brough had the greatest success at Wimbledon. However, Pauline Betz, who had won the wartime US Championships three times from 1942 to 1944 and was to win it again in 1946, was arguably as good and was lost to the amateur game only because, by the harsh rules of the day, she was declared professional merely for stating that it was her ultimate intention to be so. She won the first post-war Championship for the loss of only 20 games and no sets with a devastating display of power tennis.

Pauline and Louise, and to a lesser degree Margaret Osborne, who became Mrs du Pont, Doris Hart and Shirley Fry, were all attacking players in the mould of the last pre-war champion Alice Marble. Miss Connolly was the supreme baseliner and, like Helen Wills Moody before her, utterly ruthless as a match player, with powers of concentration and determination that intimidated her opponents. Despite her tender years, for she was 17 when she won the first of her three consecutive victories between 1952 and 1954, Maureen had a maturity and grasp of the tactical niceties of the game that were partly inborn and partly the result of careful tuition from her coach Eleanor 'Teach' Tennant, with whom she fell out immediately before her first Championship. She had already won the US Championship the previous September at the age of 16. From that victory in the course of a remarkable career, sadly cut short in 1954 by a riding accident on her beloved Colonel Merryboy, she lost only four times; twice to her great friend Doris Hart, once to Shirley Fry and once to Beverley Fleitz. None of the losses was in important events and by the end of her short but spectacular career she had collected three American, three Wimbledon, two French and one Australian titles and had remained unbeaten in nine Wightman Cup rubbers. That Australian win in 1953 initiated a Grand Slam of the four major Championships in the same year, a feat that has been equalled only once by a woman, by Margaret Smith Court in 1970.

Louise Brough, a devastating serve-volleyer whose game was mastered only by the piercing returns of Maureen Connolly, won the title three years in a row between 1948 and 1950 and extended her winning sequence to 22 matches before losing to Shirley Fry in the 1951 semi-finals. When you remember that she had been in the first post-war final against Pauline Betz and had twice lost in the final to Maureen and then won again in 1955 after the prodigy had retired, you begin to understand the quality of her game. Furthermore, she won all three titles at Wimbledon twice, in 1948 and 1950, and altogether won the mixed doubles four times and the ladies' doubles five with Margaret Osborne du Pont with whom she also won three French and twelve US doubles' titles. With a US singles' win in 1947 and a success in Australia in 1950 Miss Brough lacked only a French title to complete an otherwise perfect record which included an unbeaten run of 22 Wightman Cup rubbers between 1946 and 1957. The contribution of this likeable and talented athlete to the development of women's tennis is often overlooked.

In any other age Margaret Osborne, the winner in 1947, and Doris Hart, who won in 1951, would have been hailed as outstanding champions. Indeed they were. Margaret won three US and two French singles' titles and in 1962, at the age of 42, returned to win a last mixed title at Wimbledon with the left-handed Australian Neale Fraser. She also played an important part in those relentless US Wightman Cup teams of the day winning 18 out of 18 rubbers between 1946 and 1962.

Doris, with two French and two US wins, plus innumerable doubles and mixed titles, was equally impressive. Her success was all the more remarkable because, as a child in Florida, she had suffered an accident which had left her with a permanently deformed leg and it was only through the encouragement of her brother that she persevered with tennis as a form of therapy. She was to develop the most perfectly produced strokes in women's tennis that are still used, on film, to teach beginners. It was sad that at Wimbledon Margaret and Doris were overshadowed by Maureen and Louise.

When you consider the other fine American ladies who appeared either fleetingly or not at all in the latter stages at Wimbledon, such as Pat Todd, Dorothy Bundy, Beverley Fleitz, Barbara Scofield Davidson, Gussie Moran, Nancy Chaffee, Dorothy Knode and Betty Pratt you begin to understand the depth of talent in the American game – a depth that has never been repeated. All the more credit, then, to the British girls Angela Mortimer and Anne Shilcock who won the women's doubles together in 1955, which was the first home success of any kind since Dorothy Round's singles' win in 1937. It was a hopeful end to the decade.

BIOGRAPHIES

GENTLEMEN

Y. Petra

J. A. Kramer

R. Falkenburg

F. R. Schroeder

J. E. Patty

1946

YVON PETRA

Born: 8 March 1916; died: 12 September 1984

This tall, shambling Frenchman emerged in the first year after the Second World War as a sledgehammer of a player. In a field of unsettled form his long reach and strong muscles surprisingly gave him a win in the final when the normally hard-hitting Australian, Geoff Brown, tried to slow-ball him.

He became a professional. In later years he became a keen painter.

1947

JACK KRAMER

Born: 1 August 1921

This very considerable player was born in Las Vegas and brought up in California. But for a blistered hand it is virtually certain he would have won in 1946. His victory progress was utterly overwhelming a year later. Despite losing one set he was the easiest men's singles' winner of all time, winning 130 games and losing only 37.

His final win against compatriot Tom Brown was the briefest of the century, 48 minutes. He returned to the United States to win his national title for the second year and became a professional. Kramer also became a promoter and was the leading impresario of the pros until open tennis in 1968. In 1972 he became the first Executive Director of ATP, the players' union.

The World Grand Prix was his concept. He was, as a player, the apostle of 'percentage tennis', the exploitation of shots having the greater likelihood of success.

1948

BOB FALKENBURG

Born: 29 January 1926

Falkenburg, a tall Californian, was probably lucky to win. In his final against Australian John Bromwich, a man of high artistry, he was thrice match point behind. On each he won with a hit or miss winner.

He found it vital to conserve his energies and provoked criticism by 'throwing' whole sets while recouping. Later in his career he played in the Davis Cup for Brazil. His special shot was an angled stop volley that only he could play.

1949

TED SCHROEDER

Born: 20 July 1921

'Lucky Ted' was a pipe-smoking Californian, though born in New Jersey, with the rolling gait of a cowboy. He won the singles at his only attempt having survived a hair-raising quarter-final against the Australian Frank Sedgman. He won the fifth set 9-7 after saving two match points, on one of which he came to the net behind his second serve after being foot-faulted.

In four rounds he was taken the full distance and he lost eight sets in all, the most conceded by a champion until Boris Becker in 1985.

He played little but was an outstanding Davis Cup man for the United States and the mainstay of four victories.

1950

BUDGE PATTY

Born: 11 February 1924

He was an American in Paris, idolised in Europe but little known in his own country. Slim and handsome, his fluency was exceptional and his forehand volley a dream. His Wimbledon triumph followed his first breakthrough to a major title in the French Championships when he was 26.

Seven years later he again delighted Wimbledon by taking the doubles with the 43-year-old American Gardnar Mulloy. He must rate as the most suave champion.

1951

DICK SAVITT

Born: 4 March 1927

The fifth US winner in as many years, Savitt was an underrated player from New Jersey with a heavy and punishing backhand. He had won the Australian title early in the year but was later overlooked when the Americans selected their side for the Challenge Round of the Davis Cup.

His final against the Australian Ken McGregor was among the more one-sided.

1952

FRANK SEDGMAN

Born: 29 October 1927

An Australian who moved with the ease of a panther, he initiated a period of Australian dominance. His forehand was a classic stroke.

He first broke through in doubles and won initially with John Bromwich before his successful pairing with Ken McGregor, with whom he won the 'Grand Slam' in 1951 and added three further legs in 1952.

He became a popular professional in 1953 after the Australian Lawn Tennis Association had seemingly delayed the decision with a lavish wedding present; they had the satisfaction of seeing Sedgman lead them to Davis Cup victory for the third time.

1953

VIC SEIXAS

Born: 30 August 1923

He was the second man from Philadelphia to reach the top, Tilden being the first. If rarely inspired he was always diligent. He hewed his way to success with a 9-7 fifth-set quarter-final win against Lew Hoad and followed it with 71 games in the semi-final against another Australian, Mervyn Rose, to whom he lost the second and third sets 10-12 9-11. He was lucky to find an unseeded finalist in the Dane Kurt Nielsen.

His Davis Cup loyalty was exceptional and he played 55 rubbers for the United States between 1951 and 1957, though only once could he help them to victory. A fine, rugged and aggressive performer.

1954

JAROSLAV DROBNY

Born: 12 October 1921

He was a Czech, later to become a British citizen, who was technically an Egyptian when he had the most popular win for years. He was then living in England with a British wife. A superb hard court performer, he was the first left-hander to win since Norman Brookes in 1914.

He was in the forefront in all previous post-war meetings having also competed in 1938 and 1939, and never more so than in 1953 when he beat Budge Patty after an historic 93-game third-round match. His touch was superb, his smashing impeccable though an injured shoulder had tamed his cannonball service by the time he won. His final against Ken Rosewall was a classic and its 58 games total was then the highest ever for a final.

1955

TONY TRABERT

Born: 16 August 1930

A rugged champion from Cincinnati, who is often under-estimated. He had an outstanding backhand. He won not only Wimbledon in 1955 but the French and US titles also. His Wimbledon title was achieved without the loss of a set, a distinction which, among the play-through champions, he shares only with Don Budge, Chuck McKinley and Bjorn Borg – and Budge alone lost fewer games.

Like so many of his era he became a professional.

M. A. Trabert

R. Savitt

F. A. Sedgman

E. V. Seixas

J. Drobny

LADIES

P. M. Betz

M. E. Osborne/du Pont

A. L. Brough

D. J. Hart

M. C. Connolly

1946

PAULINE BETZ

Born: 6 August 1919; married: 2 February 1949 (to R. Addie)

This elegant American was in the vanguard of the shatteringly effective US invasion of Wimbledon in the decade after the Second World War. A rhythmic player she won at her first and only attempt, losing no set and a total of but 20 games.

She did not return because the American LTA, in an excess of amateur zeal, ruled that she had forfeited her status merely by discussing professional prospects.

1947

MARGARET OSBORNE/DU PONT

Born: 4 March 1918; married: 26 November 1947 (to W. du Pont)

A most competent all-rounder, she won the singles but once, in 1947; she took the US title the three years following and the French in 1946 and 1949.

As a doubles pair she and Louise Brough were almost invincible. Her best years were lost in the War. In 1962 at Wimbledon she won the mixed with Neale Fraser when she was 44. She never lost a Wightman Cup rubber in 18.

1948, 1949, 1950, 1955

LOUISE BROUGH

Born: 11 March 1923; married: 9 August 1958 (to A. T. Clapp)

A vigorous exponent of the serve and volley, her achievements were staggering. For three successive years she was in the final of all three events and missed being triple champion only by losing the mixed in 1949.

In that year she was on the Centre Court on finals day for more than five hours. She won the singles 10-8 1-6 10-8, the doubles 8-6 7-5 but yielded the mixed 7-9 11-9 5-7, which was

a total of 117 games when play was continuous and resting not possible.

She came back to win the singles a fourth time. She lost no Wightman Cup rubber in 22. With 13 Wimbledon titles, 17 American, 3 French and 2 Australian she was a champion extraordinary. She was Oklahoma-born but Californian by adoption.

1951

DORIS HART

Born: 20 June 1925

Born in St Louis but trained in Florida she was a superlatively graceful stroke player whose achievements would have been greater had she not flourished in the period when outstanding American women were two-a-penny. The purity and elegance of her play was despite taking up tennis as a remedial exercise for threatened deformity of her legs.

She was exceptionally gracious as well. Her 35 Grand Slam titles include singles, doubles and mixed in all four championships.

1952, 1953, 1954

MAUREEN CONNOLLY

Born: 17 September 1934; married: 11 June 1955 (to N. Brinker); died: 21 June 1969

This Californian genius was 16 when she won the US singles in 1951. She was still under 20 when a broken leg in a riding accident ended her career. By then she had won Wimbledon thrice, the US title three times also, the French twice and the Australian once. She had taken the Grand Slam in 1953, becoming the first woman to do so.

Nor had she yet become a complete player. Groundstrokes, with a backhand of gigantic dimensions, were her strength and she was still seeking comparable volleying skills in her last year. A very great player.

Sadly she died young, though a wife and mother of two.

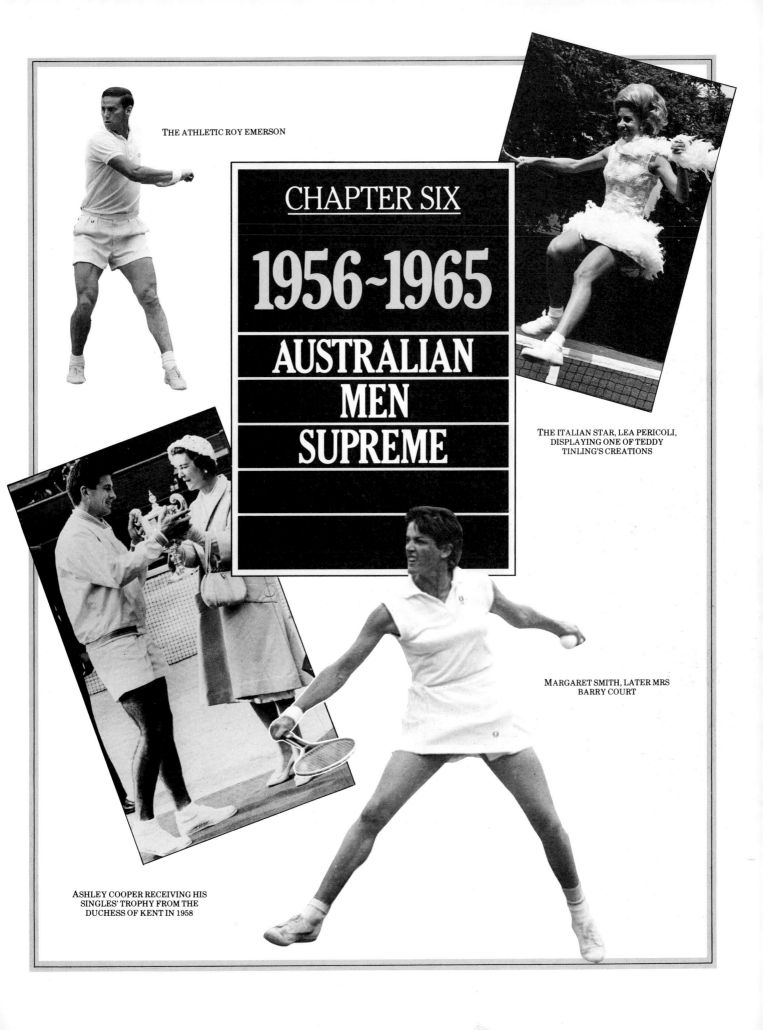

THE ATHLETIC ROY EMERSON

CHAPTER SIX

1956~1965

AUSTRALIAN MEN SUPREME

THE ITALIAN STAR, LEA PERICOLI, DISPLAYING ONE OF TEDDY TINLING'S CREATIONS

MARGARET SMITH, LATER MRS BARRY COURT

ASHLEY COOPER RECEIVING HIS SINGLES' TROPHY FROM THE DUCHESS OF KENT IN 1958

RECOVERY from the lethargy and austerity of the war years in Britain was not a fast process. Following the end of the unpopular Korean War in 1951, the Festival of Britain, which had attracted over 8 million visitors, had begun the process of belief in a brighter future. The accession of Elizabeth II in 1952, resulting from the sad death from cancer of her father, gave the country the youthful leadership that was needed to restore confidence. It seemed to be an act of providence when, the following spring, Edmund Hillary and Sherpa Tenzing conquered Everest. That mighty peak had finally been scaled on 29 May but the news was held back so that it reached London on the very eve of the emotional and colourful coronation ceremony.

In the wider world the United Nations, which had taken the initiative over Korea, was powerless to stop the Russian invasion of Hungary in November 1956 when that country, demanding greater democratic freedom, had renounced the Warsaw Pact. United Nations' entreaties to the Soviet Union were ignored. Attempts to understand the Russians, it seemed, were futile. Earlier that year Commander Crabbe, a Navy diver, had mysteriously disappeared during a visit by the Russian Navy to Portsmouth and the arrival in Britain of the Russian leaders Khrushchev and Bulganin during the de-Stalinisation period did nothing to convince the British people that the hug of the Russian bear would be any more friendly in the future.

Britain and France had troubles of their own in 1956 when President Nasser of Egypt seized the Suez Canal following the sudden decision in July by the Americans not, after all, to finance the building of the Aswan High Dam. Israel invaded and Britain and France sent troops. This prompted a threat from the Russians that they would intervene. After a short burst of fighting both sides heeded a United Nations call to end hostilities. Clearly Britain was no longer the great power it had been. Clearly, too, the effectiveness of the UN depended on the attitudes and strengths of the combatants. Some nations were more equal than others. This incident led to the resignation of Prime Minister Anthony Eden in January the following year, a tired and sick man.

Other lands had their problems too in 1956. In Algeria 400,000 French troops failed to quell a revolt. In Johannesburg there were mass arrests following the introduction of apartheid in 1952. In Ulster the IRA were engaging in murderous border raids. However, there were also more cheerful events. In the United States Dwight D. Eisenhower was re-elected as President for a second term in 1956. Pakistan became a republic within the British Commonwealth; Morocco became an independent state; the Sudan became an independent republic and was admitted to the Arab League. In Monaco the wedding of the decade between Prince Rainier III and his fairytale, filmstar princess, Grace Kelly, was presented with such glittering pomp that even the most Hollywood-hardened commentators were left misty-eyed.

Winston Churchill, having resigned from the premiership in 1955, turned to authorship and produced the first volume of his mammoth work *A History of the English Speaking Peoples*, which was not completed until 1958. These were the days of those rounded and sensual Henry Moore sculptures, of popular novelists like Hammond Innes and Rose Macaulay and of a new breed of realists like Colin Wilson whose *The Outsider* caught the flavour of class frustration as did John Osborne's play *Look Back in Anger*. This was the rock-and-roll era when Bill Haley and the Comets were straining the pelvic girdles of an entire generation and James Dean was adopted as a folk hero by the disillusioned youth of the Western world following the release of his film *Rebel without a Cause* – despite the fact that the cinema was fighting a losing battle with television. The Establishment was being challenged in Britain. A CND march from the Atomic Research Establishment's headquarters at Aldermaston following the opening of the world's first large-scale nuclear reactor at Calder Hall in Cumberland demonstrated people's fears of technological progress and of the dangers of a holocaust. However, you would never have guessed that such undercurrents were running had you been in Melbourne that summer where, for a few brief weeks, the XVIth Olympic Games unified the sporting youth of the world.

Wimbledon had always enjoyed a separate identity since the earliest times. There is evidence of a Neolithic settlement in about 2500 BC and in the Domesday Book it appears as a village that is part of the Manor of Mortlake. After 800 years of evolution, then, one can imagine the feelings of the residents when, on 1 April 1965, Wimbledon ceased to exist as an independent borough. On that day, by Act of Parliament, it was forcibly joined with the neighbouring boroughs of Merton, Mitcham and Morden to become the London Borough of Merton. To the older residents this was an unforgivable betrayal.

To the new generation of youthful tennis players Wimbledon still only meant tennis at the All England Club. The ones who captured most of the attention, and most of the men's titles, in the second post-war decade were the suntanned, Hopman-trained Australians. Led by a muscular, blond Adonis called Lew Hoad, five of them won eight Wimbledon singles' titles during this period. These engaging warriors won as many friends for their cheerful attitudes on and off the court as for their superb skills. Lew won the title twice, in 1956 and 1957, with displays of awesome power that overwhelmed first his partner and travelling companion, Ken Rosewall, who had been born 21 days before Lew and within a few miles of him in a neighbouring Sydney suburb in November 1934, and then the 20-year-old from Melbourne, Ashley Cooper. The latter match, a devastating 6-2 6-1 6-2, caused many of the old champions present to rate Lew's performance that day as the most perfect exhibition of sustained power ever played.

Hoad was a charismatic character in every way with the looks of Robert Mitchum, the physique of a middleweight boxer and the gentle charm of a genuinely shy young man. His tennis, though, was anything but gentle. Thanks to amazing strength in his arms he had the ability to wield the racket like a tooth-pick and his strong wrist enabled him to meet the ball firmly even when at full stretch or caught close to his body. The sight of Lew throwing in a heavy second serve, volleying crisply off his toes from inside the service line, and then, with perfect timing, soaring up to kill the lob with an explosive smash was to savour the movements of a born athlete. Lew loved nothing better than to work himself into a lather on court in one of those two-against-one drills that the Hopman Aussies developed into almost an art form of its own, or to work out in the gym where he enjoyed pitting his great strength against the exercise equipment.

ABOVE: Althea Gibson (left) and Darlene Hard produced an adventurous final in 1957 that was full of aggressive volleying and ambitious returns of serve that did not always find the mark. This was the first of two successive titles for Althea but Darlene, good player though she was (as her four doubles' titles with three different partners confirm), was destined never to win the singles. She was beaten in the final again two years later by Maria Bueno.

BELOW: The only demonstration there has been on the Centre Court occurred on the final day in 1957 when the Queen was visiting The Championships for the first time. During a change of ends in the doubles' final between the top seeds Hoad and Fraser against the eventual winners Mulloy and Patty, who were unseeded and whose combined ages totalled 76 years, Helen Jarvis of Croydon, founder of the 'Life, Love and Sex Appeal Party', climbed

BELOW: Australia's incredible tennis 'twins', Lew Hoad (left) and Ken Rosewall, set new standards of achievement for tennis teenagers in the 1950s. On their first visit to Wimbledon in 1952 as the finest 17-year-olds the world had ever seen, they beat the No. 2 seeds in the doubles, Gardnar Mulloy and Dick Savitt (who was the reigning singles' champion at the time), to reach the semi-finals of the doubles and the following year they won the event. Born within three weeks of each other in neighbouring Sydney suburbs, these two did more than any other players of the 1950s to glamorise tennis to the increasingly young band of tennis fans who could identify with them.

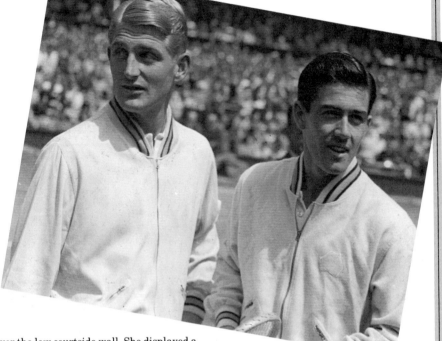

over the low courtside wall. She displayed a banner which began with the loyal message 'Save Our Queen' and started shouting about her campaign for a new banking system. In a few minutes she was hustled off the court by the Referee and a policeman.

RIGHT: The first Swede to win a Wimbledon title was not Bjorn Borg. In 1958 Sven Davidson (left) and Ulf Schmidt won the doubles together with a straight-sets' victory over the Australians Ashley Cooper and Neale Fraser. Davidson, the French Champion in 1957, had been a Wimbledon quarter-finalist in 1955 and would be again in 1958 after reaching the semi-finals in 1957. Schmidt did almost as well, finishing twice in the last eight, in 1956 and 1957.

BELOW: In 1959 only one of the eight seeded players lost in the first round. The man who beat Italy's Nicola Pietrangeli (No. 3), the reigning French champion, was the 19-year-old American 'Butch' Buchholz who, the previous year, had won all four junior titles at the major Championships, which then were still invitation events. Not until 1983 was this feat equalled when Stefan Edberg of Sweden won the first junior Grand Slam of the open era.

ABOVE: After watching Alex Olmedo, the Peruvian American, beat 20-year-old Rod Laver in the 1959 final, Princess Margaret left Wimbledon by helicopter from the golf course on the other side of Church Road. The golfers were glad to see the 'chopper' taking off for its arrival had held up play for an hour.

With singles' titles in France and Australia that same year plus three doubles' titles each in Australia and at Wimbledon, and one each in the United States and France, Lew proved his all-round ability. His 17 winning Davis Cup rubbers between 1953 and 1956 were equally important in making Lew a national hero throughout Australia. Sadly for his many fans around the world Lew suffered a severe back injury shortly after he turned pro in 1957 so that he was never completely able to fulfil his potential and when open tennis finally came in 1968 he was only a shadow of the man who had caused so much excitement 12 years earlier. Fortunately he still serves the game through his beautiful tennis ranch at Fuengirola in Southern Spain and as a member of the ITF panel that each year selects the Men's World Champion.

Lew's former tennis twin, Ken Rosewall, was his perfect complement in an amazing partnership. Small but wiry in stature and with a permanently boyish face topped with a head of sleek jet-black hair, Ken was the absolute perfectionist with immaculate footwork and flawless stroke production, devoid of a single wasted motion. Nicknamed 'muscles' (originally because of his lack of them), Ken was a natural left-hander who used to hold the racket with both hands as a youngster but made the decision to play right-handed after discussions with his father who had been his only teacher. It produced one of the best backhands the game has ever seen, hit with a flat swing and a slightly 'open' face that imparted a little natural, controlling backspin. Deceptively quick and with a speed of thought and reaction that kept him always one step ahead of the opposition, Ken turned himself into the most consistent player of the age.

One of his most remarkable performances came at Wembley in the 1959 London Professional Championships against the reigning Wimbledon champion Alex Olmedo, who had just turned professional. Playing on a fast wooden floor that should have helped his opponent's serve-volley game, Ken won the first 15 games with an astonishing display of controlled passing shots and lobs that, allied to his own quick-silver volleying, brought him a 6-0 6-0 6-3 victory containing only four unforced errors. His fellow pros that day stood leaning on the wooden barrier surrounding the court marvelling at the sheer perfection of it all.

It has been an amazingly enduring career. Consider the record. The Australian and French champion first in 1953, aged 18, he won the latter again in the first year of 'open' tennis in 1968 and the former three times more, in 1955, 1971 and 1972. That last win was achieved just 20 years after his first success, and at the age of 37! His two US titles were won 14 years apart and the first of them, in 1956, prevented Hoad from winning the elusive Grand Slam. Like Lew, Ken's best days coincided with the old pro tour on which he reigned supreme for four years from the moment he eclipsed Pancho Gonzales to the arrival of Rod Laver in 1963. And, believe it or not, he is still winning titles on the Grand Masters tour for over-45s. Seemingly he is not happy unless he is competing; only his opponents wish he would stop.

The year after Hoad's two successive victories Ashley Cooper had his hour of glory when both Hoad and Rosewall had departed to the ranks of the professionals. The man he beat in the 1958 final was the left-hander from Melbourne, Neale Fraser, who would win the singles two years later, in 1960. Fraser's opponent in that final was a carroty-haired youngster from Rockhampton, Queensland, called Rod Laver who had already been a singles' finalist the previous year. In some ways Fraser was lucky to have been in the final at all for in a remarkable quarter-final against the tall American Earl 'Butch' Buchholz, on a scorching afternoon, he had survived five match points before the American was forced to retire with cramp after 30 games of the unfinished fourth set when leading 6-4 3-6 6-4 15-15. Fraser had one of the best swinging and kicking left-handed serves since Drobny and learned to cover up a slight weakness on the backhand with some agile footwork. Fraser was five years older than Laver and sufficiently experienced to keep the 21-year-old under constant pressure. They split the opening sets and Fraser held on to win 6-4 3-6 9-7 7-5. After a distinguished playing career, which included two US titles and many doubles' successes, Neale became a worthy successor to Harry Hopman as the Australian Davis Cup captain.

In the intervening year, 1959, the tall Peruvian American Alex Olmedo had beaten Laver, who was competing at Wimbledon for the third time, in straight sets. Olmedo was a natural athlete who moved with the grace of a panther. He was the son of a groundsman in Arequipa, Peru but had won a scholarship to the University of Southern California in Los Angeles and acquired US citizenship. The Czar of Californian tennis at this time was Perry T. Jones who had watched over the young man's development at the Los Angeles Tennis Club. Jones was also the US Davis Cup captain in 1958 and believed that Olmedo's quick eye and beautifully coordinated power game would be ideal on the grass courts

in Australia. Accordingly, Jones selected him to play in the Challenge Round in Brisbane. It was an inspired decision. Olmedo's two singles' wins and a share in the doubles' win with Hamilton Richardson gave the United States a first victory since the famous upset in Sydney in 1954. 'The Chief', as Olmedo was popularly known, went on to win the Australian Championships with a four-set win over Fraser and six months later he won even more easily against Laver to win at Wimbledon. It had been a meteoric rise which immediately made him a target for the professional promoters. It was no surprise when, after Fraser had scored a revenge win against him in the final of the US Championships and another in the unsuccessful defence of the Davis Cup, Olmedo joined the professional ranks.

With the emergence of Laver at the summit we were treated to a rare blend of skill, courage and confidence that turned this 5 foot 9 inch fireball, with the bandy legs, the mop of ginger hair and the shy manner, into a relentless match-winning machine. During his junior days Laver had tried to hit with Hoad's severity but, without that champion's physique, he could not control the ball. It was not until the regime of repeated exercises and drills had transformed his slight figure into a frame as whipcord-tough as one of the drover's ponies from the Queensland outback where Rod grew up that he began to cut down the percentage of errors to an acceptable level. His ability to hit the ball early with either slice or topspin on his single-handed backhand set the pattern for others to follow. All-out attack was the name of the game, even on the heartbreakingly slow courts at the Stade Roland Garros in Paris. It made for some truly thrilling tennis that earned Rod the nickname of the

RIGHT: To the east of the Centre Court is the running track beside the lake in Wimbledon Park. South-west of the Centre Court is the covered court building that was opened in 1958, and ringing the club are the car parks. To the north of the Centre Court are the cricket pitches that were later developed for improved facilities.

BELOW: The key match for the 1960 champion, Australia's Neale Fraser, was his quarter-final against Earl 'Butch' Buchholz. After 2 hours and 50 minutes on a sweltering afternoon, the American had built a lead of 6-4 3-6 6-4 15-14 and had seen six match points come and go as he increasingly became affected by cramps. Collapsing for the second time at 15 games all Buchholz lay prone as Fraser and the physiotherapist rushed to his aid. He was carried off the court in agony and, eventually, Fraser won his title.

BELOW: The No. 2 seed, Darlene Hard of the United States, coming to the assistance of 16-year-old Frances Walton in their second-round match in 1960. With a safety-pin borrowed from a spectator, the bra-strap was repaired and Darlene completed her 6-1 6-0 victory en route to the quarter-finals where the South African Sandra Reynolds, seeded four, beat her in three sets.

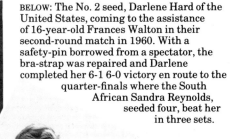

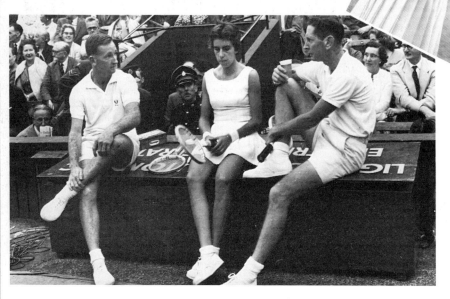

LEFT: On the last day of the same Championships in the mixed doubles' final, Darlene herself was forced to leave the court for natural reasons. Her unexplained departure totally bewildered her partner Rod Laver (left) and their opponents Bob Howe and Maria Bueno who sat and waited on the ball cooler. Eventually Maria, somewhat irritated, went off to find Darlene. When they both returned and the match was resumed the Brazilian had lost her rhythm. The spectators, though, had their money's worth as Laver and Miss Hard finally won 8-6.

BELOW: Christine Truman (left) and Angela Mortimer in 1961, the first all-British finalists since 1914 when Dorothea Lambert Chambers had beaten Ethel Larcombe for her seventh and last title. The 1961 final proved to be a close and dramatic encounter that was won eventually 4-6 6-4 7-5 by Angela, who became the first British singles' champion since Dorothy Round in 1937.

ABOVE: The Australians have always excelled in doubles on the fast grass of Wimbledon and the 1961 men's doubles final provided another thrilling all-Australian spectacle. The match ran its spectacular five-set course as Roy Emerson (far end, left) and Neale Fraser, the champions in 1959, defeated Bob Hewitt (near end, left) and Fred Stolle 6-4 6-8 6-4 6-8 8-6. However, the following year, and again in 1964, Hewitt and Stolle did claim the doubles' prize.

LEFT: Dr John and Neale Fraser came from Melbourne, the sons of a High Court Judge, and in 1962 were the first brothers ever to reach the semi-finals of the singles in the same year. They both lost – Neale to Rod Laver and John to Martin Mulligan. This was also the first time that all four semi-finalists were from Australia and the first year since 1922 that there was no American among the last eight. The nearest parallels of fraternal success occurred in the days of the Challenge Round before 1922. In 1898 Laurie Doherty had won the All-Comers' singles to challenge his brother Reggie for the title. Two years earlier Wilfred Baddeley had been the holder when his twin brother Herbert had reached the semi-finals of the All-Comers where W. V. Eaves beat him.

'Rockhampton Rocket' and helped him to build a record that may never be equalled. For in 1962, and again in 1969 when the game had gone 'open', Rod won the Grand Slam of the four major championships, all in the same year. No one before or since has achieved that feat twice.

Rod also served Australia well on Davis Cup duty, being part of Hopman's successful teams between 1959 and 1962. Returning in 1973 under the captaincy of Neale Fraser he collected three more rubbers as the Australians beat the United States in Cleveland.

Rod's Wimbledon record is outstanding. With his two wins in 1961 and 1962 before he turned professional and his third and fourth in 1968 and 1969 when he was allowed to compete there again as the game became 'open', Rod had won 28 consecutive matches at Church Road. When his progress was halted in 1970 in the fourth round by Britain's Roger Taylor he had stretched that run to 31, a figure that was to remain a modern record until the remarkable Bjorn Borg came on the scene a few years later. Between 1956 and 1971 Rod contested 55 singles' matches of which he won 49 and lost 6 and I shall always be convinced that had he not changed from his faithful wooden Dunlop Maxply frame to an American Chemold aluminium one Rod would have remained unbeatable for two or three more years. We often discussed this point and I used to ask him if he really believed that Yehudi Menuhin would ever have considered swapping his trusty Stradivarius for a tin fiddle! Although Rod minimised the effect of the switch the fact is that his timing and touch were disturbed and, once he had lost a few matches, the cloak of invincibility dropped from his shoulders. Such is the power of the almighty dollar.

Chuck McKinley's hustling, bustling win in 1963 for the United States halted the Australian steamroller, but only temporarily. Possessed of immense strength and energy Chuck bounced around the court with such speed that it was an exhausting experience merely watching him. He was one of only four men who have won The Championship without losing a set; the others are Budge (1938), Trabert (1955) and Borg (1976). His final round victim was the unfortunate Australian Fred Stolle who had the doubtful privilege of filling that role for the next two years as well when his conqueror was his Davis Cup team-mate Roy Emerson. The likeable 'Emmo' would surely have won a third consecutive title and equalled Fred Perry's post-Challenge Round record before Borg achieved it in 1978 had he not been injured in 1966.

There has surely never been a fitter or faster tennis athlete than Roy whose appetite for practice and training was legendary. Roy was the natural successor to Laver when in 1962 that far-sighted champion sensed the need to keep the pro game going before the seemingly inevitable introduction of open tennis. For Harry Hopman, Roy was a wonderful example to the younger players and a marvellously dependable rock on which to build the fortunes of four more successful Davis Cup teams in the five years up to 1967. Emerson's tally of six Australian, two American and two French titles, plus a remarkable six successive French doubles' successes with five different partners, demonstrates clearly the complete domination he achieved in the days leading up to open tennis.

The same dominance might well have occurred in the women's game if only that talented athlete Althea Gibson had decided to remain an amateur. As it was, after becoming the first black player to win a Wimbledon title – which she did twice, in 1957 and 1958 – she turned professional and toured for a time with the Harlem Globetrotters playing matches against Carol Fageros, of gold lamé panties fame, before turning to singing and then golf, at which she quickly became good enough to join the women's pro tour. In three short years Althea won the singles and doubles in France once and at Wimbledon twice, plus the US singles' title twice, making her the outstanding player of the day. She was tall, strong and talented with the 'big game' of those magnificent Americans of the previous decade, namely Pauline Betz, Louise Brough, Margaret Osborne and Doris Hart. In 1957 she overpowered the stocky American Darlene Hard and in 1958 the British girl from Torquay, Angela Mortimer, who would learn from the experience and shortly bring inspiration to a new generation of home players.

In between Louise Brough's fourth and last win in 1955 and the two Gibson successes came a most popular victor. Shirley Fry, the quiet girl from Akron, Ohio, had always been in the shadow of the other great American players but in 1956 she enjoyed her *annus mirabilis* with victories at Wimbledon (where, with Doris Hart, she had already won the doubles' title three times from five appearances in the final), and at Forest Hills, where she had won the doubles four times. On the way to the final she beat both Althea and Louise, each time in three sets, before outclassing the British No. 6 seed, Angela Buxton. Miss Buxton had benefited from a walk-over conceded by the second favourite, Beverley Fleitz of the United States, who had discovered during the course of the tournament that she was pregnant and so had retired on medical advice.

Between 1959 and 1964 we were treated to three regal wins from the artistic racket of the elegant queen of Brazilian tennis, Maria Bueno. Here was poetry in motion whose every movement combined the grace of a ballet dancer with the controlled power of a top gymnast. In that first year the luckless Darlene Hard was once again a losing finalist; the following year the delightful, elfin South African Sandra Reynolds was her victim; and in 1964 the reigning champion Margaret Smith was humbled 6-4 7-9 6-3 after a tremendous battle of power against finesse. Shown off to perfection in some stunning Tinling creations, Maria captivated the knowledgeable Wimbledon crowd until, towards the end of her reign, she appeared on Court No. 1 wearing, beneath another pretty white dress, a pair of pants in navy blue with turquoise panels that matched the coloured panels of her under-skirt. To the unpractised eyes of certain enraged committee members it appeared that Tinling had deliberately chosen the club colours of green and mauve to adorn the most shapely bottom in The Championships. Although this was clearly not the case, coming on top of the 1949 affair of Gussie Moran's lace panties, which had caused their designer to resign from his post as Wimbledon's 'call-boy' this, they felt, was too much. It took almost 20 years for the combined effects of these two incidents to be forgotten and forgiven, despite the fact that the second incident was based on incorrect information. Only when a new generation of management arrived in 1982 was it opportune to call once again on the services of someone whose unique position in tennis and unrivalled knowledge of the requirements of both players and administrators make him an indispensible part of the Wimbledon scene.

LEFT: In 1962 the title fell to the No. 8 seed, Karen Susman (right), who the previous year, as 18-year-old Karen Hantze, had caused great excitement by winning the doubles with another American teenager, a precocious 17-year-old called Billie Jean Moffitt. The girl Karen beat in the 1962 final was the unseeded Czechoslovak, Vera Sukova, the first woman from her country to reach the final and the trailblazer for Martina Navratilova, whom she used to coach, and Hana Mandlikova. Her own daughter Helena became a fine player, too, and was ranked in the world's top ten in the mid-1980s.

RIGHT: Happily, accidents at Wimbledon have been rare but in 1963 Australia's Jan Lehane twisted her ankle so badly at 1-6 2-1 against Darlene Hard in the quarter-finals that she was carried off the court and conceded the match.

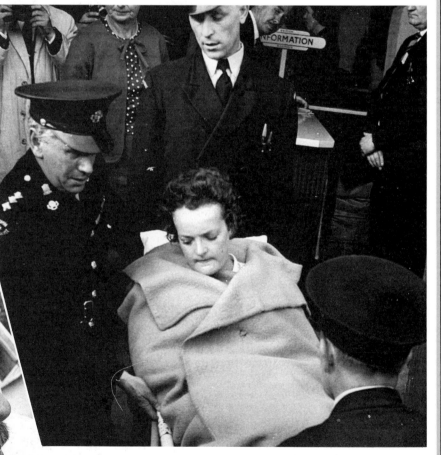

LEFT: In 1963 Captain Mike Gibson took over from his father-in-law, Colonel John Legg, as Referee and filled the post with great efficiency until 1975.

RIGHT: Despite three appearances in the final, the popular Australian Fred Stolle (left) was fated never to win the singles though he did have two doubles' successes to his credit in 1962 and 1964 in partnership with fellow countryman Bob Hewitt. In 1963 he had lost to Chuck McKinley; here in 1964 his Davis Cup team-mate Roy Emerson was his conqueror, as he was again the following year.

LEFT: It is easy to see why there was no call when Clark Graebner's shot fell over the line when he was match point down against South Africa's Abe Segal on Court No. 3 in this first-round match in 1964. Amid the confusion the ball boy awakened the embarrassed lineswoman, Dorothy Cavis Brown, whose picture was relayed round the world to make her the most famous court official of the decade. Subsequently, she was suspended from duty and soon afterwards gave up umpiring.

RIGHT: John Newcombe (left) and the left-handed Tony Roche were arguably the finest doubles' team of recent years. They won Wimbledon five times together and would surely have won more if Roche had not suffered the misfortune of tennis elbow for which he visited a faith healer in the Philippines and underwent an operation without anaesthetic that helped to cure the problem. Newcombe was so impressed that a few years later when he had golfer's elbow he visited the same healer who performed a similar operation which was equally successful. For some time afterwards John would delight in showing the tiny scar to his friends.

At last, in 1961, all the long years of waiting for another British champion were ended. We were guaranteed a first home winner since Dorothy Round in 1937 when, in the lower half, Angela Mortimer beat the No. 1 seed Sandra Reynolds to reach her second singles' final and, in the top half, Christine Truman, the favourite of all the schoolgirls, beat both the No. 2 seed, Margaret Smith of Australia and Miss Reynold's compatriot, Renée Schuurman, who had eliminated Ann Haydon, the official third favourite. This was the first all-British women's final at Wimbledon since Mrs Lambert Chambers had won the last of her seven titles by beating Ethel Larcombe in 1914 at Worple Road; and how the Centre Court crowd loved it.

In an emotional match that included a break for rain at the end of the first set and a much discussed fall by Christine in the second, which appeared to affect her psychologically more than physically, Angela finally fulfilled her life's ambition at the age of 29 and at the eleventh attempt. The 4-6 6-4 7-5 victory was fashioned as much on the strength of nerve and determination of the winner as on skill, factors which usually gave Angela victory against Christine when they met. It was a fitting reward for one of the most consistent and workmanlike baseliners of the day, who had already won the French title in 1953 (the last English girl to win there had been Peggy Scriven in 1934) and the Australian crown in 1958 (Dorothy Round had won there in 1935), after recovering from entamoebic dysentery contracted in Egypt two years earlier but not diagnosed until 1960.

The following year, 1962, saw Karen Susman who, as Miss Hantze, had won the doubles the previous year with a fellow Californian tomboy named Billie Jean Moffitt, come into her own as a singles' player. Miss Moffitt had eliminated the top seed Margaret Smith in her opening match but had then lost to Ann Haydon who, in turn, had fallen to Miss Hantze in the semi-finals. In the lower half the second favourite Darlene Hard had been surprisingly put out by the unseeded Czechoslovak Vera Sukova who then beat the No. 3 seed Maria Bueno, as well. Mrs Susman, though, served and volleyed too well for Vera Sukova in the final and won the title in two ten-game sets.

The second post-war decade ended with two majestic wins by Margaret Smith from three finals. In 1963 she beat Billie Jean and in 1965 she mastered Maria Bueno, who had beaten her the previous year. It was at once apparent that the tall, athletic Australian was something special. She played the game like a man and had a better serve than several of the lesser men. A fitness fanatic, Margaret could play all day without getting tired and had it not been for a slight temperamental weakness which caused her to tighten up occasionally on the biggest occasions, she would surely have been universally acclaimed as the greatest player who ever lived. As it was she amassed the greatest number of major titles that any player, male or female, has ever done before or since. Her 24 singles' Championships (3 Wimbledon, 5 US, 5 French and 11 Australian) plus 19 doubles and 19 mixed doubles titles bring her tally in the four major Championships to 62. If you add the three events at the Championships of Italy, Germany and South Africa, you arrive at the hardly credible figure of 88. Then you must add the 1970 Grand Slam in singles and the 1963 Grand Slam in mixed doubles (with Ken Fletcher) plus the undefeated run of 20 rubbers in eight

Federation Cup years between 1963 and 1970 fully to understand Margaret's gigantic contribution to the development of women's tennis. Motherhood (she became Mrs Barry Court in 1967) and religious visions finally ended the tournament career of one of the most remarkable ladies ever to lift a tennis racket who still enjoys imparting her vast knowledge and experience to the next generation of aspiring Australian youngsters on her private tennis court behind her beautiful home overlooking the Swan River in Perth.

So ended another decade of growth, but it was as nothing compared to the explosion that lay just around the corner as the pressure to introduce open tennis gathered irrepressible momentum.

BIOGRAPHIES

GENTLEMEN

L. A. Hoad

A. J. Cooper

A. Olmedo

N. A. Fraser

R. G. Laver

1956, 1957

LEW HOAD

Born: 23 November 1934

With a solid frame, a wrist of iron, muscles of steel and the eye of an eagle, this Australian was one of the best players of all time, albeit not a consistent match winner.

His first Wimbledon singles' final was won against his partner Ken Rosewall; a few weeks later the same man denied him the 'Grand Slam' by ousting him in the US final. The next year at Wimbledon Hoad won against another Australian, Ashley Cooper, in an utterly devastating display of power tennis.

He became a professional 48 hours later in New York. A back injury marred his later career and he settled in Spain with his wife, the Australian international Jennifer Staley, and children as owner of a tennis complex.

1958

ASHLEY COOPER

Born: 15 September 1936

Hopelessly outplayed by Lew Hoad in 1957, he came back the following year to become yet another Australian champion. In the third all-Australian final in as many years he beat the left-handed Neale Fraser over 52 games, with a fourth set of 13-11.

Few champions worked harder. He yielded seven sets in his seven matches and played a total of 322 games in all. This is the record for any champion.

Having added the American title Cooper became a professional in the autumn of 1958.

1959

ALEX OLMEDO

Born: 24 March 1936

Peruvian by race, Californian by adoption, it was for the United States that he ended a sequence of Australian victories in 1959. He was very fast and an adept volleyer.

He beat two memorable champions-to-be in the course of his success, Roy Emerson in the semi-final and Rod Laver in the final. Subsequently, the professional game took his loyalties.

1960

NEALE FRASER

Born: 3 October 1933

A distinguished Australian left-hander, he had an intimidating variety of service deliveries, including a 'googly' that confounded everyone. Having been the losing finalist in 1958, his victory two years later was adventurous. In the quarter-final against the American Earl Buchholtz he was six times match point down in the fourth set before Buchholtz, paralysed with cramp, retired at 15 games all. Rod Laver was his victim in the final.

He was twice US Champion. He remained amateur and became a notable captain of the Australian Davis Cup team.

1961, 1962, 1968, 1969

ROD LAVER

Born: 9 August 1938

Arguably the greatest singles' player of all time. This left-handed genius from Queensland won what was for him four consecutive Wimbledons. He could not play between 1963 and 1967 because he was a professional but with the open game he immediately picked up where he had left off.

Laver was twice the Grand Slam winner, in 1962 and 1969. In the first of those years he also won the Italian and German titles, which was an awesome performance. He played five Davis Cup Challenge Rounds for Australia and won them all. After his initial year, 1959, he never lost a singles, the last of which was as late as 1973. His prowess among the pros was such that one can assume that had open tennis come about earlier he could have won Wimbledon for nine successive years.

1963

CHUCK McKINLEY

Born: 5 January 1941

He was from St Louis, Missouri, and a mercurial, entertaining champion. His only major success was at Wimbledon and it came in a damp year when the seeding, then entirely a judgement by committee, was controversial.

Be that as it may, McKinley had the unique experience of never meeting another seed and winning from a field in which none of eight seeds ever met. Nor did he lose a set in any round.

1964, 1965

ROY EMERSON

Born: 3 November 1936

Like Rod Laver he was from Queensland. As a lad of 14 he ran 100 yards in 10.6 seconds and his speed about the court was always exceptional. Emerson probably changed the pattern of the men's game. Until he proved otherwise it had been assumed that it was impossible to maintain a serve-volley technique through a long five-setter. Emerson's example was similar to the psychological break-through of the four-minute mile.

His delight in running almost certainly cost him his third successive title in 1966 when he chased a drop shot too enthusiastically in the quarter-final and injured himself. His overall record was tremendous. He won the singles and doubles of all four Grand Slam titles. In the Davis Cup for Australia he lost but four out of 38 rubbers and none of nine vital Challenge Round singles.

C. R. McKinley

R. S. Emerson

LADIES

1956

SHIRLEY FRY

Born: 30 June 1927; married: 16 February 1957 (to K. E. Irving)

A diligent all-rounder from middle America, she endured the brunt of high American expertise and finally succeeded at Wimbledon at her eighth attempt.

She was content to end her career on this high note, a career that had given her the singles' and doubles' titles in all four Grand Slam tournaments.

1957, 1958

ALTHEA GIBSON

Born: 25 August 1927; married: (1) 17 October 1965, to W. A. Darben, (2) 2 April 1983, to S. Llewelyn

She was the ninth successive American women's singles champion at Wimbledon and the first black player to achieve as much. She was 29, having fought much racial prejudice as well as keen competition.

She was a virile player with athletic figure and muscle. In her triumph she not only advanced her racial cause but polished the aggressive technique of the women's game. She duplicated her Wimbledon triumphs at Forest Hills.

1959, 1960, 1964

MARIA BUENO

Born: 11 October 1939

A majestic and graceful Brazilian, she made an instant impact on the international game when she won the Italian title, her first European event, in 1958. She was 18.

Her rivalry with the athletic Margaret Smith-Court was the *motif* of the women's game for years. No one hit the ball more effectively with less apparent effort when her timing was perfect, but with no margin for error she could beat herself.

The Brazilians used her portrait on a postage stamp and erected a statue to her in her native São Paulo.

S. J. Fry

A. Gibson

M. E. Bueno

135

A. Mortimer

K. Hantze/Susman

M. Smith/Court

1961

ANGELA MORTIMER

Born: 21 April 1932; married: 3 April 1967 (to J. E. Barrett)

Born in Plymouth, she was competing for the eleventh time when at the age of 29 she became the first British winner for 27 years. She was sound more than spectacular, with the classic virtues of control and consistency.

She emerged best from the first all-British final since 1914, beating Christine Truman after averting what looked to be a winning lead against her in the second set. It capped success elsewhere, as French champion in 1955 and Australian in 1958.

1962

KAREN HANTZE/SUSMAN

Born: 11 December 1942; married: 21 September 1961 (to J. R. Susman)

A Californian, she was, like Alice Marble and Maureen Connolly, schooled by Eleanor Tennant. A deft all-court player, she had a fragile air and her energy conservation by slowness between rallies provoked comment.

She had success in her début year, 1961, when, as Miss Hantze, she won the doubles with Billie Jean Moffitt, later Mrs King. She was still a young winner when she took the singles a year later at 19.

1963, 1965, 1970

MARGARET SMITH/COURT

Born: 16 July 1942; married: 28 October 1967 (to B. M. Court)

From Albury, New South Wales, near the Victorian border, her Australian training schedules were as difficult as any man's and gym work turned her into a super athlete. Her game was vigorous and aggressive to a high degree.

Her record was unique and no player won more. Between 1961 and 1975 she won everything of consequence. She took 10 titles at Wimbledon; her total of Grand Slam titles was 66. She won the Grand Slam in 1970. There was no title in any major event she did not take. She lost none of 20 singles she played in the Federation Cup. She won what was arguably the greatest Wimbledon women's singles final when she beat Mrs King 14-12, 11-9 in 1970.

Margaret Court won her tenth and last Wimbledon title in 1975 as the mother of a baby son. Her husband, Barry Court, was an Olympic yachtsman.

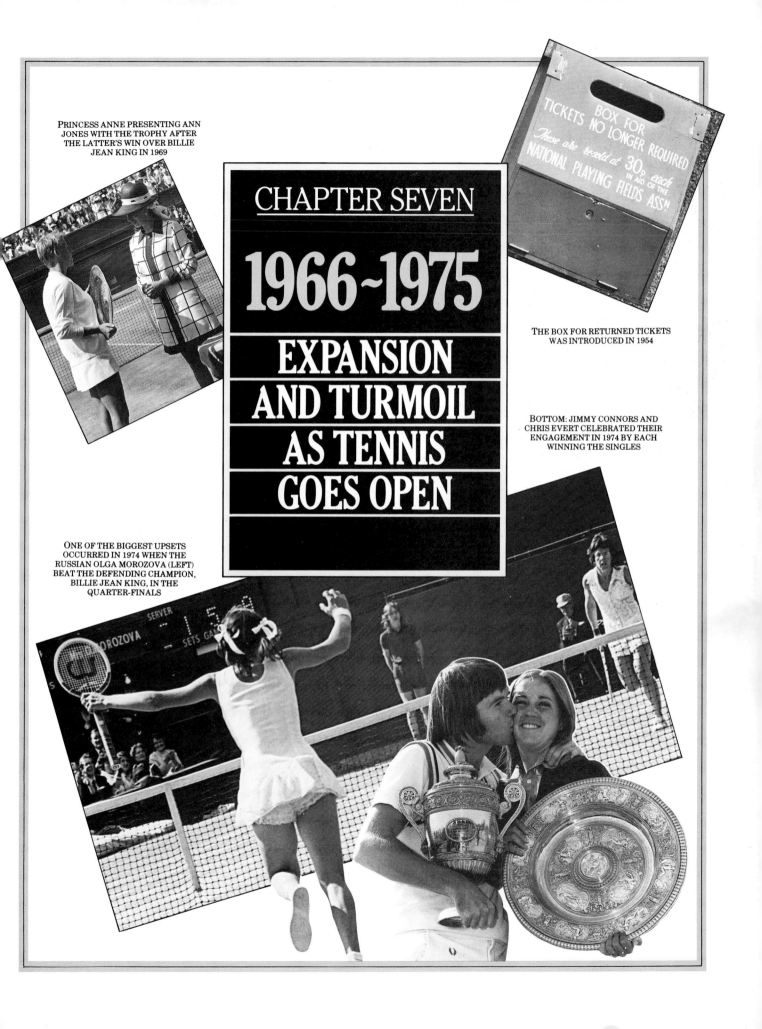

PRINCESS ANNE PRESENTING ANN
JONES WITH THE TROPHY AFTER
THE LATTER'S WIN OVER BILLIE
JEAN KING IN 1969

CHAPTER SEVEN

1966~1975

EXPANSION AND TURMOIL AS TENNIS GOES OPEN

THE BOX FOR RETURNED TICKETS
WAS INTRODUCED IN 1954

BOTTOM: JIMMY CONNORS AND
CHRIS EVERT CELEBRATED THEIR
ENGAGEMENT IN 1974 BY EACH
WINNING THE SINGLES

ONE OF THE BIGGEST UPSETS
OCCURRED IN 1974 WHEN THE
RUSSIAN OLGA MOROZOVA (LEFT)
BEAT THE DEFENDING CHAMPION,
BILLIE JEAN KING, IN THE
QUARTER-FINALS

THE final decision that tennis should become open to both amateurs and professionals was not taken until March 1968 at a Special General Meeting of the ILTF held in Paris. There had been previous attempts, led by the All England Club, to effect the change. As early as October 1959 the new Chairman, Herman David, had presided at a Special General Meeting of the club when a resolution had been passed asking the LTA to propose to the International Lawn Tennis Federation that open tennis should be introduced forthwith. In July 1960 at the fateful ILTF meeting held in Paris the resolution failed to achieve a two-thirds majority by a meagre five votes. At the time the motion was put three delegates, all in favour, were elsewhere in the building and failed to vote. By such bizarre happenings was the course of tennis history diverted.

A further attempt, led by the club, to go it alone – even if it meant that Britain would be expelled from the ILTF – was defeated by 48 votes at the Annual General Meeting of the LTA in December 1964. However, at the AGM three years later a proposal that, from April 1968, all reference to amateurs and professionals should be deleted from the rules of the LTA was passed without further overt pressure from the club. Behind the scenes, though, Herman David had convinced enough members of the hierarchy that it was time to end the 'shamateurism' that, in his words, had made international tennis during recent years 'a living lie'. The leading players were known to be making a living from under-the-table payments, some of which were being paid by those very delegates to the ILTF annual meetings who would hold their hands on their hearts and claim ignorance of the practice. Furthermore, the trickle of amateur champions to Jack Kramer's professional circus had become a flood with the appearance of World Championship Tennis Inc, the Dallas-based company that had signed eight of the top amateurs in 1967, the 'Handsome Eight', to commence a new type of spectator-involved tennis first in Australia and then in the United States.

This crucial decision by the LTA came in the wake of another momentous occasion, the staging of the first major professional tournament on the sacred lawns of the All England Club in August 1967 involving the eight leading professionals of the day – Rod Laver, Ken Rosewall, Pancho Gonzales, Lew Hoad, Fred Stolle, Dennis Ralston, Andres Gimeno and Butch Buchholz. However, this was not Wimbledon's first professional tournament. Few people know that in July 1930 the British Professional Championships were played there. The singles was won by Dan Maskell, the resident professional, who beat the Melbury Club professional Tom Jeffery 6-1 6-0 6-2 in the final on Court No. 2. The doubles, which had to be played on the hard courts, was won by Jeffery and Bill Dear who defeated the popular Queen's Club teachers Joe Pearce and Fred Poulson 6-3 6-4 6-1.

The 'Wimbledon World Lawn Tennis Professional Championships' of 1967, mounted in cooperation with BBC 2 who used the event to launch colour television, was a rather different affair. The tournament was won by Laver 6-2 6-2 12-10 in a thrilling final against Rosewall on a somewhat green and slippery Centre Court (the fertiliser had magically converted the bare brown patches of the final day of The Championships to a lush sward). Needless to say it was an immediate success. The quality of play contrasted sharply with what had been seen a few weeks earlier during a rather one-sided final between John Newcombe and the unseeded German Wilhelm Bungert. To the world at large it emphasised the determination of Britain to allow open tennis at Wimbledon whatever the rules might say.

The mood of Britain's tennis administrators coincided with the mood of the country for greater freedom of expression and the ending of outmoded attitudes. These were the Swinging Sixties, the days of the Pill (introduced from the United States in 1961 but banned to British Roman Catholics) and the Permissive Society. The Abortion and the Sexual Offences Acts of 1967 both recognised the individual's right of choice in private matters affecting their person. The phrase 'Generation Gap' was coined to describe the time-old alienation of the young who claimed that they were not understood. However, no phrase could adequately explain the worrying riots of the Mods and Rockers at south coast seaside resorts in the mid-1960s and the student riots of 1968 and 1969. The ending of the death penalty in 1965 and the passing of the Race Relations Act the same year provided further evidence of a sharper awareness of the need to be scrupulously fair and humane in our dealings with our fellow men.

In politics some fundamental changes of leadership took place in the early 1960s. In 1963 Hugh Gaitskell died and was succeeded as leader of the Labour Party by Harold Wilson. In the same year Harold Macmillan, having immortalised the material prosperity of the late 1950s in the election-winning catchphrase 'You've never had it so good', decided, at the age of 69, to retire. He was succeeded by Sir Alec Douglas-Home, the last Prime Minister to be appointed after consultation between the Queen and the leading members of the Tory party. Thereafter the party elected their leader. After a year at the helm Sir Alec lost the General Election of October, 1964 by only 13 seats as Harold Wilson kindled hopes of a Labour revival, even though their overall majority was only four.

Home's prospects had not been helped by the furore surrounding the unmasking, during the end of Macmillan's administration the previous year, of Kim Philby as the third man in the Burgess and Maclean affair. This, together with the unsavoury Vassall spy case and the resignation of the Secretary for War, John Profumo, in an adultery scandal with overtones of security risk, had seriously damaged the party's credibility. The authorities were further embarrassed by the daring Great Train Robbery in 1963 in which Ronald Biggs and his accomplices were regarded with sneaking respect by the man in the street.

After two difficult years Wilson, an astute politician, felt that the tide was running his way. At the General Election of 1966 Labour secured a respectable majority of 97 against the Tory party led now by Edward Heath, the first elected leader. In 1965, between these two Labour victories, Winston Churchill had died at the age of 90, which seemingly marked the end of Britain's role as a major world power. The further erosion of British influence had been emphasised in 1960 by the granting of independence to Nigeria, by the withdrawal of South Africa from the Commonwealth in 1961 and the granting of independence to Tanganyika (as Tanzania) the same year and Uganda the next. The process continued with the loss in 1963 of Aden to the Federation of South Arabia and the granting of independence to Kenya plus the passage to independence of Nyasaland in 1964, the year when Zambia,

RIGHT: When the attractive Australian sisters Carol (left) and Gail Sheriff met in the second round in 1966 it was the first such meeting since the first ladies singles' final in 1884 when Maud Watson had beaten her sister Lilian. Whenever the Sheriffs had met in previous tournaments they had taken it in turns to forfeit. But they agreed that Wimbledon was too important for that and duly played the match which Gail won 8-10 6-3 6-3. Although umpire Rob Cadwallader knew the girls quite well he kept getting their names muddled and had to be corrected by the players.

LEFT: The victory of the Spanish artist Manuel Santana in 1966 was as unexpected as it was refreshing. 'Manolo' had always said that 'grass is only fit for cows' but as he had shown at Forest Hills the previous September and as he demonstrated in beating the US number one Dennis Ralston at Wimbledon, it is possible to play a touch game on grass – if your timing is good enough.

BELOW: In 1967, the last year before the arrival of open tennis, there was an unseeded finalist when the German number one, Wilhelm Bungert, who had reached the last four in 1963 and 1964, beat Britain's Roger Taylor in a five-set semi-final. However, in the final he was no match for the powerful Australian John Newcombe who beat him in straight sets.

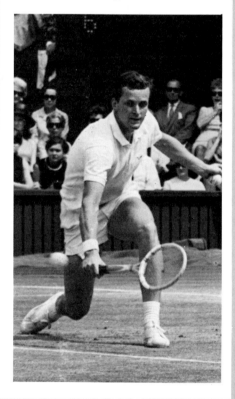

ABOVE: The performer who utterly dominated the period of the mid-1960s and mid-1970s was the aggressive American Billie Jean King who won her first singles' title when she beat Maria Bueno in 1966. Of the ten Championships between 1966 and 1975 Mrs King won six and was a losing finalist in two of the others. Her dynamic play, despite four operations on her knees, continued to influence her generation and her battle for world supremacy with that other giant of the game, Margaret Smith Court, formed the central theme of women's tennis during this period.

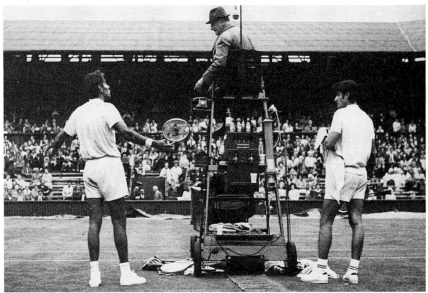

ABOVE LEFT: The two South Africans Cliff Drysdale and Jean Forbes were married at Paddington Registry office on the morning of Cliff's fourth-round match against Roger Taylor in 1967, which he lost in five sets. Jean, who was the sister of Cliff's Davis Cup colleague, Gordon Forbes, had already lost to the Russian girl Miss G. Baksheeva in the second round.

ABOVE RIGHT: On the opening day in 1969 there occurred a rare incident. The ageing lion 'Pancho' Gonzales (left), still fiercely competitive at 41, was incensed when the umpire, Harold Duncombe, three times refused his request to summon the Referee, Captain Mike Gibson, to appeal against the light during the course of a long first set which Gonzales ultimately lost 22-24 to the American Davis Cup player, Charlie Pasarell. In temper Gonzales threw the second set 1-6 before Gibson called them off court with the scoreboard lights shining like beacons in the gathering gloom. Incredibly, the next day, Gonzales saved seven match points in taking the last three sets 16-14 6-3 11-9 to win Wimbledon's longest match after 112 games and 5 hours 12 minutes of play.

RIGHT: During the course of her winning run in 1969 Britain's Ann Jones, who had been a world-class table tennis player before her tennis days, took on court a holdall with 'Pepsi' prominently displayed on it. Under pressure from the BBC, the committee asked Ann to remove the offending name which she did for the final. There had also been complaints about the labels on the bottles of soft drink that sat on the umpire's chair and ultimately plain plastic containers were used. This was rather hard on Robinsons who sent 80 dozen free bottles of their barley water each year to The Championships.

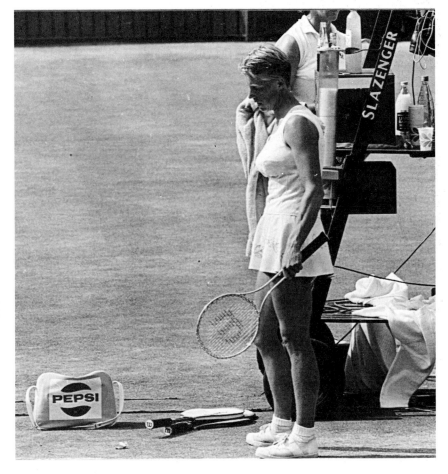

formerly Northern Rhodesia, became a Republic. It was also in 1964 that Canada's new national flag omitted the Union Jack. Another sharper, more serious change came in 1965 when Ian Smith's government in Southern Rhodesia made a Unilateral Declaration of Independence. The repercussions reverberated around the Commonwealth for years to come. Reassuringly, though, in 1967 the inhabitants of Gibraltar voted overwhelmingly to remain under British protection.

The glorious industrial past, too, was over. Insufficient investment in new plant and machinery meant that Britain was no longer the workshop of the world. By great good fortune in 1965 huge deposits of natural gas were discovered beneath the waters of the North Sea. When, in 1970, it became apparent that oil lay there, too, in equal abundance, the future looked decidedly more promising. By 1975 the oil and gas were flowing and would contribute annually some £13 billion to the national income at its peak in the 1980s.

In other lands changes were also taking place – some of them through acts of dreadful violence. Following the 1963 riots in Birmingham, Alabama, associated with Martin Luther King's Campaign for Negro Rights, the assassination of President John Kennedy in Dallas after only three promising years in office, sent shock waves throughout the entire free world. Lyndon Johnson was elected in his own right the following year, the same year which saw the resignation in Moscow of Nikita Khrushchev, the man who had ordered the building of the Berlin Wall in 1961, and the assumption of power by First Secretary Leonid Brezhnev and Prime Minister Alexei Kosygin. The two greatest powers in the world were both in new hands and, as a

first direct 'hot line' was established between them, the other nations held their breath. In 1966 France withdrew from NATO, the Red Guards engaged in Cultural Revolution in China, Negroes rioted in Chicago, Cleveland and Brooklyn and an International Treaty on the peaceful uses of outer space was signed. Three years later in 1969, with open tennis in its infancy, Neil Armstrong inspired the whole of mankind with his historic first step on the surface of the moon.

Culturally the mid-1960s was no less rewarding than the post-war era. The opening of the Harrogate Festival of Arts and Sciences plus the foundation of a rash of new universities, such as Surrey, Bradford, Brunel, Aston, the City University in London, Heriot-Watt in Edinburgh and the University of Technology in Loughborough, suggested a bright artistic and academic future that was never properly realised. The architects had other triumphs elsewhere when the Tay Road Bridge, Britain's longest, and the graceful suspension bridge over the Severn estuary were both opened and the notorious London skyscraper, Centre Point, was completed. The huge office block was still empty in 1974! In New York the Whitney Museum, designed by Marcel Breuer, and the Metropolitan Opera House were opened.

In literature Truman Capote produced his chilling 'non-fiction' novel *In Cold Blood*, Graham Greene was busy with short stories in between *A Burnt-out Case* and *The Honorary Consul*, John Updike published his two novels set in Pennsylvania – *The Centaur* and *Of the Farm* and Iris Murdoch gave us *The Time of the Angels*. As the *New York Herald Tribune* ceased publication, in London *The Times* was taken over by Lord Thomson and for the first time started to print news on the front page. Another seemingly impregnable bulwark of tradition had collapsed.

The musical world was well served with Tippett's *The Vision of St Augustine*, Britten's song cycle *The Poet's Echo* and his opera *The Burning Fiery Furnace*. In the cinema Laurence Olivier and Charlton Heston (a devoted tennis fan and later to become a temporary member of the All England Club) joined forces in *Khartoum* and Paul Schofield gave a commanding performance in *A Man for All Seasons*. The gossip columnists made much of the fact that Richard Burton and Elizabeth Taylor were together again in *Who's Afraid of Virginia Woolf?* Meanwhile, in separate football stadiums, Billy Graham was rousing the emotions of the spiritually needy with his Greater London Crusade while the England football team was creating national hysteria with their World Cup success against the West Germans in London.

Wimbledon itself was enjoying a period of prosperity and further growth as the need to preserve what was best about the old village had become apparent. By making the High Street a conservation area in 1967 the planners were ensuring that the character of the place would be preserved. They received a rapid acknowledgement of their efforts the following year when Wimbledon was awarded the Civic Trust award for the Village Improvement Scheme. Meanwhile, just above the All England Club in Somerset Road, rose the towering blocks of luxury apartments that completely changed the skyline – and, incidentally – afforded a fine view over the No. 1 and Centre Courts from the upper floors. In the town large new office blocks began to appear while the schools went comprehensive in 1969. There were celebrations, too, with the first Merton Festival

in 1972 and, four years later, the centenary of Elys department store.

During the decade 1966–75 change was the order of the day among the men at Wimbledon, though the women's game was dominated by the most dynamic and prolific winner ever to play there, Billie Jean King. In 1966 the reigning champion, Roy Emerson, who was expected to equal Fred Perry's feat of winning three titles in a row, fell victim to his own exuberance in his quarter-final against fellow Australian Owen Davidson. Speeding forward to chase a short ball he crashed into the umpire's chair and injured himself. Thereafter he could offer only token resistance as Davidson entered his first semi-final. There the 22-year-old left-hander from Melbourne who, the following year, was to be appointed the resident professional at the All England Club, lost a thrilling encounter in a 12-game final set against Manuel Santana. The artistic Spaniard, who had himself survived the previous round in an identical manner against another Australian, Ken Fletcher, went on to win the title from a rather nervous US No. 1, Dennis Ralston, who had been the surprise unseeded doubles' winner in 1960 with Rafael Osuna of Mexico, when he was only 17. Osuna's untimely death in an air crash in 1969 at the age of 30 robbed the game of one of its fastest, most skilful and colourful players.

Fletcher was one of the most underrated players of the day. Possessed of the finest forehand in the game at the time, the likeable, carefree Queenslander thus lost his greatest chance of fulfilling his considerable potential in singles. However, there was consolation in a curious way.

For the previous two years Fletcher, a truly great doubles' player who had won the mixed doubles Grand Slam with

BELOW: At 16, the youngest male player ever to qualify, Stephen Warboys of Essex, lost in the first round in 1970 to Hans-Joachim Plotz of West Germany while suffering acutely from hay fever. Warboys had an outstanding junior career following a carefully-planned upbringing by his somewhat eccentric father, Jack, who himself had once represented Essex. However, after becoming the youngest player ever to be selected for a British Davis Cup squad, Stephen failed to make progress in the senior game and turned to coaching.

ABOVE LEFT: When the rugged Yorkshire left-hander Roger Taylor knocked out the title-holder Rod Laver in the fourth round in 1970, he became a national hero overnight. When he then beat Clark Graebner to enter his second semi-final there were thoughts of a possible British victory at last. But the ageless Ken Rosewall ended those dreams in four sets before himself being worn down in five by the relentless attack of John Newcombe.

RIGHT: When he had first brought Evonne Goolagong to Europe in 1970, her legal guardian and coach Vic Edwards had predicted that Evonne would win Wimbledon within five years. Her unexpected 1971 success therefore caught Vic and everyone else by surprise. Her effortless annihilation of fellow Australian Margaret Court, who looked extremely tense throughout, was magnificent to behold. Evonne's natural and spontaneous way of playing the game and the human frailty of her occasional 'walkabouts' endeared her to fans the world over. On the eve of Wimbledon in 1975, she married Roger Cawley who had been a good English junior and severed her relationship with Edwards.

ABOVE LEFT: The 1972 final provided a beautiful contrast between the tall, fair, straight-backed American Stan Smith and the dark, round-shouldered Romanian Ilie Nastase. It was the best contest since the War and was won by Smith in five sets. It was also the first Sunday final – it had rained incessantly the day before. Smith was a corporal in the US Army at the time and Nastase an officer in the Romanian Army. In the early part of the match Nastase seemed obsessed with the tension in his rackets which he changed several times. It seemed to affect his concentration and confidence.

ABOVE RIGHT: Wimbledon's 'predominantly white' rule of dress is strictly enforced. So is the rule governing the size of advertisement on a player's clothing, which is why Rosie Casals was asked to change this Virginia Slims outfit. She did, for a blue and purple Virginia Slims scrolled dress which she wore for her Centre Court match! More recently Martina Navratilova was not allowed to wear a dress on which the Kim name was too large.

ABOVE: Players and officials are ferried between their places of residence and the club each day by a fleet of courtesy cars supplied by British Leyland, complete with lady drivers. The Referee always prefers players to use this service because he knows more or less where they are and when they will arrive. Years ago, one player who attempted to find his way by tube, got lost, arrived late and found himself scratched.

Margaret Smith in 1963, had been on the losing side in the doubles final, first with Emerson against Bob Hewitt and Fred Stolle and then with Hewitt against John Newcombe and Tony Roche. This last pair, in the opinion of many the finest ever to appear at Wimbledon, were winning the first of their five titles together. By an odd twist of fate, in 1966 on the eve of the tournament, Roche was injured and withdrew, leaving Newcombe without a partner. Fletcher's entry with Jerry Sung, his young protégé from Hong Kong, had been refused and so at the last moment he teamed with Newcombe. It was ironic that these two should meet in the third round of the singles where Fletcher won 6-3 in the fifth set after losing the first two. However, they did win the doubles together from another fine Australian pair, Bill Bowrey and Owen Davidson, the same man who had lost to Santana. That year Fletcher also claimed the third of the four mixed titles he would win with Margaret Smith Court between 1963 and 1968.

This is probably the place to digress for a moment to acknowledge the tremendous contribution made by the Australians to the art of men's doubles at Wimbledon since the War. With the enormous advantage of having some of the finest grass courts in the world in 'the sunburned country', the Australians have also been brought up on doubles competition in their inter-club and inter-State matches. From the successes of Sedgman and Bromwich in 1948 and Bromwich and Quist (aged 31 and almost 37 respectively) in 1950, through the era of Hoad and Rosewall, Hartwig and Rose, Emerson and Fraser, Hewitt and Stolle, Newcombe and Roche, to Case and Masters and those joyous extroverts McNamara and McNamee, we have been treated to some truly marvellous enter-

tainment – and always with a cheerful acceptance of the rubs of the green. Altogether, in the 41 years since the resumption of The Championships after the Second World War, there have been 22 Australian doubles' victories, plus the two won by Bob Hewitt when he had joined South African Frew McMillan. It is a remarkable record – especially when you remember that, before the supreme skill of John McEnroe was revealed in partnership with Peter Fleming during their four winning years, only five all-American pairs were successful during the same period – Tom Brown and Kramer in 1946, Falkenburg and Kramer the following year, Gonzales and Parker in 1949 (the only Wimbledon title the great Pancho ever won), Mulloy and Patty in 1957 (at the age of 42 and 33 respectively) and the young, unseeded Gerulaitis and Mayer in 1975.

But in singles the demise of Australian dominance was near. There would be only four more victories before three Americans and a Czechoslovak took the honours. The last closed Championship in 1967 has already been referred to as being a one-sided victory for Newcombe over a thoroughly satisfied Bungert. It appeared to me that the German was delighted merely to have reached the final and was quite ready to go quietly. Not so Newcombe. He was becoming paranoid about his early departures at Wimbledon in six previous attempts. Since his first challenge in 1961 the best that John had done was to reach the fourth round once. This time he took his chance, and in commanding fashion. His 6-3 6-1 6-1 win was one of the fastest finals on record.

The excitement surrounding the first year of open tennis was infectious. Great names which had disappeared into the bottomless professional void, men like

Gonzales and Segura, Hoad and Gimeno, Laver and Buchholz, had suddenly reappeared, perhaps a little fuller round the waist in some cases but nevertheless there in person with an air of the unknown surrounding them. Another was Ken Rosewall who had won the world's first open tournament, the British Hard Court Championships, at Bournemouth the previous April in four sets from Laver and had then beaten Laver again in the first French Open. Not surprisingly these two were the top seeds at Wimbledon, Laver at 1 and Rosewall 2. It was another Australian, the elegant left-hander Tony Roche, who upset that forecast by beating Rosewall in straight sets in the fourth round. However, Roche had no answer to Laver's explosive genius in the final which the 1962 champion won 6-3 6-4 6-2. Thus Laver, after five years in the professional wilderness, had proved beyond question that he was the greatest player of his generation. If anyone doubted it, he won Wimbledon again the following year from Newcombe and went on to complete a second Grand Slam. Throughout he was a tremendous ambassador for his sport and for his country, always totally in command of his emotions and always as gracious in victory as he was in the occasional defeats that he suffered in lesser events. What a player, what a champion!

In 1970 Laver at last was humbled, and in spectacular fashion by Britain's Roger Taylor in four thrilling sets on the Centre Court in the fourth round. To his credit Roger did not relax after that startling success. In the next round he beat the powerful American 'Superman' Clark Graebner (who, with his glasses, was a Clark Kent double), before Rosewall brought him down to earth in the semi-finals. With Laver gone New-

combe was not to be denied. On a hot afternoon when neither man seemed able to time the ball properly on a court that had been watered overnight Rosewall, in his third final 16 years after his first, was worn down in five gruelling sets – the last of only seven games.

The following year Newcombe won again from the tall American, Stan Smith, after trailing by one set to two. This was the year when the tie-break was introduced at eight games all in every set except the third for women and fifth for men. This system prevailed until 1979 when it came into operation at six games all. It has remained thus ever since. In the semi-finals Newcombe had again beaten Rosewall, an exhausted Rosewall this time who, in the previous round, had provided one of Wimbledon's classic matches – a recovery from two sets down against the US number one Cliff Richey – that had kept the late afternoon Centre Court crowd tied to their seats by the fluctuating drama as the little Australian finally won 6-8 5-7 6-4 9-7 7-5.

Newcombe's contribution to Wimbledon's history as thrice singles' winner and six times doubles' champion (five with Tony Roche and one with Ken Fletcher) was an important one. As the champion of 1967 he spanned the transition between amateur and open tennis. Although he had turned professional as one of Lamar Hunt's 'Handsome Eight' later that year, he was able to return for the first open meeting in 1968. Seeded 4, he lost rather unexpectedly to Arthur Ashe in five sets in the fourth round. However, the rugged, powerful Newcombe was the obvious successor to Laver and when that great champion's eclipse occurred in 1970 it was he who dominated the field for two years with his heavy, forthright game.

Newcombe was one of the few players

LEFT: A bevy of beauty – and considerable skill – on display at the Hurlingham Garden Party on the eve of Wimbledon 1972 where designer Ted Tinling collects some of the ladies who will wear his creations during the next two weeks.

BELOW: 'Borgmania' came to Wimbledon in 1973 as the boyish good looks of the Swedish teenager Bjorn Borg excited a frenzied following from the hordes of 'Teenyboppers' who besieged him at every turn. So great was the crush that Borg had to have a police escort merely to move between clubhouse and court. The following year the All England Club Secretary, Major David Mills, wrote to 60 girls' schools asking the Heads to use their influence to keep their girls under control and Borg was advised not to sign autographs. Special crush barriers were introduced and crowd control was much improved.

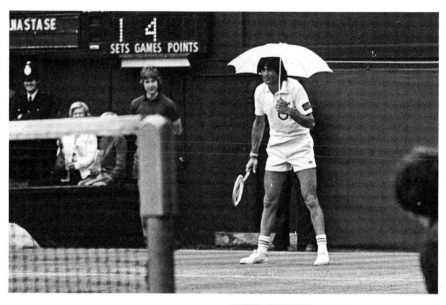

LEFT: The Clown Prince of Wimbledon – and everywhere else for that matter – was the mischievous Romanian Ilie Nastase who had grabbed this umbrella from a courtside spectator during his fourth-round match in 1974 against the American Dick Stockton who won in four sets. Nastase, one of the greatest improvisers the game has ever seen, lacked the ability to finish off the rallies – especially on the volley. Unable to decide whether he was a serious athlete or an entertainer, he never overcame the devil within him that provoked several serious confrontations with authority. It was a tragedy that this delightful, if sometimes childish, character never fulfilled his unique potential.

RIGHT: For the first and only time in 1975 a betting tent was allowed inside the grounds at Wimbledon. The man engaged by the William Hill Organisation to act as form adviser was the joint British number one Buster Mottram (left facing camera), who was injured and unable to compete. Officially the players were not allowed to place bets but because of the obvious temptations and the potential danger of matches being 'fixed' the experiment was discontinued.

LEFT: During the changes of ends through-out the 1975 final against Arthur Ashe, Jimmy Connors constantly referred to a note that he kept tucked inside his sock. It transpired that it was a message from his Grandmother. Unfortunately, the advice could not prevent his comprehensive defeat. Nor could the urgings of a fan in the crowd who yelled, at a critical moment near the end, 'Come on Jimmy'. Turning in the direction of the voice, Connors retorted: 'I'm trying for Christ's sake!'.

of the day with a good forehand, and what an overwhelming shot it was. He was also a good, natural volleyer who seldom failed to put the ball away if it was above the height of the net, and his overhead was devastating. His serve, relentlessly pounded down to a good length, was the foundation of his success and he varied its direction with discretion. Newcombe was unlucky that the 1972 ban on contract professionals prevented him from attempting to win the singles for three years in a row which he might well have done for, at the time, he was a more complete player than Stan Smith, the winner that year, who played in a similar way to Newcombe but with less flexibility. The Wimbledon crowds will probably remember him best for some truly entertaining doubles' finals with Roche, none better than the first open final in 1968 against Rosewall and Stolle that went to five long sets which were full of good-natured banter and some thrilling rallies.

In a wider context Newcombe will be remembered for his two US titles in 1967 and 1973 and the two he won in Australia in 1973 and 1975. His contribution to the success of Australian Davis Cup teams between 1963 and 1976 is also noteworthy for in that first year, aged 19, he was the youngest player who had ever played in a Challenge Round.

We could not know it then, but Newcombe's Wimbledon win in 1971 would be the last Australian men's singles success until the present day. With Harry Hopman settling in the United States to establish a coaching centre and so many of the leading players making the USA their home as they competed on the world's circuits – Laver, Newcombe, Emerson and Stolle among them – the Australian game drifted about like some rudderless vessel. Only in the last few years, with the LTAA coming up with some imaginative incentive schemes through new sponsors, and Newcombe returned and working with Roche on junior development, are there at last the signs of a revival.

The next two years were complicated by the involved politics of open tennis. Inevitably in a sport that had just drifted into the new situation without forethought or planning, there were clashes of interest between the various factions which made up the professional game. The Dallas-based promotion organisation World Championship Tennis Inc (WCT) had come into existence on the eve of open tennis and had eight of the leading players under contract, the 'Handsome Eight'. When they started to ask tournaments to pay corporation fees to guarantee the participation of their players, the national associations of the ILTF felt threatened.

The failure of any WCT men to enter the French Championships of 1971 convinced the Establishment that they had to act. They retaliated by banning all contract professionals from official ILTF tournaments in 1972, a situation that was ended by the Agreement signed between WCT and the ILTF in Copenhagen on 17 April that year. It was decided that, in 1973, the first quarter of the year would be allocated to WCT tournaments and the remaining months to ILTF events. In return WCT agreed not to sign any more players to contracts and not to renew existing ones as they expired. Unfortunately the truce came too late to secure the involvement of any contract players in Paris or at Wimbledon, though they did compete at the US Open.

In the absence of many of the stars, including Laver, Rosewall, Ashe and the holder Newcombe, Stan Smith won the Wimbledon crown against the errant genius from Romania, Ilie Nastase. Ironically in view of so many absentees, the final, won 4-6 6-3 6-3 4-6 7-5 by Smith, was by general consent the best seen at Wimbledon since the epic encounter between Crawford and Vines in 1933. Certainly it presented the classic contrast of the tall, upright, blond American with the typical Californian power game of serve and volley against the dark-haired, olive-skinned, round-shouldered Romanian with the touch of a genius and the volatile temperament of a spoilt child.

These two were destined to play out one more crucial drama later that year in the final of the Davis Cup in Bucharest. This was the first year after the abolition of the Challenge Round and it was generally expected that before a rapturous home crowd on clay courts at the Progresul Stadium the Romanians, Nastase and Ion Tiriac, would win. Clearly the opening rubber between Smith and Nastase would be crucial. On the day Nastase could never throw off the dreadful weight of national expectation that hung heavily on his shoulders and lost in straight sets. In the circumstances of acute provocation from the hostile crowd and some of the most blatantly biased line calls I can remember witnessing, Smith's performance during that tie was one of the finest sporting achievements I have ever seen. He also won the doubles with Erik van Dillen and on the final day sealed victory for his country with a win over Tiriac by 6-0 in the fifth set.

The following year, 1973, was even more fraught with political turmoil when the newly-formed Association of Tennis Professionals decided to boycott Wimbledon in support of one of their members, Nikki Pilic. The Yugoslavian number one had been suspended by his national association for allegedly not attending a Davis Cup tie, which meant that he would not be permitted to play at Wimbledon. An attempt by ATP to secure an injunction in the High Court that would have forced Wimbledon to accept Pilic's entry failed. Accordingly, to emphasise the point that their members were no longer answerable to national associations, the ATP board instructed all members not to play at Wimbledon. Ultimately 79 players withdrew but Roger Taylor, Nastase and Ray Keldie of Australia decided that the reasons in favour of their participation overrode their loyalty to ATP.

The favourite, Nastase, lost unexpectedly to the new US Intercollegiate champion Alex 'Sandy' Mayer on Court No. 2. Mayer was in turn beaten by the USSR number one Alex Metreveli. The victory of the Czechoslovak Jan Kodes that year has often been denigrated but those who saw the manner in which he faced his real test – the gruelling semi-final against Taylor which he won 8-9 9-7 5-7 6-4 7-5 amid the showers – will know that he was a player of exceptional class. He had already won two French Championships and had been in the final of the US Open on grass two years earlier and would be again later in 1973. Thus his relatively easy passage in the final against the proud Georgian, Metreveli, in what was the first Wimbledon final between members of Eastern Bloc countries, was no more than expected. Many Wimbledon finals are one-sided.

Two Americans of totally different backgrounds and different temperaments dominated the meetings of 1974 and 1975. In the first year, 21-year-old Jimmy Connors, the brash street fighter from Belleville, Illinois, thrilled onlookers with the sheer exuberance and ferocity of his all-out attacking style. A left-hander who wielded his flashing steel racket like a deadly rapier, he carved his way through the field in cavalier style, dropping sets as he went, seven of them altogether, but always on the attack. His swift, final-round execution of Rosewall, whose 39-year-old legs simply could not match the furious pace set by Connors, was utterly ruthless. As the old warrior went down 6-1 6-1 6-4, still looking so boyish, it was impossible to believe that he had played his first final against 'Old Drob' 20 years before. 'His time will come', they had said then. It never did.

The 1975 final was the first between two Americans since 1947. It resulted in a victory for the quiet American Arthur Ashe over the defending champion Connors in four fascinating sets, 6-1 6-1 5-7 6-4. This was more than just a tennis match, even though it was one of the finest tactical tennis matches I have ever seen. It was also a victory for his race and for all the dedicated people, in particular his father and mentor Dr Robert Johnson, and Donald Dell, his former Davis Cup captain and by now his manager, who had helped a poor young black boy from Richmond, Virginia to make good in a sport riddled with those same white prejudices that the late Martin Luther King (he had been assassinated in Memphis on 4 April 1968) and his followers had been trying to batter down.

The final itself was a fascinating confrontation of styles and personalities. Ashe, usually a ferocious hitter, completely changed his style. The way he swung the serve wide to the Connors backhand in the right court, the way he denied his opponent any pace and gave him lifeless, low passes and teasing shallow lobs that kept Connors off balance and trapped him into error and, above all, the way he kept the ball short and low to the vulnerable Connors forehand that

broke down completely on his approaches to the net, was quite masterly. As Connors sat slumped at the changes of ends repeatedly looking at a note that he kept tucked inside his sock, which was from his Grandmother we later discovered, Ashe would sit totally still with his eyes closed or with a towel over his head, the picture of intense, but relaxed, concentration.

To say that Billie Jean King totally dominated the years between 1966 and 1975 hardly does her justice. It would be truer to say that, during that period, women's tennis at Wimbledon was Mrs King. Let us dispose of the facts first. Of the eight singles' finals Billie Jean contested during these years she won six. Between 1961 and 1979 she also won ten ladies' doubles titles, three as Billie Jean Moffitt and seven as Mrs King. Of the first three, two were with Karen Hantze – during her first visit to Wimbledon in 1961 and the following year when she had become Mrs Susman – and one with Maria Bueno, in 1965. Of the last seven, five were with Rosie Casals (1967, 1968, 1970, 1971 and 1973), one with Betty Stove (1972), and the last, the record-breaking twentieth title, was with Martina Navratilova in 1979 against Betty Stove and Wendy Turnbull. The mixed doubles she won 'only' four times, with Owen Davidson on each occasion. Until 1979 Billie Jean's 19 titles equalled the 19 in women's and mixed doubles won by that great fellow-Californian Elizabeth Ryan between 1914 and 1934. It is one of life's ironies that Elizabeth collapsed in the clubhouse at Wimbledon and died that day on the eve of Billie Jean's twentieth win, blissfully unaware that her joint record was about to fall.

The contribution made by Billie Jean to the history of Wimbledon and her influence on the development of the sport itself have been immense. Her forceful, attacking style, bred on the fast cement courts of California, reminded a whole generation of young players that a woman could play the serve-and-volley game like the men. In fact, it was her much-publicised victory over a man at the Houston Astrodome on 20 September 1973 that really led to the explosion of interest in the game in the United States. Within a couple of years indoor centres were springing up all over the country and a survey suggested that 32 million Americans were playing tennis, a figure which I find hard to believe. However, no one can dispute that there were 30,492 spectators present at the Astrodome that day, which remains a record crowd for any tennis match, to see her beat Bobby Riggs in straight sets. There were some 50 million more watching on their television sets around the world. Phoney it might have been but the impetus created by that bizarre Battle of the Sexes in Houston can hardly be over-exaggerated.

Billie Jean was in the attacking mould of Marble and Betz, of Brough, Osborne and Hart, of Gibson and Bueno. It was Maria who was her victim in her first two singles' successes in 1966 and 1967. Billie Jean did everything just a bit faster and a bit harder than the graceful South American. The next year it was Australia's Judy Tegart who felt the power and accuracy of the dynamic American's serves and volleys.

A loss to Ann Haydon Jones (Ann had married Pip Jones in 1962) followed in 1969. This first British success since Angela Mortimer's win eight years earlier was an immense achievement for a girl who, like Fred Perry, had learnt about the psychology of match play on the table tennis table. In 1957 Ann had reached the final of all three events at the World Table Tennis Championships in Stockholm but had lost each one in five games. The extraordinary thing is that at table tennis Ann was an all-out attacking player whereas on the tennis court she preferred to defend. She had won on the clay of Paris in 1961 and 1966 but few expected her to succeed on fast grass at Wimbledon against the best serving volleyers in the business. However, that is just what she did by eliminating first Mrs Court and then Mrs King in successive rounds by being prepared to take the net position herself whenever the opportunity presented itself. These were the best British wins since the War and, like those of Angela Mortimer, were triumphs of character and concentration.

Billie Jean suffered another loss in 1970, this time to Margaret Court who, as Miss Smith, had already won the title twice, in 1963 and 1965. This thrilling 14-12 11-9 victory for the Australian was full of the most tremendous rallies, despite the fact that both girls were slightly injured.

There followed a year in which Mrs King did not feature in the final, which was a rare thing indeed. The champion in 1971 was Australia's delightful part-Aborigine, Evonne Goolagong, who surprised her coach Vic Edwards by beating Margaret Court 6-4 6-1 with one of the most fluent and natural displays of controlled aggression I have ever witnessed. To see her play was like watching a deer leaping across the veldt or a tiger pouncing on its prey, so spontaneous were the movements of this super-athlete.

For the next two years Billie Jean was back in the winning groove. In 1972 she beat the holder Evonne Goolagong who now seemed to be operating on the conscious level and was consequently much less effective. The next year it was the young Chris Evert, 18 years old, who was given a lesson by 'The Old Lady' as Billie Jean was becoming known. When, in 1974, Chris returned to take the title with a one-sided victory over Olga Morozova, the only Russian girl ever to appear in a singles' final, it was clear she had learned those lessons.

For the last time, in 1975, Billie Jean held aloft the famous silver-gilt plate after beating Evonne Cawley, as Miss Goolagong had now become after marrying an Englishman, Roger Cawley, who himself had been a useful junior player. In a superb display of sustained aggression in which she lost but one game in the second set Billie Jean closed her singles' account at Wimbledon. She could hardly have gone out on a more spectacular note.

BIOGRAPHIES

GENTLEMEN

1966

MANUEL SANTANA

Born: 10 May 1938

The only Spaniard among the men's singles champions and a popular one. His touch was exceptional and his ball control almost magical. He played an oblique forehand pass that seemed impossible. He defied his status as a hard-court specialist (he twice won the French crown) by taking the US title on grass the year before he triumphed at Wimbledon.

His final against the American Dennis Ralston was a joyous Wimbledon occasion. A year later this ever-cheerful player became the only defending champion not to survive the opening round when he lost on the Centre Court to Charles Pasarell.

1967, 1970, 1971

JOHN NEWCOMBE

Born: 23 May 1944

This Australian stands among the finest in the hierarchy of champions. He wielded heavy, punishing attacking shots and was the last of the 'amateur' winners. As soon as Rod Laver had gone over the hill he reasserted his supremacy. He might have had greater success but was barred in 1972 because of a dispute among the world administrators and did not play in 1973, the 'boycott' year.

In doubles, mainly in harness with his left-handed compatriot Tony Roche, Newcombe was also outstanding. The French singles was the only title of consequence he did not win.

1972

STAN SMITH

Born: 14 December 1946

This Californian is remembered not only for winning the first singles final to be played on Sunday (because of rain) but because he did so after a match of classic quality. In a magnificent five-setter he beat the talented Romanian, Ilie Nastase, after averting a probable fifth set deficit of 2-4 with a shot off the wood.

His greatest exploit was winning the 1972 Davis Cup final for the United States in a tempestuous tie in Bucharest, played in conditions of preposterous unfairness. It has been held to rank among the finest sporting achievements of the century.

Very much a 'gentleman' he was perhaps more diligent than inspired.

1973

JAN KODES

Born: 1 March 1946

The winner from the weakest field of modern times in the year the Association of Tennis Professionals inflicted its 'boycott' of Wimbledon. He was the first Czechoslovak champion as such, though Jaroslav Drobny was, of course, racially as Bohemian. He stands, though, more worthy than a *'faute de mieux'* champion, as his French singles' wins in 1970 and 1971 and his arrival in two US Open finals in 1971 and 1973 make evident.

The final broke new ground in being between nations of Communist States. It was against the Soviet Alex Metreveli.

1974, 1982

JIMMY CONNORS

Born: 2 September 1952

An outstandingly courageous fighter. He won Wimbledon at his third attempt then, against the odds, at his eleventh. At 32 in 1985 he reached the semi-final. In only two challenges, 1983 and 1986, did he fail to reach the last eight.

In the United States his power play was even more successful and he won the US Open five times between 1974 and 1983 and on three different surfaces, grass, clay and cement. No one else has achieved that.

Double-fisted on the backhand, his ranging depth of shot made this left-hander a permanent threat in a decade of talent that included Bjorn Borg and John McEnroe. As a competitor he seemed to loom larger than life.

M. Santana

J. D. Newcombe

S. R. Smith

J. Kodes

J. S. Connors

A. R. Ashe

B. J. Moffitt/King

A Haydon/Jones

E. F. Goolagong/ Cawley

C. M. Evert/Lloyd

1975

ARTHUR ASHE

Born: 10 July 1943

The first great black player among men, he came to a peak when he dethroned his compatriot Jimmy Connors in an intriguing final. It was a triumph of intelligence over power as Ashe exploited Connors' relative weakness on the forehand.

Ashe was the son of a policeman from Richmond, Virginia and the first winner of the US Open in 1968. In 1973 he reached the final of the South African singles (and won the doubles) after fighting against the racial prejudice which denied him entry in 1970.

He was 32 when he won Wimbledon. His later career was cut short by a heart attack.

LADIES

1966, 1967, 1968, 1972, 1973, 1975

BILLIE JEAN MOFFITT/KING

Born: 22 November 1943; married: 17 September 1965 (to L. King)

No one has played or won so much at Wimbledon as Mrs King. This ebullient Californian, expert at every facet of the game, won a record 20 titles in all; she was twice, in 1967 and 1973, triple champion. She competed every year save one between 1961 and 1983, 22 times in all, playing 265 matches. She won 224.

Her record round the world approached but did not equal that of her great rival, Margaret Court. She won twelve US titles, four French and two Australian. She was without doubt one of the great players of all time.

1969

ANN HAYDON/JONES

Born: 7 October 1938; married: 30 August 1962 (to P. F. Jones)

From Birmingham, she first achieved world-class standard at table tennis before concentrating on the broader game. She was left-handed, diligent and an intelligent tactician.

Her Wimbledon triumph came when she was 30 and playing for the fourteenth time. She reached a hitherto unsurpassed peak to beat Margaret Court and Billie Jean King in the last two rounds. To complete her Wimbledon swan song, for she did not play again, she also took the mixed. She won the French singles in 1961 and 1966.

1971, 1980

EVONNE GOOLAGONG/CAWLEY

Born: 31 July 1951; married: 19 June 1975 (to R. Cawley)

A gifted and popular Australian who captivated Wimbledon spectators, she first won at her second attempt when 19. She won again nine years later at 28 and as the mother of a son.

She sometimes lost concentration, dissipating her brilliant shot-making talent. She was a losing finalist in 1972, 1975 and 1976. She married an Englishman, Roger Cawley.

1974, 1976, 1981

CHRIS EVERT/LLOYD

Born: 21 December 1954; married: 17 April 1979 (to J. M. Lloyd)

Trained by her father on the slow courts of Florida, this much-loved champion revived the prestige of the traditional values of the women's game based on sound groundstrokes and at the same time defied orthodoxy with her double-fisted backhand. This she turned into common practice all round the world.

Between her international début in the Wightman Cup in 1971 and the end of 1985 she never failed to win a Grand Slam singles' title. Nor did she suffer defeat in any Federation or Wightman Cup singles. A model of consistency and outstanding for her sportsmanship, she stands as an exemplary champion. She married John Lloyd, the British Davis Cup player.

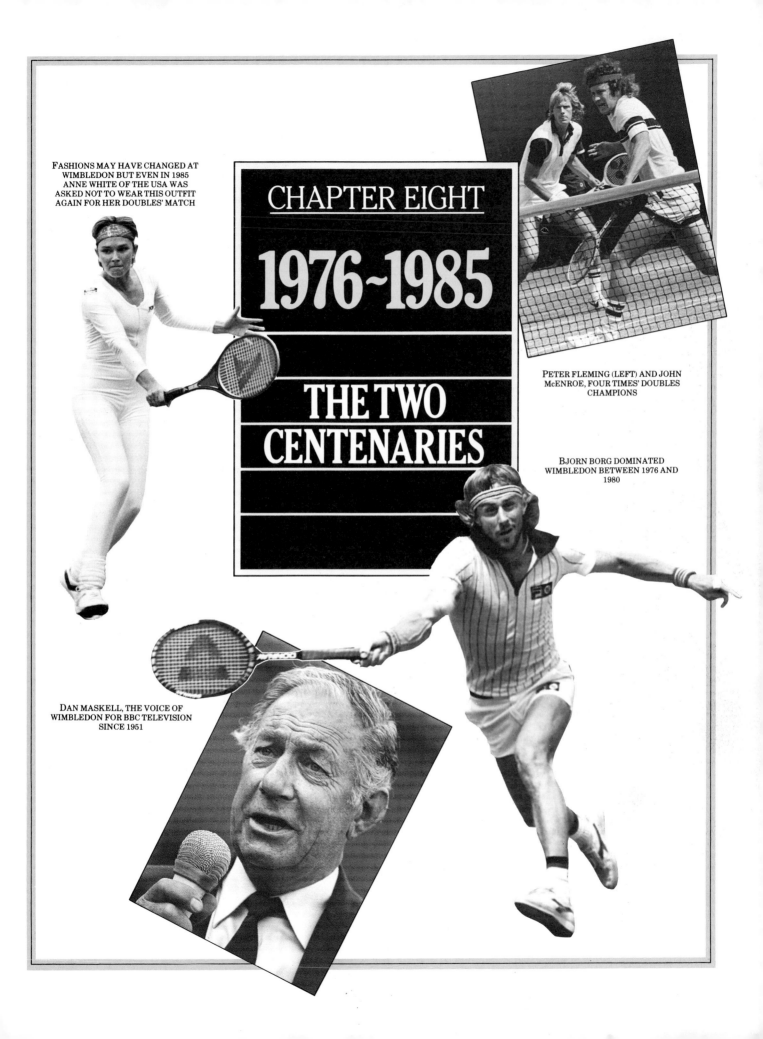

FASHIONS MAY HAVE CHANGED AT WIMBLEDON BUT EVEN IN 1985 ANNE WHITE OF THE USA WAS ASKED NOT TO WEAR THIS OUTFIT AGAIN FOR HER DOUBLES' MATCH

CHAPTER EIGHT

1976~1985

THE TWO CENTENARIES

PETER FLEMING (LEFT) AND JOHN McENROE, FOUR TIMES' DOUBLES CHAMPIONS

BJORN BORG DOMINATED WIMBLEDON BETWEEN 1976 AND 1980

DAN MASKELL, THE VOICE OF WIMBLEDON FOR BBC TELEVISION SINCE 1951

HE decade from 1976 to 1985 saw a dramatic growth in the development of tennis at all levels but it was a turbulent period for the professional game as the administrative structure was overhauled to keep pace with rapid expansion. In 1976 the two-year-old Men's International Professional Tennis Council was increased to nine members, three each from the players and the ITF who had been represented from the start, and three new members to represent the tournaments; one from North America, one from Europe and one from the Rest of the World. The same year the Women's International Professional Tennis Council was formed with ten members: four from the WTA, four from the ITF and two from the tournaments. In 1981 the MIPTC appointed a North Carolina lawyer, Marshall Happer, as Administrator for the Grand Prix and in 1985 the WIPTC appointed a Managing Director, Maidie Oliveau, who had been part of the successful Olympic Games directorate. After barely a year in office, however, she resigned to be replaced by Jane Brown.

At the highest level tennis was becoming a part of showbusiness and the stars of both sexes became multi-millionaires. The combined earnings of the top ten men and women graphically illustrate the rising levels of prize money that were now prevalent and threatening the game's stability as the superstars were marketed in special events and exhibition matches by their enterprising agents. According to official sources the top ten men in 1976 earned $2,688,171 and the women $1,107,445. By 1980 those figures had risen to $4,916,838 and $3,628,322 respectively and five years later were up to $8,106,698 and $5,056,713. A mark of the astonishing progress made by the women's game was the fact that Martina Navratilova's career earnings of $9,886,474 from official events alone was almost $1 million more than the $8,956,688 earned by the top male, John McEnroe.

The Wimbledon Championships were keeping pace with this expansion. Total prize money in 1976 was £157,740. By 1980 it had increased to £293,464 and in 1985 it was £1,934,760. There were dramatic improvements to the ground and buildings, too, that made life more comfortable for players, spectators and administrators alike. In 1977, to mark the centenary of The Championships, the Lawn Tennis Museum and the Kenneth Ritchie library were opened. Two years later the north side of the ground was developed. The roof of the Centre Court was raised 1 metre to provide 1,088 extra seats on the north side and four new courts were built though they were not used until 1980.

In 1981 the improvements continued with the rebuilding of the north and south stands of No. 1 Court. This provided an enlarged competitors' restaurant and much needed extra space for a competitors' lounge and writing room, as well as modernised offices for the Referee and his staff, the umpires and the ball boys. The following year the Barkers ground, which had been known as Aorangi Park since its purchase in 1967 when it had been leased to the New Zealand Club, was converted from the debenture holders' car park into extra facilities for the public. Tented restaurants, a picnic area, a results structure and extra entertainment marquees were some of the new features. In 1985 a large new building was completed on the east side of the Centre Court to provide 800 more seats, a superbly-appointed media centre, an enlarged museum and library and a suite of new administrative offices. In charge of this expanding empire was Christopher Gorringe, the Secretary since 1979, who in 1983 became the first Chief Executive. From 1985 his team included Robert McCowen, the ex Marketing Director of Slazengers Ltd, who had been engaged to develop the club's merchandising interests which had grown significantly since their introduction in 1978 and were now contributing towards the impressive surplus of £5,373,444 that was handed to the LTA in 1985. These were significant changes and no one could accuse the club and their partners at the LTA of not keeping up with developments. I wonder what Henry Jones, who had successfully piloted the first Championship to a profit of £10 in 1877, would have thought, or for that matter the first champion, Spencer Gore, who had been convinced that the game would never catch on!

Gore, a Wimbledon resident, would doubtless have had strong views on the changes being proposed by Merton Council. The very fabric of the town was being threatened by their plan to sell off historic Cannizaro House on Wimbledon Common as an hotel, to demolish the Town Hall so as to make way for a huge shopping precinct and office centre, and to move the Reference Library from Wimbledon to a central library in Merton. The locals were up in arms.

The glittering façade of international tennis contrasted sharply with a host of complex national and international problems at home and abroad that no one seemed capable of solving. In British politics this was a period of considerable change. There were four General Elections and three Prime Ministers between 1974 and 1986 as successive administrations tackled the problems of 'stagflation'. The last years of the 1970s were marked by the inevitable indecisiveness of minority rule. Edward Heath had taken Britain into the Common Market on New Year's Day 1973 but had fallen when he misjudged the nation's attitude over the miners' strike in 1974. Harold Wilson created the 'Social Contract' that had increased enormously the influence and power of the Trade Unions which it fell to later administrations to curb. Wilson's decision in March 1976 to retire from the Premiership was unexpected. His successor, Jim Callaghan, survived until 1979 thanks to an uneasy alliance with the Liberals during two and a half difficult years of minority government. The 'Lib-Lab pact' was the basis of a European-style coalition government that could not afford to offend the minor parties. It was the issue of devolution for Scotland and Wales that brought down Callaghan. Defeated on a vote of no confidence by a single vote (311 to 310), he became the first Prime Minister forced to call an election following defeat in the House since Ramsay MacDonald in 1924.

In the dark shadow cast over affairs by the IRA's callous murder of Airey Neave, the shadow Secretary for Northern Ireland, who died when the bomb hidden in his car exploded on the ramp of the House of Commons car park, the election of 3 May 1979 produced a handsome victory for the Conservatives. It also gave Britain her first woman Prime Minister. One of Margaret Thatcher's main aims was to restore Britain's self-confidence. She was a leader who knew what she wanted, though some thought her dogmatic and inflexible. Her later steadfastness as a wartime leader during the short, sharp engagement with Argentina over the sovereignty of the Falkland Islands in 1982 restored her popularity at a time when it had been slipping. The

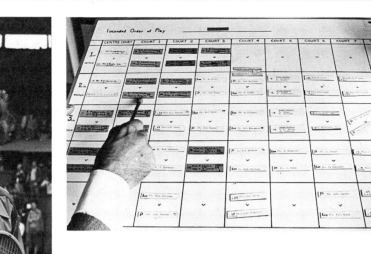

ABOVE: The Referee's-eye view of the order of play board from the Centre Court to Court No. 8. Every player is represented by a magnetic card, which starts life in a series of enlarged displays of the full draws for each event on the wall of the Referee's office. Then, each evening, the Referee presents the Order of Play Committee with these court boards containing his recommendations for the next day's programme. A representative from the media also attends these meetings.

ABOVE LEFT: For the second year in succession Australia's Evonne Cawley (right) reached the final but, as in 1975, she was thwarted in attempting to add to her 1971 success. This time Chris Evert was her conqueror, as the American number one continued her habit, begun in 1974, of winning at least one of the Grand Slam singles' titles every year.

CENTRE: In 1976, with Lincolnshire farmer Fred Hoyles as the new Referee, these deliberations took so long one day that for the first time in living memory the order of play was published too late for it to appear in the next morning's papers.

LEFT: The calm before the storm in the Wimbledon First Aid Room, staffed as always by the volunteers of the St John's Ambulance Brigade. So hot was the weather in 1976 that on one day alone over 500 people were treated for heatstroke. The only doctor on duty appealed for help as casualties were laid out on the floor, on the grass and even on the tarmac paths. In a normal year some 2,000 are treated for various ailments during the entire fortnight.

RIGHT: The Centenary of The Championships was celebrated in 1977 with a lunch for 41 of the surviving singles' champions – 27 men and 14 women – with the club's President The Duke of Kent and the Duchess of Kent on the opening day.

BELOW: An innovation in 1977 was the inclusion of ball girls, though on the outside courts only. Commander Lane, who had been training the ball boys with military precision for many years, believed that girls would not have sufficient stamina to do the job properly. However, ever since the girls have played their full part in affairs. The ball boys used to be drawn from the Dr Barnardo's Homes, later the Shaftesbury Homes. Since 1969 they have been recruited from local schools and face great competition to be finally selected for duty.

ABOVE: The 1977 semi-final between Vitas Gerulaitis (right) and his friend and regular practice partner Bjorn Borg, produced one of those classic encounters whose outcome was in doubt until the last ball had been struck. The anticipation of the two men who knew each other's games backwards contributed to a thrilling spectacle that contained many breathtaking winners and relatively few losers. Gerulaitis never did beat Borg in a live singles' match (only in exhibitions) and went down bravely, this time 8-6 in the fifth set.

election which followed in 1983 produced the biggest landslide since the War as the Conservatives swept back to power with an overall majority of 144. Although the spectre of inflation had been banished by tight fiscal control, the unemployment figures would not respond and had reached almost 3.5 million by the mid-1980s.

The ten years between 1975 and 1985 were turbulent ones both socially and economically. The topics which dominated that period were inflation, unemployment, trade union power, relations within the Common Market, feminism, race relations and the unity of Britain. The Equal Pay and the Sexual Discrimination Acts of 1975 and the Race Relations Act the following year reflected the concern for oppressed minorities and the exploitation of women. Yet many of those minority groups, especially the unemployed young, remained disenchanted. The inner city riots of 1980 in Bristol, Brighton, Scarborough and Finsbury Park, London, were preludes to much uglier scenes the following year in Toxteth, Moss Side and Brixton. Equally worrying was the violence on the picket lines during the year-long miners' strike which began on 6 March 1984 without a ballot of members.

As the bulging cells of Britain's overcrowded prisons demonstrated, this was now a more violent and less law-abiding society. Sexual attitudes were more liberal, alcoholism and drug taking among the young were no longer minor problems and the growth of fringe religions contrasted with the decline in orthodox religious observance. In this technological age people were also anxious about the misuse of electronic data banks as the microchip revolutionised the storage and use of information. The birth of the world's first test tube baby in 1979 seemed the ultimate triumph of science over nature.

Internationally the leadership changes that took place within the major powers during the second half of this period were significant for the future of the entire world. With the death of Mao Tse-tung in 1976, Deng Xiaoping assumed leadership of the largest country on earth. The Chinese, who had always patterned their economic Five-Year Plans on the Soviet system, were wise enough in 1984 to see that something new was needed. Their hybrid economic scheme, adopted for the seventh Five Year Plan (1986-90), combined community planning with a free market system that would bring greater wealth to those individuals who put in the most effort. It was a refreshing change and a bold experiment.

In the United States Ronald Reagan made the transition from Hollywood to the White House, via the governorship of California, so smoothly in 1980 that his re-election in 1984, with a record 525 votes to 13 in the Electoral College, surprised only those who had not yet appreciated the importance of good television technique in Presidential elections. In Moscow three leadership changes occurred in quick succession. On the death of Leonid Brezhnev in November 1982 Yury Andropov, the former chief of the KGB, assumed power ahead of Brezhnev's choice, Konstantin Chernenko. Fifteen months later Andropov died and was replaced by the ailing Chernenko who, himself, lasted only 13 months. The assumption of leadership by Mikhail Gorbachev on 12 March 1985, ten days after his fifty-fourth birthday, completed the shuffle and left the West in no doubt that a man of firm resolve was in command, and would be so probably for many years to come. His total opposition to Reagan's ambitious and costly 'Star Wars' defence initiative in space, which received a serious setback with the tragic loss of the space shuttle *Challenger* just after lift-off at Cape Canaveral in January 1986, set the scene for the propaganda war that seemed destined to dominate the remaining years of the twentieth century. Optimists pointed to the qualified success of the summit meeting between Reagan and Gorbachev held in Geneva in November 1985. At least the two superpowers were still talking.

What sort of a world it would be in the year 2000 was uncertain but the extrapolation of statistics that were available at the end of 1984 suggested as chilling a picture of the future as George Orwell had envisaged in his alarming novel *1984*, that had been published 35 years earlier. As 1985 dawned the planet earth contained 4.8 billion inhabitants. With population expanding faster than the food supply or the jobs available and with international debt spiralling out of control (the world's debtor nations owed $800 billion), there seemed a real possibility that the world's economic framework was heading for a total breakdown. Anarchy reigned in several countries and terrorism had become a way of life for fanatical groups of various persuasions. Nobody could suggest a way of ending it. Meanwhile, illegal immigration was happening on such a massive scale in the USA (from Mexico and the Caribbean), in Nigeria (from Ghana), in Assam (from Bangladesh) and in Venezuela (from Colombia) that no one could even roughly assess the true size of the problem.

The chief events of 1984 provided a good indication of the general state of the world. Bishop Desmond Tutu, the leader of the South African Council, was awarded the Nobel Peace Prize for his brave stand against apartheid there and went to Oslo in December to receive it. The following year a series of bloody clashes between armed police and black protesters brought further universal condemnation. China and Britain came to agreement on the terms of the handover of Hong Kong in 1997. Robert Maxwell acquired Mirror Group newspapers and two years later Rupert Murdoch set up a new printing works at Wapping for *The Times* newspaper and the other titles of his News International group.

At Bhopal in India 2,500 were killed and 100,000 suffered long-term injuries when a large cloud of isocyanate gas escaped from the Union Carbide plant. In Wilberg, Utah, 27 miners died in an underground fire. Donald Duck celebrated his fiftieth birthday and pop star Michael Jackson added to his millions from records and video-tapes with *Billie Jean* (which had no connection with tennis). Jeremy Irons had a success with Stoppard's *The Real Thing* in New York and Albert Finney returned triumphantly to the stage with *The Biko Inquest*.

Despite the Soviet-led boycott of Eastern Bloc countries, the 1984 Los Angeles Olympic Games were the most successful ever and were watched by a world-wide television audience of 2,000 million; they made a profit of $150 million, $25 million of which went to the US Olympic committee. This success also made the reputation of the organiser Peter Ueberroth who later became baseball's Commissioner in the United States. Of the athletes Britain's Daley Thompson won the Decathlon for the second time, becoming only the second man ever to do so, and fellow countryman Sebastian Coe successfully defended his 1,500 metre title. These two were the only athletes, men or

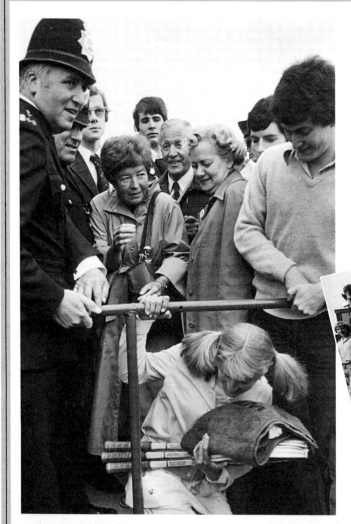

LEFT: By 1978 the fame of Tracy Austin, still only 15, had spread to such an extent that, like Borg in 1973, she and her mother needed police help to walk from clubhouse to the outside courts. Although Tracy won the US Open in 1979 and 1981 on the fast high-bouncing American hard courts, the best she did on Wimbledon's grass with its lower, skidding bounce was to reach the semi-finals twice in 1979 and 1980 and the quarter-finals twice in 1981 and 1982. Since early 1984 she has been virtually out of the game with a back problem that will not respond to treatment.

ABOVE: The number of temporary staff and officials required to run The Championships each year continues to grow as the amenities offered to the public expand. There is a team of some 37 cleaners, mostly students, who operate before the gates open at 11.30 a.m., and a further 95 who clean up round the courts after play.

LEFT: Those who believe that Ivan Lendl cannot play as well on grass should recall his performances in 1978 that gave him the Wimbledon junior title. After winning the unofficial World Junior Championships at the Orange Bowl in December 1977, Ivan proved that he was the best junior in the world in 1978 by claiming the Italian and French Open titles before his Wimbledon success. These performances earned him the official title of ITF world junior champion. Since those days Ivan has won the French Open twice, the US Open once and the Masters three times. He was also a Wimbledon finalist in 1986 and must surely now believe that he can win the Wimbledon title.

LEFT: Jana Navratilova, who had been given special permission to visit Wimbledon, shares in her daughter's joy when Martina retained the singles' title in 1979 with a 6-4 6-4 victory over the newly-married Chris Evert Lloyd. Jana's husband was not allowed to leave Czechoslovakia with her.

BELOW: The next day it was Martina's turn to share in the joy of her partner Billie Jean King whom she had just partnered to a 5-7 6-3 6-2 win over Betty Stove and Wendy Turnbull. As Billie Jean's delighted face reveals, this victory gave her a record-breaking twentieth Wimbledon title.

BELOW: It was in 1980 that 'Cyclops', the magic eye, first made its appearance. Invented by Bill Carlton, the beam device became the standard service line aid for linesmen despite some scepticism from the players. At first only the linesman could hear the bleep through headphones but later it was decided to make the signal audible to everyone. This helped to overcome the doubts about its accuracy.

ABOVE: At the age of 15 Andrea Jaeger, who played with the same double-handed backhand as Chris Evert Lloyd and Tracy Austin, became Wimbledon's fourteenth seed, the youngest player ever to be accorded that distinction. What is more she beat the No. 7 seed, Virginia Wade, to reach the quarter-finals where Mrs Lloyd was too experienced for her. Three years later in 1983, now seeded No. 3, she reached the final and the pinnacle of her short career before being overwhelmed by Martina Navratilova. In 1984 she withdrew from the circuit and returned to college.

women, successfully to defend. Michael Gross of West Germany won four medals and broke two world swimming records, Carl Lewis won four gold medals for the United States in track and field and compatriot Mary Lou Retton vaulted her way into the hearts of all who saw her complete her gold-winning gymnastic routines. Britain's South African-born Zola Budd earned unlooked-for notoriety when she accidentally tripped the American favourite Mary Decker in the 3,000 metres.

Two great tennis athletes, Bjorn Borg of Sweden and the Czechoslovak left-hander Martina Navratilova, thrilled the Wimbledon crowds of the decade 1976 to 1985 as they dominated half of the ten Championships. To a lesser degree the American left-handers John McEnroe and Jimmy Connors contributed significantly to the excitement of the men's events, while the remorselessly consistent American Chris Evert Lloyd contributed even more to the women's. In those ten years Chris appeared in the final no less than seven times and won twice. Martina was in 'only' six finals – but she won them all!

The enigmatic Borg, cool and unflappable even in the deepest crisis, of which there were several, won the first five Championships of this decade with such sharp skill, such intense competitiveness, it was difficult to remember that with his heavily-topspun groundstrokes, Western-gripped on the forehand and double-handed on the backhand, he was really a clay court player. Yet, four years earlier there had been a clue of what he might achieve on grass. In 1972, at the age of 16, Bjorn had won the junior title from Britain's Buster Mottram after trailing 2-5 in the final set. I remember speaking to him afterwards as we stood on the roof of the competitors' tea room. I asked him what his ambition was. As he gazed out across the expanse of Wimbledon's outside courts towards the spire of St Mary's Church, he answered quietly 'To be the best player in the world.' It was spoken without a trace of conceit, stated as a fact. Incredibly, within four short years he was. Already the Italian and French champion in 1974, which were his first two important titles and won either side of his eighteenth birthday, he won a second French Open in 1975 and came to Wimbledon in 1976 as the No. 4 seed. In seven astonishing rounds he demolished David Lloyd, Marty Riessen, Colin Dibley, Brian Gottfried (seeded 14), Guillermo Vilas (6), Roscoe Tanner (7) who had eliminated Connors (2), and Ilie Nastase (3) who had come through the defending champion Ashe's top quarter, all without losing a single set as only the fourth man ever to do so. It had been a devastating performance, built on the merits of a much improved first serve, which was something he had been working on hard with his omnipresent coach, Lennart Bergelin, tremendous speed about the court and those piercing topspin groundstrokes that seemed glued to the lines every time an opponent was rash enough to risk an advance to the net.

I do not suppose there has ever been a better match player than Bjorn. Five times during that majestic reign he was on the point of extinction but each time he found something extra. In 1977 out on Court 14 against Australia's Mark Edmondson, who knew all about grass court play and had won the Australian Open in 1976, he lost the first two sets but won the next three for the loss of only seven games. Bjorn's semi-final against Vitas Gerulaitis, his friend and regular practice partner at the Cumberland Club, Hampstead, that year was an outstanding battle that was remarkable for the extraordinary anticipation and the low percentage of errors from both men. Gerulaitis had a break in the final set and could certainly have won but he had never beaten Bjorn in a match and appeared to stop believing. Bjorn duly won it 8-6.

On the opening day the next year on a still greasy Centre Court the giant American, Victor Amaya, pounding down untakable left-handed serves, led two sets to one. In the fourth Bjorn faced a point that would have put him 1-4 down. Again, by sheer willpower and a stubborn refusal to give in, he survived. In 1979 there were two crises. On Court No. 1 against an inspired Vijay Amritraj he was again behind two sets to one. But the graceful, fluent Indian could not convert any of several opportunities to go a service break ahead in the fourth and eventually lost it on a tie-break. His chance had gone. Then, in the final the powerful American left-hander Roscoe Tanner failed to break Borg as the champion served at 4-3 15-40 in the final set. Had Tanner levelled at 4-4 and then held serve to lead 5-4 anything might have happened. But again Borg had the self confidence; he went for his shots and won 6-4.

The last success, in 1980, provided a final fit for the gods. The 21-year-old American left-hander John McEnroe, who had already been a semi-finalist against Connors in 1977 when he had come through from the qualifying tournament (something which no other player has ever achieved), was hot. He had revenged himself against Connors in the semi-final in four sets and took the opening set 6-1 against Borg in the final. Somehow the champion repulsed the fierce, left-handed net attack of the New Yorker to take the second set 7-5 and

then won the third 6-3. Playing largely from the baseline against the rampant volleying of his opponent, Borg was struggling to stay level. Suddenly a winning topspin backhand across the advancing McEnroe broke the serve at last. Leading 5-4, 40-15, Borg held two Championship points. McEnroe saved the first with a fearless backhand and the second with a foolhardy forehand drive-volley that was the shot of a madman or a genius – at different times in his stormy career John has been both! With a run of six superb points against a shaken champion the American drew level.

The 20-minute tie-break that ended the fourth set will be talked about for as lonng the game is played. Five more times Borg stood at Championship point, but he was denied each time by some truly brilliant, acrobatic shot-making from the American. Six times McEnroe held set points only to be thwarted by some courageous topspin passes and well-disguised low, fast lobs. On the seventh Borg at last missed a forehand volley and the match was level. In the fifth set it was the power of Borg's service that decided the issue. After the opening game, which he won from 0-30, he lost only one more point on his serve and eventually broke McEnroe to win an exhausting match 1-6 7-5 6-3 6-7 8-6. Tossing his racket skywards Borg sank to his knees on the worn turf in sheer relief. It had lasted 3 hours and 53 minutes and was as good a final as we had seen since the War, ranking with the greatest ever.

Although we did not know it then, this was the pinnacle of Borg's remarkable career. A sixth French title in 1981 was his last major achievement and after losing at last to McEnroe in the 1981 Wimbledon final and again in the US Open final, both in four sets, he decided to take

BELOW LEFT: Florida's talented teenager, Kathy Rinaldi, has been setting records of precocity all her life. In 1979 she became the youngest girl to win an American Junior Grand Slam – in the 12-and-under division – by winning the Indoor, Hard Court, Clay Court and National titles. In 1980 she became the US Junior Clay Courts 14-and-under champion; in 1981 she became the youngest player to reach the quarter-finals of the French Open; then the same year at Wimbledon she became the youngest player at 14 years 3 months ever to win a round at The Championships. By the end of 1985 she had become the eleventh ranked player in the world.

BELOW RIGHT: Hana Mandlikova's win over Martina Navratilova in 1981 put the 19-year-old Czechoslovak into the final for the first time. When she lost somewhat listlessly to Chris Evert Lloyd 6-2 6-2 there were doubts about Hana's ability to maintain her determination to win. These doubts were magnificently dispelled at the 1985 US Open where she beat Martina and Chris back-to-back to win her first US crown. She reached the Wimbledon final again in 1986.

ABOVE: It was a unique moment in Wimbledon's history when John and Tracy Austin won the mixed doubles in 1980. Never before had a brother and sister won the title though back in 1892 Lottie Dod and her brother Anthony had won the All England Mixed Championship when it was played at Manchester. However, this had no connection with Wimbledon whose Mixed Doubles' Championship did not begin until 1913.

LEFT: In 1980 a permanent refreshment building for club members was constructed on Court No. 6, just inside the Doherty Gates.

ABOVE: The second win by the energetic Australians Peter McNamara (right) and Paul McNamee in 1982 was against the holders Peter Fleming and John McEnroe. The score 6-3 6-2 is Wimbledon's only best-of-three sets men's final, occasioned by weather affected programming.

LEFT: The match of The Championships in 1983 was the semi-final between the agile New Zealander Chris Lewis and the former South African Kevin Curren. For five fluctuating sets the battle raged with daring dives from Lewis, like this one, and beautifully-struck passes from Curren that seemed to defy the laws of gravity as they squeezed over the high part of the net. At the end of a full-blooded 3-hour 43-minute battle both men were covered in glory but it was Lewis who survived to face John McEnroe in the final.

RIGHT: Finalists in 1983 were Tim (left) and Tom Gullikson, the first twins to appear in a Wimbledon doubles' final since Herbert and Wilfred Baddeley in 1897.

a break from the awful grind of hard, daily practice sessions and the constant pressure of always being expected to win. Twice he attempted a comeback, in 1982 at Monte Carlo and two years later in Stuttgart. Curiously, he lost on both occasions to the mercurial Frenchman, Henri Leconte, and wisely decided to devote himself to other interests. His legacy to the game in general and to Swedish tennis in particular was enormous. He proved that self-control and success do go hand in hand, which he had been taught by suspension as a junior for bad court behaviour, and he showed us that chivalry had not died with the arrival of open tennis. It was refreshing to discover that nice guys can still come first.

Undoubtedly, his was the inspiration that led to an explosion of interest in tennis in Sweden and to the emergence of the new wave of Swedish champions: Mats Wilander, at 17 the youngest French Open champion ever in 1982; and Anders Jarryd the French Open doubles' champion of 1983 and member of the successful 1984 Swedish Davis Cup team. There was also Henrik Sundstrom who beat McEnroe on the opening day of that 1984 final to seal the fate of the Americans as Sweden won the famous trophy for the second time; and Stefan Edberg the world junior champion of 1983 and the Australian Open champion of 1985 who won the deciding rubber of the 1985 Davis Cup final against Michael Westphal in Munich.

The arrival of McEnroe as a fully mature match player was clearly a contributory factor in Borg's decision to retire. He had always said that the American's potential was far greater than that of any player on the circuit, ever since McEnroe had become the first player younger than himself to beat him in Stockholm in 1978. The three McEnroe successes at Wimbledon, in 1981 against Borg, which was tainted by some appalling behaviour against Tom Gullikson in the opening round on Court No. 1 for which he was lucky not to have been disqualified, in 1983 against the unseeded New Zealander Chris Lewis, and in 1984 against Connors, revealed the ripening of a quite outstanding talent. It was a talent equally at home on the doubles court, as his four titles with Peter Fleming demonstrate.

There was another match in 1983 that set the pulses racing. It was the electrifying semi-final between Chris Lewis and Kevin Curren. Lewis had trained like a fanatic for Wimbledon with the help of his Davis Cup colleague Jeff Simpson. Long practice sessions on the Aorangi Park courts were followed by running and exercises to improve mobility and stamina. They would be needed. Curren, seeded 12, had caused a sensation by defeating the holder, Jimmy Connors, in the fourth round on the notoriously difficult Court No. 2 when he had delivered no fewer than 33 aces. This was the first time in 12 years that Connors had failed to reach the quarter-finals.

Curren had reached the semi-final with a wonderfully sporting four-set victory over Tim Mayotte and Lewis had beaten another American, the delightful extrovert Mel Purcell, also in four sets. Winning the first set of the semi-final on a tie-break, Curren was marginally in command with some superb down-the-line passes against an opponent who came in on everything. But the hustling tactics and courageous retrieving of Lewis, whose lighter strokes never threatened to hit his opponent off the court, began to unsettle Curren. Lewis, darting about the court like a startled gazelle and diving headlong for some remarkable volleys, took the second set 6-4 and the third 7-6 as his opponent began to look jaded. When a clearly nervous Lewis lost the fourth set on another tie-break and saw Curren move to 3-0 in the fifth it seemed that ranking seniority would prevail. Curren was the fifteenth ranked player at the time, Lewis the ninety-first. But the afternoon heat and all the nervous energy he had expended had taken their toll of the South African's stamina. His legs would not work fast enough to chase Lewis's angled volleys and the famous serve had lost its bite. In a thrilling climax with the result in doubt until the last, Lewis prevailed in a 14-game final set to win 6-7 6-4 7-6 6-7 8-6. It had lasted 3 hours and 43 minutes and had left players and spectators alike totally exhausted. It was the match of The Championships.

Lewis was utterly outclassed by McEnroe in the final. The American was at his dominating best, quick, sharp and effective. How sad, then, that the world will remember this gifted athlete more for some outrageous and offensive attacks on umpires and linesmen than for his abundant talent and impressive record. Unquestionably the pressures in the modern game had become greater than any previous generation had faced. The level of prize money had risen to heights undreamed of by the old professionals of the pre-open days. By 1985 the men's Grand Prix tour was offering prize money of more than $23 million and the rewards from the women's World Championship Series exceeded $13 million. All this did not take into account team competitions, special events or exhibition matches. Competition had become intense with a programme that offered tournaments all the year round. Tennis had become part of showbusiness and media interest had turned players'

private lives into public property. Not surprisingly the more volatile among them cracked under the strain so that it became necessary to strengthen the Code of Conduct.

In McEnroe's case the officials had only themselves to blame for not invoking the rules early in his career before the pattern had become established. Honest tennis lovers felt outraged by some of his worst excesses. The club made their feelings known by letting a year pass before awarding John the honorary membership that is customarily bestowed on every singles' champion. But they, like everyone else, marvelled at his talent.

McEnroe's ability to take even the fastest serves on the rise and project them for winners to the most acute angles or, like rifle-shots, down the line, made it difficult to serve to him. This was particularly so in doubles. Then his own left-handed delivery, hit from a closed stance with a disguised trajectory, was almost impossible to read. He could hit it flat and fast down the middle or slice it wide or into the body, all with the same action. His reflexes, too, were quite remarkable. At his best he was almost impossible to pass or lob, so quickly did he react and so fast was he to back-pedal and leap for his smashes.

All these qualities came together in the 1984 final against Connors. So perfect was his play that day, so finely tuned was every part of the delicate machinery, all operating at the speed of light, that many of us who witnessed the 6-1 6-1 6-2 destruction of so fine a player as Connors who, through no fault of his own, was rendered utterly impotent, believed we had seen the best tennis that man has ever played. It was amazing to think that Connors himself had beaten McEnroe on this same court just two years earlier in the 1982 final, coming back from two sets

ABOVE: There was a new man at the helm in 1983, the year when Alan Mills, the former British Davis Cup player and a Wimbledon doubles' semi-finalist himself with Mark Cox in 1966, replaced Fred Hoyles as the Referee.

ABOVE: Kathy Jordan, who comes from the improbably-named Pennsylvania town, King of Prussia, closed a chapter of Wimbledon history in 1983 when, in the third round, she beat a slightly ill No. 2 seed, Chris Evert Lloyd, 6-1 7-6. This was the first time since she had made her début at Wimbledon as a determined 17-year-old in 1972 that Chris had failed to reach at least the semi-finals. In fact, it was the first time in 35 consecutive Grand Slam Championships that this remarkable champion had failed to reach that stage.

LEFT: The popular Nigerian Nduka Odizor, known universally as 'The Duke', had a good run to the fourth round in 1983 with wins over Guillermo Vilas and Peter Fleming but he was no match for the speedy New Zealander Chris Lewis who beat him 6-1 6-3 6-3.

BELOW: In 1982 Pat Cash, a strapping 17-year-old from Melbourne, won Wimbledon's junior event. Two years later he beat the No. 4 seed Mats Wilander and powered on towards a meeting with John McEnroe in the semi-finals. However, he was beaten by the defending champion in three hard sets. Later in the year at Flushing Meadow, Pat beat Wilander again and had a match point against Ivan Lendl for a place in the final of the US Open. Following a serious back injury and an appendectomy on the eve of the 1986 Championships, he nevertheless reached the quarter-finals.

ABOVE: The highlight of the 1984 celebrations to mark the Centenary of women's tennis at Wimbledon was the parade of champions on the Centre Court on the second Monday. It was an emotional and nostalgic scene as 17 of the 20 surviving lady champions came forward to receive their specially-commissioned piece of Waterford Crystal from the Duke and Duchess of Kent. The biggest cheer of all was reserved for the champion of 1924 and 1926 Kitty Godfree who, at the age of 88, still enjoyed a regular game of tennis at Wimbledon. She and her husband, Leslie, are the only married couple to have won the mixed doubles' title, which they did in 1926.

Waterford Crystal from the Duke and Duchess of Kent. The biggest cheer of all was reserved for the champion of 1924 and 1926 Kitty Godfree who, at the age of 88, still enjoyed a regular game of tennis at Wimbledon. She and her husband, Leslie, are the only married couple to have won the mixed doubles' title, which they did in 1926.

RIGHT: Until the final, the man of the meeting in 1985 was undoubtedly South-African-born Kevin Curren who had become an American citizen earlier in the year. Seeded No. 8 himself, Curren eliminated in succession Stefan Edberg (14), John McEnroe (1) and Jimmy Connors (3) with a barrage of withering serves and brilliant early returns that left all three opponents flat-footed. Sadly for his supporters, he remained tense and inhibited in the final against Boris Becker who outserved him and, despite his 17 years, kept his nerve better during the critical third-set tie-break which was the turning point of the match.

to one down to impose a courageous victory 3-6 6-3 6-7 7-6 6-4. That, in its way, had been as impressive a performance for this win came a full eight years after his only previous success against Rosewall in 1974. Not since Tilden's two wins nine years apart in 1921 and 1930 had anyone achieved a comparable feat. It was also Jimmy's fifth final, for he had lost to Ashe in 1975 and to Borg in 1977 and 1978.

Connors always gave full value and saw himself as an entertainer. His rugged professionalism, his dynamic go-for-broke style with his low, fast forehand and his punishing two-handed backhand always made him an exciting player to watch though his occasional vulgar actions marred his image. Only a slight weakness on the serve, which was marvellously improved in 1982 with a toss placed further forward, prevented him from achieving even more than the record 105 tournament titles that stood against his name by the end of 1984. What a pity, then, that in centenary year, 1977, he should have elected to miss the parade of 43 former champions, which included the doubles' experts 'Toto' Brugnon of France and Elizabeth Ryan of the United States, who filed past the Duke and Duchess of Kent on the opening day to receive commemorative silver medals. Connors lost some friends that day and was mildly booed onto court for his first match.

The decade ended with the most spectacular success of even Wimbledon's rich history. When the fresh-faced West German Boris Becker, at the age of 17 years and 7 months, beat South African-born Kevin Curren, now a naturalised American, to win the ninety-ninth Championship he wrote a new page in the history books. No man so young had ever won the world's oldest title; no German man had ever achieved that feat; nor had an unseeded player ever taken the title.

If the outcome was truly historic, the manner of it was electrifying. Four times Becker was taken to four sets and twice to five as he battled past a succession of more experienced players over the course of 292 games. Only two men had played a similar number of games to win their titles. In 1958 Ashley Cooper had lost seven sets and played 322 games and in 1949 Ted Schroeder had lost eight sets, like Becker, and played one game fewer than the West German, 291, in winning. Serving explosively and going for his returns with refreshing vigour, Boris was the epitome of youthful enthusiasm. Against the seventh seed Joakim Nystrom in the third round he twice broke back in the final set when the Swede was serving for the match. Against sixteenth seeded Tim Mayotte one round later he was two sets to one down and 5-6 down in the third when he twisted an ankle and was about to retire, remembering the awful experience of the previous year when an ankle injury had forced him to default to Bill Scanlon. His coach Gunther Bosch advised him to take an injury break and afterwards, with ankle taped, he came storming back to win 6-3 4-6 6-7 7-6 6-2. Then it was the turn of Ivan Lendl's conqueror Henri Leconte and fifth seeded Anders Jarryd to feel the full force of the Becker serve. It was simply too fast for them. Similarly, in the final, Curren, who had put out both McEnroe and Connors, the first and third seeds, and so was the logical favourite, could only stand in awe as Boris, flinging himself headlong at everything with his ginger hair flying, produced some amazing mid-air volleys. It was a breathless finish to a spectacular four weeks which had begun with Boris, ranked 29 in the world, winning his first Grand Prix title at Queen's and had ended with him taking a prize of £130,000, earning a world ranking of eight and placing the world's most respected and ancient trophy on his mantlepiece. It was a romantic tale more improbable than any fairy story. The sheer youthful joy of the lad, his disarming honesty and amazing maturity at Press conferences, were like a breath of fresh air after the unpleasantness of recent years. This surely was the finest thing to have happened to Wimbledon and to tennis generally since the War.

If the sixth win by Martina Navratilova in 1985 was less spectacular it was no less impressive. Her opponent, as on four previous Wimbledon finals days, was her old friend and rival Chris Evert Lloyd. This was their eighty-sixth meeting since they had first faced each other in the opening round of a small 16-draw tournament in Akron, Ohio back in March 1973 when Chris was 18 and Martina 16. Chris had won that one, and she won again on all but two of their first 20 meetings. The Florida girl's relentlessly accurate groundstrokes were too consistent for the more powerful, but less reliable attacking game of the Czechoslovak teenager. But as Martina matured and assimilated the lessons of previous defeats her greater weight and variety of shot began to earn her more victories than losses.

Although she had left Prague to live in the United States after leading Czechoslovakia to a 3-0 victory over Australia in the 1975 Federation Cup in Aix-en-Provence, Martina did not feel fully at home there for some years. The American way of life was so different and the material wealth so enticing that she put on weight and lost some of her single-minded drive. She needed guidance. Two great American athletes from other sports helped Martina to instil that sense

of belief that all champions need and they gave her a new sense of purpose.

Sandra Haynie, the golfer, was in Martina's corner when she won her second Wimbledon title in 1979. But the year before Martina had been on her own. That 1978 win had come after a tremendous battle in the Eastbourne final which Martina had won 9-7 in the last set on a gale-swept day that was bad even by the standards of the notoriously windy south coast. It had been only her fourth win against Chris in 25 meetings and it boosted her confidence at just the right moment, particularly as she had recovered from being 1-4 down in the final set and, later, match point down, before she had won. The only previous time they had played on grass had been in the Wimbledon semi-finals of 1976, Chris's second victory year there. Thus the Eastbourne win broke the spell of Chris's invincibility on a surface that Martina knew should favour her.

Martina's parents had not been able to get permission to leave Czechoslovakia, as they would be able to do the following year, and so they travelled close to the West German border and watched the match on German television. How thrilled they must have been as Martina, having lost the opening set and won the second, came back from 2-4 and 4-5 in the decider to take the match 2-6 6-4 7-5. At last her nerve had held in an important final against her great rival. It was one of two turning points in her career.

The other turning point came with her first success in Paris in 1982. In the spring of 1981 Martina had sought the help of Nancy Lieberman, the basketball star, as a trainer. As Martina set about the tough routines a new dimension of fitness and mobility was added to her game. Another American, Renee Richards, took on the role of coach after the US Open in 1981. The combined wisdom of the two advisers helped Martina to achieve the success on clay she had for so long been seeking when she beat Andrea Jaeger for the 1982 French title. Later that year she started to follow the diet designed especially for athletes by Dr Robert Haas, the same one that Ivan Lendl was later to adopt. Gradually Martina began to look physically harder and stronger, much to the dismay of her opponents!

There had been two disappointing semi-final round losses at Wimbledon in 1980 and 1981, to Chris Lloyd and Hana Mandlikova respectively. However, Renee Richards and Nancy Lieberman restored the slipping confidence in time for that Paris win and a third victory at Wimbledon in 1982, the first of five successive titles there that stamped Martina as arguably the best woman who has ever wielded a racket. Three of those finals were against Chris Evert Lloyd but the second in 1983 was against little Andrea Jaeger, the girl whom Martina had beaten the previous year in the Paris final. Andrea had taken her chance following the surprise defeat of a below-par Mrs Lloyd in the third round by Kathy Jordan, the first occasion in the last 35 Grand Slam Championships that Chris had failed to reach at least the semi-finals. Kathy had lost to Billie Jean King who was no match for the teenager in the penultimate round. Similarly, in the final, Andrea was swept aside by Martina's power, but not before she had delighted the spectators with some beautiful passing shots and lobs.

Martina's standing as the greatest player of modern times was reinforced by her most impressive performance to date in the 1984 Paris final where all the strands of her majestic game, power, touch, athleticism and tactical awareness, came together as she beat the world's finest clay court player of the decade, Chris Evert Lloyd, 6-3 6-1.

It was after a surprise defeat at the hands of Kathy Horvath in Paris in 1983 that Martina had ended her association with Renee Richards and asked the American circuit player Mike Estep if he would give up his own career to act as her coach. After a fourth Wimbledon title that year this happy and successful partnership at last brought Martina the one success that had always eluded her, the US Open crown. Inevitably it was Chris who opposed her in the final and after the 6-1 6-3 beating it was refreshing to see how genuinely pleased this great champion was on seeing Martina at last take the title which she herself had won six times.

It was equally pleasing, two years later in Paris, to see Martina graciously acknowledge one of the greatest performances of Chris's entire career as she hung in tenaciously to record a sixth win there 6-3 6-7 7-5 in a fluctuating final that, for sheer drama, was one of the greatest matches of the decade.

Although Chris Evert Lloyd's tally of three Wimbledon singles' titles looks meagre beside those six US crowns and the seven French Opens that have fallen to her exquisite craftsmanship, let us remember that she is one of a select band of 13 women who have won the title three times or more. The first win in 1974 when, a demure 19-year-old, she had triumphed alongside her fiancé Jimmy Connors, was a romantic moment in Wimbledon's history. It was also a landmark in the game's history for, from that moment on, double-handed backhands became legitimate. A whole new generation of players all over the world would adopt that method. Chris could also exact vicarious pleasure from her husband

John's two mixed doubles successes with Wendy Turnbull in 1983 and 1984, the first Wimbledon titles won by a British man since Fred Perry in 1936.

Martina and Chris, then, have written the last decade of Wimbledon's intriguing story almost unchallenged – and how sportingly and regally have they conducted themselves. But two others in that time have each created a moment of sheer joy and emotional excitement that will live for ever in the annals of the game. When, in 1980, Evonne Cawley won a second singles' title nine years after she had first delighted us as Evonne Goolagong with her own special brand of Australian magic, the hearts of millions of fans around the world went out to her. This graceful and beautifully relaxed shot-maker had survived some cruel injuries and countless disappointments during those intervening years and had started a family too. In fact, with that second singles' victory, she became the first mother to win at Wimbledon since Dolly Lambert Chambers in 1914.

But even that joy had been surpassed in 1977, the centenary year of The Championships, when 31-year-old Virginia Wade, challenging for the sixteenth time and playing before the Queen who was visiting Wimbledon for the third time in this her Jubilee year, won the title against Betty Stove of the Netherlands in three agonising sets. Since Ann Jones' win in 1969 Virginia had maintained the respectability of British tennis practically single-handed. At the first US Open in 1968 Virginia had beaten Billie Jean King to win her first Grand Slam title and it seemed the world was at her feet. But for one so intelligent (she had earned a degree in mathematics at the University of Sus-

sex) her suicidal tactics in so many subsequent matches that she should have been capable of winning were bewildering. Thus it was an adventurous career with some spectacular highs and some depressing lows. Had Virginia ever eradicated a fundamental weakness on the forehand side she might have achieved all that her enormous potential had forecast for her in 1968. Yet the Italian Open fell to her in 1971, an impressive win this on slow clay and worth more, really, than the Australian Open on grass which she won in 1972. Her contribution to Britain's Federation Cup and Wightman Cup teams since 1965 has been immense and her present contribution to Wimbledon as the first lady committee member (she was elected to that position in 1982) has been equally important.

But at Wimbledon in 1977 it was as if the whole of her career had come to a moment of fulfilment. In the semi-finals the British girl had played at her forceful best to bring down Chris Evert 6-1 in the third set. In the final against Betty her nerves, so often the cause of her downfall, wavered for a moment as she lost the opening set. But then, lifted on a patriotic tide of emotional support she sailed majestically home 4-6 6-3 6-1, her broad smile and flashing eyes reflecting the feelings of the cheering multitude as they spontaneously sang *For She's a Jolly Good Fellow* while the Queen, looking slightly bewildered by all the fuss, handed Virginia the famous silver-gilt plate that glittered and sparkled in the sunlight as she held it triumphantly aloft.

What a decade it had been as Wimbledon, in 1986, approached its one hundredth Championship!

BIOGRAPHIES

GENTLEMEN

J. P. McEnroe

B. Becker

B. Borg

1976, 1977, 1978, 1979, 1980

BJORN BORG

Born: 6 June 1956

This Swede was one of the giants. He won his first Grand Slam title with the French in 1974 when he was barely 18. In 1981 he won it for the sixth time. At Wimbledon he controlled events for five tremendous years; curiously his initial victory was the most one-sided and it was the only occasion he did not lose a set.

He made his Davis Cup début when only 15. His double-fisted backhand combined with his heavy, topspun forehand to make him virtually invincible when on form. His Wimbledon record is unsurpassed. He won 41 successive singles' matches and his eventual defeat was in the final against John McEnroe. The US title, however, eluded him, the blot on an almost perfect record.

He retired in 1982 when only 26. He was then a millionaire but he ceased being a tax exile in Monte Carlo to return to his native Sweden.

His example created a vast school of effective Swedish players.

1981, 1983, 1984

JOHN McENROE

Born: 16 February 1959

This left-handed genius, supreme in singles and doubles, rarely ceased to be sensational. When a junior in 1977, he turned form upside down by qualifying for Wimbledon and then reaching the semi-finals.

After two stagnant years his emergence as champion in 1981 was through brilliant play combined with controversial behaviour. His readiness to argue with officials and lack of graciousness caused the All England Club to take the unprecedented step of withholding the normal honorary membership of the club after winning. The honour was given a year later when, though not winning, he had purged his offence by good behaviour.

He showed his flair equally in the US Championships where he succeeded in 1978, 1979, 1980 and 1984. In the French Championships (where he won the mixed doubles in 1977) he met with surprising failure and in 1984 actually dissipated a two sets to love lead in the final against the Czechoslovak Ivan Lendl.

1985, 1986

BORIS BECKER

Born: 22 November 1967

The ninety-ninth Wimbledon meeting produced its most remarkable winner. At 17 years 227 days, Boris Becker, from Leimen in West Germany, became the youngest men's singles winner of all time. By losing a total of eight sets (winning 166 games, losing 126) he exceeded by one game the record of Ted Shroeder 36 years before in having the most laboured victory, though Ashley Cooper in 1958 had lost 7 sets and played 322 games. He was the first German singles' winner among men. He was the first unseeded victor since seeding began in 1927.

When he successfully defended his title a year later with an impressively mature performance against World Champion Ivan Lendl, he silenced for ever those critics who had called his first win lucky.

LADIES

1977

VIRGINIA WADE

Born: 10 July 1945

Born in Bournemouth, trained in South Africa, where her father was Archdeacon of Durban, she indicated her strength of character by sitting for her science degree at Sussex University while playing in the Wightman Cup; she had success in both.

Her Wimbledon triumph was a patriotic highlight, being in front of the Queen in the Silver Jubilee Year and on Wimbledon's Centenary. She acquired the US Open title in 1968, the Australian in 1972 but her Wimbledon success was after 15 earlier failures. Her aggressive game was often costly in its mistakes.

She competed for the twenty-fourth consecutive time in 1985 in singles. She was the first woman elected to the Wimbledon Management Committee.

1978, 1979, 1982, 1983, 1984, 1985, 1986

MARTINA NAVRATILOVA

Born: 18 October 1956

She was a 16-year-old Czechoslovak when her volleying capacity was made evident in the BP Cup at Torquay in 1972. After seven Wimbledon singles' titles, after winning the Grand Slam, after dominating doubles to unsurpassed lengths, the same player, now American, had taken the women's game to new dimensions.

No woman in tennis' history has been so professional as Martina Navratilova. Her tremendous earning capacity (she won a prize of $1 million for taking the Grand Slam in 1984 and by the end of 1985 had altogether earned over $9 million) has enabled her to employ expert and continuing advice, not only in training but in matters often thought peripheral, like diet.

She turned herself into the most expert and complete woman player of all time.

S. V. Wade

M. Navratilova

WIMBLEDON'S OLDEST LIVING
CHAMPION, THE MUCH-LOVED
KITTY GODFREE, AGED 90,
PRESENTS THE FAMOUS PLATE SHE
HAD HELD IN 1924 AND 1926 TO
MARTINA NAVRATILOVA

THE FRENCH 'MUSKETEER', JEAN
BOROTRA, AND THE DUCHESS OF
KENT LEAVE THE COURT AFTER
PRESENTING BORIS BECKER WITH
THE TROPHY AND CHEQUE

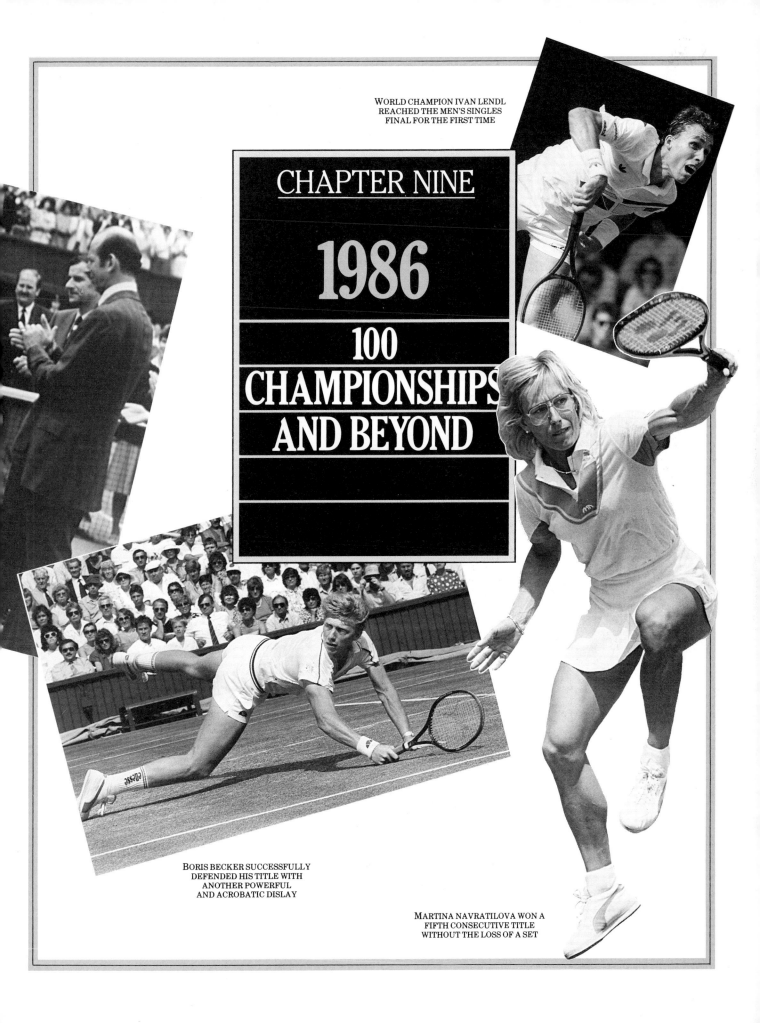

WORLD CHAMPION IVAN LENDL
REACHED THE MEN'S SINGLES
FINAL FOR THE FIRST TIME

CHAPTER NINE

1986

100 CHAMPIONSHIPS AND BEYOND

BORIS BECKER SUCCESSFULLY
DEFENDED HIS TITLE WITH
ANOTHER POWERFUL
AND ACROBATIC DISLAY

MARTINA NAVRATILOVA WON A
FIFTH CONSECUTIVE TITLE
WITHOUT THE LOSS OF A SET

THERE seemed to be a providential hand guiding the fortunes of the hundredth Championship meeting. When Martina Navratilova and Boris Becker successfully retained their titles at the end of a fortnight of blazing skies and smiling encounters, there was an unmistakable feeling that tennis had returned to its origins. Despite the total professionalism of the modern game, its gifted stars, millionaires all, had rediscovered the simple joy of competition – that same basic and compelling desire which had motivated its earliest champions. Certainly, the absence of John McEnroe in self-imposed exile and the early loss of Jimmy Connors had removed two sources of potential irritation, but the mood was much more fundamental. It was as if the players, conscious that they were all part of something much greater than themselves, could recognise greatness in one another and generously show their appreciation of it in word and gesture.

The public responded enthusiastically to the mood. The ground record was broken on the first Thursday when 39,813 attended and, altogether, 400,032 spectators thronged the grounds during the 13 days of fierce but friendly competition – more than in any previous year – and they revelled in the joyous atmosphere. The decision to use yellow balls for the first time seemed universally popular. With rain interrupting play on only the first day and the final Saturday, the head groundsman Jim Thorne was able to water the courts each night before covering them so that the Centre Court presented a greener face for the final stages than ever before.

As always at Wimbledon there were some heroic performances, particularly in the men's singles where 27 different nations were represented. On the second day a tall young American, Robert Seguso, who was the world's top-ranked doubles' player in 1985, served with consistent venom to defeat Jimmy Connors, the No. 3 seed, 6-3 3-6 7-6 7-6 initiating a slaughter of the seeds that had reduced their number to a scant seven by the fourth round.

One who narrowly survived to that stage was Mats Wilander, the No. 2 seed, who had been assaulted gloriously in the second round by a bright, 22-year-old Englishman from Taunton called Andrew Castle who was playing in only his third Grand Prix tournament and had been a wild card entry. Tiring in his first-ever five-set match, Castle went down 4-6 7-6 6-7 6-4 6-0 after 3 hours and 44 minutes but his fighting spirit and realistic attitude afterwards earned him selection for the Davis Cup match against the Australians to be played at Wimbledon in three weeks' time.

Wilander's challenge was ended two rounds later by another wild card entry. His conqueror in four serve-and-volley sets was Pat Cash, the 21-year-old Australian who, remarkably, only four weeks earlier had been on the operating table having his appendix removed. Then Cash ran into the mercurial Frenchman Henri Leconte, the seventh seed, in the quarter-finals. Here, the Australian's brave progress was halted by one of those typically explosive performances from Leconte that make every match he plays a thrilling, pyrotechnic spectacle. Had Cash been able to convert the set point he held in the second set tie-break to give himself a two sets to love lead then he might have won. But some superbly enterprising shot-making from the Frenchman, combined with those delicate touches that were once the hallmark of the great French champion,

Henri Cochet, gave Leconte a 4-6 7-6 7-6 6-3 win that had spanned three hours in the full heat of the afternoon. At the end Cash's tired body could offer only token resistance.

Three other men surpassed expectations by reaching the quarter-finals unseeded. The gentle Yugoslav giant Slobodan Zivojinovic, all 6 feet 6 inches and 14 stone 2 pounds of him, was the one who emerged to the semi-finals, the tenth unseeded semi-finalist in succession. The man whom Zivojinovic beat in four delightful sets was the Indian with the gossamer touch, Ramesh Krishnan, whose father Ramanathan had twice been a Wimbledon semi-finalist. Predictably, power overcame touch as Zivojinovic, 'Bobo' to his friends, ripped apart the Indian's defences in his 6-2 7-6 4-6 6-3 victory.

The third intruder was the bearded Czechoslovak, Miloslav Mecir, a deceptively gifted tactician with a flexible wrist who has the ability to send an opponent off in one direction while gliding the ball gently away in the other. Two seeded players, Stefan Edberg (5) and Brad Gilbert (12), became ensnared on his tactical web and gained only one set between them.

However, even Mecir (christened 'The Big Cat') could not survive the pace set by the defending champion Becker. With his serve now looking ominously grooved (there were 12 aces), the young West German was also projecting those rocket-like backhand returns which are taken so early after the bounce that incoming volleyers are left flailing at thin air. It took exactly two hours for Becker to quell the elusive Czechoslovak 6-4 6-2 7-6.

In the only quarter-final between two seeded players, the World Champion and official favourite Ivan Lendl of Czecho-slovakia defeated the tenth seed Tim Mayotte. The American had won the Stella Artois tournament at Queen's Club two weeks before The Championships and had just the sort of conventional serve-and-volley game to worry Lendl. Furthermore, he had always done well at Wimbledon having reached the semi-finals in 1982 and the quarter-finals in 1981 and 1983. But he lacks variety and flair. In the closing stages of a thrilling five-set encounter that ended on Court No. 1 in gathering darkness, Lendl could play the percentages with impunity. Perhaps the knowledge that he had never lost to Mayotte in ten previous meetings helped him to remain steadfast in the crisis as he forced the necessary break of Mayotte's serve to win confidently in the end 6-4 4-6 6-4 3-6 9-7. Still, though, Lendl did not look really at ease on grass. His coach, Tony Roche, had certainly improved his serve-and-volley game but it never seemed natural.

Both men's semi-finals were satisfying matches and, for the first time since the Challenge Round had been abolished in 1922, were contested by four Europeans. Becker played faultless tennis for two imperious sets against Leconte but lost the third on a tie-break as the Frenchman found a new level of inspiration. Although he had stemmed the German advance the brave Leconte could never halt it; the power was too great, the spirit too intense for that. So, after a feast of improvisation, Becker entered his second final in succession with his 6-2 6-4 6-7 6-3 success. But Leconte in defeat earned many new friends as he threw his arm spontaneously round Becker's neck and left the arena smiling broadly and waving to the delighted fans.

Lendl could have been excused for thinking that he might have an easy time against Zivojinovic for he had won their only previous encounter 6-4 6-0 in Indianapolis in 1985. But that had been on clay. Here the Yugoslav giant had already tasted blood – last year he had put out a surprised No. 4 seed Wilander in the first round – and he liked the taste. What a spirited challenge it was! Trailing one set to two, Zivojinovic held a point to break Lendl's serve for a 4-3 lead. When Lendl's obvious fault was overruled so that it became his thirteenth ace, Zivojinovic exploded. Refusing at first to play on, he received a delay warning. Fortunately, the incident had no effect on the outcome, except perhaps to stiffen the Yugoslav's resistance. Winning the fourth-set tie-break 7-1, Zivojinovic took the match into a fifth set. Despite 18 huge aces and many glorious volleys, Zivojinovic was forced to concede his serve in the seventh game and lost the match 6-2 6-7 6-3 6-7 6-4 to a more complete and determined player.

The men's final was another historic occasion. It was the first time that Lendl, the World Champion, had proceeded that far. Before that the best he had done was to reach the semi-finals twice, in 1983 when McEnroe had beaten him and the following year when Connors had proved too good. From nine previous Grand Slam finals he had won only three times: twice in Paris (1984 and 1986) and once in New York (1985). One of the six defeats had been on grass – in Melbourne in 1983 when Wilander had surprised him. Yet, Lendl was outstandingly the best player of the day. He had won 83 of his last 86 matches and 11 of his last 14 tournaments. Significantly, the last of those three losses since the 1985 US Open had been to Becker in the Chicago final in March when Lendl had had some doubts about a knee. This last was the only win by Becker against Lendl in five previous meetings.

On paper the defending champion seemed to have competed rather better than the No. 1 seed. On the way to his second Grand Slam final, Becker had lost his service only four times in his six winning matches, which had cost him a mere 2 sets and 73 games. Lendl, on the other hand, had conceded his service 6 times and had lost 5 sets and 103 games in reaching the final.

The match was not an epic, Becker served too well for that. But it was remarkable for the resilience of the young German when threatened and for the quality of his second serves. Lendl it was who broke first to lead 3-2 as a slightly tense Becker delivered the second of the seven double faults he would serve altogether. Despite a second ace Lendl's serve was immediately ripped from his grasp by three piercing backhand returns and a forced error on the forehand volley, which was a stroke that was to prove vulnerable all afternoon. Four more imperious winners in the tenth game, two on each wing, brought West Germany the first set 6-4 – much to the delight of President Weizsacker who had extended his state visit by one day so that he and his wife could attend the final. He sat proudly in the front row of the Royal Box alongside the Duke and Duchess of Kent, Prince and Princess Michael of Kent, King Constantine and Queen Anne-Marie of the Hellenes, Princess Alexandra and the Hon. Angus Ogilvy, The Prime Minister Margaret Thatcher and the Club Chairman 'Buzzer' Hadingham – as concentrated a collection of dignitaries as the Royal Box had seen throughout the fortnight. They all seemed to admire the youthful exuberance and stunning power of the young German – just as King George and Queen Mary had admired the grace and elegance of the only previous German finalist, Baron Gottfried von Cramm, in another age.

To signal his growing confidence Becker opened the second set with three untouchable aces, his eighth, ninth and tenth and a single break of serve in the eighth game brought Becker the second set 6-3 as a fourteenth ace thwacked against the canvas screen. When Lendl found two beautifully struck backhand returns to break the Becker serve in the second game of the third set and then built a lead of 3-0 and 4-1 it seemed he had at last come to terms with the young man's pace. Becker himself had momentarily lost his intensity. He was cruising along in second gear as if mentally satisfied with his two sets to love lead. But, as Lendl came to serve with the new balls at 4-2, you could see the determination return to Becker's face. Despite serving a fourth ace for 15-15 Lendl stood helpless once more as Becker, taking his returns almost suicidally early, whipped a forehand return, a crosscourt forehand pass and finally a crosscourt backhand return out of Lendl's reach to break back. At 4-5 and 0-40 the champion faced three set points. All were saved with positive volleys. An ace, his fifteenth and last, and another service winner 5-all. The end now seemed inevitable as the young German, swelling with confidence and performing his intense little victory shuffle with every new winner, broke again in the eleventh game and served out the match to 30.

As the Centre Court crowd rose to acclaim him, his manager Ion Tiriac and coach Gunther Bosch in the players' box finally managed to smile while his mother Elvira, sitting in the international box with his father Karl Heinz, at last opened her eyes. She had been too nervous and superstitious to watch any of the play at all! It had been another breathtaking display by a player who was still younger than any other previous male champion. The 12 months since his first, unseeded triumph had brought a noticeable maturity. The mood was just as intense but less frenetic; the tactical awareness was markedly improved so that inspiration could be summoned rather than relied on; greater physical strength had produced better court coverage; the sense of belonging on the Centre Court, that it was his stage, was also apparent. He was also aware of the effect of his successes in West Germany. Interviewed by *Time* magazine he had said: 'The Germans were waiting for somebody. They were searching for another hero. The Americans could say they were Americans and be proud. But the Germans never liked to say they were Germans outside their own country. Now it often happens that they say "We are Germans from the land of Boris Becker". That is my achievement.' But he saw the dangers: 'The Germans wanted me to live for them. They worshipped too much ... When I looked into the eyes of my fans at the Davis Cup matches last December I thought I was looking at monsters. Their eyes were fixed and had no life in them. When I saw this kind of blind, emotional devotion, I could understand what happened to us a long time ago in Nuremberg.' Yes, the young Champion had certainly matured.

While the fans cheered, Jean Borotra the French 'Musketeer' and the oldest surviving men's champion, who had won in 1924 and 1926, presented Boris with the famous silver gilt cup. Then the Duchess of Kent gave him the winner's cheque for £140,000, less the £3,080 first-round prize money Boris had donated to UNICEF on the opening day as the newly-appointed Sports Ambassador to the United Nations Children's

RIGHT: Was there ever a more attractive or more effective 16-year-old than the Argentine champion, Gabriela Sabatini, the youngest women's semi-finalist since Lottie Dod in 1887? Guided by her coach, Patricio Apey, Gabriela has made consistent progress since being the world's best junior in 1984. Her natural athleticism and her winning mentality will surely one day bring her the world's great titles.

LEFT: The expressive mannerisms of Henri Leconte endeared the extrovert Frenchman to the spectators who cheered his recovery against Pat Cash and cheered him again in defeat against Boris Becker. Leconte's dazzling left-handed genius and generous acknowledgement of his opponents' shots reawakened memories of the great French Musketeers of the 1920s, Borotra, Lacoste, Cochet and Brugnon.

ABOVE RIGHT: Andrew Castle, a 22-year-old wild card entry from Somerset who was playing in only his third Grand Prix tournament, set British pulses racing by the manner of his attack on the No. 2 seed, Mats Wilander of Sweden, in the second round. Tiring in the closing stages, Castle failed to turn a two sets to one lead into a victory but, nevertheless, earned a standing ovation for his courageous display.

LEFT: The customary curtsey to the Royal Box as the two Czechoslovak-born finalists Hana Mandlikova (left) and Martina Navratilova (right) arrive for their first Wimbledon meeting since 1981 when Hana, who had once been a ball girl for Martina, had inflicted her last Wimbledon defeat on the six times champion. With an authoritative display of aggressive tennis, Martina reversed that result to maintain her record of never losing a Wimbledon singles' final.

RIGHT: Although eclipsed in the singles where none of their four seeded representatives, Mats Wilander (2), Stefan Edberg (5), Joakim Nystrom (6) and Anders Jarryd (8), reached their appointed places, Sweden did, however, claim the men's doubles title. Wilander (right) and Nystrom (left) beat the Americans Peter Fleming and Gary Donnelly to become only the second pair from their country to win the title.

BELOW: Heinz Gunthardt (Switzerland) and Martina Navratilova (USA) (left) with the American pair who beat them in the final of the mixed doubles, Kathy Jordan and Ken Flach. So, for the sixth time since 1979, Martina had to be content with two Wimbledon titles and cannot yet join that select band of three men and five women who have won all three in the same year.

Fund. As they left the court Lendl earned much admiration by smiling and waving to the crowd. His time may yet come.

As usual, the ladies ran truer to form than the men. There were only two unseeded players in the quarter-finals, Bettina Bunge of West Germany and the black American Lori McNeil. Miss Bunge, who had done well to remove the No. 8 seed Manuela Maleeva 3-6 6-2 6-3 with her attacking net play, could gain only four games from Martina Navratilova as the four-time defending champion inflicted a fifteenth consecutive win against her. Miss McNeil of Houston, who is coached by John Wilkerson (the man who guides Zina Garrison), had put out Betsy Nagelsen, the conqueror of fifth-seeded Pam Shriver in the opening round. She took advantage of an erratic start by the No. 3 seed Hana Mandlikova to take the opening set on a tie-break but was then routed 6-0 6-2. It was the second time in three meetings that Miss McNeil had taken a set from the Czechoslovak.

In the two quarter-finals between seeded players three-time former champion Chris Evert Lloyd (2) beat the tall Czechoslovak Helena Sukova (7) 7-6 4-6 6-4 and the 16-year-old Argentine girl Gabriela Sabatini (10) prevailed at the expense of Catarina Lindqvist (15). The athletic Miss Sabatini was no doubt inspired by the success of the Argentine footballers in Mexico who had just won the World Cup as she entered the semi-final with a 6-2 6-3 victory, the youngest girl to advance as far this century – as she had been in Paris when she had reached the same stage in 1985 aged 15 years 2 months. At Wimbledon only Lottie Dod, who had won the first of her five titles aged 15 years 10 months in 1887 when the entries were small, had been younger.

Not surprisingly, Miss Sabatini could make little impression against the defending champion in the first semi-final. It was the first time they had met and the younger girl was shown the full range of Miss Navratilova's powerful game which prevailed 6-2 6-2. Four aces from Miss Sabatini's stinging delivery surprised the champion, as did the loss of her own serve for the only time in the match in the sixth game of the second set as she served her only double fault. Even in this brief encounter there was enough evidence to suggest that Miss Sabatini, along with the 17-year-old West German Steffi Graf whose virus infection had caused her to withdraw on the eve of The Championships, will be the ones most likely to supplant the present leaders.

In her forty-fifth Grand Slam semi-final of the 46 Championships she has contested since 1971 and her fourteenth at Wimbledon in 15 challenges, Mrs Lloyd had the comforting knowledge that she had beaten Miss Mandlikova in straight sets on the only two occasions they had met on Wimbledon's grass. There had also been another win on grass in Australia in 1981. Furthermore, their most recent meeting in the penultimate round of the French Open had resulted in a crushing 6-1 6-1 win for the 31-year-old American. However, Hana had won 5 of their 24 previous meetings and was the one player, apart from Miss Navratilova, who was quite capable of sweeping Mrs Lloyd (or anyone else) from the court.

So it proved. Despite some magnificently accurate driving and counter-hitting passes from Mrs Lloyd who had led 2-0 and 4-3 with a service break in the opening set, the Czechoslovak girl kept producing those glorious free-flowing patches of play that would not be denied. Recovering at once to 4-4 and holding securely thereafter she took control of the tie-break at 4-1, 5-3 and finally 7-5. Mrs Lloyd's 5-2 lead in the second set served only to inspire her opponent to another of those glittering spells when instinct takes over and frees the mind of all inhibitions. With a run of 14 consecutive points Miss Mandlikova swept to 5-5 and 0-30 against the Lloyd serve, which was wilting now, perhaps as the result of her more difficult path to the last four via Kathy Jordan and Helena Sukova. The break duly came and the match was won on the second match point with a full-blooded smash. Thus Mrs Lloyd was denied the chance of contesting an eleventh Wimbledon singles' final since 1973 that would have been her thirty-fourth in Grand Slam Championships. For her opponent it was a second appearance in the final and a chance to complete her Grand Slam hand for she had already won in Melbourne (1980), Paris (1981) and New York (1985).

The final brought out the best in Miss Navratilova. Banishing the memory of the 1981 semi-final when Hana had inflicted on her the last loss she had suffered at Wimbledon before beginning her run of 4 successive titles and 33 winning matches, Martina did not panic and could still smile when her opponent made a perfect start to lead 3-0, 4-1 and 5-2. It was at this point that Miss Mandlikova changed her shoes because she had been slipping on the drizzle-soaked surface and on the still-wet lines which Jim Thorne had marked too close to the start of the match on such a sultry day. The interruption to her concentration was fatal. With the spell broken, Martina began to assert herself. The timing and accuracy of her passing shots improved, the penetration of her service increased and all at once the match took on a different aspect. As she strode majestically to 5-5 you could see that Martina was now in total command, queen once more of the stage where she had never lost a singles' final in six previous appearances. The tie-break, won 7-1, merely underlined her supremacy and you had to feel sorry for Hana who simply was not allowed to recapture her flair.

A quick second set completed Martina's seventh triumph 7-5 6-3, a fifth consecutive win that equalled the run of Suzanne Lenglen from 1919 to 1923. How fitting that the oldest surviving champion Kitty Godfree, aged 90 now and the singles' winner in 1924 and 1926 (coincidentally the same years as Borotra), should have been invited to present Martina with her trophy. Now the record 8 wins of Helen Wills Moody between 1927 and 1938, the 41 consecutive winning matches of Bjorn Borg from the first round in 1976 to the final in 1981 (only 7 away) and the 20 Wimbledon titles of Billie Jean King (still 6 away) beckon as the ultimate challenges.

Once again Martina failed to win all three titles, a feat last achieved by Mrs King in 1973. Having regained with Pam Shriver the doubles' title they had so unexpectedly lost the previous year with a straight sets win over Miss Mandlikova and Wendy Turnbull, Martina's bid was ended at the last hurdle by the same girl who had thwarted her in 1985. Kathy Jordan had played with Elizabeth Sayers Smylie then, now in the mixed she was paired with fellow American Ken Flach who together inflicted a 6-3 7-6 defeat on Martina and her Swiss partner Heinz Gunthardt. This was the only success by American-born players. In an exciting final Heinz could not convert any of the set points that would have levelled the match. He seemed to be trying too hard.

The men's doubles fell to Joakim Nystrom and Mats Wilander who beat the Americans Gary Donnelly and four times former champion Peter Fleming 7-6 6-3 6-3. The Swedes thus atoned for disappointing performances in the singles and became the first pair from their country to win the title since Sven Davidson and Ulf Schmidt in 1958.

Another who made up for a disappointing loss was Pam Shriver who won the Ladies' Plate by beating the teenage American Stephanie Rehe 4-6 7-6 6-0. For the second year running the boys' singles was won by a Mexican. Eduardo Velez had lost in the previous year's final to Leonardo Lavalle but this time he was successful 6-3 7-5 against Javier Sanchez of Spain, the younger brother of Emilio, the world's twenty-first ranked player. Because the Americans had decided not to send their juniors to compete in Europe this year for fear of Libyan bombers, the standard of both events was probably lower than usual. Nevertheless, the fact that the girls' singles was contested by two Russians served to remind the rest of the world of the advances they have made of late. Natali Zvereva defeated Leila Meski 2-6 6-2 9-7 to become the first Russian junior to take a Wimbledon title since Natasha Chmyreva in 1976.

In the final of the over-35 invitation singles there was no consolation for Tony Roche whose charge Ivan Lendl had lost in the men's singles final. He was comprehensively beaten 6-3 6-2 by Jaime Fillol of Chile, a former President of ATP, the player's union.

So ended the hundredth Championships, a meeting that was memorable for the cheerful and friendly spirit it had engendered as well as for some outstanding performances. As usual, the organisation had been flawless thanks to meticulous planning. Since 1984 the management team has been strengthened to recognise the increasing complexity of the modern game and the growing activities of the club in the area of marketing. As Chief Executive, Christopher Gorringe is in overall command of the day-to-day activities, reporting to the Joint Championships Committee (comprising 12 AELTC members, 6 from the LTA) on anything that is connected with the tournament and to the Club Committee on club affairs. The division of responsibilities is recognised by the functions of Richard Grier, The Championships Director and Roger Ambrose, the Club Secretary. The responsibilities of the Financial Director, Tony Hughes, extend to both areas and Robert McCowen, the Marketing Director, creates extra income for The Championships account, the surplus of which each year passes to the LTA. In 1987 the governing body should expect to receive approximately £6 million from all Wimbledon sources towards the cost of financing the game in Britain.

The average age of the Club Committee itself has also fallen in recent years with the election of former players Mark Cox and Virginia Wade to membership. Miss Wade is the first and so far the only woman elected to the Committee and her voice is a welcome reminder of the changing attitude of a body that used to be regarded as the epitome of reaction. That charge can no longer be levelled. Change is a word no longer feared at Wimbledon. Indeed, the Chairman, in a lifetime associated with the commercial aspects of sport through his 50 years with Slazengers Ltd (whose Chairmanship he resigned when he took up office at the All England Club in 1983), is deeply conscious of the need to keep abreast of the rapid changes that are taking place within the international game. He has the priceless advantage of knowing personally all the personalities who have been involved in the development of international tennis from an amateur pastime into a huge industry. He also goes out of his way to get to know today's players and he encourages each member of the Committee to do the same. Accordingly, Wimbledon now presents a much friendlier face to the players and public than it ever used to when it was somewhat arrogantly assumed that simply because it was there everyone would automatically want to come and play and watch.

The club is also keenly aware of the need to assist the LTA in their own attempts to modernise. Only by a strong partnership between a dynamic governing body and the All England Club can the game in Britain begin to enjoy the boom that other countries have experienced. That is why the recently announced Indoor Tennis Initiative (ITI), a co-operative grant aid venture between the two bodies and the Sports Council which, together with contributions from the local authorities themselves, will make £20 million available to build, it is hoped, 100 indoor tennis centres throughout Britain in the next five years, is such an important first joint venture. Eventually, it may become apparent that the LTA and the All England Club should merge to give even greater unity and impetus to tennis development in Britain. This is what has happened in France which, in terms of popularity against other sports, is the foremost tennis nation in the world.

But that change, if it comes at all, lies some way in the future. Of more immediate moment are the pressures for change from within the game itself. The players, better organised than ever before, will continue to press for a higher share of the growing revenue – both through increases in prize money and in contributions to pension funds and wel-

fare schemes. These should only be met in so far as revenue is available above the continuing need to improve the ground and public facilities and to fund British tennis. If sponsorship ever becomes necessary, you can be sure that the Committee will introduce it with style. They will jealously guard the unique garden party atmosphere that is an essential part of The Championships' success.

When the Australian Open changes from grass to a new synthetic surface in 1988, pressure will grow on Wimbledon to tear up the grass. The players will say that it is unreasonable to expect them to come from European clay for only a four-week season on grass, which is a surface that increasingly few of them ever play on outside Britain. The answer to that may be to start Wimbledon two weeks later so that there are four weeks of preliminary tournaments before The Championships.

I would hate to see The Championships played on any other surface than grass, not just because it has always been played on the surface but because I still believe that a good grass court sets the sternest test for every player. Conditions are never quite the same two days running so a player must be adaptable; because of the speed of bounce a player must move fast and think fast and must get it right first time for there is no time to change one's mind. Also the grass itself adds to the garden party atmosphere. Without it, as the Americans found out to their cost when they changed from grass to clay at Forest Hills in 1975, the atmosphere is lost. It is just another tournament on the tour.

Another possible change, being freely discussed, concerns the growing domination of the service. Perhaps the time has come to restrict players to one serve or to mark a line 1 yard behind the baseline from which the serve would be delivered. Unless some action is taken there is a distinct possibility that the public will begin to shun a sport which, through the sheer perfection of its performers using modern, powerful equipment, is often boring to watch. This is something that the game's administrators should ponder most seriously.

'Wimbledon', as The Championships are universally known, has become over the years an established part of the fabric of British life. It is more than a tradition, more than just the world's most important and historic tennis tournament. It is a symbol of all that is best about sport, royal patronage, and social occasion that the British do so well, a subtle blend that the rest of the world finds irresistible.

The players feel it too, which is why they are inspired to produce their finest tennis on the famous old Centre Court. When Martina and Boris spoke at the champion's dinner on the final evening at the Savoy Hotel that ended the hundredth Championships, they both acknowledged that the Wimbledon title is the one they most wanted to win. Indeed, every player, if he were honest, would say the same.

When all the words had been said and the toasts had been drunk, the Chairman, 'Buzzer' Hadingham, stood for the last time to wind up the proceedings with a piece of verse that had come to him, he told us, in the middle of the previous night. It perfectly captured the mood of the occasion and is a fitting way to end this celebration of Wimbledon's 100 Championships.

'So, all too soon, the final curtain falls,
Each one who worked, now weary, homeward goes.
Take out the posts and stow the tennis balls
Our hundredth meeting's drawing to a close.

All Champions and competitors depart;
The work of umpires, ball boys, all is done.
Tomorrow those whose job it is will start
Preparing for our meeting 101.

Forecasting match results no mystery now,
The memories remain for us to share.
The titles won go down to history now
And we shall tell our children "We were there".

Take down the canvas, fold away each net.
Repair the courts, yes even let it rain.
Come back in '87 – don't forget!
We'll welcome you to Wimbledon again.'

AN OIL PAINTING BY LOCAL ARTIST F. RANSOM OF THE SITE OF THE NEW GROUND
IN CHURCH ROAD AS IT WAS IN 1914. THE PAINTING WAS PRESENTED TO THE WIMBLEDON LAWN
TENNIS MUSEUM IN 1979 BY MRS K. SAXBY, WHOSE FATHER WAS A FRIEND OF THE ARTIST

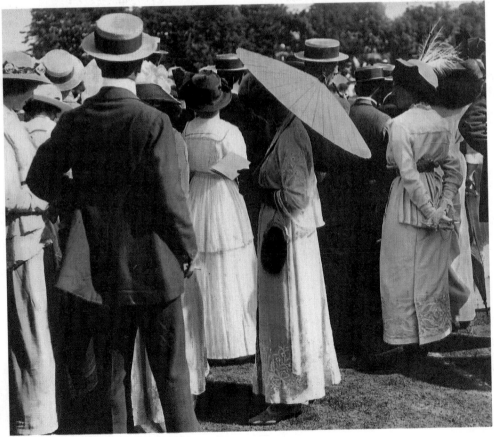

ABOVE
HELEN WILLS MOODY, WHOSE
EIGHT WINS BETWEEN 1927
AND 1938 REMAIN A RECORD
THAT MARTINA
NAVRATILOVA IS WITHIN ONE
WIN OF EQUALLING

OPPOSITE PAGE
IN 1907 THE AUSTRALIAN
LEFT-HANDER, NORMAN
BROOKES (LATER SIR
NORMAN), BECAME THE FIRST
OVERSEAS PLAYER TO WIN
THE MEN'S SINGLES STARTING
A TREND THAT WAS TO
ACCELERATE OVER THE
YEARS

THE ELEGANT
PARISIAN-AMERICAN, BUDGE
PATTY, WHO WON THE
FRENCH AND WIMBLEDON
TITLES IN 1950

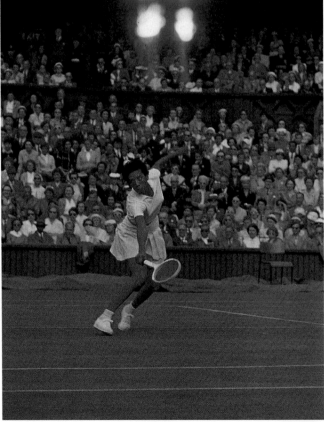

ALTHEA GIBSON, THE FIRST
BLACK CHAMPION, WON
TWICE – IN 1957 AND 1958

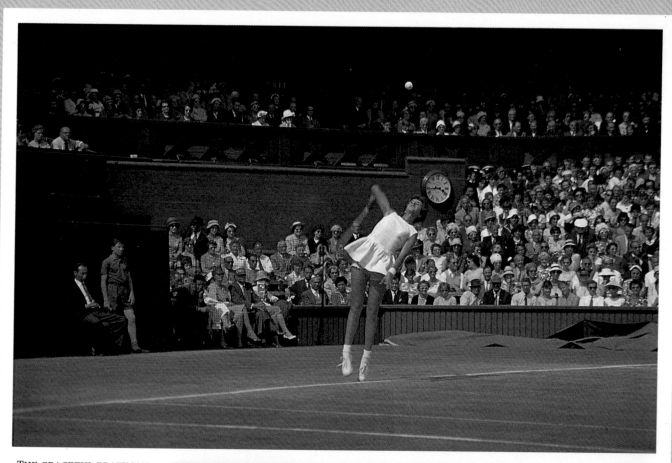

THE GRACEFUL BRAZILIAN,
MARIA BUENO, THREE TIMES A
SINGLES' WINNER

THE GREAT AUSTRALIAN
LEFT-HANDER, ROD LAVER, IS
THE ONLY PLAYER TO HAVE
WON THE GRAND SLAM TWICE,
WHICH HE DID IN 1962 AND
1969

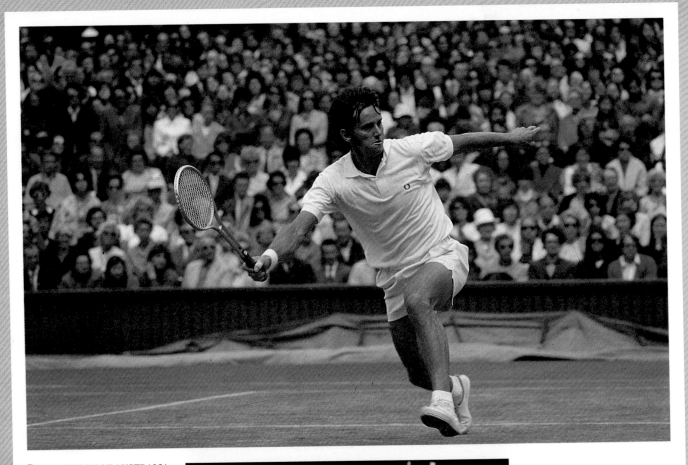

ROY EMERSON OF AUSTRALIA,
WHO WON THE SINGLES IN
1964 AND 1965, WAS ONE OF
THE FITTEST CHAMPIONS

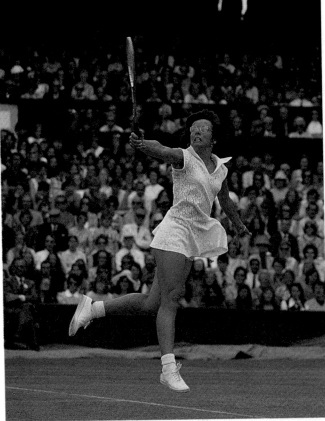

WIMBLEDON'S MOST
SUCCESSFUL PLAYER, BILLIE
JEAN KING, WON 20 TITLES
BETWEEN 1961 AND 1979

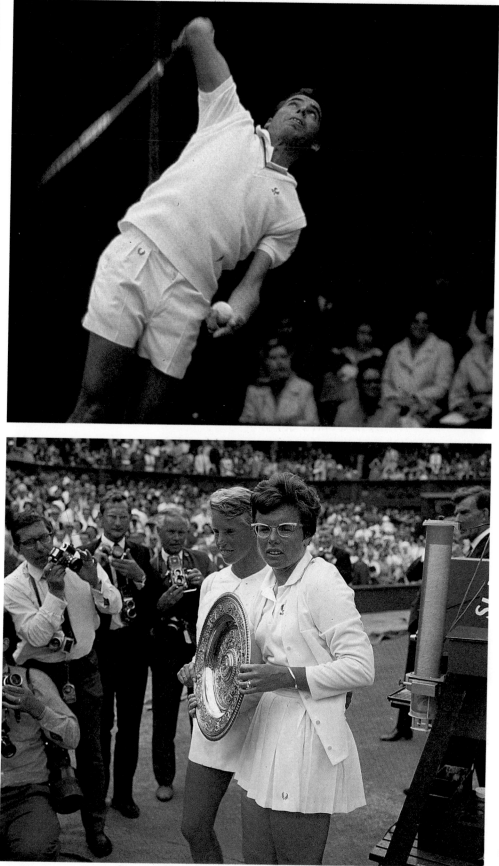

THE ARTISTIC SPANIARD, MANUEL SANTANA, WHO ONCE SAID, 'GRASS IS ONLY FOR COWS'. NEVERTHELESS, HE EVENTUALLY TRIUMPHED AT BOTH WIMBLEDON AND FOREST HILLS

THE SECOND OF BILLIE JEAN KING'S SIX SINGLES' TITLES CAME IN 1967 AGAINST BRITAIN'S ANN JONES, WHO GAINED HER REVENGE IN THE 1969 FINAL

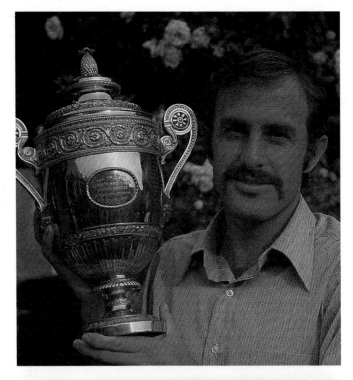

JOHN NEWCOMBE OF
AUSTRALIA, WHOSE
POWERFUL GAME WON HIM
THREE WIMBLEDONS, TWO US
AND TWO AUSTRALIAN TITLES
– ALL ON GRASS

THE GIFTED LEFT-HANDER,
TONY ROCHE, FORMED
ARGUABLY THE GREATEST
POST-WAR PARTNERSHIP
WITH JOHN NEWCOMBE. THEY
WON WIMBLEDON FIVE TIMES
TOGETHER

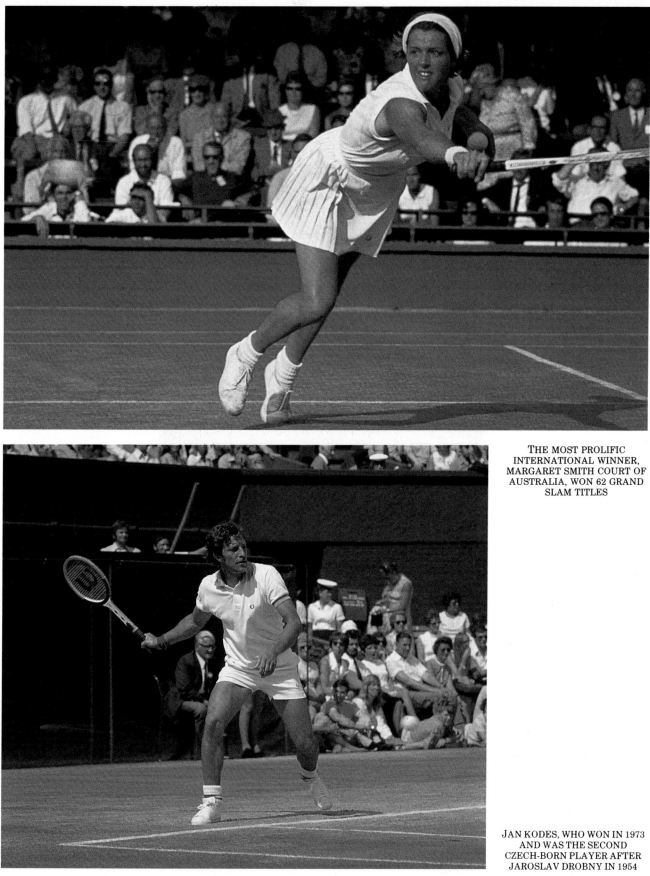

THE MOST PROLIFIC
INTERNATIONAL WINNER,
MARGARET SMITH COURT OF
AUSTRALIA, WON 62 GRAND
SLAM TITLES

JAN KODES, WHO WON IN 1973
AND WAS THE SECOND
CZECH-BORN PLAYER AFTER
JAROSLAV DROBNY IN 1954

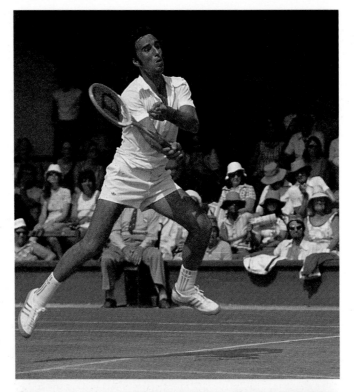

ALEX METREVELI, THE GEORGIAN WHO LOST TO JAN KODES IN 1973, IS THE ONLY MEN'S SINGLES FINALIST FROM THE SOVIET UNION

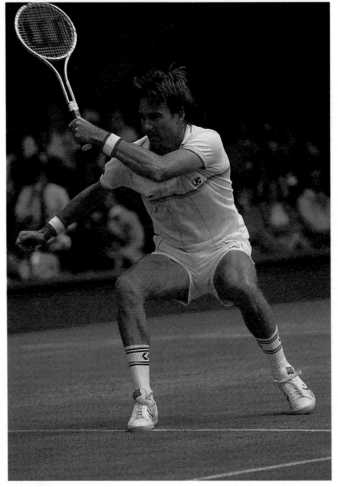

JIMMY CONNORS, THE MOST CONSISTENTLY SUCCESSFUL POST-WAR MALE PLAYER, WAS IN SIX FINALS, WON TWICE AND FAILED TO REACH THE QUARTER-FINALS ON ONLY TWO OCCASIONS IN FIFTEEN YEARS

THE CLUB'S PRESIDENT, THE DUKE OF KENT, COMMISERATES WITH KEN ROSEWALL OF AUSTRALIA WHO WAS FOUR TIMES A LOSING FINALIST BUT WAS NEVERTHELESS MADE AN HONORARY MEMBER OF THE ALL ENGLAND LAWN TENNIS CLUB

THE 1975 CHAMPION ARTHUR ASHE, THE FIRST BLACK MEN'S WINNER, SHORTLY BEFORE HIS PREMATURE RETIREMENT IN 1979 AFTER A HEART ATTACK

APPROPRIATELY, THE CENTENARY CHAMPION IN 1977 WAS BRITAIN'S VIRGINIA WADE WHO WON BEFORE THE QUEEN IN HER MAJESTY'S JUBILEE YEAR

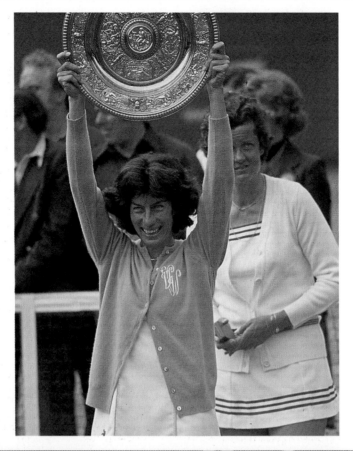

DRIVEN BY A RAGING PERFECTIONISM, JOHN McENROE, THE US LEFT-HANDER, DELIGHTED AND OFFENDED IN EQUAL MEASURE AS HE WON IN 1981, 1983 AND 1984

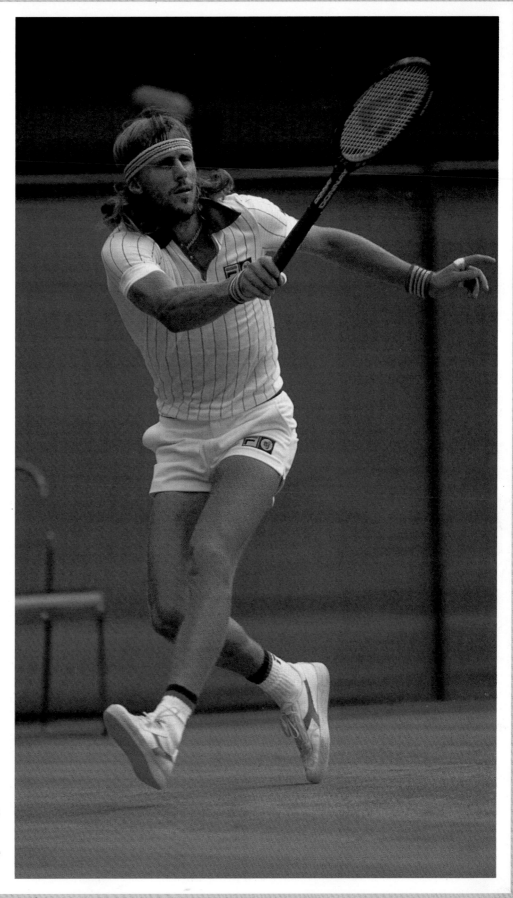

BJORN BORG – SWEDEN'S FIVE
TIMES CHAMPION AND A
MODEL SPORTSMAN, WHOSE
HEAVY TOPSPIN AND
TWO-HANDED BACKHAND SET
THE GAME IN A NEW
DIRECTION

THE 1971 CHAMPION, EVONNE
GOOLAGONG CAWLEY OF
AUSTRALIA, WON A SECOND
TITLE IN 1980 – THE SECOND
MOTHER TO DO SO SINCE MRS
LAMBERT CHAMBERS IN 1914

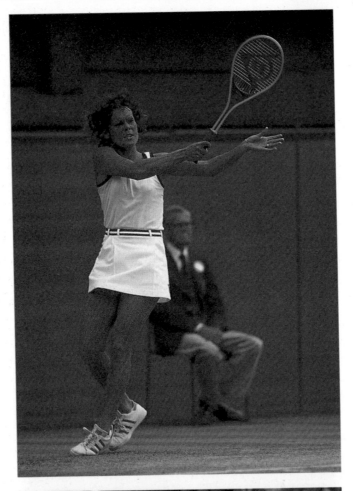

BY 1985 AMERICA'S CHRIS
EVERT LLOYD, THE MOST
CONSISTENT PLAYER OF THE
PAST DECADE, HAD BEEN IN
THE SINGLES' FINAL TEN
TIMES AND HAD WON IN 1974,
1976 AND 1981

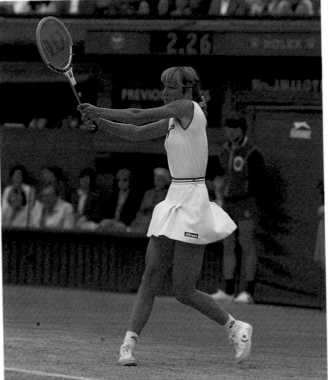

OPPOSITE PAGE
MARTINA NAVRATILOVA, THE
CZECHOSLOVAK-BORN
LEFT-HANDER WHO IS NOW A
US CITIZEN, WON HER
SEVENTH WIMBLEDON
SINGLES IN 1986 AND IS
PROBABLY THE GREATEST
ATTACKING WOMAN PLAYER
OF ALL TIME

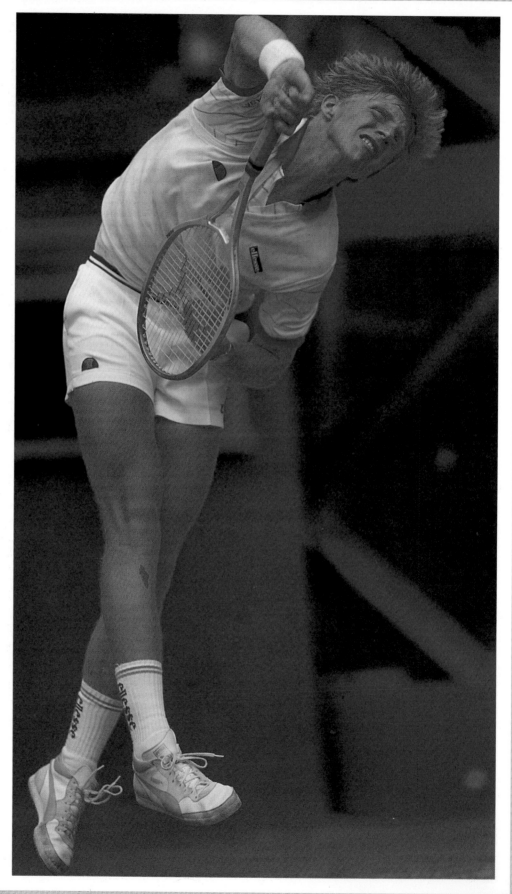

WITH THUNDEROUS SERVING
AND WHIRLWIND HITTING,
WEST GERMANY'S BORIS
BECKER, AGED 17, BECAME
WIMBLEDON'S YOUNGEST
MEN'S CHAMPION IN 1985.
WHEN HE RETAINED THE
TITLE IN 1986, HE WAS,
UNBELIEVABLY, STILL
YOUNGER THAN ANY OTHER
PREVIOUS MEN'S CHAMPION

THE GREATEST WOMEN'S DOUBLES PAIR OF MODERN TIMES, MARTINA NAVRATILOVA AND HER AMERICAN PARTNER PAM SHRIVER, WHO WON FOR THE FIFTH TIME IN SIX YEARS IN 1986

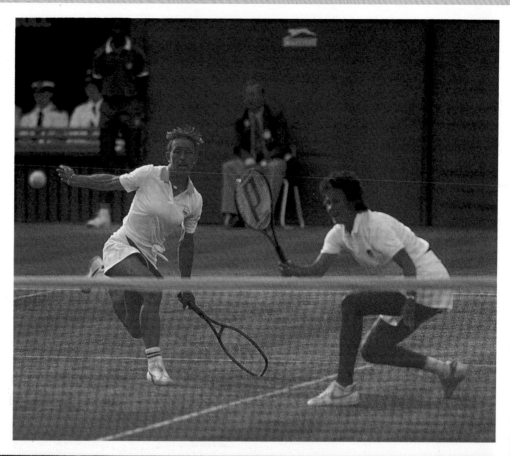

MIXED DOUBLES' WINNERS IN 1983 AND 1984, WENDY TURNBULL OF AUSTRALIA AND JOHN LLOYD, WHO IS THE FIRST BRITISH MAN TO WIN A WIMBLEDON TITLE SINCE FRED PERRY IN 1936

THE AMERICANS JOHN
McENROE AND PETER
FLEMING BECAME A GREAT
PARTNERSHIP WITH FOUR
WIMBLEDON AND SEVEN
CONSECUTIVE MASTERS'
TITLES TO THEIR CREDIT

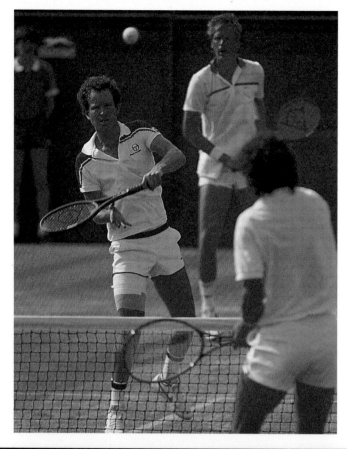

THE EXUBERANT
AUSTRALIANS PETER
McNAMARA AND PAUL
McNAMEE BROUGHT NEW JOY
TO MEN'S DOUBLES AND WON
TWICE IN 1980 AND 1982

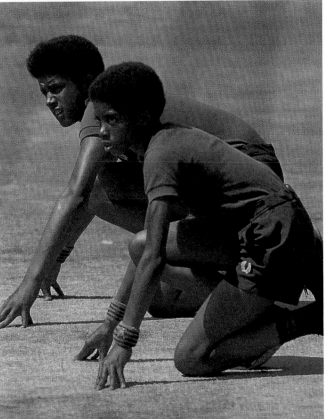

WIMBLEDON'S WELL-DRILLED BALL BOYS AND BALL GIRLS ALL COME FROM LOCAL SCHOOLS

MEMBERS OF THE BRITISH TENNIS UMPIRES' ASSOCIATION OFFICIATE AT ALL MATCHES

DURING THE EARLY ROUNDS
THE CROWDS ARE ABLE TO
HAVE A CLOSE LOOK AT THE
PLAYERS ON THE OUTSIDE
COURTS

FAR-SIGHTED PURCHASES OF
SURROUNDING LAND HAVE
PROVIDED AMPLE PARKING
SPACE, WHICH IS AUGMENTED
BY THE USE OF THE ADJACENT
GOLF AND CRICKET CLUBS

THE LONG QUEUE FOR
STANDING ROOM ON THE
CENTRE COURT OFTEN
STRETCHES DOWN THE MAIN
CONCOURSE

OPPOSITE PAGE, TOP
BANDS FROM THE SERVICES
ENTERTAIN THE CENTRE
COURT CROWDS ON THE LAST
TWO DAYS, BUT BACK IN 1906 A
VIENNESE ORCHESTRA
PLAYED AT WORPLE ROAD

BOTTOM
EVER-HOPEFUL FANS WAIT IN
THEIR SEATS FOR THE RAIN TO
STOP

THE DUKE AND DUCHESS OF KENT ENTERTAINED 17 OF THE SURVIVING LADY CHAMPIONS TO LUNCH AT THE CENTENARY CELEBRATIONS IN 1984. FRONT ROW (*FROM LEFT TO RIGHT*): ALTHEA GIBSON, DORIS HART, MARGARET OSBORNE DU PONT, ALICE MARBLE, DUCHESS OF KENT, DUKE OF KENT, KITTY GODFREE, PAULINE BETZ, LOUISE BROUGH, SHIRLEY FRY. BACK ROW: VIRGINIA WADE, EVONNE CAWLEY, ANGELA MORTIMER, MARIA BUENO, MARGARET COURT, ANN JONES, CHRIS EVERT LLOYD, MARTINA NAVRATILOVA. BILLIE JEAN KING IS MISSING FROM THE PHOTOGRAPH AND HELEN WILLS MOODY, KAREN HANTZE AND HELEN JACOBS WERE UNABLE TO ATTEND.

THE ARMED SERVICES HAVE PROVIDED STEWARDS EVER SINCE THE SECOND WORLD WAR AND THE METROPOLITAN POLICE ARE ALWAYS ON DUTY AROUND THE GROUND

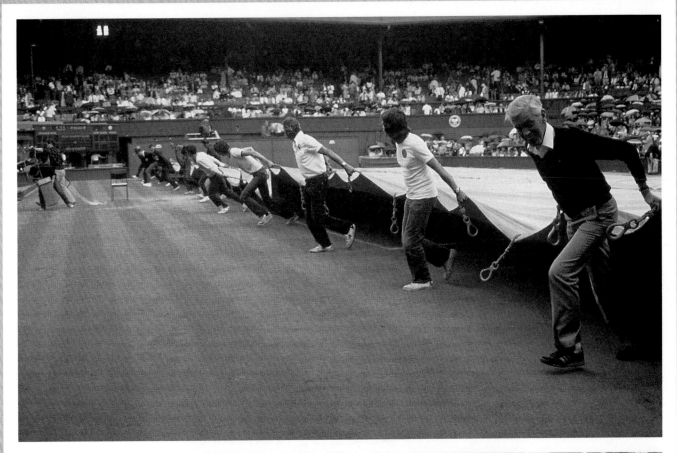

THE CENTRE COURT PARTY IN
A DEPRESSINGLY REGULAR
ROLE

PLAY CONTINUES, DESPITE
THE DRIZZLE

SINCE ITS BEGINNINGS,
WIMBLEDON HAS BEEN
FAMOUS FOR ITS
STRAWBERRIES AND CREAM
AND NOW THE PIMMS AND
CHAMPAGNE BAR AND OTHER
REFRESHMENT AREAS RETAIN
THE GARDEN PARTY
ATMOSPHERE

THE DUCHESS OF KENT, ONE
OF WIMBLEDON'S KEENEST
AND BEST-LOVED FANS

THE LADIES' DRESSING ROOM ON FINALS DAY WHERE BOUQUETS AWAIT THE ARRIVAL OF THE TWO FINALISTS

IN 1984, 50 YEARS AFTER THE FIRST OF HIS THREE SINGLES' WINS, FRED PERRY (*LEFT*) WATCHES THE DUKE OF KENT NAMING THE NEW PERRY GATES AT THE OTHER SIDE OF THE CLUB FROM THE PERRY STATUE, WHICH WAS UNVEILED THE SAME DAY

TOP LEFT
THE MEN'S SINGLES TROPHY, A SILVER GILT ONE, WAS PURCHASED BY THE CLUB IN 1887 AND IS PRESENTED ANNUALLY TO THE CHAMPION

TOP RIGHT
IN 1907 THE PRINCE OF WALES, WHO HAD BECOME PRESIDENT OF THE CLUB, PRESENTED THE PRESIDENT'S CUP FOR THE WINNER OF THE ALL-COMERS' SINGLES. SINCE THE ABOLITION OF THE CHALLENGE ROUND IN 1922, THE SINGLES' WINNER RECEIVES BOTH THE PRESIDENT'S CUP AND CHAMPION'S CUP

ABOVE LEFT
THE MEN'S SINGLES WINNER ALSO NOW RECEIVES AND KEEPS THE RENSHAW CUP, WHICH IS A TROPHY PRESENTED EACH YEAR BY THE RENSHAW FAMILY

ABOVE RIGHT
THE ORIGINAL CUP, WORTH £25 AND PRESENTED BY *THE FIELD* IN 1877, WAS WON OUTRIGHT BY WILLIAM RENSHAW IN 1883 ON HIS THIRD CONSECUTIVE WIN. THE SECOND ALL ENGLAND CLUB TROPHY WAS ALSO WON OUTRIGHT BY WILLIAM RENSHAW FOR THREE MORE WINS BUT HAS BEEN LOST

TOP LEFT
THE OXFORD UNIVERSITY DOUBLES' CUP (*LEFT*) WAS PRESENTED TO THE ALL ENGLAND CLUB WHEN THEIR DOUBLES' EVENT ENDED IN 1883. FROM 1884 TO 1937 THERE WAS ONLY ONE TROPHY UNTIL, THAT YEAR, SIR HERBERT WILBERFORCE DONATED FOR COMPETITION

A COMPANION CUP (*RIGHT*) THAT THE CLUB MEMBERS HAD PRESENTED TO HIM ON HIS RETIREMENT FROM THE CHAIRMANSHIP

TOP RIGHT
THE LADY CHAMPIONS' SILVER PARCEL GILT SALVER HAD BEEN MADE IN 1864 BUT WAS NOT PRESENTED TO THE CLUB UNTIL 1886 FROM WHICH TIME IT HAS BEEN HELD BY THE CHAMPION FOR A YEAR. SHE ALSO RECEIVES A SMALL REPLICA TO KEEP

ABOVE LEFT
THE LADIES' DOUBLES CUP WAS PRESENTED TO THE CLUB BY PRINCESS MARINA IN 1949

ABOVE RIGHT
THE MIXED DOUBLES' CUP WAS PRESENTED TO THE CLUB BY THE FAMILY OF S. H. SMITH IN 1949

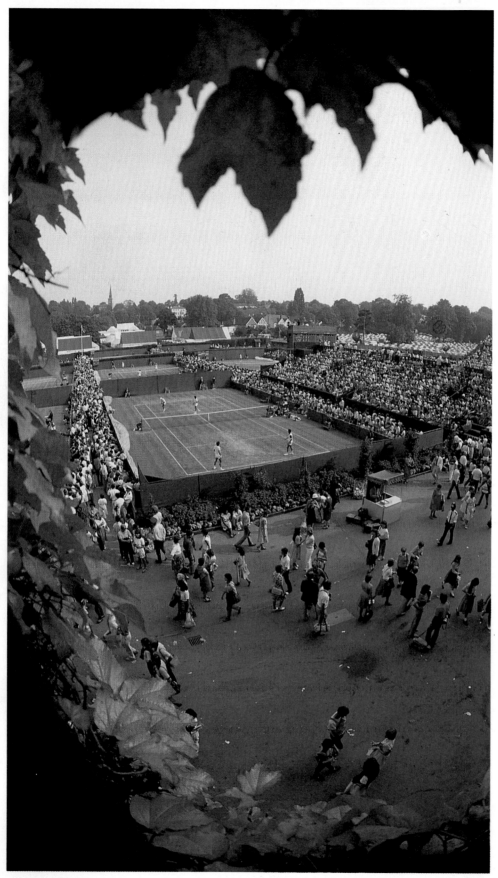

WITH SO MUCH GOOD TENNIS
TO WATCH ON THE OUTSIDE
COURTS, THE ATTRACTION OF
WIMBLEDON HAS GROWN
STEADILY OVER THE YEARS SO
THAT, FOR THE FIRST TIME,
MORE THAN 400,000
SPECTATORS ATTENDED THE
HUNDREDTH MEETING IN 1986

CHAMPIONSHIP RESULTS

CHAMPIONSHIP ROLLS

GENTLEMEN'S SINGLES

1877	Spencer W. Gore	1931	S. B. Wood
1878	P. F. Hadow	1932	H. E. Vines
1879	Revd J. T. Hartley	1933	J. H. Crawford
1880	Revd J. T. Hartley	1934	F. J. Perry
1881	W. Renshaw	1935	F. J. Perry
1882	W. Renshaw	1936	F. J. Perry
1883	W. Renshaw	1937	J. D. Budge
1884	W. Renshaw	1938	J. D. Budge
1885	W. Renshaw	1939	R. L. Riggs
1886	W. Renshaw	1940-5	not held
1887	H. F. Lawford	1946	Y. Petra
1888	E. Renshaw	1947	J. A. Kramer
1889	W. Renshaw	1948	R. Falkenburg
1890	W. J. Hamilton	1949	F. R. Schroeder
1891	W. Baddeley	1950	J. E. Patty
1892	W. Baddeley	1951	R. Savitt
1893	J. Pim	1952	F. A. Sedgman
1894	J. Pim	1953	E. V. Seixas
1895	W. Baddeley	1954	J. Drobny
1896	H. S. Mahony	1955	M. A. Trabert
1897	R. F. Doherty	1956	L. A. Hoad
1898	R. F. Doherty	1957	L. A. Hoad
1899	R. F. Doherty	1958	A. J. Cooper
1900	R. F. Doherty	1959	A. Olmedo
1901	A. W. Gore	1960	N. A. Fraser
1902	H. L. Doherty	1961	R. G. Laver
1903	H. L. Doherty	1962	R. G. Laver
1904	H. L. Doherty	1963	C. R. McKinley
1905	H. L. Doherty	1964	R. S. Emerson
1906	H. L. Doherty	1965	R. S. Emerson
1907	N. E. Brookes	1966	M. Santana
1908	A. W. Gore	1967	J. D. Newcombe
1909	A. W. Gore	1968	R. G. Laver
1910	A. F. Wilding	1969	R. G. Laver
1911	A. F. Wilding	1970	J. D. Newcombe
1912	A. F. Wilding	1971	J. D. Newcombe
1913	A. F. Wilding	1972	S. R. Smith
1914	N. E. Brookes	1973	J. Kodes
1915-18	not held	1974	J. S. Connors
1919	G. L. Patterson	1975	A. R. Ashe
1920	W. T. Tilden	1976	B. Borg
1921	W. T. Tilden	1977	B. Borg
1922	G. L. Patterson	1978	B. Borg
1923	W. M. Johnston	1979	B. Borg
1924	J. Borotra	1980	B. Borg
1925	J. R. Lacoste	1981	J. P. McEnroe
1926	J. Borotra	1982	J. S. Connors
1927	H. J. Cochet	1983	J. P. McEnroe
1928	J. R. Lacoste	1984	J. P. McEnroe
1929	H. J. Cochet	1985	B. Becker
1930	W. T. Tilden	1986	B. Becker

LADIES' SINGLES

1884	Miss M. E. E. Watson	1938	Mrs H. N. Wills/Moody
1885	Miss M. E. E. Watson	1939	Miss A. Marble
1886	Miss B. Bingley	1940-5	not held
1887	Miss C. Dod	1946	Miss P. M. Betz
1888	Miss C. Dod	1947	Miss M. E. Osborne
1889	Mrs G. W. Hillyard	1948	Miss A. L. Brough
1890	Miss H. B. G. Rice	1949	Miss A. L. Brough
1891	Miss C. Dod	1950	Miss A. L. Brough
1892	Miss C. Dod	1951	Miss D. J. Hart
1893	Miss C. Dod	1952	Miss M. C. Connolly
1894	Mrs G. W. Hillyard	1953	Miss M. C. Connolly
1895	Miss C. Cooper	1954	Miss M. C. Connolly
1896	Miss C. Cooper	1955	Miss A. L. Brough
1897	Mrs G. W. Hillyard	1956	Miss S. J. Fry
1898	Miss C. Cooper	1957	Miss A. Gibson
1899	Mrs G. W. Hillyard	1958	Miss A. Gibson
1900	Mrs G. W. Hillyard	1959	Miss M. E. Bueno
1901	Mrs A. Sterry	1960	Miss M. E. Bueno
1902	Miss M. E. Robb	1961	Miss A. Mortimer
1903	Miss D. K. Douglass	1962	Mrs J. R. Susman
1904	Miss D. K. Douglass	1963	Miss M. Smith
1905	Miss M. G. Sutton	1964	Miss M. E. Bueno
1906	Miss D. K. Douglass	1965	Miss M. Smith
1907	Miss M. G. Sutton	1966	Mrs L. W. King
1908	Mrs A. Sterry	1967	Mrs L. W. King
1909	Miss D. P. Boothby	1968	Mrs L. W. King
1910	Mrs R. Lambert Chambers	1969	Mrs P. F. Jones
1911	Mrs R. Lambert Chambers	1970	Mrs B. M. Court
1912	Mrs D. R. Larcombe	1971	Miss E. F. Goolagong
1913	Mrs R. Lambert Chambers	1972	Mrs L. W. King
1914	Mrs R. Lambert Chambers	1973	Mrs L. W. King
1915-18	not held	1974	Miss C. M. Evert
1919	Mlle S. Lenglen	1975	Mrs L. W. King
1920	Mlle S. Lenglen	1976	Miss C. M. Evert
1921	Mlle S. Lenglen	1977	Miss S. V. Wade
1922	Mlle S. Lenglen	1978	Miss M. Navratilova
1923	Mlle S. Lenglen	1979	Miss M. Navratilova
1924	Miss K. McKane	1980	Mrs R. A. Cawley
1925	Mlle S. Lenglen	1981	Mrs J. M. Lloyd
1926	Mrs L. A. Godfree	1982	Miss M. Navratilova
1927	Miss H. N. Wills	1983	Miss M. Navratilova
1928	Miss H. N. Wills	1984	Miss M. Navratilova
1929	Miss H. N. Wills	1985	Miss M. Navratilova
1930	Mrs H. N. Wills/Moody	1986	Miss M. Navratilova
1931	Frl C. Aussem		
1932	Mrs H. N. Wills/Moody		
1933	Mrs H. N. Wills/Moody		
1934	Miss D. E. Round		
1935	Mrs H. N. Wills/Moody		
1936	Miss H. H. Jacobs		
1937	Miss D. E. Round		

GENTLEMEN'S DOUBLES

1884	E. Renshaw and W. Renshaw	1915–18	not held	1955	R. N. Hartwig and L. A. Hoad
1885	E. Renshaw and W. Renshaw	1919	P. O'Hara-Wood and R. V. Thomas	1956	L. A. Hoad and K. R. Rosewall
1886	E. Renshaw and W. Renshaw	1920	C. S. Garland and R. N. Williams	1957	G. Mulloy and J. E. Patty
1887	P. Bowes-Lyon and H. W. W. Wilberforce	1921	R. Lycett and M. Woosnam	1958	S. Davidson and U. Schmidt
1888	E. Renshaw and W. Renshaw	1922	R. Lycett and J. O. Anderson	1959	R. S. Emerson and N. A. Fraser
1889	E. Renshaw and W. Renshaw	1923	R. Lycett and L. A. Godfree	1960	R. H. Osuna and R. D. Ralston
1890	J. Pim and F. O. Stoker	1924	F. T. Hunter and V. Richards	1961	R. S. Emerson and N. A. Fraser
1891	H. Baddeley and W. Baddeley	1925	J. Borotra and J. R. Lacoste	1962	R. A. J. Hewitt and F. S. Stolle
1892	H. S. Barlow and E. W. Lewis	1926	J. Brugnon and H. J. Cochet	1963	R. H. Osuna and A. Palafox
1893	J. Pim and F. O. Stoker	1927	F. T. Hunter and W. T. Tilden	1964	R. A. J. Hewitt and F. S. Stolle
1894	H. Baddeley and W. Baddeley	1928	J. Brugnon and H. J. Cochet	1965	J. D. Newcombe and A. D. Roche
1895	H. Baddeley and W. Baddeley	1929	W. L. Allison and J. Van Ryn	1966	K. N. Fletcher and J. D. Newcombe
1896	H. Baddeley and W. Baddeley	1930	W. L. Allison and J. Van Ryn	1967	R. A. J. Hewitt and F. D. McMillan
1897	H. L. Doherty and R. F. Doherty	1931	G. M. Lott and J. Van Ryn	1968	J. D. Newcombe and A. D. Roche
1898	H. L. Doherty and R. F. Doherty	1932	J. Borotra and J. Brugnon	1969	J. D. Newcombe and A. D. Roche
1899	H. L. Doherty and R. F. Doherty	1933	J. Borotra and J. Brugnon	1970	J. D. Newcombe and A. D. Roche
1900	H. L. Doherty and R. F. Doherty	1934	G. M. Lott and L. R. Stoefen	1971	R. S. Emerson and R. G. Laver
1901	H. L. Doherty and R. F. Doherty	1935	J. H. Crawford and A. K. Quist	1972	R. A. J. Hewitt and F. D. McMillan
1902	F. L. Riseley and S. H. Smith	1936	G. P. Hughes and C. R. D. Tuckey	1973	J. S. Connors and I. Nastase
1903	H. L. Doherty and R. F. Doherty	1937	J. D. Budge and C. G. Mako	1974	J. D. Newcombe and A. D. Roche
1904	H. L. Doherty and R. F. Doherty	1938	J. D. Budge and C. G. Mako	1975	V. Gerulaitis and A. Mayer
1905	H. L. Doherty and R. F. Doherty	1939	E. T. Cooke and R. L. Riggs	1976	B. E. Gottfried and R. Ramirez
1906	F. L. Riseley and S. H. Smith	1940–5	not held	1977	R. L. Case and G. Masters
1907	N. E. Brookes and A. F. Wilding	1946	T. P. Brown and J. A. Kramer	1978	R. A. J. Hewitt and F. D. McMillan
1908	M. J. G. Ritchie and A. F. Wilding	1947	R. Falkenburg and J. A. Kramer	1979	P. Fleming and J. P. McEnroe
1909	H. Roper Barrett and A. W. Gore	1948	J. E. Bromwich and F. A. Sedgman	1980	P. McNamara and P. McNamee
1910	M. J. G. Ritchie and A. F. Wilding	1949	R. A. Gonzales and F. A. Parker	1981	P. Fleming and J. P. McEnroe
1911	M. Decugis and A. H. Gobert	1950	J. E. Bromwich and A. K. Quist	1982	P. McNamara and P. McNamee
1912	H. Roper Barrett and C. P. Dixon	1951	K. McGregor and F. A. Sedgman	1983	P. Fleming and J. P. McEnroe
1913	H. Roper Barrett and C. P. Dixon	1952	K. McGregor and F. A. Sedgman	1984	P. Fleming and J. P. McEnroe
1914	N. E. Brookes and A. F. Wilding	1953	L. A. Hoad and K. R. Rosewall	1985	H. P. Gunthardt and B. Taroczy
		1954	R. N. Hartwig and M. G. Rose	1986	J. Nystrom and M. Wilander

LADIES' DOUBLES

Non-Championship Event

1899	Mrs G. W. Hillyard and Miss B. Steedman	1931	Mrs D. C. Shepherd Barron and Miss P. E. Mudford
1900	Mrs W. H. Pickering and Miss M. E. Robb	1932	Mlle D. Metaxa and Mlle J. Sigart
1901	Mrs G. W. Hillyard and Mrs A. Sterry	1933	Mme R. Mathieu and Miss E. Ryan
1902	Miss A. M. Morton and Mrs A. Sterry	1934	Mme R. Mathieu and Miss E. Ryan
1903	Miss D. K. Douglass and Mrs W. H. Pickering	1935	Miss F. James and Miss K. E. Stammers
1904	Miss W. A. Longhurst and Miss E. W. Thomson	1936	Miss F. James and Miss K. E. Stammers
1905	Miss W. A. Longhurst and Miss E. W. Thomson	1937	Mme R. Mathieu and Miss A. M. Yorke
1906	Mrs G. W. Hillyard and Miss M. G. Sutton	1938	Mrs S. P. Fabyan and Miss A. Marble
1907	Mrs R. Lambert Chambers and Miss C. M. Wilson	1939	Mrs S. P. Fabyan and Miss A. Marble
1908–12	not held	1940–5	not held
		1946	Miss A. L. Brough and Miss M. E. Osborne
		1947	Miss D. J. Hart and Mrs P. C. Todd

Full Championship Event

1913	Miss D. P. Boothby and Mrs R. J. McNair	1948	Miss A. L. Brough and Mrs W. D. du Pont
1914	Miss A. M. Morton and Miss E. Ryan	1949	Miss A. L. Brough and Mrs W. D. du Pont
1915–18	not held	1950	Miss A. L. Brough and Mrs W. D. du Pont
1919	Mlle S. Lenglen and Miss E. Ryan	1951	Miss S. J. Fry and Miss D. J. Hart
1920	Mlle S. Lenglen and Miss E. Ryan	1952	Miss S. J. Fry and Miss D. J. Hart
1921	Mlle S. Lenglen and Miss E. Ryan	1953	Miss S. J. Fry and Miss D. J. Hart
1922	Mlle S. Lenglen and Miss E. Ryan	1954	Miss A. L. Brough and Mrs W. D. du Pont
1923	Mlle S. Lenglen and Miss E. Ryan	1955	Miss A. Mortimer and Miss J. A. Shilcock
1924	Mrs G. Wightman and Miss H. N. Wills	1956	Miss A. Buxton and Miss A. Gibson
1925	Mlle S. Lenglen and Miss E. Ryan	1957	Miss A. Gibson and Miss D. R. Hard
1926	Miss M. K. Browne and Miss E. Ryan	1958	Miss M. E. Bueno and Miss A. Gibson
1927	Miss E. Ryan and Miss H. N. Wills	1959	Miss J. Arth and Miss D. R. Hard
1928	Mrs P. H. Watson and Miss P. Saunders	1960	Miss M. E. Bueno and Miss D. R. Hard
1929	Mrs P. H. Watson and Mrs L. R. C. Michel	1961	Miss K. Hantze and Miss B. J. Moffitt
1930	Mrs H. N. Wills/Moody and Miss E. Ryan	1962	Miss B. J. Moffit and Mrs J. R. Susman
		1963	Miss M. E. Bueno and Miss D. R. Hard

LADIES' DOUBLES—*continued*

1964	Miss M. Smith and Miss L. R. Turner		1976	Miss C. M. Evert and Miss M. Navratilova
1965	Miss M. E. Bueno and Miss B. J. Moffit		1977	Miss H. F. Gourlay Cawley and Miss J. C. Russell
1966	Miss M. E. Bueno and Miss N. Richey		1978	Mrs G. E. Reid and Miss W. M. Turnbull
1967	Miss R. Casals and Mrs L. W. King		1979	Mrs L. W. King and Miss M. Navratilova
1968	Miss R. Casals and Mrs L. W. King		1980	Miss K. Jordan and Miss A. E. Smith
1969	Mrs B. M. Court and Miss J. A. M. Tegart		1981	Miss M. Navratilova and Miss P. H. Shriver
1970	Miss R. Casals and Mrs L. W. King		1982	Miss M. Navratilova and Miss P. H. Shriver
1971	Miss R. Casals and Mrs L. W. King		1983	Miss M. Navratilova and Miss P. H. Shriver
1972	Mrs L. W. King and Miss B. F. Stove		1984	Miss M. Navratilova and Miss P. H. Shriver
1973	Miss R. Casals and Mrs L. W. King		1985	Miss K. Jordan and Mrs E. Smylie
1974	Miss E. F. Goolagong and Miss M. Michel		1986	Miss M. Navratilova and Miss P. H. Shriver
1975	Miss A. K. Kiyomura and Miss K. Sawamatsu			

MIXED DOUBLES

Non-Championship Event

1900	H. A. Nisbet and Mrs W. H. Pickering		1946	T. P. Brown and Miss A. L. Brough
1901	H. L. Doherty and Mrs A. Sterry		1947	J. E. Bromwich and Miss A. L. Brough
1902	H. L. Doherty and Mrs A. Sterry		1948	J. E. Bromwich and Miss A. L. Brough
1903	S. H. Smith and Miss E. W. Thomson		1949	E. W. Sturgess and Mrs S. P. Summers
1904	S. H. Smith and Miss E. W. Thomson		1950	E. W. Sturgess and Miss A. L. Brough
1905	A. W. Gore and Miss C. M. Wilson		1951	F. A. Sedgman and Miss D. J. Hart
1906	A. F. Wilding and Miss D. K. Douglass		1952	F. A. Sedgman and Miss D. J. Hart
1907	B. C. Wright and Miss M. G. Sutton		1953	E. V. Seixas and Miss D. J. Hart
1908	A. F. Wilding and Mrs R. Lambert Chambers		1954	E. V. Seixas and Miss D. J. Hart
1909	H. Roper Barrett and Miss A. M. Morton		1955	E. V. Seixas and Miss D. J. Hart
1910	S. N. Doust and Mrs R. Lambert Chambers		1956	E. V. Seixas and Miss S. J. Fry
1911	T. M. Mavrogordato and Mrs E. G. Parton		1957	M. G. Rose and Miss D. R. Hard
1912	J. C. Parke and Mrs D. R. Larcombe		1958	R. N. Howe and Miss L. Coghlan
			1959	R. G. Laver and Miss D. R. Hard
			1960	R. G. Laver and Miss D. R. Hard

Full Championship Event

1913	H. Crisp and Mrs C. O. Tuckey		1961	F. S. Stolle and Miss L. R. Turner
1914	J. C. Parke and Mrs D. R. Larcombe		1962	N. A. Fraser and Mrs W. D. du Pont
1915–18	not held		1963	K. N. Fletcher and Miss M. Smith
1919	R. Lycett and Miss E. Ryan		1964	F. S. Stolle and Miss L. R. Turner
1920	G. L. Patterson and Mlle S. Lenglen		1965	K. N. Fletcher and Miss M. Smith
1921	R. Lycett and Miss E. Ryan		1966	K. N. Fletcher and Miss M. Smith
1922	P. O'Hara-Wood and Mlle S. Lenglen		1967	O. K. Davidson and Mrs L. W. King
1923	R. Lycett and Miss E. Ryan		1968	K. N. Fletcher and Mrs B. M. Court
1924	J. B. Gilbert and Miss K. McKane		1969	F. S. Stolle and Mrs P. F. Jones
1925	J. Borotra and Mlle S. Lenglen		1970	I. Nastase and Miss R. Casals
1926	L. A. Godfree and Mrs L. A. Godfree		1971	O. K. Davidson and Mrs L. W. King
1927	F. T. Hunter and Miss E. Ryan		1972	I. Nastase and Miss R. Casals
1928	P. D. B. Spence and Miss E. Ryan		1973	O. K. Davidson and Mrs L. W. King
1929	F. T. Hunter and Miss H. N. Wills		1974	O. K. Davidson and Mrs L. W. King
1930	J. H. Crawford and Miss E. Ryan		1975	M. C. Riessen and Mrs B. M. Court
1931	G. M. Lott and Mrs L. A. Harper		1976	A. D. Roche and Miss F. Durr
1932	E. Maier and Miss E. Ryan		1977	R. A. J. Hewitt and Miss G. R. Stevens
1933	G. von Cramm and Frl H. Krahwinkel		1978	F. D. McMillan and Miss B. Stove
1934	R. Miki and Miss D. E. Round		1979	R. A. J. Hewitt and Miss G. R. Stevens
1935	F. J. Perry and Miss D. E. Round		1980	J. R. Austin and Miss T. Austin
1936	F. J. Perry and Miss D. E. Round		1981	F. D. McMillan and Miss B. Stove
1937	J. D. Budge and Miss A. Marble		1982	K. Curren and Miss A. E. Smith
1938	J. D. Budge and Miss A. Marble		1983	J. M. Lloyd and Miss W. M. Turnbull
1939	R. L. Riggs and Miss A. Marble		1984	J. M. Lloyd and Miss W. M. Turnbull
1940–5	not held		1985	P. McNamee and Miss M. Navratilova
			1986	K. Flach and Miss K. Jordan

MAIDEN NAMES OF PROMINENT MARRIED LADY COMPETITORS

Mrs D. C. Aucamp
Mrs C. M. Balastrat
Mrs I. A. R. F. Bentzer
Mme M. Billout
Mrs E. W. A. Bostock
Mrs N. W. Bolton
Mrs W. W. Bowrey
Mrs C. Brasher
Mrs T. S. Bundy
Mrs R. Cawley
Mrs R. L. Cawley
Mrs J. D. Chaloner
Mrs R. Lambert Chambers
Mrs J. B. Chanfreau
Mrs B. M. Court
Mrs B. C. Covell
Mrs P. W. Curtis
Mrs D. E. Dalton
Mrs P. Darmon
Mrs G. Davidson
Mrs P. C. Dent
Mrs G. R. Dingwall
Mrs P. M. Doerner
Mrs E. C. Drysdale
Mrs J. du Plooy
Mrs W. du Pont
Mrs K. Ebbinghaus
Mrs M. Evans
Mrs M. Fabyan
Mrs H. G. Fales
Mrs R. N. Faulkener
Mrs J. Fleitz
Mrs I. M. Fordyce
Mrs P. F. Glover
Mrs A. C. Green
Mrs L. A. Godfree
Mrs C. E. Graebner
Mrs G. Greville
Mrs T. E. Guerrant
Mrs K. S. Gunter
Mrs C. Harrison
Mrs D. M. Hayashi
Mrs P. Haygarth
Mrs E. L. Heine Miller
Mrs G. W. Hillyard
Mrs L. A. Hoad
Mrs P. D. Howard
Mrs G. T. Janes
Mrs A. M. Jarrett
Mrs P. Jauch
Mrs P. F. Jones
Mrs N. Kalogeropoulos
Mrs L. W. King
Mrs M. R. King
Mrs D. P. Knode
Mrs I. Kuhn
Mrs G. Lamplough
Mrs D. R. Larcombe
Mrs J. L. Leisk
Mrs R. D. Little

Miss C. Hanks
Miss D. L. Fromholtz
Miss I. A. R. F. Lofdahl
Mlle M. Broquedis
Miss J. Nicholl
Miss N. Wynne
Miss L. R. Turner
Miss S. J. Bloomer
Miss M. G. Sutton
Miss E. F. Goolagong
Miss H. F. Gourlay
Miss J. N. Connor
Miss D. K. Douglass
Miss G. V. Sheriff
Miss M. Smith
Miss P. L. Howkins
Miss M. A. Eisel
Miss J. A. M. Tegart
Miss R. Reyes
Miss B. Schofield
Miss B. A. Stuart
Miss A. M. Tobin
Miss C. G. Sieler
Miss J. R. Forbes
Miss A. M. van Zyl
Miss M. E. Osborne
Miss K. Burgemeister
Miss A. M. Tobin
Miss S. Palfrey
Miss D. Floyd
Miss P. McClenaughan
Miss B. Baker
Miss P. S. A. Hogan
Miss N. Lyle
Miss D. P. Boothby
Miss K. McKane
Miss C. A. Caldwell
Miss L. Austin
Miss N. Schallau
Miss N. Richey
(Mrs) B. E. Hilton
Miss A. Kiyomura
Miss R. Schuurman
Miss E. L. Heine
Miss B. Bingley
Miss J. Staley
Mlle D. Metaxa
Miss C. C. Truman
Miss D. A. Jevans
Miss P. Delhees
Miss A. S. Haydon
Miss C. A. Prosen
Miss B. J. Moffitt
Miss P. E. Mudford
Miss D. Head
Miss I. Riedel
Miss G. Eastlake Smith
Miss E. W. Thomson
Miss H. Aitchison
Miss D. E. Round

Mrs J. M. Lloyd
Mrs T. Louie-Harper
Mrs J. J. Lovera
Mrs J. F. Luard
Mrs R. Lycett
Mrs G. McDade
Frau H. Masthoff
Mrs M. Menzies
Mme J. de Meulemeester
Mrs L. R. C. Michel
Mrs A. R. Mills
Mrs H. A. Mochizuki
Mrs F. S. Moody
Mrs J. L. Moore
Mrs A. J. Mottram
Mrs V. Nelson-Dunbar
Mme H. Nicolopoulo
Mrs J. J. O'Neill
Mrs L. Orth
Mrs J. G. Paish
Mrs S. Parkhomenko
Mrs E. G. Parton
Mrs E. Peled
Mrs M. H. Pete
Mrs M. Pinterova
Mrs B. Pratt
Mrs Q. C. Pretorius
Mrs L. E. G. Price
Mrs M. Proctor
Mrs G. E. Reid
Mrs J. Rinkel-Quertier
Mrs J. D. G. Robinson
Mrs P. H. Rodriguez
Mrs W. R. Roth
Mrs A. A. Segal
Mrs V. Segal
Mrs L. A. Shaefer
Mrs R. Shaw
Mrs O. C. Shepherd Barron
Mrs L. Short
Mrs K. Skronska-Bohm
Mrs P. D. Smylie
Mrs B. Sparre-Viragh
Frau S. Sperling
Mrs A. Sterry
Mrs A. D. Stocks
Mrs V. Sukova
Mrs J. R. Susman
Mrs R. Taylor
Mrs B. Teacher
Mrs E. Vessies-Appel
Mrs J. Volovkova
Mrs T. Walhof
Mrs J. H. Wheeler
Mrs F. Whittingstall
Mrs G. M. Williams
Mrs K. Wooldridge
Mrs F. I. Wright
Mrs C. E. Zeeman

Miss C. M. Evert
Miss M. Louie
Miss G. V. Sherriff
Miss C. M. Wilson
Miss J. Austin
Miss A. J. McMillan
Frl H. Niessen
Miss K. E. Stammers
Mlle J. Sigart
Miss P. Saunders
Miss J. Rook
Miss T. B. Watanabe
Miss H. N. Wills
Miss F. M. E. Toyne
Miss J. Gannon
Miss V. Nelson
Mlle H. Contoslavlos
Miss J. Lehane
Miss H. Schildknecht
Miss W. S. Gilchrist
Miss S. Cherneva
Miss M. B. Squire
Miss P. Piesachov
Miss S. A. Walsh
Miss M. Neumannova
Miss B. Rosenquest
Miss P. M. Walkden
Miss S. Reynolds
Miss L. M. Gordon
Miss K. Melville
Miss J. Quertier
Miss L. Cochlan
Miss M. Boulle
Miss R. Tomanova
Miss H. Nicholls
Miss V. Gonzalez
Miss K. G. Jones
Miss K. K. Kemmer
Miss D. C. Shepherd
Miss L. A. Spain
Miss K. Skronska
Miss E. M. Sayers
Miss B. Sparre
Frl H. Krahwinkel
Miss C. Cooper
Miss M. McKane
Miss V. Puzejova
Miss K. Hantze
Miss F. V. M. MacLennan
Miss K. A. May
Miss E. Appel
Miss J. Horcickova
Miss T. Groenman
Miss M. Arnold
Miss E. Bennett
Miss J. C. Barclay
Miss W. M. Shaw
Miss J. S. Newberry
Miss C. E. Sheriff

THE ALL ENGLAND LAWN TENNIS & CROQUET CLUB

Patrons

1910–35 HM King George V
1936   HM King Edward VIII
1937–52 HM King George VI
1952–   HM Queen Elizabeth II

Presidents

1907–09 HRH The Prince of Wales KG KT KP GCSI GCMG GCIE GCVO ISO
1911–   A. W. Gore
1912–14 Lord Desborough KCVO
1915–20 H. Wilson Fox MP
1921–29 H. W. W. Wilberforce
1929–34 HRH The Prince George KG
1935–42 HRH The Duke of Kent KG
1943–61 HRH The Duchess of Kent CI GCVO GBE
1961–68 HRH Princess Marina, Duchess of Kent CI GCVO GBE
1969–   HRH The Duke of Kent GCMG GCVO ADC
1974–83 Air Chief Marshall Sir Brian Burnett GCB DFC AFC RAF (Retd)

Chairmen

*(Up to 1929 there was no permanently elected Chairman. The chair
at Committee Meetings was normally taken by the President.)*

1929–36 Sir Herbert Wilberforce
1937–53 Sir Louis Greig KBE CVO DL
1953–55 A. H. Riseley OBE
1955–59 Dr J. C. Gregory
1959–74 H. F. David CBE
1974–83 Air Chief Marshall Sir Brian Burnett GCB DFC AFC RAF (Ret'd)
1983–   R. E. H. Hadingham OBE MC TD

Secretaries/Chief Executives
*(Following the restructuring of the club's staff in 1983 the Secretary
became the Chief Executive.)*

1871–79   J. W. Walsh
1880–88   J. Marshall
1888–91   H. W. W. Wilberforce
1891–98   A. Chitty
1899–1906 A. Palmer
1907–24   Commander G. W. Hillyard
1925–40   Major D. R. Larcombe
1940–45   Miss N. G. Cleather (acting)
1946–63   Lieutenant Colonel A. D. C. Macaulay OBE
1963–79   Major A. D. Mills
1979–   C. J. Gorringe

Referees

1877–85   H. Jones
1886   J. Marshall
1887–89   S. A. E. Hickson
1890–1905 B. C. Evelegh
1906–14   H. S. Scrivener
1919–36   F. R. Burrow
1937–39   H. Price
1946–48   Captain A. K. Trower
1949–62   Colonel W. J. Legg
1963–75   Captain M. B. Gibson
1976–82   F. W. Hoyles
1983–   A. R. Mills

Full results of the gentlemen's and ladies' singles, plus finals of all other events

GENTLEMEN'S SINGLES   1877

FIRST ROUND	SECOND ROUND	QUARTER-FINALS	SEMI-FINALS	FINAL	CHAMPION
H. T. Gillson	Gore	Gore			
S. W. Gore	6-2 6-0 6-3	6-4 4-6 6-2 6-1			
R. D. Dalby	Hankey		Gore		
M. Hankey	6-4 6-2 3-6 6-2		6-3 6-2 5-6 6-1		
J. Baker	Baker	Langham			
J. W. Trist	6-1 6-4 6-0	6-3 4-6 6-0 6-5			
F. N. Langham	Langham			Gore d. Heathcote	
C. F. Buller	w.o.			6-2 6-5 6-2	
E. Wheeler	Erskine	Erskine			Gore
L. R. Erskine	6-2 6-5 6-2	6-2 6-1 ret'd			6-1 6-2 6-4
H. C. Soden	Lambert		W. C. Marshall		
J. Lambert	6-1 6-5 6-5		6-5 5-6 6-4 6-1		
B. N. Akroyd	Akroyd	W. C. Marshall		W. C. Marshall	
G. Nicol	6-0 6-0 6-4	6-4 6-2 6-2		bye	
W. C. Marshall	W. C. Marshall				
F. D. Jackson	6-3 6-5 6-0				
F. W. Oliver	Oliver	J. Marshall			
Major Battye	6-1 6-1 6-1	4-6 6-5 6-1 4-6 6-3			
J. Marshall	J. Marshall				
Captain Grimston	3-6 1-6 6-2 6-3 6-3		Heathcote		
C. G. Heathcote	Heathcote	Heathcote	6-3 6-3 6-5		
Captain G. F. Buxton	6-0 6-2 6-3	bye			

2nd and 3rd place play-off: Marshall d. Heathcote 6-4 6-4.

GENTLEMEN'S SINGLES   1878

FIRST ROUND	SECOND ROUND	THIRD ROUND	QUARTER-FINALS	SEMI-FINALS	FINAL	ALL-COMERS' CHAMPION
L. R. Erskine	Erskine	Erskine				
A. W. Nicholson	6-1 6-1 6-3	w.o.				
Clapham & Clum			Erskine			
(both absent)			6-1 6-3 5-6 6-1			
E. Bates	Porter	Porter				
F. W. Porter	6-0 3-6 6-0 3-6 6-3	5-6 6-5 3-6 6-2 6-1				
A. W. Crichton	S. Montgomerie			Erskine		
S. Montgomerie	6-2 6-2 6-1			6-4 3-6 6-1 3-6 6-5		
G. Montgomerie	G. Montgomerie	Hamilton				
G. E. Tabor	5-6 6-2 2-6 6-5 6-5	5-6 6-4 6-5 6-3				
C. G. Hamilton	Hamilton		Hamilton			
F. Pollock	6-1 6-1 6-3		6-0 6-2 6-2			
C. G. Heathcote	Heathcote	Brackenbury				
H. T. W. Wheeler	6-4 6-2 6-0	6-4 6-2 4-6 4-6 6-5			Erskine	
E. B. Brackenbury	Brackenbury				6-3 6-1 6-3	
G. James	6-1 2-6 6-0 6-0					
Mr Keyser	Lawford	Lawford				
H. F. Lawford	w.o.	5-6 6-4 6-4 6-5				
J. Cunningham	Grimston		Lawford			
Captain Grimston	6-3 6-2 6-0		6-4 5-6 6-5 6-4	Lawford		
H. S. Cotton	Seymour	Seymour		bye		Hadow
E. R. Seymour	6-1 6-1 ret'd	bye				6-4 6-4 6-4
A. S. Tabor	A. S. Tabor					
C. Wallis	6-0 6-0 6-0					
P. F. Hadow	P. F. Hadow	Hadow				
F. W. Oliver	6-2 6-1 6-3	6-2 6-1 6-1				
R. D. Dalby	Dalby		Hadow			
B. Smith	6-2 6-3 6-3		6-2 6-3 6-0			
F. M. Ashley	Brown	Brown		Hadow		
A. C. Brown	6-0 6-0 6-0	6-1 6-1 6-1		6-0 6-4 6-3	Hadow	
G. F. Buxton	Myers				bye	
A. T. Myers	6-5 6-4 6-0					
C. Ewbank	A. A. Hadow	Myers	Myers			
A. A. Hadow	5-6 6-1 6-1 6-2	6-1 0-6 6-4 1-6 6-2	bye			

Challenge round: P. F. Hadow (Challenger) d. S. W. Gore (Holder) 7-5 6-1 9-7.

GENTLEMEN'S SINGLES

1879

FIRST ROUND: C. L. Stephen d. H. Taylor w.o.; C. G. Heathcote d. C. J. Coventry 6-2 4-6 6-3 5-6 6-5; V. Brooke d. E. Renshaw w.o.; B. T. Cotton d. A. Schacht 6-1 3-6 6-1 6-4; J. T. Hartley d. C. J. Cole 6-0 6-0 6-3; L. R. Erskine d. F. W. Porter 6-0 6-1 6-1; G. H. Cartland d. M. L. Mulholland 6-2 2-6 6-3 1-6 6-4; W. C. Marshall d. A. H. Cochran 6-1 6-2 6-2; C. F. Parr d. G. Montgomerie 6-3 3-6 6-4 3-6 6-3; H. T. Medlicott d. E. B. Hill 6-1 6-0 4-6 6-1; E. N. Buxton d. Capt. Belson 6-1 6-5 6-2; T. Hoare d. W. F. Adams 6-5 6-1 6-5; A. Basil-Brooke d. H. T. Gillson 6-5 6-2 1-6 6-4; A. T. Myers d. W. Wells Cole 6-2 3-6 6-5 6-5; C. D. Barry d. R. Barrington 6-0 6-1 6-1; G. G. Arbuthnot d. O. E. Woodhouse 6-2 4-6 6-1 6-2; G. E. Tabor d. W. Renshaw w.o.; W. E. Martin d. L. S. F. Winslow 6-0 6-1 6-2; S. Pilkington d. E. B. Brackenbury 6-0 6-5 6-4; E. Lubbock d. H. F. Lawford 6-2 4-6 6-1 6-2; A. J. Mulholland d. A. S. Tabor 5-6 6-2 6-3 6-0; V. 'St Leger' d. F. Durant 6-1 6-2 6-3; J. D. Vans Agnew bye.

SECOND ROUND: Heathcote d. Stephen 1-6 6-2 6-1 5-6 6-1; Brooke d. Cotton 4-6 6-3 2-6 6-2 6-1; Hartley d. Erskine 6-4 6-5 5-6 0-6 6-5; Marshall d. Cartland 6-3 6-2 6-4; Parr d. Medlicott 6-5 5-6 6-2; Hoare d. Buxton 6-3 6-2 ret'd; Myers d. Basil-Brooke 6-1 6-0 6-2; Barry d. Arbuthnot 6-1 6-4 6-4; Tabor d. Martin 4-6 6-4 6-5 6-4; Lubbock d. Pilkington 6-2 6-2 6-0; Mulholland bye; 'St Leger' d. Vans Agnew 6-3 6-2 6-1.

THIRD ROUND	QUARTER-FINALS	SEMI-FINALS	FINAL	ALL-COMERS' CHAMPION
Heathcote	Heathcote			
Brooke	6-2 6-0 6-1	Hartley		
Hartley	Hartley	6-4 6-3 6-3		
Marshall	6-1 6-3 4-6 6-1		Hartley	
Parr	Parr		2-6 6-0 6-1 6-1	
Hoare	6-4 1-6 6-0 6-2	Parr		Hartley
Myers	Barry	6-2 6-5 6-4		6-2 6-4 6-2
Barry	6-3 6-2 6-2			
G. E. Tabor	G. E. Tabor			
Lubbock	5-6 4-6 6-5 6-1 6-5	'St Leger'		
Mulholland	'St Leger'	6-2 6-5 5-6 6-3	'St Leger'	
'St Leger'	6-4 2-6 6-1 6-4		bye	

Challenge round: J. T. Hartley (Challenger) d. P. F. Hadow w.o.
2nd and 3rd place play-off: 'St Leger' d. Parr 4-6 6-2 5-6 6-4 6-4.

OTHER FINAL

GENTLEMEN'S DOUBLES (Non-Championship event played at Oxford): **Final** — L. R. Erskine/H. F. Lawford d. F. Durant/G. E. Tabor 4-6 6-4 6-5 6-2 3-6 5-6 10-8.

GENTLEMEN'S SINGLES

1880

FIRST ROUND: D. Womersley d. V. Brooke 6-3 2-6 6-5 6-3; W. Renshaw d. F. B. Maddison 6-3 6-0 6-4; O. E. Woodhouse d. J. H. Brand 5-6 6-1 6-0 6-3; F. W. Monement d. B. Follett 3 sets to 1; C. H. Evill d. W. M. Bird 6-3 6-1 6-0; H. J. Medlycott d. E. N. Buxton 5-6 6-5 6-3 4-6 6-5; E. Renshaw d. F. G. Templer 6-1 6-5 6-1; C. D. Heatley d. R. C. Christian 6-1 6-2 6-1; H. L. Mulholland d. G. E. Tabor 4-6 6-3 2-6 6-3 6-3; C. J. Cole d. S. Montgomerie 6-4 5-6 5-6 6-3 6-2; G. Montgomerie d. W. Wells Cole 6-2 6-5 6-5; O. L. Stephen d. T. Taylor 6-4 4-4-6 6-3 6-5; G. Murray Hill d. H. E. Solly 6-1 6-0 6-1; R. H. Beresford d. W. S. Trollope 6-5 6-3 5-6 6-5; H. C. Jenkins d. H. R. Hallward 6-0 6-0 6-2; A. S. Tabor d. F. R. Benson 6-1 6-0 6-3; H. F. Lawford d. J. E. Eddis 6-2 6-2 6-4; W. B. Monement d. 'F. Harold' 6-0 6-0 6-3; R. T. Richardson d. A. Kaye Butterworth 6-5 6-3 6-1; K. M'Alpine d. N. L. Hallward 6-5 6-5 6-3; F. Durant d. H. Daly 6-2 6-1 6-1; F. Crowder d. W. L. Hacon w.o.; M. G. M'Namara d. J. Maxwell Scott 6-2 6-0 6-4; 'W. H. d'Esterre' d. B. F. Buxton 6-4 5-6 6-4 6-4; R. R. Farrer d. M. Hankey 6-2 6-2 6-3; W. E. Hansell d. W. C. Marshall 4-6 6-4 6-5 6-3; C. Wallis d. B. T. Cotton 6-2 6-5 4-6 6-5; C. G. Heathcote d. W. F. Clerke 6-5 5-6 2-6 6-5; G. M. Butterworth d. N. Womersley 6-2 6-2 5-6 6-5; 'J. Devans' d. W. C. Taylor 6-2 6-2 6-3.

SECOND ROUND: W. Renshaw d. Womersley 6-2 6-4 6-0; Woodhouse d. F. W. Monement 6-3 6-3 6-5; Medlycott d. Evill 6-4 6-3 6-0; E. Renshaw d. Heatley 6-2 2-6 6-4 6-2; Cole d. Mulholland w.o.; G. Montgomerie d. Stephen 6-2 6-2 6-0; Hill d. Beresford 6-3 6-1 6-3; Jenkins d. A. S. Tabor 3-6 6-3 6-2 6-2; Lawford d. W. B. Monement 6-2 6-1 6-1; Richardson d. M'Alpine 6-1 6-0 6-3; Durant d. Crowder 6-4 6-5 6-2. 'd'Esterre' d. M'Namara 6-2 6-1 2-6 6-4; Farrer d. Hansell 6-1 4-6 4-6 6-0 6-4; Heathcote d. Wallis 6-4 2-6 6-0 6-5; G. M. Butterworth d. 'Devans' 4-6 6-4 6-3 6-3.

THIRD ROUND	QUARTER-FINALS	SEMI-FINALS	FINAL	ALL-COMERS' CHAMPION
W. Renshaw	Woodhouse			
Woodhouse	5-6 6-3 6-3 6-4	Woodhouse		
Medlycott	E. Renshaw	6-3 6-3 3-6 6-0		
E. Renshaw	6-3 6-3 6-3		Woodhouse	
Cole	G. Montgomerie		6-4 2-6 6-3 5-6 6-1	
G. Montgomerie	6-0 6-1 6-1	G. Montgomerie		
Hill	Jenkins	6-3 5-6 6-2 2-6 6-3		Lawford
Jenkins	6-4 6-4 6-2			7-5 6-4 6-0
Lawford	Lawford			
Richardson	1-6 6-3 0-6 6-5 6-4	Lawford		
Durant	'd'Esterre'	6-0 6-3 6-1		
'd'Esterre'	6-3 6-2 5-6 5-6 6-1		Lawford	
Farrer	Farrer		6-2 6-3 6-3	
Heathcote	5-6 6-1 6-0 6-3	G. M. Butterworth		
G. M. Butterworth	G. M. Butterworth	1-6 6-1 6-4 6-5		
	bye			

Challenge round: J. T. Hartley (Holder) d. H. F. Lawford (Challenger) 6-3 6-2 2-6 6-3.

OTHER FINAL

GENTLEMEN'S DOUBLES (Non-Championship event played at Oxford): **Final** — W./E. Renshaw d. C. J. Cole/O. E. Woodhouse 6-1 4-6 6-0 6-8 6-3.

GENTLEMEN'S SINGLES

1881

FIRST ROUND: M. D. Buckingham d. H. Grove 6-2 6-4 6-1; O. E. Woodhouse d. H. H. Wilkes 6-4 6-5 6-0; W. Milne d. W. M. Bird 6-0 5-0 ret'd; 'Castor' d. R. W. Braddell 6-5 6-3 2-6 6-4; W. Renshaw d. W. J. Down 6-2 6-0 6-0; T. W. Gallwey d. A. J. Stanley 4-6 6-3 6-5 6-4; C. Cheales d. B. T. Cotton w.o.; E. Lubbock d. J. Rankine w.o.; C. B. Russell d. F. Pollock 6-2 6-2 6-2; H. C. Jenkins d. R. Pollock w.o.; W. H. 'Edward' d. J. M. Thornycroft 6-0 6-2 6-2; H. F. Lawford d. C. J. Cole 6-0 6-2 6-3; G. Murray-Hill d. E. S. Saxton 4-6 6-1 6-1 1-6 6-4; A. Keyser d. C. Wallis 6-3 6-5 6-2; M. Fenwick d. H. R. Hallward 6-3 6-2 2-6 6-4; A. J. Chitty d. M. L. Hallward 6-2 2-6 6-5 6-4; H. L. Mulholland d. B. Follett 2-6 6-3 6-1 ret'd; W. H. Darby d. F. H. Stokes 6-2 6-5 6-3; F. L. Rawson d. G. Montgomerie w.o.; 'Pollux' d. J. Wilkes 6-3 6-4 6-4; E. Renshaw d. J. G. Horn 6-2 6-2 6-4; J. M. Scott d. H. B. Porter 6-5 1-6 6-4 6-3; M. G. M. M'Namara d. W. C. Taylor 6-2 6-4 6-1; R. T. Richardson d. A. H. Cochran 6-0 6-1 6-2.

SECOND ROUND: Woodhouse d. Buckingham 6-1 6-0 6-0; Milne d. 'Castor' 6-2 5-6 6-2 6-4; W. Renshaw d. Gallwey 6-0 6-0 6-1; Lubbock d. Cheales 6-0 6-0 6-1; Jenkins d. Russell 6-5 6-2 6-0; Lawford d. 'Edward' 6-3 6-2 6-2; Murray-Hill d. Keyser 6-5 6-2 4-6 3-6 6-2; Fenwick d. Chitty 6-3 2-6 6-5 0-6 6-1; Darby d. Mulholland 6-3 6-5 6-2; 'Pollux' d. Rawson 6-5 6-4 ret'd; E. Renshaw d. Scott 6-0 6-0 6-3; Richardson d. M'Namara 6-2 6-1 6-2.

THIRD ROUND	QUARTER-FINALS	SEMI-FINALS	FINAL	ALL-COMERS' CHAMPION
Woodhouse	Woodhouse			
Milne	6-1 6-0 6-1	W. Renshaw		
W. Renshaw	W. Renshaw	4-6 6-4 6-0 6-3		
Lubbock	6-5 6-3 6-3		W. Renshaw	
Jenkins	Lawford		1-6 6-3 6-2 5-6 6-3	
Lawford	6-4 6-3 6-0	Lawford		W. Renshaw
Murray-Hill	Murray-Hill	6-1 6-1 6-0		6-4 6-2 6-3
Fenwick	6-2 2-6 6-5 6-4			
Darby	Darby			
'Pollux'	6-5 6-5 0-6 6-3	Richardson	Richardson	
E. Renshaw	Richardson	6-0 6-4 6-1	bye	
Richardson	2-6 6-5 6-4 6-5			

Challenge round: W. Renshaw (Challenger) d. J. T. Hartley (Holder) 6-0 6-1 6-1.
2nd and 3rd place play-off: Richardson d. Lawford 6-3 4-6 6-1 3-6 7-5.

OTHER FINAL

GENTLEMEN'S DOUBLES (Non-Championship event played at Oxford): **Final** — W./E. Renshaw d. W. J. Down/H. Vaughan 6-0 6-0 6-4.

GENTLEMEN'S SINGLES

1882

FIRST ROUND: E. de S. H. Browne d. C. E. Farrer 6-0 6-2 6-0; E. Renshaw d. W. M. Tatham 6-0 6-1 6-1; P. G. Von Donop d. G. Montgomerie 6-3 4-6 6-3 6-2; H. Berkeley d. G. G. Arbuthnot 4-6 4-6 6-3 6-2 6-4; A. J. Stanley d. H. Chipp 4-6 6-1 5-6 6-0 6-2; H. F. Lawford d. B. Follett 6-4 6-2 6-3; H. W. W. Wilberforce d. H. H. Wilkes 6-5 6-5 6-3; R. Hyde Clarke d. J. C. Maxwell-Scott w.o.; F. A. Fairlie d. W. Milne 3-6 6-4 6-2 6-2; O. E. Woodhouse d. F. J. Ridgway 6-3 6-1 6-4; G. M. Butterworth d. H. Grove 5-6 6-3 5-6 6-2 6-0; R. T. Richardson d. Stewart 6-0 6-2 6-0; J. G. Horn d. C. J. Michod 6-2 6-3 6-4; F. R. Benson d. F. A. Govett 6-5 6-3 6-4.

SECOND ROUND	QUARTER-FINALS	SEMI-FINALS	FINAL	ALL-COMER'S CHAMPION
Browne	E. Renshaw			
E. Renshaw	6-1 6-5 1-6 4-6 6-5	E. Renshaw		
Von Donop	Berkeley	6-5 6-1 6-4		
Berkeley	w.o.		E. Renshaw	
Stanley	Lawford		6-4 4-6 6-2 3-6 6-0	
Lawford	6-1 6-2 6-3	Lawford		
Wilberforce	Wilberforce	6-2 6-5 6-5		E. Renshaw
Hyde Clarke	6-4 6-2 6-1			7-5 6-3 2-6 6-3
Fairlie	Woodhouse			
Woodhouse	6-5 6-5 6-3	Richardson		
Butterworth	Richardson	6-1 6-0 6-2	Richardson	
Richardson	6-1 6-5 6-3		6-1 6-2 6-1	
Horn	Benson	Benson		
Benson	6-3 1-6 6-5 3-6 6-5	bye		

Challenge round: W. Renshaw (Holder) d. E. Renshaw (Challenger) 6-1 2-6 4-6 6-2 6-2.

OTHER FINAL

GENTLEMEN'S DOUBLES (Non-Championship event played at Oxford): **Final** — J. T. Hartley/R. T. Richardson d. J. G. Horn/C. B. Russell 6-2 6-1 6-0.

GENTLEMEN'S SINGLES

1883

FIRST ROUND: H. W. W. Wilberforce d. F. A. Govett w.o.; J. T. Hartley d. H. S. Barlow 6-1 6-3 6-1; D. Stewart d. H. Grove 6-3 3-6 3-6 6-5 6-2; C. E. Farrer d. B. Follett 2-6 6-2 6-2 6-1; F. J. Ridgway d. F. Warren 3-6 6-1 6-1 3-6 6-4; W. C. Taylor d. W. Milne 2-6 6-4 1-6 6-1 6-3; L. G. Campbell d. O. E. Woodhouse 4-6 5-6 6-1 6-5 6-4; M. Constable d. L. J. Maxse w.o.; E. Renshaw d. H. F. Lawford 5-6 6-1 3-6 6-2 7-5; G. Montgomerie d. H. H. Playford 6-1 6-3 6-0; C. W. Grinstead d. E. L. Williams 4-6 6-4 6-4 4-6 6-5; R. T. Richardson bye.

SECOND ROUND	QUARTER-FINALS	SEMI-FINALS	FINAL	ALL-COMERS' CHAMPION
Wilberforce	Wilberforce	Stewart		
Hartley	4-6 6-5 6-2 6-4	6-5 3-6 5-6 6-5 6-4		
Stewart	Stewart		Stewart	
Farrer	6-4 6-4 6-4		6-0 6-1 6-3	
Ridgway	Taylor	Taylor		E. Renshaw
Taylor	6-0 6-4 6-1	6-3 6-5 5-6 4-6 6-3		0-6 6-3 6-0 6-2
Campbell	Constable			
Constable	6-3 1-6 6-2 6-4		E. Renshaw	
E. Renshaw	E. Renshaw	E. Renshaw	bye	
Montgomerie	6-3 6-3 6-3	6-4 6-3 6-3		
Grinstead	Grinstead			
Richardson	6-3 5-6 6-5 6-2			

Challenge round: W. Renshaw (Holder) d. E. Renshaw (Challenger) 2-6 6-3 6-3 4-6 6-3.

OTHER FINAL

GENTLEMEN'S DOUBLES (Non-Championship event played at Oxford): **Final** — C. W. Grinstead/C. E. Welldon d. R. T. Milford/C. B. Russell 3-6 6-1 6-3 6-4.

GENTLEMEN'S SINGLES

1884

FIRST ROUND: W. Milne d. J. C. Maxwell-Scott 6-1 6-4 6-3; O. Milne d. W. T. Ryres 6-3 6-1 6-4; E. Renshaw d. E. L. Williams 6-3 7-5 6-1; B. Cokayne d. G. Montgomerie w.o.; A. J. Stanley d. B. Follett 6-0 6-3 6-1; C. W. Grinstead d. R. D. Sears (USA) w.o.; A. W. M. White d. C. J. Cramer-Roberts 5-7 6-0 4-6 6-2 7-5; E. de S. H. Browne d. D. Stewart 6-3 6-1 7-5; P. B. Lyon d. F. L. Rawson 5-6 6-2 3-6 6-4 6-1; W. C. Taylor d. E. Wigram 6-1 6-3 6-1; H. Chipp d. A. L. Rives (USA) 6-1 6-2 6-1; J. Dwight (USA) d. F. J. Ridgway 6-2 6-1 6-1; H. F. Lawford d. H. W. W. Wilberforce 6-1 6-3 7-5; R. C. Thompson d. J. B. Deykin w.o.

SECOND ROUND	QUARTER-FINALS	SEMI-FINALS	FINAL	ALL-COMERS' CHAMPION
W. Milne	W. Milne	E. Renshaw		
O. Milne	9-7 8-6 1-6 6-3	6-3 6-3 7-5		
E. Renshaw	E. Renshaw		Grinstead	
Cokayne	6-2 6-1 6-4		2-6 6-4 6-2 6-3	
Stanley	Grinstead	Grinstead		Lawford
Grinstead	6-8 6-4 6-3 6-3	5-7 4-6 7-5 6-4 6-1		7-5 2-6 6-2 9-7
White	Brown			
Brown	6-0 6-1 6-0		Lawford	
Lyon	Taylor	Chipp	7-5 6-4 6-4	
Taylor	3-6 3-6 7-5 6-4 9-7	10-8 6-1 6-4		
Chipp	Chipp			
Dwight	6-1 2-6 6-3 3-6 7-5			
Lawford	Lawford	Lawford		
Thompson	6-1 6-1 6-2	bye		

Challenge round: W. Renshaw (Holder) d. H. F. Lawford (Challenger) 6-0 6-4 9-7.

LADIES' SINGLES

FIRST ROUND	QUARTER-FINALS	SEMI-FINALS	FINAL	CHAMPION
M. Watson	Watson	M. Watson		
Mrs A. Tyrwhitt Drake	6-0 6-2	7-5 6-0		
B. E. Williams	Williams		M. Watson	
Mrs C. Wallis	6-2 6-1		3-6 6-4 6-2	
B. Bingley	Bingley	Bingley		M. Watson
Mrs C. J. Cole	6-3 6-3	6-0 6-8 6-3		6-8 6-3 6-3
F. M. Winckworth	Winckworth			
E. Bushell	6-0 6-1		L. Watson	
Mrs G. J. Cooper	Cooper	L. Watson	6-4 6-1	
C. Bushell	w.o.	7-5 5-7 6-3		
L. Watson	bye			
M. Leslie	Leslie	Leslie		
B. Wallis	6-2 6-1	bye		

OTHER FINAL

GENTLEMEN'S DOUBLES: Final — E./W. Renshaw d. E. W. Lewis/E. L. Williams 6-3 6-1 1-6 6-4.

GENTLEMEN'S SINGLES

1885

FIRST ROUND: W. Milne d. O. Milne 8-6 2-6 6-3 7-5; E. Renshaw d. D. Stewart 6-1 2-6 4-6 8-6 6-4; M. G. McNamara d. J. G. Rogers 6-0 6-3 6-2; E. de S. H. Browne d. G. Kerr 6-1 6-1 6-3; J. Dwight (USA) d. E. 'Cotton' 6-4 6-2 6-3; G. Montgomerie d. W. C. Taylor 7-5 6-4 2-6 6-4; H. Grove d. E. N. Stenhouse 6-4 6-0 6-0.

SECOND ROUND	QUARTER-FINALS	SEMI-FINALS	FINAL	ALL-COMERS' CHAMPION
H. Chipp	Chipp			
W. Milne	6-3 6-1 6-4	Renshaw		
O. P. Trescott	Renshaw	6-4 6-4 7-5		
Renshaw	6-2 6-0 6-1		Renshaw	
McNamara	McNamara		6-4 8-6 2-6 5-7 6-4	
E. G. Meers	6-3 6-1 6-4	Browne		
E. W. Lewis	Browne	6-1 7-5 6-2		
Browne	6-1 2-6 6-4 7-5			Lawford
Dwight	Dwight			5-7 6-1 0-6 6-2 6-4
A. A. Thomson	6-1 6-0 6-1	Dwight		
A. J. Stanley	Stanley	6-3 6-3 6-4		
Montgomerie	4-6 6-3 6-8 6-0 6-0		Lawford	
H. F. Lawford	Lawford		6-2 6-2 6-3	
Grove	6-3 6-2 6-1	Lawford		
P. B. Lyon	Lyon	6-2 7-5 6-3		
C. H. A. Ross	6-2 6-1 3-6 8-6			

Challenge round: W. Renshaw (Holder) d. H. F. Lawford (Challenger) 7-5 6-2 4-6 7-5.

LADIES' SINGLES

FIRST ROUND	QUARTER-FINALS	SEMI-FINALS	FINAL	CHAMPION
B. Bingley	Bingley			
L. M. Nash	6-2 6-2	Bingley		
Mrs Dransfield	bye	w.o.		
J. Meikle	Meikle		Bingley	
L. Watson	6-3 4-6 6-4	Gurney	6-1 6-2	
E. Gurney	bye	7-5 6-4		M. Watson
E. F. Hudson	bye	Hudson		6-1 7-5
Miss Bryan	bye	6-3 6-0	M. Watson	
M. Watson	bye	M. Watson	6-0 6-1	
B. Langrishe	bye	6-0 6-2		

OTHER FINAL

GENTLEMEN'S DOUBLES: Final — E./W. Renshaw d. C. E. Farrer/A. J. Stanley 6-3 6-3 10-8.

GENTLEMEN'S SINGLES

1886

FIRST ROUND: E. J. Avery d. C. E. Farrer 6-3 6-2 6-2; T. R. Garvey d. H. Pease 6-3 6-3 2-6 6-1; W. Milne d. E. Chatterton w.o.; W. C. Taylor d. A. R. Lewis 6-3 4-6 6-3 6-4; M. G. McNamara d. J. H. Lewis w.o.; E. Renshaw d. H. Chipp 6-1 6-3 11-13 6-3; E. W. Lewis d. C. P. Triscott 6-0 6-1 6-2.

SECOND ROUND	QUARTER-FINALS	SEMI-FINALS	FINAL	ALL-COMERS' CHAMPION
H. J. Hamilton	Hamilton			
E. G. Meers	7-5 6-4 8-6	Lawford		
H. F. Lawford	Lawford	8-6 6-1 8-6		
H. Grove	0-6 6-0 4-6 6-4 6-2		Lawford	
Avery	Garvey		6-3 6-2 6-0	
Garvey	6-4 1-6 6-4 6-3	Garvey		
Milne	Taylor	8-6 6-4 2-6 6-3		
Taylor	4-6 7-5 3-6 6-3 6-0			Lawford
McNamara	Renshaw			6-2 6-3 2-6 4-6 6-4
Renshaw	4-6 6-3 8-6 6-0	Lewis		
Lewis	Lewis	4-6 5-7 6-4 6-1 6-0		
H. S. Stone	3-6 6-0 6-0 6-3		Lewis	
C. H. A. Ross	Ross		3-6 6-2 1-6 6-1 6-3	
O. Milne	6-3 6-3 6-3	Wilberforce		
H. W. W. Wilberforce	Wilberforce	3-6 2-6 6-4 6-2 6-4		
P. B. Lyon	8-6 6-4 3-0 ret'd			

Challenge round: W. Renshaw (Holder) d. H. F. Lawford (Challenger) 6-0 5-7 6-3 6-4.

LADIES' SINGLES

FIRST ROUND	SEMI-FINALS	FINAL	CHAMPION
M. Shackle	Shackle		
J. McKenzie	6-3 6-4	Tabor	
A. Tabor	Tabor	6-4 7-5	
F. M. Pearson	6-1 6-2		Bingley
B. Bingley	Bingley		6-2 6-0
J. Shackle	6-2 6-1	Bingley	
L. Watson	Watson	6-3 8-6	
A. M. Chambers	6-3 6-3		

Challenge round: Miss B. Bingley (Challenger) d. Miss M. Watson (Holder) 6-3 6-3.

OTHER FINALS

GENTLEMEN'S DOUBLES: Final — C. E. Farrer/A. J. Stanley d. P. Bowes-Lyon/H. W. W. Wilberforce 7-5 6-3 6-1.
Challenge round — E./W. Renshaw d. Farrer/Stanley 6-3 6-3 4-6 7-5.

GENTLEMEN'S SINGLES

1887

FIRST ROUND	QUARTER-FINALS	SEMI-FINALS	FINAL	ALL-COMERS' CHAMPION
H. B. Lyon	Lyon			
M. G. McNamara	6-2 6-4 ret'd	Grove		
H. W. W. Wilberforce	Grove	6-3 6-2 10-8		
H. Grove	6-1 6-3 6-3		Lawford	
H. S. Barlow	Lawford		4-6 6-3 7-5 7-5	
H. F. Lawford	6-0 9-7 6-3	Lawford		
O. Milne	Milne	7-5 6-0 6-3		Lawford
E. V. Thompson	5-7 6-4 1-6 6-4 8-6			1-6 6-3 3-6 6-4 6-4
E. Renshaw	Renshaw			
P. B. Lyon	6-1 6-0 6-0	Renshaw		
E. W. Lewis	Lewis	7-5 6-2 6-4		
F. A. Bowlby	6-2 6-2 6-1		Renshaw	
W. Milne	Milne		w.o.	
G. Montgomerie	w.o.	Lacy Sweet		
W. C. Taylor	Lacy Sweet	6-3 6-1 6-3		
C. Lacy Sweet	6-2 6-2 4-6 6-1			

Challenge round: H. F. Lawford (Challenger) d. W. Renshaw (Holder) w.o.

LADIES' SINGLES

FIRST ROUND	SEMI-FINALS	FINAL	ALL-COMERS' CHAMPION
L. Dod	bye	Dod	
B. James	James	6-1 6-1	
M. Shackle	8-6 6-2		Dod
Mrs C. J. Cole	bye	Cole	6-2 6-3
J. Shackle	bye	6-4 6-1	

Challenge round: Miss L. Dod (Challenger) d. Miss B. Bingley (Holder) 6-2 6-0.

OTHER FINALS

GENTLEMEN'S DOUBLES: Final — P. Bowes-Lyon/H. W. W. Wilberforce d. E. Barratt-Smith/J. H. Crispe 7-5 6-3 6-2. **Challenge round** — Bowes-Lyon/Wilberforce d. E./W. Renshaw w.o.

GENTLEMEN'S SINGLES

1888

FIRST ROUND: F. A. Bowlby d. T. Campion 6-3 0-6 6-2 5-7 6-4; W. J. Hamilton d. E. G. Meers 7-5 4-6 6-4 6-2; W. Renshaw d. H. Chipp 6-4 6-4 6-2; H. Grove d. H. S. Barlow 7-5 6-4 7-5; C. G. Eames d. A. Walker 6-2 5-7 6-1 7-5; E. W. Lewis d. P. B. Lyon 6-1 6-2 6-3; C. H. A. Ross d. O. Milne 6-8 6-4 7-5 6-2; H. S. Scrivener d. M. G. McNamara 6-4 6-4 1-6 6-3.

SECOND ROUND	QUARTER-FINALS	SEMI-FINALS	FINAL	ALL-COMERS' CHAMPION
E. Renshaw	E. Renshaw			
G. R. Mewburn	6-1 6-4 7-5	E. Renshaw		
H. W. W. Wilberforce	Wilberforce	4-6 6-3 7-5 4-6 6-0		
C. Lacy Sweet	4-6 6-3 6-0 4-6 6-1		E. Renshaw	
Bowlby	Hamilton		7-5 7-5 5-7 6-3	
Hamilton	6-1 6-1 6-4	Hamilton		
W. Renshaw	W. Renshaw	5-7 7-5 6-4 6-2		E. Renshaw
Grove	5-7 14-12 6-3 6-2			7-9 6-1 8-6 6-4
Eames	Lewis			
Lewis	6-1 6-0 6-3	Lewis		
Ross	Scrivener	7-5 6-3 6-1		
Scrivener	6-3 7-5 9-7		Lewis	
W. C. Taylor	Taylor		9-7 6-4 6-4	
A. W. Gore	3-6 3-6 6-2 6-3 6-3	Taylor		
F. C. Rawson	Rawson	6-4 6-0 4-6 4-6 6-1		
A. G. Ziffo	10-8 6-3 3-0 ret'd			

Challenge round: E. Renshaw (Challenger) d. H. F. Lawford (Holder) 6-3 7-5 6-0.

LADIES' SINGLES

FIRST ROUND	SEMI-FINALS	FINAL	ALL-COMERS' CHAMPION
Miss Howes	bye	Howes	
D. Patterson	Patterson	6-4 6-2	
Miss Williams	6-0 6-3		Hillyard
Mrs G. W. Hillyard	Hillyard	Hillyard	6-1 6-2
Miss Canning	6-2 6-2	w.o.	
Miss Phillimore	bye		

Challenge round: Miss L. Dod (Holder) d. Mrs G. W. Hillyard (Challenger) 6-3 6-3.

OTHER FINALS

GENTLEMEN'S DOUBLES: Final — E./W. Renshaw d. E. G. Meers/A. G. Ziffo 6-3 6-2 6-2. **Challenge round** — E./W. Renshaw d. P. Bowes-Lyon/H. W. W. Wilberforce 2-6 1-6 6-3 6-4 6-3.

GENTLEMEN'S SINGLES

1889

FIRST ROUND: G. W. Hillyard d. L. Winslow 6-4 6-3 6-3; F. A. Bowlby d. E. G. Meers w.o.; H. S. Barlow d. F. A. Darbishire 6-4 6-1 8-6; H. Grove d. F. L. Rawson w.o.; H. W. W. Wilberforce d. A. W. Gore 6-0 6-3 6-1; W. Renshaw d. E. J. Avory 6-2 6-3 6-2; M. F. Goodbody d. H. S. Stone 6-4 4-6 6-3 6-3; W. C. Taylor d. A. Walker 6-0 3-6 3-6 6-4 6-4.

SECOND ROUND	QUARTER-FINALS	SEMI-FINALS	FINAL	ALL-COMERS' CHAMPION
E. W. Lewis	Lewis			
T. S. Campion	6-1 6-1 6-1	Hamilton		
W. J. Hamilton	Hamilton	4-6 7-5 6-3 5-7 6-4		
J. Baldwin	w.o.		Barlow	
Hillyard	Hillyard		3-6 6-3 2-6 6-3 6-3	
Bowlby	6-3 4-6 6-4 13-11	Barlow		
Barlow	Barlow	7-5 6-2 6-4		Renshaw
Grove	6-8 6-4 6-4 3-6 9-7			3-6 5-7 8-6 10-8 8-6
Wilberforce	Renshaw			
Renshaw	6-4 7-5 6-0	Renshaw		
Goodbody	Goodbody	7-5 6-4 6-4		
Taylor	3-6 6-4 9-7 6-2		Renshaw	
H. F. Lawford	Lawford		7-5 5-7 6-3 6-2	
A. W. Andrews	6-1 6-3 6-1	Lawford		
A. G. Ziffo	Ziffo	6-2 6-2 6-0		
W. H. Cohen	6-3 6-1 6-1			

Challenge round: W. Renshaw (Challenger) d. E. Renshaw (Holder) 6-4 6-1 3-6 6-0.

LADIES' SINGLES

FIRST ROUND	SEMI-FINALS	FINAL	ALL-COMERS' CHAMPION
L. Rice	bye	L. Rice	
M. Jacks	Jacks	6-2 6-0	
M. Steedman	6-4 6-2		Hillyard
Mrs G. W. Hillyard	Hillyard		4-6 8-6 6-4
A. E. Rice	6-3 6-0	Hillyard	
B. Steedman	bye	8-6 6-1	

Challenge round: Mrs G. W. Hillyard (Challenger) d. Miss L. Dod (Holder) w.o.

OTHER FINALS

GENTLEMEN'S DOUBLES: Final — G. W. Hillyard/E. W. Lewis d. A. W. Gore/G. R. Mewburn 6-2 6-1 6-3.
Challenge round — E./W. Renshaw d. Hillyard/Lewis 6-4 6-4 3-6 0-6 6-1.

GENTLEMEN'S SINGLES

1890

FIRST ROUND: J. Pim d. O. Milne 7-5 9-11 6-3 6-2; H. S. Scrivener d. H. W. W. Wilberforce 7-5 9-7 ret'd; W. V. Eaves d. F. A. Bowlby 6-4 3-6 6-0 0-6 6-4; W. C. Taylor d. F. L. Rawson w.o.; W. J. Hamilton d. A. W. Gore 6-0 6-1 6-1; G. R. Mewburn d. A. G. Ziffo 6-2 6-4 6-3; W. Baddeley d. A. W. Andrews 6-0 6-3 6-0; H. F. Lawford d. E. A. Thomson (USA) w.o.; D. Miller (USA) d. H. S. Mahony 6-4 6-1 5-7 4-6 6-2; E. W. Lewis d. H. A. B. Chapman 6-4 6-3 6-4; E. G. Meers d. A. Walker 6-1 6-1 6-2; H. Baddeley d. E. Renshaw w.o.; D. G. Chaytor d. C. Lacy Sweet 6-3 6-2 6-1; G. W. Hillyard d. C. H. A. Ross w.o.

SECOND ROUND	QUARTER-FINALS	SEMI-FINALS	FINAL	ALL-COMERS' CHAMPION
M. F. Goodbody	Pim			
Pim	w.o.	Pim		
Scrivener	Scrivener	6-3 12-10 6-0		
Eaves	6-4 6-1 4-6 9-7		Hamilton	
Taylor	Hamilton		0-6 6-4 6-4 6-2	
Hamilton	7-5 6-1 6-1	Hamilton		
Mewburn	Baddeley	6-3 6-0 6-1		Hamilton
W. Baddeley	6-4 8-6 6-2			2-6 6-4 6-4 4-6 7-5
Lawford	Miller			
Miller	w.o.	Lewis		
Lewis	Lewis	6-3 6-1 6-1		
Meers	6-3 6-2 2-6 4-6 6-2		Barlow	
H. Baddeley	Chaytor		7-5 6-4 4-6 7-5	
Chaytor	6-4 6-3 6-3	Barlow		
Hillyard	Barlow	8-10 6-4 2-6 6-1 6-1		
H. S. Barlow	6-1 6-0 6-3			

Challenge round: W. J. Hamilton (Challenger) d. W. Renshaw (Holder) 6-8 6-2 3-6 6-1 6-1.

LADIES' SINGLES

FIRST ROUND	FINAL	ALL-COMERS' CHAMPION
M. Jacks	Jacks	
Mrs C. J. Cole	6-4 7-5	Rice
L. Rice	Rice	6-4 6-1
Mrs G. W. Hillyard	7-5 6-2	

Challenge round: Miss L. Rice (Challenger) d. Mrs G. W. Hillyard (Holder) w.o.

OTHER FINALS

GENTLEMEN'S DOUBLES: Final — J. Pim/F. O. Stoker d. G. W. Hillyard/E. W. Lewis 6-0 7-5 6-4. **Challenge round —** Pim/Stoker d. E./W. Renshaw w.o.

GENTLEMEN'S SINGLES

1891

FIRST ROUND: W. W. Wilberforce d. M. F. Goodbody w.o.; W. Baddeley d. F. O. Stoker w.o.; H. Chipp d. E. W. Lewis w.o.; A. W. Gore d. H. Baddeley 5-7 10-8 6-4 4-6 6-2; H. S. Mahony d. J. E. Kingsley 6-3 6-1 6-4; H. A. B. Chapman d. A. J. Chitty 6-1 6-0 6-3.

SECOND ROUND	QUARTER-FINALS	SEMI-FINALS	FINAL	ALL-COMERS' CHAMPION
E. Renshaw	Renshaw			
W. C. Taylor	6-1 6-1 6-1	Renshaw		
H. Grove	Grove	6-3 7-5 6-2		
E. G. Meers	6-4 8-6 5-7 2-6 6-3		W. Baddeley	
A. J. Avory	Avory		6-0 6-1 6-1	
Wilberforce	6-0 6-2 6-0	W. Baddeley		
W. Baddeley	W. Baddeley	6-0 6-1 4-6 6-2		
Chipp	6-4 6-0 6-4			W. Baddeley
Gore	Mahony			6-4 1-6 7-5 6-0
Mahony	6-3 6-1 3-6 6-0	Mahony		
Chapman	Chapman	6-2 6-0 6-1		
Mewburn	7-5 6-0 6-1		Pim	
J. Pim	Pim		6-4 6-0 6-2	
O. Milne	6-3 6-3 6-4	Pim		
H. S. Barlow	Barlow	5-7 0-6 6-2 6-3 7-5		
D. G. Chaytor	6-1 6-2 7-5			

Challenge round: W. Baddeley (Challenger) d. W. J. Hamilton (Holder) w.o.

LADIES' SINGLES

FIRST ROUND	QUARTER-FINALS	SEMI-FINALS	FINAL	ALL-COMERS' CHAMPION
L. Dod	bye	Dod		
Mrs Parsons	bye	6-0 6-0	Dod	
H. Jackson	Jackson		6-3 6-1	
M. Shackle	6-4 7-5	Steedman		
B. Steedman	bye	6-2 6-2		Dod
M. Langrishe	bye			6-2 6-1
M. Jacks	bye	Langrishe	Hillyard	
Mrs G. W. Hillyard	bye	11-9 6-3	6-4 6-1	
P. Legh	bye	Hillyard		
		6-3 6-2		

Challenge round: Miss L. Dod (Challenger) d. Miss L. Rice (Holder) w.o.

OTHER FINALS

GENTLEMEN'S DOUBLES: Final — H./W. Baddeley d. H. S. Barlow/E. Renshaw 4-6 6-4 7-5 0-6 6-2. **Challenge round** — H./W. Baddeley d. J. Pim/F. O. Stoker 6-1 6-3 1-6 6-2.

GENTLEMEN'S SINGLES

1892

FIRST ROUND: W. V. Eaves d. E. Colby 6-2 6-2 6-1; H. Baddeley d. M. R. Wright 7-5 6-3 6-1; R. Gamble d. W. C. Taylor 5-7 6-4 6-4 6-0; E. J. Avory d. H. Colby 6-1 6-2 6-4; A. E. Crawley d. O. Milne 6-2 4-6 4-6 6-4 2-1 ret'd; H. A. B. Chapman d. D. Fuller 6-1 6-2 6-0; H. Grove d. N. Burlacher 6-4 1-6 6-0 6-2; H. S. Mahony d. A. J. Chitty 10-8 6-3 6-4; O. S. Campbell (USA) d. F. A. Bowlby 6-4 6-3 8-6; A. W. Gore d. J. E. Kingsley 6-3 4-6 6-2 6-2; J. Pim d. J. H. Crispe 8-10 6-1 6-4 6-3.

SECOND ROUND	QUARTER-FINALS	SEMI-FINALS	FINAL	ALL-COMERS' CHAMPION
E. W. Lewis	Lewis			
G. W. Hillyard	8-6 6-1 6-3	Lewis		
Eaves	Eaves	7-5 6-2 6-2		
Baddeley	3-6 6-2 6-0 6-1		Lewis	
Gamble	Gamble		2-6 6-3 6-1 6-2	
Avory	6-0 2-6 6-2 6-4	Chapman		
Crawley	Chapman	6-4 6-0 6-1		
Chapman	6-1 6-1 6-2			Pim
Grove	Mahony			2-6 5-7 9-7 6-3 6-2
Mahony	7-5 9-7 3-6 2-6 6-1	Mahony		
Campbell	Gore	4-6 6-2 6-3 6-4		
Gore	6-1 8-6 8-6		Pim 6-1 12-10 2-6 6-2	
Pim	Pim			
E. G. Meers	10-8 6-2 6-3	Pim		
A. Palmer	Barlow	3-6 9-7 6-2 7-5		
H. S. Barlow	6-1 7-5 6-1			

Challenge round: W. Baddeley (Holder) d. J. Pim (Challenger) 4-6 6-3 6-3 6-2.

LADIES' SINGLES

FIRST ROUND	SEMI-FINALS	FINAL	ALL-COMERS' CHAMPION
B. Steedman	Steedman		
Miss Barefoot	6-0 6-1	Shackle	
M. Shackle	Shackle	6-4 6-3	
H. Jackson	6-3 6-4		Hillyard
Mrs G. W. Hillyard	Hillyard		6-1 6-4
Mrs Draffen	6-2 6-2	Hillyard	
Miss Martin	bye	1-6 6-3 9-7	

Challenge round: Miss L. Dod (Holder) d. Mrs G. W. Hillyard (Challenger) 6-1 6-1.

OTHER FINALS

GENTLEMEN'S DOUBLES: Final — H. S. Barlow/E. W. Lewis d. H. S. Mahony/J. Pim 8-10 6-3 5-7 11-9 6-1.
Challenge round — Barlow/Lewis d. H./W. Baddeley 4-6 6-2 8-6 6-4.

GENTLEMEN'S SINGLES   **1893**

FIRST ROUND: A. W. Gore d. S. H. Hughes 6-4 6-2 6-2; H. S. Barlow d. E. G. Meers 6-2 3-6 5-7 6-4 6-3; M. F. Goodbody d. H. A. B. Chapman 6-3 6-1 6-0; G. W. Hillyard d. J. H. Crispe 6-2 7-5 6-2; J. Pim d. A. E. Crawley 6-4 2-6 6-3 6-2; S. H. Smith d. H. J. W. Fosbery 1-6 6-1 6-2 6-4; H. S. Mahony d. W. M. Cranston 4-6 6-3 6-1 6-4; E. Renshaw d. W. Renshaw w.o.; F. O. Stoker d. H. Baddeley 8-6 7-5 4-6 6-2; W. V. Eaves d. W. Escombe 6-1 6-2 6-2; N. Durlacher d. H. Grove 6-4 6-2 8-6.

SECOND ROUND	QUARTER-FINALS	SEMI-FINALS	FINAL	ALL-COMERS' CHAMPION
A. W. Hallward	Hallward			
H. Bacon	6-4 6-4 6-4	Barlow		
Gore	Barlow	7-9 6-2 10-8 6-8 6-1		
Barlow	6-4 3-6 2-6 6-2 6-2		Pim	
Goodbody	Goodbody		9-7 6-2 6-3	
Hillyard	4-6 6-3 6-8 8-6 6-2	Pim		
Pim	Pim	8-6 6-3 3-6 6-1		Pim
Smith	6-2 7-5 7-5			9-7 6-3 6-0
Mahony	Mahony			
E. Renshaw	1-6 7-5 6-1 4-6 6-3	Mahony		
Stoker	Eaves	10-8 11-9 6-0		
Eaves	7-5 6-1 1-6 11-9		Mahony	
Durlacher	Durlacher		3-6 6-3 6-3 6-1	
D. Fuller	6-1 6-3 6-3	Palmer		
T. E. Haydon	Palmer	6-3 6-4 7-5		
A. Palmer	6-1 6-3 10-12 6-3			

Challenge round: J. Pim (Challenger) d. W. Baddeley (Holder) 3-6 6-1 6-3 6-2.

LADIES' SINGLES

FIRST ROUND	SEMI-FINALS	FINAL	ALL-COMERS' CHAMPION
L. Austin	Austin		
S. Robins	6-2 6-1	Shackle	
M. Shackle	Shackle	6-0 6-2	Hillyard
P. Legh	10-8 6-1		6-3 6-2
C. Cooper	Cooper		
Mrs Horncastle	6-4 6-1	Hillyard	
Mrs G. W. Hillyard	bye	6-3 6-1	

Challenge round: Miss L. Dod (Holder) d. Mrs G. W. Hillyard (Challenger) 6-8 6-1 6-4.

OTHER FINALS

GENTLEMEN'S DOUBLES: Final – J. Pim/F. O. Stoker d. H./W. Baddeley 6-2 4-6 6-3 5-7 6-2. **Challenge round** – Pim/Stoker d. H. S. Barlow/E. W. Lewis 4-6 6-3 6-1 2-6 6-0.

GENTLEMEN'S SINGLES   **1894**

FIRST ROUND: T. Chaytor d. H. A. B. Chapman 8-6 6-1 6-0; C. Cazalet d. R. F. Doherty 6-3 6-4 2-6 6-3; E. G. Meers d. A. W. Hallward 6-3 6-2 6-3; G. C. Ball-Greene d. W. V. Eaves w.o.; H. S. Mahony d. W. M. Cranston 6-4 4-6 7-5 6-1; E. W. Lewis d. A. W. Gore 6-2 4-6 6-2 6-4; G. M. Simond d. H. A. Nisbet 6-4 6-3 6-3.

SECOND ROUND	QUARTER-FINALS	SEMI-FINALS	FINAL	ALL-COMERS' CHAMPION
J. F. Talmage (USA)	Talmage			
J. H. Crispe	w.o.	W. Baddeley		
W. Baddeley	W. Baddeley	6-2 6-1 6-3		
D. Fuller	6-3 6-2 6-0		W. Baddeley	
Chaytor	Chaytor		w.o.	
Cazalet	6-4 2-6 6-1 6-4	Chaytor		
Meers	Meers	1-6 6-1 6-8 8-6 6-4		W. Baddeley
Ball-Greene	6-3 6-0 6-2			6-0 6-1 6-0
Mahony	Lewis			
Lewis	6-1 6-1 6-3	Lewis		
Simond	Simond	6-2 6-3 6-2		
M. F. Goodbody	w.o.		Lewis	
H. S. Barlow	Barlow		2-6 7-5 6-3 1-6 7-5	
R. B. Scott	9-11 6-4 6-2 6-4	H. Baddeley		
H. Baddeley	H. Baddeley	0-6 6-3 4-6 6-1 6-1		
A. Palmer	6-3 6-1 6-3			

Challenge round: J. Pim (Holder) d. W. Baddeley (Challenger) 10-8 6-2 8-6.

LADIES' SINGLES

FIRST ROUND	QUARTER-FINALS	SEMI-FINALS	FINAL	ALL-COMERS' CHAMPION
Mrs G. W. Hillyard	bye	Hillyard		
Miss Chatterton Clarke	bye	6-1 6-0		
Miss Bryan	Bryan		Hillyard	
Miss Snook	6-2 6-4	Bryan	6-1 6-1	
Mrs Draffen	Draffen	6-3 7-5		
Miss Morgan	6-2 6-2			Hillyard
L. Austin	bye			6-1 6-1
C. Cooper	Cooper	Austin		
Mrs Horncastle	6-2 6-3	6-1 3-6 6-3	Austin	
S. Robins	bye	Robins	6-1 6-1	
Mrs Edwardes	bye	6-2 6-1		

Challenge round: Mrs G. W. Hillyard (Challenger) d. Miss L. Dod (Holder) w.o.

OTHER FINALS

GENTLEMEN'S DOUBLES: Final – H./W. Baddeley d. F. S. Barlow/C. H. Martin 5-7 7-5 4-6 6-3 8-6. **Challenge round** – H./W. Baddeley d. J. Pim/F. O. Stoker w.o.

GENTLEMEN'S SINGLES

1895

FIRST ROUND: H. A. Nisbet d. E. W. Lewis 6-2 6-3 3-0 ret'd; E. G. Meers d. M. F. Goodbody w.o.

SECOND ROUND	QUARTER-FINALS	SEMI-FINALS	FINAL	ALL-COMERS' CHAMPION
W. Baddeley	W. Baddeley			
A. W. Gore	w.o.	W. Baddeley		
H. S. Barlow	Barlow	6-1 6-4 8-6		
C. H. L. Cazalet	5-7 6-4 6-4 6-2		W. Baddeley	
H. Baddeley	H. Baddeley		w.o.	
H. A. B. Chapman	6-4 6-3 6-0	H. Baddeley		
R. F. Doherty	Doherty	6-4 6-2 6-4		W. Baddeley
N. A. Nisbet	4-6 6-4 6-4 6-4			4-6 2-6 8-6 6-2 6-3
E. G. Meers	E. G. Meers			
A. W. Hallward	7-5 6-3 6-1	E. G. Meers		
J. M. Flavelle	Flavelle	6-1 6-2 6-1		
A. W. Meers	w.o.		Eaves	
W. V. Eaves	Eaves		6-3 7-9 9-11 6-4 6-1	
W. C. Taylor	w.o.	Eaves		
G. M. Simond	Simond	6-4 6-2 7-5		
E. J. Avory	w.o.			

Challenge round: W. Baddeley (Challenger) d. J. Pim (Holder) w.o.

LADIES' SINGLES

FIRST ROUND	QUARTER-FINALS	SEMI-FINALS	FINAL	ALL-COMERS' CHAMPION
Mrs W. H. Pickering	bye	Pickering		
M. Shackle	bye	3-6 6-3 6-3	Jackson	
H. Jackson	Jackson		6-4 3-6 8-6	
J. M. Corder	7-5 6-3	Jackson		
Miss Bernard	bye	6-0 6-2		Cooper
C. Cooper	bye	Cooper		7-5 8-6
L. Patterson	bye	6-3 9-11 6-2	Cooper	
Mrs Draffen	bye	Draffen	6-2 6-8 6-1	
Mrs Horncastle	bye	6-2 6-0		

Challenge round: Miss C. Cooper (Challenger) d. Mrs G. W. Hillyard (Holder) w.o.

OTHER FINALS

GENTLEMEN'S DOUBLES: Final — W. V. Eaves/E. W. Lewis d. W. G. Bailey/C. F. Simond 6-4 6-4 6-3. **Challenge round** — H./W. Baddeley d. Eaves/Lewis 8-6 5-7 6-4 6-3.

GENTLEMEN'S SINGLES

1896

FIRST ROUND: W. Castle d. F. W. Payne 6-2 6-1 3-6 6-2; H. S. Mahony d. R. F. Doherty 6-3 5-7 6-1 3-6 6-2; F. L. Riseley d. J. M. Flavelle 6-2 6-1 7-5; A. H. Riseley d. F. J. Plaskitt 6-2 6-8 6-1 6-1; H. A. Nisbet d. W. G. Bailey 6-1 6-3 6-2; H. A. B. Chapman d. C. P. Dixon 6-3 6-3 6-2; G. M. Simond d. G. Greville 6-4 3-6 2-6 7-5 6-3; C. G. Allen d. R. B. Scott 3-6 6-0 6-4 1-6 6-4; C. H. L. Cazalet d. H. L. Doherty 6-4 4-6 6-4 7-5; A. E. Foote (USA) d. D. M. Hawes 6-4 6-3 6-3; W. V. Eaves d. A. W. Gore 5-7 6-4 6-2 6-1; E. R. Allen d. A. Kirby 6-1 6-3 7-5; H. Baddeley d. H. Marley 6-2 6-2 4-6 6-2; A. E. Crawley d. M. F. Goodbody w.o.; W. A. Larned (USA) d. A. W. Hallward 6-1 7-5 6-4.

SECOND ROUND	QUARTER-FINALS	SEMI-FINALS	FINAL	ALL-COMERS' CHAMPION
Castle	Mahony			
Mahony	6-1 11-9 6-4	Mahony		
F. L. Riseley	F. L. Riseley	7-5 5-7 7-5 6-3		
A. H. Riseley	8-8 ret'd		Mahony	
Nisbet	Nisbet		6-4 2-6 8-6 4-6 6-3	
Chapman	3-6 3-6 6-1 6-3 6-4	Nisbet		
Simond	Simond	2-6 6-4 6-4 1-6 6-3		Mahony
Allen	6-1 6-2 6-1			6-2 6-2 11-9
Cazalet	Cazalet			
Foote	6-4 9-7 6-3	Eaves		
Eaves	Eaves	7-5 6-3 6-0		
Allen	6-0 6-2 6-1		Eaves	
H. Baddeley	H. Baddeley		6-4 6-3 6-4	
Crawley	6-2 6-2 6-2	H. Baddeley		
Larned	Larned	3-6 3-6 6-4 6-4 6-3		
R. B. Hough	6-4 6-2 6-3			

Challenge round: H. S. Mahony (Challenger) d. W. Baddeley (Holder) 6-2 6-8 5-7 8-6 6-3.

LADIES' SINGLES

FIRST ROUND	SEMI-FINALS	FINAL	ALL-COMERS' CHAMPION
Mrs Horncastle	bye		
L. Austin	Austin	Austin	
L. Patterson	6-4 6-1	w.o.	
Mrs W. H. Pickering	Pickering		Pickering
Miss 'Hungerford'	6-1 6-0	Pickering	4-6 6-3 6-3
Mrs Draffen	bye	6-3 7-5	

Challenge round: Miss C. Cooper (Holder) d. Mrs W. H. Pickering (Challenger) 6-2 6-3.

OTHER FINALS

GENTLEMEN'S DOUBLES: Final — R. F. Doherty/H. A. Nisbet d. C. G./E. R. Allen 3-6 7-5 6-4 6-1. **Challenge round** — H./W. Baddeley d. Doherty/Nisbet 1-6 3-6 6-4 6-2 6-1.
GENTLEMEN'S SINGLES PLATE: Final — A. W. Gore d. H. L. Doherty 1-6 6-2 7-5.

GENTLEMEN'S SINGLES

1897

FIRST ROUND: C. H. Cazalet d. S. C. Atkey 6-2 6-2 10-8; S. H. Smith d. A. W. Hallward 7-5 8-6 6-3; G. W. Hillyard d. W. Wallace w.o.; A. E. M. Taylor d. G. E. Evered 6-1 6-3 3-6 3-6 6-4; G. Greville d. A. B. Norris 6-2 6-2 6-1; A. W. Gore d. 'J. J. Stone' 7-5 6-2 6-3; W. V. Eaves d. R. Sheldon 6-3 6-3 6-2; A. H. Riseley d. F. J. Plaskitt 6-0 6-2 6-4; H. A. Nisbet d. R. B. Hough 6-3 6-2 7-9 6-3; W. Baddeley d. D. M. Hawes w.o.; A. E. Crawley d. A. Palmer w.o.; H. L. Doherty d. H. Baddeley 6-4 6-4 8-6; R. F. Doherty d. G. M. Simond 11-9 1-6 6-4 6-3; G. Milne d. F. S. M. Bates 6-4 6-3 7-5; F. L. Riseley d. M. F. Goodbody w.o.

SECOND ROUND	QUARTER-FINALS	SEMI-FINALS	FINAL	ALL-COMERS' CHAMPION
Cazalet	Smith			
Smith	4-6 3-6 6-2 6-2 6-1	Smith		
Hillyard	Hillyard	3-6 6-4 6-2 6-4		
Taylor	6-2 6-2 6-1		Eaves	
Greville	Greville		6-2 5-7 1-6 6-2 6-1	
Gore	w.o.	Eaves		
Eaves	Eaves	6-1 6-2 8-10 6-0		R. F. Doherty
A. H. Riseley	8-10 6-3 6-1 6-4			6-3 7-5 2-0 ret'd
Nisbet	W. Baddeley			
W. Baddeley	6-2 6-2 7-5	W. Baddeley		
Crawley	H. L. Doherty	6-4 6-2 6-2		
H. L. Doherty	6-0 6-2 7-5		R. F. Doherty	
R. F. Doherty	R. F. Doherty		6-3 6-0 6-3	
Milne	6-2 6-1 9-7	R. F. Doherty		
F. L. Riseley	F. L. Riseley	w.o.		
M. J. G. Ritchie	6-3 6-2 6-1			

Challenge round: R. F. Doherty (Challenger) d. H. S. Mahony (Holder) 6-4 6-4 6-3.

LADIES' SINGLES

FIRST ROUND	SEMI-FINALS	FINAL	ALL-COMERS' CHAMPION
Mrs Horncastle	Horncastle		
E. M. Thynne	12-10 6-4	Hillyard	
Mrs G. W. Hillyard	Hillyard	w.o.	
L. Austin	6-0 6-1		Hillyard
R. Dyas	Dyas		6-2 7-5
E. J. Bromfield	6-0 6-3	Pickering	
Mrs W. H. Pickering	bye	6-4 4-6 6-1	

Challenge round: Mrs G. W. Hillyard (Challenger) d. Miss C. Cooper (Holder) 5-7 7-5 6-2.

OTHER FINALS

GENTLEMEN'S DOUBLES: Final — H. L./R. F. Doherty d. C. H. L. Cazalet/S. H. Smith 6-2 7-5 2-6 6-2. **Challenge round** — H./W. Baddeley d. H. L./R. F. Doherty 6-4 4-6 8-6 6-4.
GENTLEMEN'S SINGLES PLATE: Final — H. Baddeley d. A. E. Crawley 6-1 6-3 5-7 6-2.

GENTLEMEN'S SINGLES

1898

FIRST ROUND: A. C. Pearson d. J. H. Hechle 1-6 6-0 6-0 6-4; M. R. L. White d. A. B. J. Norris 7-5 1-6 6-0 6-0; 'E. Stanley' d. A. M. Mackay 7-5 6-2 6-4; N. A. Nisbet d. F. L. Plaskitt 7-5 6-4 8-6; A. W. Gore d. J. M. Boucher w.o.

SECOND ROUND: M. J. G. Ritchie d. H. S. Barlow 2-6 6-2 6-8 8-6 6-1; R. B. Hough d. J. Johnstone 7-5 6-0 7-5; C. Hobart (USA) d. G. E. Evered 9-7 6-1 6-3; F. W. Payn d. L. T. 'Ball' 3-6 6-4 6-4 3-6 6-4; H. Roper Barrett ('A. L. Gydear') d. G. A. Caridia 4-6 6-2 3-6 6-4 9-7; H. L. Doherty d. G. W. Hillyard 6-1 6-3 6-1; J. M. Flavelle d. Pearson 6-3 4-6 6-4 6-3; White d. 'Stanley' 3-6 6-4 6-3 4-6 6-2; Gore d. Nisbet 9-7 0-6 6-1 6-4; G. Greville d. W. C. Grant (USA) 6-1 6-0 6-1; S. H. Smith d. W. V. Eaves w.o.; D. M. Hawes d. G. R. Mewburn 6-3 4-6 12-10 7-5; H. S. Mahony d. S. Baddeley 6-3 6-3 6-2; P. G. Pearson d. R. F. Leslie 6-1 6-2 6-1; O. Milne d. H. A. B. Chapman w.o.; G. M. Simond d. J. P. Paret (USA) 9-7 3-6 6-3 12-10.

THIRD ROUND	QUARTER-FINALS	SEMI-FINALS	FINAL	ALL-COMERS' CHAMPION
Ritchie	Ritchie			
Hough	6-1 6-4 7-5	Hobart		
Hobart	Hobart	6-2 3-6 6-3 6-2		
Payn	6-1 4-6 6-3 6-3		H. L. Doherty	
Barrett	H. L. Doherty		6-1 6-4 6-3	
H. L. Doherty	6-1 6-4 6-1	H. L. Doherty		
Flavelle	Flavelle	6-2 6-3 3-6 6-0		H. L. Doherty
White	7-9 6-4 6-1 6-4			6-1 6-2 4-6 2-6 14-12
Gore	Gore			
Greville	4-6 6-4 8-6 10-8	Gore		
Smith	Smith	4-6 6-0 4-6 6-3 7-5		
Hawes	6-1 6-2 6-2		Mahony	
Mahony	Mahony		6-2 3-6 4-6 6-2 6-4	
Pearson	6-4 6-3 6-8 6-1	Mahony		
Milne	Simond	6-2 6-4 6-4		
Simond	6-2 6-4 6-1			

Challenge round: R. F. Doherty (Holder) d. H. L. Doherty (Challenger) 6-3 6-3 2-6 5-7 6-1.

continued

LADIES' SINGLES

FIRST ROUND: E. R. Morgan d. E. J. Bromfield 8-6 4-6 8-6; L. Austin d. Mrs Kirby 7-5 6-2.

SECOND ROUND	QUARTER-FINALS	SEMI-FINALS	FINAL	ALL-COMERS' CHAMPION
C. Morgan	Morgan			
B. Tulloch	6-4 6-2	Legh		
P. Legh	Legh	6-0 6-1		
Mrs Horncastle	6-2 6-2		Martin	
L. Martin	Martin		w.o.	
Miss 'Ireland'	w.o.	Martin		
E. R. Morgan	E. R. Morgan	6-2 6-0		Cooper
Miss Hitchins	6-1 6-1			6-4 6-4
Austin	Austin			
E. M. Thynne	6-1 6-0	Austin		
R. Dyas	Dyas	4-6 6-3 6-4		
Mrs W. H. Pickering	8-6 2-6 6-4		Cooper	
B. Steedman	Steedman		6-4 6-1	
H. I. Harper	6-1 6-2	Cooper		
C. Cooper	Cooper	4-6 6-3 6-4		
H. Smythe	6-2 6-4			

Challenge round: Miss C. Cooper (Challenger) d. Mrs G. W. Hillyard (Holder) w.o.

OTHER FINALS

GENTLEMEN'S DOUBLES: Final — C. Hobart (USA)/H. A. Nisbet d. G. W. Hillyard/S. H. Smith 2-6 6-2 6-2 6-3.
Challenge round — H. L./R. F. Doherty d. Hobart/Nisbet 6-4 6-4 6-2.
GENTLEMEN'S SINGLES PLATE: Final — G. W. Hillyard d. A. C. Pearson 6-3 8-6.

GENTLEMEN'S SINGLES

FIRST ROUND: G. M. Simond d. C. H. L. Cazalet w.o.; H. S. Mahony d. W. V. Doherty w.o.; D. M. Hawes d. F. W. Payn 7-5 6-0 5-7 6-3; H. A. Nisbet d. J. Johnstone 6-0 6-3 6-1; E. R. Allen d. H. N. Wright 6-4 7-5 7-5.

SECOND ROUND: P. G. Pearson d. F. J. Plaskitt 6-1 6-0 6-3; M. J. G. Ritchie d. W. V. Eaves 6-4 3-6 6-4 4-6 6-4; A. W. Gore d. A. N. Dudley 8-6 6-2 6-3; G. A. Caridia d. S. V. R. Drapes 6-2 6-4 6-1; G. Greville d. G. W. Hillyard w.o.; M. R. L. White d. A. J. McNair 5-7 7-5 6-4 6-1; Simond d. A. M. Mackay 6-1 6-0 6-1; Mahony d. Hawes 6-3 7-5 6-2; Nisbet d. E. R. Allen 6-3 6-4 6-0; M. F. Day d. A. C. Pearson 1-6 2-6 6-3 6-4 6-1; J. M. Flavelle d. R. J. McNair w.o.; S. H. Smith d. E. Reynolds 6-1 6-1 6-1; J. H. Crispe d. B. Wood-Hill 6-3 6-3 6-1; C. Hobart (USA) d. C. P. Dixon 6-3 6-1 4-6 6-2; R. B. Hough d. O. Milne 6-4 8-10 6-3 10-8; H. Roper Barrett d. C. G. Allen 6-0 6-0 6-0.

THIRD ROUND	QUARTER-FINALS	SEMI-FINALS	FINAL	ALL-COMERS' CHAMPION
Pearson	Pearson			
Ritchie	6-3 6-2 6-4	Gore		
Gore	Gore	6-3 6-2 9-7		
Caridia	6-2 6-1 6-4		Gore	
Greville	Greville		6-3 4-6 3-6 7-5 6-1	
White	6-0 6-3 6-2	Mahony		
Simond	Mahony	6-3 9-7 2-6 10-8		Gore
Mahony	6-2 4-6 8-6 6-2			3-6 6-1 6-2 6-4
Nisbet	Nisbet			
Day	6-4 6-3 6-3	Smith		
Flavelle	Smith	6-3 7-5 6-4		
Smith	4-6 4-6 6-1 7-5 6-2		Smith	
Crispe	Hobart		2-6 11-9 4-6 8-6 8-6	
Hobart	6-3 2-6 9-7 6-3	Roper Barrett		
Hough	Roper Barrett	8-6 7-5 6-4		
Roper Barrett	6-1 6-3 6-3			

Challenge round: R. F. Doherty (Holder) d. A. W. Gore (Challenger) 1-6 4-6 6-3 6-3 6-3.

LADIES' SINGLES

FIRST ROUND: Mrs R. J. Winch d. Miss C. Parsons-Smith 6-0 6-0.

SECOND ROUND	QUARTER-FINALS	SEMI-FINALS	FINAL	ALL-COMERS' CHAMPION
M. E. Robb	Robb			
H. M. Garfit	6-3 2-6 6-4	Durlacher		
Mrs N. Durlacher	Durlacher	6-1 5-7 6-3		
Mrs Tanner	6-0 6-0		Durlacher	
Mrs Kirby	Kirby		6-4 6-2	
Mrs W. H. Pickering	6-4 3-6 6-3	Steedman		
B. Steedman	Steedman	4-6 6-2 6-2		
Winch	6-2 7-9 8-6			Hillyard
Mrs G. W. Hillyard	Hillyard			7-5 6-8 6-1
H. Smythe	6-3 6-0	Hillyard		
L. Austin	Austin	8-6 6-4		
U. Templeman	6-4 6-0		Hillyard	
B. Tulloch	Tulloch		6-3 3-6 6-2	
Miss 'Ireland'	7-5 6-2	Tulloch		
E. J. Bromfield	Bromfield	3-6 6-2 6-1		
E. M. Thynne	6-5 5-7 6-2			

Challenge round: Mrs G. W. Hillyard (Challenger) d. Miss C. Cooper (Holder) 6-2 6-3.

OTHER FINALS

GENTLEMEN'S DOUBLES: Final — C. Hobart (USA)/H. A. Nisbet d. A. W. Gore/H. Roper Barrett 6-4 6-1 8-6.
Challenge round — H. L./R. F. Doherty d. Hobart/Nisbet 7-5 6-0 6-2.
LADIES' DOUBLES (Non-Championship event): **Final** — Mrs G. W. Hillyard/B. Steedman d. Mrs N. Durlacher/Mrs W. H. Pickering 6-4 2-6 6-4.
GENTLEMEN'S SINGLES PLATE: Final — W. V. Eaves d. G. W. Hillyard w.o.

GENTLEMEN'S SINGLES

1900

FIRST ROUND: N. H. Davidson d. 'S. Herbert' 6-3 6-8 6-3 4-0 ret'd; S. H. Smith d. E. D. Black 6-4 6-8 3-6 6-1 9-7.

SECOND ROUND: R. B. Hough d. F. N. Warden 5-7 6-3 3-6 7-5 6-4; F. J. Plaskitt d. O. Milne 6-3 6-4 6-3; C. H. L. Cazalet d. H. S. Mahony 7-5 6-2 6-8 8-10 6-4; A. W. Gore d. D. M. Hawes 6-1 6-2 6-3; A. C. Pearson d. F. L. Riseley w.o.; H. L. Doherty d. E. S. Wills 6-0 6-4 6-1; S. Baddeley d. 'A. Raleigh' 6-0 6-1 6-3; R. J. McNair d. Davidson 6-2 6-2 5-7 6-0; Smith d. G. Greville 6-1 6-3 5-7 3-6 6-1; G. L. Orme d. J. M. Flavelle 2-6 6-1 4-6 6-4 6-1; H. Roper Barrett ('J. Verne') d. G. M. Simond 6-3 6-1 6-2; C. P. Dixon d. B. Hillyard 3-6 6-4 6-2 6-1; G. E. Evered d. H. Chipp 6-2 7-5 6-0; H. A. Nisbet d. B. Wood-Hill w.o.; F. W. Payn d. H. Plaskitt 6-4 6-4 6-4; M. J. G. Ritchie d. L. H. Escombe 6-3 6-4 6-4.

THIRD ROUND	QUARTER-FINALS	SEMI-FINALS	FINAL	ALL-COMERS' CHAMPION
Hough	Plaskitt			
Plaskitt	3-6 6-3 6-4 6-4	Gore		
Cazalet	Gore	6-3 6-2 6-0		
Gore	6-1 5-7 6-2 6-2		Gore	
Pearson	H. L. Doherty		4-6 8-6 8-6 6-1	
H. L. Doherty	6-3 6-1 6-3	H. L. Doherty		
Baddeley	McNair	6-1 6-2 6-4		
McNair	6-1 6-1 4-6 3-6 6-3			Smith
Smith	Smith			6-4 4-6 6-2 6-1
Roper Barrett	6-1 6-2 6-2	Smith		
Dixon	Roper Barrett	6-1 4-6 7-5 6-2		
Evered	6-4 6-0 6-3		Smith	
Nisbet	Nisbet		6-0 6-1 6-1	
Payn	6-3 6-0 6-3	Nisbet		
Ritchie	Payn	6-2 6-8 6-4 3-6 6-2		
	6-3 2-6 2-6 6-4 7-5			

Challenge round: R. F. Doherty (Holder) d. S. H. Smith (Challenger) 6-8 6-3 6-1 6-2.

LADIES' SINGLES

FIRST ROUND	QUARTER-FINALS	SEMI-FINALS	FINAL	ALL-COMERS' CHAMPION
M. E. Robb	Robb			
Mrs W. H. Pickering	6-3 6-4	Cooper		
C. Cooper	Cooper	6-3 9-7		
Mrs Horncastle	7-5 6-2		Cooper	
B. Tulloch	Tulloch		6-1 6-2	
H. Smythe	6-3 2-6 6-1	Greville		
Mrs G. Greville	Greville	7-5 6-0		
E. J. Bromfield	5-7 6-4 6-3			Cooper
M. Jones (USA)	Jones			8-6 5-7 6-1
U. Templeman	6-3 6-4	Evered		
Mrs G. E. Evered	Evered	7-5 6-2		
T. Lowther	6-3 9-7		Martin	
D. K. Douglass	Douglass		6-0 6-2	
M. W. Fisher	w.o.	Martin		
L. Martin	Martin	6-4 6-3		
Miss 'Ireland'	6-0 6-2			

Challenge round: Mrs G. W. Hillyard (Holder) d. Miss C. Cooper (Challenger) 4-6 6-4 6-4.

OTHER FINALS

GENTLEMEN'S DOUBLES: Final — H. A. Nisbet/H. Roper Barrett d. F. L. Riseley/S. H. Smith 6-2 2-6 6-8 8-6 6-2. **Challenge round** — H. L./R. F. Doherty d. Nisbet/Roper Barrett 9-7 7-5 4-6 3-6 6-3. **LADIES' DOUBLES** (Non-Championship event): **Final** — Mrs W. H. Pickering/M. E. Robb d. Mrs G. W. Hillyard/L. Martin 2-6 6-4 6-4.

MIXED DOUBLES (Non-Championship event): **Final** — H. A. Nisbet/Mrs W. H. Pickering d. H. Roper Barrett/E. J. Bromfield 8-6 6-3. **GENTLEMEN'S SINGLES PLATE: Final** — G. Greville d. E. D. Black 6-2 4-6 6-3.

GENTLEMEN'S SINGLES

1901

FIRST ROUND: D. M. Hawes d. J. H. Cripps w.o.; F. W. Payn d. Capt. Barton 6-2 6-2 6-4; P. G. Pearson d. A. W. Andrews 8-6 6-2 6-3; H. Roper Barrett ('D'Agger') d. H. M. Sweetman 6-2 6-2 6-3.

SECOND ROUND: H. S. Mahony d. A. C. Pearson 8-6 6-4 5-7 6-1; C. H. L. Cazalet d. 'A. Raleigh' 6-2 6-2 6-4; R. J. McNair d. F. W. Brambeer 6-3 7-5 6-4; G. E. Evered d. R. B. Hough 8-6 6-3 4-6 7-5; G. M. Simond d. A. B. J. Norris 2-6 6-4 6-4 6-2 6-3; C. L. Nedwill d. W. Crawley 10-8 6-1 6-0 6-6 6-4; C. P. Dixon d. H. Wilson 6-3 6-3 4-6 8-6; Payn d. Hawes 6-3 6-3 6-4; Roper Barrett d. Pearson 6-4 6-4 6-3; M. J. G. Ritchie d. H. W. Davies 3-6 6-2 6-8 6-3 6-3; W. V. Eaves d. B. Wood-Hill 5-7 7-5 7-5 6-1; S. H. Smith d. S. H. Adams 6-2 6-2 6-0; H. L. Doherty d. E. S. Wills 6-1 6-0 6-2; G. W. Hillyard d. G. Greville 6-8 7-5 6-2 6-1; A. W. Gore d. E. Yatman 6-1 3-6 6-4 6-3; H. A. Parker (NZ) d. B. Hillyard 2-6 4-6 6-1 6-2 11-9.

THIRD ROUND	QUARTER-FINALS	SEMI-FINALS	FINAL	ALL-COMERS' CHAMPION
Mahony	Mahony			
Cazalet	8-6 2-6 6-1 6-0	Mahony		
McNair	McNair	6-4 6-3 3-6 6-3		
Evered	4-6 6-1 6-1 6-3		Dixon	
Simond	Simond		6-3 6-4 11-9	
Nedwill	6-1 6-3 6-3	Dixon		
Dixon	Dixon	6-4 7-5 1-6 6-3		
Payn	6-3 6-4 6-4			Gore
Roper Barrett	Roper Barrett			6-4 6-0 6-3
Ritchie	6-2 8-6 6-4	Roper Barrett		
Eaves	Smith	7-5 6-4 8-6		
Smith	6-0 6-2 6-3		Gore	
H. L. Doherty	Hillyard		8-6 6-1 7-5	
Hillyard	0-6 4-6 6-1 6-4 6-3	Gore		
Gore	Gore	6-1 2-6 4-6 8-6 6-2		
Parker	6-1 6-4 3-6 6-4			

Challenge round: A. W. Gore (Challenger) d. R. F. Doherty (Holder) 4-6 7-5 6-4 6-4.

continued

LADIES' SINGLES

FIRST ROUND: Mrs G. Greville d. C. H. E. Meyer 6-1 6-0; L. Martin d. Mrs M. Chatterton w.o.; Mrs Norton Barry d. C. B. Bell 6-3 6-0; E. Monckton d. A. Bell 8-6 7-5; A. M. Morton d. E. G. Johnston 6-2 6-2; Mrs W. H. Pickering d. E. M. Stawell-Brown 6-8 6-2 6-1; T. Lowther d. Miss Francis w.o.; Mrs. G. E. Evered d. Mrs Horncastle w.o.; M. E. Robb d. Mrs R. Winch 7-9 6-4 6-4; D. K. Douglass d. E. J. Bromfield 7-9 6-1 6-3; Mrs A. Sterry d. Mrs N. Durlacher 6-2 6-4; Miss Hughes D'Eath d. B. Tulloch 6-3 6-2; C. Parsons Smith d. C. Webber w.o.; Miss Adams d. A. Martin 6-0 6-0.

SECOND ROUND	QUARTER-FINALS	SEMI-FINALS	FINAL	ALL-COMERS' CHAMPION
Greville	Greville			
Mrs Popp	6-0 6-1	Martin		
Martin	Martin	4-6 6-3 6-4		
Barry	6-4 6-1		Martin	
Morton	Morton		7-5 6-2	
Monckton	6-1 6-2	Morton		
Pickering	Pickering	6-3 7-5		
Lowther	7-5 6-1			Sterry
Robb	Robb			6-3 6-4
Evered	6-3 4-6 6-3	Sterry		
Sterry	Sterry	6-0 6-0		
Douglass	6-4 6-2		Sterry	
Hughes D'Eath	Hughes D'Eath		6-1 6-1	
Parsons Smith	w.o.	Adams		
Adams	Adams	6-1 6-0		
D. Slater	w.o.			

Challenge round: Mrs A. Sterry (Challenger) d. Mrs G. W. Hillyard (Holder) 6-2 6-2.

OTHER FINALS

GENTLEMEN'S DOUBLES: Final — D. F. Davis (USA)/H. Ward (USA) d. H. Roper Barrett/G. M. Simond 7-5 6-4 6-4. **Challenge round** — H. L./R. F. Doherty d. Davis/Ward 4-6 6-2 6-3 9-7.
LADIES' DOUBLES (Non-Championship event): **Final** — Mrs G. W. Hillyard/Mrs A. Sterry d. Miss Adams/Mrs W. H. Pickering 6-3 6-0.

MIXED DOUBLES (Non-Championship event): **Final** — H. L. Doherty/Mrs A. Sterry d. W. V. Eaves/Mrs N. Durlacher 6-2 6-3.
GENTLEMEN'S SINGLES PLATE: Final — P. G. Pearson d. H. W. Davies 6-1 4-6 6-2 7-5.

GENTLEMEN'S SINGLES

FIRST ROUND: S. H. Smith d. R. M. Sweetman 6-3 6-0 7-5; H. M. Sweetman d. J. P. Ward 6-1 6-3 6-2; H. Roper Barrett d. G. C. Ball Greene 11-9 6-2 6-2; G. M. Simond d. E. R. Clarke 6-2 6-1 3-6 6-1; A. C. Pearson d. A. Walker 6-4 6-0 6-2; G. Greville d. B. Hillyard 6-3 6-1 4-6 6-3; W. C. Crawley d. 'A. Raleigh' 6-0 6-2 6-0; R. B. Hough d. R. F. Doherty w.o.; G. A. Caridia d. H. Whale 6-1 6-2 6-2; F. L. Riseley d. F. W. Brambeer 6-0 6-1 6-2.

SECOND ROUND: M. J. G. Ritchie d. R. J. McNair 6-3 6-0 6-1; G. W. Hillyard d. J. E. Mellor 6-3 6-0 6-1; E. Yatman d. A. W. Andrews w.o.; A. E. Crawley d. A. J. B. Norris 6-4 6-1 6-2; P. de Borman d. E. S. Salmon 6-3 7-5 6-2; Smith d. H. Pollard 6-0 6-4 6-3; Roper Barrett d. H. M. Sweetman 8-6 6-2 6-1; Simond d. Pearson 6-1 8-6 7-5; Greville d. W. C. Crawley 6-1 6-2 7-9 4-6 6-0; Caridia d. Hough 6-4 7-5 6-4; Riseley d. H. Fleming 6-0 6-0 6-2; H. L. Doherty d. L. R. Hausburg w.o.; F. W. Payn d. C. R. D. Pritchett w.o.; W. Lemaire (B) d. L. H. Escombe 6-2 6-1 6-1; H. S. Mahony d. S. H. Adams 6-3 6-1 6-4; H. Wilson-Fox d. E. S. Wills 6-0 6-2 3-6 4-6 8-6.

THIRD ROUND	QUARTER-FINALS	SEMI-FINALS	FINAL	ALL-COMERS' CHAMPION
Ritchie	Ritchie			
Hillyard	5-7 6-4 ret'd	Ritchie		
Yatman	Crawley	6-2 6-1 2-6 6-3		
Crawley	7-5 6-3 6-2		Ritchie	
de Borman	Smith		6-4 4-6 6-4 6-4	
Smith	7-5 6-4 8-6	Smith		
Roper Barrett	Roper Barrett	6-3 6-4 6-3		
Simond	6-2 6-1 9-7			H. L. Doherty
Greville	Greville			8-6 6-3 7-5
Caridia	6-4 6-3 6-0	H. L. Doherty		
Riseley	H. L. Doherty	6-1 4-6 6-3 7-5		
H. L. Doherty	6-4 6-1 6-3		H. L. Doherty	
Payn	Payn		4-6 4-6 8-6 2-0 ret'd	
Lemaire	6-2 6-0 6-3	Mahony		
Mahony	Mahony	6-2 6-2 6-4		
Wilson-Fox	6-4 6-0 6-4			

Challenge round: H. L. Doherty (Challenger) d. A. W. Gore (Holder) 6-4 6-3 3-6 6-0.

LADIES' SINGLES

FIRST ROUND: D. K. Douglass d. Mrs Horncastle w.o.; Mrs N. Durlacher d. B. Tulloch w.o.; A. N. G. Greene d. E. M. Stawell-Brown 6-1 6-3; C. H. E. Meyer d. E. G. Johnson w.o.; W. A. Longhurst d. E. Burrill w.o.; A. M. Morton d. E. W. Thomson 6-4 6-4.

SECOND ROUND	QUARTER-FINALS	SEMI-FINALS	FINAL	ALL-COMERS' CHAMPION
H. Lane	Lane			
Mrs G. W. Hillyard	6-2 6-8 9-7	Robb		
M. E. Robb	Robb	6-1 7-5		
E. J. Bromfield	6-3 4-6 6-4		Robb	
Douglass	Douglass		6-4 2-6 9-7	
E. Godfrey	w.o.	Douglass		
Durlacher	Durlacher	6-2 10-8		
Greene	6-3 6-2			Robb
Longhurst	Longhurst			7-5 6-4
Meyer	6-1 6-2	Morton		
Morton	Morton	6-3 6-4		
Mrs L. R. Hausberg	w.o.		Morton	
Mrs G. Greville	Greville		7-5 6-4	
C. B. Bell	w.o.	Greville		
B. Steedman	Steedman	6-1 3-6 6-2		
C. M. Wilson	6-3 8-10 6-4			

continued

Challenge round: Miss M. E. Robb (Challenger) d. Mrs A. Sterry (Holder) 7-5 6-1 (after being level 4-6 13-11 in a match abandoned owing to rain).

OTHER FINALS

GENTLEMEN'S DOUBLES: Final — F. L. Riseley/S. H. Smith d. C. H. L. Cazalet/G. W. Hillyard 7-5 2-6 6-8 6-3 6-1. **Challenge round** — Riseley/Smith d. H. L./R. F. Doherty 4-6 8-6 6-3 4-6 11-9.
LADIES' DOUBLES (Non-Championship event): **Final** — A. M. Morton/Mrs A. Sterry d. H. Lane/C. M. Wilson w.o.

MIXED DOUBLES (Non-Championship event): **Final** — H. L. Doherty/Mrs A. Sterry d. C. H. L. Cazalet/M. E. Robb 6-4 6-3.
GENTLEMEN'S SINGLES PLATE: Final — B. Hillyard d. C. R. D. Pritchett 8-6 6-1.

GENTLEMEN'S SINGLES

FIRST ROUND: F. W. Donisthorpe d. J. E. Mellor 6-3 6-3 6-2; S. H. Smith d. R. Williams 6-1 6-3 6-1; A. W. Gore d. F. J. Barker 6-1 6-2 6-3; H. S. Mahony d. G. C. Ball Greene 6-2 6-4 6-3; S. H. Adams d. W. C. Crawley w.o.; G. A. Caridia d. H. R. Fussell 7-5 6-1 6-2; C. Hobart (USA) d. E. S. Franklin 5-7 6-2 6-2 6-0; F. W. Payn d. E. Yatman 6-3 6-2 6-4; R. J. McNair d. F. J. Plaskitt 6-3 6-2 3-6 6-3; C. F. Simond d. P. Pinckney 6-3 5-7 6-4 6-3.

SECOND ROUND: B. Hillyard d. L. H. Escombe w.o.; D. M. Hawes d. J. M. Flavelle 7-5 3-6 6-3 6-0; A. B. J. Norris d. T. F. Vreede (NTH) 6-0 6-4 6-0; F. L. Riseley d. A. B. van Groenon (NTH) 6-0 6-2 6-0; H. Pollard d. L. L. Whiteway 6-1 6-1 6-4; Donisthorpe d. H. Wilson-Fox 6-4 2-3 6-4 6-3; Smith d. Gore 6-4 6-3 6-3; Mahony d. Adams 4-6 4-6 6-1; Caridia d. Hobart 8-6 6-2 6-1; Payn d. McNair 6-3 10-8 6-2; A. D. Prebble d. Simond 6-2 1-6 6-3 9-7; E. S. Salmon d. W. F. Martin 6-4 6-3 6-4; G. Greville d. E. R. Clarke 6-2 6-0 6-2; M. J. G. Ritchie d. C. E. Finlason 6-1 6-2 6-0; G. L. Orme d. R. B. Hough 6-1 6-1 9-7; E. S. Wills d. A. H. Greening 6-2 6-4 3-6 6-2.

THIRD ROUND	QUARTER-FINALS	SEMI-FINALS	FINAL	ALL-COMERS' CHAMPION
Hillyard	Hillyard			
Hawes	6-4 3-6 6-3 7-5	Riseley		
Norris	Riseley	6-1 6-4 6-4		
Riseley	6-2 6-0 6-3		Riseley	
Pollard	Pollard		7-5 6-3 7-9 1-6 9-7	
Donisthorpe	8-6 6-3 4-6 7-9 7-5	Smith		
Smith	Smith	6-2 6-3 6-1		
Mahony	6-3 6-4 7-5			Riseley
Caridia	Caridia			1-6 6-3 8-6 13-11
Payn	2-6 11-9 3-6 7-5 6-2	Caridia		
Prebble	Salmon	6-3 6-4 6-2		
Salmon	3-6 6-3 6-2 6-3		Ritchie	
Greville	Ritchie		6-1 6-0 4-6 6-1	
Ritchie	7-5 12-14 6-3 6-2	Ritchie		
Orme	Wills	6-1 6-2 6-2		
Wills	7-5 1-6 6-2 6-4			

Challenge round: H. L. Doherty (Holder) d. F. L. Riseley (Challenger) 7-5 6-3 6-0.

LADIES' SINGLES

FIRST ROUND: E. Walter d. B. Steedman w.o.; A. M. Morton d. C. H. E. Meyer 6-1 6-3; H. Lane d. E. M. Stawell-Brown 6-2 8-6; Mrs G. M. Houselander d. M. Stoneham 6-1 6-1; V. M. Pinckney d. A. Bell ret'd; D. K. Douglass d. Mrs Riseley w.o.; C. M. Wilson d. Mrs G. Greville 1-6 6-2 6-2; L. Ripley d. Mrs M. Chatterton w.o.; E. L. Bosworth d. Mrs Horncastle 6-1 6-1; E. W. Thomson d. B. Tulloch 6-3 6-2; H. Smythe d. C. B. Bell w.o.; E. J. Bromfield d. E. A. Longhurst 6-3 6-3.

SECOND ROUND	QUARTER-FINALS	SEMI-FINALS	FINAL	ALL-COMERS' CHAMPION
T. Lowther	Lowther			
W. A. Longhurst	8-6 6-3	Lowther		
Morton	Morton	6-1 6-0		
Walter	6-2 6-2		Douglass	
Houselander	Houselander		6-4 6-2	
Lane	1-6 6-1 9-7	Douglass		
Douglass	Douglass	6-2 6-0		
Pinckney	w.o.			Douglass
Wilson	Wilson			4-6 6-4 6-2
Ripley	6-2 6-1	Thomson		
Thomson	Thomson	6-4 8-6		
Bosworth	6-4 6-1		Thomson	
Bromfield	Bromfield		6-3 6-1	
Smythe	6-0 6-2	Greene		
A. N. G. Greene	Greene	6-0 4-6 6-3		
Mrs Newton	6-1 6-2			

Challenge round: Miss D. K. Douglass (Challenger) d. Miss M. E. Robb (Holder) w.o.

OTHER FINALS

GENTLEMEN'S DOUBLES: Final — H. L./R. F. Doherty d. H. S. Mahony/M. J. G. Ritchie 8-6 6-2 6-2. **Challenge round** — H. L./R. F. Doherty d. F. L. Riseley/S. H. Smith 6-4 6-4 6-4.
LADIES' DOUBLES (Non-Championship event): **Final** — D. K. Douglass/Mrs W. H. Pickering d. H. Lane/C. M. Wilson 6-2 6-1.

MIXED DOUBLES (Non-Championship event): **Final** — S. H. Smith/E. W. Thomson d. C. Hobart (USA)/E. J. Bromfield 6-2 6-3.
GENTLEMEN'S SINGLES PLATE: Final — A. W. Gore d. C. Hobart 7-5 6-3.

GENTLEMEN'S SINGLES

1904

FIRST ROUND: H. N. Marrett d. S. T. Watts 6-4 6-2 6-1; E. S. Franklin d. J. B. Dufall 6-3 2-6 6-0 ret'd; D. M. Hawes d. C. H. L. Cazalet w.o.; G. Greville d. G. L. Orme 6-1 6-0 6-0; F. L. Riseley d. H. R. Fussell 6-3 6-2 6-3; A. F. Wilding d. A. D. Prebble 2-6 6-2 6-4 6-2; H. S. Mahony d. F. S. Warburg 6-4 6-2 6-3; F. W. Goldberg d. R. F. Doherty w.o.; B. Hillyard d. A. W. Perceval 6-0 6-0 6-2; A. J. McNair d. E. R. Clarke 6-2 6-3 6-4; G. A. Caridia d. W. C. Crawley 1-6 12-10 6-0 6-2; E. W. Timmis d. F. H. Pearce w.o.; A. W. McGregor d. R. Kinzl (AU) w.o.; H. Pollard d. A. Herschell 6-1 6-2 3-0 ret'd; S. H. Smith d. C. R. Brown 6-3 4-6 6-4 6-1; S. H. Adams

d. A. B. J. Norris 6-4 6-3 6-2; A. E. Beamish d. F. N. Warden 6-4 4-6 6-2 6-3; W. Lemaire (B) d. C. F. Simond 6-1 6-1 6-3; W. V. Eaves d. H. I. Bury 7-5 6-2 6-3; J. M. Flavelle d. W. H. Jackson 6-1 6-1 7-5; M. J. G. Ritchie d. F. J. G. Plaskitt 6-2 6-2 6-4; A. K. Cronin d. S. R. Arthur 6-4 6-1 6-2; R. J. McNair d. S. Baddeley 7-5 3-6 6-8 6-3 6-4; C. E. Finlason d. F. M. Pearson 4-6 6-2 6-4 6-8 6-2; G. M. Simond d. E. Gwynne-Evans 7-5 6-4 6-3; R. B. Hough d. C. von Wessely (AU) w.o.; E. S. Wills d. H. Wilson-Fox 6-1 7-5 8-10 6-0; F. W. Payn d. T. M. Mavrogordato 6-2 6-2 6-2; P. de Borman (B) d. L. H. Escombe 7-5 6-2 6-3.

SECOND ROUND: A. W. Gore d. Merrett 6-3 6-2 6-3; Hawes d. Franklin 6-4 9-7 6-2; Riseley d. Greville 2-6 6-0 4-6 6-2 6-3; Mahony d. Wilding 4-6 6-4 11-9 6-1; Goldberg d. B. Hillyard w.o.; Caridia d. A. J. McNair 7-5 6-2 6-4; McGregor d. Timmis 4-6 6-4 4-6 4-6 6-1; Smith d. Pollard 6-2 6-1 6-1; Adams d. Sampson 6-4 6-4 6-4; Lemaire d.

Beamish 6-0 2-6 6-0 6-3; Eaves d. Flavelle 6-1 2-6 6-4 7-5; Ritchie d. Cronin 6-1 6-4 6-3; R. J. McNair d. Finlason 12-10 6-4 10-12 9-7; G. M. Simond d. Hough 2-9 7-6 6-2; Payn d. Wills 6-3 6-3 6-3; de Borman d. G. C. Ball Greene 6-4 6-2 3-6 6-4.

THIRD ROUND	QUARTER-FINALS	SEMI-FINALS	FINAL	ALL-COMERS' CHAMPION
Gore	Gore			
Hawes	6-2 6-4 6-0	Riseley		
Riseley	Riseley	3-6 6-1 3-6 6-4 6-3		
Mahony	6-1 6-4 6-2		Riseley	
Goldberg	Caridia		7-5 5-7 8-6 5-7 ret'd	
Caridia	7-5 6-0 6-2	Smith		
McGregor	Smith	7-5 8-6 6-3		
Smith	6-0 6-1 6-0			Riseley
Adams	Lemaire			6-0 6-1 6-2
Lemaire	6-1 6-3 6-2			
Eaves	Ritchie	Ritchie		
Ritchie	3-6 6-1 2-6 6-2 7-5	6-1 8-6 6-4		
R. J. McNair	R. J. McNair		Ritchie	
Simond	9-7 1-0 ret'd		6-3 6-1 6-1	
Payn	de Borman	de Borman		
de Borman	1-6 6-0 6-0 6-2	6-0 6-4 6-4		

Challenge round: H. L. Doherty (Holder) d. F. L. Riseley (Challenger) 6-1 7-5 8-6.

LADIES' SINGLES

FIRST ROUND: H. Lane d. C. B. Bell 6-1 6-0; E. G. Johnson d. M. Taplin 6-2 5-7 7-5; Mrs R. J. Winch d. E. M. Stawell-Brown 4-6 6-3 7-5; Mrs M. Chatterton d. C. H. E. Meyer w.o.; M. B. Squire d. M. Banks 6-0 6-2; D. P.

Boothby d. M. E. Brown 6-3 6-2; W. A. Longhurst d. L. Flemmich 6-1 6-0; A. Farrington d. Mrs Albury 6-2 6-3; Mrs G. W. Hillyard d. K. Kentish 6-0 6-2.

SECOND ROUND: Mrs A. Sterry d. L. H. Ransome ret'd; B. Tulloch d. Mrs Macaulay 2-6 6-0 6-0; Mrs G. Greville d. E. J. Bromfield w.o.; Miss Masson (F) d. Miss Benton 6-2 6-3; V. M. Pinckney d. M. L. de Pfeffel 6-0 6-3; A. N. G. Greene d. Lane 4-6 7-5 6-1; Winch d. Johnson 6-1 6-0; Squire d. Chatterton w.o.; Longhurst d. Boothby 6-2 8-6;

Hillyard d. Farrington 6-0 6-1; E. W. Thomson d. L. Ripley 6-0 6-1; A. M. Morton d. Mrs Horncastle 6-1 6-0; C. M. Wilson d. Miss de Robiglio (F) 8-6 1-6 ret'd; A. Mooijaart d. Mrs L. R. Hausberg ret'd; E. L. Bosworth d. Mrs G. D. Driver ret'd; E. E. Sargeant d. A. G. Ransome 0-6 7-5 6-4.

THIRD ROUND	QUARTER-FINALS	SEMI-FINALS	FINAL	ALL-COMERS' CHAMPION
Sterry	Sterry			
Tulloch	6-2 6-2	Sterry		
Greville	Greville	8-6 9-7		
Masson	6-0 6-1		Sterry	
Greene	Greene		6-2 6-1	
Pinckney	6-2 3-6 6-3	Greene		
Winch	Winch	6-4 6-4		
Squire	6-3 6-3			Sterry
Longhurst	Longhurst			6-3 6-3
Hillyard	6-0 6-0	Morton		
Morton	Morton	6-1 6-4		
Thomson	8-6 2-6 8-6		Morton	
Wilson	Wilson		3-6 6-4 8-6	
Mooijaart	6-4 6-0	Wilson		
Bosworth	Bosworth	6-3 6-4		
Sargeant	7-5 6-2			

Challenge round: Miss D. K. Douglass (Holder) d. Mrs A. Sterry (Challenger) 6-0 6-3.

OTHER FINALS

GENTLEMEN'S DOUBLES: Final — F. L. Riseley/S. H. Smith d. G. A. Caridia/A. W. Gore 6-3 6-4 6-3. **Challenge round** — H. L./R. F. Doherty d. Riseley/Smith 6-3 6-4 6-3.
LADIES' DOUBLES (Non-Championship event): **Final** — W. A. Longhurst/E. W. Thomson d. D. K. Douglass/Mrs A. Sterry 6-4 3-6 7-5.

MIXED DOUBLES (Non-Championship event): **Final** — S. H. Smith/E. W. Thomson d. W. V. Eaves/Mrs R. J. Winch 7-5 12-10.
GENTLEMEN'S SINGLES PLATE: Final — G. Greville d. B. Hillyard 6-3 6-0.

GENTLEMEN'S SINGLES

1905

FIRST ROUND: L. H. Escombe d. E. M. Hall 6-4 6-3 6-1; H. Wilson-Fox d. G. O. Thomas 6-1 6-2 6-0; G. A. Caridia d. C. E. Finlason 8-6 7-5 6-2; N. E. Brookes (A) d. E. S. Salmon 6-0 6-2 6-3; H. J. W. Fosbery d. C. Gouldesborough 6-2 6-2 6-4; K. Powell d. R. F. Doherty w.o.; S. H. Smith d. H. Ward (USA) 6-4 6-3 8-6.

SECOND ROUND: F. Leaver d. F. Houget (B) 6-4 6-0 6-2; A. F. Wilding (NZ) d. A. W. Dunlop (A) 6-4 7-5 6-4; W. J. Clothier (USA) d. A. W. Perceval 6-1 6-2 6-3; R. B. Hough d. B. Nehru w.o.; A. W. Gore d. S. H. Adams 6-3 1-6 6-0 6-1; T. D. Stoward d. G. M. Thomas 6-3 6-2 6-1; E. G. Parton d. W. Lemaire (B) 4-6 6-4 6-4 5-7 6-1; B. C. Wright (USA) d. G. F. Simond 6-4 6-2 6-3; E. W. Timmis d. P. de Borman (B) w.o.; F. L. Riseley d. J. M. Flavelle 6-2 6-4 6-4; A. E. M. Taylor d. E. Gwynne Evans 9-7 6-3 6-3; N. G. Davidson d. Th. Hillerup (D) w.o.; C. H. L. Cazalet d. J. B. Ward 8-6 6-3 6-0; G. W. Hillyard d. G. M. Simond 6-4 9-7 6-2; Escombe d. Wilson-Fox 2-6 6-3 6-2 7-5; Brookes d. Caridia 6-2 6-1

6-0; Fosbery d. Powell 6-4 6-3 9-7; Smith d. W. V. Eaves 6-2 6-2 6-3; H. P. Gaskell d. J. B. Dufall w.o.; T. M. Mavrogordato d. F. H. Pearce 5-7 6-2 6-3 6-2; H. A. Parker (NZ) d. K. Doust (USA) 6-3 6-2 7-5; R. J. McNair d. W. P. Groser 6-2 6-2 6-2; G. L. Orme d. H. S. Mahony w.o.; W. A. Larned (USA) d. E. Larsen (D) 6-1 6-0 6-1; E. R. Clarke d. G. C. Ball Greene w.o.; E. Yatman d. F. C. Uhl 4-6 6-2 6-4 7-5; E. S. Wills d. W. Bostrom (SW) w.o.; A. K. Cronin d. F. J. Plaskitt 6-2 6-3 6-1; M. J. G. Ritchie d. B. Murphy (A) 6-2 6-2 6-1; C. Hartley d. W. J. Lancaster 6-3 6-3 8-6; H. Pollard d. H. A. Kitson (SA) 7-5 6-4 5-7 6-2; A. E. Beamish d. D. M. Hawes 6-3 6-3 6-2.

THIRD ROUND: Wilding d. Leaver 6-4 6-0 6-1; Clothier d. Hough 6-2 6-3 6-4; Gore d. Stoward 6-4 6-2 6-2; Wright d. Parton 6-2 6-4 6-3; Riseley d. Timmis 6-2 6-2 6-1; Taylor d. Davidson w.o.; Hillyard d. Cazalet 8-10 8-6 ret'd; Brookes d. Escombe 6-3 6-4 6-4; Smith d. Fosbery 6-3 6-2 6-3; Mavrogordato d. Gaskell 6-0 6-0 6-0; Parker d.

McNair 6-4 6-4 6-3; Larned d. Orme 6-3 6-3 6-3; Yatman d. Clarke 2-6 3-6 8-6 6-4 6-1; Cronin d. Wills 6-2 6-2 6-2; Ritchie d. Hartley 6-3 6-3 6-2; Beamish d. Pollard 6-0 6-3 7-5.

continued

FOURTH ROUND	QUARTER-FINALS	SEMI-FINALS	FINAL	ALL-COMERS' CHAMPION
Wilding	Wilding			
Clothier	5-7 1-6 8-6 7-5 10-8	Gore		
Gore	Gore	8-6 6-2 6-2		
Wright	6-2 7-9 6-3 6-2		Brookes	
Riseley	Riseley		6-3 9-7 6-2	
Taylor	6-1 6-0 6-2	Brookes		
Hillyard	Brookes	6-3 6-2 6-4		
Brookes	6-3 6-1 6-3			Brookes
Smith	Smith			1-6 6-4 6-1 1-6 7-5
Mavrogordato	6-2 6-0 6-2	Smith		
Parker	Larned	6-2 6-4 6-4		
Larned	6-4 1-6 6-4 5-7 6-3		Smith	
Yatman	Cronin		6-0 3-6 6-4 4-6 6-1	
Cronin	9-7 3-6 6-2 8-6	Ritchie		
Ritchie	Ritchie	6-0 6-2 6-0		
Beamish	6-1 8-6 6-2			

Challenge round: H. L. Doherty (Holder) d. N. E. Brookes (Challenger) 8-6 6-2 6-4.

LADIES' SINGLES

FIRST ROUND: D. Spencer d. Mrs Horncastle w.o.; M. G. Sutton (USA) d. N. Meyer 6-0 6-0; E. M. Stawell-Brown d. A. Farrington 6-3 6-1; M. Coles d. E. Flemmich 6-1 6-2; E. E. Sargeant d. A. G. Ransome 6-1 6-0; E. W. Thomson d. F. Meyer 7-5 6-4; Mrs P.M. Morton d. V. M. Pinckney w.o.; B. Tulloch d. K. Kentish w.o.; L. Ripley d. Mrs Albury 6-0 5-7 6-3; H. Lane d. E. Smith 9-7 6-8 6-4; Mrs G. W. Hillyard d. M. Banks 6-0 6-0; L. H. Paterson d. M. Taplin 6-1 6-3; Mrs G. M. Houselander d. M. E. Brown 6-1 6-3.

SECOND ROUND: H. I. Harper d. Mrs Armstrong w.o.; Mrs O'Neill d. C. B. Bell w.o.; A. N. G. Greene d. Mrs G. Greville w.o.; A. M. Morton d. Mrs Macaulay 6-2 6-1; W. A. Longhurst d. Spencer 6-2 6-0; Sutton d. Stawell-Brown 6-3 6-1; Coles d. Sargeant 7-5 6-3; Thomson d. Morton 6-2 6-0; Tulloch d. Ripley 7-5 6-3; Hillyard d. Lane 6-3 6-2; Paterson d. Houselander 4-6 6-1 12-10; D. P. Boothby d. L. Flemmich 6-2 6-4; C. H. E. Meyer d. Mrs L. R. Hausberg w.o.; B. M. Holder d. E. G. Johnson 6-3 6-1; M. B. Squire d. D. Taplin 6-1 6-1; C. M. Wilson d. A. Mooijaart 6-2 6-0.

THIRD ROUND	QUARTER-FINALS	SEMI-FINALS	FINAL	ALL-COMERS' CHAMPION
Harper	Harper			
O'Neill	6-2 6-2	Morton		
Morton	Morton	6-2 6-4		
Greene	7-5 6-4		Sutton	
Sutton	Sutton		6-4 6-0	
Longhurst	6-3 6-1	Sutton		
Thomson	Thomson	8-6 6-1		
Coles	6-2 6-0			Sutton
Hillyard	Hillyard			6-3 8-6
Tulloch	6-0 6-8 7-5	Hillyard		
Boothby	Boothby	6-3 6-2		
Paterson	3-6 6-3 6-3		Wilson	
Holder	Holder		7-5 9-11 6-2	
C. H. E. Meyer	8-6 2-6 6-4	Wilson		
Wilson	Wilson	6-2 6-0		
Squire	w.o.			

Challenge round: Miss M. G. Sutton (Challenger) d. Miss D. K. Douglass (Holder) 6-3 6-4.

OTHER FINALS

GENTLEMEN'S DOUBLES: Final — F. L. Riseley/S. H. Smith d. N. E. Brookes (A)/A. W. Dunlop (A) 6-2 1-6 6-2 6-3.
Challenge round — H. L./R. F. Doherty d. Riseley/Smith 6-2 6-4 6-8 6-3.
LADIES' DOUBLES (Non-Championship event): **Final** — W. A. Longhurst/E. W. Thomson d. A. M. Morton/M. G. Sutton (USA) 6-3 6-3.

MIXED DOUBLES (Non-Championship event): **Final** — A. W. Gore/C. M. Wilson d. A. F. Wilding (NZ)/E. W. Thomson 8-6 6-4.
GENTLEMEN'S SINGLES PLATE: Final — W. V. Eaves d. B. Murphy 6-3 6-2.

GENTLEMEN'S SINGLES

FIRST ROUND: T. M. Mavrogordato d. L. Kulenkampff (G) w.o.; K. Ingram d. W. V. Eaves w.o.; C. Hartley d. E. E. White 7-5 6-2 3-6 6-1; R. D. Little (USA) d. A. R. Sawyer 6-1 6-2 6-1; P. T. G. Pipon d. D. H. Rutherglen 4-6 6-3 7-5 4-6 9-7.

SECOND ROUND: P. Hicks d. L. Powell 3-6 7-5 4-6 9-7 6-1; A. E. Beamish d. W. P. Groser 6-2 6-3 6-4; R. B. Hough d. R. F. Kalberer (G) w.o.; A. F. Wilding (NZ) d. H. J. W. Fosbery 6-1 6-0 6-1; A. L. Bentley d. R. J. McNair 7-5 6-1 6-4; M. J. G. Ritchie d. A. E. M. Taylor 6-1 6-4 6-0; C. Zenger d. G. A. Caridia w.o.; A. D. Prebble d. A. H. Lowe 6-2 6-4 6-4; E. W. Timmis d. E. R. Clarke 7-5 1-6 6-3 6-2; L. H. Escombe d. G. L. Orme 6-2 6-2 6-4; A. W. Gore d. J. B. Ward 6-1 6-2 6-1; G. C. Ball Greene d. G. A. Thomas w.o.; F. W. Goldberg d. W. E. Lane 6-1 6-4 9-7; F. G. Lowe d. C. Gouldesborough 6-0 6-2 6-3; A. E. Crawley d. Mavrogordato 4-6 6-4 6-3 6-3; Hartley d. Ingram 6-4 6-2 2-6 4-6 6-4; Little d. Pipon 6-1 6-4 7-5; S. F. Card d. D. R. Larcombe w.o.; J. K. Frost d. E. Warnant w.o.; T. D. Stoward d. E. M. Hall 6-0 6-2 6-0; K. Collins (USA) d. E. R. Patterson 6-1 6-2; K. Powell d. C. F. Simond 4-6 8-6 6-3 6-1; F. L. Riseley d. J. S. Talbot 6-0 6-1 6-1; H. Schomburgk (G) d. G. W. Hillyard w.o.; J. M. Flavelle d. H. Comyn 6-0 6-1 6-3; G. M. Simond d. N. G. Davidson 6-3 6-1 6-3; S. H. Smith d. D. M. Hawes 6-2 6-1 6-2; T. E. Haydon d. H. Pollard w.o.; S. H. Adams d. E. Gwynne Evans 3-6 6-4 6-3 3-6 6-4; C. H. L. Cazalet d. W. J. Lancaster 6-4 6-2 6-3; E. S. Wills d. F. H. Pearce 6-2 6-3 6-0; E. L. Bristow d. E. S. Franklin 7-5 6-3 3-0 ret'd.

THIRD ROUND: Beamish d. Hicks 6-3 6-4 7-5; Wilding d. Hough 6-0 6-3 6-2; Ritchie d. Bentley 6-0 6-1 6-2; Prebble d. Zenger 6-0 6-1 6-1; Escombe d. Timmis 6-1 9-7 6-2; Gore d. Ball Greene 6-4 7-5 6-3; Goldberg d. F. G. Lowe 6-4 6-1 6-2; Crawley d. Hartley 6-2 6-4 6-0; Little d. Card w.o.; Stoward d. Frost 6-2 6-3 6-1; K. Powell d. Collins 6-4 3-6 6-4 4-6 6-2; Riseley d. Schomburgk 6-1 6-2 6-0; Flavelle d. G. M. Simond 6-2 6-4 7-5; Smith d. Haydon 6-1 6-1 6-2; Cazalet d. Adams 6-4 7-5 6-4; Bristow d. Wills 4-6 3-6 12-10 ret'd.

continued

FOURTH ROUND	QUARTER-FINALS	SEMI-FINALS	FINAL	ALL-COMERS' CHAMPION
Beamish	Wilding			
Wilding	6-1 6-3 6-4	Wilding		
Ritchie	Ritchie	6-4 6-1 4-6 3-6 6-2		
Prebble	6-2 6-1 6-3		Gore	
Escombe	Gore		9-7 6-1 8-6	
Gore	8-6 6-4 1-6 6-3	Gore		
Goldberg	Crawley	6-0 6-1 8-6		
Crawley	7-5 6-1 6-0			Riseley
Little	Little			6-3 6-3 6-4
Stoward	6-0 8-6 6-4			
Powell	Riseley	Riseley		
Riseley	6-1 6-2 6-2	6-3 6-1 6-4		
Flavelle	Smith		Riseley	
Smith	6-0 6-1 6-4		8-6 2-6 6-2 6-4	
Cazalet	Cazalet	Smith		
Bristow	6-2 6-3 3-6 4-6 6-2	6-2 4-6 7-5 ret'd		

Challenge round: H. L. Doherty (Holder) d. F. L. Riseley (Challenger) 6-4 4-6 6-2 6-3.

LADIES' SINGLES

FIRST ROUND: Mrs Armstrong d. A. Andrews w.o.; B. Tulloch d. Mrs D. Snowden 6-3 6-3; E. L. Bosworth d. S. Benton 6-1 6-2; I. Huleatt d. E. M. Mayne w.o.; F. Meyer d. B. Rowlandson w.o.; Mrs G. W. Hillyard d. A. Mooijaart 6-0 6-0; E. G. Johnson d. H. I. Harper 6-4 6-4; Mrs E. B. Hawker d. C. B. Bell 6-4 6-1; E. E. Sargeant d. B. Holder w.o.; V. M. Pinckney d. E. J. Bromfield 6-0 3-6 7-5; H. Lane d. W. M. Slocock 6-1 6-1; M. Coles d. Mrs Houselander 6-2 6-4; A. M. Morton d. M. Bloxsome 6-1 6-1; Mrs E. G. Parton d. Mrs C. Whyte 6-1 6-2; Mrs A. Sterry d. D. P. Boothby 8-6 6-2; Mrs P. N. Morton d. K. Kentish w.o.

SECOND ROUND: W. A. Longhurst d. R. Elliott 6-2 6-3; A. N. G. Greene d. M. Perceval w.o.; C. H. E. Meyer d. M. E. Brown 6-1 6-1; D. K. Douglass d. E. W. Thomson 6-2 6-1; Tulloch d. Armstrong w.o.; Bosworth d. Huleatt 6-2 4-6 7-5; Hillyard d. F. Meyer 6-0 6-0; Johnson d. Hawker 6-1 6-4; Pinckney d. Sargeant 6-1 6-4; Lane d. Coles 6-3 6-2; Miss Morton d. Parton 6-0 6-3; Sterry d. Mrs Morton 6-0 6-3; Mrs C. Bagenal d. L. Smith w.o.; T. Lowther d. G. M. Carver 6-0 6-2; Mrs G. Greville d. Mrs R. J. Winch 6-2 6-2; G. S. Eastlake Smith d. C. Cassel w.o.

THIRD ROUND	QUARTER-FINALS	SEMI-FINALS	FINAL	ALL-COMERS' CHAMPION
Longhurst	Longhurst			
Greene	7-5 6-4	Douglass		
Douglass	Douglass	6-4 6-3		
C. H. E. Meyer	6-3 6-1		Douglass	
Tulloch	Tulloch		6-2 6-2	
Bosworth	6-0 6-3	Tulloch		
Hillyard	Hillyard	6-3 6-1		
Johnson	6-3 6-4			Douglass
Pinckney	Pinckney			6-2 6-2
Lane	7-5 6-1			
Sterry	Sterry	Sterry		
Morton	6-0 6-3	6-4 6-2		
Lowther	Lowther		Sterry	
Bagenal	6-0 6-0		4-6 8-6 6-4	
Eastlake Smith	Eastlake Smith	Lowther		
Greville	6-2 6-3	6-3 6-3		

Challenge round: Miss D. K. Douglass (Challenger) d. Miss M. G. Sutton (USA) (Holder) 6-3 9-7.

OTHER FINALS

GENTLEMEN'S DOUBLES: Final – F. L. Riseley/S. H. Smith d. C. H. L. Cazalet/G. M. Simond 6-2 6-2 5-7 6-4. **Challenge round** – Riseley/Smith d. H. L./R. F. Doherty 6-8 6-4 5-7 6-3 6-3.
LADIES' DOUBLES (Non-Championship event): **Final** – Mrs G. W. Hillyard/M. G. Sutton (USA) d. A. M. Morton/Mrs A. Sterry 6-4 6-3.

MIXED DOUBLES (Non-Championship event): **Final** – A. F. Wilding (NZ)/D. K. Douglass d. A. W. Gore/E. W. Thomson 4-6 6-2 6-3.
GENTLEMEN'S SINGLES PLATE: Final – G. W. Hillyard d. T. M. Mavrogordato 6-2 6-4.

GENTLEMEN'S SINGLES

FIRST ROUND: R. H. Hotham d. E. R. Clarke 6-2 7-5 5-7 6-4; L. H. Escombe d. W. P. Haviland 6-1 8-6 9-7; D. P. Fitton d. H. Comyn 6-1 6-2 6-0; E. S. Wills d. C. Hartley w.o.; A. L. Bentley d. E. E. White 6-0 6-1 6-3; T. D. Stoward d. E. G. Parton 4-6 6-3 6-4 6-4; C. H. G. Mackintosh d. H. P. Gaskell 6-0 6-8 4-6 6-3 6-3; W. V. Eaves d. H. J. W. Fosbery 6-0 6-2 6-3; X. Casdagli d. E. W. Timmis 8-6 6-3 6-1 6-3; W. S. Andrews d. H. B. Routledge 6-4 6-3 4-6 6-2; F. G. Lowe d. A. E. Crawley w.o.; J. C. S. Rendall d. C. Wyllie 2-6 6-2 6-1 1-6 6-1; J. Powell d. R. C. Punnett w.o.; K. Behr (USA) d. T. M. Mavrogordato 6-2 6-8 6-4 6-4; H. Wilson Fox d. C. F. Simond 6-4 6-3 6-0; A. F. Wilding (NZ) d. B. C. Wright (USA) 6-2 8-6 7-5; N. E. Brookes (A) d. J. E. Boyd 6-0 6-1 6-1; A. H. Lowe d. P. Corlett w.o.; P. J. G. Pipon d. A. Palmer w.o.; H. Pollard d. R. Boucher 6-4 6-2 6-2; A. E. M. Taylor d. N. D. Malcolm 6-3 6-2 6-2.

SECOND ROUND: S. N. Doust (A) d. C. D. Beater 1-6 6-2 6-3 6-3; J. H. Winston d. C. H. Ridding w.o.; S. J. Watts d. D. M. Hawes w.o.; A. W. Gore d. W. E. Lane 6-1 6-3 6-1; R. J. McNair d. R. Gamble w.o.; J. B. Ward d. G. A. Thomas 6-2 6-3 3-0 ret'd; A. R. Sawyer d. H. Behr (USA) 6-0 6-2 6-2; P. Hicks d. J. A. Randall 6-0 6-2 8-6; F. H. Pearce d. E. S. Franklin 6-0 6-2 8-6; F. Chesterton d. A. D. Prebble w.o.; R. B. Powell (C) d. Hotham 8-6 6-3 6-2; Escombe d. Fitton 7-5 6-2 8-6; Bentley d. Wills 6-0 6-3 6-1; Stoward d. Mackintosh 6-0 6-3 6-1; Eaves d. Casdagli 6-4 6-2 6-3; F. G. Lowe d. Andrews 6-3 6-1 6-4; Rendall d. J. Powell 1-6 2-6 6-1; K. Behr (USA) d. Wilson Fox 6-2 6-2 6-4; Brookes d. Wilding 4-6 6-2 6-3 2-6 6-3; A. H. Lowe d. Pipon 6-3 6-3 6-4; Pollard d. Taylor 10-8 6-0 3-6 6-4; D. P. Rhodes (USA) d. A. G. Plante 6-2 6-4; K. Powell d. E. G. Levien 6-2 6-2 6-2; S. H. Adams d. J. B. Dufall w.o.; K. J. Ingram d. N. Durlacher 4-6 6-3 3-6 6-2 4-2 ret'd; F. W. Goldberg d. G. R. Bennett 6-1 6-1 6-0; M. J. G. Ritchie d. C. von Wessely (AU) 6-2 6-0 6-2; R. Kinzl (AU) d. C. O. Tuckey 4-6 6-4 4-6 6-2 6-4; E. P. Corlett d. T. 'Jones' w.o.; E. M. Hall d. A. K. Cronin 6-3 6-1 2-6 4-6 6-1; W. C. Crawley d. G. W. Pratt 6-3 6-1 6-2; O. Kreuzer (G) d. P. M. Davson 6-3 6-4 7-5.

THIRD ROUND: Doust d. Winston w.o.; Gore d. Watts 6-4 6-1 6-0; Ward d. McNair 6-2 5-7 6-2 6-3; Sawyer d. Hicks 6-2 6-1 6-3; Pearce d. Chesterton 6-1 6-2 6-4; Escombe d. R. B. Powell 6-4 4-6 6-4 6-3; Bentley d. Stoward 6-0 6-2 9-7; Eaves d. F. G. Lowe 8-6 6-3 6-0; Behr d. Rendall 6-2 9-7 4-6 6-3; Brookes d. A. H. Lowe 6-3 6-2 6-0; Rhodes d. Pollard 6-2 2-6 6-4 6-4; Adams d. Powell 4-6 6-2 7-5 7-5; Ingram d. Goldberg 2-6 1-6 6-2 6-4 6-4; Ritchie d. Kinzl 6-1 6-4 6-2; Corlett d. Hall 7-5 6-1 6-3; Kreuzer d. Crawley 6-3 6-4 6-4.

FOURTH ROUND	QUARTER-FINALS	SEMI-FINALS	FINAL	ALL-COMERS' CHAMPION
Doust	Gore			
Gore	6-1 10-8 6-4	Gore		
Ward	Sawyer	6-0 6-3 6-0		
Sawyer	5-7 7-5 6-8 6-4 6-3		Gore	
Pearce	Escombe		9-7 7-5 6-2	
Escombe	6-1 6-2 6-2	Eaves		
Bentley	Eaves	6-0 4-6 6-3 1-6 6-3		
Eaves	6-2 6-4 0-6 6-4			Brookes
Behr	Brookes			6-4 6-2 6-2
Brookes	6-4 6-2 2-6 3-6 6-1			
Rhodes	Adams	Brookes		
Adams	8-6 6-4 0-6 6-2	6-1 6-3 6-3		
Ingram	Ritchie		Brookes	
Ritchie	6-2 6-0 6-3		6-0 6-1 6-4	
Corlett	Kreuzer	Ritchie		
Kreuzer	6-1 6-4 6-1	6-4 6-1 6-2		

Challenge round: N. E. Brookes (Challenger) d. H. L. Doherty (Holder) w.o.

LADIES' SINGLES

FIRST ROUND: C. H. E. Meyer d. F. Walter 6-3 6-2; M. G. Sutton (USA) d. W. M. Slocock 6-2 6-1; T. Lowther d. D. P. Boothby 7-5 6-3; A. M. Morton d. W. Klima (AU) 6-0 6-2; M. Coles d. M. Taplin 6-2 6-2; C. M. Wilson d. Mrs Armstrong 6-1 6-1; E. E. Sargeant d. V. M. Pinckney w.o.; Mrs N. Durlacher d. Miss Adams 6-3 6-1; G. S. Eastlake Smith d. Mrs A. Sterry 6-3 9-7; Mrs O'Neill d. K. Klima (AU) 6-1 6-2.

SECOND ROUND: E. L. Bosworth d. M. Boadle 6-1 6-3; J. Coles d. M. Bloxsome 7-5 6-3; D. Johnston d. V. Summerhayes (C) 6-2 6-1; M. E. Brown d. H. Lane 5-7 8-6 8-6; A. G. Ransome d. D. Boadle 6-4 7-5; Meyer d. J. Tripp 6-2 6-2; Sutton d. Lowther 6-4 6-4; Morton d. M. Coles 6-1 6-2; Wilson d. Sargeant 6-1 6-0; Eastlake Smith d. Durlacher 1-6 6-1 6-4; A. N. G. Greene d. O'Neill 6-3 6-0; Mrs E. B. Hawker d. W. Boadle 6-1 6-3; Mrs E. G. Parton d. Miss Groombridge 6-2 6-2; Mrs G. W. Hillyard d. H. I. Harper 6-1 6-1; E. G. Johnson d. Mrs Speck 6-3 6-2; D. Taplin d. Mrs N. Quicke w.o.

THIRD ROUND	QUARTER-FINALS	SEMI-FINALS	FINAL	ALL-COMERS' CHAMPION
Bosworth	Bosworth			
J. Coles	6-3 6-3	Bosworth		
Brown	Brown	6-1 6-2		
Johnston	6-3 7-5		Sutton	
Meyer	Meyer		6-2 6-2	
Ransome	8-6 6-4	Sutton		
Sutton	Sutton	6-0 6-3		Sutton
Morton	6-0 6-2			6-4 6-2
Wilson	Wilson			
Eastlake Smith	6-1 6-4	Wilson		
Greene	Greene	6-2 9-7		
Hawker	6-1 6-2		Wilson	
Hillyard	Hillyard		6-3 6-2	
Parton	6-4 6-3	Hillyard		
Johnson	Johnson	6-2 6-3		
D. Taplin	6-3 6-0			

Challenge round: Miss M. G. Sutton (Challenger) d. Mrs R. Lambert Chambers (Holder) 6-1 6-4.

OTHER FINALS

GENTLEMEN'S DOUBLES: Final — N. E. Brookes (A)/A. F. Wilding (NZ) d. K. Behr (USA)/B. C. Wright (USA) 6-4 6-4 6-2. **Challenge round** — Brookes/Wilding d. F. L. Riseley/S. H. Smith w.o.
LADIES' DOUBLES (Non-Championship event): **Final** — Mrs R. Lambert Chambers/C. M. Wilson d. A. M. Morton/Mrs A. Sterry 7-9 6-3 6-2.

MIXED DOUBLES (Non-Championship event): **Final** — B. C. Wright/M. G. Sutton d. A. D. Prebble/D. P. Boothby 6-1 6-3.
GENTLEMEN'S SINGLES PLATE: Final — A. F. Wilding (NZ) d. C. von Wesseley (AU) 6-3 6-4.

GENTLEMEN'S SINGLES

FIRST ROUND: P. M. Davson d. E. von Bissing (G) 6-4 10-8 6-3; R. J. McNair d. E. S. Wills 6-3 6-1 6-1; F. N. Warden d. C. H. L. Cazalet 6-4 3-6 6-4 3-6 6-4; H. Pollard d. O. Froitzheim (G) w.o.; A. R. Sawyer d. F. H. Bryant 2-6 6-2 7-9 6-4 6-3; H. Wilson Fox d. Sirdar Nihal Singh (IN) 11-9 6-2 6-4.

SECOND ROUND: C. S. Gordon Smith d. P. Verde Delisle 6-1 6-4 6-3; W. C. Grant (USA) d. J. B. Ward 6-3 8-10 7-5 6-3; F. H. Pearce d. G. M. Simond w.o.; W. Lemaire (B) d. H. A. Kitson (SA) 6-1 2-6 6-2 9-7; F. W. Rahe (G) d. E. S. Franklin w.o.; G. C. Ball Greene d. R. H. Hotham 6-3 6-2 3-6 6-0; R. B. Powell (C) d. Count de Lastours 6-0 6-2 6-2; C. O. Tuckey d. A. E. M. Taylor 7-5 4-6 7-5 4-6 6-3; C. P. Dixon d. F. W. Goldberg 6-4 6-4 6-1; C. H. Ridding d. V. O. C. Miley 6-3 6-3 6-2; G. A. Caridia d. W. P. Haviland 6-1 6-2 6-2; J. F. Foulkes (C) d. A. W. Andrews 6-3 4-6 7-5 6-0; J. Richardson (SA) d. E. W. Timmis 6-4 6-3 1-6 2-6 6-4; A. W. Gore d. L. H. Escombe 6-2 6-1 7-5; K. Powell d. Davson 7-5 6-4 6-1; McNair d. Warden 6-3 6-3 7-5; Pollard d. Sawyer 6-0 7-5 6-1; W. C. Crawley d. Wilson Fox 6-0 6-2 6-0; A. D. Prebble d. P. Hicks 6-3 6-8 6-3 0-6 6-1; G. A. Thomas d. J. M. Flavelle 6-2 6-0 4-6 6-3; M. J. G. Ritchie d. V. R. Gauntlett (SA) 6-3 1-6 6-2 6-4; C. W. Blackwood Price d. S. J. Watts 6-1 3-6 7-5 6-4; T. D. Stoward d. D. W. Kitching 6-2 2-6 5-7 6-4 6-0; W. V. Eaves d. E. Yatman 6-1 6-1 6-3; T. M. Mavrogordato d. C. R. D. Pritchett 6-1 6-2 6-2; A. F. Wilding (NZ) d. O. Kreuzer (G) 3-6 6-0 6-2 7-5; E. Morris Hall d. D. Rhodes 6-3 6-3 5-7 6-3; F. M. Pearson d. A. E. Beamish 9-11 6-1 3-6 6-4 6-3; M. Germot (F) d. F. G. Lowe w.o.; A. H. Lowe d. W. G. Milburn 6-2 4-6 4-8 6-8 6-1; H. Roper Barrett d. W. S. Andrews 6-3 6-2 6-4; O. G. Toler d. 'A. N. Other' w.o.

THIRD ROUND: Grant d. Gordon Smith 4-6 6-3 7-5 6-2; Lemaire d. Pearce 6-3 6-3 6-2; Ball Greene d. Rahe 6-2 9-7 6-1; R. B. Powell d. Tuckey 6-1 6-2 6-2; Dixon d. Ridding 6-3 6-2 6-3; Caridia d. Foulkes 6-1 6-2 6-1; Gore d. Richardson 6-2 6-4 6-0; K. Powell d. McNair 6-1 7-5 6-4; Crawley d. Pollard 1-6 6-4 6-1 6-1; Thomas d. Prebble w.o.; Ritchie d. Blackwood Price 6-2 6-0 6-2; Eaves d. Stoward 6-1 6-2 8-6; Wilding d. Mavrogordato 6-0 6-3 6-3; Pearson d. Hall 6-1 6-4 6-2; A. H. Lowe d. Germot w.o.; Roper Barrett d. Toler 6-0 6-0 6-1.

FOURTH ROUND	QUARTER-FINALS	SEMI-FINALS	FINAL	ALL-COMERS' CHAMPION
Grant	Lemaire	Powell		
Lemaire	3-6 4-6 6-4 6-2 6-2	6-4 8-6 6-4		
Ball Greene	Powell		Gore	
Powell	6-3 8-6 ret'd		10-8 6-4 6-2	
Dixon	Dixon	Gore		
Caridia	1-6 6-3 6-3 6-3	10-8 6-3 3-6 6-0		
Gore	Gore			Gore
Powell	6-2 9-7 7-5			6-3 6-2 4-6 3-6 6-4
Crawley	Crawley	Ritchie		
Thomas	6-1 6-4 6-1	6-1 6-3 6-2		
Ritchie	Ritchie		Roper Barrett	
Eaves	7-5 6-3 3-1 ret'd		6-3 6-1 3-6 6-1	
Wilding	Wilding	Roper Barrett		
Pearson	6-1 6-1 6-1	2-6 6-4 6-4 6-0		
Lowe	Roper Barrett			
Roper Barrett	9-7 6-1 6-3			

Challenge round: A. W. Gore (Challenger) d. N. E. Brookes (A) (Holder) w.o.

LADIES' SINGLES

FIRST ROUND: Countess Schulenburg d. E. E. Sargeant 6-1 6-2; M. Coles d. A. N. G. Greene 6-8 6-3 6-4; V. M. Pinckney d. E. L. Bosworth 6-3 6-2; Mrs R. J. Winch d. Mrs C. Whyte 4-6 2-6; Mrs R. Lambert Chambers d. Mrs Paine 6-0 6-0; Mrs A. Sterry d. Mrs Perrett 6-2 6-0; Mrs J. F. Luard d. N. Stevens w.o.; C. B. Bell d. E. M. Boucher w.o.; A. M. Morton d. Mrs E. G. Parton 2-6 6-0 6-2; Mrs G. W. Hillyard d. E. G. Johnson 6-2 6-3; B. Tulloch d. H. I. Harper 6-4 6-0; Mrs O'Neill d. Mrs R. J. McNair 4-6 6-0 6-3; Mrs H. W. Lamplough d. A. G. Ransome 6-1 6-2; Mrs C. O. Tuckey d. Mrs Armstrong 6-1 6-2.

continued 1908

SECOND ROUND	QUARTER-FINALS	SEMI-FINALS	FINAL	ALL-COMERS' CHAMPION
D. P. Boothby	Boothby			
Schulenburg	5-7 6-3 6-1	Boothby		
Pinckney	Pinckney	6-1 6-4		
Coles	7-5 6-2		Sterry	
Lambert Chambers	Lambert Chambers		6-2 6-4	
Winch	6-3 6-3	Sterry		
Sterry	Sterry	6-3 7-5		
Luard	6-3 6-4			Sterry
Morton	Morton			6-4 6-4
Bell	w.o.	Morton		
Tulloch	Tulloch	7-5 6-1		
Hillyard	7-5 3-6 6-4		Morton	
Lamplough	Lamplough		6-3 6-4	
O'Neill	6-2 6-1	Lamplough		
Tuckey	Tuckey	6-3 6-1		
L. Flemmich	7-5 6-1			

Challenge round: Mrs A. Sterry (Challenger) d. Miss M. G. Sutton (USA) (Holder) w.o.

OTHER FINALS

GENTLEMEN'S DOUBLES: Final — M. J. G. Ritchie/A. F. Wilding (NZ) d. A. W. Gore/H. Roper Barrett 6-1 6-2 1-6 1-6 9-7. **Challenge round** — Ritchie/Wilding d. N. E. Brookes (A)/A. F. Wilding (NZ) w.o.
MIXED DOUBLES (Non-Championship event): **Final** — A. F. Wilding (NZ)/Mrs R. Lambert Chambers d. H. Roper Barrett/Mrs A. Sterry 6-4 6-3.

GENTLEMEN'S SINGLES PLATE: Final! — O. Kreuzer (G) d. V. R. Gauntlett (SA) 6-3 6-4.

GENTLEMEN'S SINGLES

1909

FIRST ROUND: T. R. Quill (NZ) d. R. H. Hotham 11-9 7-5 6-4; F. W. Goldberg d. L. E. Milburn 7-5 6-1 6-0; E. S. Knight (ARG) d. R. D. Nolan 6-4 1-6 6-2 6-1; S. N. Doust (A) d. E. von Bissing (G) 4-6 6-2 10-8 6-2; H. B. Knight (ARG) d. W. E. Lane w.o.; M. J. G. Ritchie d. H. B. Routledge 6-1 6-1 6-2; H. A. Parker d. H. S. Fellowes 6-1 6-3 6-3; H. Wilson Fox d. A. D. Prebble w.o.; P. M. Davson d. B. C. Hopson 7-5 6-3 5-7 6-2; C. Gordon Smith d. C. J. Adams 6-1 6-0; J. M. Flavelle d. R. Quennessen 4-6 6-2 11-9 5-7 6-0; W. J. B. Blew d. E. Gwynne Evans w.o.; C. H. Ridding d. C. F. Simon 6-1 7-5 6-4; E. S. Franklin d. E. S. Wills 4-6 4-6 6-4 8-6 6-3; G. Coulson d. Otto Blom 6-3 7-5 4-6 6-3; E. W. Timmis d. R. W. Dudley 6-0 7-5 5-7 6-3; S. G. Walker d. L. Bidlake 6-4 6-1 6-4; L. Trasenster (B) d. E. Yatman 6-3 7-5 6-3; L. H. Escombe d. D. M. Hawes 6-0 6-0 6-2; J. C. Parke d. A. Hendriks 6-2 6-0 6-2; H. Roper Barrett d. J. Powell 6-1 6-1 6-1.

SECOND ROUND: G. A. Thomas d. Sirdar Nihal Singh (IN) 4-6 6-2 6-2 7-5; G. Watson (B) d. K. J. Ingram 7-5 6-4 6-4; D. Rhodes d. R. B. Gurney 9-7 6-0 6-3; T. M. Mavrogordato d. 'T. Ennis' 6-0 6-4 6-0; C. O. Tuckey d. E. Morris Hall w.o.; D. W. Kitching d. L. O. S. Poidevin (A) 5-7 6-2 6-4 6-4; G. A. Caridia d. A. E. Crawley 6-0 6-4 8-6; W. V. Eaves d. C. H. L. Cazalet 6-4 6-3 ret'd; C. P. Dixon d. W. Lemaire (B) 6-2 6-2 4-6 6-4; J. B. Ward d. S. J. Watts 6-2 6-4 7-5; Quill d. R. Storms w.o.; Goldberg d. E. S. Knight 6-3 4-6 6-0 6-3; Doust d. H. B. Knight 6-1 6-4 3-6 3-6 6-4; Ritchie d. Parker 0-6 6-2 6-3 6-3; Davson d. Wilson Fox 6-2 6-2 7-5; Flavelle d. Gordon Smith 6-2 6-0 6-0; Ridding d. Blew 6-2 3-6 8-6 6-3; Franklin d. Coulson 3-6 3-6 6-3 6-4 6-1; Timmis d. Walker 6-1 6-1 3-6 8-6; Escombe d. Trasenster 3-6 3-6 6-0 6-4; Roper Barrett d. Parke 6-3 6-2 6-4; G. T. Watt d. G. P. Allen 6-2 6-4 8-6; A. W. Andrews d. B. Hillyard 6-3 6-3 6-3; D. P. Rhodes (USA) d. H. Pollard 4-6 6-1 6-3 6-2; A. H. Lowe d. A. E. M. Taylor 6-2 6-2 8-6; F. G. Lowe d. A. L. Prinsep 6-4 6-4 6-3; R. S. Barnes d. H. L. Brutton 6-4 6-3 6-3; A. E. Beamish d. A. C. Butler 6-2 ret'd; K. Powell d. R. B. Powell (C) 6-1 6-3 6-4; P. de Borman (B) d. G. E. Fowler 6-1 9-7 0-6 7-5; F. W. Rahe (G) d. 'T. Edmett' (H. T. Haydon) 4-6 6-1 6-4 8-6; J. Robinson d. R. J. McNair 9-7 3-6 6-0 8-6.

THIRD ROUND: Thomas d. Watson 7-5 6-3 3-6 6-3; Mavrogordato d. Rhodes 6-0 6-0 6-1; Kitching d. Tuckey 2-6 6-2 6-1 2-6 6-3; Caridia d. Eaves 4-6 6-3 6-1 6-2; Dixon d. Ward 9-7 6-1 6-8 6-0; Goldberg d. Quill 6-2 1-6 6-0 6-4; Ritchie d. Doust 7-5 6-3 7-5; Davson d. Flavelle 8-6 2-6 2-4 ret'd; Ridding d. Franklin 6-1 6-1 6-1; Escombe d. Timmis 6-4 6-2 6-3; Roper Barrett d. Watt 6-1 6-1 6-1; Rhodes d. Andrews 6-2 6-4 6-1; F. G. Lowe d. A. H. Lowe 3-6 6-2 6-3 6-2; Barnes d. Beamish 3-6 6-0 6-4 7-5; Powell d. de Borman 3-6 6-1 6-1 6-2; Rahe d. Robinson 6-1 6-2 6-2.

FOURTH ROUND	QUARTER-FINALS	SEMI-FINALS	FINAL	ALL-COMERS' CHAMPION
Thomas	Mavrogordato			
Mavrogordato	7-5 6-4 6-4	Mavrogordato		
Kitching	Caridia	6-1 9-7 2-6 4-6 6-4		
Caridia	6-1 6-3 6-2		Ritchie	
Dixon	Dixon		3-6 6-3 6-3 6-2	
Goldberg	11-9 6-3 6-3	Ritchie		
Ritchie	Ritchie	8-10 6-1 6-1 6-4		
Davson	6-2 6-2 2-0 ret'd			Ritchie
Ridding	Escombe			6-2 6-3 4-6 6-4
Escombe	6-3 4-6 3-6 6-4 6-3	Roper Barrett		
Roper Barrett	Roper Barrett	4-6 7-5 11-9 ret'd		
Rhodes	6-3 5-7 6-3 6-1		Roper Barrett	
F. G. Lowe	F. G. Lowe		6-4 6-2 6-8 7-5	
Beamish	0-6 6-3 6-4 1-6 6-3	Rahe		
Powell	Rahe	12-10 6-0 6-4		
Rahe	6-3 3-6 0-6 6-3 6-3			

Challenge round: A. W. Gore (Holder) d. M. J. G. Ritchie (Challenger) 6-8 1-6 6-2 6-2 6-2.

LADIES' SINGLES

FIRST ROUND: A. M. Morton d. J. Tripp 6-2 5-7 7-5; A. G. Ransome d. Mrs Armstrong w.o.; Mrs R. J. Winch d. M. Bloxsome 6-0 6-1; Miss Attfield d. L. Boustead 2-6 6-2 6-2; Mrs E. G. Parton d. L. Everts w.o.

SECOND ROUND: Mrs L. R. Hausberg d. W. A. Longhurst w.o.; Mrs O'Neill d. C. B. Bell w.o.; M. Brooksmith d. Mrs Woodhouse w.o.; Mrs H. Edgington d. Mrs G. W. Hillyard 6-3 6-4; E. G. Johnson d. M. Bjurstedt 6-1 7-5; E. J. Bromfield d. Mrs D. K. Hole 6-4 6-0; Morton d. Mrs Robinson 6-0 6-0; Winch d. Ransome 6-2 6-3; Parton d. Attfield 6-3 6-2; H. Lane d. Mrs R. J. McNair 5-7 6-1 7-5; H. M. Garfit d. W. Evens w.o.; B. Tulloch d. E. E. Sargeant 6-0 6-2; D. P. Boothby d. A. N. G. Greene 6-4 6-2; M. Coles d. M. Messom 1-6 6-1 6-3; H. Aitchison d. Mrs G. Greville 6-2 4-6 7-5; Mrs C. O. Tuckey d. V. E. R. Aitken 6-0 6-2.

THIRD ROUND	QUARTER-FINALS	SEMI-FINALS	FINAL	ALL-COMERS' CHAMPION
O'Neill	O'Neill			
Hausberg	6-3 6-4	Edgington		
Edgington	Edgington	7-5 6-4		
Brooksmith	w.o.		Morton	
Johnson	Johnson		6-0 6-2	
Bromfield	6-3 6-4	Morton		
Morton	Morton	6-0 6-3		
Winch	5-7 6-3 8-6			Boothby
Parton	Parton			6-4 4-6 8-6
Lane	6-3 6-3	Garfit		
Garfit	Garfit	6-3 6-4		
Tulloch	6-4 3-6 6-4		Boothby	
Boothby	Boothby		6-2 6-1	
Coles	6-2 6-4	Boothby		
Aitchison	Aitchison	6-4 3-0 ret'd		
Tuckey	4-6 6-1 13-11			

continued

Challenge round: Miss D. P. Boothby (Challenger) d. Mrs A. Sterry (Holder) w.o.

OTHER FINALS

GENTLEMEN'S DOUBLES: Final — A. W. Gore/H. Roper Barrett d. S. N. Doust (A)/H. A. Parker (A) 6-2 6-1 6-4.
Challenge round — Gore/Roper Barrett d. M. J. G. Ritchie/A. F. Wilding (NZ) w.o.

MIXED DOUBLES (Non-Championship event): **Final** — H. Roper Barrett/A. M. Morton d. A. D. Prebble/D. P. Boothby 6-2 7-5.
GENTLEMEN'S SINGLES PLATE: Final — R. B. Powell (C) d. H. A. Parker (NZ) 3-6 6-3 6-1.

GENTLEMEN'S SINGLES

FIRST ROUND: R. J. McNair d. D. Rhodes 6-2 6-0 6-1; R. R. W. Dudley d. A. L. Prinsep 6-2 6-3 2-6 3-6 6-1; M. J. G. Ritchie d. A. Sawyer 6-2 6-0 6-2; D. M. Hawes d. J. Arenholt 6-3 6-1 6-3; J. B. Ward d. W. P. Wise 8-6 6-0 7-5; A. F. Wilding (NZ) d. H. Roper Barrett 4-6 6-4 6-1 6-4; A. Hendriks d. H. Price 6-1 7-5 5-7 6-2; H. W. D. Gallwey d. W. St J. Pym w.o.; K. Powell d. J. Ganzoni 6-3 6-0 6-0; H. W. Sevenoaks d. S. J. Watts 6-3 6-2 1-6 8-6; O. Froitzheim (G) d. A. A. Fyzee (IN) 4-6 6-3 6-3 4-0 ret'd; A. H. Fyzee (IN) d. N. G. Deed 6-1 6-4 5-7 7-5; E. W. Timmis d. E. M. Hall 6-1 3-6 6-2 4-6 7-5; W. V. Eaves d. E. G. Parton 6-1 6-2 6-2; H. Pollard d. A. C. Holland 6-4 6-2 7-5; W. C. H. Tripp d.

C. F. Simond 6-3 11-9 7-5; O. Blom d. A. K. Cronin 6-3 9-11 4-6 6-2 6-2; G. H. Nettleton (USA) d. R. A. Pfleiderer (NTH) 6-2 6-3 6-2; C. P. Dixon d. V. O. C. Miley 7-5 6-4 4-6 6-3; R. D. Nolan d. W. D. Waller w.o.; P. M. Davson d. S. Hardy (USA) 6-3 0-6 6-3 6-0; A. H. Lowe d. A. C. Butler 6-2 6-2 6-2; S. N. Doust (A) d. A. H. Gobert (F) 6-2 6-2 6-1; E. O. Pockley d. H. Clement w.o.; F. Good d. G. P. Allen 6-2 6-2 6-1; 'T. Edmett' (H. T. Haydon) d. A. L. H. Mulcahy 6-2 6-1 6-1; C. S. Gordon Smith d. E. Scott 9-7 6-1 6-3; W. G. Milburn d. N. Malcolm 6-3 6-2 9-7.

SECOND ROUND: A. E. Beamish d. H. Wilson Fox 6-2 6-3 6-4; H. S. Fellows d. E. S. Franklin 6-4 4-6 9-7 6-3; F. M. Pearson d. W. J. Lancaster 6-2 6-0 6-3; R. S. Barnes d. J. Robinson 6-2 6-2 6-1; O. Frederiksen (D) d. C. J. Adams 6-3 6-2 6-0; T. M. Mavrogordato d. L. O. S. Poidevin (A) 4-6 6-4 ret'd; G. M. Simond d. A. F. Stephen w.o.; J. C. Parke d. J. M. Flavelle 6-1 6-1 6-1; L. E. Milburn d. L. Rovsing (D) 5-7 4-6 6-1 6-1; McNair d. Dudley 6-2 6-1 6-3; Ritchie d. Hawes 6-0 6-1 6-1; Wilding d. Ward 6-1 6-0 6-0; Hendriks d. Gallwey 6-1 2-6 6-2 6-4; K. Powell d. Sevenoaks 6-1 6-1 6-2; Froitzheim d. A. H. Fyzee 6-1 4-6 6-2 6-4; Eaves d. Timmis 2-6 6-0 6-0 6-2; Tripp d. Pollard 2-6 4-2 6-6 6-8 6-2

6-1; Blom d. Nettleton 6-3 6-2 2-6 7-5; Dixon d. Nolan 6-3 6-2 11-9; A. H. Lowe d. Davson 6-8 6-2 4-6 4-5 7-6-3; Doust d. Pockley 6-4 6-1 6-2; 'Edmett' d. Good 0-6 6-2 6-4 6-3; Gordon Smith d. W. G. Milburn 6-2 6-2 6-2; T. D. Stoward d. O. Kreuzer (G) w.o.; F. G. Lowe d. A. W. Andrews 6-3 6-3 6-1; B. C. Wright (USA) d. W. C. Crawley 6-1 7-5 3-6 6-2; G. D. Roberts d. J. Powell 8-6 6-3 6-2; Sirdar Nihal Singh (IN) d. A. C. Bostwick 6-1 6-0 6-2; G. A. Thomas d. P. Groes-Petersen (D) 6-1 6-4 6-4; A. D. Prebble d. A. Holmes (USA) 4-6 10-8 6-4; R. B. Powell (C) d. C. E. Fox w.o.; B. Hillyard d. B. J. Pfleiderer (NTH) 6-2 6-1 6-1.

THIRD ROUND: Beamish d. Fellows 6-4 4-6 6-2; Barnes d. Pearson 4-6 6-2 6-4 6-3; Mavrogordato d. Frederiksen 6-1 6-1 6-3; Parke d. Simond 6-2 6-3 ret'd; McNair d. Milburn 6-3 10-8 7-5; Wilding d. Ritchie 6-2 6-3 5-7 6-2; Powell d. Hendriks 6-1 6-4 6-2; Froitzheim d. Eaves 9-7 6-3 6-2; Blom d. Tripp 7-5 8-6 5-7 6-3; A. H. Lowe d. Dixon

6-3 6-3; Doust d. 'Edmett' 6-3 6-3 6-3; Gordon Smith d. Stoward 6-3 7-5 6-4; Wright d. F. G. Lowe 6-1 6-3 6-0; Roberts d. Singh 6-4 7-5 6-4; Thomas d. Prebble 5-7 6-3 4-6 6-2 6-4; Powell d. Hillyard 7-5 6-1 6-4.

FOURTH ROUND	QUARTER-FINALS	SEMI-FINALS	FINAL	ALL-COMERS' CHAMPION
Beamish	Beamish			
Barnes	6-2 6-4 11-9	Parke		
Mavrogordato	Parke	8-6 5-7 6-4 6-3		
Parke	1-6 8-6 2-6 7-5 6-4		Wilding	
McNair	Wilding		7-5 6-1 6-2	
Wilding	6-0 6-0 6-0	Wilding		
Powell	Froitzheim	6-1 6-1 6-2		
Froitzheim	8-6 6-3 7-5			Wilding
Blom	A. H. Lowe			4-6 4-6 6-3 6-2 6-3
A. H. Lowe	6-2 6-2 6-1	A. H. Lowe		
Doust	Doust	6-3 6-3 2-6 6-4		
Gordon Smith	6-3 6-0 6-2		Wright	
Wright	Wright		6-3 3-6 6-4 6-4	
Roberts	6-1 6-2 6-2	Wright		
Thomas	Powell	6-3 6-1 6-1		
Powell	6-4 9-7 4-6 6-4			

Challenge round: A. F. Wilding (Challenger) d. A. W. Gore (Holder) 6-4 7-5 4-6 6-2.

LADIES' SINGLES

FIRST ROUND: M. Messom d. W. G. Ramsey 5-4 6-2.

SECOND ROUND: Miss Castenschiold (D) d. Mrs Armstrong w.o.; Mrs O'Neill d. Mrs V. Tabbush 1-6 6-4 6-0; Mrs H. W. Lamplough d. Mrs F. Good w.o.; B. Tulloch d. Mrs L. R. Hausberg w.o.; E. D. Holman d. E. Peterson 6-0 6-2; E. G. Johnson d. Mrs Schmitz 6-3 6-4; Mrs E. G. Parton d. M. Coles 6-4 7-5; O. B. Manser d. Messom 6-1 6-1; A. G.

Ransome d. M. Boadle 6-3 6-1; H. Aitchison d. M. Brooksmith 6-4 6-3; V. E. R. Aitken d. J. Tripp w.o.; Mrs R. Lambert Chambers d. Mrs Nesham 6-1 6-0; Mrs H. Edgington d. Mrs A. Sterry w.o.; D. Boadle d. L. Flemmich 9-7 6-4; Mrs G. W. Hillyard d. V. E. M. Evans 6-1 6-1; Mrs R. J. McNair d. R. V. Salusbury 1-6 6-4 6-1.

THIRD ROUND	QUARTER-FINALS	SEMI-FINALS	FINAL	ALL-COMERS' CHAMPION
Castenschiold	Castenschiold			
O'Neill	6-3 6-3	Lamplough		
Lamplough	Lamplough	7-9 6-4 6-3		
Tulloch	w.o.		Johnson	
Johnson	Johnson		1-6 6-0 6-3	
Holman	5-7 6-0 6-0	Johnson		
Parton	Parton	7-5 6-4		
Manser	6-2 8-6			Lambert Chambers
Aitchison	Aitchison			6-4 6-2
Ransome	6-1 6-3	Lambert Chambers		
Lambert Chambers	Lambert Chambers	6-2 6-1		
Aitken	6-1 6-0		Lambert Chambers	
Edgington	Edgington		6-1 6-0	
D. Boadle	6-1 6-4	McNair		
McNair	McNair	2-6 6-3 6-3		
Hillyard	5-7 6-3 6-3			

Challenge round: Mrs R. Lambert Chambers (Challenger) d. Miss D. P. Boothby 6-2 6-2.

OTHER FINALS

GENTLEMEN'S DOUBLES: Final — M. J. G. Ritchie/A. F. Wilding (NZ) d. K./R. B. Powell (C) 9-7 6-0 6-4.
Challenge round — Ritchie/Wilding d. A. W. Gore/H. Roper Barrett 6-1 6-1 6-2.

MIXED DOUBLES (Non-Championship event): **Final** — S. N. Doust (A)/Mrs R. Lambert Chambers d. R. B. Powell (C)/Mrs A. Sterry 6-2 7-5.
GENTLEMEN'S SINGLES PLATE: Final — A. H. Gobert (F) d. P. M. Davson 6-4 6-4.

GENTLEMEN'S SINGLES

FIRST ROUND: S. N. Doust (A) d. S. M. Edwards 6-2 6-1 6-2; R. D. Pritchett d. R. W. F. Harding 6-2 8-6 6-4; A. W. Gore d. A. Popp 6-0 6-0 6-0; A. H. Gobert (F) d. W. S. Cushing 6-2 6-0 7-5; C. P. Dixon d. L. E. Milburn 6-1 6-3 3-6 6-2; C. S. Grace d. A. H. Green w.o.; T. R. Quill d. G. Gault w.o.; C. J. Adams d. C. Van Lennep w.o.; E. G. Parton d. C. F. Ryder 7-9 6-3 5-7 6-3 6-4; E. O. Pockley d. H. W. D. Gallwey 6-2 6-2 6-1; P. M. Davson d. A. W. Dunlop (A) 2-6 6-4 6-3 9-7; M. J. G. Ritchie d. J. R. Brinkley 6-2 6-0 6-0; A. S. Reid d. J. Powell 6-2 7-5 6-3; M. H. Marsh d. G. Stoddart 6-4 6-4 5-7 5-7 6-3; E. S. Franklin d. 'R. Otter' 6-1 6-0 6-3; A. D. Prebble d. A. J. Jimenez 6-3 6-0 6-2; E. W. Timmis d. P. V. Tabbush 9-7 4-6 6-3 6-4; G. A. Thomas d. C. Scott 6-3 8-6 6-4; K. Powell d. G. A. Caridia 6-0 6-1 6-2; W. V. Eaves d. D. H. Rutherglan 7-5 6-1 6-4; F. H. Jarvis d. C. Brooke Leggatt w.o.; C. Moore d. H. Crisp 3-6 7-5 7-5 6-4; A. E. Beamish d. W. J. Lancaster 6-3 6-1 6-3; G. D. Roberts d. S. H. V. Dillon w.o.; R. R. W. Dudley d. A. F. Stephen 2-6 0-6 6-4 6-2 7-5; D. P. Rhodes d. H. Galsworthy w.o.; R. J. McNair d. F. Good 5-7 6-2 6-1 6-2; F. H. Bryant d. E. Gordon Cleather 6-4 6-3 3-6 6-3; C. S. Gordon Smith d. J. B. Ward 10-8 7-5 6-4; M. R. L. White d. S. Hawksworth 6-0 6-0 6-1; T. M. Mavrogordato d. H. Kleinschroth (G) 6-3 4-6 7-5 3-6 6-3; R. S. Barnes d. E. M. Hall 6-0 6-3 6-4; H. Roper Barrett d. J. C. Parke 6-3 6-1 6-4; R. H. Hotham d. L. S. Deane 8-6 6-1 8-6; A. R. Sawyer d. R. A. Gamble 6-1 6-3 6-4; P. Hicks d. F. B. Clogg 6-1 3-6 6-3 6-2; R. B. Powell (C) d. 'H. Wilson' 6-2 6-1 5-7 6-1; F. W. Rahe (G) d. R. Somers Lewis 6-2 6-1 6-1; T. D. Stoward d. E. J. Sampson 6-2 6-4 6-2; A. Hendriks d. G. de Martino (IT) 3-6 6-3 6-4 8-6.

SECOND ROUND: A. C. Hunter d. F. W. Last 6-1 6-2 6-4; R. Heath (A) d. N. D. Malcolm w.o.; F. E. Cochran (SA) d. H. G. Bache 6-3 7-9 6-3 6-3; T. G. Helding d. R. P. Anceau w.o.; A. L. Bentley d. G. R. Johnson w.o.; M. Decugis (F) d. E. Larsen (D) 7-9 6-3 6-3 6-0; Pritchett d. Doust 6-3 2-6 2-6 6-3 6-4; Gore d. Gobert 6-3 6-3 6-2; Dixon d. Grace 6-1 6-2 6-4; Quill d. Adams 6-3 6-1 6-0; Pockley d. Parton 6-2 6-3 6-2; Ritchie d. Davson 6-2 3-6 6-1 6-4; Marsh d. Reid 6-3 6-4 7-5; Franklin d. Prebble 0-6 3-6 7-5 6-0 6-3; Thomas d. Timmis 9-7 6-0 6-2; K. Powell d. Eaves 10-8 6-3 ret'd; Moore d. Jarvis 3-6 6-3 6-1 2-6 6-2; Beamish d. Roberts 6-3 6-2 3-6 6-3; Dudley d. Rhodes w.o.; McNair d. Bryant 6-2 6-2 6-0; Gordon Smith d. White 6-4 7-5 2-6 6-2; Mavrogordato d. Barnes 7-5 2-6 6-3 9-7; Roper Barrett d. Hotham 6-3 6-2 6-0; Sawyer d. Hicks 6-1 4-6 6-1 6-3; Rahe d. R. B. Powell 6-4 4-6 4-6 6-6 7-5; Stoward d. Hendriks 2-6 6-1 6-2 6-3; P. de Borman (B) d. W. P. Barringer 6-0 6-0 6-1; S. J. Watts d. 'E. A. Ess' 6-2 6-1 3-6 6-3; C. Gouldesbrough d. W. S. Slade 6-4 6-4 5-7 1-6 6-1; F. G. Lowe d. A. H. Lowe 5-7 7-5 6-4 ret'd; G. P. Allen d. F. C. Budd 6-2 8-6 7-5; 'T. Edmett' d. C. Biddle (USA) 3-6 7-5 6-2 6-2.

THIRD ROUND: Heath d. Hunter 6-0 6-2 6-1; Cochran d. Heldring 6-3 6-2 6-3; Decugis d. Bentley 6-2 6-3 6-1; Gore d. Pritchett d. Gore 6-1 8-6 6-3; Dixon d. Quill 8-6 6-4 6-3; Ritchie d. Pockley 6-1 6-3 7-5; Marsh d. Franklin 6-4 6-4 4-0 ret'd; Thomas d. Powell 11-9 5-7 6-2 6-3; Beamish d. Moore 6-4 6-2 6-1; McNair d. Dudley 6-1 9-7 5-7 7-9 6-2; Mavrogordato d. Gordon Smith 6-3 6-4 7-5; Roper Barrett d. Sawyer 6-0 6-3 6-1; Rahe d. Stoward 7-5 3-6 3-6 6-1 9-7; de Borman d. Watts 6-2 6-2 6-3; F. G. Lowe d. Gouldesbrough 6-2 6-0 6-3; 'Edmett' d. Allen 6-3 7-5 6-0.

FOURTH ROUND	QUARTER-FINALS	SEMI-FINALS	FINAL	ALL-COMERS' CHAMPION
Heath	Heath			
Cochran	6-1 6-2 6-2	Decugis		
Decugis	Decugis	10-8 6-4 7-5		
Gore	2-6 6-4 6-4 8-6		Dixon	
Dixon	Dixon		6-2 5-7 6-2 6-3	
Ritchie	8-6 6-4 6-8 6-4	Dixon		
Marsh	Thomas	6-4 5-7 8-6 6-3		
Thomas	9-7 4-6 5-7 6-1 6-3			Roper Barrett
Beamish	Beamish			5-7 4-6 6-4 6-3 6-1
McNair	6-1 6-2 7-5	Roper Barrett		
Mavrogordato	Roper Barrett	6-1 1-6 6-4 6-3		
Roper Barrett	6-3 3-6 8-6 8-6		Roper Barrett	
Rahe	Rahe		6-2 6-3 6-2	
de Borman	6-3 6-2 6-4	F. G. Lowe		
F. G. Lowe	F. G. Lowe	5-7 6-3 6-2 9-7		
'Edmett'	6-2 6-3 4-6 6-2			

Challenge round: A. F. Wilding (NZ) (Holder) d. H. Roper Barrett (Challenger) 6-4 4-6 2-6 6-2 ret'd.

LADIES' SINGLES

FIRST ROUND: Mrs Hazel d. B. Tulloch 4-6 6-4 6-4; Mrs H. Edgington d. C. Antrobus w.o.

SECOND ROUND: Mrs F. J. Hannam d. E. C. Attfield w.o.; Mrs O'Neill d. Mrs A. Sterry w.o.; M. Coles d. Miss Dudley w.o.; Mrs Gracey d. Mrs Ritchie w.o.; H. Aitchison d. E. Dillon 6-1 6-3; A. M. Morton d. M. Rieck (G) 6-2 6-4; R. V. Salusbury d. D. Elliadi w.o.; Hazel d. W. G. Ramsey 6-2 7-5; Edgington d. H. Lane 6-4 6-3; P. H. Carr d. M. Dillon 7-9 6-3 8-6; E. G. Johnson d. Mrs A. H. Crosfield 6-4 6-2; D. P. Boothby d. C. Castenschiold (D) 6-3 8-6; Mrs E. G. Parton d. Mrs Lent 6-2 6-2; Mrs E. G. McNair d. Mrs E. Bousfield 6-2 6-2; V. E. Spofforth d. Mrs Armstrong w.o.; E. D. Holman d. Mrs Nutcombe Quicke 6-0 6-2.

THIRD ROUND	QUARTER-FINALS	SEMI-FINALS	FINAL	ALL-COMERS' CHAMPION
Hannam	Hannam			
O'Neill	6-1 6-1	Hannam		
Coles	Coles	6-4 4-6 7-5		
Gracey	6-1 6-1		Hannam	
Aitchison	Aitchison		6-3 6-8 7-5	
Morton	6-4 ret'd	Aitchison		
Hazel	Hazel	6-0 6-3		
Salusbury	w.o.			Boothby
Edgington	Edgington			6-2 7-5
Carr	8-6 6-4	Boothby		
Boothby	Boothby	6-2 6-4		
Johnson	6-3 6-3		Boothby	
Parton	Parton		6-3 6-4	
McNair	6-2 7-5	Parton		
Holman	Holman	6-0 8-6		
Spofforth	6-1 6-0			

Challenge round: Mrs R. Lambert Chambers (Holder) d. Miss D. P. Boothby (Challenger) 6-0 6-0.

OTHER FINALS

GENTLEMEN'S DOUBLES: Final — M. Decugis (F)/H. Gobert (F) d. S. Hardy (USA)/J. C. Parke 6-2 6-1 6-2.
Challenge round — Decugis/Gobert d. M. J. G. Ritchie/A. F. Wilding (NZ) 9-7 5-7 6-3 2-6 6-2.

MIXED DOUBLES (Non-Championship event): **Final** — T. M. Mavrogordato/Mrs E. G. Parton d. S. N. Doust (A)/Mrs R. Lambert Chambers 6-2 6-4.
GENTLEMEN'S SINGLES PLATE: Final — A. H. Lowe d. J. C. Parke 6-0 8-6.

GENTLEMEN'S SINGLES

1912

FIRST ROUND: S. N. Doust (A) d. F. Good 6-3 6-2 8-6; F. R. Crawford d. G. H. Cartwright 5-7 6-0 6-4 6-3; M. J. G. Ritchie d. G. Stoddart 6-0 6-4 6-1; W. A. Ingram d. H. F. Hunt w.o.; C. P. Dixon d. F. W. Goldberg 6-4 6-1 6-3; H. Roper Barrett d. A. Zorab 6-1 6-2 7-5; A. Dudley d. H. A. Davis 6-2 9-7 6-1; C. Scott d. N. Willford 6-3 6-4 6-3; P. H. Robbs (SA) d. H. W. Brown (SA) 6-3 6-4 6-2; F. G. Lowe d. S. J. Watts 6-4 6-4 6-2; O. von Bissing (G) d. E. W. Timmis 6-4 6-4 6-3; A. L. Bentley d. S. T. de Jakimowicz 6-1 6-0 6-3; A. H. Lowe d. E. Larsen (D) 9-7 6-4 5-7 1-6 6-2; R. J. McNair d. M. Germot (F) w.o.; M. D. Hick d. W. P. Haviland 6-2 6-1 6-2; A. E. Beamish d. A. Wallis Myers 9-11 6-4 6-1 2-0 ret'd; R. 'Trebor' d. C. E. Leo Lyle 4-6 3-6 6-2 6-3 6-3.

SECOND ROUND: C. Gouldesbrough d. G. T. C. Watt 6-3 8-6 6-3; T. M. Mavrogordato d. G. F. Anson 6-3 6-2 6-3; F. W. Rahe (G) d. A. Hendriks 7-9 6-3 8-6 6-3; W. G. Milburn d. A. C. Hunter 6-4 6-8 7-5 6-4; A. H. Gobert (F) d. E. U. Williams 6-0 6-4 6-0; J. C. Parke d. J. C. S. Rendall 6-3 6-4 2-6 6-2; P. R. Hewlett d. E. J. Sampson w.o.; A. D. Prebble d. J. Spalding w.o.; M. Decugis (F) d. G. A. Thomas 6-2 6-0 6-3; A. J. Ross d. A. W. Maloney w.o.; O. Froitzheim (G) d. G. Gault w.o.; Doust d. F. E. Barritt (A) 6-1 6-0 6-1; Ritchie d. Crawford 6-1 6-2 6-3; Dixon d. Ingram 6-3 6-3 6-3; Roper Barrett d. Dudley 6-2 6-1 6-0; Robbs d. Scott 6-1 6-4 6-3; F. G. Lowe d. von Bissing 6-3 6-0 6-3; A. H. Lowe d. Bentley 6-0 6-3 6-0; Hick d. McNair 6-1 6-4 6-4; Beamish d. 'Trebor' 6-1 6-0 6-3; T. D. Stoward d. J. H. Harris 6-2 6-1 6-1; J. E. H. Zimmermann d. H. 'Wilson' 4-6 6-0 6-2 6-3; C. J. Adams d. F. Poulin w.o.; P. Hicks d. W. H. Warman 7-5 6-3 6-4; C. F. Simond d. C. H. Hole 7-5 8-6 4-6 6-4; C. Moore d. F. M. Pearson 4-6 7-5 6-4 6-3; C. Bergmann (G) d. P. de Borman (B) 6-0 0-6 6-2 10-8; A. W. Gore d. L. E. Milburn 6-2 6-2 6-4; R. B. Powell (C) d. L. Bonnington 6-2 6-2 6-4; E. G. Parton d. A. J. Jimenez 6-3 8-6 6-0; F. N. Warden d. C. Macleod w.o.; R. W. Harding d. H. Price 6-3 6-3 6-2.

THIRD ROUND: Mavrogordato d. Gouldesbrough 6-4 6-1 6-3; Rahe d. W. G. Milburn 6-2 6-2 6-1; Gobert d. Parke 6-3 6-4 6-4; Prebble d. Hewlett 6-0 6-0 6-2; Decugis d. Ross 6-0 6-1 7-5; Doust d. Froitzheim 6-4 7-5 6-3; Ritchie d. Dixon 6-4 7-5 6-0; Roper Barrett d. Robbs 2-6 3-6 8-6; F. G. Lowe d. A. H. Lowe 2-6 6-2 6-1 6-3; Beamish d. Hick 6-2 6-8 6-2 6-0; Zimmermann d. Stoward 6-1 4-6 6-3 6-2; Hicks d. Adams 6-0 6-1 6-2; Moore d. Simond 7-5 8-6 3-6 7-5; Gore d. Bergmann 6-4 6-4 6-4; Powell d. Parton 6-2 6-1 6-1; Warden d. Harding 5-7 6-1 4-6 6-3 6-1.

FOURTH ROUND	QUARTER-FINALS	SEMI-FINALS	FINAL	ALL-COMERS' CHAMPION
Mavrogordato	Rahe			
Rahe	6-3 6-3 6-8 6-4	Gobert		
Gobert	Gobert	6-1 6-2 7-5		
Prebble	6-1 6-4 6-4		Gobert	
Decugis	Decugis		6-3 6-3 1-6 4-6 6-4	
Doust	6-3 6-3 7-5	Decugis		
Ritchie	Roper Barrett	6-3 7-5 4-6 6-4		Gore
Roper Barrett	8-6 3-6 6-2 3-6 6-4			9-7 2-6 7-5 6-1
F. G. Lowe	Beamish			
Beamish	11-9 6-1 6-2	Beamish		
Zimmermann	Zimmermann	6-4 6-3 6-1		
Hicks	3-6 6-0 6-1 6-2		Gore	
Moore	Gore		6-2 0-6 11-9 6-4	
Gore	8-6 8-6 6-4	Gore		
Powell	Powell	6-3 6-2 4-6 6-2		
Warden	6-1 6-1 8-6			

Challenge round: A. F. Wilding (NZ) (Holder) d. A. W. Gore (Challenger) 6-4 6-4 4-6 6-4.

LADIES' SINGLES

FIRST ROUND: O. B. Manser d. Mrs Hollick 6-1 5-7 6-4; J. Coles d. E. A. Longhurst 6-3 6-4.

SECOND ROUND: Mrs C. O. Tuckey d. Mrs V. Woodhouse w.o.; W. A. Longhurst d. Mrs Satterthwaite 6-4 6-2; D. P. Boothby d. E. G. Johnson 6-4 6-3; Mrs A. Sterry d. Mrs E. G. Parton 12-10 7-5; H. Aitchison d. Mrs Scott w.o.; E. D. Holman d. B. Tulloch 6-0 6-2; Mrs O'Neill d. J. Tripp 6-3 7-5; A. M. Morton d. Manser 7-5 6-2; Mrs F. J. Hannam d. Coles 6-1 6-1; Mrs D. R. Larcombe d. H. Lane w.o.; Mrs E. S. Hall d. Mrs Armstrong w.o.; Mrs R. J. McNair d. V. E. Spofforth 6-3 6-2; Mrs G. W. Hillyard d. Mrs A. E. Beamish 2-6 6-1 7-5; Miss Kribben d. Miss Schultz w.o.; D. Allen d. Mrs M. Decugis (F) 8-6 5-7 6-3; E. Ryan (USA) d. J. Liebrechts (B) 7-5 6-3.

THIRD ROUND	QUARTER-FINALS	SEMI-FINALS	FINAL	ALL-COMERS' CHAMPION
W. A. Longhurst	Longhurst			
Tuckey	8-6 3-6 6-1	Sterry		
Sterry	Sterry	6-1 6-3		
Boothby	6-2 4-6 6-1		Sterry	
Holman	Holman		6-3 4-6 7-5	
Aitchison	w.o.	Holman		
Morton	Morton	7-5 6-2		Larcombe
O'Neill	6-2 6-1			6-3 6-1
Larcombe	Larcombe			
Hannam	7-5 8-6	Larcombe		
McNair	McNair	6-2 5-7 6-0		
Hall	6-1 6-2		Larcombe	
Hillyard	Hillyard		6-1 6-0	
Kribben	w.o.	Hillyard		
Ryan	Ryan	3-6 8-6 6-3		
Allen	6-1 6-2			

Challenge round: Mrs D. R. Larcombe (Challenger) d. Mrs R. Lambert Chambers (Holder) w.o.

OTHER FINALS

GENTLEMEN'S DOUBLES: Final – C. P. Dixon/H. Roper Barrett d. A. E. Beamish/J. C. Parke 6-8 6-4 3-6 6-3 6-4.
Challenge round – Dixon/Roper Barrett d. M. Decugis (F)/A. H. Gobert (F) 3-6 6-3 6-4 7-5.

MIXED DOUBLES (Non-Championship event): **Final** – J. C. Parke/Mrs D. R. Larcombe d. A. D. Prebble/D. P. Boothby 6-4 6-2.
GENTLEMEN'S SINGLES PLATE: Final – F. M. Pearson d. F. E. Barritt (A) 6-0 10-8.

GENTLEMEN'S SINGLES

FIRST ROUND: F. F. Roe d. H. F. Guggenheim 6-3 6-1 6-0; W. A. Ingram d. B. Wood Hill 4-6 1-6 6-2 6-1; A. H. Glendinning d. A. J. Jimenez 6-2 6-3 6-8 6-2; M. E. McLoughlin (USA) d. H. Roper Barrett 4-6 8-6 1-6 6-2 8-6; T. M. Mavrogordato d. H. Kleinschroth (G) 6-4 6-2 6-1; A. E. Crawley d. E. F. Herring 6-4 7-5 6-2; R. N. Williams (USA) d. P. V. Tabbush w.o.; R. M. K. Turnbull d. S. Thol 6-4 6-4 2-6 6-1; H. Nickerson d. C. A. Patterson 3-6 7-5 7-5 3-6 6-3; R. F. Le Sueur (SA) d. A. H. Davis 4-6 6-2 6-3 8-6; R. D. Watson d. M. D. Hick 6-4 6-1 4-6 6-1; G. Zinn d. J. S. de Morpurgo 6-4 6-2 9-7; F. W. Goldberg d. 'E. A. Ess' 6-3 6-4 6-2; W. H. Warman d. M. Germot (F) w.o.; G. A. Caridia d. G. Boustead 6-3 6-3 6-4; W. G. Milburn d. S. H. Cole 6-1 7-5 6-3; H. C. Webb d. J. D. Fuller 6-3 5-7 9-7 7-5; W. F. Johnson d. A. W. Andrews 6-1 6-0 6-3; J. 'Robinson' d. L. S. Hunter 3-6 6-2 6-2 7-5; G. H. Cartwright d. F. R. Price 6-4 7-5 7-5; A. H. Lowe d. G. A. Thomas 6-4 6-0 6-3; F. G. Lowe d. H. B. Bland 6-0 6-0 6-0; S. P. O'Donnell d. E. S. Franklin w.o.; J. C. Parke d. R. D. Nolan w.o.; H. M. Rice (A) d. O. G. N. Turnbull 6-3 6-4 8-6; A. E. Beamish d. L. E. Milburn 6-2 6-2 6-1; E. W. Hicks d. F. N. Thorne 5-7 6-1 2-6 6-3 10-8; C. R. Leach (SA) d. P. de Borman (B) 4-6 7-5 11-9 ret'd; G. T. C. Watt d. R. W. F. Harding w.o.; O. Kreuzer (G) d. C. F. Simond 6-4 5-7 6-2 6-1; B. P. Schwengers (C) d. C. S. Grace 6-3 6-2 2-6 4-6 8-6; R. J. McNair d. L. S. Lee 6-1 6-0 6-1; A. W. Gore d. S. J. Watts 7-5 6-4 6-2; C. J. Tindell Green d. S. Hardy w.o.; F. Good d. H. J. Gilbert 6-3 4-6 10-8 3-6 6-1; G. Stoddart d. E. W. Timmis 6-2 6-3 6-3; N. Willford d. A. B. Jones (A) 5-7 6-4 6-2 ret'd; C. P. Dixon d. J. E. Boyd 6-2 6-0 6-3; V. R. Gauntlett (SA) d. A. Wallis Myers 6-2 6-0 6-0; Count Salm d. E. L. Jones w.o.; R. A. Gamble d. 'F. Karl' 6-2 6-1 6-4; K. Powell d. P. Hicks 7-5 7-5 6-4; E. Williams d. J. F. Foulkes (C) w.o.; D. M. Field d. Wilson Fox 6-4 6-3 5-7 6-1; M. R. L. White d. M. Decugis (F) w.o.; E. Larsen (D) d. A. Hendriks 6-0 6-2 6-1; P. M. Davson d. A. Traill 6-0 5-7 6-0 6-1; J. E. H. Zimmermann d. N. S. B. Kidson 5-7 6-4 6-1 6-2; S. N. Doust (A) d. C. J. Adams 6-1 6-2 6-0; R. H. Hotham d. A. C. Simon (SWZ) 12-14 6-2 9-7 6-2; W. C. Crawley d. G. Gault w.o.; F. W. Rahe (G) d. F. V. Kirk 6-0 6-0 6-4.

SECOND ROUND: C. Biddle (USA) d. H. G. Mayers (C) 7-5 6-4 6-3; F. H. Jarvis d. A. C. Hunter 6-4 6-2 6-2; F. S. Wilding d. H. S. Owen 6-1 6-1 7-5; Ingram d. Roe 4-7-9 6-4 2-6 8-6; McLoughlin d. Glendinning 6-2 6-0 6-3; Mavrogordato d. A. E. Crawley 6-2 6-0 6-4; R. N. Williams d. R. M. K. Turnbull 6-1 6-4 6-3; Le Sueur d. Nickerson 6-0 6-4 6-3; Watson d. Zinn 6-2 6-1 6-2; Goldberg d. Warman 12-10 6-0 6-3; Caridia d. W. G. Milburn 6-2 3-6 7-5 8-6; Johnson d. Webb 6-2 6-1 7-5; 'Robinson' d. Cartwright 6-4 6-4 6-4; A. H. Lowe d. F. G. Lowe w.o.; Parke d. O'Donnell 6-1 6-4 6-4; Beamish d. Rice 4-6 6-1 6-4; Leach d. E. W. Hicks 3-6 6-4 7-5 4-6 6-1; Kreuzer d. Watt 6-2 6-2 6-3; Schwengers d. McNair 4-6 7-5 6-1 6-2; Gore d. Green 2-6 7-9 6-3 6-2 6-3; Stoddart d. Good 3-6 2-6 6-1 7-5 6-2; Dixon d. Willford 6-0 6-4 6-3; Gauntlett d. Salm 3-6 6-4 6-3 6-3; K. Powell d. Gamble 6-1 6-1 6-2; Field d. E. Williams 6-3 6-2 4-6 6-3; Larsen d. White 6-3 6-3 6-3; Davson d. Zimmermann 7-5 6-4 7-5; Doust d. Hotham 6-0 6-1 6-2; W. C. Crawley d. Rahe 10-8 0-6 4-9 7; R. B. Powell d. J. B. Ward (C) 7-5 9-7 3-6 6-1; H. Crisp d. B. S. Foster 6-4 6-2 6-0; J. M. Flavelle d. H. C. Eltringham 5-7 6-4 6-3 6-0.

THIRD ROUND: Biddle d. Jarvis 6-1 6-3 7-5; Ingram d. Wilding 6-0 6-3 6-4; McLoughlin d. Mavrogordato 6-4 6-3 6-2; R. N. Williams d. Le Sueur 8-6 8-6 7-5; Watson d. Goldberg 6-3 6-3 8-6; Johnson d. Caridia w.o.; A. H. Lowe d. 'Robinson' 6-3 6-1 6-2; Parke d. Beamish 6-2 4-6 6-3 6-3; Kreuzer d. Leach w.o.; Gore d. Schwengers 6-1 6-3 4-6 11-9; Dixon d. Stoddart 6-2 6-2 6-4; K. Powell d. Gauntlett 4-6 6-1 6-3 7-5; Larsen d. Field 4-6 6-2 6-4 6-2; Doust d. Davson 6-2 6-4 1-6 1-6 10-8; R. B. Powell d. Crawley 6-2 6-4 6-2; Crisp d. Flavelle 6-2 6-2 6-1.

FOURTH ROUND	QUARTER-FINALS	SEMI-FINALS	FINAL	ALL-COMERS' CHAMPION
Biddle	Ingram			
Ingram	6-3 6-2 1-6 6-1	McLoughlin		
McLoughlin	McLoughlin	6-1 6-2 6-4		
R. N. Williams	6-4 6-4 3-6 ret'd		McLoughlin	
Watson	Watson		6-4 7-5 6-4	
Johnson	2-6 8-6 6-1 7-5	Parke		
A. H. Lowe	Parke	6-4 6-1 6-4		McLoughlin
Parke	7-5 6-0 7-5			6-3 6-4 7-5
Kreuzer	Kreuzer			
Gore	3-6 7-5 6-2 6-0	Kreuzer		
Dixon	K. Powell	6-4 6-1 5-7 6-0		
K. Powell	6-3 3-6 3-6 6-3 11-9		Doust	
Larsen	Doust		6-3 6-2 6-3	
Doust	4-6 2-6 6-1 6-0 6-4	Doust		
R. B. Powell	Crisp	7-5 6-3 3-6 11-9		
Crisp	6-4 7-5 6-3			

Challenge round: A. F. Wilding (NZ) (Holder) d. M. E. McLoughlin (Challenger) 8-6 6-3 10-8.

LADIES' SINGLES

FIRST ROUND: Mrs H. Edgington d. Mrs A. A. Hall 6-1 6-3; M. Rieck (G) d. B. M. Warren 6-1 6-1; H. Lane d. E. F. Rose 6-3 6-3; D. P. Boothby d. E. Ryan (USA) 6-4 4-6 6-3; Mrs Satterthwaite d. O. B. Manser 7-5 6-1; B. Tulloch d. Mrs C. E. Hunter w.o.; Mrs Hazel d. Mrs W. E. Hudleston 6-3 6-8 6-2; Mrs A. E. Beamish d. E. G. Johnson w.o.; M. Coles d. Miss Brooksmith 7-5 6-2; A. M. Morton d. Mrs H. W. Lamplough 6-2 6-4.

SECOND ROUND: Mrs A. Sterry d. Mrs Colston 4-6 6-2 6-2; Mrs F. J. Hannam d. Mrs G. W. Hillyard 4-6 6-2 6-0; Mrs G. Greville d. Mrs Perrett 6-0 5-7 6-2; Mrs R. J. McNair d. J. Coles 6-1 6-0; Mrs Nesham d. G. B. Foster 10-8 6-1; E. D. Holman d. Edgington 4-6 6-2 6-1; Rieck d. Lane 2-6 6-1 6-2; Satterthwaite d. Boothby 6-3 6-4; Tulloch d. Hazel 2-6 7-5 7-5; M. Coles d. Beamish 7-9 8-6 6-4; Morton d. K. M. Allen 6-1 6-2; Mrs R. Lambert Chambers d. Mrs C. O. Tuckey 6-2 6-3; Mrs O'Neill d. Mrs E. G. Parton 6-4 1-6 6-2; V. E. Spofforth d. B. M. S. Lee 6-3 6-2; H. Aitchison d. J. Greene 7-9 6-0 6-0; Mrs E. S. Hall d. D. Boadle w.o.

THIRD ROUND	QUARTER-FINALS	SEMI-FINALS	FINAL	ALL-COMERS' CHAMPION
Sterry	Sterry			
Hannam	6-1 2-6 6-2	McNair		
McNair	McNair	0-6 6-4 9-7		
Greville	6-3 6-2		McNair	
Holman	Holman		2-6 6-2 7-5	
Nesham	6-1 6-0	Holman		
Satterthwaite	Satterthwaite	6-4 6-1		
Rieck	6-1 6-2			Lambert Chambers
M. Coles	M. Coles			6-0 6-4
Tulloch	6-2 6-0	Lambert Chambers		
Lambert Chambers	Lambert Chambers	6-1 6-0		
Morton	6-1 6-3		Lambert Chambers	
O'Neill	O'Neill		6-2 6-3	
Spofforth	6-2 6-3	Aitchison		
Aitchison	Aitchison	6-2 6-0		
S. Hall	6-1 6-2			

Challenge round: Mrs R. Lambert Chambers (Challenger) d. Mrs D. R. Larcombe (Holder) w.o.

OTHER FINALS

GENTLEMEN'S DOUBLES: Final — H. Kleinschroth (G)/F. W. Rahe (G) d. A. E. Beamish/J. C. Parke 6-3 6-2 6-4.
Challenge round — C. P. Dixon/H. Roper Barrett d. Kleinschroth/Rahe 6-2 6-4 4-6 6-2.
LADIES' DOUBLES: Final — Mrs R. J. McNair/D. P. Boothby d. Mrs A. Sterry/Mrs R. Lambert Chambers 4-6 2-4 ret'd.

MIXED DOUBLES: Final — H. Crisp/Mrs C. O. Tuckey d. J. C. Parke/Mrs D. R. Larcombe 3-6 5-3 ret'd.
GENTLEMEN'S SINGLES PLATE: Final — F. G. Lowe d. F. F. Roe 8-10 6-3 6-3.

GENTLEMEN'S SINGLES

1914

FIRST ROUND: J. C. Parke d. C. P. Dixon 11-9 6-1 6-3; F. G. Lowe d. S. M. Jacob 6-2 6-4 8-6; T. B. Nicholson d. D. A. Weatherhead 6-4 6-3 8-6; N. Willford d. W. P. Pinckney 6-3 9-7 6-4; C. Scott d. F. Good 6-1 8-6 6-3; R. H. Hotham d. E. J. Whittall w.o.; H. C. Eltringham d. H. Kleinschroth (G) w.o.; T. M. Mavrogordato d. O. G. N. Turnbull 6-4 6-0 6-4; S. J. Watts d. Baron G. Franckenstein w.o.; C. J. T. Green d. R. J. McNair 6-2 6-1 6-3; S. N. Doust (A) d. E. S. Franklin 6-1 6-2 6-2; M. Germot (F) d. H. A. Davis 6-4 6-4 6-0; A. Moss d. R. M. Kidston 4-6 8-6 6-2 3-1 ret'd; C. F. Simond d. A. C. Hunter 6-4 6-2 6-2; G. Stoddart d. J. E. Boyd 6-3 6-3 6-4; L. M. Hayden d. L. Harvey 2-6 6-1 6-3 6-4; M. D. Hick d. R. F. Baird 6-0 6-0 6-3; H. M. 'Robin' d. E. T. Barnard w.o.; A. W. Dunlop (A) d. H. Wilson Fox 6-1 6-3 6-2; R. W. F. Harding d. C. N. Thompson 6-3 6-2 6-2; E. Larsen (D) d. C. Gouldesbrough 6-2 6-3 6-1; R. D. Watson d. E. D. Yencken 6-3 6-1 6-3; A. J. Jimenez d. C. O. Tuckey 6-8 7-5 1-6 0-5 ret'd; H. Aitken d. R. H. Somers Lewis 6-2 6-4 6-1; M. Decugis (F) d. S. F. Thol 6-2 6-2 6-1; P. M. Davson d. T. D. Stoward 6-2 6-2 4-6 6-0; P. Hicks d. F. W. Last 6-3 6-4 6-1; A. J. Ross d. P. V. Tabbush 6-1 7-5 6-2; W. C. Crawley d. H. S. Owen 3-6 8-6 6-2 6-2; J. B. Ward d. L. S. Lee 6-4 4-6 6-4 6-2; F. W. Goldberg d. J. D. Fuller 6-1 6-1 9-7; A. M. Cooper d. E. A. Stoner 6-2 6-2 7-5; J. M. Flavelle d. C. R. D. Pritchett 4-6 6-3 6-3 6-3; E. G. Parton d. A. F. Yencken 6-2 6-0 7-5; A. E. Beamish d. E. W. Timmis 6-2 6-1 6-2; A. R. F. Kingscote d. W. D. Barber 6-2 6-2 6-0; A. W. Gore d. G. A. Thomas 6-3 6-2 7-5; F. H. Jarvis d. R. C. Spies 6-3 8-6 3-6 6-4.

SECOND ROUND: R. Dash d. C. H. Hole w.o.; O. Froitzheim (G) d. H. Crisp 6-2 3-6 6-2 6-2; A. H. Lowe d. B. Wood Hill 6-2 6-0 6-1; C. Biddle (USA) d. L. G. O. Woodhouse w.o.; C. A. Caridia d. S. E. Charlton 6-2 5-7 6-2 6-3; R. M. K. Turnbull d. J. G. Bill w.o.; Parke d. G. T. C. Watt 6-2 6-0 ret'd; F. G. Lowe d. Nicholson 6-3 6-4 6-2; Scott d. Willford 7-5 6-3 6-8 6-4; Eltringham d. Hotham 6-3 8-10 6-2 6-1; Mavrogordato d. Watts 6-2 6-3 6-3; Doust d. Green 6-1 2-6 2-6 6-1 6-4; Germot d. Moss 6-4 6-2 6-4; Stoddart d. Simond 6-0 6-4 6-2; Hayden d. Hick 6-2 6-2 6-4; Dunlop d. 'Robin' 7-9 6-2 6-2 6-1; Larsen d. Harding 6-3 7-5 6-3; Watson d. Jimenez 6-4 6-4 6-2; Decugis d. Aitken 6-2 6-1 6-3; P. M. Davson d. Hicks 10-8 6-2 6-4; W. C. Crawley d. Ross 6-1 6-3 6-2; Goldberg d. Ward 6-2 6-3 6-2; Flavelle d. Cooper 13-11 6-1 3-6 5-7 7-5; Beamish d. Parton 6-1 6-1 6-3; Gore d. Kingscote 6-4 6-3 6-3; Jarvis d. H. T. L. Speer 6-2 6-4 6-4; E. H. Pooley d. A. E. Crawley 7-5 1-6 5-2 ret'd; C. E. L. Lyle d. A. W. Davson 9-7 6-4 6-4; W. L. Clements d. W. A. Ingram 6-2 12-10 6-0; C. Gordon Smith d. P. de Borman (B) 7-5 6-2 10-8; N. E. Brookes (A) d. L. F. Davin 6-0 6-0 6-0; M. J. G. Ritchie d. H. Roper Barrett 4-6 6-1 6-4 6-3.

THIRD ROUND: Froitzheim d. Dash 6-3 6-3 6-2; A. H. Lowe d. Biddle w.o.; Caridia d. Turnbull 7-9 6-2 6-3 6-4; Parke d. F. G. Lowe 6-1 6-3 6-4; Scott d. Eltringham 10-8 9-7 4-6 6-4; Mavrogordato d. Doust 6-0 6-4 6-4; Germot d. Stoddart 5-7 6-2 6-0 7-5; Dunlop d. Hayden 8-6 0-6 7-5 6-1; Watson d. Larsen 6-1 2-6 2-6 6-0 6-3; Davson d. Decugis 6-4 4-6 6-1 6-3; Crawley d. Goldberg 6-2 6-1 0-6 6-4; Beamish d. Flavelle 6-2 6-2 6-0; Gore d. Jarvis 6-3 6-3 6-2; Lyle d. Pooley 6-1 6-0 6-4; Clements d. Gordon Smith 6-3 3-6 6-4 3-6 6-3; Brookes d. Ritchie 6-1 6-0 6-1.

FOURTH ROUND	QUARTER-FINALS	SEMI-FINALS	FINAL	ALL-COMERS' CHAMPION
Froitzheim	Froitzheim	Froitzheim		
A. H. Lowe	6-3 6-4 5-7 10-8	5-7 6-2 9-7 6-2		
Caridia	Parke		Froitzheim	
Parke	6-2 6-2 6-1		6-3 6-2 7-5	
Scott	Mavrogordato			
Mavrogordato	6-4 6-1 6-4	Mavrogordato		
Germot	Germot	6-3 2-6 6-4 6-1		
Dunlop	6-8 6-4 6-1 4-1 ret'd			Brookes
Watson	Davson			6-2 6-1 5-7 4-6 8-6
Davson	6-2 6-4 5-7 6-1	Beamish		
Crawley	Beamish	6-4 6-2 6-1		
Beamish	6-2 7-5 6-4		Brookes	
Gore	Gore		6-0 6-3 6-2	
Lyle	6-2 6-0 6-2	Brookes		
Clements	Brookes	7-5 6-1 6-2		
Brookes	6-3 6-0 6-0			

Challenge round: N. E. Brookes (Challenger) d. A. F. Wilding (NZ) (Holder) 6-4 6-4 7-5.

LADIES' SINGLES

FIRST ROUND: H. Lane d. E. F. Rose 3-6 6-4 6-4; Mrs H. Edgington d. Mrs Harding 6-0 6-1; Mrs C. O. Tuckey d. Mrs F. Schmidt 6-4 6-2; Miss Broquedis (F) d. Mrs Parbury 6-4 6-2; E. D. Holman d. Miss Hill w.o.; Mrs A. E. Beamish d. Miss Elliadi w.o.; Mrs G. C. Hampton d. Mrs Jacob w.o.; Mrs D. R. Larcombe d. Miss Baldwin 6-2 6-2; Mrs A. Sterry d. M. L. Fison 6-2 6-2; Mrs R. J. McNair d. B. M. S. Lee 2-4 6-4 6-3; B. Leader d. Mrs Barclay 6-3 6-0; Mrs A. Mitchell d. D. K. Betty 6-0 6-1; J. Green d. Mrs Williams 6-2 3-6 6-4; Mrs Holloway d. Mrs Greenough Smith 6-0 6-4; V. M. Pinckney d. Mrs Baker 6-1 6-1; H. Aitchison d. Mrs E. G. Parton 6-2 6-4; B. Tulloch d. Mrs F. J. Hannam 2-6 7-5 6-4; A. M. Morton d. Mrs Satterthwaite 6-2 6-3; E. Ryan (USA) d. E. Nash 6-0 6-1.

SECOND ROUND: Mrs Craddock d. M. H. Davy 6-0 6-3; G. B. Palmer d. Mrs Ritchie w.o.; Mrs O'Neill d. V. E. Spofforth 7-5 9-7; Edgington d. Lane 6-4 2-6 6-4; Tuckey d. Broquedis 6-1 5-7 6-2; Holman d. Beamish 6-1 5-7 8-6; Larcombe d. Hampton 6-2 6-3; Sterry d. McNair 6-4 7-5; Leader d. Mitchell 6-4 6-3; Green d. Holloway 6-4 1-6 6-3; Aitchison d. Pinckney 6-3 6-0; Morton d. Tulloch 6-1 6-3; Ryan d. Mrs Hole w.o.; E. G. Johnson d. Countess of Drogheda 6-0 6-0; C. M. Douglass d. Mrs Nesham 3-6 6-3 6-2; Mrs Crundall Punnett d. Mrs N. Willford 6-2 8-6.

THIRD ROUND	QUARTER-FINALS	SEMI-FINALS	FINAL	ALL-COMERS' CHAMPION
Craddock	Craddock	Edgington		
Palmer	4-6 6-2 8-6	6-1 6-3		
Edgington	Edgington		Larcombe	
O'Neill	6-3 6-3		4-6 6-3	
Tuckey	Tuckey			
Holman	8-6 3-6 6-4	Larcombe		
Larcombe	Larcombe	w.o.		
Sterry	6-2 6-1			Larcombe
Leader	Leader			6-3 6-2
Green	7-5 6-3	Aitchison		
Aitchison	Aitchison	6-2 6-0		
Morton	7-5 6-3		Ryan	
Ryan	Ryan		4-6 6-3	
Johnson	6-2 6-3	Ryan		
Crundall Punnett	Crundall Punnett	6-0 6-3		
Douglass	6-1 6-4			

Challenge round: Mrs R. Lambert Chambers (Holder) d. Mrs D. R. Larcombe (Challenger) 7-5 6-4.

OTHER FINALS

GENTLEMEN'S DOUBLES: Final — N. E. Brookes (A)/A. F. Wilding (NZ) d. A. H./F. G. Lowe 6-2 8-6 6-1.
Challenge round — Brookes/Wilding d. C. P. Dixon/H. Roper Barrett 6-1 6-1 5-7 8-6.
LADIES' DOUBLES: Final — A. M. Morton/E. Ryan (USA) d. Mrs D. R. Larcombe/Mrs G. Hannam 6-1 6-3.

MIXED DOUBLES: Final — J. C. Parke/Mrs D. R. Larcombe d. A. F. Wilding (NZ)/M. Broquedis (F) 4-6 6-4 6-2.
GENTLEMEN'S SINGLES PLATE: Final — C. P. Dixon d. R. W. F. Harding 6-1 6-2.

GENTLEMEN'S SINGLES

1919

FIRST ROUND: H. J. P. Thompson d. N. G. Deed 6-4 2-6 6-4 5-7 7-5; D. Beningfield d. W. P. Haviland 6-4 6-3 6-2; C. P. Dixon d. W. A. Ingram 6-4 6-4 6-1; N. Field d. R. D. England w.o.; L. Raymond (SA) d. S. Glen Walker 6-0 6-1 6-1; D. Mathey d. J. C. F. Simpson 6-3 6-0 6-0; J. S. Brown d. A. C. Wiswell 7-5 6-3 4-6 6-2; S. P. O'Donnell d. G. Wrenn (USA) w.o.; H. Sharpe d. F. Thomasson 6-3 6-2 10-8; H. L. Addison d. P. F. Glover w.o.; G. T. C. Watt d. Ivor Evans 6-3 6-1 6-2; F. H. Jarvis d. A. W. Gore 2-6 4-6 7-5 6-4 6-2; C. Tindell Green d. A. H. West 8-6 8-6 7-5; M. J. G. Ritchie d. J. 'Robinson' 6-2 6-1 6-0; J. S. Cannon d. H. A. Davis 7-5 6-4 6-3; B. E. Henty d. L. F. Davin w.o.; A. M. Lovibond d. J. M. Flavelle 6-1 2-2 ret'd; A. H. Gobert d. N. Mishu (RU) 6-1 6-4 6-4; M. D. Hick d. C. L. Philcox 8-10 6-8 6-3 6-2; F. W. Donisthorpe d. G. B. Youll 6-0 6-0 6-0; M. Woosnam d. W. C. Youll 6-2 8-6 6-2; R. W. Heath (A) d. E. S. Franklin w.o.; G. F. Birtles d. P. Byrne 6-2 6-1 6-2; B. I. C. Norton (SA) d. C. E. Leo Lyle 6-1 6-2 6-1; A. H. Lowe d. H. R. Fussell w.o.; T. M. Mavrogordato d. F. Laxon 6-1 6-2 6-1; G. L. Patterson (A) d. H. J. Gilbert 6-0 6-4 6-0; H. Roper Barrett d. L. A. Nypels 6-3 6-4 6-3; E. G. Bisseker d. A.H. Erskine Lindop 6-0 6-4 6-0; A. W. Asthalter d. A. W. Davson 6-1 1-6 2-6 6-2 6-4; S. N. Doust (A) d. G. W. Chesterman 6-0 6-2 2-1 ret'd; F. L. Riseley d. C. G. McIlquham 6-1 6-3 6-2; A. C. Hunter d. B. Wood Hill 6-3 6-3 6-2; V. S. Erskine Lindop d. H. G. Maves w.o.; A. R. F. Kingscote d. W. H. Laurentz (F)

7-5 6-3 6-1; O. G. N. Turnbull d. H. B. Silver 6-1 6-1 6-1; M. Decugis (F) d. S. F. Thol 4-6 6-0 6-4; F. R. L. Crawford d. E. Morris Hall 5-7 3-6 6-2 6-1 6-3; R. 'James' d. C. A. McConchie 7-5 6-0 6-1; C. S. Grace d. J. H. King 6-1 6-1 6-0 6-3; G. H. Dodd (SA) d. R. M. K. Turnbull 6-1 6-2 6-2; H. S. Owen d. R. H. Hotham 6-8 0-6 6-2 7-5 6-2; R. Walker d. H. C. Breck w.o.; P. O'Hara Wood (A) d. G. A. Thomas 6-1 6-8 6-4 5-7 6-3; A. Zorab d. M. R. L. White 6-4 6-2 6-4; E. G. Parton d. M. T. McAvity 6-3 6-4 6-4; H. J. P. Aitken d. P. V. Tabbush 6-2 6-3 6-1; W. M. Washburn (USA) d. D. H. Mellet 6-1 6-3 3-6 6-1; W. C. Crawley d. A. N. W. Dudley 6-1 6-1 6-3; G. H. M. Cartwright d. G. J. Scheurleer w.o.; L. Graves d. N. Willford 6-4 6-3 6-3; C. B. Smith-Bingham d. W. M. Swinden 4-6 6-2 6-4 3-6 6-4; R. Dash d. C. W. Tabbush 6-2 6-1 6-0; H. R. C. Martin d. V. Crawshaw 4-6 6-3 6-1; F. M. B. Fisher (NZ) d. E. D. Black 6-2 6-2 6-4; C. Garland (USA) d. E. Borrett 6-0 6-0 6-1; R. V. Thomas (A) d. J. C. Masterman 6-4 2-6 6-3 6-8 9-7; C. J. Griffin d. J. B. Ward 6-2 6-2 6-2; C. N. Thompson d. L. D. Edwards 6-0 6-2 6-2; E. Seale d. E. G. de Seriere 6-0 8-6 6-4; F. H. Teall d. J. H. Harris 6-1 6-4 6-0; W. Davis d. P. M. Davson 6-2 5-7 2-6 6-2 6-2; G. Stoddart d. E. C. Williams 11-9 6-3 6-2; B. V. Stacy d. W. C. Bersey w.o.

SECOND ROUND: Beningfield d. Thompson 7-5 6-1 6-3; Dixon d. Field 6-1 6-2 6-2; Mathey d. Raymond 3-6 6-2 6-4 6-1; Brown d. O'Donnell 4-6 7-5 6-4 6-4; Sharpe d. Addison 6-2 4-6 8-6 6-3; Jarvis d. Watt 6-3 6-3 ret'd; Ritchie d. Tindell Green 7-5 6-8 6-2 6-2; Cannon d. Henty 7-5 6-1 1-6 6-1; Gobert d. Lovibond 6-2 6-2 6-4; Donisthorpe d. Hick 3-6 7-5 7-5 6-3; Heath d. Woosnam 4-6 6-3 7-5; Norton d. Birtles 6-2 6-0 6-0; Mavrogordato d. A. H. Lowe 5-7 9-11 6-2 6-1 6-3; Patterson d. Roper Barrett 7-5 6-2 7-5; Bisseker d. Asthalter 9-7 6-4 6-4; Doust d. Riseley 1-6 9-7 6-8 6-4

6-1; Hunter d. Lindop 6-2 6-2 6-4; Kingscote d. O. G. N. Turnbull 6-0 6-3 6-1; Decugis d. Crawford 6-2 4-6 5-7 10-8 6-1; Grace d. James 6-3 6-4 6-2; Dodd d. Owen 6-1 6-4 6-2; O'Hara Wood d. Walker 6-1 6-0 6-2; Parton d. Zorab 9-7 2-6 6-3 6-4; Washburn d. Aitken 8-6 6-8 6-0 6-4; Crawley d. Cartwright 6-2 6-4 6-1; Graves d. Smith-Bingham 6-4 6-4 6-0; Dash d. Martin 6-1 6-4 6-3; Garland d. Fisher w.o.; R. V. Thomas d. Griffin 5-7 2-6 6-4 7-5 7-5; Thompson d. Seale 6-2 6-1 7-5; Davis d. Teall 6-0 5-7 6-4 6-0; Stoddart d. Stacy 6-1 6-1 4-6 6-1.

THIRD ROUND: Dixon d. Beningfield 6-2 6-4 6-1; Mathey d. Brown 6-3 7-5 6-0; Jarvis d. Sharpe 6-2 6-4 6-3; Ritchie d. Cannon 6-2 6-1 6-4; Gobert d. Donisthorpe 10-12 6-2 6-0 6-2; Heath d. Norton 5-7 3-6 6-1 6-4 6-2; Patterson d. Mavrogordato 6-0 6-3 7-5; Doust d. Bisseker 6-4 6-1 7-5; Kingscote d. Hunter 6-1 6-2 6-2; Decugis d.

Grace 6-0 6-1 6-3; O'Hara Wood d. Dodd 5-7 8-6 6-4 6-1; Washburn d. Parton 6-3 7-5 6-8 6-3; Graves d. Crawley 6-0 8-6 8-6; Garland d. Dash 3-6 6-0 6-2; R. V. Thomas d. Thompson 6-2 8-6 6-2; Davis d. Stoddart 6-2 6-4 6-2.

FOURTH ROUND	QUARTER-FINALS	SEMI-FINALS	FINAL	ALL-COMERS' CHAMPION
Dixon	Dixon			
Mathey	6-4 7-5 5-7 6-3			
Jarvis	Ritchie	Ritchie		
Ritchie	6-1 6-4 4-6 6-2	4-6 6-4 6-3 6-3		
Gobert	Gobert		Patterson	
Heath	3-6 6-4 6-4 6-1		6-1 7-5 1-6 6-3	
Patterson	Patterson	Patterson		
Doust	6-2 6-0 6-2	10-8 6-3 6-2		Patterson
Kingscote	Kingscote			6-2 6-1 6-3
Decugis	6-2 4-6 4-6 8-6 8-6	Kingscote		
O'Hara Wood	O'Hara Wood	6-4 3-6 6-3 1-6 6-4		
Washburn	12-14 6-3 6-4 4-6 6-3		Kingscote	
Graves	Garland		6-1 6-4 2-6 5-7 6-4	
Garland	6-0 8-6 3-6 6-2	Garland		
R. V. Thomas	R. V. Thomas	6-4 6-0 6-1		
Davis	2-6 7-5 7-5 6-2			

Challenge round: G. L. Patterson (Challenger) d. N. E. Brookes (A) (Holder) 6-3 7-5 6-2.

LADIES' SINGLES

FIRST ROUND: Mrs Winch d. Mrs Silver w.o.; N. B. Palmer d. Mrs Leisk w.o.; L. M. Addison d. Mrs C. O. Tuckey 6-3 6-1; Mrs R. J. McNair d. Mrs Lamb 6-4 6-0; Mrs Satterthwaite d. Mrs A. Hall 6-0 6-0; Mrs Lamplough d. Mrs S. Hall 6-3 6-2; Mrs C. A. Beck d. Mrs Willford 8-6 6-3; Mrs Craddock d. E. Tighe 6-1 6-3; Mrs D. R. Larcombe d. A. G. Ransome 6-0 6-1; S. Lenglen (F) d. Mrs Cobb 6-0 6-1; K. McKane d. O. B. Manser 6-3 7-5.

SECOND ROUND: Mrs A. G. Wilkinson d. G. B. Foster 6-8 6-2 6-4; Mrs A. E. Beamish d. Mrs Wolfson 6-2 6-4; Mrs A. Sterry d. Mrs O'Neill 6-3 8-6; Mrs H. Edgington d. Mrs Greville 6-4 6-2; P. Dransfield d. L. C. Radeglia 4-6 8-6 6-3; Winch d. Palmer 6-0 6-2; McNair d. Addison 12-10 6-2; Satterthwaite d. Lamplough 8-6 6-4; Craddock d. Beck 4-6 4-6 6-0; Lenglen d. Larcombe 6-2 6-1; K. McKane d. Mrs Colston 6-2 6-2; Mrs E. King d. Mrs A. Green w.o.; E. Ryan (USA) d. M. McKane 6-1 6-4; E. D. Holman d. M. A. Wright w.o.; D. Ballingal d. Mrs Hextall w.o.; Mrs E. G. Parton d. Mrs Perrett 6-1 6-4.

THIRD ROUND	QUARTER-FINALS	SEMI-FINALS	FINAL	ALL-COMERS' CHAMPION
Wilkinson	Beamish			
Beamish	7-5 14-12	Beamish		
Sterry	Edgington	6-8 6-3 6-2		
Edgington	8-6 9-11 6-3		Satterthwaite	
Dransfield	Winch		6-4 10-8	
Winch	6-2 6-2	Satterthwaite		
McNair	Satterthwaite	6-3 6-4		Lenglen
Satterthwaite	6-2 6-3			6-1 6-1
Craddock	Lenglen			
Lenglen	6-0 6-1	Lenglen		
K. McKane	K. McKane	6-0 6-1		
King	6-1 6-2		Lenglen	
Ryan	Ryan		6-4 7-5	
Holman	8-6 6-4	Ryan		
Ballingal	Parton	6-2 6-3		
Parton	6-0 6-2			

Challenge round: Miss S. Lenglen (F) (Challenger) d. Mrs R. Lambert Chambers (Holder) 10-8 4-6 9-7.

OTHER FINALS

GENTLEMEN'S DOUBLES: Final – P. O'Hara Wood (A)/R. V. Thomas (A) d. R. W. Heath (A)/R. Lycett 6-4 6-2 4-6 6-2. **Challenge round** – O'Hara Wood/Thomas d. N. E. Brookes (A)/A. F. Wilding (NZ) w.o.
LADIES' DOUBLES: Final – S. Lenglen (F)/E. Ryan (USA) d. Mrs R. Lambert Chambers/Mrs D. Larcombe 4-6 7-5 6-3.

MIXED DOUBLES: Final – R. Lycett/E. Ryan (USA) d. A. D. Prebble/Mrs R. Lambert Chambers 6-0 6-0.
GENTLEMEN'S SINGLES PLATE: Final – F. R. L. Crawford d. M. Woosnam 6-3 5-7 7-5.

GENTLEMEN'S SINGLES

FIRST ROUND: T. M. Mavrogordato d. G. T. C. Watt 6-0 6-2 6-1; F. M. B. Fisher (NZ) d. Col. Day 6-4 6-2 6-3; C. P. Dixon d. T. A. Fuller 9-7 6-2 8-6; P. M. Davson d. B. Hillyard 6-0 6-1 6-4; A. C. Hunter d. E. G. Parton 6-3 7-5 3-6 6-1; A. W. Macpherson d. W. C. Crawley 6-1 6-3 6-4; B. I. C. Norton (SA) d. J. C. F. Simpson 6-2 7-5 6-2; R. H. Hotham d. I. S. White 6-4 6-4 6-1; E. Tegner (D) d. M. Temple 6-4 6-2 6-0; A. B. Gravem d. J. A. Frost 6-3 6-4 6-2; R. N. Williams d. N. Field 6-2 6-1 6-3; G. Boustead d. J. W. O'Farrell w.o.; A. W. Gore d. G. R. Sherwell 9-7 6-2 6-4; J. Brugnon (F) d. J. T. Baines 6-8 6-4 6-4 6-0; L. Raymond (SA) d. B. E. Henty 6-3 6-4 6-3; W. H. Laurentz (F) d. L. F. Davin 6-2 6-3 6-1; W. Lock Wei d. V. Burr 3-6 6-4 8-6 2-6 6-4; C. L. Philcox d. F. Roche 6-2 6-2 6-4; S. Malmstrom (SW) d. B. C. Covell 6-1 6-3 5-7 6-2; A. G. Zerlendi (GR) d. C. E. Leo Lyle 6-4 6-3 6-3; H. S. Owen d. C. Van Lennep (NTH) w.o.; A. H. Gobert (F) d. P. Portlock 6-1 6-2 7-5; F. G. Lowe d. P. F. Glover w.o.; Z. Shimidzu (J) d. A. C. Belgrave 6-3 6-3 6-1; W. P. Pinckney d. N. G. Deed 6-4 6-4 6-1; M. Blythman d. S. H. G. Dillon w.o.; H. G. Mayes d. P. M. Dixon 3-6 6-4 6-3 6-2; R. Walker d. J. B. Ward 5-7 6-0 2-6 6-3 6-2; R. J. McNair d. H. J. Gilbert 6-3 1-6 6-1 6-0; N. Willford d. W. M. Swinden 6-2 6-2 6-4; M. R. L. White d. F. A. Lindeman w.o.; J. E. Hogan d. G. B. Youll 3-6 6-1 2-6 6-2; S. Hardy (USA)

d. T. Moss 6-0 6-3 6-2; S. N. Doust (A) d. R. M. K. Turnbull 6-1 6-2 6-0; R. Lycett d. C. Hopkins 6-2 6-0 6-4; G. A. Thomas d. W. A. Ingram 2-6 6-2 6-3 6-3; A. E. Beamish d. S. F. Thol 6-4 6-2 6-2; H. S. Milford d. L. de Olivares 6-3 5-7 2-6 6-1 6-4; P. de Borman (B) d. A. J. Gerbault 6-1 6-4 3-6 8-6; M. J. G. Ritchie d. H. G. Stoker 6-1 6-3 7-5; F. C. Inman d. L. Robinson 6-1 6-1 7-5; A. R. F. Kingscote d. E. Coutts w.o.; A. H. Lowe d. A. M. Lovibond 6-3 8-6 6-3; E. Morris Hall d. F. Wallers w.o.; J. C. Parke d. D. Kingdon 6-4 6-2 6-3; W. M. Johnston d. J. M. Flavelle 6-2 6-4 6-2; W. T. Tilden (USA) d. H. R. Fussell 6-3 6-2 6-1; A. Dudley d. C. W. Murray 6-4 6-4 10-8; C. R. Blackbeard (SA) d. Mohamed Yasin 6-0 6-1 6-0; G. Stoddart d. B. Wood Hill 6-3 6-3 6-2; G. H. Dodd (SA) d. E. A. Niles 6-2 6-3 6-1; N. Mishu (RU) d. C. E. von Braun 6-4 6-1 6-2; G. J. Scheurleer d. A. Wallis Myers 7-9 4-6 6-2 6-4 4-3 ret'd; F. H. Jarvis d. C. S. Grace 6-4 6-1 6-3; J. M. Bell d. M. D. Hick 5-7 8-6 6-4 4-6 6-1; E. T. Lamb d. C. S. Galbraith w.o.; J. C. Masterman d. E. U. Williams 3-6 6-4 6-3 6-6 6-3; C. L. Winslow (SA) d. E. B. Milner 6-2 6-2 6-2; C. S. Garland (USA) d. O. G. N. Turnbull 7-5 6-8 6-3 6-3; A. S. Drew d. R. S. Barnes 12-10 8-6 6-4; M. Decugis (F) d. A. W. Davson 6-0 6-1 6-3; J. M. Hillyard d. A. W. Asthalter w.o.; L. A. Godfree d. P. E. Harrison 6-1 6-0 6-2.

SECOND ROUND: Mavrogordato d. Fisher 6-4 6-2 6-3; P. M. Davson d. Dixon 6-3 6-2 5-7 6-0; Macpherson d. Hunter 6-4 6-2 7-5; Norton d. Hotham 6-2 13-11 6-2; Gravem d. Tegner 5-7 2-6 6-3 6-4 7-5; R. N. Williams d. Boustead 6-2 6-2 6-1; Brugnon d. Gore 6-2 6-4 2-6 0-6 6-3; Laurentz d. Raymond 6-4 6-3 4-6 6-3; Philcox d. Lock Wei 3-6 4-6 6-4 6-4 6-4; Zerlendi d. Malmstrom 6-1 6-0 6-1 6-4; Gobert d. Owen 6-4 6-2 6-3; Shimidzu d. F. G. Lowe 6-2 6-2 6-8 6-2; Pinckney d. Blythman 6-2 6-1 6-1; Mayes d. Walker 6-1 6-2 4-6 6-4; Willford d. McNair 0-6 6-4 6-4 6-4; Hogan d. White 3-3 ret'd; Doust d. Hardy 2-6 6-1 6-3 6-8 ret'd; Lycett d. Thomas 2-6 6-1 6-3 8-6; Beamish d. Milford

6-0 6-2 6-1; Ritchie d. de Borman 6-4 6-1 6-2; Kingscote d. Inman 6-2 6-0 6-0; A. H. Lowe d. Hall 6-1 6-2 6-2; Parke d. Johnston 7-5 2-6 6-2 8-6; Tilden d. Franklin 6-1 6-1 6-0; Blackbeard d. Dudley 6-3 4-6 2-6 6-4 6-3; Dodd d. Stoddart 6-2 8-6 6-0; Scheurleer d. Mishu 7-5 6-4 4-6 6-3; Jarvis d. Bell 3-6 6-4 4-6 7-5 6-2; Masterman d. Lamb 5-7 6-1 6-2 6-2; Garland d. Winslow 6-4 6-1 6-3; Drew d. Decugis 6-4 9-7 6-8 6-2; Hillyard d. Godfree 6-4 5-7 4-6 6-2 6-3.

THIRD ROUND: Mavrogordato d. P. M. Davson 3-6 7-5 6-3 7-5; Norton d. Macpherson 4-6 6-4 6-2 6-2; R. N. Williams d. Gravem 7-5 6-0 6-1; Brugnon d. Laurentz 6-4 3-6 6-3 6-2; Zerlendi d. Philcox 6-3 2-6 6-3 6-2; Shimidzu d. Gobert 6-4 10-8 4-6 2-6 6-4; Mayes d. Pinckney 6-0 5-7 7-5 6-3; Willford d. Hogan 6-2 1-6 6-1 6-2; Lycett d. Doust

6-2 5-7 6-3 6-4; Beamish d. Ritchie 6-4 6-4 3-6 6-3; Kingscote d. A. H. Lowe 8-6 6-4 6-0; Tilden d. Parke 6-3 6-2 6-4; Blackbeard d. Dodd 6-2 8-6 4-6 6-3; Jarvis d. Scheurleer 6-3 6-4 6-0; Garland d. Masterman 6-4 6-2 6-1; Drew d. Hillyard 4-6 6-1 6-4 6-4.

FOURTH ROUND	QUARTER-FINALS	SEMI-FINALS	FINAL	ALL-COMERS' CHAMPION
Mavrogordato	Mavrogordato			
Norton	6-1 7-5 8-6	Mavrogordato		
R. N. Williams	R. N. Williams	6-3 4-6 9-7 7-5		
Brugnon	6-0 6-2 6-2		Shimidzu	
Zerlendi	Shimidzu		3-6 6-4 6-0 6-2	
Shimidzu	6-3 6-4 6-3	Shimidzu		
Mayes	Willford	6-0 6-1 6-2		
Willford	8-6 6-1 7-5			Tilden
Lycett	Lycett			6-4 6-4 13-11
Beamish	6-2 6-0 4-6 6-0	Tilden		
Kingscote	Tilden	7-5 4-6 6-4 7-5		
Tilden	6-3 5-7 6-4 5-7 6-3		Tilden	
Blackbeard	Blackbeard		6-4 8-6 6-2	
Jarvis	6-2 6-1 6-4	Garland		
Garland	Garland	4-6 6-1 6-3 6-1		
Drew	6-4 6-2 6-1			

Challenge round: W. T. Tilden (USA) (Challenger) d. G. L. Patterson (A) (Holder) 2-6 6-2 6-3 6-4.

LADIES' SINGLES

FIRST ROUND: E. Ryan (USA) d. Mrs E. H. Berthoud w.o.; Mrs Satterthwaite d. D. K. Betty 6-1 6-1; Mrs Winch d. I. E. Ward 6-2 6-2; E. D. Holman d. Mrs R. C. Middleton 6-2 ret'd; Mrs Davis d. Mrs A. A. Hall 6-4 6-2; Mrs E. G. Parton d. Mrs C. E. Hunter 6-1 6-2; M. B. Holmes d. N. Durlacher 6-3 6-1; Mrs D. R. Larcombe d. E. Tighe w.o.; E. F. Rose d. Mrs H. C. Hextall 6-4 4-6 6-4; S. Lance (A) d. Mrs L. H. Wimble 1-6 6-2 6-1; D. C. Shepherd d. Mrs C. L. Winslow 11-9

6-3; Mrs H. Leisk d. Mrs R. C. Cole w.o.; P. L. Howkins d. O. B. Manser 6-2 6-1; Mrs F. Mallory (USA) d. E. G. Johnson w.o.; Mrs Geen d. Mrs Craddock 6-3 6-4; M. McKane d. N. E. Black 6-3 8-6; P. H. Dransfield d. Mrs M. Decugis (F) 6-3 6-1; Mrs Lamplough d. Mrs O'Neill 5-7 6-3 6-3.

SECOND ROUND: V. Pinckney d. Mrs F. S. Warburg 6-1 6-2; Mrs R. W. F. Harding d. A. Currie 11-9 6-4; Mrs A. E. Beamish d. Mrs J. S. Youle 6-3 6-2; Ryan d. Mrs H. Edgington 6-1 6-2; Satterthwaite d. Winch 6-1 6-1; Holman d. Davis 6-0 6-1; Parton d. Holmes 6-1 2-6 6-2; Tighe d. Rose 6-4 0-6 7-5; Shepherd d. Lance 6-2 6-4; Leisk d. Howkins

8-6 1-6 6-2; Mallory d. Geen 6-3 7-5; Dransfield d. M. McKane 6-2 6-2; Mrs R. Lambert Chambers d. Lamplough 6-0 6-1; Mrs C. O. Tuckey d. C. M. Everard w.o.; Mrs R. J. McNair d. Mrs D. K. Hole 6-3 6-2; K. McKane d. E. L. Colyer 6-1 4-6 6-3.

THIRD ROUND	QUARTER-FINALS	SEMI-FINALS	FINAL	ALL-COMERS' CHAMPION
Pinckney	Pinckney			
Harding	6-0 6-0	Ryan		
Beamish	Ryan	w.o.		
Ryan	9-7 6-4		Ryan	
Satterthwaite	Satterthwaite		6-4 6-2	
Holman	6-2 6-3	Parton		
Parton	Parton	6-4 6-4		
Tighe	6-3 6-2			Lambert Chambers
Shepherd	Leisk			6-2 6-1
Leisk	6-3 6-4	Mallory		
Mallory	Mallory	6-3 6-1		
Dransfield	5-7 6-0 6-1		Lambert Chambers	
Lambert Chambers	Lambert Chambers		6-0 6-3	
Tuckey	7-5 6-2	Lambert Chambers		
McNair	McNair	3-6 6-0 6-2		
K. McKane	6-3 4-6 6-2			

Challenge round: Miss S. Lenglen (F) (Holder) d. Mrs R. Lambert Chambers (Challenger) 6-3 6-0.

OTHER FINALS

GENTLEMEN'S DOUBLES: Final — C. S. Garland (USA)/R. N. Williams (USA) d. A. R. F. Kingscote/J. C. Parke 4-6 6-4 7-5 6-2. **Challenge round** — Garland/Williams d. P. O'Hara Wood (A)/R. V. Thomas (A) w.o.
LADIES' DOUBLES: Final — S. Lenglen (F)/E. Ryan (USA) d. Mrs R. Lambert Chambers/Mrs D. Larcombe 6-4 6-0.

MIXED DOUBLES: Final — G. L. Patterson (A)/S. Lenglen (F) d. R. Lycett/E. Ryan (USA) 7-5 6-3.
GENTLEMEN'S SINGLES PLATE: Final — F. G. Lowe d. C. P. Dixon 1-6 8-6 6-3.

GENTLEMEN'S SINGLES

FIRST ROUND: H. Roper Barrett d. J. B. Gilbert 3-6 6-3 6-3 6-1; F. T. Stowe d. M. E. Nigel Jones 6-3 5-7 7-5 6-4; H. S. Owen d. G. C. Golding 6-4 6-2 6-2; G. T. C. Watt d. E. S. Franklin w.o.; Z. Shimidzu (J) d. R. H. Hotham 6-1 6-1 6-0; V. de Bousies d. J. D. E. Jones w.o.; C. F. Roupell d. C. S. Grace 8-6 9-7 6-4; O. G. N. Turnbull d. R. J. McNair 6-3 7-5 6-1; A. E. Beamish d. C. Ramaswami 6-3 6-2 6-2; G. R. Ashton d. A. Dudley w.o.; C. F. Scroope d. F. H. Teall 6-3 6-0 6-4; M. J. G. Ritchie d. C. E. von Braun 6-4 6-2 6-0; E. U. Williams d. P. M. Dixon 2-6 6-3 7-5; G. Stoddart d. A. C. Hunter w.o.; A. C. Belgrave d. G. Towle 6-0 6-4 6-1; R. Lycett d. L. E. Gaunt 6-0 6-2 6-4; G. R. Sherwell d. H. E. Pervin 6-1 6-2 6-2; M. Temple d. W. P. Pinckney 6-1 4-1 ret'd; W. Radcliffe d. W. L. Hollick 6-2 5-7 8-6 6-2; G. F. Birtles d. H. S. Job 6-8 6-4 6-4 6-4; H. G. Stoker d. L. M. Andrews 0-6 9-7 6-3 6-2; A. Wallis Myers d. E. G. Parton 6-4 6-3 6-1; M. Alonso (SP) d. H. L. Askham 6-3 6-3; L. F. Davin d. T. B. Nicholson 6-3 7-5 6-3; A. M. Lovibond d. T. Moss 6-2 9-7 6-4; 'J. Sydney' d. J. Evers 6-4 6-3 10-8; T. M. Mavrogordato d. N. G. Deed 6-2 6-1; A. W. Davson d. E. M. Hall 6-1 6-0 6-2; A. R. F. Kingscote d. F. M. B. Fisher (NZ) 6-2 6-1 7-5; C. P. Dixon d. G. L. A. Brian 6-4 6-3 6-1; F. G. Lowe d. W. C. Crawley 6-2 6-4; A. H. Fyzee (IN) d. C. S. Gordon Smith 6-1 6-1 6-2; M. Woosnam d. G. D. H. Alston 6-3 6-2 6-3; A. S. Drew d. H. P. Greenwood 7-5 6-3; C. Campbell d. B. Hillyard 6-2 7-5 6-1; A. J. Gerbault d.

A. A. Fyzee (IN) 4-6 6-4 10-8 6-4; A. Diemer Kool d. A. B. Gravem 6-4 4-6 5-7 6-4 6-3; D. H. Kleinman d. R. de Grenus 0-6 6-3 4-6 6-3 9-7; A. H. Gobert (F) d. W. H. Laurentz (F) w.o.; F. W. Donisthorpe d. H. I. P. Aitken 4-6 4-6 6-3 6-0; L. A. Godfree d. H. C. Eltringham 6-3 6-2 6-3; P. M. Davson d. J. A. Frost 6-2 3-6 6-1 6-4; B. Haughton d. J. L. Holt 6-4 6-4 6-1; F. T. Hunter (USA) d. J. M. Hillyard 6-3 6-2 6-0; M. Sleem (IN) d. J. C. F. Simpson 6-1 6-0 6-2; G. H. M. Cartwright d. A. K. Davis 2-6 1-6 3; R. D. Watson d. M. D. Hick 6-4 6-2 2-6 6-4; U. Kramet d. D. Browne 6-3 6-3 7-9 6-3; E. D. Black d. F. de Saram 6-2 2-6 6-1 7-5; J. D. P. Wheatley d. L. S. Deane 6-4 4-6 6-2; H. B. Harrison d. J. Nathan 6-4 6-2 6-4; B. I. C. Norton (SA) d. J. C. F. Masterman 6-4 4-10 12-6 2; A. H. Lowe d. C. E. Leo Lyle 4-6 6-3 6-4 6-1; P. de Borman (B) d. F. de Weck 6-2 7-5 6-1; S. M. Jacob d. A. W. Gore 6-3 6-2 6-2; G. A. Thomas d. H. S. Milford 5-7 6-4 7-5 7-5; C. Van Lennep (NTH) d. E. J. Bunbury 6-0 6-2 6-4; W. A. Ingram d. A. Jones 6-1 6-2 4-6 6-3; O. C. Johnson d. J. W. O'Farrell 6-2 6-0 6-0; T. Bevan d. R. Walker 6-1 6-0 1-6 6-2; E. G. Bisseker d. G. M. Boustead 6-4 6-3 6-1; H. G. Mayes d. F. P. Down 6-2 6-1 6-2; F. H. Jarvis d. R. S. Barnes 4-4 5-7 6-2 6-2; R. Dash d. J. T. Baines 6-4 6-3 9-7.

SECOND ROUND: Roper Barrett d. Stowe 2-6 4-6 6-3; Owen d. Watt 6-1 6-3 6-4; Shimidzu d. de Bousies 6-0 6-2 6-0; Turnbull d. Roupell 6-0 6-3 6-3; Beamish d. Ashton w.o.; Ritchie d. Scroope 6-3 8-6 6-0; Williams d. Stoddart w.o.; Lycett d. Belgrave 6-3 6-2 6-4; Sherwell d. Temple 1-6 5-7 7-5 7-5 6-2; Birtles d. Radcliffe 1-6 6-4 6-1 4-6 6-1; Stoker d. Wallis Myers 1-6 6-3 6-2 8-6; Alonso d. Davin 6-2 6-0 6-3; Lovibond d. 'Sydney' 6-3 6-0 6-1; Mavrogordato d. A. W. Davson 6-0 6-0 7-5; Kingscote d. Dixon 6-1 6-0 6-0; F. G. Lowe d. A. H. Fyzee 2-6 6-4 6-3 6-1; Woosnam d.

Drew 5-7 1-6 6-3 6-2 7-5; Campbell d. Gerbault 6-2 6-3 6-2; Diemer Kool d. Kleinman 8-6 6-1 6-3; Gobert d. Donisthorpe 6-0 4-6 6-1 6-0; P. M. Davson d. Godfree 6-0 9-7 6-1; Hunter d. Haughton 4-6 6-3 3-6 7-5 6-2; Sleem d. Cartwright 6-3 6-0 6-1; Watson d. Kramet 6-2 9-7 6-2; Wheatley d. Black 7-5 6-2 6-3; Norton d. Harrison 6-3 6-2 6-1; A. H. Lowe d. de Borman 6-2 6-0 6-1; Jacob d. Thomas 6-3 6-3 6-1; Van Lennep d. Ingram 6-1 6-1 6-3; Bevan d. Johnson 4-6 6-2 6-1 6-1; Mayes d. Bisseker 6-2 6-1 6-4; Jarvis d. Dash 5-7 6-2 1-6 6-3 6-4.

THIRD ROUND: Roper Barrett d. Owen 6-0 6-1 6-3; Shimidzu d. Turnbull 6-3 7-5 6-1; Beamish d. Ritchie 6-3 6-2 8-6; Lycett d. Williams 6-2 6-2 6-0; Sherwell d. Birtles 6-2 6-4 8-6; Alonso d. Stoker 6-3 6-1 6-2; Mavrogordato d. Lovibond 6-3 6-4 6-3; Kingscote d. F. G. Lowe 6-2 6-3 6-3; Campbell d. Woosnam 7-5 6-3 5-7 2-6 6-4; Gobert d.

Diemer Kool 6-3 4-6 6-1 6-4; Hunter d. P. M. Davson 7-5 6-3 1-6 5-7 9-7; Sleem d. Watson 6-4 6-4 6-2; Norton d. Wheatley 6-4 6-4 6-3; Jacob d. A. H. Lowe 1-6 6-3 6-2 6-2; Van Lennep d. Bevan 6-4 4-6 6-1 6-2; Mayes d. Jarvis 6-3 5-7 6-4 6-3.

FOURTH ROUND	QUARTER-FINALS		SEMI-FINALS		FINAL		ALL-COMERS' CHAMPION
Roper Barrett	Shimidzu						
Shimidzu	6-3 6-3 6-1		Shimidzu				
Beamish	Lycett		6-3 9-11 3-6 6-2 10-8				
Lycett	8-6 8-6 6-4				Alonso		
Sherwell	Alonso				3-6 7-5 3-6 6-4 8-6		
Alonso	6-0 6-2 6-2		Alonso				
Mavrogordato	Kingscote		6-1 6-3 2-6 6-2				
Kingscote	6-0 10-8 6-4						Norton
Campbell	Campbell						5-7 4-6 7-5 6-3 6-3
Gobert	9-7 1-6 4-6 4-2 ret'd		Hunter				
Hunter	Hunter		6-2 7-5 3-6 6-4				
Sleem	2-6 7-5 6-3 7-5				Norton		
Norton	Norton				6-0 6-3 5-7 5-7 6-2		
Jacob	6-1 6-1 6-2		Norton				
Van Lennep	Mayes		4-6 6-2 6-2 6-2				
Mayes	w.o.						

Challenge round: W. T. Tilden (USA) (Holder) d. B. I. C. Norton (SA) (Challenger) 4-6 2-6 6-1 6-0 7-5.

LADIES' SINGLES

FIRST ROUND: Mrs Leisk d. Mrs Davis w.o.; Mrs H. F. Cobb d. Mrs Perrett 3-6 7-5 6-2; M. W. Haughton d. Mrs Parbury 3-6 6-4 6-3; D. C. Shepherd d. B. W. Donaldson 6-0 6-0; Mrs Hollick d. M. Thom 7-5 6-2; E. F. Rose d. Mrs de Borman 6-3 6-4; Mrs Satterthwaite d. Mrs Lamplough 6-3 0-6 6-4; Mrs Craddock d. Mrs A. A. Hall 6-2 6-1; P. H. Dransfield d. Mrs Marriott 4-6 6-2 6-1; P. L. Howkins d. Mrs Alston 6-1 6-0; E. E. Tanner d. N. B. Palmer 6-1 6-2; M. M. Fergus d. R. Foulger 6-3 6-1; L. Bull d. Mrs R. R. W. Jackson 6-2 6-1; Mrs R. J. McNair d. Mrs E. G. Parton 6-1

6-0; Mrs R. C. Middleton d. E. Sigourney (USA) 6-2 6-4; K. A. H. Todd d. Mrs Crundall Punnett 6-3 6-2; Mrs S. W. Gracey d. E. Tighe 6-4 6-1; E. M. Head d. Mrs Rowan Harker 4-6 7-5 6-4; Mrs G. Peacock (SA) d. Mrs O. Bruce 6-1 6-0; Mrs O'Neill d. E. L. Colyer 5-7 6-0 6-2; Mrs A. E. Beamish d. M. Smailes 6-0 6-0; E. D. Holman d. Mrs H. B. Weston 11-9 6-4; K. McKane d. Mrs H. Edgington 6-2 6-4; E. Ryan (USA) d. D. Kemmis Betty 6-3 6-1.

SECOND ROUND: Mrs Clayton d. M. McKane 6-1 2-6 6-3; E. Kelsey d. P. Ingram 7-5 7-5; Leisk d. Cobb 6-3 6-1; Shepherd d. Haughton 4-6 6-4 6-0; Rose d. Hollick 6-1 6-2; Satterthwaite d. Craddock 6-1 2-6 7-5; Howkins d. Dransfield 6-4 9-7; Fergus d. Tanner 5-7 7-5 6-4; McNair d. Bull 6-4 6-4 6-3; Middleton d. Todd 8-6 6-3; Gracey d.

Head 6-4 4-6 7-5; Peacock d. O'Neill 6-1 6-2; Beamish d. Holman 6-1 7-5; Ryan d. K. McKane 6-4 6-2; Mrs Geen d. Mrs Colston 6-1 6-3; Mrs F. Mallory (USA) d. E. G. Johnson w.o.

THIRD ROUND	QUARTER-FINALS		SEMI-FINALS		FINAL		ALL-COMERS' CHAMPION
Clayton	Clayton						
Kelsey	6-1 6-0		Clayton				
Leisk	Shepherd		6-3 6-2				
Shepherd	7-5 4-6 6-1				Satterthwaite		
Rose	Satterthwaite				8-6 6-2		
Satterthwaite	6-2 6-1		Satterthwaite				
Howkins	Howkins		6-1 6-8 6-1				
Fergus	6-0 6-4						Ryan
McNair	McNair						6-1 6-0
Middleton	7-5 6-2		Peacock				
Gracey	Peacock		7-5 2-6 6-4				
Peacock	6-0 6-4				Ryan		
Beamish	Ryan				8-6 6-4		
Ryan	7-5 6-4		Ryan				
Geen	Mallory		0-6 6-4 6-4				
Mallory	6-3 6-2						

Challenge round: Miss S. Lenglen (F) (Holder) d. Miss E. Ryan (USA) (Challenger) 6-2 6-0.

OTHER FINALS

GENTLEMEN'S DOUBLES: Final — R. Lycett/M. Woosnam d. A. H./F.G. Lowe 6-3 6-0 7-5. **Challenge round** — Lycett/Woosnam d. C. S. Garland (USA)/R. N. Williams (USA) w.o.
LADIES' DOUBLES: Final — S. Lenglen (F)/E. Ryan (USA) d. Mrs A. E. Beamish/Mrs G. Peacock (SA) 6-1 6-2.

MIXED DOUBLES: Final — R. Lycett/E. Ryan (USA) d. M. Woosnam/P. L. Howkins 6-3 6-1.
GENTLEMEN'S SINGLES PLATE: Final — J. B. Gilbert d. F. M. B. Fisher (NZ) 7-5 4-6 6-0.

From 1922 onwards the Challenge rounds were abolished.

GENTLEMEN'S SINGLES

1922

FIRST ROUND: M. Alonso (SP) d. E. G. Bisseker 6-1 7-5 3-6 2-6 6-3; J. Brugnon (F) d. J. C. F. Masterman 9-7 4-6 5-7 6-2 6-2; J. M. Alonso (SP) d. H. P. Greenwood 5-7 4-6 7-5 9-7 7-5; M. J. G. Ritchie d. A. W. Asthalter 6-2 6-4 6-2; G. C. Golding d. O. G. Miller 6-3 7-5 5-7 4-6 6-2; R. Lycett d. C. Colombo 6-4 5-7 6-4 6-4; P. F. Glover d. M. D. Hick 6-3 7-5 6-3; H. L. de Morpurgo (IT) d. P. de Becker w.o.; C. F. Roupell d. J. M. Lowry 6-1 6-4 2-6 6-3; A. S. Drew d. H. O. Dixon 6-1 6-4 6-2; A. H. Lowe d. B. Haughton 6-4 6-2 6-2; M. Dupont (F) d. C. P. Dixon 6-4 7-5 2-6 6-3; T. Bevan d. E. L. Bartleet 6-1 3-6 6-3 6-4; P. M. Davson d. A. N. W. Dudley 6-4 5-7 6-3 4-6 6-4; D. Greig d. L. Ricciardi 6-1 6-0 6-1; G. C. Caner d. R. R. P. Barbour 6-1 6-1 11-9; T. M. Mavrogordato d. G. R. Sherwell 6-2 6-1 6-1; A. N. Wilder d. W. A. Ingram 3-6 4-6 6-1 7-5 6-2; C. E. Leo Lyle d. M. Temple 6-1 6-3 6-3; C. G. McIlquham d. C. S. Gordon Smith 6-4 6-4 ret'd; C. E. von Braun d. J. Weakley 6-3 6-1 6-1; P. C. Chase d. W. L. van Ryn 6-1 2-6 6-2 6-3; D. L. Craig d. J. J. Lezard 6-1 8-6 9-7; H. R. Fussell d. H. S. Milford 7-9 4-6 6-1 6-3 7-5; H. S. L. Barclay d. V. A. Cazalet 6-2 6-3 6-2; C. A. Belgrave d. F. Vasconcelos w.o.; F. M. B. Fisher (NZ) d. A. J. Gerbault (F) 6-3 6-0 6-0; J. B. Gilbert d. C. S. Grace 6-4 4-6 6-3 7-5; S. M. Hadi d. H. S. Owen 3-6 4-6 6-4 6-1 6-2; A. Blair d. P. de Borman (B) 6-1 6-2 6-3; R. Dash d. A. M. D. Pitt 6-4 6-2 2-6 6-4; G. A. Thomas d. A. W. Davson 2-6 6-4 6-3 6-3; A. H. Fyzee (IN) d. A. W. Gore 6-2 6-2 6-4; S. F.

Hepburn d. C. Balbi de Robecco w.o.; B. I. C. Norton (SA) d. W. M. Swinden 6-4 6-2 7-5; J. O. Anderson (A) d. O. G. N. Turnbull 7-5 7-5 6-3; Dean Mathey d. J. Washer (B) 0-6 6-2 6-2 7-5; H. Cochet (F) d. W. C. Crawley 4-6 3-6 6-4 7-5 6-2; N. Mishu (RU) d. S. D. Casanovas 6-2 6-1 6-3; C. Ramaswami d. E. U. Williams 5-7 8-10 6-0 14-12 6-3; E. Flaquer d. N. Willford 6-4 6-4 5-7 6-3; M. Wallenberg (SW) d. M. D. Horn 6-2 6-3 6-3; C. H. Kingsley d. S. D. de Verda w.o.; W. Radcliffe d. R. Peyrelongue 4-6 6-4 6-4 9-7; P. O'Hara Wood (A) d. R. Lacoste (F) 6-1 6-1 6-3; Count de Gomar (SP) d. G. L. Brian 6-3 6-0 6-1; J. M. Hillyard d. F. R. L. Crawford 1-6 6-3 6-3 9-7; A. Zerlendi (GR) d. W. L. Hollick 6-2 6-4 6-4; G. L. Patterson (A) d. D. L. Morgan w.o.; A. B. Gravem d. A. G. Watson (B) 6-4 6-2 4-6 7-5; J. Borotra (F) d. F. H. Jarvis 6-1 6-4 6-3; Dean Mathey d. N. Mishu (RU) d. S. D. Casanovas 6-2 6-1 6-3; C. Ramaswami d. E. U. Williams 5-7 8-10 6-0 14-12 6-3; A. J. Gore d. E. Coutts w.o.; R. C. Wertheim (A) d. R. H. Hotham 6-2 6-1 6-0; A. H. Gobert (F) d. N. G. Deed 6-2 6-1 6-2; D. R. Rutnam d. W. P. Pinckney 6-3 6-3 7-5; F. G. Lowe d. A. A. Fyzee (IN) 6-3 6-0 2-0 ret'd; C. Campbell d. G. W. V. Hurst 3-6 6-1 6-3 6-2; L. A. Meldon d. J. H. van Alen (USA) 6-3 6-4 5-7 6-2; W. H. M. Aitken d. F. Rattigan 6-2 8-10 5-7 4-2 ret'd; G. Stoddart d. S. F. Thol 6-0 5-7 6-2 7-5; H. G. Stoker d. S. J. Watts 6-4 6-2 6-2; C. J. Tindell Green d. G. M. Elliott 3-6 6-4 6-3 6-3.

SECOND ROUND: Brugnon d. M. Alonso 6-3 6-4 4-6 6-3; Ritchie d. J. M. Alonso 6-3 7-5 2-6 6-1; Lycett d. Golding 6-2 6-2 6-4; de Morpurgo d. Glover 7-5 6-1 6-3; Drew d. Roupell 7-5 6-3 7-9 6-2; A. H. Lowe d. Dupont 6-8 4-6 6-1 6-0 6-4; P. M. Davson d. Bevan 8-6 6-1 3-6 4-6 8-6; Caner d. Greig 7-5 2-6 2-6 6-1 6-4; Mavrogordato d. Wilder 6-1 6-0 6-1; Leo Lyle d. McIlquham 6-4 6-4 6-1; von Braun d. Chase 6-4 7-5 6-3; Fussell d. Craig 6-4 6-2 6-3; Barclay d. Belgrave 6-4 6-4 6-2; Gilbert d. Fisher 6-4 6-3 6-1; Hadi d. Blair 2-6 7-5 6-4 6-4; Thomas d. Dash 0-6 6-2 6-3 6-4;

A. H. Fyzee d. Hepburn 6-1 3-6 6-2 6-2; Anderson d. Norton 6-2 6-3 6-2; Cochet d. Mathey 6-2 3-6 6-4 6-2; Mishu d. Ramaswami 6-1 4-6 6-3; Flaquer d. Wallenberg 7-5 6-3 2-6 6-8 6-4; Radcliffe d. Kingsley 6-3 6-2 6-4; O'Hara Wood d. de Gomar 6-1 6-3 6-4; Hillyard d. Zerlendi 6-2 0-6 6-4 5-7 6-3; Patterson d. Gravem 6-1 6-1 6-4; Borotra d. Eltringham 6-2 6-2 6-2; Kingscote d. A. J. Gore 6-3 6-2 6-1; Gobert d. Wertheim 6-4 6-4 6-2; F. G. Lowe d. Rutnam 6-3 6-1 6-3; Campbell d. Meldon 6-4 6-3 6-1; Aitken d. Stoddart 2-6 6-2 6-3 7-5; Tindell Green d. Stoker 6-3 7-5 6-4.

THIRD ROUND: Brugnon d. Ritchie 8-6 6-2 6-1; Lycett d. de Morpurgo 4-6 6-3 6-0 6-0 6-3; Drew d. A. H. Lowe 4-6 6-2 7-5 8-6; P. M. Davson d. Caner 6-4 6-3 7-5; Mavrogordato d. Leo Lyle 6-2 1-6 6-3; Fussell d. von Braun 6-3 6-2 7-5; Gilbert d. Barclay 6-3 2-6 7-5 6-3; Thomas d. Hadi 8-6 4-6 6-4 7-5; Anderson d. A. H. Fyzee 6-2 2-6 6-2 6-3;

Cochet d. Mishu 3-6 6-3 6-3 4-6 6-2; Flaquer d. Radcliffe 6-2 7-5 6-2; O'Hara Wood d. Hillyard 6-3 4-6 6-2 6-0; Patterson d. Borotra 6-0 6-1 6-3; Kingscote d. Gobert 4-6 6-4 6-2 6-2; Campbell d. F. G. Lowe 15-13 6-2 6-4; Tindell Green d. Aitken 6-1 6-1 6-1.

FOURTH ROUND	QUARTER-FINALS	SEMI-FINALS	FINAL	CHAMPION
Brugnon	Lycett			
Lycett	6-2 1-6 7-5 6-3	Lycett		
Drew	Davson	2-6 6-1 6-4 8-6		
P. M. Davson	6-0 6-4 6-3		Lycett	
Mavrogordato	Mavrogordato		8-6 9-7 6-3	
Fussell	6-1 7-5 6-4	Gilbert		
Gilbert	Gilbert	6-4 3-6 6-3 3-6 6-2		
Thomas	9-11 6-2 3-6 6-2 6-0			Patterson
Anderson	Anderson			6-3 6-4 6-2
Cochet	6-3 6-0 6-4	Anderson		
Flaquer	O'Hara Wood	6-3 6-3 2-6 2-6 6-4		
O'Hara Wood	6-2 6-4 11-9		Patterson	
Patterson	Patterson		6-1 3-6 7-9 6-1 6-3	
Kingscote	6-4 3-6 5-7 6-4 6-3	Patterson		
Campbell	Campbell	7-9 6-3 6-2 6-1		
Tindell Green	2-6 6-2 9-7 6-0			

LADIES' SINGLES

FIRST ROUND: E. Ryan (USA) d. E. M. Head 6-3 6-0; Mrs R. J. McNair d. O. B. Manser 8-6 6-1; E. H. Harvey d. Mrs R. R. W. Jackson 7-5 4-6 6-2; Mrs Rawson Wood d. D. Fenwick 1-6 6-4 6-4; E. L. Colyer d. M. L. Stevenson 6-3 7-5; P. M. Stevenson d. S. C. Lumley Ellis 8-6 6-4; K. McKane d. E. Sears (USA) 6-1 6-0; S. Lenglen (F) d. Mrs M. F. Ellis 6-0 6-0; Mrs Anstey d. Mrs Winch w.o.; Mrs Colston d. P. Ingram 6-3 6-4; P. H. Dransfield d. Mrs H. F. Cobb w.o.; Mrs Leisk d. Mrs Welsh 8-6 6-2; Mrs Middleton d. Mrs Hextall 8-6 6-8 6-1; Mrs G. Peacock (SA) d. 'M. Coles' 6-2 6-1; Mrs Macready d. Mrs A. A. Hall 6-3 2-6 6-2; E. D. Holman d. V. Pinckney 6-1 6-2; C. Rimington d. E. Sigourney

(USA) 6-4 3-6 6-4; Mrs Elliot d. Mrs Johnstone Brown 6-2 6-2; Mrs O'Neill d. Mrs Perrett 7-5 3-6 6-2; L. Bull d. P. Alison 8-6 6-1; A. Rodocanachi d. Mrs E. S. Graham 6-4 6-4; Mrs A. E. Beamish d. D. Kemmis Betty 6-2 6-4; Mrs H. B. Weston d. M. W. Haughton 2-6 6-3 7-5; Mrs Stocks d. M. H. Bain 6-0 6-0; Mrs J. S. Youle d. M. S. Scott 7-5 7-5; Mrs Edgington d. Mrs Craddock 6-1 6-0; E. Z. Stokes d. A. M. Hogg 6-3 6-4; E. F. Rose d. E. Goss (USA) 6-2 6-0; Mrs E. G. Parton d. Mrs B. May 6-2 6-4; Mrs Satterthwaite d. Mrs F. T. Walker 6-0 3-6 6-1; Mrs F. Mallory (USA) d. Mrs Keays 6-0 6-3; Mrs Hollick d. J. Hextall 6-3 6-3.

SECOND ROUND: Ryan d. McNair 4-6 6-3 6-0; Harvey d. Rawson Wood 6-2 6-1; Colyer d. P. M. Stevenson 6-3 6-3; Lenglen d. McKane 6-1 7-5; Colston d. Anstey 2-3 6-3 6-4; Dransfield d. Leisk 8-2 6-4; Peacock d. Middleton 6-2 6-0; Holman d. Macready 6-3 6-0; Elliot d. Rimington 7-5 6-3; O'Neill d. Bull 6-2 8-6; Beamish d.

Rodocanachi 6-2 6-2; Weston d. Stocks 6-4 6-4; Edgington d. Youle 6-2 6-3; Rose d. Stokes 7-5 6-1; Parton d. Satterthwaite 6-4 6-1; Mallory d. Hollick 6-1 6-2.

THIRD ROUND	QUARTER-FINALS	SEMI-FINALS	FINAL	CHAMPION
Ryan	Ryan			
Harvey	6-3 6-3	Lenglen		
Colyer	Lenglen	6-1 8-6		
Lenglen	6-0 6-0		Lenglen	
Colston	Dransfield		6-4 6-1	
Dransfield	w.o.	Peacock		
Peacock	Peacock	6-2 6-2		
Holman	7-5 6-0			Lenglen
Elliot	Elliot			6-2 6-0
O'Neill	6-4 6-3	Beamish		
Beamish	Beamish	8-6 6-1		
Weston	6-3 6-4		Mallory	
Edgington	Edgington		6-2 6-2	
Rose	6-1 3-6 6-3	Mallory		
Parton	Mallory	6-2 6-4		
Mallory	6-2 6-1			

OTHER FINALS

GENTLEMEN'S DOUBLES: Final — J. O. Anderson (A)/R. Lycett d. P. O'Hara Wood (A)/G. L. Patterson (A) 3-6 7-9 6-4 6-3 11-9.
LADIES' DOUBLES: Final — S. Lenglen (F)/E. Ryan (USA) d. K. McKane/Mrs A. D. Stocks 6-0 6-4.

MIXED DOUBLES: Final — P. O'Hara Wood (A)/S. Lenglen (F) d. R. Lycett/E. Ryan (USA) 6-4 6-3.
GENTLEMEN'S SINGLES PLATE: Final — B. I. C. Norton (SA) d. R. C. Wertheim (A) 6-2 6-2.

GENTLEMEN'S SINGLES

FIRST ROUND: E. O. Anderson d. L. W. Alderson w.o.; C. Brierley d. H. K. Lester 6-1 6-2 3-6 10-8; J. M. Hillyard d. A. J. Villegas 6-3 6-2 7-5; J. M. Bell d. S. M. Lahey Bean 6-0 6-2 6-2; J. A. Dean d. C. E. Leo Lyle w.o.

SECOND ROUND: R. Lacoste (F) d. D. S. Menda 6-0 6-4 6-1; R. Dash d. A. H. McCormick 6-4 6-0 6-2; L. F. Davin d. F. R. Scovel 6-2 6-4 4-6 6-3; A. W. Davson d. H. C. Fisher (NZ) 6-4 6-4 3-6 2-6 9-7; S. M. Hadi d. P. C. Chase 6-1 6-2 6-4; A. W. Macpherson d. R. H. Hotham 6-3 6-0 6-2; C. Campbell d. T. R. Quill w.o.; G. R. Sherwell d. R. F. Scovell 7-5 6-3 6-2; N. Willford d. G. Stoddart 2-6 3-6 6-1 3-1 ret'd; J. Brugnon (F) d. B. E. Henty 6-4 6-4 6-3; S. M. Jacob (IN) d. W. Robson 6-0 6-1 6-2; V. Richards (USA) d. J. Washer (B) 6-1 6-3 6-2; M. Fox d. W. Radcliffe 2-6 7-5 6-0 3-6 6-4; P. D. B. Spence (SA) d. G. Millard 7-5 2-6 6-4 7-5; R. D. Watson d. F. R. L. Crawford 5-7 6-3 7-5 4-1 ret'd; W. M. Johnston (USA) d. E. Higgs 6-4 6-2 6-1; J. D. P. Wheatley d. N. H. Latchford 6-1 6-3 6-1; H. S. Milford d. J. P. Carleton 6-2 7-5 6-1; B. I. C. Norton (SA) d. M. J. G. Ritchie 6-2 6-4 6-3; V. R. Penman d. R. Wilkinson 6-3 6-2 2-6 6-2; F. T. Stowe d. G. W. Grounsell 3-6 6-2 6-4 6-1 6-4; W. C. Crawley d. H. S. Owen 6-0 6-2 6-2; H. R. Fussell d. P. Marsden 6-4 6-3 6-2; J. Borotra (F) d. J. Legg 6-4 6-1 1-6 9-7; H. G. Mayes d. A. C. Belgrave 6-3 6-4 6-4; F. M. B. Fisher (NZ) d. E. G. Bisseker 6-2 7-5 6-4; C. Caminos d. J. van Ryn (USA) w.o.; J. T. Baines d. D. Browne 5-7 6-1 6-2 6-0; T. M. Mavrogordato d. G. P. Sayers 6-3 6-3 6-1; M. Woosnam d. H. R. Price 6-0 6-2 6-3; W. H. M. Aitken d. Alderson 6-2 6-3 6-0; Hillyard d. Brierley 6-1 6-2 6-4; Bell d. Dean 9-7 7-5 6-3; H. Larsen d. T. Moss 6-4 8-6 6-2; J. C.
Masterman d. H. W. Standring 6-2 6-0 6-1; C. E. von Braun d. J. F. Phillpotts 6-1 6-0 6-0; C. H. Kingsley d. A. S. Drew 4-6 6-2 6-4 6-4; D. M. Evans d. A. A. Fyzee (IN) 2-6 6-4 6-2 6-3; D. R. Rutnam d. L. S. Deane (IN) 7-5 6-1 3-6 6-3; A. Dudley d. N. Field 6-2 7-5 2-6 4-6 6-4; R. D. Poland d. A. F. Yencken 1-6 6-0 6-3 7-5; L. A. Godfree d. N. Mishu (RU) 1-6 6-4 0-6 6-2 9-7; A. Berger d. V. A. Cazalet 6-3 3-6 6-1 1-6 6-3; U. Kramet d. E. Portlock 7-5 6-3 4-6 3-6 6-1; J. B. Gilbert d. F. Crosbie 6-0 9-7 6-2; F. G. Lowe d. S. J. Watts 6-3 6-2 6-0; M. Temple d. S. Simons 6-3 6-0 6-3; R. Lycett d. E. U. Williams 6-3 6-3 1-6 6-1; V. Burr d. E. Crawshay Williams 4-6 6-3 10-12 6-1 6-4; F. T. Hunter (USA) d. E. Flaquer (SP) 7-5 6-4 6-1; A. H. Fyzee (IN) d. R. R. Boyd 6-0 6-0 6-0; P. Feret d. C. P. Dixon 6-3 6-2 ret'd; N. Dicks d. A. Gentien 10-8 6-4 6-0; P. M. Davson d. N. M. Heath 1-6 7-5 6-2 6-3; H. A. Carless d. O. G. N. Turnbull 1-6 6-3 6-4 6-1; H. G. Stoker d. A. Blair 2-6 7-5 8-10 6-1 6-3; C. J. Tindell Green d. B. D. Helmore 9-7 6-1 6-3; W. M. Swinden d. C. G. McIlquham 6-3 6-4 6-4; Conde de Gomar (SP) d. T. Bevan 4-6 6-2 6-2 6-3; W. A. Ingram d. G. C. Golding 6-1 3-6 6-1 3-6 7-5; D. M. Greig d. G. A. Thomas 6-4 6-4 6-2; R. B. N. Taylor d. C. Branfoot 6-3 2-6 6-8 6-1 6-4; C. F. Roupell d. R. Bernard 6-0 7-5 6-2; C. P. Luck d. M. D. Hick 6-3 6-4 7-5.

THIRD ROUND: Lacoste d. Dash 6-1 6-3 6-4; A. W. Davson d. Davin 8-6 6-2 7-5; Macpherson d. Hadi 6-1 2-6 3-6 6-3 7-5; Campbell d. Sherwell 7-5 6-1 8-6; Brugnon d. Willford 6-3 6-3 6-2; Richards d. Jacob 6-2 6-3 8-6; Spence d. Fox 6-1 6-4 8-6; Johnston d. Watson 6-1 6-2 9-7; Wheatley d. Milford 6-3 9-7 6-4; Norton d. Penman 6-0 6-3 6-1; Crawley d. Stowe 6-2 6-3 6-2; Borotra d. Fussell 6-3 7-5 8-6; Mayes d. F. M. B. Fisher 6-2 6-2 6-0; Baines d. Caminos 6-4 6-4 6-4; Woosnam d. Mavrogordato 5-7 6-1 6-3 10-8; Hillyard d. Aitken 7-5 7-5 6-2; Larsen d. Bell 4-6 7-5 6-3
6-3; Masterman d. von Braun 4-6 6-4 1-6 6-0 6-3; Evans d. Kingsley 6-3 6-2 6-8 6-8 6-1; Dudley d. Rutnam 6-4 9-7 6-4; Godfree d. Poland 6-4 9-7 6-3; Berger d. Kramet 6-1 6-2 3-6 4-6 8-6; Lowe d. Gilbert 7-5 6-4 8-6; Lycett d. Temple 6-4 6-4 6-2; Hunter d. Burr 5-7 6-0 6-5 7-6 2; Dicks d. P. M. Davson 6-8 6-3 6-2 1-6 9-7; Carless d. Stoker 6-0 6-0 3-6 5-7 6-2; Tindell Green d. Swinden 6-4 6-0 6-4; de Gomar d. Ingram 6-4 6-4 7-5; Greig d. Taylor 6-4 6-2 6-4; Luck d. Roupell 3-6 6-2 4-6 6-4 6-3.

FOURTH ROUND: Lacoste d. A. W. Davson 6-2 6-2 6-0; Campbell d. Macpherson 6-3 6-1 6-4; Richards d. Brugnon 6-4 6-1 6-2; Johnston d. Spence 6-0 6-1 6-4; Norton d. Wheatley 3-6 8-6 6-1 6-2; Borotra d. Crawley 3-6 6-2 3-6 7-5 6-0; Mayes d. Baines 6-1 6-4 6-3 6-3; Woosnam d. Hillyard 6-4 6-3 6-3; Masterman d. Larsen 6-4 6-4 6-1; Evans d.
Dudley 7-5 6-3 4-6 6-4; Berger d. Godfree 6-4 7-5 6-1; Lowe d. Lycett 6-1 8-6 3-6 6-3; Hunter d. A. H. Fyzee 8-6 6-3 7-5; Dicks d. Carless 7-5 6-4 7-5; de Gomar d. Tindell Green 8-6 6-4 6-2; Greig d. Luck 6-1 6-4 6-3.

FIFTH ROUND	QUARTER-FINALS	SEMI-FINALS	FINAL	CHAMPION
Lacoste	Campbell			
Campbell	1-6 3-6 6-3 6-2 6-3	Johnston		
Richards	Johnston	6-1 5-7 6-2 6-2		
Johnston	6-4 6-3 7-5		Johnston	
Norton	Norton		6-4 6-2 6-4	
Borotra	6-3 7-5 6-3	Norton		
Mayes	Woosnam	7-5 6-3 6-2		
Woosnam	6-4 8-6 6-1			Johnston
Masterman	Evans			6-0 6-3 6-1
Evans	5-7 6-0 6-1 5-7 9-7	Lowe		
Berger	Lowe	6-2 8-6 7-5		
Lowe	6-4 3-6 6-1 8-6		Hunter	
Hunter	Hunter		6-3 7-5 6-4	
Dicks	9-7 6-4 8-6	Hunter		
de Gomar	de Gomar	3-6 4-6 6-1 6-3 6-2		
Greig	4-6 6-0 6-1 6-4			

LADIES' SINGLES

FIRST ROUND: L. Bancroft d. Mrs McIlquham 2-6 6-0 8-6; M. P. Bayard d. L. Cadle 6-0 6-4; E. R. Clarke d. C. Rimington 7-5 3-6 6-1; A. Rodocanachi d. K. M. Marriott 2-6 6-2 6-3; Mrs Gunter d. Mrs Golding (F) w.o.; K. McKane d. K. L. Gardner 6-1 6-0.

SECOND ROUND: S. Lenglen d. P. Ingram 6-0 6-0; Mrs B. C. Covell d. P. Dransfield 6-4 6-2; Mrs N. McArthur d. Mrs Grisar 6-2 5-7 6-2; Miss Vlasto (F) d. Mrs R. R. W. Jackson 6-2 6-3; Mrs M. B. Reckitt d. K. Bouman (NTH) 6-0 6-3; Mrs Cobb d. Mrs Perrett 6-4 6-1; Mrs Satterthwaite d. E. D. Holman 6-1 0-6 6-3; Mrs Hazel d. Mrs B. May 2-6 6-1 6-4; Mrs F. Mallory (USA) d. H. L. Eddis 6-3 6-2; Mrs Edgington d. Mrs R. Welsh 6-2 7-9 6-4; Mrs W. L. Hollick d. J. Reid-Thomas 6-2 6-2; K. Lidderdale d. V. M. Pinckney 7-9 6-2 7-5; Mrs H. B. Weston d. L. Bull 7-5 6-1; Mrs A. E. Beamish d. J. Hextall 6-3 6-2; Bancroft d. Mrs E. G. Parton 9-7 6-0; Clarke d. Bayard 6-3 6-4; Rodocanachi d. Gunter
1-6 6-4 11-9; McKane d. P. Holcroft 6-1 6-2; Mrs R. C. Clayton d. E. McDonald 6-3 6-1; S. C. Lumley Ellis d. Miss Woolrych 5-7 1-2 ret'd; Mrs J. S. Youle d. E. L. Colyer 6-3 0-6 6-4; E. Goss (USA) d. B. W. Donaldson 6-4 6-1; E. M. Beckingham d. S. M. Fison 6-3 6-4; Mrs Colston d. E. M. Head 6-0 6-3; Mrs Macready d. J. L. Mumford 6-2 6-3; F. M. Haldane d. C. Tyrrell 3-6 7-5 6-2; J. W. Austin d. Mrs Elliot 5-7 6-3 8-6; E. F. Rose d. C. Beckingham 6-4 6-0; E. Ryan (USA) d. Mrs G. B. Goodes 6-0 6-1; Mrs Craddock d. Mrs G. S. Colegate 9-7 6-3; E. H. Harvey d. Mrs Middleton 6-4 6-2; Mrs D. C. Shepherd Barron d. Miss Sears (USA) 6-3 6-2.

THIRD ROUND: Lenglen d. Covell 6-0 6-0; Vlasto d. McArthur 6-2 6-0; Reckitt d. Cobb 6-2 6-2; Hazel d. Satterthwaite 12-14 6-2 6-0; Mallory d. Edgington 6-4 6-0; Lidderdale d. Hollick 8-6 6-3; Beamish d. Weston 6-4 6-2; Clarke d. Bancroft 6-4 1-6 6-4; McKane d. Rodocanachi 6-0 6-1; Clayton d. Lumley Ellis 6-1 6-3; Goss d. Youle
8-6 6-4; E. M. Beckingham d. Colston w.o.; Haldane d. Macready 6-0 6-0; Rose d. Austin 8-6 6-0; Ryan d. Craddock 6-1 6-4; Shepherd Barron d. Harvey 8-6 6-3.

FOURTH ROUND	QUARTER-FINALS	SEMI-FINALS	FINAL	CHAMPION
Lenglen	Lenglen			
Vlasto	6-1 6-0	Lenglen		
Reckitt	Hazel	6-2 6-1		
Hazel	w.o.		Lenglen	
Mallory	Mallory		6-0 6-0	
Lidderdale	6-3 6-3	Beamish		
Beamish	Beamish	4-6 7-5 6-4		
Clarke	6-0 6-1			Lenglen
McKane	McKane			6-2 6-2
Clayton	6-4 6-1	McKane		
Goss	Goss	6-2 6-2		
E. M. Beckingham	6-2 6-2		McKane	
Haldane	Rose		1-6 6-2 6-4	
Rose	4-6 6-2 9-7	Ryan		
Ryan	Ryan	6-0 6-0		
Shepherd Barron	6-1 6-1			

OTHER FINALS

GENTLEMEN'S DOUBLES: Final – L. A. Godfree/R. Lycett d. E. Flaquer (SP)/Count de Gomar (SP) 6-3 6-4 3-6 6-3.
LADIES' DOUBLES: Final – S. Lenglen (F)/E. Ryan (USA) d. J. Austin/E. L. Colyer 6-3 6-1.

MIXED DOUBLES: Final – R. Lycett/E. Ryan (USA) d. L. S. Deane (IN)/Mrs D. C. Shepherd Barron 6-4 7-5.
GENTLEMEN'S SINGLES PLATE: Final – J. Washer (B) d. M. J. G. Ritchie 6-3 6-4.

GENTLEMEN'S SINGLES

1924

FIRST ROUND: S. M. Hadi (IN) d. C. H. Kingsley 6-8 6-4 6-4 6-1; K. Hooi-Hye (CH) d. L. F. Davin w.o.; M. Alonso (SP) d. J. C. Gregory 6-1 6-3 6-4; R. Lacoste (F) d. S. Okamoto (J) 6-2 4-6 6-3 6-4; G. Leembruggen (NTH) d. G. W. Todd 1-6 3-6 6-4 6-0 6-1; J. Weakley d. W. D. K. Thellusson 6-8 8-6 6-3 4-6 6-4; J. B. Gilbert d. O. G. N. Turnbull 6-3 6-4 6-4; J. Condon (SA) d. A. N. Wilder 7-5 6-0 6-2; W. A. Ingram d. F. Canto (M) 4-6 6-1 9-7 6-1; J. Washer (B) d. P. E. Allison (NZ) 6-4 6-3 6-3; R. Lycett d. F. Crosbie 6-3 7-5 6-4; J. M. Bayley d. G. S. Fletcher 8-6 6-4 6-3; F. T. Hunter (USA) d. J. F. Park 6-1 6-2 6-2; J. M. Hillyard d. W. H. M. Aitken 6-2 6-3 7-5; D. R. Rutnam (IN) d. J. Legg 6-1 6-2 6-3; N. E. Brookes (A) d. H. C. Fisher (NZ) 6-2 6-2 6-3; M. Fukuda (J) d. D. Browne 6-4 9-11 6-3 6-2; T. M. Mavrogordato d. G. Stoddart 6-3 3-6 7-5 6-1; S. M. Jacob (IN) d. E. Higgs 6-4 6-0 6-0; H. G. Stoker d. B. D. Helmore 3-6 5-7 6-3 6-0 6-3; N. Dicks d. T. A. Digby 6-0 6-2 6-1; M. J. G. Ritchie d. C. E. von Braun (SW) 6-1 6-0 ret'd; G. R. O. Crole-Rees d. L. W. Alderson 6-3 3-6 6-4 6-2; A. R. F. Kingscote d. F. H. Jarvis 6-0 6-2 6-4; A. N. W. Dudley d. A. J. Gerbault (F) w.o.; V. Burr d. B. M. Clark 5-7 7-5 6-2 3-6 6-4; P. Feret (F) d. C. G. Eames 6-0 10-8 6-4; R. N. Williams d. E. A. McGuire (IRE) 6-1 6-4 6-2; W. M. Swinden d. H. J. F. Hunter (USA) 6-3 6-4 7-5; N. Mishu (RU) d. J. C. Masterman w.o.; I. Richardson (SA) d. J. C. Peacock (NZ) 2-6 6-1 6-1 10-8; H. K. Lester d. C. E. S. Evers 6-4 6-2 6-1; M. Sleem (IN) d. A. W. Davson 6-2 6-1 6-1; L. J. Hill d. A. K. Evans 6-3 6-2 9-7; P. D. B. Spence (SA) d. M. Lozano 6-1 6-2 6-0; C. Bryan d. C. S. Grace 3-6 1-6 6-4 6-2 6-3; J. Borotra (F) d. N. Willford 9-11 6-4 6-3 6-3; M. Woosnam d. N. C. Abrams 6-2 6-1 6-3; C. Fischer (USA) d. V. Rudolf 7-5 6-3 6-3; F. G. Lowe d. H. R. Fussell 6-1 6-4 6-1; J. M. Bell d. E. B. N. Taylor 6-2 6-3 3-6 6-3; A. H. Lowe d. J. H. Van Alen (USA) 7-5 3-6 4-6 7-5 6-1; R. D. Poland d. W. Radcliffe 6-1 7-5 6-3; D. M. Greig d. E. G. Bisseker 2-6 6-2 6-2 6-4; R. Dash d. J. M. Alonso (SP) 7-5 6-2 6-2; V. Richards (USA) d. A. E. Park 6-1 6-1 6-0; E. Crawshay-Williams d. R. G. Stone 6-0 6-3 6-2; T. Harada (J) d. N. G. Deed 6-4 6-1 6-3; W. M. Washburn (USA) d. L. A. Godfree 6-4 6-0 0-7; H. G. Mayes (C) d. M. D. Hick 6-1 6-1 6-3; G. Watson (B) d. J. J. Lezard 3-6 6-1 3-6 6-3 6-0; F. R. L. Crawford d. G. A. Thomas 6-3 3-6 15-13 6-3; C. F. Roupell d. P. M. Davson 7-5 5-7 7-5 2-6 6-1; A. S. Watt d. M. Temple 6-4 6-0 6-4; H. S. Owen d. A. H. Fyzee (IN) w.o.; H. W. Standring d. C. W. Leslie (C) 6-1 6-2 6-0; H. Timmer (NTH) d. F. M. B. Fisher (NZ) 7-5 2-6 9-7 6-3; L. Raymond (SA) d. L. R. C. Mitchell 6-1 6-2 6-2; A. S. Drew d. A. C. Belgrave 7-9 3-6 6-3 6-0 6-2; J. Brugnon (F) d. R. G. MacInnes 6-3 7-5 6-1; A. A. Fyzee (IN) d. G. R. Sherwell 6-2 6-1 6-2; W. C. Crawley d. H. V. S. Dillon 11-9 6-1 9-7; J. D. P. Wheatley d. G. Millard 11-9 8-6 6-1; A. J. Willard (C) d. A. Blair 6-4 6-3 6-1.

SECOND ROUND: Hadi d. Hooi-Hye 7-5 6-3 6-2; Lacoste d. Alonso 2-6 6-2 13-15 6-3 6-2; Weakley d. Leembruggen 6-1 6-1 6-2; Gilbert d. Condon 5-7 6-2 9-7 6-2; Washer d. Ingram 6-3 8-6 3-6 2-6 6-3; Bayley d. Lycett 7-5 6-4 3-6 6-3; Hunter d. Hillyard 6-3 6-2 6-2; Brookes d. Rutnam 6-2 6-2 2-6 6-1; Fukuda d. Mavrogordato 1-6 7-5 6-4 6-4; Jacob d. Stoker 6-3 7-5 6-2; Ritchie d. Dicks 4-6 7-5 7-5 4-6 6-4; Kingscote d. Crole-Rees 6-2 7-5 8-6; Dudley d. Burr 6-2 6-2 5-7 8-6; Williams d. Feret 6-4 4-6 8-6 6-4; Mishu d. Swinden 6-2 6-2 6-4; Richardson d. Lester 6-4 6-2 6-2; Sleem d. Hill 6-3 6-3 6-1; Spence d. Bryan 6-3 7-5 6-4; Borotra d. Woosnam 6-3 7-5 2-6 6-4; F. G. Lowe d. Fischer 6-1 6-3 6-3; A. H. Lowe d. Bell 3-6 6-1 6-1 6-1; Greig d. Poland 6-4 6-0 6-3; Richards d. Dash 6-0 6-4 6-3; Harada d. Crawshay-Williams 6-2 6-1 6-4; Washburn d. Mayes 4-6 6-4 6-0 5-7 6-4; Crawford d. Watson 2-6 6-3 6-0; Watt d. Roupell 6-2 6-4 0-6 2-6 6-3; Standring d. Owen 4-6 4-7 6-5; Raymond d. Timmer 6-4 6-4 6-4; Brugnon d. Drew 6-0 6-3 6-1; Crawley d. A. A. Fyzee 6-3 7-5 6-4; Wheatley d. Willard 4-6 7-5 5-7 7-5 2-1 ret'd.

THIRD ROUND: Lacoste d. Hadi 7-5 6-3 6-3; Gilbert d. Weakley 6-0 6-2 6-0; Washer d. Bayley 6-4 0-6 6-2 6-8 7-5; Brookes d. Hunter 3-6 6-3 6-4 5-7 6-3; Jacob d. Fukuda 6-0 6-2 6-4; Kingscote d. Ritchie 6-4 6-3 6-3; Williams d. Dudley 6-3 6-0 6-4; Richardson d. Mishu 2-6 6-3 3-1 ret'd; Spence d. Sleem 6-4 1-6 6-3 6-2; Borotra d. F. G. Lowe 6-1 6-3 6-4; Greig d. A. H. Lowe 2-6 6-2 6-2 6-2 6-4; Richards d. Harada 6-4 6-1 6-2; Washburn d. Crawford 6-4 6-4 4-6 6-2; Watt d. Standring 6-3 6-4 6-3; Raymond d. Brugnon 8-6 2-6 4-6 12-10 6-4; Wheatley d. Crawley 6-3 6-4 8-6.

FOURTH ROUND	QUARTER-FINALS	SEMI-FINALS	FINAL	CHAMPION
Lacoste	Lacoste			
Gilbert	6-3 6-3 6-2	Lacoste		
Washer	Washer	6-1 5-7 6-4 6-2		
Brookes	6-2 7-5 6-4		Lacoste	
Jacob	Kingscote		6-1 3-6 6-2 6-3	
Kingscote	6-3 6-3 6-0	Williams		
Williams	Williams	5-7 6-4 6-3 6-4		
Richardson	6-1 6-1 6-4			Borotra
Spence	Borotra			6-1 3-6 6-1 3-6 6-4
Borotra	6-2 14-12 3-6 6-0	Borotra		
Greig	Richards	6-4 4-6 6-0 6-3		
Richards	6-2 4-6 6-2 7-5		Borotra	
Washburn	Washburn		6-2 6-4 7-5	
Watt	0-6 6-3 6-4 6-4	Raymond		
Raymond	Raymond	6-0 7-5 17-15		
Wheatley	7-5 6-0 6-0			

LADIES' SINGLES

FIRST ROUND: Mrs Hazel d. R. Watson 6-1 4-6 6-1; E. F. Rose d. G. C. Hutchings 6-3 6-0; Mrs D. C. Shepherd Barron d. Mrs J. Hill 8-6 6-0; H. Wallis d. Miss Sigourney (USA) 3-6 6-2 8-6; Mrs Satterthwaite d. E. Goss (USA) 6-4 6-4; C. Tyrrell d. J. M. Coote 6-2 6-3; K. Lidderdale d. Mrs C. O. Tuckey 2-6 6-4 ret'd; Mrs Craddock d. J. C. Ridley 6-4 6-3; H. N. Wills (USA) d. L. Scharman 6-1 6-0; P. H. Dransfield d. L. Bull (USA) 4-6 6-1 6-4; Mrs McIlquham d. H. L. Eddis 6-1 6-2; Mrs H. Edgington d. Mrs Jackson Feilden 6-3 6-1; Mrs Colegate d. Mrs H. B. Weston 6-4 6-3; A. Rodocanachi d. C. J. Walters w.o.; E. L. Colyer d. Mrs Macready (F) 8-6 6-1; Mrs A. E. Beamish d. Mrs R. C. Middleton 6-0 6-0; Mrs J. B. Jessup (USA) d. Mrs Hasler 6-1 6-2; Mrs Barrett d. Mrs L. C. Pitman 6-1 6-3; P. Holcroft d. M. K. Taylor 6-4 6-3; M. W. Haughton d. J. W. Austin 2-6 6-3 6-2; K. McKane d. Mrs Colston 6-4 4-6 6-1; Mrs F. Mallory (USA) d. E. H. Harvey 7-5 6-3; Miss Woolrych d. Mrs Monk (SWZ) 6-1 6-4; M. Coles d. Mrs R. Welsh 6-3 6-2; E. R. Clarke d. E. R. Sears (USA) 6-1 6-2; S. Lenglen (F) d. S. C. Lumley Ellis 6-0 6-0; Mrs G. Wightman (USA) d. Mrs R. J. McNair 6-2 7-5; Mrs Saunders-Taylor d. I. Haselden (C) 6-0 6-0; Mrs B. C. Covell d. E. D. Holman 4-6 6-4 6-0; J. Reid-Thomas d. K. M. Marriott 9-7 6-4; Mrs E. G. Parton d. K. Bouman (NTH) 6-1 2-6 8-6; E. Ryan (USA) d. Mrs P. Bouverie 6-0 6-0.

SECOND ROUND: Rose d. Hazel 6-1 6-1; Shepherd Barron d. Wallis 6-0 6-1; Satterthwaite d. Tyrrell 6-1 6-4; Craddock d. Lidderdale 6-1 6-3; Wills d. Dransfield 6-0 6-2; Edgington d. McIlquham 6-8 6-3 7-5; Colegate d. Rodocanachi 6-0 6-0; Colyer d. Beamish 6-3 6-4; Jessup d. Barrett 6-0 6-2; Holcroft d. Haughton 6-1 9-7; McKane d. Mallory 6-1 6-0; Woolrych d. Coles 12-10 2-6 6-3; Lenglen d. Clarke 6-0 6-0; Wightman d. Saunders-Taylor 6-0 6-2; Covell d. Reid-Thomas 6-1 6-1; Ryan d. Parton 6-4 8-6.

THIRD ROUND	QUARTER-FINALS	SEMI-FINALS	FINAL	CHAMPION
Rose	Shepherd Barron			
Shepherd Barron	6-2 6-4	Satterthwaite		
Satterthwaite	Satterthwaite	6-4 10-8		
Craddock	6-1 6-1		Wills	
Wills	Wills		6-2 6-1	
Edgington	6-2 6-2	Wills		
Colegate	Colegate	6-1 6-0		
Colyer	6-3 6-3			McKane
Jessup	Jessup			4-6 6-4 6-4
Holcroft	6-1 6-3	McKane		
McKane	McKane	6-1 6-3		
Woolrych	4-6 6-0 6-0		McKane	
Lenglen	Lenglen		w.o.	
Wightman	6-0 6-0	Lenglen		
Covell	Ryan	6-2 6-8 6-4		
Ryan	6-4 7-5			

OTHER FINALS

GENTLEMEN'S DOUBLES: Final — F. T. Hunter (USA)/V. Richards (USA) d. W. M. Washburn (USA)/R. N. Williams (USA) 6-3 3-6 8-10 8-6 6-3.
LADIES' DOUBLES: Final — Mrs G. Wightman (USA)/H. N. Wills (USA) d. Mrs B. C. Covell/K. McKane 6-4 6-4.

MIXED DOUBLES: Final — J. B. Gilbert/K. McKane d. L. A. Godfree/Mrs D. C. Shepherd Barron 6-3 3-6 6-3.
GENTLEMEN'S SINGLES PLATE: Final — J. Condon (SA) d. J. M. Hillyard 7-5 6-2.

GENTLEMEN'S SINGLES

FIRST ROUND: W. E. N. Kelly d. E. U. Williams 6-4 5-7 6-4 6-4; B. Hillyard d. E. Salmond w.o.; H. Cochet (F) d. J. C. Gregory 6-4 6-2 6-0; A. Zerlendi (GR) d. N. G. Deed 4-6 6-2 6-2 6-2; R. Jagmohan d. A. H. Gobert (F) w.o.; Jagat Mohan Lal (IN) d. E. M. Jonklaas 6-4 6-3 4-6 6-2; W. A. Ingram d. D. Powell 4-6 6-3 6-1 6-1; J. Pennycuick d. H. G. Stoker 6-3 7-5 6-2; F. H. Jarvis d. J. F. Park 8-6 6-4 10-8; F. G. Lowe d. F. S. Burnett 6-1 4-6 6-1 6-1; N. Sharpe d. L. A. Godfree 2-6 6-4 6-1 6-2; C. J. Tindell Green d. A. A. Fyzee (IN) 6-3 6-3 4-6 6-3; G. R. O. Crole Rees d. F. R. L. Crawford 8-6 7-5 6-3; C. H. Kingsley d. L. C. Terrey 6-2 6-2 6-2; J. Hennessey (USA) d. M. van der Feen 6-3 4-6 6-1 6-2; N. Dicks d. C. F. Roupell 6-2 3-6 6-4 6-0; C. G. Eames d. W. J. Melody 6-2 6-2 6-1; C. S. Garland (USA) d. Lord Cholmondeley 4-6 6-4 2-6 6-4 6-3; J. B. Gilbert d. S. M. Hadi 6-3 6-3 6-4; M. Ferrier d. G. R. Ashton 6-4 6-2 6-4; J. Borotra (F) d. R. W. Heath (A) 6-1 6-3 6-1; O. G. N. Turnbull d. E. Vulliemin w.o.; L. B. Dailey, Junr. d. J. B. Fenno 3-6 6-3 6-3 6-1; W. H. M. Aitken d. P. R. R. Hurditch 6-3 6-4 6-0; P. M. Davson d. G. Stoddart 6-4 6-2 7-5; A. H. Lowe d. E. N. W. Oliver 6-0 6-4 6-0; H. S. L. Barclay d. T. M. Mavrogordato 12-14 7-5 6-1 3-6 6-3; M. Temple d. H. A. Lake 6-2 6-2 6-0; B. de Kehrling (HU) d. J. G. Hogan 6-2 6-4 1-6 7-5; H. G. Mayes d. J. P. Carleton 6-1 6-1 2-6 8-6; G. Thomas d. R. Powell 0-6 11-13 6-0 7-5 7-5; L. E. Williams d. A. Casanovas 6-1 6-4 4-6 6-2; L. W. Alderson d. L. J.

Carr 6-0 6-4 6-2; A. H. Fyzee (IN) d. J. M. Hillyard 6-4 6-4 6-3; H. Timmer (NTH) d. D. Stralem 6-0 6-3 7-5; P. Feret (F) d. J. Nicholson w.o.; H. C. Fisher d. M. D. Hick 6-0 6-1 9-7; A. Berger d. N. Willford 6-2 6-1 6-3; P. F. Glover d. H. S. Owen 7-5 5-7 6-4 6-1; L. A. Meldon d. N. Mishu (RU) 7-5 6-4 6-3; P. D. B. Spence (SA) d. R. D. Poland 6-1 7-5 6-4; J. D. P. Wheatley d. R. Dash 6-2 6-2 7-5; V. Burr d. Baron de Banfield 6-8 6-2 6-2 4-6 6-3; J. O. Anderson (A) d. E. B. Andreae 2-6 3-6 8-6 6-3 6-3; J. Brugnon (F) d. N. Cruz 6-2 6-1 6-3; W. B. Stott d. W. M. Swinden 6-3 6-4 4-6 6-3; D. J. R. Sumner d. S. R. Cargill 4-6 6-2 6-1 6-3; L. B. Rice d. W. E. T. Cole 6-4 4-6 6-2 6-2; M. V. Summerson d. R. George 6-0 3-6 6-3 6-4; R. Lacoste (F) d. E. Higgs 6-4 6-2 6-2; C. F. Scroope d. H. S. Utz 6-4 8-6 6-4; R. Lycett d. N. H. Latchford 6-1 6-1 6-1; E. T. Hollins d. J. H. van Alen (USA) w.o.; R. Casey d. C. Bryan 3-2 6-6 6-0 6-3; G. Leembruggen d. C. E. Leo Lyle 4-6 7-5 6-4 6-3; C. E. von Braun d. D. L. Craig 3-6 7-5 6-2 8-6; W. A. Fotheringham d. M. Pan w.o.; S. M. Jacob (IN) d. G. M. Thomas 5-0 6-1 6-1; A. C. Belgrave d. F. M. B. Fisher (NZ) 6-3 2-6 6-1 8-10 6-3; C. G. McIlquham d. J. J. Lezard w.o.; J. Washer (B) d. M. Wallenberg (SW) 6-2 6-4 6-8 8-6; V. S. E. Lindop d. J. Weakley 6-4 6-8 2-6 6-3 6-2; H. L. de Morpurgo d. A. N. W. Dudley 6-0 6-2 6-2; G. R. Sherwell d. H. K. Lester 3-6 6-4 7-5 10-8.

SECOND ROUND: B. Hillyard d. Kelly 6-2 6-3 13-15 6-0; Cochet d. Zerlendi 6-3 6-1 3-6 6-0; Jagat Mohan Lal d. Jagmohan 6-2 6-1 6-3; Pennycuick d. Ingram 2-6 6-4 6-3 6-1; F. G. Lowe d. Jarvis 6-0 6-3 6-4; Tindell Green d. Sharpe 6-2 6-4 6-4; Crole Rees d. Kingsley 3-6 6-1 6-4 6-4; Hennessey d. Dicks 8-6 6-3 6-4; Garland d. Eames 2-6 6-3 4-6 6-4 6-4; Gilbert d. Ferrier 6-1 6-3 6-3; Borotra d. Turnbull 10-8 5-7 7-5 10-8; Dailey d. Aitken 6-2 6-3 6-4; Davson d. A. H. Lowe 2-6 6-1 6-1 6-3; Barclay d. Temple 6-3 6-3 6-3; Mayes d. de Kehrling 7-5 7-5 6-4; L. E. Williams

d. G. Thomas 6-1 6-2 6-2; A. H. Fyzee d. Alderson 6-1 4-6 6-3 6-2; Timmer d. Feret w.o.; H. C. Fisher d. Berger 6-3 3-6 2-6 4-6; Meldon d. Glover 6-0 8-10 6-1 6-1; Spence d. Wheatley 5-6 6-4; Anderson d. Burr 6-0 6-2 6-1; Brugnon d. Stott 4-6 6-2 6-0 6-0; Rice d. Sumner 6-4 6-3 6-1; Lacoste d. Summerson 4-6 2-7 5; Lycett d. Scroope 6-3 6-2 6-1; Casey d. Hollins 6-1 6-2 6-4; von Braun d. Leembruggen 9-7 6-1 6-0; Jacob d. Fotheringham 6-2 7-5 6-0; Belgrave d. McIlquham 6-3 6-2 4-6 6-4; Washer d. Lindop 6-1 6-2 6-3; Sherwell d. de Morpurgo 1-6 6-2 7-5 2-6 8-6.

THIRD ROUND: Cochet d. B. Hillyard 8-6 6-3 6-3 8-6; Jagat Mohan Lal d. Pennycuick 6-2 6-2 6-3; F. G. Lowe d. Tindell Green 6-1 6-2 6-2; Hennessey d. Crole Rees 8-6 2-3 6-3 6-4 6-4; Gilbert d. Garland 8-6 6-1 6-1; Borotra d. Dailey 6-2 6-4 7-5; Barclay d. Davson 7-5 6-0 6-3; Mayes d. L. E. Williams 4-6 4-6 6-3; A. H. Fyzee d. Timmer 4-6 12-10 6-4;

H. C. Fisher d. Meldon 6-2 6-3 6-0; Anderson d. Spence 6-3 8-10 6-2 6-3; Brugnon d. Rice 6-1 6-4 6-1; Lacoste d. Lycett 6-3 4-6 7-5 6-4; Casey d. von Braun 6-3 6-3 6-3; Jacob d. Belgrave 6-1 9-7 6-3; Washer d. Sherwell 6-0 6-3 6-1.

FOURTH ROUND	QUARTER-FINALS	SEMI-FINALS	FINAL	CHAMPION
Cochet	Cochet			
Jagat Mohan Lal	6-2 1-6 6-2 6-3	Cochet		
F. G. Lowe	Hennessey	7-9 4-6 6-1 6-3 6-0		
Hennessey	9-7 8-6 6-4		Borotra	
Gilbert	Borotra		5-7 8-6 6-4 6-1	
Borotra	6-1 7-5 6-3	Borotra		
Barclay	Barclay	6-3 5-7 6-3 6-3		
Mayes	6-2 1-6 4-6 6-3 6-1			Lacoste
A. H. Fyzee	H. C. Fisher			6-3 6-3 4-6 8-6
H. C. Fisher	6-4 8-6 7-5	Anderson		
Anderson	Anderson	6-1 6-1 6-4		
Brugnon	3-6 7-9 6-4 7-5 6-2		Lacoste	
Lacoste	Lacoste		6-4 7-5 6-1	
Casey	8-6 6-4 6-1	Lacoste		
Jacob	Jacob	6-3 6-8 6-0 6-4		
Washer	2-6 1-6 10-8 6-4 7-5			

LADIES' SINGLES

FIRST ROUND: Mrs Satterthwaite d. Mrs Seel 6-1 6-2; B. C. Brown d. Miss Canters 3-6 6-1 6-0; Mrs A. V. Bridge d. Mrs Melody 3-6 6-0; K. McKane d. G. R. Sterry 6-3 6-1; Mrs C. K. Pitt d. L. Dixon w.o.; E. Boyd d. C. Hardie 6-2 6-0; Mrs C. O. Tuckey d. P. Dransfield 6-3 7-5; Mrs Mavrogordato d. C. Beckingham 7-5 2-6 6-2; E. Ryan (USA) d. J. E. Brown 6-3 6-4; S. Lenglen (F) d. Mrs Edgington w.o.; E. A. Goldsack d. Mrs Colston w.o.; L. Bull d. Mrs Jackson Feilden 2-6 6-1 6-0; Mrs Gough d. A. B. Townsend 6-3 7-5; E. M. Head d. Mrs M. B. Reckitt 6-2 6-2; M. Cambridge d. Mrs H. S. Utz w.o.; Mrs A. E. Beamish d. I. A. Maltby 6-0 6-2; J. Fry d. Mrs R. C. Middleton 6-3 6-2; P. Saunders d.

J. C. Ridley 6-1 6-0; C. Tyrrell d. E. Bennett 7-5 6-8 7-5; Mrs W. G. Lowe d. J. Reid Thomas 8-6 13-11; Mrs J. L. Colegate d. Mrs B. May 6-2 6-4; E. L. Colyer d. E. H. Harvey 6-2 2-6 8-6; D. Akhurst (A) d. Mrs H. B. Weston 6-3 7-5; Mrs Craddock d. Mrs Tomlinson 6-2 2-6 6-2; Mrs Billout (F) d. Mrs Lycett 4-6 6-3 11-9; V. M. Pinckney d. V. B. Southam 9-7 6-2; F. St George d. S. K. Johnson 2-6 6-2 6-2; Mrs Hazel d. E. R. Clarke 6-4 6-3; Mrs C. G. McIlquham d. R. Watson 4-5 7-7 5; E. F. Rose d. Mrs R. C. Clayton 6-3 5-7 6-3; Mrs Harper d. Mrs Holcroft Watson 6-2 8-6; K. Bouman (NTH) d. S. C. Lumley Ellis 4-6 6-3 6-1.

SECOND ROUND: Satterthwaite d. Brown 6-2 6-1; McKane d. Bridge 6-0 6-1; Boyd d. Pitt 6-0 6-2; Tuckey d. Mavrogordato 6-2 ret'd; Lenglen d. Ryan 6-2 6-0; Goldsack d. Bull 6-2 6-3; Head d. Gough 6-2 6-0; Beamish d. Cambridge 6-0 6-0; Fry d. Saunders 6-1 6-4; Lowe d. Tyrrell 7-5 8-6; Colyer d. Colegate 2-6 10-8 6-2; Akhurst d.

Craddock 7-5 5-7 6-4; Billout d. Pinckney 6-4 6-2; Hazel d. St George 4-6 7-5 6-3; McIlquham d. Rose 6-4 6-2; Harper d. Bouman 6-3 6-1.

THIRD ROUND	QUARTER-FINALS	SEMI-FINALS	FINAL	CHAMPION
Satterthwaite	McKane			
McKane	6-3 6-1	McKane		
Boyd	Boyd	6-1 6-1		
Tuckey	3-6 6-1 6-3		Lenglen	
Lenglen	Lenglen		6-0 6-0	
Goldsack	6-1 6-0	Lenglen		
Head	Beamish	6-0 6-0		
Beamish	6-4 6-4			Lenglen
Fry	Fry			6-2 6-0
Lowe	7-5 6-1	Fry		
Colyer	Akhurst	2-6 6-4 6-3		
Akhurst	4-6 6-4 6-4		Fry	
Billout	Billout		6-2 4-6 6-3	
Hazel	6-3 3-6 6-2	Billout		
McIlquham	McIlquham	6-3 6-3		
Harper	6-4 1-6 13-11			

OTHER FINALS

GENTLEMEN'S DOUBLES: Final — J. Borotra (F)/R. Lacoste (F) d. R. Casey (USA)/ J. Hennessey (USA) 6-4 11-9 4-6 1-6 6-3.
LADIES' DOUBLES: Final — S. Lenglen (F)/E. Ryan (USA) d. Mrs A. V. Bridge/Mrs C. G. McIlquham 6-2 6-2.

MIXED DOUBLES: Final — J. Borotra (F)/S. Lenglen (F) d. H. L. de Morpurgo (IT)/E. Ryan (USA) 6-3 6-3.
GENTLEMEN'S SINGLES PLATE: Final — B. von Kehrling (HU) d. R. George (F) 6-3 6-4.

GENTLEMEN'S SINGLES

1926

FIRST ROUND: E. Zemla d. N. H. Latchford 1-6 7-5 6-2 6-2; N. Dicks d. J. Weakley 6-4 6-0 6-4; J. Brugnon (F) d. N. Mishu (RU) 4-6 6-4 6-4 6-2 6-1; D. A. Hodges (IN) d. S. W. Bobb (IN) 6-4 6-2 6-2; R. Lycett d. F. Glanz (AU) 6-1 6-2 6-4; J. F. Park d. W. Foley (C) w.o.; W. H. M. Aitken d. E. L. Jones (A) 6-0 1-6 8-6 6-0; G. Leembruggen (NTH) d. R. Lacoste (F) w.o.; C. H. Kingsley d. W. Robson (ARG) 6-2 1-6 6-2 6-4; H. C. Fisher (NZ) d. R. D. Watson 7-5 1-6 7-5 6-4; M. Decugis (F) d. F. R. L. Crawford 2-6 6-4 8-6 1-6 7-5; G. Greville d. R. R. T. Young 6-2 6-3 6-1; H. G. Mayes d. J. E. Pogson-Smith 6-2 6-1 6-3; H. Timmer (NTH) d. D. Stralem 6-2 6-2 6-1; C. F. Aeschliman (SWZ) d. J. N. Lowry (NZ) 7-5 6-1 6-2; F. S. Burnett d. A. C. Crossley 6-2 8-6 6-3; A. A. Fyzee (IN) d. E. L. Sarkies 6-3 4-6 6-2 6-3; E. C. Peters d. T. M. Mavrogordato 4-6 6-3 6-3 2-6 8-6; C. Bryan (NTH) d. Count Salm (AU) w.o.; R. Dash d. C. L. Philcox 4-6 6-2 6-0 7-5; J. B. Gilbert d. C. H. Campbell 7-5 2-6 4-6 6-3 6-2; H. Kinsey (USA) d. C. P. Dixon 6-2 6-1 6-1; E. Flaquer (SP) d. J. Olmsted 8-6 6-4 3-6 7-5; W. C. Crawley d. M. V. Summerson 6-2 6-3 6-2; N. Sharpe d. M. J. G. Ritchie 6-3 6-4 4-6 6-2; Lord Cholmondeley d. F. Bryans 6-1 6-2 6-1; A. Petersen (D) d. E. J. Mockler (IRE) 6-4 6-1 7-5; P. D. B. Spence (SA) d. R. D. N. Pryce Jones 7-5 11-9 6-3; D. M. Greig d. M. Temple 6-4 6-2 6-4; B. D. Helmore d. E. Obarrio (ARG) 6-1 6-4 6-4; O. G. N. Turnbull d. G. R. O. Crole Rees 6-3 6-3 6-2; B. de Kehrling (HU) d. P. Feret (F) 7-5 8-6 6-3; R.

Bernard (IN) d. A. Blair 4-6 7-5 6-3 6-1; M. van der Feen (NTH) d. F. H. Jarvis 6-8 5-7 7-5 6-1 6-1; V. Richards (USA) d. A. F. Yencken 6-0 6-0 6-0; H. Cochet (F) d. A. N. W. Dudley 6-1 7-5 6-3; H. K. Lester d. C. G. McIlquham 8-6 9-7 6-8 6-4; E. Higgs d. J. R. Sumner 6-3 6-2 7-5; F. G. Lowe d. E. Crawshay Williams 6-4 6-2 6-2; R. Boyd (ARG) d. W. H. Powell 7-5 3-6 6-4 8-6; J. C. Gregory d. R. D. Poland 6-3 6-4 6-8 6-3; B. Hillyard d. A. Rodzianko w.o.; G. R. Sherwell d. A. Dungyersky 6-8 6-3 6-4 6-2; F. Crosbie d. H. Lewis Philipps 6-2 6-3 6-3; P. M. Davson d. D. H. Williams 6-1 6-1 6-2; L. J. Aslangul d. W. A. Ingram 9-7 6-4 4-6 6-2; J. D. P. Wheatley d. C. J. Tindell Green 6-4 6-1 6-2; H. G. Mackintosh d. P. Brick (AU) 2-6 6-2 1-6 6-3 6-2; A. H. Gobert (F) d. D. Powell 2-6 6-3 6-0 6-3; C. van Lennep (NTH) d. A. Berger 6-0 7-5 6-3; C. G. Eames d. J. C. F. Simpson 4-6 6-4 6-3 6-1; H. W. Austin d. B. R. Lawrence 6-1 6-0 7-5; H. W. Standring d. N. Willford 6-1 6-3 6-2; J. Kozeluh (CZ) d. G. A. Thomas 6-0 6-2 6-2; J. Pennycuick d. L. W. Alderson w.o.; C. F. Roupell d. W. B. Stott 6-4 6-0 2-6 4-6 6-3; J. Borotra (F) d. L. A. Godfree 6-3 6-4 6-4; A. H. Fyzee (IN) d. G. P. Hughes 7-5 6-2 2-6 6-4; A. H. Lowe d. G. Watson 6-2 6-2 6-1; V. E. Lindop d. R. de Castro Pereira 6-3 6-3 6-2; L. F. Davin d. P. Papadopoulo (GR) w.o.; E. Ulrich (D) d. D. R. Morrice (C) 4-6 6-4 6-1 6-4; H. Cattaruzza (ARG) d. F. M. B. Fisher (NZ) 6-2 6-0 9-7; W. Radcliffe d. I. de Borbolla (M) 8-6 7-5 8-6.

SECOND ROUND: Zemla d. Dicks 2-6 6-3 6-3 2-0 ret'd; Brugnon d. Hodges 7-5 6-2 6-2; Lycett d. Park 6-1 6-1 6-0; Aitken d. Leembruggen 6-1 5-7 6-4 6-0; Kingsley d. Fisher 11-9 6-2 6-2; Decugis d. Greville 6-3 7-5 4-6 6-4; Mayes d. Timmer 6-3 4-6 6-4 6-3; Aeschliman d. Burnett 6-4 6-2 6-4; A. A. Fyzee d. Peters 6-3 3-6 6-3 6-1; Bryan d. Dash 2-6 6-1 6-3 5-7 6-4; Kinsey d. Gilbert 6-1 6-1 6-4; Flaquer d. Crawley 2-6 9-7 9-7 7-5; Sharpe d. Lord Cholmondeley 4-6 6-4 6-1 6-3; Spence d. Petersen 6-3 2-6 2-6 6-2 6-2; Greig d. Helmore 6-4 6-2 6-4; Turnbull d. de Kehrling 6-2 7-5 6-3; Bernard d. van der Feen 8-6 8-10 7-5 6-4; Cochet d. Richards 4-6 6-3 6-4 6-2; Lester d. Higgs 6-3 6-3 17-15; F. G. Lowe d. Boyd 6-3 6-2 3-6 6-3; Gregory d. Hillyard 8-6 6-2 6-2; Sherwell d. Crosbie 6-4 6-0 6-1; Davson d. Aslangul 6-2 6-1 4-6 6-4; Wheatley d. Mackintosh 6-3 6-1 5-7 6-1; van Lennep d. Gobert 2-6 7-5 7-5 8-6; Austin d. Eames 5-7 6-4 6-0 4-1 ret'd; Kozeluh d. Standring 4-6 6-2 6-3 6-2; Pennycuick d. Roupell 6-3 9-7 4-6 6-2; Borotra d. A. H. Fyzee 3-6 6-4 7-5 6-4; A. H. Lowe d. Lindop 6-1 6-1 6-2; Ulrich d. Davin 7-5 8-6 3-6 6-4; Cattaruzza d. Radcliffe 4-6 6-3 4-6 6-1 6-2.

THIRD ROUND: Brugnon d. Zemla 6-3 6-0 6-2; Lycett d. Aitken 6-3 6-1 7-5; Kingsley d. Decugis 6-2 6-2 9-7; Mayes d. Aeschliman 2-6 5-7 6-1 6-1 6-4; Bryan d. A. A. Fyzee 6-8 6-4 6-1 6-4; Kinsey d. Flaquer 6-2 6-2 4-6 3-6 6-1; Spence d. Sharpe 8-6 3-6 7-5 6-3; Greig d. Turnbull 6-4 3-6 6-2 6-0; Cochet d. Bernard 6-1 6-3 6-3; Lester d. F. G. Lowe 6-3 6-4 6-3; Gregory d. Sherwell 6-0 4-6 3-6 6-4 7-5; Wheatley d. Davson 1-6 6-4 5-7 6-0 6-3; Austin d. van Lennep 6-0 4-6 6-4 6-1; Kozeluh d. Pennycuick 6-1 6-1 6-3; Borotra d. A. H. Lowe 6-3 6-4 7-5; Ulrich d. Cattaruzza 7-5 6-1 8-6.

FOURTH ROUND	QUARTER-FINALS	SEMI-FINALS	FINAL	CHAMPION
Brugnon				
Lycett	Brugnon			
Kingsley	6-4 6-1 6-3	Brugnon		
Mayes	Kingsley	6-2 4-6 6-2 4-6 6-4		
Bryan	6-2 1-6 6-1 2-6 6-3		Kinsey	
Kinsey	Kinsey		6-4 4-6 6-3 3-6 9-7	
Spence	6-4 6-2 6-4	Kinsey		
Greig	Spence	6-3 6-3 3-6 6-3		
Cochet	4-6 5-7 6-2 6-3 6-0			Borotra
Lester	Cochet			8-6 6-1 6-3
Gregory	6-2 7-5 6-4	Cochet		
Wheatley	Gregory	3-6 6-4 6-2 4-6 6-3		
Austin	6-4 4-6 6-2 5-7 6-1		Borotra	
Kozeluh	Kozeluh		2-6 7-5 2-6 6-3 7-5	
Borotra	2-6 6-0 6-1 6-3	Borotra		
Ulrich	Borotra	6-4 4-6 9-7 6-1		
	6-1 2-6 6-4 7-5			

LADIES' SINGLES

FIRST ROUND: C. Beckingham d. Mrs C. G. McIlquham 7-5 6-1; Mrs R. E. Haylock d. Mrs D. K. Craddock 6-2 6-3; S. Lenglen (F) d. M. K. Browne (USA) 6-2 6-3; Mrs G. J. Dewhurst d. M. E. Dix 11-9 6-4; E. de Alvarez (SP) d. W. M. Haughton (IRE) 6-2 6-0; E. D. Holman d. E. Norman 6-3 6-2; Mrs Holcroft Watson d. R. Watson 6-0 8-6; B. Nuthall d. M. Elliott 6-4 5-7 6-2; J. Fry d. Mrs Marshall (NZ) 6-1 6-0; E. Bennett d. Mrs Crawshay Williams 6-3 6-2; Mrs H. Edgington d. Mrs P. J. Whitley 6-2 6-2; Mrs F. Mallory (USA) d. L. V. McCune (USA) 6-1 6-2; G. J. Gilder 6-1 6-2; Mrs H. F. Wright (C) w.o.; Mrs J. Hill d. P. Saunders 6-1 7-5; K. Bouman (NTH) d. E.A. Goldsack 6-0 6-1; Lady Crosfield (GR) d. H. N. Wills (USA) w.o.; E. L. Colyer d. M. V. Chamberlain 7-5 6-2; Miss Vlasto (F) d. P. Dransfield 6-1 6-2; G. Sterry d. Mrs M. B. Reckitt 6-1 6-3; Mrs R. R. W. Jackson (IRE) d. Mrs Strawson 3-6 6-3 7-5; Mrs Jessup (USA) d. Mrs Mavrogordato 6-2 6-4; H. Contostavlos (GR) d. E. Morle 6-4 6-1; Mrs A. E. Beamish d. Mrs D. C. Shepherd Barron 6-1 6-1; R. Stephens (A) d. J. C. Ridley 5-7 7-5 6-2; C. Tyrrell d. Miss MacFarlane (NZ) 6-4 6-4; C. Hardie d. Mrs McC. Harper 6-4 6-4; E. F. Rose d. Mrs Broadbridge 6-4 6-0; S. C. Lumley Ellis d. Mrs Mathieu (F) 6-8 6-4 6-2; E. R. Clarke d. E. H. Harvey 7-5 7-5; E. Ryan (USA) d. Mrs Colegate 6-0 6-4; H. Woolrych d. D. E. Rendall (A) w.o.; Mrs L. A. Godfree d. Mrs Von Ellisen (A) 6-0 6-0.

SECOND ROUND: Beckingham d. Haylock 6-4 6-2; Lenglen d. Dewhurst 6-2 6-2; de Alvarez d. Holman 6-4 3-6 6-2; Holcroft Watson d. Nuthall 6-3 6-0; Fry d. Bennett 6-3 4-6 7-5; Mallory d. Edgington 6-2 6-1; Hill d. Gilder 3-6 6-1 6-2; Bouman d. Lady Crosfield 6-0 6-0; Vlasto d. Colyer 6-4 7-5; Sterry d. Jackson 6-4 6-2; Contostavlos d. Jessup 2-6 6-4 6-4; Beamish d. Stephens 6-0 6-3; Tyrrell d. Hardie 4-6 6-2 6-4; Lumley Ellis d. Rose 2-6 6-1 6-1; Ryan d. Clarke 6-3 6-2; Godfree d. Woolrych 6-2 6-0.

THIRD ROUND	QUARTER-FINALS	SEMI-FINALS	FINAL	CHAMPION
Beckingham				
Lenglen	Beckingham			
de Alvarez	w.o.	de Alvarez		
Holcroft Watson	de Alvarez	6-2 6-2		
Fry	6-1 6-3		de Alvarez	
Mallory	Mallory		6-2 6-2	
Hill	4-6 6-4 7-5	Mallory		
Bouman	Bouman	3-6 7-5 6-3		
Vlasto	6-3 6-2			Godfree
Sterry	Vlasto			6-2 4-6 6-3
Contostavlos	3-6 6-3 6-3	Vlasto		
Beamish	Contostavlos	6-3 6-3		
Tyrrell	7-5 6-4		Godfree	
Lumley Ellis	Tyrrell		6-4 6-0	
Ryan	6-2 1-6 6-0	Godfree		
Godfree	Godfree	6-2 6-0		
	1-6 6-4 6-0			

OTHER FINALS

GENTLEMEN'S DOUBLES: Final — J. Brugnon (F)/H. Cochet (F) d. H. Kinsey (USA)/V. Richards (USA) 7-5 4-6 6-3 6-2.

LADIES' DOUBLES: Final — M. K. Browne (USA)/E. Ryan (USA) d. Mrs L. A. Godfree/E. L. Colyer 6-1 6-1.

MIXED DOUBLES: Final — L. A./Mrs Godfree d. H. O. Kinsey (USA)/M. K. Browne (USA) 6-3 6-4.

GENTLEMEN'S SINGLES PLATE: Final — J. B. Gilbert d. F. R. L. Crawford 10-8 6-2.

From 1927 onwards full seeding was introduced.

GENTLEMEN'S SINGLES

FIRST ROUND: W. T. Tilden (2) (USA) d. G. A. Pratt 6-2 6-1 6-0; R. D. Poland d. R. C. Wackett 1-6 6-3 6-4 6-3; R. E. Worthington d. E. Crawshay Williams 6-1 6-3 7-5; G. P. Hughes d. N. Mishu (RU) 6-3 2-6 6-0 3-6 7-5; Lord Cholmondeley d. E. A. Dearman 6-8 6-8 6-3 6-1 8-6; E. A. McGuire (IRE) d. T. M. Mavrogordato 6-2 9-7 1-6 7-5; H. C. Fisher d. C. B. de Ricou 6-3 4-6 6-1 11-9; C. Boussus (F) d. J. M. Hillyard 9-7 7-5 6-4; **J. Brugnon** (7) (F) d. F. M. B. Fisher (NZ) 8-6 6-4 6-4; H. J. F. Hunter d. A. W. Buzzard 6-4 6-3 4-6 6-4; E. C. Peters d. G. Stoddart 6-2 6-2 6-2; O. Froitzheim (G) d. I. G. Collins 11-9 6-3 3-6 6-3; A. E. Browne d. E. C. Penny 6-2 9-7 6-2; N. G. Holmes d. P. D. B. Spence (SA) w.o.; K. Prasada (IN) d. A. F. Yencken 7-5 6-1 6-4; C. H. Kingsley d. W. Legg 6-2 6-0 6-2; **H. Cochet** (4) (F) d. F. S. Burnett 6-4 6-3 6-4; O. G. N. Turnbull d. C. W. Banks 6-2 7-5 6-1; L. G. Owen d. C. Bryan (NTH) w.o.; H. Kleinschroth (G) d. H. R. Price 6-3 6-3 6-4; R. D. England d. J. Miley, (IRE) 2-6 7-5 7-5 6-3; N. H. Latchford d. E. Gottlieb (CZ) w.o.; W. H. Powell d. H. G. Stoker 6-8 6-3 11-9 2-6 6-1; B. de Kehrling (HU) d. J. Pennycuick 6-1 6-3 3-6 7-5; **L. Raymond** (6) (SA) d. C. F. Roupell 6-4 7-5 8-6; G. R. O. Crole-Rees d. D. M. Evans (IN) 6-1 7-5 2-6 6-3; F. R. L. Crawford d. J. E. Pogson-Smith 2-6 11-9 6-1 3-6 8-6; J. C. Gregory d. M. V. Summerson 10-8 6-0 6-3; A. H. Lowe d. R. Lycett 6-2 6-4 6-4; B. Hillyard d. E. R. Avory 6-3 8-6 3-6 6-0; F. T. Hunter (USA) d. Y. Ohta (J) 6-1 6-4 6-3; A. R. F.

Kingscote d. W. H. Standring 10-8 6-3 6-0; **R. Lacoste** (1) (F) d. S. B. Wood (USA) 6-1 6-3 6-1; S. M. Jacob (IN) d. B. D. Helmore 6-1 6-3 6-1; H. G. Mackintosh G. Greville 6-4 6-3 5-7 7-5; M. Danet d. C. J. Brierley (IN) w.o.; J. Condon (SA) d. G. O. Jameson 6-2 6-0 6-4; A. Gentien (F) d. D. Powell 7-9 6-2 6-1 5-7 6-2; H. C. Walsh d. A. A. Fyzee (IN) w.o.; H. G. Mayes d. A. Berger 6-1 6-3 6-2; **J. Kozeluh** (8) (CZ) d. R. Dash 6-7 6-4 6-1 6-2; H. H. S. Hillier d. L. Wahid (F) w.o.; A. St J. Mahoney (IRE) d. L. W. Alderson 7-5 6-4 9-7; C. H. Campbell d. H. Muller (SW) 6-3 6-4 4-6 6-3; D. M. Greig d. D. A. Hodges 6-4 6-1 7-5; N. Sharpe d. C. J. Tindell Green 6-2 6-1 6-1; O. Kreuzer (G) d. N. G. Deed 6-2 6-2 6-3; H. K. Lester d. L. A. Godfree 6-4 6-4 5-7 6-3; **J. Borotra** (3) (F) d. A. C. Belgrave 7-5 7-5 9-7; W. Radcliffe d. E. L. Sarkies 6-2 6-1 6-3; W. A. R. Collins d. J. B. Gilbert w.o.; E. Higgs d. H. Artens (HU) 2-6 3-6 6-2 7-5 8-6; N. G. Farquharson (SA) d. C. G. McIlquham 5-7 0-6 6-3 6-3 6-4; A. N. W. Dudley d. A. H. Fyzee (IN) w.o.; D. H. Williams d. P. R. R. Hurditch 9-7 6-4 6-4; C. Campbell (IRE) d. W. B. Stott 6-1 6-1 6-0; P. Landry (F) d. **T. Harada** (5) (J) 4-6 6-4 6-1 1-6 6-2; N. Dicks d. F. Crosbie 6-3 8-6 4-6 6-1; H. Timmer (NTH) d. W. Washburn 6-1 8-6 8-6; W. C. Crawley d. J. D. F. Fisher 6-1 6-3 6-0; F. H. Jarvis d. R. D. N. Pryce-Jones 2-8 6-6 4-2; C. L. Philcox d. W. H. M. Aitken 2-6 6-3 6-3 6-4; H. G. N. Lee d. M. Temple 6-3 6-4 6-1; C. G. Eames d. G. R. Sherwell 6-1 4-6 6-1 6-3.

SECOND ROUND: Tilden (2) d. Poland 6-3 6-0 6-1; Hughes d. Worthington 6-2 8-6 6-2; McGuire d. Lord Cholmondeley 6-4 6-3 6-1; Boussus d. H. C. Fisher 2-6 7-9 6-3 6-4 6-2; **Brugnon** (7) d. H. J. F. Hunter 7-5 6-1 6-3; Froitzheim d. Peters 6-0 6-3 12-10; Browne d. Holmes 6-4 10-8 3-6 4-6 6-2; Kingsley d. Prasada 6-1 6-1 6-2; **Cochet** (4) d. Turnbull 6-2 0-6 6-2 6-3; Kleinschroth Owen 6-4 2-6 6-1 6-3; England d. Latchford 4-6 1-6 8-6 6-4 6-3; de Kehrling d. Powell 4-6 6-0 10-8 6-1; **Raymond** (6) 2-6 6-3 4-6 7-5 6-2; Gregory d. Crawford 6-3 6-1 6-3; A. H. Lowe d. B. Hillyard 6-4 6-4 6-0; F. T. Hunter d. Kingscote 6-3 6-3 6-4; **Lacoste** (1) d. Jacob 6-2 6-0 6-3 6-4;

Mackintosh d. Danet 4-4 6-3 6-4; Condon d. Gentien 6-3 9-7 6-4; Mayes d. Walsh 6-2 4-6 6-1 6-0; **Kozeluh** (8) d. Hillier d. Mahony d. C. H. Campbell 10-8 7-5 6-1; Greig d. Sharpe 4-1 6-4 6-3 6-4; Lester d. Kreuzer 6-1 6-0 6-3; **Borotra** (3) d. Radcliffe 7-5 3-6 6-4 6-3; Higgs d. W. A. R. Collins 6-3 6-0 4-6 6-4; Farquharson d. Dudley 10-8 4-6 5-7 6-4 6-3; C. Campbell d. D. H. Williams 6-1 6-1 6-0; Landry d. Dicks 6-1 2-6 6-1 6-2; Timmer d. Crawley 6-4 6-4 6-2; Philcox d. Jarvis 6-3 6-3 6-3; Lee d. Eames 3-6 6-4 7-5 6-2.

THIRD ROUND: Tilden (2) d. Hughes 6-3 6-4 6-0; Boussus d. McGuire 6-2 5-7 6-0 6-1; **Brugnon** (7) d. Froitzheim 6-1 6-2 4-6 6-3; Kingsley d. Browne 6-3 4-6 7-5 6-2; **Cochet** (4) d. Kleinschroth 7-5 9-7 6-0; de Kehrling d. England 6-1 6-1 6-2; Gregory d. Crole-Rees 3-6 3-6 6-3 6-1; F. T. Hunter d. A. H. Lowe 6-2 8-6 6-3; **Lacoste** (1) d. Mackintosh 6-0

6-2 6-2; Condon d. Mayes 9-7 4-6 6-2 4-6 6-2; **Kozeluh** (8) d. Mahony 6-2 6-4 6-4. Greig d. Lester 3-6 3-6 6-4 6-4 6-4; **Borotra** (3) d. Higgs 6-1 2-6 1-6 6-2 6-2; C. Campbell d. Farquharson 6-1 6-4 6-1; Timmer d. Landry 7-5 6-4 3-6 8-6; Philcox d. Lee 7-9 5-7 6-1 6-2 6-4.

FOURTH ROUND	QUARTER-FINALS	SEMI-FINALS	FINAL	CHAMPION
Tilden (2)	**Tilden** (2)			
Boussus	6-1 7-5 6-2			
Brugnon (7)	**Brugnon** (7)	**Tilden** (2)		
Kingsley	4-6 6-3 6-2 6-2	6-3 6-1 3-6 7-5		
Cochet (4)	**Cochet** (4)		**Cochet** (4)	
de Kehrling	8-6 6-3 6-2		2-6 4-6 7-5 6-4 6-3	
Gregory	F. T. Hunter	**Cochet** (4)		
F. T. Hunter	4-6 7-5 6-2 4-6 6-3	3-6 3-6 6-2 6-2 6-3		**Cochet** (4)
Lacoste (1)	**Lacoste** (1)			4-6 4-6 6-3 6-4 7-5
Condon	6-0 6-3 6-3			
Kozeluh (8)	**Kozeluh** (8)	**Lacoste** (1)		
Greig	6-4 3-0 ret'd	6-4 6-3 6-4		
Borotra (3)	**Borotra** (3)		**Borotra** (3)	
C. Campbell	6-8 8-6 6-0 6-1		6-4 6-3 1-6 1-6 6-2	
Timmer	Timmer	**Borotra** (3)		
Philcox	6-3 6-3 6-0	6-1 3-6 6-3 6-0		

LADIES' SINGLES

FIRST ROUND: E. L. Heine (7) (SA) d. E. F. Rose 4-3 6-4; E. Hemmant d. W. M. C. Bower 5-7 6-2 6-0; Mrs R. R. W. Jackson (IRE) d. Mrs D. K. Craddock 6-3 6-1; Mrs Holcroft Watson d. P. von Reznicek (G) w.o.; M. V. Chamberlain d. G. J. Gilder 6-3 6-2; Mrs Macready d. M. Slaney 7-9 6-3 6-1; C. Tyrrell d. Mrs Bruce-May 2-6 6-3 6-1; Mrs A. V. Bridge d. S. K. Johnson 6-2 0-6 6-3; **H. N. Wills** (1) (USA) d. G. R. Sterry 3-3 6-3 6-3; S. C. Lumley Ellis

d. Mrs C. M. B. Marriott 6-3 6-2; C. Hardie d. Mrs A. D. Stocks 6-3 6-2; E. Bennett d. Mrs C. O. Tuckey (IRE) 7-5 6-4; D. Gordon d. J. E. Brown 6-3 6-2; E. A. Goldsack d. R. Watson 3-6 6-0; Mrs R. Lycett d. Mrs C. G. McIlquham 1-6 6-0 6-4; Mrs A. E. Beamish d. Mrs D. Munro 6-1 6-1.

SECOND ROUND: Mrs L. A. Godfree (2) d. N. Trentham 6-2 6-2; R. D. Tapscott (SA) d. G. Cousin (F) 7-5 6-4; E. L. Colyer d. Mrs Satterthwaite 6-8 6-2 7-5; J. C. Ridley d. Mrs Bordes (F) 6-0 7-5; **E. Ryan** (5) d. Mrs C. Connell 6-2 6-4; Mrs H. G. Broadbridge d. M. Macfarlane (NZ) 6-3 6-4; E. H. Harvey d. Mrs I. Friedleben (G) 6-4 8-6; H. Contostavlos (GR) d. D. Alexander 6-1 6-1; **E. de Alvarez** (4) (SP) d. Mrs M. B. Reckitt 6-2 6-3; P. Dransfield d. V. Gallay 6-4 6-1; Mrs Mavrogordato d. E. Norman 4-6 6-4; M. Valantine d. Mrs J. L. Colegate 6-2 6-3; **Heine** (7) d. Hemmant 6-3 6-2; Holcroft Watson d. Jackson 6-0 6-2; Chamberlain d. Macready 6-3 6-2; Tyrrell d. Bridge 6-2 6-1;

Wills (1) d. Lumley Ellis 6-3 6-2; Bennett d. Hardie 6-4 3-6 6-2; Goldsack d. Gordon 6-3 6-4; Lycett d. Beamish 6-4 6-3; **Mrs Peacock** (8) (SA) d. B. Feltham 6-0 6-1; E. R. Clarke d. M. P. Davies 6-2 6-3; I. A. Maltby d. Mrs R. E. Haylock 6-1 2-6 6-3; Mrs H. Edgington d. C. Beckingham 7-5 3-6 6-4; **K. Bouman** (3) (NTH) d. D. Busby 6-0 6-3; Mrs B. C. Covell d. D. A. Shaw 6-3 6-3; J. Fry d. Mrs Mathieu (F) 6-3 6-2; Mrs M. L. Morison d. Mrs Hazel 6-4 6-4; **Mrs F. Mallory** (6) (USA) d. B. Boas 6-3 6-2; B. Nuthall d. C. Aussem 6-3 6-2; Mrs J. Hill d. H. L. Eddis 6-1 6-2; P. Saunders d. M. E. Dix 6-4 6-3.

THIRD ROUND: Godfree (2) d. Tapscott 6-2 10-8; Colyer d. Ridley 6-4 6-3; **Ryan** (5) d. Broadbridge 6-2 6-3; Harvey d. Contostavlos 6-4 6-4; **de Alvarez** (4) d. Dransfield 6-0 6-4; Mavrogordato d. Valantine 9-11 6-4 6-4; Holcroft Watson d. Heine (7) 4-6 6-3 7-5; Chamberlain d. Tyrrell 6-3 2-6 6-4; **Wills** (1) d. Bennett 7-5 6-3; Goldsack

d. Lycett 6-8 8-6 6-3; **Peacock** (8) d. Clarke 6-3 6-1; Maltby d. Edgington 3-6 6-4 6-4; **Bouman** (3) d. Covell 7-5 6-3; Fry d. Morison 6-2 6-2; Nuthall d. **Mallory** (6) 2-6 6-2 6-0; Hill d. Saunders 6-2 6-4.

FOURTH ROUND	QUARTER-FINALS	SEMI-FINALS	FINAL	CHAMPION
Godfree (2)	**Godfree** (2)			
Colyer	6-2 6-2			
Ryan (5)	**Ryan** (5)	**Ryan** (5)		
Harvey	7-5 6-1	3-6 6-4 6-4		
de Alvarez (4)	**de Alvarez** (4)		**de Alvarez** (4)	
Mavrogordato	6-3 6-0		2-6 6-0 6-4	
Holcroft Watson	Holcroft Watson	**de Alvarez** (4)		
Chamberlain	6-1 7-5	6-3 3-6 8-6		**Wills** (1)
Wills (1)	**Wills** (1)			6-2 6-4
Goldsack	6-1 6-3			
Peacock (8)	**Peacock** (8)	**Wills** (1)		
Maltby	6-3 6-2	6-3 6-1		
Bouman (3)	Fry		**Wills** (1)	
Fry	2-6 6-4 9-7		6-3 6-1	
Nuthall	Nuthall	Fry		
Hill	6-3 6-3	1-6 6-3 6-4		

OTHER FINALS

GENTLEMEN'S DOUBLES: Final — F. T. Hunter (USA)/W. T. Tilden (USA) d. J. Brugnon (F)/H. Cochet (F) 1-6 4-6 8-6 6-3 6-4.
LADIES' DOUBLES: Final: — H. N. Wills (USA)/E. Ryan (USA) d. E. L. Heine (SA)/Mrs G. Peacock 6-3 6-2.

MIXED DOUBLES: Final — F. T. Hunter (USA)/E. Ryan (USA) d. L. A./Mrs Godfree 8-6 6-0.
GENTLEMEN'S SINGLES PLATE: Final — A. Gentien (F) d. O. G. N. Turnbull 1-6 6-2 6-0.

GENTLEMEN'S SINGLES

1928

FIRST ROUND: H. Cochet (1) (F) d. M. Sleem (IN) 6-2 8-6 6-2; H. C. Hopman d. E. Higgs 6-2 6-4 7-5; H. G. Mayes d. R. O. Cummings 6-3 6-2 6-1; G. V. Hurst d. F. H. Jarvis 7-5 6-1 7-9 1-6 6-1; **E. Borotra** (F) d. A. Lacroix (B) 7-5 4-6 6-1 8-6; C. F. Scroope d. A. Aroa w.o.; R. Boyd d. L. A. Godfree 6-3 6-2 6-2; A. M. D. Pitt d. A. Zappa 6-3 6-2 3-6 6-2; **J. F. Hennessey** (6) (USA) d. E. O. Mather 6-1 6-0 6-2; N. H. Latchford d. T. M. Mavrogordato 6-3 6-0 6-1; G. R. Sherwell d. B. Hillyard 6-3 0-6 3-6 6-1 9-7; C. G. Eames d. C. L. Philcox 6-4 7-9 6-3 6-1; E. C. Peters d. G. R. O. Crole-Rees 6-2 6-2 6-1; F. Frens d. P. Gaslini w.o.; N. Dicks d. J. C. Peacock 6-4 3-6 1-6 6-2 6-3; R. Danet d. A. C. Belgrave 6-3 6-1 0-6 3-6 6-3; R. D. Andrews d. **F. T. Hunter** (4) (USA) 6-4 5-7 6-4 2-6 7-5; C. Boussus (F) d. H. F. David 6-1 6-3 6-2; P. F. Glover d. N. Jones 6-1 6-1 1-6 6-2; J. W. Olmsted d. R. Menzel w.o.; R. Lycett d. W. H. Powell 6-4 4-6 7-5 6-8 6-2; E. F. Moon (A) d. J. B. Gilbert 5-7 6-1 6-0 6-4; Y. Ohta (J) d. G. de Stefani (IT) 6-3 1-6 6-1 6-3; A. Zerlendi (GR) d. C. B. de Ricou 6-4 8-6 6-4; **G. L. Patterson** (8) (A) d. F. R. L. Crawford 6-2 4-6 6-3 7-5; H. Kleinschroth (G) d. W. A. R. Collins 6-4 6-2 6-1; J. S. Olliff d. E. du Plaix (B) 6-1 1-6 1-6 6-3 7-5; C. H. Kingsley d. O. G. N. Turnbull 6-2 1-6 6-3 6-2; C. H. C. O'Callaghan d. R. Pickersgill 6-4 6-3 6-0; W. Robson d. R. Dash 6-3 6-2 6-3; J. Brugnon (F) d. U. Kramet 6-0 6-0 6-1; J. Holthouse d. J. H. Frowen 7-9 6-4 6-2 6-8 6-4; **R. Lacoste** (2) (F) d. H. L. Walcott 6-0 6-0 6-2; J. B. Hawkes

(A) d. H. Artens 6-3 6-4 6-1; G. M. Lott, Jnr d. F. Crosbie 6-2 6-0 6-0; H. K. Lester d. J. Koseluh (CZ) w.o.; W. F. Coen (USA) d. A. Petersen (D) 7-5 6-3 6-3; E. V. Bobb d. J. M. Hillyard 6-4 6-2 3-6 6-4; H. W. Austin d. S. M. Jacob (IN) 6-1 6-3 6-1; J. D. P. Wheatley d. Capt. Cazalet 7-5 8-6 6-2; **H. L. de Morpurgo** (7) (IT) d. W. L. Breese 6-2 9-7 6-1; D. H. Williams d. D. H. Kleinman 6-1 6-4 7-5; E. R. Avory d. R. C. Wackett 4-6 6-4 6-1 6-4; F. Matejka d. F. W. Rahe 6-3 8-10 8-6 6-3; H. Cattaruzza d. R. E. Worthington 6-1 7-5 6-2; H. G. N. Lee d. B. D. Helmore 6-2 6-3 6-3; I. G. Collins d. M. Bally 6-3 6-3 6-3; R. de Buzelet d. A. St J. Mahony 5-7 6-2 7-5 9-7; **W. T. Tilden** (3) (USA) d. M. V. Summerson 6-0 6-1 6-0; H. C. Fisher d. G. O. Jameson 6-3 6-2 6-4; B. R. Lawrence d. H. S. L. Barclay w.o.; B. de Kehrling (HU) d. H. L. Soni 6-2 7-9 6-2 6-2; C. Campbell d. C. Bocciardo 6-4 4-6 6-4 3-6 7-5; P. Landry (F) d. D. M. Greig 6-3 6-8 6-4 4-6 3-2 ret'd; S. B. Wood (USA) d. N. Sharpe 10-6 6-1 12-10; H. C. Brunie d. A. Gentien (F) 3-6 3-6 6-3 6-3 6-4; **J. Borotra** (5) (F) d. A. H. Lowe 6-2 8-6 6-4; G. P. Hughes d. R. R. T. Young 6-1 6-4 6-4; H. Timmer (NTH) d. G. E. L. Rogers 8-6 6-4 6-3; P. D. B. Spence (SA) d. H. G. Mackintosh 6-1 10-8 2-6 6-3; J. Pennycuick d. N. G. Farquharson (SA) 8-6 6-3 6-3; J. Crawford (A) d. D. A. Hodges 6-1 6-3 6-2; J. C. Gregory d. F. Hartz 6-2 5-7 6-3 6-4; C. Morea d. W. E. Lingelbach 4-6 6-3 10-6 4-6 6-4.

SECOND ROUND: Cochet (1) d. Hopman 6-1 6-4 8-6; Mayes d. Hurst 6-1 6-2 6-2; Scroope d. E. Borotra 8-6 1-6 12-10 6-4; Boyd d. Pitt 6-3 6-3 7-5; **Hennessey** (6) d. Latchford 6-2 6-4 6-2; Sherwell d. Eames 3-6 6-3 6-3 5-7 7-5; Frenz d. Peters 6-2 2-6 2-6 12-10 7-5; Dicks d. Danet 6-2 6-1 6-1; Boussus d. Andrews 4-6 6-1 6-1; Olmsted d. Glover 9-7 6-1 7-5; Moon d. Lycett 9-7 4-6 7-5 5-7 6-0; Ohta d. Zerlendi 6-1 8-6 6-3; **Patterson** (8) d. Kleinschroth 6-0 6-2 6-1; Kingsley d. Olliff 6-1 10-12 6-2 6-2; O'Callaghan d. Robson 7-5 6-3 1-6 6-4; Brugnon d. Holthouse 6-2 6-4 6-2; **Lacoste** (2) d. Hawkes 6-3 4-6 6-3 6-4; Lott Jnr d. Lester 6-1 7-5 7-5; Coen d. Bobb 6-3 6-3 6-3; Austin d. Wheatley

6-2 6-8 6-8 6-2 6-1; **de Morpurgo** (7) d. Williams 6-2 6-4 6-2; Matejka d. Avory 3-6 3-6 6-0 6-3 6-0; Lee d. Cattaruzza 1-6 6-2 6-3 10-8 6-4 6-2; de Buzelet d. I. G. Collins 3-6 10-8 6-4 6-2; **Tilden** (3) d. Fisher 6-1 6-3 6-1; de Kehrling Lawrence 6-0 6-2 6-3; Landry d. Campbell 6-2 4-6 6-4 6-3; Wood d. Brunie 1-6 4-6 6-3 6-4 6-2; **J. Borotra** (5) d. Hughes 1-6 6-4 6-3 8-6; Spence d. Timmer 6-1 4-6 4-8 10 6-3; J. Crawford d. Pennycuick 6-4 2-6 6-3 12-10; Gregory d. Morea 6-3 3-6 8-6 4-6 6-1.

THIRD ROUND: Cochet (1) d. Mayes 6-1 6-8 7-5 6-2; Boyd d. Scroope 6-3 8-6 6-0; **Hennessey** (6) d. Sherwell 6-4 7-5 6-2; Frenz d. Dicks 6-3 8-6 6-3; Boussus d. Olmsted 9-7 6-1 6-2; Moon d. Ohta 6-4 6-2 7-9 6-4; **Patterson** (8) d. Kingsley 10-8 9-11 10-8 5-7 6-2; Brugnon d. O'Callaghan 6-2 6-2 6-4; **Lacoste** (2) d. Lott Jnr 6-1 9-7 6-8 6-2; Austin

d. Coen 6-4 3-6 6-4 3-6 6-1; **de Morpurgo** (7) d. Matejka 6-2 9-7 3-6 7-5; de Buselet d. Lee 2-6 6-3 6-4 13-11; **Tilden** (3) d. de Kehrling 6-2 6-3 6-1; Landry d. Wood 4-6 6-1 6-1 8-6; **J. Borotra** (5) d. Spence 7-5 7-5 6-3; J. Crawford d. Gregory 9-7 6-4 6-3.

FOURTH ROUND	QUARTER-FINALS	SEMI-FINALS	FINAL	CHAMPION
Cochet (1)	**Cochet** (1)			
Boyd	6-4 6-1 6-3	**Cochet** (1)		
Hennessey (6)	**Hennessey** (6)	6-4 6-1 5-7 6-3		
Frenz	6-4 6-1 6-3		**Cochet** (1)	
Boussus	Boussus		11-9 3-6 6-2 6-3	
Moon	6-0 6-4 2-6 6-2	Boussus		
Patterson (8)	Brugnon	12-10 10-8 6-2		
Brugnon	6-3 5-7 6-4 6-2			**Lacoste** (2)
Lacoste (2)	**Lacoste** (2)			6-1 4-6 6-4 6-2
Austin	6-4 6-4 6-8 1-6 6-2	**Lacoste** (2)		
de Morpurgo (7)	**de Morpurgo** (7)	6-2 6-3 6-4		
de Buselet	6-4 6-2 6-2		**Lacoste** (2)	
Tilden (3)	**Tilden** (3)		2-6 6-4 2-6 6-4 6-3	
Landry	6-4 2-6 2-6 6-1 6-4	**Tilden** (3)		
J. Borotra (5)	**Borotra** (5)	8-6 3-6 6-3 6-2		
J. Crawford	3-6 6-4 6-2 7-9 6-3			

LADIES' SINGLES

FIRST ROUND: K. Bouman (5) (NTH) d. C. Beckingham 6-2 7-5; Mrs von Reznicek (G) d. D. E. Anderson 6-1 6-4; S. C. Lumley Ellis d. E. Hemmant 4-6 6-3 6-3; Mrs Nicolopoulo (F) d. Mrs Bordes (F) 6-4 6-4; P. Anderson d. C. Hardie 6-4 6-4; M. P. Davies d. Princess von Lobkowitz w.o.; N. Trentham d. D. Round 2-6 8-8 6; Mrs P. J. Whitley d. B.

Nuthall w.o.; **E. de Alvarez** (2) (SP) d. Mrs R. Lycett 6-2 6-2; Mrs B. C. Covell d. Mrs Mavrogordato 6-3 6-0; E. L. Colyer d. P. Saunders 7-5 6-4; J. Fry d. D. Busby w.o.; Miss Couquerque (NTH) d. C. Tyrrell 6-8 6-3 6-0; E. F. Rose d. M. Cambridge 6-2 6-0; L. Bickerton d. Mrs F. Mallory (USA) 6-3 4-6 6-4; D. Gordon d. J. Sigart (B) 11-9 6-4.

SECOND ROUND: H. N. Wills (1) (USA) d. E. A. Goldsack 6-2 6-1; V. Gallay (F) d. Mrs S. Sperling 6-4 0-6 6-3; E. H. Harvey d. Mrs H. V. Edwards 6-2 6-1; P. E. Mudford d. Mrs Macready 6-2 3-6 7-5; **Mrs Holcroft Watson** (6) d. B. Feltham 6-2 6-2; Mrs P. O'Hara Wood (A) d. M. Canters 6-1 6-2; Mrs H. Edgington d. D. A. Shaw 6-2 7-5 6-2; E. Hoffman (G) d. M. Slaney 2-6 8-6 6-4; **E. Ryan** (4) (USA) d. Mrs A. V. Bridge 6-1 6-4; J. Gallay d. M. E. Dix 6-2 4-6 6-4; E. Boyd (A) d. G. R. Sterry 6-3 10-8; H. Evelyn Jones d. Mrs W. D. List 6-4 6-2; **Bouman** (5) d. von Reznicek 6-3 6-2; Nicolopoulo d. Lumley Ellis 6-2 6-1; Anderson d. Davies 6-2 6-4; Trentham d. Whitley 6-2 4-6 6-4; **de Alvarez**

(2) d. Covell 4-6 6-3 7-5; Colyer d. Fry 4-6 6-3 6-4; Rose d. Couquerque 6-4 6-2; Bickerton d. Gordon 6-1 6-4; **C. Aussem** (7) (G) d. M. V. Chamberlain 6-2 6-4; Mrs Satterthwaite d. R. Watson 4-6 7-5 6-3; Mrs A. E. Beamish d. K. T. Annington 6-4 6-2; Mrs F. M. Strawson v. Marshall 6-2 6-3; **E. Bennett** (3) d. Mrs D. C. Shepherd Barron 6-3 9-7; Mrs C. G. McIlquham d. Miss Rost (G) 6-2 6-4; Mrs J. L. Colegate d. Mrs C. O. Tuckey 6-3 6-1; L. Valerio (IT) d. Mrs B. May 6-3 6-0; **H. Jacobs** (8) (USA) d. J. C. Ridley 6-0 6-2; D. Akhurst (A) d. H. Bourne 6-4 6-2; Mrs R. E. Haylock d. Y. Bourgeois (F) 6-4 4-6 6-4; E. R. Clarke d. B. C. Brown 6-0 6-1.

THIRD ROUND: Wills (1) d. Gallay 6-0 6-0; Harvey d. Mudford 6-2 6-2; **Holcroft Watson** (6) d. O'Hara Wood 6-0 6-1; Edgington d. Hoffman 7-9 6-1 8-6; **Ryan** (4) d. Gallay 6-4 6-1; Boyd d. Evelyn Jones 6-0 6-1; Nicolopoulo d. **Bouman** (5) 12-10 8-6; Trentham d. Anderson 3-6 6-4 6-4; **de Alvarez** (2) d. Colyer 6-4 6-4; Bickerton d. Rose 6-3

6-1; **Aussem** (7) d. Satterthwaite 6-4 7-5; Strawson d. Beamish 4-6 6-1 6-1; **Bennett** (3) d. McIlquham 6-3 6-3; Colegate d. Valerio 6-2 7-5; Akhurst d. Jacobs (8) 6-8 6-1 8-6; Haylock d. Clarke 10-8 6-0.

FOURTH ROUND	QUARTER-FINALS	SEMI-FINALS	FINAL	CHAMPION
Wills (1)	**Wills** (1)			
Harvey	6-2 6-3	**Wills** (1)		
Holcroft Watson (6)	**Holcroft Watson** (6)	6-3 6-0		
Edgington	6-0 6-0		**Wills** (1)	
Ryan (4)	**Ryan** (4)		6-1 6-1	
Boyd	6-0 6-2	**Ryan** (4)		
Nicolopoulo	Nicolopoulo	6-1 4-6 6-2		
Trentham	5-7 6-2 6-1			**Wills** (1)
de Alvarez (2)	**de Alvarez** (2)			6-2 6-3
Bickerton	9-7 6-4	**de Alvarez** (2)		
Aussem (7)	**Aussem** (7)	7-5 6-2		
Strawson	6-1 4-6 6-1		**de Alvarez** (2)	
Bennett (3)	**Bennett** (3)		6-2 6-0	
Colegate	6-3 6-2	Akhurst		
Akhurst	Akhurst	2-6 6-3 6-2		
Haylock	6-4 8-10 6-0			

OTHER FINALS

GENTLEMEN'S DOUBLES: Final — J. Brugnon (F)/H. Cochet (F) d. J. B. Hawkes (A)/G. L. Patterson (A) 13-11 6-4 6-4.

LADIES' DOUBLES: Final — Mrs Holcroft Watson/P. Saunders d. E. Bennett/E. H. Harvey 6-2 6-3.

MIXED DOUBLES: Final — P. D. B. Spence (SA)/E. Ryan (USA) d. J. H. Crawford (A)/D. Akhurst (A) 7-5 6-4.

GENTLEMEN'S SINGLES PLATE: Final — M. Sleem (IN) d. J. B. Gilbert 6-3 6-3.

GENTLEMEN'S SINGLES

FIRST ROUND: H. **Cochet** (1) (F) d. A. C. Crossley 6-3 6-4 6-3; K. C. Gandar Dower d. A. H. Fyzee (IN) 6-3 4-6 4-6 9-7 8-6; G. L. Rogers (IRE) d. J. F. G. Lysaght 6-3 7-5 6-3; W. H. Powell d. H. G. Mackintosh 6-1 6-4 4-6 6-4; D. H. Williams d. C. Ostberg (SW) 6-3 6-4 6-4; J. H. Frowen d. S. W. Harris 6-4 7-5 6-2; J. Hennessey (USA) d. R. Malcolm (SA) 6-3 6-0 6-3; R. E. Worthington d. F. Sindreu (SP) w.o.; **H. L. de Morpurgo** (5) (IT) d. G. R. Ashton 6-3 6-0 6-0; H. Moldenhauer (G) d. R. Bernard 6-1 6-2 6-4; N. Sharpe d. I. G. Collins 6-2 6-1 3-6 6-2; J. L. Chamberlain d. N. G. Holmes 6-2 4-6 6-2 6-1; E. Ulrich (D) d. H. B. Purcell 7-5 9-7 6-1; R. de Buzelet d. A. W. Vinall 6-0 0-6 5-7 6-1 7-5; J. M. Hillyard d. C. F. Efstratiades (GR) 6-2 6-2 6-3; H. Timmer (NTH) d. W. E. Lingelbach 6-0 6-2 6-3; **W. T. Tilden** (3) (USA) d. H. V. S. Dillon (IRE) 6-1 6-1 6-2; C. H. Campbell d. R. Menzel (CZ) 3-6 4-6 8-6 8-6 6-3; A. del Bono (IT) d. E. C. Peters 6-4 6-3 4-6 6-3; D. Prenn (G) d. H. F. David 6-2 6-2 6-3; W. F. Coen (USA) d. J. A. Wright (C) 2-6 9-7 6-4 6-2; C. J. Robbins (USA) d. E. Nourney (G) 6-4 6-4 6-4; C. Boussus (F) d. N. H. Latchford 6-4 6-0 6-3; G. R. O. Crole-Rees d. V. A. Cazalet 6-3 3-6 6-2 4-6 6-2; **J. C. Gregory** (8) d. H. K. Lester 4-6 6-3 6-3 7-5; F. R. L. Crawford d. F. H. D. Wilde w.o.; R. Rodel (F) d. B. D. Helmore 4-6 3-4 6-4 6-2; J. Kuhlmann (G) d. L. A. Godfree w.o.; E. D. Andrews (NZ) d. P. Leiner (HU) 6-1 6-1 6-0; P. Landry (F) d. Count E. Salm (AU) 6-4 6-0 6-0; Y. Ohta (J) d. P. Lacroix (B) 4-6 6-1 2-6 6-2 6-3; H. G. N. Lee d. A. Brown 6-4 1-7 5-; **J. Borotra** (2) (F) d. G. R. Sherwell 3-6 6-4 6-4; W. A. R. Collins d. F. H.

Jarvis 6-1 6-3 8-6; O. G. N. Turnbull d. S. M. Hadi (IN) 6-2 6-1 6-4; G. P. Hughes d. N. G. Farquharson (SA) 6-8 6-1 6-2 2-6 6-2; J. D. P. Wheatley d. I. de Takats (HU) 6-4 6-2 6-3; C. S. Higgins d. D. H. Balfour 5-7 6-2 7-5 6-2; H. G. N. Cooper d. H. C. Dhanda 6-2 6-2 6-2; W. Allison (USA) d. E. G. Chandler (USA) 2-6 6-3 6-3 6-3; **G. M. Lott** (6) (USA) d. E. du Plaix (F) 6-4 6-3 6-2; L. de Borman (B) d. G. Grandguillot (E) w.o.; L. Bonzi d. C. F. Aeschlimann (SWZ) w.o.; D. M. Greig d. H. S. L. Barclay 6-2 6-1 6-4; H. S. Burrows d. E. Maier (SP) w.o.; C. Campbell (IRE) d. N. Mishu (RU) 6-2 6-4 5-7 6-1; J. Kozeluh (CZ) d. W. Dessart (G) 5-7 6-0 6-0 6-2; A. Zerlendi (GR) d. B. Hillyard 6-2 6-3 4-6 6-2; **F. T. Hunter** (4) (USA) d. R. Miki (J) 6-1 7-5 6-3; H. W. Austin d. J. B. Gilbert 3-6 6-3 6-2 6-4; J. Brugnon (F) d. J. H. Shales (USA) 1-6 6-3 3-6 6-4 6-3; J. Van Ryn (USA) d. A. Gentien (F) 6-2 6-0 6-2; K. Wetzel (G) d. F. R. Price 6-1 6-2 6-2; D. R. Fussell d. A. J. Smith 8-6 4-6 3-6 6-4 6-1; C. H. Kingsley d. F. Matejka (AU) 4-6 6-3 6-2 6-3; H. Kleinschroth (G) d. E. A. McGuire (IRE) 1-6 6-3 3-6 6-4 6-3; **B. von Kehrling** (7) (HU) d. W. Radcliffe 6-2 6-1 6-1; C. S. Colvin d. H. Ramberg (SW) 6-3 6-2 6-1; R. Lycett d. C. L. Philcox 6-1 6-1 6-3; L. Raymond (SA) d. A. H. Lowe 6-1 6-3; F. J. Perry d. C. Bocciardo (IT) 7-5 2-6 6-4 3-6 9-7; N. Dicks d. F. Frenz (G) 6-3 6-4 3-6 6-4; J. S. Olliff d. G. Glasser (F) 6-4 2-6 6-3 6-3; W. F. Crocker (C) d. J. S. Harrison 9-7 7-5 8-6.

SECOND ROUND: Cochet (1) d. Gandar Dower 6-4 6-4 4-6 6-4; Rogers d. Powell 3-6 6-1 6-4 7-5; Frowen d. Williams 6-4 6-2 6-3; Hennessey d. Worthington 6-4 6-4 6-3; **de Morpurgo** (5) d. Moldenhauer 3-6 6-4 6-3 2-6 6-4; Sharpe d. Chamberlain 6-2 7-5 7-5; de Buzelet d. Ulrich 4-6 7-5 6-0 6-4; Timmer d. J. M. Hillyard 3-6 6-0 6-2; **Tilden** (3) d. C. H. Campbell 6-2 6-2 6-0; Prenn d. del Bono 6-1 6-1 7-9 6-1; Coen d. Robbins 6-1 6-1 7-9 6-1; Boussus d. Crole-Rees 6-4 6-4 6-3; **Gregory** (8) d. Crawford 1-6 6-0 6-1 6-2; Rodel d. Kuhlmann 6-4 6-8 6-2 6-1; Landry d. Andrews 4-6 7-5 6-0 6-1; Lee d. Ohta 5-7 6-4 6-4 7-5; **Borotra** (2) d. W. A. R. Collins 6-3 6-4 6-2; Turnbull d. Hughes

1-6 6-4 7-5 6-0; Wheatley d. Higgins 5-7 6-4 6-3 7-5; Allison d. Cooper 6-3 3-6 6-3 6-2; **Lott** (6) d. de Borman 6-1 6-1 6-2; Bonzi d. Greig 6-2 6-4 6-3; C. Campbell d. Burrows 6-0 6-1 6-2; Kozeluh d. Zerlendi 6-1 6-4 6-8 4-6 6-3; Austin d. **Hunter** (4) 6-3 6-2 4-6 6-3; Brugnon d. Van Ryn 1-6 6-3 6-2 6-4; Wetzel d. Fussell 6-2 6-2 8-6; Kingsley d. Kleinschroth 6-1 6-1 6-2; **von Kehrling** (7) d. Colvin 6-3 6-1 6-4; Raymond d. Lycett 6-3 6-3 6-0; Perry d. Dicks 3-6 6-2 6-2 6-4; Olliff d. Crocker 6-3 6-3.

THIRD ROUND: Cochet (1) d. Rogers 5-7 6-0 9-7 4-6 6-3; Hennessey d. Frowen 6-2 6-1 7-5; Sharpe d. **de Morpurgo** (5) 6-2 6-4 4-6 6-3; Timmer d. de Buzelet 2-6 4-6 6-3 6-2 6-3; **Tilden** (3) d. Prenn 6-4 6-0 8-6; Boussus d. Coen 6-1 10-8 7-5; **Gregory** (8) d. Rodel 2-6 6-2 6-4 6-0; Landry d. Lee 5-7 4-6 6-4 6-2 6-3; **Borotra** (2) d. Turnbull

6-2 6-1 5-7 6-4; Allison d. Wheatley 6-1 6-1 6-1; **Lott** (6) d. Bonzi 6-1 6-0 6-3; Kozeluh d. C. Campbell 6-3 6-4 6-2; Austin d. Brugnon 6-3 6-4 6-0; Kingsley d. Wetzel 6-3 4-6 6-3 6-0; **von Kehrling** (7) d. Raymond 6-3 7-5 6-3; Olliff d. Perry 6-4 6-2 2-6 6-3.

FOURTH ROUND	QUARTER-FINALS	SEMI-FINALS	FINAL	CHAMPION
Cochet (1)	**Cochet** (1)			
Hennessey	6-1 6-4 9-7	**Cochet** (1)		
Sharpe	Timmer	6-4 7-5 6-2		
Timmer	6-1 3-6 6-0 11-9		**Cochet** (1)	
Tilden (3)	**Tilden** (3)		6-4 6-1 7-5	
Boussus	6-3 9-7 6-4	**Tilden** (3)		
Gregory (8)	Landry	6-4 2-6 6-3 7-5		**Cochet** (1)
Landry	8-6 6-4 3-6 6-3			6-4 6-3 6-4
Borotra (2)	**Borotra** (2)			
Allison	6-3 6-1 4-6 6-3	**Borotra** (2)		
Lott (6)	**Lott** (6)	6-3 6-3 6-4		
Kozeluh	6-4 6-1 6-4		**Borotra** (2)	
Austin	Austin		6-1 10-8 5-7 6-1	
Kingsley	6-2 4-6 6-1 4-6 11-9	Austin		
von Kehrling (7)	**von Kehrling** (7)	6-2 8-6 6-3		
Olliff	9-7 7-5 6-4			

LADIES' SINGLES

FIRST ROUND: B. **Nuthall** (3) d. V. Marshall 6-1 6-4; D. E. Round d. Mrs Friedleben (G) 6-3 4-6 8-6; E. R. Clarke d. E. Cross (USA) 3-6 6-4 7-5; Mrs L. R. C. Michell d. M. E. Dix 4-6 6-2 7-5; E. A. Goldsack d. H. Bourne 6-3 6-4; Mrs E. Dam (D) d. W. M. C. Bower 6-4 6-1; C. Hardie d. Mrs J. L. Colegate 6-2 7-5; Mrs R. E. Haylock d. Mrs Blair White (IRE) 5-7 6-3 6-2; S. Barbier (F) d. J. Sandison (IN) 6-2 6-3; R. Tapscott (SA) d. B. Feltham 7-5 6-3; S. K. Johnson d. B. Boas 6-3 6-1; Mrs Satterthwaite d. M. Slaney 7-5 4-6 6-2; D. Gordon d. Mrs A. Mellows 6-2 1-8 10-8; M. V. Chamberlain d. Mrs H. Edgington 6-3 6-2; **E. de Alvarez** (2) (SP) d. Mrs B. May 6-4; Mrs Serpieri (IT) d. I. Lenos (GR) 6-0 6-3; Mrs J. Hill

d. M. Heeley 6-1 6-8 6-0; E. Ryan (USA) d. D. Anderson 6-1 6-1; E. F. Rose d. Mrs H. V. Edwards 6-2 6-3; Mrs C. G. McIlquham d. D. Cole (SA) 6-0 10-8; E. Hemmant d. Mrs A. D. Stocks w.o.; P. E. Mudford d. F. Pearson (IRE) 6-2 6-1; **H. Jacobs** (5) (USA) d. Mrs Neave (SA) 6-0 6-3; Miss Rost (G) d. V. Gallay (F) 6-0 12-10; Mrs R. Lycett d. E. Goldsworth 6-4 6-4; V. Montgomery d. Mrs Vaussard (F) w.o.; J. Fry d. Mrs H. G. Broadbridge 6-2 7-5; Mrs D. C. Shepherd Barron d. Mrs Macready 6-4 6-2; Mrs C. H. Jameson d. L. Payot (SWZ) w.o.; Mrs Holcroft Watson d. E. L. Colyer 7-5 6-2.

SECOND ROUND: H. N. **Wills** (1) (USA) d. G. E. Tomblin 6-0 6-0; Mrs I. Schomburgk (G) d. Miss Valerio (IT) w.o.; G. R. Sterry d. Mrs C. M. B. Marriott 6-4 4-6 6-2; J. Sigart (B) d. Mrs F. M. Strawson 6-2 6-8 9-7; **E. L. Heine** (6) (SA) d. G. M. Thompson 6-3 6-3; Mrs Kleinadel (F) d. Mrs C. Campbell (IRE) 6-2 3-6 6-3; Mrs B. C. Covell d. M. Canters (NTH) w.o.; Mrs A. E. Beamish d. J. Gallay (F) 6-1 6-2; **Nuthall** (3) d. Round 6-1 6-1; Michell d. Clarke 2-6 6-3 6-4; Goldsack d. Dam 6-3 6-3; Haylock d. Hardie 6-2 8-6; **Mathieu** (7) d. Whitley 7-5 6-4; Tapscott d. Barbier 4-6 6-1 6-1; Satterthwaite d. Johnson 7-5 6-3; Chamberlain d. Gordon 6-1 2-6 6-3; **de Alvarez** (2) d. Serpieri 6-2 6-2; Ryan d.

Hill 6-0 6-2; McIlquham d. Rose 6-1 6-2; Mudford d. Hemmant 6-3 6-0; **H. Jacobs** (5) d. Rost 6-3 6-0; Lycett d. Montgomery 7-5 6-3; Fry d. Shepherd Barron 6-3 6-4; Holcroft Watson d. Jameson 6-4 7-5; **E. Bennett** (4) d. Mrs la Besnerais (F) 6-3 6-1; M. Morrill (USA) d. Mrs D. Munro 6-0 6-1; Mrs Bundy (USA) d. Mrs E. Robertson w.o.; E. H. Harvey d. N. Trentham 6-2 6-2; **C. Aussem** (8) (G) d. C. Tyrrell 6-0 6-2; Mrs M. Mallory (USA) d. A. de Smidt (SA) 6-3 3-6 7-5; J. C. Ridley d. Y. Sigart (B) 6-0 6-1; K. Bouman (NTH) d. N. Lyle 8-6 6-1.

THIRD ROUND: Wills (1) d. Schomburgk 6-0 6-0; Sigart d. Sterry 8-6 6-4; **Heine** (6) d. Kleinadel 6-2 6-3; Covell d. Beamish 6-4 4-6 6-3; Michell d. **Nuthall** (3) 6-3 6-3; Goldsack d. Haylock 6-3 6-0; Tapscott d. **Mathieu** (7) 5-7 6-1 6-3; Chamberlain d. Satterthwaite 6-3 9-7; **de Alvarez** (2) d. Ryan 6-4 8-6; McIlquham d. Mudford 3-6 6-0 6-2;

Jacobs (5) d. Lycett 6-2 6-2; Fry d. Holcroft Watson 6-1 6-4; **Bennett** (4) d. Morrill 6-3 6-3; Bundy d. Harvey 6-2 4-6 6-4; **Aussem** (8) d. Mallory 6-4 6-1; Ridley d. Bouman 6-4 6-3.

FOURTH ROUND	QUARTER-FINALS	SEMI-FINALS	FINAL	CHAMPION
Wills (1)	**Wills** (1)			
Sigart	6-2 6-3	**Wills** (1)		
Heine (6)	**Heine** (6)	6-2 6-4		
Covell	6-2 7-5		**Wills** (1)	
Michell	Goldsack		6-2 6-0	
Goldsack	4-6 7-5 6-0	Goldsack		
Tapscott	Tapscott	6-3 6-3		**Wills** (1)
Chamberlain	6-3 5-7 6-4			6-1 6-2
de Alvarez (2)	McIlquham			
McIlquham	6-4 4-6 6-2			
Jacobs (5)	**Jacobs** (5)	**Jacobs** (5)		
Fry	6-3 6-4	6-1 6-0		
Bennett (4)	Bundy		**Jacobs** (5)	
Bundy	3-6 6-4 6-4		6-2 6-2	
Aussem (8)	Ridley	Ridley		
Ridley	8-6 6-1	6-3 6-2		

OTHER FINALS

GENTLEMEN'S DOUBLES: Final — W. L. Allison (USA)/J. Van Ryn (USA) d. I. G. Collins/J. C. Gregory 6-4 5-7 6-3 10-12 6-4.

LADIES' DOUBLES: Final — Mrs Holcroft Watson/Mrs L. R. C. Michell d. Mrs B. C. Covell/Mrs D. C. Shepherd Barron 6-4 8-6.

MIXED DOUBLES: Final — F. T. Hunter (USA)/H. N. Wills (USA) d. I. G. Collins/J. Fry 6-1 6-4.

GENTLEMEN'S SINGLES PLATE: Final — E. G. Chandler (USA) d. W. H. Powell 6-4 6-1.

GENTLEMEN'S SINGLES

1930

FIRST ROUND: H. Cochet (1) (F) d. H. Timmer (NTH) 6-4 9-11 4-6 6-4 6-2; C. E. Malfroy (NZ) d. P. Gaslini (IT) 6-3 6-1 6-1; R. Menzel (CZ) d. J. R. Reddall 3-6 6-3 6-1 6-2; B. Bell (USA) d. A. W. Vinall 5-7 6-4 6-3 6-1; H. K. Lester d. E. H. McCauliffe (USA) 6-2 7-5 0-6 6-4; R. D. Poland d. L. de Borman (B) 6-4 6-3 6-4; J. W. Nuthall d. A. H. Fyzee (IN) 6-4 1-6 6-4 6-2; J. B. Gilbert d. J. H. Shales 6-4 7-5 2-6 2-6 6-0; W. Allison (USA) d. **E. F. Moon** (A) 6-1 6-3 6-3; S. W. Harris d. N. Mishu (RU) 6-3 6-4 6-4; E. C. Peters d. A. J. Smith 1-6 2-6 6-1 6-1; G. L. Rogers (IRE) d. H. Satoh (J) 1-6 6-2 6-3 6-4; G. H. Perkins d. A. J. Gerbault (F) 4-6 6-2 6-4 6-0; D. Prenn (G) d. G. O. Jameson 9-7 6-0 6-1; I. H. Wheatcroft d. H. J. F. Hunter 6-2 6-8 6-2 6-2; G. P. Hughes d. J. D. P. Wheatley 6-2 6-2 4-6 6-4; **J. H. Doeg** (4) (USA) d. N. Sharpe 6-3 6-1 4-6 4-6 6-1; A. L. Della Porta d. M. Ferrier (SWZ) 6-2 6-4 6-0; E. Flury d. E. C. Metcalf 6-3 4-6 10-8 6-2; C. Boussus (F) d. M. S. Ellmer (SWZ) 6-2 6-2 6-4; M. Mohan (IN) d. R. J. Ritchie 6-1 6-1 0-7 5; J. Crawford (A) d. M. Malecek (CZ) 6-0 6-3 8-6; H. Kleinschroth (G) d. J. S. Harrison 6-2 2-6 6-2 7-5; H. F. David d. B. M. Clark (JAM) 3-6 9-7 6-2 6-4; **H. W. Austin** (6) d. E. R. Avory 2-6 7-5 6-3 6-2; J. Grandguillot (E) d. L. M. Williams (ARG) 6-1 6-1 6-4; P. Landry (F) d. G. R. Sherwell (SA) 6-3 6-0 6-3; G. Glasser (F) d. H. B. Purcell (IRE) 6-3 4-6 6-2 6-4; O. G. N. Turnbull d. Count L. Salm (AU) w.o.; G. S. Mangin (USA) d. Y. Ohta (J) 6-4 6-2 6-1; R. Miki (J) d. J. M. Hillyard 6-1 6-3 11-13 8-6; W. A. R. Collins d. I. G. Collins 6-2 6-4 1-6 6-4; **W. T. Tilden** (2) (USA) d. A. A. Fyzee (IN) 6-1 6-0 6-2;

E. O. Mather (USA) d. J. H. Frowen 6-4 8-6 7-5; J. Van Ryn (USA) d. W. A. H. Duff (C) 6-1 6-1 7-5; J. L. Chamberlain d. H. Chiesa (SWZ) w.o.; J. Pennycuick d. G. R. Williams (ARG) 6-4 6-2 3-6 9-7; D. M. Greig d. J. Charanjiva (IN) 6-4 7-5 4-6 8-6; J. Brugnon (F) d. F. Kuhlmann (G) 6-2 6-0 4-6 8-6; E. D. Andrews (NZ) d. A. J. Willard (A) 6-2 7-5 6-3; **H. L. de Morpurgo** (7) (IT) d. G. E. M. de Ste Croix 6-2 6-1 6-1; J. F. G. Lysaght d. R. K. Tinkler 6-2 9-7 12-10; O. Wright d. P. B. de Ricou (F) w.o.; F. J. Perry d. B. Hillyard 6-3 6-4 6-2; J. C. Gregory d. H. S. Lewis-Barclay 6-0 6-2 7-5; V. Landau (M) d. L. A. Godfree 8-6 4-6 3-6 6-4 6-2; C. S. Higgins d. D. M. Evans 6-2 6-2 6-1; T. Harada (J) d. E. N. W. Oliver (MAL) 6-0 6-3 6-4; **J. Borotra** (3) (F) d. F. Crosbie (IRE) 6-0 6-4 6-2; H. G. N. Lee d. W. H. Powell 6-4 5-7 6-2 6-4; K. C. Gandar Dower d. W. G. Curtis Morgan 6-4 4-6 6-1 6-2; J. S. Olliff d. B. D. Helmore 6-0 9-11 3-6 6-4 6-0; V. A. Cazalet d. J. Van der Heide (NTH) 6-2 6-2 7-5; B. de Kehrling (HU) d. R. Rodel (F) 2-6 8-6 6-3 6-3; P. F. Glover d. G. L. Tuckett 6-4 6-3 6-4; J. Kozeluh (CZ) d. N. H. Latchford 2-6 7-5 6-4 6-1; **G. M. Lott** (5) (USA) d. H. L. Soni (IN) 6-1 6-3 6-1; C. H. Kingsley d. G. R. O. Crole-Rees 7-5 6-2 6-2; H. C. Hopman d. d. Leahong (JAM) 6-0 6-0 6-2; F. H. D. Wilde d. H. Lacroix (B) 6-3 6-3 6-1; E. du Plaix (F) d. D. R. Rutnam (IN) 7-5 6-2 9-7; P. D. B. Spence (SA) d. J. C. Masterman 6-4 4-6 4-6 6-4; G. E. Godsell d. H. W. Artens (AU) w.o.; T. Abé (J) d. D. H. Williams 4-6 5-7 6-1 6-2 6-2.

SECOND ROUND: Cochet (1) d. Malfroy 6-4 6-1 6-1; Bell d. Menzel 6-1 6-2 6-2; Lester d. Poland 6-1 6-2 7-5; Gilbert d. Nuthall 6-1 6-2 6-1; Allison d. Harris 6-3 8-6 6-4; Rogers d. Peters 1-6 6-0 7-5 6-4; Prenn d. Perkins 6-3 6-3 6-3; Hughes d. Wheatcroft 6-1 6-2 6-2; **Doeg** (4) d. Della Porta 6-1 6-2 6-2; Boussus d. Flury 5-7 6-4 6-2; J. Crawford d. Mohan 6-2 3-6 6-3 6-2; David d. Kleinschroth 6-7 5-6 4-6 1; **Austin** (6) d. Grandguillot 6-2 7-5 6-1; Landry d. Glasser 6-0 7-5 0-6 3-6 6-0; Mangin d. Turnbull 6-2 7-5 6-0; Miki d. W. A. R. Collins 6-0 6-3 7-5; **Tilden** (2) d. Mather 6-2 6-2

6-1; Van Ryn d. Chamberlain 6-2 6-2 6-2; Greig d. Pennycuick 6-3 6-4 6-2; Andrews d. Brugnon 6-3 5-7 6-3 6-0; **de Morpurgo** (7) d. Lysaght 4-6 6-2 6-1; Perry d. Wright 6-1 6-2 6-3; Gregory d. Landau 6-1 6-3 10-8; Harada d. Higgins 6-4 6-2 6-3; **Borotra** (3) d. lee 5-7 3-6 6-3 6-3 6-1; Gandar Dower d. Olliff 5-7 6-4 9-7 6-3; de Kehrling d. Cazalet 6-2 6-3 6-3; Kozeluh d. Glover 6-2 1-6 4-6 9-7 6-1; **Lott** (5) d. Kingsley 6-3 6-4 6-4; Hopman d. Wilde 3-6 6-0 6-0 4-6 6-1; Spence d. du Plaix 6-8 6-4 6-3 6-2; Abé d. Godsell 6-1 3-6 6-2 6-4.

THIRD ROUND: Cochet (1) d. Bell 6-2 6-2 5-7 4-6 6-1; Lester d. Gilbert 6-1 6-3 3-6 8-6; Allison d. Rogers 6-3 6-3 6-2; Hughes d. Prenn 5-7 6-4 6-1 6-3; **Doeg** (4) d. Boussus 5-7 6-1 12-14 6-0 6-2; David d. J. Crawford 6-2 6-3 3-6 6-4; **Austin** (6) d. Landry 6-0 6-3 6-2; Mangin d. Miki 6-4 6-3 6-2; **Tilden** (2) d. Van Ryn 7-5 6-4 6-1; Andrews d.

Greig 6-3 7-5 6-2; Perry d. **de Morpurgo** (7) 10-8 4-6 6-1 6-2; Gregory d. Harada 6-3 6-2 7-5; **Borotra** (3) d. Gandar Dower 6-4 9-7 10-8; de Kehrling d. Kozeluh 6-3 6-4 13-11; **Lott** (5) d. Hopman 7-5 6-3 6-3; Spence d. Abé 6-1 6-4 5-7 6-3.

FOURTH ROUND	QUARTER-FINALS	SEMI-FINALS	FINAL	CHAMPION
Cochet (1)	**Cochet** (1)			
Lester	6-3 4-6 6-2 6-1			
Allison	Allison	Allison		
Hughes	4-6 6-1 6-2 6-3	6-4 6-4 6-3		
Doeg (4)	**Doeg** (4)		Allison	
David	6-3 6-3 6-1		6-3 4-6 8-6 3-6 7-5	
Austin (6)	Mangin	**Doeg** (4)		
Mangin	9-7 10-8 6-0	6-3 1-6 6-3 6-4		
Tilden (2)	**Tilden** (2)			**Tilden** (2)
Andrews	6-4 6-4 6-2	**Tilden** (2)		6-3 9-7 6-4
Perry	Gregory	6-1 6-2 6-3		
Gregory	3-6 9-7 6-1 3-6 6-1		**Tilden** (2)	
Borotra (3)	**Borotra** (3)		0-6 6-4 4-6 6-0 7-5	
de Kehrling	6-2 6-2 2-6 6-1	**Borotra** (3)		
Lott (5)	**Lott** (5)	2-6 6-3 6-3 6-4		
Spence	6-1 6-3 10-8			

LADIES' SINGLES

FIRST ROUND: M. Palfrey (USA) d. **E. de Alvarez** (4) (SP) w.o.; M. E. Dix d. E. H. Smith 6-0 6-3; Mrs E. Robertson (A) d. C. Tyrrell 6-3 6-1; C. Hardie d. G. Harry 4-6 6-1 6-4; A. Peitz (G) d. Mrs H. Ryland 6-2 6-3; Mrs J. B. Pittman d. J. Morfey 6-3 3-6 6-2; J. C. Ridley d. Mrs A. D. Stocks 1-6 6-1 7-5; S. Palfrey (USA) d. Mrs I. D. Brumwell 6-2 6-2; Mrs Fearnley Whittingstall d. Mrs L. G. Owen 6-1 7-5; E. M. Dearman d. D. V. Eastley 6-1 8-6; J. Fry d. R. Watson 1-6 6-2 6-4; G. R. Sterry d. Mrs Charpenel (F) 6-2 6-3; B. Feltham d. O. L. Webb 6-3 4-6 6-2; M. Heeley d. Mrs E. S. Law 6-1 6-4; Mrs Satterthwaite d. Mrs J. L. Colegate 6-0 6-3; **Mrs Holcroft Watson** (2) d. B. Nuthall w.o.; N. M. Lyle d. M. R. Couquerque (NTH) 7-5 6-4; Mrs C. H. Jameson d. Mrs R. E.

Haylock 6-4 3-6 6-3; E. Hemmant d. Mrs E. Dam (D) 6-2 6-1; N. Trentham d. Mrs F. M. Strawson 6-4 6-4; E. H. Harvey d. Mrs Henrotin (F) 6-8 6-0 7-5; Mrs H. V. Edwards d. Mrs M. A. O. Mayne 6-2 4-6 6-4; Mrs C. G. McIlquham d. V. Marshall 6-2 6-0; **E. Ryan** (8) (USA) d. H. M. Brooke 6-2 6-3; V. H. Montgomery d. Mrs J. Sigart 6-2 6-2; B. E. Cross (USA) d. M. Scriven 6-3 6-3; D. Gordon d. Mrs Dudley Cox 6-3 6-4; L. Payot (SWZ) d. R. Vlasto (GR) 6-4 6-1; M. Elton d. Mrs M. Stork 3-6 6-3 6-2; K. Le Messurier (A) d. M. C. Scriven 10-8 6-1; M. Greef (USA) d. Mrs T. Wolf (AU) 6-1 6-1.

SECOND ROUND: Mrs H. N. Wills Moody (1) (USA) d. H. Krahwinkel (G) 6-2 6-1; E. Goldsworth d. E. R. Clarke 6-4 6-2; L. Johnstone d. Mrs B. May 6-3 3-6 7-5; M. Canters (NTH) d. M. G. Hargreaves 6-2 6-4; **P. E. Mudford** (7) d. C. F. C. Turner 6-1 6-1; Mrs H. G. Broadbridge d. G. N. Thompson 8-6 4-6 6-2; G. Vaughton d. Mrs A. E. Beamish 2-6 6-0 6-4; Mrs H. S. Uber d. E. Stockel (D) 6-2 7-5; Dix d. M. Palfrey 3-6 6-4 6-2; Robertson d. Hardie 6-2 6-4; Pittman d. Peitz 3-6 6-2 6-4; Ridley d. S. Palfrey 3-6 6-4 6-1; **Mathieu** (5) d. Fearnley Whittingstall d. Fry d. Dearman 6-4 6-8 6-4; Sterry d. Feltham 2-6 6-1 6-3; Satterthwaite d. Heeley 6-3 6-0; Nuthall d. Lyle 6-3 6-4;

Jameson d. Hemmant 6-2 6-3; Harvey d. Trentham 9-11 6-1 6-3; McIlquham d. Edwards 6-2 6-1; **Ryan** (8) d. Montgomery 6-2 6-4; Sigart d. Gordon 6-1 6-2; Payot d. Elton 6-2 8-10 6-3; Greef d. Le Messurier 6-2 2-6 7-5; **H. Jacobs** (3) (USA) d. Mrs A. H. Mellows 6-3 6-1; M. Slaney d. J. Sandison (IN) 6-0 2-6 6-1; Mrs W. D. List d. S. Barbier (F) 6-2 6-4; S. K. Johnson d. D. Anderson 6-2 6-1; **C. Aussem** (6) (G) d. W. M. C. Bower 6-3 6-0; Mrs A. V. Bridge d. V. Gallay 6-1 6-1; F. James d. Mrs R. Lycett 6-3 6-3; D. E. Round d. J. Gallay (F) 6-1 6-4.

THIRD ROUND: Wills Moody (1) d. Goldsworth 6-1 6-2; Canters d. Johnstone 6-4 6-2; **Mudford** (7) d. Broadbridge 6-2 6-2; Uber d. Vaughton 6-3 6-2; Robertson d. Dix 3-6 6-2 6-1; Ridley d. Pittman 7-5 5-7 7-5; **Mathieu** (5) d. Fry 6-2 6-1; Satterthwaite d. Sterry 2-6 7-5 6-3; Nuthall d. Jameson 6-4 6-3; McIlquham d. Harvey

2-6 8-6 4-2 ret'd; **Ryan** (8) d. Sigart 6-3 6-4; Payot d. Greef 6-4 6-3; **Jacobs** (3) d. Slaney 6-3 6-0; List d. Johnson 6-1 6-2; **Aussem** (6) d. Bridge 6-3 6-2; James d. Round 4-6 6-3 6-4.

FOURTH ROUND	QUARTER-FINALS	SEMI-FINALS	FINAL	CHAMPION
Wills Moody (1)	**Wills Moody** (1)			
Canters	6-0 6-1			
Mudford (7)	**Mudford** (7)	**Wills Moody** (1)		
Uber	6-0 6-0	6-1 6-2		
Robertson	Ridley		**Wills Moody** (1)	
Ridley	6-4 6-1		6-3 3-6 6-2	
Mathieu (5)	**Mathieu** (5)	**Mathieu** (5)		
Satterthwaite	6-4 7-5	6-2 6-1		
Nuthall	Nuthall			**Wills Moody** (1)
McIlquham	6-2 6-3			6-2 6-2
Ryan (8)	**Ryan** (8)	**Ryan** (8)		
Payot	6-0 3-6 8-6	6-2 2-6 6-0		
Jacobs (3)	**Jacobs** (3)		**Ryan** (8)	
List	6-0 6-1		6-3 0-6 4-4 ret'd	
Aussem (6)	**Aussem** (6)	**Aussem** (6)		
James	6-2 6-1	6-2 6-1		

OTHER FINALS

GENTLEMEN'S DOUBLES: Final — W. L. Allison (USA)/J. Van Ryn (USA) d. J. H. Doeg (USA)/G. M. Lott (USA) 6-3 6-3 6-2.

LADIES' DOUBLES: Final — Mrs H. Wills Moody (USA)/E. Ryan (USA) d. E. Cross (USA)/S. Palfrey (USA) 6-2 9-7.

MIXED DOUBLES: Final — J. H. Crawford (A)/E. Ryan (USA) d. D. Prenn(G)/H. Krahwinkel (G) 6-1 6-3.

GENTLEMEN'S SINGLES PLATE: Final — E. du Plaix (F) d. C. E. Malfroy (NZ) 6-1 8-6.

GENTLEMEN'S SINGLES

1931

FIRST ROUND: N. Sharpe d. **H. Cochet** (2) (F) 6-1 6-3 6-2; H. B. Purcell d. E. E. R. Whitehouse 6-2 6-1 9-7; J. D. P. Wheatley d. W. E. Attewell 6-3 6-0 6-1; J. W. Nuthall d. P. Goldschmidt (F) 6-8 6-3 2-6 14-12 6-3; J. C. Gregory d. F. H. D. Wilde 6-3 6-3 2-6 6-2; P. F. Glover d. G. P. Hughes 6-1 6-4 6-3; L. Hecht (CZ) d. O. Wright 7-5 6-8 6-3 7-5; L. del Castillo (ARG) d. A. L. Della Porta 6-3 6-4 6-3; **S. B. Wood** (7) (USA) d. R. Singh (IN) 6-4 6-2 6-2; A. C. Crossley d. J. H. Frowen 1-6 8-6 8-4 7-5; E. Maier (SP) d. N. G. Farquharson (SA) 9-7 6-3 5-7 4-6 6-4; W. H. Powell d. B. Panker (D) 6-3 6-4 6-3; C. N. O. Ritchie d. V. A. Cazalet 6-3 5-7 6-1 6-4; O. Koopman (HU) d. E. Flury (SWZ) 0-6 4-6 6-1 2-6 6-2; S. W. Harris (SA) d. N. G. Holmes 6-2 4-6 6-1 6-4; C. E. Malfroy (NZ) d. S. Rodzianko (RU) w.o.; **C. Boussus** (4) (F) d. L. Raymond (SA) 7-5 6-0 8-6; H. S. Lewis Barclay d. R. D. Poland 2-6 3-6 6-3 6-4 7-5; A. R. Sissener (ARG) d. W. F. Freeman 5-7 6-4 6-4 9-7; M. Kawachi (J) d. A. A. Fyzee (IN) 6-0 6-0 6-4; D. H. Williams d. J. F. G. Lysaght 1-6 4-6 8-6 6-3 6-3; F. W. Matejka (AU) d. W. Washburn (USA) 6-3 6-2 6-4; A. Merlin (F) d. V. Landau (M) 2-6 7-5 6-3 6-2; J. Van Ryn (USA) d. F. Schaeffer (YU) 6-0 6-2 6-1; **F. J. Perry** (5) d. J. Cummins 6-1 3-6 3-1; I. Aoki (J) d. E. M. du Plaix (F) 6-3 6-3 6-3; E. R. Avory d. F. Marsalek (CZ) 7-5 4-6 8-6 5-7 6-1; A. Gentien (F) d. G. E. Godsell 6-1 7-5 6-3; C. H. Kingsley d. N. Van Chim (AN) w.o.; R. J. Ritchie d. H. S. L. Soni (IN) 6-2 8-6 6-2; C. F. Scroope (IRE) d. W. H. Smith 6-3 6-1 8-6; G. von Cramm d. G. B. de Kehrling (HU) 6-8 6-1 2-6 6-2 6-3; **J. Borotra** (1) (F) d. A. J. Smith 8-6 6-4 8-6; A.

Brown d. B. C. Law (USA) 7-5 7-5 7-5; W. Legg d. H. Van Giao (AN) w.o.; R. Miki (J) d. S. M. Hadi (IN) 6-3 6-4 6-2; H. W. Artens (AU) d. O. G. N. Turnbull 2-6 6-2 4-6 6-3 6-3; H. G. N. Cooper d. J. Novotny (CZ) 6-1 6-4 6-0; G. O. Jameson d. W. A. R. Collins 6-3 6-4 6-2; I. Tloczynski (POL) d. P. H. Partridge 6-2 6-1 6-1; **J. Satoh** (8) (J) d. V. G. Kirby (SA) 6-3 6-2 6-4; G. E. L. Rogers (IRE) d. G. S. Mangin (USA) 0-8 8-6 6-3 6-3; A. Madan Mohan (IN) d. N. H. Latchford 6-1 6-0 6-2; R. Boyd (ARG) d. K. C. Gandar Dower 9-7 2-6 7-5 6-1; A. W. Vinall d. G. E. M. de Ste Croix 6-3 11-9 6-4; H. G. N. Lee d. M. V. Callendar 6-2 3-6 6-2 4-6 6-1; G. M. Lott (USA) d. B. Berthet (F) 3-6 6-3 6-0 6-2; P. Landry (F) d. H. S. Burrows 6-3 6-2 6-2; **F. X. Shields** (3) (USA) d. P. D. B. Spence (SA) 6-1 6-1 6-2; H. F. David d. J. R. Reddall 6-4 6-3 6-2; J. H. Knottenbelt (NTH) d. P. Grandguillot (E) 6-4 7-5 3-6 4-6 9-7; H. Plougmann (D) 6-2 6-1 6-4; J. B. Gilbert d. A. Zappa (ARG) 6-2 6-2 5-7 3-6 6-1; J. Lesueur (F) d. J. Pennycuick 8-6 3-6 6-3 6-1; J. S. Olliff d. G. R. Ashton 8-6 1-6 6-0 6-0; C. R. D. Tuckey d. D. M. Greig w.o.; **H. W. Austin** (6) d. J. Malecek (CZ) 6-3 6-1 6-4; H. Satoh (J) d. Prince N. Magaloff (RU) w.o.; J. Brugnon d. H. K. Lester 7-9 6-4 4-6 7-5 6-3; E. C. Peters d. R. Rodel (F) w.o.; R. K. Tinkler d. J. Charanjiva (IN) 7-5 6-4 8-6; F. Kukuljevich (YU) d. E. M. Buzzard 6-4 0-6 3-6 6-3 7-5; E. A. McGuire (IRE) d. E. Higgs 6-4 2-6 6-3 ret'd; I. G. Collins d. H. Kleinschroth (G) 6-3 6-2 ret'd.

SECOND ROUND: Sharpe d. Purcell 6-0 6-3 6-2; Wheatley d. Nuthall 5-7 7-5 6-2 6-2; Hughes d. Gregory 3-6 1-6 6-2 6-3 6-2; del Castillo d. Hecht 7-5 6-4 5-7 2-6 6-2; **Wood** (7) d. Crossley 6-3 6-1 6-2; Maier d. Powell 6-4 5-7 6-2 1-6 8-6; Koopman d. C. N. O. Ritchie 4-6 2-6 6-3 6-3 6-3; Malfroy d. Harris 6-4 6-1 7-5; **Boussus** (4) d. Lewis Barclay 6-3 6-1 6-3; Kawachi d. Sissener 6-2 6-0 6-1; Matejka d. Williams 6-2 1-6 6-2 6-4; Van Ryn d. Merlin 6-2 6-3 6-3; **Perry** (5) d. Aoki 7-5 6-2 6-2; Gentien d. Avory 1-6 6-3 6-2 6-1; Kingsley d. R. J. Ritchie 4-6 4-6 6-3 6-4 6-4; von Cramm d. Scroope 6-1 2-6 7-5 6-4; **Borotra** (1) d. Brown 1-6 6-4 6-1 8-6; Miki d. Legg 9-7 6-2 8-6; Artens d. Cooper

9-7 6-2 6-3; Tloczynski d. Jameson 5-7 6-4 6-4 6-4; **J. Satoh** (8) d. Rogers 4-6 7-5 6-3 6-2; Madan Mohan d. Boyd 6-1 6-2 6-1; Lee d. Vinall 7-5 6-3 6-3; Lott d. Landry 6-4 11-9 6-2; **Shields** (3) d. David 2-6 6-0 6-3 6-4; Nourney d. Knottenbelt 10-8 2-6 6-0 11-9; Lesueur d. Gilbert 6-1 4-6 6-3 6-2; Olliff d. Tuckey 7-5 8-10 6-2 6-4; **Austin** (6) d. H. Satoh 6-1 6-3 6-0; Brugnon d. Peters 6-3 8-6 6-2; Tinkler d. Kukuljevich 10-8 1-6 6-4 6-4; I. G. Collins d. McGuire 7-5 5-7 3-6 6-2 6-3.

THIRD ROUND: Sharpe d. Wheatley 6-1 7-5 6-4; Hughes d. del Castillo 6-4 6-2 6-2; **Wood** (7) d. Maier 8-6 6-3 6-2; Malfroy d. Koopman 7-5 6-3 6-4; **Boussus** (4) d. Kawachi 6-3 6-3 6-4; Van Ryn d. Matejka 6-3 3-6 6-1 6-4; **Perry** (5) d. Gentien 6-2 6-3 8-6; von Cramm d. Kingsley 7-5 6-4 6-2; **Borotra** (1) d. Miki 6-4 6-1 6-2; Artens d. Tloczynski 6-3

6-2 4-6 6-4; **J. Satoh** (8) d. Madan Mohan 6-3 6-2 6-3; Lee d. Lott 7-5 7-5 7-5; **Shields** (3) d. Nourney 6-1 6-1 6-2; Olliff d. Lesueur 6-2 6-4 7-5; **Austin** (6) d. Brugnon 6-3 6-4 6-0; I. G. Collins d. Tinkler 8-6 6-1 6-3.

FOURTH ROUND	QUARTER-FINALS	SEMI-FINALS	FINAL	CHAMPION
Sharpe	Hughes			
Hughes	4-6 6-2 6-4 6-3	**Wood** (7)		
Wood (7)	**Wood** (7)	4-6 6-4 6-3 6-1		
Malfroy	6-3 10-12 10-8 6-4		**Wood** (7)	
Boussus (4)	Van Ryn		4-6 6-2 6-4 6-2	
Van Ryn	6-2 1-6 6-2 6-1	**Perry** (5)		
Perry (5)	**Perry** (5)	6-4 8-6 7-5		
von Cramm	7-5 6-2 6-4			**Wood** (7)
Borotra (1)	**Borotra** (1)			w.o.
Artens	6-4 6-2 6-3	Borotra (1)		
J. Satoh (8)	**J. Satoh** (8)	6-2 6-3 4-6 6-4		
Lee	8-6 6-4 6-3		**Shields** (3)	
Shields (3)	**Shields** (3)		7-5 3-6 6-4 6-4	
Olliff	6-2 6-0 6-2	Shields (3)		
Austin (6)	**Austin** (6)	6-3 2-6 5-7 7-5 6-1		
I. G. Collins	6-3 6-3 6-4			

LADIES' SINGLES

FIRST ROUND: **Mrs Mathieu** (3) (F) d. Mrs A. E. Beamish 6-3 7-5; J. Morfey d. Mrs J. G. Stephens 6-1 6-2; Miss Sander (G) d. V. Nicolopoulo (GR) d. Mrs V. Burr 6-0 3-6 6-2; Mrs R. E. Haylock d. M. E. Rudd 6-4 4-6 6-0; Mrs J. Van Ryn (USA) d. E. R. Clarke 6-3 6-3; F. James d. Mrs C. G. McIlquham 6-1 7-5; N. Trentham d. Mrs I. H. Wheatcroft 6-3 6-2; **P. E. Mudford** (7) d. E. M. Dearman 6-0 6-2; N. M. Lyle d. D. E. Anderson 6-3 6-3; J. C. Ridley d. Mrs H. S. Uber 6-3 6-2; M. E. Dix d. Mrs H. G. Broadbridge 6-3 6-3; Mrs D. C. Shepherd Barron d. J. Couchman 6-3 6-2; M. Heeley d. Mrs G. Lucas 6-2 6-4; E. H. Harvey d. V. H. Montgomery 6-2 6-2; M. C. Scriven

d. J. Sigart (B) 7-5 0-6 6-2; **B. Nuthall** (2) d. R. Berthet (F) 6-0 6-2; B. Feltham d. E. Hemmant 6-2 6-4; A. Peitz (G) d. Mrs Satterthwaite 6-2 6-4; H. M. Brooke d. R. Watson 2-6 8-6 7-5; V. Marshall d. V. Gallay (F) 6-4 6-2; Mrs L. A. Harper (USA) d. M. A. Thomas 6-3 6-4; M. E. Nonweiler d. E. Goldsworth 6-0 10-8; O. L. Webb d. J. Gallay (F) 2-6 6-4 6-1; **H. Jacobs** (6) (USA) d. Mrs Pons (SP) w.o.; B. Yorke d. S. K. Hewitt 6-2 6-1; Mrs J. B. Pittman d. G. Harry 6-1 6-2; J. Lawson d. A. D. Stocks 4-6 6-3 6-2; Mrs J. S. Kirk d. Mrs Dros-Canters (NTH) 6-3 6-4; Mrs E. S. Law d. R. Belliard (F) w.o.; Mrs L. A. Godfree d. J. Jedrzejowska (POL) 2-6 6-4 6-3; I. Adamoff (F) d. Mrs A. T. Price (A) 6-1 6-3.

SECOND ROUND: **C. Aussem** (1) (G) d. J. Goldschmidt (F) 6-4 6-1; E. Alexandroff (E) d. Mrs R. A. Seel 6-4 6-4; A. Neufeld (F) d. Mrs P. Thomas 4-6 6-3 7-5; B. Soames d. J. Marshall 6-3 6-1; **Mrs E. Fearnley Whittingstall** (8) d. Mrs H. A. Lewis 6-1 6-2; Mrs L. R. C. Michell d. Mrs A. V. Bridge 6-3 6-4; F. K. Scott d. G. Vaughton w.o.; L. Payot (SWZ) d. M. Elton (IN) 6-4 6-2; **Mathieu** (3) d. Morfey 6-2 6-4; Nicolopoulo d. Sander 6-3 6-2; Van Ryn d. Haylock 6-2 3-6 8-6; Trentham d. James 6-1 8-6; **Mudford** (7) d. Lyle 6-3 6-1; Ridley d. Dix 6-3 6-3; Heeley d. Shepherd Barron 7-5 7-5; Scriven d. Harvey 9-7 6-4; **Nuthall** (2) d. Feltham 6-2 6-2; Peitz d. Brooke 6-3 1-6 6-0; Harper d.

Marshall 6-3 6-2; Webb d. Nonweiler 6-3 11-13 7-5; **Jacobs** (6) d. Yorke 6-2 7-5; Pittman d. Lawson 6-0 6-4; Kirk d. Law 6-2 5-7 7-5; Godfree d. Adamoff 6-3 6-4; **H. Krahwinkel** (4) d. M. Slaney 6-2 6-1; Mrs C. H. Jameson d. Mrs H. G. Townsend 7-5 7-5; D. Metaxa (F) d. Mrs W. D. List 6-2 10-8; G. R. Sterry d. Mrs F. M. Strawson 6-2 6-4; **E. de Alvarez** (5) (SP) d. Mrs R. Lycett 2-6 6-1 6-2; D. E. Round d. K. E. Stammers 6-0 6-4; S. K. Johnson d. W. M. C. Bower 6-0 3-6 6-3; M. Sachs (USA) d. E. Perry 6-2 6-4.

THIRD ROUND: Aussem (1) d. Alexandroff 6-2 6-3; Neufeld d. Soames 6-1 6-4; **Fearnley Whittingstall** (8) d. Michell 6-4 6-1; Payot d. Scott 6-4 6-4; **Mathieu** (3) d. Nicolopoulo 6-3 6-0; Van Ryn d. Trentham 7-5 6-2; Ridley d. **Mudford** (7) 10-8 1-6 6-4; Scriven d. Heeley 6-4 8-6; **Nuthall** (2) d. Peitz 4-6 6-0 6-1; Harper d. Webb 6-0 6-4;

Jacobs (6) d. Pittman 6-3 6-4; Godfree d. Kirk 6-2 6-0; **Krahwinkel** (4) d. Jameson 6-3 6-4; Sterry d. Metaxa 7-5 4-6 6-3; Round d. **de Alvarez** (5) 6-3 6-3; Johnson d. Sachs 6-2 3-6 7-5.

FOURTH ROUND	QUARTER-FINALS	SEMI-FINALS	FINAL	CHAMPION
Aussem (1)	**Aussem** (1)			
Neufeld	6-0 6-2	**Aussem** (1)		
Fearnley Whittingstall (8)	Payot	2-6 6-2 6-1		
Payot	6-2 6-2		**Aussem** (1)	
Mathieu (3)	**Mathieu** (3)		6-0 2-6 6-3	
Van Ryn	6-4 6-3	**Mathieu** (3)		
Ridley	Scriven	1-6 6-2 7-5		
Scriven	6-1 6-4			**Aussem** (1)
Nuthall (2)	**Nuthall** (2)			6-2 7-5
Harper	6-4 6-2	Jacobs (6)		
Jacobs (6)	**Jacobs** (6)	6-2 6-3		
Godfree	6-2 6-1		**Krahwinkel** (4)	
Krahwinkel (4)	**Krahwinkel** (4)		10-8 0-6 6-4	
Sterry	8-6 6-0	**Krahwinkel** (4)		
Round	Round	7-5 6-3		
Johnson	6-0 6-1			

OTHER FINALS

GENTLEMEN'S DOUBLES: Final — G. M. Lott (USA)/J. Van Ryn (USA) d. J. Brugnon (F)/H. Cochet (F) 6-2 10-8 9-11 3-6 6-3.
LADIES' DOUBLES: Final — Mrs D. C. Shepherd Barron/P. E. Mudford d. D. Metaxa (F)/J. Sigart (B) 3-6 6-3 6-4.

MIXED DOUBLES: Final — G. M. Lott (USA)/Mrs L. A. Harper (USA) d. I. G. Collins/J. C. Ridley 6-3 1-6 6-1.
GENTLEMEN'S SINGLES PLATE: Final — V. G. Kirby (SA) d. G. E. L. Rogers (IRE) 2-6 6-3 6-3.

GENTLEMEN'S SINGLES

1932

FIRST ROUND: H. E. Vines (2) (USA) d. E. du Plaix (F) 7-5 6-3 6-4; H. S. Burrows d. G. Van Zuylen (B) 5-7 6-1 6-8 6-2 6-4; H. C. Hopman (A) d. J. W. Nuthall 6-3 6-1 8-6; C. E. Malfroy (NZ) d. P. Graves 6-1 6-1 6-0; C. R. D. Tuckey d. A. T. England 6-3 6-4 6-2; J. Siba (CZ) d. J. F. G. Lysaght 3-6 6-4 7-5 5-7 6-2; H. Kinzel (AU) d. W. H. S. Michelmore 6-2 8-10 3-6 6-4 6-3; I. Aoki (J) d. P. Landry (F) 6-4 6-4 6-3; **J. Borotra** (7) (F) d. A. Merlin (F) 0-6 6-1 1-6 6-4 6-2; C. N. O. Ritchie d. J. H. Knottenbelt (NTH) 6-1 6-2 6-4; R. J. Ritchie d. M. V. Callendar 6-4 6-4 6-2; H. G. N. Lee d. P. F. Glover 6-3 8-6 6-4; E. Maier (SP) d. B. de Kehrling (HU) 6-3 7-5 6-4; A. L. Della Porta d. L. Haensch (G) 4-6 6-4 6-3 0-6 6-2; G. E. L. Rogers (IRE) d. Prince N. Magaloff (RU) 10-8 9-7 6-2; F. H. D. Wilde d. G. E. M. de Ste Croix 6-2 6-1 6-2; **F. J. Perry** (4) d. G. O. Jameson 6-3 6-2 6-4; H. F. David d. H. L. Soni (IN) 6-3 6-0 6-3; J. D. P. Wheatley d. C. H. E. Betts 6-2 6-1 6-0; J. Van Ryn (USA) d. C. H. Kingsley 6-3 7-5 2-6 8-6; A. W. Hill d. A. Hyat 6-1 6-2 6-1; R. Miki (J) d. A. V. Rasmussen (D) 6-3 4-6 6-4 6-1; W. Allison (USA) d. G. L. Tuckett 6-3 4-6 6-1 3-6 6-2; I. Tloczynski (POL) d. G. E. Godsell 6-1 6-3 7-5; **J. H. Crawford** (8) (A) d. A. W. Vinall 6-4 6-3 6-3; J. C. Gregory d. V. Landau (M) 6-3 8-6 7-5; G. von Cramm d. A. A. Fyzee (IN) 6-4 6-3 6-1; C. Boussus (F) d. A. Madan Mohan (IN) 8-6 6-2 4-6 6-3; F. W. Matejka (AU) d. W. H. Powell 6-0 6-3 6-3; J. S. Olliff d. W. A. R. Collins 0-4 6-0 6-1; R. Bernard d. J. H. Shales 5-7 8-6 6-3 3-6 6-1; J. G. Grandguillot (E) d. H. C. Fisher (SWZ) w.o.; S. Rodzianko (R) d. E. M. Buzzard 4-6 8-6 11-9 6-1; P. Feret (F) d.

R. C. Wackett 3-6 7-5 0-1 ret'd; A. Brown d. H. W. Artens (AU) 5-7 6-2 6-3 3-6 7-5; J. Clemenger (A) d. H. K. Lester 0-6 6-2 6-2 6-2; E. C. Peters d. D. H. Williams 6-2 6-4 4-6 6-4; W. E. Attewell d. C. M. Jones Jnr 7-5 4-6 6-1 6-4; K. C. Gandar Dower d. A. C. Crossley 6-0 6-3 6-0; **H. W. Austin** (6) d. M. A. Young (NZ) 6-2 9-7 6-3; B. W. Finnigan d. H. D. Mackinnon 6-4 6-3 2-6 9-7; J. Cummins d. H. R. Price 11-9 6-8 3-6 6-2 6-3; G. P. Hughes d. T. Kuwabara (J) 4-6 2-6 6-3 6-2 6-2; R. Menzel (CZ) d. J. T. B. Leader 6-0 6-1 6-0; E. D. Andrews (NZ) d. J. Brugnon (F) 6-4 6-3 6-3; R. K. Tinkler d. J. R. Reddall 6-3 6-3 3-6 6-4; N. Taylor d. N. G. Holmes (IRE) w.o.; **F. X. Shields** (3) (USA) d. P. Grandguillot (E) 6-1 6-3 6-3; G. S. Mangin (USA) d. L. Hecht (CZ) 6-1 6-0 6-3; C. Sproule (A) d. W. F. Freeman 4-6 6-0 6-2; E. Higgs d. J. Charanjiva (IN) 6-4 6-2 6-0; E. R. Avory d. N. Sharpe 6-4 1-6 6-4 10-8; A. Gentien (F) d. S. W. Harris 6-2 6-2; A. Jacobsen (D) d. H. E. Weatherall 6-2 1-6 6-1 4-6 7-5; I. H. Wheatcroft d. J. M. Hillyard w.o.; **S. B. Wood** (5) (USA) d. A. M. Wedd 6-2 6-2 8-6; J. B. Gilbert d. G. Palmieri (IT) w.o.; H. Timmer (NTH) d. O. Wright w.o.; C. A. Magrane (ARG) d. H. B. Purcell (IRE) 4-6 6-1 6-1 4-6 6-2; H. Kleinschroth (G) d. D. G. Freshwater 6-3 1-6 9-7 2-6 6-2; P. V. V. Sherwood d. F. R. L. Crawford 6-1 6-3 6-3; J. Satoh (J) d. N. H. Latchford 6-2 6-3 6-2; I. G. Collins d. W. H. Smith 6-1 6-1 7-5; **H. Cochet** (1) (F) d. P. H. Partridge 7-5 6-3 6-2.

SECOND ROUND: Vines (2) d. Burrows 6-1 6-2 3-6 6-3; Hopman d. Malfroy 3-6 6-1 6-2; Tuckey d. Siba 7-5 6-2 6-4; Aoki d. Kinzel 6-3 6-0 6-4; **Borotra** (7) d. C. N. O. Ritchie 6-4 6-1 3-6 6-1; Lee d. R. J. Ritchie 6-3 7-5 6-4; Maier d. Della Porta 6-1 6-0 6-3; Wilde d. Rogers 7-5 6-4 6-4; **Perry** (4) d. David 6-4 6-3 7-5 6-1; Van Ryn d. Wheatley 6-3 6-4 7-5; Miki d. Hill 7-5 6-3 6-2; Allison d. Tloczynski 8-6 6-3 6-2; **Crawford** (8) d. Gregory 2-6 6-2 8-6 6-4; Boussus d. von Cramm 4-6 8-6 6-0 6-4; Olliff d. Matejka 6-1 6-4 6-2; J. G. Grandguillot d. Bernard 8-6 6-3 5-7 6-2; Feret d.

Rodzianko 5-7 6-4 4-6 6-3 6-4; Clemenger d. Brown 6-4 6-1 9-7; Peters d. Attewell 6-4 6-4 6-3; **Austin** (6) d. Gandar Dower 6-2 4-6 6-3 6-2; Finnigan d. Cummins 6-0 6-4 6-2; Menzel d. Hughes 8-6 1-6 6-4 6-2; Andrews d. Tinkler 10-8 6-2; **Shields** (3) d. Taylor 6-3 6-4 6-1; Mangin d. Sproule 6-2 6-2 9-7; Avory d. Higgs 6-3 6-4 8-6; Gentien d. Jacobsen 7-9 8-6 6-4 8-6; **Wood** (5) d. Wheatcroft 6-3 7-5 6-1 6-3; Timmer d. Gilbert 6-2 6-3 6-2; Kleinschroth d. Magrane 6-1 8-6 4-6 14-12; Satoh d. Sherwood 10-8 6-4 6-4; I. G. Collins d. **Cochet** (1) 6-2 8-6 0-6 6-3.

THIRD ROUND: Vines (2) d. Hopman 7-5 6-2 7-5; Aoki d. Tuckey 6-2 6-3 6-2; **Borotra** (7) d. Lee 6-3 7-5 6-1; Maier d. Wilde 6-4 6-3 6-3; **Perry** (4) d. Van Ryn 6-3 6-4 6-0; Allison d. Miki 6-4 6-0 2-6 6-1; **Crawford** (8) d. Boussus 9-7 6-4 6-2; Olliff d. J. G. Grandguillot 6-2 6-0 6-3; Feret d. Clemenger 4-6 6-1 4-6 6-0 6-3; **Austin** (6) d. Peters 6-1 6-4

6-2; Menzel d. Finnigan 6-2 6-3 6-1; **Shields** (3) d. Andrews 4-6 13-15 6-3 7-5 6-2; Mangin d. Avory 7-5 6-1 6-4; **Wood** (5) d. Gentien 6-2 6-3 6-2; Timmer d. Kleinschroth 6-2 2-3 ret'd; Satoh d. I. G. Collins 6-4 6-4 6-2.

FOURTH ROUND	QUARTER-FINALS	SEMI-FINALS	FINAL	CHAMPION
Vines (2)	**Vines** (2)			
Aoki	6-2 3-6 6-3 6-2	**Vines** (2)		
Borotra (7)	Maier	6-2 6-3 6-2		
Maier	6-3 6-3 2-6 6-2		**Vines** (2)	
Perry (4)	**Perry** (4)		6-2 6-1 6-3	
Allison	6-4 6-1 4-6 6-2	**Crawford** (8)		
Crawford (8)	**Crawford** (8)	7-5 8-6 2-6 8-6		
Olliff	6-3 6-4 3-6 6-1			**Vines** (2)
Feret	**Austin** (6)			6-4 6-2 6-0
Austin (6)	6-4 8-6 4-6 6-3	**Austin** (6)		
Menzel	**Shields** (3)	6-1 9-7 5-7 6-1		
Shields (3)	6-3 6-4 10-12 6-4		**Austin** (6)	
Mangin	**Wood** (5)		7-5 6-2 6-1	
Wood (5)	6-1 9-7 6-3	Satoh		
Timmer	Satoh	7-5 7-5 2-6 6-4		
Satoh	6-3 6-2 6-4			

LADIES' SINGLES

FIRST ROUND: Mrs E. Fearnley Whittingstall (4) d. N. M. Lyle 9-7 4-6 6-0; Mrs S. K. Edwards d. P. G. Brazier 6-3 6-2; Mrs A. H. Mellows d. J. Goldschmidt (F) 6-2 0-6 6-1; B. Feltham d. G. Vaughton 6-4 6-1; M. C. Scriven d. B. Boas 6-0 6-2; V. H. Montgomery d. J. Morfey 6-0 6-3; Mrs J. B. Pittman d. Mrs E. C. Peters 6-3 6-4; Mrs J. Lycett d. Mrs J. H. Crawford (A) 7-5 6-2; **L Payot** (7) (SWZ) d. M. E. Nonweiler 6-2 6-4; N. Trentham d. M. Horn (G) 6-4 7-5; Mrs M. Stork d. Mrs I. H. Wheatcroft 6-3 8-6; K. E. Stammers d. Mrs L. A. Harper (USA) 1-6 6-0 7-5; E. H. Harvey d. Mrs P. Thomas 6-1 6-2; Mrs L. R. C. Michell d. M. E. Dix 6-3 6-3; M. Heeley d. E. Ryan (USA) w.o.; Mrs S. Peacock d. S. K. Hewitt 6-2 6-2; Mrs Satterthwaite d. J. Ingram 6-1 7-5; E. Goldsworth d. E. R. Clarke 9-11 6-4 6-4 ret'd; C.

Rosambert (F) d. Mrs H. S. Uber 6-4 6-4; Mrs C. H. Jameson d. F. K. Scott 6-4 6-4; Mrs Macready d. Mrs H. G. Broadbridge 6-0 6-2; Mrs D. C. Shepherd Barron d. B. Soames 6-0 6-1; Mrs B. C. Covell d. Mrs W. D. List 6-1 2-1 ret'd; **H. Jacobs** (5) (USA) d. G. M. Southwell 6-1 6-1; Mrs E. Seel d. Mrs L. G. Owen 6-3 7-5; H. M. Brooke d. B. G. Beazley 6-1 6-3; F. James d. C. Aussem (G) w.o.; Mrs H. Martin d. B. Holly 6-2 6-1; J. Jedrzejowska (POL) d. Mrs E. S. Law 6-3 6-4; J. C. Ridley d. Mrs H. G. Townsend 2-6 6-4 6-2; G. R. Sterry d. Mrs J. S. Kirk 8-6 4-6 6-4; **H. Krahwinkel** (3) d. Mrs M. R. King 6-2 6-3.

SECOND ROUND: Mrs H. N. Wills Moody (1) (USA) d. M. R. Couquerque (NTH) 6-1 6-1; W. M. C. Bower d. J. Couchman 6-4 6-4; Mrs H. A. Lewis d. D. E. Anderson 6-1 6-2; Mrs L. A. Godfree d. Mrs R. E. Haylock 6-2 6-8 6-3; **D. E. Round** (8) d. J. Sigart (B) 6-2 6-0; M. Slaney d. M. A. Thomas 6-3 6-2; D. Metaxa (F) d. Mrs R. C. Clayton 5-7 6-1 6-2; Mrs D. A. Burke (USA) d. Mrs W. J. Dyson 6-2 4-6 6-2; **Fearnley Whittingstall** (4) d. Edwards 6-3 6-4; Mrs Feltham d. Mellows 4-6 6-4 6-3; Montgomery d. Scriven 3-6 6-3 7-5; Pittman d. Lycett 6-3 7-5; **Payot** (7) d. Trentham 7-5 6-4; Stammers d. Stork 7-5 6-3; Michell d. Harvey 6-0 6-1; Heeley d. Peacock 6-3 6-1; Satterthwaite

d. Goldsworth 6-2 6-2; Jameson d. Rosambert 6-3 6-1; Shepherd Barron d. Macready 6-0 6-3; **Jacobs** (5) d. Covell 6-1 6-2; Seel d. Brooke 6-4 6-3; James d. Martin 6-2 6-1; Jedrzejowska d. Ridley 6-2 6-4; **Krahwinkel** (3) d. Sterry 4-6 7-5 6-0; S. Palfrey (USA) d. E. M. Dearman 6-4 6-2; O. L. Webb d. E. Belzer (NTH) 6-4 6-2; S. Noel d. Mrs G. Lucas 6-3 6-4; **B. Nuthall** (6) d. S. Mavrogordato 6-1 6-1; D. V. Eastley d. M. G. Hargreaves 6-0 2-6 6-4; Mrs W. G. Lowe (SA) d. Mrs B. Pons (SP) 6-4 2-6 10-8; L. Valerio (IT) d. O. Wade (C) w.o.; **R. Mathieu** (2) (F) d. D. Crichton 6-1 6-1.

THIRD ROUND: Wills Moody (1) d. Bower 6-1 6-0; Godfree d. Lewis 6-4 6-2; **Round** (8) d. Slaney 6-3 6-3; Metaxa d. Burke 4-6 6-3 6-3; **Fearnley Whittingstall** (4) d. Feltham 6-2 6-2; Pittman d. Montgomery 6-1 8-6; Stammers d. Payot (7) 8-6 6-1; Heeley d. Michell 6-2 4-6 6-2; Jameson d. Satterthwaite 7-5 7-5; **Jacobs** (5) d.

Shepherd Barron 6-2 6-2; James d. Seel 6-2 6-2; **Krahwinkel** (3) d. Jedrzejowska 6-4 6-4; Palfrey d. Webb 6-2 6-3; **Nuthall** (6) d. Noel 6-2 4-6 6-2; Lowe d. Eastley 7-5 6-3; **Mathieu** (2) d. Valerio 5-7 6-1 6-2.

FOURTH ROUND	QUARTER-FINALS	SEMI-FINALS	FINAL	CHAMPION
Wills Moody (1)	**Wills Moody** (1)			
Godfree	6-3 6-0	**Wills Moody** (1)		
Round (8)	**Round** (8)	6-0 6-1		
Metaxa	6-1 6-3		**Wills Moody** (1)	
Fearnley Whittingstall (4)	**Fearnley Whittingstall** (4)		6-2 6-0	
Pittman	10-8 6-2	Heeley		
Stammers	Heeley	3-6 6-4 6-0		
Heeley	6-4 6-3			**Wills Moody** (1)
Jameson	**Jacobs** (5)			6-3 6-1
Jacobs (5)	6-1 6-2	**Jacobs** (5)		
James		6-2 6-4		
Krahwinkel (3)	**Krahwinkel** (3)		**Jacobs** (5)	
Palfrey	6-4 6-2		7-5 6-1	
Nuthall (6)	**Nuthall** (6)	Mathieu (2)		
Lowe	8-6 9-7	6-0 6-3		
Mathieu (2)	**Mathieu** (2)			
	6-4 8-6			

OTHER FINALS

GENTLEMEN'S DOUBLES: Final — J. Borotra (F)/J. Brugnon (F) d. G. P. Hughes/F. J. Perry 6-0 4-6 3-6 7-5 7-5.
LADIES' DOUBLES: Final — D. Metaxa (F)/J. Sigart (B) d. H. Jacobs (USA)/E. Ryan (USA) 6-4 6-3.

MIXED DOUBLES: Final — E. Maier (SP)/E. Ryan (USA) d. H. C. Hopman (A)/J. Sigart (B) 7-5 6-2.
GENTLEMEN'S SINGLES PLATE: Final — H. Cochet (F) d. T. Kuwabara (J) 6-2 6-4.

237

GENTLEMEN'S SINGLES

1933

FIRST ROUND: H. E. **Vines** (1) (USA) d. G. R. B. Meredith 6-1 6-2 6-0; A. T. England d. G. O. Jameson 10-8 6-2 8-6; R. Miki (J) d. R. K. Tinkler 11-9 6-1 8-6; W. L. Breese (USA) d. H. K. Lester 3-6 8-6 6-4 6-4; D. Prenn (G) d. C. M. Jones Jnr 6-4 6-2 6-1; E. M. D. Vanderspar d. H. Larsen (D) 11-9 3-6 6-2 6-3; E. Sertorio (IT) d. G. W. Gibbs 6-1 6-3 6-2; D. P. Turnbull (A) d. H. G. N. Cooper 6-2 6-1 6-1; **F. J. Perry** (6) d. A. Lacroix (B) 6-3 6-3 6-2; N. G. Farquharson (SA) d. J. R. Reddall 6-0 6-3 6-2; J. C. Gregory d. C. N. O. Ritchie 10-8 7-5 7-9 3-6 6-1; R. Menzel (CZ) d. E. D. Andrews (NZ) 9-7 0-6 6-1 6-3; G. L. Rogers (IRE) d. M. Bernard (F) 2-6 6-2 6-8 6-3 6-3; F. H. D. Wilde d. V. A. Cazalet 7-5 6-3 7-5; P. H. Partridge d. W. F. Freeman 6-0 0-6 6-3 3-6 9-7; K. Lund (G) d. E. C. Peters 4-6 6-3 8-6 6-2; **H. Cochet** (3) (F) d. H. S. Burrows 6-2 6-2 6-1; C. R. D. Tuckey d. G. L. France 6-4 6-2 6-2; C. L. Burwell (USA) d. H. Kleinschroth 6-0 6-1 6-2; H. Timmer (NTH) d. P. V. V. Sherwood 6-2 6-3 6-3; C. J. J. Robbins (SA) d. D. Macphail 6-0 12-10 6-4; A. Brown d. F. Bryans (ARG) d. J. E. Giesen (NZ) 6-2 6-2 6-4; D. H. Williams d. E. Nourney (G) 10-8 4-6 4-6 6-1; G. de Stefani (IT) d. H. F.

David 6-0 6-3 6-2; A. Merlin (F) d. W. H. Smith 6-3 6-1 6-4; R. Journu (F) d. E. Stanham (UR) 7-5 4-6 6-3 6-1; J. F. G. Lysaght d. J. B. Gilbert 6-3 6-2 6-1; H. F. Cronin (IRE) d. J. H. Shales 12-10 6-4 9-7; S. W. Harris d. J. H. O'Shea (SA) 6-3 6-3 1-6 10-8; **J. Satoh** (7) (J) d. V. Landau (M) 6-4 6-2 6-1; A. Jacobsen (D) d. I. M. Bailey 6-3 6-2 6-4; P. D. B. Spence (SA) d. L. Hecht (CZ) 6-4 5-3 ret'd; E. Higgs d. G. L. Tuckett 6-3 6-3 6-2; V. G. Kirby (SA) d. G. E. Godsell 6-2 6-4 6-0; A. K. Quist (A) d. A. A. Fyzee (IN) 6-2 6-4 6-4; K. Gledhill (USA) d. F. W. Matejka (AU) w.o.; J. Brugnon (F) d. B. W. Finnigan 6-3 6-3 6-4; **H. W. Austin** (4) d. W. A. R. Collins 6-1 6-0 6-1; I. Aoki (J) d. J. Cummins 6-4 7-5 9-7; J. D. Morris d. P. Graves 6-3 1-6 6-1 3-0 ret'd; G. P. Hughes d. P. Grandguillot (E) 6-0 4-6 6-0 6-2; R. J. Ritchie d. G. Jason (USA) 6-3 6-2 6-4; G. von Cramm (G) d. C. H. E. Betts 4-6 6-0 6-0 6-2; H. B. Purcell (IRE) d. S. M. Hadi (IN) 6-4 6-0 6-4; C. Boussus (F) d. A. L. Della Porta 6-1 6-0 6-4; **C. Sutter** (5) (USA) d. E. Itoh (J) 6-2 8-6 6-1; L. de Borman (B) d. S. Rodzianko (RU) 6-8 6-2 6-3 6-4; J. Mohnstone (M) d. A. Jacobsen (D) a. I. M. Bailey 6-3 6-2 6-4; P. D. B. Spence (SA) d. L. Hecht (CZ) 6-4 5-3 ret'd; de Borman 7-5 7-5 6-1; Condon (SA) d. J. Malacek (CZ) 7-5 6-4 6-3; A. W. Vinall d. A. Bawarowski (AU) 6-2 6-4 8-6; B. de Kehrling (HU) d. D. M. Frame (USA) 2-6 6-4 6-4 6-4; A. Gentien (F) d. A. del Bono (IT) 6-3 5-7 6-2 6-4; A. Martin-Legeay (F) 7-5 6-4 6-2; **J. H. Crawford** (2) (A) d. E. Maier (SP) 7-5 6-4 2-6 3-6 6-4.

SECOND ROUND: Vines (1) d. England 6-1 4-6 7-5 6-1; Miki d. Breese 6-2 6-2 6-1; Prenn d. Vanderspar 6-0 6-2 6-3; Turnbull d. Sertorio 6-3 6-4 6-2; Farquharson d. **Perry** (6) 7-5 6-1 3-6 4-6 6-4; Menzel d. Gregory 9-7 6-3 6-4; Rogers d. Wilde 7-5 3-6 5-7 8-6 6-2; Lund d. Partridge 6-8 6-4 6-3 6-2; C. L. Burwell d. **Cochet** (3) d. Tuckey 4-6 6-2 6-1 6-4; Burwell d. Timmer 1-6 7-5 ret'd; Robbins d. Brown 6-3 8-6 3-6 2-6 6-4; D. N. Jones d. Weatherall 9-7 6-4 6-4; **Lee** (8) d. Fisher 6-8 6-3 6-3 6-3; McGrath d. Siba 7-5 6-3 3-6 7-9 7-5; Powell d. Glover 6-0 10-8 6-4; Stoefen d. Nunoi 9-7 2-6

9-7 1-6 6-2; de Stefani d. Williams 6-2 6-3 11-9; Merlin d. Journu 6-0 6-0 4-6 6-3; Lysaght d. Croning 6-1 6-0 6-3; **Satoh** (7) d. Harris 6-3 6-3 7-5; Spence d. Jacobsen 4-6 7-5 6-4 6-4; Kirby d. Higgs 7-5 3-4 6-4 6-3; Gledhill d. Quist 6-3 9-7 6-2; **Austin** (4) d. Brugnon 6-3 7-5 6-0; Aoki d. Morris 6-1 6-3 6-2; Hughes d. R. J. Ritchie 6-3 6-4 6-4; von Cramm d. Purcell 6-0 6-2 6-3; **Sutter** (5) d. Boussus 4-6 10-8 6-4 6-2; Stedman d. de Borman 7-5 7-5 6-1; Condon d. Vinall 6-2 6-1 6-1; Gentien d. de Kehrling 5-7 6-2 6-1 6-3; **Crawford** (2) d. Martin-Legeay 6-2 6-8 6-0 6-1.

THIRD ROUND: Vines (1) d. Miki 6-2 6-4 6-4; Prenn d. Turnbull 7-5 6-0 6-2; Menzel d. Farquharson 6-3 6-3 6-2; Rogers d. Lund 3-4 6-3 6-3 1-6 7-5; **Cochet** (3) d. Burwell 2-6 6-3 7-5 7-6 3; D. N. Jones d. Robbins 7-5 6-2 11-9; **Lees** (8) d. McGrath 6-4 6-3 6-1; Stoefen d. Powell 6-2 6-4 6-2; de Stefani d. Merlin 6-4 6-2 6-1; **Satoh** (7) d.

Lysaght 4-6 6-3 6-0 6-2; Spence d. Kirby 7-9 6-4 4-6 6-4 6-2; **Austin** (4) d. Gledhill 6-3 10-8 6-1; Hughes d. Aoki 6-2 6-1 6-0; von Cramm 6-3 6-4 9-7; Stedman d. Condon 9-11 3-6 2-5 7-5; **Crawford** (2) d. Gentien 6-3 6-4 8-6.

FOURTH ROUND	QUARTER-FINALS	SEMI-FINALS	FINAL	CHAMPION
Vines (1)	**Vines** (1)	**Vines** (1)		
Prenn		6-2 6-4 3-6 6-3		
Menzel	Menzel		**Vines** (1)	
Rogers	6-1 6-1 12-10		6-2 8-6 3-6 6-1	
Cochet (3)	**Cochet** (3)	**Cochet** (3)		
D. N. Jones	6-4 6-8 8-6 6-0	3-6 6-4 6-3 6-1		
Lee (8)	Stoefen			
Stoefen	5-7 2-6 7-5 7-5 6-3			**Crawford** (2)
de Stefani	**Satoh** (7)			4-6 11-9 6-2 2-6 6-4
Satoh (7)	6-2 6-4 3-6 6-3	**Satoh** (7)		
Spence		7-5 6-3 2-6 2-6 6-2		
Austin (4)	**Austin** (4)		**Crawford** (2)	
Hughes	6-2 6-2 6-4		6-3 6-4 2-6 6-4	
Sutter (5)	Hughes			
Stedman	9-7 7-5 6-3	**Crawford** (2)		
Crawford (2)	**Crawford** (2)	6-1 6-1 7-5		
	6-1 6-4 6-2			

LADIES' SINGLES

FIRST ROUND: Mrs R. **Mathieu** (4) (F) d. J. Ingram 6-1 6-2; R. M. Hardwick d. B. I. E. Drew 3-6 1; E. H. Harvey d. N. Adamson (B) 6-4 6-0; B. Feltham d. Mrs E. S. Law 9-7 7-5; G. Harry d. B. G. Beazley 6-1 8-6; Mrs B. Pons (SP) d. D. E. Anderson 1-6 6-2 8-6; K. E. Stammers d. Mrs B. C. Covell 6-1 6-2; J. Saunders d. Mrs A. H. Mellows 6-4 5-7 6-2; N. Trentham d. A. M. Knapp 5-7 7-5 6-2; M. R. Couquerque (NTH) d. Mrs I. H. Wheatcroft 6-2 6-1; Mrs P. J. Whitley d. Mrs H. Martin 10-8 7-5; Mrs L. R. C. Michell d. G. M. Southwell 6-3 6-4; D. H. Crichton d. Mrs G. Lucas 6-3 2-6 6-2; Mrs D. A. Burke (USA) d. Mrs L. G. Owen 9-7 4-6 6-1; Mrs M. R. King d. Mrs E. C. Peters 6-2 6-1; O. L. Webb d. F. K. Scott 6-4 3-3

ret'd; Mrs J. S. Kirk d. I. Adamoff (F) w.o.; Mrs J. B. Pittman d. S. Noel 7-5 5-7 6-2; Mrs D. C. Shepherd Barron d. N. C. Case 6-1 10-8; F. James d. V. H. Montgomery 6-1 6-8 6-4; J. L. Seymour d. D. M. S. White 6-2 6-3; **H. Krahwinkel** (6) d. K. E. Robertson 6-2 6-1; Mrs I. Ridley d. Miss A. A. Wright 6-0 6-1; B. Nuthall d. M. Slaney 6-2 6-2; M. A. Thomas d. M. Wilson (A) 6-0 6-3; N. M. Lyle d. Mrs M. Stork 6-0 6-2; E. Goldsworth d. J. E. Cunningham 6-8 6-0 6-4; Mrs L. A. Godfree d. S. Rosambert (F) 5-7 6-2 6-4; **M. C. Scriven** (3) d. J. Sigart (B) 7-5 7-5.

SECOND ROUND: D. E. **Round** (2) d. J. Morfey 6-2 6-3; Mrs Nicolopoulo (GR) d. A. M. Yorke 10-8 6-4; Mrs M. M. Moss d. J. Harman (IRE) 6-2 10-8; Mrs S. K. Edwards d. M. Whitmarsh 7-5 2-6 6-2; **J. Jedrzejowska** (7) (POL) d. Mrs G. Maclean 3-6 6-0 6-2; M. Horn (G) d. J. Goldschmidt (F) 2-6 7-5 10-8; F. S. Ford d. A. E. L. McOstrich (USA) 6-1; L. Valerio (IT) d. Mrs R. E. Haylock 6-2 6-2; **Mathieu** (4) d. Hardwick 6-3 4-6 6-3; Feltham d. Harvey 6-1; Harry d. Pons 4-6 6-4 6-2; Stammers d. Strawson 6-3 6-3; **Jacobs** (5) d. Saunders 6-1 6-3; Trentham d. Couquerque 6-3 1-6 9-7; Michell d. Whitley 6-3 6-3; Burke d. Crichton 6-4 6-4; King d. Webb 6-1 6-1; Kirk d. Pittman 6-1 6-4; James d.

Shepherd Barron 7-5 6-3; **Krahwinkel** (6) d. Seymour 6-3 6-3; Ridley d. Johnstone 6-1 6-4; Nuthall d. Thomas 6-4 6-2; Lyle d. Goldsworth 6-1 6-2; **Scriven** (3) d. Godfree 6-2 1-6 6-3; E. M. Dearman d. Mrs W. J. Dyson 3-6 6-2 6-0; Mrs E. Fearnley Whittingstall d. M. E. Nonweiler 6-0 6-2; W. A. Mason d. M. E. Rudd 7-5 8-6; **L. Payot** (8) (SWZ) d. W. M. C. Bower 6-0 6-3; Miss Von Ende-Pflugner (G) d. V. Rice (USA) 6-4 6-4; Mrs Henrotin (F) d. Mrs P. Satterthwaite 6-3 6-0; M. Heeley d. P. G. Brazier 6-1 6-1; **Mrs H. N. Wills Moody** (1) (USA) d. Mrs E. Macready 6-0 6-0.

THIRD ROUND: Round (2) d. Nicolopoulo 6-4 6-3; Edwards d. Moss 6-1 6-4; Horn d. **Jedrzejowska** (7) 6-3 6-3; Valerio d. Ford 6-2 3-6 6-1; **Mathieu** (4) d. Feltham 4-6 8-6 6-2; Stammers d. Harry 6-1 8-6; **Jacobs** (5) d. Trentham 6-2 6-1; Burke d. Michell 3-6 6-3 6-2; King d. Kirk 6-0 6-1; **Krahwinkel** (6) d. James 6-3 6-4; Nuthall d. Ridley 6-1

6-3; **Scriven** (3) d. Lyle 4-6 6-1 9-7; Fearnley Whittingstall d. Dearman 6-3 4-6 6-2; **Payot** (8) d. Mason 7-5 7-5; Henrotin d. Von Ende-Pflugner 7-5 6-1; **Wills Moody** (1) d. Heeley 6-2 6-1.

FOURTH ROUND	QUARTER-FINALS	SEMI-FINALS	FINAL	CHAMPION
Round (2)	**Round** (2)	**Round** (2)		
Edwards	6-4 6-2	6-3 6-2		
Horn	Valerio		**Round** (2)	
Valerio	6-3 8-6		4-6 6-4 6-2	
Mathieu (4)	**Mathieu** (4)			
Stammers	6-4 6-0	**Jacobs** (5)		
Jacobs (5)	**Jacobs** (5)	6-1 1-6 6-2		
Burke	6-0 6-4			**Wills Moody** (1)
King				6-4 6-8 6-3
Krahwinkel (6)	**Krahwinkel** (6)			
Nuthall	6-2 7-5	**Krahwinkel** (6)		
Scriven (3)	**Scriven** (3)	6-4 3-6 6-1		
Fearnley Whittingstall	3-6 6-0 6-4		**Wills Moody** (1)	
Payot (8)	**Payot** (8)		6-4 6-3	
Henrotin	8-6 5-7 7-5	**Wills Moody** (1)		
Wills Moody (1)	**Wills Moody** (1)	6-4 6-1		
	6-3 6-0			

OTHER FINALS

GENTLEMEN'S DOUBLES: Final — J. Borotra (F)/J. Brugnon (F) d. R. Nunoi (J)/J. Satoh (J) 4-6 6-3 6-3 7-5.
LADIES' DOUBLES: Final — Mrs R. Mathieu (F)/E. Ryan (USA) d. F. James/A. M. Yorke 6-2 9-11 6-4.
MIXED DOUBLES: Final — G. von Cramm (G)/H. Krahwinkel (G) d. N. G. Farquharson (SA)/M. Heeley 7-5 8-6.

GENTLEMEN'S SINGLES PLATE: Final — F. H. D. Wilde d. J. D. P. Wheatley 6-4 6-4.
LADIES' SINGLES PLATE: Final — C. Rosambert (F) d. J. Goldschmidt (F) 6-4 6-1.

GENTLEMEN'S SINGLES

FIRST ROUND: J. H. Crawford (1) (A) d. I. Tloczynsky (POL) 6-2 7-5 8-6; H. Henkel (G) d. H. Kleinschroth (G) 6-3 6-4 6-3; A. W. Vinall d. E. C. Peters 6-4 6-8 8-6 4-6 6-2; I. G. Collins d. L. Shaffi 6-3 6-6 4-6-4; P. V. V. Sherwood d. L. de Borman (B) 7-5 4-6 6-3 1-6 6-3; H. K. Lester d. G. W. Gibbs 6-2 6-3 6-4; J. Lesueur (F) d. C. Oestberg (SW) 6-4 6-2 6-1; J. Yamagishi (J) d. W. Hines (USA) w.o.; **L. R. Stoefen** (6) (USA) d. P. Grandguillot (E) 6-2 7-5 11-9; J. S. Olliff d. P. H. Partridge 6-4 6-4 6-2; M. Bernard (F) d. W. L. Breese (USA) 6-1 6-1 6-2; C. H. Kingsley d. I. H. Wheatcroft 6-1 3-6 6-2 6-1; E. Sertorio (IT) d. J. B. Sturgeon 6-4 6-0 6-2; H. G. N. Lee d. H. S. Burrows 6-3 6-4 10-8; J. F. G. Lysaght d. G. M. Leembruggen (NTH) 6-4 4-6 6-3; F. von Rohrer (CZ) d. D. H. Williams 6-2 8-6 2-6 6-1; **H. W. Austin** (4) d. M. Sleem (IN) 6-3 6-1 6-2; H. Denker (G) d. H. Billington 6-1 3-6 6-3 1-6 6-3; D. P. Turnbull (A) d. H. Culley (USA) 6-4 6-2 6-8; R. Miki (J) d. G. E. Godsell 6-4 6-3 6-1; W. F. Freeman d. S. Rodzianko (RU) w.o.; E. R. Avory d. H. F. David 5-7 6-4 6-4 4-6 8-6; E. Maier (SP) d. H. B. Purcell (IRE) 6-3 13-11 6-0; L. Hecht (CZ) d. C. L. Burwell (USA) 6-3 6-2; **F. X. Shields** (5) (USA) d. D. Prenn (G) 6-3 6-3 6-4; P. Landry (F) d. R. J. Ritchie 3-6 11-9 6-3 6-3; H. C. Fisher (SWZ) d. I. Aoki (J) 6-3 6-1 6-3; G. C. Frank d. B. de Kehrling (HU) 3-6 4-6 6-1 6-3 ret'd; C. Boussus (F) d. C. E. Hare 6-3 6-1 6-4; H. W. Artens (AU) d. H. Timmer (NTH) 6-2 7-9 6-3 7-5; C. E. Malfroy (NZ) d. P. D. B. Spence (SA) 6-4 7-5 7-5; P. Geelhand (B) d. R. K. Tinkler 2-6 8-10 6-4 ret'd; **F. J. Perry** (2) d. C. R. D. Tuckey 6-2 6-2 5-7 6-0; R. N. Williams (USA)

d. Prince of Cutch (IN) 6-1 6-3 6-3; R. Menzel (CZ) d. A. C. Stedman (NZ) 6-1 7-5 8-6; A. Gentien (F) d. J. H. Knottenbelt (NTH) 4-6 9-7 6-3 6-1; G. R. B. Meredith d. A. Brown 3-6 9-7 2-6 6-2 6-0; G. L. Rogers (IRE) d. J. D. Morris 6-1 4-6 4-6 6-2 6-4; K. Schroeder (SW) d. C. F. Aeschliman (SWZ) 6-1 6-1 6-4; A. K. Quist (A) d. J. Kitson (SA) 6-1 6-2 12-10; **G. de Stefani** (8) (IT) d. V. Landau (M) 7-5 10-8 7-9 7-5; G. M. Lott (USA) d. R. O. Williams 6-3 6-1 5-7 7-5; N. Sharpe d. A. T. England 6-1 6-3 6-4; J. Fujikura (J) d. R. du Plaix (F) 6-2 6-3 8-6; A. Lacroix (B) d. D. G. Freshwater 6-3 6-3 6-3; H. C. Hopman (A) d. W. Menzel (G) 6-2 6-3 1-6 6-3; J. Brugnon (F) d. P. Feret (F) w.o.; A. Merlin (F) d. G. Von Metaxa (A) 6-3 6-4 6-4; **G. von Cramm** (3) d. J. Hebda (POL) w.o.; A. Jacobsen (D) d. D. R. Rutnam (IN) 11-9 6-4 6-1; C. M. Jones d. McPhail 6-1 6-0 6-2; E. D. Andrews (NZ) d. F. H. D. Wilde 8-6 6-4 6-2; E. Gabrowitz (HU) d. C. N. O. Ritchie 4-6 6-3 6-1 6-4; F. Matejka (AU) d. J. R. Reddall 2-6 9-7 6-1 6-0; A. Martin-Legeay (F) d. N. Taylor 7-5 6-1 0-6 6-2; V. G. Kirby (SA) d. A. del Bono (IT) 6-3 6-1; **S. B. Wood** (7) (USA) d. V. B. McGrath (A) 10-8 6-4 6-4; M. Ellmer (SWZ) d. M. Bhandari (IN) 6-1 6-2 6-2; D. B. Jarvis d. W. E. Attewell 7-5 2-6 6-4 6-0; H. G. N. Cooper d. J. Clynton Reed 6-3 6-4 6-3; G. P. Hughes d. R. M. Turnbull 6-0 6-1 6-0; D. N. Jones (USA) d. C. Naeyaert (B) 6-1 6-1 6-1; H. Nishimura (J) d. K. C. Gandar Dower 4-6 7-5 6-4 6-1; J. Siba (CZ) d. O. Koopman (NTH) 6-0 6-2 6-3.

SECOND ROUND: Crawford (1) d. Henkel 6-2 6-3 3-6 6-4; Collins d. Vinall 6-2 6-3 6-4; Lester d. Sherwood 3-6 6-4 6-4 6-3; Yamagishi d. Lesueur 6-1 6-2 6-3; **Stoefen** (6) d. Olliff 6-1 6-2 6-2; Bernard d. Kingsley 6-3 6-4 5-7 4-6 6-3; Lee d. Sertorio 6-4 6-3; Lysaght d. von Rohrer 6-3 6-1 6-3; **Austin** (4) d. Denker 6-1 6-1 6-2; D. P. Turnbull d. Miki 6-3 6-1 6-1; Avory d. Freeman 6-4 6-4 6-1; Hecht d. Maier 6-3 6-2; **Shields** (5) d. Landry 6-4 6-4 6-0; Fisher d. Frank 6-3 6-3 6-0; Boussus d. Artens 6-3 6-3 7-5; Malfroy d. Geelhand 6-3 6-1 6-2; **Perry** (2) d. R. N. Williams 6-2

6-2 6-0; R. Menzel d. Gentien 6-1 6-1 6-2; Rogers d. Meredith 7-5 6-4 7-5; Quist d. Schroeder 6-3 1-6 6-2 6-2; Lott d. **de Stefani** (8) 3-6 6-3 6-4 6-4; Sharpe d. Fujikura 6-4 3-6 1-6 7-5 6-4; Hopman d. Lacroix 6-1 7-5 2-6 6-4; Merlin d. Brugnon 6-2 3-6 6-4 6-3; **von Cramm** (3) d. Jacobsen 6-2 6-3 9-7; Andrews d. C. M. Jones 6-2 6-2 8-6; Matejka d. Gabrowitz 6-8 6-1 6-2 6-3; Kirby d. Martin-Legeay 4-6 6-4 2-6 7-5 6-0; **Wood** (7) d. Ellmer 6-3 5-7 6-0 7-5; Cooper d. Jarvis 6-3 6-2 6-3; D. N. Jones d. Hughes 2-6 6-4 7-5 1-6 6-4; Siba d. Nishimura 8-6 4-6 8-6 2-6 9-7.

THIRD ROUND: Crawford (1) d. Collins 4-6 6-2 6-0 6-1; Yamagishi d. Lester 9-7 7-5 6-4; **Stoefen** (6) d. Bernard 6-4 6-4 6-3; Lee d. Lysaght 6-1 10-8 7-5; **Austin** (4) d. D. P. Turnbull 6-1 6-4 6-3; Hecht d. Avory 7-5 6-2 6-1; **Shields** (5) d. Fisher w.o.; Boussus d. Malfroy 6-1 6-2 6-3; **Perry** (2) d. R. Menzel 0-6 6-3 5-7 6-4 6-2; Quist d. Rogers 7-5 6-1

7-5; Lott d. Sharpe 7-5 2-6 6-3 1-6 6-4; Hopman d. Merlin 7-5 6-2 6-2; **von Cramm** (3) d. Andrews 6-1 6-4 6-4; Kirby d. Matejka 3-6 6-4 6-8 7-5 6-4; **Wood** (7) d. Cooper 4-6 6-2 6-2 6-1; D. N. Jones d. Siba 4-6 4-6 6-4 6-1 6-3.

FOURTH ROUND	QUARTER-FINALS	SEMI-FINALS	FINAL	CHAMPION
Crawford (1)	**Crawford** (1)			
Yamagishi	4-6 6-4 6-2 6-2	**Crawford** (1)		
Stoefen (6)	**Stoefen** (6)	7-5 2-6 7-5 6-0		
Lee	6-2 6-4 6-4		**Crawford** (1)	
Austin (4)	**Austin** (4)		2-6 4-6 6-4 6-3 6-4	
Hecht	6-3 6-1 6-2	**Shields** (5)		
Shields (5)	**Shields** (5)	4-6 2-6 7-5 6-3 7-5		
Boussus	6-4 3-6 6-4 7-9 8-6			**Perry** (2)
Perry (2)	**Perry** (2)			6-3 6-0 7-5
Quist	6-2 6-3 6-4	**Perry** (2)		
Lott	Lott	6-4 2-6 7-5 10-8		
Hopman	4-6 6-3 6-2 6-2		**Perry** (2)	
von Cramm (3)	Kirby		6-3 3-6 7-5 5-7 6-3	
Kirby	6-2 2-6 6-4 6-2	**Wood** (7)		
Wood (7)	**Wood** (7)	6-1 6-4 3-6 6-0		
D. N. Jones	6-3 6-3 6-4			

LADIES' SINGLES

FIRST ROUND: D. E. Round (2) d. J. C. Ridley 6-2 6-0; M. Heeley d. P. G. Brazier 6-3 6-2; M. R. Couquerque (NTH) d. Mrs M. Molesworth (A) 6-4 7-5; Mrs M. R. King d. M. G. Hargreaves 6-0 6-1; **L. Payot** (6) (SWZ) d. N. M. Lyle 3-6 6-3 6-1; Mrs Henrotin d. R. Haylock 7-5 1-6 6-2; J. de Chavarri (SP) d. J. Cruickshank (USA) w.o.; Mrs P. D. Howard (F) d. J. Cunningham 6-1 6-0; **S. Palfrey** (3) (USA) d. R. Smith 6-3 6-1; Mrs L. A. Godfree d. J. Saunders 6-3 8-6; R. M. Hardwick d. G. Harry 6-3 7-5; Mrs M. M. Moss d. G. A. Clarke-Jervoise 6-2 6-4; **Mrs R. Mathieu** (8) (F) d. Mrs R. Robertson 6-4 6-0; Mrs H. C. Hopman d. E. N. S. Dickin 6-1 6-2; M. Horn (G) d. Mrs Slaney 7-5 6-4; Mrs E. Fearnley Whittingstall d. B. Nuthall 2-6 6-3 6-4; **H. Jacobs** (1) (USA) d. Mrs E. C. Peters 6-1 6-1; J. Ingram d. Mrs P.

Satterthwaite 6-0 6-3; M. A. Thomas d. S. Mavrogordato 6-2 7-5; M. E. Rudd d. Mrs H. S. Uber 4-6 6-1 7-5; **C. Aussem** (7) (G) d. Mrs P. J. Whitley 6-0 6-0; Mrs J. B. Pittman d. M. E. Nonweiler 8-6 8-6; F. James d. Mrs G. G. Honeyman 6-0 1-6 6-3; Mrs F. M. Strawson d. Mrs G. Lucas 6-2 6-3; **Mrs H. Sperling** (4) (D) d. D. H. Crichton 6-2 6-2; Mrs S. K. Edwards d. M. Riddell 4-6 6-4 7-5; L. Row (IN) d. G. M. Southwell 4-6 10-8 6-2; J. Hartigan (A) d. A. A. Wright 6-3 7-5; **M. C. Scriven** (5) d. G. K. Osborne 6-1 6-2; A. E. L. McOstrich d. D. Kitson (SA) 7-5 8-6; Mrs A. H. Mellows d. G. Szapary (AU) 6-1 8-6; C. Rosambert (F) d. M. Burgess-Smith 6-1 6-3.

SECOND ROUND: Round (2) d. V. H. Montgomery 6-0 6-1; Heeley d. Mrs W. J. Dyson 6-2 6-2; Couquerque d. J. Mowbray Green 4-6 6-4 6-4 6-3; King d. B. E. Frye 6-2 6-0; **Payot** (6) d. S. G. Chuter 6-1 8-6; Henrotin d. L. Valerio (IT) 6-3 6-4; A. M. Yorke d. de Chavarri 6-2 8-6; S. Howard d. Mrs I. H. Wheatcroft 6-4 6-1; **Palfrey** (3) d. E. M. Dearman 6-3 6-2; Godfree d. F. S. Ford 6-1 6-0; Hardwick d. J. Morfey 6-4 6-1; J. Jedrzejowska (POL) d. Moss 6-4 6-4; **Mathieu** (8) d. P. L. F. Thomson 6-0 6-2; Hopman d. V. Rice (USA) 6-4 10-8; Horn d. S. Noel 6-2 6-2; Fearnley Whittingstall d. F. K. Scott 6-0 5-7 6-1; **Jacobs** (1) d. Mrs D. Andrus (USA) 6-2 6-1; Ingram d. Mrs M. A. V. Russell

3-6 6-4 6-1; J. Goldschmidt (F) d. Thomas 6-4 6-0; K. E. Stammers d. Rudd 6-1 6-1; **Aussem** (7) d. Mrs R. M. Turnbull 6-0 6-4 6-1; E. H. Harvey d. Pittman 6-3 3-6 6-2; James d. M. Whitmarsh 3-6 6-3 6-4; Strawson d. M. T. Ricketts 6-2 3-6 6-1; **Sperling** (4) d. Mrs R. A. Chamberlain 6-4 6-4; S. K. Edwards d. Mrs D. C. Shepherd Barron 7-9 7-5 8-6; I. Adamoff (F) d. Row 6-3 5-7 6-4; Hartigan d. M. Baumgarten (HU) 7-5 6-2; **Scriven** (5) d. Mrs J. S. Kirk 6-0 6-1; Mrs E. S. Law d. McOstrich 6-4 5-7 6-1; Mellows d. N. Adamson (B) 6-1 6-2; C. Babcock (USA) d. Rosambert 7-5 6-2.

THIRD ROUND: Round (2) d. Heeley 6-3 6-0; King d. Couquerque 6-4 6-3; **Payot** (6) d. Henrotin 4-6 6-3 6-4; Yorke d. Howard w.o.; **Palfrey** (3) d. Godfree 6-3 6-1; Jedrzejowska d. Hardwick 8-6 3-6 8-6; **Mathieu** (8) d. Hopman 3-6 6-1 6-3; Horn d. Fearnley Whittingstall 5-7 6-0 6-2; **Jacobs** (1) d. Ingram 4-6 6-4 6-1; Goldschmidt d. Stammers 7-5

9-7; **Aussem** (7) d. Harvey 6-1 6-0; James d. Strawson 6-1 8-6; **Sperling** (4) d. Edwards 6-2 6-4; Hartigan d. Adamoff 7-5 6-4; **Scriven** (5) d. Law 6-3 6-2; Babcock d. Mellows 6-1 6-3.

FOURTH ROUND	QUARTER-FINALS	SEMI-FINALS	FINAL	CHAMPION
Round (2)	**Round** (2)			
King	6-3 2-6 6-3	**Round** (2)		
Payot (6)	**Payot** (6)	6-4 6-2		
Yorke	6-3 6-0		**Round** (2)	
Palfrey (3)	**Palfrey** (3)		6-4 5-7 6-2	
Jedrzejowska	6-2 6-2	**Mathieu** (8)		
Mathieu (8)	**Mathieu** (8)	6-3 6-8 6-2		
Horn	7-5 6-2			**Round** (2)
Jacobs (1)	**Jacobs** (1)			6-2 5-7 6-3
Goldschmidt	6-2 6-3	**Jacobs** (1)		
Aussem (7)	**Aussem** (7)	6-0 6-2		
James	6-2 6-1		**Jacobs** (1)	
Sperling (4)	Hartigan		6-2 6-2	
Hartigan	6-4 5-7 6-4	Hartigan		
Scriven (5)	**Scriven** (5)	3-6 6-3 6-1		
Babcock	9-7 6-8 6-2			

OTHER FINALS

GENTLEMEN'S DOUBLES: Final — G. M. Lott (USA)/L. R. Stoefen (USA) d. J. Borotra (F)/J. Brugnon (F) 6-2 6-3 6-4.

LADIES' DOUBLES: Final — Mrs R. Mathieu (F)/E. Ryan (USA) d. Mrs D. B. Andrus (USA)/Mrs S. Henrotin (F) 6-3 6-3.

MIXED DOUBLES: Final — R. Miki (J)/D. E. Round d. H. W. Austin/Mrs D. C. Shepherd Barron 3-6 6-4 6-0.
GENTLEMEN'S SINGLES PLATE: Final — H. W. Artens (AU) d. C. R. D. Tuckey 5-7 7-5 6-1.
LADIES' SINGLES PLATE: Final — L. Valerio (IT) d. J. Saunders 7-5 6-3.

GENTLEMEN'S SINGLES

1935

FIRST ROUND: F. J. Perry (1) d. M. Rainville (C) 6-1 6-1 6-3; W. Hines (USA) d. A. Lacroix (B) 4-6 6-1 3-6 6-3 6-4; F. Smith (NOR) d. G. L. Rogers (IRE) 5-7 6-1 6-3 9-11 6-4; J. Van Ryn (USA) d. D. P. Turnbull (A) 6-2 6-3 8-6; J. Lesueur (F) d. E. J. Filby 6-3 6-2 6-4; J. Pallada (YU) d. C. H. E. Betts 6-4 6-3 6-3; H. Timmer (NTH) d. A. Brown 6-3 6-1 6-1; C. N. O. Ritchie d. H. W. Artens (AU) 6-4 6-3 9-7; **R. Menzel** (7) (CZ) d. L. E. Cater 6-1 4-6 6-2 6-0; J. Borotra (F) d. H. Henkel (G) 6-4 1-6 8-6 2-6 6-2; G. Palmieri (IT) d. H. Nishimura (J) 6-2 3-6 6-3 6-4; C. E. Malfroy (NZ) d. W. C. Choy (CHI) 6-2 6-2 6-1; J. Hendrie (SA) d. A. T. England 5-7 7-5 6-2 6-2; A. Gentien (F) d. H. S. Burrows 3-6 6-1 6-4 6-4; E. Maier (SP) d. W. Robertson (USA) 6-2 6-3 6-3; G. R. B. Meredith d. H. G. N. Cooper 4-6 6-3 6-1 6-0; **J. H. Crawford** (3) (A) d. J. Brugnon (F) 6-3 6-1 6-4; V. G. Kirby (SA) d. J. M. Hunt 6-1 6-2 6-3; P. Landry (F) d. L. Watt (C) 8-6 1-6 6-2 5-7 7-5; L. Hecht (CZ) d. M. Bernard (F) 6-4 2-6 5-7 6-4 7-5; H. Plougmann (D) d. K. Lasn (E) w.o.; G. P. Hughes d. H. M. Culley (USA) 6-3 11-9 6-2; F. Kukuljevic (YU) d. E. Straub (HU) 6-3 6-3 6-4; K. Lund (G) d. L. de Borman (B) 4-6 4-6 6-0 2-0 ret'd; **S. B. Wood** (6) (USA) d. E. Itoh (J) 6-2 6-2 6-0; G. E. Godsell d. C. F. Aeschliman (SWZ) 6-2 6-4 4-6 6-4; D. H. Williams d. C. H. Kingsley 6-3 7-5 4-6 2-6 6-4; L. Shaffi d. C. L. Burwell (USA) 8-6 4-6 8-6 7-5; D. MacPhail d. W. Muir (SA) 8-6 6-2 6-4; A. del Bono (IT) d. H. Pietzner w.o.; H. C. Hopman (A) d. D. G. Freshwater 6-1 7-5 6-0; A. C. Stedman (NZ) d. J. B. Sturgeon 6-3 6-0 6-1; A. K. Quist (A) d. P. H. Partridge 6-2 6-1

7-5; M. Ellmer (SWZ) d. C. Naeyaert (B) 6-4 6-4 6-1; D. Budge (USA) d. F. H. D. Wilde 8-6 6-2 6-1; M. Bertram (SA) d. N. Taylor 8-6 6-1 6-1; J. F. G. Lysaght d. E. Wittman (POL) w.o.; R. Gabrowitz (HU) d. H. B. Purcell (IRE) 8-6 4-6 6-1 6-3; F. Puncec (YU) d. H. Kleinschroth (G) 6-1 6-2 6-2; **C. Boussus** (8) (F) d. I. G. Collins 1-6 6-0 2-6 6-4 6-1; D. W. Butler d. V. Taroni (IT) 5-7 3-6 6-3 7-5 6-3; E. D. Andrews (NZ) d. H. F. David 6-1 7-5 6-1; J. S. Olliff d. R. Longtin (C) 6-4 5-7 2-6 6-0 6-4; G. von Metaxa (AU) d. D. Teschmacher (NTH) w.o.; H. Billington d. L. J. Aslangul (F) 6-0 7-5 6-1; W. Musgrove (SA) d. L. W. J. Newman 6-1 6-4 6-3; J. Haanes (NOR) d. J. S. Harrison 6-4 6-4 0-6 6-4; **H. W. Austin** (4) d. E. R. Avory 6-3 6-1 6-3; N. Sharpe d. D. Prenn (G) 6-2 6-3 3-6 6-2; R. K. Tinkler d. H. C. Fisher (SWZ) 1-6 4-6 6-3 6-3; J. Van den Eynde (B) d. A. Martin Legeay (F) d. R. J. Ritchie 10-8 6-2 7-5; H. G. N. Lee d. R. M. Turnbull 6-3 6-1 6-1; C. R. D. Tuckey d. P. D. B. Spence (SA) 4-6 2-6 7-5 6-3; V. B. McGrath (A) d. **W. Allison** (5) (USA) 6-4 6-3 7-9 7-5; R. Murray (C) d. G. Troncin (F) 7-5 6-3 6-0; N. G. Farquharson (SA) d. R. E. Mulliken 6-1 6-0 6-3; J. Yamagishi (J) d. H. L. de Morpurgo (IT) 6-3 6-1 6-1; G. Mako (USA) d. D. N. Jones (USA) 7-5 6-3 4-6 6-4; P. V. V. Sherwood d. J. L. Chamberlain 6-0 6-2 11-13 2-6 8-6; J. Caska (CZ) d. H. A. Hare 4-6 6-3 6-3 6-1; C. M. Jones d. F. W. Matejka (AU) 7-5 6-3 8-6; **G. von Cramm** (2) (G) d. P. de Leon (UR) 6-1 6-0 6-3.

SECOND ROUND: Perry (1) d. Hines 6-1 7-5 6-3; Van Ryn d. Smith 6-3 6-0 6-2; Pallada d. Lesueur 3-6 6-3 7-5 6-2; Timmer d. C. N. O. Ritchie 7-5 5-7 6-2 6-3; **Menzel** (7) d. Borotra 5-7 6-4 6-2 2-6 11-9; Palmieri d. Malfroy 11-13 1-6 6-3 6-4 7-5; Gentien d. Hendrie 6-3 7-5 7-5; Maier d. Meredith 6-1 8-6 6-2; **Crawford** (3) d. Kirby 6-1 6-0 5-7 6-2; Hecht d. Landry 6-4 1-6 6-4 6-2; Hughes d. Plougmann 6-2 6-3 6-2; Kukuljevic d. Lund 6-3 6-4; **Wood** (6) d. Godsell 6-3 6-3 6-2; D. H. Williams d. Shaffi 2-6 6-2 4-6 6-1 7-5; MacPhail d. del Bono 6-1 6-2 6-0; Hopman d. Stedman 6-4 3-6 6-4 6-0; Quist d. Ellmer 6-3 7-5 3-6 6-3; Budge d. Bertram 6-4 6-2 6-3; Gabrowitz d. Lysaght 6-4 6-3

6-2, **Boussus** (8) d. Puncec 7-5 6-8 6-2 6-2; Andrews d. Butler 6-2 9-7 6-4; Olliff d. von Metaxa 6-3 6-2 5-7 6-2; Musgrove d. Billington 7-5 6-3 10-8; **Austin** (4) d. Haanes 6-2 6-0 6-0; Sharpe d. Tinkler 5-7 6-3 6-1 4-6 8-6; de Stefani d. Van den Eynde 4-6 4-6 6-0; Martin Legeay d. Lee 7-5 1-6 6-2 2-6 6-4; McGrath d. Tuckey 6-4 6-2 6-4; Mako d. Yamagishi 2-6 2-6 6-1 6-1 6-2; Caska d. Sherwood 1-6 6-2 6-2 8-6; **von Cramm** (2) d. C. M. Jones 6-2 6-3 6-1.

THIRD ROUND: Perry (1) d. Van Ryn 4-6 6-1 6-3 10-8; Pallada d. Timmer 6-3 6-4 6-4; **Menzel** (7) d. Palmieri 10-8 6-0 6-4; Maier d. Gentien 7-5 6-0 6-3; **Crawford** (3) d. Hecht 11-9 6-4 6-8 6-2; Hughes d. Kukuljevic 3-6 6-3 3-6 6-4 6-4; **Wood** (6) d. D. H. Williams 6-3 9-7 6-3; Hopman d. MacPhail 6-1 6-3 6-1; Budge d. Quist 8-6 6-3 6-3; **Boussus** (8) d. Gabrowitz 8-6 6-3 6-4; Andrews d. Olliff 11-9 6-8 6-3; **Austin** (4) d. Musgrove 6-3 6-0 3-6 6-0; Sharpe d. de Stefani 8-6 3-6 6-3 3-6 7-5; McGrath d. Martin Legeay 6-3 6-2 6-4; Mako d. Farquharson 2-6 6-4 2-6 6-4 6-1; **von Cramm** (2) d. Caska 6-1 8-6 6-4.

FOURTH ROUND	QUARTER-FINALS	SEMI-FINALS	FINAL	CHAMPION
Perry (1)	**Perry** (1)			
Pallada	6-2 6-2 0-6 6-2	**Perry** (1)		
Menzel (7)	**Menzel** (7)	9-7 6-1 6-1		
Maier	6-3 6-0 0-6 6-3		**Perry** (1)	
Crawford (3)	**Crawford** (3)		6-2 3-6 6-4 6-4	
Hughes	7-5 4-6 6-4 6-2	**Crawford** (3)		
Wood (6)	**Wood** (6)	6-4 6-3 6-8 5-7 6-1		**Perry** (1)
Hopman	6-1 6-4 3-6 6-3			6-2 6-4 6-4
Budge	Budge			
Boussus (8)	6-3 6-2 3-6 6-0	Budge		
Andrews	**Austin** (4)	3-6 10-8 6-4 7-5		
Austin (4)	4-6 6-1 6-4 6-0		**von Cramm** (2)	
Sharpe	McGrath		4-6 6-4 6-4 6-2	
McGrath	6-1 6-3 7-5	**von Cramm** (2)		
Mako	**von Cramm** (2)	6-4 6-2 4-6 6-1		
von Cramm (2)	6-0 6-1 3-6 6-1			

LADIES' SINGLES

FIRST ROUND: Mrs H. N. Wills Moody (4) (USA) d. A. Baumgarten (HU) 6-0 6-1; A. M. Yorke d. J. Morfey 6-2 6-3; E. de Alvarez (SP) d. M. A. Thomas 8-6 4-6 7-5; S. Noel d. P. M. Weeks 6-3 6-3; V. H. Montgomery d. B. W. List 6-4 8-6; J. Mowbray Green d. Mrs W. F. Freeman 6-2; J. E. Cunningham d. Mrs J. S. Kirk 7-5 6-2; E. Cepkova (CZ) d. M. E. Lumb 6-3 11-9 6-2; F. R. M. Hardwick 7-5 6-4; S. G. Chuter d. J. Dawbarn 6-1 6-2; M. Kraus (AU) d. A. A. Wright 6-2 4-6 6-2; F. K. Scott d. M. E. Rudd 4-6 6-1 6-1; Mrs J. B. Pittman d. G. M. Southwell 6-4 7-5; J. Ingram d. E. H. Harvey 6-0 6-4; Mrs P. D. Howard d. F. James 6-2 3-6 6-4; Mrs M. R. King d. Mrs G. Lucas 7-5 6-3; F. S. Ford d. G. K. Osborne 6-2 6-1; E. M. Dearman d. L. Row (IN) 6-2 6-1; J. Jedrzejowska (POL) d. B. Soames

7-5 6-4; L. Valerio (IT) d. S. Mavrogordato 6-2 6-2; Mrs E. Fearnley Whittingstall d. Mrs S. K. Edwards 6-2 6-2; Mrs H. C. Hopman (A) d. Mrs E. S. Law 6-2 6-1; Mrs D. C. Shepherd Barron d. M. Whitmarsh 6-4 4-6; **M. C. Scriven** (7) d. Mrs R. E. Haylock 6-2 7-5; E. Belliard (F) d. R. J. Smith 6-0 7-5; P. G. Brazier d. W. St John Maule 7-5 7-5 6-2; Mrs E. C. Peters d. B. I. E. Drew 6-1 7-5; E. N. S. Dickin d. B. M. Watson (B) 6-3 6-1; N. M. Lyle d. G. Harry 6-0 4-6 6-4; M. Slaney d. Mrs P. J. Whitley 6-1 6-4; M. R. Couquerque (NTH) d. Mrs F. M. Strawson 6-2 6-2; **H. Jacobs** (3) (USA) d. N. Adamson (B) 6-3 6-2.

SECOND ROUND: D. E. Round (1) d. A. E. L. McOstrich 8-6 6-3; M. G. Hargreaves d. P. L. F. Thomson 6-0 4-6 6-4; M. Heeley d. Mrs M. M. Moss 6-3 6-0; J. Saunders d. Mrs S. Andrus (USA) 6-1 3-6 6-3; **J. Hartigan** (8) (A) d. Mrs R. Henrotin (F) 10-8 6-8 6-3; Mrs J. de Meulemeester (B) d. E. Young (C) 6-1 6-4; Mrs W. G. Lowe (SA) d. G. Terwindt (NTH) 6-2 9-7; M. Burgess Smith d. L. Payot (SWZ) w.o.; **Wills Moody** (4) d. Yorke 6-3 6-1; Noel d. de Alvarez w.o.; Montgomery d. Mowbray Green 5-7 8-6 7-5; Cepkova d. Cunningham 6-3 6-8 8-6 6-4; **Mathieu** (5) d. Chuter 6-3 6-2; Ingram d. Pittman 6-1 6-3; Ford d. Dearman 8-11 9-6 1-5; Jedrzejowska d. Valerio 6-4 6-2; Fearnley Whittingstall d. Hopman 6-0 6-2; **Scriven** (7) d. Shepherd Barron 13-11 6-3; Belliard d. Brazier 9-7 8-6; Peters d. Dickin 6-4 5-7 6-4; Lyle d. Slaney 6-3 4-6 6-2; Jacobs (3) d. Couquerque 8-6 6-4; J. C. Ridley d. G. A. Clarke-Jervoise 6-4 6-4; M. Riddell d. C. Deacon (C) 6-1 6-4; A. Lizana (CH) d. Mrs A. Werring (NOR) 6-3 6-0; **K. Stammers** (6) d. J. Goldschmidt (F) 6-2 9-7; Mrs I. H. Wheatcroft d. P. Xydis (GR) 6-2 6-4; P. J. Owen d. J. de Chavarri (SP) w.o.; M. Horn d. S. Travers 6-2 6-2; **Mrs S. Sperling** (2) (G) d. B. G. Beazley 6-0 6-2.

THIRD ROUND: Round (1) d. Hargreaves 6-2 6-2; Saunders d. Heeley 6-2 6-4; **Hartigan** (8) d. de Meulemeester 4-6 6-1 10-8; Lowe d. Burgess Smith 6-4 6-3; **Wills Moody** (4) d. Noel 6-1 6-3; Cepkova d. Montgomery 7-5 6-1; **Mathieu** (5) d. Scott 3-4 6-4; King d. Ingram 9-7 6-4; Jedrzejowska d. Ford 6-0 9-7; Fearnley Whittingstall d. Scriven (7) 6-3 6-2; Peters d. Belliard 6-4 6-4; Jacobs (3) d. Lyle 7-5 6-1; Ridley d. Riddell 2-6 6-2 7-5; **Stammers** (6) d. Lizana 6-2 8-6; Wheatcroft d. Owen 6-2 7-5; Sperling (2) d. Horn 6-3 6-0.

FOURTH ROUND	QUARTER-FINALS	SEMI-FINALS	FINAL	CHAMPION
Round (1)	**Round** (1)			
Saunders	6-3 6-1			
Hartigan (8)	**Hartigan** (8)	**Hartigan** (8)		
Lowe	5-7 7-5 6-1	4-6 6-4 6-3		
Wills Moody (4)	**Wills Moody** (4)		**Wills Moody** (4)	
Cepkova	3-6 6-4 6-3	**Wills Moody** (4)	6-3 6-3	
Mathieu (5)	**Mathieu** (5)	6-3 6-0		
King	8-6 3-6 6-4			**Wills Moody** (4)
Jedrzejowska	Jedrzejowska			6-3 3-6 7-5
Fearnley Whittingstall	6-2 6-2			
Peters	**Jacobs** (3)	**Jacobs** (3)		
Jacobs (3)	6-2 6-1	6-1 9-7		
Ridley			**Jacobs** (3)	
Stammers (6)	**Stammers** (6)		6-3 6-0	
Wheatcroft	6-0 8-6	**Sperling** (2)		
Sperling (2)	**Sperling** (2)	7-5 7-5		
	6-1 6-1			

OTHER FINALS

GENTLEMEN'S DOUBLES: Final — J. H. Crawford (A)/A. K. Quist (A) d. W. L. Allison (USA)/J. Van Ryn (USA) 6-3 5-7 6-2 5-7 7-5.
LADIES' DOUBLES: Final — F. James/K. E. Stammers d. Mrs R. Mathieu (F)/Mrs S. Sperling (D) 6-1 6-4.

MIXED DOUBLES: Final — F. J. Perry/D. E. Round d. H. C./Mrs Hopman (A) 7-5 4-6 6-2.
GENTLEMEN'S SINGLES PLATE: Final — J. Yamagishi (J) d. J. Lesueur (F) 6-2 6-2.
LADIES' SINGLES PLATE: Final — L. Valerio (IT) d. A. E. L. McOstrich 6-2 1-6 6-0.

GENTLEMEN'S SINGLES

FIRST ROUND: **F. J. Perry** (1) d. G. D. Stratford (USA) 6-4 6-3 6-1; K. Chartikavanij (SIAM) d. J. R. Reddall 10-8 8-10 7-5 6-3; J. Van Ryn (USA) d. R. Morton 6-3 8-6 6-2; H. Timmer (NTH) d. D. H. Williams 6-2 6-0 6-2; C. E. Malfroy (NZ) d. F. Kukuljevic (YU) 8-6 7-5 6-4; J. F. G. Lysaght d. J. D. Anderson 6-2 6-3; J. Jamain (F) d. J. Borotra (F) w.o.; C. F. O. Lister d. R. K. Tinkler 2-6 3-6 6-3 6-2 6-2; **B. M. Grant** (8) (USA) d. H. Henkel (G) 5-7 3-6 7-5 6-4 6-2; M. D. Deloford d. A. T. England 6-4 6-4 6-1; E. R. Avory d. H. Billington 5-7 1-6 6-4 6-1 6-3; B. Maneff (SWZ) d. J. H. Ho (CHI) 7-5 9-7 1-6 6-1; P. Landry (F) d. G. E. Godsell 5-7 6-4 ret'd; V. B. McGrath (A) d. H. B. Purcell (IRE) 8-6 6-0 9-7; L. de Borman (B) d. W. W. Robertson (USA) 2-6 2-6 6-3 6-4 6-4; L. del Castillo (ARG) d. W. C. Choy (CHI) 6-0 1-6 6-1 6-4; **A. K. Quist** (3) (A) d. N. Taylor 6-2 6-0 6-4; M. Ellmer (SWZ) d. G. L. Rogers (IRE) 6-3 3-6 6-1; E. Itoh (J) d. T. Hughan (NTH) 6-1 6-2 6-3; J. Haanes (NOR) d. A. Baworowski (AU) 6-3 3-6 4-6 6-2 6-3; Y. Petra (F) d. D. MacPhail 6-4 6-2 6-4; M. Bhandari (IN) d. J. Pallada (YU) w.o.; N. Sharpe d. H. Surface (USA) 6-4 6-3 6-2; D. W. Butler d. L. Watt (C) 7-5 6-2 6-3; **D. Budge** (5) (USA) d. H. A. Hare 6-1 6-1 6-4; I. G. Collins d. S. Stewart 6-4 6-3 6-2; J. Brugnon (F) d. R. J. Ritchie 5-7 4-6 8-6 6-0 6-0; J. Lesueur (F) d. I. H. Wheatcroft 6-3 10-8 4-6 6-1; G. P. Hughes d. S. K. Kho (CHI) 9-11 6-4 3-6 6-3 8-6; H. G. N. Cooper d. G. Nicolaides (GR) 7-5 6-3 7-5; J. Caska (CZ) d. H. S. Burrows 8-6 6-2 1-6 6-1; H. A. Coldham d. L. W. J. Newman 4-6 8-6 7-5 6-0; E. D. Andrews (NZ) d. C. F. Aeschliman (SWZ) 6-1 6-1

6-2; P. Feret (F) d. J. S. Olliff 6-4 8-6 8-6; A. Martin Legeay (F) d. H. F. David 7-5 2-6 6-4 7-5; J. Siba (CZ) d. G. Lum (CHI) 6-2 6-2 6-2; B. Destremau (F) d. J. S. Comery 3-6 4-6 6-1 6-0 6-3; C. R. D. Tuckey d. G. Metaxa (AU) 8-10 6-2 6-3 6-4; C. Sproule (A) d. C. N. O. Ritchie 6-4 6-4 4-6 6-3; **H. W. Austin** (7) d. P. D. B. Spence 5-7 6-0 6-3 6-1; K. Lund (G) d. P. V. V. Sherwood 2-6 6-3 6-3 6-4; C. M. Jones d. H. Plougmann (D) 6-4 6-4 6-2; P. Pelizza (F) d. L. Stalios (GR) 6-2 6-2 6-2; W. H. S. Michelmore (IN) d. V. Landau (M) 6-4 2-6 6-4 6-3; E. C. Peters d. J. H. Knottenbelt (NTH) 6-4 6-3 6-2; J. Van den Eynde (B) d. J. S. Harrison 6-8 6-0 6-3 6-3; D. N. Jones (USA) d. E. J. David 6-3 6-1 5-7 6-2; **W. L. Allison** (4) (USA) d. R. E. Mulliken 6-4 6-3; H. C. Fisher (SWZ) d. E. Gabrowitz (HU) 6-4 6-7 7-5; A. C. Stedman (NZ) d. F. H. D. Wilde 4-6 6-2 4-6 8-6; H. van Swol (NTH) d. A. M. Cunninggim (USA) 6-1 6-2 6-8 3-6 6-3; H. G. N. Lee d. W. L. Breese (USA) 6-4 6-1 6-1; R. M. Turnbull d. A. Gentien (F) w.o.; K. C. Gandar Dower d. T. G. McVeagh (IRE) 6-1 4-6 6-3 6-1; C. E. Hare d. J. Hebda (POL) 6-4 6-3 6-2; **J. H. Crawford** (6) (A) d. D. Prenn (G) 6-4 6-2 6-4; E. G. Maier (SP) d. A. Zappa (ARG) 6-1 6-3 6-4; H. E. Weatherall d. C. H. Kingsley 2-6 6-2 6-3 6-0; R. A. Shayes d. E. J. Filby 6-0 3-6 6-2 5-7 6-4; G. R. B. Meredith d. J. Puncec (YU) w.o.; G. Mako (USA) d. L. Shaffi 6-3 6-0 6-4; C. Boussus (F) d. F. Jenssen (NOR) 6-4 6-3 6-2; L. Hecht (CZ) d. R. Murray (C) 6-4 6-3 6-4 6-2; **G. von Cramm** (2) (G) d. G. L. France 6-2 6-0 6-1.

SECOND ROUND: Perry (1) d. Chartikavanij 6-3 6-2 6-2; Van Ryn d. Timmer 6-4 8-6 6-3; Malfroy d. Lysaght 6-3 8-6 9-11 6-2; Jamain d. Lister 7-5 6-2 6-3; Grant (8) d. Deloford 4-6 6-2 6-2 6-1; Avory d. Maneff 4-6 6-4 6-4 8-6; McGrath d. Landry 5-7 6-4 6-3 6-1; del Castillo d. de Borman 6-4 6-3 6-4; **Quist** (3) d. Ellmer 6-4 6-4 6-4; Itoh d. Haanes 6-2 6-2 6-2; Petra d. Bhandari 6-3 6-3 6-2; Butler d. Sharpe 7-5 3-6 4-6 6-2 10-8; **Budge** (5) d. Collins 6-2 6-2 6-1; Lesueur d. Brugnon 5-7 6-3 4-6 7-5 1-0 ret'd; Cooper d. Hughes 3-6 7-5 2-6 ret'd; Caska d. Coldham 6-2 6-1

6-1; Feret d. Andrews 3-6 6-3 6-4 ret'd; Martin Legeay d. Siba 3-6 6-4 6-4 6-1; Tuckey d. Destremau 7-5 3-6 7-5 6-2; **Austin** (7) d. Sproule 6-3 6-4 6-1; C. M. Jones d. Lund 6-3 4-6 6-3 6-2; Pelizza d. Michelmore 6-0 6-1 6-0; Van den Eynde d. Peters 3-6 6-2 7-5 6-3; **Allison** (4) d. D. N. Jones 14-12 6-3 6-4; Stedman d. Fisher 6-1 6-1 6-2; Lee d. van Swol 6-2 6-3 6-4; Gandar Dower d. Turnbull 8-6 6-4 6-0; **Crawford** (6) d. C. E. Hare 6-3 6-2 8-6; Maier d. Weatherall 6-4 6-3 6-1; Meredith d. Shayes 6-4 9-7 7-5; Boussus d. Mako w.o.; **von Cramm** (2) d. Hecht 6-4 6-3 6-4.

THIRD ROUND: Perry (1) d. Van Ryn 6-3 6-2 6-0; Malfroy d. Jamain 6-0 6-4 7-5; **Grant** (8) d. Avory 6-4 6-2 6-4; McGrath d. del Castillo 6-4 2-6 6-3 12-10; **Quist** (3) d. Itoh 6-0 6-0 6-3; Butler d. Petra 3-6 8-6 6-0 8-6; **Budge** (5) d. Lesueur 6-1 6-1 6-1; Caska d. Cooper 6-1 6-1 2-6 6-3; Martin Legeay d. Feret 6-1 8-6 8-6; **Austin** (7) d. Tuckey 6-2

6-1 6-3; C. M. Jones d. Pelizza 7-5 7-5 6-2; **Allison** (4) d. Van den Eynde 8-6 7-5 7-5; Lee d. Stedman 6-3 6-4 6-4; **Crawford** (6) d. Gandar Dower 6-1 6-2 6-3; Maier d. Meredith 6-1 6-2 6-2; **von Cramm** (2) d. Boussus 6-4 6-3 6-2.

FOURTH ROUND	QUARTER-FINALS	SEMI-FINALS	FINAL	CHAMPION
Perry (1)	**Perry** (1)			
Malfroy	6-2 6-2 6-4	**Perry** (1)		
Grant (8)	**Grant** (8)	6-4 6-3 6-1		
McGrath	6-3 6-4 6-0		**Perry** (1)	
Quist (3)	**Quist** (3)		5-7 6-4 6-3 6-4	
Butler	6-3 7-5 9-7	**Budge** (5)		
Budge (5)	**Budge** (5)	6-2 6-4 6-4		
Caska	6-3 6-0 6-4			**Perry** (1)
Martin Legeay	**Austin** (7)			6-1 6-1 6-0
Austin (7)	6-4 6-1 6-2	**Austin** (7)		
C. M. Jones	**Allison** (4)	6-1 6-4 7-5		
Allison (4)	10-8 6-4 1-6 7-5		**von Cramm** (2)	
Lee	**Crawford** (6)		8-6 6-3 2-6 6-3	
Crawford (6)	7-5 6-4 9-7	**von Cramm** (2)		
Maier	**von Cramm** (2)	6-1 7-5 6-4		
von Cramm (2)	10-8 6-2 2-6 6-2			

LADIES' SINGLES

FIRST ROUND: **K. E. Stammers** (4) d. V. K. King 6-1 6-2; A. A. Wright d. R. J. M. Smith 6-4 6-2; Mrs J. de Meulemeester (B) d. E. Belliard (F) 6-1 8-10 8-6; A. M. Yorke d. Mrs J. Van Ryn (USA) 6-3 6-4; J. Saunders d. M. C. Scriven 6-1 6-2; J. E. Cunningham d. E. Ford 3-6 6-4 6-4; F. James d. Mrs E. S. Law 6-4 6-3; P. M. Weekes d. M. Trouncer 6-2 2-6 6-3; **J. Jedrzejowska** (7) (POL) d. M. Riddell 6-4 6-4; J. Mowbray Green d. P. L. F. Thomson 6-4 6-1; A. E. L. Westrich d. F. S. Ford 3-6 6-4 7-5; Mrs M. R. King d. L. Green 6-4 1-5; S. Noel d. Mrs R. Allister (SA) 6-3 6-1; M. Slaney d. T. Kingsbury 6-3 6-1; G. M. Southwell d. G. Terwindt (NTH) 4-6 6-1 6-4; M. E. Lumb d. P. J. Owen 7-5 8-6; M. G. Hargreaves d. Mrs A. Werring (NOR) w.o.; Mrs G. Lucas d. N. B. Brown 1-6 6-0 6-3; R. M. Hardwick d.

D. A. Huntbach 6-1 6-2; J. Ingram d. N. Stoker (IRE) 6-3 7-5; Mrs K. Bowden d. Mrs H. G. Broadbridge 6-2 6-3; Mrs D. B. Andrus (USA) d. G. Harry 6-4 8-6; E. M. Dearman d. S. G. Chuter 6-2 6-4; **Mrs R. Mathieu** (6) (F) d. E. H. Harvey 6-0 6-1; Mrs F. M. Strawson d. M. E. Rudd 4-6 6-2 6-2; Mrs J. B. Pittman d. Mrs J. N. C. Couper 6-2 6-3; A. G. Curtis d. S. Paterson 2-6 6-2; Mrs E. C. Peters d. Mrs I. H. Wheatcroft 6-3 6-3; M. R. Couquerque (NTH) d. B. G. Beazley 6-0 6-4; J. Morfey d. Mrs D. J. P. O'Meara 6-8 6-3 6-2; V. E. Scott d. Mrs M. M. Moss 6-4 6-3; M. Horn (G) d. **Mrs M. Fabyan** (3) (USA) 6-3 7-5.

SECOND ROUND: **H. Jacobs** (2) d. Mrs M. Cable 6-1 6-0; J. Goldschmidt (F) d. N. M. Lyle 6-3 6-2; Mrs E. W. A. Luxton d. P. Xydis (GR) 6-0 8-6; Countess de la Valdène (F) d. Mrs J. S. Kirk 6-3 6-2; **A. Lizana** (8) (CH) d. M. Baumgarten (HU) d. F. Wallis (IRE) d. M. Wittenstrom (SW) 6-4 6-2; M. Heeley d. Mrs R. E. Haylock 6-3 6-4; E. N. S. Dickin d. S. Mavrogordato 6-1 6-1; **Stammers** (4) d. Wright 6-3 6-0; de Meulemeester d. Yorke 6-4 6-1; Saunders d. Jarvis 4-6 6-4 6-1; James d. Weekes 7-9 6-3 6-2; **Jedrzejowska** (7) d. Mowbray Green 6-2 6-2; King d. McOstrich 6-0 4-6 6-3; Noel d. Slaney 6-2 6-2; Lumb d. Southwell 6-3 6-3; Lucas d. Hargreaves 6-3 6-2; Hardwick

d. Ingram 6-1 7-5; Andrus d. Bowden 6-4 7-5; **Mathieu** (6) d. Dearman 6-3 6-2; Pittman d. Strawson 6-3 7-5; Curtis d. Peters 6-2 6-3; Couquerque d. Morfey 6-4 6-1; Horn d. Scott 8-6 6-2; Mrs S. Henrotin (F) d. G. K. Osborne 6-4 6-2; N. Adamson (B) d. Mrs W. D. List 6-3 6-3; C. Babcock (USA) d. Mrs R. V. Fontes 6-2 6-3; **Mrs S. Sperling** (5) (D) d. Page P. O'Connell 7-5 6-2; M. Whitmarsh d. Mrs D. Trentham 2-6 6-1 6-2; M. B. Hobson d. A. Page (USA) 6-0 7-5; R. Kraus (AU) d. P. N. Morison 7-5 7-5; **D. E. Round** (1) d. B. Nuthall 9-7 6-3.

THIRD ROUND: Jacobs (2) d. Goldschmidt 6-1 6-0; de la Valdène d. Luxton 6-2 6-1; **Lizana** (8) d. Wallis w.o.; Heeley d. Dickin 6-3 2-2 ret'd; **Stammers** (4) d. Meulemeester 6-4 6-0; James d. Saunders 3-6 6-4 6-3; **Jedrzejowska** (7) d. King 6-3 6-2; Noel d. Lumb w.o.; Hardwick d. Lucas 8-6 6-3; **Mathieu** (6) d. Andrus 6-4 4-6

6-3; Curtis d. Pittman 6-3 7-5; Horn d. Couquerque 6-3 6-0; Adamson d. Henrotin 6-4 4-6 9-7; **Sperling** (5) d. Babcock 7-5 6-1; Whitmarsh d. Hobson 6-3 7-5; **Round** (1) d. Kraus 6-1 6-3.

FOURTH ROUND	QUARTER-FINALS	SEMI-FINALS	FINAL	CHAMPION
Jacobs (2)	**Jacobs** (2)			
de la Valdène	6-4 6-3	**Jacobs** (2)		
Lizana (8)	**Lizana** (8)	6-2 1-6 6-4		
Heeley	6-3 6-3		**Jacobs** (2)	
Stammers (4)	**Stammers** (4)		6-4 6-2	
James	7-5 6-2	**Jedrzejowska** (7)		
Jedrzejowska (7)	**Jedrzejowska** (7)	6-2 6-3		
Noel	6-1 4-6 6-2			**Jacobs** (2)
Hardwick	**Mathieu** (6)			6-2 4-6 7-5
Mathieu (6)	6-2 4-6 7-5	**Mathieu** (6)		
Curtis	Horn	7-5 6-3		
Horn	6-3 6-3		**Sperling** (5)	
Adamson	**Sperling** (5)		6-3 6-2	
Sperling (5)	6-1 6-0	**Sperling** (5)		
Whitmarsh	**Round** (1)	6-3 8-6		
Round (1)	6-4 6-2			

OTHER FINALS

GENTLEMEN'S DOUBLES: Final — G. P. Hughes/C. R. D. Tuckey d. C. E. Hare/F. H. D. Wilde 6-4 3-6 7-9 6-1 6-4.
LADIES' DOUBLES: Final — F. James/K. E. Stammers d. Mrs M. Fabyan (USA)/H. Jacobs (USA) 6-2 6-1.
MIXED DOUBLES: Final — F. J. Perry/D. E. Round d. J. D. Budge (USA)/Mrs M. Fabyan (USA) 7-9 7-5 6-4.

GENTLEMEN'S SINGLES PLATE: Final — D. N. Jones (USA) d. I. G. Collins 6-0 6-2.
LADIES' SINGLES PLATE: Final — F. S. Ford d. M. Riddell 6-4 6-4.

GENTLEMEN'S SINGLES

1937

FIRST ROUND: G. von Cramm (2) (G) d. J. F. G. Lysaght 3-6 6-1 6-2 6-0; C. R. D. Tuckey d. R. V. Fontes 6-2 6-1 6-1; H. F. David d. T. Hughan (NTH) 6-4 6-4 6-2; J. Yamagishi (J) d. E. P. K. Hansom 6-0 6-0 6-0; F. H. D. Wilde d. Y. Petra (F) 6-3 5-7 6-4 6-0 7-5; S. K. Kho (CHI) d. R. E. Mulliken 6-3 6-2 6-3; G. Mako (USA) d. J. Jamain (F) 6-4 5-7 6-3 6-3; H. C. Fisher (SWZ) d. L. de Borman (B) 8-6 6-4 6-1; J. H. Crawford (A) d. **R. Menzel** (6) (CZ) 6-4 7-9 4-6 6-3 6-4; E. D. Andrews (NZ) d. F. Jenssen (NOR) 6-1 6-2 6-1; H. Surface (USA) d. S. Martenson (SW) 6-0 6-2 6-1; F. Kukuljevic (YU) d. H. A. Hare 6-2 6-2 6-2; L. Shaffi d. L. B. Hall (USA) 6-3 6-4 12-10; D. M. Bull d. A. T. England 10-8 6-3 6-3; J. Van den Eynde (B) d. H. B. Purcell (IRE) 4-6 6-3 6-4 6-2; C. J. Eedes (SA) d. G. de Stefani (IT) 6-1 2-6 7-5 6-4; **H. W. Austin** (4) d. G. L. Rogers (IRE) 3-6 8-6 6-1 6-2; W. Sabin (USA) d. R. J. Ritchie 6-4 6-3 6-4; J. Bromwich (A) d. J. S. Comery 6-3 10-8 6-1; V. G. Kirby (SA) d. G. Nicolaides (GR) 6-0 11-9 7-5; G. L. France d. J. R. Fawcus 6-4 6-1 6-4; H. G. N. Lee d. M. E. Lucking 7-5 6-3 6-3; H. A. Coldham d. A. H. F. C. Horne 6-8 6-4 6-3 6-3; A. Lacroix (B) d. J. R. Reddall 6-2 7-5 6-3; **B. M. Grant** (5) (USA) d. J. M. Hunt 3-6 4-7 7-5; R. Morton d. H. Rothwell 6-3 6-2 6-4; N. Taylor d. D. J. Cook 6-2 7-5 6-2; E. R. Avory d. J. A. S. Collins 3-6 6-4 2-7-5; M. Bernard (F) d. R. M. Turnbull 6-4 6-1 6-2; D. MacPhail d. V. M. Landau (M) 6-4 6-1 6-1; A. C. Stedman (NZ) d. A. Brown 6-1 6-3 6-3; N. Sharpe d. P. V. V. Sherwood 6-8 6-3 6-3 7-5; H. G. N. Cooper d. M. A. Young 6-4 6-3 6-3; D. Prenn (G) d. W. Robertson (USA) 7-5 6-1

6-2; P. Geelhand (B) d. H. E. Weatherall 6-4 6-1 6-0; G. E. Godsell d. R. E. Boone (A) 6-3 6-2 6-2; M. D. Deloford d. G. L. Tuckett 11-13 6-0 6-3 4-6 7-5; H. D. Mackinnon d. J. D. Anderson 12-10 1-6 6-0 6-2; J. Brugnon (F) d. L. E. King (A) 7-5 6-1 6-4; **F. Parker** (8) (USA) d. J. H. Ho (CHI) 6-1 6-1 6-3; C. E. Hare d. G. von Metaxa (AU) 6-0 4-6 3-6 6-0 6-3; H. Billington d. I. H. Wheatcroft 6-0 6-3 1-6 6-3; C. Sproule (A) d. J. B. Sturgeon 2-6 6-3 6-4 6-2; E. E. Fannin (SA) d. S. C. Clark 2-6 6-1 6-4 6-2; F. Puncec (YU) d. B. Maneff (SWZ) 6-3 6-3 6-2; K. Schroeder (SW) d. E. A. Barlow 2-6 6-0 6-3; R. K. Tinkler d. G. M. T. Zarifi (F) 6-3 2-6 6-4 7-5; **H. Henkel** (3) (G) d. L. W. J. Newman 6-1 6-0 6-3; W. C. Choy (CHI) d. H. J. Whitney 7-5 6-4 6-0; R. A. Shayes d. T. G. McVeagh (IRE) 1-6 6-3 6-1 6-4; F. Quintavalle (IT) d. J. S. Harrison 6-4 6-4 11-9; F. Nakano (J) d. C. R. Harris (USA) 3-6 6-2 6-2 2-6 6-4; E. J. David d. I. G. Collins 7-5 6-3 4-6 4-6 10-8; J. Pallada (YU) d. J. S. Olliff 2-6 2-6 6-4 6-0 6-2; D. C. Coombe (NZ) d. P. H. Partridge 6-1 6-2 10-8; **V. B. McGrath** (7) (A) d. M. Ellmer (SWZ) 0-6 6-4 6-4 9-7; L. Hecht (CZ) d. E. J. Filby 6-4 6-1 7-5; C. F. O. Lister d. H. Plougmann (D) 6-2 6-2 4-6 6-3; D. W. Butler d. E. C. Peters 6-3 5-7 6-2 6-2; C. M. Jones d. H. S. Burrows 6-4 6-4; C. Boussus (F) d. C. N. O. Ritchie 6-1 6-2 5-7 6-3; H. van Swol (NTH) d. G. R. B. Meredith 6-4 6-2 6-2; G. P. Hughes d. C. H. E. Betts 6-0 6-0 8-6; **D. Budge** (1) (USA) d. N. G. Farquharson (SA) 6-3 6-2 6-1.

SECOND ROUND: von Cramm (2) d. Tuckey 6-2 6-0 6-4; Yamagishi d. H. F. David 6-1 6-4 6-3; Kho d. Wilde 6-4 4-6 6-2 3-6 6-3; Mako d. H. C. Fisher 6-1 6-2 6-1; Crawford d. Andrews 6-4 8-6 6-1; Kukuljevic d. Surface 5-7 6-3 2-6 6-3 9-7; Shaffi d. Bull 6-4 6-4 8-10 6-3; Van den Eynde d. Eedes 7-5 6-4; **Austin** (4) d. Sabin 6-2 6-3 6-0; Bromwich d. Kirby 7-5 2-6 6-4 6-3; Lee d. France 6-3 6-2 6-3; Lacroix d. Coldham 6-2 7-5 6-4; **Grant** (5) d. Morton 6-2 3-6 6-3 6-0; Avory d. Taylor 6-3 4-6 6-4 5-7 7-5; Bernard d. MacPhail 3-6 6-2 0-6 6-1 6-4; Stedman d. Sharpe 6-4 6-4 ret'd; Prenn d. Cooper 6-1 2-6 4-2; Godsell d. Geelhand 5-7 6-3 6-4 6-2; Deloford d. Mackinnon 6-2 3-6 6-2 5-7 6-3; **Parker** (8) d.

Brugnon 6-0 6-3 6-1; C. E. Hare d. Billington 2-6 6-2 7-5 6-4; Fannin d. Sproule 7-5 3-6 1-6 8-6 6-0; Puncec d. Schroeder 10-8 6-2 6-3; **Henkel** (3) d. Tinkler 2-6 7-5 3-6 6-0 6-3; Shayes d. Choy 3-1 6-5 7-5 7-5 6-1; Nakano d. Quintavalle 6-3 4-3 4-6 6-4; Pallada d. E. J. David 6-1 6-1 7-5; **McGrath** (7) d. Coombe 6-3 6-3 5-7 6-2; Hecht d. Lister 6-1 6-0 9-7; C. M. Jones d. Butler 3-6 4-6 6-3 6-3; Boussus d. van Swol 6-2 6-1 6-2; **Budge** (1) d. Hughes 6-2 6-2 6-2.

THIRD ROUND: von Cramm (2) d. Yamagishi 6-4 6-4 3-6 6-4; Mako d. Kho 3-6 6-1 6-2 6-4; Crawford d. Kukuljevic 6-3 6-2 10-8; Shaffi d. Van den Eynde 2-6 6-2 7-5 6-4; **Austin** (4) d. Bromwich 6-2 4-6 6-0 8-6; Lacroix d. Lee 4-6 6-4 6-2 6-4; **Grant** (5) d. Avory 6-3 6-4 2-6 6-2; Stedman d. Bernard 6-4 6-2 6-3; Prenn d. Godsell 6-4 6-1 6-2; **Parker** (8)

d. Deloford 6-0 6-1 5-7 8-6; C. E. Hare d. Fannin 6-0 6-1 10-8; **Henkel** (3) d. Puncec 6-2 6-2 6-1; Shayes d. Nakano 6-8 10-8 6-3 6-1; **McGrath** (7) d. Pallada 4-6 6-3 7-5 6-2; Hecht d. C. M. Jones 8-6 6-4 6-3; **Budge** (1) d. Boussus 6-1 6-4 6-2.

FOURTH ROUND	QUARTER-FINALS	SEMI-FINALS	FINAL	CHAMPION
von Cramm (2)	**von Cramm** (2)	**von Cramm** (2)		
Mako	6-0 6-2 6-3	6-3 8-6 3-6 2-6 6-2		
Crawford	Crawford			
Shaffi	6-4 6-3 8-6		**von Cramm** (2)	
Austin (4)	**Austin** (4)	**Austin** (4)	8-6 6-3 12-14 6-1	
Lacroix	6-2 6-1 6-0	6-1 7-5 6-4		
Grant (5)	**Grant** (5)			
Stedman	4-6 6-8 6-1 6-4 6-3			**Budge** (1)
Prenn	**Parker** (8)			6-3 6-4 6-2
Parker (8)	6-4 7-5 6-2	**Parker** (8)		
C. E. Hare	**Henkel** (3)	6-3 7-5 4-6 4-6 6-2		
Henkel (3)	6-4 3-6 3-6 6-2 6-3			
Shayes	**McGrath** (7)		**Budge** (1)	
McGrath (7)	6-2 6-1 6-3	**Budge** (1)	2-6 6-4 6-4 6-1	
Hecht	**Budge** (1)	6-3 6-1 6-4		
Budge (1)	6-4 6-2 6-2			

LADIES' SINGLES

FIRST ROUND: Mrs R. E. Haylock d. S. G. Chuter 6-8 6-2 6-3; **J. Jedrzejowska** (4) (POL) d. S. Noel 6-2 6-0; B. G. Beazley d. Mrs J. N. C. Couper 6-3 7-5; G. M. Southwell d. M. Whitmarsh 3-6 4-4; A. E. P. K. Hansom 6-0 6-0 6-0; D. Trentham d. A. Samuelson (SW) 4-6 10-8 6-3; F. S. Ford d. Mrs E. O. Moss 6-1 6-1; J. Goss d. W. M. C. Bower 7-5 6-2; A. M. Yorke d. T. R. Jarvis 6-3 6-3; Mrs D. B. Andrus (USA) d. E. N. S. Dickin 6-4 6-2; Mrs N. M. Lyle 6-2 6-2; Mrs H. S. Uber d. M. G. Norman 4-6 6-4 6-4; K. Winthrop (USA) d. M. B. Hobson 7-5 6-4; P. O'Connell d. G. C. Hoahing 8-6 6-4; Mrs E. C. Peters d. J. Ingram 6-1 6-1; Mrs F. M. Strawson d. Mrs K. J. Underwood 7-5 6-4; M. C. Scriven d. J. Harman (IRE) 6-0 6-2; V. E. Scott d. S. Paterson 6-2 6-2; Mrs J. Selwyn James d. Mrs O. Haycraft 6-2

6-4; Mrs J. B. Pittman d. V. K. King 6-3 6-3; Mrs M. R. King d. B. Batt 6-0 6-1; Mrs K. Bowden d. Lady D. Pleydell Bouverie 6-4 6-3; Mrs R. G. MacInnes d. J. Marquis 6-3 2-6 6-4; E. M. Dearman d. P. C. Grover 6-2 6-2; K. Bowden (YU) d. A. P. Cardinall 6-3 6-3; **Mrs R. Mathieu** (6) (F) d. Mrs C. Boegner (F) 6-1 6-0; P. N. Morison d. M. Slaney 6-4 6-3; Mrs E. S. Law d. Mrs M. B. Lewis 6-3 6-3; P. L. F. Thomson d. K. Keith-Steele 6-2 7-5; B. Nuthall d. M. Trouncer 6-8 6-0 6-2; J. Saunders d. M. Stewart 6-1 6-4; M. Riddell d. Mrs E. H. Fenwick 6-2 6-3; M. E. Lumb d. N. B. Brown 6-4 4-6 6-3; **A. Lizana** (3) (CH) d. G. K. Osborne 6-2 6-2.

SECOND ROUND: **Mrs S. Sperling** (2) (D) d. M. Baumgarten (HU) 6-2 6-0; M. Horn (G) d. C. M. Burrows 6-1 7-9 7-5; D. A. Huntbach d. Mrs A. T. P. Luxton 3-6 7-5 6-3; A. G. Curtis d. V. G. Valentine-Brown 6-3 6-3; **A. Marble** (5) (USA) d. R. M. Hardwick 9-11 6-4 6-3; W. M. Lincoln d. R. Kraus (AU) 6-4 6-3; M. R. Couquerque (NTH) d. Mrs S. Henrotin (F) 6-1 6-1; Haylock d. E. A. Middleton 6-2 6-1; **Jedrzejowska** (4) d. Beazley 6-1 6-2; Southwell d. Trentham 6-2 6-2; Ford d. Goss 6-4 6-4; Andrus d. Yorke 6-3 6-4; **Stammers** (8) d. Uber 9-7 6-2; Winthrop d. O'Connell 4-6 8-6 6-1; Peters d. Strawson 6-4 4-6 6-2; Scriven d. Scott 6-2 6-2; Pittman d. Selwyn James 7-5 6-4

King d. Bowden 6-0 6-0; Dearman d. MacInnes 6-3 7-5; **Mathieu** (6) d. Kovac 6-2 6-3; Law d. Morison 6-2 6-1; Nuthall d. Thomson 6-1 6-2; Saunders d. Riddell 8-6 6-4; **Lizana** (3) d. Lumb 1-6 6-1 6-2; A. E. L. McOstrich d. Mrs Myerscough (IRE) 6-1 6-2; Countess de la Valdène (F) d. F. James 6-4 6-0; G. Terwindt (NTH) d. Mrs E. Hollis (D) 2-6 7-5 6-4; **D. E. Round** (7) d. Mrs I. H. Wheatcroft 6-1 6-1; R. J. M. Smith d. R. Jarvis 9-7 6-2; A. A. Wright d. P. Xydis (GR) 7-5 6-1; M. Heeley d. Mrs J. S. Kirk 6-2 6-1; **H. Jacobs** (1) (USA) d. E. H. Harvey 6-2 6-1.

THIRD ROUND: Sperling (2) d. Horn 6-2 6-0; Curtis d. Huntbach 8-6 8-6; **Marble** (5) d. Lincoln 6-1 6-0; Couquerque d. Haylock 6-4 6-4; **Jedrzejowska** (4) d. Southwell 6-1 6-1; Andrus d. Ford 6-4 6-4; **Stammers** (8) d. Winthrop 6-3 6-3; Scriven d. Peters 6-2 6-1; King d. Pittman 6-1 6-4; **Mathieu** (6) d. Dearman 6-0 6-3; Nuthall d.

Law 2-6 6-4 6-2; **Lizana** (3) d. Saunders 6-4 6-1; de la Valdène d. McOstrich 6-4 6-2; **Round** (7) d. Terwindt 6-2 6-0; Wright d. Smith 6-4 3-6 7-5; **Jacobs** (1) d. Heeley 6-3 6-1.

FOURTH ROUND	QUARTER-FINALS	SEMI-FINALS	FINAL	CHAMPION
Sperling (2)	**Sperling** (2)			
Curtis	6-4 6-4	**Marble** (5)		
Marble (5)	**Marble** (5)	7-5 2-6 6-3		
Couquerque	6-0 6-2		**Jedrzejowska** (4)	
Jedrzejowska (4)	**Jedrzejowska** (4)		8-6 6-2	
Andrus	6-0 6-2	**Jedrzejowska** (4)		
Stammers (8)	Scriven	6-1 6-2		
Scriven	7-5 6-3			**Round** (7)
King	**Mathieu** (6)			6-2 2-6 7-5
Mathieu (6)	1-6 6-2 6-0	**Mathieu** (6)		
Nuthall	**Lizana** (3)	6-3 6-3		
Lizana (3)	6-3 6-2		**Round** (7)	
de la Valdène	**Round** (7)		6-4 6-0	
Round (7)	6-1 6-0	**Round** (7)		
Wright	**Jacobs** (1)	6-4 6-2		
Jacobs (1)	6-0 6-3			

OTHER FINALS

GENTLEMEN'S DOUBLES: Final — J. D. Budge (USA)/G. Mako (USA) d. G. P. Hughes/C. R. D. Tuckey 6-0 6-4 6-8 6-1.

LADIES' DOUBLES: Final — Mrs R. Mathieu (F)/A. M. Yorke d. Mrs M. R. King/Mrs J. B. Pittman 6-3 6-3.

MIXED DOUBLES: Final — J. D. Budge (USA)/A. Marble (USA) d. Y. Petra (F)/Mrs R. Mathieu (F) 6-4 6-1.

GENTLEMEN'S SINGLES PLATE: Final — W. Sabin (USA) d. N. G. Farquharson (SA) 2-6 6-0 6-3.

LADIES' SINGLES PLATE: Final — F. James d. M. E. Lumb 6-0 7-5.

GENTLEMEN'S SINGLES

FIRST ROUND: H. W. Austin (2) d. E. J. Filby 4-6 6-1 3-6 6-4 6-3; J. Darkins d. H. S. Burrows 6-3 7-5 6-3; R. F. Bessemer Clark d. L. E. J. King (A) 2-6 6-1 1-6 6-4 6-2; J. S. Comery d. J. Mehta (IN) 6-2 6-2 6-4; G. Mako (USA) d. D. J. Cook 6-1 6-2 6-0; C. E. Malfroy (NZ) d. J. A. Moore 6-1 6-2 6-2; T. B. Henderson Brooks d. D. R. Rutnam (IN) 6-1 6-2 7-5; E. Koch (G) d. A. del Bono (IT) 6-2 2-6 6-3 6-1; **D. Mitic** (6) (YU) d. M. G. Weston (A) 3-6 6-4 6-1 6-4; A. D. Russell (ARG) d. J. Drobny (CZ) 10-8 6-4 7-9 6-3; A. Procopio (BR) d. L. de Borman (B) 6-3 7-5 6-0; S. Harreguy (U) d. R. F. Egan (IRE) 11-9 6-4 9-7; M. Ellmer (SWZ) d. Y. Kuramitu (J) 6-4 7-5 6-4; R. Morton d. K. Lavarack 6-1 6-2 6-2; J. B. Sturgeon d. H. G. N. Cooper 6-1 6-1 6-3; S. L. R. Sawhney (IN) d. M. E. Lucking 6-3 7-5 6-3; **H. Henkel** (4) (G) d. D. M. Bull 6-2 6-0 6-2; M. D. Deloford d. D. Prenn 4-6 4-6 7-5 6-1 6-4; C. Boussus (F) d. L. Shaffi 6-3 6-1 7-5; G. R. B. Meredith d. O. Szigeti (HU) 3-6 6-1 6-2 2-6 6-3; B. Maneff (SWZ) d. W. Robertson (USA) 6-3 6-4 6-2; W. T. Anderson d. C. H. E. Betts 6-4 8-6 9-7; E. C. Peters d. R. E. Mulliken 3-6 6-4 3-1 6-6 4-1; R. Singh (IN) d. J. H. Ho (CHI) 6-1 6-3 2-6 7-5; **L. Hecht** (7) (CZ) d. F. D. Leyland 6-4 6-3 6-4; J. Van den Eynde (B) d. J. A. S. Collins 6-2 6-3 6-3; N. Sharpe d. E. J. David 7-5 6-1 6-2; R. K. Tinkler d. H. F. David 6-3 6-2 2-6 7-5; F. Nakano (J) d. G. Medecin (M) 6-1 6-1 6-2; G. L. Tuckett d. T. Hughan (NTH) 1-8 8-6 1-6 6-4 6-4; F. Kukuljevic (YU) d. D. W. Butler 2-6 2-6 6-3 6-4 6-2; L. Nelson (USA) d. W. Musgrove (SA) 3-6 6-3 6-4 6-2; C. N. O. Ritchie d. H. J. Etchart (ARG) 6-4 8-6 2-6 6-2; R. Gõpfert

(G) d. Y. Singh (IN) 6-2 3-6 6-3 4-6 6-3; T. Abe (J) d. D. H. Williams 6-0 8-6 6-3; J. S. Olliff d. R. J. Ritchie 6-1 6-4 4-6 6-2; M. Caikos (HU) d. G. Nicolaides (GR) 6-4 4-6 3-6 6-3 7-5; O. Anderson (USA) d. H. A. Coldham (A) 6-2 6-4 4-6 6-3; S. Rinde (NOR) d. J. M. Hunt 4-6 6-1 6-3 6-1; **F. Puncec** (5) (YU) d. J. Brugnon (F) 6-3 6-2 6-4; E. R. Avory d. H. E. Weatherall 6-1 6-3 6-2; P. Geelhand (B) d. F. J. Piercy 6-4 6-4 6-2; D. MacPhail d. H. van Swol (NTH) 6-3 4-6 6-2; H. G. N. Lee d. A. D. Brown (NZ) 6-4-6 3-6 6-3; C. M. Jones d. N. Taylor 6-1 8-6 6-3; C. F. O. Lister d. W. Steiner (SWZ) 4-6 6-4 2-6 6-2 6-2; W. C. Choy (CHI) d. A. M. Hamburger (RU) 6-4 2-6 6-2 6-3; **R. Menzel** (3) (CZ) d. G. W. S. Fitt 6-3 7-5 6-3; D. C. Coombe (NZ) d. C. J. Hovell 6-3 4-6 6-3 4-6 6-3; F. Cejnar (CZ) d. V. Landau (M) 6-2 6-4 6-2; Ghaus Mohammed (IN) d. R. de Brauw (NTH) 6-3 6-1 6-4; H. Bolelli (F) d. L. Brooke Edwards (IN) 6-4 6-2 6-1; R. W. Higgin d. J. Moreau (B) 3-6 6-3 6-2; I. G. Collins d. H. J. Whitney 6-1 6-4 6-1; G. von Metaxa (G) d. F. H. D. Wilde 4-6 6-3 9-7 7-5; **Kho Sin Kie** (8) (CHI) d. H. A. Hare 6-3 6-4 6-4; G. E. Godsell d. I. H. Wheatcroft 6-4 6-3 6-4; A. T. England d. P. D. Eeman 3-6 6-4 6-1 6-4; J. F. G. Lysaght d. G. Dallos (HU) 1-6 6-2 6-1 6-4; R. A. Shayes d. P. V. V. Sherwood 6-0 2-6 6-3 7-5; G. L. Rogers (IRE) d. S. C. Clark 6-4 2-6 6-1 6-3; J. Pallada (YU) d. H. C. Fisher (SWZ) 6-1 3-6 6-3 6-4; H. Billington d. J. S. Harrison 6-4 6-3 6-4; **J. D. Budge** (1) (USA) d. K. C. Gandar Dower 6-2 6-3 6-3.

SECOND ROUND: Austin (2) d. Darkins 6-4 6-4 6-4; Comery d. Bessemer Clark 6-0 6-4 6-1; Mako d. Malfroy 4-6 6-3 6-4 4-6 6-2; Henderson Brooks d. Koch 6-4 1-6 4-6 9-7 6-0; **Mitic** (6) d. Russell 6-8 6-0 6-3 3-6 6-4; Procopio d. Harreguy 2-6 7-5 6-4 7-5; Ellmer d. Morton 7-5 6-0 6-1; Sawhney d. Sturgeon 3-6 6-4 6-3 6-2; **Henkel** (4) d. Deloford 6-3 6-1 6-3; Boussus d. Meredith 6-4 6-3 6-3; Maneff d. W. T. Anderson 6-1 5-7 6-2 6-4; R. Singh d. Peters 6-2 4-6 7-5 6-3; **Hecht** (7) d. Van den Eynde 6-2 6-4 6-4; Sharpe d. Tinkler 6-3 6-3 9-7; Nakano d. Tuckett 6-3 6-4 12-10; Kukuljevic d. Nelson 6-1 6-1 6-4; Gõpfert d. C. N. O. Ritchie 6-2 6-3 6-0; Olliff d. Abe 6-4 9-7 6-3; O. Anderson

d. Caikos 6-2 6-0 6-4; **Puncec** (5) d. Rinde 6-1 6-4 6-1; Avory d. Geelhand 6-4 10-8 7-5; MacPhail d. Lee 6-3 6-3 2-6 6-1; Jones d. Lister 6-2 6-3 6-4; **Menzel** (3) d. Choy 7-5 4-6 6-2 8-6; Cejnar d. Coombe 6-0 4-3 6-4 6-8; Ghaus Mohammed d. Bolelli 2-6 6-2 6-3 6-2; I. G. Collins d. Higgin 8-6 6-2 6-4; **Kho Sin Kie** (8) d. von Metaxa 6-4 3-6 6-4 6-4; Godsell d. England 6-2 6-4 6-0; Shayes d. Lysaght 6-4 6-4 6-4; Rogers d. Pallada 7-5 0-6 6-4 6-3; **Budge** (1) d. Billington 7-5 6-1 6-1.

THIRD ROUND: Austin (2) d. Comery 6-1 6-1 6-3; Mako d. Henderson Brooks 6-2 6-3 5-7 6-2; **Mitic** (6) d. Procopio 4-6 6-2 6-0 6-0; Ellmer d. Sawhney 6-2 6-2 6-1; **Henkel** (4) d. Boussus d. R. Singh 6-3 3-6 6-2 6-1; **Hecht** (7) d. Sharpe 3-6 6-4 5-7 6-1; Kukuljevic d. Nakano 6-3 7-5 6-8 6-2 6-3; Olliff d. Gõpfert 6-2 2-6 6-4 6-3; **Puncec** (5) d. O. Anderson 7-5 6-3 4-6 3-6 6-4; MacPhail d. Avory 6-2 6-3 6-1; **Menzel** (3) d. Jones 6-3 6-2 4-6 8-10 7-5; Cejnar d. Ghaus Mohammed 6-2 6-4 11-9; **Kho Sin Kie** (8) d. I. G. Collins 8-10 6-2 8-6 6-2; Shayes d. Godsell 2-6 6-3 6-4 6-4; **Budge** (1) d. Rogers 6-0 7-5 6-1.

FOURTH ROUND	QUARTER-FINALS	SEMI-FINALS	FINAL	CHAMPION
Austin (2)	**Austin** (2)			
Mako	6-4 4-6 9-7 0-6 6-4	**Austin** (2)		
Mitic (6)	Ellmer	6-2 6-1 6-2		
Ellmer	3-6 6-2 7-5 1-6 6-2		**Austin** (2)	
Henkel (4)	**Henkel** (4)		6-2 6-4 6-0	
Maneff	6-3 6-1 6-1	**Henkel** (4)		
Hecht (7)	**Hecht** (7)	7-5 6-1 6-2		
Kukuljevic	6-4 3-6 6-3 6-4			**Budge** (1)
Olliff	**Puncec** (5)			6-1 6-0 6-3
Puncec (5)	6-3 6-3 6-0	**Puncec** (5)		
MacPhail	MacPhail 6-8 9-7 ret'd	6-2 6-1 6-1		
Menzel (3)	Cejnar		**Budge** (1)	
Cejnar	7-5 3-6 3-6 6-1 6-3		6-2 6-1 6-4	
Kho Sin Kie (8)	**Budge** (1)	**Budge** (1)		
Shayes	6-3 6-4 6-1	6-3 6-0 7-5		
Budge (1)				

LADIES' SINGLES

FIRST ROUND: J. Jedrzejowska (3) (POL) d. D. Stevenson (A) 6-1 3-6 6-3; Mrs M. R. King d. D. A. Huntbach 6-4 6-2; F. B. Cooke d. N. K. Maingay 7-5 6-2; Mrs W. H. Durlac d. Mrs R. G. MacInnes 6-4 6-4; M. Morphew (SA) d. R. J. M. Smith 3-6 6-2 6-2; E. H. Harvey d. Mrs E. S. Law 7-5 2-6 6-2; S. Noel d. M. Wilson (A) 6-2 6-3; Mrs J. Paksy (HU) d. J. Milne (C) 6-2 7-5; **M. C. Scriven** (8) d. T. R. Jarvis 6-2 6-4; V. E. Scott d. M. Slaney 6-3 6-4; M. Riddell d. B. Batt 6-4 3-6 6-4; M. R. Coquerque (NTH) d. M. Macfarlane (NZ) 6-4 6-2; M. Whitmarsh 6-3 6-3; J. Ingram d. Mrs J. S. Kirk 6-4 6-2; F. James d. E. M. Dearman 8-2 8-6; Mrs J. de Meulemeester (B) d. B. G. Beazley 6-0 6-2; J. Saunders d. P. L. F. Thomson 6-3 4-6 6-2; R. Thomas d. J. M. Lacy 10-8 7-5; D. Bundy (USA) d. P. N.

Morison 6-2 6-2; F. S. Ford d. Mrs C. F. Myerscough (IRE) 6-2 6-0; G. M. Southwell d. M. G. N. Norman 5-7 6-4 6-2; M. Trouncer d. L. Valerio (IT) 6-3 6-3; Mrs R. E. Haylock d. R. Jarvis 6-4 0-6 6-0; **Mrs S. P. Fabyan** (7) (USA) d. B. Enger (G) 6-2 6-3; M. E. Lumb d. O. Craze (SA) 6-0 6-3; M. Heeley d. B. M. Smith 6-3 6-3; E. M. Hamilton d. E. E. Curtis 2-6 7-5 6-3; S. G. Chuter d. Mrs W. S. Thompson 6-2 6-2; T. Coyne (A) d. A. M. Yorke 7-5 6-1; G. C. Hoahing d. E. A. Middleton 6-2 3-6 6-1; G. Wheeler (USA) d. C. M. Burrows 6-3 6-0; **Mrs S. Sperling** (4) (D) d. H. Kovac (YU) 6-1 6-2.

SECOND ROUND: A. Marble (2) (USA) d. M. Cootes (USA) 6-0 6-2; S. Piercey (SA) d. Mrs E. Hollis (D) 6-4 7-5; R. M. Hardwick d. J. Hartigan (A) 6-4 6-2; Mrs R. D. McKelvie d. Mrs G. Deutschova (CZ) 6-4 6-4; **Mrs R. Mathieu** (5) (F) d. A. Lizana (CH) d. A. G. Curtis d. Mrs W. D. Porter 5-7 6-2 6-3; R. Kraus (G) d. P. A. O'Connell 6-3 1-6 6-3; N. Wynne (A) d. Mrs J. B. Pittman 6-3 6-0; Jedrzejowska (3) d. King 6-2 6-4 6-4; Durlac d. Cooke 6-2 6-1 6-4; Morphew d. Harvey 6-3 9-7; Noel d. Paksy 7-5 6-3; **Scriven** (8) d. Scott 6-3 6-4; Coquerque d. Riddell 6-3 8-10 6-3; Jacobs d. Ingram 9-7 6-3; James d. de Meulemeester 6-0 6-8 7-5; Saunders d. Thomas 6-3 6-3; Bundy d. Ford 6-2

6-2; Southwell d. Trouncer 6-3 1-6 7-5; **Fabyan** (7) d. Haylock 6-2 6-4; Lumb d. Heeley 7-5 6-3; Chuter d. Hamilton 6-3 6-4; Coyne d. Hoahing 6-3 6-0; **Sperling** (4) d. Wheeler 6-0 6-0; B. Nuthall d. Mrs D. B. Andrus (USA) 2-6 6-4; M. Stewart d. N. B. Brown 6-1 7-5; **K. E. Stammers** (6) d. Mrs L. R. C. Michell 6-3 6-2; Mrs P. Knight d. M. Baumgarten (HU) 10-8 7-5; Mrs E. L. Heine Miller (SA) d. D. Kitson (SA) 6-1 6-2; Mrs P. F. Glover d. Mrs S. Henrotin (F) 3-6 6-4 6-4; **Mrs H. N. Wills Moody** (1) (USA) 6-3 6-4.

THIRD ROUND: Marble (2) d. Piercey 6-4 6-0; Hardwick d. McKelvie 6-3 6-3; **Mathieu** (5) d. Curtis 6-0 6-3; Wynne d. Kraus 6-3 7-5; **Jedrzejowska** (3) d. Durlac 6-1 6-3; Morphew d. Noel 3-6 6-2 6-3; **Scriven** (8) d. Coquerque 6-2 6-3; Jacobs d. James 6-4 6-2; Bundy d. Saunders 6-4 6-2; **Fabyan** (7) d. Southwell 6-1 6-0; Lumb d.

Chuter 6-2 6-2; **Sperling** (4) d. Coyne 6-4 6-2; Nuthall d. Macpherson-Grant 6-2 2-6 6-4; **Stammers** (6) d. Stewart 6-4 6-1; Heine Miller d. Knight 6-0 6-2; **Wills Moody** (1) d. Glover 6-4 7-5.

FOURTH ROUND	QUARTER-FINALS	SEMI-FINALS	FINAL	CHAMPION
Marble (2)	**Marble** (2)			
Hardwick	7-5 6-4	**Marble** (2)		
Mathieu (5)	**Mathieu** (5)	6-2 6-3		
Wynne	1-6 6-2 6-0		Jacobs	
Jedrzejowska (3)	**Jedrzejowska** (3)		6-4 6-4	
Morphew	6-3 6-2	Jacobs		
Scriven (8)	Jacobs	6-2 6-3		
Jacobs	6-3 6-0			**Wills Moody** (1)
Bundy				6-4 6-0
Fabyan (7)	**Fabyan** (7)			
Lumb	3-6 6-3 6-4	**Sperling** (4)		
Sperling (4)	**Sperling** (4)	4-6 6-4 6-4		
Nuthall	7-5 6-1		**Wills Moody** (1)	
Stammers (6)	**Stammers** (6)		12-10 6-4	
Heine Miller	6-3 6-0	**Wills Moody** (1)		
Wills Moody (1)	**Wills Moody** (1)	6-2 6-1		
	8-6 6-4			

OTHER FINALS

GENTLEMEN'S DOUBLES: Final — J. D. Budge (USA)/G. Mako (USA) d. H. Henkel (G)/G. von Metaxa (G) 6-4 3-6 6-3 8-6.

LADIES' DOUBLES: Final — A. Marble (USA)/Mrs S. P. Fabyan (USA) d. Mrs R. Mathieu (F)/A. M. Yorke 6-2 6-3.

MIXED DOUBLES: Final — J. D. Budge (USA)/A. Marble (USA) d. H. Henkel (G)/Mrs S. P. Fabyan (USA) 6-1 6-4.

GENTLEMEN'S SINGLES PLATE: Final — D. W. Butler d. O. Szigeti (HU) 6-1 8-10 6-3.

LADIES' SINGLES PLATE: Final — D. Stevenson (A) d. J. Hartigan (A) 6-4 6-4.

GENTLEMEN'S SINGLES

1939

FIRST ROUND: H. W. Austin (1) d. J. Asboth (HU) 6-1 6-4 12-10; O. Anderson (USA) d. M. E. Lucking 7-5 6-1 7-5; J. Drobny (BM) d. J. H. Ho (CHI) 6-1 6-2 6-4; H. E. Weatherall d. G. M. Hone (A) 6-4 6-3 7-5; J. Darkins d. D. G. Snart 8-6 6-4 8-6; D. W. Butler d. C. Caralulis (RU) 6-4 6-2 7-9 6-0; J. Van den Eynde (B) d. H. J. Whitney 6-2 6-3 6-2; R. Goepfert (G) d. A. Najar (E) 6-3 6-3 6-1; **E. T. Cooke** (6) (USA) d. C. Boussus (F) 1-6 6-4 6-0 6-3; G. E. Godsell d. J. Spitzer (SWZ) 6-3 4-6 6-1 6-1; C. J. Hovell d. H. T. Baxter 0-6 7-9 6-0 8-6 6-3; G. L. Rogers (IRE) d. I. Ahmad (IN) 6-3 9-7 10-8; A. D. Brown (NZ) d. H. Guicz (G) 6-2 6-2 6-4; I. G. Collins d. R. W. D. Higgin 6-1 6-2 6-2; J. S. Olliff d. D. Prenn 3-6 4-6 6-1 6-4 ret'd; B. Maneff (SWZ) d. J. Charanjiva (IN) 6-2 6-4 6-1; **D. McNeill** (3) (USA) d. K. Aschner (HU) 6-1 6-1 6-0; F. Kukuljevic (YU) d. T. Hughan (NTH) 6-1 4-6 6-1 6-0; C. M. Jones d. W. F. Anderson 6-1 6-0 6-3; W. C. Choy (CHI) d. R. F. Egan (IRE) 5-7 1-6 6-4 6-2 6-3; H. F. David d. G. S. W. Fitt 6-2 6-1 5-7 6-3; D. Mitic (YU) d. D. C. Coombe (NZ) 6-4 11-13 6-3 6-1; H. J. Etchart (ARG) d. B. Royds 7-5 6-1 6-2; M. Deloford d. A. T. England 7-5 8-6 6-4; **H. Henkel** (5) (G) d. F. J. Piercy 9-7 6-0 6-0; J. S. Comery d. G. Dallos (HU) 6-3 7-9 6-4 6-4; H. Pfaff (SWZ) d. D. K. Bose (IN) 6-2 4-6 6-1 1-6 6-2; L. Shaffi d. J. B. Sturgeon 6-1 6-2 3-6 7-5; J. Brugnon (F) d. F. H. D. Wilde 6-1 6-3 3-6 6-3; R. E. Mulliken d. R. F. Bessemer-Clark 7-5 6-1 8-6; G. de Stefani (IT) d. A. Baworowski (POL) 3-6 6-4 7-5 7-5; L. de Borman (B) d. C. N. O. Ritchie 6-4 7-5 3-6 0-6 7-5; E. Gabory (HU) d. J. S. Harrison 6-4 6-2 6-2; J. W. Gunn (NZ) d. Kho Sin Kie (CHI) w.o.; V. Canepele (IT) d. H. G. N. Cooper 7-5 6-4 6-3; Y. Savur (IN) d. P. Geelhand (B) 7-5 9-7 6-1; F. Cejnar (BM) d. A. Gentien (F) 6-1 9-7 6-2; M. Csikos (HU) d. M. D. Maclagan 6-2 7-5 9-7; E. Smith (USA) d. E. D. Andrews (NZ) 3-6 6-2 6-3 6-4; **R. Menzel** (7) (G) d. E. C. Peters 6-1 6-2 6-2; H. A. Coldham (A) d. G. L. Tuckett 6-3 6-4 6-3; A. D. Russell (ARG) d. W. D. Muspratt 6-4 6-3 6-4; A. Schmidt (RU) d. H. A. Hare 2-6 6-3 8-6 0-6 6-3; A. J. Mottram d. E. J. Filby 6-8 6-3 4-6 6-1 7-5; H. C. Fisher (SWZ) d. R. Morton 3-6 6-3 3-6 6-2 6-1; D. MacPhail d. G. R. B. Meredith 6-2 6-1 6-3; P. V. V. Sherwood d. H. Billington 6-3 6-2 11-9; **F. Puncec** (4) (YU) d. N. V. Edwards (NZ) 6-2 6-2 6-3; H. Plougmann (D) d. G. Medecin (M) 9-7 1-6 6-2 6-1; O. Szigeti (HU) d. W. Robertson (USA) 12-10 6-4 6-4; H. Van Swol (NTH) d. J. F. G. Lysaght 6-4 6-3 6-4; M. Ellmer (SWZ) d. A. M. Hamburger (RU) 6-1 6-0 6-3; R. K. Tinkler d. C. F. O. Lister 6-1 4-6 6-3 6-1; Ghaus Mohammed (IN) d. N. Taylor 6-3 6-1 6-2; D. H. Slack d. H. S. Burrows 6-8 6-4 5-7 7-5 6-3; **I. Tloczynski** (8) (POL) d. E. C. Peters 6-1 6-2 6-2; R. Abdesselam (F) d. G. von Metaxa (G) 6-2 6-4 3-6 6-4; J. Siba (BM) d. A. E. Fannin (IRE) 6-3 6-2 6-1; R. A. Shayes d. G. Nicolaides (GR) 2-6 6-2 7-5 4-6 6-2; J. Pallada (YU) d. J. C. Warboys 6-0 6-0 6-0; H. G. N. Lee d. E. J. David 6-2 7-5 7-5; C. E. Malfroy (NZ) d. N. Sharpe 6-4 6-3 2-6 4-6 6-0; E. R. Avory d. F. D. Leyland 6-3 1-6 6-4 4-6 6-4; **R. L. Riggs** (2) (USA) d. J. N. Dhamija (IN) 6-3 6-0 6-4.

SECOND ROUND: Austin (1) d. O. Anderson 6-3 6-4 6-4; Drobny d. Weatherall 6-2 6-2 6-4; Butler d. Darkins 9-7 4-6 6-3 6-1; Goepfert d. Van den Eynde 7-5 6-4 6-2; **Cooke** (6) d. Godsell 6-1 7-5 7-5; Rogers d. Hovell 6-2 10-8 8-6; Collins d. Brown 6-3 1-6 6-4 6-1; Olliff d. Maneff 6-2 7-9 6-2; **McNeill** (3) d. Choy 6-4 7-5 6-1; Choy d. Jones 6-3 2-6 6-2 6-4; Mitic d. H. F. David 6-4 7-5 6-4; Deloford d. Etchart 4-3 2-6 6-2; **Henkel** (5) d. Comery 6-1 6-2 6-4; Shaffi d. Pfaff 3-6 6-3 6-3 6-4; Brugnon d. Mulliken 6-4 6-2 6-4; de Stefani d. de Borman 6-2 10-8 6-1; Gabory d. Gunn 7-5 9-7 5-7 6-2; Canepele d. Savur 6-2 6-4 7-5; Cejnar d. Csikos 6-4 7-5 6-3; Smith d. **Menzel** (7) 6-1 3-6 6-3 7-5; Russell d. Coldham 6-8 6-4 11-9 6-2; Mottram d. Schmidt 3-6 6-3 6-1 6-1; MacPhail d. Fisher 3-6 6-1 6-2 6-0; **Puncec** (4) d. Sherwood 6-3 5-7 6-3 7-5; Van Swol d. Ellmer 6-2 6-3 4-6 6-4; Ghaus Mohammed d. Tinkler 6-4 6-3 6-2; **Tloczynski** (8) d. Slack 6-3 6-1 6-1; Siba d. Abdesselam 7-5 6-1 6-4; Shayes d. Pallada 6-4 3-6 9-7 2-6 8-6; Malfroy d. Lee 6-2 6-4 7-5; **Riggs** (2) d. Avory 6-4 6-4 6-2.

THIRD ROUND: Austin (1) d. Drobny 7-5 9-7 ret'd; Butler d. Goepfert 4-6 6-2 4-6 6-3 6-3; **Cooke** (6) d. Rogers 7-5 6-1 6-4; Olliff d. Collins 8-6 5-7 6-2 6-4; Kukuljevic d. Choy 6-4 7-5 6-4; Deloford d. Mitic 7-5 6-4 2-6 2-6 6-3; **Henkel** (5) d. Shaffi 6-4 4-6 6-4 6-1; Brugnon d. de Stefani 6-4 4-6 8-6 6-4; Gabory d. Canepele 6-4 6-1 2-6 6-1; Smith d. Cejnar 6-3 6-2 5-7 1-6 6-1; Russell d. Mottram 10-8 6-4 6-1; **Puncec** (4) d. MacPhail 6-3 6-3 7-5; Szigeti d. Van Swol 8-6 6-4 6-3; Ghaus Mohammed d. **Tloczynski** (8) 6-0 6-3 6-4; Shayes d. Siba 7-5 6-4 9-7; **Riggs** (2) d. Malfroy 8-6 11-9 6-2.

FOURTH ROUND	QUARTER-FINALS	SEMI-FINALS	FINAL	CHAMPION
Austin (1)	**Austin** (1)			
Butler	8-6 6-4 6-4	**Cooke** (6)		
Cooke (6)	**Cooke** (6)	6-3 6-0 6-1		
Olliff	6-1 6-1 6-4		**Cooke** (6)	
Kukuljevic	Kukuljevic		6-3 4-6 6-4 6-4	
Deloford	6-4 6-3 6-1	**Henkel** (5)		
Henkel (5)	**Henkel** (5)	6-1 6-3 6-2		
Brugnon	6-1 6-3 6-0			
Gabory	Smith			**Riggs** (2)
Smith	6-0 6-4 6-3			2-6 8-6 3-6 6-3 6-2
Russell	**Puncec** (4)	**Puncec** (4)		
Puncec (4)	6-3 8-6 6-1	6-0 6-2 6-2		
Szigeti	Ghaus Mohammed		**Riggs** (2)	
Ghaus Mohammed	6-4 14-16 2-6 6-3 6-4		6-2 6-3 6-4	
Shayes	**Riggs** (2)	**Riggs** (2)		
Riggs (2)	7-5 6-8 6-4 6-3	6-2 6-2 6-2		

LADIES' SINGLES

FIRST ROUND: Mrs R. Mathieu (4) (F) d. E. Porokova (CZ) 6-4 6-1; Mrs M. R. King d. Mrs D. Roberts 7-5 6-1; C. Somogyi (HU) d. B. M. Smith 6-4 6-4; A. M. Yorke d. P. C. Grover 6-0 12-10; V. E. Scott d. Mrs L. Herbst (CZ) 6-2 6-0; E. M. Hamilton d. Mrs K. J. Underwood 6-2 7-5; S. Noel d. P. L. F. Thomson 6-1 6-2; I. Schumann (G) d. N. Lieber 7-5 7-5; **Mrs S. P. Fabyan** (8) (USA) d. M. G. N. Norman 6-2 6-2; Mrs S. H. Hammersley d. B. Batt 6-3 6-2; Mrs H. J. Sargeant d. M. Whitmarsh 4-6 7-5 8-6; D. A. Huntbach d. J. Nicoll 6-8 6-4 6-2; M. Slaney d. N. K. Maingay 6-3 6-1; R. J. M. Smith d. A. P. Cardinall 6-1 7-5; Mrs D. B. Andrus (USA) d. J. Goss 6-3 7-5; Mrs D. L. Little d. M. Stewart 6-1 8-6; Mrs E. G. Macpherson-Grant d. M. I. Harris 6-1 6-3; B. E. Clements d. O. V. Cooper 7-5 2-6 6-2; R. Jarvis d. Mrs E. Pittman 6-1 7-5; G. M. Southwell d. Mrs M. B. Lewis 6-4 7-5; Mrs R. T. Ellis d. Mrs R. D. McKelvie 9-7 6-2; G. Wheeler (USA) d. B. Nuthall 7-5 2-6 6-2; A. Weiwers (LUX) d. Mrs E. S. Law 6-1 6-0; **R. M. Hardwick** (7) d. R. Thomas 10-8 6-4; J. Saunders d. S. Mavrogordato 6-2 6-1; M. Trouncer d. Mrs F. M. Strawson 6-3 6-1; M. Berescu (RU) d. E. H. Harvey 2-6 6-1 6-4; P. A. O'Connell d. E. M. Dearman 6-4 3-6 6-4; D. M. Wood d. Mrs J. S. James 6-1 6-2; S. Pannetier (F) d. Mrs P. R. Goodwyn (IRE) 0-6 6-0 6-3; Mrs E. C. Peters d. A. G. Curtis 7-5 6-0; **Mrs S. Sperling** (3) (D) d. G. C. Hoahing 6-2 6-0.

SECOND ROUND: H. Jacobs (2) (USA) d. Mrs R. E. Haylock 6-0 6-2; J. P. Curry d. Mrs W. H. Durlac 6-4 5-7 10-8; M. E. Lumb d. A. Florian (YU) 6-1 6-2; F. B. Cooke d. J. Ingram 6-4 7-5; **K. E. Stammers** (6) d. E. A. Middleton 6-0 6-2; N. B. Brown d. Mrs M. R. Couquerque (NTH) 11-9 6-1; W. San Donnino (IT) d. M. F. Brace 6-4 6-2; Mrs S. Henrotin (F) d. Mrs T. Dietz (G) 7-5 6-3; **Mathieu** (4) d. King 6-1 6-0; Somogyi d. Yorke 6-3 6-3; Scott d. Hamilton 3-6 6-0 6-2; Noel d. Schumann 6-4 10-8; **Fabyan** (8) d. Hammersley 6-2 6-3; Huntbach d. Sargeant 6-3 10-8; Slaney d. Smith 6-3 6-3; Little d. Andrus 6-3 6-0; Macpherson-Grant d. Clements 6-3 1-6 6-4; Jarvis d. Southwell 4-6 8-6 6-2; Wheeler d. Ellis 6-3 7-5; **Hardwick** (7) d. Weiwers 6-2 6-4; Saunders d. Trouncer 8-6 7-5; O'Connell d. Berescu 6-3 6-2; Wood d. Pannetier 7-5 4-6 6-1; **Sperling** (3) d. Peters 6-3 6-0; Mrs D. F. Cartwright d. T. R. Jarvis 6-0 6-3; M. C. Scriven d. A. Ullstein (G) 6-3 6-3; H. Kovac (YU) d. V. Tonolli (IT) 6-2 6-8 6-1; **J. Jedrzejowska** (5) (POL) d. Mrs J. de Meulemeester (B) 6-3 8-6; Mrs A. Halff (F) d. Mrs P. D. Howard 6-4 6-2; Mrs P. F. Glover d. Mrs G. A. Smith 7-5 6-0; B. G. Beazley d. B. Rodway 5-7 6-1 6-0; **A. Marble** (1) (USA) d. Mrs J. S. Kirk 6-3 6-2.

THIRD ROUND: Jacobs (2) d. Curry 6-3 6-2; Lumb d. Cooke 6-3 6-3; **Stammers** (6) d. Brown 6-2 6-2; Henrotin d. San Donnino 6-1 6-1; **Mathieu** (4) d. Somogyi 6-0 6-8 6-3; Scott d. Noel 6-3 3-6 6-0; **Fabyan** (8) d. Huntbach 6-2 6-3; Little d. Slaney 3-6 6-0 6-1; Macpherson-Grant d. Jarvis 4-6 8-6 7-5; **Hardwick** (7) d. Wheeler 7-5 9-7; Saunders d. O'Connell 6-2 3-6 6-2; **Sperling** (3) d. Wood 6-3 6-1; Scriven d. Cartwright 6-3 6-3; **Jedrzejowska** (5) d. Kovac 6-4 6-3; Halff d. Glover 6-3 4-6 6-1; **Marble** (1) d. Beazley 6-4 6-3.

FOURTH ROUND	QUARTER-FINALS	SEMI-FINALS	FINAL	CHAMPION
Jacobs (2)	**Jacobs** (2)			
Lumb	6-2 7-5	**Stammers** (6)		
Stammers (6)	**Stammers** (6)	6-2 6-2		
Henrotin	7-5 6-2		**Stammers** (6)	
Mathieu (4)	**Mathieu** (4)		7-5 2-6 6-3	
Scott	6-3 4-6 6-2	Fabyan (8)		
Fabyan (8)	**Fabyan** (8)	6-4 6-2		
Little	6-1 3-6 6-2			**Marble** (1)
Macpherson-Grant	**Hardwick** (7)			6-2 6-0
Hardwick (7)	6-4 8-6	**Sperling** (3)		
Saunders	**Sperling** (3)	6-4 6-0		
Sperling (3)	6-2 6-4		**Marble** (1)	
Scriven	**Jedrzejowska** (5)		6-0 6-0	
Jedrzejowska (5)	6-3 6-2	**Marble** (1)		
Halff	**Marble** (1)	6-1 6-4		
Marble (1)	6-1 6-1			

OTHER FINALS

GENTLEMEN'S DOUBLES: Final — E. T. Cooke (USA)/R. L. Riggs (USA) d. C. E. Hare/F. H. D. Wilde 6-3 3-6 6-3 9-7.
LADIES' DOUBLES: Final — A. Marble (USA)/Mrs S. P. Fabyan (USA) d. H. Jacobs (USA)/A. M. Yorke 6-1 6-0.
MIXED DOUBLES: Final — R. L. Riggs (USA)/A. Marble (USA) d. F. H. D. Wilde/N. B. Brown 9-7 6-1.

GENTLEMEN'S SINGLES PLATE: Final — D. McNeill (USA) d. J. Van den Eynde (B) 8-6 6-2.
LADIES' SINGLES PLATE: Final — Mrs R. D. McKelvie d. A. Weiwers (LUX) 6-4 4-6 6-2.

1946

GENTLEMEN'S SINGLES

FIRST ROUND: **D. Pails** (1) (A) d. A. R. Hammersley (CH) 6-2 6-2 6-0; H. Wilton (NTH) d. H. Billington 6-4 6-4 7-5; D. W. Butler d. D. Scharenguivel (CEY) 6-2 6-1 6-2; F. E. Mehner (USA) d. R. Morton 6-3 6-1 7-5; J. A. Moore d. W. T. Anderson 6-2 6-4 6-3; P. Geelhand (NTH) d. E. D. Andrews (NZ) 6-4 6-3 6-4; H. Bolelli (F) d. F. Carlson 6-3 6-3 6-1; B. Patty (USA) d. J. Thomas (F) 4-6 6-3 6-2 6-2; **Y. Petra** (5) (F) d. J. Vodicha (CZ) 6-2 8-6 7-5; J. Pallada (YU) d. R. F. Egan (IRE) 6-0 6-3 6-4; A. Shaffei (E) d. G. E. Godsell 3-6 5-7 6-3 6-4 6-3; R. W. Baker (A) d. J. Clynton-Reed (A) 6-8 9-7 6-2 5-7 6-4; T. Johansson (SW) d. K. Lo (CHI) w.o.; P. E. Hare d. G. S. W. Fitt 6-1 3-6 10-8 6-3; R. Buser (SWZ) d. G. R. B. Meredith 6-3 6-4 3-6 4-6 6-2; G. Gremillet (F) d. G. L. Paish 7-5 2-6 7-5 6-0; **F. Segura** (4) (EC) d. H. A. Clark 6-1 6-1 6-1; J. S. Comery d. S. Webster (USA) 1-6 7-9 6-3 6-1 7-5; T. Brown (USA) d. M. D. Deloford 6-4 10-8 6-2; E. Carter d. C. F. O. Lister 6-4 6-4 11-9; J. Siba (CZ) d. H. Huonder (SWZ) 2-6 4-6 6-1 6-4 6-3; A. J. Mottram d. S. Laslo (YU) 6-2 6-1 6-1; J. Van den Eynde (B) d. R. Abdesselam (F) 4-6 6-1 4-6 4-6 6-1; F. H. D. Wilde d. D. H. Slack 3-6 6-2 0-6 6-3 6-3; **F. Puncec** (7) (YU) d. G. L. Tuckett 6-2 6-2 6-3; J. Ipsen (D) d. T. G. McVeagh (IRE) 7-5 6-4 6-3; E. Buse (PE) d. F. Wallis 2-6 7-5 6-4 4-6 6-2; F. Vrba (CZ) d. H. G. N. Cooper 3-6 2-6 6-0 6-3; Kho Sin Kie (CHI) d. P. J. A. Feret (F) 6-4 6-1 6-4; H. A. Coldham (A) d. D. R. Bocquet 6-1 5-7 6-2; J. E. Harper (A) d. L. de Borman (B) 6-2 6-2; A. C. Van Swol (NTH) d. R. K. Tinkler 6-1 6-3 6-0; F. D. Leyland d. J. E. Slater (USA) 6-3 6-4 6-3; J. Sanglier (F) d. J. Haanes

(NOR) 6-2 6-4 6-4; W. W. Robertson (USA) d. A. L. Van Meegeren (NTH) 6-4 5-7 6-2 6-2; C. A. Kemp (IRE) d. W. C. Choy (CHI) 6-4 6-4 0-6 11-13 6-2; D. W. Barton d. C. Grandet (F) 6-2 6-4 6-3; A. T. England d. J. K. Drinkall 6-4 6-1 7-5; M. E. Lucking d. D. C. Coombe (NZ) 6-8 6-4 3-6 6-2 8-6; **L. Bergelin** (8) (SW) d. P. Washer (B) 6-4 3-6 6-1 2-6 7-5; B. Destremau (F) d. J. Caska (CZ) 7-5 8-6 4-6 6-0; J. Darkins d. M. Talaat (E) 4-6 6-3 6-2 7-5; E. Morea (ARG) d. H. R. Marsland 6-3 6-3 8-6; J. Spitzer (SWZ) d. R. C. Nicoll 6-2 6-1 6-3; S. Drobac (USA) d. F. Davidson (CO) 5-7 2-6 7-5 6-4 7-5; E. Wittmann (POL) d. H. F. Beeman (USA) 6-1 6-2 6-2; H. Marriner d. D. Clayton (A) 4-6 6-0 6-2 6-0; **G. E. Brown** (3) (A) d. B. K. Burnett 6-0 6-3 6-0; H. F. David d. D. N. Hardwick 8-6 9-7 6-2; I. Rinkel (NTH) d. N. R. Lewis 7-5 6-4 7-5; G. Pellizza (F) d. R. C. Smith 6-2 6-1 6-0; H. C. Hopman (A) d. A. Najar (E) 6-4 6-0 6-2; R. Dubuc (F) d. M. Stolarow (POL) w.o.; C. H. E. Betts d. J. M. Cope (NZ) 6-3 6-1 6-2; D. Macphail d. H. Pellizza (F) 6-2 6-3 6-2; **D. Mitic** (6) (YU) d. J. B. Wilkinson (USA) 6-1 6-2 6-0; C. Spychalla (POL) d. C. M. Jones 6-1 6-4 9-7; J. Drobny (CZ) d. E. J. Filby 6-4 6-2 6-3; H. T. Baxter d. G. Medecin (M) 6-1 6-0 6-3; J. Peten (B) d. H. Pfaff (SWZ) 3-8 6-7 5-7; I. Tloczynski d. J. Lesueur (F) 6-2 4-6 6-3 6-4; C. J. Hovell d. H. F. Walton 6-3 6-4 6-4; E. R. Avory d. H. Johansen (D) 6-3 6-2 6-1; **J. Kramer** (2) (USA) d. R. J. Sandys (IRE) 6-0 6-2 6-0.

SECOND ROUND: Pails (1) d. Wilton 6-0 6-4 6-1; Butler d. Mehner 6-4 4-6 6-4 4-6 6-4; Geelhand d. Moore 6-1 6-2 8-6; Patty d. Bolelli 6-3 8-6 9-7; **Petra** (5) d. Pallada 9-7 6-4 6-0; Shaffei d. Baker 6-3 6-2 6-2; Johansson d. Fitt 6-3 6-4 3-6 6-3; Buser d. Gremillet 6-3 6-1 3-6 4-6; Comery 6-1 6-1 6-1; T. Brown d. Carter 6-1 6-4 6-1; Mottram d. Siba 3-6 6-1 10-8 6-4; Van den Eynde d. Wilde 6-2 5-7 7-9 6-3; **Puncec** (7) d. Ipsen 6-3 6-0; Vrba d. Buse 4-6 6-3 6-4 6-3; Kho Sin Kie d. Coldham 6-1 4-6 6-4 7-5; Van Swol d. Harper 4-6 8-6 7-5 6-3; Sangliar d.

Leyland 6-1 6-1 12-10; Robertson d. Kemp 4-6 8-6 6-4 4-6 6-0; Barton d. England 6-3 8-6 6-2; **Bergelin** (8) d. Lucking 6-0 6-0 6-0; Destremau d. Darkins 6-1 6-0 6-3; Morea d. Spitzer 6-2 6-1 6-2; Wittmann d. Drobac 6-2 6-1 6-1; **G. E. Brown** (3) d. Marriner 6-0 6-0 6-1; Rinkel d. David 6-4 9-11 6-3 4-6 6-3; Pellizza d. Hopman 4-6 4-6 6-3 6-4 6-1; Dubec d. Betts 6-2 7-5 6-0; **Mitic** (6) d. Macphail 2-6 6-3 6-0 6-2; Drobny d. Spychalla 6-4 6-4 6-2; Peten d. Baxter 7-5 8-6 6-2; Tloczynski d. Hovell 6-3 6-2 6-1; **Kramer** (2) d. Avory 6-1 6-1 6-0.

THIRD ROUND: Pails (1) d. Butler 6-1 6-4 6-2; Patty d. Geelhand 6-8 6-1 6-3 6-4; **Petra** (5) d. Shaffei 6-2 6-2 6-2; Buser d. Johansson 3-6 6-3 10-8 7-5 6-4; T. Brown d. **Segura** (4) 4-6 6-3 6-3 6-3; Mottram d. Van den Eynde 6-3 6-1 6-2; **Puncec** (7) d. Vrba 6-3 6-0 0-5 7-6 3; Van Swol d. Kho Sin Kie 1-6 6-4 6-2 7-5; Sanglier d. Robertson 7-5 6-2 4-6

1-6 7-5; Bergelin (8) d. Barton 10-8 6-3 6-4; Morea d. Destremau 2-6 6-0 6-2 10-8; **G. E. Brown** (3) d. Wittmann 6-0 6-0 6-2; Pellizza d. Rinkel 6-2 6-4 6-3; **Mitic** (6) d. Dubuc 6-2 6-4 6-3; Drobny d. Peten 6-2 6-2 6-3; **Kramer** (2) d. Tloczynski 6-1 6-0 6-0.

FOURTH ROUND	QUARTER-FINALS	SEMI-FINALS	FINAL	CHAMPION
Pails (1)	**Pails** (1)			
Patty	6-2 6-1 7-5			
Petra (5)	**Petra** (5)	**Petra** (5)		
Buser	6-4 4-6 6-0 6-1	7-5 7-5 6-8 6-4		
T. Brown	T. Brown		**Petra** (5)	
Mottram	6-1 6-1 6-3		4-6 4-6 6-3 7-5 8-6	
Puncec (7)	**Puncec** (7)	T. Brown		
Van Swol	6-1 6-2 6-2	6-2 8-6 6-4		
Sanglier	**Bergelin** (8)			**Petra** (5)
Bergelin (8)	6-2 6-4 6-1			6-2 6-4 7-9 5-7 6-4
Morea	**G. E. Brown** (3)	**G. E. Brown** (3)		
G. E. Brown (3)	6-2 6-1 6-3	13-11 11-9 6-4		
Pellizza	Pellizza		**G. E. Brown** (3)	
Mitic (6)	7-9 3-6 7-5 6-4 6-2		6-4 7-5 6-2	
Drobny	Drobny	Drobny		
Kramer (2)	2-6 17-15 6-3 3-6 6-3	6-4 6-4 6-4		

LADIES' SINGLES

FIRST ROUND: **Mrs M. Menzies** (4) d. P. A. O'Connell 6-1 6-1; Mrs E. S. Law d. G. E. Woodgate 6-1 6-3; A. M. Yorke d. E. M. Wilford 6-2 6-2; L. M. Godefroy (NTH) d. Mrs S. H. Hammersley w.o.; Mrs E. G. Macpherson-Grant d. Mrs R. A. Chamberlain 6-1 6-4; A. J. Wenyon d. Mrs J. N. Goodwyn 6-1 5-7 6-4; D. R. Herbst (CZ) d. V. Nielsen (D) 6-3 6-2; Mrs Y. Vincart (B) d. Mrs W. D. Porter 6-4 3-6 6-4; **D. Bundy** (5) (USA) d. Mrs E. E. Murdock 6-0 6-1; Mrs N. Passingham d. Mrs L. J. Osborne 6-4 6-2; Mrs G. Blaisse (NTH) d. Mrs J. N. C. Couper 6-1 6-1; K. Winthrop (USA) d. N. K. Maingay 6-0 6-1; W. M. Lincoln d. D. M. Litherland 6-3 6-4; Mrs T. Kenyon d. Mrs J. S. James 6-3 6-4; Mrs D. L. Coutts d. E. De Roberts 6-2 6-3; B. Nuthall d. Mrs R. Mathieu (F) 7-5 3-6 6-2; Mrs P. F. Glover d. Mrs

S. R. Mason 7-5 6-0; Mrs G. R. Lines d. Mrs F. E. Heppenstall 6-4 6-4; Mrs F. H. Vivian d. L. Anderson 6-1 6-1; J. Quertier d. J. Marcellin (F) 6-2 6-4; Mrs E. C. Peters d. Mrs P. Knight 6-1 6-3; M. Inglebert (F) d. N. Liebert 6-4 6-2; R. F. Woodgate d. Mrs E. W. Dawson Scott 4-6 7-5 6-4; Mrs C. Boegner (F) d. Mrs A. T. P. Luxton 6-4 6-2; Mrs H. S. Uber 6-1 11-9; Mrs W. C. J. Halford d. T. R. Jarvis 6-1 6-3; Mrs C. Boegner (F) d. Mrs A. T. P. Luxton 6-4 6-2; Mrs H. M. Strawson d. Mrs J. Macnair (J) 6-3 6-0; Mrs P. C. Todd (USA) d. V. S. Dace 6-1 4-6 6-4; Mrs R. E. Haylock d. R. M. Mechel (NTH) 8-6 4-6 6-1; Mrs N. Landry (F) d. M. R. Couquerque (NTH) 7-5 1-6 6-3; **L. Brough** (3) (USA) d. A. Burton (A) w.o.

SECOND ROUND: **P. Betz** (1) (USA) d. Mrs J. de Meulemeester (B) 6-3 6-1; J. Gannon d. Mrs J. Poynder 6-2 6-2; O. V. Cooper d. Y. L. Webster 6-1 8-6; Mrs R. D. McKelvie d. Mrs R. F. Chandler (IRE) 7-5 6-4; **Mrs S. Laffargue** (8) (F) d. J. Jedrzejowska (POL) 6-4 6-4; J. R. M. Morgan d. Mrs E. G. Lister 5-7 9-7 6-3; H. Straubeova (CZ) d. J. Van der Wal (NTH) 6-4 6-4; P. J. Curry d. Countess Russocki (POL) 6-1 6-1; **Menzies** (4) d. Law 6-1 6-3; Yorke d. Godefroy 6-2 6-2; Macpherson-Grant d. Wenyon 6-3 2-6 6-1; Vincart d. Herbst 1-6 6-2 6-0; **Bundy** (5) d. Passingham 6-4 6-1; Winthrop d. Blaisse 2-6 6-0 6-1; Lincoln d. Kenyon 2-6 6-2 6-3; Nuthall d. Coutts 6-0 7-5; Lines

d. Glover 5-7 6-0 6-3; Vivian d. Quertier 6-0 6-3; Inglebert d. Peters 7-5 2-6 6-4; **Bostock** (6) d. Woodgate 6-0 6-3; Halford d. Powell 3-6 6-3 6-2; Boegner d. Strawson 6-0 6-1; Todd d. Haylock 6-1 6-0; **Brough** (3) d. Landry 6-2 6-1; G. C. Hoahing d. P. Rodgers 2-6 6-2 6-2; Mrs B. Carris d. Mrs J. H. Mobbs 5-7 8-6 6-2; Mrs R. C. Panton d. Mrs P. Belin (USA) 7-5 6-3; **D. Hart** (7) (USA) d. J. Ingram 6-0 6-1; Mrs J. Patorni (F) d. P. Hermsen (NTH) 6-2 6-1; Mrs B. E. Hilton d. Mrs M. B. Lewis 6-3 6-2; S. Pannetier (F) d. M. de Borman (B) 6-4 6-0; **M. Osborne** (2) (USA) d. J. W. K. Stork 6-2 6-0.

THIRD ROUND: Betz (1) d. Gannon 6-1 6-0; Cooper d. McKelvie 0-6 7-5 6-4; **Laffargue** (8) d. Morgan 6-1 7-5; Curry d. Straubeova 6-0 6-2; **Menzies** (4) d. Yorke 6-1 6-2; Macpherson-Grant d. Vincart 3-6 6-2 6-4; **Bundy** (5) d. Winthrop 9-7 6-0; Nuthall d. Lincoln 6-1 4-6 6-1; Vivian d. Lines 6-8 6-1 6-2; **Bostock** (6) d. Inglebert 6-2 6-2;

Halford d. Boegner 6-8 6-4 7-5; **Brough** (3) d. Todd 2-6 9-7 6-1; Carris d. Hoahing 6-2 1-6 6-1; **Hart** (7) d. Panton 6-1 6-4; Hilton d. Patorni 6-3 6-2; **Osborne** (2) d. Pannetier 6-0 6-0.

FOURTH ROUND	QUARTER-FINALS	SEMI-FINALS	FINAL	CHAMPION
Betz (1)	**Betz** (1)			
Cooper	6-1 6-0			
Laffargue (8)	Curry	**Betz** (1)		
Curry	6-3 6-3	6-0 6-3		
Menzies (4)	**Menzies** (4)		**Betz** (1)	
Macpherson-Grant	6-0 6-2		6-2 6-3	
Bundy (5)	**Bundy** (5)	**Bundy** (5)		
Nuthall	6-3 6-2	4-6 6-1 6-3		
Vivian	**Bostock** (6)			**Betz** (1)
Bostock (6)	6-0 6-1			6-2 6-4
Halford	**Brough** (3)	**Brough** (3)		
Brough (3)	6-1 6-3	6-1 6-2		
Carris	**Hart** (7)		**Brough** (3)	
Hart (7)	6-8 6-2 6-2		8-6 7-5	
Hilton	**Osborne** (2)	**Osborne** (2)		
Osborne (2)	6-1 6-1	5-7 6-4 6-4		

OTHER FINALS

GENTLEMEN'S DOUBLES: Final — T. Brown (USA)/J. A. Kramer (USA) d. G. E. Brown (A)/D. Pails (A) 6-4 6-4 6-2.
LADIES' DOUBLES: Final — A. L. Brough (USA)/M. E. Osborne (USA) d. P. M. Betz (USA)/D. J. Hart (USA) 6-3 2-6 6-3.

MIXED DOUBLES: Final — T. Brown (USA)/A. L. Brough (USA) d. G. E. Brown (A)/D. Bundy (USA) 6-4 6-4.
GENTLEMEN'S SINGLES PLATE: Final — R. Abdesselam (F) d. C. Spychala (POL) 7-5 6-3.
LADIES' SINGLES PLATE: Final — J. Jedrzejowska (POL) d. P. A. O'Connell 6-4 7-5.

GENTLEMEN'S SINGLES

1947

FIRST ROUND: J. E. Bromwich (2) (A) d. J. Spitzer (SWZ) 6-1 6-2 6-4; L. Bergelin (SW) d. R. Guise 6-2 6-3 6-1; B. Destremau (F) d. A. G. Roberts 6-1 6-1 6-4; C. A. Kemp (IRE) d. A. J. N. Starte 7-5 6-3 6-4; B. Patty (USA) d. O. W. Sidwell (A) 4-6 6-3 3-6 6-2 6-3; Man Mohan (IN) d. R. J. Sandys 6-2 6-4 6-3; D. W. Barton d. N. E. Hessen (NOR) 6-2 6-4 6-2; H. Billington d. G. S. W. Fitt 6-4 7-5 6-3; **J. Drobny** (6) (CZ) d. F. Segura (EC) 7-5 7-5 6-3; J. M. Mehta (IN) d. J. Sanglier (F) 6-1 3-6 3-6 9-7 6-3; Y. Finkelkraut (PA) d. C. E. Malfroy (NZ) 6-1 8-6 6-1; W. Skonecki (POL) d. T. Frigyesy (HU) 6-4 6-3 6-4 6-3; J. Peten (B) d. W. C. Shute 6-3 9-7 6-0; A. Najar (E) d. G. L. Emmett 6-2 6-2 6-1; R. McKenzie (NZ) d. L. Carles (SP) 6-4 6-0 6-3; E. Morea (ARG) d. M. Del Bello (IT) 6-3 6-2 6-8 9-7; **T. Brown** (3) (USA) d. E. W. Sturgess (SA) 7-5 5-7 6-2 2-6 8-6; C. Grandet (F) d. P. E. Hare 13-11 6-8 6-2 6-3; I. F. Rinkel (NTH) d. J. R. Mansell 6-3 8-6 6-2; H. T. Baxter d. C. J. Hovell 5-7 6-3 3-6 6-3 6-4; Y. Rurac (RU) d. D. G. C. Mockridge 6-0 6-1 6-4; I. Tloczynski (POL) d. J. A. Moore 6-3 6-1 6-0; I. Harper (A) d. J. Brichant (B) 6-1 6-1 6-2; C. F. Long (A) d. K. B. Hansen (D) 6-1 6-1 6-0; **Y. Petra** (7) (F) d. D. W. Butler 6-2 7-5 6-0; H. F. Walton d. J. S. Comery 6-3 5-7 8-6; D. K. Bose (IN) d. G. D. Oakley 6-2 6-3 6-0; J. Van den Eynde (B) d. J. B. Griffith 6-4 6-3 6-4; J. E. Robson (NZ) d. A. T. England (A) 6-2 1-6 6-0; F. J. Piercy d. R. K. Tinkler 6-1 5-7 6-3 6-3; E. Buchi (SWZ) d. G. E. Godsell 6-4 7-5 4-6 5-7 6-4; C. M. Jones d. F. Wallis 6-3 7-5 6-4; H. Redl (AU) d. J. N. Archer 6-4; M. Ellmer (SWZ) d. J. H. Crawford (A) 5-7 8-6 8-6 6-0; J. Barry (NZ) d. G. L. Paish 0-6 4-6 8-6 6-4 6-4; D. H. Slack d. D. G. Snart 4-6 6-2 11-9 6-3; J. Hebda (POL) d. F. Carlson 4-6 6-1 6-2 6-3; C. F. O. Lister d. M. Appel (PA) 6-4 6-3 7-5; R. E. Carter d. C. Caralulis (RU) 6-3 9-7 4-6 4-6 8-6; **R. Falkenburg** (8) (USA) d. P. Washer (B) 6-2 6-2 6-2; K. I. Ahmed (IN) d. H. A. Coldham 6-2 6-2 6-4; J. Michelmore d. R. F. Egan (IRE) 6-8 6-0 6-2 3-6 6-1; E. E. Fannin (SA) d. J. Eros (HU) 6-0 6-3 6-2; R. Abdesselam (F) d. F. D. Leyland 6-4 6-3 6-4; A. A. Stolpa (HU) d. R. G. Reeve 6-2 6-2 6-2; S. C. Misra (IN) d. H. F. David 4-8 6-6 6-2 6-3; J. Staubo (NOR) d. H. G. N. Cooper 6-2 7-5 6-2; **D. Pails** (4) (A) d. L. E. Cater 6-1 6-0 6-1; W. C. Choy (CHI) d. S. Nimr (E) 6-2 6-0; M. D. Deloford d. G. P. Jackson 8-6 1-6 6-3 8-6; A. J. Mottram d. N. G. Farquharson (SA) 8-6 7-5 7-5; P. Pellizza (F) d. D. M. Bull 6-2 6-1 6-0; E. Bjerre (D) d. N. R. Lewis 6-3 6-3 4-6 6-1; G. R. B. Meredith d. E. Wittman 4-6 8-6 7-5 6-4; V. Cernik (CZ) d. A. Hamburger 6-1 6-2 7-5; **G. E. Brown** (5) (A) d. W. Robertson (USA) 6-1 6-0 6-3; P. Geelhand (B) d. E. J. David 6-1 6-3 8-10 6-4; T. Johansson (SW) d. B. Royds 6-0 6-0 6-0; J. Asboth (HU) d. A. C. Van Swol (NTH) 7-9 6-4 6-3 5-7 6-1; G. Mohammed Khan (IN) d. G. L. Tuckett 6-2 6-2 6-3; O. M. Bold (NZ) d. J. L. Morea (ARG) 9-7 6-3 2-6 6-2; C. Cucelli (IT) d. N. Kitovitz 6-3 6-4 6-1; C. Spychala (POL) d. J. K. Drinkall 7-5 6-0 6-4; **J. Kramer** (1) (USA) d. W. J. Moss 6-0 6-1 6-0.

SECOND ROUND: Bromwich (2) d. Bergelin 6-0 6-4 11-9; Destremau d. Kemp 4-6 6-3 4-6 6-3 6-4; Patty d. Man Mohan 7-5 1-6 6-2 5-7 6-3; Barton d. Billington 3-6 6-2 6-2 6-1; **Drobny** (6) d. Mehta 6-2 6-1 6-2; Skonecki d. Finkelkraut 6-0 6-4 6-3; Peten d. Najar 6-8 6-1 6-2 6-2; Morea d. McKenzie 2-6 6-3 6-4 6-4; **T. Brown** (3) d. Grandet 6-3 6-4 6-4; Baxter d. Rinkel 3-6 6-2 6-3 6-1; Rurac d. Tloczynski 7-5 3-6 7-5 6-4 6-4; Long d. Harper 6-2 6-2 6-4; **Petra** (7) d. Walton 6-2 6-2 6-2; Bose d. Van den Eynde 2-6 6-1 6-4 3-6 6-4; Robson d. Piercy 7-5 2-6 4-6 6-3 13-11; Jones d. Buchi 4-6 6-3 6-2 6-3; Redl d. Ellmer 6-2 2-6 6-3 6-4; Slack d. Barry 7-5 6-2 7-5; Lister d. Hebda 1-6 6-3 6-3 6-2; **Falkenburg** (8) d. Carter 6-2 6-1 7-5; Ahmed d. Michelmore 6-0 6-1 6-3; Abdesselam d. Fannin 11-9 6-3 2-6 6-4; Misra d. Stolpa 6-4 7-5 6-1; **Pails** (4) d. Staubo 6-2 6-1 6-1; Deloford d. Choy 3-6 4-6 6-4 6-3; Pellizza d. Mottram 7-5 6-3 8-10 6-4; Meredith d. Bjerre 2-6 6-4 3-1 ret'd; **G. E. Brown** (5) d. Cernik 2-6 6-1 4-6 6-1; Johansson d. Geelhand 6-0 6-0 6-0; Asboth d. Mohammed Khan 6-3 6-2 6-4; Cucelli d. Bold 6-0 6-4 6-8 6-3; **Kramer** (1) d. Spychala 6-2 6-2 6-2.

THIRD ROUND: Bromwich (2) d. Destremau 6-1 6-1 6-1; Patty d. Barton 6-3 6-4 3-6 6-1; **Drobny** (6) d. Skonecki 6-3 6-1 6-3; Morea d. Peten 1-6 6-2 6-3 6-3; **T. Brown** (3) d. Baxter 6-2 6-2 10-12 6-4; Long d. Rurac 6-3 6-2 6-3; **Petra** (7) d. Bose 6-3 6-4 6-3; Robson d. Jones 6-4 2-6 6-8 6-4 10-8; Redl d. Slack 1-6 6-3 7-5 0-6 6-3; **Falkenburg** (8) d. Lister 7-5 6-3 6-1; Abdesselam d. Ahmed 9-7 6-4 7-9 4-6 6-4; **Pails** (4) d. Misra 6-4 6-3 6-2; Pellizza d. Deloford 4-6 9-7 6-3 6-3; **G. E. Brown** (5) d. Meredith 6-2 6-1 6-3; Johansson d. Asboth 8-6 5-7 6-2 6-2; **Kramer** (1) d. Cucelli 6-0 6-2 6-0.

FOURTH ROUND	QUARTER-FINALS	SEMI-FINALS	FINAL	CHAMPION
Bromwich (2)	Patty			
Patty	6-4 0-6 6-4 1-6 6-4	Patty		
Drobny (6)	**Drobny** (6)	3-6 6-4 7-9 6-2 6-3		
Morea	w.o.		**T. Brown** (3)	
T. Brown (3)	**T. Brown** (3)		6-3 6-3 6-3	
Long	3-6 13-11 3-6 6-1 6-0	**T. Brown** (3)		
Petra (7)	**Petra** (7)	7-5 6-2 6-4		
Robson	6-2 6-3 4-6 6-3			**Kramer** (1)
Redl	**Falkenburg** (8)			6-1 6-3 6-2
Felkenburg (8)	6-3 6-3 6-4	**Pails** (4)		
Abdesselam	**Pails** (4)	4-6 4-6 6-3 6-0 6-2		
Pails (4)	6-2 6-1 6-4		**Kramer** (1)	
Pellizza	**G. E. Brown** (5)		6-1 3-6 6-1 6-0	
G. E. Brown (5)	6-3 6-2 1-6 6-3	**Kramer** (1)		
Johansson	**Kramer** (1)	6-0 6-1 6-3		
Kramer (1)	7-5 6-2 6-3			

LADIES' SINGLES

FIRST ROUND: D. Hart (3) (USA) d. Mrs M. D. Muller (SA) 6-1 6-1; Mrs W. C. J. Halford d. V. S. Dace 6-2 6-1; B. Gullbrandsson (SW) d. Mrs D. R. Bocquet 6-1 7-5; Mrs M. R. Couquerque (NTH) d. M. Hamelin (F) 6-4 6-4; Mrs M. Rurac (RU) d. Mrs R. W. Baker (A) 6-4 6-0; O. V. Cooper d. N. Liebert 6-2 6-2; Mrs E. W. Dawson-Scott d. Mrs R. C. Panton 6-1 6-3; Mrs B. Carris d. Mrs N. W. Blair 3-6 6-1 10-8; **Mrs E. W. A. Bostock** (8) d. Mrs S. Kormoczy (HU) 6-4 6-3; Mrs F. O. Lister d. L. Studer (SWZ) 6-1 6-2; Mrs G. R. Lines d. E. M. Wilford 6-4 6-3; Mrs R. McKelvie d. P. A. O'Connell 6-4 4-3 ret'd; M. Slaney d. D. R. Herbst 6-1 6-2; P. J. Curry d. P. Cowney 6-0 6-1; E. F. Lombard (IRE) d. K. L. A. Tuckey w.o.; Mrs M. R. King d. M. de Borman (B) 6-2 6-4; Mrs H. Doleschell (AU) d. B. Knapp 6-1 8-6; A. Weiwers (F) d. Mrs F. M. Strawson 6-4 6-0; Mrs L. J. Osborne d. Mrs T. A. Morris 6-1 6-1; A. M. Yorke d. M. E. Parker 3-6 6-3 9-7; G. E. Woodgate d. E. Sutton 6-0 6-1; J. Quertier d. Mrs E. C. Peters 6-4 6-1; Mrs E. Hamilton d. Mrs A. T. P. Luxton 6-3 6-2; Mrs S. P. Summers (7) (SA) d. Mrs M. B. Lewis 6-3 6-1; Mrs B. E. Hilton d. Mrs J. B. Walker-Smith 6-4 6-3; J. Jedrzejowska (POL) d. Mrs P. Knight 6-2 6-3; J. Gannon d. Mrs Saladin (F) w.o.; G. Kornfeld (PA) d. Mrs D. W. Pritchard 6-4 6-2; Mrs F. H. Vivian d. Mrs J. David 6-1 6-1; Mrs J. de Meulemeester (B) d. L. Churcher 6-0 6-1; Mrs R. T. Ellis d. H. H. Straubeova (CZ) 6-4 6-2; **Mrs P. C. Todd** (4) (USA) d. H. S. Morgan 6-3 6-0.

SECOND ROUND: L. Brough (2) (USA) d. Mrs P. F. Glover 6-1 6-0; Mrs E. E. Pool d. D. J. Fry 5-7 8-6 6-2; Mrs J. Bathurst (A) d. Mrs G. F. Powell 3-6 6-2 6-1; P. C. Grover d. V. S. White 6-3 6-3; **Mrs N. W. Bolton** (5) (A) d. J. Coles 6-1 6-0; Mrs D. L. Coutts d. Mrs D. B. E. Walton 6-1 6-2; J. R. M. Morgan d. M. Carlisle 6-3 1-6 6-4; J. W. K. Stork d. Mrs H. R. Philips 3-6 6-4 6-2; **Hart** (3) d. Halford 6-0 7-5; Gullbrandsson d. Couqerque 6-4 6-4; Rurac d. Cooper 6-3 9-7; Dawson-Scott d. Carris 4-6 6-4 6-2; **Bostock** (8) d. Lister 6-2 6-3; Lines d. McKelvie 6-3 7-5; Curry d. Slaney 6-3; Lombard d. King 4-0 6-4 6; Weiwers d. Doleschell 6-4 6-2; Osborne d. Yorke 8-6 7-5; Quertier d. Woodgate 6-3 3-6 6-3; **Summers** (7) d. Hamilton 0-6 6-0; Hilton d. Jedrzejowska 6-4 9-7; Gannon d. Kornfeld 6-3 6-3; Vivian d. de Meulemeester 6-4 9-7; **Todd** (4) d. Ellis 6-3 6-2; G. C. Hoahing d. W. M. Peterdy (HU) 8-6 6-2; Mrs H. C. Hopman (A) d. K. Keith Steele 6-3 6-0; Mrs R. H. Chapman d. E. A. Middleton 6-2 8-6; **Mrs M. Menzies** (6) d. M. C. Mary Nielsen (D) 6-2 6-1; Mrs A. Bossi (IT) d. P. Rodgers 6-3 7-5; Mrs C. Boegner (F) d. Mrs J. A. Hibbert 4-6 6-2 6-1; Mrs W. H. Durlac d. Mrs T. Kenyon 7-5 6-2; **M. Osborne** (1) (USA) d. Mrs R. F. Chandler 6-3 6-2.

THIRD ROUND: Brough (2) d. Pool 6-1 6-0; Grover d. Bathurst 6-3 4-6 6-3; **Bolton** (5) d. Coutts 6-1 6-1; Stork d. Morgan 6-0 6-1; **Hart** (3) d. Gullbrandsson 6-3 6-0; Rurac d. Dawson-Scott 7-5 6-2; **Bostock** (8) d. Lines 6-3 6-1; Curry d. Lombard 6-3 3-6 6-2; Osborne d. Weiwers 7-5 2-6 6-4; **Summers** d. Quertier 11-9 6-1; Hilton d. Gannon 7-5 6-3; **Todd** (4) d. Vivian 6-1 6-3; Hopman d. Hoahing 6-4 6-2; **Menzies** (6) d. Chapman 6-0 6-1; Bossi d. Boegner 3-6 6-3 6-3; **Osborne** (1) d. Durlac 6-3 6-0.

FOURTH ROUND	QUARTER-FINALS	SEMI-FINALS	FINAL	CHAMPION
Brough (2)	**Brough** (2)			
Grover	6-0 6-1	**Brough** (2)		
Bolton (5)	**Bolton** (5)	6-2 6-3		
Stork	6-1 6-2		**Hart** (3)	
Hart (3)	**Hart** (3)		2-6 8-6 6-4	
Rurac	6-4 8-6	**Hart** (3)		
Bostock (8)	**Bostock** (8)	4-6 6-1 6-2		
Curry	6-3 6-3			**Osborne** (1)
Osborne	**Summers** (7)			6-2 6-4
Summers (7)	7-5 6-1	**Summers** (7)		
Hilton	**Todd** (4)	7-5 6-4		
Todd (4)	6-1 6-2		**Osborne** (1)	
Hopman	**Menzies** (6)		6-1 6-2	
Menzies (6)	6-2 6-2	**Osborne** (1)		
Bossi	**Osborne** (1)	6-2 6-4		
Osborne (1)	6-3 7-5			

OTHER FINALS

GENTLEMEN'S SINGLES PLATE: Final — E. W. Sturgess (SA) d. A. J. Mottram 6-3 6-3.
LADIES' SINGLES PLATE: Final — J. Jedrzejowska (POL) d. Mrs N. W. Blair 6-2 7-5.
BOYS' INVITATION SINGLES (Round Robin): **Final** — K. Nielsen (D) d. S. Davidsson (SW) 8-6 6-1 9-7.
GIRLS' INVITATION SINGLES (Round Robin): **Final** — Miss Domken (B) d. Miss Wallen (SW) 6-1 6-4.

GENTLEMEN'S SINGLES PLATE: Final — E. W. Sturgess (SA) d. A. J. Mottram 6-3 6-3.
LADIES' SINGLES PLATE: Final — J. Jedrzejowska (POL) d. Mrs N. W. Blair 6-2 7-5.
BOYS' INVITATION SINGLES (Round Robin): **Final** — K. Nielsen (D) d. S. Davidsson (SW) 8-6 6-1 9-7.
GIRLS' INVITATION SINGLES (Round Robin): **Final** — Miss Domken (B) d. Miss Wallen (SW) 6-1 6-4.

1948

GENTLEMEN'S SINGLES

FIRST ROUND: J. E. Bromwich (2) (A) d. J. Van den Eynde (B) 6-2 6-4 8-6; G. P. Jackson (IRE) d. Z. Katona (HU) 4-6 4-6 6-2 6-2 6-2; D. G. Snart d. H. C. Bernstein 3-6 6-1 6-1 6-3; V. Cernik (CZ) d. F. Quintavalle (IT) 6-2 6-1 6-2; A. C. Van Swol (NTH) d. C. Spychala (POL) 9-7 6-3 3-6 2-6 6-2; F. Ampon (PH) d. J. Bartroli (SP) 6-1 6-0 6-1; R. E. Carter d. F. Wallis 8-6 6-1 6-4; N. Nath (IN) d. A. Najar (E) 6-4 6-2 6-1; **B. Patty** (6) (USA) d. T. Ulrich (D) 6-4 6-4 7-5; R. Abdesselam (F) d. E. Donnell (USA) 4-6 8-6 6-0 6-3; C. Sada (IT) d. T. R. Miles 7-5 6-2 6-3; F. Puncec (YU) d. W. Robertson (USA) 8-6 6-3 6-2; H. T. Baxter d. E. Buchi (SWZ) 6-4 6-0 4-6 6-2; C. M. Jones d. W. J. Moss 9-7 6-1 6-2; G. R. B. Meredith d. J. Ducos (F) 1-6 7-5 3-6 6-0 6-4; C. Jones (USA) d. J. Morison (USA) 7-9 6-2 6-1 6-1; **T. Brown** (4) (USA) d. D. W. Butler 5-7 6-1 4-6 6-2 9-7; H. F. Walton d. J. P. MacHale (LUX) 6-4 7-5 6-1; F. Fornstedt (SW) d. R. Bossi (IT) 8-6 6-2 8-6; A. G. Roberts d. J. W. Spence (A) 11-9 7-5 4-6 6-8 8-6; D. K. Bose (IN) d. C. F. O. Lister 6-0 6-1 6-4; H. C. Hopman (A) d. W. K. Young (USA) 6-2 9-11 8-6 6-2; H. Billington d. A. T. England 6-0 6-1 6-1; J. A. Moore d. J. R. Mansell 6-4 5-7 6-4 6-3; **E. W. Sturgess** (8) (SA) d. R. Van Meegeren (NTH) 6-2 6-0 6-3; J. Peten (B) d. K. B. Madan (IN) 6-3 6-4 8-6; E. Morea (ARG) d. E. Mandelbaum (E) 6-3 6-1 6-3; C. Grandet (F) d. E. Wittmann 6-4 1-6 6-4 6-3; J. Asboth (HU) d. J. S. Comery 6-3 6-0 6-2; J. Haanes (NOR) d. N. R. Lewis 6-4 1-6 6-2; E. J. David d. A. J. N. Starte 8-6 3-6 8-6 6-4; J. Pallada (YU) d. D. Scharenguivel 6-3 6-2 6-4; R. J. E. Mayers (K) d. M. Murphy (IRE) 6-4 6-1

8-6; D. M. Bull d. H. G. N. Cooper 6-4 6-3 6-1; R. G. Reeve d. G. Eros (HU) 6-4 6-4 6-3; P. Washer (B) d. A. H. Khokhar (PAK) 6-0 6-0 6-2; A. J. Mottram d. N. Kitovitz 6-1 6-4 6-2; K. Nielsen (D) d. F. Kukuljevic (IN) 2-6 6-3 6-3 6-2; C. Cucelli (IT) d. R. J. MacCabe (IRE) 6-2 6-4 6-1; **J. Drobny** (5) (CZ) d. W. C. Choy (CHI) 6-1 6-3 6-3; I. Rinkel (NTH) d. R. Guise 6-0 7-5 6-2; J. Delire (B) d. A. L. Proctor 6-1 6-2 6-4; L. E. Cater d. D. G. C. Mockridge 6-1 6-2 6-4; J. E. Harper (A) d. B. Destremau (F) 6-2 0-6 6-3 5-7 6-0; Q. S. W. Fitt d. W. Muller (SA) 6-1 5-7 6-1 6-2; S. C. Misra (IN) d. M. Szavoszt (SP) 6-1 6-4 3-6 6-3; H. Redl (AU) d. A. C. Dobbs 6-4 6-4 3-6 8-6; **G. Mulloy** (3) (USA) d. A. D. Russell (ARG) 6-2 6-4 6-3; R. Deyro (PH) d. D. H. Slack 6-3 6-2 6-3; Lord Ronaldshay d. G. L. Tuckett 6-4 7-9 6-3 6-2; F. Sedgman (A) d. S. L. R. Sawhney (IN) 6-2 7-5 6-4; M. Del Bello (IT) d. P. Remy (F) 6-2 7-5 2-6 6-4; D. Mitic (YU) d. I. Tloczynski (POL) 6-3 7-5 8-6; G. L. Paish d. V. Vodicha (CZ) 6-2 0-6 6-1 7-5; A. Hamburger d. G. E. Godsell 7-5 10-8 1-6 6-0; **R. Falkenburg** (7) (USA) d. J. Brichant (B) 6-1 6-2 6-3; W. Coen d. Alam 9-7 6-4 5-7 6-3; Bergelin d. Weiss 4-6 6-1 6-1 7-5; Kemp d. Coldham 6-2 6-2 7-5; **Parker** (1) d. Carlson 6-0 6-0 6-2.

SECOND ROUND: Bromwich (2) d. Jackson 6-0 6-0 6-2; Cernik d. Snart 7-5 6-4 6-2. Van Swol d. Ampon 8-6 6-2 7-5; Nath d. Carter 6-1 6-1 6-1; **Patty** (6) d. Abdesselam 6-1 6-1 6-1; Puncec d. Sada 2-6 6-2 6-3 6-2; Jones d. Baxter 3-6 6-2 6-4 6-3; Meredith d. Jones 7-5 6-3 6-1; **Brown** (4) d. Walton 6-2 6-2 7-5; Fornstedt d. Roberts 6-2 6-4 6-2; Bose d. Hopman 6-4 0-3 6-8 6-8 8-6; Billington d. Moore 7-5 4-6 6-2; **Sturgess** (8) d. Peten 6-4 7-5 6-2; Morea d. Grandet 6-2 5-7 6-4 6-3; Asboth d. Haanes 7-5 6-4 6-1; Pallada d. David 6-4 6-0 6-2; Mayers d. Bull 6-4 5-7 2-6 7-5

6-4; Washer d. Reeve 6-1 6-1 6-1; Mottram d. Nielsen 6-2 6-4 6-1; Cucelli d. Drobny (5) 6-4 16-14 1-6 2-6 6-3; Delire d. Rinkel 5-7 1-6 6-3 7-5 8-6; Harper d. Cater 6-2 6-2 6-1; Misra d. Fitt 6-2 6-1 6-4; **Mulloy** (3) d. Redl 6-1 6-4 6-4; Deyro d. Lord Ronaldshay 6-0 6-3 6-3; Sedgman d. Del Bello 6-3 6-2 6-8 5-7 7-5; Mitic d. Paish 8-6 6-8 6-2 6-1; **Falkenburg** (7) d. Hamburger 6-2 6-2 6-3; Coen d. Alam 9-7 6-4 5-7 6-3; Bergelin d. Weiss 4-6 6-1 6-1 7-5; Kemp d. Coldham 6-2 6-2 7-5; **Parker** (1) d. Carlson 6-0 6-0 6-2.

THIRD ROUND: Bromwich (2) d. Cernik 6-4 6-1 6-2; Van Swol d. Nath 8-6 1-6 6-3 6-1; **Patty** (6) d. Puncec 6-3 ret'd; Meredith d. Jones 4-6 6-3 3-7 5-7 5-7; **Brown** (4) d. Fornstedt 4-3 6-3 6-3 6-2; Bose d. Billington 6-3 6-3 6-1; **Sturgess** (8) d. Morea 7-5 6-4 5-7 6-2; Asboth d. Pallada 6-3 6-4 6-4; Washer d. Mayers 6-4 6-2 6-4; Mottram d.

Cucelli 6-8 6-3 10-12 9-7 6-2; Harper d. Delire 6-2 6-3 6-3; **Mulloy** (3) d. Misra 2-6 6-4 6-1 3-6 6-4; Sedgman d. Deyro 0-8 6-6 6-3 6-1; **Falkenburg** (7) d. Mitic 5-7 6-3 4-6 6-3 6-4; Bergelin d. Coen 6-1 6-1 7-5; **Parker** (1) d. Kemp 6-0 6-1 6-0.

FOURTH ROUND	QUARTER-FINALS	SEMI-FINALS	FINAL	CHAMPION
Bromwich (2)	**Bromwich** (2)			
Van Swol		**Bromwich** (2)		
Patty (6)	6-4 6-3 6-4	6-4 7-5 6-1		
Meredith	**Patty** (6)		**Bromwich** (2)	
Brown (4)	6-3 6-3 8-6		6-3 14-12 6-2	
Bose	**Brown** (4)			
Sturgess (8)	4-6 8-6 6-4 6-4	Asboth		
Asboth	Asboth	4-6 6-3 4-6 6-1 6-1		
Washer	2-6 9-7 7-5 2-6 6-1			**Falkenburg** (7)
Mottram	Mottram			7-5 0-6 6-2 3-6 7-5
Harper	10-8 6-1 7-5			
Mulloy (3)	**Mulloy** (3)	**Mulloy** (3)		
Sedgman	7-5 6-0 6-4	6-2 1-6 7-5 6-1		
Falkenburg (7)	**Falkenburg** (7)		**Falkenburg** (7)	
Bergelin	6-1 6-2 6-4		6-4 6-4 8-6	
Parker (1)		**Falkenburg** (7)		
	5-7 7-5 9-7 0-6 10-8	6-4 6-2 3-6 6-4		

LADIES' SINGLES

FIRST ROUND: D. Hart (4) (USA) d. J. Gannon 4-6 6-0 6-1; Mrs H. P. Rihbany (USA) d. F. B. Cooke 6-4 6-0; Mrs G. R. Lines d. N. Hermsen (NTH) 6-0 6-4; E. Sutz (SWZ) d. Mrs A. Bossi (IT) 6-4 6-4; P. J. Curry d. A. Rice (USA) 6-2 8-6; Mrs R. F. Chandler d. Mrs J. David 6-4 6-1; B. Scofield (USA) d. V. Mattar (LUX) 6-1 6-1; Mrs H. Weiss (ARG) d. K. G. E. Woodgate 8-6 6-3; **Mrs N. Landry** (7) (F) d. L. Schou-Nilsen (NOR) 6-1 6-3; P. A. O'Connell d. J. W. K. Stork 6-4 4-6 6-3; K. L. A. Tuckey d. A. M. Carlisle 6-4 6-1; P. Rodgers d. V. S. White 6-3 6-1; G. P. Butler (USA) d. Mrs E. E. Pool 8-6 6-2; Mrs A. Thomas d. Mrs T. S. Wallace 6-2 6-3; Mrs W. M. Peterdy (HU) d. Mrs J. J. FitzGibbon (IRE) 6-8 6-4 6-1; M. de Borman d. A. L. Morgan 6-1 6-2; Mrs L. G. Andersen (D) d. Mrs J. Hibbert 6-2; J. Quertier d. M. Cary

(USA) 6-2 3-6 6-1; Mrs J. B. Fulton d. M. Brennan (IRE) 6-3 4-6 6-3; Mrs N. W. Blair d. E. M. Percival 6-4 7-5; A. Weiwers (F) d. M. R. Couquerque (NTH) 5-7 6-0 6-2; Mrs O. Anderson (USA) d. Mrs R. C. Panton 6-1 6-4; M. E. Parker d. P. Fisher 6-2 6-1; **Mrs S. P. Summers** (6) (SA) d. Mrs H. R. Phillips 7-5 6-1; E. M. S. Andrews d. Mrs M. B. Lewis 4-6 6-2 6-1; Mrs N. Passingham d. Mrs L. Lind (NOR) 6-3 6-3; Mrs W. C. J. Halford d. Mrs L. J. Osborne 6-4 6-2; Mrs J. S. James d. P. C. Grover 2-6 6-2 6-1; Mrs D. R. Bocquet d. Mrs C. F. O. Lister 6-4 6-3; J. R. M. Morgan d. D. R. Herbst 6-4 6-3; B. N. Knapp d. Mrs E. C. Peters 6-3 6-0; **Mrs P. C. Todd** (3) (USA) d. Mrs J. J. Walker-Smith 6-2 6-1.

SECOND ROUND: Mrs W. du Pont (1) (USA) d. O. V. Cooper 6-3 6-0; Mrs G. Blaisse-Terwindt (NTH) d. Mrs H. E. F. Behr 7-5 6-4; K. Keith-Steele d. Mrs R. A. Bain (IRE) 9-7 6-3; Mrs E. W. Dawson-Scott d. Mrs W. H. Durlac 7-5 6-2; C. G. Hoahing d. Mrs P. J. Kerr 6-3 6-1; Mrs M. D. Muller d. Mrs R. M. Dowdeswell (K) 2-6 6-2 6-3; Mrs C. Boegner (F) d. P. Cowney 6-1 8-6; **Hart** (4) d. Rihbany 6-0 6-1; Lines d. Sutz 0-3 6-6 2; Curry d. Chandler 6-4 6-3; Scofield d. Weiss 6-3 7-5; **Landry** (7) d. O'Connell w.o.; Tuckey d. Rodgers 6-8 8-6 6-2; Thomas d. Butler 6-2 6-3; Peterdy d. de Borman 6-3 7-5; Quertier d. Andersen 6-0

6-1; Blair d. Fulton 6-1 6-2; Weiwers d. Anderson 8-10 14-12 6-4; **Summers** (6) d. Parker 6-4 6-3; Passingham d. Andrews 7-5 4-6 9-7; Halford d. James 6-3 6-0; Bocquet d. Morgan 6-2 6-3; **Todd** (3) d. Knapp 6-1 8-6; Mrs S. Kormoczy (HU) d. G. Jucker 6-2 6-2; Mrs J. de Meulemeester (B) d. Mrs T. Lubbers-Fischer (NTH) 6-2 6-1; Mrs B. E. Hilton d. Mrs M. Wavish 6-0 6-1; **S. Fry** (8) (USA) d. M. Slaney 6-1 6-1; E. A. Middleton d. Mrs B. Carris 6-8 6-4 6-1; Mrs A. C. Brighton d. Mrs J. B. Parker 6-3 6-4; Mrs M. A. Prentiss (USA) d. E. M. Wilford 6-4 6-2; **L. Brough** (2) (USA) d. E. F. Lombard (IRE) 6-1 6-1.

THIRD ROUND: du Pont (1) d. Blaisse-Terwindt 6-2 6-2; Dawson-Scott d. Keith-Steele 6-2 6-4; **Bostock** (5) d. Hoahing 6-1 6-2; Muller d. Boegner 2-6 6-4 7-5; **Hart** (4) d. Lines 6-1 6-4; Curry d. Scofield 7-5 6-4; **Landry** (7) d. Tuckey 6-1 6-1; Thomas d. Peterdy 6-1 4-6 6-1; Quertier d. Blair 6-8 6-0 ret'd; **Summers** (6) d. Weiwers 6-0 6-1;

Halford d. Passingham 6-3 6-0; **Todd** (3) d. Bocquet 6-4 6-0; Kormoczy de Meulemeester 3-6 6-2 6-1; **Fry** (8) d. Hilton 6-1 1-6 6-2; Middleton d. Brighton 3-6 6-2 6-2; **Brough** (2) d. Prentis 6-1 4-6 6-1.

FOURTH ROUND	QUARTER-FINALS	SEMI-FINALS	FINAL	CHAMPION
du Pont (1)	**du Pont** (1)			
Dawson-Scott	6-2 6-2	**du Pont** (1)		
Bostock (5)	**Bostock** (5)	7-5 6-3		
Muller	6-2 2-6 7-5		**Hart** (4)	
Hart (4)	**Hart** (4)		6-4 2-6 6-3	
Curry	6-2 6-3	**Hart** (4)		
Landry (7)	**Landry** (7)	6-0 6-2		
Thomas	6-3 8-6			**Brough** (2)
Quertier	Quertier			6-3 8-6
Summers (6)	7-5 6-2	**Todd** (3)		
Halford	**Todd** (3)	6-2 6-4		
Todd (3)	6-3 6-3		**Brough** (2)	
Kormoczy	**Fry** (8)		6-3 7-5	
Fry (8)	4-6 6-4 6-4	**Brough** (2)		
Middleton	**Brough** (2)	3-1 ret'd		
Brough (2)	6-0 6-1			

OTHER FINALS

GENTLEMEN'S DOUBLES: Final — J. E. Bromwich (A)/F. A. Sedgman (A) d. T. Brown (USA)/G. Mulloy (USA) 5-7 7-5 7-5 9-7.

LADIES' DOUBLES: Final — A. L. Brough (USA)/Mrs W. du Pont (USA) d. D. J. Hart (USA)/Mrs P. C. Todd (USA) 6-3 3-6 6-3.

MIXED DOUBLES: Final — J. E. Bromwich (A)/A. L. Brough (USA) d. F. A. Sedgman (A)/D. J. Hart (USA) 6-2 3-6 6-3.

GENTLEMEN'S SINGLES PLATE: Final — F. Ampon (PH) d. H. Weiss (ARG) 11-9 6-4.

LADIES' SINGLES PLATE: Final — Mrs H. Weiss (ARG) d. E. M. Wilford 6-1 5-7 7-5.

BOYS' INVITATION SINGLES (Round Robin): **Final** — S. Stockenberg (SW) d. D. Vad (HU) 6-0 6-8 5-7 6-4 6-2.

GIRLS' INVITATION SINGLES (Round Robin): **Final** — O. Miskova (CZ) d. V. Rigollet (SWZ) 6-4 6-2.

GENTLEMEN'S SINGLES

1949

FIRST ROUND: R. Gonzales (2) (USA) d. J. Brichant (B) 6-3 6-2 6-3; C. Grandet (F) d. N. R. Lewis 2-6 6-3 1-6 6-2 7-5; N. Kitovitz d. H. Billington 6-4 3-6 1-6 6-3 6-4; M. Coen (E) d. N. E. Hessen (NOR) 6-4 0-6 6-3 6-4; G. E. Brown (A) d. F. Wallis 6-0 6-3 6-1; F. Beernink (NTH) d. A. T. England 0-6 7-5 4-6 7-5 6-0; G. P. Jackson (IRE) d. E. Mandelbaum (E) 6-1 6-3 7-5; F. Ampon (PH) d. J. R. Mansell 6-0 6-2 6-2; **J. Drobny** (CZ) d. L. E. Cater 6-0 6-2 6-2; J. Thomas (F) d. A. Hamburger 8-6 6-1 6-2; B. Patty (USA) d. M. Kizlink 6-1 6-4 6-3; Lord Ronaldshay d. b. Royds 2-6 6-4 6-1 7-5; M. del Bello (IT) d. W. Skonecki (POL) w.o.; A. Stolpa (HU) d. J. Ducos (F) 6-3 6-1 5-7 6-4; J. Bartroli (SP) d. P. Milojkovic (YU) w.o.; N. M. Cockburn (SA) d. A. D. L. Hunter (NZ) 6-1 6-2 6-0; **R. Falkenburg** (4) (USA) d. D. Mitic (YU) 6-2 2-6 8-6 6-4; E. J. David d. G. E. Godsell 6-4 3-6 7-9 6-2 3-2 ret'd; M. Matous (CZ) d. E. C. Ford 3-6 6-4 6-2 6-3; J. Asboth (HU) d. B. Kozeluh (D) 6-2 6-1 6-3; A. C. Van Swol (NTH) d. H. F. Walton 4-6 7-5 6-1 6-3; R. Abdesselam (F) d. H. Huonder (SWZ) 6-3 6-3 3-6 6-2; R. Balbiers (IN) d. H. Redl (A) 6-1 6-0; T. Haanes (NOR) d. P. Geelhand (B) 1-6 6-2 11-9 5-7 6-4; **J. E. Bromwich** (5) (A) d. J. J. McArdle (IRE) 6-1 6-1 6-0; J. Krajcik (CZ) d. R. Colin (F) 2-6 4-6 6-4 6-4 6-3; H. T. Baxter d. M. F. Mohtadi (IN) 8-6 6-3 6-4; E. E. Fannin (SA) d. E. Cochell (USA) 5-7 7-5 6-4 9-7; N. Kumar (IN) d. G. D. Oakley 6-4 11-9 6-4; A. Shaffei (E) d. D. M. Bull 6-4 6-4 5-7 6-4; D. Vad (HU) d. M. F. Ellmer (SWZ) 6-2 6-2 0-6 8-6; R. del Bello (IT) d. S. Salo (FIN) 6-3 6-4 4-6 6-1; J. Peten (B) d. A. Kalman (HU) 6-4 6-3 6-1; A. G.

Roberts d. M. D. Deloford 13-15 6-0 6-2 4-6 6-4; G. Cucelli (IT) d. A. Huber (AU) 6-3 6-1 6-4; A. J. Mottram d. M. Taverne (CH) 6-1 6-1 6-1; J. Palada (YU) d. D. G. Snart 4-6 10-8 1-6 6-0 6-3; J. Morison (USA) d. C. Maas (C) 6-2 6-3 6-3; T. Johansson (SW) d. J. Staubo (NOR) 4-6 6-3 6-4 6-1; **E. W. Sturgess** (7) (SA) d. C. Spychala (PA) 6-0 6-2 6-3; G. Worthington (A) d. A. L. Van Meegeren (NTH) 6-0 6-1 8-6; W. Destremau (F) d. E. Bjerre (D) 6-2 6-3 3-6 4-6 6-3; P. Forsman (FIN) d. P. E. Hare 6-2 4-6 4-6 6-4 6-0; J. E. Harper (A) d. D. A. Samaai (SA) 6-1 6-4 6-3; S. L. R. Sawhney (IN) d. D. V. Connor (SA) 6-4 6-2 6-3; R. P. Hanna (USA) d. R. F. Egan (IRE) 6-3 6-4 3-6 6-3; O. W. Sidwell (A) d. S. G. F. Nimr (E) 6-1 6-1; **F. Parker** (3) (USA) d. H. Weiss (ARG) 6-0 6-1 6-2; C. A. Kemp (IRE) d. G. R. B. Meredith 6-2 6-0 6-2; P. Washer (B) d. D. C. Coombe (NZ) 6-1 6-0; H. E. Weatherall d. W. A. Manahan 6-1 6-1 6-1; C. F. O. Lister d. J. Charanjiva (IN) 6-4 6-4 6-1; D. W. Butler d. M. Branovic (YU) 6-3 6-3 7-5; V. Canepele (IT) d. R. G. Reeve 6-2 6-2 6-2; F. Puncec (YU) d. W. C. Choy (CHI) 6-4 6-2 6-0; **F. Sedgman** (8) (A) d. G. B. Leyton 6-1 6-3 6-2; W. Robertson (USA) d. A. J. N. Starte 6-4 9-7 6-0; V. Cernik (CZ) d. G. L. Paish 8-6 6-3 1-6 6-2; P. Remy (F) d. C. J. Hovell 6-1 6-3 6-0; S. Levy (SA) d. E. Sohikish (IN) 6-0 6-2 6-0; R. E. Carter d. W. J. Moss 3-6 1-6 1; R. Buser (SWZ) d. R. V. Gotto (IRE) 6-2 6-1; K. Feher (HU) d. J. R. Frolik (USA) 6-2 6-3 6-1; **F. R. Schroeder** (1) (USA) d. G. Mulloy (USA) 3-6 9-11 6-1 6-0 7-5.

SECOND ROUND: Gonzales (2) d. Grandet 6-4 6-3 6-4; Coen d. Kitovitz 6-1 6-3 4-6 8-6; Brown d. Beernink 6-0 6-2 6-1; Ampon d. Jackson 6-2 7-5 6-1; **Drobny** (6) d. Thomas 9-7 6-2 6-1; Patty d. Lord Ronaldshay 7-5 6-2 6-1; M. del Bello d. Stolpa 6-3 6-4; Cockburn d. Bartroli 6-1 6-3 6-2; **Falkenburg** (4) d. David 6-3 6-1 6-2; Asboth d. Matous 7-5 6-1 6-1; Van Swol d. Abdesselam 3-6 1-6 6-2 7-5 13-11; Balbiers d. Haanes 6-4 6-0 3-6 6-1; **Bromwich** (5) d. Krajcik 6-1 6-1 6-1; Fannin d. Baxter 6-3 6-4 6-2; Kumar d. Shaffei 6-3 1-6 6-4 7-9 6-1; R. del Bello d. Vad 6-0

6-1 3-6 6-4; Peten d. Roberts 6-4 7-5 6-4; Cucelli d. Mottram 5-7 11-9 8-6 6-2; Palada d. Morison 6-4 6-4 6-1; **Sturgess** (7) d. Johansson 4-6 6-4 6-2 8-6; Worthington d. Destremau 6-2 6-0 6-3; Harper d. Forsman 8-6 6-3 6-2; **Parker** (3) d. Sidwell 4-6 6-4 6-3 6-4; Washer d. Kemp 6-2 6-4 6-3; Lister d. Weatherall 6-2 8-6 6-4; Canepele d. Butler 6-4 6-4 7-5; **Sedgman** (8) d. Puncec 6-2 6-4 6-0; Cernik d. Robertson 6-2 6-1 6-3; Levy d. Remy 6-3 3-6 4-6 6-1 6-0; Buser d. Carter 5-7 6-1 6-1 6-2; **Schroeder** (1) d. Feher 6-0 6-1 6-4.

THIRD ROUND: Gonzales (2) d. Coen 6-1 6-2 6-4; Brown d. Ampon 6-4 6-2 7-5; **Drobny** (6) d. Patty 6-4 6-8 7-9 6-0 6-2; Cockburn d. M. del Bello 6-0 6-2 6-3; **Falkenburg** (4) d. Asboth 6-4 7-5 2-6 0-6 6-4; Van Swol d. Balbiers 6-3 1-6 7-5 6-4; **Bromwich** (5) d. Fannin 6-1 6-4 6-1; R. del Bello d. Kumar 6-4 6-4 6-0; Cucelli d. Peten 6-3 6-0 6-3;

Sturgess (7) d. Palada 6-2 6-2 6-4; Worthington d. Harper 6-2 5-7 2-6 6-0 6-2; **Parker** (3) d. Hanna 6-2 6-0 6-4; Washer d. Lister 6-1 6-1 6-2; **Sedgman** (8) d. Canepele 6-2 6-2 6-4; Cernik d. Levy 6-2 3-6 6-4 8-6; **Schroeder** (1) d. Buser 6-2 6-3 7-5.

FOURTH ROUND	QUARTER-FINALS	SEMI-FINALS	FINAL	CHAMPION
Gonzales (2)	Brown			
Brown	2-6 6-3 6-2 6-1			
Drobny (6)	**Drobny** (6)	**Drobny** (6)		
Cockburn	6-2 6-3 6-2	2-6 7-5 1-6 6-2 6-4		
Falkenburg (4)	**Falkenburg** (4)		**Drobny** (6)	
Van Swol	7-5 6-0 6-4		6-1 6-3 6-2	
Bromwich (5)	**Bromwich** (5)	**Bromwich** (5)		
R. del Bello	6-1 6-1 6-0	3-6 9-11 6-0 6-0 6-4		**Schroeder** (1)
Cucelli	**Sturgess** (7)			3-6 6-0 6-3 4-6 6-4
Sturgess (7)	6-2 6-4 6-1	**Sturgess** (7)		
Worthington	**Parker** (3)	3-6 6-4 3-6 6-1 6-3		
Parker (3)	6-2 6-3 6-1		**Schroeder** (1)	
Washer	**Sedgman** (8)		3-6 7-5 5-7 6-1 6-2	
Sedgman (8)	6-4 6-4 7-5	**Schroeder** (1)		
Cernik	**Schroeder** (1)	3-6 6-8 6-3 6-2 9-7		
Schroeder (1)	6-3 8-6 8-6			

LADIES' SINGLES

FIRST ROUND: Mrs P. C. Todd (3) (USA) d. N. C. Potts 6-0 6-1; R. F. Woodgate d. V. Boyer (USA) 6-4 5-7 6-2; Mrs O. Anderson (USA) d. Mrs H. Doleschell (AU) 2-6 6-3 6-4; Mrs R. M. Dowdeswell (K) d. Z. J. Lusty w.o.; J. Marcellin (F) d. Mrs J. B. Fulton 6-3 3-6 6-4; M. E. Parker d. Mrs J. J. FitzGibbon (IRE) 6-2 6-2; Mrs B. I. S. Gourlay d. Mrs A. C. Brighton 10-8 2-6 6-2; V. S. White d. V. Rigollet (SWZ) 6-4 6-8 6-3; **P. J. Curry** (8) d. Mrs M. R. King 6-1 6-4; Mrs S. P. Summers (SA) d. Mrs A. Bossi (IT) 7-5 6-3; Mrs J. J. Walker-Smith d. Mrs J. M. Beswick 6-3 6-3; B. Gullbrandsson (SW) d. E. M. Stephens 6-1 6-3; Mrs H. Weiss (ARG) d. B. Venter (SA) 11-9 6-0; Mrs W. H. L. Gordon d. P. Rodgers 6-0 6-2; Mrs T. Long (A) d. Mrs W. H. Durlac 6-1 6-1; M. de Borman (B) d. G. P. Butler (USA) 9-7 6-2; H.

Straubeova (CZ) d. Mrs L. F. Byrne 6-1 6-3; J. R. M. Morgan d. Mrs J. David 3-6 6-3 6-4; Mrs E. Watermeyer (SA) d. Mrs B. N. Quelch 6-3 6-0; Mrs H. R. Phillips d. E. M. Fog (D) 8-6 6-3; Mrs J. B. Parker d. P. Cowney 6-4 3-6 6-2; Mrs C. Boegner (F) d. P. E. Ward 6-0 6-0; Mrs E. W. Dawson-Scott d. A. G. Bates 6-2 6-2; **J. Quertier** (6) d. Mrs N. Scott 6-2 6-2; Mrs H. P. Rihbany (USA) d. Mrs R. Stone 6-1 6-2; K. L. A. Tuckey d. Mrs J. Hibbert 6-1 6-3; J. Gannon d. Mrs H. Bathurst (AU) 6-1 6-2; G. E. Woodgate d. Mrs K. F. Knight 6-3 6-2; G. Hoahing d. J. W. K. Stork 2-6 6-4 6-2; Mrs J. Boutin (F) d. Mrs E. C. Peters 6-2 6-4; E. M. Wilford d. A. V. Mothersole 6-2 5-7 6-1; **G. Moran** (4) (USA) d. Mrs G. Walter 3-6 6-2 6-3.

SECOND ROUND: L. Brough (1) (USA) d. E. A. Middleton 6-1 6-1; Mrs W. C. J. Halford d. Mrs D. L. Coutts 6-3 9-7; E. Sutton d. Mrs F. D. M. Flowerdew 3-6 6-2 6-3; R. Walsh d. M. Buxton-Knight (E) 6-4 3-6 10-8; **Mrs N. Adamson** (7) (F) d. L. Schou-Nielsen (D) 6-1 6-4; Mrs N. W. Blair d. B. Knapp 3-6 7-5 6-1; E. M. Percival d. E. Sutz (SWZ) 6-4 2-6 7-5; Mrs S. H. Hammersley d. H. Stoodley Morgan 7-5 6-3; **Todd** (3) d. Woodgate 6-1 6-2; Dowdeswell d. Anderson 6-3 2-6 6-2; Marcellin d. Parker 6-4 6-2; White d. Gourlay 5-7 6-3 6-2; Summers d. Curry (8) 6-3 7-5; Walker-Smith d. Gullbrandsson 6-1 6-3; Weiss d. Gordon 5-7 8-6 6-2; Long d. de Borman 6-0 6-2; Straubeova d. Morgan 7-5 2-6

7-5; Watermeyer d. Phillips 6-1 6-2; Boegner d. Parker 6-1 6-0; Dawson-Scott d. **Quertier** (6) 6-4 6-4; Rihbany d. Tuckey 6-3 3-6 8-6; Gannon d. Woodgate 6-3 6-0; Hoahing d. Boutin 6-4 6-0; **Moran** (4) d. Wilford 6-1 6-4; Mrs B. E. Hilton d. Mrs A. M. Seghers (F) 7-5 6-2; S. N. Andrews d. K. Keith-Steele 6-3 6-2; A. McGuire (USA) d. A. R. N. Feiron 6-2 6-2; **S. Fry** (5) d. Mrs M. Lagerborg (SW) 6-2 6-2; P. F. Hermsen (NTH) d. E. F. Lombard (IRE) 6-3 6-2; J. Fitch (A) d. P. A. O'Connell 4-6 6-0 6-1; Mrs R. F. Chandler d. F. B. Cooke 6-1 9-7; **Mrs W. du Pont** (2) (USA) d. Mrs G. R. Lines 6-2 6-1.

THIRD ROUND: Brough (1) d. Halford 6-1 6-0; Walsh d. Sutton 6-4 6-4; Blair d. **Adamson** (7) 6-2 7-5; Hammersley d. Percival 7-5 6-2; **Todd** (3) d. Dowdeswell 6-1 6-0; Marcellin d. White 4-6 6-3 6-4; Walker-Smith d. Summers 6-2 6-2; Long d. Weiss 3-6 7-5 6-3; Watermeyer d. Straubeova 6-1 6-2; Dawson-Scott d. Boegner 11-9

0-6 7-5; Rihbany d. Gannon 7-5 7-5; Hoahing d. **Moran** (4) 6-2 5-7 6-3; Hilton d. Andrews 6-1 3-6 6-3; **Fry** (5) d. McGuire 6-3 6-4; Fitch d. Hermsen 6-1 6-1; **du Pont** (2) d. Chandler 6-1 6-1.

FOURTH ROUND	QUARTER-FINALS	SEMI-FINALS	FINAL	CHAMPION
Brough (1)	**Brough** (1)			
Walsh	6-1 6-2	**Brough** (1)		
Blair	Blair	6-2 6-3		
Hammersley	6-3 6-1		**Brough** (1)	
Todd (3)	**Todd** (3)		6-3 6-0	
Marcellin	6-2 6-1	**Todd** (3)		
Walker-Smith	Walker-Smith	3-6 6-4 6-3		
Long	6-1 6-3			**Brough** (1)
Watermeyer	Dawson-Scott			10-8 1-6 10-8
Dawson-Scott	6-4 7-5			
Rihbany	Rihbany	Rihbany		
Hoahing	6-4 6-4	7-5 7-5		
Hilton	Hilton		**du Pont** (2)	
Fry (5)			6-2 6-2	
Fitch	**du Pont** (2)	**du Pont** (2)		
du Pont (2)	6-0 6-1	6-1 6-3		

OTHER FINALS

GENTLEMEN'S DOUBLES: Final — R. A. Gonzales (USA)/F. A. Parker (USA) d. G. Mulloy (USA)/F. R. Schroeder (USA) 6-4 6-4 6-2.
LADIES' DOUBLES: Final — A. L. Brough (USA)/Mrs W. du Pont (USA) d. G. Moran (USA)/Mrs P. C. Todd (USA) 8-6 7-5.
MIXED DOUBLES: Final — E. W. Sturgess (SA)/Mrs S. P. Summers (SA) d. J. E. Bromwich (A)/A. L. Brough (USA) 9-7 9-11 7-5.

GENTLEMEN'S SINGLES PLATE: Final — E. H. Cochell (USA) d. G. P. Jackson (IRE) 4-6 6-3 6-1.
LADIES' SINGLES PLATE: Final — Mrs A. Bossi (IT) d. B. Gullbrandson (SW) 6-0 7-5.
BOYS' INVITATION SINGLES: Final — S. Stockenberg (SW) d. J. A. T. Horn 6-2 6-1.
GIRLS' INVITATION SINGLES: Final — C. Mercelis (B) d. S. Partridge 6-4 6-2.

GENTLEMEN'S SINGLES

FIRST ROUND: F. A. Sedgman (1) (A) d. H. F. Walton 6-4 7-5 6-4; R. Haillet (F) d. R. Guise 4-6 6-2 4-6 6-1 6-3; G. Caccia (IT) d. F. Olozaga (SP) 6-2 6-0 6-1; P. Washer (B) d. J. E. Harper (A) w.o.; **F. Kovaleski** (13) (USA) d. R. G. Reeve 6-2 7-5 9-11 6-2; H. T. Baxter d. J. Delire (B) 6-3 7-5 6-0; N. Nath (IN) d. J. Sanglier (F) 6-4 6-1 6-0; G. Delhomme (F) d. A. Kalman (HU) 6-3 6-1 6-2; **A. Larsen** (7) (USA) d. V. Cernik (E) 8-6 7-5 6-2; L. Bergelin (SW) d. C. A. Kemp (IRE) 6-2 6-3 6-4; P. Molloy (A) d. R. K. Kaley 6-2 4-6 6-4 4-6 7-5; W. J. Smith (NZ) d. E. Mandelbaum (E) 4-6 6-1 6-4 6-2; C. Carmona (PH) d. A. W. Tills (NZ) 5-7 6-3 6-3 5-7 6-2; A. L. van Meegeren (NTH) d. E. C. Ford 2-6 6-4 5-7 6-3 6-4; J. C. Molinari (F) d. C. M. Jones 8-6 8-6 6-0; C. J. Hovell d. P. Milojkovic (YU) 7-5 6-3 8-6; **J. Drobny** (3) (E) d. C. Grandet (F) 6-4 6-3 6-1; D. W. Butler d. Lord Ronaldshay 6-4 7-5 6-2; H. Ampon (PH) d. I. Rinkel (NTH) 6-1 6-1 6-0; T. Ulrich (D) d. J. G. Rutherglen 6-4 6-4 7-5; **K. McGregor** (10) (A) d. D. G. Snart 6-0 6-3 7-5; A. J. N. Starte d. E. J. Filby 7-5 6-2 6-3; A. Huber (AU) d. J. Staubo (NOR) 6-4 7-9 7-5 6-2; I. Tloczynski (POL) d. P. Geelhand (B) 6-4 6-4 6-1; **G. Mulloy** (6) (USA) d. J. Palada (YU) 3-6 6-1 6-1 6-1; N. Kumar (IN) d. G. E. Godsell 6-2 3-6 6-3 6-2; G. L. Paish d. J. D. Hackett (IRE) 2-6 6-2 6-3 6-3 6-0; B. Destremau (F) d. C. Spychala (POL) 6-2 6-2 6-2 6-4; **O. W. Sidwell** (11) (A) d. C. F. O. Lister (D) d. D. Lurie (SA) 6-4 4-6 6-2 6-1; M. G. Rose (A) d. M. Matous 6-3 6-4 6-4; H. Weiss (ARG) d. K. H. Ip (M) 6-8 6-3 6-3 6-4; J. P. A. Linck (NTH) d. D. G. C. Mockridge 6-4 6-1 6-3; A. Najar (E) d. B.

Berthet (F) 7-5 6-3 2-6 1-6 6-1; J. Brichant (B) d. M. Branovic (YU) 0-6 6-4 6-1 6-1; **V. Seixas** (12) (USA) d. S. Davidson (SW) 6-4 3-6 6-1 6-3; S. C. Misra (IN) d. G. R. B. Meredith 6-3 6-2 6-1; H. Hopman (A) d. K. Nielsen (D) 8-6 6-3 6-3; P. E. Hare d. L. E. Cater 6-3 6-3 6-1; **J. E. Bromwich** (8) (A) d. M. Murphy (IRE) 6-0 6-2 6-2; A. J. Mottram d. G. L. Ward 6-0 6-0 6-1; T. Trabert (USA) d. B. W. Rooke (SA) 6-4 6-4 6-2; J. Haanes (NOR) d. R. E. Carter 6-3 6-3 6-1; **G. E. Brown** (9) (A) d. A. Shafei (E) 6-1 6-1 6-2 6-3; H. Billington d. B. E. Crouch 6-3 6-2 8-6; H. Wilton (NTH) d. C. R. Fawcus 6-3 2-6 6-8 6-1 6-3; A. G. Roberts d. P. Chatrier (F) 3-6 6-2 6-2 3-6 6-4; **E. W. Sturgess** (4) (SA) d. J. A. T. Horn 6-2 6-2 6-0; N. E. Hessen (NOR) d. H. Redl (AU) 3-6 6-3 6-4 6-1; S. Lie (NOR) d. E. J. David 6-4 8-4 6-6-3 6-1 7-5; A. C. van Swol (NTH) d. V. Canepele (IT) 6-2 9-7 5-7 2-6 6-4; **D. K. Bose** (15) (IN) d. F. R. Mott-Trille (JAM) 6-3 11-9 6-1; D. M. Bull d. H. E. Weatherall 4-6 4-6 6-2; J. Ducos (F) d. G. I. Pettigrew 12-14 6-3 6-3 6-2; S. L. R. Sawhny (IN) d. F. Wallis 2-6 6-3 6-2; **B. Patty** (5) (USA) d. Mrs Deyro (PH) 3-6 6-1 6-2 9-7; A. K. Quist (A) d. D. Mitic (YU) 6-0 6-2 6-3; D. Scharenguivel d. J. P. Blondel (SWZ) 5-7 8-6 7-5 6-3; E. Morea (ARG) d. A. M. Hamburger 6-1 6-3 6-3; **I. Dorfman** (14) (USA) d. J. Bartroli (SP) 6-0 6-3 6-2; T. Johansson (SW) d. J. Peten (B) 6-3 6-0 6-4; G. Worthington (A) d. G. D. Oakley 7-5 6-2 6-2; M. Coen (E) d. M. F. Mohtadi (IN) 3-6 6-3 6-1 4-6 6-2; **W. Talbert** (2) (USA) d. N. Kitovitz 6-2 6-2 6-4.

SECOND ROUND: Sedgman (1) d. Haillet 6-4 8-6 6-2; Washer d. Caccia 8-6 6-3 6-4; **Kovaleski** (13) d. Baxter 3-6 6-2 6-2 6-4; Nath d. Delhomme 6-1 6-2 6-3; **Larsen** (7) d. Bergelin 6-3 5-7 7-5 7-5; Molloy d. Smith 8-6 6-0 2-6 6-3; Carmona d. van Meegeren 6-4 7-5 3-6 6-1; Molinari d. Hovell 6-3 7-5 6-4; **Drobny** (3) d. Butler 6-4 6-2 6-4; Ampon d. Ulrich 6-8 6-3 6-0 6-4; **McGregor** (10) d. Starte 6-1 6-3 6-3; Huber d. Tloczynski 6-3 7-5 8-6; **Mulloy** (6) d. Kumar 6-2 6-4 12-10; Destremau d. Paish 6-4 6-1 6-4; **Sidwell** (11) d. del Bello 6-4 6-1 6-2; Rose d. Weiss 6-4 6-4 7-5;

Linck d. Najar 6-4 6-3 6-4; **Seixas** (12) d. Brichant 6-4 6-3 6-3; Hopman d. Misra 1-6 6-3 6-1 4-6 8-6; **Bromwich** (8) d. Hare 6-2 6-0 6-0; Mottram d. Trabert 6-1 6-4 6-1; **Brown** (9) d. Haanes 10-8 6-2 6-3; Billington d. Wilton 6-1 7-5 11-9; **Sturgess** (4) d. Roberts 7-5 6-4 6-1; van Swol d. Bose 6-3 6-1 6-4 ret'd; **Patty** (5) d. Sawhny 6-2 6-0 6-4; Quist d. Scharenguivel 3-6 6-4 7-5; **Dorfman** (14) d. Morea 6-4 6-2 6-4; Johansson d. Worthington 7-5 2-6 6-4 2-6 8-6; **Talbert** (2) d. Coen 6-1 6-3 6-0.

THIRD ROUND: Sedgman (1) d. Washer 6-3 6-2 6-3; **Kovaleski** (13) d. Nath 6-4 8-6 6-3; **Larsen** (7) d. Molloy 6-2 6-3 7-5; Molinari d. Carmona 7-5 1-6 6-2 6-2; **Drobny** (3) d. Ampon 6-3 6-4 6-2; **McGregor** (10) d. Huber 6-1 6-2 6-3; **Mulloy** (6) d. Destremau 6-3 6-2 6-3; **Sidwell** (11) d. Rose 9-7 6-4 4-6 7-5; **Seixas** (12) d. Linck 6-1 6-4 6-3;

Bromwich (8) d. Hopman 6-0 6-1 6-3; **Brown** (9) d. Mottram 1-6 6-2 5-7 6-4 6-3; **Sturgess** (4) d. Billington 6-1 6-3 6-2; van Swol d. Lie 6-1 6-2 6-4; **Patty** (5) d. Bull 6-3 7-5; Quist d. **Dorfman** (14) 6-4 6-2 6-2; **Talbert** (2) d. Johansson 6-1 3-6 6-2 6-2.

FOURTH ROUND	QUARTER-FINALS	SEMI-FINALS	FINAL	CHAMPION
Sedgman (1)	**Sedgman** (1)			
Kovaleski (13)	6-3 6-3 6-4	**Sedgman** (1)		
Larsen (7)	**Larsen** (7)	8-10 5-7 7-5 6-3 7-5		
Molinari	6-1 6-3 6-1		**Sedgman** (1)	
Drobny (3)	**Drobny** (3)		3-6 3-6 6-3 7-5 6-2	
McGregor (10)	6-3 6-2 7-5	**Drobny** (3)		
Mulloy (6)	**Mulloy** (6)	6-3 6-4 6-4		
Sidwell (11)	6-4 6-3 7-5			**Patty** (5)
Seixas (12)	**Seixas** (12)			6-1 8-10 6-2 6-3
Bromwich (8)	6-1 7-5 4-6 6-3	**Seixas** (12)		
Brown (9)	**Sturgess** (4)	9-7 6-8 3-6 6-2 7-5		
Sturgess (4)	6-2 3-6 6-3 6-4		**Patty** (5)	
van Swol	**Patty** (5)		6-3 5-7 6-2 7-5	
Patty (5)	8-6 6-4 8-6	**Patty** (5)		
Quist	**Talbert** (2)	3-6 6-4 6-2 6-3		
Talbert (2)	6-3 6-3 6-2			

LADIES' SINGLES

FIRST ROUND: D. Hart (3) (USA) d. K. L. A. Tuckey 6-4 8-6; Mrs B. Sanden (SW) d. Mrs R. M. Dowdeswell 6-3 6-4; G. C. Hoahing d. Mrs M. Dubois (F) 6-2 6-3; Mrs P. M. Johns d. Mrs J. David 6-4 6-0; Mrs H. P. Rihbany (USA) d. Mrs E. C. Peters 6-0 6-4; N. Chaffee (USA) d. M. Barnett (USA) 6-3 6-3; Mrs S. H. Hammersley d. Mrs G. Walter 6-3 6-4; Mrs J. Hibbert d. Mrs D. L. Coutts 6-3 6-4; Mrs H. Weiss (ARG) d. **Mrs A. Bossi** (8) (IT) 6-1 5-7 6-3; Mrs A. Varin (F) d. R. Walsh 8-6 10-8; Mrs D. R. Bocquet d. J. W. K. Stork 6-4 6-8 9-7; R. F. Woodgate d. Mrs G. R. Lines 8-6 9-7; R. Bulleid d. Mrs M. Galtier (F) 3-6 6-2 6-3; B. Scofield (USA) d. H. Stoodley-Morgan 6-4 6-1; Mrs E. W. Dawson Scott d. Mrs A. T. P. Luxton 6-3 7-5; Mrs G. Jamain (F) d. A. Ross Dilley 6-4 7-5; P. E. Ward d. Mrs M. Van Leer (B) 6-3 6-1;

Mrs T. Long (A) d. E. A. Middleton 6-0 6-0; Mrs L. Schmier (NTH) d. A. M. Carlisle 2-6 6-3 6-4; D. Head (USA) d. Mrs H. E. F. Behr 6-2 6-2; G. E. Woodgate d. Mrs L. F. Byrne 6-4 6-2; Mrs J. M. Wagstaff d. Mrs J. B. Parker 6-1 2-6 7-5; N. Morrison (USA) d. P. L. Cowley 6-1 6-2; Mrs J. M. Knapp 6-3 6-1; Mrs R. D. McKelvie d. A. G. Bates 6-4 6-3; J. R. M. Morgan d. M. E. Parker 9-7 6-4; Mrs R. F. Chandler d. Mrs J. M. Beswick 6-3 6-4; Mrs M. R. King d. M. A. Emerson 5-7 7-5 6-0; E. M. Wilford d. Mrs H. R. Phillips 7-5 6-4; P. Rodgers d. H. M. Fletcher 6-3 6-0; L. M. Cornell d. N. Liebert 6-2 6-4; **Mrs P. C. Todd** (4) (USA) d. Mrs G. M. Worrall 6-0 6-0.

SECOND ROUND: L. Brough (1) (USA) d. Mrs A. C. Brighton 6-0 6-1; Mrs A. J. Mottram d. P. F. Hermsen (NTH) 6-2 6-1; E. M. S. Andrews d. Mrs C. G. Moeller 4-6 6-2 6-4; Mrs G. Bucaille (F) d. B. Rosenquest (USA) 8-6 7-5; **S. Fry** (5) (USA) d. J. S. V. Partridge 6-3 6-4; Mrs R. Anderson (USA) d. Mrs J. A. Quelch 6-2 6-1; E. F. Lombard (IRE) d. Mrs B. W. Knott 9-7 5-7 6-1; P. J. Curry d. J. M. Trower 4-6 6-2 6-1; **Hart** (3) d. Sanden 6-1 6-0; Hoahing d. Johns 6-4 6-3; Chaffee d. Rihbany 6-1 6-3; Hammersley d. Hibbert 7-5 6-1; Weiss d. Varin 6-1 6-1; Bocquet d. Woodgate 6-2 6-1; Scofield d. Bulleid 6-0 6-1; Dawson Scott d. Jamain 6-0 6-3; Long d. Ward 6-2 6-2; Head d. Schmier 6-2 6-0;

Woodgate d. Wagstaff 6-1 6-0; **Harrison** (6) d. Morrison 6-3 7-5; McKelvie d. Morgan 4-0 6-3; King d. Chandler 6-2 6-3; Rodgers d. Wilford 5-7 6-2 6-4; **Todd** (4) d. Cornell 6-1 6-2; Mrs W. C. J. Halford d. Mrs J. J. Fitzgibbon (IRE) 7-5 6-1; Mrs J. Amouretti (F) d. S. Glietenberg (SA) 6-4 6-2; Mrs A. M. Seghers (F) d. E. Neumann (AU) 6-0 7-5; **G. Moran** (7) (USA) d. Mrs M. Lagerborg (SW) 6-4 8-6; L. Manfredi (IT) d. G. Kornfeld (IS) 6-2 4-6 6-3; J. Quertier d. Mrs M. Matous 6-2 6-2; Mrs J. J. Walker-Smith d. V. Rigollet (SWZ) 6-2 6-2; **Mrs W. du Pont** (2) (USA) d. F. B. Cooke 6-0 6-3.

THIRD ROUND: Brough (1) d. Mottram 9-7 6-2; Andrews d. Bucaille 2-6 7-5 6-2; **Fry** (5) d. Anderson 6-1 6-1; Curry d. Lombard 6-4 7-5; **Hart** (3) d. Hoahing 6-2 6-3; Chaffee d. Hammersley 6-2 6-0; Weiss d. Bocquet 6-4 6-3; Scofield d. Dawson Scott 6-1 7-5; Head d. Long 6-3 5-7 6-2; **Harrison** (6) d. Woodgate 9-7 7-5; McKelvie d. King 6-4 6-4;

Todd (4) d. Rodgers 6-0 6-1; Halford d. Amouretti 6-2 6-3; **Moran** (7) d. Seghers 6-4 6-2; Quertier d. Manfredi 6-0 6-0; **du Pont** (2) d. Walker-Smith 6-3 6-3.

FOURTH ROUND	QUARTER-FINALS	SEMI-FINALS	FINAL	CHAMPION
Brough (1)	**Brough** (1)			
Andrews	6-0 6-0	**Brough** (1)		
Fry (5)	**Fry** (5)	2-6 6-3 6-0		
Curry	6-2 7-5		**Brough** (1)	
Hart (3)	**Hart** (3)		6-4 6-3	
Chaffee	6-2 6-2	**Hart** (3)		
Weiss	Scofield	6-1 6-1		
Scofield	6-4 8-6			**du Pont** (2)
Head	**Harrison** (6)			6-1 3-6 6-1
Harrison (6)	6-3 6-2	**Todd** (4)		
McKelvie	**Todd** (4)	6-2 6-2		
Todd (4)	6-1 6-2		**du Pont** (2)	
Halford	**Moran** (7)		8-6 4-6 8-6	
Moran (7)	6-2 6-1	**du Pont** (2)		
Quertier	**du Pont** (2)	6-4 6-4		
du Pont (2)	6-2 6-2			

OTHER FINALS

GENTLEMEN'S DOUBLES: Final — J. E. Bromwich (A)/A. K. Quist (A) d. G. E. Brown (A)/O. W. Sidwell (A) 7-5 3-6 6-3 3-6 6-2.

LADIES' DOUBLES: Final — A. L. Brough (USA)/Mrs W. du Pont (USA) d. S. J. Fry (USA)/D. J. Hart (USA) 6-4 5-7 6-1.

MIXED DOUBLES: Final — E. W. Sturgess (SA)/A. L. Brough (USA) d. G. E. Brown (A)/Mrs P. C. Todd (USA) 11-9 6-1 6-4.

GENTLEMEN'S SINGLES PLATE: Final — G. L. Paish d. J. Brichant (B) 6-4 6-4.

LADIES' SINGLES PLATE: Final — K. L. A. Tuckey d. B. Rosenquest (USA) 6-4 6-1.

BOYS' INVITATION SINGLES: Final — J. A. T. Horn d. K. Moubarek (E) 6-0 6-2.

GIRLS' INVITATION SINGLES: Final — L. Cornell d. A. Winther (NOR) 6-3 6-2.

GENTLEMEN'S SINGLES

1951

FIRST ROUND: F. A. Sedgman (1) (A) d. R. Deyro (PH) 6-4 6-3 6-4; S. Davidson (SW) d. H. C. Bernstein 6-2 6-0 3-6 6-3; S. Lie (NOR) d. G. P. Jackson (IRE) 6-8 3-6 7-5 6-3 6-1; S. Clark (USA) d. R. Sibert (USA) 6-0 6-0 6-2; **G. Mulloy** (9) (USA) d. P. Washer (B) 13-15 4-6 6-3 6-4 6-1; J. A. T. Horn d. D. Scharenguivel (CEY) 6-2 6-1 3-6 7-5; H. Weiss (ARG) d. M. D. Deloford 6-4 2-6 9-7 6-2; F. Gardini (IT) d. H. T. Baxter 4-6 6-2 6-1 6-2; **H. Flam** (5) (USA) d. N. Kumar (IN) 6-1 6-2 6-2; C. Spychala (POL) d. G. L. Ward 6-2 6-3 6-3; H. Billington d. P. E. Hare 6-4 6-2 6-1; J. Molinari (F) d. S. Levy (SA) 3-6 6-4 4-6 6-0 6-4; P. Chatrier (F) d. J. Bartroli (SP) 8-6 8-6 4-6 6-3; A. Huber (AU) d. P. Milojkovic (YU) 6-2 6-1 3-6 2-6 6-3; A. C. van Swol (NTH) d. D. G. Snart 6-0 6-1 10-8; A. Shafei (E) d. A. Kalman (HU) 6-4 6-4 6-4; **A. Larsen** (3) (USA) d. M. G. Rose (A) 6-1 6-2 0-6 6-1; G. L. Paish d. H. Burrows (USA) 6-3 6-3 6-2; W. E. Garrett (USA) d. M. del Bello (IT) d. K. 6-4 6-0 7-5; J. Palada (YU) d. W. T. Hough 6-1 6-0 6-1; M. Matous d. R. Haillet (F) 1-6 2-6 6-2 6-1 6-0; H. F. Walton d. R. G. Reeve 6-3 11-9 6-4; T. Johansson (SW) d. E. Balestra (SWZ) 6-0 6-0 6-1; D. M. Bull d. M. F. Mohtadi (IN) 4-6 2-6 9-7 6-3 6-3; **R. Savitt** (6) (USA) d. N. M. Cockburn (SA) 6-2 6-2 6-2; E. J. David d. Lord Ronaldshay 6-0 6-4 6-4; K. Nielsen (D) d. B. H. Macken (C) 6-3 7-9 6-3 6-2; J. Peten (B) d. C. R. Fawcus 6-2 4-6 6-2 6-3; V. Skonecki d. J. R. Mansell 7-5 6-1 6-1; I. Tloczynski (POL) d. J. Roquette (POR) w.o.; J. Asboth (HU) d. E. Buchholtz (G) 4-6 10-8 6-3 6-2; V. Cernik (E) d. K. H. Ip (HK) 6-4 4-6 4-6 7-5 6-2; B. Destremau (F) d. I. Devroe (B) 6-2

6-3 6-2; R. del Bello (IT) d. C. Carmona (PH) 1-6 6-3 6-8 6-4 6-2; D. H. Shaw d. J. Morison (USA) 3-6 6-4 6-2 5-7 6-1; G. D. Oakley d. C. B. Ong (M) 6-3 6-4 8-6; B. Axelsson (SW) d. B. E. Crouch 6-1 6-2 6-4; S. Davidson (SA) d. F. R. Mott-Trille (JAM) 6-4 6-4 6-4; D. W. Candy (A) d. A. G. Roberts 8-6 6-2 6-3; **E. W. Sturgess** (8) (SA) d. R. E. Carter 6-1 6-0 6-3; S. Stockenberg (SW) d. J. D. Hackett (IRE) 6-4 6-4 6-7 7-5; A. Segal (SA) d. J. Spitzer (SWZ) 6-4 6-3 6-4; C. F. O. Lister d. M. Coen (E) 6-0 6-1 6-4; A. Vieira (BR) d. D. P. Tregonning (A) 7-5 6-4 8-6; W. T. Anderson d. H. A. Clark 4-6 6-2 6-3; V. Petrovic (YU) d. R. T. Connor (SA) 7-5 2-6 6-1 5-7 6-4; H. Richardson (USA) d. A. E. Dehnert (NTH) 6-2 6-3 6-2; **B. Patty** (4) (USA) d. D. A. Lurie (SA) 6-1 6-1 6-4; I. F. Rinkel (NTH) d. B. P. Hyks 6-2 6-0 6-0; L. H. Norgarb (SA) d. J. F. Kupferburger (SA) 7-5 6-3 6-0; P. Remy (F) d. M. Branovic (YU) 6-3 7-5 6-2; J. W. Cawthorn (A) d. B. A. Haughton (IRE) 6-2 8-6 7-5; H. Redl (AU) d. P. Becker (F) 6-1 1-4 6-6 6-0; D. A. Samaai (SA) d. M. Lemasson (F) 6-4 4-6 6-3 2-6 6-4; L. Main (E) d. J. E. Barrett 6-0 6-2 6-1; **K. McGregor** (7) (A) d. N. Nath (IN) 8-6 6-1 3-6 6-2; G. Cucelli (IT) d. N. Kitovitz 6-2 6-2 6-3; A. W. Tills (NZ) d. G. E. Godsell 6-1 6-4 1-6 6-4; F. Ampon (PH) d. R. Guise 6-1 6-0 6-0; **L. Bergelin** (10) (SW) d. A. J. N. Starte 6-2 6-1 6-0; A. J. Mottram d. F. Soehol (NOR) 6-2 6-2 6-4; H. Rochon (C) d. T. A. Slawek 6-0 6-2 6-0; T. Ulrich (D) d. J. Brichant (B) 7-5 6-4 6-3; **J. Drobny** (2) (E) d. G. von Cramm (G) 9-7 6-4 6-4.

SECOND ROUND: Sedgman (1) d. Davidson 6-4 7-9 6-4 6-2; Clark d. Lie 6-4 6-4 7-5; **Mulloy** (9) d. Horn 6-4 6-0 6-4; Gardini d. Weiss 2-3 8-6 6-4; **Flam** (5) d. Spychala 6-0 6-1 6-2; Billington d. Molinari 6-2 6-3 4-6 8-6; Chatrier d. Huber 6-4 2-6 1-6 8-6; van Swol d. Shafei 7-5 6-3 6-1; **Larsen** (3) d. Paish 6-3 6-7; Garrett d. Palada 6-3 6-2; Matous d. Walton 6-1 6-3 6-2; Johansson d. Bull 6-1 5-7 6-4 6-4; **Savitt** (6) d. David 6-1 6-1 6-1; Nielsen d. Peten 6-4 6-1 7-5; Skonecki d. Tloczynski 6-3 6-4 6-4; Asboth d. Cernik 6-1 9-11 1-6 11-9 6-3; Destremau

d. del Bello 2-6 6-4 6-4 9-7; Oakley d. Shaw 6-1 6-4 6-3; Axelsson d. Davidson 6-3 6-3 6-2; **Sturgess** (8) d. Candy 6-3 4-6 8-6 6-2; Stockenberg d. Segal 6-1 7-5 4-6 6-4; Vieira d. Lister 6-4 6-4 1-6 6-3; Petrovic d. Anderson 2-6 8-6 6-0 6-6 6-1; Richardson d. Patty 2-6 6-0 6-2 7-5; Remy d. Norgarb 3-6 6-4 6-4 3-3 6-2; **McGregor** (7) d. Samaai 8-1 6-4 6-1; Cucelli d. Tills 1-6 6-1 6-4; **Bergelin** (10) d. Ampon 2-6 2-6 6-2 9-7 6-3; Mottram d. Rochon 6-0 6-3 7-5; **Drobny** (2) d. Ulrich 11-9 1-6 6-3 6-4.

THIRD ROUND: Sedgman (1) d. Clark 8-6 11-9 6-3; Gardini d. Mulloy (9) 7-5 3-6 6-4 6-4; **Flam** (5) d. Billington 6-3 6-4 6-4; van Swol d. Chatrier 6-4 6-3 6-4; **Larsen** (3) d. Garrett 6-3 3-6 6-3; Johansson d. Matous 6-3 9-7 6-4; **Savitt** (6) d. Nielsen 6-4 1-6 6-3 8-10 6-4; Asboth d. Skonecki 7-5 3-6 10-8 4-6 6-2; Destremau d. Oakley 6-4 6-1 6-4;

Sturgess (8) d. Axelsson 4-6 6-0 6-4 6-2; Vieira d. Stockenberg 8-6 6-3 8-6; Richardson d. Petrovic 2-6 6-0 6-2 7-5; Remy d. Norgarb 3-6 6-4 6-3 3-3 6-2; **McGregor** (7) d. Samaai 8-1 6-4 6-1; **Bergelin** (10) d. Cucelli 5-7 6-2 6-4 6-3; Mottram d. **Drobny** (2) 5-7 6-4 2-6 7-5 8-6.

FOURTH ROUND	QUARTER-FINALS	SEMI-FINALS	FINAL	CHAMPION
Sedgman (1)	**Sedgman** (1)			
Gardini	6-0 6-2 6-1			
Flam (5)	**Flam** (5)	**Flam** (5)		
van Swol	6-2 6-2 6-3	2-6 1-6 6-3 6-4 7-5		
Larsen (3)	**Larsen** (3)		**Savitt** (6)	
Johansson	6-3 7-5 6-4		1-6 15-13 6-3 6-2	
Savitt (6)	**Savitt** (6)	**Savitt** (6)		
Asboth	6-4 6-2 6-3	6-1 6-4 6-4		
Destremau				**Savitt** (6)
Sturgess (8)	**Sturgess** (8)			6-4 6-4 6-4
Vieira	6-2 6-3 6-2	**Sturgess** (8)		
Richardson	Vieira	6-2 6-0 6-3		
Remy	6-3 1-6 6-3 6-0		**McGregor** (7)	
McGregor (7)	**McGregor** (7)		6-4 3-6 6-3 7-5	
Bergelin (10)	6-4 3-6 6-3 6-4	**McGregor** (7)		
Mottram	**Bergelin** (10)	6-0 4-6 5-7 6-2 6-4		
	6-1 6-0 6-2			

LADIES' SINGLES

FIRST ROUND: D. Hart (3) (USA) d. J. Marcellin (F) 6-2 6-0; Mrs H. Weiss (ARG) d. M. E. Parker 8-6 6-1; Mrs N. M. Bolton (A) d. Mrs N. W. Blair 6-1 6-2; P. J. Curry d. Mrs C. G. Moeller 6-2 6-1; M. P. Harrison d. Mrs J. B. Parker 6-2 7-5; Mrs W. H. L. Gordon (UG) d. E. M. Wilford 6-2 6-1; R. J. Bulleid d. Mrs J. Hibbert 6-4 7-5; J. Quertier d. Mrs R. Hauknes (NOR) 6-1 6-3; **N. Chaffee** (7) (USA) d. Mrs J. M. Lloyd 4-6 6-2 6-3; E. G. Attwood (NZ) d. M. S. White 6-3 3-6 6-2; A. McGuire (USA) d. Mrs A. H. Thomas 6-2 12-10; Mrs F. Bartlett (SA) d. Mrs D. W. Gotla 6-3 6-2; R. Walsh d. A. G. Bates 2-6 6-4 6-4; Mrs W. C. J. Halford d. C. Mercelis (B) 6-3 6-4; H. M. Fletcher d. M. A. Emerson 4-6 6-3; Mrs B. Sanden (SW) d. J. R. M. Morgan 3-6 6-0 6-4; R. F. Woodgate d. Mrs M. A. Schmier (NTH) 6-3 6-1; Mrs R.

Anderson (USA) d. Mrs G. R. Lines 6-1 6-4; J. W. K. Stork d. Mrs A. C. Brighton 4-6 6-3 6-2; N. Liebert d. Mrs K. F. Knight 6-4 6-4; Mrs D. R. Bocquet d. Mrs H. R. Phillips 6-2 6-2; Mrs S. H. Hammersley d. J. M. Trower 4-6 6-4 6-3; V. Rigollet (SWZ) d. J. Ross Dilley 6-4 6-3; **Mrs J. J. Walker-Smith** (8) d. G. E. Woodgate 6-0 6-4; Mrs P. M. Johns d. B. N. Knapp 2-6 6-4 6-3; L. M. Cornell d. Mrs B. W. Knott 6-2 6-2; Mrs C. F. O. Lister d. Mrs R. A. Gilbert 3-6 6-4 6-1; C. Procter (A) d. Mrs R. D. McKelvie 6-3 6-1; Mrs M. A. Downey (IRE) d. F. Walthew 7-5 6-3; S. Schmitt (F) d. Mrs T. D. Long (A) w.o.; B. Rosenquest (USA) d. Mrs J. A. Starling 6-1 6-2; **S. Fry** (4) (USA) d. J. S. V. Partridge 6-3 6-1.

SECOND ROUND: Mrs W. du Pont (2) (USA) d. Mrs A. J. Mottram 6-3 6-4; Mrs B. Kormoczy (HU) d. B. Penrose (A) 6-4 6-0; E. M. S. Andrews d. S. Speight 8-6 7-5; Mrs E. W. Dawson Scott d. Mrs H. Strecker (AU) w.o.; **B. Baker** (5) (USA) d. A. L. Morgan 6-2 6-0; A. Gibson (USA) d. P. E. Ward 6-0 2-6 6-4; Mrs N. Migliori (IT) d. Mrs R. M. Dowdeswell 6-4 6-3; Mrs M. Matous d. Mrs E. Broz (AU) 6-1 6-4; **Hart** (3) d. Weiss 6-0 7-5; Bolton d. Curry 6-1 6-1; Gordon d. Harrison 7-5 6-3; Quertier d. Bulleid 6-3 6-3; **Chaffee** (7) d. Attwood 6-1 6-0; McGuire d. Bartlett 6-3 3-6 6-4; Halford d. Walsh 6-8 6-2 6-0; Sanden d. Fletcher 6-1 6-1; Anderson d. Woodgate 7-5 6-3; Stork d.

Liebert 6-0 6-2; Bocquet d. Hammersley 6-3 4-6 6-2; **Walker-Smith** (8) d. Rigollet 6-2 6-4; Cornell d. Johns 6-2 2-6 6-0; Procter d. Lister 6-3 7-5; Schmitt d. Downey 2-6 6-2 6-0; **Fry** (4) d. Rosenquest 6-3 7-5; P. F. Hermsen (NTH) d. A. Mortimer 6-2 6-2; Mrs G. Davidson (USA) d. A. M. Carlisle 7-5 6-1; Mrs R. F. Chandler d. Mrs A. T. P. Luxton 6-4 6-3; K. L. A. Tuckey d. M. R. Couquerque (NTH) 6-3 6-2; Mrs J. M. Wagstaff d. Mrs D. L. Coutts 6-2 3-6 6-2; P. A. Lewis d. Mrs E. C. Peters 6-0 9-7; G. C. Hoahing d. V. S. White 6-2 6-2; **L. Brough** (1) (USA) d. Mrs R. L. Scott 6-1 6-2.

THIRD ROUND: du Pont (2) d. Kormoczy 6-1 6-1; Dawson Scott d. Andrews 5-7 6-1 6-3; **Baker** (5) d. Gibson 6-1 6-3; Matous d. Migliori 8-6 6-4; **Hart** (3) d. Bolton 6-4 7-5; Quertier d. Gordon 6-4 6-1; **Chaffee** (7) d. McGuire 6-3 6-3; Sanden d. Halford 6-2 6-1; Anderson d. Stork 2-6 8-6; **Walker-Smith** (8) d. Bocquet 6-3 6-4; Cornell d. Procter

6-4 6-4; **Fry** (4) d. Schmitt 6-1 6-0; Davidson d. Hermsen 6-1 6-2; Tuckey d. Chandler 6-2 6-3; Lewis d. Wagstaff 6-2 6-2; **Brough** (1) d. Hoahing 6-1 6-3.

FOURTH ROUND	QUARTER-FINALS	SEMI-FINALS	FINAL	CHAMPION
du Pont (2)	**du Pont** (2)			
Dawson Scott	7-5 6-2			
Baker (5)	**Baker** (5)	**Baker** (5)		
Matous	10-8 6-3	6-1 4-6 6-3		
Hart (3)	**Hart** (3)		**Hart** (3)	
Quertier	6-4 6-3		6-3 6-1	
Chaffee (7)	**Chaffee** (7)	**Hart** (3)		
Sanden	6-0 6-3	6-3 6-3		
Anderson				**Hart** (3)
Walker-Smith (8)	**Walker-Smith** (8)			6-1 6-0
Cornell	6-4 6-1			
Fry (4)	**Fry** (4)	**Fry** (4)		
Davidson	6-0 6-1	8-6 6-4		
Tuckey	Tuckey		**Fry** (4)	
Lewis	6-2 3-6 6-1		6-4 6-2	
Brough (1)	**Brough** (1)	**Brough** (1)		
	6-1 6-0	5-7 6-1 6-3		

OTHER FINALS

GENTLEMEN'S DOUBLES: Final – K. McGregor (A)/F. A. Sedgman (A) d. J. Drobny (E)/E. W. Sturgess (SA) 3-6 6-2 6-3 3-6 6-3.
LADIES' DOUBLES: Final – S. J. Fry (USA)/D. J. Hart (USA) d. A. L. Brough (USA)/Mrs W. du Pont (USA) 6-3 13-11.
MIXED DOUBLES: Final – F. A. Sedgman (A)/D. J. Hart (USA) d. M. G. Rose (A)/Mrs N. W. Bolton (A) 7-5 6-2.

GENTLEMEN'S SINGLES PLATE: Final – N. M. Cockburn (SA) d. K. H. Ip (HK) 7-5 5-7 10-8.
LADIES' SINGLES PLATE: Final – Mrs F. Bartlett (SA) d. Mrs G. E. Woodgate 3-6 6-1 6-2.
BOYS' INVITATION SINGLES: Final – J. Kupferburger (SA) d. K. Moubarek (E) 8-6 6-4.
GIRLS' INVITATION SINGLES: Final – L. Cornell d. S. Lazzarino (IT) 6-3 6-4.

GENTLEMEN'S SINGLES

1952

FIRST ROUND: F. A. **Sedgman** (1) (A) d. J. Bartroli (SP) 6-1 6-0 6-2; B. J. Katz (SR) d. H. Weiss (ARG) w.o.; P. Washer (B) d. K. H. Ip (HK) 6-1 6-4 6-4; H. Billington d. A. B. Martin (USA) w.o.; F. Ampon (PH) d. **H. Richardson** (11) (USA) 1-6 5-7 6-2 6-3 6-0; D. W. Candy (A) d. R. J. Lee 6-1 6-1 6-0; R. Balbiers (CH) d. S. Salo (FIN) 6-4 6-1 6-4; C. F. O. Lister d. M. Branovic 6-3 6-4 6-3; **E. W. Sturgess** (7) (SA) d. H. Redl (AU) 8-6 6-2 6-0; R. J. E. Mayers (K) d. V. Petrovic (YU) 6-1 6-4 3-6 1-6 6-1; G. Cucelli (IT) d. J. M. Gracie 6-1 6-3 6-1; A. J. Mottram d. H. T. Baxter 6-2 6-4 6-1; T. Johansson (SW) d. **A. Larsen** (9) (USA) 10-8 2-6 6-4 6-2; P. J. Brophy (A) d. J. D. Hackett (IRE) 4-6 6-3 6-4 6-2; H. F. Walton d. A. E. Dehnert (NTH) 4-6 6-3 6-3 6-4; G. Golden (USA) d. P. Guimaraes (BR) 6-2 6-1 6-0; **R. Savitt** (4) (USA) d. N. Kumar (IN) 6-1 6-2 6-0; G. D. Oakley (A) d. C. V. Irvine (SR) 6-3 7-9 6-3 6-2; L. Ayala (CH) d. M. Matous 8-6 7-9 6-2 6-0; H. Likas (USA) d. J. W. Cawthorn (A) 6-2 0-6 6-0 6-2; J. Brichant (B) d. D. W. Butler 6-1 6-3 6-3; I. Tloczynski (POL) d. P. Chatrier (F) 4-6 4-6 6-2 6-0 6-4; D. Capell (SA) d. J. W. Ager (USA) 6-0 6-0 4-6 6-1; B. M. Woodroffe (SA) d. M. F. Mohtadi (IN) 6-4 6-3 5-7 6-2; **M. G. Rose** (8) (A) d. I. G. Ayre (A) 7-5 7-5 8-6; H. Hermann (d) d. P. S. Eisenberg (USA) 6-2 3-6 4-6 6-3 6-4; K. Nielsen (D) d. B. Destremau (F) 6-0 6-1 6-4; J. Palada (YU) d. M. Hime 6-4 6-2 6-4; H. C. Bernstein d. E. Balestra (SWZ) 6-1 3-6 6-1 6-3; F. Gardini (IT) d. E. Saller (BR) 7-5 7-5 6-3; I. F. Rinkel (NTH) d. A. Specht (AU) 6-2 6-1 6-4; S. Clark (USA) d. D. Mitic 6-1 6-2 7-5; M. del Bello (IT) d. I. Adel (E) 6-3 4-6 6-1 6-0; S.

Stockenberg (SW) d. S. Soriano (ARG) 4-6 6-3 6-3 6-3; K. R. Rosewall (A) d. J. E. Barrett 6-2 6-2 6-0; **G. Mulloy** (9) (USA) d. V. Skonecki 6-1 6-3 8-6; G. Garrett (USA) d. C. A. Kemp (IRE) 6-1 6-0 6-2; T. Ulrich (D) d. J. Aguero (BR) 6-0 6-2 6-3; G. L. Paish d. D. M. Bull 6-3 6-2 6-1; **H. Flam** (6) (USA) d. O. G. Williams (SA) 6-3 8-6 6-4; T. T. Fancutt (SA) d. J. Peten (B) 7-5 2-6 7-5 6-1; J. A. T. Horn d. P. Milojkovic (YU) 6-0 6-2 6-4; L. Norgarb (SA) d. C. Sanhueza (CH) 6-2 3-6 8-6 6-3; **B. Patty** (12) (USA) d. A. W. Tills (NZ) 6-1 6-2 6-1; R. Haillet (F) d. E. Tsai (HK) 6-2 6-4 10-8 4-6 6-1; A. D. Russell (ARG) d. S. D. Potts (USA) 6-1 6-2 6-0; E. Buchholz (G) d. D. G. Snart 6-2 3-6 6-4 6-1; **V. Seixas** (3) (USA) d. N. Nath (IN) 7-5 6-2 6-2; J. C. Molinari (F) d. P. E. Hare 6-2 6-1 6-3; A. Vieira (BR) d. N. Rohisson (SW) 6-3 6-4 6-4; D. Scharenguivel (CEY) d. D. P. Tregonning (A) 6-2 6-3 6-4; I. Dorfman (USA) d. S. C. Clark 6-2 6-4 6-4; E. J. David d. D. H. Shaw 6-0 7-5 8-10 6-2; N. M. Cockburn (SA) d. R. Becker 6-1 6-1 6-2; E. Morea (ARG) d. G. E. Godsell 6-2 6-4 6-4; **K. McGregor** (5) (A) d. A. J. N. Starte 6-0 6-2 6-2; G. P. Jackson (IRE) d. J. U. Spitzer (SWZ) 5-7 7-5 7-5 6-2; A. Huber (Au) d. M. Taverne (CH) 6-2 6-4 1-6 6-4; R. del Bello (IT) d. W. T. Anderson 6-3 6-4 6-0; L. A. Hoad (A) d. G. Merlo (IT) 4-6 7-5 2-6 6-2 6-2; A. C. van Swol (NTH) d. H. C. Hopman (A) 6-1 7-5 6-3; C. Spychala (POL) d. E. R. Bulmer 6-3 3-6 6-1 6-3; R. K. Wilson d. J. Moreau (B) 6-2 6-4 7-5; **J. Drobny** (2) (E) d. W. A. Knight 6-0 6-1 6-3.

SECOND ROUND: Sedgman (1) d. Katz 6-1 6-1 6-0; Washer d. Billington 6-2 6-4 6-2; Candy d. Ampon 6-4 4-6 7-5 7-5; Balbiers d. Lister 8-6 6-1 6-2; **Sturgess** (7) d. Mayers 6-1 6-0 6-1; Mottram d. Cucelli 6-2 6-4 9-7; Johansson d. Brophy 6-4 6-0 6-3; Golden d. Walton 7-5 6-1 6-0; **Savitt** (4) d. Oakley 6-1 6-4 8-6; Likas d. Ayala 6-4 7-5 6-4; Brichant d. Tloczynski 6-3 6-3 3-6 7-5; Capell d. Woodroffe 6-3 2-2-6 6-2; **Rose** (8) d. Hermann 6-8 6-1 7-5 6-0; Nielsen d. Palada 6-3 6-4 6-3 6-0; Gardini d. Bernstein 6-3 6-0; Clark d. Rinkel 6-1 6-0 6-0; S. Stockenberg d. del Bello

7-5 6-4 8-6; **Mulloy** (9) d. Rosewall 9-7 6-3 8-6; Ulrich d. Garrett 6-4 6-3 6-0; **Flam** (6) d. Paish 6-2 8-6 7-5; Horn d. Fancutt 6-4 6-3 7-9 6-3; **Patty** (12) d. Norgarb 6-4 6-3 6-4; Russell d. Haillet 5-7 6-4 3-6 6-3; **Seixas** (3) d. Buchholz 6-2 6-1 6-4; Vieira d. Molinari 6-4 6-4 6-3; Dorfman d. Scharenguivel 6-1 6-1 8-6; Cockburn d. David 6-2 6-3 6-3; **McGregor** (5) d. Morea 7-5 6-4 6-4; Huber d. Jackson 4-6 6-3 6-1 10-8; Hoad d. del Bello 6-3 8-6 6-4; van Swol d. Spychala 10-12 6-0 6-2 6-2; **Drobny** (2) d. Wilson 6-0 6-1 6-3.

THIRD ROUND: Sedgman (1) d. Washer 6-3 4-6 6-3 6-3; Candy d. Balbiers 6-0 6-1 6-4; **Sturgess** (7) d. Mottram 6-4 6-3 6-4; Golden d. Johansson 6-3 4-6 6-1 4-6 6-1; **Savitt** (4) d. Likas 6-1 6-3 3-6 6-3; Brichant d. Capell 6-3 3-6 6-8 6-2 6-4; **Rose** (8) d. Nielsen 8-6 6-4 6-3; Clark d. Gardini 6-1 6-1 6-2; **Mulloy** (9) d. Stockenberg 7-5 4-6 3-6 6-2

4-2 ret'd; **Flam** (6) d. Ulrich 7-5 6-2 8-6; **Patty** (12) d. Horn 6-1 6-1 6-1; **Seixas** (3) d. Russell 6-3 6-2 6-4; Vieira d. Dorfman 11-9 6-1 7-5; **McGregor** (5) d. Cockburn 6-0 4-6 6-4 6-3; Hoad d. Huber 4-6 6-3 6-1; **Drobny** (2) d. van Swol 6-0 6-1 6-4.

FOURTH ROUND	QUARTER-FINALS	SEMI-FINALS	FINAL	CHAMPION
Sedgman (1)	**Sedgman** (1)			
Candy	6-2 6-1 6-0	**Sedgman** (1)		
Sturgess (7)	**Sturgess** (7)	7-5 6-1 6-0		
Golden	4-6 6-3 6-1 7-9 6-4		**Sedgman** (1)	
Savitt (4)	**Savitt** (4)		6-4 6-4 7-5	
Brichant	6-3 6-3 6-3			
Rose (8)	**Rose** (8)	**Rose** (8)		
Clark	6-2 6-2 6-4	6-4 3-6 6-4 4-6 6-2		**Sedgman** (1)
Mulloy (9)	**Flam** (6)			4-6 6-2 6-3 6-2
Flam (6)	6-4 7-5 6-1			
Patty (12)	**Seixas** (3)	**Flam** (6)		
Seixas (3)	7-5 4-6 6-3 7-5	6-4 3-6 6-3 7-5		
Vieira	**McGregor** (5)		**Drobny** (2)	
McGregor (5)	5-7 6-3 6-1 6-3		6-2 6-4 0-6 8-10 6-4	
Hoad	**Drobny** (2)	**Drobny** (2)		
Drobny (2)	6-3 3-6 8-6 6-3	6-0 3-6 2-6 7-5 7-5		

LADIES' SINGLES

FIRST ROUND: S. **Fry** (3) (USA) d; Mrs W. C. J. Halford 6-0 6-0; E. G. Attwood (NZ) d. Mrs J. M. Beswick 6-2 6-2; J. R. M. Morgan d. S. J. Bloomer 6-1 6-4; E. F. Lombard (IRE) d. N. de Ridder (B) 6-2 6-2; J. M. Trower d. Mrs D. W. Gotla 6-3 6-3; E. M. Watson d. Mrs H. Strecker (AU) 2-6 6-2 6-3; N. C. Potts d. Mrs J. M. Wagstaff 1-6 7-5 7-5; Mrs J. Bourbonnais (F) d. Mrs R. C. Panton 6-4 6-3; **Mrs J. J. Walker-Smith** (6) d. S. Schmitt (F) 6-2 6-1; H. Redick-Smith (SA) d. A. L. Morgan 6-1 6-2; M. P. Harrison d. R. J. R. Bulleid 3-6 6-1 6-2; Mrs B. Abbas (EG) d. Mrs B. Wedderburn (SA) 6-3 6-4; Mrs J. F. van der Wal Roos (NTH) d. Mrs A. T. P. Luxton 6-1 6-2; P. E. Ward d. Mrs M. Matous 6-2 6-3; G. E. Woodgate d. Mrs K. F. Knight 6-4 6-2; V. M. Lewis d. A. Buxton 3-6 6-3 6-3; Mrs E. W. Dawson

Scott d. Mrs K. Pohmann (G) 6-4 3-6 6-1; Mrs H. R. Phillips d. Mrs B. W. Knott 2-2 6-6 6-4; R. F. Woodgate d. Mrs E. Broz (AU) 6-3 4-6 6-1; Mrs H. C. Hopman (A) d. M. Carlisle 6-0 6-0; H. M. Fletcher d. J. A. MacLeod 6-2 6-4; Mrs F. J. Bartlett (SA) d. Mrs V. E. A. Morris 6-2 6-1; Mrs R. B. R. Wilson d. Mrs R. L. Scott 6-1 6-2; **Mrs J. Rinkel-Quertier** (8) d. Mrs R. Cooper 6-1 6-3; Mrs A. H. Thomas d. P. F. Hermsen (NTH) 6-3 6-1; S. Speight d. Mrs E. C. Peters 2-6 7-5 6-3; M. E. Parker d. A. G. Bates 4-6 6-3 6-1; Mrs N. Adamson (F) d. C. G. Hoahing 6-3 6-2; G. Love (SA) d. J. M. Petchell 7-5 6-3; B. Penrose (A) d. R. Walsh 6-4 6-2; Mrs R. F. Chandler d. Mrs C. F. O. Lister 4-6 6-4 5-3 ret'd; **L. Brough** (4) (USA) d. P. A. Lewis 6-1 6-0.

SECOND ROUND: M. **Connolly** (2) (USA) d. Mrs C. G. Moeller 6-2 6-0; A. Mortimer d. Mrs R. Anderson (USA) 6-2 6-2; B. M. Knapp d. L. M. Cornell 6-3 4-6 6-0; J. S. V. Partridge d. J. Kermina (F) 8-6 6-2; **Mrs T. D. Long** (7) (A) d. Mrs H. M. Proudfoot 6-1 6-0; V. Rigollet (SWZ) d. E. M. Wilford 6-3 6-4; Mrs H. Weiss (ARG) d. M. E. Morgan 6-2 6-2; V. S. White d. C. B. Decker (USA) 6-2 6-4; **Fry** (3) d. Attwood 6-2 6-4; Lombard d. Morgan 6-2 6-2; Watson d. Trower 7-5 6-2; Bourbonnais d. Potts 6-2 6-1; **Walker-Smith** (6) d. Redick-Smith 6-1 6-4; Harrison d. Abbas 6-4 5-7 6-4; Ward d. van der Wal Roos 8-6 6-2; G. E. Woodgate d. Lewis 6-3 6-4; Dawson Scott d. Phillips 6-3 6-2; Hopman

d. R. F. Woodgate 6-3 6-0; Fletcher d. Bartlett 4-6 6-3 6-0; **Rinkel-Quertier** (8) d. Wilson 6-1 6-3; Thomas d. Speight 4-6 8-6 6-2; Adamson d. Parker 6-4 6-1; Penrose d. Love 6-2 6-1; **Brough** (4) d. Chandler 6-0 6-0; F. Walthew d. Mrs P. J. Kerr 6-4 3-0 ret'd; D. Head (USA) d. Mrs S. Salo (FIN) 6-3 6-2; P. J. Curry d. Mrs G. R. Lines 6-1 6-3; **Mrs P. C. Todd** (5) (USA) d. A. McGuire (USA) 6-0 6-2; Mrs A. C. Brighton d. M. Harris 7-5 6-3; Mrs J. Wipplinger (SA) d. C. Mercelis (B) 4-6 6-4 7-5; Mrs B. M. Lewis (USA) d. E. Lehmann (ARG) 6-3 6-1; **D. Hart** (1) (USA) d. S. I. Odling 6-1 6-0.

THIRD ROUND: Connolly (2) d. Mortimer 6-4 6-3; Partridge d. Knapp 6-4 9-7; Long (7) d. Rigollet 6-1 6-4; White d. Weiss 6-4 4-1 ret'd; Fry (3) d. Lombard 6-2 6-1; Bourbonnais d. Watson 6-3 6-4; **Walker-Smith** (6) d. Harrison 6-1 6-3; G. E. Woodgate d. Ward 7-5 4-6 6-1; Dawson Scott d. Hopman 6-2 3-6 6-2; **Rinkel-Quertier** (8) d. Fletcher

6-0 6-4; Adamson d. Thomas 8-6 6-3; **Brough** (4) d. Penrose 6-2 6-1; Head d. Walthew 6-0 6-0; **Todd** (5) d. Curry 6-3 6-3; Wipplinger d. Brighton 6-4 6-1; **Hart** (1) d. Lewis 6-1 2-6 6-1.

FOURTH ROUND	QUARTER-FINALS	SEMI-FINALS	FINAL	CHAMPION
Connolly (2)	**Connolly** (2)			
Partridge	6-3 5-7 7-5	**Connolly** (2)		
Long (7)	**Long** (7)	5-7 6-2 6-0		
White	6-2 6-1		**Connolly** (2)	
Fry (3)	**Fry** (3)		6-4 6-3	
Bourbonnais	6-4 6-0	**Fry** (3)		
Walker-Smith (6)	**Walker-Smith** (6)	6-3 6-3		
G. E. Woodgate	6-1 6-1			**Connolly** (2)
Dawson Scott	**Rinkel-Quertier** (8)			7-5 6-3
Rinkel-Quertier (8)	6-1 6-2			
Adamson	**Brough** (4)	**Brough** (4)		
Brough (4)	1-6 6-1 6-2	6-1 9-7		
Head	**Todd** (5)		**Brough** (4)	
Todd (5)	6-4 6-3		6-3 3-6 6-1	
Wipplinger	**Hart** (1)	**Todd** (5)		
Hart (1)	6-4 4-6 6-3	6-8 7-5 6-4		

OTHER FINALS

GENTLEMEN'S DOUBLES: Final — K. McGregor (A)/F. A. Sedgman (A) d. E. V. Seixas (USA)/E. W. Sturgess (SA) 6-3 7-5 6-4.
LADIES' DOUBLES: Final — S. J. Fry (USA)/D. J. Hart (USA) d. A. L. Brough (USA)/M. Connolly (USA) 8-6 6-3.
MIXED DOUBLES: Final — F. A. Sedgman (A)/D. J. Hart (USA) d. E. Morea (ARG)/Mrs T. D. Long (A) 4-6 6-3 6-4.

GENTLEMEN'S SINGLES PLATE: Final — L. Ayala (CH) d. N. Kumar (IN) 8-6 6-2.
LADIES' SINGLES PLATE: Final — Mrs B. Abbas (E) d. G. C. Hoahing 0-6 6-4 6-3.
BOYS' INVITATION SINGLES: Final — R. K. Wilson d. T. Fancutt (SA) 6-3 6-2.
GIRLS' INVITATION SINGLES: Final — F. ten Bosch (NTH) d. R. Davar (IN) 5-7 6-1 7-5.

251

GENTLEMEN'S SINGLES

1953

FIRST ROUND: V. Seixas (2) (USA) d. R. J. Lee 6-3 6-0 6-1; V. Skonecki d. F. R. Kipping 6-2 6-4 6-2; T. L. Tan (INDO) d. D. Scharenguivel (CEY) 6-4 4-5 7 1-6 6-3 6-2; P. Washer (B) d. J. J. McArdle (IRE) 6-0 6-3 6-4; G. A. Worthington (NZ) d. A. Vieira (BR) 6-0 5-7 6-1 6-1; L. Bergelin (SW) d. J. Ulrich (D) 6-3 7-5 6-3; Z. Katona (HU) d. A. L. van Meegeren (NTH) 6-2 6-8 6-4 6-1; F. Ampon (PH) d. G. Pilet (F) 6-1 6-1 6-1; **L. A. Hoad** (6) (A) d. W. R. Seymour (SA) 6-4 6-2 7-5; N. Nath (IN) d. H. C. Bernstein 7-5 6-3 6-3; S. Laslo (YU) d. G. Clerici (IT) 8-6 6-8 6-2 6-4; J. E. Barrett d. R. G. Reeve 6-1 6-3 6-4; Z. Nikolitch (YU) d. G. Snart 6-0 8-6 4-6 6-3; H. W. Stewart (USA) d. A. J. Mottram 6-4 3-6 4-6 6-3 6-4; B. E. Crouch d. E. J. David 6-3 6-3 6-3; H. Redl (AU) d. P. E. Hare 6-0 6-3 8-6; **M. G. Rose** (3) (A) d. R. Krishnan (IN) 8-6 6-4 4-6 6-1; N. R. Lewis d. C. W. Hannam 6-3 7-5 3-6 6-3; J. Peten (B) d. R. S. Condy (IRE) 6-1 6-2 6-2; J. C. Molinari (F) d. G. L. Ward 8-6 6-1 8-6; J. A. T. Horn d. G. Sturdza (NOR) 6-0 6-2 6-2; D. L. M. Black (RH) d. C. Spychala (POL) 9-7 6-1 6-2; J. Brichant (B) d. R. Becker 3-6 9-7 6-3 6-0; C. F. O. Lister d. H. Hermann (G) 6-4 6-2 6-0; **A. Larsen** (7) (USA) d. A. Jancso (HU) 6-2 4-8 6-6; D. W. Butler d. C. Ferrer (SP) 6-3 6-3 3-6 6-4; J. Michelmore d. R. Oliver 6-3 8-6 8-6; J. Palada (YU) d. W. A. Knight 6-2 6-2 7-5; J. N. Grinda (F) d. J. F. Kupferburger (SA) 7-5 6-3 6-3; T. Johansson (SW) d. P. Chatrier (F) 6-3 6-0; T. Ulrich (D) d. A. L. Proctor 6-1 6-1 6-3; G. Merlo (IT) d. G. P. Jackson (IRE) 6-4 6-4 7-5; R. K. Wilson d. C. J. Hovell 4-6 2-6 6-2; R. Buser (SWZ) d. J. van Dalsum (NTH) 0-6 6-4 6-2 7-5; S.

Davidson (SW) d. D. H. Shaw 6-2 11-9 7-5; G. Golden (USA) d. V. Petrovic (YU) 6-1 7-5 6-1; C. E. Wilderspin (A) d. E. Buchholz (G) 6-4 6-2 6-4; E. R. Bulmer d. R. V. Gotto (IRE) 6-2 6-2 6-0; I. G. Ayre (A) d. J. Asboth (HU) 4-6 9-7 6-2 6-2; **E. Morea** (8) (ARG) d. I. A. McDonald (TRIN) 6-4 8-6 6-0; R. Hartwig (A) d. W. van Voorhees (USA) 6-3 6-2 6-1; G. L. Paish d. I. C. Vermaak (SA) 6-4 6-4 6-3; I. Tloczynski (POL) d. E. P. Argon (UR) 3-6 6-2 6-3 6-2; A. J. N. Starte d. S. Hojberg (D) 6-2 6-3 5-7 6-2; B. Patty (USA) d. J. Thomas (F) 6-2 6-4 6-4; E. Tsai (HK) d. H. T. Baxter 6-1 6-8 6-3 6-3; B. Bartzen (USA) d. H. F. Walton 6-2 6-2 6-0; **J. Drobny** (4) (E) d. B. Destremau (F) 6-0 6-1 6-2; K. Nielsen (D) d. B. Green (A) 6-3 6-2 4-6 7-5; K. R. Malcolm (SA) d. J. D. Hackett (IRE) 7-5 6-4 1-6 6-3; B. M. Woodroffe (SA) d. G. D. Oakley 6-2 6-2 6-3; I. Sikorski (HU) d. F. Gardini (IT) 7-5 6-3 6-1; S. Stockenberg (SW) d. M. F. Mohtadi (IN) 6-2 6-4 6-2; J. W. Ager (USA) d. G. de Kermadec (F) 3-6 6-2 6-3 6-3; A. Huber (AU) d. G. Mezzi (B) 6-4 7-5 4-6 8-6; **G. Mulloy** (5) (USA) d. A. Arkinstall (A) d. N. Kumar (IN) 3-6 4-6 6-3 6-2 6-2; A. E. Dehnert (NTH) d. I. Panajotovic (YU) 6-3 6-4 3-6 6-4; J. A. Pickard d. C. A. Kemp (IRE) 3-6 8-6 6-3 6-8 6-2; R. Deyro (PH) d. H. Billington 8-6 6-0 8-6; J. Bartroli (SP) d. J. I. Devroe (B) 6-3 6-2 6-2; I. J. Warwick d. A. Wellford (USA) 6-4 4-6 6-2 6-3; R. Abdesselam (F) d. J. M. Gracie 6-3 6-4 6-4; **K. R. Rosewall** (1) (A) d. M. D. Davies 6-2 6-4 6-2.

SECOND ROUND: Seixas (2) d. Skonecki 6-2 6-2 7-5; Washer d. Tan 6-3 6-0 6-3; Worthington d. Bergelin 2-6 6-0 6-3 6-2; Ampon d. Katona 6-4 6-3 6-1; **Hoad** (6) d. Nath 6-0 6-4 6-1; Barrett d. Laslo 6-1 6-3 6-8 14-12; Stewart d. Nikolitch 6-4 6-2 6-2; Redl d. Crouch 6-2 6-3 5-7 6-4; **Rose** (3) d. Lewis 6-3 6-3 6-2; Molinari d. Peten 6-1 3-6 6-0 6-0; Black d. Horn 3-6 4-6 7-5 7-5 8-6; Brichant d. Lister 8-6 6-3 6-0; **Larsen** (7) d. Butler 6-4 6-2 7-5; Palada d. Michelmore 6-4 6-1 6-2; Johansson d. Grinda 3-6 6-1 6-4 6-2; Ulrich d. Merlo 6-3 4-6 6-2 6-3; Wilson d. Buser 6-4

6-3 6-3; Davidson d. Golden 6-3 6-4 6-4; Wilderspin d. Bulmer 6-2 6-3 7-5; Ayre d. **Morea** (8) 6-8 6-4 11-9 6-2; Hartwig d. Paish 6-8 6-3 6-3 6-2; Tloczynski d. Starte 6-4 4-6 6-4 7-5; Patty d. Tsai 7-5 6-2 6-0; **Drobny** (4) d. Bartzen 6-4 6-3 6-3; Nielsen d. Malcolm 6-1 6-1 8-6; Woodroffe d. Sikorski 5-7 6-1 6-0 6-3; Stockenberg d. Ager 7-5 8-6 6-4; **Mulloy** (5) d. Huber 6-2 6-2 3-6 6-4; Arkinstall d. Dehnert 6-1 6-3 6-1; Deyro d. Pickard 6-2 6-3 6-0; Warwick d. Bartroli 8-6 6-3 7-9 5-7 10-8; **Rosewall** (1) d. Abdesselam 6-3 6-1 4-6 6-2.

THIRD ROUND: Seixas (2) d. Washer 6-3 6-1 6-3; Worthington d. Ampon 6-2 6-2 8-6; **Hoad** (6) d. Barrett 6-2 6-2 6-1; Stewart d. Redl 6-3 6-1 6-0; **Rose** (3) d. Molinari 6-4 6-0 6-4; Brichant d. Black 7-5 10-8 6-3; **Larsen** (7) d. Palada 6-1 6-2 7-5; Johansson d. Ulrich 7-5 6-3 2-6 7-5; Davidson d. Wilson 6-3 4-6 8-10 6-0 6-2; Ayre d. Wilderspin

7-5 6-2 7-5; Hartwig d. Tloczynski 6-1 6-1 6-3; **Drobny** (4) d. Patty 8-6 16-18 3-6 8-6 12-10; Nielsen d. Woodroffe 6-4 3-6 6-3 6-2; **Mulloy** (5) d. Stockenberg 4-6 3-6 6-3 6-3 9-7; Arkinstall d. Deyro 7-5 2-6 4-6 6-3 6-2; **Rosewall** (1) d. Warwick 6-3 6-2 6-2.

FOURTH ROUND	QUARTER-FINALS	SEMI-FINALS	FINAL	CHAMPION
Seixas (2)	Seixas (2)			
Worthington	10-8 7-5 6-3	Seixas (2)		
Hoad (6)	Hoad (6)	5-7 6-4 6-3 1-6 9-7		
Stewart	6-0 6-3 6-2		Seixas (2)	
Rose (3)	Rose (3)		6-4 10-12 9-11 6-4 6-3	
Brichant	6-4 6-4 8-6	Rose (3)		
Larsen (7)	Larsen (7)	6-3 6-3 16-14		Seixas (2)
Johansson	8-6 6-2 6-0			9-7 6-3 6-4
Davidson	Davidson			
Ayre	6-3 6-4 6-4			
Hartwig	Drobny (4)	Drobny (4)		
Drobny (4)	6-3 7-5 7-5	7-5 6-4 6-0		
Nielsen	Nielsen		Nielsen	
Mulloy (5)	10-8 6-3 7-5		6-4 6-3 6-2	
Arkinstall	Rosewall (1)	Nielsen		
Rosewall (1)	4-6 3-6 6-1 6-1 6-2	7-5 4-6 6-8 6-0 6-2		

LADIES' SINGLES

FIRST ROUND: Mrs D. Knode (4) (USA) d. G. E. Woodgate 6-2 6-2; K. Fageros (USA) d. V. A. Pitt 6-1 4-6 6-1; Mrs B. Davidson (USA) d. M. E. Fisher (A) 6-2 6-1; Mrs E. Broz (AU) d. Mrs M. Lagerborg (SW) w.o.; Mrs N. W. Blair d. N. Liebert 6-3 6-4; R. Walsh d. Mrs A. C. Brighton 6-3 6-3; Mrs E. W. Dawson Scott d. Mrs A. H. Thomas 6-4 2-6 9-7; R. H. Bentley d. S. G. Mackay 2-6 6-2 7-5; **A. Mortimer** (5) d. Mrs J. Drobny 6-1 6-4; S. Schmitt (F) d. J. M. Scott (SA) 6-0 1-6 6-1; P. E. Ward d. Mrs E. C. Peters 6-0 6-2; Mrs K. F. Knight d. V. M. Lewis 3-7 7-5 7-5; Mrs M. C. Cheadle d. E. F. Lombard (IRE) 4-6 6-3 6-1; J. A. MacLeod d. J. de Riba (SP) 7-5 6-2; M. Bourbonnais (F) d. Mrs A. C. Gray (USA) 6-4 6-3; V. S. White d. E. G. Attwood (NZ) 6-3 3-6 6-2; Mrs H. Weiss (ARG) d. A. L. Morgan 6-1 6-2; Mrs M. A.

Downey (IRE) d. S. Speight 6-3 6-4; J. Sampson (USA) d. Mrs D. W. Gotla 6-1 6-2; L. van der Westhuizen (SA) d. D. Herbst 6-4 9-7; P. J. Curry d. B. N. Knapp 6-4 6-2; Mrs H. C. Hopman (A) d. Mrs J. M. Wagstaff 6-0 5-7 6-2; R. J. R. Bulleid d. Mrs H. M. Proudfoot 4-6 6-1 6-2; **Mrs N. Adamson** (8) (F) d. R. F. Woodgate 2-6 6-0 6-3; Mrs A. Dawes d. F. J. I. ten Bosch (NTH) 8-6 6-4; Mrs B. M. Lewis (USA) d. M. P. Harrison 8-6 6-3; S. J. Bloomer d. N. C. Potts 7-5 6-4; Mrs V. Alvensleben (SWZ) d. J. M. Middleton 4-6 6-4 6-3; M. Harris d. J. M. Boundy 6-4 6-1; Mrs J. Rinkel-Quertier d. M. E. Parker 2-6 6-0 6-1; F. W. Walthew d. Mrs G. R. Lines 2-6 6-0 8-6. **S. Fry** (3) (USA) d. Mrs B. Gullbrandsson-Sanden (SW) w.o.

SECOND ROUND: D. Hart (2) (USA) d. J. R. M. Morgan 6-0 6-0; T. Zehden d. Mrs W. H. L. Gordon (UG) 7-5 6-4; A. Buxton d. Mrs C. F. O. Lister 7-5 5-7 6-1; A. J. Goldsworthy d. J. E. Bowyer (RH) 6-3 6-3; **H. M. Fletcher** (6) d. D. Midgley 6-2 6-0; C. Mercelis (B) d. Mrs R. B. R. Wilson 6-0 6-2; E. M. Watson d. Mrs P. J. Kerr 6-1 11-9; Mrs Z. Koermoczi (HU) d. A. V. Houseley 6-0 6-0; **Knode** (4) d. Fageros 8-6 6-3; Davidson d. Broz 6-4 6-3; Walsh d. Blair 6-2 2-6 9-7; Dawson Scott d. Bentley 6-2 6-2; **Mortimer** (5) d. Schmitt 2-6 6-0 6-1; Ward d. Knight 6-0 6-1; Cheadle d. MacLeod 7-5 6-1; Bourbonnais d. White 6-1 6-4; Weiss d. Downey 6-3 6-1; Sampson d. van der Westhuizen 6-1

6-3; Hopman d. Curry 9-11 6-2 1-0 ret'd; **Adamson** (8) d. Bulleid 1-6 6-3 6-3; Lewis d. Dawes 6-1 6-3; Bloomer d. Alvensleben 6-4 8-6; Rinkel-Quertier d. Harris 6-3 6-2; **Fry** (3) d. Walthew 6-2 6-2; Mrs H. Strecker (AU) d. J. S. Reid 2-6 6-1 6-4; Mrs E. Vollmer (G) d. P. A. Hird 6-3 6-3; Mrs W. Brewer (BER) d. A. M. Carlisle 6-2 6-1; **Mrs P. Chatrier** (7) d. C. G. Hoahing 6-1 6-3; J. A. Shilcock d. Mrs M. R. King 6-3 6-2; Mrs M. Peterdi (HU) d. J. de Ridder (B) 6-4 4-6 6-4; J. M. Petchell d. Mrs H. L. K. Brock 6-4 6-1; **M. Connolly** (1) (USA) d. D. Kilian (SA) 6-0 6-0.

THIRD ROUND: Hart (2) d. Zehden 6-0 6-0; Buxton d. Goldsworthy 6-4 6-2; **Fletcher** (6) d. Mercelis 6-3 6-3; Koermoczi d. Watson 6-3 6-2; **Knode** (4) d. Davidson 6-3 6-0; Dawson Scott d. Walsh 6-2 9-7; **Mortimer** (5) d. Ward 6-3 6-3; Cheadle d. Bourbonnais 6-4 6-4; Sampson d. Weiss 11-9 7-5; **Adamson** (8) d. Hopman 1-6 6-2 6-1;

Lewis d. Bloomer 6-3 6-2; **Fry** (3) d. Rinkel-Quertier 3-6 6-4 6-1; Vollmer d. Strecker 6-2 6-2; Brewer d. **Chatrier** (7) 7-5 6-3; Shilcock d. Peterdi 6-2 6-0; **Connolly** (1) d. Petchell 6-1 6-1.

FOURTH ROUND	QUARTER-FINALS	SEMI-FINALS	FINAL	CHAMPION
Hart (2)	Hart (2)			
Buxton	6-3 6-1	Hart (2)		
Fletcher (6)	Koermoczi	7-5 7-5		
Koermoczi	6-3 6-4		Hart (2)	
Knode (4)	Knode (4)		6-2 6-2	
Dawson Scott	6-2 6-1	Knode (4)		
Mortimer (5)	Mortimer (5)	6-4 6-3		
Cheadle	6-2 6-1			Connolly (1)
Sampson	Sampson			8-6 7-5
Adamson (8)	4-6 6-3 6-3			
Lewis	Fry (3)	Fry (3)		
Fry (3)	6-1 6-3	6-4 6-2		
Vollmer	Vollmer		Connolly (1)	
Brewer	6-2 6-1		6-1 6-1	
Shilcock	Connolly (1)	Connolly (1)		
Connolly (1)	6-0 6-1	6-3 6-0		

OTHER FINALS

GENTLEMEN'S DOUBLES: Final — L. A. Hoad/K. R. Rosewall (A) d. R. N. Hartwig (A)/M. G. Rose (A) 6-4 7-5 4-6 7-5.
LADIES' DOUBLES: Final — S. J. Fry (USA)/D. Hart (USA) d. M. Connolly (USA)/J. Sampson (USA) 6-0 6-0.
MIXED DOUBLES: Final — E. V. Seixas (USA)/D. Hart (USA) d; E: Morea (ARG)/S. J. Fry (USA) 9-7 7-5.

GENTLEMEN'S SINGLES PLATE: Final — G. L. Paish d. J. W. Ager (USA) 4-6 6-0 7-5.
LADIES' SINGLES PLATE: Final — M. P. Harrison d. E. F. Lombard (IRE) 1-6 6-3 6-3.
BOYS' INVITATION SINGLES: Final — W. A. Knight d. R. Krishnan (IN) 7-5 6-4.
GIRLS' INVITATION SINGLES: Final — D. Killian (SA) d. V. A. Pitt 6-4 4-6 6-1.

GENTLEMEN'S SINGLES

FIRST ROUND: L. A. Hoad (2) (A) d. G. Fachini (IT) 6-3 6-2 7-5; I. Tloczynski (POL) d. W. Van Voorhees (USA) 6-2 9-7 8-6; R. Bedard (CAN) d. G. L. Forbes (SA) 6-3 7-9 6-1 6-3; E. P. Argon (UR) d. C. A. Kemp (IRE) 6-3 6-1 6-3; **G. Mulloy** (12) (USA) d. N. R. Lewis 6-4 6-0 7-5; B. E. Crouch d. S. Nikolitch (YU) w.o.; I. J. Warwick d. A. Lemyze (F) 8-6 6-3 2-6 6-1; B. P. Molloy (A) d. I. Panajotovic (YU) 4-6 6-1 6-1 6-2; **A. Larsen** (6) (USA) d. H. C. Bernstein 6-2 6-4 10-8; N. Nath (IN) d. R. Howe (A) 4-6 3-6 6-3 6-4 6-2; K. H. Ip (HK) d. J. C. Molinari (F) 6-3 1-6 4-6 10-8 6-0; P. Washer (B) d. F. Soehol (NOR) 6-1 6-2 6-3; **J. Drobny** (11) (E) d. J. Arkinstall (A) 6-3 6-3 6-3; T. Ulrich (D) d. W. A. Knight 2-6 6-4 3-6 6-2 6-1; C. Spychala (POL) d. F. Saiko (AU) 6-3 6-1 3-6 6-1; L. Bergelin (SW) d. P. Guimaraes (BR) 6-1 6-2 6-1; **V. Seixas** (4) (USA) d. G. A. Cass 6-1 6-0 6-1; N. Pietrangeli (IT) d. M. Murphy 6-2 9-7 6-0; B. J. Katz (RH) d. A. L. Proctor 6-3 6-1 4-6 6-3; M. A. Otway (NZ) d. C. Grandet (F) 6-1 6-4 6-2; J. Brichant (B) d. J. D. Heldman (USA) 6-1 6-4 12-10; G. L. Paish d. F. R. Kipping 6-2 8-6 6-2; S. Stockenberg (SW) d. R. Moreira (BR) 6-1 6-4; D. A. Samaai (SA) d. R. Huber (G) 6-2 6-1 6-2; **B. Patty** (7) (USA) d. B. J. Bucknell 6-1 6-0 6-0; H. W. Stewart (USA) d. L. H. Norgarb (SA) 6-4 6-3 6-1; N. Kumar (IN) d. G. B. Robinson 4-6 6-0 6-0 6-3; J. Palada (YU) d. J. A. Pickard 6-4 4-6 6-2 4-6 6-1; M. G. Davies d. E. R. Bulmer 6-3 6-2 6-1; J. M. Ward d. C. F. O. Lister 6-3; R. Becker d. E. Balestra (SW) 6-0 6-1 6-3; F. Nys (F) d. P. Wooldridge 6-2 6-0 6-2; G. J. Shea (USA) d. C. W. Hannam 6-1 6-3 8-6; G. D. Oakley d. O. Sirola (IT)

6-4 9-7 7-9 6-4; L. Main (C) d. H. Billington 6-2 6-3 6-2; A. Hammersley (CH) d. J. E. Robson (NZ) 6-3 4-6 2-6 6-3 6-4; J. W. Ager (USA) d. H. F. Walton 4-6 3-6 6-0 6-3 6-3; H. Burrows (USA) d. G. L. Ward 6-4 8-6 6-4; E. Tsai (HK) d. M. F. Mohtadi (IN) 6-3 6-3 6-4; **R. N. Hartwig** (8) (A) d. H. Redl (AU) 6-0 6-1 6-3; A. Cooper (A) d. I. Plecevic (YU) 6-0 6-2 6-4; R. Emerson (A) d. M. Fox (USA) 6-1 6-3 8-6; T. Vincent (USA) d. I. Devroe (B) 6-2 6-4 3-6 6-3; N. Kitovitz d. M. Hime 6-2 6-2 6-3; P. Remy (F) d. D. R. Oliver 6-0 6-2 6-2; R. Falkenburg (BR) d. B. Pottinger (G) 6-4 6-4 6-1; H. Flam (USA) d. D. H. Shaw 6-4 6-3 8-6; **K. R. Rosewall** (3) (A) d. A. Segal (SA) 7-5 4-6 8-6 8-6; D. C. Hamilton (A) d. J. Bartroli (SP) 6-0 6-2 6-3; J. E. Barrett d. D. H. Reid (A) 6-0 6-2 9-7; W. A. Paton (USA) d. P. Moys 8-6 7-9 6-3 4-6 6-3; **K. Nielsen** (10) (D) d. A. E. Dehnert (NTH) 6-4 6-4 6-4; D. Scharenguivel (CEY) d. D. W. Butler 6-1 8-6 3-6 6-3; R. Krishnan (IN) d. G. Garrett (USA) 6-3 6-3 6-2; N. G. Fraser (A) d. R. J. Lee 6-2 6-3 6-3; **M. G. Rose** (5) (A) d. A. J. Mottram 6-1 6-2 6-3; G. C. Pryor (A) d. R. S. Condy (IRE) 3-6 6-4 1-6 6-4 6-4; J. Grinda (F) d. G. P. Jackson (IRE) 6-4 6-4 8-10 3-6 7-5; J. Peten (B) d. L. M. Black (RH) 6-3 2-6 6-3 ret'd; **S. Davidson** (9) (SW) d. I. A. McDonald (TRIN) 6-2 7-5 6-3; A. Vieira (BR) d. J. A. Barry (NZ) 7-5 3-6 6-4 6-1; R. K. Wilson, V. Petrovic (YU) 6-4 6-3 6-1; O. G. Williams (SA) d. P. Chatrier (F) 6-4 6-0 6-3; **T. Trabert** (1) (USA) d. P. Wooller 6-0 6-2 6-2.

SECOND ROUND: Hoad (2) d. Tloczynski 6-0 6-3 6-1; Bedard d. Argon 2-6 6-4 6-3; **Mulloy** (12) d. Crouch 6-2 6-4 6-1; Molloy d. Warwick 6-4 0-6 7-5 6-4; **Larsen** (6) d. Nath 7-5 6-3 6-3; Washer d. Ip 9-7 6-2 5-7 6-1; **Drobny** (11) d. Ulrich 6-4 6-2; Brichant d. Bergelin 6-1 6-2 6-2; **Seixas** (4) d. Pietrangeli (IT) d. M. Murphy 7-5 9-7 3-6 6-3; **Patty** (7) d. Stewart 10-8 4-6 6-3 6-4; Kumar d. Palada 6-4 6-4 6-0; Davies d. Ward 4-6 7-5 10-8 6-1; Becker d. Nys 6-3 6-0 6-2; Shea d. Oakley 4-6 4-6 6-1

6-4 6-4; Main d. Hammersley 6-1 6-3 7-9 7-5; Burrows d. Ager 6-4 3-6 6-2 6-3; **Hartwig** (8) d. Tsai 6-1 7-5 6-3; Cooper d. Emerson 6-1 6-1 6-2; Vincent d. Kitovitz 6-4 6-2 6-3; Falkenburg d. Remy 6-4 6-4 8-6; **Rosewall** (3) d. Flam 6-1 6-4 6-2; Main d. Paton 6-3 12-10 4-6 4-6 6-4; Krishnan d. Scharenguivel 6-2 6-3 6-2; **Rose** (5) d. Fraser 8-6 6-3 6-1; Grinda d. Pryor 0-6 7-5 6-4 8-6; **Davidson** (9) d. Peten 6-4 6-1 6-2; Wilson d. Vieira 7-5 6-3 6-3; **Trabert** (1) d. Williams 7-5 6-2 7-5.

THIRD ROUND: Hoad (2) d. Bedard 6-3 6-0 1-6 6-1; **Mulloy** (12) d. Molloy 6-4 10-8 8-6; Washer d. **Larsen** (6) 10-12 7-5 6-2 9-7; **Drobny** (11) d. Bergelin 6-4 6-2 6-2; **Seixas** (4) d. Otway 6-3 6-4 9-7; Brichant d. Stockenberg 7-5 6-1 6-1; **Patty** (7) d. Kumar 6-1 6-3 6-4; Davies d. Becker 4-6 6-4 6-1 6-3; Shea d. Main 6-1 7-5 5-7 1-6 6-1; **Hartwig**

(8) d. Burrows 6-3 6-4 6-3; Cooper d. Vincent 6-3 7-5 11-9; **Rosewall** (3) d. Falkenburg 6-2 4-6 6-1 6-4; **Nielsen** (10) d. Barrett 4-6 6-3 6-4 6-4; **Rose** (5) d. Krishnan 6-3 6-1 6-3; **Davidson** (9) d. Grinda 6-1 6-2 6-4; **Trabert** (1) d. Wilson 10-8 8-6 6-2.

FOURTH ROUND	QUARTER-FINALS	SEMI-FINALS	FINAL	CHAMPION
Hoad (2)	**Hoad** (2)			
Mulloy (12)	4-6 6-0 7-5 6-3	**Drobny** (11)		
Washer	**Drobny** (11)	6-4 6-3 6-3		
Drobny (11)	8-6 10-8 6-3		**Drobny** (11)	
Seixas (4)	**Seixas** (4)		6-2 6-4 4-6 9-7	
Brichant	6-8 7-5 6-2 5-7 6-2	**Patty** (7)		
Patty (7)	**Patty** (7)	7-5 4-6 6-3 6-2		**Drobny** (11)
Davies	7-5 6-1 7-5			13-11 4-6 6-2 9-7
Shea	**Hartwig** (8)			
Hartwig (8)	6-4 1-6 6-1 6-4	**Rosewall** (3)		
Cooper	**Rosewall** (3)	6-3 3-6 3-6 6-3 6-1		
Rosewall (3)	6-2 6-3 4-6 10-8		**Rosewall** (3)	
Nielsen (10)	**Rose** (5)		3-6 6-3 4-6 6-1 6-1	
Rose (5)	4-6 6-3 9-7 6-4	**Trabert** (1)		
Davidson (9)	**Trabert** (1)	6-2 6-2 7-5		
Trabert (1)	3-6 12-10 6-0 7-9 6-3			

LADIES' SINGLES

FIRST ROUND: L. Brough (4) (USA) d. Mrs D. W. Gotla 6-1 6-1; Mrs E. Vollmer (G) d. S. E. Waters 6-1 9-7; Mrs A. H. Thomas d. S. Schmitt (F) 6-3 6-1; J. A. Fitzpatrick (IRE) d. Mrs H. C. Hopman (A) 3-6 6-2 6-3; M. P. Harrison d. M. K. Morris (USA) d. G. A. Cheadle d. R. Walsh 6-2 6-2; B. J. Bradley (USA) d. J. M. Petchell 9-7 6-1; F. J. I. ten Bosch (NTH) d. Mrs M. C. Cheadle 6-4 6-1; **A. Mortimer** (6) d. Mrs R. W. Stone 6-0 6-1; Mrs J. Kemsey-Bourne d. Mrs H. L. K. Brock 6-2 6-4; Mrs J. E. Robson (NZ) d. Mrs J. D. Heldman (USA) 6-0 6-0; Mrs G. Bucaille (F) d. V. A. Pitt 6-3 6-3; Mrs A. C. Brighton d. Z. J. Lusty 6-1 6-0; M. Bonstrom d. Mrs K. F. Knight 1-8 6-4 4-5 ret'd; M. Ramirez (M) d. E. E. Ruffin (A); E. Lehmann (ARG) d. Mrs A. Coessens (B) 6-1 6-1; K. Hubbell (USA) d. K. M. Stott 9-7

6-1; J. A. Shilcock d. A. I. Bilse (SA) 7-5 6-3; R. J. R. Bulleid d. M. E. Parker 6-3 6-2; P. J. Curry d. E. G. Attwood (NZ) 6-3 6-2; Mrs B. M. Lewis (USA) d. Mrs J. A. Quelch 6-1 6-3; J. Knight d. Mrs J. A. Collier 5-7 6-4 6-3; Mrs N. Adamson (F) d. G. C. F. Rhodes 6-1 6-4; **Mrs C. Pratt** (8) (USA) d. J. de Riba (SP) 6-1 6-2; P. E. Ward d. Mrs C. G. Moeller 6-1 6-1; P. A. Hird d. Mrs J. W. Cawthorn 6-4 6-1; M. Harris d. M. Dittmeyer (G) 9-7 6-0; C. G. Hoahing d. S. Lazzarino (IN) 6-1 6-1; Mrs J. Roos (NTH) d. Mrs C. F. O. Lister 6-3 6-3; Mrs D. W. Levine (USA) d. Mrs R. B. R. Wilson 6-4 6-0; J. Kermina (F) d. Mrs J. P. Vogler (G) 6-4 6-1; **S. Fry** (3) (USA) d. Mrs L. Alvensleben-Rigollet (SWZ) 6-4 6-4.

SECOND ROUND: D. Hart (2) (USA) d. G. E. Woodgate 6-1 6-1; J. F. Burke (NZ) d. E. M. Watson 5-7 6-4 6-1; S. Kamo (J) d. Mrs H. Strecker (AU) 6-3 7-5; Mrs N. Migliori (IT) d. Mrs H. Praczukowski (JAM) 6-4 6-0; **H. M. Fletcher** (7) d. Mrs H. Sladek (C) 6-3 5-7 6-3; Mrs H. Kaufmann (SWZ) d. J. M. Boundy 6-0 6-0; Mrs E. W. Dawson-Scott d. M. E. Govett 6-2 6-2; B. N. Knapp d. R. F. Woodgate 6-1 6-2; **Brough** (4) d. Vollmer 6-3 6-3; Thomas d. Fitzpatrick 6-0 7-5; Harrison d. Kimbrell 7-5 5-7 6-4; Bradley d. ten Bosch 9-7 2-0 ret'd; **Mortimer** (6) d. Kemsey-Bourne 6-0 6-2; Bucaille d. Robson 6-3 6-1; Bonstrom d. Brighton 3-6 6-3 6-3; Ramirez d. Lehman 6-0 7-5; Shilcock d. Hubbell

6-2 6-4; Curry d. Bulleid 6-3 6-2; Lewis d. Knight 6-0 8-6; **Pratt** (8) d. Adamson 2-1 ret'd; Ward d. Hird 6-3 6-1; Hoahing d. Harris 6-1 6-2; Levine d. Roos 6-4 6-1; **Fry** (3) d. Kermina 6-2 6-1; C. Mercelis (B) d. R. Davar (IN) 6-1 6-0; J. R. M. Morgan d. Mrs E. Broz (AU) 6-4 7-5; Mrs B. Abbas (E) d. V. S. White 6-1 6-0; A. Buxton d. V. M. Lewis 6-1 6-1; Mrs W. Brewer (BER) d. J. M. Middleton 6-4 3-6 7-5; E. Buding (ARG) d. Mrs F. W. Byrne 6-0 6-3; **M. Connolly** (1) (USA) d. J. Scott (SA) 6-0 6-3.

THIRD ROUND: Hart (2) d. Burke 6-1 6-2; Migliori d. Kamo 6-3 11-9; **Fletcher** (7) d. Kaufmann 6-3 6-1; Dawson-Scott d. Knapp 9-7 8-6; **Brough** (4) d. Thomas 6-2 6-2; Bradley d. Harrison 6-3 8-6; **Mortimer** (6) d. Bucaille 6-0 6-2; Ramirez d. Bonstrom 6-4 6-2; Curry d. Shilcock 6-3 6-3; **Pratt** (8) d. Lewis 6-1 9-7; Ward d. Hoahing

6-0 6-1; **Fry** (3) d. Levine 6-4 6-4; Mercelis d. Morgan 6-3 6-1; **du Pont** (5) d. Abbas 6-0 6-4; Buxton d. Brewer 6-1 3-6 6-3; **Connolly** (1) d. Buding 6-2 6-3.

FOURTH ROUND	QUARTER-FINALS	SEMI-FINALS	FINAL	CHAMPION
Hart (2)	**Hart** (2)			
Migliori	6-1 6-1	**Hart** (2)		
Fletcher (7)	**Fletcher** (7)	6-1 6-3		
Dawson-Scott	6-0 6-1		**Brough** (4)	
Brough (4)	**Brough** (4)		2-6 6-3 6-3	
Bradley	6-1 6-1	**Brough** (4)		
Mortimer (6)	**Mortimer** (6)	6-1 6-3		
Ramirez	5-7 6-4 6-2			**Connolly** (1)
Curry	**Pratt** (8)			6-2 7-5
Pratt (8)	6-3 3-6 6-3	**Pratt** (8)		
Ward	**Fry** (3)	6-4 9-11 6-3		
Fry (3)	6-3 6-1		**Connolly** (1)	
Mercelis	**du Pont** (5)		6-1 6-1	
du Pont (5)	6-1 8-6	**Connolly** (1)		
Buxton	**Connolly** (1)	6-1 6-1		
Connolly (1)	6-0 6-0			

OTHER FINALS

GENTLEMEN'S DOUBLES: Final – R. N. Hartwig (A)/M. G. Rose (A) d. E. V. Seixas (USA)/M. A. Trabert (USA) 6-4 6-4 3-6 6-4.

LADIES' DOUBLES: Final – A. L. Brough (USA)/Mrs W. du Pont (USA) d. S. J. Fry (USA)/D. J. Hart (USA) 4-6 9-7 6-3.

MIXED DOUBLES: Final – E. V. Seixas (USA)/D. Hart (USA) d. K. R. Rosewall (A)/Mrs W. du Pont (USA) 5-7 6-4 6-3.

GENTLEMEN'S SINGLES PLATE: Final – H. W. Stewart (USA) d. A. Vieira (BR) 8-6 6-4.
LADIES' SINGLES PLATE: Final – R. Walsh d. P. A. Hird 6-2 7-5.
BOYS' INVITATION SINGLES: Final – R. Krishnan (IN) d. A. Cooper (A) 6-2 7-5.
GIRLS' INVITATION SINGLES: Final – V. A. Pitt d. C. Monnot (F) 5-7 6-3 6-2.

GENTLEMEN'S SINGLES

FIRST ROUND: K. R. Rosewall (2) (A) d. G. D. Owen 6-4 6-4 6-1; G. A. Worthington (A) d. T. Vincent (USA) 6-1 6-2 6-1; J. E. Barrett d. G. A. Cass (IRE) 6-3 4-6 8-6 9-7; J. Palada (YU) d. J. M. Draper (SP) 4-6 6-2 6-3 6-1; M. G. Davies d. H. C. Bernstein 6-1 6-1 6-4; W. Van Voorhees (USA) d. C. Figueira (POR) 6-0 6-1 6-1; C. V. Botha (SA) d. J. Bartroli (SP) 6-3 6-1 6-3; G. Merlo (IT) d. I. A. McDonald (TRIN) 6-0 6-2 6-4; **S. Davidson** (8) (SW) d. H. Richardson (USA) 4-6 6-3 6-4 4-6 8-6; E. Morea (ARG) d. A. Gubb (A) 6-2 8-6 6-1; F. Saiko (AU) d. J. A. Pickard 4-6 7-5 6-4 4-6 6-3; W. A. Knight d. G. Mezzi (B) w.o.; R. Krishnan (IN) d. E. R. Bulmer 6-1 6-3 6-3; W. R. Seymour (SA) d. H. W. Sweeney (USA) 8-6 6-1 7-5; I. Gulyas (HU) d. R. Huber (G) 7-9 10-8 6-4 9-7; L. Ayala (CH) d. C. H. Mason (A) 6-2 6-3 7-5; **V. Seixas** (3) (USA) d. A. J. Clayton 6-3 6-0 6-0; G. Shea (USA) d. T. Johansson (SW) 4-6 6-1 4-6 6-3 6-4; A. L. Proctor d. J. I. Devroe (B) 6-4 3-6 6-2 6-2; A. K. Quist (A) d. D. A. Fontana (C) 6-0 7-5 6-2; N. Pietrangeli (IT) d. J. N. Grinda (F) 6-2 4-6 8-6 6-3; A. J. Mottram d. G. Mulloy (USA) 6-1 6-4 6-1; C. W. Hannam d. J. J. F. Robinson 4-6 6-4 6-1; J. M. Ward d. J. W. Ager (USA) 4-6 6-0 6-2 6-3; **R. N. Hartwig** (5) (A) d. R. J. Lee 6-2 6-1 6-2; G. D. Oakley d. D. R. Oliver 6-4 6-2 6-4; A. Segal (SA) d. G. de Kermadec (F) 6-0 6-0 6-3; A. D. Russell (ARG) d. I. J. Warwick 3-6 6-1 6-4 7-5; R. T. Potter (A) d. H. F. Walton 2-6 4-7 5-; K. Nielsen (D) d. A. D. Marshall (A) 6-2 6-4 8-6; J. van Dalsum (NTH) d. K. Saeed (PAK) 6-2 6-1 6-4; I. Froman (SA) d. S. Laslo (YU) 9-11 7-5 6-4 2-0 ret'd; A. Huber (AU) d. G. L. Ward 6-3 3-6 6-2 11-13

7-5; I. Panajotovic (YU) d. R. Ahmad (PAK) 6-2 6-3 6-4; G. Forbes (SA) d. L. Bergelin (SW) 4-6 2-6 6-2 12-10 9-7; H. Flam (USA) d. R. Bedard (C) 6-3 6-2 6-2; S. Schwartz (USA) d. E. J. della Paolera (ARG) 6-3 7-5 3-6 6-3; R. K. Wilson d. S. Hoiberg (D) 6-4 6-1 6-3; P. Scholl (G) d. F. R. Kipping 6-1 6-2 6-4; **B. Patty** (7) (USA) d. G. W. Druliner (USA) 6-4 6-3 6-1; A. Larsen (USA) d. O. Sirola (IT) 6-4 7-5 6-3; M. Fox (USA) d. I. Sikorski (HU) 11-9 6-3 8-6; O. G. Williams (SA) d. A. Motolko (UR) 6-2 6-1 7-5; M. Hime d. D. G. Flye (USA) 2-6 7-5 6-1 2-6 6-4; V. Skonecki d. A. E. Dehnert (NTH) 6-3 6-2 6-2; G. L. Paish d. J. C. Molinari (F) 3-6 6-4 1-5 7-6 3; P. Washer (B) d. E. J. Filby 6-3 8-10 6-0 6-3; **L. A. Hoad** (4) d. R. N. Howe (A) 7-5 7-5 6-2; R. M. Perry (USA) d. M. F. Mohtadi (IN) 6-4 6-2 5-7 6-2; H. Redl (AU) d. L. T. Tan (INDO) 6-2 7-5 4-6 6-2; S. Stockenberg (SW) d. P. S. Eisenberg (USA) 6-3 6-2 1-6 6-4; J. A. T. Horn d. J. D. Forbes (SA) 6-3 6-4 6-2; R. Haillet (F) d. G. E. Mudge 6-3 6-4 6-0; J. Arkinstall (A) d. A. R. Mills 6-2 6-3 6-2; M. G. Rose (A) d. A. J. Cooper (A) 6-4 7-5 6-2; J. Drobny (6) (E) d. R. Buser (SWZ) 6-3 6-1 6-2; P. Chatrier (F) d. E. Martinez (SP) 4-6 6-3 2-6 6-3 6-3; I. Vermaak (SA) d. A. Hammersley (CH) 4-6 6-3 6-4 6-3; N. Kumar (IN) d. I. Pimentel (VEN) 6-3 6-1 8-6; W. W. Gilmour (SA) d. J. D. Hackett (IRE) 6-0 6-4 6-1; H. W. Stewart (USA) d. N. A. Fraser (A) 6-2 8-6 6-4; J. Brichant (B) d. A. J. N. Starte 6-3 6-1 6-3; T. T. Fancutt (SA) d. R. Becker 3-6 6-3 6-4 6-2; **T. Trabert** (1) (USA) d. M. J. Anderson (A) 6-3 6-4 6-2.

SECOND ROUND: Rosewall (2) d. Worthington 6-0 5-7 6-1 6-2; Barrett d. Palada 6-3 6-3; Davies d. Van Voorhees 6-4 6-2 10-8; Merlo d. Botha 6-1 6-4 3-6 6-1; **Davidson** (8) d. Morea 6-4 6-4 6-2; Knight d. Saiko 6-3 6-2 6-2; Krishnan d. Seymour 6-2 6-1 5-7 7-5; Ayala d. Gulyas 6-2 6-1 6-3; Shea d. Quist 6-3 3-6 6-4 4-6 6-4; Quist d. Proctor 6-2 6-0 6-2; Pietrangeli d. Mottram 7-5 5-7 11-9 5-7 6-2; Ager d. Hannam 6-1 3-6 8-6 6-1; **Hartwig** (5) d. Oakley 6-0 6-4 6-3; Segal d. Russell 6-3 6-2 6-0; Nielsen d. Potter 4-6 6-2 6-2 9-7; Froman d. van Dalsum 3-6 3-6 6-2

6-1 6-4; Huber d. Panajotovic 6-4 6-4 3-6 6-3; Flam d. Forbes w.o.; Wilson d. Schwartz 6-1 6-4 6-2; **Patty** (7) d. Scholl 6-0 6-4 6-3; Larsen d. Fox 6-2 7-5 7-5; Williams d. Hime 4-6 7-5 6-2; Skonecki d. Paish 6-4 6-4 6-3; **Hoad** (4) d. Washer 6-1 6-4 6-2; Drobny (6) d. Rose 6-4 3-6 11-9 6-4; Vermaak d. Chatrier 6-1 6-1; Kumar d. Gilmour 3-6 6-4 8-6 6-2; Stewart d. Brichant 6-2 3-6 6-3 8-6; **Trabert** (1) d. Fancutt 6-1 6-2 6-2.

THIRD ROUND: Rosewall (2) d. Barrett 6-3 6-2 6-2; Merlo d. Davies 8-6 1-6 6-4 3-6 8-6; **Davidson** (8) d. Knight 6-3 6-3 2-6 4-6 6-3; Ayala d. Krishnan 6-2 8-6 4-6 10-12 6-2; Shea d. Quist 6-2 5-7 7-5 6-3; Pietrangeli d. Ager 1-6 6-4 7-5 6-4; Segal d. **Hartwig** (5) 8-6 6-4 6-4; Nielsen d. Froman 6-3 6-1 6-2; Flam d. Huber 4-6 6-2 6-4 6-2; **Patty** (7)

d. Wilson 6-4 7-9 6-4 6-1; Larsen d. Williams 6-2 10-8 6-2; **Hoad** (4) d. Skonecki 6-3 6-3 6-4; Perry d. Stockenberg 2-6 6-2 6-4 4-6 6-4; **Drobny** (6) d. Arkinstall 6-4 2-6 6-2 11-9; Kumar d. Vermaak 6-3 6-2 3-6 9-7; **Trabert** (1) d. Stewart 6-4 6-3 6-1.

FOURTH ROUND	QUARTER-FINALS	SEMI-FINALS	FINAL	CHAMPION
Rosewall (2)	**Rosewall** (2)			
Merlo	6-4 6-1 2-1 ret'd	**Rosewall** (2)		
Davidson (8)	**Davidson** (8)	6-4 6-1 6-2		
Ayala	4-6 6-1 7-5 6-4		Nielsen	
Shea	Pietrangeli		11-9 6-2 2-6 6-4	
Pietrangeli	2-6 6-4 6-4 6-4	Nielsen		
Segal	Nielsen	1-6 6-3 5-7 6-2 7-5		
Nielsen	4-6 6-1 6-4 6-3			**Trabert** (1)
Flam	**Patty** (7)			6-3 7-5 6-1
Patty (7)	6-1 6-3 4-6 1-6 6-4	**Patty** (7)		
Larsen	**Hoad** (4)	6-4 6-4 6-4		
Hoad (4)	6-4 6-4 6-8 6-3		**Trabert** (1)	
Perry	**Drobny** (6)		8-6 6-2 6-2	
Drobny (6)	8-6 6-3 6-4	**Trabert** (1)		
Kumar	**Trabert** (1)	8-6 6-1 6-4		
Trabert (1)	6-4 6-2 6-2			

LADIES' SINGLES

FIRST ROUND: Mrs J. Fleitz (3) (USA) d. Mrs I. Pohmann (G) 6-0 6-2; R. F. Woodgate d. P. A. Hird 1-6 6-4 6-1; S. Schmitt (F) d. V. A. Pitt 6-3 6-0; D. Spiers d. Mrs E. W. Dawson-Scott 3-6 6-2 6-4; Mrs P. Chatrier (F) d. J. A. MacLeod 6-1 6-1; Mrs J. Kemsey-Bourne d. Mrs P. Coessens (B) 6-3 6-2; R. H. Bentley d. Mrs J. W. Cawthorn 6-4 6-4; J. Knight d. Mrs B. Gullbrandsson (SW) 3-6 12-10 6-4; **A. Buxton** (8) d. Mrs A. H. Thomas w.o.; L. L. Felix (USA) d. C. G. Hoahing 6-3 7-5; Mrs M. C. Cheadle d. Mrs J. A. Quelch 6-1 6-1; S. E. Waters d. Mrs J. W. Bee 6-3 13-11; V. J. Nichols (A) d. Mrs R. W. Baker (A) 6-2 6-0; H. Pascoe (SA) d. Mrs I. Wrede-Holm (NOR) 4-6 4-6 6-1; Mrs L. A. Hoad (A) d. A. McGuire (USA) 7-5 6-8 7-5; A. M. Gibb d. A. M. Price 13-11 6-4; M. P. Harrison d. B. N. Knapp 5-7 6-4 6-3; F.

J. I. ten Bosch (NTH) d. Mrs V. E. A. Morris 6-1 6-3; M. Carter (A) d. Mrs R. C. Panton 6-1 6-2; Mrs M. T. Weiss (ARG) d. Mrs G. Walter 6-3 3-6 7-5; Mrs R. Kaufmann (SWZ) d. E. E. Ruffin (A) 6-2 6-1; J. A. Shilcock d. P. J. Curry 6-1 6-2; Mrs A. C. Brighton d. Mrs G. C. Davidson (USA) 7-7 ret'd; **D. R. Hard** (6) (USA) d. D. Seeney (A) 6-3 6-6 0; Mrs G. Bucaille (F) d. G. E. Woodgate 6-2 5-7 6-4; J. M. Middleton d. Mrs J. A. Collier 6-0 8-6; C. Mercelis (B) d. Mrs E. Vollmer (G) 4-6 9-7 6-3; J. M. Boundy d. S. M. Griffin 6-2 7-5; Mrs E. Broz (AU) d. Mrs N. Migliori (IT) 4-6 6-1 6-2; V. Koortzen (SA) d. N. A. Schuurman (SA) 1-6 6-3 6-3; Mrs Z. Kormoczi (HU) d. R. J. R. Bulleid 6-1 6-1; **A. Mortimer** (4) d. D. L. Luxton (NZ) 6-0 6-2.

SECOND ROUND: D. Hart (1) (USA) d. Mrs H. C. Hopman (A) 6-1 6-0; D. Kilian (SA) d. K. M. Hubbell 6-2 6-1; M. E. Parker d. A. K. Clarke (IRE) 6-1 6-2; J. de Riba (SP) d. L. Pericoli (IT) 5-7 6-1 6-2; **Mrs D. P. Knode** (5) (USA) d. F. Muller (A) 6-4 2-6 7-5; M. Dittmeyer (G) d. Mrs K. S. Stott 6-4 1-6 6-3; S. J. Bloomer d. H. M. Macfarlane 6-3 6-3; V. M. Lewis d. Mrs M. P. O. Shuh-Proxauf (AU) 6-2 6-2; **Fleitz** (3) d. Woodgate 6-3 6-1; Spiers d. Schmitt 6-4 6-1; Chatrier d. Kemsey-Bourne 6-1 6-2; Knight d. Bentley 6-3 6-2; **Buxton** (8) d. Felix 5-7 6-4 6-1; Cheadle d. Waters 6-2 4-6 6-4; Nichols d. Pascoe 3-6 6-4 6-3; Hoad d. Gibb 6-1 3-6 6-3; ten Bosch d. Harrison 6-1 8-6; Carter d. Weiss 9-7

6-2; Shilcock d. Kaufman 6-1 3-6 6-3; **Hard** (6) d. Brighton 6-2 6-2; Middleton d. Bucaille 5-7 6-2 6-1; Mercelis d. Boundy 0-6 7-5 8-6; Koortzen d. Broz 6-2 6-4; Kormoczi d. **Mortimer** (4) 7-5 6-2; V. S. White d. M. Craig-Smith 6-3 2-6 6-4; Mrs H. Redick-Smith (SA) d. R. Davar (IN) 6-1 6-3; F. Lemal (F) d. M. E. Govett 6-1 6-2; **B. Penrose** (7) (A) d. Mrs C. Ball 6-2 4-6 6-3; Mrs H. Brewer (BER) d. P. E. Ward 4-6 6-3 8-6; E. M. Watson d. S. Speight 6-2 6-3; J. R. M. Morgan d. S. F. Pool 6-2 4-6 6-3; **A. L. Brough** (2) (USA) d. R. Walsh 6-0 6-2.

THIRD ROUND: Hart (1) d. Kilian 6-2 6-1; de Riba d. Parker 6-2 6-4; **Knode** (5) d. Dittmeyer 6-3 4-6 6-3; Bloomer d. Lewis 4-6 6-1; **Fleitz** (3) d. Spiers 6-4 6-1; Chatrier d. Knight 6-2 6-0; **Buxton** (8) d. Cheadle 6-4 6-3; Hoad d. Nichols 4-6 6-3 6-3; Carter d. ten Bosch 6-4 6-2; **Hard** (6) d. Shilcock 6-0 6-4; Mercelis d. Middleton 2-6 6-4; Kormoczi d.

Koortzen 6-1 6-3; Redick-Smith d. White 6-2 6-2; **Penrose** (7) d. Lemal 6-1 6-2; Brewer d. Watson 6-4 6-1; **Brough** (2) d. Morgan 6-0 6-0.

FOURTH ROUND	QUARTER-FINALS	SEMI-FINALS	FINAL	CHAMPION
Hart (1)	**Hart** (1)			
de Riba	6-1 6-3	**Hart** (1)		
Knode (5)	**Knode** (5)	6-4 6-3		
Bloomer	6-2 6-2		**Fleitz** (3)	
Fleitz (3)	**Fleitz** (3)		6-3 6-0	
Chatrier	6-3 6-0	**Fleitz** (3)	1	
Buxton (8)	**Buxton** (8)	6-2 6-2		
Hoad	6-1 6-0			**Brough** (2)
Carter	**Hard** (6)			7-5 8-6
Hard (6)	6-3 6-3	**Hard** (6)		
Mercelis	Kormoczi	6-2 6-3		
Kormoczi	6-1 6-2		**Brough** (2)	
Redick-Smith	**Penrose** (7)		6-3 8-6	
Penrose (7)	4-6 6-2 6-3	**Brough** (2)		
Brewer	**Brough** (2)	6-2 6-0		
Brough (2)	6-2 6-2			

OTHER FINALS

GENTLEMEN'S DOUBLES: Final – R. N. Hartwig (A)/L. A. Hoad (A) d. N. A. Fraser (A)/K. R. Rosewall (A) 7-5 6-4 6-3.
LADIES' DOUBLES: Final – A. Mortimer/J. A. Shilcock d. S. J. Bloomer/P. E. Ward 7-5 6-1.
MIXED DOUBLES: Final – E. V. Seixas (USA)/D. J. Hart (USA) d. E. Morea (ARG)/A. L. Brough (USA) 8-6 2-6 6-3.

GENTLEMEN'S SINGLES PLATE: Final – N. A. Fraser (A) d. R. N. Howe (A) 6-2 7-5.
LADIES' SINGLES PLATE: Final – F. Muller (A) d. L. L. Felix (USA) 6-4 6-4.
BOYS' INVITATION SINGLES: Final – M. P. Hann d. J. E. Lundquist (SW) 6-0 11-9.
GIRLS' INVITATION SINGLES: Final – S. M. Armstrong d. B. de Chambre (F) 6-2 6-4.

GENTLEMEN'S SINGLES

FIRST ROUND: L. A. **Hoad** (1) (A) d. D. A. Fontana (C) 9-7 6-2 6-0; T. T. Fancutt (SA) d. P. Wooller 6-3 6-3 6-2; D. B. Hughes d. D. Brinkman (USA) 6-3 4-6 11-9 6-3; J. Fleitz (USA) d. E. Martinez (SP) 6-3 1-6 2-6 6-4 6-3; G. J. Shea (USA) d. O. H. Garrido (CU) 6-4 6-4 8-6; R. M. Perry (USA) d. S. Hoiberg (D) 6-3 6-4 6-4; P. S. Eisenberg (USA) d. J. Palada (YU) 6-2 6-4 6-2; J. F. O'Brien (A) d. W. A. Knight 6-4 6-2 6-2; R. Krishnan (IN) d. J. **Drobny** (5) (E) 6-1 4-6 6-1 6-4; D. W. Candy (A) d. P. Darmon (F) 12-10 6-2 6-2; M. J. Anderson (A) d. G. Mezzi (B) 6-1 6-2 6-4; G. Sjowall (NOR) d. K. Saeed (PAK) 7-5 6-3 6-1; N. Pietrangeli (IT) d. B. C. Bowman (A) 6-2 6-4 7-5; I. Pimental (VEN) d. G. L. Paish 6-4 6-3 3-6 4-6 6-1; W. S. Farrer (SA) d. R. T. Potter (A) 6-4 6-1 6-4; S. Stockenberg (SW) d. A. E. Dehnert (NTH) 1-6 6-4 6-2 4-6 6-4; **B. Patty** (4) (USA) d. A. Huber (AU) 6-2 6-4 9-7; R. K. Wilson d. P. A. Willey (A) d. G. Mulloy (USA) 13-11 6-4 6-1; N. A. Fraser (A) d. B. E. Page (SA) 6-1 6-1 6-2; J. A. Pickard d. D. R. Collins 6-3 6-2 6-2; R. N. Howe (A) d. R. Abdesselam (F) 6-1 6-4 6-4; F. Feldbausch (G) d. E. C. Ford 7-5 5-7 6-0 6-8 6-2; **H. Richardson** (6) (USA) d. J. Arkinstall (A) 6-4 9-7 11-13 8-6; G. E. Mudge d. S. D. Lester 6-1 6-3 6-1; B. MacKay (USA) d. G. A. Cass 6-1 6-2 6-4; T. Ulrich (D) d. V. Petrovic 6-1 6-2; A. R. Mills d. J. Parma (CZ) 6-4 7-5 6-2; A. Segal d. B. Destremau (F) 6-3 6-1 6-0; A. D. Marshall (A) d. K. Moubarek (E) 6-0 6-1 6-1; M. Pirzada (PAK) d. R. T. White 6-3 6-1 8-6; I. J. Warwick d. I. Panajotovic (YU) 6-4 6-2 4-6

6-1; J. A. T. Horn d. H. Redl (AU) 6-2 6-3 6-1; S. Giammalva (USA) d. E. P. Argon (UR) 6-3 6-3 6-2; G. L. Forbes (SA) d. W. Van Voorhees (USA) 6-1 6-1 6-4; T. Vincent (USA) d. P. Scholl (G) 6-3 6-3 1-6 4-6 6-3; H. Flam d. I. Dorfman (USA) 6-4 6-4 6-3; J. C. Molinari (F) d. H. F. Walton 6-4 6-4 6-1; **V. Seixas** (8) (USA) d. M. Fox (USA) 6-1 6-2 6-3; M. P. Hann d. R. Goosen (SA) 3-6 6-3 6-4 6-2; F. R. Kipping d. K. Keretic (YU) 4-6 1-6 8-6 6-4 6-4; B. Gulley (A) d. R. D. Bennett 6-4 1-6 6-0 7-5; J. A. Morris (USA) d. E. R. Bulmer 7-5 6-3 5-7 6-4; O. S. Prenn d. P. Moys 7-5 8-6 5-7 6-2; D. L. M. Black (RH) d. G. D. Oakley 6-2 3-6 6-4 10-8; A. J. Cooper (A) d. M. G. Davies 4-6 6-4 2-6 6-4 6-3; **S. Davidson** (3) (SW) d. G. D. Owen 7-5 6-1 6-3; A. Gimeno (SP) d. F. Soehol (NOR) 6-0 6-4 6-1; G. A. Regan (A) d. J. Van Dalsum (NTH) 6-3 6-3 1-6 8-6; I. C. Vermaak (SA) d. J. C. Mayers (SA) 6-1 6-2 7-5; U. Schmidt (SW) d. H. W. Sweeney (USA) 6-0 6-3 6-3; L. Ayala (CH) d. S. Badr-el-Din (E) 6-1 6-3 6-4; R. Becker d. J. D. Hackett (IRE) 6-4 6-1 6-3; A. Ali (IN) d. A. J. Clayton (USA) 6-4 6-3 12-10; **K. Nielsen** (7) (D) d. R. Mark (A) 6-0 6-2 6-3; H. W. Stewart (USA) d. K. J. Meyer (USA) 6-3 6-3 6-4; A. Larsen (USA) d. A. R. Holmberg (USA) 5-7 6-3 6-4 6-3; L. E. Barcley (C) d. M. Belkhodja (F) 6-1 7-5 1-6 6-3; J. Brichant (B) d. J. M. Ward 6-4 6-2 6-2; O. Sirola (IT) d. R. Laver (A) 7-5 4-6 6-2; N. Kumar (IN) d. A. Vieira (BR) w.o.; G. L. Ward d. H. C. Bernstein 6-3 2-6 6-3 6-2; **K. R. Rosewall** (2) (A) d. J. E. Barrett 6-2 6-1 2-6 6-1.

SECOND ROUND: Hoad (1) d. Fancutt 9-7 6-3 7-5; Fleitz d. Hughes 6-2 6-4 6-4; Perry d. Shea 4-6 7-5 6-4; O'Brien d. Eisenberg 6-0 6-1 6-4; Krishnan d. Candy 1-6 7-5 2-6 6-3 6-3; Anderson d. Sjowall 6-1 6-1 7-5; Pietrangeli d. Pimental 7-5 6-3 6-3; Stockenberg d. Farrer 6-4 6-2 12-10; Wilson d. **Patty** (4) 12-10 2-6 6-3 6-4; Fraser d. Blatchford 6-1 6-1 6-4; Emerson d. Pickard 6-1 4-3 6-6 6-3; Howe d. Feldbausch 6-1 6-4; **Richardson** (6) d. Mudge 6-1 6-0; Ulrich d. MacKay 7-5 6-4 6-2; Segal d. Mills 6-3 6-2 6-3; Marshall d. Pirzada 6-0 6-2 6-3; Warwick d. Horn 10-8

6-2 6-1; Forbes d. Giammalva 6-1 9-7 6-4; Flam d. Vincent 6-3 5-7 6-3 6-1; **Seixas** (8) d. Molinari 7-5 6-3 6-2; Kipping d. Hann 7-5 7-5 6-4; Morris d. Gulley 6-2 6-3 6-3; Black d. Prenn 4-6 6-4 6-0 7-9 6-1; Cooper d. **Davidson** (3) 6-3 2-6 6-3 1-6 6-4; Schmidt d. Vermaak 8-6 1-6 5-7 6-3; Ayala d. Becker 1-6 4-6 12-10 6-2 6-3; **Nielsen** (7) d. Ali 6-1 8-10 6-2 6-1; Larsen d. Stewart 6-3 6-2 6-0; Brichant d. Barclay 6-4 9-7 7-5; Sirola d. Kumar 2-6 7-5 6-2 4-6 8-6; **Rosewall** (2) d. Ward 6-2 6-1 6-3.

THIRD ROUND: Hoad (1) d. Fleitz 6-3 6-2 6-0; O'Brien d. Perry 2-6 8-6 2-6 6-4; Anderson d. Krishnan 6-4 6-4 6-1; Pietrangeli d. Stockenberg 9-7 6-4 6-4; Fraser d. Wilson 8-6 7-5 6-3; Howe d. Emerson 6-2 2-6 6-1 6-4; **Richardson** (6) d. Ulrich 10-8 6-3; Segal d. Marshall 6-0 6-2 22-20; Forbes d. Warwick 6-0 6-2 6-1; **Seixas** (8)

d. Flam 4-6 6-1 6-1 10-8; Morris d. Kipping 6-4 7-5 9-7; Cooper d. Black 2-4 6-6 1-4 6-9 9-7; Schmidt d. Gimeno 4-6 6-3 6-1 6-4; Ayala **Nielsen** (7) 5-7 6-4 6-4 5-7 6-4; Larsen d. Brichant 6-3 6-3 6-1; **Rosewall** (2) d. Sirola 7-5 6-4 9-7.

FOURTH ROUND	QUARTER-FINALS	SEMI-FINALS	FINAL	CHAMPION
Hoad (1)	**Hoad** (1)			
O'Brien	6-4 6-1 6-4	**Hoad** (1)		
Anderson	Anderson	4-6 6-1 6-1 13-11		
Pietrangeli	9-7 3-6 6-3 4-6 6-2		**Hoad** (1)	
Fraser	Fraser		3-6 6-4 6-2 6-4	
Howe	6-2 6-4 7-5	**Richardson** (6)		
Richardson (6)	**Richardson** (6)	6-3 9-11 7-5 6-4		
Segal	7-5 ret'd			**Hoad** (1)
Forbes	**Seixas** (8)			6-2 4-6 7-5 6-4
Seixas (8)	6-2 6-1 8-6	**Seixas** (8)		
Morris	Morris	13-11 6-0 6-3		
Cooper	1-6 12-10 8-6 3-6 6-3		**Rosewall** (2)	
Schmidt	Schmidt		6-3 3-6 6-8 6-3 7-5	
Ayala	7-5 5-7 6-4 6-2	**Rosewall** (2)		
Larsen	**Rosewall** (2)	6-1 6-3 6-2		
Rosewall (2)	7-5 7-5 6-3			

LADIES' SINGLES

FIRST ROUND: A. **Mortimer** (3) d. Mrs T. D. Long (A) 6-1 4-6 6-3; Mrs R. C. Panton d. A. M. Gibb 6-4 6-3; H. Moorley d. Mrs P. C. Bramley 7-5 6-4; D. Hard (USA) d. Mrs J. A. Collier 6-2 6-2; Mrs G. Walter d. Mrs J. L. Deloford 0-6 6-4 6-1; Mrs G. Davidson (USA) d. Mrs B. Gullbrandsson-Sanden (USA) 8-6 7-5; Mrs J. F. Hale (SA) d. G. Evans 6-2 6-2; F. de la Courtie (F) d. J. Godfrey (A) 6-2; **Mrs D. P. Knode** (7) d. S. E. Waters 8-6 6-2; V. Puzejova (CZ) d. V. M. Lewis 1-6 6-0 6-3; D. Spiers d. Mrs V. A. Roberts 8-6 5-7 6-4; Mrs E. Vollmer (G) d. Mrs H. L. K. Brock 6-1 6-1; E. Becroft (NZ) d. S. M. Armstrong 6-0 7-5; J. Clarke (USA) d. E. Van Tonder (SA) 6-1 7-5; P. E. Ward d. H. M. Macfarlane 6-3 6-2; B. L. Carr (SA) d. J. Rook 6-0 6-0; Mrs L. A. Hoad (A) d. G. E. Woodgate 6-3 3-6 6-2; Mrs A. H.

Thomas d. Mrs J. W. Cawthorn (A) 6-2 6-2; J. A. MacLeod d. V. S. White 2-6 6-2 9-7; S. G. Waddington (SA) d. J. R. M. Morgan 6-4 4-6 9-7; Mrs W. Brewer (BER) d. Mrs C. J. Van der Storm (NTH) 6-1 6-3; M. J. de Riba (SP) d. J. M. Boundy 7-5 6-2; Mrs G. Bucaille (F) d. A. Winther (NOR) 6-4 6-1; **S. Fry** (5) (USA) d. C. Mercelis (B) 6-2 6-1; Mrs G. Holt d. M. H. O'Donnell (A) 4-6 7-5 6-4; L. Snow (USA) d. S. Speight 6-0 6-3; P. A. Hird d. J. A. Fitzpatrick (IRE) 2-6 6-3 6-2; I. Metzner (BR) d. Mrs E. Schmith (D) 6-3 6-4; J. A. Shilcock d. I. Buding (G) 6-3 6-2; A. S. Haydon d. K. Newcombe (A) 6-0 6-2; P. J. A. Wheeler d. M. E. Parker 2-6 6-0 6-2; **A. Gibson** (4) (USA) d. E. Buding (G) 6-4 6-2.

SECOND ROUND: **Mrs J. Fleitz** (2) (USA) d. P. Barril (SP) 6-4 6-3; C. G. Hoahing d. J. R. Edmondson (A) 6-4 6-2; D. G. Seeney (A) d. Mrs A. C. Brighton 6-2 6-3; Mrs Z. Kormoczi (HU) d. Mrs H. C. Hopman (A) 6-1 6-4; **A. Buxton** (6) d. Mrs S. le Besnarais (F) 6-4 6-2; Mrs L. Gram Andersen (D) d. Mrs J. Kemsey-Bourne 6-4 6-1; Mrs J. A. Roos (NTH) d. Mrs R. B. R. Wilson 4-6 6-2 6-2; E. M. Watson d. J. Curry 6-2 6-4; **Mortimer** (3) d. Panton 6-1 6-2; Hard d. Moorley 6-2 6-3; Davidson d. Walter 6-3 7-9 6-4; Hale d. de la Courtie 7-5 4-6 8-6; Puzejova d. **Knode** (7) 6-4 7-9 6-1; Vollmer d. Spiers 6-2 6-0; Becroft d. Clarke 6-3 3-6 7-5; Ward d. Carr 12-10 4-6 6-2; Hoad d. Thomas 8-6 6-4;

Waddington d. MacLeod 6-4 6-0 10-8; Brewer d. de Riba 6-4 6-0; **Fry** (5) d. Bucaille 6-3 6-2; Snow d. Holt 6-3 6-1; Hird d. Metzner 3-6 6-0 7-5; Shilcock d. Haydon 3-6 6-3 6-2; **Gibson** (4) d. Wheeler 6-1 6-2; Mrs J. H. Brown d. S. Reynolds (SA) 6-4 6-3; Mrs E. Gustafsson (SW) d. Mrs E. C. S. Pratt (USA) d. Mrs Craig-Smith 6-4 6-3; **S. J. Bloomer** (8) d. J. Knight 6-0 6-0; C. Yates-Bell d. N. Knapp 6-8 6-4; F. Muller (A) d. C. Monnot (F) 6-3 6-2; J. M. Middleton d. P. Edwards 6-2 6-4; **A. L. Brough** (1) (USA) d. J. R. Forbes (SA) 6-0 6-0.

THIRD ROUND: Fleitz (2) d. Hoahing 6-1 6-3; Kormoczi d. Seeney 6-2 6-3; **Buxton** (6) d. Gram Andersen 6-3 6-2; Watson d. Roos 10-8 6-2; **Mortimer** (3) d. Hard 6-3 7-5; Hale d. Davidson w.o.; Puzejova d. Vollmer 10-8 6-3; Ward d. Becroft 6-4 6-4; Hoad d. Waddington 6-0 6-2; **Fry** (5) d. Brewer 6-3 6-4; Hird d. Snow 3-6 6-1 6-2; **Gibson** (4) d.

Shilcock 4-6 6-2 6-1; Brown d. Gustafsson 6-1 6-3; **Bloomer** (8) d. Pratt 4-6 6-2 8-6; Muller d. Yates-Bell 6-0 6-0; **Brough** (1) d. Middleton 6-0 6-4.

FOURTH ROUND	QUARTER-FINALS	SEMI-FINALS	FINAL	CHAMPION
Fleitz (2)	**Fleitz** (2)			
Kormoczi	6-0 8-6	**Buxton** (6)		
Buxton (6)	**Buxton** (6)	w.o.		
Watson	6-4 6-4		**Buxton** (6)	
Mortimer (3)	**Mortimer** (3)		6-1 6-4	
Hale	6-2 6-0	Ward		
Puzejova	Ward	6-3 6-0		
Ward	6-3 6-2			**Fry** (5)
Hoad	**Fry** (5)			6-3 6-1
Fry (5)	6-2 6-2	**Fry** (5)		
Hird	**Gibson** (4)	4-6 6-3 6-4		
Gibson (4)	6-0 6-4		**Fry** (5)	
Brown	**Bloomer** (8)		6-4 4-6 6-3	
Bloomer (8)	6-2 7-5	**Brough** (1)		
Muller	**Brough** (1)	5-7 6-1 6-3		
Brough (1)	6-3 6-1			

OTHER FINALS

GENTLEMEN'S DOUBLES: Final — L. A. Hoad (A)/K. R. Rosewall (A) d. N. Pietrangeli (IT)/O. Sirola (IT) 7-5 6-2 6-1.
LADIES' DOUBLES: Final — A. Buxton/A. Gibson (USA) d. F. Muller (A)/D. G. Seeney (A) 6-1 8-6.
MIXED DOUBLES: Final — E. V. Seixas (USA)/S. J. Fry (USA) d. G. Mulloy (USA)/A. Gibson (USA) 2-6 6-2 7-5.
GENTLEMEN'S SINGLES PLATE: Final — H. W. Stewart (USA) d. G. Mulloy (USA) 4-6 6-4 6-4.

LADIES' SINGLES PLATE: Final — Mrs T. D. Long (A) d. I. Buding (G) 6-3 6-4.
BOYS' INVITATION SINGLES: Final — R. Holmberg (USA) d. R. G. Laver (A) 6-1 6-1.
GIRLS' INVITATION SINGLES: Final — A. S. Haydon d. I. Buding (G) 6-3 6-4.

GENTLEMEN'S SINGLES

FIRST ROUND: A. J. Cooper (2) (A) d. A. E. Dehnert (NTH) 6-2 6-1 9-7; J. Drobny (E) d. S. Stockenberg (SW) 6-2 6-2 6-3; R. Haillet (F) d. G. Sjowall (NOR) 6-4 11-9 6-3; A. Segal (SA) d. L. A. Gerrard (NZ) 6-3 6-3 15-13; N. C. Gibson (A) d. W. Skonecki (POL) 6-4 5-7 6-3 2-6 6-1; M. E. Green (USA) d. R. Mark (A) 6-2 6-4 6-2; H. W. Stewart (USA) d. J. I. Tattersall 6-2 6-2 6-4; E. Reyes (M) d. F. R. Kipping 5-7 0-6 6-0 6-3 6-4; **H. Flam** (7) (USA) d. P. Blondel (SWZ) 6-3 6-4 7-5; R. Krishnan (IN) d. N. Pietrangeli (IT) 6-4 6-3 6-4; J. Brichant (B) d. R. Garrido (CU) 7-5 6-2 6-2; R. Bedard (C) d. T. Ulrich (D) 9-7 3-6 7-5 6-1; J. M. Ward d. O. S. Prenn 4-6 6-1 9-7 6-3; W. A. Knight d. R. Huber (G) 6-2 6-4 4-6 6-3; G. D. Oakley d. R. K. Nyysonen (FIN) 6-1 2-6 11-9 6-3; A. Jancso d. A. J. Clayton 3-6 4-6 6-2 6-0 6-2; I. Ayala (CH) d. **H. Richardson** (3) (USA) 3-6 6-4 7-5 6-4; U. Schmidt (SW) d. I. Ribeiro (BR) 6-2 6-2 8-6 6-3; P. B. Frankland d. H. F. Walton 6-3 3-6 8-6 6-0; P. Remy (F) d. S. Hoiberg (D) 6-4 7-5; A. R. Mills d. J. D. Hackett (IRE) 6-2 6-1 6-3; E. Martinez (SP) d. D. L. M. Black (RH) 6-3 8-6 6-2; E. P. Argon (UR) d. G. N. Bassett (USA) 8-6 6-4 6-3; **N. A. Fraser** (5) (A) d. E. Aguirre (CH) 6-1 6-2 6-0; R. Becker d. G. L. Forbes (SA) 6-4 6-3 6-3; M. G. Davies d. J. Arkinstall 6-2 6-0 6-3; G. D. Owen d. I. Panajotovic (YU) 6-2 6-1 9-7; B. Patty (USA) d. A. Huber (AU) 6-4 6-1; F. Contreras (M) d. G. Mezzi (B) 9-7 6-1 6-3; M. J. Franks (USA) d. G. Fachini (IT) w.o.; W. W. Woodcock (A) d. M. P. Hann 6-1 6-3 4-6 6-2; M. J. Anderson d. J. E. Robson (NZ) 1-6 7-5 7-5 6-4; J. C. Molinari (F)

d. G. L. Ward 6-4 9-7 11-9; K. Nielsen (D) d. P. Scholl (G) 6-4 6-4 6-4; P. Washer (B) d. R. D. Bennett 9-7 6-4 5-7 6-4; A. Palafox (M) d. C. V. Baxter 6-4 6-3 6-3; K. Kamo (J) d. C. Crawford (USA) 6-3 6-3 6-3; N. Kumar (IN) d. R. N. Howe (A) 8-6 9-7 7-5; **V. Seixas** (6) (USA) d. C. P. Mayne (USA) 6-3 6-4 6-2; R. K. Wilson d. O. H. Garrido (CU) 6-3 6-2 6-3; A. Hammersley (CH) d. A. Gimeno (SP) 6-2 6-4 3-6 6-4; D. R. Oliver d. J. J. F. Robinson 3-6 4-6 6-3; G. Mulloy (USA) d. D. J. Lawer (SA) 6-4 6-1 3-6 6-4; P. S. Eisenberg (USA) d. A. Licis (P) 6-1 6-3 8-6; S. Schwartz (USA) d. D. Gunson 7-5 7-5 6-4; H. R. Buttimer (USA) d. A. A. Charnock (SA) 6-4 6-4 6-2; **S. Davidson** (4) (SW) d. A. Bey (RH) 6-3 9-7 7-5; F. Saiko (AU) d. G. Koenig (SA) 9-7 9-7 6-4; I. Pimental (VEN) d. W. Alwarez (COL) 6-4 6-2 4-6 6-2; J. Ulrich (D) d. C. Fernandes (BR) 3-6 5-7 6-3 8-6 6-4; J. M. Cranston (USA) d. J. Javorsky (CZ) 6-4 6-4 6-4; N. Kitovitz d. G. L. Paish 3-6 6-3 6-3 6-3; M. Froesch (SWZ) d. I. Piecevic (YU) 7-5 7-5 6-0; B. J. Katz (RH) d. P. G. Nicholls (NZ) 6-4 6-4 6-3; **M. G. Rose** (8) (A) d. A. Olmedo (PE) 7-5 7-5; O. Sirola (IT) d. E. R. Bulmer 6-4 6-3 4-6 6-3; J. E. Barrett d. R. V. Sherman (USA) 4-6 10-12 7-5 6-3 6-1; R. Emerson (A) d. G. J. Shea (USA) 8-6 6-3 6-1; J. J. Lesch (USA) d. M. Llamas 6-2 6-1 6-4; C. T. Parker (NZ) d. D. B. Hughes 3-6 8-6 6-3 6-4; T. T. Fancutt (SA) d. C. W. Hannam 6-3 7-5 6-8 6-3; **L. A. Hoad** (1) (A) d. P. Darmon (F) 6-2 6-4 6-3.

SECOND ROUND: Cooper (2) d. Drobny 6-1 6-3 6-3; Haillet d. Segal 4-6 6-4 6-4 9-7; Green d. Gibson 6-4 7-5 6-2; Stewart d. Reyes 6-2 6-4 3-6 6-3; **Flam** (7) d. Krishnan 3-6 6-2 7-5 5-7 6-2; Brichant d. Bedard 6-2 8-6 6-4; Knight d. Ward 6-1 6-3 4-6 6-1; Oakley d. Jancso 6-3 6-4 6-4; Schmidt d. Ayala 6-4 1-6 6-4 6-4; Remy d. Frankland 6-3 6-2 6-0; Mills d. Martinez 6-4 6-3 6-3; Candy d. Argon 6-1 1-6 6-3 6-2; **Fraser** (5) d. Becker 6-3 6-4 6-3; Davies d. Owen 6-3 7-5 3-6 7-5; Patty d. Contreras 6-4 6-4 6-0; Franks d. Woodcock 2-6 6-4 2-6 6-0 9-7; Anderson d. Molinari 4-6 6-2

6-2 6-4; Nielsen d. Washer w.o.; Kamo d. Palafox 6-1 7-9 6-3 6-3; **Seixas** (6) d. Kumar 6-4 6-1 6-4; Wilson d. Hammersley 6-2 6-3 3-6 6-2; Mulloy d. Oliver 6-2 6-3 6-1; Schwartz d. Eisenberg 1-6 15-13 7-5 6-1; **Davidson** (4) d. Buttimer 6-4 6-4 6-2; Pimental d. Saiko 6-2 6-2 6-3; Ulrich d. Cranston 6-4 4-6 4-6 6-3 7-5; **Rose** (8) d. Katz 6-1 7-5 7-5; Sirola d. Pickard 6-8 6-3 8-6 6-3; Emerson d. Barrett 6-1 6-1 6-4; Lesch d. Parker 8-6 3-6 6-4 6-3; **Hoad** (1) d. Fancutt 6-2 6-1.

THIRD ROUND: Cooper (2) d. Haillet 6-0 6-2 6-4; Green d. Stewart 6-4 1-0 ret'd; **Flam** (7) d. Brichant 1-6 6-2 6-1 6-4; Knight d. Oakley 10-8 3-6 9-7 6-1; Schmidt d. Remy 6-4 6-1 1-6 1-6 6-4; Candy d. Mills 2-6 6-3 6-2 6-4; **Fraser** (5) d. Davies 6-2 6-3 1-6 1-6 6-2; Patty d. Franks 6-4 6-3 6-4; Anderson d. Nielsen 7-9 6-2 6-0 4-6 6-3; **Seixas** (6) d.

Kamo 6-2 6-2 5-7 6-3; Wilson d. Mulloy 4-6 6-3 6-3 7-5; **Davidson** (4) d. Schwartz 6-1 6-4 7-5; Pimental d. Ulrich 6-2 6-2 3-6 6-2; **Rose** (8) d. Froesch 6-2 6-4 6-2; Emerson d. Sirola 6-3 3-2 6-1 6-4; **Hoad** (1) d. Lesch 6-3 9-7 6-4.

FOURTH ROUND	QUARTER-FINALS	SEMI-FINALS	FINAL	CHAMPION
Cooper (2)	**Cooper** (2)	**Cooper** (2)		
Green	6-2 6-3 9-7	6-3 7-5 6-1		
Flam (7)	**Flam** (7)			
Knight	6-3 6-1 6-3		**Cooper** (2)	
Schmidt	Schmidt		1-6 14-12 6-3 8-6	
Candy	6-4 2-6 6-2 11-9	**Fraser** (5)		
Fraser (5)	**Fraser** (5)	1-6 6-4 6-8 6-4 6-4		
Patty	6-3 6-4 10-12 6-4			**Hoad** (1)
Anderson	**Seixas** (6)			6-2 6-1 6-2
Seixas (6)	4-6 6-3 6-2 6-2	**Davidson** (4)		
Wilson	**Davidson** (4)	5-7 6-4 6-4 6-4		
Davidson (4)	3-6 6-1 8-6 6-4			
Pimental	**Rose** (8)		**Hoad** (1)	
Rose (8)	6-3 6-3 6-4	**Hoad** (1)	6-4 6-4 7-5	
Emerson	**Hoad** (1)	6-4 4-6 10-8 6-3		
Hoad (1)	6-4 6-4 6-2			

LADIES' SINGLES

FIRST ROUND: Mrs D. P. Knode (4) (USA) d. Mrs L. A. Hoad (A) 4-6 9-7 6-1; C. Mercelis (B) d. Mrs I. J. Warwick 6-2 6-0; Mrs P. Chatrier (F) d. B. N. Knapp 6-2 6-4; Mrs R. C. Panton d. J. A. Fulton 6-3 7-5; P. Edwards d. Mrs P. C. Bramley 6-1 5-7 6-2; Mrs M. Sladek (C) d. J. A. MacLeod 8-6 8-6; P. A. Hird d. Mrs V. A. Roberts 6-1 6-1; Mrs J. A. Collier d. B. M. Horton 6-2 6-1; **A. Mortimer** (7) d. Mrs C. T. Clark 6-0 6-1; Mrs I. Vogler (G) d. Mrs J. M. Wagstaff 6-3 6-2; K. Fageros (USA) d. P. J. A. Wheeler 4-6 6-3 6-2; I. Buding (G) d. Mrs H. Kaufmann (USA) 6-0 6-3; M. Arnold (USA) d. P. M. Burrell 6-0 6-0; V. S. White d. Mrs H. G. Macintosh 7-5 6-4; R. Schuurman (SA) d. Mrs M. Weiss (SP) 6-4 6-2; R. M. Reyes (M) d. Mrs J. W. Cawthorn 6-3 6-2; Mrs M. C. Cheadle d. H. M. Macfarlane 6-0 6-1; G. E.

Woodgate d. Mrs J. G. Holt 6-0 7-5; R. M. Morrison (NZ) d. M. Craig-Smith 6-3 6-2; P. J. Curry d. P. Barril (SP) 6-4 6-3; Mrs E. C. S. Pratt (USA) d. S. E. Waters 6-1 6-0; G. Evans d. Mrs G. E. Marshall (KEN) 5-7 6-3 6-3; Mrs B. I. Shenton d. Mrs A. H. Thomas 2-6 7-5 9-7; Mrs T. T. Fancutt (SA) d. **Mrs T. D. Long** (6) (A) 6-8 9-7 9-7; Mrs G. Walter d. P. A. Ingram 6-0 8-6; C. C. Truman d. Mrs M. Cranadak-Milonja (YU) 6-1 6-1; S. M. Cox d. Mrs A. Enzen (SWZ) 6-1 7-9 10-8; Mrs Z. J. Van der Storm (NTH) d. H. Moorley 6-3 4-6 6-1; J. Rook d. J. E. Lintern 6-4 6-4; Mrs S. le Besnerais (F) d. J. A. Fitzpatrick (IRE) 6-2 6-4; R. F. Woodgate d. Mrs A. Bernheim (B) 2-6 6-2 6-0; **S. J. Bloomer** (3) d. P. E. Ward 6-1 6-3.

SECOND ROUND: A. L. Brough (2) (USA) d. Mrs K. Hawton (A) 6-2 6-0; F. de la Courtie (F) d. Mrs B. S. Worrall 6-4 6-1; Mrs J. E. Robson (NZ) d. Mrs E. Broz (AU) 6-1 6-2; Mrs W. Brewer (BER) d. Mrs E. Van Nielsen (D) 6-0 6-0; **D. R. Hard** (5) (USA) d. R. H. Bentley 6-2 6-0; Mrs L. B. E. Thung (NTH) d. M. H. de Amorim (BR) 6-3 4-6 6-1; E. Buding (G) d. M. O. Bouchet (F) 6-4 6-1; A. S. Haydon d. Mrs G. L. Forbes (SA) 6-4 6-1; **Knode** (4) d. Mercelis 6-4 5-7 6-4; Chatrier d. Panton 6-1 6-1; Edwards d. Sladek 6-4 5-7 6-1; Hird d. Collier 6-1 6-2; **Mortimer** (7) d. Vogler 6-1 6-1; Fageros d. Buding 4-6 6-3 7-5; Arnold d. White 6-4 6-0; Reyes d. Schuurman 7-5 6-1; Woodgate d. Cheadle 6-1 6-4; Morrison

d. Curry w.o.; Pratt d. Evans 6-3 6-1; Fancutt d. Shenton 6-4 6-0; Truman d. Walter 6-3 6-2; Cox d. Van der Storm 7-5 3-6 6-2; Rook d. le Besnerais 6-4 4-6 6-0; **Bloomer** (3) d. Woodgate 6-0 6-1; Mrs E. Vollmer (G) d. M. E. Morgan 6-1 6-0; S. Reynolds (SA) d. J. A. Shilcock 4-6 9-7 6-4; S. M. Armstrong d. Mrs J. L. Deloford 10-8 3-6 6-2; **V. Puzejova** (8) (CZ) d. Mrs G. Bucaille (F) 6-1 6-2; C. G. Hoahing d. Y. Ramirez (M) 9-7 3-6 8-6; J. Knight d. K. Newcombe (A) 9-7 4-6 6-2; M. Hellyer (A) d. M. J. de Riba (SP) 6-1 6-0; **A. Gibson** (1) (USA) d. Mrs Z. Kormoczy (HU) 6-4 6-4.

THIRD ROUND: Brough (2) d. de la Courtie 6-2 6-0; Brewer d. Robson 6-1 6-2; **Hard** (5) d. Thung 6-1 6-1; Buding d. Haydon 3-6 6-4 6-3; **Knode** (4) d. Chatrier 6-0 6-2; Edwards d. Hird 7-5 3-6 6-4; Fageros d. **Mortimer** (7) 6-3 4-6 6-3; Reyes d. Arnold 6-3 6-3; Morrison d. Woodgate 2-6 6-3 6-1; Pratt d. Fancutt 6-4 6-3; Truman d. Cox 6-1 6-1;

Bloomer (3) d. Rook 6-1 6-2; Reynolds d. Vollmer 7-5 3-6 13-11; Armstrong d. **Puzejova** (8) 6-4 1-6 6-1; Hoahing d. Knight 6-3 6-1; **Gibson** (1) d. Hellyer 6-4 6-2.

FOURTH ROUND	QUARTER-FINALS	SEMI-FINALS	FINAL	CHAMPION
Brough (2)	**Brough** (2)	**Hard** (5)		
Brewer	7-5 6-1	6-2 6-2		
Hard (5)	**Gard** (5)			
Buding	3-6 7-5 6-3		**Hard** (5)	
Knode (4)	**Knode** (4)		6-2 6-3	
Edwards	6-3 6-3	**Knode** (4)		
Fageros	Reyes	6-4 6-0		
Reyes	7-5 6-4			**Gibson** (1)
Morrison	Pratt			6-3 6-2
Pratt	6-4 11-9	Truman		
Truman	Truman	9-7 5-7 6-4		
Bloomer (3)	6-3 6-3		**Gibson** (1)	
Reynolds	Reynolds		6-1 6-1	
Armstrong	6-3 8-6	**Gibson** (1)		
Hoahing	**Gibson** (1)	6-3 6-4		
Gibson (1)	6-1 6-1			

OTHER FINALS

GENTLEMEN'S DOUBLES: Final – G. Mulloy (USA)/J. E. Patty (USA) d. N. A. Fraser (A)/L. A. Hoad (A) 8-10 6-4 6-4 6-4.

LADIES' DOUBLES: Final – A. Gibson (USA)/D. R. Hard (USA) d. Mrs K. Hawton (A)/Mrs T. D. Long (A) 6-1 6-2.

MIXED DOUBLES: Final – M. G. Rose (A)/D. R. Hard (USA) d. N. A. Fraser (A)/A. Gibson (USA) d. 6-4 7-5.

GENTLEMEN'S SINGLES PLATE: Final – G. L. Forbes (SA) d. A. Segal (SA) 10-8 11-13 6-3.

LADIES' SINGLES PLATE: Final – M. B. Hellyer (A) d. R. Schuurman (SA) 6-4 6-4.

BOYS' INVITATION SINGLES: Final – J. I. Tattersall d. I. Ribeiro (BR) 6-2 6-1.

GIRLS' INVITATION SINGLES: Final – M. Arnold d. R. M. Reyes (M) 8-6 6-2.

GENTLEMEN'S SINGLES

1958

FIRST ROUND: M. J. Anderson (2) (A) d. P. J. Lal (IN) 6-4 6-4 7-5; A. Gimeno (SP) d. H. F. Walton 6-4 6-3 6-3; J. E. Barrett d. R. E. Hull 6-1 7-5 6-2; P. F. Hearnden (A) d. E. L. Scott (USA) 6-8 6-0 6-2 6-4; R. Laver (A) d. E. Balestra (SWZ) 6-0 6-2 6-2; C. D. Carter (USA) d. R. D. Bennett 6-3 4-6 6-4 6-0; A. Licis (POL) d. J. I. Tattersall 3-6 6-2 6-3 3-6 6-2; J. Drobny (E) d. R. Haillet (F) 2-6 6-3 3-6 6-3 6-2; **K. Nielsen** (6) (D) d. J. Van de Weg (NTH) 6-2 6-4 6-0; G. L. Ward d. P. Rodriguez (CH) 6-4 6-3 6-4; I. Panajotovic (YU) d. Gunson 4-6 15-13 6-2 6-3; A. Ali (IN) d. A. J. Clayton 6-1 8-6 6-4; J. Brichant (B) d. E. P. Argon (UR) 6-2 7-5 6-3; M. G. Davies d. A. Palafox (M) 6-2 4-6 6-2 6-2; O. Sirola (IT) d. A. W. Gaertner (SA) 6-2 10-8 3-6 10-8; U. Schmidt (SW) d. G. J. Shea (USA) 1-6 6-4 6-2 6-4; **N. A. Fraser** (4) (A) d. V. Petrovic 6-3 6-1 6-0; F. Mei (CHI) d. F. Hainka (AU) 6-2 6-2 6-1; P. Scholl (G) d. J. M. Ward 7-5 6-4 6-4; A. Maggi (IT) d. E. C. Ford 1-6 6-3 6-4 5-7 7-5; D. W. Candy (A) d. W. A. Knight 7-5 5-7 13-15 6-3 12-10; M. Fox (USA) d. W. Van Voorhees 2-6 11-9 6-0 6-1; P. Darmon (F) d. E. Aguirre (CH) 6-1 6-1 6-4; R. Garrido (CU) d. N. Kitovitz 6-3 7-5 2-6 6-4; **S. Davidson** (7) (SW) d. J. N. Grinda (F) 6-1 7-5 6-3; F. Contreras (M) d. R. K. Stilwell (RH) 6-3 6-0 6-3; I. Pimental (VEN) d. G. Stewart (A) 7-5 6-4 6-2; N. Kumar (IN) d. I. Ribeiro (BR) 6-1 10-8 6-2; R. M. Perry (USA) d. L. A. Gerrard (NZ) 6-4 6-1 3-6 8-6; J. Patty (USA) d. A. C. Kendall (A) 6-3 6-3 6-4; W. W. Woodcock (A) d. J. A. Pickard 3-6 6-2 11-3 6-1 8-6; T. Ulrich (D) d. A. Arilla (SP) 6-1 6-1 6-2; I. J. Warwick d. M. Llamas (M) 8-6 9-7 6-2; R. Krishnan (IN)

d. J. M. Cranston (USA) 6-3 6-4 1-6 6-3; J. C. Molinari (F) d. O. H. Garrido (CU) 8-6 6-3 6-2; R. Becker d. P. Newman (A) 6-2 6-2 6-1; R. Mark (A) d. D. R. Collins 6-1 6-1 6-2; G. Grant (USA) d. M. J. Sangster 6-4 6-4 4-6 8-6; E. R. Bulmer d. I. Gulyas (HU) w.o.; **B. MacKay** (8) (USA) d. E. Martinez (SP) 4-6 6-2 6-3 6-1; B. M. Kearney (A) d. S. Hoiberg (D) 6-1 6-2 6-3 6-1; M. E. Green (USA) d. A. Lazzarino (IT) 4-6 6-2 3-6 6-1 6-2; G. Mulloy (USA) d. A. Hammersley (CH) 6-2 6-2 4-6 6-3; E. J. Hurry (SA) d. C. V. Baxter 6-1 6-2 6-3; R. W. Barnes (BR) d. G. D. Oakley 3-6 3-6 6-4 6-2 8-6; O. S. Prenn d. J. D. Hackett (IRE) 6-4 6-2 9-7; J. Frost (USA) d. P. J. O'Kane (A) 7-5 8-6 6-2; **M. G. Rose** (3) (A) d. W. Skonecki (POL) 6-3 6-4 6-1; W. V. Reid (A) d. P. Van Eysden (NTH) 7-5 7-5 6-2; R. K. Wilson d. W. Bungert (G) 6-0 6-3 6-2; W. W. Quillian (USA) d. P. G. Nicholls (NZ) 6-3 6-4 6-2; M. P. Hann d. R. H. Dabbs 6-3 6-1 5-7 6-3; G. L. Paish d. I. Sikorski (POL) 6-3 6-1 6-4; N. Pietrangeli (IT) d. A. Jancso 10-8 6-4 10-8; E. Buchholz (USA) d. C. A. Fernandes (BR) 6-4 6-4 6-3; **L. Ayala** (5) (CH) d. K. Keretic (YU) 6-3 6-2 6-3; A. R. Mills d. P. Remy (F) 4-6 6-3 1-6 6-2 7-5; W. F. Jacques (A) d. N. Nath (IN) 8-6 6-4 6-4; W. Alwarez (COL) d. M. S. Santana (SP) 6-3 10-8 6-3; A. Segal (SA) d. J. E. Lundquist (SW) 3-6 3-6 6-3 6-2 6-3; R. N. Howe (A) d. R. W. T. Cawthorn (A) 6-2 6-1 6-2; J. Ulrich (D) d. P. Wooller 8-6 6-1 4-6 7-5; F. Saiko (AU) d. A. J. Udaykumar (IN) 6-3 6-4 6-2; **A. J. Cooper** (1) (A) d. G. D. Owen 10-8 3-6 6-4 6-1.

SECOND ROUND: Anderson (2) d. Gimeno 6-4 6-4 6-4; Barrett d. Hearnden 6-3 6-1 5-7 6-3; Laver d. Carter 4-6 6-3 12-10 6-4; Drobny d. Licis 6-4 8-6 6-4; **Nielsen** (6) d. Ward 8-6 4-6 4-8 10-8 6-2; Panajotovic d. Ali 8-6 6-4 6-8 6-3 7-5; Brichant d. Davies 6-3 8-6 2-6 5-7 6-1; Schmidt d. Sirola 11-9 6-3 1-6 2-6 7-5; **Fraser** (4) d. Mei 6-1 6-1 6-1; Maggi d. Scholl 6-2 6-4 6-2; Candy d. Fox 6-4 10-8 6-4; Darmon d. Garrido 3-6 6-2 6-7 5-7; **Davidson** (7) d. Contreras 6-2 10-8 8-6; Pimental d. Kumar 7-9 8-6 10-8 6-3; Patty d. Perry 6-4 6-3 3-6 4-6 6-4; Ulrich d. Woodcock

6-4 6-1 6-2; Krishnan d. Warwick 6-1 14-12 6-0; Molinari d. Becker 6-3 6-3 6-4; Mark d. Grant 15-13 0-6 8-6 6-2; **MacKay** (8) d. Bulmer 6-1 9-7 6-2; Green d. Kearney 7-5 6-1 6-4; Mulloy d. Barnes 7-5 9-7 2-6 6-4; **Rose** (3) d. Frost 6-4 10-8 6-4; Wilson d. Reid 7-5 6-0 7-5; Hann d. Quillian 11-9 1-6 6-3 6-4; Pietrangeli d. Paish 6-2 6-0 4-6 4-6 6-3; **Ayala** (5) d. Buchholz 6-4 8-6 8-6; Jacques d. Mills 8-10 7-5 7-9 6-4 6-1; Segal d. Alwarez 6-4 6-1 6-2; Ulrich d. Howe 6-2 4-6 7-5 8-6; **Cooper** (1) d. Saiko 6-3 6-4 6-1.

THIRD ROUND: Anderson (2) d. Barrett 3-6 6-0 6-2 6-3; Drobny d. Laver 6-1 6-1 6-4; **Nielsen** (6) d. Panajotovic 6-1 6-4 6-2; Schmidt d. Brichant 3-6 6-3 7-5 4-6 7-5; **Fraser** (4) d. Maggi 6-0 6-4 6-3; Darmon d. Candy w.o.; **Davidson** (7) d. Pimental 6-3 3-6 6-1 6-4; Patty d. Ulrich 4-6 7-5 6-1 6-2; Krishnan d. Molinari 8-6 6-1 6-0; **MacKay**

(8) d. Mark 4-6 10-8 6-4 6-4; Mulloy d. Green 3-6 6-4 6-4 6-2; **Rose** (3) d. Barnes 6-3 9-7 6-4; Wilson d. Hann 8-6 6-4 6-0; Pietrangeli d. **Ayala** (5) 6-4 6-4 6-3; Segal d. Jacques 6-3 6-1 6-4; **Cooper** (1) d. Ulrich 9-7 6-2 3-6 6-3.

FOURTH ROUND	QUARTER-FINALS	SEMI-FINALS	FINAL	CHAMPION
Anderson (2)	**Anderson** (2)			
Drobny	6-3 10-8 6-2			
Nielsen (6)	**Nielsen** (6)	**Nielsen** (6)		
Schmidt	6-4 15-13 6-4	6-2 6-3 ret'd		
Fraser (4)	**Fraser** (4)		**Fraser** (4)	
Darmon	6-4 6-3 6-3		6-4 6-4 17-19 6-4	
Davidson (7)	**Davidson** (7)	**Fraser** (4)		
Patty	6-4 2-6 4-6 9-7 6-4	6-4 6-8 6-2 3-6 8-6		**Cooper** (1)
Krishnan	**MacKay** (8)			3-6 6-3 6-4 13-11
MacKay (8)	6-3 11-9 6-2			
Mulloy		**Rose** (3)		
Rose (3)	**Rose** (3)	6-2 6-4 6-4		
Wilson	6-2 6-3 6-1		**Cooper** (1)	
Pietrangeli	Wilson		7-9 6-2 6-2 6-3	
Segal	11-9 6-2 6-2	**Cooper** (1)		
Cooper (1)	**Cooper** (1)	6-4 6-2 3-6 4-6 7-5		
	13-11 6-3 3-6 14-12			

LADIES' SINGLES

FIRST ROUND: Mrs D. P. Knode (3) (USA) d. Mrs V. A. Roberts 7-5 6-2; C. Mercelis (B) d. S. E. Waters 6-2 6-1; Mrs I. J. Warwick d. Mrs P. Chatrier (F) w.o.; S. M. Cox d. Mrs B. S. Worrall 8-6 2-6 6-1; E. Buding d. C. G. Hoahing 6-0 6-1; Mrs A. H. Thomas d. Mrs P. I. Vogler (G) 1-6 9-7 6-2; S. Reynolds (SA) d. M. Solsona (SP) 6-0 6-2; A. Mortimer d. C. Ibarra (CH) 6-0 6-2; **J. S. Hopps** (7) (USA) d. Mrs E. W. A. Bostock 6-3 6-3; N. S. Marsh (A) d. M. O. Bouchet (F) 6-2 6-2; J. A. Fulton d. J. A. Fitzpatrick (IRE) 6-2 6-2; Mrs W. du Pont (USA) d. R. C. Panton 6-3 6-0; C. M. Leather d. S. M. Hannah 8-6 7-5; R. M. Reyes (M) d. R. H. Bentley 1-6 6-6 6-0; S. H. Cox (NZ) d. Mrs W. S. Smith (USA) 6-4 7-5; F. Muller (A) d. J. Knight 6-0 6-1; A. S. Haydon d. J. M. Young 6-1 6-1; M. Varner (USA) d. I. Buding (G)

7-5 6-4; P. Barril (SP) d. M. Grace 3-6 6-0 6-1; J. Forbes (SA) d. G. Evans 6-1 6-4; P. E. Ward d. P. A. Hird 6-3 6-2; Mrs C. F. O. Lister d. Mrs R. B. R. Wilson 6-4 7-9 7-5; S. Lazzarino (IT) d. Mrs A. Bernheim (B) 6-1 6-2; **K. Fageros** (8) (USA) d. S. M. Moore (USA) 6-3 7-5; V. S. White d. M. M. Carter (A) 6-3 2-6 6-4; Mrs T. D. Long (A) d. J. A. Shilcock 6-1 5-7 6-2; R. M. Morrison (NZ) d. L. Snow (USA) 11-9 6-3; S. M. Armstrong d. I. Troccole (USA) 6-1 9-7; Mrs M. Galtier (F) d. Mrs I. Wrede-Holm (NOR) w.o.; P. J. Curry d. P. C. Drew 6-3 6-2; R. Schuurman (SA) d. Mrs P. Rushton 6-4 8-6; **M. E. Bueno** (4) (BR) d. Mrs M. C. Cheadle 6-1 6-2.

SECOND ROUND: C. C. Truman (2) d. Mrs J. L. Deloford 6-0 6-1; J. Rook d. P. M. Nettleton (NZ) 6-4 8-6; M. Arnold (USA) d. P. J. A. Wheeler 2-6 6-3 6-0; Mrs E. Vollmer (G) d. V. Studer (SW) 6-4 6-4; **Mrs Z. Kormoczy** (6) (HU) d. F. de la Courtie (F) 6-2 6-4; Mrs A. Segal (SA) d. S. Pachta (AU) 6-4 6-1; Mrs G. E. Marshall (K) 6-2 6-4; Mrs K. Hawton (A) d. Mrs J. F. Roos (NTH) 6-2 6-0; Mercelis d. **Knode** (3) 6-3 7-5; Warwick d. Cox 6-4 1-6 6-2; Buding d. Thomas 6-3 6-1; Mortimer d. Reynolds 6-8 6-2 6-0; Marsh d. **Hopps** (7) 7-5 9-7; du Pont d. Fulton 6-1 6-0; Reyes d. Leather 6-1 10-8; Muller d. Cox 7-5 6-3; Haydon d. Varner 6-3 1-6 6-2; Forbes d. Barril 6-1 5-7 6-3;

Ward d. Lister 6-3 7-5; **Fageros** (8) d. Lazzarino 6-1 7-5; Long d. White 6-3 6-2; Morrison d. Armstrong 2-6 6-3 6-3; Curry d. Galtier 6-4 6-2; **Bueno** (4) d. Schuurman 6-0 6-2; Mrs H. E. Kaufmann (SWZ) d. M. Catt 5-7 8-6 6-2; B. Carr (SA) d. F. Marinkelle (NTH) 6-1 9-7; M. Dittmeyer (G) d. Mrs J. M. Wagstaff 6-4 8-6; **S. J. Bloomer** (5) d. A. Guri (SP) 6-1 6-2; R. Courteix (F) d. Mrs E. Broz (AU) 6-8 6-3 6-2; L. Coghlan (A) d. Mrs C. D. Carter (USA) 6-0 6-3; Y. Ramirez (M) d. J. M. Trewby 6-0 6-2; **A. Gibson** (1) (USA) d. M. G. Hellyer (A) 6-0 6-2.

THIRD ROUND: Truman (2) d. Rook 6-3 6-1; Arnold d. Vollmer 6-2 8-6; **Kormoczy** (6) d. Segal 6-2 6-3; Hawton d. Weiss 6-4 6-1; Mercelis d. Warwick 6-0 6-2; Mortimer d. Buding 6-4 6-1; du Pont d. Marsh 6-3 3-6 8-6; Muller d. Reyes 6-3 7-5; Haydon d. Forbes 3-6 6-2 7-5; Ward d. **Fageros** (8) 2-6 6-4 6-4; Long d. Morrison 6-4 6-3; **Bueno** (4)

d. Curry 6-0 6-2; Carr d. Kaufmann 6-4 6-4; **Bloomer** (5) d. Dittmeyer 6-1 6-2; Coghlan d. Courteix 6-0 6-3; **Gibson** (1) d. Ramirez 9-7 6-2.

FOURTH ROUND	QUARTER-FINALS	SEMI-FINALS	FINAL	CHAMPION
Truman (2)	Arnold			
Arnold	10-8 6-3	**Kormoczy** (6)		
Kormoczy (6)	**Kormoczy** (6)	6-1 5-7 8-6		
Hawton	6-2 6-1		Mortimer	
Mercelis	Mortimer		6-0 6-1	
Mortimer	6-3 6-4	Mortimer		
du Pont	du Pont	4-6 6-3 10-8		
Muller	6-3 6-2			**Gibson** (1)
Haydon	Haydon			8-6 6-2
Ward	1-6 6-3 6-1	Haydon		
Long	**Bueno** (4)	6-3 7-5		
Bueno (4)	6-2 6-3		**Gibson** (1)	
Carr	**Bloomer** (5)		6-2 6-0	
Bloomer (5)	6-3 6-4	**Gibson** (1)		
Coghlan	**Gibson** (1)	6-3 6-8 6-2		
Gibson (1)	6-0 6-2			

OTHER FINALS

GENTLEMEN'S DOUBLES: Final — S. Davidson (SW)/U. Schmidt (SW) d. A. J. Cooper (A)/N. A. Fraser (A) 6-4 6-4 8-6.
LADIES' DOUBLES: Final — M. E. Bueno (BR)/A. Gibson (USA) d. Mrs W. du Pont (USA)/M. Varner (USA) 6-3 7-5.
MIXED DOUBLES: Final — R. N. Howe (A)/L. Coghlan (A) d. K. Nielsen (D)/A. Gibson (USA) 6-3 13-11.

GENTLEMEN'S SINGLES PLATE: Final — P. Remy (F) d. J. N. Grinda (F) 6-3 11-9.
LADIES' SINGLES PLATE: Final — S. Reynolds (SA) d. M. B. Hellyer (A) 6-2 6-2.
BOYS' INVITATION SINGLES. Final — E. Buchholz (USA) d. P. Lall (IN) 6-1 6-3.
GIRLS' INVITATION SINGLES: Final — S. M. Moore (USA) d. A. Dmitrieva (USSR) 6-2 6-4.

257

GENTLEMEN'S SINGLES

FIRST ROUND: N. A. Fraser (2) (A) d. P. Darmon (F) 6-4 6-4 6-2; C. A. Fernandes (BR) d. F. Saiko (AU) 10-8 6-3 4-6 6-2; A. E. G. Bailey (A) d. R. V. Sherman (USA) 4-6 6-4 7-5 7-9 8-6; M. P. Hann d. G. Sjowall (NOR) 6-1 10-8 6-3; A. C. Kendall (A) d. E. P. Argon (UR) 6-4 6-8 2-6 7-5 8-6; O. Sirola (IT) d. J. H. Maloney (SA) 6-4 6-2 6-4; M. Santana (SP) d. A. Bresson (F) 6-0 6-0 6-1; J. Grigry (USA) d. R. W. Dixon 3-6 11-13 6-4 9-7 6-4; **B. Mackay** (5) (USA) d. I. C. Vermaak (SA) 6-2 6-2 3-6 6-3; W. Skonecki (POL) d. J. Mukherjea (IN) 6-3 7-9 6-4 7-5; I. Panajotovic (YU) d. J. I. Tattersall 6-4 4-6 6-3 6-1; I. Leschly (D) d. G. L. Ward 6-3 6-2 3-6 9-7; W. A. Knight d. J. E. Barrett 6-2 6-0 6-3; J. E. Lundquist (SW) d. R. Becker 6-3 9-7 6-4; R. Hewitt (A) d. M. A. Otway 6-4 6-4 6-0; J. A. Douglas (USA) d. B. Patty (USA) 4-6 6-1 6-1 6-0; E. Buchholz (USA) d. **N. Pietrangeli** (3) (IT) 6-4 3-6 7-5 7-5; G. L. Forbes (SA) d. P. Blondel (SWZ) 6-3 6-0 6-1; G. Mulloy (USA) d. A. Jancso 6-3 6-3 6-2; L. A. Gerrard (NZ) d. N. B. Nette (A) 9-11 6-3 10-8 6-4; J. M. Couder (SP) d. W. F. Jacques (A) 4-6 6-3 6-4 2-6 6-3; S. Davidson (SW) d. A. J. Lane (A) 7-5 6-2 1-6 6-0; M. Fox (USA) d. S. Nikolic (YU) 6-4 6-2 11-13 6-1; J. C. Molinari (F) d. C. Chu (CHI) 4-6 6-3 7-5 6-4; **K. Nielsen** (7) (D) d. M. Mulligan (A) 6-4 1-6 6-3 7-5; R. Laver (A) d. J. E. Mandarino (BR) d. S. W. Hicks (A) 6-2 4-6 6-8 6-3; J. M. Ward d. G. D. Owen 6-3 7-5 5-7 6-2; A. R. Mills d. J. Drobny (A) 14-12 3-6 10-8 8-6; O. S. Prenn d. P. Rodriguez (CH) 6-3 6-8 6-2 6-3; W. Maris (NTH) d. A. F. M. Dillon 6-1 6-3 6-2; R. N. Howe (A) d. P. J. Lal (IN) 10-8 6-3 9-7; G. Merlo (IT) d. D.

Ecklebe (G) 6-4 2-6 6-3 6-1; J. W. Frost (USA) d. T. A. Adamson 6-1 6-1 6-1; J. Ulrich (D) d. R. Weedon (SA) 6-3 6-4 6-2; R. F. Sanders (SA) d. M. Branovic (G) 6-4 6-1 6-1; I. A. McDonald (BG) d. P. Van Eysden (NTH) 6-3 4-6 6-4 6-3; A. Gimeno (SP) d. U. Schmidt (SW) 7-5 11-9 8-6; F. Gorman (A) d. K. Keretic (YU) 6-3 6-4 6-1; **R. Emerson** (8) (A) d. W. Alvarez (COL) 6-3 6-3; M. J. Franks (USA) d. F. Hainka (AU) 6-4 2-6 6-2 6-2; J. N. Grinda (F) d. A. Potanin (USSR) 6-1 6-3 6-1; J. M. Gracie d. D. Reilly (A) 6-4 6-3 6-2; K. Fletcher (A) d. W. Gasiorek (POL) 6-2 6-1 6-3; C. V. Baxter d. J. D. Hackett (IRE) 3-6 8-6 6-3 6-4; D. W. Candy (A) d. G. N. Bassett (USA) 6-4 6-1 6-2; J. A. Pickard d. C. W. Hannam 2-6 4-7 7-5; **R. K. Wilson** (4) d. I. J. Warwick 6-3 6-0 6-4; G. D. Oakley d. P. Willey (C) 6-3 7-5 6-3; S. Stockenberg (SW) d. J. Hammill (SA) 4-6 6-2 6-4 8-10 6-3; A. Bey (RH) d. O. H. Garrido (CU) 1-6 7-5 7-5 6-2; F. D. Jagge (NOR) d. D. R. Oliver 2-6 4-6 8-6 6-3 6-2; J. Brichant (B) d. A. J. Clayton 6-2 6-1 6-3; G. L. Paish d. L. Legenstein 6-1 12-10 2-6 2-6 6-2; **L. Ayala** (6) (CH) d. J. Javorsky (CZ) d. 6-3 6-0 6-3; M. G. Davies d. B. E. Woolf (NZ) 6-1 6-8 6-4 6-2; B. Jovanovic (YU) d. I. Gulyas (HU) 6-3 6-4 6-3; F. Mei (CHI) d. R. W. Barnes (BR) 3-6 9-11 11-9 6-1 6-1; T. Ulrich (D) d. R. Mark (A) 6-4 6-8 6-4 6-3; R. Krishnan (IN) d. T. W. Heckler (SA) 6-3 6-1 6-0; B. Phillips-Moore d. J. L. Arilla (SP) 4-6 6-4 3-7 5; A. R. Mandelstam (SA) d. A. Maggi (C) 6-4 6-1 6-2; **A. Olmedo** (1) (USA) d. W. W. Woodcock (A) 6-2 6-4 6-3.

SECOND ROUND: Fraser (2) d. Fernandes 6-3 6-1 6-2; Hann d. Bailey 6-2 4-6 6-1 6-3; Sirola d. Kendall 9-7 6-1 1-6 10-8; Santana d. Grigry 6-2 4-6 4-6 9-7 6-1; **Mackay** (5) d. Skonecki 6-4 6-3 3-6 6-1; Leschly d. Panajotovic 6-4 3-6 4-6 7-5 3-6 4-4 7-5; Knight d. Lundquist 6-3 3-6 6-1 6-4; Hewitt d. Douglas 6-1 8-6 6-4; Buccholz d. Forbes 3-6 7-5 11-9 10-8; Mulloy d. Gerrard 6-3 7-5 6-4; Davidson d. Couder 6-1 4-6 6-1 6-2; Molinari d. Fox 6-3 3-6 6-3 6-2; Laver d. **Nielsen** (7) 10-8 6-4 7-5; Ward d. Mandarino 6-4 6-4 3-6 6-0; Mills d. Prenn 6-4 6-1 6-1; Howe d. Maris 7-5 6-4 6-1; Frost d.

Merlo 6-0 6-0 6-3; Ulrich d. Sanders 6-2 6-3 6-2; Gimeno d. McDonald 6-3 6-2 6-1; **Emerson** (8) d. Gorman 6-1 4-6 8-6 6-3; Grinda d. Franks 3-6 3-6 7-5 6-4 7-5; Fletcher d. Gracie 6-2 6-1 6-0; Candy d. Baxter 3-6 2-6 2; **Wilson** (4) d. Pickard 6-3 8-6 6-4; Oakley d. Stockenberg 6-2 9-7; Bey d. Jagge 7-5 6-2 6-2; Segal d. Brichant 6-4 4-6 8-6 6-2; **Ayala** (6) d. Paish 6-3 6-1 6-4; Davies d. Jovanovic 6-1 3-6 6-3 6-2; Ulrich d. Mei 6-1 6-1 6-1; Krishnan d. Phillips-Moore 6-2 6-2 6-3; **Olmedo** (1) d. Mandelstam 6-1 6-1 6-3.

THIRD ROUND: Fraser (2) d. Hann 7-5 8-4 6-2; Sirola d. Santana 6-4 9-7 3-6 6-3; **Mackay** (5) d. Leschly 6-3 6-2 6-4; Knight d. Hewitt 6-3 7-5 6-3; Mulloy d. Buchholz 4-7 5-6 6-4; Molinari d. Davidson 9-7 6-1 11-13 4-6 6-4; Laver d. Ward 6-2 6-3 7-5; Mills d. Howe 9-11 6-4 7-5 6-2; Ulrich d. Frost 9-7 7-5 6-1; **Emerson** (8) d. Gimeno 6-2 3-6 6-4

6-1; Grinda d. Fletcher 6-2 7-5 6-4; **Wilson** (4) d. Candy 6-4 6-3 1-6 6-4; Bey d. Oakley 4-9 7-4 6-6 6-4; **Ayala** (6) d. Segal 6-3 8-10 6-4 6-2; Ulrich d. Davies 3-6 6-4 8-6 1-6 6-1; **Olmedo** (1) d. Krishnan 6-4 3-6 6-4 7-5.

FOURTH ROUND	QUARTER-FINALS	SEMI-FINALS	FINAL	CHAMPION
Fraser (2)	**Fraser** (2)			
Sirola	3-6 6-3 14-12 8-10 6-3	**Mackay** (5)		
Mackay (5)	**Mackay** (5)	5-7 10-8 0-6 6-3 6-1		
Knight	6-2 8-6 10-8		Laver	
Mulloy	Molinari		11-13 11-9 10-8 7-9 6-3	
Molinari	6-1 6-2 7-9 6-2	Laver		
Laver	Laver	6-3 6-3 6-0		
Mills	6-3 3-6 6-3 6-4			**Olmedo** (1)
Ulrich	**Emerson** (8)			6-4 6-3 6-4
Emerson (8)	7-9 6-3 10-8 6-1	**Emerson** (8)		
Grinda	**Wilson** (4)	6-3 6-4 6-2		
Wilson (4)	6-3 17-15 6-1		**Olmedo** (1)	
Bey	**Ayala** (6)		6-4 6-0 6-4	
Ayala (6)	6-2 6-1 6-0	**Olmedo** (1)		
Ulrich	**Olmedo** (1)	7-5 3-6 6-3 6-3		
Olmedo (1)	6-3 6-3 6-2			

LADIES' SINGLES

FIRST ROUND: D. R. Hard (4) (USA) d. U. Hultkrantz (SW) 6-1 6-0; R. Ostermann (G) d. Mrs J. M. Wagstaff 6-3 6-3; Mrs J. L. Deloford d. Mrs R. B. R. Wilson 6-4 10-8; M. R. O'Donnell d. C. Webb 6-2 6-2; A. Guri (SP) 6-2 7-5; R. H. Bentley d. Mrs L. Gram Andersen (D) 6-3 6-2; Mrs A. C. Brighton d. S. Pachta (AU) 9-7 6-2; M. Hammill (SA) d. Mrs V. A. Roberts 3-6 6-4 6-4 4; **A. S. Haydon** (8) d. D. Thomas (A) 6-1 6-0; J. M. Young d. Mrs P. Chatrier (F) 6-4 6-2; J. Rees Lewis (F) d. Mrs M. C. Cheadle 2-6 6-1 7-5; J. Rook d. Mrs G. E. Marshall (K) 6-1 7-5; N. Marsh (A) d. G. Thomas (USA) 6-2 2-6 6-4; Mrs H. C. Hopman (A) d. H. J. M. Durose 5-7 6-2 6-4; K. Fageros (USA) d. Mrs C. T. Clark 6-3 7-5; Mrs A. H. Thomas d. J. E. Lintern 6-4 6-1; Mrs C. Brasher d. E. T. Court 6-3 6-1; B. Gunderson

(USA) d. J. Gencic (YU) ret'd; J. D. Johnson (USA) d. J. A. Shilcock 1-3 6-6 2; R. Morrison (NZ) d. Mrs R. C. Panton 6-3 7-5; M. Arnold (USA) d. J. A. Fulton 6-3 6-1; D. M. Catt d. L. Vail (USA) 6-3 6-1; M. Dittmeyer (G) d. M. M. Carter (A) 6-2 6-3; **M. E. Bueno** (6) (BR) d. P. Edwards 6-1 6-3; P. J. A. Wheeler d. A. Dmitrieva (USSR) 6-4 6-4; Mrs S. J. Reitano (A) d. V. S. White 6-3 6-3; E. Buding (G) d. S. M. Hannah 6-2 6-4; F. de la Courtie (F) d. F. Marinkelle (NTH) 6-0 3-6 6-2; P. Barril (SP) d. M. Grace 6-3 6-2; C. Mercelis (B) d. L. M. Grundy 6-1 6-4; S. Lazzarino (IT) d. C. Lampe (USA) 8-6 5-7 8-6; **Mrs J. G. Fleitz** (3) (USA) d. R. Schuurman (SA) 2-6 6-4 6-4.

SECOND ROUND: A. Mortimer (2) d. Mrs M. T. Weiss (SP) 6-0 6-0; M. Moritz (NTH) d. Mrs H. L. K. Brock 6-8 7-5 6-4; V. Puzejova (CZ) d. M. B. Hellyer (A) 9-7 6-2; P. A. Hird d. Mrs B. I. Shenton 6-2 6-4; **S. Reynolds** (5) (SA) d. J. M. Trewby 6-3 6-2; L. Pericoli (IT) d. Mrs M. Sladek (C) 6-2 7-5; R. M. Reyes (M) d. J. Arth (USA) 6-1 6-4; M. L. Gerson (SA) d. P. M. Nettleton (NZ) 3-6 8-6 6-4; **Hard** (4) d. Ostermann 7-5 6-2; Deloford d. O'Donnell 6-4 8-6; Bentley d. Buding 6-3 6-4; Hammill d. Brighton 6-2 6-0; **Haydon** (8) d. Young 6-0 6-3; Rees Lewis d. Rook 4-6 7-5 7-5; Marsh d. Hopman 6-4 6-4; Fageros d. Thomas 6-2 6-2; Gunderson d. Brasher 6-8 6-2 6-2; Morrison d. Johnson 3-4 6-4 6-0;

Arnold d. Catt 2-6 6-3 6-4; **Bueno** (6) d. Dittmeyer 4-6 6-1 6-1; Reitano d. Wheeler 4-6 6-1 6-3; Buding d. de la Courtie 6-3 6-3; Mercelis d. Barril 6-1 6-1; **Fleitz** (3) d. Lazzarino 4-6 6-4 6-2; Mrs E. Launert (G) d. A. Heegewaldt 6-1 6-4; J. S. Hopps (USA) d. J. Cross (SA) 6-3 6-1; P. Courteix (F) d. P. A. Stewart (USA) 6-2 6-3; **S. M. Moore** (7) (USA) d. E. F. Muller (A) 5-7 8-6 6-4; Y. Ramirez (M) d. C. Yates-Bell 6-2 6-1; S. M. Armstrong d. Mrs B. Byrne (IRE) 6-2 6-3; P. E. Ward d. Mrs J. W. Cawthorn 6-3 6-4; **C. C. Truman** (1) d. S. E. Waters 6-3 7-5.

THIRD ROUND: Mortimer (2) d. Moritz 6-0 6-1; Hird d. Puzejova 9-7 6-4; **Reynolds** (5) d. Pericoli 3-6 7-5 6-3; Reyes d. Gerson 6-2 2-8 6-4; **Hard** (4) d. Deloford 6-0 6-2; Bentley d. Hammill 6-2 6-2; **Haydon** (8) d. Rees Lewis 6-1 6-4; Marsh d. Fageros w.o.; Morrison d. Gunderson 3-6 6-3 6-3; **Bueno** (6) d. Arnold 5-7 6-3 6-1; Buding d. Reitano

6-1 2-6 6-4; **Fleitz** (3) d. Mercelis 4-6 6-1 6-4; Hopps d. Launert 6-1 6-4; **Moore** (7) d. Courteix 6-4 6-4; Ramirez d. Armstrong 7-5 6-1; **Truman** (1) d. Ward 4-6 6-4 6-3.

FOURTH ROUND	QUARTER-FINALS	SEMI-FINALS	FINAL	CHAMPION
Mortimer (2)	**Mortimer** (2)			
Hird	6-1 6-2	**Reynolds** (5)		
Reynolds (5)	**Reynolds** (5)	7-5 8-6		
Reyes	6-4 6-2		**Hard** (4)	
Hard (4)	**Hard** (4)		6-4 6-4	
Bentley	6-2 6-4	**Hard** (4)		
Haydon (8)	**Haydon** (8)	1-6 6-4 7-5		
Marsh	8-6 6-2			**Bueno** (6)
Morrison	**Bueno** (6)			6-4 6-3
Bueno (6)	6-1 7-5	**Bueno** (6)		
Buding	Buding	6-3 6-3		
Fleitz (3)	8-6 2-6 7-5		**Bueno** (6)	
Hopps	**Moore** (7)		6-2 6-4	
Moore (7)	7-5 2-6 6-4	**Moore** (7)		
Ramirez	Ramirez	6-3 6-2		
Truman (1)	6-3 6-2			

OTHER FINALS

GENTLEMEN'S DOUBLES: Final — R. S. Emerson (A)/N. A. Fraser (A) d. R. G. Laver (A)/R. Mark (A) 8-6 6-3 14-16 9-7.
LADIES' DOUBLES: Final — J. Arth (USA)/D. R. Hard (USA) d. Mrs J. Fleitz (USA)/C. C. Truman 2-6 6-2 6-3.
MIXED DOUBLES: Final — R. G. Laver (A)/D. R. Hard (USA) d. N. A. Fraser (A)/M. E. Bueno (BR) 6-4 6-3.

GENTLEMEN'S SINGLES PLATE: Final — J. Javorsky (CZ) d. M. Fox (USA) 6-3 6-2.
LADIES' SINGLES PLATE: Final — Mrs C. Brasher d. Mrs M. Sladek (C) 3-6 6-3 7-5.
BOYS' INVITATION SINGLES: Final — T. Lejus (USSR) d. R. Barnes (BR) 6-2 6-4.
GIRLS' INVITATION SINGLES: Final — J. Cross (SA) d. Schuster (AU) 6-1 6-1.

GENTLEMEN'S SINGLES

1960

FIRST ROUND: B. MacKay (2) (USA) d. J. L. Arilla (SP) 6-2 6-4 7-5; A. Bey (RH) d. P. Eisenberg (USA) 6-4 6-4 6-4; U. Schmidt (SW) d. G. P. Jackson (IRE) 6-1 6-2 6-2; J. C. Molinari (F) d. F. Soehol (NOR) 6-2 7-5 6-4; G. L. Paish d. W. Alvarez (COL) 6-4 3-6 6-4 6-4; J. Ulrich (D) d. G. Koenig (SA) 6-1 6-2 6-3; R. H. Osuna (M) d. P. van Eysden (NTH) 6-1 6-3 6-4; L. A. Gerrard (NZ) d. I. Plecevic (YU) 6-2 6-0 6-2; **N. Pietrangeli** (5) (IT) d. B. Patty (USA) 6-3 9-7 6-3; M. Mulligan (A) d. J. Mukerjea (IN) 6-4 6-2; R. K. Wilson d. R. W. Barnes (BR) 6-2 6-3 6-3; P. Rodriguez (CH) d. A. Licis (POL) 11-9 6-1 1-6 1-6 6-4; I. Gulyas (HU) d. R. Aubone (ARG) 6-3 6-3 6-4; W. Bungert (G) d. J. F. O'Brien (A) 5-7 13-11 6-4 6-4; J. W. Frost (USA) d. C. V. Baxter 6-2 6-4 6-1; R. Nyyssonen (FIN) d. A. Ochoa (M) 3-6 6-1 6-4 6-1; **R. Laver** (3) (A) d. G. L. Ward d. 6-3 6-0 6-2; H. Flam (USA) d. N. B. Nette (A) 6-3 6-4 2-6 6-4; A. J. Lane (A) d. F. Saiko (AU) 6-3 1-6 6-4 6-4; M. Santana (SP) d. S. Stockenberg (SW) 6-2 6-3 6-2; P. Darmon (F) d. J. R. McDonald (NZ) d. F. M. Aly (E) 6-2 6-1; M. J. Sangster d. G. D. Oakley 6-4 6-4 6-4; **R. Emerson** (6) (A) d. T. Ulrich (D) 6-1 6-4 6-4; J. Javorsky (CZ) d. M. Mozer (USSR) 7-9 6-3 4-6 6-2 6-3; N. Pilic (YU) d. C. Kuhnke (G) 10-8 6-3 6-3; **J. Lehane** (7) (A) w.o.; R. M. Morrison (SA) d. J. A. Douglas (USA) 5-7 7-5 5-7 6-4 6-2; R. Becker d. A. Segal (SA) 11-9 3-6 6-4 6-3; G. Merlo (IT) d. J. Brichant (B) 6-3 6-4 6-3; W. W. Woodcock (A) d. M. Hann 6-2 6-2 6-2; M. Llamas (M) d. B. Phillips-Moore (A) 7-5 2-6 7-5 3-6 6-1; A. R. Mandelstam (SA) d. C. R. Applewhaite 6-3 6-0 6-2; I. C. Vermaak (SA) d. F. A. Froehling (USA) 4-6 8-6 6-3 6-4; R.

Hewitt (A) d. B. E. Woolf (NZ) 6-4 6-4 6-4; R. Haillet (F) d. R. Taylor 6-4 2-6 3-6 7-5; W. Stuck (G) d. J. Drobny 3-6 7-5 6-1 6-2; C. A. Fernandes (BR) d. L. Legenstein (AU) 4-6 7-5 3-6 6-4 6-3; A. Gimeno (SP) d. A. B. Krikorian (USA) 6-3 6-2 8-6; **R. Krishnan** (7) (IN) d. J. B. Hillebrand (A) 6-4 6-3 2-6 3-6 6-1; J. E. Lundquist (SW) d. R. N. Howe (A) 2-6 1-6 6-3 6-3 6-3; R. D. Ralston (USA) d. T. Moe (NOR) 6-3 6-2 6-4; K. Nielsen (D) d. R. Holmberg (USA) 4-6 8-6 6-3 10-8; W. A. Knight d. A. Palafox (M) 6-3 10-12 6-2 7-5; A. R. Mills d. W. G. Coghlan (A) 4-6 6-4 3-6 8-6 7-5; J. J. Pearce (A) d. V. Presecki (YU) 6-2 6-1 6-3; S. Tacchini (IT) d. J. M. Ward 6-1 4-6 7-5 4-6 8-6; **L. Ayala** (4) (CH) d. R. F. Sanders (SA) 9-7 6-2 8-6; J. N. Grinda (F) d. B. Sayed (E) 6-3 6-2 6-4; M. Fox (USA) d. H. W. Ditzler (USA) 3-6 3-3 6-0 6-3; F. Contreras (M) d. J. Leschly (D) 5-7 6-4 3-6 6-2; A. W. Gaertner (SA) d. C. Holm (SW) 6-4 6-0 6-4; R. Mark (A) d. N. Kumar (IN) 6-0 6-2 6-1; B. Jovanovic (YU) d. C. P. Mayne (USA) 8-6 5-7 6-4 7-5; J. M. Cranston (USA) d. J. E. Barrett 6-2 6-4 6-1; **E. Buchholz** (8) (USA) d. J. M. Couder (SP) 6-3 9-7 2-6 6-2; G. Mulloy (USA) d. J. A. Pickard 7-5 6-4 15-17 6-3; M. G. Davies d. P. Moys 6-4 8-6 4-6 2; D. W. Candy (A) d. R. J. Siska (USA) 2-6 6-3 6-1 6-1; O. Sirola (IT) d. I. Buding 0-6 8-6 6-1 6-1; T. Lejus (USSR) d. W. Gasiorek (POL) 6-2 6-3 6-4; D. Ecklebe (G) d. J. Hammill (SA) 2-6 6-3 13-11 3-6 10-8; W. Maris (NTH) d. J. E. Mandarino (BR) 6-4 6-3 2-6 6-4; **N. A. Fraser** (1) (A) d. F. Hainka (AU) 6-2 6-0 6-4.

SECOND ROUND: MacKay (2) d. Bey 6-2 8-6 6-4; Schmidt d. Molinari 4-6 6-4 7-5 6-2; Ulrich d. Paish 7-5 3-6 6-1 6-3; Osuna d. Gerrard 6-4 8-6 6-2; **N. Pietrangeli** (5) d. Mulligan 6-1 6-4 9-7; Wilson d. Rodriguez 6-2 6-0 7-5; Gulyas d. Bungert 11-9 6-4 6-3; Frost d. Nyyssonen 6-3 6-3 6-8 8-6; **Laver** (3) d. Flam 6-2 6-2 6-2; Santana d. Lane 6-3 5-7 10-12 6-4 8-6; Darmon d. McKinley 6-4 6-2 3-6 4-6 6-1; Sangster d. McDonald 6-4 6-3 7-5; **Emerson** (6) d. Javorsky 4-6 1-6 6-1 6-0 6-3; Otway d. Pilic 8-6 6-3 6-2; Becker d. Merlo 7-6 3-6 6-2; Llamas d. Woodcock

6-3 7-5 6-2; Vermaak d. Mandelstam 5-7 6-3 7-5 7-5; Hewitt d. Haillet 9-7 6-3 6-4; Stuck d. Fernandes 7-5 6-1 7-5; **Krishnan** (7) d. Gimeno 2-6 6-3 6-0 2-6 6-3; Lundquist d. Ralston 6-4 6-1 9-7; Nielsen d. Knight 2-6 6-4 2-6 11-9 6-3; Mills d. Pearce 3-6 6-0 10-8 6-3; **Ayala** (4) d. Tacchini 6-1 6-1 6-3; Grinda d. Fox 6-0 6-1 6-2; Gaertner d. Contreras 6-1 8-6 6-2; Mark d. Jovanovic 8-6 6-3 6-0; **Buchholz** (8) d. Cranston 6-4 6-3 6-1; Mulloy d. Davies 6-3 6-3 6-4; Candy d. Sirola 6-0 6-8 6-1 6-1; Lejus d. Ecklebe 6-4 8-6 9-7 6-4; **Fraser** (1) d. Maris 6-2 6-3 6-2.

THIRD ROUND: MacKay (2) d. Schmidt 6-4 6-3 11-9; Ulrich d. Osuna 9-7 7-5 4-6 6-1; **Pietrangeli** (5) d. Wilson 6-2 4-6 13-11 6-8 6-3; Frost d. Gulyas 7-5 6-4 6-4; **Laver** (3) d. Santana 3-6 6-1 6-4 6-4; Darmon d. Sangster 6-1 8-6 6-2; **Emerson** (6) d. Otway 13-11 4-6 6-3 7-5; Llamas d. Becker 6-2 6-4 4-6 8-6; Vermaak d. Hewitt 6-4 4-3 6-3 6-1;

Krishnan (7) d. Stuck 6-0 6-1 6-1; Lundquist d. Nielsen 13-11 6-1 4-6 4-6 9-7; **Ayala** (4) d. Mills 8-7 ret'd; Gaertner d. Grinda 6-3 3-6 8-6 6-4; **Buchholz** (8) d. Mark 6-4 15-13 7-5; Candy d. Mulloy 6-4 7-5 3-6 6-2; **Fraser** (1) d. Lejus 6-4 6-1 6-8 6-3.

FOURTH ROUND	QUARTER-FINALS	SEMI-FINALS	FINAL	CHAMPION
MacKay (2)	**MacKay** (2)			
Ulrich	6-2 6-2 8-6			
Pietrangeli (5)	**Pietrangeli** (5)	**Pietrangeli** (5)		
Frost	6-4 6-1 6-2	16-14 6-2 3-6 6-4		
Laver (3)	**Laver** (3)		**Laver** (3)	
Darmon	6-2 2-6 6-1 8-6		4-6 6-3 8-10 6-2 6-4	
Emerson (6)	**Emerson** (6)	**Laver** (3)		
Llamas	2-6 6-0 6-2 9-7	6-4 5-7 6-4 6-4		
Vermaak	**Krishnan** (7)			**Fraser** (1)
Krishnan (7)	3-6 8-6 6-0 5-7 6-2			6-4 3-6 9-7 7-5
Lundquist	**Ayala** (4)	**Krishnan** (7)		
Ayala (4)	9-11 0-6 6-1 10-8 6-4	7-5 10-8 6-2		
Gaertner	**Buchholz** (8)		**Fraser** (1)	
Buchholz (8)	6-2 6-4 7-5		6-3 6-2 6-2	
Candy	**Fraser** (1)	**Fraser** (1)		
Fraser (1)	6-2 6-3 6-2	4-6 6-3 4-6 15-15 ret'd		

LADIES' SINGLES

FIRST ROUND: C. C. Truman (3) d. P. J. A. Wheeler 6-1 6-2; Mrs R. Hales d. I. Rjazanova (USSR) 6-2 3-6 6-1; Mrs J. Bryan (USA) d. P. A. Hird 3-6 7-5 6-1; Mrs D. P. Knode (USA) d. Mrs D. K. Illingworth 6-3 6-3; V. Puzejova (CZ) d. J. A. Fulton 7-5 6-2; Mrs A. Segal (SA) d. C. M. Leather 6-0 6-1; M. L. Hammill (SA) d. C. Hernandez-Coronado (SP) 6-2 6-1; L. Pericoli (IT) d. Mrs C. F. O. Lister 6-3 6-1; D. E. Starkie (A) d. M. R. Morrison (NZ) d. J. M. Young 6-0 6-4; L. M. Grundy d. Mrs H. E. Kaufmann (SWZ) 1-6 11-9 2-0 ret'd; L. M. Hutchings (SA) d. Mrs J. M. Wagstaff 6-1 6-2; Mrs A. H. Thomas d. Mrs R. B. R. Wilson 6-0 6-3; K. Hantze (USA) d. Mrs D. P. Flinn (IRE) 6-0 6-3; Mrs A. Nenot (F) d. D. Thomas 6-4 6-2 d. C. Yates-Bell d. Mrs A. C. Brighton 6-1 6-2; S. Pachta (AU) d. Mrs A. R.

Mills 2-6 8-6 6-4; Y. Ramirez (M) d. J. E. Kemp 6-4 6-4; R. Schuurman (SA) d. Mrs R. C. Panton 6-2 6-2; Mrs K. Hawton (A) d. G. M. O'Brien (A) 6-0 6-1; F. de la Courtie (F) d. Mrs V. A. Roberts 6-2 7-5; M. L. Gerson (SA) d. Mrs P. Chatrier (F) 6-8 6-3 6-0; J. S. Hopps (USA) d. Mrs P. C. Bramley 6-2 6-0; **Mrs Z. Kormoczy** (6) (HU) d. D. M. Catt 6-4 6-3; Mrs J. L. Deloford d. Mrs M. Peterdi 8-6 6-3; S. M. Armstrong d. J. M. Langley (A) 6-3 6-3; R. H. Bentley d. S. E. Waters 6-2 6-0; G. Thomas d. Mrs L. Ayala (CH) 3-6 6-1 6-2; J. Knight d. Mrs I. J. Warwick 6-1 4-6 6-1; Mrs B. I. Shenton d. C. Webb 6-3 6-2; Mrs M. C. Cheadle d. H. J. M. Durose 6-2 6-1; **A. S. Haydon** (4) d. Mrs J. W. Cawthorn 6-1 6-1.

SECOND ROUND: M. E. Bueno (1) (BR) d. C. Mercelis (B) 6-3 6-2; T. Schirmer (NOR) d. Mrs S. Rosin (SW) 7-5 4-6 6-2; Mrs H. G. Macintosh d. M. R. Burrell 3-6 6-1 6-3; M. B. Hellyer (A) d. M. Arnold (USA) 3-6 6-2 6-2; **A. Mortimer** (5) d. J. M. Trewby 6-2 6-1; Mrs V. Vukovich (SA) d. S. M. Moore (A) 6-4; R. Ostermann (G) d. E. Herdy (AU) 6-2 6-3; D. Wild (F) d. M. L. Hunt (SA) 6-3 7-5; **Truman** (3) d. Hales 8-6 6-3; Knode d. Bryan 6-2 6-2; Puzejova d. Segal 4-6 6-3 7-5; Pericoli d. Hammill 6-4 6-4; Morrison d. Starkie 6-1 6-0; Hutchings d. Grundy 6-0 6-0; Hantze d. Thomas 6-1 6-2; Nenot d. Yates-Bell 6-1 6-4; Ramirez d. Pachta 6-1 6-0; Schuurman d. Hawton 6-2 4-6 6-1; de la Courtie d.

Gerson 6-2 2-6 6-3; Hopps d. **Kormoczy** (6) 6-3 3-6 9-7; Armstrong d. Deloford 6-2 6-1; Bentley d. Thomas 6-2 7-5; Shenton d. Knight 4-6 6-3 6-2; **Haydon** (4) d. Cheadle 6-0 6-2; M. Dittmeyer d. G. P. Barril (SP) 6-3 2-6 6-2; E. Buding (G) d. Mrs M. Cox 6-1 6-2; Mrs C. W. Brasher d. N. Marsh (A) 6-4 6-3; **S. Reynolds** (8) (SA) d. M. Bourbonnais (F) 7-5 6-3; S. Lazzarino (IT) d. Mrs G. E. Marshall (KEN) 6-2 6-4; A. Dmitrieva (USSR) d. K. Frendelius (SW) 6-2 6-0; F. E. Walton d. R. A. Blakelock 6-3 5-7 6-2; **D. R. Hard** (2) (USA) d. J. A. Shilcock 6-1 6-4.

THIRD ROUND: Bueno (1) d. Schirmer 6-2 6-1; Hellyer d. Macintosh 6-0 6-2; **Mortimer** (5) d. Vukovich 6-2 6-3; Ostermann d. Wild 6-3 6-2; **Truman** (3) d. Knode 1-6 6-0 6-3; Puzejova d. Pericoli 6-1 6-4; Hutchings d. Morrison 2-6 6-4 6-2; Hantze d. Nenot 6-2 6-1; Schuurman d. Ramirez 6-2 6-2; Hopps d. de la Courtie 6-4 6-1; Bentley d.

Armstrong 4-6 6-3 6-3; **Haydon** (4) d. Shenton 6-2 6-0; Dittmeyer d. Buding 6-4 6-4; **Reynolds** (8) d. Brasher 6-1 6-2; Dmitrieva d. Lazzarino 6-4 6-1; **Hard** (2) d. Walton 6-1 6-0.

FOURTH ROUND	QUARTER-FINALS	SEMI-FINALS	FINAL	CHAMPION
Bueno (1)	**Bueno** (1)			
Hellyer	6-0 6-0			
Mortimer (5)	**Mortimer** (5)	**Bueno** (1)		
Ostermann	6-2 6-4	6-1 6-1		
Truman (3)	**Truman** (3)		**Bueno** (1)	
Puzejova	7-5 6-3		6-0 5-7 6-1	
Hutchings	Hantze	**Truman** (3)		
Hantze	6-2 6-8 8-1	4-6 6-4 6-4		
Schuurman	Schuurman			**Bueno** (1)
Hopps	6-3 6-4			8-6 6-0
Bentley	**Haydon** (4)	**Haydon** (4)		
Haydon (4)	8-6 6-0	7-5 1-6 6-2		
Dittmeyer	**Reynolds** (8)		**Reynolds** (8)	
Reynolds (8)	6-3 6-3		6-3 2-6 6-4	
Dmitrieva	**Hard** (2)	**Reynolds** (8)		
Hard (2)	5-7 6-2 6-1	6-1 2-6 6-1		

OTHER FINALS

GENTLEMEN'S DOUBLES: Final – R. H. Osuna (M)/R. D. Ralston (USA) d. M. G. Davies/R. K. Wilson 7-5 6-3 10-8.
LADIES' DOUBLES: Final – M. E. Bueno (BRI)/D. R. Hard (USA) d. S. Reynolds (SA)/R. Schuurman (SA) 6-4 6-0.
MIXED DOUBLES: Final – R. G. Laver (A)/D. R. Hard (USA) d. R. N. Howe (A)/M. E. Bueno (BR) 13-11 3-6 8-6.
GENTLEMEN'S SINGLES PLATE: Final – T. Ulrich (D) d. O. Sirola (IT) 6-4 7-5.

LADIES' SINGLES PLATE: Final – D. M. Catt d. Mrs J. W. Cawthorn 6-3 6-2.
BOYS' INVITATION SINGLES: Final – A. R. Mandelstam (SA) d. J. Mukerjea (IN) 1-6 8-6 6-4.
GIRLS' INVITATION SINGLES: Final – K. Hantze (USA) d. L. M. Hutchings (SA) 6-4 6-4.

GENTLEMEN'S SINGLES

FIRST ROUND: R. Laver (2) (A) d. T. Lejus (USSR) 6-4 6-1 6-1; P. Darmon (F) d. B. Jovanovic (YU) 9-7 6-3 10-8; W. Bungert (G) d. G. Merlo (IT) 5-7 8-6 7-5 6-4; K. E. Diepraam (SA) d. A. J. Lane (A) d. A. Brichant (B) d. W. Skonecki (POL) 6-2 3-6 6-2 6-2; W. Alvarez (COL) d. A. Arilla (SP) 4-6 8-6 6-3 4-6 6-2; R. E. Holmberg (USA) d. E. Morea (ARG) 7-5 7-5 6-3; R. Hewitt (A) d. S. Stockenberg (SW) 6-3 6-2 6-4; **L. Ayala** (2) (CH) d. R. F. Sanders (SA) 6-3 6-2 6-2; J. Javorsky (CZ) d. P. van Eysden (NTH) 2-11-9 6-4; M. Llamas (M) d. R. W. Barnes (BR) 6-3 9-7 1-6 10-12 6-4; F. A. Froehling (USA) d. J. E. Barrett 6-2 4-6 6-2 6-3; W. E. Bond (USA) d. L. Legenstein (AU) 6-4 12-10 6-2; I. Gulyas (HU) d. M. A. Otway (NZ) 3-6 6-4 6-0 0-6 6-4; W. A. Knight d. T. Moe (NOR) 7-5 9-7 9-7; P. Lall (IN) d. L. P. Coni 15-13 6-1 6-0; **R. Emerson** (4) (A) d. N. Kumar (IN) 6-2 6-1 6-3; C. I. Henry (USA) d. M. P. Hann 4-6 6-2 6-4 6-4; G. Mulloy (USA) d. J. M. Ward 6-2 6-8 1-6 6-4 6-4; J. A. Douglas (USA) d. J. B. Hillebrand (A) 6-0 6-4 3-6 6-1; R. D. Bennett d. E. L. Scott (USA) 6-4 4-6 6-4 6-4; M. Belkhodja (TUN) d. T. A. Adamson 6-2 4-6 11-13 6-2 6-4; W. W. Woodcock (A) d. A. R. Mandelstam (SA) 12-10 3-6 4-6 6-4 6-3; R. Taylor d. O. H. Garrido (CU) 6-4 6-4 10-8; **R. Krishnan** (7) (IN) d. F. Jauffret (F) 6-0 6-4 6-1; M. Riessen (USA) d. J. C. Mayers (SA) 3-6 7-5 4-6 6-3 7-5; O. Sirola (IT) d. F. Godbout (C) 6-3 6-4 6-3; K. Fletcher (A) d. U. Schmidt (SW) 6-2 6-2 9-7; O. Ishiguro (J) d. A. R. Mills 7-5 4-6 6-4 7-5; J. A. Pickard d. J. Renavand (F) 6-2 6-4 6-4; F. Saiko (AU) d. G. Palafox (M) 6-4 6-0 6-2; G. K. Pares (A) d. N. C. Gibson (A) 6-3 3-6 6-3 5-7 8-6; M. J. Sangster d. R. Bedard (C) 6-3 6-2

6-4; J. E. Lundquist (SW) d. J. Newcombe (A) 10-8 6-4 3-6 2-6 6-4; R. D. Ralston (USA) d. P. Rodriguez (CH) 3-6 6-1 6-0 6-3; R. N. Howe (A) d. J. J. Lesch (USA) 4-6 1-6 6-1; A. Bey (RH) d. E. Reyes (M) 6-1 4-6 6-3 4-6 6-2; A. Segal (SA) d. S. Likhachev (USSR) 1-6 6-2 6-3 6-0; **M. Santana** (5) (SP) d. W. Maris (NTH) 6-2 6-0 6-2; N. Pilic (YU) d. R. J. Siska (USA) 4-6 6-3 6-2 6-8 7-5; F. Hainka (AU) d. P. Washer (B) 6-0 6-4 6-4; I. Pimentel (VEN) d. G. Pilet (F) 6-1 6-2 3-6 6-4; W. G. Coghlan (A) d. C. Kuhnke (G) 4-6 6-4 6-4 6-3; C. L. Crawford (USA) d. N. Kitovitz 6-1 6-2 6-3; M. Fox (USA) d. F. D. McMillan (SA) 6-4 9-7 6-4; B. J. Phillips-Moore (A) d. J. E. Mandarino (BR) 6-3 3-6 6-1 4-6 6-3; **N. Pietrangeli** (3) (IT) d. A. Ali (IN) 6-4 6-2 6-1; J. C. Barclay (F) d. G. J. Hughes (A) 6-2 7-5 6-0; D. L. Dell (USA) d. D. Contet (F) 4-6 6-2 6-3; W. F. Jacques (A) d. J. Ulrich (G) 6-3 6-2 3-6 7-5; I. Buding (G) d. I. Ingvarsson (SW) 6-2 6-4 6-3; W. Gasiorek (POL) d. F. D. Jagge (NOR) 7-5 6-2 6-4; G. L. Ward 5-7 6-2 6-3 2-6 6-3; F. A. Gaertner (SA) d. R. K. Nyyssonen (FIN) 5-7 6-3 3-6 6-2 7-5; **C. R. McKinley** (8) (USA) d. S. Tacchini (IT) 6-2 6-2 4-6 6-4; J. W. Frost (USA) d. W. Stuck (G) 6-2 6-2; R. Mark (A) d. L. A. Gerrard (NZ) 10-8 6-3 2-6 6-1; C. A. Fernandes (BR) d. R. W. Dixon 6-2 6-3 6-3; R. K. Wilson d. E. Soriano (ARG) 6-2 4-6 5-7 16-14 6-3; F. Stolle (A) d. J. Mukerjea (IN) 6-3 6-4 3-6 6-3; M. F. Mulligan (A) d. H. E. Truman 7-5 6-1 6-1; W. Reed (USA) d. H. Elschenbroich (G) 6-2 6-4 6-4; **N. A. Fraser** (1) (A) d. R. Hernando (USA) 6-3 6-1 6-1.

SECOND ROUND: Laver (2) d. Darmon 8-6 2-6 6-3 4-6 6-4; Bungert d. Diepraam 10-12 11-9 6-0 6-4; Brichant d. Alvarez 2-6 6-1 6-0 7-9 6-2; Hewitt d. Holmberg 10-8 8-6 2-6 6-4; **Ayala** (6) d. Javorsky 7-5 6-4 6-2; Froehling d. Llamas 1-6 6-2 6-2 4-6 6-1; Bond d. Gulyas 6-1 6-1 6-4; Knight d. Lall 6-3 8-6 8-6; **Emerson** (4) d. Henry 6-2 6-4 6-4; Douglas d. Mulloy 6-2 6-2 4-6 6-1; Belkhodja d. Bennett 6-2 9-7 4-6 6-3; Taylor d. Woodcock 6-1 6-2 3-6 6-3; **Krishnan** (7) d. Riessen 6-3 6-2 11-9; Sirola d. Fletcher 6-4 0-6 3-6 7-5 6-0; Palafox d. Ishiguro 6-2 6-3 6-8 6-3; Pickard d. Saiko 6-4 11-9 3-6 6-2; Sangster d. Pares 6-3 4-6 6-3 6-3; Ralston d. Lundquist 6-4 6-2 3-6 16-14; Bey d.

Howe 6-4 10-8 9-11 6-4; Segal d. **Santana** (5) 6-4 6-4 12-10; Pilic d. Hainka 7-5 4-6 6-3 8-6; Pimentel d. Coghlan 6-4 3-6 6-3 11-9; Crawford d. Fox 6-2 6-2 6-2; **Pietrangeli** (3) d. Phillips-Moore 6-3 6-4 1-6 6-3; Dell d. Barclay 6-3 6-4 6-2; Jacques d. Buding 7-5 6-0 6-4; Gasiorek d. Paish 6-2 6-1 4-6 6-4 6-2; **McKinley** (8) d. Gaertner 6-2 6-1 6-3; Frost d. Mark 6-4 6-4 6-4; Wilson d. Fernandes 6-3 8-6 6-4; Mulligan d. Stolle 6-1 6-4 1-0 ret'd; **Fraser** (1) d. Reed 5-7 6-4 4-6 6-1 7-5.

THIRD ROUND: Laver (2) d. Bungert 6-3 6-1 8-10 4-6 6-3; Hewitt d. Brichant 6-2 6-3 6-4; **Ayala** (6) d. Froehling 6-2 7-5 6-4; Knight d. Bond 12-10 5-7 2-6 9-7 6-0; **Emerson** (4) d. Douglas 6-3 6-0 5-7 6-4; Taylor d. Belkhodja 8-10 6-1 6-4 6-3; **Krishnan** (7) d. Sirola 6-4 3-6 6-3 6-1; Palafox d. Pickard 6-3 6-3 6-2; Sangster d. Ralston 6-8 4-6 6-3 6-3

6-4; Segal d. Bey 6-3 6-4 6-4; Pimentel d. Pilic 4-6 7-5 6-3 1-6 7-5; Crawford d. **Pietrangeli** (3) 2-6 6-3 6-4 6-4; Jacques d. Dell 6-8 6-4 8-6 9-7; **McKinley** (8) d. Gasiorek 6-3 4-6 6-0 6-2; Wilson d. Frost 6-2 6-4 6-4; **Fraser** (1) d. Mulligan 6-2 3-6 6-2 6-1.

FOURTH ROUND	QUARTER-FINALS	SEMI-FINALS	FINAL	CHAMPION
Laver (2)	**Laver** (2)	**Laver** (2)		
Hewitt	6-4 6-4 6-2	6-1 6-3 6-2		
Ayala (6)	**Ayala** (6)		**Laver** (2)	
Knight	9-7 6-4 6-2		6-2 8-6 6-2	
Emerson (4)	**Emerson** (4)			
Taylor	6-3 6-1 6-1	**Krishnan** (7)		**Laver** (2)
Krishnan (7)	**Krishnan** (7)	6-1 6-4 6-4		6-3 6-1 6-4
Palafox	4-6 6-1 6-3 6-1			
Sangster	Sangster			
Segal	8-6 8-6 6-4	Sangster		
Pimentel	Pimentel	6-2 6-2 6-4		
Crawford	6-4 6-2 12-10		**McKinley** (8)	
Jacques	**McKinley** (8)		6-4 6-4 8-6	
McKinley (8)	8-6 6-1 7-5	**McKinley** (8)		
Wilson	Wilson	6-4 6-4 4-6 6-4		
Fraser (1)	1-6 6-0 13-11 9-7			

LADIES' SINGLES

FIRST ROUND: A. S. Haydon (3) d. J. Bourgnon (SWZ) 6-0 6-0; C. Mercelis (B) d. S. M. Moore (USA) 7-5 7-5; C. Webb d. D. Wild (F) 6-4 6-4; Mrs M. P. Pombo (SP) d. J. E. Scoble 6-3 3-6 10-8; P. J. A. Wheeler d. F. V. M. MacLennan 6-3 6-3; R. Schuurman (SA) d. R. H. Bentley 7-5 6-3; F. Gordigiani (IT) d. E. M. O'Neill (IRE) 6-2 6-2; Mrs V. A. Roberts d. F. E. Walton 6-0 6-4; **K. Hantze** (8) (USA) d. Mrs P. Darmon (M) 6-2 6-2; V. H. Dennis d. J. M. Tee 1-6 6-3 6-3; R. A. Blakelock d. Mrs O. Peterdy-Wolf (Stateless) 6-3 7-5; E. R. Duldig (A) d. R. Ostermann (G) 6-4 4-6 6-2; Mrs C. W. Brasher d. J. Seven (NTH) 6-0 3-6 6-2; J. Lehane d. A. Dmitrieva (USSR) 6-4 6-0; E. Dodge (C) d. M. Bourbonnais (F) 4-6 7-5 7-5; Mrs A. R. Mills d. C. Yates-Bell 6-3 6-4; Mrs J. L. Deloford d. Mrs H. C. Hopman (A) 6-3

8-6; A. J. Stroud d. G. M. Houlihan (IRE) 6-1 6-3; J. Bricka (USA) d. Mrs S. Rosin (SW) 6-4 6-3; D. Floyd (USA) d. Mrs V. Kuzmenko-Titova (USSR) 6-1 6-3; Mrs M. G. Davies d. M. M. Lee 5-7 6-4 6-1; D. Schuster (AU) d. C. Hanks (USA) 6-3 6-3; H. J. M. Durose d. Mrs J. M. Wagstaff 1-6 12-10 7-5; **A. Mortimer** (7) d. J. S. Barclay w.o.; Mrs R. Mark (SA) d. G. Thomas (USA) 6-3 1-6 8-6; L. M. Hutchings (SA) Mrs M. Sladek (C) 5-7 6-2 6-2; Mrs V. Sukova (CZ) d. M. Dittmeyer (G) 6-0 6-0; Mrs D. K. Illingworth d. M. L. Gerson (SA) 9-7 5-7 6-1; K. Herich (G) d. P. Barril (SP) 3-6 6-4 7-5; T. Schirmer (NOR) d. Mrs N. C. Gibson (A) 6-2 6-4; M. G. Arnold (USA) d. J. M. Trewby 7-5 6-0; **L. Turner** (4) (A) d. D. C. Tuckey 6-1 6-2.

SECOND ROUND: M. Smith (2) (A) d. N. Richey (USA) 3-6 6-3 6-4; P. A. Stewart (USA) d. Mrs P. Chatrier (F) 3-6 6-0 6-3; C. H. Coronado (SP) d. B. Gunderson (USA) 6-0 1-6 6-4; Mrs Z. Kormoczy (HU) d. S. Lazzarino (IT) 6-2 6-2; **C. C. Truman** (6) d. M. B. Hellyer (A) 6-4 6-4; Mrs N. B. de Somoza (ARG) d. P. A. Hird 6-1 4-6 6-4; M. L. Hunt (SA) d. S. Pachta (AU) 6-1 6-3; E. Buding (G) d. Mrs R. Hales 6-1 6-1; **Haydon** (3) d. Mercelis 6-2 6-1; Webb d. Pombo 6-4 6-1; Schuurman d. Wheeler 6-2 6-0; Gordigiani d. Roberts 6-2 3-6 6-4; **Hantze** (8) d. Dennis 6-1 6-1; Duldig d. Blakelock 6-1 9-7; Lehane d. Brasher 6-0 6-3; Mills d. Dodge 6-4 1-6 6-4; Deloford d. Stroud 6-8 6-1 6-2; Bricka d. Floyd 6-1

9-7; Schuster d. Davies 6-4 6-3; **Mortimer** (7) d. Durose 6-0 6-0; Hutchings d. Mark 6-2 6-3; Sukova d. Illingworth 6-3 6-1; Herich d. Schirmer 7-5 6-2; Arnold d. **Turner** (4) 7-5 6-4; D. E. Starkie d. R. Ebbern (A) 6-2 8-6; H. Schultze (G) d. V. S. White 8-6 6-2; M. Datt d. M. R. O'Donnell 6-2 6-2; **Ramirez** (5) (M) d. B. J. Moffitt (USA) 11-9 1-6 6-2; F. de la Courtie (F) d. C. A. Rosser 6-3 6-2; A. M. Estalella (SP) d. Mrs S. Reitano w.o.; D. S. Butt (C) d. L. Pericoli (IT) 6-4 6-3; **S. Reynolds** (1) (SA) d. Mrs J. W. Cawthorn 6-1 6-0.

THIRD ROUND: Smith (2) d. Stewart 6-3 6-0; Kormoczy d. Coronado 6-3 6-0; **Truman** (6) d. de Somoza 6-2 6-2; Hunt d. Buding 6-2 1-6 6-4; **Haydon** (3) d. Webb 6-1 6-1; Schuurman d. Gordigiani 0-6 6-0 6-3; **Hantze** (8) d. Duldig 6-3 6-2; Lehane d. Mills 6-1 6-4; Bricka d. Deloford 6-1 6-3; **Mortimer** (7) d. Schuster 6-2 6-0; Sukova d. Hutchings

6-2 7-5; Arnold d. Herich 6-2 6-1; Starkie d. Schultze 6-0 6-1; **Ramirez** (5) d. Catt 3-6 6-1 6-3; de la Courtie d. Estalella 6-4 6-3; **Reynolds** (1) d. Butt 6-3 6-2.

FOURTH ROUND	QUARTER-FINALS	SEMI-FINALS	FINAL	CHAMPION
Smith (2)	**Smith** (2)	**Truman** (6)		
Kormoczy	6-2 6-1	3-6 6-3 9-7		
Truman (6)	**Truman** (6)		**Truman** (6)	
Hunt	6-3 6-2		6-4 6-4	
Haydon (3)	Schuurman			
Schuurman	3-6 6-4 6-2	Schuurman		
Hantze (8)	**Hantze** (8)	6-4 2-6 7-5		
Lehane	6-3 6-2			**Mortimer** (7)
Bricka	**Mortimer** (7)			4-6 6-4 7-5
Mortimer (7)	6-4 9-7	**Mortimer** (7)		
Sukova	Sukova	6-3 6-4		
Arnold	7-5 6-2		**Mortimer** (7)	
Starkie	**Ramirez** (5)		11-9 6-3	
Ramirez)5(	8-6 6-1	**Reynolds** (1)		
de la Courtie	**Reynolds** (1)	4-6 6-3 6-0		
Reynolds (1)	6-1 6-3			

OTHER FINALS

GENTLEMEN'S DOUBLES: Final — R. S. Emerson (A)/N. A. Fraser (A) d. R. A. J. Hewitt (A)/F. S. Stolle (A) 6-4 6-8 6-4 6-8 8-6.
LADIES' DOUBLES: Final — K. Hantze (USA)/B. J. Moffitt (USA) d. J. Lehane (A)/M. Smith (A) 6-3 6-4.
MIXED DOUBLES: Final — F. S. Stolle (A)/L. R. Turner (A) d. R. N. Howe (A)/E. Buding (G) 11-9 6-2.

GENTLEMEN'S SINGLES PLATE: Final — T. Ulrich (D) d. N. Kumar (IN) 6-4 10-12 6-3.
LADIES' SINGLES PLATE: Final — R. H. Bentley d. A. Dmitrieva (USSR) 6-4 3-6 6-3.
BOYS' INVITATION SINGLES: Final — C. E. Graebner (USA) d. E. Blanke (AU) 6-3 9-7.
GIRLS' INVITATION SINGLES: Final — G. Baksheeva (USSR) d. K. D. Chabit (USA) 10-8 3-6 6-4.

1962

GENTLEMEN'S SINGLES

FIRST ROUND: R. Laver (1) (A) d. N. Kumar (IN) 7-5 6-1 6-2; J. A. Pickard d. M. Fujii (J) 2-6 6-1 6-3 6-1; W. Reed (USA) d. F. Saiko (AU) 6-3 6-2 6-3; F. D. McMillan (SA) d. J. Reyes (M) 6-2 6-2 7-5; I. Pimentel (VEN) d. S. Jacobini (IT) 6-3 6-4 6-1; T. Moe (NOR) d. E. Zuleta (EC) 6-4 10-8 6-1; P. Rodriguez (CH) d. W. W. Woodcock (A) 6-0 4-6 6-4 7-5; P. Darmon (F) d. M. A. Otway (NZ) 6-3 6-4 1-6 6-4; **M. Santana** (6) (SP) d. C. Drysdale (SA) 6-3 6-1 6-3; T. Lejus (USSR) d. J. Brichant (B) 7-5 3-6 6-1 12-10; J. Renavand (F) d. L. P. Coni 6-1 6-3 6-1; G. Hernandez (PH) d. H. E. Truman 5-7 4-6 6-4 14-12 6-2; O. Davidson (A) d. D. Ecklebe (G) 6-4 6-2 6-2; R. K. Nyyssonen (FIN) d. A. Ali (IN) 3-6 4-6 6-4 6-0 6-2; W. Bowrey (A) d. G. Palafox (M) 15-13 6-3 6-2; F. A. Froehling (USA) d. R. Becker 16-14 4-6 6-4 6-4; **N. A. Fraser** (3) (A) d. E. A. Neely (USA) 6-0 6-4 6-3; G. K. Pares (A) d. N. T. Holland (A) 5-7 10-8 6-3 6-0; G. Pilet (F) d. J. R. McDonald (NZ) 6-3 7-5 8-6; W. A. Knight d. E. Soriano (ARG) 6-3 17-15 6-2; J. Mukerjea (IN) d. A. C. Kendall (A) 6-0 6-3 6-1; D. L. Dell (USA) d. J. P. Lemann (SWZ) 6-2 6-4 6-1; J. M. Couder (SP) d. F. Godbout (F) 9-7 7-5 6-2; C. Kuhnke (G) d. W. Gasiorek (POL) 6-2 6-1 6-1; **N. Pietrangeli** (7) (IT) d. A. Lane (A) 10-8 6-2 6-3; N. Pilic (YU) d. J. M. Gracie 6-4 6-1 6-4; M. Fox (USA) d. G. Mulloy (USA) 6-3 6-3 6-4; A. R. Mills d. R. W. Dixon 3-6 6-2 6-2 6-2; J. Newcombe (A) d. E. L. Scott (USA) 8-6 7-5 6-4; R. H. Osuna (M) d. J. E. Mandarino (BR) 8-10 1-6 6-4 6-3 6-3; R. F. Sanders (SA) d. G. L. Paish 6-4 6-2 6-4; G. L. Forbes (SA) d. P. V. Palmer (USA) 6-3 6-1 6-4; I. S. Crookenden (NZ) d. L. Legenstein (AU)

6-3 1-6 12-10 6-3; F. S. Salomon (RH) d. J. E. Barrett 4-6 6-3 11-13 12-10 6-2; R. Talor d. M. Belkhodja (TUN) w.o.; J. F. Shepherd (A) d. J. I. Tattersall 6-4 6-4 7-5; K. Fletcher (A) d. B. J. Phillips-Moore (A) 6-2 6-3 6-3; O. Ishiguro (J) d. P. Jalabert (F) 4-6 6-4 6-2 6-1; M. P. Hann d. G. J. Hughes (A) 6-4 6-4 5-7 7-5; **C. R. McKinley** (5) (USA) d. O. K. French (A) 6-1 6-2 6-1; I. Buding (G) d. W. F. Jacques (A) 2-6 6-4 4-6 6-4 6-4; A. Palafox (M) d. W. Alvarez (COL) 6-3 6-2 6-3; O. Sirola (IT) d. B. Jovanovic (YU) 10-8 5-7 2-6 7-5 6-4; M. J. Sangster d. C. I. Henry (USA) 3-6 6-3 11-9 6-0; C. L. Crawford (USA) d. A. Arilla (SP) 6-4 6-3 6-4; J. G. Fraser (A) d. C. A. Fernandes (BR) 1-6 6-4 6-3 6-4; K. E. Diepraam (SA) d. J. B. Hillebrand (A) 6-4 6-2 6-4; **R. Krishnan** (4) (IN) d. E. Drossart (B) 6-2 6-3 7-5; J. L. Arilla (SP) d. I. Gulyas (HU) 4-6 6-4 6-2 1-6 6-2; R. N. Howe d. M. Cox 7-5 6-2 6-2; J. N. Grinda (F) d. M. Olvera (EC) 3-6 9-7 6-1 6-2; P. Lall (IN) d. F. Hainka (AU) 6-3 4-6 6-2 6-2; R. K. Wilson d. J. W. Frost (USA) 6-4 6-2 6-2; M. Llamas (M) d. R. J. Siska (USA) 8-6 6-4 4-4 6-7 5; J. Ulrich (D) d. E. G. Rubinoff (USA) 6-3 7-5 6-8 1-6 6-2; **R. Hewitt** (8) (A) d. B. W. Geraghty (A) 6-1 3-6 6-3 6-2; M. F. Mulligan (A) d. W. V. Reid (A) 6-4 6-3 4-6 6-1; J. E. Sharpe (A) d. J. Javorsky (CZ) 6-2 6-3 12-10; R. D. Ralston (USA) d. B. G. Knox (A) 6-2 6-2 6-2; S. Likhachev (USSR) d. R. W. Barnes (BR) 2-6 4-6 6-1 6-4 6-4; F. Stolle (A) d. A. Segal (SA) 6-2 2-6 6-4 3-6 6-3; S. Tacchini (IT) d. J. Gisbert (SP) 9-7 7-5 4-6 7-5; W. P. Bungert (G) d. J. Tiriac (RU) 7-5 6-2 6-2; **R. Emerson** (2) (A) d. J. A. Douglas (USA) 6-3 6-4 8-6.

SECOND ROUND: Laver (1) d. Pickard 6-1 6-2 6-2; Reed d. McMillan 8-6 4-6 6-2 6-4; Moe d. Pimentel 2-6 7-5 6-3 6-3; Darmon d. Rodriguez 6-0 6-2 6-2; **Santana** (6) d. Lejus 6-2 6-3 6-4; Renavand d. Hernandez 6-0 6-3 7-5; Davidson d. Nyyssonen 11-9 2-6 6-1 6-4; Froehling d. Bowrey 7-5 6-3 6-4; **Fraser** (3) d. Pares 6-0 6-3 6-4; Knight d. Pilet 6-4 7-5 6-4; Mukerjea d. Dell 6-4 3-6 3-6 6-4 6-2; Kuhnke d. Couder 6-1 6-1 6-4; **Pietrangeli** (7) d. Pilic 24-22 6-2 6-4; Mills d. Fox 9-7 6-3 6-2; Osuna d. Newcombe 6-4 3-6 7-5 6-3; Forbes d. Sanders 6-1 6-3 6-1; Crookenden d. Salomon 3-6 6-3 3-6 6-2 6-3; Taylor d. Shepherd 9-7 13-11 19-17; Fletcher d. Ishiguro 6-2 3-6 6-4 5-7 6-4; Hann d.

McKinley (5) 6-3 6-2 6-2; Palafox d. Buding 6-3 4-6 7-5 6-3; Sirola d. Sangster 2-6 2-6 6-3 6-2 6-0; Fraser d. Crawford 9-7 4-6 6-4 6-4; **Krishnan** (4) d. Diepraam 6-2 7-5 6-4; Howe d. Arilla 4-6 5-7 6-3 6-2 7-5; Lall d. Grinda 3-6 8-6; Wilson d. Llamas 7-5 3-6 6-4 6-4; **Hewitt** (8) d. Ulrich 9-7 6-1 5-7 1-6 6-4; Mulligan d. Sharpe 6-1 7-5 6-4; Ralston d. Likhachev 6-4 6-3 6-3; Stolle d. Tacchini 2-6 6-3 6-4 6-2; **Emerson** (2) d. Bungert 13-15 4-6 6-3 6-0 6-4.

THIRD ROUND: Laver (1) d. Reed 6-4 6-1 6-4; Darmon d. Moe 6-3 6-4 6-4; **Santana** (6) d. Renavand 6-3 3-4 6-4 6-1; Froehling d. Davidson 8-6 7-5 6-8 6-4 6-1; **Fraser** (3) d. Knight 6-4 16-14 10-8; Kuhnke d. Mukerjea 9-7 6-4 7-5; Mills d. Pietrangeli (7) 6-4 2-6 4-6 7-5 6-1; Osuna d. Forbes 6-2 9-11 8-6 6-4; Taylor d. Crookenden 6-3 4-6 9-7 6-4;

Fletcher d. Hann 6-3 6-3 6-1; Sirola d. Palafox 6-3 1-6 6-2 6-1; Fraser d. **Krishnan** (4) 5-2 ret'd; Howe d. Lall 5-7 4-6 6-4 6-3 6-3; **Hewitt** (8) d. Wilson 2-6 8-6 2-6 6-4 7-5; Mulligan d. Ralston 3-6 9-7 6-3 2-6 7-5; **Emerson** (2) d. Stolle 6-4 6-4 6-0.

FOURTH ROUND	QUARTER-FINALS	SEMI-FINALS	FINAL	CHAMPION
Laver (1)	**Laver** (1)			
Darmon	6-3 6-2 13-11	**Laver** (1)		
Santana (6)	**Santana** (6)	14-16 9-7 6-2 6-2		
Froehling	12-10 6-3 8-10 6-3		**Laver** (1)	
Fraser (3)	**Fraser** (3)		10-8 6-1 7-5	
Kuhnke	8-6 8-10 6-1 6-3	**Fraser** (3)		
Mills	Osuna	6-3 6-1 4-6 4-6 6-2		**Laver** (1)
Osuna	6-3 6-3 6-2			6-2 6-2 6-1
Taylor	Fletcher			
Fletcher	2-6 6-3 6-8 6-4 6-4	Fraser		
Sirola	Fraser	1-6 7-9 6-4 6-1 6-2		
Fraser	6-4 6-4 6-2		Mulligan	
Howe	**Hewitt** (8)		6-3 6-2 6-2	
Hewitt (8)	3-6 1-6 6-4 6-3 10-8	Mulligan		
Mulligan	Mulligan	6-8 6-4 6-3 6-4		
Emerson (2)	3-6 6-1 ret'd			

LADIES' SINGLES

FIRST ROUND: R. Schuurman (4) (SA) d. F. V. M. MacLennan 6-0 6-4; Mrs V. A. Roberts d. Mrs D. H. Roberts 6-2 6-3; J. M. Alvarez (USA) d. M. A. Smith (NZ) 9-7 6-4; Mrs J. W. Cawthorn d. Mrs D. P. Courteix (F) 6-3 6-1; R. H. Bentley d. C. A. Rosser 6-3 6-2; Mrs O. Peterdy-Wolf (Stateless) d. Mrs J. L. Deloford 4-6 7-5 7-5; J. A. Blackman (A) d. C. Mercelis (B) 2-6 7-5 6-0; M. Schacht (A) d. C. Yates-Bell 7-5 6-2; **Mrs J. R. Susman** d. A. M. Estalella (SP) 6-2 6-1; P. A. Hird d. M. T. Riedl (IT) 8-2 8-6; D. E. Starkie d. Mrs M. C. Cheadle 6-1 6-1; G. Thomas d. F. E. Walton w.o.; S. V. Wade d. Mrs J. H. Edrich (USA) 4-6 6-4 6-2; J. A. M. Tegart (A) d. A. J. Stroud 6-4 6-1; Mrs G. L. Forbes (SA) d. A. G. McAlpine 6-1 6-1; H. Schildknecht (G) d. R. A. Blakelock 6-1 12-10; J. R. Forbes (SA) d. Mrs J. M.

Wagstaff 7-5 6-1; C. H. Coronado (SP) d. Mrs A. Wavre (SWZ) 6-1 6-3; L. Bassi (IT) d. E. M. O'Neill (IRE) 6-3 6-1; M. M. Lee d. Mrs J. W. Cawthorn (A) 6-2 6-3; C. C. Truman d. Mrs W. du Pont (USA) 6-2 6-4; E. A. Green (NZ) d. I. Overgaard (D) 6-4 6-0; K. Dening (A) d. M. L. Gerson (SA) 7-5 6-3; **L. Turner** (7) (A) d. Mrs A. R. Mills 6-4 6-1; Mrs K. Hawton (A) d. H. Ross (A) 3-6 6-3 6-1; N. Richey (USA) d. D. Floyd (USSR) 11-9 10-8; Mrs Z. Kormoczy (HU) d. Mrs P. Chatrier (F) 2-6 6-4 7-5; D. M. Catt d. Mrs V. Vukovich (SA) 6-2 6-4; A. Dmitrieva (USSR) d. C. Webb 6-1 6-2; R. Ostermann (G) d. K. Herich (G) 8-6 6-2; E. Buding (G) d. F. Gordigiani (IT) 6-2 6-3; **M. E. Bueno** (3) (BR) d. M. Varner (USA) 6-3 6-4.

SECOND ROUND: B. J. Moffitt (USA) d. **M. Smith** (1) (A) 1-6 6-3 7-5; C. A. Caldwell (USA) d. F. de la Courtie (F) 4-6 6-2 8-6; A. Sturm (G) d. M. Arnold (USA) 6-0 4-6 6-3; S. Pachta (AU) d. P. A. Belton (NZ) 6-1 6-2; **A. S. Haydon** (5) d. S. Lazzarino (IT) 6-1 6-2; Mrs L. E. G. Price (SA) d. M. B. Hellyer (A) 6-2 1-6 8-6; V. Palmer (USA) d. P. Barril (SP) 6-1 6-1; R. Ebbern (A) d. J. Knight 6-0 6-0; **Schuurman** (4) d. Roberts 6-2 6-2; Bricka d. Alvarez 6-4 6-3; Bentley d. Peterdy-Wolf 6-1 6-3; Schacht d. Blackman 3-6 8-7-5; Starkie d. Thomas 5-7 6-4 6-2; **Susman** (8) d. Hird 8-6 6-4; Starkie d. Thomas 5-7 6-4 6-2; Tegart d. Wade 4-6 6-3 6-1; Forbes d. Schildknecht 6-3 6-3; Forbes d. Coronado 6-3 6-1; Bassi d. Lee 6-1 4-6 6-4;

Truman d. Green 6-1 6-0; **Turner** (7) d. Dening 6-4 6-1; Richey d. Hawton 7-5 7-5; Catt d. Kormoczy 7-5 6-1; Dmitrieva d. Ostermann 8-6 5-7 7-5; **Bueno** (3) d. Buding 6-4 4-6 6-3; Mrs V. Sukova (CZ) d. D. Schuster (AU) 6-1 6-3; J. Lehane d. C. A. Loop (USA) 6-3 6-1; J. Davidson (NZ) d. M. Bourbonnais (F) 6-2 8-6; **A. Mortimer** (6) d. M. Grace 6-2 6-2; H. Schultze (G) d. V. R. Cox 2-6 6-4 6-1; Mrs A. Segal (SA) d. Mrs P. Darmon (M) 6-3 6-1; Mrs H. de Jong (NTH) d. L. Pericoli (IT) 6-3 6-4; **D. R. Hard** (2) (USA) d. Mrs D. K. Illingworth 6-0 6-2.

THIRD ROUND: Moffitt d. Caldwell 7-5 6-3; Pachta d. Sturm 6-4 2-6 6-1; **Haydon** (5) d. Price 6-4 6-4; Palmer d. Ebbern 2-6 6-0 7-5; **Schuurman** (4) d. Bricka 2-6 6-1 6-4; Schacht d. Bentley 6-4 6-1; **Susman** (8) d. Starkie 7-5 10-8; Tegart d. Forbes 6-3 6-3; Forbes d. Bassi 6-3 6-3; **Turner** (7) d. Truman 7-5 6-4; Catt d. Richey 7-5 8-6; Bueno

(3) d. Dmitrieva 3-6 6-1 6-1; Sukova d. Lehane 8-6 6-3; **Mortimer** (6) d. Davidson 6-1 6-1; Schultze d. Segal 6-4 1-6 6-3; Hard (2) d. de Jong 6-0 6-0.

FOURTH ROUND	QUARTER-FINALS	SEMI-FINALS	FINAL	CHAMPION
Moffitt	Moffitt			
Pachta	6-1 6-2	**Haydon** (5)		
Haydon (5)	**Haydon** (5)	6-3 6-1		
Palmer	6-2 6-2		**Susman** (8)	
Schuurman (4)	**Schuurman** (4)		8-6 6-1	
Schacht	5-7 6-4 6-1	**Susman** (8)		
Susman (8)	**Susman** (8)	6-4 6-4		**Susman** (8)
Tegart	6-4 6-2			6-4 6-4
Forbes	**Turner** (7)			
Turner (7)	6-1 6-2	**Bueno** (3)		
Catt	**Bueno** (3)	2-6 6-4 6-2		
Bueno (3)	6-2 6-4		Sukova	
Sukova	Sukova		6-4 6-3	
Mortimer (6)	1-6 6-4 6-3	Sukova		
Schultze	**Hard** (2)	6-4 6-3		
Hard (2)	6-1 6-0			

OTHER FINALS

GENTLEMEN'S DOUBLES: Final – R. A. J. Hewitt (A)/F. S. Stolle (A) d. B. Jovanovic (YU)/N. Pilic (YU) 6-2 5-7 6-2 6-4.
LADIES' DOUBLES: Final – B. J. Moffitt (USA)/Mrs J.R. Susman (USA) d. Mrs L. E. G. Price (SA)/R. Schuurman (SA) 5-7 6-3 7-5.
MIXED DOUBLES: Final – N. A. Fraser (A)/Mrs W. du Pont (USA) d. R. D. Ralston (USA)/A. S. Haydon 2-6 6-3 13-11.

GENTLEMEN'S SINGLES PLATE: Final – J. A. Douglas (USA) d. A. Segal (SA) 3-6 6-2 6-3.
LADIES' SINGLES PLATE: Final – M. L. Gerson (SA) d. M. B. Hellyer (A) 6-2 6-1.
BOYS' INVITATION SINGLES: Final – S. J. Matthews d. A. Metreveli (USSR) 10-8 3-6 6-4.
GIRLS' INVITATION SINGLES: Final – G. Baksheeva (USSR) d. E. Terry (NZ) 6-4 6-2.

GENTLEMEN'S SINGLES

1963

FIRST ROUND: R. Emerson (1) (A) d. W. J. Lenoir (USA) 6-0 6-4 6-3; O. Sirola (IT) d. G. Mulloy (USA) 6-3 1-6 6-3 3-6 7-5; O. K. Davidson (A) d. E. L. Scott (USA) 9-7 6-4 9-7; R. J. Carmichael (A) d. J. M. Gracie 6-1 2-6 6-3 6-4; R. W. Barnes (BR) d. J. M. Couder (SP) 6-1 7-5 6-1; K. E. Diepraam (SA) d. H. S. Matheson 3-6 6-4 6-3 6-3; R. D. Ralston (USA) d. L. Legenstein (AU) 6-4 6-4 6-3; R. Krishnan (IN) d. I. S. Crookenden (NZ) 6-1 6-1 6-4; W. P. Bungert (G) d. **M. J. Sangster** (8) 6-3 7-5 6-3; E. Drossart (B) d. P. Beust (F) 6-4 3-6 6-3 14-12; I. Gulyas (HU) d. J. N. Grinda (F) 6-8 10-8 6-1 6-0; T. Lejus (USSR) d. W. F. Jacques (A) 6-1 6-4 6-4; W. Stuck (G) d. J. D. C. Crump 9-11 6-4 6-2 6-2; J. A. Pickard d. E. Soriano (ARG) 6-4 1-6 4-6 6-3 6-2; J. L. Arilla (SP) d. A. Kreinberg (G) 6-3 9-7 4-6 6-4; B. Jovanovic (YU) d. C. Duxin (F) 6-2 7-5 6-1; **C. R. McKinley** (4) (USA) d. E. C. Drysdale (SA) 6-3 6-3 8-6; A. J. Lane (A) d. J. G. Fraser (A) 6-2 6-4 6-4; A. R. Ashe (USA) d. C. A. Fernandes (BR) 3-6 4-6 6-4 6-4 6-1; J. B. Hillebrand (A) d. J. D. Newcombe (A) 14-12 9-7 4-6 6-4; A. R. Mills d. T. Moe (NOR) 6-4 6-1 13-11; J. Mukerjea (IN) d. P. Rodriguez (CH) 6-2 6-4 6-8 8-10 6-4; O. Ishiguro (J) d. I. Buding (G) 6-3 6-2 4-2 ret'd; A. K. Carpenter (C) d. A. Ochoa (M) 7-5 6-4 6-1; **M. F. Mulligan** (5) (A) d. M. Belkhodja (TUN) 6-1 6-2 6-2; J. Gisbert (SP) d. M. Pirro (IT) 6-2 11-9 3-6 6-2; R. A. J. Hewitt (A) d. A. Metreveli (USSR) 6-3 6-3 6-4; D. D. Phillips (SA) d. G. Majoli (IT) 6-3 6-3 7-5; E. G. Rubinoff (C) d. D. Contet (F) 8-6 6-1 6-3; J. Ulrich (D) d. W. E. Bond (USA) 6-4 6-0 6-4; R. K. Wilson d. J. Renavand (F) 6-2 6-0 6-2; R. McKenzie (A) d. P. Barthes (F) 6-3 6-8 6-2 6-4; R. Taylor d. A. Segal (SA) 3-6 6-2 6-3 6-0; P. Lall (IN) d. R. K. Nyyssonen (FIN) 6-3

6-4 6-1; F. D. McMillan (SA) d. D. Ecklebe (G) 6-4 2-6 7-5 6-4; J. W. Frost (USA) d. T. Koch (BR) 3-6 7-5 9-7 13-11; W. Geraghty (A) d. A. Bresson (F) 6-2 3-6 6-2 6-2; F. A. Froehling (USA) d. D. L. Dell (USA) 1-6 8-6 6-3 3-6 6-3; R. N. Howe (A) d. A. Maggi (IT) 6-3 6-3 6-3; **P. Darmon** (6) (F) d. N. Pilic (YU) 6-4 7-9 8-6 8-6; A. Palafox (M) d. R. J. Moore (SA) 6-0 8-6 6-4; W. H. Hoogs (USA) d. A. Arilla (SP) 8-10 6-0 6-0 6-4; D. Sturdza (SWZ) d. J. E. Baker (HAI) 20-18 6-3 6-4; S. Likhachev (USSR) d. J. H. McManus (USA) 2-6 6-4 6-4 5-7 6-3; N. Pietrangeli (IT) d. C. M. Buchholz (USA) 6-3 3-6 4-6 6-3 6-3; M. P. Hann d. W. Alvarez (COL) 6-1 6-4 6-3; F. S. Stolle (A) d. K. Wooldridge 6-1 6-2 6-1; **K. N. Fletcher** (3) (A) d. G. Sjowall (NOR) 7-5 6-4 6-4; M. Cox d. R. W. Fisher (USA) 4-6 6-4 6-3 7-5; C. Kuhnke (G) d. J. C. Barclay (F) 6-4 6-3 10-8; W. A. Knight d. G. Hernandez (PH) 6-3 6-4 6-2; G. L. Forbes (SA) d. N. Kumar (IN) 6-4 6-4 6-3; T. Edelfsen (USA) d. A. C. Kendall (A) 3-6 6-3 7-5 1-6 6-4; C. M. Pasarell (USA) d. F. Hainka (A) 6-3 6-3 7-5; F. Jauffret (F) d. S. Matthews (A) 6-3 6-2 6-4; **J. E. Lundquist** (7) (SW) d. N. T. Holland (A) 6-2 6-1 6-2; G. Merlo (IT) d. G. R. Stilwell 6-4 6-2; R. J. Siska d. I. Tiriac (RU) 6-4 7-5; A. Bey (RH) d. A. Fox (USA) 6-4 12-10 6-4; H. Flam (USA) d. G. B. Knox 7-5 4-6 6-2 4-6 6-3; R. H. Osuna (M) d. M. Mozer (USSR) 6-4 9-7 6-3; S. Matthews d. S. Tacchini (IT) 6-4 6-3 6-1; J. E. Mandarino (BR) d. M. Fujii (J) 6-4 6-1 6-1; **M. Santana** (2) (SP) d. A. D. Roche (A) 6-4 6-4 6-1.

SECOND ROUND: Emerson (1) d. Sirola 8-6 7-5 6-2; Davidson d. Carmichael 7-5 6-3 6-1; Barnes d. Diepraam 6-2 2-6 10-8 6-0; Krishnan d. Ralston 6-3 6-3 3-6 12-10; Bungert d. Drossart 6-3 6-3 6-3; Lejus d. Gulyas 6-3 12-10 6-2; Pickard d. Stuck 6-2 4-6 6-3 9-11 8-6; Arilla d. Jovanovic 6-1 7-5 6-2; **McKinley** (4) d. Lane 7-5 6-4 8-6; Ashe d. Hillebrand 5-7 7-5 11-9 3-6 6-3; Mukerjea d. Mills 7-5 9-7 2-6 12-10; Ishiguro d. Carpenter 6-2 3-6 6-3 17-15; **Mulligan** (5) d. Gisbert 6-1 6-2 6-3; Hewitt d. Phillips 6-1 6-3 6-2; Ulrich d. Rubinoff 6-1 6-7 6-3; Wilson d. McKenzie 6-4 6-1 6-4; Taylor d. Lall 6-3 6-4 6-4; Frost d. McMillan 6-4 6-1 7-5; Froehling d. Geraghty 3-6 15-13 4-6

6-1 6-2; Howe d. **Darmon** (6) 3-6 1-6 6-3 6-4 6-3; Palafox d. Hoogs 6-2 6-2 8-10 1-6 6-2; Likhachev d. Sturdza 6-3 6-4 4-6 9-7; Pietrangeli d. Hann 5-7 7-5 6-2 6-4; Stolle d. **Fletcher** (3) 7-5 9-7 13-15 6-0; Kuhnke d. Cox 2-6 6-4 6-3 6-4; Knight d. Forbes 1-6 7-5 6-4 9-11 6-3; Edelfsen d. Pasarell 6-3 9-11 10-8 6-3; **Lundquist** (7) d. Jauffret 8-6 6-4 3-6 6-3; Merlo d. Siska 6-3 6-2 6-3; Bey d. Flam 6-1 13-11 2-6 4-6 12-10; Osuna d. Matthews 7-5 4-6 8-6 6-2; **Santana** (2) d. Mandarino 6-3 6-3 6-3.

THIRD ROUND: Emerson (1) d. Davidson 6-4 8-6 6-2; Krishnan d. Barnes 6-4 6-0 6-4; Bungert d. Lejus 6-4 6-3 6-4; Arilla d. Pickard 12-10 6-2 6-3; **McKinley** (4) d. Ashe 6-3 6-2 6-2; Mukerjea d. Ishiguro 6-3 6-3 10-8; **Mulligan** (5) d. Hewitt 6-4 6-3 13-11; Wilson d. Ulrich 6-2 6-2 6-3; Taylor d. Frost 6-2 7-5 4-6 3-6 9-7; Froehling d. Howe 6-3

6-4 3-2 ret'd; Palafox d. Likhachev 6-4 4-6 6-3 6-3; Stolle d. Pietrangeli 6-3 4-3 ret'd; Kuhnke d. Knight 12-10 6-4; **Lundquist** (7) d. Edelfsen 6-2 6-4 6-0; Bey d. Merlo 6-2 6-3 6-3; **Santana** (2) d. Osuna 2-6 0-6 6-1 6-3 6-4.

FOURTH ROUND	QUARTER-FINALS	SEMI-FINALS	FINAL	CHAMPION
Emerson (1)	**Emerson** (1)			
Krishnan	6-1 6-4 6-0			
Bungert	Bungert	Bungert		
Arilla	4-6 6-3 6-0 10-12 7-5	8-6 3-6 6-3 4-6 6-3		
McKinley (4)	**McKinley** (4)		**McKinley** (4)	
Mukerjea	6-3 8-6 6-3		6-2 6-4 8-6	
Mulligan (5)	Wilson	**McKinley** (4)		
Wilson	6-4 6-1 9-7	8-6 6-4 6-2		
Taylor	Froehling			**McKinley** (4)
Froehling	2-6 6-4 7-9 6-2 15-13			9-7 6-1 6-4
Palafox	Stolle	Stolle		
Stolle	7-5 6-3 6-3	9-7 7-5 6-4		
Kuhnke	Kuhnke		Stolle	
Lundquist (7)	6-4 6-3 6-2		8-6 6-1 7-5	
Bey	**Santana** (2)	**Santana** (2)		
Santana (2)	6-3 6-1 11-13 6-3	6-3 6-4 6-4		

LADIES' SINGLES

FIRST ROUND: D. R. Hard (4) (USA) d. J. A. Fulton 6-0 6-0; C. Yates-Bell d. M. M. Lee 6-1 6-2; H. Schultze (G) d. P. Barril (SP) 6-2 6-0; Mrs M. C. Cheadle d. H. Schildknecht (G) 6-4 7-5; Mrs Z. Kormoczy (HU) d. Mrs J. H. Edrich (USA) 6-1 6-1; C. C. Truman d. Mrs A. Ochoa (M) d. J. A. M. Tegart (A) d. L. Bassi (IT) 6-1 7-5; A. Dmitrieva (USSR) d. R. Beltrame (IT) 6-1 6-2; **J. P. Lehane** (5) (A) d. S. J. Holdsworth 6-2 6-0; S. Barclay d. U. Sandulf (SW) 2-6 5-2 ret'd; T. Fretz (USA) d. C. A. Prosen (USA) 6-1 6-1; F. Durr (F) d. D. C. Tuckey 6-4 6-1; R. H. Bentley d. A. Sturm (G) 6-1 6-1; M. L. Hunt (SA) d. Mrs V. A. Roberts 6-2 6-1; C. E. Hanks (USA) d. P. Watermeyer (SA) 6-2 6-2; Mrs C. W. Brasher d. Mrs A. R. Mills 7-5 6-3; S. Lazzarino (IT) d. E. B. Rigby (SA) 6-0 6-4; Mrs D. P. Knode (USA) d. A. G.

McAlpine 6-2 6-1; H. Niessen (G) d. C. A. Newman (A) 6-3 4-6 6-4; Mrs J. W. Cawthorn d. M. E. Habicht (USA) 6-4 6-0; N. A. Turner (A) d. C. A. Rosser 6-2 7-9 8-6; Mrs H. G. Fales (USA) d. A. L. K. Barclay (C) 6-3 6-2; C. H. Coronado (SP) d. C. J. Jaster (USA) 6-2 4-6 6-0; **Mrs V. Sukova** (6) (CZ) d. J. Albert (USA) 6-4 6-4; I. de Lansalut (F) d. H. W. A. Hira 3-6 6-3 6-3; R. Lesh (A) d. J. M. Alvarez (USA) 8-6 6-4; R. A. Ebbern (A) d. M. B. H. McAnally 6-0 6-1; J. M. Barnes (A) d. K. Bardoczy (HU) 6-1 6-4; Mrs M. Sladek (C) d. Mrs M. Peterdy-Wolf (Stateless) 6-2 6-3; J. Knight d. J. M. Trewby 7-5 6-2; S. V. Wade d. Mrs A. Segal (SA) 8-6 6-4; **Mrs P. F. Jones** (3) d. J. A. Blackman (A) 6-3 6-2.

SECOND ROUND: **M. Smith** (1) (A) d. Mrs R. W. Brown (C) 6-1 6-1; Mrs K. Bartholdson (SW) d. M. Bourbonnais (A) 6-4 6-1; C. A. Caldwell (USA) d. C. Mercelis (B) 6-1 6-2; N. Baylon (ARG) d. J. Lieffrig (F) 6-4 3-6 6-2; **R. Schuurman** (8) (SA) d. D. M. Catt 4-6 6-4 6-4; F. Gordigiani (IT) d. Mrs G. Rosin (SW) 8-6 6-3; R. Ostermann (G) d. Mrs J. M. Wagstaff (A) 6-2 6-0; J. Bourgnon (SWZ) d. Mrs F. W. Ridderhof (NTH) 5-7 6-4 7-5; **Hard** (4) d. Yates-Bell 6-2 6-1; Schultze d. Cheadle 6-1 6-3; Truman d. Kormoczy 6-1 6-3; Tegart d. Dmitrieva 6-3; **Lehane** (5) d. Barclay 6-3 6-2; Fretz d. Durr 8-6 1-6 9-7; Hunt d. Bentley 6-2 6-3; Hanks d. Brasher 6-0 6-2; Knode d. Lazzarino 6-4 3-6 6-4;

Cawthorn d. Niessen 6-2 7-5; Fales d. Turner 6-1 6-1; **Sukova** (6) d. Coronado 2-6 6-1 6-4; Lesh d. de Lansalut 6-2; Ebbern d. Barnes 6-0 6-2; Sladek d. Knight 3-6 6-3 6-3; **Jones** (3) d. Wade 6-3 9-7; D. E. Starkie d. A. M. Estalella (SP) 6-4 6-0; Mrs H. de Jong (NTH) d. Mrs Z. Brossmann (HU) 4-6 7-5 6-4; A. M. Van Zyl (SA) d. Mrs J. L. Deloford 6-3 6-4; **M. E. Bueno** (7) (BR) d. Mrs P. N. Ahmed (PA) 6-0 6-0; B. J. Moffitt (USA) d. S. Pachta (AU) 6-4 6-4; L. Pericoli (IT) d. P. A. Hird 6-2 6-1; E. Buding (G) d. J. M. Tee 6-1 6-3; **L. R. Turner** (2) (A) d. Mrs M. Dohrer (G) 6-1 6-3.

THIRD ROUND: Smith (1) d. Bartholdson 6-1 6-0; Baylon d. Caldwell 0-6 6-3 6-3; **Schuurman** (8) d. Gordigiani 6-2 6-1; Ostermann d. Bourgnon 6-1 6-2; **Hard** (4) d. Schultze 6-3 6-0; Truman d. Tegart 8-6 0-6 6-1; **Lehane** (5) d. Fretz 8-6 6-4; Hunt d. Hanks 4-6 6-2 8-6; Cawthorn d. Knode 6-3 7-5; Fales d. **Sukova** (6) w.o.; Ebbern d. Lesh 6-3 8-6;

Jones (3) d. Sladek 6-1 6-0; Starkie d. de Jong 6-0 6-1; **Bueno** (7) d. Van Zyl 6-2 6-0; Moffitt d. Pericoli 7-9 6-4 6-0; **Turner** (2) d. Buding 6-4 6-3.

FOURTH ROUND	QUARTER-FINALS	SEMI-FINALS	FINAL	CHAMPION
Smith (1)	**Smith** (1)			
Baylon	6-3 6-3			
Schuurman (8)	**Schuurman** (8)	**Smith** (1)		
Ostermann	6-4 6-2	3-6 6-0 6-1		
Hard (4)	**Hard** (4)		**Smith** (1)	
Truman	3-6 6-3 8-6		6-3 6-3	
Lehane (5)	**Lehane** (5)	**Hard** (4)		
Hunt	6-1 6-3	6-1 1-2 ret'd		
Cawthorn	Fales			**Smith** (1)
Fales	6-0 6-4			6-3 6-4
Ebbern	**Jones** (3)	**Jones** (3)		
Jones (3)	6-2 6-4	6-4 6-1		
Starkie	**Bueno** (7)		Moffitt	
Bueno (7)	6-1 7-5		6-4 6-4	
Moffitt	Moffitt	Moffitt		
Turner (2)	4-6 6-4 7-5	6-2 7-5		

OTHER FINALS

GENTLEMEN'S DOUBLES: Final – R. H. Osuna (M)/A. Palafox (M) d. J. C. Barclay (F)/P. Darmon (F) 4-6 6-2 6-2 6-2.

LADIES' DOUBLES: Final – M. E. Bueno (BR)/D. R. Hard (USA) d. R. A. Ebbern (A)/M. Smith (A) 8-6 9-7.

MIXED DOUBLES: Final – K. N. Fletcher (A)/M. Smith (A) d. R. A. J. Hewitt (A)/D. R. Hard (USA) 11-9 6-4.

GENTLEMEN'S SINGLES PLATE: Final – E. L. Scott (USA) d. J. S. Crookenden (NZ) w.o.

LADIES' SINGLES PLATE: Final – F. Durr (F) d. A. Dmitrieva (USSR) 6-1 6-0.

BOYS' INVITATION SINGLES: Final – N. Kalogeropoulos (GR) d. I. El Shafei (E) 6-4 6-3.

GIRLS' INVITATION SINGLES: Final – D. Salfati (F) d. K. Dening (A) 6-4 6-1.

GENTLEMEN'S SINGLES

1964

FIRST ROUND: R. Emerson (1) (A) d. D. L. Dell (USA) 6-3 6-1 6-0; N. Pilic (YU) d. O. Ishiguro (J) 6-3 3-6 6-3 6-2; D. Sturdza (SWZ) d. A. R. Russell (JAM) 6-1 6-4 6-8 10-8; H. W. Stewart (USA) d. R. D. Senkowski (USA) 6-4 6-2 6-8 6-2; A. R. Ashe (USA) d. M. Holecek (CZ) 3-6 6-4 10-8 6-1; C. Richey (USA) d. A. Licis (Stateless) 6-4 3-6 6-4 8-10 6-3; L. A. Gerrard (NZ) d. D. Contet (F) 6-4 6-1 6-0; W. E. Bond (USA) d. R. W. Dixon 6-4 6-4 5-7 6-2; **M. F. Mulligan** (8) (A) d. W. Stuck (G) 8-6 6-4 6-2; R. A. J. Hewitt (A) d. G. Majoli (IT) 6-0 6-2 6-0; E. C. Drysdale (SA) d. C. M. Buchholz (USA) 6-2 6-4 3-6 2-6 6-4; M. I. Belkin (C) d. C. de Gronckel (B) 6-3 4-8 6-6 6-3; S. P. Misra (IN) d. E. A. Neely (USA) 6-2 6-4 6-4; J. Mukerjea (IN) d. R. Taylor 4-6 6-2 6-3 3-6 6-4; P. Darmon (F) d. M. Leclercq (F) 6-1 6-3 6-1; R. W. Barnes (BR) d. S. Likhachev (USSR) 6-4 7-5 6-1; **R. H. Osuna** (4) (M) d. L. H. Nagier (USA) 6-4 6-4 6-4; E. A. Zuleta (E) d. J. Hajer (NTH) 6-4 6-4 6-2; M. C. Riessen (USA) d. R. W. Fisher (USA) 6-3 3-6 14-12 6-2; R. Holmberg (USA) d. M. Belkhodja (TUN) 6-4 6-4 6-2; J. L. Arilla (SP) d. R. S. Werksman (USA) 3-6 6-3 6-4 4-6 6-2; J. E. Mandarino (BR) d. R. McKenzie (A) 8-6 7-5 6-3; I. Gulyas (HU) d. J. R. McDonald (NZ) 2-6 6-4 8-6 4-6 6-2; I. Pimentel (VEN) d. W. H. Hoogs (USA) 6-4 2-6 7-5 6-4; J. A. Pickard d. **R. D. Ralston** (5) (USA) 3-6 3-6 6-4 7-5 9-7; T. P. Brown (USA) d. G. R. Stilwell 8-10 6-2 6-2 5-7 8-6; J. Ulrich (D) d. C. M. Pasarell (USA) 7-9 9-11 6-4 9-7 8-6; F. Godbout (C) d. G. Battrick 6-3 6-2 8-6; K. E. Diepraam (C) d. R. Applewhaite (A) 6-4 3-8-6; W. P. Bungert (G) d. R. J. Moore (SA) 8-6 7-5 1-6 3-6 6-2; F. Jauffret (F) d. M. Pirro (IT) w.o.; M. J. Sangster d. R. K. Nyyssonen (FIN) 6-4 6-4 6-2; R. Kalogeropoulos (GR) d. F. A.

Froehling (USA) 13-11 3-6 6-2 0-6 6-4; R. J. Carmichael (A) d. J. Saul 6-2 6-1 7-9 2-6 9-7; K. Wooldridge d. B. Jovanovic (YU) 6-4 6-1 6-3; E. Drossart (B) d. J. E. Robson (NZ) 6-1 6-8 10-8 6-1; J. A. Stephens (A) d. M. L. Waters 6-2 6-2 6-1; A. R. Palafox (M) d. J. D. C. Crump (A) 6-2 3-6 6-3 6-4; K. N. Fletcher (A) d. J. Javorsky (CZ) 7-5 6-2 6-4; **F. S. Stolle** (6) (A) d. J. D. Newcombe (A) 8-6 7-5 6-3; C. Kuhnke (G) d. R. K. Wilson 6-3 6-4 1-6 6-2; A. K. Carpenter (C) d. G. C. Bluett 6-2 6-4 6-2; A. Bey (RH) d. J. B. Hillebrand (A) 3-6 2-6 11-9 6-3 6-3; C. S. Brebnor (SA) d. J. Leschly (D) 7-5 11-9 6-4; C. A. Fernandes (BR) d. J. C. Barclay (F) 7-5 6-4 6-1; E. L. Scott (USA) d. P. Rodriguez (CH) 7-5 16-14 6-4; T. Leyus (USSR) d. A. E. Fox (USA) 6-3 6-2 6-2; **M. Santana** (3) (SP) d. P. Lall (IN) 6-2 2-6 6-3 7-5; R. N. Howe (A) d. A. Bresson (F) 6-1 6-4 9-7; A. Segal (SA) d. C. E. Graebner (USA) 6-2 7-5 6-2; T. Okker (NTH) d. F. D. McMillan (SA) 6-3 5-7 6-3 3-2 ret'd; A. Metreveli (USSR) d. E. Soriano (ARG) 6-3 3-6 6-1 6-4; J. H. McManus (USA) d. I. S. Crookenden (NZ) 8-6 8-6 6-3; M. J. Franks (USA) d. E. N. Newman (USA) 8-6 1-3 6-6 6-4 6-4; P. Barthes (F) d. G. Hernandez (PH) 9-7 6-4 6-3; **N. Pietrangeli** (7) (IT) d. W. W. Bowrey (A) 6-3 4-6 9-7 7-5; C. E. Zeeman (SA) d. C. Iles 6-2 3-6 2-6 6-1 6-4; D. D. Phillips (SA) d. K. Andersson (SW) 3-6 7-5 6-3 6-4 6-2; W. A. Knight d. A. R. Mills 6-1 6-2 6-4; M. Cox d. W. Alvarez (COL) 4-6 6-1 8-6 6-3; A. D. Roche (A) d. J. M. Gisbert (SP) 6-1 6-4 6-4; T. Ulrich (D) d. S. J. Matthews 11-9 6-3 6-2; T. Koch (BR) d. O. Bengtson (SW) 6-1 7-5 6-3; **C. R. McKinley** (2) (USA) d. T. J. Ryan (SA) 6-2 6-1 6-3.

SECOND ROUND: Emerson (1) d. Pilic 6-3 11-9 3-6 6-4; Stewart d. Sturdza 6-4 6-4 7-5; Ashe d. Richey 4-6 4-6 6-3 6-2 6-2; Bond d. Gerrard 7-5 6-3 6-2; Hewitt d. **Mulligan** (8) 6-4 6-2 6-4; Belkin d. Drysdale 7-5 3-6 6-4 6-4; Mukerjea d. Misra 2-6 6-1 1-2-6 6-4; Darmon d. Barnes 4-6 6-3 7-5 4-6 6-1; **Osuna** (4) d. Zuleta 6-2 6-1 6-3; Holmberg d. Riessen 14-16 11-13 6-4 6-2 10-8; Arilla d. Mandarino 9-7 3-6 11-9 6-3; Pimental d. Gulyas 3-6 6-2 8-6 6-3; Pickard d. Brown 6-4 6-2 4-6 6-4; Ulrich d. Godbout 2-6 6-4 8-6 6-2; Bungert d. Diepraam 5-7 6-3 3-6 8-6 6-2; Sangster d. Jauffret 7-5 9-7 6-4; Kalogeropoulos d. Carmichael 6-8 4-6 6-3 13-11 6-4; Wooldridge d. Drossart

6-3 6-4 10-8; Palafox d. Stephens 7-5 3-6 6-3 6-2; **Stolle** (6) d. Fletcher 13-11 4-6 6-3 6-4; Kuhnke d. Carpenter 6-3 6-1; Bey d. Brebnor 4-6 5-7 6-3 6-4 6-1; Scott d. Fernandes 6-2 6-4 3-6 6-1; **Santana** (3) d. Leyus 6-4 6-2 6-2; Segal d. Howe 6-2 1-6 6-3 5-7 8-6; Metreveli d. Okker 2-6 7-5 6-4 6-2; Franks d. McManus 6-3 2-6 6-4 10-12 6-4; Barthes d. **Pietrangeli** (7) 6-3 7-5 6-4; Phillips d. Zeeman 6-3 6-4 6-2; Knight d. Cox 6-4 6-4 11-9; Ulrich d. Roche 9-7 6-2 5-7 7-5; **McKinley** (2) d. Koch 3-6 6-3 6-4 5-7 6-4.

THIRD ROUND: Emerson (1) d. Stewart 6-3 6-3 6-3; Ashe d. Bond 6-4 6-4 6-0; Hewitt d. Belkin 6-4 6-0 6-1; Mukerjea d. Darmon 6-0 4-6 6-8 6-3 7-5; **Osuna** (4) d. Holmberg 6-4 6-4 3-6 6-3; Arilla d. Pimentel 6-4 6-4 5-7 6-4; Ulrich d. Pickard 3-6 6-4 6-4 6-1; Bungert d. Sangster 6-4 4-6 6-3 6-3; Kalogeropoulos d. Wooldridge 3-6 7-5 6-1 2-6

6-4; **Stolle** (6) d. Palafox 6-0 6-2 3-6 4-6 11-9; Kuhnke d. Bey 6-1 6-4 6-4; **Santana** (3) d. Scott 6-3 4-6 3-6 6-3 9-7; Segal d. Metreveli w.o.; Barthes d. Franks 12-10 7-9 15-17 6-3 6-4; Knight d. Phillips 6-2 6-0 6-2; **McKinley** (2) d. Ulrich 7-5 6-3 2-6 7-5.

FOURTH ROUND	QUARTER-FINALS	SEMI-FINALS	FINAL	CHAMPION
Emerson (1)	**Emerson** (1)			
Ashe	6-3 6-2 7-5	**Emerson** (1)		
Hewitt	Hewitt	6-1 6-4 6-4		
Mukerjea	6-4 6-2 6-1		**Emerson** (1)	
Osuna (4)	**Osuna** (4)		6-3 15-13 6-0	
Arilla	6-4 6-4 10-12 6-3	Bungert		
Ulrich	Bungert	6-4 6-2 6-3		**Emerson** (1)
Bungert	3-6 6-2 6-3 6-4			6-1 12-10 4-6 6-3
Kalogeropoulos	**Stolle** (6)			
Stolle (6)	6-2 6-3 6-0	**Stolle** (6)		
Kuhnke	Kuhnke	6-3 7-5 6-3		
Santana (3)	6-3 7-5 6-8 6-4		**Stolle** (6)	
Segal	Segal		4-6 10-8 9-7 6-4	
Barthes	6-2 4-6 6-3 6-4	**McKinley** (2)		
Knight	**McKinley** (2)	6-3 6-3 4-6 6-4		
McKinley (2)	8-6 6-4 2-6 6-4			

LADIES' SINGLES

FIRST ROUND: B. J. Moffitt (3) (USA) d. R. Beltrame (IT) 7-5 4-6 6-3; Mrs H. G. Fales (USA) d. F. M. E. Toyne (A) 6-3 6-1; M. M. Lee d. A. J. Stroud 6-4 4-6 6-4; D. C. Tuckey d. A. M. Estalella (SP) 6-2 6-3; J. Rees-Lewis (F) d. C. L. Crosby (USA) 6-1 6-3; Mrs A. Segal (SA) d. J. Knight (A) 8-6 6-2; C. Yates-Bell d. F. E. Walton 2-6 6-3 6-0; L. Pericoli (IT) d. H. W. Allen 6-2 6-2; **Mrs P. F. Jones** (6) d. L. L. Crosby (USA) 6-0 6-0; Mrs J. A. G. Lloyd d. G. M. Houlihan (IRE) 4-6 7-5 11-9; Mrs J. W. Cawthorn 6-0 3-6 6-4; C. A. Rosser d. I. de Lansalut (F) 8-6 8-6; B. Stove (NTH) d. P. R. McClenaughan (A) 6-4 6-3; J. A. M. Tegart d. Mrs G. M. Williams 6-2 6-1; T. A. Fretz (USA) d. H. Schultze (G) 2-6 6-4; H. Schildknecht (G) d. M. E. Habicht (USA) 6-4 0-6 6-3; S. Pachta (AU) d. S. R. de Fina (USA) 6-3

8-6; R. H. Bentley d. R. Ostermann (G) 6-4 6-1; J. M. Alvarez (USA) d. J. Lieffrig (F) 0-6 8-6 7-5; S. V. Wade d. J. A. Garner (SA) 9-7 6-2; J. M. Trewby d. Mrs P. J. Kerr 6-1 6-3; D. E. Starkie d. M. Fourie (SA) 6-2 6-3; Mrs P. Haygarth (SA) d. M. B. H. McAnally (SA) 6-3 6-4; **N. Richey** (5) (USA) d. J. Bricka (USA) 6-0 6-2; G. Swan (SA) d. Mrs J. Ridderhof-Seven (NTH) 10-8 6-2; V. H. Dennis d. Mrs Z. Kormoczy (HU) 1-0 ret'd; Mrs G. Rosin (SW) d. M. T. Riedl (IT) 6-2 4-6 6-2; P. Kellmeyer (USA) d. A. L. Owen 6-4 9-7; M. A. Eisel (USA) d. Mrs M. C. Cheadle 7-5 6-1; R. Lesh (A) d. N. Truman 6-3 6-3; C. E. Hanks (USA) d. Mrs B. I. Shenton 6-3 6-3; **L. R. Turner** (4) (A) d. J. M. Tee 6-3 6-3.

SECOND ROUND: M. Smith (1) (A) d. A. M. van Zyl (SA) 6-2 6-1; Mrs J. R. Susman (USA) d. A. Dmitrieva (USSR) 4-6 6-3 7-5; F. Gordigiani (IT) d. M. R. O'Donnell 6-4 6-2; A. Lepoutre (NTH) d. Mrs K. Bartholdson (SW) 4-6 7-5 6-0; **J. P. Lehane** (7) (A) d. F. Durr (F) 6-2 6-1; N. Baylon (ARG) d. C. H. Coronado (SP) 6-4 7-5; H. Niessen (G) d. Mrs P. Darmon (M) 2-6 6-4 6-4; D. M. Catt d. Mrs V. Sukova (CZ) 6-4 6-2; **Moffitt** (3) d. Fales 6-2 6-2; Lee d. Tuckey 6-3 7-5; Rees-Lewis d. Segal 4-6 6-4 6-4; Pericoli d. Yates-Bell 6-1 6-3; **Jones** (6) d. Lloyd 6-1 7-5; Rosser d. Roberts 6-4 6-4; Tegart d. Stove 6-4 6-3; Fretz d. Schildknecht 7-5 3-6 6-1; Bentley d. Pachta 6-3 6-3; Alvarez d. Wade 7-9 6-3

8-6; Starkie d. Trewby 6-1 6-2; **Richey** (5) d. Haygarth 6-1 6-2; Swan d. Dennis 6-2 7-5; Rosin d. Kellmeyer 6-1 6-2; Eisel d. Lesh 0-6 6-2 6-2; **Turner** (4) d. Hanks 6-2 6-0; U. K. Sandulf (SW) d. C. C. Truman w.o.; C. A. Caldwell (USA) d. H. N. Plaisted (A) 6-3 6-4; M. Schacht (A) d. A. Sturm (G) 6-4 6-3; **R. A. Ebbern** (8) (A) d. M. Salfati (F) 6-2 6-4; T. Groenman (NTH) d. V. Palmer (USA) 2-6 6-2 6-4; V. Kodesova (CZ) d. P. Barril (SP) 4-4-6 6-1; C. Mercelis (B) d. L. Paldan (NOR) 6-1 6-2; **M. E. Bueno** (2) (BR) d. C. A. Prosen (USA) 6-0 6-3.

THIRD ROUND: Smith (1) d. Susman 11-9 6-0; Lepoutre d. Gordigiani 6-3 4-6 6-1; Baylon d. **Lehane** (7) 6-3 2-6 7-5; Catt d. Niessen 6-4 6-0; **Moffitt** (3) d. Lee 3-6 6-4 6-2; Rees-Lewis d. Pericoli 1-6 6-1 7-5; **Jones** (6) d. Rosser 6-4 6-4; Tegart d. Fretz 6-2 6-1; Alvarez d. Bentley 6-2 6-3; **Richey** (5) d. Starkie 6-1 10-8; Swan d. Rosin 6-4 6-4;

Turner (4) d. Eisel 6-3 6-2; Caldwell d. Sandulf 6-2 6-2; **Ebbern** (8) d. Schacht 6-3 6-2; Groenman d. Kodesova 6-4 6-2; **Bueno** (2) d. Mercelis 6-1 6-1.

FOURTH ROUND	QUARTER-FINALS	SEMI-FINALS	FINAL	CHAMPION
Smith (1)	**Smith** (1)			
Lepoutre	6-1 6-1	**Smith** (1)		
Baylon	Baylon	6-0 2-0 ret'd		
Catt	4-6 6-0 6-3		**Smith** (1)	
Moffitt (3)	**Moffitt** (3)		6-3 6-4	
Rees-Lewis	6-4 6-4	**Moffitt** (3)		
Jones (6)	**Jones** (6)	6-3 6-3		
Tegart	10-8 6-3			**Bueno** (2)
Alvarez	**Richey** (5)			6-4 7-9 6-3
Richey (5)	6-2 6-2	**Turner** (4)		
Swan	**Turner** (4)	6-3 6-4		
Turner (4)	6-0 5-7 6-2		**Bueno** (2)	
Caldwell	**Ebbern** (8)		3-6 6-4 6-4	
Ebbern (8)	6-4 6-0	**Bueno** (2)		
Groenman	**Bueno** (2)	6-4 6-1		
Bueno (2)	6-1 6-1			

OTHER FINALS

GENTLEMEN'S DOUBLES: Final — R. A. J. Hewitt (A)/F. S. Stolle (A) d. R. S. Emerson (A)/K. N. Fletcher (A) 7-5 11-9 6-4.
LADIES' DOUBLES: Final — M. Smith (A)/L. R. Turner (A) d. B. J. Moffitt (USA)/Mrs J. R. Susman (USA) 7-5 6-2.
MIXED DOUBLES: Final — F. S. Stolle (A)/L. R. Turner (A) d. K. N. Fletcher (A)/M. Smith (A) 6-4 6-4.
GENTLEMEN'S SINGLES PLATE: Final — R. K. Wilson d. W. W. Bowrey (A) 6-4 6-3.

LADIES' SINGLES PLATE: Final — Mrs V. Sukova (CZ) d. J. Bricka (USA) 0-6 6-3 6-3.
BOYS' INVITATION SINGLES: Final — I. El Shafei (E) d. V. Korotkov (USSR) 6-2 6-3.
GIRLS' INVITATION SINGLES: Final — J. Bartkowicz (USA) d. E. Subirats (M) 6-3 6-1.
VETERANS' MEN'S DOUBLES: Final — B. Destremau (F)/W. F. Talbert (USA) d. G. R. MacCall (USA)/A. V. Martini (USA) 7-5 6-3.

GENTLEMEN'S SINGLES

FIRST ROUND: R. Emerson (1) (A) d. I. S. Pimentel (VEN) 6-3 6-2 6-2; M. J. Sangster d. F. A. Froehling (USA) 6-4 6-2 18-16; J. R. Cooper d. J. A. Pickard 3-6 4-6 9-7 6-2 6-2; R. F. Sanders (USA) d. W. Gasiorek (POL) 6-2 6-8 6-4 5-7 7-5; G. Mulloy (USA) d. J. M. Couder (SP) w.o.; P. Lall (IN) d. G. Merlo (IT) 6-0 6-2 4-6 7-5; A. R. Mills d. J. E. Sharpe (A) 3-6 6-3 10-8 6-3; K. N. Fletcher (A) d. R. S. Werksman (USA) 6-4 6-3 2-6 6-2; **A. D. Roche** (7) (A) d. R. O. Ruffels (A) 6-2 12-10 6-4; M. F. Mulligan (A) d. H. Elschenbroich (G) 6-3 6-2 7-5; I. S. Crookenden (NZ) d. E. A. Beards 6-4 6-1 7-5; J. H. McManus (A) d. C. Duxin (F) 6-3 6-0 6-3; R. W. Barnes (BR) d. A. Licis (Stateless) 6-4 6-3 6-3; F. Jauffret (F) d. F. Guzman (E) 7-5 6-2 6-0; C. W. Stubs d. W. J. Lenoir (USA) 6-4 2-6 4-6 6-4 6-3; K. E. Diepraam (SA) d. K. Watanabe (J) 9-7 6-2 6-3; **R. D. Ralston** (4) d. H. Richardson (USA) 15-13 9-7 6-2; M. Leclercq (F) d. M. Holecek (CZ) 6-4 9-7 6-4; R. Krishnan (IN) d. L. A. Gerrard (NZ) 6-2 6-3 6-2; T. Koch (BR) d. W. W. Bowrey (A) 6-1 8-6 3-6 6-2; P. Barthes (F) d. T. Okker (NTH) 10-12 14-12 9-7 6-3; **W. P. Bungert** (5) d. A. R. Palafox (M) 6-3 6-2 1-6 6-3; R. K. Wilson d. C. M. Pasarell (USA) 6-2 8-6 7-5; S. Tacchini (IT) d. C. E. Zeeman (SA) 6-3 6-3 6-2; M. C. Riessen (USA) d. N. Kalogeropoulos (GR) 6-4 6-4 3-6 6-3; R. N. Howe (A) d. B. Holmstrom (SW) 6-3 8-6 6-4; G. C. Bluett d. A. Kreinberg (G) 6-4 3-6 6-4 6-3; J. E. Barrett d. J. Gisbert (SP) 6-3 6-4 7-5; H. S. FitzGibbon (USA) d. C. S. Brebnor (SA) 9-7 6-2 6-3; E. C. Drysdale (SA) d. V. Zarazua (M) 6-1 6-3 6-0;

J. Mukerjea (IN) d. O. Ishiguro (J) 6-3 6-4 6-2; M. P. Hann d. J. L. Moore (A) 6-8 6-0 6-2 6-8 8-6; H. C. Kuhnke (G) d. J. E. Mandarino (BR) 12-10 6-4 6-3; C. Richey (USA) d. W. Alvarez (COL) 2-6 6-3 7-5; J. C. Barclay (F) d. P. H. Rodriguez (CH) 6-4 7-5 3-6 12-10; T. Brown (USA) d. G. Battrick 6-4 6-3 6-2; **J. D. Newcombe** (6) (A) d. E. Soriano (ARG) 6-2 6-1 8-6; R. R. Dowdeswelt (RH) d. F. Bautista (PH) 6-3 6-2 7-5; N. Pietrangeli (IT) d. T. J. Ryan (SA) 7-5 6-4 7-5; E. Zuleta (E) 6-1 6-0 6-0; D. L. Dell (USA) d. W. H. Hoogs (USA) 5-7 11-13 6-1 6-2 6-4; T. Lejus (USSR) d. F. D. McMillan (SA) 6-1 3-6 6-3 6-4; E. L. Scott (USA) d. S. J. Matthews 6-4 6-2 7-5; A. E. Fox (USA) d. T. B. Edlefsen (USA) 5-7 6-0 6-2 6-4; **J. E. Lundquist** (3) (SW) d. J. R. McDonald (NZ) 6-2 6-4 6-0; A. R. Ashe (USA) d. D. H. Kelso (A) 3-6 6-2 6-3 6-3; P. Darmon (F) d. C. R. Applewhaite 6-2 6-2 3-6 6-4; R. J. Carmichael (A) d. S. P. Misra (IN) 6-4 4-6 8-6 4-6 6-3; A. A. Segal (SA) d. O. Pabst (CH) 6-4 7-5 6-3; I. Buding (G) d. O. K. Davidson 6-8 6-1 8-6 4-6 6-4; A. K. Carpenter (C) d. P. J. Cramer (SA) 8-6 5-7 6-3 7-5; S. R. Smith (USA) d. J. Hajer (NTH) 6-4 2-3 6-6 6-4; **R. H. Osuna** (8) (M) d. I. Gulyas (HU) 6-4 6-3 6-4; N. A. Fraser (SA) d. R. J. Moore (SA) 2-6 6-1 6-4 10-8; T. Ulrich (D) d. J. L. Arilla (SP) 9-7 6-0 6-4; G. R. Stilwell (SA) d. D. D. Phillips (SA) 6-0 9-7 7-5; R. A. J. Hewitt (SA) d. J. R. Parker (USA) 6-3 6-1 6-0; W. A. Knight d. K. E. Wooldridge 6-2 6-1 6-3; J. Javorsky (CZ) d. I. Watanabe (J) 2-6 6-4 6-1 6-1; C. de Gronckel (B) d. D. Sturdza (SWZ) 6-2 9-7 8-6; **F. S. Stolle** (2) (A) d. V. Egorov (USSR) 6-3 6-4 7-5.

SECOND ROUND: Emerson (1) d. Sangster 8-6 6-3 6-2; Cooper d. Sanders 9-7 6-1 6-4; Lall d. Mulloy 8-6 6-2 6-2; Fletcher d. Mills 6-1 6-0 3-6 6-1; Mulligan d. **Roche** (7) 6-4 6-2 6-8 7-5; Newcombe d. Crookenden 6-2 6-3 1-6 6-4; Jauffret d. Barnes 7-5 6-4 6-4; Diepraam d. Stubs 3-6 6-3 6-2 6-2; **Ralston** (4) d. Leclercq 6-3 6-2 6-2; Krishnan d. Graebner 7-5 1-6 6-4 6-2; Metreveli d. Contet 6-3 8-6 10-8; Koch d. Barthes 3-6 6-2 6-3 7-5; **Bungert** (5) d. Wilson 6-4 6-3 2-6 5-7 6-2; Riessen d. Tacchini 6-3 6-4 6-3; Howe d. Bluett 6-2 6-1 8-6; FitzGibbon d. Barrett 4-6 7-5 6-3

6-2; Drysdale d. Mukerjea 6-2 6-3 8-6; Kuhnke d. Hann 7-5 6-2 6-3; Richey d. Barclay 4-6 3-6 6-1 6-0 7-5; **Newcombe** (6) d. Brown 6-4 6-2 7-5; Pietrangeli d. Dowdeswell 6-3 6-4 7-5; Taylor d. Dell 6-2 7-5 6-4; Scott d. Lejus 6-2 9-7 7-9 4-6 6-4; Fox d. **Lundquist** (3) 7-9 7-5 6-2 7-5; Ashe d. Darmon 6-8 6-4 6-2 7-5 7-5; Fraser d. Ulrich 10-8 4-6 2-6 7-5 7-5; **Osuna** (8) d. Smith 4-6 6-2 6-3 6-3; Buding d. Carpenter 9-7 6-2 6-4; Stilwell d. Phillips 6-0 9-7 7-5; Hewitt d. Stilwell 7-5 6-3 6-2 6-1; Knight d. Javorsky 6-3 6-2 6-1; **Stolle** (2) d. de Gronckel 6-3 6-2 8-6.

THIRD ROUND: Emerson (1) d. Cooper 6-3 6-4 6-4; Fletcher d. Lall 6-3 6-2 6-1; McManus d. Mulligan 6-4 6-2 6-2; Diepraam d. Jauffret 6-0 6-2 6-2; **Ralston** (4) d. Krishnan 9-7 6-1 6-4; Koch d. Metreveli 7-5 3-6 15-17 6-3 8-6; Riessen d. **Bungert** (5) 6-2 7-5 8-6; Howe d. FitzGibbon 6-3 6-2 6-4; Drysdale d. Kuhnke 7-5 6-2 3-6 6-1; **Newcombe** (6) d. Richey 6-4 6-2 6-2; Pietrangeli d. Taylor 7-5 2-6 4-6 6-2 6-3; Fox d. Scott 4-6 7-5 6-2; Ashe d. Carmichael 7-5 6-3 8-6; **Osuna** (8) d. Buding 6-4 6-4 7-5; Hewitt d. Fraser 6-0 8-6 8-6; **Stolle** (2) d. Knight 6-4 6-4 6-8 6-4.

FOURTH ROUND	QUARTER-FINALS	SEMI-FINALS	FINAL	CHAMPION
Emerson (1)	**Emerson** (1)			
Fletcher	10-8 6-4 3-6 11-9	**Emerson** (1)		
McManus	Diepraam	4-6 6-3 6-1 6-1		
Diepraam	5-7 6-4 6-4 6-2		**Emerson** (1)	
Ralston (4)	**Ralston** (4)		6-1 6-2 7-9 6-1	
Koch	6-3 6-3 6-1	**Ralston** (4)		
Riessen	Riessen	3-6 2-6 6-4 6-2 6-2		**Emerson** (1)
Howe	6-2 6-2 6-1			6-2 6-4 6-4
Drysdale	Drysdale			
Newcombe (6)	9-7 6-4 11-13 11-9	Drysdale		
Pietrangeli	Fox	4-6 6-2 7-5 7-5		
Fox	5-7 7-5 6-2 6-4		**Stolle** (2)	
Ashe	**Osuna** (8)		6-3 6-4 7-5	
Osuna (8)	8-6 6-4 6-4	**Stolle** (2)		
Hewitt	**Stolle** (2)	11-13 6-3 6-1 6-2		
Stolle (2)	6-3 6-4 6-4			

LADIES' SINGLES

FIRST ROUND: L. R. Turner (3) (A) d. J. Lieffrig (F) 6-0 6-1; G. V. Sherrif (A) d. Mrs W. A. Tym (USA) 9-7 6-3; K. A. Blake (USA) d. A. M. Estalella (SP) 6-4 6-3; P. R. McClenaughan (ET) 8-6 6-3; T. A. Fretz (USA) d. J. P. Bartkowicz (USA) 10-8 6-3; Mrs J. Volavkova (CZ) d. Mrs K. Bartholdson (SW) 6-3 6-1; C. H. Sherrif (A) d. Mrs J. A. Bennett 8-11 9-11; L. Pericoli (IT) d. H. Schildknecht (USA) 6-3 6-3; **B. J. Moffitt** (5) d. E. M. Spruyt (USA) 6-2 6-3; D. E. Starkie d. F. M. E. Toyne (A) 4-6 6-4 6-2; J. A. Blackman (A) d. V. H. Dennis 6-2 6-1; I. de Lansalut (F) d. B. Stove (NTH) 6-3 1-6 8-6; E. Krocke (NTH) d. V. M. Wiggill (SA) 7-5 6-1; S. Pachta (AU) d. S. M. Tutt 2-6 6-2 6-1; Mrs L. M. Cawthorn d. D. A. Whitely (A) 9-7 6-3; R. Lesh (A) d. C. A. Prosen (USA) 6-0 6-4; J. Heldman (USA) d. Mrs J.

Ridderhof-Seven (NTH) 2-6 6-0 6-0; A. L. Owen d. Mrs D. K. Illingworth 6-4 13-11; Mrs J. A. G. Lloyd d. M. B. H. McAnally 6-3 6-3; L. Bassi (IT) d. P. Barril (SP) 7-5 6-1; A. Dmitrieva (USSR) d. A. Rigby 6-2 6-3; J. A. M. Tegart (A) d. Mrs A. R. Mills 6-2 6-1; C. C. Truman d. S. Lazzarino (IT) 6-0 6-0; **Mrs C. E. Graebner** (6) (USA) d. P. M. Walkden (RH) 7-5 6-3; Mrs G. M. Williams d. Mrs P. Darmon (M) 6-2 8-6; I. A. R. F. Lofdahl (SW) d. J. Rees-Lewis (F) 1-6 6-3 8-6; N. Truman d. E. Buding (G) 4-6 6-3 6-1; C. A. Rosser d. Mrs V. Vopickova (CZ) 6-1 6-1; Mrs J. L. Deloford d. A. G. Sturm (G) 6-4 6-4; Mrs M. R. O'Donnell d. V. A. Berner (C) 6-3 6-1; Mrs V. A. Roberts d. Mrs A. A. Segal (SA) 6-4 6-2; **N. Richey** (4) d. E. Emanuel (USA) 6-3 6-0.

SECOND ROUND: M. E. Bueno (1) (BR) d. W. M. Shaw 6-3 6-2; M. Schacht (A) d. M. C. Riedl (IT) 6-2 6-0; C. Sandberg (SW) d. M. Hassmann (AU) 6-3 6-4; Mrs P. F. Jones d. M. E. Habicht (USA) 6-2 6-2; **F. Durr** (8) (F) d. C. H. Coronado (SP) 6-4 6-2; G. S. Swan (SA) d. M. A. Eisel (USA) 6-3 3-6 6-2; J. T. Albert (USA) d. N. Baylon (ARG) 6-3 6-4; H. Schultze (G) d. H. W. Allen 7-5 6-2; **Turner** (3) d. Sherriff 6-1 6-3; McClenaughan d. Blake 4-6 7-5 6-2; Fretz d. Volavkova 6-4 6-4; Pericoli d. Sherriff 4-3 6-9 7; **Moffitt** (5) d. Starkie 6-4 3-6 6-3; Blackman d. de Lansalut 6-3 6-2; Krocke d. Pachta 6-2 6-1; Lesh d. Cawthorn 6-1 6-0; Heldman d. Owen 6-1 6-1; Lloyd d. Bassi 6-1 6-1; Tegart d.

Dmitrieva 6-4 4-6 8-6; Truman d. **Graebner** (6) 5-7 8-6 6-1; Williams d. Lofdahl 6-1 6-4; Rosser d. Truman 6-2 10-8; Deloford d. O'Donnell 6-3 6-4; **Richey** (4) d. Roberts 6-4 6-3; J. Bricka (USA) d. F. Gordigiani (IT) 7-5 6-2; M. Salfati (F) d. L. Paldan (NOR) 6-1 7-5; S. V. Wade d. Mrs O. Peterdy-Wolf (F) 6-1 6-3; M. Boulle (F) d. C. Mercelis (B) 3-6 6-1 6-3; F. V. M. MacLennan d. U. K. Sandulf (SW) 6-4 6-3; M. M. Lee d. H. Niessen (G) 6-3 6-1; R. H. Bentley d. T. Groenman (NTH) 4-6 7-5 9-7; **M. Smith** (2) (A) d. L. M. Leyrer (AU) 6-0 6-1.

THIRD ROUND: Bueno (1) d. Schacht 6-4 7-5; Jones d. Sandberg 6-0 6-3; **Durr** (8) d. Swan 6-1 6-2; Albert d. Schultze 6-4 6-3; **Turner** (3) d. McClenaughan 7-5 6-2; Pericoli d. Fretz 8-6 3-6 6-4; **Moffitt** (5) d. Blackman 7-5 12-10; Lesh d. Krocke 6-2 6-4; Heldman d. Lloyd 6-2 6-2; Truman d. Tegart 6-4 6-2; Williams d. Rosser 3-6 6-2 6-2; **Richey** (4) d. Deloford 6-1 6-0; Bricka d. Salfati 6-2 3-6 7-5; Wade d. Boulle 6-0 6-2; MacLennan d. Lee 6-3 6-4; **Smith** (2) d. Bentley 6-0 6-1.

FOURTH ROUND	QUARTER-FINALS	SEMI-FINALS	FINAL	CHAMPION
Bueno (1)	**Bueno** (1)			
Jones	6-4 7-5	**Bueno** (1)		
Durr (8)	Albert	6-2 6-2		
Albert	6-4 7-5		**Bueno** (1)	
Turner (3)	**Turner** (3)		6-4 5-7 6-3	
Pericoli	6-0 6-4	**Moffitt** (5)		
Moffitt (5)	**Moffitt** (5)	6-2 6-1		**Smith** (2)
Lesh	6-2 6-0			6-4 7-5
Heldman	Truman			
Truman	3-6 6-2 6-2	Truman		
Williams	**Richey** (4)	6-4 1-6 7-5		
Richey (4)	6-0 6-3		**Smith** (2)	
Bricka	Bricka		6-4 6-0	
Wade	5-7 6-4 8-6	**Smith** (2)		
MacLennan	**Smith** (2)	6-3 6-0		
Smith (2)	6-2 6-1			

OTHER FINALS

GENTLEMEN'S DOUBLES: Final — J. D. Newcombe (A)/A. D. Roche (A) d. K. N. Fletcher (A)/R. A. J. Hewitt (A) 7-5 6-3 6-4.
LADIES' DOUBLES: Final — M. E. Bueno (BR)/B. J. Moffitt (USA) d. F. Durr/J. Lieffrig (F) 6-2 7-5.
MIXED DOUBLES: Final — K. N. Fletcher (A)/M. Smith (A) d. A. D. Roche (A)/J. A. M. Tegart (A) 12-10 6-3.
GENTLEMEN'S SINGLES PLATE: Final — O. K. Davidson d. T. S. Okker (NTH) 6-3 8-6.

LADIES' SINGLES PLATE: Final — A. Dmitrieva (USSR) d. F. E. Truman 6-1 6-2.
BOYS' INVITATION SINGLES: Final — V. Korotkov (USSR) d. G. Goven (F) 6-2 3-6 6-3.
GIRLS' INVITATION SINGLES: Final — O. Morozova (USSR) d. R. Giscafre (ARG) 6-3 6-3.
VETERANS' MEN'S DOUBLES: Final — G. Mulloy (USA)/W. F. Talbert (USA) d. A. V. Martini (USA)/G. R. MacCall 6-1 2-6 6-2.

GENTLEMEN'S SINGLES

1966

FIRST ROUND: R. Emerson (1) (A) d. H. E. Fauquier (C) 6-0 6-1 6-2; W. P. Bungert (G) d. B. Montrenaud (F) 1-6 6-4 8-6 6-4; C. M. Pasarell (USA) d. P. Pokorny (AU) 6-3 6-1 6-3; J. E. Barrett d. J. R. Pinto Bravo (CH) 6-2 7-5 6-1; K. Watanabe (J) d. S. Tacchini (IT) 6-1 4-6 6-0 6-1; S. R. Smith (USA) d. R. R. Maud (SA) 6-0 7-5 6-4; W. H. Hoogs (USA) d. J. F. Guzman (E) 6-3 6-1 6-2; K. E. Wooldridge d. J. H. McManus (USA) 9-7 6-2 9-7; **C. E. Graebner** (8) (USA) d. M. F. Mulligan (A) 6-4 6-4 6-3; O. K. Davidson (A) d. N. Pilic (YU) 6-4 6-4 6-4; P. Beust (F) d. E. Davidman (IS) 6-2 5-7 6-1 6-3; D. Sturdza (SWZ) d. K. Yanagi (J) 3-6 4-6 6-3 6-4 6-2; T. Okker (NTH) d. A. R. Mills (A) 6-4 6-1 6-1; C. Iles d. P. D. Van Lingen (SA) 8-6 6-2 6-4; M. J. Sangster d. P. Saila (FIN) 6-2 6-2 6-4; R. W. Barnes (BR) d. W. I. Alvarez (COL) 6-1 6-3 6-2; **M. Santana** (4) (SP) d. I. Watanabe (J) 5-7 3-0 ret'd; M. Belkin (C) d. J. L. Moore (USA) 6-4 6-1 6-1; M. C. Riessen (USA) d. B. Phillips-Moore (A) w.o.; E. L. Scott (USA) d. L. A. Gerrard (NZ) 9-7 13-11 7-5; D. Contet (F) d. I. Gulyas (HU) 6-4 6-0 8-6; O. Bengtson (SW) d. J. H. Osborne (USA) 6-4 6-1 1-6 6-1; J. L. Cromwell (USA) d. C. de Gronckel (B) 6-4 6-3 6-2; R. K. Wilson d. J. A. Cottrill (A) 6-0 9-7 6-3; **J. D. Newcombe** (5) (A) d. R. O. Ruffels (A) 6-3 4-6 6-3 6-3; T. Koch (BR) d. I. Nastase (RU) 6-2 6-0 6-0; K. N. Fletcher (A) d. R. J. Carmichael (A) 6-1 6-3 6-4; F. D. McMillan (SA) d. B. Paul (F) 6-2 8-6 3-6 6-2; R. E. Holmberg (USA) d. G. Maioli (IT) 6-3 6-4 3-6 6-4; G. Battrick d. J. Javorsky (CZ) 6-1 6-4 7-5; T. Ulrich (D) d. G. di Maso (IT) 9-7 5-7 6-3 6-4; J. Mukerjea (IN) d. S. Likhachev (USSR) 2-6 7-5 7-5 6-3; E.

Zuleta (E) d. G. B. Primrose (A) 8-6 7-5 3-6 9-7; P. Darmon (F) d. D. L. Dell (USA) 7-5 6-3 6-0; J. Saul (SA) d. O. Ishiguro (J) 6-1 6-4 3-6 4-6 12-10; I. El Shafei (UAR) d. S. J. Matthews 6-2 6-8 6-4 7-5; K. E. Diepraam (SA) d. M. Leclercq (F) 6-8 6-2 6-2 6-2; A. K. Carpenter (C) d. G. Mulloy (USA) 6-3 9-7 9-7; A. Metreveli (USSR) d. R. Taylor 6-3 0-6 6-0 6-2; **R. D. Ralston** (6) (USA) d. R. C. Lutz (USA) 7-5 6-2 3-6 6-4; J. Ulrich (D) d. D. A. R. Russell (JAM) 6-3 6-3 6-2; J. E. Mandarino (BR) d. J. B. Chanfreau (F) 7-5 6-4 6-0; M. Cox d. S. P. Misra (IN) 6-8 6-3 6-4 6-4; W. W. Bowrey (A) d. W. Gasiorek (POL) 6-2 6-4 6-4; T. J. Ryan (SA) d. N. Pietrangeli (IT) 6-2 6-8 3-6 6-3 6-2; I. Konishi (J) d. J. C. Barclay (F) 1-6 6-4 6-1 6-0; R. A. J. Hewitt (A) d. L. E. Lumsden (JAM) 6-2 6-4 6-3; **F. S. Stolle** (3) (A) d. I. D. Buding (G) 6-2 6-2 4-6 6-2; J. L. Arilla (SP) d. P. H. Rodriguez (CH) 20-22 4-6 6-2 6-2 6-2; W. A. Knight d. R. D. Crealy (A) 6-4 6-2 12-10; A. A. Segal (SA) d. I. Tiriac (RU) 6-4 6-2 6-3; J. Leschly (D) d. F. Salomon (RH) 6-4 9-7 6-4; R. J. Moore (SA) d. J. G. Clifton 2-6 6-2 10-8 6-1; J. A. Pickens (USA) d. G. C. Bluett 6-3 1-5 7-7 5; P. Lall (IN) d. C. E. Zeeman (SA) 6-3 6-4 6-1; **E. C. Drysdale** (7) (SA) d. J. Kodes (CZ) 4-6 4-7 5; G. C. Richey (USA) d. G. R. Stilwell 6-4 6-2 3-6 15-13; T. W. Addison d. R. A. Weedon (SA) 6-4 9-7 3-6 4-6 6-2; G. Goven (F) d. E. Soriano (ARG) 6-3 6-4 7-5; R. N. Howe (A) d. R. E. Puddicombe (C) 6-1 6-2 6-4; E. Drossart (B) d. P. R. Hutchins 6-3 6-3 6-4; P. W. Curtis d. B. R. Butcher (SA) 6-1 6-4 6-3; A. J. Stone (A) d. M. Olvera (E) 5-7 6-2 2-6 7-5 6-0; **A. D. Roche** (2) (A) d. E. A. Beards (A) 6-4.

SECOND ROUND: Emerson (1) d. Bungert 6-2 6-3 6-1; Pasarell d. Barrett 9-7 1-6 8-10 6-4 6-3; Smith d. Watanabe 4-6 10-8 6-2 6-2; Wooldridge d. Hoogs 9-7 7-5 4-6 4-6 6-4; Davidson d. **Graebner** (8) 6-3 3-6 8-6 6-1; Beust d. Sturdza 6-4 9-7 6-4; Okker d. Iles 6-1 2-0 ret'd; Barnes d. Sangster 6-3 8-6 6-4; **Santana** (4) d. Belkin 6-0 6-1 6-2; Riessen d. Scott 6-3 6-3 13-11; Bengtson d. Contet 3-6 6-3 6-4 6-4; Wilson d. Cromwell 6-1 6-4 6-0; **Newcombe** (5) d. Koch 7-5 7-5 6-4; Fletcher d. McMillan 6-4 6-3 1-6 6-3; Holmberg d. Battrick 6-1 6-1 6-4; Mukerjea d. Ulrich 6-3

6-4 7-5; Darmon d. Zuleta 6-2 6-0 6-1; Saul d. El Shafei 6-3 6-3 5-7 5-7 7-5; Dieraam d. Carpenter 11-13 10-8 6-1 6-0; **Ralston** (6) d. Metreveli 6-0 4-6 6-4 6-4; Ulrich d. Mandarino 7-9 2-6 6-3 6-4 6-4; Bowrey d. Cox 6-4 4-6 4-6 6-2 6-3; Ryan d. Konishi 6-4 7-5 6-4; Hewitt d. **Stolle** (3) 6-2 6-3 4-6 6-2; Arilla d. Knight 4-6 7-5 6-4 6-2; Leschly d. Segal 8-6 6-2 3-6 6-4; Pickens d. Moore 7-5 6-2 6-2; **Drysdale** (7) d. Lall 8-6 4-6 6-2 6-0; Richey d. Addison 5-7 6-2 6-4 6-4; Goven d. Howe 2-6 7-5 6-3 6-4 6-1; Curtis d. Drossart 6-1 6-2 12-10; **Roche** (2) d. Stone 6-1 10-8 6-4.

THIRD ROUND: Emerson (1) d. Pasarell 7-5 6-2 7-5; Smith d. Wooldridge 6-3 6-2 6-3; Davidson d. Beust 6-1 6-2 6-2; Okker d. Barnes 6-0 6-1 3-6 9-7; **Santana** (4) d. Riessen 6-3 6-2 10-8; Wilson d. Bengtson 4-6 11-9 6-4 6-4; Fletcher d. **Newcombe** (5) 8-10 4-6 6-3 6-4 6-3; Mukerjea d. Holmberg 6-8 6-2 8-6 7-5; Darmon d. Saul 6-1 6-2 6-1;

Ralston (6) d. Diepraam 6-2 4-6 6-1 6-1; Bowrey d. Ulrich 10-8 5-7 6-3 6-3; Hewitt d. Ryan 6-3 6-4 2-6 3-6 6-1; Leschly d. Arilla 6-3 6-2 8-6; **Drysdale** (7) d. Pickens 6-3 6-2 6-2; Richey d. Goven 6-2 7-5 9-7; **Roche** (2) d. Curtis 6-2 4-6 8-6 6-2.

FOURTH ROUND	QUARTER-FINALS	SEMI-FINALS	FINAL	CHAMPION
Emerson (1)	**Emerson** (1)			
Smith	6-2 6-2 6-2	Davidson		
Davidson	Davidson	1-6 6-3 6-4 6-4		
Okker	6-1 2-6 6-3 6-3		**Santana** (4)	
Santana (4)	**Santana** (4)		6-2 4-6 9-7 3-6 7-5	
Wilson	6-3 6-2 1-2 ret'd	**Santana** (4)		
Fletcher	Fletcher	6-2 3-6 8-6 4-6 7-5		**Santana** (4)
Mukerjea	2-6 10-8 9-7 3-6 6-1			6-4 11-9 6-4
Darmon	**Ralston** (6)			
Ralston (6)	4-6 6-3 6-4 6-4	**Ralston** (6)		
Bowrey	Hewitt	7-5 6-2 11-9		
Hewitt	4-6 6-4 7-5 6-1		**Ralston** (6)	
Leschly			6-8 8-6 3-6 7-5 6-3	
Drysdale (7)	**Drysdale** (7)	**Drysdale** (7)		
Richey	3-6 6-1 8-6 3-6 8-6	9-7 6-2 6-2		
Roche (2)	**Roche** (2)			
	6-4 6-4 6-4			

LADIES' SINGLES

FIRST ROUND: Mrs L. W. King (4) (USA) d. W. M. Shaw 2-6 8-6; F. E. Truman d. M. T. Riedl (IT) 6-1 6-2; C. Mercelis (B) d. L. M. Bellamy (A) 6-1 6-1; B. Stove (NTH) d. M. S. Delport (SA) 7-5 6-2; Mrs H. G. Fales (USA) d. E. Lundquist (SW) 6-1 6-3; K. Krantzcke (A) d. H. Niessen (G) 6-4 6-8 6-4; H. C. Sherriff (A) d. A. Soady 6-1 6-4; G. V. Sherriff (A) d. J. A. Blackman (A) 6-4 3-6 6-4; A. M. van Zyl (SA) d. V. H. Dennis 6-1 6-0; G. Baksheeva (USSR) d. K. A. Blake w.o.; M. E. Habicht (USA) d. M. B. H. McAnally 8-6 6-1; Mrs D. P. Knode (USA) d. Mrs W. A. Tym (USA) 10-8 6-2; M. G. Arnold (USA) d. T. M. Van Haren (B) 8-6; H. Gourlay (A) d. Mrs J. L. Deloford (USA) 6-3; L. A. Roussouw (SA) d. A. L. Surbeek (NTH) 3-6 8-6 6-2; C. A. Rosser d. H. W. Allen 2-6 6-3 6-3; H. Schultze (G) d. J.

Lieffrig (F) 4-6 11-9 12-10; G. S. Swan (SA) d. J. C. L. Poynder 6-2 6-4; K. M. Harter (USA) d. I. A. R. F. Lofdahl (SW) 6-4 6-2; D. A. Whitely (A) d. Mrs C. Rouchon (F) 7-9 7-5 6-4; R. H. Bentley d. R. Beltrame (IT) 6-3 6-2; Mrs A. A. Segal (SA) d. S. S. Behlmar (USA) 6-2 6-4; P. M. Walkden (RH) d. O. Morozova (USSR) 6-1 6-3; **N. Richey** (5) (USA) d. F. M. E. Toyne (A) 1-6 6-3 6-0; Mrs P. Darmon (F) d. E. Spruyt (NTH) 6-2 7-5; Y. Ramirez (USA) d. A. Pickens (USA) 6-3; J. A. M. Tegart (A) d. S. V. Wade 6-1 8-6; T. A. Fretz (USA) d. Mrs L. Orth-Schildknecht (G) 6-3 6-2; **M. E. Bueno** (2) (BR) d. S. R. De Fina (SA) 6-1 6-2.

SECOND ROUND: M. Smith (1) (A) d. D. E. Starkie 8-6 6-2; J. T. Albert (USA) d. Mrs J. Volavkova (CZ) 6-2 6-3; S. Pachta (AU) d. U. K. Sandulf (SW) 6-1 6-4; E. Buding (G) d. Mrs R. N. Faulkner (A) 6-4 6-3; **N. Baylon** (8) (ARG) d. F. Urban (C) 6-3 6-0; T. Groenman (NTH) d. F. Gordigiani (IT) 6-4 6-4; A. E. Jansen Venneboer (NTH) d. I. de Lansalut (F) 6-3 4-6 6-3; M. Schacht (A) d. E. Emanuel (SA) 6-3 7-5; **King** (4) d. Truman 6-4 6-1; Mrs W. D. Greville Collins d. Mrs V. A. Roberts 6-8 6-1 6-4; Mrs C. W. Brasher d. Mrs V. Vopickova (CZ) 6-4 6-1; M. A. Eisel (USA) d. E. Krocke (NTH) 6-8 6-1 6-2; **F. Durr** (7) (F) d. L. M. Godwin (SA) 6-4 7-5; J. M. Heldman (USA) d. S. Lazzarino (IT) 6-3 6-2; J. A. M. Tegart d. S. V. Wade 6-1 8-6; **M. E. Bueno** (2) (BR) d. S. R. De Fina (SA) 6-1 6-2.

THIRD ROUND: Smith (1) d. Albert 6-1 6-2; Buding d. Pachta 6-1 6-4; Groenman d. **Baylon** (8) 4-6 6-4 6-4; Schacht d. Jansen Venneboer 6-0 6-3; **King** (4) d. Stove 6-4 6-3; Krantzcke d. Sherriff 11-9 6-3; **van Zyl** (6) d. Habicht 6-3 6-1; Arnold d. Rossouw 6-1 7-5; Harter d. Schultze 6-3 6-2; **Richey** (5) d. Bentley 3-6 6-4 6-2; Casals d.

Melville 1-6 7-5 6-4; **Jones** (3) d. MacLennan 6-0 6-2; Brasher d. Greville Collins 6-4 6-2; **Durr** (7) d. Eisel 6-4 7-5; Tegart d. Heldman 6-1 6-1; **Bueno** (2) d. Fretz 6-2 6-0.

FOURTH ROUND	QUARTER-FINALS	SEMI-FINALS	FINAL	CHAMPION
Smith (1)	**Smith** (1)			
Buding	6-1 6-2	**Smith** (1)		
Groenman	Groenman	6-0 6-4		
Schacht	6-1 6-2		**King** (4)	
King (4)	**King** (4)		6-3 6-3	
Krantzcke	9-7 6-2	**King** (4)		
van Zyl (6)	**van Zyl** (6)	1-6 6-2 6-4		**King** (4)
Arnold	6-1 6-2			6-3 3-6 6-1
Harter	**Richey** (5)			
Richey (5)	6-2 6-4	**Jones** (3)		
Casals	**Jones** (3)	4-6 6-1 6-1		
Jones (3)	6-2 6-3		**Bueno** (2)	
Brasher	**Durr** (7)		6-3 9-11 7-5	
Durr (7)	6-2 6-2	**Bueno** (2)		
Tegart	**Bueno** (2)	6-4 6-3		
Bueno (2)	6-3 4-6 6-2			

OTHER FINALS

GENTLEMEN'S DOUBLES: Final – K. N. Fletcher (A)/J. D. Newcombe (A) d. W. M. Bowrey (A)/O. K. Davidson (A) 6-3 6-4 3-6 6-3.
LADIES' DOUBLES: Final – M. E. Bueno (BR)/N. Richey (USA) d. M. Smith (A)/J. A. M. Tegart (A) 6-3 4-6 6-4.
MIXED DOUBLES: Final – K. N. Fletcher (A)/M. Smith (A) d. R. D. Ralston (USA)/Mrs L. W. King (USA) 4-6 6-3 6-3.
GENTLEMEN'S SINGLES PLATE: Final – R. Taylor d. R. N. Howe 6-4 2-6 7-5.

LADIES' SINGLES PLATE: Final – P. M. Walkden (RH) d. Mrs J. G. A. Lloyd 6-4 6-0.
BOYS' INVITATION SINGLES: Final – V. Korotkov (USSR) d. B. Fairlie (NZ) 6-3 11-9.
GIRLS' INVITATION SINGLES: Final – B. Lindstrom (FIN) d. J. Congdon 7-5 6-3.
VETERANS' MEN'S DOUBLES: Final – G. Mulloy (USA)/W. F. Talbert (USA) d. R. J. Freedman (USA)/R. V. Sherman (USA) 6-8 6-2 6-3.

GENTLEMEN'S SINGLES

1967

FIRST ROUND: C. M. Pasarell (USA) d. **M. Santana** (1) (SP) 10-8 6-3 2-6 8-6; R. A. J. Hewitt (SA) d. G. C. Garner (SA) 8-6 6-4 6-4; K. Yanagi (J) d. W. Gasiorek (POL) 6-4 6-1 8-6; F. Tutvin (C) d. S. Tacchini (IT) 3-6 6-1 6-3 6-4; T. Koch (BR) d. J. Kukal (CZ) 6-4 13-11 6-4; I. Gulyas (HU) d. L. Olander (SW) 4-6 7-5 6-3 4-6 6-2; J. E. Barrett d. B. Montrenaud (F) 6-3 4-6 1-6 6-3 8-6; C. W. Stubs (A) d. T. Ulrich (D) 1-6 5-7 6-2 7-5 6-2; **W. W. Bowrey** (8) (A) d. P. Beust (F) 8-6 6-4 6-3; T. Lejus (USSR) d. A. Licis (Stateless) 6-3 6-2 6-4; R. K. Wilson d. J. G. Clifton 6-4 6-4 6-3; R. J. Carmichael (A) d. F. D. McMillan (SA) 5-2 6-3 6-4; A. A. Segal (SA) d. B. Jovanovic (YU) 6-4 6-4 7-5; E. L. Scott (USA) d. D. L. Dell (USA) 6-4 8-10 6-3 7-5; F. A. Froehling (USA) d. D. Sturdza (SWZ) 6-4 6-4 6-2; W. P. Bungert (G) d. R. J. Wilson (A) 8-6 8-6 7-5; **A. D. Roche** (4) (A) d. J. Kodes (CZ) 4-6 6-1 6-2 8-6; C. Richey (USA) d. R. W. Barnes (BR) 6-2 6-4 6-2; I. D. Buding (G) d. A. Szikszai (HU) 6-1 9-7 6-4; R. O. Ruffels (A) d. G. Battrick 6-1 9-7 6-4; K. Watanabe (J) d. P. Hombergen (B) 6-2 7-5 6-0; I. Tiriac (RU) d. G. di Maso (IT) 6-2 6-1 6-4; J. A. Cottrill (A) d. Z. Franulovic (YU) 6-4 2-6 7-5 6-4; D. Contet (F) d. G. B. Primrose (A) 6-3 10-8 4-6 6-3; **E. C. Drysdale** (5) (SA) d. S. J. Matthews 8-6 6-3 6-4; G. R. Stilwell d. R. G. Summers (SA) 2-6 6-4 7-5; J. Hajer (NTH) d. R. N. Howe (A) 8-6 5-7 11-9 6-2; J. Mukerjea (IN) d. R. McKenzie (A) 2-6 6-2 4-6 8-6 6-3; R. Taylor d. C. D. Steele (NTH) 6-1 6-2 6-1; M. F. Mulligan (A) d. V. Korotkov (USSR) 6-2 10-8 6-1; R. Saila (FIN) d. C. Iles 6-4 4-6 7-5 7-5; P. Cornejo (CH) d. R. Mori (J) 4-6 6-2 6-1 9-7; E. V. Seixas (USA) d. J. Ulrich (D) 6-3 4-3 4-6 6-3; G. Maioli (IT) d. J. Javorsky (CZ) 6-2 6-1 6-4; H. J. Plotz (G) d. J. A. Pickens (USA) 6-3

7-5 3-6 6-3; O. Parun (NZ) d. R. C. Lutz (USA) 14-12 11-9 3-6 6-4; M. J. Sangster d. T. W. Addison (A) 7-5 8-6 6-2; P. Lall (IN) d. J. F. Guzman (E) 6-1 6-4 6-0; O. K. Davidson (A) d. R. J. Moore (SA) 8-6 7-5 6-4; **K. N. Fletcher** (6) (A) d. W. Hoogs (USA) 6-0 6-3 8-6; O. Bengtson (SW) d. P. H. Rodriguez (CH) 6-4 3-6 6-4 6-4; C. E. Graebner (USA) d. N. Spear (YU) 6-3 6-1 6-1; J. E. Mandarino (BR) d. B. Weinmann (G) 6-4 4-4 4-6 6-1; T. Okker (NTH) d. K. Wooldridge 6-0 6-1 6-2; R. H. Osuna (M) d. I. Konishi (J) 6-4 11-9 12-10; S. R. Smith (USA) d. J. M. Gisbert (SP) 10-8 6-4 6-4; B. E. Fairlie (NZ) d. A. Metreveli (USSR) 1-6 6-8 6-3 8-6 6-4; **J. D. Newcombe** (3) (A) d. F. Jauffret (F) 6-2 10-8 6-3; R. D. Crealy (A) d. D. A. R. Russell (JAM) 6-3 2-6 6-3 6-4; N. Pietrangeli (IT) d. M. Cox 6-4 6-4 4-4 6-6 6-4; J. B. Chanfreau (F) d. M. Holecek (CZ) 2-6 6-4 1-6 6-3 6-4; S. Likhachev (USSR) d. T. Akbari (IRAN) 6-3 6-3 6-0; J. R. Cooper (A) d. H. Elschenbroich (G) 6-2 6-4 0-6 6-4; M. Leclercq (F) d. J. R. Pinto Bravo (CH) 4-6 4-6 6-4 13-11 6-4; M. C. Riessen (USA) d. R. Krishnan (IN) 4-6 6-4 6-3 8-6; J. Saul (SA) d. J. H. McManus (USA) 6-8 14-12 7-5 6-2; S. Minotra (IN) d. R. F. Keldie (A) 6-4 11-9 6-0; R. R. Maud (SA) d. J. H. Osborne (USA) 3-6 2-6 6-3 6-2 6-4; J. Saul (SA) d. A. J. Stone (A) 6-1 6-3 6-3; P. W. Curtis d. I. Nastase (RU) 6-4 6-4 6-2; **R. Emerson** (2) (A) d. A. K. Carpenter (C) 6-3 6-3 6-2.

SECOND ROUND: Pasarell d. Hewitt 6-3 6-8 6-2 6-4; Tutvin d. Yanagi 6-1 9-7 2-6 6-4; Koch d. Gulyas 6-2 6-2 6-2; Stubs d. Barrett 12-10 7-5 6-0; **Bowrey** (8) d. Lejus 4-6 13-11 6-2 6-2; Wilson d. Carmichael 3-8 10-4 6-4 6-4; Segal d. Scott 6-4 4-6 6-4 6-3; Bungert d. Froehling 10-8 6-3 1-6 3-6 7-5; Richey d. **Roche** (4) 3-6 3-6 19-17 14-12 6-3; Ruffels d. Buding 2-6 6-3 6-2 7-5; Tiriac d. Watanabe 7-5 6-4 9-7; Contet d. Contrill 6-3 8-6 6-1; **Drysdale** (5) d. Stilwell 6-1 6-2 6-3; Mukerjea d. Hajer 3-6 6-8 6-0 6-1 6-3; Taylor d. Mulligan 6-1 6-2 6-4; Saila d. Cornejo 5-7 11-9 6-4 11-13 6-4; Maioli d. Seixas 6-1 2-6 7-9 6-2 6-2; Plotz d. Parun 7-5 14-12 9-7; Sangster d. Lall 6-8 6-4 9-7 16-14;

Fletcher (6) d. Davidson 7-5 6-2 6-1; Graebner d. Bengtson 6-1 6-4 6-3; Mandarino d. Okker 6-1 0-6 6-4 4-6 6-4; Smith d. Osuna 6-4 7-5 6-3; **Newcombe** (3) d. Fairlie 6-4 6-4 8-6; Crealy d. Pietrangeli 8-6 6-3 6-4; Likhachev d. Chanfreau 6-4 6-4 6-3; Cooper d. Leclercq 4-6 6-4 6-3 6-4; Riessen d. **Leschly** (7) 1-6 6-3 3-6 6-1 6-4; Darmon d. Kalogeropoulos 7-5 6-2 5-7 6-3; Pilic d. Minotra 6-3 6-2 6-1; Maud d. Saul 6-4 6-4 6-4; **Emerson** (2) d. Curtis 7-5 6-3 6-4.

THIRD ROUND: Pasarell d. Tutvin 6-1 6-3 6-1; Koch d. Stubs 6-1 6-3 6-2; Wilson d. **Bowrey** (8) 4-6 7-5 4-6 6-3 6-2; Bungert d. Segal 6-2 3-6 6-2 6-3; Ruffels d. Richey 6-4 6-2 6-4; Tiriac d. Contet 6-4 6-1 6-2; **Drysdale** (5) d. Mukerjea 6-3 6-4 6-3; Taylor d. Saila 6-2 6-1 6-3; Plotz d. Maioli 6-4 7-5 3-6 6-3; **Fletcher** (6) d. Sangster 12-10 11-9

6-3; Graebner d. Mandarino 6-3 6-3 11-9. **Newcombe** (3) d. Smith 6-4 4-6 6-4 6-3; Likhachev d. Crealy 10-8 6-4 6-2; Cooper d. Riessen 11-9 6-3 11-13 8-6; Pilic d. Darmon 6-2 6-8 6-2 6-3; **Emerson** (2) d. Maud 6-3 9-7 6-4.

FOURTH ROUND	QUARTER-FINALS	SEMI-FINALS	FINAL	CHAMPION
Pasarell	Koch			
Koch	6-4 4-6 3-6 6-4 8-6	Bungert		
Wilson	Bungert	6-4 4-6 4-6 6-1 6-3		
Bungert	1-6 5-7 6-1 7-5 9-7		Bungert	
Ruffels	Ruffels		6-4 6-8 2-6 6-4 6-4	
Tiriac	9-7 6-3 6-4	Taylor 6-4 8-6 6-4		
Drysdale (5)	Taylor			**Newcombe** (3)
Taylor	3-6 11-9 6-4 4-6 6-4			6-3 6-1 6-1
Plotz	**Fletcher** (6)	**Newcombe** (3)		
Fletcher (6)	6-1 3-6 6-3 6-0	6-4 6-2 6-4		
Graebner	**Newcombe** (3)			
Newcombe (3)	17-15 6-3 6-4		**Newcombe** (3)	
Likhachev	Cooper	Pilic	9-7 4-6 6-3 6-4	
Cooper	6-4 6-3 6-1	14-12 8-10 6-1 4-6 6-2		
Pilic	Pilic			
Emerson (2)	6-4 5-7 6-3 6-4			

LADIES' SINGLES

FIRST ROUND: F. Durr (4) (F) d. C. C. Truman 6-3 3-6 6-3; A. Bakker (NTH) d. Mrs D. P. Knode (USA) 6-1 6-0; Mrs J. J. O'Neill d. Mrs N. Kalogeropoulos (USA) 6-0 6-1; R. Beltrame (IT) d. Mrs D. C. Aucamp (USA) 6-4 6-4; J. C. L. Poynder d. B. Lindstrom (FIN) 3-6 7-5 6-3; E. Buding (G) d. T. A. Fretz (USA) 6-3 6-4; Mrs J. A. G. Lloyd d. Mrs P. Islanova (USSR) 2-6 6-3 6-4; K. M. Harter (USA) d. G. V. Sherriff (A) 6-3 6-3; **L. R. Turner** (6) (A) d. Mrs E. C. S. Pratt (USA) 7-5 6-2; F. E. Truman d. F. F. Urban (C) 6-1 6-1; M. J. Aubet (SP) d. G. S. Swan (SA) 6-1 6-2; K. A. Blake (USA) d. M. O. Harris (A) 4-6 9-7 6-4; G. Baksheeva (USSR) d. Mrs H. G. Fales (USA) 6-3 6-1; J. R. Forbes (SA) d. Mrs A. A. Segal (SA) 7-5 3-6 6-4; Mrs W. A. Tym (USA) d. S. Lazzarino (A) w.o.; T. Groenman (NTH) d. P. S. A. Hogan (USA) 6-3

6-2; H. C. Sherriff (A) d. A. T. Mackay (A) 6-1 6-4; M. A. Eisel (USA) d. J. A. Congdon 6-1 6-3; I. Loeys (B) d. Mrs J. E. Richey (USA) 5-0 (USA) d. H. F. Gourlay (A) 6-1 6-1; L. Jansen Venneboer (NTH) d. F. M. E. Toyne (A) 6-2 6-4; S. R. De Fina (USA) d. I. de Lansalut (F) 6-2 6-3; E. Lundquist (SW) d. H. W. Allen 6-1 9-7; K. M. Krantzcke (A) d. M. M. Lee 6-4 6-2; E. Emanuel (SA) d. K. Seelbach (G) 6-3 6-1; Mrs V. Vopickova (CZ) d. J. Venturino (F) 6-4 6-2; Mrs C. E. Graebner (USA) d. V. A. Coombs 7-5 6-4; **Mrs P. F. Jones** (3) d. Mrs W. D. Greville Collins 6-1 6-2.

SECOND ROUND: Mrs L. W. **King** (1) (USA) d. I. A. R. F. Lofdahl (SW) 8-6 6-2; Mrs E. Veentjer-Spruyt (NTH) d. C. Mercelis (B) w.o.; L. M. Godwin (SA) d. A. L. Suurbeek (NTH) 6-4 6-4; T. Pericoli (IT) d. F. V. M. MacLennan (USA) 6-3 6-1; **S. V. Wade** (8) d. W. V. Hall 6-2 6-3; K. A. Melville (A) d. M. Salfati (F) 7-5 7-5; M. S. Delport (SA) d. D. S. Butt (C) 6-4 6-1; Mrs J. Volavkova (CZ) d. S. J. Alexander (A) 6-3 6-3; **Durr** (4) d. Bakker 6-3 6-2; O'Neill d. Beltrame 6-3 6-3; Buding d. Poynder 6-3 6-3; Harter d. Lloyd 3-6 6-1 6-4; **Turner** (6) d. Truman 6-1 7-5; Blake d. Aubet 6-2 7-5; Baksheeva d. Forbes 6-1 6-2; Groenman d. Tym 6-2 6-3; Eisel d. H. C. Sherriff 6-3 6-3; Martinez d. Loeys 6-1 6-4;

Dmitrieva d. Gordigiani 6-2 6-2; **Richey** (5) d. Williams 6-0 7-5; De Fina d. Jansen Venneboer 6-3 12-10; Krantzcke d. Lundquist 6-1 6-2; Emanuel d. Vopickova 2-6 6-3 6-3; **Jones** (3) d. Graebner 4-6 6-3 6-4; J. A. M. Tegart (A) d. A. Soady 6-4 6-3; P. M. Walkden (RH) d. M. M. Henreid (USA) 6-1 6-0; Mrs J. A. Cottrill (A) d. B. Stove (NTH) 6-0 6-1; **A. M. van Zyl** (7) (SA) d. S. S. Behlmar (USA) 6-4 6-4; W. M. Shaw d. R. H. Bentley 6-0 4-6 6-3; R. Casals (USA) d. E. Terras (F) 6-1 6-3; L. Abbes (USA) d. M. Giorgi (IT) 6-4 6-0; **M. E. Bueno** (2) (BR) d. L. A. Rossouw (SA) 6-3 6-1.

THIRD ROUND: King (1) d. Veentjer-Spruyt w.o.; Pericoli d. Godwin 6-1 6-2; **Wade** (8) d. Melville 7-5 6-2; Volavkova d. Delport 7-5 6-2; O'Neill d. **Durr** (4) 6-4 9-7; Harter d. Buding 6-2 6-3; **Turner** (6) d. Blake 6-1 6-2; Baksheeva d. Groenman 6-3 6-4; Eisel d. Martinez 3-6 6-1 6-0; **Richey** (5) d. Dmitrieva 6-4 6-4; De Fina d. Krantzcke

6-0 8-6; **Jones** (3) d. Emanuel 6-3 6-1; Tegart d. Walkden 8-6 6-0; **van Zyl** (7) d. Cottrill 6-3 3-6 6-0; Casals d. Shaw 6-1 8-6; **Bueno** (2) d. Abbes 6-4 6-0.

FOURTH ROUND	QUARTER-FINALS	SEMI-FINALS	FINAL	CHAMPION
King (1)	**King** (1)			
Pericoli	6-1 6-2	**King** (1)		
Wade (8)	**Wade** (8)	7-5 6-2		
Volavkova	6-2 8-6		**King** (1)	
O'Neill	Harter		6-0 6-3	
Harter	6-2 4-6 6-3	Harter		
Turner (6)	**Turner** (6)	7-5 1-6 6-2		**King** (1)
Baksheeva	11-9 5-7 6-1			6-3 6-4
Eisel	Eisel			
Richey (5)	9-7 3-6 6-4	**Jones** (3)		
De Fina	**Jones** (3)	6-2 4-6 7-5		
Jones (3)	6-1 6-1		**Jones** (3)	
Tegart	Tegart		2-6 6-3 7-5	
van Zyl (7)	6-4 3-6 6-1	Casals		
Casals	Casals	7-5 6-4		
Bueno (2)	2-6 6-2 6-3			

OTHER FINALS

GENTLEMEN'S DOUBLES: Final — R. A. J. Hewitt (SA)/F. D. McMillan (SA) d. R. S. Emerson (A)/K. N. Fletcher (A) 6-2 6-3 6-4.

LADIES' DOUBLES: Final — R. Casals (USA)/Mrs L. W. King (USA) d. M. E. Bueno (BR)/N. Richey (USA) 9-11 6-4 6-2.

MIXED DOUBLES: Final — O. K. Davidson (A)/Mrs L. W. King (USA) d. K. N. Fletcher (A)/M. E. Bueno (BR) 7-5 6-2.

GENTLEMEN'S SINGLES PLATE: Final — J. H. McManus (USA) d. E. L. Scott (USA) 6-3 6-2.

LADIES' SINGLES PLATE: Final — P. S. A. Hogan (USA) d. G. V. Sherriff (A) 6-2 9-7.

BOYS' INVITATION SINGLES: Final — M. Orantes (SP) d. M. Estep (USA) 6-2 6-2.

GIRLS' INVITATION SINGLES: Final — J. Salome (NTH) d. M. Strandberg (SW) 6-4 6-2.

VETERANS' MEN'S DOUBLES: Final — J. Drobny/A. V. Martini (USA) d. R. J. Freedman (USA)/R. V. Sherman (USA) 6-2 6-4.

GENTLEMEN'S SINGLES

1968

FIRST ROUND: R. G. Laver (1) (A) d. E. L. Scott (USA) 6-3 4-6 6-3 6-2; S. R. Smith (USA) d. G. Merlo (IT) 6-4 6-3 6-0; M. C. Riessen (USA) d. J. Kodes (CZ) 6-2 6-3 6-2; B. E. Fairlie (NZ) d. D. L. Dell (USA) 3-6 6-3 6-4; H. S. FitzGibbon (USA) d. **N. Pilic** (16) (YU) 3-6 7-5 6-3 6-2; M. Cox d. G. L. Forbes (SA) 7-9 8-6 6-3 6-4; A. E. Fox (USA) d. R. Becker 6-2 6-4 7-5; D. Contet (F) d. H. Rahim (PAK) 3-6 7-5 7-5 7-9 6-2; **R. Gonzales** (8) (USA) d. R. Krishnan (IN) 6-2 6-4 6-3; R. R. Maud (SA) d. D. W. Schroder (SA) 3-6 2-6 6-2; A. Metreveli (USSR) d. M. Orantes (SP) 2-6 2-6 2-4 6-10 8; P. Beust (F) d. P. C. Dent (A) 4-6 6-3 6-4 7-5; **R. D. Ralston** (9) (USA) d. J. F. Brown (A) 6-1 7-5 8-6; C. Richey (USA) d. B. J. Phillips-Moore (A) 6-2 8-6 7-5; J. Leschly (D) d. C. W. Stubs (A) 6-2 3-6 8-6 6-1; J. E. Mandarino (BR) d. A. Palafox (M) 6-3 7-5 2-6 6-4; **J. D. Newcombe** (4) (A) d. O. K. Davidson (A) 4-6 6-3 6-4 6-3; J. G. Alexander (A) d. F. D. McMillan (SA) 5-7 9-7 6-3 9-7; D. A. Lloyd d. P. Darmon (F) 6-4 6-4 10-12 6-1; T. J. Ryan (SA) d. K. Wooldridge 6-4 6-4 4-6 2-6 8-6; **A. R. Ashe** (13) (USA) d. E. A. Zuleta (E) 6-1 6-2 6-3; I. El Shafei (UAR) d. P. Lall (IN) 6-4 6-4 11-13 6-3; **R. Emerson** (5) (A) d. R. E. Holmberg (USA) 6-2 6-2 6-4; I. Tiriac (RU) d. D. A. R. Russell (JAM) 7-5 6-2 8-6; K. N. Fletcher (A) d. J. H. McManus (USA) 6-4 2-6 6-1 6-3; A. Olmedo (PE) d. P. H. Rodriguez (CH) 12-10 7-5 6-3; **T. S. Okker** (12) (NTH) d. P. W. Curtis 7-5 3-6 6-2 6-2; M. J. Sangster d. C. Fernandez (BR) 6-0 6-4 6-4; V. Korotkov (USSR) d. S. J. Matthews 6-4 7-9 6-4 6-4; P. Barthes (F) d. L. Ayala (CH) 9-11 6-2 6-4 8-6; T. W. Addison (A) d. R. Haillet (F) 11-9 6-3

6-2; N. Kalogeropoulos (GR) d. R. A. Peralta (ARG) 6-1 6-4 6-3; R. N. Howe (A) d. G. Battrick 6-4 8-6 7-5; **F. S. Stolle** (11) (A) d. J. C. Barclay (F) 6-1 6-2 6-2; C. E. Graebner (USA) d. R. R. Barth (USA) 6-4 6-3 6-8 6-8 11-9; J. Ulrich (D) d. K. Watanabe (J) 6-2 6-4 7-5; G. R. Stilwell d. S. Likhachev (USSR) 3-6 5-7 6-2 6-1 6-2; **M. Santana** (6) (SP) d. H. J. Plotz (G) 6-0 6-4 6-2; T. B. Edelsen (USA) d. J. Fassbender (G) 6-2 7-5 7-5; G. C. Bluett d. N. Pietrangeli (IT) 6-4 6-2 2-6 2-6 6-4; G. C. Garner (SA) d. L. E. Lumsden (JAM) 2-6 6-2 6-4 7-5; **E. C. Drysdale** (14) (SA) d. R. K. Wilson 9-7 6-3 6-2; R. D. Crealy (A) d. J. Kukal (CZ) 6-3 6-4 6-2; R. J. Moore (SA) d. N. Spear (YU) 6-1 6-2 9-7; W. W. Bowrey (A) d. W. Gasiorek (POL) 6-3 6-1 7-5; **A. Gimeno** (3) (SP) d. I. Gulyas (HU) 6-3 7-5 6-4; G. Goven (F) d. P. Castillo (COL) 9-7 6-4 6-2; T. Ulrich (D) d. T. Lejus (USSR) 4-6 6-1 10-8 6-2; R. J. Carmichael (A) d. M. Holecek (CZ) 6-8 4-6 6-4 6-2 7-5; **E. Buchholz** (10) (USA) d. A. J. Stone (A) 6-4 6-2 10-12 6-4; R. A. J. Hewitt (SA) d. J. E. Barrett 6-3 8-6 6-4; T. Koch (BR) d. G. di Maso (IT) 6-3 6-2 11-13 6-0; J. F. Guzman (E) d. R. C. Lutz (USA) 11-13 1-6 8-6 6-3 6-4; **L. A. Hoad** (7) (A) d. J. Mukerjea (IN) 6-3 6-4 6-2; C. Iles d. J. P. Courcol (F) 7-5 3-6 6-3 7-5; R. O. Ruffels (A) d. P. Cornejo (CH) 6-2 6-1 6-2; J. H. Osborne (USA) d. M. G. Davies 4-6 7-9 10-8 6-1 6-3; **A. D. Roche** (15) (A) d. R. F. Keldie (A) 6-3 6-1 7-5; O. Parun (NZ) d. P. R. Hutchins 6-3 9-7 12-10; R. Taylor d. A. R. Mills 6-4 6-2 6-3; C. M. Pasarell (USA) d. P. Hombergen (B) 6-3 7-5 3-6 6-3; **K. R. Rosewall** (2) (A) d. A. A. Segal (SA) 6-3 6-4 6-4.

SECOND ROUND: Laver (1) d. Smith 6-3 6-4 6-4; Riessen d. Fairlie w.o.; Cox d. FitzGibbon 4-6 6-3 7-9 9-7 12-10; Contet d. Fox w.o.; **Gonzales** (8) d. Maud 6-2 6-4 9-7; Metreveli d. Beust 6-1 6-1 6-1; **Ralston** (9) d. Richey 6-3 6-3 7-9 6-3 13-11; Mandarino d. Leschly 11-9 10-8 6-3; **Newcombe** (4) d. Alexander 6-1 6-3 6-4; Lloyd d. Ryan 6-4 3-6 0-6 6-3 7-5; **Ashe** (13) d. El Shafei 6-1 6-2 9-7; Bengtson d. Arilla 6-0 5-7 6-4 3-6 12-10; **Emerson** (5) d. Tiriac 5-7 6-1 6-2 6-0; Olmedo d. Fletcher 6-4 5-7 6-4 6-3; **Okker** (12) d. Sangster 3-6 0-7 5; Korotkov d. Barthes 2-6 7-5 4-6 7-5 7-5; Addison d. Kalogeropoulos 4-6 6-1 3-6 6-4 6-3; **Stolle** (11) d. Howe 6-1 6-1 6-1; Graebner d. Ulrich 6-2 6-0

6-4; **Santana** (6) d. Stilwell 5-7 10-8 6-0 6-4; Edlefsen d. Bluett 7-5 4-6 6-1 6-2; **Drysdale** (14) d. Garner 6-2 7-5 8-6; Moore d. Crealy 3-6 7-5 6-3 6-4; **Gimeno** d. Bowrey 6-2 4-6 9-7 6-3; Goven 6-3 6-3 8-6; **Buchholz** (10) d. Carmichael 11-13 6-4 6-4 1-6 6-2; Hewitt d. Koch 3-6 6-4 3-6 6-3 12-10; **Hoad** (7) d. Guzman 8-6 6-1 6-4; Ruffels d. Iles 6-4 6-2 6-3; **Roche** (15) d. Osborne 6-4 6-0 6-2; Parun d. Taylor 2-6 3-6 14-12 6-4 6-4; **Rosewall** (2) d. Pasarell 7-9 6-1 6-8 6-2 6-3.

THIRD ROUND: Laver (1) d. Riessen 6-4 3-6 7-5 6-3; Cox d. Contet 6-3 6-4 6-4; Metreveli d. **Gonzales** (8) 4-6 6-4 6-3 7-5; **Ralston** (9) d. Mandarino 6-2 6-4 6-2; **Newcombe** (4) d. Lloyd 7-5 6-0 6-1; **Ashe** (13) d. Bengtson 11-9 6-4 6-1; **Emerson** (5) d. Olmedo 7-5 6-1 6-1; **Okker** (12) d. Korotkov 8-10 6-2 6-1 6-2; **Stolle** (11) d. Addison 6-3 8-6

6-2; Graebner d. **Santana** (6) 9-7 6-2 6-1; Edlefsen d. **Drysdale** (14) 9-7 4-6 1-6 6-4 6-4; Moore d. **Gimeno** (3) 4-6 6-3 7-5 2-6 6-2; **Buchholz** (10) d. Ulrich 5-7 6-2 6-3 6-1; Hewitt d. **Hoad** (7) 6-3 9-11 1-6 6-3 6-3; **Roche** (15) d. Ruffels 6-4 6-1 6-3; **Rosewall** (2) d. Parun 6-4 3-6 6-3 6-2.

FOURTH ROUND	QUARTER-FINALS	SEMI-FINALS	FINAL	CHAMPION	PRIZE MONEY	
Laver (1)	**Laver** (1)				Champion	£2,000
Cox					Runner-up	1,300
Metreveli	9-7 5-7 6-2 6-0	**Laver** (1)			Semi-finals	750
Ralston (9)	**Ralston** (9)	4-6 6-3 6-1 4-6 6-2			Quarter-finals	400
Newcombe (4)	6-3 7-5 6-2		**Laver** (1)		Fourth round	150
Ashe (13)	**Ashe** (13)		7-5 6-2 6-4		Third round	100
Emerson (5)	6-4 6-4 4-6 1-6 6-3	**Ashe** (13)			Second round	75
Okker (12)	**Okker** (12)	7-9 9-7 9-7 6-2			First round	50
Stolle (11)	6-3 9-11 7-5 7-5			**Laver** (1)		
Graebner	Graebner			6-3 6-4 6-2		
Edlefsen	6-1 7-5 7-5	Graebner				
Moore	Moore	6-2 6-0 9-7				
Buchholz (10)	6-4 2-6 6-1 3-6 6-4					
Hewitt	**Buchholz** (10)		**Roche** (15)			
Roche (15)	6-4 3-6 6-2 6-2	**Roche** (15)	9-7 8-10 6-4 8-6			
Rosewall (2)	**Roche** (15)	3-6 7-5 6-4 6-4				
	9-7 6-3 6-2					

LADIES' SINGLES

FIRST ROUND: Mrs P. F. Jones (4) d. K. M. Harter (USA) 6-0 4-6 6-4; Mrs L. A. Hoad (A) d. L. Bassi 6-3 6-4; E. Emanuel (SA) d. M. Giorgi (IT) 6-3 6-2; P. M. Walkden (SA) d. Mrs P. Darmon (F) 3-6 6-0 8-6; H. Niessen (G) d. Mrs A. A. Segal (SA) 6-2 7-5; H. F. Gourlay (A) d. O. Morozova (USSR) 6-4 6-4; C. A. Martinez (USA) d. E. Subirats (M) 6-8 6-3 6-4; J. A. Congdon d. C. Spinoza (F) 6-2 4-6 6-4; C. E. M. Sandberg (SW) d. **S. V. Wade** (5) 6-4 6-3; M. J. Aschner (USA) d. R. H. Bentley (?) 6-4 6-4; C. Molesworth d. Mrs J. H. Wheeler (USA) 6-4 6-4; P. S. A. Hogan (USA) d. Mrs E. C. Drysdale (SA) 6-1 6-2; F. Durr (F) d. C. Mercelis (B) 6-4 6-2; J. H. Townsend d. Mrs W. A. Tym (USA) 6-2 6-4; P. Lamm (USA) d. L. Jansen Venneboer (NTH) 6-3 9-7; K. A. Melville (A) d. K. Sawamatsu (J) 6-2 6-2; K. M. Krantzcke d. K.

S. Schediwy (G) 6-1 10-8; R. Casals (USA) d. V. J. Ziegenfuss (USA) 6-3 7-5; F. V. M. MacLennan d. G. V. Sherriff (A) 6-4 6-4; G. Baksheeva (USSR) d. I. A. R. F. Lofdahl (SW) 11-9 6-2; F. F. Urban (C) d. M. M. Lee 5-7 6-0 7-5; J. M. Heldman (USA) d. Mrs J. E. Mandarino (BR) 6-1 6-4; H. C. Sherriff (A) d. Mrs E. C. S. Pratt (USA) 8-6 6-4; **M. E. Bueno** (6) (BR) d. L. Pericoli (IT) w.o.; N. E. Netter (USA) d. I. Loeys (B) 6-2 6-3; Mrs L. Orth-Schildknecht (G) d. Mrs L. de la Courtie-Billat (F) 1-6 8-6 6-1; Mrs V. Vukovich (SA) d. Mrs P. M. Roberts 7-5 6-2; K. Pigeon (USA) d. M. Salfati (F) 6-4 3-6 7-5; A. Suurbeek (NTH) d. Mrs W. D. Greville Collins 6-3 7-5; W. M. Shaw d. F. E. Truman (A) 6-4 4-6 6-3; H. J. Amos (A) d. W. V. Hall 3-6 6-4 6-3; **N. Richey** (3) (USA) d. L. M. Godwin (SA) 6-1 6-3.

SECOND ROUND: Mrs L. W. King (1) (USA) d. P. Bartkowicz (USA) 7-5 6-4; S. R. De Fina (USA) d. L. A. Rossouw (SA) 6-3 6-4; Mrs J. L. Moore (A) d. L. E. Hunt (A) 2-6 6-2 6-3; M. Jansen (NTH) d. Mrs G. T. Janes 6-4 6-2; **Mrs W. W. Bowrey** (8) (A) d. E. B. Lundquist (SW) 6-2 6-1; H. Schultze (G) d. F. Gordigiani (IT) 6-1 6-3; Mrs G. M. Williams d. Mrs V. Vopickova (CZ) 6-2 7-5; J. P. Lieffrig (F) d. A. Soady 10-8 6-3; **Jones** (4) d. Hoad 6-0 6-1; Walkden d. Emanuel 6-2 6-3; Gourlay d. Niessen 3-6 8-6 8-6; Martinez d. Congdon 6-1 7-5; Sandberg d. Aschner 6-2 7-5; Hogan d. Molesworth 3-6 6-3 6-3; Durr d. Townsend 6-0 6-4; Melville d. Lamm 6-4 6-4; Casals d. Krantzcke 9-7 6-3;

Baksheeva d. MacLennan 7-5 6-1; Heldman d. Urban 5-7 7-5 6-2; **Bueno** (6) d. H. C. Sherriff 6-4 6-1; Orth-Schildknecht d. Netter 6-2 6-1; Pigeon d. Vukovich 6-1 6-3; Shaw d. Suurbeek 6-0 4-6 6-2; **Richey** (3) d. Amos 6-1 6-3; Mrs C. W. Brasher d. R. Giscafre (ARG) 4-6 6-3 6-4; J. V. Rogers (USA) d. Mrs J. A. G. Lloyd 6-1 6-3; M. A. Eisel (USA) d. M. T. Riedl (IT) 6-1 6-4; **J. A. M. Tegart** (7) d. Mrs J. Volavkova (CZ) 6-0 6-1; K. Seelbach (G) d. M. O. Harris (A) 6-3 6-2; E. Buding (G) d. K. Harris (A) 6-1 6-1; A. Bakker (NTH) d. E. Terras (F) 4-6 6-3 6-1; **Mrs B. M. Court** (2) (A) d. Mrs J. du Plooy (SA) 6-1 6-0.

THIRD ROUND: King (1) d. De Fina 6-2 7-5; Moore d. Jansen 2-6 6-4 6-1; **Bowrey** (8) d. Schultze 6-4 6-2; Williams d. Lieffrig 7-5 4-6 6-4; **Jones** (4) d. Walkden 6-2 7-5; Gourlay d. Martinez 6-4 6-0; Hogan d. Sandberg 6-4 6-4; Durr d. Melville 6-3 8-6; Casals d. Baksheeva 8-6 3-6 7-5; **Bueno** (6) d. Heldman 6-4 6-1; Pigeon d.

Orth-Schildknecht 6-2 6-0; **Richey** (3) d. Shaw 6-1 6-2; Brasher d. Rogers 6-2 9-7; **Tegart** (7) d. Eisel 6-2 8-6; Buding d. Seelbach 6-1 6-1; **Court** (2) d. Bakker 6-0 6-2.

FOURTH ROUND	QUARTER-FINALS	SEMI-FINALS	FINAL	CHAMPION	PRIZE MONEY	
King (1)	**King** (1)				Champion	£750
Moore	6-2 6-4	**King** (1)			Runner-up	450
Bowrey (8)	**Bowrey** (8)	6-3 6-4			Semi-finals	300
Williams	6-3 6-1		**King** (1)		Quarter-finals	150
Jones (4)	**Jones** (4)		4-6 7-5 6-2		Fourth round	90
Gourlay	6-3 6-1	**Jones** (4)			Third round	50
Hogan	Durr	6-2 6-2			Second round	35
Durr	6-2 6-2			**King** (1)	First round	25
Casals	**Bueno** (6)			9-7 7-5		
Bueno (6)	5-7 6-4 6-3	**Richey** (3)				
Pigeon	**Richey** (3)	6-4 6-2				
Richey (3)	7-5 7-5		**Tegart** (7)			
Brasher	**Tegart** (7)		6-3 6-1			
Tegart (7)	6-2 6-2	**Tegart** (7)				
Buding	**Court** (2)	4-6 8-6 6-1				
Court (2)	6-2 6-3					

OTHER FINALS

GENTLEMEN'S DOUBLES: Final — J. D. Newcombe (A)/A. D. Roche (A) d. K. R. Rosewall (A)/F. S. Stolle (A) 3-6 8-6 5-7 14-12 6-3.

LADIES' DOUBLES: Final — R. Casals (USA)/Mrs L. W. King (USA) d. F. Durr (F)/Mrs P. F. Jones 3-6 6-4 7-5.

MIXED DOUBLES: Final — K. N. Fletcher (A)/Mrs B. M. Court (A) d. A. Metreveli (USSR)/O. Morozova (USSR) 6-1 14-12.

GENTLEMEN'S SINGLES PLATE: Final — G. Battrick d. H. S. FitzGibbon (USA) 6-4 3-6 7-5.

LADIES' SINGLES PLATE: Final — S. V. Wade d. K. M. Harter (USA) 6-2 12-10.

BOYS' INVITATION SINGLES: Final — J. D. Alexander (A) d. J. Thamin (F) 6-1 6-2.

GIRLS' INVITATION SINGLES: Final — K. Pigeon (USA) d. L. Hunt (A) 6-4 6-3.

VETERANS' MEN'S DOUBLES: Final — J. Drobny/A. V. Martini (USA) d. S. Match (USA)/G. Mulloy (USA) 6-2 7-5.

GENTLEMEN'S SINGLES

1969

FIRST ROUND: R. G. Laver (1) (A) d. N. Pietrangeli (IT) 6-1 6-2 6-2; P. Lall (IN) d. C. D. Steele (USA) 6-4 10-12 10-8 8-6; J. Leschly (D) d. K. N. Fletcher (A) 6-4 7-5 6-2; J. L. Rouyer (F) d. W. B. Geraghty (A) 6-2 5-7 6-4 5-7 6-3; **S. R. Smith** (16) (USA) d. A. J. Stone (A) 20-22 6-4 9-7 4-6 6-3; D. A. Lloyd d. I. Gulyas (HU) 8-6 6-4 7-5; W. W. Bowrey (A) d. D. L. Dell (USA) 6-3 3-6 6-2 6-1; G. Goven (F) d. T. Koch (BR) 6-8 6-3 5-7 6-3 6-4; **E. C. Drysdale** (8) (SA) d. P. Hombergen (B) 7-5 7-5 9-7; O. K. Davidson (A) d. J. G. Paish 6-1 6-2 6-3; I. Tiriac (RU) d. B. J. Phillips-Moore (A) 7-5 6-4 4-6 6-1; M. Cox d. M. Orantes (SP) 7-5 6-4 6-3; **R. Emerson** (9) (A) d. P. Pokorny (AU) 6-1 6-1 6-1; S. J. Matthews d. J. G. Clifton 6-4 3-6 6-4 2-6 7-5; V. Korotkov (USSR) d. M. J. Sangster 6-4 6-3 8-6; N. Kalogeropoulos (GR) d. J. Fillol (CH) 6-2 6-2 6-4; **K. R. Rosewall** (4) (A) d. W. Gasiorek (POL) 6-1 6-1 6-2; R. Taylor d. E. V. Seixas (USA) 6-4 13-11 6-2; R. C. Lutz (USA) d. S. Koudelka (Stateless) 6-1 6-1 6-0; J. Kodes (CZ) d. P. Cornejo (CH) 6-3 3-6 5-7 6-3 6-1; J. G. Alexander d. **R. J. Moore** (13) (USA) d. 6-3 6-2 9-11 6-4; O. Parun (NZ) d. G. L. Forbes (SA) 4-6 8-6 6-3; J. P. Courcol (F) d. A. J. McDonald (A) 7-5 7-5 8-6; T. W. Addison d. E. A. Zuleta (E) 9-7 6-3 6-3; **A. R. Ashe** (5) (USA) d. M. C. Riessen (USA) 1-6 11-9 6-3 7-5; T. J. Ryan (SA) d. T. Ulrich (D) 4-6 6-4 6-4 9-7; G. R. Stilwell d. K. Wooldridge 6-2 3-6 8-6 4-6 6-1; I. D. Buding (G) d. A. R. Mills 2-6 6-2 4-6 7-5 14-12; **R. Gonzales** (12) (USA) d. C. M. Pasarell (USA) 22-24 1-6 16-14 6-3 11-9; O. Bengtson (SW) d. J. E. Barrett 6-4 6-4 6-2; T. B. Edlefsen (USA) d. R. R. Barth (USA) 6-3 3-6 9-7 6-3; R. F. Keldie (A) d. S. Likhachev (USSR) 12-10 4-6 6-4 6-4; G. Battrick d. T. Nowicki (POL) 6-4 3-6

4-6 6-4 6-4; M. Holecek (CZ) d. E. J. van Dillen (USA) 6-3 5-7 11-9 6-4; R. R. Maud (SA) d. K. Yanagi (J) 6-4 6-1 6-2; **F. S. Stolle** (11) (A) d. P. R. Hutchins 6-4 10-8 6-4; M. Anderson (A) d. D. Contet (F) 6-4 11-9 6-8 6-4; J. R. Cooper (A) d. J. Ulrich (D) 6-1 6-4 1-6 6-4; B. E. Fairlie (NZ) d. P. H. Rodriguez (CH) 6-2 8-6 6-3; **J. D. Newcombe** (6) (A) d. N. Pilic (YU) 12-10 6-4 4-6 7-5; R. K. Wilson d. W. C. Higgins (USA) 6-4 6-2 6-0; Z. Franulovic (YU) d. T. Lejus (USSR) 7-5 6-8 6-3 7-9 10-8; R. J. Carmichael (A) d. J. E. Mandarino (BR) 5-7 6-1 7-5 6-4; G. C. Richey (USA) d. **R. A. J. Hewitt** (14) (SA) 0-6 6-4 6-8 6-2 9-7; R. D. Crealy (A) d. R. Seegers (SA) 7-5 6-3 6-1; D. A. R. Russell (JAM) d. D. Sturdza (SWZ) 4-6 14-12 5-7 6-3 6-4; R. E. Holmberg (USA) d. A. Olmedo (PE) 8-6 4-6 6-4 2-6 7-5; **T. S. Okker** (3) (NTH) d. I. El Shafei (UAR) 6-3 10-8 6-4; P. C. Dent (A) d. J. F. Guzman (CH) 6-4 6-2 6-3; F. Jauffret (F) d. R. Giltinan (A) 7-5 6-4 6-2; A. Metreveli (USSR) d. N. Spear (YU) 6-4 6-1 6-1; **A. Gimeno** (10) (SP) d. F. D. McMillan (SA) 6-3 6-4 3-6 6-1; P. Barthes (F) d. E. L. Scott (USA) 18-16 6-4 6-1; I. Nastase (RU) d. T. Gorman (USA) 6-3 4-6 6-3 6-8 6-4; J. F. Brown (USA) d. J. D. Bartlett (A) 9-7 6-2 7-5; **C. E. Graebner** (7) (USA) d. R. O. Ruffels (A) 6-4 8-6 6-3; E. Buchholz (USA) d. J. H. McManus (USA) 6-2 4-6 1-6 6-4 8-6; L. Ayala (CH) d. R. N. Howe (A) 6-4 6-2 12-10; J. Kukal (CZ) d. J. Krinsky (SA) 16-14 6-3 8-6; **R. D. Ralston** (15) (USA) d. J. Mukerjea (IN) 6-2 8-6 7-5; H. J. Plotz (D) d. P. W. Curtis 6-2 3-6 6-4 6-1; K. Watanabe (J) d. P. Beust (F) 6-3 7-5 6-3; A. A. Segal (SA) d. E. Castagliano (IT) 6-2 6-1 6-3; **A. D. Roche** (2) (A) d. J. C. Barclay (F) 7-5 4-6 6-3 6-2.

SECOND ROUND: Laver (1) d. Lall 3-6 4-6 6-3 6-0 6-0; Leschly d. Rouyer 6-4 22-20 6-4; **Smith** (16) d. Lloyd 6-3 7-5 6-1; Bowrey d. Goven 8-6 6-4 6-3; **Drysdale** (8) d. Davidson 6-4 4-11 13-6 2; Cox d. Tiriac 2-6 10-8 9-7 12-10; **Emerson** (9) d. Matthews 6-3 6-1 6-2; Kalogeropoulos d. Korotkov 2-6 6-4 6-3 3-6 6-3; **Rosewall** (4) d. Taylor 6-1 6-4 8-4 6; Lutz d. Kodes 2-6 4-6 6-1 6-2 7-5; Alexander d. Parun 7-5 6-4 6-3; Addison d. Courcol 6-3 6-2 3-6 7-5; **Ashe** (5) d. Ryan 3-6 4-6 4-6 6-1; Stilwell d. Buding 6-3 6-2 9-11 6-4; **Gonzales** (12) d. Bengtson 6-4 7-5; Edlefsen d. Keldie 8-6 6-3 4-6 5-7 6-4; Holecek d. Battrick 6-3 5-7 6-1 4-6 6-3; **Stolle** d. Maud 19-17 2-6 6-0 7-5; Anderson

d. Cooper 13-11 8-6 6-4; **Newcombe** (6) d. Fairlie 7-5 6-4 6-4; Wilson d. Franulovic 6-4 3-6 7-5 5-7 6-0; Carmichael d. Richey 2-6 6-4 7-5 6-4; Crealy d. Russell 9-7 6-4 6-4; **Okker** (3) d. Holmberg 3-6 2-6 6-1 6-4 6-2; **Gimeno** (10) d. Metreveli 6-3 3-6 6-1 3-6 6-3; Nastase d. Barthes 6-2 6-4 3-6 6-3; **Graebner** (7) d. Brown 6-2 3-0 ret'd; Buchholz d. Ayala 8-6 6-2 6-4; **Ralston** (15) d. Kukal 7-5 6-2 6-4; Plotz d. Watanabe 9-7 3-6 9-7 9-7; **Roche** (2) d. Segal 6-1 6-2 6-0.

THIRD ROUND: Laver (1) d. Leschly 3-6 6-3 6-3; **Smith** (16) d. Bowrey 3-6 9-7 6-3 6-4; **Drysdale** (8) d. Cox 6-2 11-9 6-4; **Emerson** (9) d. Kalogeropoulos 7-5 6-3 6-2; Lutz d. **Rosewall** (4) 8-6 7-9 6-3 6-2; Alexander d. Addison 6-3 8-10 13-11 3-6 6-3; **Ashe** (5) d. Stilwell 6-2 1-6 6-2 13-15 12-10; **Gonzales** (12) d. Edlefsen 6-4 6-3 6-2; **Stolle**

(11) d. Holecek 6-2 6-4 6-2; **Newcombe** (6) d. Anderson 2-6 6-3 6-3; Wilson d. Carmichael 6-1 6-4 15-13; **Okker** (3) d. Crealy 4-6 6-3 6-2 6-4; **Gimeno** (10) d. Dent 2-6 6-8 6-3 6-4; **Graebner** (7) d. Nastase 7-5 8-6 6-4; **Ralston** (15) d. Buchholz 6-4 6-2 7-5; **Roche** (2) d. Plotz 6-1 9-7 6-4.

FOURTH ROUND	QUARTER-FINALS	SEMI-FINALS	FINAL	CHAMPION	PRIZE MONEY	
Laver (1)	**Laver** (1)				Champion	£3,000
Smith (16)	6-4 6-2 7-9 3-6 6-3	**Laver** (1)			Runner-up	1,500
Drysdale (8)	**Drysdale** (8)	6-4 6-2 6-3			Semi-finals	800
Emerson (9)	6-4 6-8 0-6 6-3 9-7		**Laver** (1)		Quarter-finals	450
Lutz	Lutz		2-6 6-2 9-7 6-0		Fourth round	175
Alexander	9-7 4-6 3-6 6-4 6-4	**Ashe** (5)			Third round	125
Ashe (5)	**Ashe** (5)	6-4 6-2 4-6 7-5			Second round	80
Gonzales (12)	7-5 4-6 6-3 6-3				First round	50
Stolle (11)	**Newcombe** (6)			**Laver** (1)		
Newcombe (6)	6-4 7-5 3-6 6-3			6-4 5-7 6-4 6-4		
Wilson	**Okker** (3)	**Newcombe** (6)				
Okker (3)	11-9 6-4 6-2	8-6 3-6 6-1 7-5				
Gimeno (10)	**Graebner** (7)		**Newcombe** (6)			
Graebner (7)	7-9 6-5 ret'd		3-6 6-1 14-12 6-4			
Ralston (15)	**Roche** (2)	**Roche** (2)				
Roche (2)	6-3 4-6 7-5 8-10 6-2	4-6 4-6 6-3 6-4 11-9				

LADIES' SINGLES

FIRST ROUND: Mrs P. F. Jones (4) d. Mrs J. E. Mandarino (SP) 6-0 6-1; S. M. Tutt d. J. M. Boundy 6-2 6-0; J. M. Wilshere (SA) d. B. Kirk (SA) 6-3 2-6 6-4; Mrs P. Darmon (F) d. R. Giscafre (ARG) 6-1 6-2; A. L. van Deventer (SA) d. C. Molesworth (SA) d. L. Liem (INDO) d. W. Hall 6-4; C. E. M. Sandberg (SW) d. Mrs R. Taylor 9-7 6-1; M. Michel (USA) d. L. E. Hunt (A) 6-1 6-4; **N. Richey** (5) (USA) d. B. Lindstrom (FIN) 6-1 6-2; W. L. Tomlinson d. J. A. Young (A) 2-6 9-7 6-3; P. Bartkowicz (USA) d. L. Bassi (IT) 6-1 6-2; Mrs G. M. Williams d. S. J. Holdsworth 6-1 6-1; Mrs C. W. Brasher d. M. E. Guzman (E) 6-1 6-4; K. M. Krantzcke d. K. Sawamatsu (J) 11-9 6-4; Mrs N. Schaar (NTH) d. Mrs R. A. Lloyd 6-4 3-6 7-5; P. A. Teeguarden (USA) d. M. J. Aschner (USA) 6-3 6-2; H. J. Amos (SA) d.

Soady 6-2 6-4; S. Petersen (BR) d. E. B. Lundquist (SW) 6-4 7-9 6-2; K. Harris (A) d. S. E. Grant (USA) 9-7 2-6 6-1; T. A. Fretz (USA) d. H. C. Sherriff (A) 6-0 6-1; F. Durr (F) d. J. H. Townsend 6-2 6-3; J. K. Anthony (USA) d. J. H. Salome (NTH) 6-1 6-0; R. Casals (USA) d. V. J. Ziegenfuss (USA) 6-1 7-5; **K. A. Melville** (A) d. L. Rossouw (SA) 6-3 6-1; Mrs J. B. Chanfreau (F) d. A. M. Estalella (SP) 6-0 6-1; Mrs P. W. Curtis (USA) d. M. T. Riedl (IT) 6-3 6-1; Mrs W. W. Bowrey (A) d. E. M. Ernest 4-6 8-6; A. Suurbeek (NTH) d. A. M. Arias (ARG) 6-1 4-6 6-1; P. M. Walkden (SA) d. C. A. Martinez (USA) 8-6 6-1; P. S. A. Hogan (USA) d. K. Kaligis (INDO) 6-2 6-3; Mrs J. L. Moore (A) d. K. Seelbach (G) 6-3 6-3; **S. V. Wade** (3) d. L. Tuero (USA) 6-2 6-1.

SECOND ROUND: Mrs B. M. Court (1) (A) d. B. A. Grubb (USA) 6-3 6-0; H. F. Gourlay (A) d. B. Stove (NTH) 4-6 6-3 6-4; A. Palmeova (CZ) d. C. Spinoza (F) 3-6 8-6 7-5; Mrs G. T. Janes d. E. Emanuel (SA) 6-3 5-7 6-1; **J. M. Heldman** (7) (USA) d. J. P. Cooper 6-2 6-3; D. Carter (USA) d. F. F. Urban (C) 4-6 6-2 6-2; O. Morozova (USSR) d. T. Zwaan (NTH) 6-3 6-4; Mrs M. Procter (SA) d. G. Moran (ARG) 6-4 6-3; Mrs S. V. Hall 6-1 6-4; Damon d. Wilshere 6-2 6-1; **Jones** (4) d. Tutt 6-1 6-2; **Richey** (5) d. Tomlinson 6-3 6-4; Bartkowicz d. van Deventer d. Liem 6-0 2-6 8-6; Michel d. Sandberg 6-3 6-0; **Richey** (5) d. Tomlinson 6-3 6-4; Bartkowicz d. Williams 6-2 6-0; Krantzcke d. Brasher 6-1 6-4; Teeguarden d. Schaar 2-6 6-4 6-1; Amos d. Petersen 6-4 3-6 6-4;

Harris d. Fretz 6-4 3-6 7-5; Anthony d. Durr 0-6 6-3 6-4; Casals d. **Melville** (6) 6-2 7-5; Curtis d. Chanfreau 7-5 6-2; Bowrey d. Suurbeek 6-1 6-3; Walkden d. Hogan 6-4 7-5; **Wade** (3) d. Moore 6-1 6-2; W. S. Gilchrist (A) d. A. Bakker (NTH) 6-3 5-7 9-7; F. E. Truman d. J. A. Congdon 6-1 6-2; W. M. Shaw d. I. L. Loeys (B) 6-1 6-1; **J. A. M. Tegart** (8) d. Mrs Vopickova (CZ) 6-1 6-0; K. Pigeon (USA) d. M. Chuvirina (USSR) 6-2 6-3; L. Pericoli (IT) d. Mrs C. E. Graebner (USA) 6-1 6-3; M. Brummer (SA) d. E. Terras (F) 6-4 4-6 7-5; **Mrs L. W. King** (2) (USA) d. Mrs V. Vukovich (SA) 6-2 6-1.

THIRD ROUND: Court (1) d. Gourlay 6-1 6-0; Janes d. Palmeova 6-1 6-1; **Heldman** (7) d. Carter 6-2 6-3; Morozova d. Procter 6-3 1-6 6-4; **Jones** (4) d. Darmon 6-1 6-2; Michel d. van Deventer 6-4 6-2; **Richey** (5) d. Bartkowicz 6-4 8-6; Krantzcke d. Teeguarden 6-0 6-0; Harris d. Amos 6-1 6-4; Casals d. Anthony 6-1 6-3; Bowrey d. Curtis 8-10 6-4

6-2; Walkden d. Wade (3) 7-5 6-1; Truman d. Gilchrist 3-6 6-4 6-1; **Tegart** (8) d. Shaw 6-0 7-5; Pigeon d. Pericoli 4-6 6-1 6-2; **King** (2) d. Brummer 6-0 6-4.

FOURTH ROUND	QUARTER-FINALS	SEMI-FINALS	FINAL	CHAMPION	PRIZE MONEY	
Court (1)	**Court** (1)				Champion	£1,500
Janes	6-2 6-0	**Court** (1)			Runner-up	750
Heldman (7)	**Heldman** (7)	4-6 6-3 6-3			Semi-finals	350
Morozova	6-4 6-3		**Jones** (4)		Quarter-finals	200
Jones (4)	**Jones** (4)		10-12 6-3 6-2		Fourth round	125
Michel	6-0 9-7	**Jones** (4)			Third round	90
Richey (5)	**Richey** (5)	6-2 7-5			Second round	70
Krantzcke	4-6 6-3 7-5				First round	50
Harris	Casals			**Jones** (4)		
Casals	6-2 6-2			3-6 6-3 6-2		
Bowrey	Bowrey	Casals				
Walkden	6-3 1-6 8-6	3-6 9-7 7-5				
Truman	**Tegart** (8)		**King** (2)			
Tegart (8)	6-4 6-4		6-1 6-0			
Pigeon	**King** (2)	**King** (2)				
King (2)	6-3 6-2	4-6 7-5 8-6				

OTHER FINALS

GENTLEMEN'S DOUBLES: Final – J. D. Newcombe (A)/A. D. Roche (A) d. T. S. Okker (NTH)/M. C. Riessen (USA) 7-5 11-9 6-3.
LADIES' DOUBLES: Final – Mrs B. M. Court (A)/J. A. M. Tegart (A) d. P. S. A. Hogan (USA)/M. Michel (USA) 9-7 6-2.
MIXED DOUBLES: Final – F. S. Stolle (A)/Mrs P. F. Jones d. A. D. Roche (A)/J. A. M. Tegart (A) 6-3 6-2.
GENTLEMEN'S SINGLES PLATE: Final – T. Koch (BR) d. R. O. Ruffels (A) 6-1 6-3.

LADIES' SINGLES PLATE: Final – B. A. Grubb (USA) d. L. A. Rossouw (SA) 6-3 4-6 6-4.
BOYS' INVITATION SINGLES: Final – B. Bertram (SA) d. J. D. Alexander (A) 6-3 1-6 7-5.
GIRLS' INVITATION SINGLES: Final – K. Sawamatsu (J) d. B. Kirk (SA) 6-3 1-6 7-5.
VETERANS' MEN'S DOUBLES: Final – J. Drobny/E. V. Seixas (USA) d. E. G. Slack (USA)/R. C. Sorlein (USA) 9-7 8-6.

GENTLEMEN'S SINGLES

FIRST ROUND: R. G. Laver (1) (A) d. G. Seewagen (USA) 6-2 6-0 6-2; J. G. Alexander (A) d. H. Kary (AU) 7-5 3-6 6-3 6-4; R. G. Giltinan (A) d. H. S. FitzGibbon (USA) 8-6 8-6 5-7 6-4; F. D. McMillan (SA) d. J. L. Rouyer (F) 7-5 6-4 11-9; **R. Taylor** (16) d. B. E. Fairlie (NZ) 1-6 6-3 8-6 3-6 6-4; J. Mukerjea (IN) d. H. Rahim (PAK) w.o.; M. Holecek (CZ) d. J. G. Paish 6-2 6-2 4-6 7-5; C. M. Pasarell (USA) d. A. Munoz (SP) 6-4 7-5 6-3; **I. Nastase** (8) (RU) d. O. Parun (NZ) 6-8 6-0 7-5 8-6; G. C. Richey (USA) d. I. Gulyas (HU) 6-2 6-8 6-4 6-4; T. J. Ryan (SA) d. P. M. Doerner (A) 9-7 6-4 3-6 6-3; S. Koudelka (Stateless) d. S. Baranyi (HU) 7-5 6-3 6-2; D. W. Schroder (SA) d. F. J. Guzman (E) 6-2 6-2 6-0; P. Lall (IN) d. G. Vilas (ARG) 6-1 6-2 6-4; **A. D. Roche** (4) (A) d. R. R. Maud (S) 6-1 6-4 6-2; R. O. Ruffels (A) d. R. R. Dowdeswell (RH) 5-7 6-1 3-6 6-1 7-5; A. J. Pattison (SA) d. E. J. van Dillen (USA) 8-6 6-1 4-6 3-6 6-3; M. Cox d. D. Irvine (RH) 6-2 4-6 6-3 6-4; A. Metreveli (USSR) d. **J. Kodes** (13) (CZ) 6-2 7-5 3-6 2-6 7-5; J. E. Mandarino (BR) d. F. Pala (CZ) 6-4 6-4 6-2; E. L. Scott (USA) d. R. Krog 8-6 6-2 14-12; M. C. Riessen (USA) d. J. H. McManus (USA) 6-0 6-2 6-2; **K. R. Rosewall** (5) (A) d. C. S. Dibley (A) 6-3 7-5 6-4; J. C. Barclay (F) d. P. Proisy (F) 6-8 12-10 6-3 6-4; Addison d. Bowrey (A) 3-6 10-8 12-10 6-3; **E. C. Drysdale** (12) (SA) d. F. S. Stolle (A) 7-5 9-11 8-6 3-6 6-3; N. Spear (YU) d. M. T. Akbari (IRAN) 6-2 6-3 6-3; T. W. Gorman (USA) d. J. B. Chanfreau (F) 6-2 8-6 7-5; P. W. Curtis d. J. H. Osborne (USA) 6-3 6-3 1-6 6-4; R. C. Lutz (USA)

d. G. Goven (F) 4-6 6-3 6-3 6-4; P. C. Dent (A) d. P. Hombergen (B) 6-2 6-3 6-2; R. A. J. Hewitt (SA) d. D. Contet (F) 6-2 6-3 6-4; **T. S. Okker** (11) (NTH) d. J. Ulrich (D) 11-9 4-6 6-1 6-3; R. J. Carmichael (A) d. C. D. Steele (USA) 3-6 10-8 6-3 6-1; R. D. Crealy (A) d. E. A. Zuleta (E) 6-3 6-2 6-2; K. E. Diepraam (SA) d. D. A. R. Russell (JAM) 7-5 13-11 6-2; **Z. Franulovic** (6) (YU) d. D. A. Lloyd 6-2 6-4 6-4; T. Ulrich (D) d. P. Marmureanu (RU) 6-2 7-5 6-4; I. D. Buding (D) d. K. Watanabe (J) 7-5 6-3 4-6 6-3; A. J. Stone (A) d. R. K. Wilson 6-3 6-4 6-2; **A. Gimeno** (14) (SP) d. P. Barthes (F) 4-6 6-1 6-4 6-2; I. El Shafei (UAR) d. S. J. Matthews 6-4 12-10 8-6; L. A. Hoad (A) d. D. Sturdza (SWZ) 6-4 6-4 7-9 6-4; N. Pilic (YU) d. G. Battrick 4-6 6-1 6-1 4-6 6-3; **A. R. Ashe** (3) (USA) d. G. R. Stilwell 6-3 6-2 6-1; J. Saul (SA) d. J. D. Bartlett (A) 5-7 6-2 6-4 6-4; B. Bertram (SA) d. F. Jauffret (F) 6-4 1-6 6-3 6-3; J. Leschly (D) d. T. Lejus (USSR) 6-3 6-4 11-9; **R. S. Emerson** (10) (A) d. A. Volkov (USSR) 6-4 6-2 6-0; M. Orantes (SP) d. S. Ball (A) 6-2 6-2 7-9 6-4; J. Kukal (CZ) d. B. Montrenaud (F) 6-2 7-5 7-9 3-6 7-5; H. J. Plotz (G) d. S. A. Warboys 6-4 6-4 6-4; **S. R. Smith** (7) (USA) d. J. Fillol (CH) 7-5 2-6 6-3 6-4; J. Loyo Mayo (M) d. M. F. Mulligan (A) 7-5 6-1 8-6; V. Korotkov (USSR) d. A. J. McDonald (A) 5-7 8-10 6-3 6-4 6-4; I. G. Fletcher (A) d. J. G. Clifton 6-3 6-2 6-4; **R. D. Ralston** (15) (USA) d. N. Pietrangeli (IT) w.o.; O. K. Davidson (A) d. A. Panatta (IT) 6-1 6-3 5-7 8-6; R. E. Holmberg d. R. J. Moore (USA) 11-9 6-4 2-6 6-1; N. Kalogeropoulos (GR) d. R. F. Keldie (A) 4-6 6-2 6-3 6-1; **J. D. Newcombe** (2) (A) d. R. R. Barth (USA) 6-2 6-3 6-4.

SECOND ROUND: Laver (1) d. Alexander 6-1 6-3 6-3; McMillan d. Giltinan 3-6 5-7 6-4 6-1 6-2; **Taylor** (16) d. Mukerjea 3-6 6-3 6-2 6-4; Pasarell d. Holecek 6-1 6-2 6-4; **Nastase** (8) d. Richey 7-5 1-6 2-6 6-4 6-3; Ryan d. Koudelka 4-6 6-2 6-4 3-6 6-3; **Graebner** (9) d. Tiriac 4-16 14-12 6-2 ret'd; Lall d. Schroder 6-4 7-9 6-2; **Roche** (4) d. Ruffels 6-4 6-3 6-2; Cox d. Pattison 3-6 4-9 7; Mandarino d. Metreveli 5-7 6-4 6-4 6-4; Riessen d. Scott 6-4 6-2 6-3; **Rosewall** (5) d. Barclay 6-2 6-1 6-3; Addison d. Bowrey 6-4 6-4 6-4; **Drysdale** (12) d. Spear 6-4 6-4 6-4; Gorman d. Curtis 6-2 4-6 6-4 6-1; Lutz d. Dent 6-2 6-1 6-2; Hewitt d. **Okker** (11) 6-3 6-4 6-3; Carmichael d.

Crealy 4-6 6-3 6-4 3-6 6-3; **Franulovic** (6) d. Diepraam 6-3 6-4 2-6 6-1; Ulrich d. Buding 6-2 6-3 6-3; **Gimeno** (14) d. Stone 7-5 4-6 6-3 6-4; El Shafei d. Hoad 6-3 6-3 4-6 6-1; **Ashe** (3) d. Pilic 9-7 11-13 6-4 6-3; Bertram d. Saul 6-3 6-1 6-4; **Emerson** (10) d. Leschly 6-3 6-3 6-4; Orantes d. Kukal 3-6 11-9 6-3 6-4; **Smith** (7) d. Plotz 6-2 6-2 6-4; Loyo Mayo d. Korotkov 3-6 6-1 6-2 2-6 6-4; **Ralston** (15) d. Fletcher 4-6 6-3 7-5 6-2; Davidson d. Holmberg 6-4 6-4 6-2; **Newcombe** (2) d. Kalogeropoulos 6-1 6-2 6-1.

THIRD ROUND: Laver (1) d. McMillan 6-2 3-6 6-0 6-2; **Taylor** (16) d. Pasarell 8-6 17-15 6-4; **Nastase** (8) d. Ryan 6-3 6-1 6-8 4-6 6-1; **Graebner** (9) d. Lall 6-0 6-2 6-1; **Roche** (4) d. Cox 6-2 9-7 6-3; Riessen d. Mandarino 4-6 7-5 7-5 6-1; **Rosewall** (5) d. Addison 6-2 6-4 6-0; Gorman d. Drysdale (12) 6-3 6-3 6-2; Hewitt d. Lutz 1-6 5-7 7-5 9-7 6-3; Carmichael d. **Franulovic** (6) 6-3 6-2 6-0; **Gimeno** (14) d. Ulrich 4-6 6-1 6-2 6-2; **Ashe** (3) d. El Shafei 6-3 6-1 2-6 6-0; **Emerson** (10) d. Bertram 8-10 6-0 6-3 6-1; **Smith** (7) d. Orantes 4-6 6-3 8-6 6-0; **Ralston** (15) d. Loyo Mayo 6-0 6-0 6-1; **Newcombe** (2) d. Davidson 9-7 6-3 7-5.

FOURTH ROUND	QUARTER-FINALS	SEMI-FINALS	FINAL	CHAMPION	PRIZE MONEY	
Laver (1)	**Taylor** (16)				Champion	£3,000
Taylor (16)	4-6 6-4 6-2 6-1	**Taylor** (16)			Runner-up	1,500
Nastase (8)	**Graebner** (9)	6-3 11-9 12-10			Semi-finals	800
Graebner (9)	6-3 6-0 4-6 6-3		**Rosewall** (5)		Quarter-finals	450
Roche (4)	**Roche** (4)		6-3 4-6 6-3 6-3		Fourth round	220
Riessen	6-4 8-10 6-4 6-2	**Rosewall** (5)			Third round	165
Rosewall (5)	**Rosewall** (5)	10-8 6-1 4-6 6-2			Second round	125
Gorman	6-2 6-2 3-6 7-5			**Newcombe** (2)	First round	100
Hewitt	Carmichael			5-7 6-3 6-3 3-6 6-1		
Carmichael	6-4 9-7 6-2	**Gimeno** (14)				
Gimeno (14)	**Gimeno** (14)	6-1 6-2 6-4				
Ashe (3)	7-5 7-5 6-2		**Newcombe** (2)			
Emerson (10)	**Emerson** (10)		6-3 8-6 6-0			
Smith (7)	2-6 6-3 6-4 6-2					
Ralston (15)	**Newcombe** (2)	**Newcombe** (2)				
Newcombe (2)	14-12 9-7 6-2	6-1 5-7 3-6 6-2 11-9				

LADIES' SINGLES

FIRST ROUND: K. A. Melville (4) (A) d. J. H. Townsend 6-4 6-1; O. Morozova (USSR) d. J. Szorenyi (HU) 6-2 6-3; M. Brummer (SA) d. J. E. O'Hara (C) 6-4 6-3; M. E. Greenwood d. P. A. Edwards (A) 6-0 6-3; A. Palmeova (CZ) d. S. Petersen (BR) 6-2 6-3; M. Michel (USA) d. Mrs T. W. Cowie 6-3 6-2; W. M. Shaw d. K. Harris (A) 6-3 6-4; L. E. Hunt (A) d. Mrs R. M. Johnson (USA) 7-5 6-4; **R. Casals** (5) (USA) d. K. M. Harter (USA) 8-6 1-6 6-1; W. A. Overton (USA) d. Mrs K. W. Crooke (A) 6-3 7-5; L. A. Rossouw (SA) d. M. Nasuelli (IT) 6-0 6-2; D. Carter (USA) d. P. M. Walkden (SA) 6-3 3-6 6-3; Mrs C. W. Brasher d. M. J. Pryde (NZ) 9-7 6-0; L. J. Beaven d. A. M. Wilshere (SA) 6-4 2-6 6-3; C. Murakami (J) d. C. M. F. Spinoza (F) 8-10 6-2 8-6; C. M. Sandberg (SW) d. J. A. Fayter 10-8 6-0; S. Walsh (USA) d.

P. S. A. Hogan (USA) 8-6 6-3; H. F. Gourlay d. L. Liem (INDO) 6-0 2-6 6-4; Mrs P. W. Curtis (USA) d. M. Neumannova (CZ) 7-5 4-6 6-3; F. Durr (F) d. L. Kaligis (INDO) 6-2 6-3; V. J. Ziegenfuss (USA) d. S. H. Walsham (A) 7-5 6-2; Mrs T. Walhof (NTH) d. D. H. Botha (SA) 6-3 6-4; H. J. Amos (A) d. M. Giorgi (IT) 6-0 6-2; **J. M. Heldman** (6) (USA) d. Mrs J. L. Moore (USA) 6-1; C. A. Martinez (SA) d. K. Hatanaka (J) 6-2 6-0; P. A. Cody (USA) d. W. L. Tomlinson (SA) 1-6 8-6 6-2; P. R. H. Bentley d. W. V. Hall 6-1 6-1; V. A. Burton d. E. Isopaitis (USSR) 2-6 9-7 6-4; E. F. Goolagong (A) d. O. de Roubin (F) 6-1 6-2; P. Bartkowicz (USA) d. K. Pigeon (USA) 6-3 6-9 7-6-1; Mrs J. Du Plooy (SA) d. B. I. Kirk (SA) 2-6 6-3 6-4; **S. V. Wade** (3) d. S. J. Holdsworth 6-1 6-4.

SECOND ROUND: Mrs B. M. Court (1) (A) d. S. J. Alexander (A) 6-0 6-1; M. E. Guzman (E) d. Mrs J. A. Bentzer (SW) 4-6 6-3 6-3; Mrs V. Vopickova (CZ) d. Mrs J. A. G. Lloyd 6-0 6-3; J. P. Cooper d. C. Molesworth 6-1 6-3; **H. Niessen** (8) (G) d. A. M. Arias (ARG) 6-3 6-0; G. Hansen (USA) d. E. Terras (F) 6-4 6-4 11-9; M. A. Bakker (NTH) d. Mrs L. Orth-Schildknecht (G) 5-7 6-4 11-9; B. A. Grubb (USA) d. P. A. Teeguarden (USA) 4-6 8-6 6-1; **Melville** (4) d. Morozova 11-9 7-5; Brummer d. Greenwood 4-7 5; Michel d. Palmeova 6-0 6-0; Shaw d. Hunt 6-4 6-2; **Casals** (5) d. Overton 6-3 6-1; Carter d. Rossouw 6-3 6-3; Brasher d. Beaven 6-4 6-4; Sandberg d. Murakami 6-2 6-2; Walsh d. Hogan 6-2 6-4; Ziegenfuss d. Walhof 6-4 7-5; **Heldman** (6) d. Amos 6-4 6-2; Martinez d. Cody 6-3 6-1; Bentley d. Burton 8-6 1-6 10-8; Bartkowicz d. Goolagong 6-4 6-0; **Wade** (3) d. Du Plooy 6-4 7-5; Mrs J. B. Chanfreau (F) d. Mrs G. M. Williams 6-3 6-2; Mrs D. E. Dalton (A) d. Mrs P. J. Northen 6-2 6-0; Mrs K. Sawamatsu (J) d. F. Luff (A) 6-1 6-2; **K. M. Krantzcke** (7) (A) d. F. E. Truman 6-1 6-8 7-5; L. Pericoli (IT) d. E. M. Ernest 6-4 7-5; E. Emanuel (SA) d. Mrs C. E. Graebner (USA) 7-5 5-7 6-3; Mrs N. Schaar (NTH) d. B. F. Stove (NTH) 6-2 3-6 9-7; **Mrs L. W. King** (2) (USA) d. F. Bonicelli (PE) 6-2 6-1.

THIRD ROUND: Court (1) d. Guzman 6-0 6-1; Vopickova d. Cooper 5-7 10-8 6-2; **Niessen** (8) d. Hansen 8-6 6-1; Grubb d. Bakker 7-5 6-2; **Melville** (4) d. Brummer 6-4 3-6 6-2; Shaw d. Michel 6-3 6-0; **Casals** (5) d. Carter 6-3 8-6; Sandberg d. Brasher 6-4 7-9 6-4; Durr d. Walsh 7-5 6-1; **Heldman** (6) d. Ziegenfuss 3-6 2-6; Martinez d. Bentley 9-7 9-7; **Wade** (3) d. Bartkowicz 6-4 6-4; Dalton d. Chanfreau 6-2 6-0; **Krantzcke** (7) d. Sawamatsu 6-2 6-3; Pericoli d. Emanuel 6-2 6-2; **King** (2) d. Schaar 6-4 6-0.

FOURTH ROUND	QUARTER-FINALS	SEMI-FINALS	FINAL	CHAMPION	PRIZE MONEY	
Court (1)	**Court** (1)				Champion	£1,500
Vopickova	6-3 6-3	**Court** (1)			Runner-up	750
Niessen (8)	**Niessen** (8)	6-8 6-0 6-0			Semi-finals	400
Grubb	6-1 6-3		**Court** (1)		Quarter-finals	225
Melville (4)	Shaw		6-4 6-1		Fourth round	150
Shaw	6-2 6-4	**Casals** (5)			Third round	125
Casals (5)	**Casals** (5)	6-2 6-0			Second round	100
Sandberg	6-1 6-0			**Court** (1)	First round	75
Durr	Durr			14-12 11-9		
Heldman (6)	6-2 6-4	Durr				
Martinez	Martinez	6-0 6-4				
Wade (3)	6-1 6-4		**King** (2)			
Dalton	**Krantzcke** (7)		6-3 7-5			
Krantzcke (7)	6-4 6-3	**King** (2)				
Pericoli	**King** (2)	3-6 6-3 6-2				
King (2)	6-1 6-2					

OTHER FINALS

GENTLEMEN'S DOUBLES: Final — J. D. Newcombe (A)/A. D. Roche (A) d. K. R. Rosewall (A)/F. S. Stolle (A) 10-8 6-3 6-1.
LADIES' DOUBLES: Final — R. Casals (USA)/Mrs L. W. King (USA) d. F. Durr (F)/S. V. Wade 6-2 6-3.
MIXED DOUBLES: Final — I. Nastase (RU)/R. Casals (USA) d. A. Metreveli (USSR)/O. Morozova (USSR) 6-3 4-6 9-7.

GENTLEMEN'S SINGLES PLATE: Final — R. R. Maud (S) d. R. R. Barth (USA) 6-4 6-3.
LADIES' SINGLES PLATE: Final — E. F. Goolagong (A) d. L. Liem (INDO) 6-2 6-1.
BOYS' INVITATION SINGLES: Final — B. Bertram (SA) d. F. Gebert (G) 6-0 6-3.
GIRLS' INVITATION SINGLES: Final — S. Walsh (USA) d. M. V. Kroschina (USSR) 8-6 6-4.
VETERANS' MEN'S DOUBLES: Final — J. Drobny/R. L. Riggs (USA) d. G. R. MacCall (USA)/P. Segura (EC) 6-2 6-2.

GENTLEMEN'S SINGLES

1971

FIRST ROUND: R. G. **Laver** (1) (A) d. R. N. Howe (A) 6-2 6-0 6-1; R. J. Moore (SA) d. A. J. Stone (A) 6-1 3-6 8-9 6-4 9-7; C. E. Graebner (USA) d. A. J. McDonald (A) 6-4 6-2 6-2; Z. Franulovic (YU) d. I. Gulyas (HU) 6-2 6-4 6-8 6-2; T. S. Okker (NTH) d. J. Kodes (CZ) 6-3 6-3 6-3; R. O. Ruffels (A) d. E. L. Scott (USA) 4-6 4-6 6-3 6-0 6-3; N. Pilic (YU) d. T. J. Ryan (SA) 6-3 9-8 5-7 6-4; N. Kalogeropoulos (GR) d. P. J. Cramer (SA) 8-9 8-9 6-3 6-2 9-7; T. W. Gorman (USA) d. **E. C. Drysdale** (8) (SA) 2-6 6-8 6-3 6-4 7-5; E. Di Matteo (IT) d. P. W. Curtis 6-4 6-3 8-6; I. Tiriac (RU) d. A. Amritraj (IN) 9-8 6-3 6-1; B. E. Fairlie (NZ) d. R. R. Barth (USA) 8-6 9-8 6-4; J. Ulrich (D) d. S. Koudelka (Stateless) 1-6 6-1 4-6 6-4 6-4; R. L. Case (A) d. J. Simpson (NZ) 6-4 7-5 7-5; D. Irvine (RH) d. W. Schroder (SW) 6-1 6-3 3-6 6-4; T. W. Addison (A) d. W. N'Godrella (F) 6-3 9-8 9-7; S. R. **Smith** (4) (USA) d. M. Leclercq (F) 6-2 6-4 6-3; J. G. Paish d. A. Gimeno (SP) 6-3 1-6 6-4 6-4; O. Bengtson (SW) d. J Fassbender (G) 6-4 6-4 7-9 7-9 7-5; A. J. Pattison (RH) d. J. Kuki (J) 6-2 6-1 6-0; R. C. Lutz (USA) d. F. A. Froehling (USA) 8-6 8-9 4-6 6-2 12-10; J. G. Clifton d. P. Marmureanu (RU) 6-2 6-1 6-2; P. M. Doerner (A) d. K. Yanagi (J) 6-2 6-3 3-6 6-0; R. S. Emerson (A) d. M. Holecek (CZ) 6-4 6-4 6-4; **A. R. Ashe** (5) (USA) d. J. E. van Dillen (USA) 3-6 6-3 6-4 7-5; P. Proisy (F) d. H. Eischenbroich (G) 3-6 7-5 6-3 6-1; J. G. Alexander (A) d. W. W. Bowrey (A) 6-0 6-2 6-2; M. C. Riessen (USA) d. J. H. McManus (USA) 9-8 6-4 8-6; R. Gonzales (USA) d. M. Orantes (SP) 6-4 6-4 7-5; P. Barthes (F) d. K. Meiler (G) 6-4 8-9 6-3 9-7; O. Parun (NZ) d. J. L. Rouyer (F) 6-2 2-6 6-4 6-3; H. J. Plotz (G) d. F. Pala (CZ) 6-1 6-2 6-3

2-6 6-3; F. A. Sedgman (A) d. J. Kukal (CZ) 3-6 6-3 6-2 6-1; J. Borowiak (USA) d. F. Jauffret (F) 4-6 2-6 6-3 6-4 6-2; B. J. Phillips-Moore (A) d. S. J. Matthews 6-3 8-6 8-6; C. M. Pasarell (USA) d. A. D. Roche (A) 9-7 4-6 8-6 9-8; A. Panatta (IT) d. G. Seewagen (USA) 6-3 3-6 6-3 6-4; R. Taylor d. M. Lara (USA) 6-2 6-3 6-4; **G. C. Richey** (6) (USA) d. R. D. Crealy (A) 6-3 9-7 2-6 6-3; F. S. Stolle (A) d. K. G. Warwick (A) 6-4 3-6 9-7 4-6 6-3; T. Koch (BR) d. P. Szoke (HU) 7-5 6-2 6-2; F. D. McMillan (SA) d. T. Sakai 6-4 6-2 6-1; O. K. Davidson (A) d. J. Leschly (D) 3-6 6-3 6-3 6-3; J. de Mendoza d. J. B. Chanfreau (F) 8-9 6-3 6-3 6-4; J. Fillol (CH) d. I. El Shafei (UAR) 6-4 5-7 4-6 6-0 6-2; R. J. Carmichael (A) d. J. S. Connors (USA) w.o.; **K. R. Rosewall** (3) (A) d. P. Hombergen (B) 6-3 6-3 6-1; C. S. Dibley (A) d. H. Kary (AU) 7-5 6-2 6-2; G. R. Stilwell d. J. C. Barclay (F) 8-6 6-0 1-6 7-5; R. D. Ralston (USA) d. T. Ulrich (D) 8-6 6-3 6-2; G. Masters (A) d. N. Spear (YU) 7-5 6-0 6-2; J. Loyo-Mayo (M) d. S. Baranyi (HU) 1-6 6-1 6-4 6-2; B. M. Bertram (SA) d. V. Zednik (CZ) 6-3 6-2 6-0; G. Goven (F) d. P. Cornejo (CH) 6-4 6-2 7-5; **I. Nastase** (7) (RU) d. R. F. Keldie (A) 6-2 6-1 6-3 4-6 10-8; P. C. Dent (A) d. P. Lall (IN) 6-4 5-7 6-4 7-5; A. Metreveli (USSR) d. J. Mukerjea (IN) 6-2 6-4 6-4; J. E. Mandarino (BR) d. A. Munoz (SP) 6-4 8-9 6-4 6-2; J. Reese (USA) d. J. W. Feaver 7-5 6-2 6-2; A. Fox (USA) d. S. Ball (A) 2-6 9-7 1-6 6-1 7-5; G. Battrick d. J. D. Bartlett (A) 2-6 6-4 6-3 6-1; I. G. Fletcher (A) d. M. Cox 8-6 7-5 1-6 6-4; **J. D. Newcombe** (2) (A) d. R. A. J. Hewitt (SA) 6-4 6-3 7-5.

SECOND ROUND: Laver (1) d. Moore 6-8 6-3 6-2 7-5; Graebner d. Franulovic 6-3 6-1 6-1; Okker d. Ruffels 8-9 6-4 6-3 6-4; Pilic d. Kalogeropoulos 6-2 6-3 4-6 6-1; Gorman. Di Matteo 2-6 6-2 6-2 6-1; Tiriac d. Fairlie 6-3 6-3 7-9 8-6; Case d. Ulrich 6-3 2-6 5-7 6-3 6-1; Irvine d. Addison 6-2 8-6 6-4; **Smith** (4) d. Paish 6-1 6-4 6-4; Pattison Bengtson 4-6 4-6 6-4 9-7; Lutz d. Clifton 6-3 6-1 6-4; Emerson d. Doerner 4-6 6-2 8-6 6-1; Ashe (5) d. Proisy 6-4 6-4 6-4; Riessen d. Alexander 9-8 6-2 6-3; Barthes d. Gonzales 7-5 8-9 3-6 6-3 6-4; Parun d. Plotz 6-0 6-2 6-2; Sedgman d. Maud 6-4 5-7 6-4 2-6 6-4; Borowiak d. Phillips-Moore 6-2 9-7 8-6; Panatta d. Pasarell 6-3 6-3 3-6 6-3;

Richey (6) d. Taylor 6-2 3-6 2-6 6-4 11-9; Stolle d. Koch 6-3 6-4 6-4; Davidson d. McMillan 9-7 3-6 6-1 6-4; Fillol d. Chanfreau 9-8 6-3 9-8; **Rosewall** (3) d. Carmichael 9-7 2-6 6-4 6-3; Dibley d. Stilwell 2-6 6-3 3-6 9-8 6-4; Ralston d. Masters 6-1 6-4 5-7 9-7; Loyo-Mayo d. Bertram 9-8 6-3 6-2; Goven d. **Nastase** (7) 6-4 6-4 6-2; Metreveli d. Dent 9-7 6-3 6-4; Hrebec d. Mandarino 6-4 6-4 6-3; Battrick d. Fox 6-4 6-2 6-2; **Newcombe** (2) d. Fletcher 7-5 6-4 6-2.

THIRD ROUND: Laver (1) d. Graebner 9-8 6-2 7-5; Okker d. Pilic 3-6 6-3 6-4 8-6; Gorman d. Tiriac 6-4 6-3 7-5; Case d. Irvine 6-3 6-4 6-3; **Smith** (4) d. Pattison 2-6 6-4 7-5; Emerson d. Lutz 8-9 6-3 9-8 9-8; Riessen d. Ashe (5) 6-1 9-8 8-9 6-4; Parun d. Barthes 6-2 4-6 9-7 6-1; Borowiak d. Sedgman 6-2 4-6 6-3 6-4; **Richey** (6) d. Panatta 6-2 6-2 6-4;

Stolle d. Davidson 9-8 6-1 6-2; **Rosewall** (3) d. Fillol 6-3 6-1 6-4; Dibley d. Ralston 3-6 8-9 6-3 6-0 10-8; Loyo-Mayo d. Goven 4-6 9-7 6-4 6-4; Metreveli d. Hrebec 6-4 7-5 6-4; **Newcombe** (2) d. Battrick 6-4 6-4 6-4.

FOURTH ROUND	QUARTER-FINALS	SEMI-FINALS	FINAL	CHAMPION	PRIZE MONEY	
Laver (1)	**Laver** (1)				Champion	£3,750
Okker	7-5 6-1 2-6 7-5	Gorman			Runner-up	2,250
Gorman	Gorman	9-7 8-6 6-3			Semi-finals	750
Case	6-3 8-6 6-4		**Smith** (4)		Quarter-finals	415
Smith (4)	**Smith** (4)		6-3 8-6 6-2		Fourth round	225
Emerson	2-6 6-1 6-3 9-7	**Smith** (4)			Third round	150
Riessen	Parun	8-6 6-3 6-4			Second round	95
Parun	9-8 6-3 3-6 6-3				First round	75
Borowiak	**Richey** (6)			**Newcombe** (2)		
Richey (6)	6-4 4-6 6-4 6-4	**Rosewall** (3)		6-3 5-7 2-6 6-4 6-4		
Stolle	**Rosewall** (3)	6-8 5-7 6-4 9-7 7-5				
Rosewall (3)	6-4 7-5 7-9 6-4		**Newcombe** (2)			
Dibley	Dibley		6-1 6-1 6-3			
Loyo-Mayo	6-3 8-6 6-3	**Newcombe** (2)				
Metreveli	**Newcombe** (2)	6-1 6-2 6-3				
Newcombe (2)	9-8 6-3 4-6 6-3					

LADIES' SINGLES

FIRST ROUND: R. **Casals** (4) (USA) d. Mrs P. Darmon (F) 6-0 6-0; K. A. Melville (A) d. H. F. Gourlay (A) 6-3 6-2; B. I. Kirk (SA) d. A. T. Coleman (A) 6-2 6-2; B. F. Stove (NTH) d. A. Martin (C) 6-1 6-1; K. Ebbinghaus (G) d. H. J. Amos (A) 6-3 6-3; C. E. M. Sandberg (SW) d. K. Pigeon (USA) 6-4 7-5; J. P. Cooper d. Mrs E. S. Kay (A) 6-3 6-3; C. E. M. Sandberg (SW) d. Mrs P. W. Curtis (USA) 6-2 6-3; **S. V. Wade** (5) d. P. S. A. Hogan (USA) 7-5 6-2; M. E. Greenwood d. O. de Roubin (F) 6-3 5-7 6-4; L. A. Rossouw (S) d. T. A. Fretz (USA) 9-7 6-4; Mrs J. M. Carter-Triolo (USA) d. M. J. Pryde (NZ) 6-8 6-4 6-3; V. J. Ziegenfuss (USA) d. M. Nasuelli (IT) w.o.; Mrs D. E. Dalton (A) d. Mrs G. M. Williams 9-7 6-4; O. Morozova (USSR) d. E. Emanuel (SA) 6-0 6-3; L. Pericoli (IT) d. Mrs J. A. Bentzer (SW) 5-7

9-8 6-4; F. E. Truman d. V. A. Burton 6-2 6-3; S. Yansone (USSR) d. F. Bonicelli (PE) 6-3 6-3; S. J. Alexander (A) d. Mrs P. H. Rodriguez (F) 6-4 6-3; B. Hawcroft (A) d. S. J. Hudson-Beck (RH) 6-2 6-2; J. Newberry (USA) d. G. L. Coles 6-2 8-6; K. Sawamatsu (J) d. V. Lancaster (A) 6-0 6-3; P. A. Reese (USA) d. L. Kaligis (INDO) 6-2 3-6 6-4; **Mrs K. Gunter** (6) (USA) d. L. Liem (INDO) 6-2 6-1; J. A. Fayter d. C. Molesworth 5-7 6-2 6-3; L. A. Tuero (USA) d. J. E. O'Hara (C) 6-2 6-2; L. E. Hunt (A) d. Mrs M. R. Wainwright 4-6 6-3 7-5; K. Harris (A) d. B. M. Lindstrom (FIN) 6-1 6-0; D. H. Botha (SA) d. M. Neumannova (CZ) 6-4 6-4; J. M. Heldman (A) d. K. Pigeon (USA) 4-6 6-2 6-2; K. K. Kemmer (USA) d. P. Bartkowicz (USA) 7-5 6-0; **E. F. Goolagong** (3) (A) d. G. Hansen (USA) 6-0 6-2.

SECOND ROUND: Mrs B. M. **Court** (1) (A) d. Mrs J. D. G. Robinson (A) 6-0 6-0; C. A. Martinez (USA) d. S. H. Minford (IRE) 6-2 7-5; Mrs N. Schaar (NTH) d. Mrs C. W. Brasher 7-5 6-3; R. H. Bentley d. S. J. Holdsworth 6-3 6-3; **Mrs H. Masthoff** (8) (G) d. Mrs J. B. Chanfreau (F) 1-6 6-2 6-4; Mrs W. W. Bowrey (A) d. B. Vest (USA) 6-1 6-1; W. M. Shaw d. I. Fernandez (COL) 6-4 6-2; E. Pande (USA) d. Mrs T. Walhof (NTH) 6-3 1-6 6-0; Melville d. **Casals** (4) 7-5 6-4; Kirk d. Stove 6-4 6-8 6-3; Sandberg d. Ebbinghaus 4-6 6-0 7-5; Curtis d. Cooper 6-1 6-3; **Wade** (5) d. Greenwood 1-6 6-4; Carter-Triolo d. Rossouw 9-8 6-3; Dalton d. Ziegenfuss 6-4 6-4; Morozova d. Pericoli 6-3 6-3;

Yansone d. Truman 1-6 7-5 7-5; Hawcroft d. Alexander 5-7 6-3 6-0; Sawamatsu d. Newberry 6-2 6-8 6-4; **Gunter** (6) d. Reese 6-0 6-1; Tuero d. Fayter 6-1 6-3; Hunt d. Harris 9-8 6-2; Heldman d. Botha 6-1 6-0; **Goolagong** (3) d. Kemmer 6-4 6-1; Mrs W. S. Palmeova-West (CZ) d. Mrs K. R. James 8-6 6-2; L. J. Beaven d. Mrs R. Faulkner (A) 6-2 6-2; A. Bakker (NTH) d. M. Kroshina (USSR) 2-6 6-2 6-1; **F. Durr** (7) (F) d. M. Holubova (CZ) 6-2 6-4; Mrs G. T. Janes d. Mrs J. L. Moore (A) 6-1 6-4; P. A. Teeguarden (USA) d. Mrs T. W. Cowie 6-1 7-5; Mrs A. Bouteleux (F) d. M. E. Guzman (E) 2-6 6-1 8-6; **Mrs L. W. King** (2) (USA) d. W. S. Gilchrist (A) 4-6 6-1 6-0.

THIRD ROUND: **Court** (1) d. Martinez 6-1 6-1; Schaar d. Bentley 3-6 6-1 6-2; Bowrey d. **Masthoff** (8) 6-3 6-1; Shaw d. Pande 6-4 6-1; Melville d. Kirk 9-8 6-1; Curtis d. Sandberg 8-6 6-4; **Wade** (5) d. Carter-Triolo 6-1 6-1; Dalton d. Morozova 6-3 7-5; Yansone d. Hawcroft 6-4 1-6 6-4; **Gunter** (6) d. Sawamatsu 6-2 6-2; Hunt d. Tuero 6-1

6-2; **Goolagong** (3) d. Heldman 6-3 6-3; Beaven d. Palmeova-West 6-4 6-1; **Durr** (7) d. Bakker 6-0 6-1; Janes d. Teeguarden 6-2 6-3; **King** (2) d. Bouteleux 6-2 6-0.

FOURTH ROUND	QUARTER-FINALS	SEMI-FINALS	FINAL	CHAMPION	PRIZE MONEY	
Court (1)	**Court** (1)				Champion	£1,800
Schaar	6-2 6-1	**Court** (1)			Runner-up	1,000
Bowrey	Shaw	6-2 6-1			Semi-finals	450
Shaw	1-6 9-7 6-3		**Court** (1)		Quarter-finals	265
Melville	Melville		4-6 6-1 6-0		Fourth round	150
Curtis	6-1 6-4 6-1	Dalton			Third round	115
Wade (5)	Dalton	6-2 3-6 6-3			Second round	75
Dalton	9-8 6-3				First round	55
Yansone	**Gunter** (6)			**Goolagong** (3)		
Gunter (6)	6-3 6-2	**Goolagong** (3)		6-4 6-1		
Hunt	**Goolagong** (3)	6-3 6-2				
Goolagong (3)	1-6 6-2 6-1		**Goolagong** (3)			
Beaven	**Durr** (7)		6-4 6-4			
Durr (7)	6-8 6-1 6-1	**King** (2)				
Janes	**King** (2)	2-6 6-2 6-2				
King (2)	6-2 7-5					

OTHER FINALS

GENTLEMEN'S DOUBLES: Final — R. S. Emerson (A)/R. G. Laver (A) d. A. R. Ashe (USA)/R. D. Ralston (USA) 4-6 9-7 6-8 6-4 6-4.

LADIES' DOUBLES: Final — R. Casals (USA)/Mrs L. W. King (USA) d. Mrs B. M. Court (A)/E. F. Goolagong (A) 6-3 6-2.

MIXED DOUBLES: Final — O. K. Davidson (A)/Mrs L. W. King (USA) d. M. C. Riessen (USA)/Mrs B. M. Court (A) 3-6 6-2 15-13.

GENTLEMEN'S SINGLES PLATE: Final — R. D. Crealy (A) d. P. Cornejo (CH) 6-3 6-4.

LADIES' SINGLES PLATE: Final — Mrs M. R. Wainwright d. B. F. Stove (NTH) 6-4 0-6 6-2.

BOYS' INVITATION SINGLES: Final — R. Kreiss (USA) d. S. A. Warboys 2-6 6-4 6-3.

GIRLS' INVITATION SINGLES: Final — M. Kroschina (USSR) d. S. Minford (IRE) 6-4 6-4.

VETERANS' MEN'S DOUBLES: Final — G. Mulloy (USA)/A. Vincent (USA) d. L. S. Clark (USA)/E. V. Seixas (USA) 6-3 6-2.

GENTLEMEN'S SINGLES

1972

FIRST ROUND: S. R. Smith (1) (USA) d. H. J. Plotz (G) 6-1 6-1 6-3; D. Irvine (RH) d. A. R. Gardiner (A) 6-2 7-9 6-2 5-7 6-4; T. Sakai (J) d. P. Cornejo (CH) 6-4 9-8 6-3; A. Mayer (USA) d. S. J. Matthews 4-6 6-3 6-3 5-7 6-3; I. G. Fletcher (A) d. J. L. Rouyer (F) 6-4 6-3 6-3; A. Olmedo (PE) d. J. Ulrich (D) 4-6 6-3 6-3 6-4; F. Pala (CZ) d. W. R. Durham (A) 6-3 9-8 6-4; H. Kary (AU) d. P. Szoke (HU) 8-6 6-3 8-9-3-6 6-0; **A. Metreveli** (8) (USSR) d. P. Marzano (IT) 6-2 8-6 6-4; P. Dominguez (F) d. J. Simpson (NZ) 6-3 4-6 6-1 7-5; T. Ulrich (D) d. J. G. Clifton 6-2 3-0 ret'd; J. G. Paish d. E. L. Scott (USA) 7-9 6-4 9-8 6-3; P. Proisy (F) d. S. Likhachev (USSR) 6-4 9-8 8-9 6-4; P. J. Cramer (SA) d. I. Gulyas (HU) 6-4 7-5 6-4; M. Estep (USA) d. J. C. Barclay (F) 6-3 7-5 6-8 6-4; J. Kamiwazumi (J) d. P. R. Hutchins 6-3 8-6 7-5; **A. Gimeno** (4) (SP) d. K. F. Weatherley 6-1 6-2 6-4; O. Parun (NZ) d. A. Van der Merwe (SA) 6-2 7-5 6-2; J. R. Cooper (A) d. J. de Mendoza 2-6 6-3 6-2 7-5; W. P. Bungert (G) d. E. Di Matteo (IT) 6-3 1-6 4-6 6-4 6-3; J. Hrebec (CZ) d. G. Vilas (ARG) 7-5 7-5 7-5; S. Baranyi (HU) d. P. Marmureanu (RU) 6-3 6-4 6-0; **J. Kodes** (5) (CZ) d. P. H. Rodriguez (CH) 1-4 6-6 6-1 6-1; G. Seewagen (USA) d. P. M. Doerner (SA) 6-2 7-9 9-8 6-4; M. Holecek (CZ) d. J. P. Meyer (F) 6-3 3-6 9-8 9-7; D. Bleckinger (USA) d. D. W. Schroder (SA) 8-6 6-2 6-3; V. Amritraj (IN) d. W. J. Austin (USA) 7-5 9-8 3-6 2-6 6-4; J. H. McManus (USA) d. P. Bertolucci (IT) 6-2 6-3 6-3; W. N'Godrella (F) d. W. L. Lloyd (A) 4-6 8-9 6-4 7-5 11-9; P. Hombergen (B) d. R. L. Bohrnstedt (USA) 5-7 6-1 5-7 6-4 6-3; C. S. Dibley (A) d. T. J. Ryan (SA) 6-3 6-4 6-3;

Gonzales (USA) d. A. Munoz (SP) 6-2 7-5 6-1; R. Tanner (USA) d. J. Velasco (COL) 6-3 2-6 6-4 7-9 7-5; A. J. McDonald (A) d. J. R. Pinto Bravo (CH) 6-4 3-6 6-3 6-0; C. J. Mottram d. J. H. Osborne (USA) 6-4 6-2 3-6 2-6 7-5; R. L. Stockton (USA) d. T. Koch (BR) 8-9 4-6 6-3 6-2 6-4; J. Gisbert (SP) d. H. Solomon (USA) 6-3 2-6 6-2 6-0; **P. Barthes** (6) (F) d. J. B. Chanfreau (F) 7-5 9-8 6-3; B. J. Phillips-Moore (A) d. J. Loyo-Mayo (M) 6-3 6-2 6-2; S. Ball (A) d. F. D. McMillan (SA) 4-6 7-5 6-3; I. Tiriac (RU) d. A. Zugarelli (IT) 6-4 6-2 5-7 7-5; B. E. Gottfried (USA) d. V. Zednik (CZ) 6-2 6-2 9-7; N. Pietrangeli (IT) d. R. Stock (USA) 6-4 6-3 6-4; I. Molina (COL) d. A. J. Pattison (RH) 3-6 6-2 4-6 6-3; R. D. Crealy (A) d. N. Spear (YU) 9-7 6-2 1-6 7-5; **M. Orantes** (3) (SP) d. G. Goven (F) 8-6 7-5 6-4; K. Meiler (G) d. J. E. Mandarino (BR) 6-2 6-1; E. J. van Dillen (USA) d. S. E. Stewart (USA) 7-5 8-6 6-1; F. Jauffret (F) d. O. Bengtson (SW) 1-6 7-5 8-9 6-1 7-5; J. W. Feaver d. C. Barazzutti (IT) 4-6 9-8 6-2 3-6 6-0; J. Kukal (CZ) d. M. Vasquez (ARG) 4-6 8-9 6-4 6-4 8-6; A. Panatta (IT) d. N. A. Fraser (A) 6-4 8-9 4-6 6-4 6-1; N. Kalogeropoulos (GR) d. S. A. Warboys 6-1 1-6 6-3 6-4; J. S. Connors (USA) d. **R. A. J. Hewitt** (7) (SA) 6-3 9-7 7-5; R. J. Moore (SA) d. R. G. Clarke (NZ) 6-2 6-1 6-0; T. W. Gorman (USA) d. B. Mignot (B) 6-4 6-2; J. Fillol (CH) d. K. G. Warwick (A) 6-0 9-7 4-6 6-3; G. Masters (A) d. A. Amritraj (IN) 8-9 8-6 4-6 6-3 12-10; J. Fassbender (G) d. L. A. Hoad (A) 4-6 7-5 7-5 6-4; P. Lall (IN) d. P. Gerken (USA) 5-7 6-3 6-2 3-6 6-3; C. E. Graebner (USA) d. J. Mukerjea (IN) 6-2 3-6 6-4 6-3; **I. Nastase** (2) (RU) d. J. D. Bartlett (A) 6-4 9-8 6-4.

SECOND ROUND: Smith (1) d. Irvine 6-4 9-8 6-3; Mayer d. Sakai 9-6 3-6 2-6 6-4; Fletcher d. Olmedo 6-0 6-4 1-6 6-3; Pala d. Kary 6-4 7-5 2-6 7-5 6-2; **Metreveli** (8) d. Dominguez 7-9 6-1 6-4 6-4; Paish d. Ulrich 6-3 7-5 6-2; Cramer d. Proisy 3-7 5-6 4; Estep d. Kamiwazumi 6-4 6-2 6-2; Parun d. **Gimeno** (4) 6-4 8-6 6-8 8-9 6-4; Bungert d. Cooper 5-7 6-4 0-6 6-2 6-3; Kakoulia d. Lloyd 9-8 4-6 6-3 6-4; Hrebec d. Baranyi 6-2 6-2 6-4; **Kodes** (5) d. Seewagen 6-0 6-1 6-2; Bleckinger d. Holecek 4-6 6-4 1-6 9-7; McManus d. Amritraj 6-1 6-2 8-6; Hombergen d. N'Godrella 5-7 8-6 6-3

6-4; Dibley d. Gonzales 6-3 6-3 8-6; Tanner d. McDonald 2-6 6-2 6-4; Stockton d. Mottram 9-8 6-1 6-4; **Barthes** (6) d. Gisbert 6-4 6-2 6-4; Phillips-Moore d. Ball 9-8-1-3-6 6-2; Tiriac d. Gottfried 6-4 9-7 9-8; Pietrangeli d. Molina 2-6 8-6 6-3 7-5; **Orantes** (3) d. Crealy 6-2 6-3 6-2; van Dillen d. Meiler 3-6 4-6 6-1 6-4 6-4; Jauffret d. Feaver 6-2 6-3 6-4; Panatta d. Kukal 9-8 8-9 6-8 9-8; Connors d. Kalogeropoulos 6-3 7-5 8-6; Gorman d. Moore 6-4 6-4 7-5; Fillol d. Masters 6-4 6-4 6-8 9-7 7-5; Fassbender d. Lall 2-6 6-4 6-3; **Nastase** (2) d. Graebner 6-3 4-6 6-1 6-2.

THIRD ROUND: Smith (1) d. Mayer 6-3 7-5 3-6 9-7; Fletcher d. Pala 6-1 6-0 6-1; **Metreveli** (8) d. Paish 7-5 6-3 3-6 6-4; Cramer d. Estep 9-8 6-4 9-7; Parun d. Bungert 6-4 4-6 9-7 9-7; Hrebec d. Kakoulia 4-6 6-3 8-6 6-1; **Kodes** (5) d. Bleckinger 6-0 6-3 6-2; McManus d. Hombergen 6-0 6-4 6-1; Dibley d. Tanner 9-8 6-4 9-8; **Barthes** (6) d. Stockton

6-3 6-3-5-7 6-4; Tiriac d. Phillips-Moore 8-6 6-1 6-2; **Orantes** (3) d. Pietrangeli 6-2 6-2 6-1; Jauffret d. van Dillen 8-6 6-1 6-4; Connors d. Panatta 6-3 0-6 6-4 8-6; Gorman d. Fillol 6-4 7-5 2-6 4-6 8-6; **Nastase** (2) d. Fassbender 9-8 6-3 6-4.

FOURTH ROUND	QUARTER-FINALS	SEMI-FINALS	FINAL	CHAMPION
Smith (1)	**Smith** (1)			
Fletcher	8-6 4-6 6-2 6-4	**Smith** (1)		
Metreveli (8)	**Metreveli** (8)	6-2 8-6 6-2		
Cramer	6-3 6-1 6-3		**Smith** (1)	
Parun	Parun		3-6 6-4 6-1 7-5	
Hrebec	8-9 6-4 6-4 ret'd	**Kodes** (5)		**Smith** (1)
Kodes (5)	**Kodes** (5)	6-2 6-3 6-4		4-6 6-3 6-3 4-6 7-5
McManus	6-2 6-4 6-4			
Dibley	Dibley			
Barthes (6)	8-9 6-3 6-2 6-1	**Orantes** (3)		
Tiriac	**Orantes** (3)	6-2 6-0 6-2		
Orantes (3)	6-4 4-6 6-3 4-6 6-3		**Nastase** (2)	
Jauffret	Connors		6-3 6-4 6-4	
Connors	6-2 6-3 8-6	**Nastase** (2)		
Gorman	**Nastase** (2)	6-4 6-4 6-1		
Nastase (2)	6-3 3-6 8-6 6-1			

PRIZE MONEY

Champion	£5,000
Runner-up	3,000
Semi-finals	1,000
Quarter-finals	550
Fourth round	300
Third round	200
Second round	125
First round	100

LADIES' SINGLES

FIRST ROUND: C. M. Evert (4) (USA) d. V. J. Ziegenfuss (USA) 1-6 6-3 6-3; J. Newberry (USA) d. Mrs K. Ebbinghaus (G) 6-3 6-1; Mrs C. W. Brasher d. Mrs C. E. Graebner (USA) 6-1 9-8; M. A. Eisel (USA) d. M. Gurdal (B) 6-2 6-4; J. Anthony (USA) d. O. de Roubin (F) 6-1 3-6 6-0; V. A. Burton d. L. J. Beaven 2-6 6-2 6-4; J. P. Cooper d. Mrs R. N. Faulkner (A) 6-0 6-3; Mrs V. Vopickova (CZ) d. T. E. O'Shaughnessy (USA) 6-1 6-2; **K. A. Melville** (5) (A) d. V. A. Berner (G) 6-2 6-2; S. Pachta (AU) d. S. Mappin (NZ) 6-3 7-5; L. A. Tuero (USA) d. J. A. Fayter 6-1 6-3; P. S. A. Hogan (USA) d. W. Appleby (USA) 6-4 8-6; L. A. Rossouw (SA) d. Mrs J. B. Chanfreau (F) 7-5 6-0; Mrs Q. C. Pretorius (SA) d. W. M. Turnbull (A) 6-0 6-3; C. E. M. Sandberg (SW) d. M. Neumannova (CZ) 6-4 6-2; **Mrs K. S. Gunter** (3) (USA) d. V. Lancaster (A) 6-2 6-1.

[Note: continues...] G. L. Coles 6-3 4-6 6-3; R. C. Giscafre (ARG) d. D. J. Riste 6-4 6-2; P. A. Teeguarden (USA) d. C. Molesworth 9-8 6-1; Mrs T. Walhof (NTH) d. Mrs W. S. Palmeova-West (CZ) 6-3 6-1; W. S. Gilchrist (A) d. K. S. Pigeon (USA) 4-6 6-4 6-3;

L. E. Hunt (A) d. B. I. Kirk (SA) 7-5 6-4; B. F. Stove (NTH) d. L. Bassi (IT) 6-3 6-0; B. Hawcroft (A) d. S. H. Minford (IRE) 6-4 6-4; E. Biriukova (USSR) d. M. E. Guzman (E) 6-4 6-1; Mrs P. M. Doerner (A) d. S. J. Hudson-Beck (RH) 6-4 3-6 6-4; **R. Casals** (6) (USA) d. L. Kaligis (INDO) 6-4 6-3; L. J. Charles d. N. Fuchs (F) 6-2 6-3; L. Liem (INDO) d. Mrs N. Schaar (NTH) 7-5 7-9 6-3; Mrs T. W. Cowie d. Mrs J. M. Carter-Triolo (USA) 6-3 6-2; K. Harris (A) d. K. K. Kemmer (USA) 8-6 3-6 7-5; H. J. Amos (A) d. Mrs J. R. Pinto Bravo (CH) 7-5 6-3; Mrs Q. C. Pretorius (SA) d. W. M. Turnbull (A) 6-0 6-3; C. E. M. Sandberg (SW) d. M. Neumannova (CZ) 6-4 6-2; **Mrs K. S. Gunter** (3) (USA) d. V. Lancaster (A) 6-2 6-1.

SECOND ROUND: E. F. Goolagong (1) (A) d. M. J. Pryde (NZ) 6-3 6-4; S. Stap (USA) d. A. Bakker (NTH) 6-0 5-7 6-1; Mrs O. Morozova (USSR) d. F. Bonicella (UR) 7-5 7-5; W. A. Overton (A) d. K. Schediwy (G) 6-1 6-4; **F. Durr** (8) (F) d. E. Emanuel (SA) 6-1 6-1; F. E. Truman d. I. Fernandez (COL) 6-2 6-4; L. Du Pont (USA) d. Mrs G. M. Williams 7-9 8-6 6-2; M. Kroshina (USSR) d. M. Schallau 4-6 6-2 6-1; **Evert** (4) d. Newberry 6-3 6-0; Eisel d. Brasher 6-2 4-6 6-3; Anthony d. Burton 7-5 2-6 6-2; Cooper d. Vopickova 6-3 6-2; **Melville** (5) d. Pachta 6-0 9-7; Hogan d. Tuero 6-1 6-4; Rossouw d. Pattison 4-6 6-3 7-5; Teeguarden d. Giscafre 6-0 1-0 ret'd; Walhof d. Gilchrist 6-3 6-4; Stove d.

Hunt 5-7 7-5 6-2; Hawcroft d. Biriukova 6-3 2-6 6-4; **Casals** (6) d. Doerner 6-2 6-8 6-0; Liem d. Charles 7-5 4-6 7-5; Harris d. Cowie 8-6 6-2; Pretorius d. Amos 6-1 6-2; **Gunter** (3) d. Sandberg 5-7 6-1 6-2; Mrs D. E. Dalton (A) d. K. Sawamatsu (J) 6-3 7-9 9-7; H. F. Gourlay (A) d. K. Blake (USA) 7-5 6-4; Mrs J. A. Bentzer (SW) d. P. G. A. Coleman (A) 6-3 6-3; **S. V. Wade** (7) d. K. M. Krantzcke (A) 6-8 6-2 6-3; W. M. Shaw d. Mrs H. Masthoff (G) 6-3 6-2; M. Louie (USA) d. J. M. Heldman (USA) 7-5 4-6 10-8; C. A. Martinez (USA) d. N. J. Ornstein (USA) 7-5 6-3; **Mrs L. W. King** (2) (USA) d. S. A. Walsh (USA) 6-2 6-0.

THIRD ROUND: Goolagong (1) d. Stap 6-2 6-0; Morozova d. Overton 6-4 6-1; **Durr** (8) d. Truman 6-0 6-1; Du Pont d. Kroshina 9-8 6-4; **Evert** (4) d. Eisel 8-6 8-6; Anthony d. Cooper 6-1 6-2; Hogan d. **Melville** (5) 6-4 6-4; Teeguarden d. Rossouw 6-2 6-2; Stove d. Walhof 6-2 9-8; **Casals** (6) d. Hawcroft 6-0 6-1; Harris d. Liem 3-6 6-2

6-2; **Gunter** (3) d. Pretorius 6-2 4-6 6-2; Gourlay d. Dalton 7-5 6-2; **Wade** (7) d. Bentzer 6-1 6-1; Shaw d. Louie 6-2 6-2; **King** (2) d. Martinez 6-1 6-3.

FOURTH ROUND	QUARTER-FINALS	SEMI-FINALS	FINAL	CHAMPION
Goolagong (1)	**Goolagong** (1)			
Morozova	3-6 6-0 9-7	**Goolagong** (1)		
Durr (8)	**Durr** (8)	8-6 7-5		
Du Pont	6-1 6-2		**Goolagong** (1)	
Evert (4)	**Evert** (4)		4-6 6-3 6-4	
Anthony	6-3 6-2	**Evert** (4)		
Hogan	Hogan	6-2 4-6 6-1		**King** (2)
Teeguarden	6-3 6-4			6-3 6-3
Stove	**Casals** (6)			
Casals (6)	6-3 6-2	**Casals** (6)		
Harris	**Gunter** (3)	3-6 6-4 6-0		
Gunter (3)	6-3 7-5		**King** (2)	
Gourlay	**Wade** (7)		6-2 6-4	
Wade (7)	6-3 6-2	**King** (2)		
Shaw	**King** (2)	6-1 3-6 6-3		
King (2)	6-4 6-2			

PRIZE MONEY

Champion	£2,400
Runner-up	1,330
Semi-finals	600
Quarter-finals	350
Fourth round	200
Third round	150
Second round	100
First round	75

OTHER FINALS

GENTLEMEN'S DOUBLES: Final — R. A. J. Hewitt (SA)/F. D. McMillan (SA) d. S. R. Smith (USA)/E. J. van Dillen (USA) 6-2 6-2 9-7.
LADIES' DOUBLES: Final — Mrs L. W. King (USA)/B. F. Stove (NTH) d. Mrs D. E. Dalton (A)/F. Durr (F) 6-2 4-6 6-3.
MIXED DOUBLES: Final — I. Nastase (RU)/R. Casals (USA) d. K. Warwick (A)/E. F. Goolagong (A) 6-4 6-4.
GENTLEMEN'S SINGLES PLATE: Final — K. G. Warwick (A) d. I. Molina (COL) w.o.

LADIES' SINGLES PLATE: Final — K. M. Krantzcke (A) d. S. A. Walsh (USA) 6-4 6-1.
BOYS' INVITATION SINGLES: Final — B. Borg (SW) d. C. J. Mottram 6-3 4-6 7-5.
GIRLS' INVITATION SINGLES: Final — I. Kloss (SA) d. G. L. Coles 6-4 4-6 6-4.
VETERANS' MEN'S DOUBLES: Final — L. S. Clark (USA)/E. V. Seixas (USA) d. G. Mulloy (USA)/A. Vincent (USA) 6-3 9-8.

271

1973

GENTLEMEN'S SINGLES

FIRST ROUND: I. Nastase (1) (RU) d. H. J. Plotz (G) 6-3 7-5 6-2; I. Molina (COL) d. W. L. Brown (USA) 6-4 9-7 8-9 6-3; H. Kary (AU) d. P. Siviter 6-4 7-9 6-1 6-2; T. Sakai (J) d. K. McMillan (USA) 6-1 3-6 9-8 6-4; R. Chavez (M) d. I. Santeiu (RU) 5-7 4-6 6-4 7-5 7-5; A. Mayer (USA) d. R. A. Lewis 7-5 6-4 6-3; C. Iles d. S. G. Messmer (USA) 7-5 6-2 6-4; V. Zednik (CZ) d. G. Misra (IN) 6-4 6-4 6-1; **J. Fassbender** (8) (G) d. I. Gulyas (HU) 8-6 6-8 6-3 6-3; J. Moreno (SP) d. M. W. Collins 6-4 6-3 6-3; R. F. Keldie (A) d. R. L. Bohrnstedt (USA) 7-5 6-3 4-6 6-3; T. Svensson (SW) d. F. Gebert (G) 6-8 9-8 7-5 9-7; J. G. Simpson (NZ) d. N. Pietrangeli (IT) 8-6 2-6 7-5 3-6 7-5; J. Hagey (USA) d. N. A. Fraser (A) 6-4 7-5 8-6; M. Lara (M) d. J. G. Paish 5-7 6-4 7-5 6-2; H. J. Pohmann (G) d. C. E. McHugo 6-3 6-4 6-4; **A. Metreveli** (4) (USSR) d. S. J. Matthews 6-3 6-4 9-8; R. G. Giltinan (A) d. R. Machan (HU) 6-4 6-3; A. J. McDonald (A) d. G. Braun (A) d. J. R. Cooper (A) d. H. S. FitzGibbon (USA) 6-3 8-9 6-4 9-7; F. P. Walthall (USA) d. T. Nowicki (POL) 4-6 3-6 6-8 6-3 6-2; C. Mukerjea (IN) d. H. Engert (G) 6-4 7-5 8-9 6-4; J. W. Feaver d. E. L. Scott (USA) 8-9 6-3 6-8 6-4 6-4; C. L. Letcher (A) d. R. H. Stock (USA) 5-7 6-4 6-3 6-1; **J. S. Connors** (5) (USA) d. M. J. Farrell 6-4 6-3 6-4; D. A. Lloyd d. C. Barazzutti (IT) 6-2 0-6 6-1 6-1; W. R. Durham (A) d. S. Likhachev (USSR) 6-3 6-4 3-6 6-4; R. J. Simpson (USA) d. T. B. Karp (USA) 6-4 8-6 6-3; J. R. Pinto Bravo (CH) d. J. G. Clifton 6-4 3-6 2-6 6-4 6-3; D. Joubert (SA) d. C. Dowdeswell (RH) 6-3 4-6 6-4 7-5; B. Mitton (SA) d. T. Bernasconi (F) 8-6 6-1 6-3; Z. Guerry (USA) d. J.

Hordijk (NTH) 9-7 6-2 6-2; S. Ball (A) d. B. Jovanovic (YU) 7-5 8-6 6-3; S. Baranyi (HU) d. J. L. Rouyer (F) 6-0 6-2 6-2; P. Kanderal (SWZ) d. K. Tanabe (J) 6-4 6-3 6-4; W. J. Austin (USA) d. T. Kakulia (USSR) 3-6 4-6 6-3 6-0 6-4; K. Meiler (G) d. G. Peebles (USA) 9-7 6-4 6-2; B. Martin (USA) d. J. Singh (IN) 6-3 9-7 2-6 6-3; P. Hombergen (B) d. S. E. Myers (A) 6-3 6-3 6-1; **B. Borg** (6) (SW) d. P. Lall (IN) 6-3 6-4 9-8; F. Pala (CZ) d. D. J. Bleckinger (USA) 6-3 1-6 6-3 7-5; N. Holmes (USA) d. D. T. Crawford (USA) 6-4 6-2 6-4; R. E. McKinley (USA) d. P. F. McNamee (A) 6-4 6-1 6-0; J. Kuki (J) d. E. Russo (A) 1-6 6-2 8-9 6-4 9-7; J. Hrebec (CZ) d. F. A. Sedgman (A) 6-0 6-4 7-5; A. Zugarelli (IT) d. D. Stojovic (YU) 6-1 W. Elschenbroich (G) d. J. W. James (A) 5-7 6-2 3-6 8-6 6-2; **R. Taylor** (3) d. J. L. Haillet (F) 6-2 6-3 6-3; J. M. Lloyd d. J. F. Caujolle (F) 8-9 4-6 6-3 6-3; K. N. Hancock (A) d. P. C. Kronk (A) 5-7 7-5 6-4 3-6 6-4; B. Mignot (B) d. P. Pokorny (AU) 6-1 6-1 6-3; V. Amritraj (IN) d. H. W. Turnbull (A) 6-4 6-2 6-4; E. W. Ewert (A) d. K. Pugaev (USSR) 3-6 6-1 7-5 6-8 6-4; W. Machette (USA) d. D. A. Parun (NZ) 6-4 6-2 6-4; B. J. Phillips-Moore d. R. W. Drysdale 6-3 9-7 7-5; **O. K. Davidson** (7) (A) d. P. Joly (F) 6-4 6-4 6-4; A. Amritraj (IN) d. S. S. Meer (POL) 6-4 6-4 9-8; J. Mukerjea (IN) d. E. A. Zuleta (E) 7-5 6-1 6-3; R. A. Buwalda (SA) d. M. Iqbal (P) 5-7 6-3 6-2 6-4; G. W. Perkins (A) d. J. Kamiwazumi (J) 6-4 3-6 9-7; J. Yuill (SA) d. S. A. Warboys 2-4 6-9 7-4 6-4; P. W. Curtis d. G. S. Thomson (A) 6-4 6-4 6-2; P. Marzano (IT) d. R. Ramirez (M) 6-3 6-4 2-6 6-2; **J. Kodes** (2) (CZ) d. K. Hirai (J) 4-6 6-4 6-1 6-3.

SECOND ROUND: Nastase (1) d. Molina 6-2 7-9 7-5 6-1; Sakai d. Kary 6-1 6-3 3-6 6-3; Mayer d. Chavez 7-9 6-1 9-7 6-2; Zednik d. Iles 6-3 6-3 4-6 6-2; **Fassbender** (8) d. Moreno 6-3 6-4 6-4; Keldie d. Svensson 6-4 8-9 6-0 6-4; Simpson d. Hagey 8-6 6-4 8-9 6-3; Pohmann d. Lara 2-6 7-5 2-6 6-1 7-5; **Metreveli** (4) d. Giltinan 6-4 6-2 6-2; Cooper d. McDonald 6-4 4-6 4-6 7-5 9-7; Walthall d. Mukerjea 3-6 6-1 6-1 9-8; Feaver d. Letcher 9-8 6-4 9-8; **Connors** (5) d. Lloyd 6-4 6-3 5-7 6-2; Simpson d. Durham 9-8 7-9 7-5 3-6 6-2; Joubert d. Pinto Bravo 2-6 4-6 6-2 6-2 2-6 6-3; Mitton d. Guerry 7-5 2-6 4-6 7-5 6-3; Baranyi d. Ball 1-0 ret'd; Austin d. Kanderal 9-8 6-3 6-3; Meiler d. Martin

6-1 6-4 9-8; **Borg** (6) d. Hombergen 6-4 6-2 6-4; Holmes d. Pala 8-6 2-6 6-0 1-6 7-5; McKinley d. Kuki 6-4 3-6 6-2 6-2; Hrebec d. Zugarelli 7-5 1-6 4-6 7-5 6-2; **Taylor** (3) d. Elschenbroich 6-3 6-2 6-2; Lloyd d. Hancock 7-5 6-4 6-4; Amritraj d. Mignot 6-1 6-4 6-2; Ewert d. Machette 7-5 6-2 6-3; **Davidson** (7) d. Phillips-Moore 6-3 6-4 6-3; Mukerjea d. Amritraj 3-6 6-3 6-2 6-4; Perkins d. Buwalda 4-6 6-3 3-6 6-1 10-8; Yuill d. Curtis 4-6 6-3 1-6 6-2 6-3; **Kodes** (2) d. Marzano 6-0 6-4 6-3.

THIRD ROUND: Nastase (1) d. Sakai 7-5 6-2 6-4; Mayer d. Zednik 8-6 7-5 6-0; **Fassbender** (8) d. Keldie 6-2 5-7 4-6 7-5 15-13; Pohmann d. Simpson 4-6 7-5 6-3 6-4; **Metreveli** (4) d. Cooper 6-2 6-3 6-1; Feaver d. Walthall 7-5 6-1 9-8; **Connors** (5) d. Simpson 6-2 6-1 6-2; Mitton d. Joubert 4-6 8-9 6-4 6-1 9-7; Baranyi d. Austin 2-6 5-7 6-3 6-4

6-4; **Borg** (6) d. Meiler 6-4 6-4 3-6 2-6 6-3; McKinley d. Holmes 6-2 3-6 7-5 7-5; **Taylor** (3) d. Hrebec 6-1 5-7 6-4 6-2; Amritraj d. Lloyd 7-5 6-4 3-6 2-6 7-5; **Davidson** (7) d. Ewert 6-1 6-4 3-6 6-3; Mukerjea d. Perkins 9-8 6-4 6-3; **Kodes** (2) d. Yuill 6-1 7-5 6-2.

FOURTH ROUND	QUARTER-FINALS	SEMI-FINALS	FINAL	CHAMPION	PRIZE MONEY	
Nastase (1)	Mayer				Champion	£5,000
Mayer	6-4 8-6 6-8 6-4	Mayer			Runner-up	3,000
Fassbender (8)	**Fassbender** (8)	3-6 4-6 6-3 6-4 6-4			Semi-finals	1,000
Pohmann	6-2 7-5 6-3				Quarter-finals	550
Metreveli (4)	**Metreveli** (4)		**Metreveli** (4)		Fourth round	300
Feaver	8-6 6-4 6-1	**Metreveli** (4)	6-3 3-6 6-3 6-4		Third round	200
Connors (5)	**Connors** (5)	8-6 6-2 5-7 6-4			Second round	125
Mitton	6-3 6-3 6-2				First round	100
Baranyi	**Borg** (6)			**Kodes** (2)		
Borg (6)	6-3 6-2 6-8 5-7 6-1			6-1 9-8 6-3		
McKinley	**Taylor** (3)	**Taylor** (3)				
Taylor (3)	6-1 7-5 6-8 7-5	6-1 6-8 3-6 6-3 7-5				
Amritraj	**Davidson** (7)		**Kodes** (2)			
Davidson (7)	7-5 8-9 6-3 6-4	**Kodes** (2)	8-9 6-7 5-7 6-4 7-5			
Mukerjea	**Kodes** (2)	6-4 3-6 4-6 6-3 7-5				
Kodes (2)	6-4 3-6 6-4 6-3					

LADIES' SINGLES

FIRST ROUND: C. M. Evert (4) (USA) d. F. Bonicelli (UR) 6-3 6-3; Mrs J. Gohn (RU) d. R. Tomanova (CZ) 6-4 6-0; J. M. Heldman (USA) d. Mrs K. Wooldridge 6-1 8-6; Mrs N. Schaar (NTH) d. M. Neumannova (CZ) 6-3 6-3; S. Barker d. Mrs R. M. Sugiarto-Liem (INDO) 6-0 6-4; L. D. Blachford d. Mrs C. W. Brasher 6-0 2-6 6-2; M. Redondo (USA) d. Mrs K. Ebbinghaus (G) 6-1 2-6 6-2; J. A. Young (A) d. V. A. Burton 6-4 7-5; **R. Casals** (5) (USA) d. B. I. Kirk (SA) 6-0 6-1; S. Mappin d. L. A. Rossouw (SA) 6-4 6-2; T. A. Fretz (USA) d. L. J. Mottram 6-1 6-3; V. A. Berner (C) d. M. Simionescu (RU) 6-4 6-2; V. J. Ziegenfuss (USA) d. M. Gurdal (B) 6-2 8-9 6-3; L. Fleming (USA) d. L. M. Tenney (USA) 6-0 8-6; K. K. Kemmer (USA) d. H. F. Gourlay (A) 6-1 6-3; L. Boshoff (SA) d. J. Anthony (USA) 9-8 6-4; F. Durr (F) d. C. S. Colman

6-3 6-0; Mrs V. Vopickova (CZ) d. C. Molesworth 6-3 1-6 8-6; M. Kroshina (USSR) d. J. Dixon (USA) 6-3 6-4; M. B. K. Wikstedt (SW) d. A. M. Coe 6-0 8-9 9-7; K. Sawamatsu (J) d. S. Pachta (AU) 6-2 6-2; P. A. Teeguarden (USA) d. O. de Roubin (F) 6-4 6-2; P. L. Bostrom (USA) d. K. S. Pigeon (USA) 6-3 7-5; **S. V. Wade** (6) d. D. L. Fromholtz (A) 3-6 6-2 6-1; N. Fuchs (F) d. L. A. Tuero (USA) 1-6 6-3 6-2; P. S. A. Hogan (USA) d. Mrs P. M. Doerner (A) 7-9 6-4 6-4; M. Navratilova (CZ) d. Mrs G. T. Janes 6-1 6-4; L. Du Pont (USA) d. H. Goto (J) 6-2 6-2; I. Fernandez (COL) d. S. A. Walsh (USA) 7-9 6-2 6-4; W. M. Turnbull (A) d. J. L. Tindle (C) 4-6 6-1 6-4; J. P. Cooper d. B. A. Downs (USA) 6-0 6-4; **E. F. Goolagong** (3) (A) d. B. F. Stove (NTH) 6-3 6-3.

SECOND ROUND: Mrs B. M. Court (1) d. K. M. Krantzcke (A) 6-2 6-3; K. Latham (USA) d. M. J. Pryde (NZ) 6-1 6-1; G. L. Coles d. J. A. Fayter 6-3 6-3; P. J. Moor d. L. Kaligis (INDO) 8-9 6-2 6-3; **Mrs O. Morozova** (8) (USSR) d. P. G. A. Coleman (A) 7-5 6-2; Mrs J. S. Williams d. R. C. Giscafre (ARG) 6-4 9-8; J. S. Newberry (USA) d. Mrs C. G. Walhof (NTH) 9-7 6-1; Mrs J. A. Bentzer (SW) d. J. Charles 6-4 6-2; **Evert** (4) d. Gohn 6-0 6-1; Heldman d. Schaar 6-2 6-1; Blachford d. Barker 3-6 6-4 6-3; Young d. Redondo 6-3 6-1; **Casals** (5) d. Mappin 6-3 6-4; Fretz d. Berner 6-4 6-3; Ziegenfuss d. Fleming 6-4 2-6 6-3; Kemmer d. Boshoff 7-5 6-4; Durr d. Vopickova 6-2 6-1; Kroshina

d. Wikstedt 3-6 6-0 6-2; Teeguarden d. Sawamatsu 5-7 7-5 7-5; **Wade** (6) d. Bostrom 7-5 6-2; Hogan d. Fuchs 6-3 6-2; Navratilova d. Du Pont 8-6 6-4; Turnbull d. Fernandez 6-3 6-2; **Goolagong** (3) d. Cooper 6-3 6-1; C. E. M. Sandberg (SW) d. L. J. Beaven 6-2 4-6 7-5; M. Michel (USA) d. S. Stap 6-4 6-4; Mrs Q. C. Pretorius (SA) d. W. A. Overton (USA) 6-2 5-7 6-2; **K. A. Melville** (7) (A) d. I. S. Kloss (SA) 6-1 6-4; L. E. Hunt (A) d. Mrs J. G. Paish (A) 6-3 6-2; M. Schallau d. A. K. Kiyomura (USA) 1-6 6-2 6-4; K. Harris (A) d. V. Ruzici (RU) 6-1 6-3; **Mrs L. W. King** (2) (USA) d. L. Bassi (IT) 6-0 6-2.

THIRD ROUND: Court (1) d. Latham 6-2 6-3; Coles d. Moor 6-2 6-1; **Morozova** (8) d. Williams 7-5 6-3; Bentzer d. Newberry 6-1 4-6 6-3; **Evert** (4) d. Heldman 6-3 6-1; Young d. Blachford 7-5 4-6 6-0; **Casals** (5) d. Fretz 7-5 7-5; Kemmer d. Ziegenfuss 8-9 6-4 6-3; Durr d. Kroshina 6-4 2-6 6-0; **Wade** (6) d. Teeguarden 6-2 6-3; Hogan d.

Navratilova 6-4 6-4; **Goolagong** (3) d. Turnbull 6-4 6-1; Michel d. Sandberg 6-1 6-0; **Melville** (7) d. Pretorius 6-1 6-1; Hunt d. Schallau 6-2 6-3; **King** (2) d. Harris 6-2 6-3.

FOURTH ROUND	QUARTER-FINALS	SEMI-FINALS	FINAL	CHAMPION	PRIZE MONEY	
Court (1)	**Court** (1)				Champion	£3,000
Coles	6-1 6-4	**Court** (1)			Runner-up	2,000
Morozova (8)	**Morozova** (8)	4-6 6-4 6-1			Semi-finals	700
Bentzer	7-5 6-1				Quarter-finals	400
Evert (4)	**Evert** (4)		**Evert** (4)		Fourth round	250
Young	6-3 3-6 8-6	**Evert** (4)	6-1 1-6 6-1		Third round	150
Casals (5)	**Casals** (5)	6-2 4-6 6-2			Second round	100
Kemmer	6-3 6-3				First round	70
Durr	**Wade** (6)			**King** (2)		
Wade (6)	4-6 6-3 7-5			6-0 7-5		
Hogan	**Goolagong** (3)	**Goolagong** (3)				
Goolagong (3)	6-0 6-1	6-3 6-3				
Michel	**Melville** (7)		**King** (2)			
Melville (7)	6-2 3-6 6-4	**King** (2)	6-3 5-7 6-3			
Hunt	**King** (2)	9-8 8-6				
King (2)	6-4 5-7 6-0					

OTHER FINALS

GENTLEMEN'S DOUBLES: Final — J. S. Connors (USA)/I. Nastase (RU) d. J. R. Cooper (A)/N. A. Fraser (A) 3-6 6-3 6-4 8-9 6-1.
LADIES' DOUBLES: Final — R. Casals (USA)/Mrs L. W. King (USA) d. F. Durr (F)/B. F. Stove (NTH) 6-1 4-6 7-5.
MIXED DOUBLES: Final — O. K. Davidson (A)/Mrs L. W. King (USA) d. R. Ramirez (M)/J. S. Newberry (USA) 6-3 6-2.
GENTLEMEN'S SINGLES PLATE: Final — J. G. Clifton d. S. G. Messmer (USA) 6-4 4-6 6-1.

LADIES' SINGLES PLATE: Final — H. F. Gourlay (A) d. V. A. Burton 6-1 4-6 6-1.
BOYS' INVITATION SINGLES: Final — W. Martin (USA) d. C. Dowdeswell (RH) 6-2 6-4.
GIRLS' INVITATION SINGLES: Final — A. Kiyomura (USA) d. M. Navratilova (CZ) 6-4 7-5.
VETERANS' MEN'S DOUBLES: Final — J. D. Budge (USA)/F. A. Sedgman (A) d. L. Bergelin (SW)/J. Drobny 4-6 6-3 6-4.

GENTLEMEN'S SINGLES

1974

FIRST ROUND: J. D. Newcombe (1) (A) d. G. Goven (F) 6-3 6-2 8-6; G. Masters (A) d. B. Mitton (SA) 6-4 6-3 7-5; N. Pilic (YU) d. M. Estep (USA) 4-6 3-6 6-4 6-2; E. Dibbs (USA) d. H. J. Plotz (G) 2-6 6-1 6-4 6-2; G. Vilas (ARG) d. V. Zednik (CZ) 6-2 9-8 6-4; M. C. Riessen (USA) d. T. Nowicki (POL) 6-4 7-5 7-5; H. Elschenbroich (G) d. J. E. Mandarino (BR) 7-5 6-2 6-1; E. J. van Dillen (USA) d. J. Singh (IN) 7-9 6-3 4-6 7-5 6-3; **A. R. Ashe** (8) (USA) d. H. Kary (AU) 6-4 6-2 6-4; T. I. Kakulia (USSR) d. W. W. Martin (USA) 8-6 6-1 5-7 6-4; R. Tanner (USA) d. R. P. Dell (USA) 6-4 6-3 6-4; K. Meiler (G) d. V. Gerulaitis (USA) 6-8 6-4 6-2 6-1; **K. R. Rosewall** (9) (A) d. B. J. Phillips-Moore (A) 6-4 6-3 6-3; V. Amritraj (IN) d. R. C. Lutz (USA) 7-5 6-4 8-6; R. G. Giltinan (A) d. W. N'Godrella (F) 6-3 3-6 6-4 6-2; P. Kanderal (SWZ) d. M. Lara (M) 4-6 8-6 6-2 ret'd; **S. R. Smith** (4) (USA) d. G. E. Reid (A) 6-3 6-3 6-2; R. R. Maud (SA) d. B. Taroczy (HU) 4-6 4-6 9-8 6-4 6-1; N. A. Fraser (A) d. D. A. Lloyd 4-6 8-9 7-5 6-4 11-9; J. Borowiak (USA) d. U. Pinner (G) 6-3 6-3 9-8; P. Dominquez (F) d. I. Tiriac (RU) 6-3 6-0 8-6; R. Ramirez (M) d. P. Cornejo (CH) 9-7 8-9 6-4 5-7 6-3; J. B. Chanfreau (F) d. G. Seewagen (USA) 9-8 5-7 9-8 1-6 9-7; D. E. Deblicker (F) d. H. Rahim (P) w.o.; **B. Borg** (5) (SW) d. G. R. Stilwell 6-1 4-6 6-4 6-1; R. L. Case (A) d. J. G. Simpson (NZ) 6-3 9-8 6-3; J. Fassbender (G) d. M. Cox 6-2 6-4 7-9 7-5; I. El Shafei (E) d. O. Parun (NZ) 6-1 4-6 8-9 7-5 9-7; **M. Orantes** (12) (SP) d. H. Solomon (USA) 6-3 6-2 6-1; T. Koch (BR) d. J. F. Caujolle (F) 6-4 1-6 4-6 6-4 8-6; A. D. Roche (A) d. O. K. Davidson (A) 6-2 6-4 7-5; J. G. Alexander (A) d. P. Szoke (HU) 6-2 7-5 8-6; A. A. Mayer (USA) d. F. D. McMillan (SA) 3-6 9-7 5-7 6-2 6-4; R. Thung (NTH) d. R. Seegers (SA) 6-1 6-4 6-4; J. M. Yuill (SA) d. R. R. Dowdeswell (RH) 6-3 6-2 4-6 3-6 6-3; **T. W. Gorman** (11) (USA) d. A. Amritraj (IN) 6-4 7-5 3-6 4-6 8-6; R. D. Crealy (A) d. R. Taylor 4-6 9-8 6-3 9-8; R. A. J. Hewitt (SA) d. J. R. Pinto Bravo (CH) 6-4 6-1 2-6 6-3; L. Johansson (SW) d. J. M. Lloyd 6-3 6-3 6-2; **J. Kodes** (6) (CZ) d. S. E. Stewart (USA) 6-3 6-4 9-7; J. Higueras (SP) d. A. Zugarelli (IT) 4-6 6-2 6-3 4-6 6-1; K. G. Warwick (A) d. A. C. Neely (USA) 9-8 7-5 6-1; J. Fillol (CH) d. F. Pala (CZ) 6-4 6-1 6-4; J. R. Ganzabal (ARG) d. J. I. Muntanola (SP) 9-7 9-8 6-0; A. Panatta (IT) d. H. J. Pohmann (G) 4-6 6-2 6-3 6-3; P. Proisy (F) d. P. C. Kronk (A) 6-3 6-4 6-4; P. C. Dent (A) d. C. S. Dibley (A) 4-6 4-6 9-8 6-4 11-9; **J. S. Connors** (3) (USA) d. O. Bengtson (SW) 6-1 7-9 6-2 6-4; A. J. Pattison (RH) d. J. G. Paish 6-2 6-3 6-8 6-3; K. Johansson (SW) d. P. R. Gerken (USA) 7-9 3-6 6-2 6-1 14-12; S. Krulevitz (USA) d. R. I. Kreiss (USA) 6-3 3-6 7-5 4-6 6-4; **A. Metreveli** (10) (USSR) d. J. W. Feaver 6-2 6-3 3-6 6-1; W. J. Austin (USA) d. M. J. Farrell 5-7 6-3 6-2 6-0; E. C. Drysdale (SA) d. I. Molina (COL) 6-0 6-3 6-3; S. Baranyi (HU) d. P. Barthes (F) 6-2 6-2 6-0 6-3; **T. S. Okker** (7) (NTH) d. R. D. Ralston (USA) 6-1 6-3 4-6 6-3; G. Battrick d. T. Svensson (SW) 9-8 6-4 6-2; R. L. Stockton (USA) d. T. Sakai (J) 6-4 6-3 6-2; C. M. Pasarell (USA) d. C. E. Graebner (USA) 6-3 0-6 6-3 4-6 6-3; C. J. Mottram (USA) d. S. Ball (A) 6-4 6-3 7-9 6-3; I. G. Fletcher (A) d. S. A. Warboys 7-5 3-6 6-3 6-3; F. Jauffret (F) d. M. Holecek (Stateless) 1-6 4-6 4-6 8-6 6-4; B. E. Gottfried (USA) d. R. J. Moore (SA) 6-3 4-6 7-5 2-6 10-8; **I. Nastase** (2) (RU) d. J. Hrebec (CZ) 8-9 6-3 6-4 6-2.

SECOND ROUND: Newcombe (1) d. Masters 9-8 6-3 8-6; Pilic d. Dibbs 6-4 8-6 6-4; Vilas d. Riessen 7-9 6-1 6-4 3-6 6-1; van Dillen d. Elschenbroich 6-4 7-5 6-4; **Ashe** (8) d. Kakulia 6-1 6-4 6-3; Tanner d. Meiler 8-6 6-4 8-6; **Rosewall** (9) d. Amritraj 6-2 5-7 9-8 6-1; Kanderal d. Giltinan 7-5 9-8 7-5; **Smith** (4) d. Maud 6-1 6-2 6-7; Borowiak d. Fraser 8-9 6-3 8-6 1-0 ret'd; Dominguez d. Ramirez 3-6 6-3 7-5 6-3; Chanfreau d. Deblicker 2-6 7-5 6-3 9-8; **Borg** (5) d. Case 3-6 6-1 8-6 9-7; El Shafei d. Fassbender 7-5 8-6 6-4; **Orantes** (12) d. Koch 6-4 7-5 6-2; Roche d. Alexander 8-6 6-4 4-6 8-9 6-3; Thung d. Mayer 9-7 6-2 6-3; **Gorman** (11) d. Yuill 6-3 7-9 8-6 6-3; Crealy d. Hewitt 2-6 0-6 6-4 6-4 6-4; **Kodes** (6) d. Johansson 3-6 7-5 6-3 4-6 6-4; Warwick d. Higueras 6-3 6-0 8-6; Fillol d. Ganzabal 6-2 6-3 6-4; **Metreveli** (10) d. Krulevitz 6-1 1-6 6-3 6-4; Drysdale d. Austin 0-6 6-2 6-4 6-3; **Okker** (7) d. Baranyi 6-2 6-2 6-4; Stockton d. Battrick 3-6 6-3 6-4 4-6 6-4; Mottram d. Pasarell 6-2 9-8 9-7; Fletcher d. Jauffret 6-3 6-4 9-7; **Nastase** (2) d. Gottfried 3-6 6-2 9-8.

THIRD ROUND: Newcombe (1) d. Pilic 6-2 7-5 7-5; van Dillen d. Vilas 6-3 6-4 1-6 7-5; Tanner d. **Ashe** (8) 7-5 6-3 8-9 6-3; **Rosewall** (9) d. Kanderal 6-2 6-3 6-3; **Smith** (4) d. Borowiak 8-9 6-3 6-4 8-6; Dominguez d. Chanfreau 7-5 6-1 6-4; El Shafei d. **Borg** (5) 6-2 6-3 6-1; **Orantes** (12) d. Roche 2-6 5-7 7-5 6-4 8-6; **Gorman** (11) d. Thung 8-6 6-1 6-1; **Kodes** (6) d. Crealy 4-6 6-4 6-3 2-6 7-5; Fillol d. Warwick 6-3 4-6 6-1 6-4; **Connors** (3) d. Panatta 6-2 7-5 6-2; **Metreveli** (10) d. Pattison 3-6 6-4 7-5 4-6 6-3; **Okker** (7) d. Drysdale 4-6 6-3 6-3; Stockton d. Mottram w.o.; **Nastase** (2) d. Fletcher 7-5 6-3 6-4.

FOURTH ROUND	QUARTER-FINALS	SEMI-FINALS	FINAL	CHAMPION
Newcombe (1)	**Newcombe** (1)			
van Dillen	7-5 6-3 6-4	**Rosewall** (9)		
Tanner	**Rosewall** (9)	6-1 1-6 6-0 7-5		
Rosewall (9)	2-6 9-7 6-3 7-5		**Rosewall** (9)	
Smith (4)	**Smith** (4)		6-8 4-6 9-8 6-1 6-3	
Dominguez	6-3 6-4 7-5	**Smith** (4)		
El Shafei	El Shafei	9-8 7-5 6-8 7-5		
Orantes (12)	6-4 3-6 6-3 7-5			**Connors** (3)
Gorman (11)	**Kodes** (6)			6-1 6-1 6-4
Kodes (6)	6-8 2-6 6-3 9-7 6-4			
Fillol	**Connors** (3)	**Connors** (3)		
Connors (3)	6-3 5-7 6-0 6-1	3-6 6-3 6-3 6-8 6-3		
Metreveli (10)	**Metreveli** (10)		**Connors** (3)	
Okker (7)	9-8 3-6 6-4 6-2		4-6 6-2 6-3 6-4	
Stockton	Stockton	Stockton		
Nastase (2)	5-7 6-4 6-3 9-8	6-4 7-5 6-1		

PRIZE MONEY

Champion	£10,000
Runner-up	6,000
Semi-finals	2,000
Quarter-finals	1,000
Fourth round	600
Third round	300
Second round	200
First round	150

LADIES' SINGLES

FIRST ROUND: R. Casals (4) (USA) d. P. J. Moor 6-2 6-1; P. A. Teeguarden (USA) d. H. Anliot (SW) 8-6 6-2; S. Mappin d. C. E. M. Sandberg (SW) 9-8 6-1; M. Jausovec (YU) d. M. Navratilova (CZ) 4-3 6-3 6-3; M. Gurdal (B) d. Mrs V. Vopickova (CZ) w.o.; L. Boshoff (SA) d. S. Barker 6-0 9-7; H. F. Gourlay (A) d. M. Michel (USA) 6-4 6-1; R. Tomanova (CZ) d. L. D. Blachford 6-2 3-6 6-3; **S. V. Wade** (5) d. V. A. Burton 6-0 6-0; J. Anthony (USA) d. O. de Roubin (F) 6-3 6-3; B. Nagelsen (USA) d. L. M. Tenney (USA) 6-1 8-9 6-4; Mrs J. B. Chanfreau (F) d. B. M. Araujo (ARG) 6-1 6-0; A. K. Kiyomura (USA) d. J. A. Fayter 6-0 9-8; M. V. Kroschina (USSR) d. L. Fromholtz (A) 6-4 6-1; P. S. A. Hogan (USA) d. W. A. Overton (USA) 8-6 8-6; B. Cuypers (SA) d. C. S. Colman 6-1 6-2; G. R. Stevens (SA) d. S. A. Stap (USA) 1-6 6-1 6-1; M. B. Wikstedt (SW) d. E. Appel (NTH) 6-3 4-6 6-4; T. A. Fretz (USA) d. Mrs J. Gohn (RU) 2-6 6-1 6-2; W. M. Turnbull (A) d. B. A. Downs (USA) 6-2 6-2; J. M. Heldman (USA) d. L. J. Fleming (USA) 6-3 6-0; K. Sawamatsu (J) d. P. L. Bostrom (USA) 6-2 6-2; R. J. Tenney (USA) d. C. Molesworth 6-2 6-3; **K. A. Melville** (6) d. B. F. Stove (NTH) 4-6 6-4 6-4; K. K. Kemmer (USA) d. L. J. Mottram 6-0 6-3; S. A. Walsh (USA) d. J. C. Evert 8-6 6-4; F. Bonicelli (UR) d. M. Neumannova (CZ) 6-3 6-4; K. D. Latham (USA) d. S. Greer (USA) 6-1 9-8; P. Peisachov (IS) d. C. Meyer (USA) 6-4 6-3; K. Harris (A) d. L. J. Beaven 6-2 6-3; I. S. Kloss (SA) d. L. Kaligis (INDO) 6-1 6-2; **E. F. Goolagong** (3) (A) d. Mrs N. Schaar (NTH) 6-1 6-1.

SECOND ROUND: Mrs L. W. King (1) d. K. May (USA) 6-1 6-1; F. Durr (F) d. M. Simionescu (RU) 6-2 6-0; Mrs G. T. Janes d. V. Ruzici 6-4 6-2; L. J. Charles d. E. S. Weisenberger (ARG) 6-8 6-4 6-2; **Mrs O. Morozova** (8) (USSR) d. Mrs V. W. Brasher 6-1 6-0; Mrs J. G. Paish (A) d. Mrs J. A. Bentzer (SW) 6-3 6-2; Mrs K. Wooldridge d. N. F. Gregory (A) 6-0 6-0; K. M. Krantzcke (A) d. L. A. Rossouw (SA) 6-0 6-3; **Casals** (4) d. Teeguarden 2-6 9-8; Jausovec d. Mappin 6-4 6-1; Boshoff d. Gurdal 6-3 7-5; Gourlay d. Tomanova 6-4 6-2; **Wade** (5) d. Anthony 7-5 6-3; Nagelsen d. Chanfreau 7-5 6-3; Kiyomura d. Kroschina 6-2 6-2 6-3; Hogan d. Cuypers 6-3 6-0; Stevens d. Wikstedt 6-3 6-3; Fretz d. Turnbull 7-5 6-3; Sawamatsu d. Heldman 6-4 6-4; **Melville** (6) d. R. J. Tenney 6-4 6-1; Kemmer d. Walsh 1-6 6-2 6-3; Bonicelli d. Latham 2-6 7-5 6-2; Harris d. Peisachov 6-3 6-3; **Goolagong** (3) d. Kloss 6-2 6-4; J. A. Young (A) d. Mann 6-4 6-2; Mrs H. Masthoff (G) d. Mrs I. Hume 9-8 6-3; R. C. Giscafre (ARG) d. V. J. Ziegenfuss (USA) 1-6 6-1 6-2; T. Zwaan (NTH) d. G. L. Coles 6-3 5-7 6-2; C. M. O'Neill d. R. A. Whitehouse (SA) 1-6 6-2 6-2; M. Schallau (USA) d. N. Fuchs (F) 6-0 6-0; I. Fernandez (COL) d. C. F. Matison (A) 6-2 5-7 6-3; **C. M. Evert** (2) (USA) d. L. E. Hunt (A) 8-6 5-7 11-9.

THIRD ROUND: King (1) d. Durr 6-1 7-5; Charles d. Janes 4-6 6-3 6-0; **Morozova** (8) d. Paish 2-6 6-0 9-7; Krantzcke d. Wooldridge 6-2 9-7; **Casals** (4) d. Jausovec 6-3 6-4; Boshoff d. Gourlay 6-3 5-7 9-7; **Wade** (5) d. Nagelsen 6-3 6-2; Hogan d. Kiyomura 6-4 6-2; Fretz d. Stevens 6-3 6-2; **Melville** (6) d. Sawamatsu 6-2 6-3; Kemmer d. Bonicelli 6-4 3-6 8-6; **Goolagong** (3) d. Harris 4-6 7-5 6-4; Masthoff d. Young 5-7 9-8 7-5; Giscafre d. Zwaan 6-3 6-2; Schallau d. O'Neill 6-2 6-3; **Evert** (2) d. Fernandez 6-1 6-1.

FOURTH ROUND	QUARTER-FINALS	SEMI-FINALS	FINAL	CHAMPION
King (1)	**King** (1)			
Charles	6-3 6-0	**Morozova** (8)		
Morozova (8)	**Morozova** (8)	7-5 6-2		
Krantzcke	9-7 6-4		**Morozova** (8)	
Casals (4)	Boshoff		1-6 7-5 6-4	
Boshoff	6-2 6-3	**Wade** (5)		
Wade (5)	**Wade** (5)	6-3 6-2		
Hogan	6-3 6-1			**Evert** (2)
Fretz	**Melville** (6)			6-0 6-4
Melville (6)	5-1 ret'd	**Melville** (6)		
Kemmer	**Goolagong** (3)	9-7 1-6 6-2		
Goolagong (3)	6-1 6-4		**Evert** (2)	
Masthoff	Masthoff		6-2 6-3	
Giscafre	6-2 6-4	**Evert** (2)		
Schallau	**Evert** (2)	6-4 6-2		
Evert (2)	7-5 6-1			

PRIZE MONEY

Champion	£7,000
Runner-up	4,000
Semi-finals	1,500
Quarter-finals	750
Fourth round	500
Third round	250
Second round	175
First round	150

OTHER FINALS

GENTLEMEN'S DOUBLES: Final — J. D. Newcombe (A)/A. D. Roche (A) d. R. C. Lutz (USA)/S. R. Smith (USA) 8-6 6-4 6-4.
LADIES' DOUBLES: Final — E. F. Goolagong (A)/M. Michel (USA) d. H. F. Gourlay (A)/K. Krantzcke (A) 2-6 6-4 6-3.
MIXED DOUBLES: Final — O. K. Davidson (A)/Mrs L. W. King (USA) d. M. J. Farrell/L. J. Charles 6-3 9-7.
GENTLEMEN'S SINGLES PLATE: Final — T. I. Kakulia (USSR) d. P. C. Kronk (A) 6-3 7-5.

LADIES' SINGLES PLATE: Final — M. V. Kroschina (USSR) d. L. J. Beaven 6-3 8-6.
BOYS' INVITATION SINGLES: Final — W. Martin (USA) d. Ashok Amritraj (IN) 6-2 6-1.
GIRLS' INVITATION SINGLES: Final — M. Jausovec (YU) d. M. Simionescu (RU) 7-5 6-4.
VETERANS' MEN'S DOUBLES: Final — R. Dunas (USA)/G. Mulloy (USA) d. H. K. Richards (USA)/R. C. Sorlein (USA) 6-3 6-2.

273

GENTLEMEN'S SINGLES

1975

FIRST ROUND: J. S. Connors (1) (USA) d. J. M. Lloyd 6-2 6-3 6-1; V. Amritraj (IN) d. B. J. Phillips-Moore (A) 7-5 6-3 6-4; M. Cox d. I. Tiriac (RU) 6-2 6-2 7-5; J. Loyo-Mayo (M) d. A. G. Fawcett (RH) 6-3 6-3 8-6; R. O. Ruffels (A) d. **V. Gerulaitis** (14) (USA) 3-6 6-4 6-2 3-6 6-1; B. Mitton (SA) d. J. Molina (COL) 6-3 6-4 6-4; R. D. Crealy (A) d. W. L. Brown (USA) 8-6 8-9 6-2 3-6 6-3; P. C. Dent (A) d. J. Pisecky (CZ) 7-5 3-6 6-4 6-2; **R. Ramirez** (8) (M) d. N. Spear (YU) 6-4 6-0 6-2; J. Borowiak (USA) d. A. J. Stone (A) 6-3 6-3 6-2; I. El Shafei (E) d. T. W. Gorman (USA) 6-1 6-2 6-4; A. Panatta (IT) d. L. Alvarez (ARG) 6-4 2-6 6-2 6-3; **J. Kodes** (12) (CZ) d. G. Goven (F) 8-6 6-2 6-3; G. Masters d. J. K. Holladay (USA) 6-3 6-1 6-3; G. C. Richey (USA) d. C. Dowdeswell (RH) 6-3 6-3 6-3; B. Taroczy (HU) C. M. Robinson 8-9 8-6 6-3 6-4; **G. Vilas** (4) (ARG) d. R. J. Simpson (NZ) 7-5 6-4 6-4 3-6 6-4; R. J. Moore (SA) d. J. M. Yuill (SA) 4-6 6-3 6-4 6-1; U. Pinner (G) d. P. Cornejo (CH) 6-8 7-5 9-8 6-4; W. J. Austin (USA) d. J. G. Paish 4-6 6-4 3-6 7-5 6-2; **O. Parun** (15) (NZ) d. N. A. Fraser (A) 6-3 6-2 9-7; T. Svensson (SW) d. J. K. Andrews (USA) 9-7 18-16; A. A. Mayer (USA) d. A. R. Gardiner (A) 6-3 6-1 6-0; M. R. Edmondson (A) d. P. B. McNamara (A) 6-1 6-2 7-5; **I. Nastase** (5) (RU) d. T. I. Kakulia (USSR) 6-2 6-4 6-2; S. E. Stewart (USA) d. K. Meiler (G) 6-2 6-4 7-5; M. Estep (USA) d. D. T. Crawford (USA) 6-4 6-4 9-8; R. W. Drysdale d. R. P. Dell (USA) 8-9 5-7 6-1 6-4 6-4; **R. Tanner** (11) (USA) d. R. C. Lutz (USA) 8-6 6-1 8-9 6-4; V. Pecci (PA) d. M. J. Farrell 4-6 1-6 6-4 7-5 6-4; J. Fassbender (G) d. H. Kary (AU) 5-7 6-3 6-4 6-2; C. W. Owens (USA) d. B. Mignot (B) 6-3 7-5 6-4; G. R. Stilwell d. G. Battrick 6-3 6-4 6-4; G. E. Reid (USA) d. F. D. McMillan

(SA) 6-1 6-4 6-4; P. C. Kronk (A) d. H. J. Pohmann (G) 3-6 1-6 6-1 6-3 6-2; **J. G. Alexander** (10) (A) d. J. Kuki (J) 6-3 6-4 6-4; C. Kirmayr (BR) d. J. Velasco (COL) 6-0 6-1 6-2; B. E. Gottfried (USA) d. R. A. Lewis 6-3 6-1 6-1; J. Kamiwazumi (J) d. E. J. van Dillen (USA) 9-8 3-6 9-7 7-5; **A. R. Ashe** (6) (USA) d. R. A. J. Hewitt (SA) 7-5 3-6 6-2 6-4; C. M. Pasarell (USA) d. J. W. Blocher (USA) 6-3 7-5 6-3; P. Gerken (USA) d. J. E. Mandarino (BR) 3-6 3-6 6-1 6-3 17-15; C. S. Dibley (A) d. T. H. Waltke (USA) 7-5 6-3 6-3; **M. C. Riessen** (13) (USA) d. P. Proisy (F) 6-3 6-2 6-2; C. Mukerjea (IN) d. W. Fibak (POL) 4-6 7-5 9-7 6-4; J. Fillol (CH) d. R. Taylor 6-3 8-6 6-4; M. Holecek (Stateless) d. H. Elschenbroich (G) 6-2 6-4 6-4; **B. Borg** (3) (SW) d. J. Andrew 6-2 6-4 6-4; P. Dominguez (F) d. R. Fisher (USA) 3-6 7-5 6-0 6-4 6-2; K. G. Warwick (A) d. R. J. Carmichael (A) 6-4 7-5 6-1; H. Rahim (P) d. A. Zugarelli (IT) 6-0 6-4 6-2; **T. S. Okker** (9) (NTH) d. N. Pilic (YU) 3-6 8-6 6-3; J. Caujolle (F) d. R. Thung (NTH) 6-4 9-8 6-4; A. Metreveli (USSR) d. A. Amritraj 6-4 6-1 6-2; A. J. Pattison (RH) d. T. Koch (BR) 6-4 7-5 6-3; B. M. Bertram (SA) d. **S. R. Smith** (7) (USA) 6-1 6-2 6-1; F. V. McNair (USA) d. S. Krulevitz (USA) 6-4 9-7 6-4; R. L. Case d. R. I. Kreiss (USA) 7-9 6-3 6-1 8-9 6-1; **M. C. Riessen** (13) (USA) d. P. J. Hrebec (CZ) 6-3 6-3 6-3; H. Hose (V) d. S. Ball 6-0 1-6 8-6 6-3; B. Andersson (SW) d. T. Vazquez (ARG) 7-5 9-7 6-8 6-2; J. W. Feaver d. M. Lara (M) 6-1 5-7 5-7 6-3 6-3; **K. R. Rosewall** (2) (A) d. C. Barazzutti (IT) 7-5 6-3 6-2.

SECOND ROUND: Connors (1) d. Amritraj 9-8 6-0 8-6; Cox d. Loyo-Mayo 6-3 3-6 6-1 6-2; Mitton d. Ruffels 6-4 2-0 ret'd; Dent d. Crealy 5-7 7-5 6-3 7-5; **Ramirez** (8) d. Borowiak 1-6 9-8 9-7 6-3; Panatta d. El Shafei 4-6 6-4 6-4 3-6 6-3; Master d. **Kodes** (12) 2-6 2-6 6-4 8-6 6-4; Richey d. Taroczy 9-7 6-4 9-8; **Vilas** (4) d. Moore 6-4 6-3 6-1; Pinner d. Austin 6-3 6-4 9-8 4-6 6-3; **Parun** (15) d. Svensson 6-2 1-0 ret'd; Mayer d. Edmondson 6-3 6-0 8-9 6-2; Stewart d. **Nastase** (5) 8-6 6-8 6-2 1-6 6-3; Estep d. Drysdale 5-7 6-4 6-4; **Tanner** (11) d. Pecci 6-3 6-4 9-8; Owens d. Fassbender 2-6 6-1 6-3 6-1; Stilwell d. Reid 5-7 6-3 7-5 6-8 6-3; Kronk d. **Alexander** (10) 1-6 9-8 9-8 9-8; Gottfried

d. Kirmayr 4-6 7-5 9-8 4-6 6-4; **Ashe** (6) d. Kamiwazumi 6-2 7-5 6-4; Pasarell d. Gerken 6-3 6-3 6-1; **Riessen** (13) d. Dibley 9-8 6-2 6-3; Fillol d. Mukerjea 6-3 3-6 6-2 6-3; Warwick d. Dominguez 4-6 6-4 7-5 4-6 6-1; **Okker** (9) d. Rahim 8-9 4-6 9-7 6-3 6-0; Metreveli d. Caujolle 5-7 6-4 6-2 6-2; Pattison d. Bertram 9-7 4-6 1-6 8-6 6-1; Case d. McNair 6-3 9-8 8-6; **Roche** (16) d. Ganzabal 6-3 6-2 6-4; Andersson d. Hose 4-6 6-3 8-6 6-4; **Rosewall** (2) d. Feaver 6-4 6-4 6-4.

THIRD ROUND: Connors (1) d. Cox 6-4 6-2 6-2; Dent d. Mitton 3-6 6-3 6-4 2-6 6-4; **Ramirez** (8) d. Panatta 6-4 7-5 7-5; Richey d. Masters 3-6 6-3 6-3 4-6 6-3; **Vilas** (4) d. Pinner 6-2 9-7 6-4; Mayer d. **Parun** (15) 6-4 9-8 6-2; Estep d. Stewart 2-6 8-6 8-9 6-4 8-6; **Tanner** (11) d. Owens 9-8 9-8 6-1; Stilwell d. Kronk 6-4 7-5 9-8; **Ashe** (6) d. Gottfried

6-2 6-3 6-1; **Riessen** (13) d. Pasarell 6-4 6-4 1-6 9-8; **Borg** (3) d. Fillol 0-6 6-4 6-4 6-3; **Okker** (9) d. Warwick 6-3 6-2 6-4; Metreveli d. Pattison 6-4 6-1 6-3; **Roche** (16) d. Case 6-2 6-0 6-3; **Rosewall** (2) d. Andersson 6-2 6-2 6-2.

FOURTH ROUND	QUARTER-FINALS	SEMI-FINALS	FINAL	CHAMPION
Connors (1)	**Connors** (1)			
Dent	6-1 6-2 6-2	**Connors** (1)		
Ramirez (8)	**Ramirez** (8)	6-4 8-6 6-2		
Richey	6-2 6-3 6-2		**Connors** (1)	
Vilas (4)	**Vilas** (4)		6-4 6-1 6-4	
Mayer	2-6 7-5 9-8 6-3	**Tanner** (11)		
Estep	**Tanner** (11)	6-4 5-7 6-8 6-2 6-2		
Tanner (11)	9-8 6-4 6-2			**Ashe** (6)
Stilwell	**Ashe** (6)			6-1 6-1 5-7 6-4
Ashe (6)	6-2 5-7 6-4 6-2	**Ashe** (6)		
Riessen (13)	**Borg** (3)	2-6 6-4 8-6 6-1		
Borg (3)	6-2 8-6 4-6 6-1		**Ashe** (6)	
Okker (9)	**Okker** (9)		5-7 6-4 7-5 8-9 6-4	
Metreveli	6-0 6-2 8-6	**Roche** (16)		
Roche (16)	**Roche** (16)	2-6 9-8 2-6 6-4 6-2		
Rosewall (2)	6-3 6-8 8-6 6-1			

PRIZE MONEY

Champion	£10,000
Runner-up	6,000
Semi-finals	2,000
Quarter-finals	1,000
Fourth round	600
Third round	300
Second round	200
First round	150

LADIES' SINGLES

FIRST ROUND: C. M. Evert (1) (USA) d. C. M. O'Neil (A) 6-0 6-2; K. Sawamatsu (J) d. L. M. Tenney (USA) 6-3 6-3; Mrs D. E. Dalton (A) d. A. M. Coe 9-7 6-3; L. J. Mottram d. R. Stark 4-6 6-4 6-0; **Mrs G. E. Reid** (8) (A) d. Y. Granaturova (USSR) 6-2 2-6 6-4 6-2; B. F. Stove (NTH) d. H. Anliot (SW) 6-2 6-8 6-2; Mrs K. Wooldridge d. C. Vlotman (SA) 6-1 6-4; J. K. Anthony (USA) d. Mrs M. Fosgardh (SW) 6-3 6-2; M. Gurdal (B) d. J. Young 6-1 6-0; **Mrs L. W. King** (3) (USA) d. Mrs C. Vlotman (SA) 6-1 6-4; J. K. Anthony (USA) d. Mrs M. Fosgardh (SW) 6-3 6-2; M. Gurdal (B) d. J. Young 6-1 6-1; Mrs P. Darmon (F) d. V. Ruzici (RU) 6-8 6-2 9-7; F. Durr (F) d. M. Simionescu (RU) 6-4 7-5; T. Zwaan (NTH) d. M. Nasuelli (IT) 7-5 6-2; P. A. Teeguarden (USA) d. D. Ganz (USA) 6-2 6-4; P. A. Reese (USA) d. C. F. Matison (A) 3-6 6-2 6-1; Mrs J. B.

Chanfreau (F) d. R. Casals (USA) 6-2 2-6 6-1; L. Boshoff (SA) d. Mrs M. N. Pinter (CZ) 6-0 6-4; J. S. Newberry (USA) d. Mrs N. Schaar (NTH) 6-2 6-1; I. Riedel (G) d. B. A. Downs (USA) 5-7 6-0 7-5; J. A. Fayter d. H. Eisterlehner (G) 6-2 2-6 6-2; Mrs P. M. Doerner (A) d. Mrs J. G. Paish (A) 8-6 6-0; L. A. Rupert (USA) d. J. B. Haas (USA) 4-6 6-4; H. F. Gourlay (A) d. Mrs I. Hume 7-5 6-4; P. S. A. Hogan (USA) d. A. K. Kiyomura (USA) 6-2 6-2; F. Bonicelli (UR) Y. Vermaak (SA) 4-6 6-2 6-0; J. N. Connor (NZ) d. F. Guedy (F) 6-3 2-6 14-12; **Mrs B. M. Court** (5) (A) d. D. L. Fromholtz (A) 6-1 6-2; N. Y. Chmyreva (USSR) d. C. Meyer (USA) 6-3 6-4; R. A. Whitehouse (SA) d. T. Holladay (USA) 6-3 6-4; G. R. Stevens (SA) d. Mrs J. A. Bentzer (SW) 6-2 6-2; **M. Navratilova** (2) (CZ) d. W. M. Turnbull (A) 6-2 8-6.

SECOND ROUND: Evert (1) d. Appel (NTH) 6-0 6-1; Sawamatsu d. R. J. Tenney (USA) 6-4 6-3; L. J. Beaven d. Dalton 6-3 6-1; Mottram d. B. Cuypers (SA) 6-3 6-3; S. Barker d. **Reid** (8) 6-4 1-0 ret'd; Stove d. B. Nagelsen (USA) 7-5 6-1; Wooldridge d. S. A. Walsh (USA) 9-7 6-3; Michel d. Mrs L. Pericoli (IT) 6-1 6-4; **King** (3) d. V. A. Burton 6-1 6-3; Anthony d. Mrs P. Peisachov (IS) 6-3 6-2; Gurdal d. O. de Roubin (F) 6-0 6-1; V. J. Ziegenfuss d. Darmon 8-6 6-3; **Mrs O. Morozova** (7) (USSR) d. Durr 6-3 4-6 6-1; K. A. May (USA) d. Zwaan 6-1 6-1; M. Jausovec (YU) d. Teeguarden 3-6 6-1 11-9; Reese d. N. Fuchs (F) 0-6 6-2 ret'd; Casals d. L. E. Hunt (A) 5-7 6-3 8-6; Boshoff d. Mrs K. S.

Gunter (USA) 3-6 6-2 6-4; Newberry d. M. B. E. Kaligis (INDO) 6-3 6-1; **S. V. Wade** (6) d. Riedel 6-1 6-3; J. L. Dimond (A) d. Fayter 6-3 6-2; M. Tyler d. Doerner 0-6 9-7 6-4; I. S. Kloss (SA) d. Rupert 6-3 7-5; **Mrs R. Cawley** (4) (A) d. Gourlay 3-6 6-1 6-1; Hogan d. R. C. Giscafre (ARG) 6-2 6-2; G. L. Coles d. Bonicelli 7-5 6-4; R. Tomanova (CZ) d. Connor 6-0 6-2; **Court** (5) d. S. A. Greer (USA) 6-2 6-3; Chmyreva d. C. Molesworth 6-0 6-4; L. J. Charles d. Whitehouse 6-2 6-4; Stevens d. L. Du Pont (USA) 8-6 6-1; **Navratilova** (2) d. S. Mappin 6-1 6-2.

THIRD ROUND: Evert (1) d. Sawamatsu 6-2 6-2; Beaven d. Mottram 6-4 6-2; Stove d. Barker 6-0 4-6 6-2; Wooldridge d. Michel 6-4 6-4; **King** (3) d. Anthony 6-2 6-3; Gurdal d. Ziegenfuss 6-3 6-3; **Morozova** (7) d. May 4-6 9-7 6-1; Jausovec d. Reese 6-2 9-7; Casals d. Boshoff 6-2 6-1; **Wade** (6) d. Newberry 6-2 6-8 8-6; Dimond d. Tyler

6-4 6-4; **Cawley** (4) d. Kloss 6-3 6-2; Coles d. Hogan 7-5 6-3; **Court** (5) d. Tomanova 6-0 6-0; Chmyreva d. Charles 8-6 7-5; **Navratilova** (2) d. Stevens 6-4 6-3.

FOURTH ROUND	QUARTER-FINALS	SEMI-FINALS	FINAL	CHAMPION
Evert (1)	**Evert** (1)			
Beaven	6-2 6-4	**Evert** (1)		
Stove	Stove	5-7 7-5 6-0		
Wooldridge	9-7 6-3		**King** (3)	
King (3)	**King** (3)		2-6 6-2 6-3	
Gurdal	6-1 6-2	**King** (3)		
Morozova (7)	**Morozova** (7)	6-3 6-3		
Jausovec	6-4 6-2			**King** (3)
Casals	**Wade** (6)			6-0 6-1
Wade (6)	6-4 4-6 6-4	**Cawley** (4)		
Dimond	**Cawley** (4)	5-7 6-3 9-7		
Cawley (4)	6-2 6-4		**Cawley** (4)	
Coles	**Court** (5)		6-4 6-4	
Court (5)	6-2 6-2	**Court** (5)		
Chmyreva	**Navratilova** (2)	6-3 6-4		
Navratilova (2)	6-1 6-0			

PRIZE MONEY

Champion	£7,000
Runner-up	4,200
Semi-finals	1,500
Quarter-finals	750
Fourth round	500
Third round	250
Second round	175
First round	150

OTHER FINALS

GENTLEMEN'S DOUBLES: Final — V. Gerulaitis (USA)/A. Mayer (USA) d. C. Dowdeswell (RH)/A. J. Stone (A) 7-5 8-6 6-4.
LADIES' DOUBLES: Final — A. K. Kiyomura (USA)/K. Sawamatsu (J) d. F. Durr (F)/B. F. Stove (NTH) 7-5 1-6 7-5.
MIXED DOUBLES: Final — M. C. Riessen (USA)/Mrs B. M. Court (A)/d. A. J. Stone (A)/B. F. Stove (NTH) 6-4 7-5.
GENTLEMEN'S SINGLES PLATE: Final — T. Koch (BR) d. V. Gerulaitis (USA) 6-3 6-2.

LADIES' SINGLES PLATE: Final — D. L. Fromholtz (A) d. V. A. Burton 6-4 6-2.
BOYS' SINGLES: Final — C. J. Lewis (NZ) d. R. Ycaza (EC) 6-1 6-4.
GIRLS' SINGLES: Final — N. Y. Chmyreva (USSR) d. R. Marsikova (CZ) 6-4 6-3.
VETERANS' MEN'S DOUBLES: Final — L. Bergelin (SW)/B. Patty (USA) d. J. D. Budge (USA)/G. Mulloy (USA) 6-3 6-3.

1976

GENTLEMEN'S SINGLES

FIRST ROUND: A. R. Ashe (1) (USA) d. F. Taygan (USA) 7-5 6-4 7-5; A. J. Stone (A) d. J. M. Yuill (SA) 6-4 4-6 6-1 6-3; M. R. Edmondson (A) d. R. J. Moore (SA) 7-5 4-6 8-9 7-5 6-2; M. J. Farrell d. J. Royappa (IN) 6-4 6-2 6-4; V. Gerulaitis (USA) d. M. Holecek (Stateless) 7-5 6-1 7-5; M. Cox d. A. Munoz (SP) 6-4 9-8 6-4; W. W. Martin (USA) d. S. E. Stewart (USA) 7-9 6-2 8-6 6-4; S. Krulevitz (USA) d. C. Dowdeswell (RH) 3-6 6-3 6-2 8-6; **R. Ramirez** (8) (M) d. C. P. Kachel (A) 6-3 6-4 9-8; M. D. Wayman d. N. J. Holmes (USA) 6-3 6-4 3-6 6-0; K. Meiler (G) d. M. Cahill (USA) 6-8 9-7 3-6 6-3 6-4; R. O. Ruffels (A) d. J. H. McManus (USA) 9-7 6-1 6-1; **J. D. Newcombe** (10) (A) d. J. S. Hagey (USA) 8-9 8-6 4-6 6-1; J. W. Feaver d. H. J. Bunis (USA) 6-1 1-6 6-2 7-5; B. Mitton (SA) d. E. Deblicker (F) 7-5 6-2 1-6 6-4; S. Menon (IN) d. R. Taylor 5-7 6-2 9-8 2-6 10-8; **I. Nastase** (3) (RU) d. N. Spear (YU) 6-2 6-3 6-2; Z. Franulovic (YU) d. L. Alvarez (SP) 6-2 6-4 6-2; G. Masters (A) d. B. E. Fairlie (NZ) 6-4 6-2 6-0; K. G. Warwick (A) d. R. Cano (ARG) 6-4 6-2 6-1; **J. Fillol** (13) (CH) d. R. Thung (NTH) 6-1 6-2 6-3; R. L. Case d. P. F. McNamee (A) 3-6 9-8 6-2; C. J. Lewis (NZ) d. J. Hrebec (CZ) 8-6 3-6 7-5 ret'd; O. Parun (NZ) d. J. G. Alexander (A) 2-6 9-8 9-7 1-6 8-6; **A. Panatta** (5) (IT) d. J. Andrew (V) 4-6 6-4 7-5 6-4; D. H. Collings (A) d. R. A. J. Hewitt (SA) 4-6 7-5 2-0 ret'd; V. Amritraj (IN) d. F. Jauffret (F) 9-8 6-3 6-4; C. M. Pasarell (USA) d. J. Kamiwazumi (J) 6-3 6-1 6-3; **T. S. Okker** (9) (NTH) d. A. A. Mayer (USA) 6-3 6-2 6-4; V. C. Amaya (USA) d. J. R. Ganzabal (ARG) 6-3 6-4 6-4; A. J. Pattison (RH) d. E. J. van Dillen (USA) 6-3 3-6 7-5 6-3; P. C. Dent d. J. M. Lloyd 4-6 5-7 6-3 9-8 7-5; W. Fibak (POL) d. J. T. Whitlinger (USA) 8-6 6-1 3-6 6-1; U.

Pinner (G) d. H. Kary (AU) 6-8 6-1 6-4 7-9 6-4; G. E. Reid (USA) d. I. Molina (COL) 6-4 5-7 6-3 6-4; **A. D. Roche** (12) (A) d. S. Ball (A) 9-8 9-8 6-4; A. Metreveli (USSR) d. G. Mayer (USA) 6-2 5-0 ret'd; R. L. Stockton (USA) d. W. Lloyd (A) 6-3 6-4 6-3; H. Rahim (P) d. G. Goven (F) 7-5 6-2 6-4; **G. Vilas** (6) (ARG) d. B. J. Phillips-Moore (A) 6-3 6-1 6-4; T. W. Gorman (USA) d. M. Estep (USA) 7-9 6-2 6-4 9-7; R. C. Lutz (USA) d. J. Borowiak (USA) 4-6 6-4 6-4 6-4; J. K. Andrews (USA) d. R. J. Simpson (NZ) 7-5 6-4 6-4; **B. E. Gottfried** (14) (USA) d. Tim Gullikson (USA) 4-6 6-3 6-2 9-7; J. Delaney (USA) d. J. Fassbender (G) 6-2 3-6 6-8 6-3 6-3; C. S. Dibley (A) d. P. C. Kronk (A) 6-2 6-3 6-2; M. C. Riessen (USA) d. F. McMillan (SA) 9-8 6-3 6-8 6-3; **B. Borg** (4) (SW) d. D. A. Lloyd 6-3 6-3 6-1; N. Pilic (YU) d. B. M. Bertram (SA) 6-2 7-5 6-2; V. Pecci (PA) d. P. J. Cramer (SA) 6-3 6-3 6-4; R. A. Lewis d. P. Proisy (F) 6-4 2-6 6-2 1-6 8-6; B. Teacher (USA) d. J. K. Holladay (USA) 9-7 3-6 9-8 6-4; C. Kirmayr (BR) d. J. R. Smith 6-3 9-7 5-7 6-2; H. J. Pohmann (G) d. J. Mottram 9-8 6-1 ret'd; K. Hirai (J) d. V. Borisov (USSR) 6-3 6-4 6-0; **R. Tanner** (7) (USA) d. C. M. Robinson 8-6 7-5 6-4; T. I. Kakulia (USSR) d. B. Taroczy (HU) 6-1 9-8 6-2; E. C. Drysdale (SA) d. R. W. Drysdale 6-2 6-3 6-4; G. Battrick d. H. J. Plotz (G) 6-3 6-3 7-5; **S. R. Smith** (16) (USA) d. P. Cornejo (CH) 6-1 6-2 6-1; P. Dominguez (F) d. D. Crealy (A) 4-6 6-2 6-1 4-6 7-5; I. El Shafei (E) d. J. F. Caujolle (F) 9-8 6-3 6-4; S. A. Warboys (A) d. J. M. P. Marks (A) 5-7 7-5 3-6 6-4 6-3; **J. S. Connors** (2) (USA) d. A. Zugarelli (IT) 6-1 6-3 6-2.

SECOND ROUND: Ashe (1) d. Stone 7-5 8-9 9-7 7-5; Edmondson d. Farrell 9-8 9-7 6-4; Gerulaitis d. Cox 6-3 6-4 6-4; Krulevitz d. Martin 6-2 6-3 4-6 9-8; **Ramirez** (8) d. Wayman 6-4 8-9 6-4 6-3; Meiler d. Ruffels 6-8 6-4 8-9 8-6; **Newcombe** (10) d. Feaver 6-3 3-6 8-9 6-4 6-4; Mitton d. Menon 8-6 6-2 6-1; **Nastase** (3) d. Franulovic 6-1 7-5 6-3; Warwick d. Masters 7-5 6-4 6-4; **Fillol** (13) d. Case 8-9 6-4 6-8 9-8 6-2; Parun d. C. J. Lewis 6-3 6-4 6-2; **Panatta** (5) d. Collings 9-7 2-6 3-6 8-6 6-1; Pasarell d. Amritraj 6-4 6-2 6-4; **Okker** (9) d. Amaya 9-7 6-2 6-3; Dent d.

Pattison 6-2 6-2 7-5; Pinner d. Fibak 6-3 9-8 6-3; **Roche** (12) d. Reid 6-4 6-2 6-4; Metreveli d. Stockton 6-8 6-3 6-3 3-6 11-9; **Vilas** (6) d. Rahim 9-7 6-3 6-4; Lutz d. Gorman 6-1 8-9 6-3 2-6 6-4; **Gottfried** (14) d. Andrews 8-6 7-9 2-6 6-4 6-2; Dibley d. Delaney 8-6 7-5 8-6; **Borg** (4) d. Riessen 6-2 6-2 6-4; Pilic d. Pecci 8-9 9-8 6-3 5-7 6-4; R. A. Lewis d. Teacher 3-6 9-7 9-8 9-8; Kirmayr d. Pohmann 8-6 6-3 6-3; **Tanner** (7) d. Hirai 6-3 6-4 9-7; Kakulia d. Drysdale 6-1 6-3 6-4; **Smith** (16) d. Battrick 6-0 6-8 6-2 6-3; El Shafei d. Carmichael 8-6 6-4 6-4; **Connors** (2) d. Warboys 6-3 6-2 6-3.

THIRD ROUND: Ashe (1) d. Edmondson 7-5 6-2 8-6; Gerulaitis d. Krulevitz 6-2 6-2 6-1; **Ramirez** (8) d. Meiler 6-2 7-5 6-1; Mitton d. **Newcombe** (10) 3-6 6-3 9-8 9-8; **Nastase** (3) d. Warwick 8-6 7-5 6-4; Parun d. **Fillol** (13) 7-5 6-4 6-4; Pasarell d. **Panatta** (5) 8-9 4-6 6-4 7-5 6-4; Dent d. **Okker** (9) 6-4 9-8 6-4; **Roche** (12) d. Pinner 6-4 3-6 6-2 6-1;

Vilas (6) d. Metreveli 2-6 7-5 6-2 6-4; **Gottfried** (14) d. Lutz 6-3 6-1 3-6 4-6 6-1; **Borg** (4) d. Dibley 6-4 6-4 6-4; Pilic d. R. A. Lewis 3-6 6-4 3-6 6-3 6-2; **Tanner** (7) d. Kirmayr 9-9 9-8 6-3 6-2; **Smith** (16) d. Kakulia 8-6 3-6 6-1 6-1; **Connors** (2) d. El Shafei 6-4 6-0 6-3.

FOURTH ROUND	QUARTER-FINALS	SEMI-FINALS	FINAL	CHAMPION	PRIZE MONEY	
Ashe (1)	Gerulaitis				Champion	£12,500
Gerulaitis	4-6 8-9 6-4 6-3 6-4	Ramirez (8)			Runner-up	7,000
Ramirez (8)	Ramirez (8)	4-6 6-4 6-2 6-4			Semi-finals	3,000
Mitton	9-8 3-6 6-1 6-1		Nastase (3)		Quarter-finals	1,500
Nastase (3)	Nastase (3)		6-2 9-7 6-3		Fourth round	1,100
Parun	7-5 6-4 6-3	Nastase (3)			Third round	550
Pasarell	Pasarell	6-4 6-2 6-3			Second round	300
Dent	2-6 4-6 6-4 6-0 7-5			Borg (4)	First round	150
Roche (12)	Vilas (6)			6-4 6-2 9-7		
Vilas (6)	6-4 3-6 5-7 6-3 6-4	Borg (4)				
Gottfried (14)	Borg (4)	6-3 6-0 6-2				
Borg (4)	6-2 6-2 7-5		Borg (4)			
Pilic	Tanner (7)		6-4 9-8 6-4			
Tanner (7)	6-3 6-4 6-4	Tanner (7)				
Smith (16)	Connors (2)	6-4 6-2 8-6				
Connors (2)	6-4 6-1 6-3					

LADIES' SINGLES

FIRST ROUND: C. M. Evert (1) (USA) d. Mrs T. J. Thomas (USA) 6-1 6-1; Mrs K. Wooldridge d. M. Simionescu (RU) 7-5 6-0; B. F. Stove (NTH) d. B. Nagelsen (USA) 6-3 6-1; B. Norton (USA) d. C. F. Marikian (A) 7-5 6-3; **Mrs O. Morozova** (5) (USSR) d. A. K. Kiyomura (USA) 6-3 6-1; T. A. Fretz (USA) d. L. D. Blachford 7-5 7-5; M. J. Louie (USA) d. Mrs H. E. Lancaster-Kerr (A) 6-3 6-3; N. Chmyreva (USSR) d. B. R. Thompson 6-1 6-1; **M. Navratilova** (4) d. M. L. Du Pont (USA) 3-6 6-1 6-3; L. Antonoplis d. S. Mehmedbasich (USA) 6-3 6-1; J. A. Fayter d. T. Zwaan (NTH) 6-2 6-4; J. A. Russell (USA) d. L. J. Charles 6-3 5-7 6-4; **S. Barker** (7) d. M. Wikstedt (SW) 6-1 7-5; V. J. Ziegenfuss (USA) d. L. M. Tenney (USA) 6-3 6-4; Mrs T. E. Guerrant (USA) d. Mrs J. J. Lovera (F) 9-7 6-2; M. E. Bueno (BR) d. R. J.

Tenney (USA) 6-4 6-4; K. M. Harter (USA) d. F. Mihai (RU) 6-4 7-5; G. R. Stevens (SA) d. L. J. Mottram 6-3 6-4; Mrs P. M. Doerner (A) d. J. L. Dimond (A) 6-2 6-2; **Mrs G. E. Reid** (8) (A) d. M. Redondo (USA) 6-4 6-4; M. Kruger (SA) d. V. Ruzici (RU) 6-2 6-4; P. S. A. Hogan (USA) d. D. A. Boshoff (SA) 6-4 5-7 6-2; B. Cuypers (SA) d. Mrs J. G. Paish (A) 6-2 6-4; **S. V. Wade** (3) d. M. Tyler 6-3 6-3; A. Spex (CU) d. C. E. M. Sandberg (SW) 6-3 8-6; Mrs I. A. Lofdahl-Bentzer (SW) d. G. Coles 6-4 8-6; T. A. Holladay (USA) d. S. P. Simmonds (IT) 6-2 6-2; **R. Casals** (6) (USA) d. L. J. Beaven 6-3 6-2; J. K. Anthony (USA) d. A. P. Cooper 6-2 6-2; D. L. Fromholtz (A) d. Y. Vermaak (SA) 6-1 6-4; C. Molesworth d. R. A. Whitehouse (SA) 6-3 8-6; **Mrs R. Cawley** (2) (A) d. Mrs E. Vessies-Appel (NTH) 6-2 7-5.

SECOND ROUND: C. M. Evert (1) d. A. M. Coe 6-0 6-0; L. E. Hunt (A) d. Wooldridge 6-0 6-4; Stove d. S. E. Saliba (A) 6-1 6-2; Norton d. Mrs C. C. G. Vlotman (SA) 6-3 9-8; **Morozova** (5) d. M. McLean (USA) 6-3 6-1; **Navratilova** (4) d. M. Gurdal (B) 6-2 6-1; Antonoplis d. I. Riedel (G) 6-3 6-2; T. Durr (F) d. Fayter 3-6 6-3 7-5; Russell d. J. M. Metcalf (USA) 6-4 9-8; **Barker** (7) d. C. A. Martinez 6-4 7-5; Ziegenfuss d. K. Kuykendall 3-6 6-3 6-1; Guerrant d. C. J. Newton (NZ) 6-1 6-1; Bueno d. B. Bruning (USA) 6-4 3-6 8-6; R. Tomanova (CZ) d. Harter 6-3 3-6 9-7; Stevens d. F.

Bonicelli (UR) 6-0 6-1; Doerner d. V. A. Burton (A) 6-2 6-1; **Reid** (8) d. P. A. Teegarden (USA) 6-4 1-6 6-2; Kruger d. H. M. Eisterlehner (G) 6-3 9-8 6-4; W. M. Turnbull (A) d. Hogan 6-2 6-4; M. Michel (USA) d. Cuypers 6-3 6-4; **Wade** (3) d. S. Mappin 6-1 6-0; Spex d. I. Fernandez (COL) 6-3 6-4; M. Jausovec (YU) d. Lofdahl-Bentzer 4-6 6-4 6-2; Holladay d. A. J. McMillan (SA) 6-4 9-8; **Casals** (6) d. P. L. Bostrom (USA) 6-2 6-4; Anthony d. N. Sato (J) 6-2 6-4; Fromholtz d. K. A. May (USA) 6-0 6-4; Molesworth d. Mrs J. L. Du Plooy (SA) 2-6 7-5 7-5; **Cawley** (2) d. S. A. Walsh (USA) 6-0 7-5.

THIRD ROUND: C. M. Evert (1) d. Hunt 6-1 6-0; Stove d. Norton 6-3 6-2; **Morozova** (5) d. Marsikova 6-4 6-1; Chmyreva d. Kloss 7-5 6-4; **Navratilova** (4) d. Antonoplis 6-1 6-4; Durr d. Russell 6-4 6-4; **Barker** (7) d. Ziegenfuss 3-6 7-5 6-2; Bueno d. Guerrant 6-4 3-6 6-3; Stevens d. Tomanova 6-2 5-7 9-7; **Reid** (8) d. Doerner 7-5 4-2 ret'd;

Kruger d. Turnbull 8-6 6-4; **Wade** (3) d. Michel 6-3 6-3; Jausovec d. Spex 8-6 6-0; **Casals** (6) d. Holladay 6-4 6-2; Fromholtz d. Anthony 6-4 9-8; **Cawley** (2) d. Molesworth 6-1 6-1.

FOURTH ROUND	QUARTER-FINALS	SEMI-FINALS	FINAL	CHAMPION	PRIZE MONEY	
C. M. Evert (1)	C. M. Evert (1)				Champion	£10,000
Stove	6-2 6-2	C. M. Evert (1)			Runner-up	5,600
Morozova (5)	Morozova (5)	6-3 6-0			Semi-finals	2,400
Chmyreva	6-4 4-6 6-1		C. M. Evert (1)		Quarter-finals	1,200
Navratilova (4)	Navratilova (4)		6-3 4-6 6-4		Fourth round	600
Durr	2-6 6-3 7-5	Navratilova (4)			Third round	300
Barker (7)	Barker (7)	6-3 3-6 7-5			Second round	200
Bueno	2-6 6-2 6-1			C. M. Evert (1)	First round	150
Stevens	Reid (8)			6-3 4-6 8-6		
Reid (8)	3-6 6-3 6-4	Wade (3)				
Kruger	Wade (3)	6-4 6-2				
Wade (3)	2-6 6-3 7-5		Cawley (2)			
Jausovec	Casals (6)		6-1 6-2			
Casals (6)	6-2 7-5	Cawley (3)				
Fromholtz	Cawley (2)	7-5 6-3				
Cawley (2)	6-3 6-0					

OTHER FINALS

GENTLEMEN'S DOUBLES: Final — B. E. Gottfried (USA)/R. Ramirez (M) d. R. L. Case (A)/G. Masters (A) 3-6 6-3 8-6 2-6 7-5.
LADIES' DOUBLES: Final — C. M. Evert (USA)/M. Navratilova (CZ) d. Mrs L. W. King (USA)/B. Stove (NTH) 6-1 3-6 7-5.
MIXED DOUBLES: Final — A. D. Roche (A)/F. Durr (F) d. R. L. Stockton (USA)/R. Casals (USA) 6-3 2-6 7-5.
GENTLEMEN'S SINGLES PLATE: Final — B. E. Fairlie (NZ) d. R. Taylor 4-6 6-3 6-4.

LADIES' SINGLES PLATE: Final — M. Wikstedt (SW) d. B. Bruning (USA) 4-6 6-3 6-3.
BOYS' SINGLES: Final — H. P. Gunthardt (SWZ) d. P. Elter (G) 6-4 7-5.
GIRLS' SINGLES: Final — N. Y. Chmyreva (USSR) d. M. Kruger (SA) 6-3 2-6 6-1.
VETERANS' MEN'S DOUBLES: Final — L. Bergelin (SW)/B. Patty (USA) d. H. K. Richards (USA)/R. C. Sorlein (USA) 6-1 4-6 6-1.

GENTLEMEN'S SINGLES

1977

FIRST ROUND: J. S. Connors (1) (USA) d. R. A. Lewis 6-3 6-2 6-4; M. C. Riessen (USA) d. C. J. Lewis (NZ) 6-3 1-6 8-6 6-1; E. C. Drysdale (SA) d. J. Borowiak (USA) 8-9 6-3 7-5 6-2; M. Estep (USA) d. J. Granat (CZ) 6-3 6-3 4-6 7-9 6-2; R. J. Simpson (NZ) d. W. Scanlon (USA) 6-3 7-5 7-5; O. Parun (NZ) d. G. W. Seewagen (USA) 8-6 7-5 9-8; C. M. Pasarell (USA) d. B. Teacher (USA) 6-2 6-1 6-4; **S. R. Smith** (11) (USA) d. R. D. Crealy (A) 6-4 6-2 6-2; **R. C. Lutz** (15) (USA) d. B. Mitton (SA) 6-3 6-4 6-3; R. D. Ralston (USA) d. T. H. Waltke (USA) 5-7 6-4 6-2 9-8; D. A. Lloyd d. R. E. Ycaza (EC) 6-4 3-6 6-3 3-6 6-4; K. G. Warwick (A) d. G. Masters (A) 6-2 6-2 6-3; P. C. Kronk (A) d. J. Delaney (USA) 7-5 6-3 3-6 1-6 6-4; D. Palm (SW) d. F. Gebert (G) 6-3 6-4 6-1; B. M. Bertram (SA) d. C. S. Dibley (A) 6-4 3-6 2-6 6-3 6-2; **B. E. Gottfried** (5) (USA) d. R. Benavides (BOL) 6-3 6-4 6-4; J. M. Lloyd d. **R. Tanner** (4) (USA) 3-6 6-4 6-4 8-6; K. Meiler (G) d. R. A. J. Hewitt (SA) 7-5 4-6 6-1 7-5; C. Dowdeswell (RH) d. J. W. Feaver 6-1 2-6 2-6 6-1 6-3; J. P. McEnroe (USA) d. I. El Shafei (E) 6-0 7-5 6-4; K. B. Walts (USA) d. J. M. P. Marks (A) 6-4 9-8 5-7 8-9 8-6; J. Andrew (V) d. S. W. Carnahan (USA) 6-4 6-2 6-4; A. A. Mayer (USA) d. D. Joubert (SA) 6-2 3-6 6-2 8-9 7-5; **A. Panatta** (10) (IT) d. E. J. van Dillen (USA) 6-4 9-8 4-6 6-3; **P. C. Dent** (13) (A) d. W. Lofgren (USA) 6-1 6-2 6-2; A. Amritraj (IN) d. J. E. Mandarino (BR) 7-5 6-1 6-2; R. J. Moore (SA) d. A. M. Jarrett 6-3 6-3 6-4; L. Alvarez (SP) d. R. Thung (NTH) 6-4 4-6 6-3 6-3; B. E. Fairlie (NZ) d. V. C. Amaya (USA) 8-9 7-5 8-6 6-4; R. J. Carmichael (A) d. M. H. Machette (USA) 4-6 6-3 9-8 6-3; Tim Gullikson (USA) d. S. Krulevitz (USA) 6-2 6-4 6-3; **R. Ramirez** (7) (M) d. P. Fleming (USA) 6-4 3-6 6-2 6-3; **V. Gerulaitis** (8) (USA) d. T. W. Gorman (USA) 6-1 9-8 6-3; G. Mayer (USA) d. J. K. Holladay (USA) 6-4 6-2 6-4; J. R. Smith d. W. P. O. Prinsloo (SA) 6-4 6-4 6-2; H. J. Bunis (USA) d. G. E. Reid (USA) 8-9 6-4 6-8 9-8 8-6; H. G. Gildemeister (CH) d. B. Prajoux (CH) 4-6 6-4 6-8 6-4 6-3; F. V. McNair (USA) d. N. Saviano (USA) 6-3 4-6 6-3 8-9 16-14; R. G. Laver (A) d. S. Sorensen (IRE) 6-0 6-2 6-2; **R. L. Stockton** (9) (USA) d. R. W. Drywdale 6-3 9-8 6-3; **M. Cox** (14) d. R. J. Chappell (SA) 6-4 7-5 8-6; J. G. Alexander (A) d. A. H. Lloyd 6-3 6-4 6-2; R. L. Bohrnstedt (USA) d. A. R. Gardiner (A) 8-9 9-8 6-1 6-4; P. Dominguez (F) d. S. Menon (IN) 6-4 4-6 6-2 6-4; W. W. Martin (USA) d. D. Schneider (SA) 6-4 6-4 6-1; R. O. Ruffels (A) d. R. Taylor 7-5 8-6 2-6 9-7; J. M. Yuill (SA) d. A. Betancur (COL) 6-3 6-4 6-3; **G. Vilas** (3) (ARG) d. J. Kodes (CZ) 9-8 7-5 6-4; **I. Nastase** (6) (RU) d. Tom Gullikson (USA) 6-2 6-1 3-6 6-3; A. J. Pattison (USA) d. E. Montano (M) 6-1 6-4 6-4; E. Teltscher (USA) d. C. Letcher (A) 6-3 0-6 6-3 6-2; P. Dupre (USA) d. T. Smid (CZ) 6-4 6-4 5-7 8-6; C. P. Kachel (A) d. R. Fisher (USA) 6-3 6-3 6-4; A. J. Stone (A) d. C. Kirmayr (BR) 9-8 7-5 6-2; T. S. Okker (NTH) d. R. L. Case (A) 6-2 6-1 6-1; S. Docherty (USA) d. **H. Solomon** (16) (USA) 6-4 4-6 7-5 7-5; **W. Fibak** (12) (POL) d. J. Fillol (CH) 6-3 4-6 4-6 9-8 6-4; J. E. Norback (SW) d. J. H. McManus (USA) 6-1 3-6 6-4 6-2; F. D. McMillan (SA) d. J. Fassbender (G) 6-4 6-4 6-4; C. J. Mottram d. J. S. Hagey (USA) 4-6 6-4 6-4 6-2; N. Pilic (YU) d. H. Pfister (USA) 6-4 6-4 6-1; V. Amritraj (IN) d. S. E. Stewart (USA) 4-6 6-4 6-3 7-5; M. R. Edmondson (A) d. M. D. Wayman 6-4 2-6 6-4 8-9 7-5; **B. Borg** (2) (SW) d. A. Zugarelli (IT) 6-4 6-2 9-7.

SECOND ROUND: Connors (1) d. Riessen 6-4 8-9 6-1 8-6; Drysdale d. Estep 6-3 6-4 6-3; Parun d. Simpson 9-8 6-3 6-4; **S. R. Smith** (11) d. Pasarell 6-4 6-3 7-5; **Lutz** (15) d. Ralston 5-7 6-3 7-5 6-2; Warwick d. D. A. Lloyd 8-6 6-1 6-4; Kronk d. Palm 5-7 6-4 6-8 6-3 6-1; Bertram d. **Gottfried** (5) 6-2 4-6 6-4 6-3; Meiler d. J. M. Lloyd 2-6 3-6 6-2 6-4 9-7; McEnroe d. Dowdeswell 9-7 6-3 6-1; Andrew d. Walts 6-2 8-6 6-4; Mayer d. **Panatta** (10) 8-9 6-0 6-2 6-4; **Dent** (13) d. Amritraj 2-6 9-8 6-3 4-6 6-4; Moore d. Alvarez 6-4 6-4 6-3; Fairlie d. Carmichael 8-6 4-6 6-4 6-3; Tim Gullikson d. **Ramirez** (7) 6-3 6-4 3-6 8-9 6-4; **Gerulaitis** (8) d. Mayer 6-3 6-1 6-1; J. R. Smith d. Bunis 6-3 7-5 1-6 6-4; McNair d. Gildemeister 6-3 6-8 6-2 7-5; **Stockton** (9) d. Laver 3-6 9-7 6-4 7-5; **Cox** (14) d. Alexander 8-6 6-4 7-5; Dominguez d. Bohrnstedt 6-2 9-8 6-3; Martin d. Ruffels 3-6 2-6 9-8 6-2 10-8; **Vilas** (3) d. Yuill 6-3 6-2 3-6 8-6; **Nastase** (6) d. Pattison 7-9 3-6 7-5 8-6 6-3; Teltscher d. Dupre w.o.; Stone d. Kachel 6-2 8-6 6-3; Okker d. Docherty 8-9 7-5 6-3 7-5; **Fibak** (12) d. Norback 6-3 6-0 6-2; Mottram d. McMillan 6-4 7-5 7-5; Pilic d. V. Amritraj 9-8 6-3 6-2; **Borg** (2) d. Edmondson 3-6 7-9 6-2 6-4 6-1.

THIRD ROUND: Connors (1) d. Drysdale 6-2 7-5 6-4; **S. R. Smith** (11) d. Parun 6-3 5-7 9-8 7-5; Warwick d. **Lutz** (15) 6-4 3-6 6-4 2-6 8-6; Bertram d. Kronk 6-4 6-0 6-2; McEnroe d. Meiler 6-2 6-2 5-7 6-3; Mayer d. Andrew 6-4 9-7 6-4; **Dent** (13) d. Moore 8-6 3-6 6-4 7-5; Tim Gullikson d. Fairlie 9-8 6-3 8-9 6-3; **Gerulaitis** (8) d. J. R. Smith 6-3 8-6 6-4; **Stockton** (9) d. McNair 6-4 6-3 6-2; **Cox** (14) d. Dominguez 6-4 6-1 8-6; Martin d. **Vilas** (3) 6-2 6-4 6-2; **Nastase** (6) d. Teltscher 6-4 6-3 6-1; Okker d. Stone 4-6 2-6 9-8 7-5 6-4; **Fibak** (12) d. Mottram 3-6 9-8 6-3 3-6 6-2; **Borg** (2) d. Pilic 9-7 7-5 6-3.

FOURTH ROUND	QUARTER-FINALS	SEMI-FINALS	FINAL	CHAMPION
Connors (1)	**Connors** (1)			
S. R. Smith (11)	7-9 6-2 3-6 6-3 6-3	**Connors** (1)		
Warwick	Bertram	6-4 3-6 6-4 6-2		
Bertram	6-3 6-2 7-5		**Connors** (1)	
McEnroe	McEnroe		6-3 6-3 4-6 6-4	
Mayer	7-5 4-6 6-3 6-1	McEnroe		
Dent (13)	**Dent** (13)	6-4 8-9 4-6 6-3 6-4		
Tim Gullikson	6-3 3-6 9-8 1-6 9-7			**Borg** (2)
Gerulaitis (8)	**Gerulaitis** (8)			3-6 6-2 6-1 5-7 6-4
Stockton (9)	6-1 6-4 3-6 6-4	**Gerulaitis** (8)		
Cox (14)	Martin	6-2 8-9 6-2 6-2		
Martin	3-6 6-3 6-4 0-6 9-7		**Borg** (2)	
Nastase (6)	**Nastase** (6)		6-4 3-6 6-3 3-6 8-6	
Okker	6-8 6-4 6-4 6-4	**Borg** (2)		
Fibak (12)	**Borg** (2)	6-0 8-6 6-3		
Borg (2)	7-5 6-4 6-2			

PRIZE MONEY	
Champion	£15,000
Runner-up	8,000
Semi-finals	4,000
Quarter-finals	2,000
Fourth round	1,200
Third round	600
Second round	350
First round	200

LADIES' SINGLES

FIRST ROUND: C. M. Evert (1) (USA) d. R. Gerulaitis (USA) 6-0 6-3; Mrs E. Vessies-Appel (NTH) d. M. K. Hamm (USA) 6-4 3-6 6-2; B. R. Thompson d. E. M. Dignam (USA) 2-6 7-5 6-1; G. R. Stevens (SA) d. M. Struthers (USA) 6-1 6-0; A. Smith (USA) d. M. Wikstedt (SW) 4-6 6-2 6-0; J. S. Newberry (USA) d. R. C. Giscafre (ARG) 6-4 6-2; W. M. Turnbull (A) d. H. Eisterlehner (G) 6-2 6-1; M. Kruger (SA) d. M. Tyler 6-4 2-6 6-2; **S. V. Wade** (3) d. J. M. Durie 6-2 6-2; J. A. Fayter d. N. U. Bohm (SW) 2-6 6-3 6-2; Mrs E. Peled (IS) d. Mrs M. Pinterova (CZ) 6-1 6-1; M. Simionescu (RU) d. S. Tolleson (USA) 6-2 6-3; **R. Casals** (6) (USA) d. T. J. Harford (SA) 6-3 6-1; J. C. Russell (USA) d. S. Mappin 8-6 6-2; **F. Durr** (11) d. L. Forood (USA) 6-0 8-6; D. A. Boshoff (SA) d. P. J. Whytcross (A) 6-4 6-4; Mrs P. M. Doerner (A) d. B. Bruning (USA) 6-3 6-1; **K. A. May** (12) (USA) d. L. J. Mottram 6-3 6-1; J. K. Anthony (USA) d. N. Sato (J) 6-1 6-3; **Mrs G. E. Reid** (8) (A) d. M. Carillo (USA) 2-6 6-4 7-5; Antonoplis (USA) d. P. L. Bostrom (USA) 6-3 6-4; Mrs J. R. Susman (USA) d. S. E. Saliba (A) 6-1 7-5; A. K. Kiyomura (USA) d. C. Meyer (USA) 6-1 7-5; Mrs H. Masthoff (G) d. F. M. Bonicelli (UR) 2-6 7-5 7-5; Mrs H. F. Gourlay Cawley (A) d. S. A. Walsh (USA) 6-4 6-2; J. Stratton (USA) d. Mrs I. M. Fordyce (USA) 4-6 9-7 6-1; B. Cuypers (SA) d. R. Marsikova (CZ) 6-0 6-4; **B. F. Stove** (7) (NTH) d. S. P. Simmonds (IT) 6-3 6-1; M. Gurdal (B) d. L. Du Pont (USA) 6-2 6-4; T. A. Holladay (US) d. L. J. Beaven 6-3 6-3; L. J. Charles d. B. Simon (F) 6-4 1-6 6-3; **M. Navratilova** (2) (USA) d. G. L. Coles 6-3 6-0.

SECOND ROUND: Evert (1) d. Mrs K. Wooldridge 6-0 6-2; T. A. Austin (USA) d. Vessies-Appel 6-3 6-3; Mrs K. Ebbinghaus (G) d. Thompson 6-2 6-0; Stevens d. A. Spex (USA) 4-6 6-0 6-2; **Mrs L. W. King** (5) (USA) d. Smith 6-8 6-0 6-3; M. E. Bueno (BR) d. Newberry 1-6 8-6 8-6; **M. Jausovec** (10) (YU) d. Turnbull 6-4 6-3; Kruger d. F. Guedy (F) 6-3 6-2; **Wade** (3) d. B. Nagelsen (USA) 6-2 6-1; Y. Vermaak (SA) d. Fayter 6-3 6-1; R. S. Fox (USA) d. Peled 6-4 4-6 6-4; Simionescu d. C. S. Reynolds (USA) 6-4 7-5; **Casals** (6) d. V. J. Ziegenfuss (USA) 6-3 6-3; Russell d. S. H. Hagey (USA) 6-3 7-5; **Durr** (11) d. V. Ruzici (RU) 6-3 7-5; Boshoff d. L. E. Hunt (A) 6-3 6-2; Doerner d. K. M. Harter (USA) 6-3 6-2; **May** (12) d. C. Molesworth 6-2 6-4; Anthony d. I. Reidel (G) 6-2 6-1; **Reid** (8) d. Mrs J. J. Lovera (F) 6-1 6-1; Antonoplis d. C. F. Matison (A) 7-5 6-1; Mrs B. Sparre-Viragh (D) d. Susman 6-3 6-2; Kiyomura d. I. S. Kloss (SA) 6-3 6-4; **S. Barker** (4) d. Masthoff 6-1 6-3; Gourlay Cawley d. A. E. Hobbs 6-4 6-3; Stratton d. C. M. O'Neill 7-9 9-8 6-3; R. Tomanova (CZ) d. Cuypers 6-4 2-6 6-3; **Stove** (7) d. P. A. Teeguarden (USA) 3-6 6-3 6-2; Mrs G. McDade (SA) d. Gurdal 1-6 8-6 6-3; Holladay d. Mrs R. Shaw (USA) 7-5 6-4; Charles d. F. Mihai (RU) 6-2 6-4; **Navratilova** (2) d. Mrs I. A. Lofdahl-Bentzer (SW) 6-0 6-3.

THIRD ROUND: Evert (1) d. Austin 6-1 6-1; Stevens d. Ebbinghaus 6-1 6-3; **King** (5) d. Bueno 6-2 7-5; Kruger d. **Jausovec** (10) 6-4 6-4; **Wade** (3) d. Vermaak 6-1 6-2; Simionescu d. Fox 7-5 6-2; **Casals** (6) d. Russell 6-1 6-1; Boshoff d. **Durr** (11) 6-3 9-7; **May** (12) d. Doerner 6-0 6-2; **Reid** (8) d. Anthony 6-3 9-7; Antonoplis d. Sparre-Viragh 6-4 6-1; **Barker** (4) d. Kiyomura 6-2 6-1; Gourlay Cawley d. Stratton 9-7 6-3; **Stove** (7) d. Tomanova 6-1 6-2; Holladay d. McDade 6-4 6-0; **Navratilova** (2) d. Charles 6-2 6-2.

FOURTH ROUND	QUARTER-FINALS	SEMI-FINALS	FINAL	CHAMPION
Evert (1)	**Evert** (1)			
Stevens	8-6 6-4	**Evert** (1)		
King (5)	**King** (5)	6-1 6-2		
Kruger	4-6 6-0 6-1		**Wade** (3)	
Wade (3)	**Wade** (3)		6-2 4-6 6-1	
Simionescu	9-7 6-3	**Wade** (3)		
Casals (6)	**Casals** (6)	7-5 6-2		
Boshoff	8-6 6-3			**Wade** (3)
May (12)	**Reid** (8)			4-6 6-3 6-1
Reid (8)	6-2 6-1	**Barker** (4)		
Antonoplis	**Barker** (4)	6-3 6-4		
Barker (4)	6-0 6-4		**Stove** (7)	
Gourlay Cawley	**Stove** (7)		6-4 2-6 6-4	
Stove (7)	6-4 6-2	**Stove** (7)		
Holladay	**Navratilova** (2)	9-8 3-6 6-1		
Navratilova (2)	6-4 6-4			

PRIZE MONEY	
Champion	£13,500
Runner-up	7,000
Semi-finals	3,500
Quarter-finals	1,600
Fourth round	925
Third round	460
Second round	270
First round	150

OTHER FINALS

GENTLEMEN'S DOUBLES: Final – R. L. Case (A)/G. Masters (A) d. J. G. Alexander (A)/P. C. Dent (A) 6-3 6-4 3-6 8-9 6-4.
LADIES' DOUBLES: Final – Mrs H. F. Gourlay Cawley (A)/J. C. Russell (USA) d. M. Navratilova (USA)/B. Stove (NTH) 6-3 6-3.
MIXED DOUBLES: Final – R. A. J. Hewitt (SA)/G. Stevens (SA) d. F. D. McMillan (SA)/B. Stove (NTH) 3-6 7-5 6-4.
GENTLEMEN'S SINGLES PLATE: Final – M. C. Riessen (USA) d. G. E. Reid (USA) 6-4 5-7 9-7.
LADIES' SINGLES PLATE: Final – Y. Vermaak (SA) d. S. Mappin 6-2 7-5.
BOYS' SINGLES: Final – V. Winitsky (USA) d. T. E. Teltscher (USA) 6-1 1-6 8-6.
GIRLS' SINGLES: Final – L. Antonoplis (USA) d. M. Louie (USA) 7-5 6-1.
VETERANS' MEN'S DOUBLES: Final – S. Davidson (SW)/T. Ulrich (D) d. R. N. Hartwig (A)/E. V. Seixas (USA) 8-6 6-4.

GENTLEMEN'S SINGLES

1978

FIRST ROUND: B. Borg (1) (SW) d. V. C. Amaya (USA) 8-9 6-1 1-6 6-3 6-3; P. McNamara (A) d. C. Roger-Vasselin (F) 8-6 6-3 5-7 6-3; J. Fillol (CH) d. J. Kodes (CZ) 6-2 6-1 2-0 ret'd; R. W. Drysdale d. J. Hrebec (CZ) 2-6 2-6 6-4 6-3 6-2; O. Bengtson (SW) d. F. S. Stolle (A) 6-4 6-4 7-5; G. Masters (A) d. W. Scanlon (USA) 7-5 6-8 6-3 6-2; F. D. McMillan (SA) d. R. Fagel (USA) 6-1 6-1 6-2; **C. J. Mottram** (12) d. D. Palm (SW) 7-5 6-2 6-2; **W. Fibak** (13) (POL) d. J. L. Clerc (ARG) 6-3 7-5 7-5; J. C. Kriek (SA) d. T. Wilkison (USA) 6-4 7-5 6-3; R. O. Ruffels (A) d. J. G. Paish 6-3 6-4 6-2; T. Moor (USA) d. M. Lara (M) 6-2 6-4 9-8; V. Winitsky (USA) d. B. Manson (USA) 6-1 6-3 4-6 6-3; M. C. Riessen (USA) d. M. J. Fishbach (USA) 6-1 6-2 6-2; M. R. Edmondson (A) d. R. J. Moore (SA) 3-6 2-6 6-4 6-2 6-4; **A. A. Mayer** (8) (USA) d. T. Smid (CZ) 7-5 6-4 6-3; **G. Vilas** (4) (ARG) d. S. R. Smith (USA) 6-4 6-3 6-3; J. W. Feaver d. J. M. Bailey (USA) 6-4 6-4 6-4; T. S. Okker (NTH) d. O. Parun (NZ) 6-8 6-3 6-3 6-2; Y. Noah (F) d. R. E. Ycaza (EC) 8-9 3-6 6-2 6-1 10-8; A. Zugarelli (IT) d. C. P. Kachel (A) 7-5 4-6 2-6 9-8 6-1; T. Leonard (USA) d. P. McNamee (A) 6-3 6-4 6-3; B. E. Fairlie (NZ) d. S. Krulevitz (USA) 6-3 6-3 7-5; S. Docherty (USA) d. **A. R. Ashe** (15) (USA) 8-9 9-8 6-3 5-7 7-5; **I. Nastase** (9) (RU) d. J. M. Yuill (SA) 6-2 6-2 5-7 6-3; G. Ocleppo (IT) d. S. Birner (CZ) 6-3 4-6 6-4 8-6; M. H. Machette (USA) d. V. Zednik (CZ) 9-7 4-6 6-3 6-3; Tom Gullikson (USA) d. R. J. Carmichael (A) 6-3 6-4 8-6; P. Fleming (USA) d. J. Granat (CZ) 9-8 9-8 6-4; F. V. McNair (USA) d. C. Letcher (A) 6-3 7-5 6-4; R. G. Giltinan (A) d. D. A. Lloyd 6-2 6-1 9-8; **R. Tanner** (6) (USA) d. I. El Shafei (E) 8-9 1-6 6-2 9-7 6-2; **B. E. Gottfried** (5) (USA) d. J. M. Lloyd 6-1 6-8 8-6 6-4; B. Teacher (USA) d. R. C. Lutz (USA) 6-4 6-4 3-6 6-1; A. J. Stone (A) d. T. Rocavert (A) 6-1 6-4 6-4; B. Mitton (SA) d. M. J. Farrell 6-1 5-7 6-1 6-4; J. Simbera (CZ) d. A. M. Jarrett 7-5 8-6 3-6 6-3; Tim Gullikson (USA) d. A. J. Pattison (USA) 6-4 3-6 6-1 6-0; W. W. Martin (USA) d. J. Borowiak (USA) 5-7 6-4 6-4 6-4; E. J. van Dillen (USA) d. **J. P. McEnroe** (11) (USA) 7-5 1-6 8-9 6-4 6-3; J. M. P. Marks (A) d. **R. L. Stockton** (10) (USA) 6-2 9-8 7-5; N. Saviano (USA) d. C. Bradnam 6-4 6-2 3-6 6-1; H. Pfister (USA) d. A. Fillol (CH) 6-1 6-1 6-2; D. Carter (A) d. R. A. Lewis 8-6 6-4 9-8; S. E. Stewart (USA) d. M. D. Wayman 6-4 9-8 6-3; R. Fisher (USA) d. J. F. Caujolle (F) 6-3 6-3 6-1; J. Royappa (IN) d. G. Halder (C) 2-6 6-3 6-2 6-2; **V. Gerulaitis** (3) (USA) d. H. P. Gunthardt (SWZ) 6-2 6-2 4-6 6-1; **R. Ramirez** (7) (M) d. C. S. Dibley (A) 9-7 9-8 6-3; D. Schneider (SA) d. R. D. Crealy (A) 6-2 6-4 9-8; R. J. Frawley (A) d. I. Tiriac (RU) 3-6 6-3 6-4 6-4; E. Deblicker (F) d. L. Sanders (NTH) 6-2 8-9 6-3 3-6 6-3; P. C. Dent (A) d. A. D. Roche (A) 6-4 7-5 4-6 4-6 7-5; V. Amritraj (IN) d. C. Kirmayr (BR) 6-1 6-3 9-8; R. L. Case (A) d. B. Prajoux (CH) 7-5 4-6 7-9 6-1 6-4; **J. D. Newcombe** (16) (A) d. D. H. Collings (A) 4-6 7-5 7-5 6-3; **J. G. Alexander** (14) (A) d. V. Pecci (PA) 7-5 4-6 9-8 8-9 12-10; Anand Amritraj (IN) d. J. R. Smith 6-3 6-0 6-4; R. A. J. Hewitt (SA) d. G. Hardie (USA) 3-6 5-7 6-4 6-3 6-2; C. Dowdeswell (SWZ) d. R. Taylor 5-7 6-3 6-4 4-6 6-2; T. W. Gorman (USA) d. C. J. Lewis (NZ) 0-6 6-2 4-6 7-5 6-3; M. Cox d. J. James (A) 6-4 3-6 6-4 6-4; K. G. Warwick (A) d. G. Mayer (USA) 7-5 0-6 6-0 2-6 6-4; **J. S. Connors** (2) (USA) d. R. J. Simpson (NZ) 7-5 9-8 6-1.

SECOND ROUND: Borg (1) d. McNamara 6-2 6-2 6-4; Fillol d. Drysdale 6-3 6-3 6-2; Masters d. Bengtson 6-0 6-8 9-8 6-4; McMillan d. **Mottram** (12) 9-8 6-4 6-3; **Fibak** (13) d. Kriek 8-6 4-6 6-2 6-4; Moor d. Ruffels 7-5 7-5 9-8; Riessen d. Winitsky 6-3 6-2 4-6 9-7; **Mayer** (8) d. Edmondson 6-4 6-2 4-6 6-2; **Vilas** (4) d. Feaver 6-3 2-6 6-4 6-3; Okker d. Noah 6-2 6-3 6-2; Leonard d. Zugarelli 6-2 6-4 9-8; Fairlie d. Docherty 6-3 6-4 6-3; **Nastase** (9) d. Ocleppo 6-3 6-4 9-7; Tom Gullikson d. Machette 6-4 6-4 6-2; McNair d. Fleming 9-8 6-8 4-6 8-6 6-3; **Tanner** (6) d. Giltinan 6-2 6-2 6-4; **Gottfried** (5) d. Teacher 6-2 7-5 6-3; Stone d. Mitton 6-1 2-6 6-8 6-1 10-8; Tim Gullikson d. Simbera 6-2 6-3 6-4; Martin d. van Dillen 5-7 7-5 6-8 6-4 7-5; Saviano d. Marks 6-3 6-2 6-3; Pfister d. Carter 6-3 6-4 9-8; Stewart d. Fisher 6-4 9-7 9-7; **Gerulaitis** (3) d. Royappa 6-3 7-5 6-2; **Ramirez** (7) d. Schneider 6-1 6-0 6-2; Frawley d. Deblicker 7-9 6-0 6-0 6-3; Dent d. Amritraj 3-6 6-3 6-3 4-6 7-5; **Newcombe** (16) d. Case 6-4 6-2 9-8; **Alexander** (14) d. Anand Amritraj 5-7 6-3 7-5 6-2; Hewitt d. Dowdeswell 6-4 4-6 6-2 6-4; Gorman d. Cox 4-6 8-6 8-6 7-5; **Connors** (2) d. Warwick 6-3 7-5 2-6 6-4.

THIRD ROUND: Borg (1) d. Fillol 6-4 6-2 6-8 6-4; Masters d. McMillan 6-3 7-5 6-1; **Fibak** (13) d. Moor 6-1 4-6 7-5 9-7; **Mayer** (8) d. Riessen 8-6 7-5 6-3; Okker d. **Vilas** (4) 6-3 6-4 6-2; Leonard d. Fairlie 6-2 4-6 8-6 6-3; **Nastase** (9) d. Tom Gullikson 6-4 6-3 1-6 6-3; **Tanner** (6) d. McNair 6-4 6-2 6-2; **Gottfried** (5) d. Stone 6-8 9-7 6-2 6-1; Tim Gullikson d. Martin 6-3 9-7 7-5; Pfister d. Saviano 9-7 8-9 6-2 6-2; **Gerulaitis** (3) d. Stewart 9-8 6-0 6-2; **Ramirez** (7) d. Frawley 6-4 7-5 6-3; **Newcombe** (16) d. Dent 6-1 1-6 6-4 6-4; **Alexander** (14) d. Hewitt 8-6 ret'd; **Connors** (2) d. Gorman 6-4 8-6 8-9 6-3.

FOURTH ROUND	QUARTER-FINALS	SEMI-FINALS	FINAL	CHAMPION
Borg (1)	**Borg** (1)			
Masters	6-2 6-4 8-6	**Borg** (1)		
Fibak (13)	**Mayer** (8)	7-5 6-4 6-3		
Mayer (8)	6-4 6-2 6-8 1-6 7-5		**Borg** (1)	
Okker	Okker		6-4 6-4 6-4	
Leonard	6-1 9-8 6-1	Okker		
Nastase (9)	**Nastase** (9)	7-5 6-1 2-6 6-3		
Tanner (6)	2-6 6-4 6-2 6-3			**Borg** (1)
Gottfried (5)	**Gottfried** (5)			6-2 6-2 6-3
Tim Gullikson	6-2 6-4 6-2	**Gerulaitis** (3)		
Pfister	**Gerulaitis** (3)	7-5 4-6 9-7 6-2		
Gerulaitis (3)	6-3 3-6 6-2 6-3		**Connors** (2)	
Ramirez (7)	**Ramirez** (7)		9-7 6-2 6-1	
Newcombe (16)	6-2 9-8 6-3	**Connors** (2)		
Alexander (14)	**Connors** (2)	6-4 6-4 6-2		
Connors (2)	6-2 6-2 6-4			

PRIZE MONEY	
Champion	£19,000
Runner-up	9,600
Semi-finals	4,800
Quarter-finals	2,400
Fourth round	1,440
Third round	720
Second round	420
First round	250

LADIES' SINGLES

FIRST ROUND: H. Anliot (SW) d. F. Thibault (F) 6-4 6-2; Mrs J. D. Chaloner (NZ) d. S. McInerney (USA) 9-7 6-4; Mrs B. Sparre-Viragh (D) d. G. L. Coles 6-3 6-4; **Mrs G. E. Reid** (10) (A) d. L. Antonoplis (USA) 6-2 6-4; **S. Barker** (14) d. A. K. Kiyomura (USA) 6-4 6-1; P. H. Shriver (USA) d. M. Wikstedt (SW) 6-3 6-3; R. Tomanova (CZ) d. L. J. Mottram 6-1 6-4; **Mrs L. W. King** (5) (USA) d. M. Gurdal (B) 6-0 6-2; **S. V. Wade** (4) d. E. Ekblom (SW) 6-1 6-2; Y. Vermaak (SA) d. D. L. Ganz (USA) 6-1 6-4; R. Gerulaitis (USA) d. S. Tolleson (USA) 6-4 6-2; **M. Redondo** (16) (USA) d. J. A. Fayter 6-1 7-5; **M. Jausovec** (12) (YU) d. F. Mihai (RU) 6-3 6-1; Mrs R. L. Cawley (A) d. W. Barlow (C) 6-1 6-3; H. Strachonova (CZ) d. C. S. Reynolds (USA) 6-1 7-5; S. Mappin d. Mrs E. Peled (IS) 6-2 6-4; S. A. Margolin (USA) d. A. E. Hobbs 6-1 6-2; F. Durr (F) d. F. M. Bonicelli (UR) 6-1 6-0; B. Cuypers (SA) d. K. M. Harter (USA) 9-8 6-0; **V. Ruzici** (13) (RU) d. Mrs K. Wooldridge 6-1 6-2; **R. Marsikova** (15) (CZ) d. V. J. Ziegenfuss (USA) 6-0 7-5; K. A. May (USA) d. P. A. Teeguarden (USA) 6-1 8-6; J. S. Newberry (USA) d. J. Stratton (USA) 7-5 6-4; L. Forood (USA) d. B. Simon (F) 6-0 6-1; **D. L. Fromholtz** (8) (A) d. Mrs K. Ebbinghaus (G) 8-6 6-3; T. A. Holladay (USA) d. K. D. Latham (USA) 6-4 7-5; I. S. Kloss (SA) d. C. M. O'Neil (A) 6-1 6-1; P. G. Smith (USA) d. J. M. Durie 6-1 9-7; **T. Austin** (9) (USA) d. D. Desfor (USA) 6-1 6-8 6-4; J. DuVall (USA) d. S. L. Collins (USA) 5-7 7-5 6-1; B. K. Jordan (USA) d. M. Louie (USA) 6-2 9-8; **M. Navratilova** (2) (USA) d. J. K. Anthony (USA) 6-1 6-3.

SECOND ROUND: C. M. Evert (1) (USA) d. Anliot 6-1 6-0; L. Du Pont (USA) d. Chaloner 6-2 6-0; Sparre-Viragh d. I. Riedel (G) 4-6 6-2 6-1; **Reid** (10) d. M. Simionescu (RU) 6-1 6-0; **Barker** (14) d. T. J. Harford (SA) 6-1 6-3; Shriver d. R. M. Harris (USA) 6-0 6-0; Tomanova d. D. R. Evers (A) 5-7 6-3 6-2; **King** (5) d. Mrs M. Pinterova (CZ) 6-3 6-2; **Wade** (4) d. Mrs W. W. Bowrey (A) 6-1 6-4; Vermaak d. B. C. Potter (USA) 6-0 4-6 6-2; Gerulaitis d. H. Ludloff (USA) 6-0 6-0; **Redondo** (16) d. S. A. Walsh (USA) 6-2 6-2; **Jausovec** (12) d. J. C. Russell (USA) 9-8 7-9 6-4; M. Tyler d. Mrs R. L. Cawley 6-3 6-4; C. Meyer (USA) d. Strachonova 9-8 6-1; **W. M. Turnbull** (7) (A) d. Mappin 8-9 6-3 6-4; **B. F. Stove** (6) (NTH) d. Margolin 6-1 6-3; Durr d. L. J. Charles 6-2 6-2; Cuypers d. M. L. Blackwood (C) 7-5 6-2; **Ruzici** (13) d. R. C. Giscafre (ARG) 6-3 7-5; **Marsikova** (15) d. L. E. Hunt (A) 9-8 4-6 6-3; May d. C. L. Stoll (USA) 6-2 6-3; Newberry d. S. Hanika (G) 6-3 9-8; **Mrs R. A. Cawley** (3) (A) d. Forood 6-0 6-2; **Fromholtz** (8) d. Mrs T. E. Guerrant (USA) 6-3 6-2; Holladay d. B. Bruning (USA) 3-6 7-5 6-4; Kloss d. Mrs P. M. Doerner (A) 6-3 6-1; **M. Kruger** (11) (SA) d. Smith 6-4 6-4; **Austin** (9) d. B. Nagelsen (USA) 6-2 6-1; B. Hallquist (USA) d. DuVall 2-6 7-5 6-3; Jordan d. V. Gonzalez (ARG) 6-2 6-0; **Navratilova** (2) d. P. J. Whytcross (A) 7-5 6-1.

THIRD ROUND: Evert (1) d. Du Pont 6-1 4-6 6-0; **Reid** (10) d. Sparre-Viragh 6-0 6-4; **Barker** (14) d. Shriver 2-6 8-6 7-5; **King** (5) d. Tomanova 4-6 6-3 6-3; **Wade** (4) d. Vermaak 6-4 4-6 7-5; Gerulaitis d. **Redondo** (16) 6-0 6-2; **Jausovec** (12) d. Tyler 2-6 6-2 6-3; **Turnbull** (7) d. Meyer 6-2 8-6; **Stove** (6) d. Durr 6-3 6-2; **Ruzici** (13) d. Cuypers 8-6 6-4; **Marsikova** (15) d. May 4-6 6-2 13-11; **Mrs R. A. Cawley** (3) d. Newberry 6-4 6-3; **Fromholtz** (8) d. Holladay 3-6 6-2 7-5; **Kruger** (11) d. Kloss 6-4 6-4; **Austin** (9) d. Hallquist 6-3 6-3; **Navratilova** (2) d. Jordan 3-6 6-1 6-4.

FOURTH ROUND	QUARTER-FINALS	SEMI-FINALS	FINAL	CHAMPION
Evert (1)	**Evert** (1)			
Reid (10)	6-3 6-4	**Evert** (1)		
Barker (14)	**King** (5)	6-3 3-6 6-2		
King (5)	6-2 6-2		**Evert** (1)	
Wade (4)	**Wade** (4)		8-6 6-2	
Gerulaitis	7-5 6-4	**Wade** (4)		
Jausovec (12)	**Jausovec** (12)	6-0 6-4		
Turnbull (7)	8-6 4-6 6-3			**Navratilova** (2)
Stove (6)	**Ruzici** (13)			2-6 6-4 7-5
Ruzici (13)	5-7 6-4 6-3	**Mrs R. A. Cawley** (3)		
Marsikova (15)	**Mrs R. A. Cawley** (3)	7-5 6-3		
Mrs R. A. Cawley (3)	6-2 6-1		**Navratilova** (2)	
Fromholtz (8)	**Kruger** (11)		2-6 6-4 6-4	
Kruger (11)	4-6 6-4 6-3	**Navratilova** (2)		
Austin (9)	**Navratilova** (2)	6-2 6-4		
Navratilova (2)	6-2 6-3			

PRIZE MONEY	
Champion	£17,100
Runner-up	8,400
Semi-finals	4,200
Quarter-finals	1,920
Fourth round	1,110
Third round	552
Second round	324
First round	188

OTHER FINALS

GENTLEMEN'S DOUBLES: Final – R. A. J. Hewitt (SA)/F. D. McMillan (SA) d. P. Fleming (USA)/J. P. McEnroe (USA) 6-1 6-4 6-2.
LADIES' DOUBLES: Final – Mrs G. E. Reid (A)/W. M. Turnbull (A) d. M. Jausovec (YU)/V. Ruzici (RU) 4-6 9-8 6-3.
MIXED DOUBLES: Final – F. D. McMillan (SA)/B. F. Stove (NTH) d. R. O. Ruffels (A)/Mrs L. W. King (USA) 6-2 6-2.
GENTLEMEN'S SINGLES PLATE: Final – D. H. Collings (A) d. T. Wilkison (USA) 3-6 9-8 6-4.
LADIES' SINGLES PLATE: Final – Mrs T. E. Guerrant (USA) d. H. Strachonova (CZ) 6-2 8-6.
BOYS' SINGLES: Final – I. Lendl (CZ) d. J. Turpin (USA) 6-3 6-4.
GIRLS' SINGLES: Final – T. Austin (USA) d. H. Mandlikova (CZ) 6-0 3-6 6-4.

GENTLEMEN'S SINGLES

1979

FIRST ROUND: B. Borg (1) (SW) d. T. W. Gorman (USA) 3-6 6-4 7-5 6-1; V. Amritraj (IN) d. M. R. Edmondson (A) 6-7 4-6 6-3 6-2 6-2; H. Pfister (USA) d. J. Kodes (CZ) 6-3 3-6 7-6 7-6; P. Fleming (USA) d. J. Fillol (CH) 3-6 6-3 6-2 6-4; D. Schneider (SA) d. R. J. Carmichael (A) 6-4 7-6 6-1; B. Teacher (USA) d. C. S. Dibley (A) 6-4 3-6 6-3 7-5; J. Borowiak (USA) d. P. C. Kronk (A) 6-2 6-2 6-4; **B. E. Gottfried** (9) (USA) d. A. M. Jarrett 6-2 7-6 6-1; **J. G. Alexander** (11) (A) d. R. L. Stockton (USA) 6-1 7-6 4-6 7-5; H. P. Gunthardt (SWZ) d. B. Mitton (SA) 6-4 6-1 6-3; O. Parun (NZ) d. D. A. Lloyd 6-2 4-6 7-5 6-3; G. Mayer (USA) d. V. C. Amaya (USA) 3-6 6-3 6-4 7-5; T. S. Okker (NTH) d. R. Guedes (BR) 6-1 7-5 6-1; J. R. Austin (USA) d. E. C. Drysdale 6-2 7-6 6-3; T. Wilkison (USA) d. N. R. Phillips (A) 6-2 6-2 6-2; **G. Vilas** (6) (ARG) d. R. Taylor 6-3 6-2 6-4; **J. S. Connors** (3) (USA) d. J. F. Caujolle (F) 6-2 6-7 6-1 6-3; M. C. Riessen (USA) d. U. Eriksson (SW) 6-3 6-4 7-5; J. C. Kriek (SA) d. P. Feigl (AU) 4-6 6-3 6-0; J. E. Norback (SW) d. A. Fillol (CH) 7-5 6-1 3-6 6-3; B. Taroczy (HU) d. R. Crawford (USA) 6-2 6-2 6-4; M. Cox d. K. Meiler (G) 7-5 6-3 6-3; G. Moretton (F) d. J. A. Cortes (COL) 7-5 6-7 6-2 1-0 ret'd; **M. Orantes** (13) (SP) d. R. J. Moore (SA) 7-6 6-7 7-6 4-6 6-4; A. J. Pattison (USA) d. **C. Barazzutti** (16) (IT) 6-3 6-4 5-7 6-4; C. Dowdeswell (SWZ) d. J. B. Fitzgerald (A) 6-4 6-7 7-6 6-2; F. Gonzalez (USA) d. R. C. Beven 4-6 6-2 6-2 6-4; W. Scanlon (USA) d. R. W. Drysdale 6-3 6-3 7-5; B. Drewett (A) d. J. M. P. Marks (A) 7-5 2-6 7-6 6-2; J. James (A) d. V. E. Iskersky (USA) 6-2 6-1 6-4; P. C. Dent (A) d. R. Fisher (USA) 7-5 6-1 7-6; **V. Pecci** (8) (PA) d. S. E. Stewart (USA) 7-5 6-2 6-3; C. P. Kachel (A) d. **A. R. Ashe** (7) (USA) 6-4 7-6 6-3; O.

Bengtson (SW) d. J. M. Lloyd 6-3 6-4 6-1; J. R. Smith d. A. R. Gardiner (A) 1-6 4-6 6-3 6-2 6-4; A. Panatta (IT) d. A. Gimenez (SP) 6-3 6-3 6-4; A. A. Mayer (USA) d. C. M. Pasarell (USA) 6-1 6-7 6-3 6-3; R. Ramirez (M) d. J. Andrew (V) 6-2 6-3 6-1; J. Sadri (USA) d. I. El Shafei (E) 3-6 6-3 7-6 6-7 6-4; **J. Higueras** (12) (SP) d. J. M. Yuill (SA) 6-2 7-5 5-7 3-6 6-4; B. Manson d. **W. Fibak** (10) (POL) 4-6 6-7 6-4 6-2 9-7; F. Buehning (USA) d. R. Meyer (USA) 6-3 6-4 6-4; R. C. Lutz (USA) d. R. Genois (C) 6-3 6-2 6-2; R. E. Ycaza (EC) d. D. P. Whyte (A) 6-4 1-6 6-2 6-0; Y. Noah (F) d. R. Krishnan (IN) 7-6 6-3 7-5; N. Saviano (USA) d. R. Fagel (USA) 6-0 6-1 6-2; C. Kirmayr (BR) d. J. W. Feaver 6-1 4-6 3-6 6-3 6-4; P. Dupre (USA) d. **V. Gerulaitis** (4) (USA) 7-6 6-3 3-6 6-3; **R. Tanner** (5) (USA) d. V. Winitsky (USA) 6-1 6-2 6-3 6-1; P. McNamara (A) d. I. Lendl (CZ) 6-3 6-2 6-3; P. Portes (F) d. F. Taygan (USA) 1-6 6-4 4-6 6-4 7-5; R. L. Case (A) d. W. W. Martin (USA) 7-5 6-7 6-2 6-2; J. L. Damiani (UR) d. C. Motta (BR) 7-5 6-3 6-4; S. R. Smith (USA) d. D. Carter (A) 6-4 3-6 6-3 3-6 6-3; **Tim Gullikson** (15) (USA) d. M. Cahill (USA) 6-4 6-2 6-4; T. Smid (CZ) d. H. Ismail (RH) 7-5 7-6 6-2; C. Letcher (A) d. K. G. Warwick (A) 7-6 6-1 2-6 7-6; P. Dominguez (F) d. P. Hutka (CZ) 6-3 6-3 6-4; A. Maurer (G) d. Anand Amritraj (IN) 6-3 6-3; **J. L. Clerc** (14) (ARG) d. R. G. Giltinan (A) 6-4 3-6 6-3 3-6 6-3; Tom Gullikson (USA) d. P. Slozil (CZ) 4-6 6-2 6-1 3-6 6-1; C. J. Mottram d. R. A. Lewis 6-4 6-3 7-5; **J. P. McEnroe** (2) (USA) d. T. Moor 7-5 6-1 6-4.

SECOND ROUND: Borg (1) d. V. Amritraj 2-6 6-4 4-6 7-6 6-2; Pfister d. Fleming 6-1 6-3 3-6 6-4; Teacher d. Schneider 6-4 6-4 6-4; **Gottfried** (9) d. Borowiak 6-4 6-4 6-4; Alexander (11) d. Gunthardt 6-3 6-4 6-3; Mayer d. Parun 6-4 6-1 6-2; Okker d. Austin 7-6 6-4 3-6 6-2; Wilkison d. **Vilas** (6) 5-7 6-2 6-1 7-6; **Connors** (3) d. Riessen 6-7 6-3 7-6 6-0; Kriek d. Norback 6-1 3-6 6-4; Cox d. Taroczy 6-4 4-6 6-3 7-6; Moretton d. Orantes (13) 7-6 3-6 7-6 3-6 6-1; Pattison d. Dowdeswell 6-3 6-4 6-0; Scanlon d. Gonzalez 7-6 6-4 6-2; Drewett d. James 7-5 7-5 6-3; **Pecci** (8) d. Dent 6-4 7-6 6-3; Bengtson d. Kachel 7-5 6-3 0-6 6-7 6-4; Panatta d. Smith 2-6 6-2 6-7 7-5 6-3; Mayer d.

Ramirez 6-3 7-6 4-6 7-6; Sadri d. **Higueras** (12) 6-3 5-7 6-4 7-5; Manson d. Buehning 7-6 4-6 6-4 6-4; Lutz d. Ycaza 6-0 6-3 6-2; Noah d. Saviano 6-1 7-6 6-3 6-4; Dupre d. Kirmayr 4-6 7-6 6-3 6-4; **Tanner** (5) d. McNamara 6-1 7-6 6-4; Case d. Portes 6-2 6-1 7-5; Smith d. Damiani 6-3 6-2 7-6; **Clerc** (14) d. Munoz 6-1 6-3 6-4; **Tim Gullikson** (15) d. Smid 7-5 6-7 6-2 6-4; Letcher d. Dominguez 6-1 3-6 6-3 6-4; Tom Gullikson d. Maurer 6-1 6-4 6-4; **McEnroe** (2) d. Mottram 6-7 6-2 7-6 6-2.

THIRD ROUND: Borg (1) d. Pfister 6-4 6-1 6-3; Teacher d. Gottfried (9) 6-3 7-5 5-7 6-3; Mayer d. Alexander (11) 6-4 6-4 6-4; Okker d. Wilkison 7-5 7-5 6-4; Connors (3) d. Kriek 6-4 6-1 7-6; Cox d. Moretton 3-6 6-4 7-5; Scanlon d. Pattison 7-6 4-6 6-4 6-2; Drewett d. Pecci (8) 4-6 7-6 7-6 6-4; Panatta d. Bengtson 7-6 7-6 7-6; Mayer d. Sadri 6-7 7-5 7-6 6-2; Lutz d. Manson 6-7 6-4 6-3 6-2; Dupre d. Noah 7-5 1-6 6-3 6-1; **Tanner** (5) d. Case 6-4 7-5 7-6; **Clerc** (14) d. Smith 6-7 7-6 6-3 7-5; **Tim Gullikson** (15) d. Letcher 6-0 6-4 6-1; **McEnroe** (2) d. Tom Gullikson 6-4 6-4 7-6.

FOURTH ROUND	QUARTER-FINALS	SEMI-FINALS	FINAL	CHAMPION	PRIZE MONEY	
Borg (1)	**Borg** (1)				Champion	£20,000
Teacher	6-4 5-7 6-4 7-5	**Borg** (1)			Runner-up	10,000
Mayer	Okker	6-2 6-1 6-3			Semi-finals	5,000
Okker	7-6 5-7 6-4 6-4		**Borg** (1)		Quarter-finals	2,500
Connors (3)	**Connors** (3)		6-2 6-3 6-2		Fourth round	1,500
Cox	6-2 6-1 6-1	**Connors** (3)			Third round	760
Scanlon	Scanlon	6-3 4-6 7-6 6-4		**Borg** (1)	Second round	440
Drewett	6-4 6-4 6-7 7-5			6-7 6-1 3-6 6-3 6-4	First round	265
Panatta	Panatta					
Mayer	7-6 6-3 7-6	Dupre				
Lutz	Dupre	3-6 6-4 6-7 6-4 6-3				
Dupre	3-6 7-5 4-6 6-4 8-6		**Tanner** (5)			
Tanner (5)	**Tanner** (5)		6-3 7-6 6-3			
Clerc (14)	6-7 7-6 6-4 6-1	**Tanner** (5)				
Tim Gullikson (15)	**Tim Gullikson** (15)	6-1 6-4 6-7 6-2				
McEnroe (2)	6-4 6-2 6-4					

LADIES' SINGLES

FIRST ROUND: M. Navratilova (1) (USA) d. T. J. Harford (SA) 4-6 6-2 6-1; R. Casals (USA) d. H. Eisterlehner (G) 7-6 7-6; R. Gerulaitis (USA) d. A. P. Cooper 6-3 6-4; G. L. Coles d. M. Kruger (SA) 5-7 6-4 7-5; **B. F. Stove** (15) (NTH) d. J. DuVall (USA) 6-4 6-1 6-4; K. McDaniel (USA) d. Mrs K. Ebbinghaus (G) 7-5 4-6 6-1; D. Porzio (IT) d. K. D. Latham (USA) 6-4 6-1; B. Stuart (USA) d. D. R. Evers (A) 4-6 6-4 6-1; M. B. K. Wikstedt (SW) d. S. A. Walsh (USA) 6-2 7-6; S. L. Collins (USA) d. I. Budarova (CZ) 6-4; A. E. Hobbs d. L. J. Charles 6-2 7-5; H. Mandlikova (CZ) d. D. Morrison (USA) 6-3 6-4; M. Jausovec (YU) d. S. Simmonds (IT) 6-2 6-2; **Mrs L. W. King** (7) d. Y. Vermaak (SA) 6-4 6-1;

S. V. Wade (5) d. P. Louie (USA) 6-0 6-4; S. Hanika (G) d. B. C. Potter (USA) 6-4 6-3; I. Riedel (G) d. F. Thibault (F) 2-6 6-1 6-3; I. Madruga (ARG) d. **S. Barker** (12) 6-3 4-6 8-6; B. Bunge (G) d. M. Pakker (NTH) 3-6 7-6 8-6; P. A. Teeguarden (USA) d. R. Tomanova (CZ) 7-6 6-4; Mrs P. M. Doerner (A) d. E. Raponi (ARG) 6-2 6-4; **Mrs R. A. Cawley** (3) (A) d. M. Louie (USA) 6-0 6-3; L. Forood (USA) d. F. Gilbert (USA) 4-6 7-5 7-5; M. Carillo (USA) d. A. K. Kiyomura (USA) 6-2 3-6 6-4; R. S. Fox (USA) d. Mrs J. J. Lovera (F) 6-4 6-2; **Mrs G. E. Reid** (9) (A) d. R. L. Blount (USA) 6-1 6-0; **P. H. Shriver** (16) (USA) d. P. S. Medrado (BR) 6-4 6-3; S. A. Margolin (USA) d. J. C. Russell (USA) 7-5 6-2; A. A. Moulton (USA) d. M. Tyler (A) 6-4 6-3; **Mrs J. M. Lloyd** (2) (USA) d. M. Redondo (USA) 6-4 6-2.

SECOND ROUND: Navratilova (1) d. J. M. Durie 6-4 6-1; Casals d. F. Durr (F) 7-5 6-2; Gerulaitis d. V. Gonzalez (ARG) 3-6 6-3 6-1; **G. R. Stevens** (11) (SA) d. Coles 6-0 6-3; **Stove** (15) d. C. M. O'Neil (A) 6-3 6-1; McDaniel d. Mrs M. Pinterova (CZ) 7-6 6-2; M. A. Mesker (NTH) d. Porzio 7-6 7-5; **Fromholtz** (6) d. M. L. Blackwood (C) 6-2 6-3; **T. Austin** (4) (USA) d. Cuypers (SA) 6-4 6-2; Stuart d. I. S. Kloss (SA) 7-5 3-6 6-4; Wikstedt d. A. E. Smith (USA) 6-3 6-4; **V. Ruzici** (10) (RU) d. Collins 6-3 6-4; **R. Marsikova** (13) (CZ) d. Hobbs 6-3 5-7 9-7; Mandlikova d. A. M. Fernandez (USA) 7-5 6-1; D. Desfor (USA) d. Jausovec 7-5 6-4; **King** (7) d. L. R. Siegel (USA) 6-1 6-3; **Wade** (5) d. B. K. Jordan

(USA) 6-0 6-1; Hanika d. L. Antonoplis (USA) 7-5 7-6; D. A. Jevans d. Riedel 6-1 3-6 6-1; A. M. Tobin (A) d. Madruga 4-6 7-6 7-5; **K. Jordan** (14) d. Bunge 6-1 6-4; H. Strachonova (CZ) d. Teeguarden 2-6 6-4 7-5; Doerner d. B. R. Thompson 5-7 6-3 6-0; **Cawley** (3) d. S. L. Acker (USA) 6-3 6-1; **W. M. Turnbull** (8) (A) d. Forood 6-3 6-3; Carillo d. B. Nagelsen (USA) 6-0 6-2; Fox d. M. Simionescu (RU) 6-4 6-1; **Reid** (9) d. C. Meyer (USA) 6-1 6-2; L. Du Pont (USA) d. **Shriver** (16) w.o.; W. White (USA) d. Margolin 6-1 3-6 9-7; Mrs B. Teacher (USA) d. Moulton 6-1 7-5; **Lloyd** (2) d. A. Whitmore (USA) 6-1 6-2.

THIRD ROUND: Navratilova (1) d. Casals 6-3 6-3; **Stevens** (11) d. Gerulaitis 6-3 6-2; **Stove** (15) d. McDaniel 2-6 6-3 6-2; **Fromholtz** (6) d. Mesker 7-5 6-4; **Austin** (4) d. Stuart 6-2 6-3; **Ruzici** (10) d. Wikstedt 6-3 6-0; Mandlikova d. **Marsikova** (13) 6-3 6-2; **King** (7) d. Desfor 6-3 6-2; **Wade** (5) d. Hanika 6-3 7-6; Jevans d. Tobin 3-6 7-5 6-2; **K. Jordan** (14) d. Strachonova 6-2 6-2; **Cawley** (3) d. Doerner 7-5 6-2; **Turnbull** (8) d. Carillo 6-1 6-3; **Reid** (9) d. Fox 6-3 6-1; Du Pont d. White 7-5 6-3; **Lloyd** (2) d. Teacher 6-4 6-3.

FOURTH ROUND	QUARTER-FINALS	SEMI-FINALS	FINAL	CHAMPION	PRIZE MONEY	
Navratilova (1)	**Navratilova** (1)				Champion	£18,000
Stevens (11)	7-6 6-7 6-3	**Navratilova** (1)			Runner-up	8,750
Stove (15)	**Fromholtz** (6)	2-6 6-3 6-0			Semi-finals	4,375
Fromholtz (6)	7-6 7-6		**Navratilova** (1)		Quarter-finals	2,000
Austin (4)	**Austin** (4)		7-5 6-1		Fourth round	1,160
Ruzici (10)	6-2 6-4	**Austin** (4)			Third round	858
Mandlikova	**King** (7)	6-4 6-7 6-2		**Navratilova** (1)	Second round	340
King (7)	6-4 6-3			6-4 6-4	First round	200
Wade (5)	**Wade** (5)					
Jevans	6-1 6-2	**Cawley** (3)				
K. Jordan (14)	**Cawley** (3)	6-4 6-0				
Cawley (3)	7-6 6-7 6-1		**Lloyd** (2)			
Turnbull (8)	**Turnbull** (8)		6-3 6-2			
Reid (9)	6-3 4-6 6-3	**Lloyd** (2)				
Du Pont	**Lloyd** (2)	3-6 6-4				
Lloyd (2)	6-2 6-1					

OTHER FINALS

GENTLEMEN'S DOUBLES: Final – P. Fleming (USA)/J. P. McEnroe (USA) d. B. E. Gottfried (USA)/R. Ramirez (M) 4-6 6-4 6-2 6-2.
LADIES' DOUBLES: Final – Mrs L. W. King (USA)/M. Navratilova (USA) d. B. F. Stove (NTH)/W. M. Turnbull (A) 5-7 6-3 6-2.
MIXED DOUBLES: Final – R. A. J. Hewitt (SA)/G. R. Stevens (SA) d. F. D. McMillan (SA)/B. F. Stove (NTH) 7-5 7-6.
GENTLEMEN'S SINGLES PLATE: Final – P. C. Kronk (A) d. M. R. Edmondson (A) 6-7 6-2 6-4.

LADIES' SINGLES PLATE: Final – S. Barker d. S. Simmonds (IT) 7-6 6-0.
BOYS' SINGLES: Final – R. Krishnan (IN) d. D. Siegler (USA) 6-0 6-2.
GIRLS' SINGLES: Final – M. L. Piatek (USA) d. A. A. Moulton (USA) 6-1 6-3.
GRAND MASTERS/SENIORS INVITATION MEN'S DOUBLES: Final – R. N. Hartwig (A)/F. A. Sedgman (A) d. N. A. Fraser (A)/R. Gonzales (USA) 6-3 3-6 6-4.

GENTLEMEN'S SINGLES

FIRST ROUND: B. Borg (1) (SW) d. I. El Shafei (E) 6-3 6-4 6-4; S. Glickstein (IS) d. R. Ramirez (M) 4-6 6-2 3-6 7-5 8-6; R. J. Frawley (A) d. P. Hjertquist (SW) 6-2 6-1 6-2; T. Graham (USA) d. H. D. Schoenfield (USA) 6-2 6-4 6-1; R. Krishnan (IN) d. W. Scanlon (USA) 6-4 6-4 6-4; M. Cox d. G. Moretton (F) 3-6 6-1 6-4 6-4; B. Taroczy (HU) d. C. Delaney (USA) 6-3 3-6 6-4 6-4 6-2; T. H. Waltke (USA) d. W. D. Hampson (A) 3-6 6-4 6-4 6-2; **I. Lendl** (10) (CZ) d. M. C. Riessen (USA) 6-3 4-6 6-2 6-4; J. Sadri (USA) d. W. W. Martin (USA) 4-6 2-6 6-4; C. S. Dibley (A) d. T. Leonard (USA) 6-1 6-2 7-6; G. Masters (A) d. R. J. Moore (SA) 2-6 6-2 6-0 6-2; C. Barazzutti (IT) d. S. E. Davis (USA) 5-7 6-4 6-2 6-3; A. Panatta (IT) d. E. J. van Dillen (USA) 3-6 2-6 7-6 7-5 9-7; A. M. Jarrett d. C. Mayotte (USA) 7-6 6-7 6-4; **G. Mayer** (6) (USA) d. C. M. Johnstone (A) 6-3 4-6 6-1 6-2; **V. Gerulaitis** (4) (USA) d. S. Simonsson (SW) 6-0 6-4 6-2; S. Menon (IN) d. R. W. Drysdale 6-7 4-6 6-0 6-4 6-4; R. L. Case (A) d. F. Gonzalez (USA) 7-6 6-4 6-3; B. Manson (USA) d. Tom Gullikson (USA) 7-6 6-7 7-6 6-4; J. R. Austin (USA) d. A. Gomez (EC) 6-2 6-1 7-6; J. C. Kriek (SA) d. F. Buehning (USA) 6-3 7-6 6-2; R. J. Simpson (NZ) d. D. Bedel (F) 6-7 6-4 6-4 7-6; **W. Fibak** (13) (POL) d. M. R. Edmondson (A) 5-7 6-4 3-6 7-6 6-0 8; **S. R. Smith** (15) (USA) d. A. J. Pattison (USA) 2-6 7-6 6-3 6-4; A. Kiyomura (USA) d. P. Feigl (AU) 6-4 6-1 6-6-3 3-6 6-3; B. E. Gottfried (USA) d. C. P. Kachel (A) 7-5 6-3 6-1; C. J. Lewis (NZ) d. L. Palin (FIN) 6-4 3-6 7-5 5-7 6-4; P. C. Dent (A) d. R. Trogolo (SA) 4-6 7-6 3-6 6-3 6-4; B. M. Mitton (SA) d. J. R. Smith 6-2 6-3 3-6 6-3; J. Kodes (CZ) d. A. Giammalva (USA) 7-6 5-7 6-3 6-3; **V. Pecci** (8) (PA) d. M. Mitchell (USA) 5-7 6-1 7-6; **R. Tanner** (5) d. J. Hrebec (CZ) 6-2 6-0 6-4; J. B. Fitzgerald (A) d. T. Koch (BR) 7-6 6-7 6-2 6-3; P. McNamee (A) d. P. Doohan (A) 6-2 7-6 6-3; R. Van't Hof (USA) d. F. Taygan (USA) 7-6 2-6 7-5 6-4; C. J. Mottram d. J. M. Lloyd 6-4 6-2 6-2; N. Saviano (USA) d. E. Edwards (USA) 6-4 6-4 6-2; E. C. Drysdale (SA) d. B. M. Bertram (SA) 6-3 3-6 3-6 7-6 6-4; **P. Dupre** (9) (USA) d. V. Van Patten (USA) 6-4 3-6 6-1 6-4; H. Pfister (USA) d. **V. C. Amaya** (14) (USA) 3-6 6-4 6-0 3-6 6-3; R. C. Lutz (USA) d. G. Hardie (USA) 7-6 6-7 6-1 7-5; Tim Gullikson (USA) d. B. Prajoux (CH) 7-5 6-3 6-1; K. G. Warwick (A) d. B. J. E. Boileau (B) 4-6 6-1 6-3 6-3; H. P. Gunthardt (SWZ) d. J. M. Yuill (SA) 7-5 6-3 7-6; W. Maher (A) d. P. McNamara (A) 2-6 6-1 6-3 6-2; S. E. Stewart (USA) d. P. Rennert (USA) 7-6 6-7 6-4 6-3; **J. S. Connors** (3) (USA) d. R. A. Lewis 6-0 6-3 6-1; **P. Fleming** (7) (USA) d. C. Dowdeswell (SWZ) 7-5 6-3 6-4; S. Birner (CZ) d. T. W. Gorman (USA) 6-4 7-5 6-4; I. Nastase (RU) d. J. W. Feaver 6-2 6-3 7-6; R. L. Stockton (USA) d. A. A. Mayer (USA) 7-6 3-6 4-6 6-3 6-2; P. Portes (F) d. V. Winitsky (USA) 6-4 3-6 6-7 9-7; O. Parun (NZ) d. C. Gattiker (ARG) 6-1 5-7 6-1 6-1; B. Fritz (F) d. J. G. Paish 6-4 7-6 7-6; **J. L. Clerc** (16) (ARG) d. V. Amritraj (IN) 1-6 3-6 7-5 7-5 6-4; K. Curren (USA) d. M. N. Doyle (USA) 6-4 6-3 6-7 6-2; B. Drewett (A) d. D. D. Schneider (IS) 4-6 6-3 6-3 6-7 6-3; S. Krulevitz (USA) d. M. Mir (SP) 6-2 6-3 6-0; B. Teacher (USA) d. T. Wilkison (USA) 6-4 7-6 7-5; T. S. Okker (NTH) d. J. James (A) 6-3 7-6 6-3; P. Dominguez (F) d. S. Sorensen (IRE) 6-2 7-6 6-1; T. J. Rocavert (A) d. R. Taylor 6-1 3-6 2-6 6-4 6-3; **J. P. McEnroe** (2) (USA) d. B. Walts (USA) 6-3.

SECOND ROUND: Borg (1) d. Glickstein 6-3 6-1 7-5; Frawley d. Graham 6-7 2-6 6-1 6-2 13-11; Krishnan d. Cox 6-7 7-5 7-5 6-1; Taroczy d. Waltke 6-3 6-2 6-2; Lendl (10) d. Sadri 6-3 6-4 6-3; Dibley d. Masters 2-6 6-2 7-6 6-7 8-6; Panatta d. Barazzutti 1-6 6-3 6-4 3-6 6-1; **Mayer** (6) d. Jarrett 6-4 6-4 6-1; **Gerulaitis** (4) d. Menon 6-7 6-4 7-5 6-2; Manson d. Case 7-6 7-6 4-6 6-3; Kriek d. Austin 6-4 6-3 6-4; **Smith** (15) d. Feigl 4-6 6-1 7-6 6-1; Gottfried d. Lewis 6-3 6-4 6-3; Dent d. Mitton 7-5 6-3 6-3; **Pecci** (8) d. Kodes 6-3 6-4 6-4; **Tanner** (5) d. Fitzgerald 6-1 3-6 6-3 7-6; McNamee d. Van't Hof 6-1 6-1 6-3; Saviano d. Mottram 6-7 7-6 6-3 4-6 13-11; **Dupre** (9) d. Drysdale 6-2 6-3 6-0; Pfister d. Lutz 6-2 6-3 6-1; Tim Gullikson d. Warwick 3-6 6-3 6-2 7-6; Gunthardt d. Maher 7-5 6-4 6-2; **Connors** (3) d. Stewart 6-0 6-2 6-1; **Fleming** (7) d. Birner 4-6 6-3 6-4 6-2; Nastase d. Stockton 4-6 6-2 5-7 6-2 6-2; Parun d. Portes 7-5 6-3 6-4; **Clerc** (16) d. Fritz 6-4 7-6 3-6 6-0; Curren d. Drewett 7-6 6-7 6-4 6-4; Teacher d. Krulevitz 4-6 6-2 6-1 6-1; Okker d. Dominguez 7-6 7-6 1-6 2-6 6-3; **McEnroe** (2) d. Rocavert 4-6 7-5 6-7 7-6 6-3.

THIRD ROUND: Borg (1) d. Frawley 6-4 6-7 6-1 7-5; Taroczy d. Krishnan 6-3 7-6 6-2; Dibley d. **Lendl** (10) 4-6 6-3 6-4 7-6; **Mayer** (6) d. Panatta 6-3 6-3 6-2; **Gerulaitis** (4) d. Manson 6-4 4-6 7-5 6-4; **Fibak** (13) d. Kriek 6-1 6-4 6-1; Gottfried d. Smith (15) 6-2 6-3 6-2; Dent d. Pecci (8) 3-6 6-2 6-3 6-1; **Tanner** (5) d. McNamee 7-6 6-4 6-4; Saviano d. **Dupre** (9) 7-6 1-6 4-6 7-5 11-9; Pfister d. Tim Gullikson 4-6 6-3 7-5 1-6 6-2; **Connors** (3) d. Gunthardt 7-6 6-2 6-1 6-4; **Fleming** (7) d. Nastase 6-4 3-6 7-6 7-6; Parun d. **Clerc** (16) 3-6 7-6 6-4 6-3; Curren d. Teacher 5-7 6-2 6-3 6-1; **McEnroe** (2) d. Okker 6-0 7-6 6-1.

FOURTH ROUND	QUARTER-FINALS	SEMI-FINALS	FINAL	CHAMPION	PRIZE MONEY	
Borg (1)	**Borg** (1)				Champion	£20,000
Taroczy		**Borg** (1)			Runner-up	10,000
Dibley	6-1 7-5 6-2	7-5 6-3 7-5			Semi-finals	5,000
Mayer (6)	**Mayer** (6)		**Borg** (1)		Quarter-finals	2,500
Gerulaitis (4)	3-6 7-5 4-6 6-1 6-2		6-2 4-6 6-2 6-0		Fourth round	1,600
Fibak (13)	**Fibak** (13)				Third round	850
Gottfried	3-6 4-6 6-3 6-3 8-6	Gottfried			Second round	500
Dent	Gottfried	6-4 7-6 6-2			First round	300
Tanner (5)	6-1 6-2 6-2			**Borg** (1)		
Saviano	**Tanner** (5)			1-6 7-5 6-3 6-7 8-6		
Pfister	7-6 3-6 6-3 6-4					
Connors (3)	**Connors** (3)	**Connors** (3)				
Fleming (7)	6-4 6-7 6-1 7-6	1-6 6-2 4-6 6-2 6-2				
Parun	**Fleming** (7)		**McEnroe** (2)			
Curren	6-3 6-2 6-7 7-6		6-3 3-6 6-3 6-4			
McEnroe (2)	**McEnroe** (2)	**McEnroe** (2)				
	7-5 7-6 7-6	6-3 6-2 6-2				

LADIES' SINGLES

FIRST ROUND: M. Navratilova (1) (USA) d. I. S. Kloss (SA) 6-0 6-3; T. J. Harford (SA) d. Y. Vermaak (SA) 6-1 6-4; P. A. Teeguarden (USA) d. M. Carillo (USA) 6-2 6-1; **K. Jordan** (10) (USA) d. K. Y. Sands (USA) 6-1 6-1; P. H. Shriver (USA) d. H. Eisterlehner (G) 6-4 3-6 6-1; K. J. Brasher d. D. F. Gilbert (USA) 6-3 6-3 8-6; A. K. Kiyomura (USA) d. Y. Brzakova (CZ) 6-3 6-1; A. E. Smith (USA) d. J. DuVall (USA) 6-2 6-2; C. Jolissaint (SWZ) d. N. S. Yeargin (USA) 6-2 6-4; Mrs B. Teacher (USA) d. R. Tomanova (CZ) 3-6 6-3 6-4; N. U. Bohm (SW) d. I. Budarova (CZ) 6-3 6-4; **V. Ruzici** (12) (RU) d. S. Simmonds (IT) 7-6 6-4; **A. Jaeger** (14) (USA) d. A. P. Cooper (A) 6-3 6-2; D. Desfor (USA) d. S. L. Collins (USA) 6-3 6-2; K. D. Latham (USA) d. G. L. Coles (USA) 6-0 6-4; **S. V. Wade** (7) (USA) d. I. Madruga (ARG) 6-4 6-4; E. Ekblom (SW) d. L. E. Allen (USA) 6-3 6-7 6-3; D. A. Jevans d. M. L. Piatek (USA) 6-2 4-6 6-1; L. K. Forood (USA) d. Mrs M. Tobin Evans (A) 6-3 6-4; Mrs P. C. Dent (USA) d. L. Geeves 3-6 6-3 6-3; W. E. White (USA) d. P. J. Whytcross (A) 6-2 6-3; R. D. Fairbank (SA) d. T. A. Lewis (USA) 6-4 6-4; B. F. Stove (NTH) d. L. Antonoplis (USA) 7-5 6-3; **Mrs R. Cawley** (4) (A) d. S. A. Walsh (USA) 6-1 6-2; **D. L. Fromholtz** (8) (A) d. R. E. McCallum (USA) 7-5 6-5; L. J. Charles d. J. A. Harrington (USA) 6-3 5-7 6-1; B. Bunge (G) d. J. M. Durie 6-4 4-6 6-4; **G. R. Stevens** (11) (SA) d. P. G. Smith (USA) 6-1 6-4; S. E. Saliba (A) d. F. Mihai (RU) 6-1 6-1; T. Holladay (USA) d. S. L. Rollinson (SA) 6-2 6-2; R. L. Blount (USA) d. R. Gerulaitis (USA) 6-3 7-6; **T. Austin** (2) (USA) d. A. A. Moulton (USA) 6-1 6-2.

SECOND ROUND: Navratilova (1) d. R. S. Fox (USA) 6-1 6-1; Harford d. R. Casals (USA) 6-3 4-6 8-6; Teeguarden d. M. A. Mesker (NTH) 6-0 7-6; **K. Jordan** (10) d. K. McDaniel (USA) 6-3 6-1; Shriver d. **S. Hanika** (16) (G) 6-3 1-6 9-7; B. K. Jordan (USA) d. Brasher 6-4 6-0; P. Louie (USA) d. Kiyomura 3-6 6-2 8-6; A. K. Kiyomura (USA) 6-3 6-2; **Mrs L. W. King** (5) (USA) d. A. J. Walker (A) 6-2 6-0; **Mrs J. M. Lloyd** (3) d. Jolissaint 6-0 6-1; L. E. Morse (USA) d. Teacher 6-4 6-4; Bohm d. D. C. Morrison (USA) 4-6 6-2 6-3; J. C. Russell (USA) d. **Ruzici** (12) 6-2 3-6 6-4; **Jaeger** (14) d. M. Redondo (USA) 6-2 6-3; J. Stratton (USA) d. Desfor 7-5 4-6 7-5; B. Nagelsen (USA) d. Latham 4-6 6-1 6-4; **Wade** (7) d. H. Anliot (SW) 6-1 6-3; **W. M. Turnbull** (6) d. A. Ekblom 6-1 6-4; S. L. Acker (USA) d. Jevans 1-3 6-6 6-2; Forood d. D. H. Lee (KOR) 6-4 6-1; Dent d. **S. Barker** (13) 3-6 7-5 6-2; **H. Mandlikova** (9) (CZ) d. White 6-4 6-7 6-4; Fairbank d. A. Buchanan 6-2 6-0; **Cawley** (4) d. Charles 2-6 7-6 6-3; Bunge d. B. Norton (USA) 6-4 6-0; **Stevens** (11) d. M. L. Blackwood (C) 6-3 6-1; Saliba d. **R. Marsikova** (15) 6-2 3-6 6-1; Holladay d. S. E. Mascarin (USA) 6-1 6-0; B. C. Potter (USA) d. Blount 7-6 7-5; **Austin** (2) d. N. F. Gregory (A) 6-1 6-2.

THIRD ROUND: Navratilova (1) d. Harford 6-3 3-6 6-3; **K. Jordan** (10) d. Teeguarden 6-4 6-3; Shriver d. B. K. Jordan 6-4 6-4; King (5) d. Louie 6-2 6-2; **Lloyd** (3) d. Morse 6-1 6-4; Russell d. Bohm 6-1 3-6 6-3; **Jaeger** (14) d. Stratton 6-1 6-1; **Wade** (7) d. Nagelsen 6-7 7-5 6-3; Turnbull (6) d. Acker 6-3 6-2; Forood d. Dent 6-2 2-6 6-3; **Mandlikova** (9) d. Fairbank 6-2 6-4; **Cawley** (4) d. Stove 3-6 6-2 6-3; **Fromholtz** (8) d. Margolin 6-4 6-2; **Stevens** (11) d. Bunge 6-4 6-3; Holladay d. Saliba 6-3 6-4; **Austin** (2) d. Potter 6-2 6-7 6-2.

FOURTH ROUND	QUARTER-FINALS	SEMI-FINALS	FINAL	CHAMPION	PRIZE MONEY	
Navratilova (1)	**Navratilova** (1)				Champion	£18,000
K. Jordan (10)	6-4 6-2	**Navratilova** (1)			Runner-up	8,750
Shriver	**King** (5)	7-6 1-6 10-8			Semi-finals	4,375
King (5)	5-7 7-6 10-8		**Lloyd** (3)		Quarter-finals	2,000
Lloyd (3)	**Lloyd** (3)		4-6 6-4 6-2		Fourth round	1,245
Russell	6-3 6-2	**Lloyd** (3)			Third round	660
Jaeger (14)	**Jaeger** (14)	6-1 6-1			Second round	390
Wade (7)	6-2 7-6				First round	230
Turnbull (6)	**Turnbull** (6)			**Cawley** (4)		
Forood	6-0 6-2			6-1 7-6		
Mandlikova (9)	**Cawley** (4)	**Cawley** (4)				
Cawley (4)	6-7 6-3 6-1	6-3 6-2				
Fromholtz (8)	**Stevens** (11)		**Cawley** (4)			
Stevens (11)	6-2 6-2		6-3 0-6 6-4			
Holladay	**Austin** (2)	**Austin** (2)				
Austin (2)	6-2 6-3	6-3 6-3				

OTHER FINALS

GENTLEMEN'S DOUBLES: Final — P. McNamara (A)/P. McNamee (A) d. R. C. Lutz (USA)/S. R. Smith (USA) 7-6 6-3 6-7 6-4.
LADIES' DOUBLES: Final — K. Jordan (USA)/A. E. Smith (USA) d. R. Casals (USA)/W. M. Turnbull (A) 4-6 7-5 6-1.
MIXED DOUBLES: Final — J. R. (USA)/T. Austin (USA) d. M. R. Edmondson (A)/D. L. Fromholtz (A) 4-6 7-6 6-3.
GENTLEMEN'S SINGLES PLATE: Final — S. Glickstein (IS) d. P. Dominguez (F) 6-3 7-6.

LADIES' SINGLES PLATE: Final — R. D. Fairbank (SA) d. S. A. Walsh (USA) 6-4 6-2.
BOYS' SINGLES: Final — T. Tulasne (F) d. H. D. Beutel (G) 6-4 3-6 6-4.
GIRLS' SINGLES: Final — D. Freeman (A) d. S. Leo (A) 7-6 7-5.
INVITATION VETERANS' DOUBLES: Final — R. K. Wilson/R. Becker d. O. Williams (SA)/A. Segal (SA) 6-2 6-2.

GENTLEMEN'S SINGLES

1981

FIRST ROUND: B. Borg (1) (SW) d. P. Rennert (USA) 7-6 6-3 6-1; M. Purcell (USA) d. D. H. Collings (A) 6-4 6-3 6-3; F. Taygan (USA) d. N. Saviano (USA) 7-5 6-1 6-2; R. Gehring (G) d. U. Marten (G) 7-6 6-2 6-7 6-3; V. C. Amaya (USA) d. P. Feigl (AU) 6-4 7-6 6-7 7-6; C. J. Mottram d. R. W. Drysdale 6-1 6-4 4-6 6-3; K. Curren (SA) d. J. M. Bailey (USA) 6-7 4-6 6-3 7-6 6-4; **V. Gerulaitis** (16) (USA) d. G. S. Holroyd (USA) 6-3 6-4 7-6; **P. McNamara** (12) (A) d. H. P. Gunthardt (SWZ) 6-1 6-2 2-6 7-5; S. E. Stewart (USA) d. J. Delaney (USA) 7-5 6-3 6-7 6-3; A. Gimenez (SP) d. J. Windahl (SW) 6-3 7-5 6-2; A. J. Pattison (USA) d. S. Giammalva (USA) 6-3 6-7 6-3 7-6; Tim Gullikson (USA) d. G. Rinaldini (IT) 6-1 6-2 6-3; P. Fleming (USA) d. S. Docherty (USA) 7-6 6-2 2-6 7-6; J. Borowiak (USA) d. E. J. van Dillen (USA) 6-2 6-4 4-6 6-2; **B. E. Gottfried** (7) (USA) d. B. Walts (USA) 6-3 6-3 6-2; **J. S. Connors** (3) (USA) d. R. L. Stockton (USA) 6-1 6-2 6-4; C. J. Lewis (NZ) d. C. M. Dunk (USA) 6-7 7-6 6-0 6-4 6-4; P. Dupre (USA) d. T. Smid (CZ) 7-5 6-3 3-6 6-2; A. Giammalva (USA) d. S. E. Davis (USA) 6-2 7-6 6-2; C. J. Wittus (USA) d. E. Edwards (USA) 6-4 6-4; B. Drewett (A) d. M. Hocevar (BR) 7-6 4-6 6-4 6-3; M. Davis (USA) d. S. Glickstein (IS) 7-5 5-7 2-6 7-5 6-4; **W. Fibak** (14) (POL) d. M. N. Doyle (USA) 6-3 6-4; **J. L. Clerc** (9) (ARG) d. A. Fillol (CH) 3-6 6-3 2-6 6-4 9-7; J. M. Lloyd d. P. C. Dent 4-6 4-3 6-4 6-3 6-4; W. R. Pascoe (A) d. P. Portes (F) 5-7 7-6 6-2 7-6; P. C. Kronk (A) d. W. W. Martin (USA) 6-2 6-3 3-6 6-4; R. Van't Hof (USA) d. K. Eberhard (G) 6-4 6-4 6-4; T. Wilkison (USA) d. T. S. Okker (NTH) 7-5 5-7 7-4 7-6; V. Amritraj (IN) d. J. Kodes (CZ) 6-0 6-1 7-5; **B. Teacher** (6) (USA) d. R. Stadler (SWZ) 4-6 6-0 6-3

6-3; **R. Tanner** (8) (USA) d. B. Manson (USA) 6-1 6-4 6-4; C. Kirmayr (BR) d. M. Cox 6-3 6-7 6-4 6-4; C. Letcher (A) d. L. Stefanki (USA) 6-1 7-6 6-3; R. J. Frawley (A) d. T. Tulasne (F) 4-6 6-2 6-3 6-0; M. Wilander (SW) d. J. R. Austin (USA) 6-7 6-2 6-2 6-2; H. Leconte (F) d. J. G. Alexander (A) 6-4 2-6 6-4 6-2; J. B. Fitzgerald (A) d. S. McCain (USA) 5-7 7-6 6-2 6-3; W. Scanlon (USA) d. **V. Pecci** (11) (PA) 7-6 6-0 6-0; M. R. Edmondson (A) d. **G. Vilas** (10) (ARG) 6-4 6-1 1-6 4-6 6-3; F. Buehning (USA) d. R. A. Lewis 7-5 4-6 6-4 6-4; H. Simonsson (SW) d. S. Krulevitz (USA) 4-6 2-6 6-4 6-4 6-3; A. A. Mayer (USA) d. I. Nastase (RU) 6-4 4-6 4-6 6-4 6-4; J. Sadri (USA) d. A. M. Jarrett 6-3 6-7 6-3 7-6; C. Roger-Vasselin (F) d. J. Lopez-Maeso (SP) 6-4 6-4 7-6; T. S. Mayotte (USA) d. B. M. Mitton (SA) 6-3 6-4 6-2; T. C. Fancutt (A) d. **I. Lendl** (4) (CZ) 4-6 6-3 6-4 1-6 6-3; J. C. Kriek (SA) d. M. Estep (USA) 6-0 6-3 6-7 6-3; J. Nystrom (SW) d. S. Menon (IN) 6-4 6-3 6-4; R. J. Simpson (NZ) d. S. Denton (USA) 7-6 3-6 7-6; G. Moretton (F) d. J. Fillol (CH) 4-6 6-3 6-2 6-3; P. McNamee (A) d. P. Slozil (CZ) 6-3 6-4 6-2; C. M. Johnstone (A) d. A. Miller (USA) 4-6 1-6 6-4 6-3; F. Gonzalez (USA) d. C. C. Freyss (F) 6-0 7-5 6-2; E. H. Fromm (USA) d. **Y. Noah** (13) (F) 6-4 4-6 6-3; **B. Taroczy** (15) (HU) d. A. Jarryd (SW) 7-6 6-4 6-3; R. Meyer (USA) d. R. J. Hightower (USA) 6-2 6-2 6-4; S. R. Smith (USA) d. H. Ismail (ZIM) 6-3 6-1 6-3; R. L. Case (A) d. R. Fagel (USA) 6-1 6-2 6-1; R. C. Lutz (USA) d. D. Carter (A) 3-6 7-4 6-6 6-1 6-3; J. W. Feaver d. F. Maynetto (PE) 7-6 6-2 6-1; R. Ramirez (M) d. R. J. Moore (SA) 6-4 7-5 6-2; **J. P. McEnroe** (2) (USA) d. Tom Gullikson (USA) 7-6 7-5 6-3.

SECOND ROUND: Borg (1) d. Purcell 6-4 6-1 6-3; Gehring d. Taygan 7-6 7-6; Amaya d. Mottram 6-3 6-4 6-2; **Gerulaitis** (16) d. Curren 6-3 6-7 6-3 6-3; **McNamara** (12) d. Stewart 5-4 6-0 6-1; Pattison d. Gimenez 4-6 7-6 6-7 6-1 6-4; Tim Gullikson d. Fleming 3-6 7-6 7-6 6-3; Borowiak d. **Gottfried** (7) 6-4 7-6 6-4; **Connors** (3) d. Lewis 7-6 7-6 6-3; Giammalva d. Dupre 6-4 6-4 7-6; Drewett d. Wittus 6-3 6-0 6-4; **Fibak** (14) d. Davis 6-4 6-4 6-4; **Clerc** (9) d. Lloyd 4-6 6-3 6-4 6-4; Kronk d. Pascoe 7-5 6-3 6-4; Wilkison d. Van't Hof 6-4 6-2; Amritraj d. **Teacher** (6) 6-4 2-6 2-6 6-2 6-1; Kirmayr d. **Tanner** (8) 6-4 6-4 3-6 6-2; Frawley d. Letcher 6-3 6-1 6-3; Wilander d. Leconte 4-6

6-4 6-2 6-2; Fitzgerald d. Scanlon 6-1 6-2 6-2; Buehning d. Edmondson 6-4 6-3 5-7 7-5; Mayer d. Simonsson 6-2 6-1 7-6; Sadri d. Roger-Vasselin 7-6 6-7 6-3 6-4; Mayotte d. Fancutt 4-6 6-4 7-6 6-3; Kriek d. Nystrom 6-2 6-4 6-7 6-3; Simpson d. Moretton 6-4 3-6 6-3; McNamee d. Johnstone 6-2 6-1 6-2; Gonzalez d. Fromm 6-3 6-7 7-5 6-3; **Taroczy** (15) d. Meyer 7-6 6-3 7-6; Smith d. Case 6-3 7-6 7-6; Lutz d. Feaver 6-3 7-5 6-1; **McEnroe** (2) d. Ramirez 6-3 6-7 6-3 7-6.

THIRD ROUND: Borg (1) d. Gehring 6-4 7-5 6-0; **Gerulaitis** (16) d. Amaya 4-6 6-4 3-6 6-3 7-5; **McNamara** (12) d. Pattison 6-1 6-0 7-5; Borowiak d. Tim Gullikson 6-3 7-6 4-6 6-3; **Connors** (3) d. Giammalva 6-4 6-4 6-0; **Fibak** (14) d. Drewett 7-6 6-1 3-6 3-6 6-4; Kronk d. **Clerc** (9) 2-6 6-4 6-1 7-6; Amritraj d. Wilkison 6-3 6-2 3-6 6-4; Frawley d.

Kirmayr 7-6 6-3 6-3; Fitzgerald d. Wilander 6-0 4-6 6-2 6-2; Mayer d. Buehning 6-4 2-6 7-6 5-7 6-1; Mayotte d. Sadri 7-6 4-3 7-5; Kriek d. Simpson 7-6 3-6 6-2 7-5; Gonzalez d. McNamee 6-4 6-2 6-2; Smith d. **Taroczy** (15) 6-3 6-2 6-3; **McEnroe** (2) d. Lutz 6-4 6-2 6-0.

FOURTH ROUND	QUARTER-FINALS	SEMI-FINALS	FINAL	CHAMPION
Borg (1)	**Borg** (1)			
Gerulaitis (16)	7-6 7-5 7-6	**Borg** (1)		
McNamara (12)	**McNamara** (12)	7-6 6-2 6-3		
Borowiak	7-6 6-0 7-6		**Borg** (1)	
Connors (3)	**Connors** (3)		0-6 4-6 6-3 6-0 6-4	
Fibak (14)	6-3 6-2 6-4			
Kronk	Amritraj	**Connors** (3)		
Amritraj	6-3 6-3 6-2	2-6 5-7 6-4 6-3 6-2		
Frawley	Frawley			**McEnroe** (2)
Fitzgerald	6-4 6-3 7-6			4-6 7-6 7-6 6-4
Mayer	Mayotte	Frawley		
Mayotte	6-3 6-4 7-6	4-6 7-6 7-6 6-3		
Kriek	Kriek		**McEnroe** (2)	
Gonzalez	3-6 6-3 7-6 6-1		7-6 6-4 7-5	
Smith	**McEnroe** (2)	**McEnroe** (2)		
McEnroe (2)	7-5 3-6 6-1 6-2	6-1 7-5 6-1		

PRIZE MONEY

Champion	£21,600
Runner-up	10,800
Semi-finals	5,400
Quarter-finals	2,700
Fourth round	1,730
Third round	920
Second round	540
First round	325

LADIES' SINGLES

FIRST ROUND: Mrs J. M. Lloyd (1) (USA) d. C. M. O'Neil (A) 6-3 6-0; K. Y. Sands (USA) d. S. Jaeger (USA) 6-1 6-2; K. S. Rinaldo (USA) d. S. L. Rollinson (SA) 6-3 2-6 9-7; P. Delhees (SWZ) d. L. J. Charles 7-5 7-6; **M. Jausovec** (10) (YU) d. P. Louie (USA) 0-6 6-2 6-4; T. J. Harford (SA) d. A. H. White (USA) 6-3 6-2; L. E. Allen (USA) d. A. P. Cooper 6-1 6-3; **A. Jaeger** (5) (USA) d. N. F. Gregory (A) 6-1 6-1; **T. A. Austin** (3) (USA) d. J. A. Mundel (SA) 6-0 6-2; S. J. Leo (A) d. I. Madruga (ARG) 6-3 2-6 6-4; S. L. Collins (USA) d. R. Casals (USA) 6-4 6-3; C. Kohde (G) d. A. K. Kiyomura (USA) 6-3 6-0; L. Romanov (RU) d. **R. Marsikova** (15) (CZ) 5-7 6-1 6-3; P. Casale (USA) d. K. J. Brasher 7-5 6-3; G. L. Coles d. T. A. Holladay (USA) 7-5 6-4; **P. H. Shriver** (7) (USA) d. E. Ekblom (SW) 3-6 6-1 6-2; **V. Ruzici** (8)

(RU) d. K. B. Cummings (USA) 6-3 6-4; N. U. Bohm (SW) d. S. A. Margolin (USA) 6-0 6-7 6-3; H. Strachonova (SWZ) d. C. C. Casabianca (ARG) 6-1 6-4; M. A. Mesker (NTH) d. K. G. Jones (USA) 6-2 6-3; S. Barker d. M. L. Blackwood (C) 6-1 6-0; D. Desfor (USA) d. I. Villiger (SW) 6-2 6-0; S. Norton (USA) 6-2 7-6; **M. Navratilova** (4) (USA) d. J. Portman (USA) 6-4 6-0; **W. M. Turnbull** (6) (A) d. D. Desfor (USA) 7-5 6-3; R. D. Fairbank (USA) d. C. S. Reynolds (USA) 6-4 6-0; E. S. Pfaff (G) d. D. Freeman (USA) 6-3 6-2; P. A. Teeguarden (USA) d. **J. C. Russell** (16) (USA) 6-2 6-7 11-9; M. L. Piatek (USA) d. **S. Hanika** (9) (G) 6-4 7-5; A. E. Hobbs d. Mrs I. Riedel Kuhn (G) 6-1 6-1; B. L. Hallquist (USA) d. Mrs E. Vessies (NTG) 3-6 6-4 6-3; **H. Mandlikova** (2) (CZ) d. C. Vanier (F) 6-3 7-5.

SECOND ROUND: Lloyd (1) d. Y. Vermaak (SA) 6-1 6-2; L. K. Forood (USA) d. Sands 6-1 7-5; C. Pasquale (SWZ) d. Rinaldi 3-6 6-0 6-0; **D. L. Fromholtz** (11) (A) d. Delhees 7-6 6-2; **Jausovec** (10) d. C. Jolissaint (SWZ) 6-3 6-3; R. L. Blount (USA) d. Harford 2-6 7-6 6-3; Allen d. Mrs M. Pinterova (CZ) 4-6 6-2; Jaeger (5) d. B. F. Stove (NTH) 4-6 6-4 6-3; **Austin** (3) d. L. Antonoplis (USA) 6-1 6-1; Leo d. G. Langela (BR) 6-1 4-6 6-2; Collins d. S. E. Saliba (USA) 3-6 7-5 6-2; Coles d. P. G. Smith (USA) 3-6 6-0 6-0 6-4; **Shriver** (7) d. E. M. Little (A) 6-0 6-3; **Ruzici** (8) d. M. B. K. Wikstedt

(SW) 4-6 7-6 6-4; Bohm d. H. Eisterlehner (G) 7-6 4-6 6-2; S. L. Acker (USA) d. Strachonova 4-6 6-1 6-4; **K. Jordan** (12) (USA) d. Mesker 6-4 6-3; Barker d. **B. Bunge** (13) (G) 6-7 6-3 6-3; Nagelsen d. E. M. Gordon (SA) 6-0 2-6 6-2; Walsh d. E. Sayers (A) 7-5 6-3; **Navratilova** (4) d. S. Mascarin (USA) 6-0 6-1; **Turnbull** (6) d. D. A. Jevans 6-2 6-2; Fairbank d. D. H. Lee (KOR) 6-3 6-1; R. Tomanova (CZ) d. Pfaff 6-2 1-6 6-2; Teeguarden d. L. Du Pont (USA) 6-3 3-6 6-4; Piatek d. L. E. Morse (USA) 7-6 6-1; Hobbs d. S. V. Wade 6-1 7-6; A. Buchanan (USA) d. Hallquist 0-6 6-3 6-3; **Mandlikova** (2) d. A. E. Smith (USA) 6-1 6-4.

THIRD ROUND: Lloyd (1) d. Forood 6-2 7-6; Pasquale d. **Fromholtz** (11) 3-6 6-2 7-5; **Jausovec** (10) d. Blount 6-2 7-5; Jaeger (5) d. Allen 6-1 6-2; **Austin** (3) d. Leo 4-6 7-6; **Potter** (14) d. Collins 6-4 6-1; Durie d. White 7-5 6-2; **Shriver** (7) d. Coles 6-0 6-3; **Ruzici** (8) d. Bohm 3-6 7-6 8-6; **Jordan** (12) d. Acker 6-3 6-4; Nagelsen d. Barker

2-6 6-2 6-3; **Navratilova** (4) d. Walsh 6-1 2-6 6-0; **Turnbull** (6) d. Fairbank 6-3 6-2; Teeguarden d. Tomanova 6-4 6-3; Hobbs d. Piatek 7-6 1-6 7-5; **Mandlikova** (2) d. Buchanan 6-3 6-0.

FOURTH ROUND	QUARTER-FINALS	SEMI-FINALS	FINAL	CHAMPION
Lloyd (1)	**Lloyd** (1)			
Pasquale	6-0 6-0	**Lloyd** (1)		
Jausovec (10)	**Jausovec** (10)	6-2 6-2		
Jaeger (5)	6-4 7-6		**Lloyd** (1)	
Austin (3)	**Austin** (3)		6-3 6-1	
Potter (14)	6-4 6-0	**Shriver** (7)		
Durie	**Shriver** (7)	7-5 6-4		
Shriver (7)	6-3 6-4			**Lloyd** (1)
Ruzici (8)	**Ruzici** (8)			6-2 6-2
Jordan (12)	3-6 6-4 6-3	**Navratilova** (4)		
Nagelsen	**Navratilova** (4)	6-2 6-3		
Navratilova (4)	6-3 6-1		**Mandlikova** (2)	
Turnbull (6)	**Turnbull** (6)		7-5 4-6 6-1	
Teeguarden	6-4 6-1	**Mandlikova** (2)		
Hobbs	**Mandlikova** (2)	6-0 6-0		
Mandlikova (2)	6-3 6-2			

PRIZE MONEY

Champion	£19,440
Runner-up	9,450
Semi-finals	4,725
Quarter-finals	2,160
Fourth round	1,345
Third round	715
Second round	420
First round	250

OTHER FINALS

GENTLEMEN'S DOUBLES: Final – P. Fleming (USA)/J. P. McEnroe (USA) d. R. C. Lutz (USA)/S. R. Smith (USA) 6-4 6-4 6-4.

LADIES' DOUBLES: Final – M. Navratilova (USA)/P. H. Shriver (USA) d. K. Jordan (USA)/A. E. Smith (USA) 6-3 7-6.

MIXED DOUBLES: Final – F. D. McMillan (SA)/B. Stove (NTH) d. J. R. Austin (USA)/T. Austin (USA) 4-6 7-6 6-3.

GENTLEMEN'S SINGLES PLATE: Final – D. Carter (A) d. C. M. Johnstone (A) 6-3 6-4.

LADIES' SINGLES PLATE: Final – S. E. Saliba (A) d. P. Casale (USA) 6-3 6-3.

BOYS' SINGLES: Final – M. Anger (USA) d. P. Cash (A) 7-6 7-5.

GIRLS' SINGLES: Final – Z. Garrison (USA) d. R. Uys (SA) 6-4 3-6 6-0.

GENTLEMEN'S SINGLES

1982

FIRST ROUND: J. P. McEnroe (1) (USA) d. V. Winitsky (USA) 6-2 6-2 6-1; E. Edwards (USA) d. G. J. Whitecross (A) 6-4 6-7 6-2 7-5; C. Motta (BR) d. F. Sauer (SA) 3-6 6-2 6-4 6-4; L. R. Bourne (USA) d. I. Nastase (RU) 6-1 6-3 3-6 6-4; R. L. Stockton (USA) d. B. Manson (USA) 6-3 6-4 7-6; J. B. Fitzgerald (A) d. J. Granat (CZ) 6-2 7-6 6-4; H. Pfister (USA) d. M. Purcell (USA) 6-2 6-3 6-4; S. R. Smith (USA) d. **A. Gomez** (9) (EC) 6-4 6-3 5-7 7-6; **B. E. Gottfried** (13) (USA) d. G. Moretton (F) 7-6 7-6 6-2; N. Saviano (USA) d. A. Gimenez (SP) 6-2 6-1 7-6; D. Carter (A) d. J. Potier (F) 6-2 6-3 6-4; A. Andrews (USA) d. T. C. Fancutt (A) 6-1 7-6 7-6; P. Rennert (USA) d. D. Tarr (SA) 6-3 3-6 3-6 6-2 6-4; J. R. Smith d. J. Avendano (SP) 2-6 6-1 6-4 7-6; P. Elter (G) d. C. M. Dunk (USA) 6-4 7-6 6-3; **J. C. Kriek** (5) (SA) d. C. J. Wittus (USA) 6-7 6-3 6-1 6-0; **A. A. Mayer** (4) (USA) d. H. Ismail (ZIM) 7-5 6-2 6-3; C. Dowdeswell (SWZ) d. G. Goven (F) 6-2 3-6 6-3 6-2; T. S. Mayotte (USA) d. P. Fleming (USA) 6-7 6-4 6-3 6-4; S. Menon (IN) d. P. Slozil (CZ) 6-2 7-6 6-0; C. M. Johnstone (A) d. D. Schneider (IS) 7-6 6-3 7-6; J. J. Lapidus (USA) d. Z. Kuharsky (HU) 3-6 7-5 6-3 6-0; V. C. Amaya (USA) d. N. Brown 7-6 6-3 6-3; **C. J. Mottram** (15) d. A. Jarryd (SW) 6-7 6-1 6-3 6-2; **B. Teacher** (11) (USA) d. S. Glickstein (IS) 3-6 7-6 6-4 4-6 6-2; R. J. Frawley (A) d. P. Dupre (USA) 6-7 6-3 7-6 6-3; S. Simonsson (SW) d. W. Scanlon (USA) 7-5 6-4 6-1; L. Palin (FI) d. C. A. Miller (A) 3-6 6-2 7-6 4-6 6-4; S. Birner (CZ) d. R. Evett (USA) 6-4 6-4 2-6 6-2; C. Panatta (IT) d. R. Fagel (USA) 2-6 6-0 6-1 6-2; N. Odizor (NI) d. J. Lopez-Maeso (SP) 4-6 7-6 7-5 7-6; **M. Wilander** (7) (SW) d. H. P. Guenthardt (SWZ) 6-4 6-3 3-6 6-3; C. Hooper (USA) d. **P. McNamara** (8) (A) 7-6 3-6 6-2 6-4; R. J. Simpson (NZ) d. J. M. Lloyd 3-6 4-6 7-6 6-4 6-4; M. Hocevar (BR) d. S. Krulevitz (USA) 6-4 6-2 6-3; F. Gonzalez (USA) d. S. McCain (USA) 6-3 6-2 6-7 5-7 6-1; D. Dowlen (USA) d. J. Nystrom (SW) 6-3 3-6 6-1 6-3; R. Krishnan (IN) d. A. M. Jarrett 6-4 2-6 4-6 7-6 6-2; J. Soares (BR) d. H. Sundstrom (SW) 7-6 6-3 6-2; **M. R. Edmondson** (12) (A) d. M. Davis (USA) 7-6 7-5 7-5; **R. Tanner** (14) (USA) d. H. Leconte (F) 6-4 7-5 6-4; F. Buehning (USA) d. M. Estep (USA) 6-3 6-3 7-6; P. Portes (F) d. J. R. Austin (USA) 7-6 6-2 6-2; V. Amritraj (IN) d. J. Borowiak (USA) 6-7 4-6 6-3 6-4 6-3; B. Fritz (F) d. S. Casal (SP) 6-2 7-5 4-6 6-7 6-3; T. Smid (CZ) d. R. A. Lewis 6-3 7-6 6-0; B. P. Derlin (NZ) d. D. T. Visser (SA) 5-7 7-6 6-3 7-5; **V. Gerulaitis** (3) (USA) d. O. B. Pirow (SA) 6-4 6-1 6-1; **G. Mayer** (6) (USA) d. Tim Gullikson (USA) 5-7 6-4 6-1 7-5; B. D. Drewett (A) d. P. Doohan (A) 7-6 6-2 6-4; L. Stefanki (USA) d. A. Cortes (COL) 6-4 6-2 6-1; E. H. Fromm (USA) d. S. Ball (A) 6-4 3-6 7-6 6-2; C. J. Lewis (NZ) d. J. Goes (BR) 6-2 6-3 6-2; Tom Gullikson (USA) d. M. J. Bates 6-4 6-4 6-3; S. W. Van der Merwe (SA) d. T. Moor (USA) 6-4 6-2 7-6; **S. Denton** (16) (USA) d. J. Sadri (USA) 6-7 7-6 6-4 3-6 6-3; R. C. Lutz (USA) d. R. Meyer (USA) 2-6 6-3 6-2 6-7 6-4; P. McNamee (A) d. M. N. Doyle (IRE) 5-7 6-3 7-6 7-6; B. J. E. Boileau (B) d. V. Van Patten (USA) 6-4 3-6 2-6 7-5 6-1; K. Curren (SA) d. J. W. Feaver 6-2 6-2 6-2; T. Tulasne (F) d. M. T. Fancutt (A) 6-3 6-4 3-6 7-6; D. Gitlin (USA) d. A. Maurer (G) 7-5 7-5 6-4; J. G. Alexander (A) d. K. Warwick (A) 2-6 5-7 7-6 6-3 7-5; **J. S. Connors** (2) (USA) d. M. P. Myburg (SA) 6-0 6-2 6-2.

SECOND ROUND: McEnroe (1) d. Edwards 6-3 6-3 7-5; Bourne d. Motta 6-4 6-4 1-6 5-7 6-3; Fitzgerald d. Stockton 6-4 6-3 6-1; Pfister d. Smith 6-4 7-6 7-6; Saviano d. **Gottfried** (13) 6-7 6-7 7-5 6-4 6-1; Carter d. Andrews 3-6 7-5 6-7 6-3 9-7, Rennert d. Smith 7-6 7-6 4-6 6-3; **Kriek** (5) d. Elter 4-6 6-3 3-6 6-0 6-4; **Mayer** (4) d. Dowdeswell 6-2 6-2 6-3; Mayotte d. Menon 6-4 6-2 3-6 7-5; Johnstone d. Lapidus 6-2 6-7 6-4 6-4; **Mottram** (15) d. Amaya 6-4 5-7 6-4 6-4; **Teacher** (11) d. Frawley 7-5 6-3 4-6 6-3; Simonsson d. Palin 6-3 6-4 6-7 7-5; Birner d. Panatta 6-4 3-6 3-6 6-1 6-4; **Wilander** (7) d. Odizor 7-6 6-4 6-0; Simpson d. Hooper 6-3 1-6 6-3 6-7 11-9; Hocevar d. Gonzalez 7-6 4-6 7-6 7-6; Krishnan d. Dowlen 6-4 7-5 6-0; **Edmondson** (12) d. Soares 6-3 7-5 6-3; **Tanner** (14) d. Buehning 6-3 6-3 6-7 6-4; Amritraj d. Portes 6-2 6-3 6-2; Smid d. Fritz 6-4 6-4 6-3; **Gerulaitis** (3) d. Derlin 7-5 6-2 6-3; **Mayer** (6) d. Drewett 6-7 6-3 6-2 6-1; Stefanki d. Fromm 6-3 4-6 6-4 7-6; Lewis d. Tom Gullikson 7-6 7-6 7-6; **Denton** (16) d. Van der Merwe 6-7 7-5 3-6 6-4 13-11; McNamee d. Lutz 6-1 1-6 6-3 7-6; Curren d. Boileau 6-4 6-3 6-2; Gitlin d. Tulasne 6-3 6-4 6-2; **Connors** (2) d. Alexander 6-3 4-6 6-1 7-6.

THIRD ROUND: McEnroe (1) d. Bourne 6-2 6-2 6-0; Pfister d. Fitzgerald 6-4 5-7 6-4 5-7 6-2; Saviano d. Carter 6-4 6-4 6-4; **Kriek** (5) d. Rennert 4-6 6-3 6-4 6-1; Mayotte d. **Mayer** (4) 3-6 6-7 6-4 6-2 6-4; **Mottram** (15) d. Johnstone 6-1 6-3 6-2; **Teacher** (11) d. Simonsson 7-6 4-6 6-3 6-3; **Wilander** (7) d. Birner 6-3 6-4 6-4; Simpson d. Hocevar 3-6 5-7 6-3 7-6 6-3; **Edmondson** (12) d. Krishnan 6-3 1-6 6-1 6-4; **Tanner** (14) d. Amritraj 6-4 6-4 4-6 4-6 6-3; **Gerulaitis** (3) d. Smid 6-7 3-6 6-3 6-4 6-2; **Mayer** (6) d. Stefanki 7-6 6-3 6-0; **Denton** (16) d. Lewis 7-6 7-5 6-7 7-5; McNamee d. Curren 7-6 3-6 3-6 6-4 6-1; **Connors** (2) d. Gitlin 6-2 6-7 7-5 7-5.

FOURTH ROUND	QUARTER-FINALS	SEMI-FINALS	FINAL	CHAMPION
McEnroe (1)	**McEnroe** (1)			
Pfister	6-4 6-4 6-4	**McEnroe** (1)		
Saviano	**Kriek** (5)	4-6 6-2 7-5 6-3		
Kriek (5)	6-2 6-3 7-5		**McEnroe** (1)	
Mayotte	Mayotte		6-3 6-1 6-2	
Mottram (15)	6-2 7-5 6-3	Mayotte		
Teacher (11)	**Teacher** (11)	6-7 7-6 7-5 3-6 6-1		
Wilander (7)	6-4 6-4 6-3			**Connors** (2)
Simpson	**Edmondson** (12)			3-6 6-3 6-7 7-6 6-4
Edmondson (12)	6-4 7-6 7-6	**Edmondson** (12)		
Tanner (14)	**Gerulaitis** (3)	7-6 3-6 6-4 6-3		
Gerulaitis (3)	6-3 6-4 6-3		**Connors** (2)	
Mayer (6)	**Mayer** (6)		6-4 6-3 6-1	
Denton (16)	6-3 6-4 6-4	**Connors** (2)		
McNamee	**Connors** (2)	6-1 6-2 7-6		
Connors (2)	6-2 6-3 6-1			

PRIZE MONEY

Champion	£41,667
Runner-up	20,833
Semi-finals	10,417
Quarter-finals	5,278
Fourth round	3,056
Third round	1,667
Second round	972
First round	556

LADIES' SINGLES

FIRST ROUND: B. Norton (USA) d. E. S. Jones 6-2 4-6 6-4; A. H. White (USA) d. L. Du Pont (USA) 2-6 7-6 9-7; L. Romanov (RU) d. A. N. Croft 1-6 6-3 6-1; Z. L. Garrison (USA) d. L. A. Thompson (USA) 6-0 6-2; P. G. Smith (USA) d. S. A. Walpole 6-0 6-2; A. Temesvari (HU) d. D. Desfor (USA) 7-6 7-6; P. Casale (USA) d. E. K. Horvath (USA) 6-4 6-1; J. C. Russell (USA) d. S. Mascarin (USA) 4-6 7-5 6-2; D. H. Lee (KOR) d. G. L. Coles 4-6 6-4 6-1; R. D. Fairbank (SA) d. S. L. Rollinson (SA) 6-3 6-2; W. E. White (USA) d. B. J. Remilton (A) 6-3 6-4; S. J. Leo (A) d. C. C. Monteiro (BR) 6-3 2-6 6-3; L. E. Allen (USA) d. C. Tanvier (F) 6-4 4-6 8-6; S. V. Wade d. J. M. Durie 3-6 7-6 6-2; B. K. Jordan (USA) d. L. J. Bonder (USA) 6-3 6-3; C. S. Reynolds (USA) d. R. L. Blount (USA) 7-6 6-3; M. A. Mesker (NTH) d. E. M. Burgin (USA) 6-2 6-2; E. S. Pfaff (G) d. E. M. Sayers (A) 7-6 6-0; T. J. Harford (SA) d. L. Antonoplis (USA) 6-2 6-4; C. Pasquale (SWZ) d. Mrs M. Pinterova (CZ) 7-6 6-2; C. Kohde (G) d. D. A. Jevans 6-1 6-3; S. A. Walsh (USA) d. S. Barker 6-0 6-4; N. S. Yeargin (USA) d. I. Budarova (CZ) 7-5 4-6 7-5; A. A. Moulton (USA) d. H. Sukova (CZ) 3-6 6-3 6-4; K. G. Jones (USA) d. S. L. Collins (USA) 6-4 6-3; K. Rinaldi (USA) d. S. A. Margolin (USA) 6-2 7-6; M. Maleeva (BUL) d. V. Nelson (USA) 2-6 6-4 6-4; K. A. Steinmetz (USA) d. P. Louie (USA) 4-6 6-3 7-5; P. Delhees (SWZ) d. K. J. Brasher 6-4 6-2; S. Simmonds (IT) d. K. Sands (USA) 6-1 6-3; B. L. Hallquist (USA) d. J. Klitch (USA) 7-6 6-3; K. D. Latham (USA) d. A. K. Kiyomura (USA) 6-4 6-7 6-0.

SECOND ROUND: M. Navratilova (1) (USA) d. Norton 6-3 6-3; White d. A. L. Minter (A) 7-5 6-3; Romanov d. A. E. Hobbs 3-6 6-1 7-5; Garrison d. **Mrs R. Cawley** (16) (A) 6-4 6-2; **S. Hanika** (9) (G) d. Smith 6-2 6-4; Temesvari d. R. Tomanova (CZ) 6-4 3-6 7-5; Casale d. R. Casals (USA) 7-6 6-2; Russell d. **M. Jausovec** (8) (YU) 6-7 6-3 7-5; **A. Jaeger** (4) (USA) d. Lee 4-6 6-4 7-5; Fairbank d. E. D. Lightbody 6-0 6-4; C. Vanier (F) d. White 6-7 7-6 7-5; **A. E. Smith** (13) (USA) d. Leo 6-4 6-4; **B. Bunge** (11) (G) d. Allen 6-3 7-5; M. L. Blackwood (C) d. Wade 7-6 7-5; P. A. Teeguarden (USA) d. B. K. Jordan 6-4 6-4; Reynolds d. **H. Mandlikova** (5) (CZ) 6-3 2-6 6-4; **W. M. Turnbull** (6) (A) d. Mesker 6-4 7-6; P. S. Medrado (BR) d. Pfaff 6-3 7-6; Harford d. E. M. Gordon (SA) 6-4 6-2; **Mrs L. W. King** (12) (USA) d. Pasquale 6-3 6-2; Kohde d. **A. Leand** (14) (USA) 7-5 6-2; Y. Vermaak (SA) d. Walsh 6-3 6-3; K. Jordan (USA) d. Yeargin 6-3 6-4; **T. A. Austin** (3) (USA) d. Moulton 6-4 7-5; **P. H. Shriver** (7) (USA) d. Jones 6-1 6-1; Rinaldi d. B. Nagelsen (USA) 6-2 6-3; J. B. Preyer (USA) d. Maleeva 6-3 6-3; **B. C. Potter** (10) (USA) d. Steinmetz 6-2 6-3; **V. Ruzici** (15) (RU) d. Delhees 6-3 7-5; Simmonds d. M. L. Piatek (USA) 7-5 6-4; Latham d. Hallquist 7-6 6-3; **Mrs J. M. Lloyd** (2) (USA) d. B. S. Gerken (USA) 6-0 6-4.

THIRD ROUND: Navratilova (1) d. White 6-1 6-4; Garrison d. Romanov 6-0 6-4; **Hanika** (9) d. Temesvari 6-2 6-2; Russell d. Casale 1-6 7-6 6-4; **Jaeger** (4) d. Fairbank 6-3 7-5; **Smith** (13) d. Vanier 6-3 6-2; **Bunge** (11) d. Blackwood 6-3 2-1 ret'd; Reynolds d. Teeguarden 5-7 6-3 8-6; **Turnbull** (6) d. Medrado 6-2 6-4; **King** (12) d. Harford 5-7 7-6 6-3; Kohde d. Vermaak 4-6 6-0 9-7; **Austin** (3) d. Jordan 4-6 6-1 6-2; **Shriver** (7) d. Rinaldi 6-4 6-1; **Potter** (10) d. Preyer 6-4 6-4; **Ruzici** (15) d. Simmonds 6-7 7-6 7-5; **Lloyd** (2) d. Latham 6-1 6-1.

FOURTH ROUND	QUARTER-FINALS	SEMI-FINALS	FINAL	CHAMPION
Navratilova (1)	**Navratilova** (1)			
Garrison	6-3 6-2	**Navratilova** (1)		
Hanika (9)	Russell	6-3 6-4		
Russell	6-4 6-7 6-3		**Navratilova** (1)	
Jaeger (4)	**Smith** (13)		6-2 6-2	
Smith (13)	6-4 6-2	**Bunge** (11)		
Bunge (11)	**Bunge** (11)	6-3 2-6 6-0		
Reynolds	6-2 6-3			**Navratilova** (1)
Turnbull (6)	**King** (12)			6-1 3-6 6-2
King (12)	6-2 6-3	**King** (12)		
Kohde	**Austin** (3)	3-6 6-4 6-2		
Austin (3)	6-3 6-3		**Lloyd** (2)	
Shriver (7)	**Potter** (10)		7-6 2-6 6-3	
Potter (10)	6-2 6-4	**Lloyd** (2)		
Ruzici (15)	**Lloyd** (2)	6-2 6-1		
Lloyd (2)	6-7 6-3 6-1			

PRIZE MONEY

Champion	£37,500
Runner-up	18,750
Semi-finals	9,125
Quarter-finals	4,222
Fourth round	2,445
Third round	1,300
Second round	755
First round	428

OTHER FINALS

GENTLEMEN'S DOUBLES: Final – P. NcNamara (A)/P. McNamee (A) d. P. Fleming (USA)/J. P. McEnroe (USA) 6-3 6-2.
LADIES' DOUBLES: Final – M. Navratilova (USA)/P. H. Shriver (USA) d. K. Jordan (USA)/A. E. Smith (USA) 6-4 6-1.
MIXED DOUBLES: Final – K. Curren (SA)/A. E. Smith (USA) d. J. M. Lloyd/W. M. Turnbull (A) 2-6 6-3 7-5.
LADIES' SINGLES PLATE: Final – C. C. Monteiro (BR) d. R. L. Blount (USA) 6-3 2-6 6-2.
BOYS' SINGLES: Final – P. Cash (A) d. H. Sundstrom (SW) 6-4 6-7 6-3.
GIRLS' SINGLES: Final – C. Tanvier (F) d. H. Sukova (CZ) 6-2 7-5.
BOYS' DOUBLES: Final – P. Cash (A)/J. Frawley (A) d. R. Leach (USA)/J. Ross (USA) 6-3 6-4.
GIRLS' DOUBLES: Final – B. Herr (USA)/P. Barg (USA) d. B. S. Gerken (USA)/G. Rush (USA) 6-1 6-4.
35 AND OVER GENTLEMEN'S INVITATION SINGLES: Final – J. D. Newcombe (A) d. F. D. McMillan (SA) 6-4 7-6.

GENTLEMEN'S SINGLES

1983

FIRST ROUND: J. S. Connors (1) (USA) d. E. Edwards (USA) 6-4 7-5 6-3; W. Masur (A) d. L. R. Bourne (USA) 4-6 4-6 6-4 6-3 6-2; H. Sundstrom (SW) d. V. Van Patten (USA) 6-4 6-0 2-6 7-5; S. Edberg (SW) d. C. Roger-Vasselin (F) 6-2 7-6 6-1; B. D. Drewett (A) d. A. Tous (SP) 6-3 6-1 6-1; R. Harmon (USA) d. R. Venter (SA) 6-2 6-3 3-6 7-6; S. Casal (SP) d. H. Simonsson (SW) 3-6 6-3 6-2 3-6 6-3; **K. Curren** (12) (SA) d. J. Borowiak (USA) 6-7 6-3 7-5 1-0 ret'd; **T. S. Mayotte** (16) (USA) d. M. Dickson (USA) 7-5 6-3 6-3; A. Andrews (USA) d. A. Jarryd (SW) 6-4 7-6 6-3; B. Teacher (USA) d. M. Hocevar (BR) 6-4 6-0 2-6 6-4; W. Fibak (POL) d. C. J. Mottram 4-6 6-4 7-6 6-2; Tom Gullikson (USA) d. S. Menon (IN) 6-2 6-1 6-2; C. Motta (BR) d. R. Ramirez (M) 7-6 6-1 2-6 3-2 ret'd; J. C. McCurdy (A) d. J. Avendano (SP) 6-3 6-4 6-2; C. Panatta (IT) d. **J. L. Clerc** (7) (ARG) 6-1 6-4 6-2; N. Odizor (NI) d. **G. Vilas** (4) (ARG) 3-6 5-7 7-6 7-5 6-2; P. Fleming (USA) d. M. J. Bates 7-6 6-3 6-2; L. Courteau (F) d. M. Tideman (SW) 7-5 6-4 7-5; A. M. Jarrett d. B. Foxworth (USA) 4-6 6-2 7-5 6-1; T. C. Fancutt (A) d. C. Bradnam 6-4 6-4 7-6; M. Bauer (USA) d. D. Keretic (G) 7-5 7-5 7-5; B. Dyke (A) d. G. Forget (F) 6-2 6-2 3-6 6-2; C. J. Lewis (NZ) d. **S. Denton** (9) (USA) 6-4 4-6 7-6 4-6 6-3; **B. E. Gottfried** (13) (USA) d. S. Glickstein (IS) 6-1 6-4 6-4; M. N. Doyle (IRE) d. L. Pimek (CZ) 6-2 6-1 6-1; A. Giammalva (USA) d. J. Turpin (USA) 6-1 7-6 3-6 7-6; J. Soares (BR) d. E. H. Fromm (USA) 6-4 6-3 6-4; S. M. Bale d. M. Mitchell (USA) 7-6 6-7 5-7 6-4 12-10; M. Purcell (USA) d. T. Wilkison (USA) 6-2 4-6 6-2 6-1; A. Maurer (G) d. M. Brunnberg (USA) 3-6 6-1 6-4 5-7 6-4; V. C. Amaya (USA) d. R. B. Kleege (USA) 6-4 6-3 6-4; **M. Wilander** (5) (SW) d. J. B. Fitzgerald (A) 6-4 6-1 4-6 6-7 6-4; C. R. O. Viljoen (SA) d. R. J. Frawley (A) 7-6 2-6 7-6 5-7 9-7; J. G. Alexander (A) d. T. Hogstedt (SW) 6-7 6-3 6-1 7-6; R. Tanner (USA) d. J. Gunnarsson (SW) 6-4 6-3 6-2; R. Van't Hof (USA) d. C. M. Johnstone (A) 4-6 6-1 3-6 7-6 6-4; H. Leconte (F) d. D. T. Visser (SA) 6-3 4-6 6-2 4-6 7-5; N. Saviano (USA) d. J. R. Smith 7-5 6-3 6-2; **J. C. Kriek** (11) (SA) d. S. Giammalva (USA) 6-4 6-3 6-2; **H. Pfister** (15) (USA) d. T. Smid (CZ) 6-3 6-4 3-6 6-3; R. Acuna (CH) d. G. Barbosa (BR) 6-7 6-4 7-6 6-3; F. Buehning (USA) d. C. J. Wittus (USA) 6-4 6-4 3-6 6-4; P. Cash (A) d. J. Goes (BR) 6-0 6-0 6-3; C. A. Miller (A) d. J. M. Lloyd 6-1 6-7 2-6 6-3 6-1; J. Hlasek (SWZ) d. S. Birner (CZ) 6-2 6-1 6-3; T. Waltke (USA) d. S. R. Smith (USA) 6-4 3-6 2-6 6-3 2-0 ret'd; **I. Lendl** (3) (CZ) d. B. M. Mitton (SA) 7-6 6-1 6-0; **V. Gerulaitis** (8) (USA) d. R. Krishnan (IN) 5-7 7-5 7-6 5-7 6-3; M. R. Edmondson (A) d. V. Amritraj (IN) 6-3 6-4 7-6; M. Leach (USA) d. R. A. Lewis 7-6 2-6 7-6 6-4; P. McNamee (A) d. E. Korita (USA) 6-1 3-6 6-4 6-7 9-7; M. Depalmer (USA) d. W. D. Hampson (A) 7-6 6-3 5-7 6-4; S. Simonsson (SW) d. P. Dupre (USA) 6-3 7-6 6-4; G. Ocleppo (IT) d. M. C. Strode (USA) 6-4 3-6 6-3 3-6 6-2; A. A. Mayer (USA) d. S. Davis (USA) 6-2 6-4 6-2; **W. Scanlon** (14) (USA) d. G. Moretton (F) 7-6 6-3 7-6; C. Hooper (USA) d. P. Hjertquist (SW) 6-2 6-4 6-4; Tim Gullikson (USA) d. T. Cain (USA) 6-1 3-0 ret'd; P. Elter (G) d. M. Schapers (NTH) 6-2 6-2 6-4; D. Gitlin (USA) d. J. Sadri (USA) 7-5 6-7 6-1 7-5; B. Gilbert (USA) d. R. J. Simpson (NZ) 4-6 6-3 6-3 6-3; F. Segarceanu (RU) d. J. Fillol (CH) 6-3 6-1 1-6 6-4; **J. P. McEnroe** (2) (USA) d. B. Testerman (USA) 6-4 7-6 6-2.

SECOND ROUND: Connors (1) d. Masur 6-4 7-6 6-0; Sundstrom d. Edberg 2-6 7-6 7-6 4-6 8-6; Harmon d. Drewett 6-2 6-4 6-4; **Curren** (12) d. Casal 7-6 6-4 6-3; **Mayotte** (16) d. Andrews 6-1 6-2 6-2; Teacher d. Fibak 7-6 2-6 4-6 7-5 6-1; Motta d. Tom Gullikson 3-6 7-6 6-4 6-4; McCurdy d. Panatta 7-6 6-3 7-6; Odizor d. Fleming 6-4 4-6 6-4 6-2; Courteau d. Jarrett 6-2 7-5 6-3; Bauer d. Fancutt 6-4 6-4 6-0; Lewis d. Dyke 7-6 6-1 6-3; **Gottfried** (13) d. Doyle 7-5 4-6 7-6 6-4; Soares d. Giammalva 7-6 6-7 7-6 6-4; Purcell d. Bale 7-6 6-4 6-3; Maurer d. Amaya 6-3 6-4 7-6; **Wilander** (5) d. Viljoen 6-3 6-2 6-1; Tanner d. Alexander 6-2 7-6 4-6 6-3; Van't Hof d. Leconte 3-6 6-4 4-6 6-3 6-2; **Kriek** (11) d. Saviano 6-4 3-6 5-7 6-3 6-2; Acuna d. **Pfister** (15) 3-6 7-6 7-6 4-6 6-4; Cash d. Buehning 6-3 6-0 6-2; Hlasek d. Miller 6-4 6-4 6-7 3-6 6-1; **Lendl** (3) d. Waltke 6-4 6-2 6-3; Edmondson d. **Gerulaitis** (8) 7-6 7-5 7-5; Leach d. McNamee 6-4 3-6 7-6 6-7 6-3; Depalmer d. Simonsson 6-4 6-4 6-3; Mayer d. Ocleppo 7-6 6-2 3-6 6-7 6-3; **Scanlon** (14) d. Hooper 7-6 6-0 7-6; Tim Gullikson d. Elter 5-7 6-1 6-4 6-4; Gilbert d. Gitlin 6-7 6-3 7-5 7-5; **McEnroe** (2) d. Segarceanu 4-6 6-2 6-3 6-3.

THIRD ROUND: Connors (1) d. Sundstrom 6-1 7-6 6-2; **Curren** (12) d. Harmon 6-4 7-5 6-2; **Mayotte** (16) d. Teacher 7-6 6-4 6-7 6-3; McCurdy d. Motta 6-0 6-4 3-6 6-1; Odizor d. Courteau 3-6 7-6 6-4 3-6 6-3; Lewis d. Bauer 6-4 3-6 7-5 6-7 6-4; **Gottfried** (13) d. Soares 7-6 6-2 6-2; Purcell d. Maurer 5-7 6-3 6-2 6-2; Tanner d. **Wilander** (5) 6-7 7-5 6-3 6-4; Van't Hof d. **Kriek** (11) 6-3 7-6 6-1; Cash d. Acuna 6-3 6-4 6-4; **Lendl** (3) d. Hlasek 6-1 6-2 6-7 6-4; Leach d. Edmondson 6-3 3-6 6-4 4-6 6-4; Mayer d. Depalmer 7-6 6-2 6-1; **Scanlon** (14) d. Tim Gullikson 6-4 6-4 6-3; **McEnroe** (2) d. Gilbert 6-2 6-2 6-2.

FOURTH ROUND	QUARTER-FINALS	SEMI-FINALS	FINAL	CHAMPION
Connors (1)	**Curren** (12)			
Curren (12)	6-3 6-7 6-3 7-6	**Curren** (12)		
Mayotte (16)	**Mayotte** (16)	4-6 7-6 6-2 7-6		
McCurdy	6-0 6-2 6-4		Lewis	
Odizor	Lewis		6-7 6-4 7-6 6-7 8-6	
Lewis	6-1 6-3 6-3	Lewis		
Gottfried (13)	Purcell	6-7 6-0 6-4 7-6		
Purcell	4-6 6-3 6-3 6-2			**McEnroe** (2)
Tanner	Tanner			6-2 6-2 6-2
Van't Hof	6-2 6-3 6-3	**Lendl** (3)		
Cash	**Lendl** (3)	7-5 7-6 6-3		
Lendl (3)	6-4 7-6 6-1		**McEnroe** (2)	
Leach	Mayer		7-6 6-4 6-4	
Mayer	6-1 7-6 6-1	**McEnroe** (2)		
Scanlon (14)	**McEnroe** (2)	6-3 7-5 6-0		
McEnroe (2)	7-5 7-6 7-6			

PRIZE MONEY

Champion	£66,600
Runner-up	33,300
Semi-finals	16,650
Quarter-finals	8,430
Fourth round	4,880
Third round	2,660
Second round	1,553
First round	888

LADIES' SINGLES

FIRST ROUND: M. Navratilova (1) (USA) d. B. A. Mould (SA) 6-1 6-0; S. L. Acker (USA) d. C. Tanvier (F) 6-4 6-2; M. Jausovec (YU) d. A. N. Croft 6-1 6-2; E. M. Burgin (USA) d. C. C. Monteiro (BR) 6-2 6-4; B. K. Jordan (USA) d. C. M. O'Neil (A) 6-3 6-3; C. Vanier (F) d. T. Lewis (USA) 6-1 1-6 8-6; P. Hy (HK) d. A. K. Kiyomura (USA) 6-1 7-6; **C. Kohde-Kilsch** (16) (G) d. H. Sukova (CZ) 6-3 7-6; **S. Hanika** (9) (G) d. B. A. Bowes (USA) 6-3 6-2; R. D. Fairbank (SA) d. Mrs L. A. Shaefer (USA) 6-7 6-2 6-0; B. Randall (A) d. L. A. Bernstein (USA) 6-4 6-0; J. A. Mundel (SA) d. N. F. Gregory (A) 6-1 6-4; C. Suire (F) d. A. M. Fernandez (USA) 6-7 6-3 6-0; L. K. Allen (USA) d. K. J. Brasher 6-2 6-1; R. Mentz (SA) d. H. A. Ludloff (USA) 7-6 6-7 6-4; **H. Mandlikova** (8) (CZ) d. R. L. Einy 7-5 6-3; B. L. Hallquist (USA) d. M. Schropp (G) 6-3 6-3; A. Leand (USA) d. P. G. Smith (USA) 6-1 6-3; R. Reggi (IT) d. M. Schillig (USA) 3-6 6-3 7-5; S. V. Wade d. A. M. Tobin (A) 1-6 7-5 6-4; E. S. Pfaff (G) d. B. J. Remilton (A) 7-5 6-2; Z. L. Garrison (USA) d. A. E. Holton (USA) 7-6 7-5; Mrs H. A. Mochizuki (USA) d. C. J. Drury 7-6 4-6 6-1; **J. M. Durie** (13) d. Y. Brzakova (CZ) 6-4 6-2; **V. Ruzici** (12) (RU) d. C. Lindqvist (SW) 6-0 6-2; N. S. Yeargin (USA) d. Mrs A. M. Jarrett 6-1 6-1; S. Simmonds (IT) d. J. Hepner (USA) 6-0 6-1; A. J. Brown d. L. A. Spain (USA) 6-4 6-2; Y. Vermaak (SA) d. S. L. Gomer 4-6 6-2 6-2; K. Sands (USA) d. L. K. Forood (USA) 7-6 6-4; I. Budarova (CZ) d. Mrs W. R. Tomanova-Roth (CZ) 6-1 6-3; **P. H. Shriver** (5) (USA) d. P. A. Fendick (USA) 6-2 6-2; C. Jolissaint (SWZ) d. **B. Bunge** (6) (G) 3-6 7-6 11-9; A. L. Minter (A) d. B. C. Bramblett (USA) 7-5 6-2; A. B. Henricksson (USA) d. E. Ekblom (SW) 6-4 5-7 6-3; L. J. Bonder (USA) d. C. Dries (G) 6-3 7-5; C. Banjamin (USA) d. L. Romanov (RU) 6-3 7-6; J. D. Davis (USA) d. H. A. Crowe (USA) 7-5 6-4; M. Torres (USA) d. J. B. Preyer (USA) 6-4 6-2; **B. C. Potter** (11) (USA) d. P. S. Medrado (BR) 7-5 6-1; **A. Temesvari** (14) (HU) d. V. Nelson (USA) 6-0 6-1; M. Maleeva (BUL) d. S. Barker 6-3 6-2; S. A. Walsh (USA) d. C. S. Reynolds (USA) 6-4 6-4; C. Bassett (C) d. J. C. Russell (USA) 6-3 7-5; S. L. Collins (USA) d. K. A. Steinmetz (USA) 6-3 6-0; S. J. Leo (A) d. R. L. Blount (USA) 7-6 6-2; P. Casale (USA) d. E. Minter (A) 5-7 7-5 6-3; **A. Jaeger** (3) (USA) d. S. K. Rimes (USA) 6-1 7-6; **W. M. Turnbull** (7) (A) d. D. L. Fromholtz (A) 6-1 6-1; A. H. White (USA) d. E. Inoue (J) 6-1 6-3; K. D. Latham (USA) d. P. A. Teeguarden (USA) 6-7 7-6 7-5; W. E. White (USA) d. J. A. Salmon 7-6 6-4; R. Casals (USA) d. M. L. Piatek (USA) 3-6 7-6 6-3; P. Delhees (SWZ) d. L. Antonoplis (USA) 6-4 6-2; B. Herr (USA) d. T. Phelps (USA) 4-6 6-2 6-1; **Mrs L. W. King** (10) (USA) d. E. M. Sayers (A) 7-5 6-3; **K. Rinaldi** (15) (USA) d. K. Skronska (CZ) 4-6 6-1 6-4; L. Sandin (SW) d. C. Jexell (SW) 6-1 6-4; C. Pasquale (SWZ) d. D. Freeman (A) 6-2 6-3; B. Nagelsen (USA) d. J. Klitch (USA) 6-4 6-7 6-3; K. Jordan (USA) d. J. Golder (USA) 6-0 6-0; D. K. Lee (KOR) d. M. Skuherska (CZ) 6-1 4-6 6-4; M. A. Mesker (NTH) d. A. E. Hobbs 6-3 7-5; **Mrs J. M. Lloyd** (2) (USA) d. A. A. Moulton (USA) 6-2 6-1.

SECOND ROUND: Navratilova (1) d. Acker 7-6 6-3; Jausovec d. Burgin 6-1 6-3; B. K. Jordan d. Vanier 6-3 6-2; **Kohde-Kilsch** (16) d. Hy 6-3 6-3; **Hanika** (9) d. Fairbank 3-6 6-2 6-3; Mundel d. Randall 6-1 6-1; Allen d. Suire 6-2 6-4; **Mandlikova** (8) d. Mentz 6-2 6-3; Leand d. Hallquist 7-6 4-6 6-4; Wade d. Reggi 6-1 6-2; Pfaff d. Garrison 3-6 7-6 6-4; **Durie** (13) d. Mochizuki 6-4 6-0; **Ruzici** (12) d. Yeargin 6-1 6-4; Simmonds d. Brown 6-3 6-4; Vermaak d. Sands 7-6 1-6 6-3; Budarova d. **Shriver** (5) 2-6 7-6 6-4; Minter d. Jolissaint 6-3 6-3; Bonder d. Henricksson 6-4 7-6; Benjamin d. Davis 6-2 6-7 11-9; **Potter** (11) d. Torres 6-1 6-4; **Temesvari** (14) d. Maleeva 7-5 6-4; Bassett d. Walsh 6-2 6-3; Leo d. Collins 6-2 6-3; **Jaeger** (3) d. Casale 6-3 6-2; **Turnbull** (7) d. A. H. White 6-3 6-3; W. E. White d. Latham 7-6 6-1; Casals d. Delhees 6-3 3-6 6-2; **King** (10) d. Herr 6-7 6-2 8-6; **Rinaldi** (15) d. Sandin 6-4 6-3; Nagelsen d. Pasquale 6-3 7-5; K. Jordan d. Lee 6-1 6-1; **Lloyd** (2) d. Mesker 6-4 6-2.

THIRD ROUND: Navratilova (1) d. Jausovec 6-2 6-1; **Kohde-Kilsch** (16) d. B. K. Jordan 6-2 6-3; Mundel d. **Hanika** (9) 2-6 6-4 6-3; **Mandlikova** (8) d. Allen 6-1 6-3; Wade d. Leand 3-6 7-6 6-2; Pfaff d. **Durie** (13) 7-6 7-5; **Ruzici** (12) d. Simmonds 6-1 3-6 6-2; Vermaak d. Budarova 5-7 6-4 6-2; Bonder d. Minter 6-1 6-3; **Potter** (11) d. Benjamin 6-7 6-2 6-1; Bassett d. **Temesvari** (14) 6-3 7-6; **Jaeger** (3) d. Leo 6-3 6-2; **Turnbull** (7) d. W. E. White 6-3 6-4; **King** (10) d. Casals 6-3 6-4; **Rinaldi** (15) d. Nagelsen 6-0 6-7 6-4; K. Jordan d. **Lloyd** (2) 6-1 7-6.

FOURTH ROUND	QUARTER-FINALS	SEMI-FINALS	FINAL	CHAMPION
Navratilova (1)	**Navratilova** (1)			
Kohde-Kilsch (16)	6-1 6-2	**Navratilova** (1)		
Mundel	Mundel	6-3 6-1		
Mandlikova (8)	5-7 6-4 6-4		**Navratilova** (1)	
Wade	Wade		6-1 6-1	
Pfaff	3-6 7-6 7-5	Vermaak		
Ruzici (12)	Vermaak	6-3 2-6 6-2		
Vermaak	6-3 6-2			**Navratilova** (1)
Bonder	**Potter** (11)			6-0 6-3
Potter (11)	7-5 6-4	**Jaeger** (3)		
Bassett	**Jaeger** (3)	6-4 6-1		
Jaeger (3)	6-4 6-3		**Jaeger** (3)	
Turnbull (7)	**King** (10)		6-1 6-1	
King (10)	7-5 6-3	**King** (10)		
Rinaldi (15)	K. Jordan	7-5 6-4		
K. Jordan	6-2 6-4			

PRIZE MONEY

Champion	£60,000
Runner-up	30,000
Semi-finals	14,585
Quarter-finals	7,123
Fourth round	3,904
Third round	2,048
Second round	1,196
First round	684

OTHER FINALS

GENTLEMEN'S DOUBLES: Final – P. Fleming (USA)/J. P. McEnroe (USA) d. Tim Gullikson (USA)/Tom Gullikson (USA) 6-4 6-3 6-4.
LADIES' DOUBLES: Final – M. Navratilova (USA)/P. H. Shriver (USA) d. R. Casals (USA)/W. M. Turnbull (A) 6-2 6-2.
MIXED DOUBLES: Final – J. M. Lloyd/W. M. Turnbull (A) d. S. Denton (USA)/Mrs L. W. King (USA) 6-7 7-6 7-5.
LADIES' SINGLES PLATE: Final – A. Brown d. A. M. Tobin (A) 3-6 6-3 6-4.
BOYS' SINGLES: Final – S. Edberg (SW) d. J. Frawley (A) 6-3 7-6.
GIRLS' SINGLES: Final – P. Paradis (F) d. P. Hy (HK) 6-2 6-1.
BOYS' DOUBLES: Final – S. Kratzman (A)/S. Youl (A) d. M. Nastase (RU)/O. Rahnasto (FIN) 6-4 6-4.
GIRLS' DOUBLES: Final – P. Fendick (USA)/P. Hy (HK) d. C. Anderholm (SW)/H. Olsson (SW) 6-1 7-5.
35 AND OVER GENTLEMEN'S INVITATION SINGLES: Final – C. S. Dibley (A) d. R. J. Moore (SA) 6-2 6-2.
35 AND OVER GENTLEMEN'S INVITATION DOUBLES: Final – S. E. Stewart (USA)/F. S. Stolle (A) d. O. K. Davidson (A)/E. C. Drysdale (SA) 7-6 6-2.

GENTLEMEN'S SINGLES

1984

FIRST ROUND: J. P. McEnroe (1) (USA) d. P. McNamee (A) 6-4 6-4 6-7 6-1; R. Harmon (USA) d. E. Sanchez (SP) 7-6 6-3 4-6 5-7 6-3; J. Hlasek (SWZ) d. W. Fibak (POL) 7-5 4-6 6-2 6-1; W. Masur (A) d. S. Youl (A) 6-4 4-6 6-4 4-6 6-3; B. Becker (G) d. B. Willenborg (USA) 6-0 6-0 6-4; N. Odizor (NI) d. J. Turpin (USA) 6-2 7-5 7-6; S. Perkis (IS) d. M. Freeman (USA) 6-3 4-6 6-1 7-5; **W. Scanlon** (14) (USA) d. E. Korita (USA) 7-6 6-7 6-2 3-6 13-11; **V. Gerulaitis** (15) (USA) d. A. Giammalva (USA) 3-6 6-1 6-4 6-7 7-5; B. Taroczy (HU) d. R. A. Lewis 6-4 4-6 6-4 7-6; E. Edwards (SA) d. C. Hooper (USA) 7-6 3-6 6-1 6-3; B. Gilbert (USA) d. P. Fleming (USA) 4-6 4-6 6-4 6-2 6-3; J. Sadri (USA) d. J. Gunnarsson (SW) 6-3 6-7 6-2 6-3; M. Leach (USA) d. P. Arraya (PE) 7-6 6-3 6-7 6-4; R. Acuna (CH) d. J. Soares (BR) 7-6 1-6 4-6 6-4 6-4; C. A. Miller (A) d. C. Mezzadri (SWZ) 6-3 3-6 6-3 6-4; **M. Wilander** (4) (SW) d. S. E. Stewart (USA) 6-4 6-4 6-7 7-5; P. Cash (A) d. R. Seguso (USA) 7-6 6-4 6-4; J. B. Fitzgerald (A) d. D. Pate (USA) 6-3 6-4 6-4; C. Motta (BR) d. M. J. Bates 6-3 6-3 6-1; R. Krishnan (IN) d. S. Colombo (IT) 4-6 6-2 7-6 6-4; C. J. Lewis (NZ) d. R. Stadler (SWZ) 6-3 6-2 6-2; B. Testerman (USA) d. C. Dowdeswell 6-4 6-3 6-3; **K. Curren** (11) (SA) d. S. Denton (USA) 6-4 3-6 4-6 7-6 6-4; **H. Sundstrom** (9) (SW) d. B. J. E. Boileau (B) 6-4 7-6 7-5; M. R. Edmondson (A) d. M. Purcell (USA) 6-4 6-3 6-4; K. Flach (USA) d. R. Van't Hof (USA) 2-6 6-4 7-6 6-3; T. Moor (USA) d. V. Van Patten (USA) 4-6 6-3 6-2 6-2; G. Michibata (C) d. B. Teacher (USA) 7-6 2-6 6-3 2-6 6-4; G. Forget (F) d. H. P. Gunthardt (SWZ) 6-2 6-0 6-3; S. M. Shaw d. C. Panatta (IT) 6-4 6-2 6-4; **A. Gomez** (6) (EC) d. M. Mitchell (USA) 3-6 7-6 6-1 7-6; P. Annacone (USA) d. J. R. Smith 7-6 6-3 6-4; M. Dickson (USA) d. C. Kirmayr (BR) 4-6 7-6 3-6 6-2 6-3; C. Van Rensburg (SA) d. M. Ostoja (YU) 6-2 6-2 6-3; M. N. Doyle (IRE) d. A. A. Mayer (USA) 3-6 7-5 6-3 6-7 7-5; H. Schwaier (G) d. V. Amritraj (IN) 6-3 6-4 6-2; S. Meister (USA) d. H. D. Beutel (G) 6-2 3-6 7-6 7-5; S. Edberg (SW) d. B. D. Drewett (A) 6-4 3-6 7-6 6-2; **J. C. Kriek** (12) (USA) d. M. Westphal (G) 6-3 6-0 2-6 6-7 6-2; **T. S. Mayotte** (16) (USA) d. M. Hocevar (BR) 7-5 7-6 6-1; F. Gonzalez (PA) d. B. E. Gottfried (USA) 6-2 1-6 6-2 6-7 6-2; Tim Gullikson (USA) d. R. J. Simpson (NZ) 7-6 4-6 6-7 6-1 6-3; L. Shiras (USA) d. M. Schapers (NTH) 6-2 6-7 7-6 7-6; M. Davis (USA) d. B. Manson (USA) 6-3 7-6 6-3; C. J. Wittus (USA) d. C. H. Cox (USA) 6-4 6-3 5-7 2-6 6-4; S. Simonsson (SW) d. S. Glickstein (IS) 4-6 6-2 3-6 6-3 6-4; **J. S. Connors** (3) (USA) d. L. R. Bourne (USA) 7-5 7-5 6-4; **J. Arias** (5) (USA) d. B. M. Mitton (SA) 3-6 6-3 6-2 6-4; G. Ocleppo (IT) d. V. Winitsky (USA) 6-4 6-3 4-6 6-0; M. Mecir (CZ) d. T. Cain (USA) 6-3 4-3 ret'd; D. T. Visser (SA) d. J. Gurfein (USA) 6-2 6-4 6-1; S. M. Bale d. J. G. Alexander (A) 7-6 3-6 4-6 7-6 6-2; Tom Gullikson (USA) d. H. Pfister (USA) 6-3 6-4 5-7 6-2; M. Kratzman (A) d. N. A. Fulwood 6-7 6-4 6-2 6-1; **T. Smid** (13) (CZ) d. L. Stefanki (USA) 6-4 6-7 0-6 6-4 6-2; S. E. Davis (USA) d. **A. Jarryd** (10) (SW) 4-6 6-4 6-3 6-2; J. Nystrom (SW) d. T. Wilkison (USA) 5-7 7-6 6-4 7-5; G. Holmes (USA) d. J. W. Feaver 6-1 6-3 6-7 6-2; J. M. Lloyd d. A. Maurer (G) 3-6 6-3 3-6 6-4 6-3; R. Gehring (G) d. P. Slozil (CZ) 6-4 6-7 7-5 6-2; Z. Kuharszky (HU) d. G. Mayer (USA) 7-6 6-2 4-6 1-6 8-6; D. Tarr (SA) d. C. Roger-Vasselin (F) 6-4 1-6 6-2 6-1; **I. Lendl** (2) (CZ) d. R. L. Stockton (USA) 4-6 6-0 6-3 5-7 6-4.

SECOND ROUND: McEnroe (1) d. Harmon 6-1 6-3 7-5; Masur d. Hlasek 6-4 6-2 7-5; Becker d. Odizor 6-3 6-4 4-2 ret'd; **Scanlon** (14) d. Perkis 6-2 6-3 6-3; **Gerulaitis** (15) d. Taroczy 6-3 7-5 4-6 6-4; Gilbert d. Edwards 6-3 7-6 3-6 4-6 8-6; Sadri d. Leach 7-6 3-6 6-4 6-4; Acuna d. Miller 3-6 6-3 6-2 6-4; Cash d. **Wilander** (4) 6-7 6-4 6-2 6-4; Motta d. Fitzgerald 7-6 4-6 6-4 6-1; Krishnan d. C. J. Lewis 6-3 6-3 6-3; **Curren** (11) d. Testerman 7-6 6-1 4-6 6-2; Edmondson d. **Sundstrom** (9) 6-7 7-6 6-4 6-7 8-6; Moor d. Flach 6-4 7-5 6-2; Forget d. Michibata 7-6 6-3 6-4; **Gomez** (6) d. Shaw 7-6 7-6 6-2; Annacone d. Dickson 7-6 7-6 3-6 6-1; Van Rensburg d. Doyle 4-6 6-2 7-5 7-6; Meister d. Schwaier 6-1 6-3 7-5; **Kriek** (12) d. Edberg 4-6 6-7 6-4 6-1 6-1; **Mayotte** (16) d. Gonzalez 7-5 7-6 7-6; Tim Gullikson d. Shiras 3-6 6-3 6-4 6-4; Davis d. Wittus 6-3 6-4 6-3; **Connors** (3) d. Simonsson 6-2 6-1 6-3; **Arias** (5) d. Ocleppo 7-5 5-7 3-6 7-6 6-4; Visser d. Mecir 6-3 6-2 6-4; Tom Gullikson d. Bale 7-5 6-3 6-4; **Smid** (13) d. Kratzman 6-3 2-6 6-7 7-6 8-6; Davis d. Nystrom 6-1 7-5 6-7 6-1; Lloyd d. Holmes 4-6 6-3 6-4 6-1; Gehring d. Kuharszky 7-6 7-5 6-3; **Lendl** (2) d. Tarr 6-3 6-1 6-3.

THIRD ROUND: McEnroe (1) d. Masur 6-0 6-4 6-3; **Scanlon** (14) d. Becker 6-2 2-6 7-6 1-2 ret'd; **Gerulaitis** (15) d. Gilbert 7-6 6-1 3-6 6-4; Sadri d. Acuna 7-5 7-6 7-5; Cash d. Motta 6-1 6-2 6-4; **Curren** (11) d. Krishnan 6-2 3-6 7-6 7-6; Moor d. Edmondson 6-3 6-4 3-6 4-6 6-2; **Gomez** (6) d. Forget 6-3 6-4 4-6 1-6 9-7; Annacone d. Van Rensburg 6-3 4-6 6-4 6-2; **Kriek** (12) d. Meister 6-2 5-7 6-4 6-1; **Mayotte** (16) d. Tim Gullikson 6-4 6-3 6-4; **Connors** (3) d. Davis 6-4 6-7 6-3 6-4; **Arias** (5) d. Visser 5-7 6-3 7-6 6-1; **Smid** (13) d. Tom Gullikson 7-5 7-6 6-2; Davis d. Lloyd 6-4 6-4 7-6; **Lendl** (2) d. Gehring 6-4 6-2 7-6.

FOURTH ROUND	QUARTER-FINALS	SEMI-FINALS	FINAL	CHAMPION
McEnroe (1)	**McEnroe** (1)			
Scanlon (14)	6-3 6-3 6-1	**McEnroe** (1)		
Gerulaitis (15)	Sadri	6-3 6-3 6-1		
Sadri	6-3 7-5 6-7 4-6 6-3		**McEnroe** (1)	
Cash	Cash		6-3 7-6 6-4	
Curren (11)	4-6 6-2 7-6 6-1	Cash		
Moor	**Gomez** (6)	6-4 6-4 6-7 7-6		
Gomez (6)	6-0 6-1 7-6			**McEnroe** (1)
Annacone	Annacone			6-1 6-1 6-2
Kriek (12)	6-3 6-2 6-4	**Connors** (3)		
Mayotte (16)	**Connors** (3)	6-2 6-4 6-2		
Connors (3)	6-7 6-2 6-0 6-2		**Connors** (3)	
Arias (5)	**Smid** (13)		6-7 6-3 7-5 6-1	
Smid (13)	7-5 6-4 6-3	**Lendl** (2)		
Davis	**Lendl** (2)	6-1 7-6 6-3		
Lendl (2)	4-6 6-4 6-4 5-7 7-5			

PRIZE MONEY	
Champion	£100,000
Runner-up	50,000
Semi-finals	25,000
Quarter-finals	12,500
Fourth round	6,850
Third round	3,850
Second round	2,200
First round	1,300

LADIES' SINGLES

FIRST ROUND: M. Navratilova (1) (USA) d. M. Louie (USA) 6-4 6-0; A. E. Holton (USA) d. S. T. Mair 6-4 7-6; A. A. Moulton (USA) d. T. Scheuer-Larsen (D) 6-4 6-1; I. Budarova (CZ) d. M.A. Mesker (NTH) 7-6 6-2; G. A. Rush (USA) d. B. Herr (USA) 4-6 6-4 6-1; E. M. Sayers (A) d. R. M. White (USA) 6-2 6-3; B. Gerken (USA) d. C. Vanier (F) 6-1 6-2; **L. Bonder** (11) (USA) d. J. Louis 2-6 6-3 6-3; **C. Bassett** (16) (C) d. S. A. Walsh (USA) 6-1 3-6 6-3; M. C. Calleja (F) d. N. Herreman (F) 5-7 6-3 6-2; M. L. Piatek (USA) d. S. Hanika (G) 6-2 2-6 10-8; A. E. Hobbs d. C. S. Reynolds (USA) 6-2 7-6; J. L. Klitch (USA) d. S. L. Collins (USA) 6-3 6-2; Y. Vermaak (SA) d. P. G. Smith (USA) 7-6 6-1; N. Reva (USSR) d. P. Paradis (F) 6-3 7-6; **M. Maleeva** (7) (BUL) d. J. A. Mundel (SA) 6-4 6-1; **P. H. Shriver** (4) (USA) d. E. S. Pfaff (G) 6-0 6-4; G. Fernandez (PR) d. L. Drescher (SWZ) 7-6 6-4; W. E. White (USA) d. M. Jausovec (YU) 7-6 7-6; C. Benjamin (USA) d. A. C. Leand (USA) 6-3 6-4; M. L. Brown (USA) d. R. Uys (SA) 7-5 1-6 6-4; M. Skuherska (CZ) d. L. Savchenko (USSR) 6-1 6-2; G. M. Kim (USA) d. E. Inoue (J) 7-6 1-6 6-0; **B. C. Potter** (13) (USA) d. C. Suire (F) 7-5 6-3; **W. M. Turnbull** (9) (A) d. S. A. Walpole 6-3 6-2; A. J. Brown d. V. L. Nelson (USA) 6-4 6-1; F. Raschiatore (USA) d. C. Jexell (SW) 6-4 6-4; S. Cherneva (USSR) d. L. Romanov (RU) 1-6 6-4 6-4; J. A. Salmon d. L. Arraya (PE) 6-4 6-3; B. A. Mould (SA) d. K. J. Brasher 6-3 6-4; V. Ruzici (RU) d. R. D. Fairbank (SA) 6-1 6-4; **K. Jordan** (6) (USA) d. H. A. Ludloff (USA) 6-1 6-1; **E. K. Horvath** (8) (USA) d. G. Purdy (USA) 6-4 6-3; B. Bunge (G) d. H. Pelletier (C) 6-1 6-2; S. Barker d. R. Mentz (SA) 2-6 6-4 6-4; S. Graf (G) d. S. E. Mascarin (USA) 6-4 5-7 10-8; K. A. Steinmetz (USA) d. K. Rinaldi (USA) 6-4 6-2; Mrs H. A. Mochizuki (USA) d. K. Skronska (CZ) 7-6 6-0; E. M. Burgin (USA) d. K. Y. Sands (USA) 7-6 3-6 6-2; **J. M. Durie** (10) d. Mrs L. A. Shaefer (USA) 6-2 6-7 6-0; **H. Sukova** (14) (CZ) d. R. Reggi 6-3 6-4; A. M. Cecchini (IT) d. K. B. Cummings (USA) 4-6 6-4 6-0; P. Casale (USA) d. P. Huber (AU) 6-1 6-4; P. Vasquez (PE) d. S. L. Acker (USA) 7-5 7-6; P. A. Teeguarden (USA) d. K. Kinney (USA) 7-6 7-6; C. Tanvier (F) d. S. E. Reeves 6-7 6-4 8-6; C. Lindqvist (SW) d. L. E. Allen (USA) 6-3 7-6; **H. Mandlikova** (3) (CZ) d. E. Eliseenko (USSR) 6-1 6-0; **Z. L. Garrison** (5) (USA) d. R. L. Einy 6-0 6-0; S. V. Wade d. A. B. Henricksson (USA) 3-6 6-3 6-4; C. Jolissaint (SWZ) d. L. McNeil (USA) 7-5 2-6 6-3; C. Karlsson (SW) d. A. H. White (USA) 7-5 2-6 8-6; S. Amiach (F) d. L. Antonoplis (USA) 6-3 6-1; S. J. Leo (A) d. T. A. Holladay (USA) 2-6 6-3 6-4; C. C. Monteiro (BR) d. A. M. Fernandez (USA) 4-6 6-2 9-7; **A. Temesvari** (15) (HU) d. J. S. Golder (USA) 6-4 6-1; **C. Kohde-Kilsch** (12) (G) d. B. C. Bramblett (USA) 6-1 6-4; S. Simmonds (IT) d. T. Phelps (USA) 7-6 6-4; Mrs D. M. Kiyomura Hayashi (USA) d. S. L. Gomer 6-2 7-6; A. L. Minter (A) d. N. S. Yeargin (USA) 6-1 6-4; M. Y. Torres (USA) d. P. S. Medrado (BR) 6-2 6-7 10-8; A. N. Croft d. Mrs P. Delhees Jauch (SWZ) 6-3 6-0; B. Nagelsen (USA) d. R. Casals (USA) 6-3 6-1; **Mrs J. M. Lloyd** (2) (USA) d. S. Goles (YU) 6-1 6-1.

SECOND ROUND: Navratilova (1) d. Holton 6-2 7-5; Budarova d. Moulton 6-4 6-4; Sayers d. Rush 6-4 3-6 6-2; **Bonder** (11) d. Gerken 7-6 6-2; **Bassett** (16) d. Calleja 6-1 6-4; Hobbs d. Piatek 6-4 6-3; Vermaak d. Klitch 6-3 6-2; **Maleeva** (7) d. Reva 6-2 6-2; **Shriver** (4) d. Fernandez 3-6 6-3 9-7; Benjamin d. White 7-5 6-3; Skuherska d. Brown 6-4 6-4; **Potter** (13) d. Kim 6-3 6-0; **Turnbull** (9) d. Brown 6-3 6-4; Cherneva d. Raschiatore 6-3 6-4; Salmon d. Mould 6-4 7-6; **K. Jordan** (6) d. Ruzici 6-4 6-4; Bunge d. **Horvath** (8) 6-0 6-4; Graf d. Barker 7-6 6-3; Steinmetz d. Mochizuki 7-6 6-3; **Durie** (10) d. Burgin 6-1 6-3; **Sukova** (14) d. Cecchini 6-3 6-0; Casale d. Vasquez 6-2 6-0; Tanvier d. Teeguarden 6-1 6-4; **Mandlikova** (3) d. Lindqvist 7-5 6-3; Wade d. **Garrison** (5) 3-6 6-4 7-5; Karllson d. Jolissaint 2-6 6-3 6-4; Leo d. Amiach 4-1 ret'd; **Temesvari** (15) d. Monteiro 6-4 6-1; **Kohde-Kilsch** (12) d. Simmonds 6-1 6-2; Kiyomura Hayashi d. Minter 6-3 1-6 12-10; Croft d. Torres 6-3 2-6 7-5; **Lloyd** (2) d. Nagelsen 6-2 4-6 6-2.

THIRD ROUND: Navratilova (1) d. Budarova 6-2 6-2; Sayers d. **Bonder** (11) 6-4 6-2; Hobbs d. **Bassett** (16) 7-6 3-6 6-4; **Maleeva** (7) d. Vermaak 6-4 6-4; **Shriver** (4) d. Benjamin 6-0 6-2; **Potter** (13) d. Skuherska 6-1 6-3; **Turnbull** (9) d. Cherneva 6-3 4-6 6-4; **K. Jordan** (6) d. Salmon 6-4 6-3; Graf d. Bunge 7-5 6-3; **Durie** (10) d. Steinmetz 6-4 6-2; **Sukova** (14) d. Casale 7-6 6-7 6-4; **Mandlikova** (3) d. Tanvier 6-4 7-6; Karlsson d. Wade 6-2 4-6 11-9; **Temesvari** (15) d. Leo 6-2 6-2; **Kohde-Kilsch** (12) d. Kiyomura Hayashi 6-3 6-1; **Lloyd** (2) d. Croft 6-3 6-4.

FOURTH ROUND	QUARTER-FINALS	SEMI-FINALS	FINAL	CHAMPION
Navratilova (1)	**Navratilova** (1)			
Sayers	6-0 ret'd	**Navratilova** (1)		
Hobbs	**Maleeva** (7)	6-3 6-2		
Maleeva (7)	6-2 3-6 6-3		**Navratilova** (1)	
Shriver (4)	**Shriver** (4)		6-3 6-4	
Potter (13)	6-4 6-3	**K. Jordan** (6)		
Turnbull (9)	**K. Jordan** (6)	2-6 6-3 6-4		
K. Jordan (6)	6-2 6-3			**Navratilova** (1)
Graf	**Durie** (10)			7-6 6-2
Durie (10)	3-6 6-3 9-7	**Mandlikova** (3)		
Sukova (14)	**Mandlikova** (3)	6-1 6-4		
Mandlikova (3)	6-4 6-1		**Lloyd** (2)	
Karlsson	Karlsson		6-1 6-2	
Temesvari (15)	6-4 7-5	**Lloyd** (2)		
Kohde-Kilsch (12)	**Lloyd** (2)	6-2 6-2		
Lloyd (2)	6-2 6-4			

PRIZE MONEY	
Champion	£90,000
Runner-up	45,000
Semi-finals	21,900
Quarter-finals	10,704
Fourth round	5,866
Third round	3,080
Second round	1,796
First round	1,027

OTHER FINALS

GENTLEMEN'S DOUBLES: Final – P. Fleming (USA)/J. P. McEnroe (USA) d. P. Cash (A)/P. McNamee (A) 6-2 5-7 6-2 3-6 6-3.
LADIES' DOUBLES: Final – M. Navratilova (USA)/P. H. Shriver (USA) d. K. Jordan (USA)/A. E. Smith (USA) 6-3 6-4.
MIXED DOUBLES: Final – J. M. Lloyd/W. M. Turnbull (A) d. S. Denton (USA)/K. Jordan (USA) 6-3 6-3.
LADIES' SINGLES PLATE: Final – M. L. Brown (USA) d. R. M. White (USA) 6-2 7-5.
BOYS' SINGLES: Final – M. Kratzman (A) d. S. Kruger (SA) 6-4 4-6 6-3.
GIRLS' SINGLES: Final – A. N. Croft d. E. Reinach (SA) 3-6 6-3 6-2.
BOYS' DOUBLES: Final – R. Brown (USA)/R. Weiss (USA) d. M. Kratzman (USA)/J. Svensson (SW) 1-6 6-4 11-9.
GIRLS' DOUBLES: Final – C. Kuhlman (USA)/S. Rehe (USA) d. V. Milvidskaya (USSR)/L. Savchenko (USSR) 6-3 5-7 6-4.
35 AND OVER GENTLEMEN'S INVITATION SINGLES: Final – S. R. Smith (USA) d. C. S. Dibley (A) 7-6 6-3.
35 AND OVER GENTLEMEN'S INVITATION DOUBLES: Final – M. C. Reissen (USA)/S. E. Stewart (USA) d. C. S. Dibley (A)/J. Fillol (CH) 6-3 3-6 10-8.

GENTLEMEN'S SINGLES

1985

FIRST ROUND: J. P. McEnroe (1) (USA) d. P. McNamara (A) 6-4 6-3 6-4; N. Odizor (NI) d. G. Muller (SA) 6-7 6-7 7-6 6-3 6-3; C. J. Lewis (NZ) d. S. M. Shaw 6-4 6-2 6-3; C. Steyn (SA) d. G. Barbosa (BR 6-4 6-4 6-2; A. Maurer (G) d. J. Frawley (A) 7-5 6-3 7-5; H. Schwaier (G) d. R. Van't Hof (USA) 6-3 6-2 6-4; J. B. Fitzgerald (A) d. A. Giammalva (USA) 6-4 7-5 6-1; **J. C. Kriek** (9) (USA) d. V. Pecci (PA) 6-4 6-0 4-6 7-5; **S. Edberg** (14) (SW) d. P. Doohan (A) 6-2 6-3 6-4; T. Wilkison (USA) d. M. Ostoja (YU) 6-4 6-0 2-6 7-6; T. Moor (USA) d. J. Hlasek (SWZ) 6-3 3-6 6-7 7-6 7-5; C. Hooper (USA) d. B. Taroczy (HU) 7-5 7-6 6-3; D. G. C. Mustard (NZ) d. S. M. Bale 7-6 6-2 4-6 6-4; M. Flur (USA) d. M. J. Bates 6-4 6-3 6-4; M. Depalmer (USA) d. R. Viver (EC) 6-3 6-3 3-6 6-3; **K. Curren** (8) (USA) d. L. Stefanki (USA) 7-6 6-3 6-4; **J. S. Connors** (3) (USA) d. S. Simonsson (SW) 6-1 6-3 6-4; K. Evernden (NZ) d. J. Navratil (CZ) 6-4 6-4 6-4; R. Krishnan (IN) d. B. P. Derlin (NZ) 6-2 7-5 4-6 7-6; L. R. Bourne (USA) d. G. Forget (F) 3-6 6-3 6-3 6-4; L. Shiras (USA) d. L. Alfred 6-3 7-6 6-3; B. Testerman (USA) d. C. A. Miller (A) 3-6 6-3 6-4 6-2; S. Giammalva (USA) d. C. H. Cox (USA) 6-0 6-4 5-7 6-4; **T. Smid** (15) (CZ) d. R. Simpson (NZ) 6-4 6-7 7-5 7-6; Tom Gullikson (USA) d. **M. Mecir** (12) (CZ) 4-6 6-3 6-4 6-7 6-3; J. Lapidus (USA) d. J. Arias (USA) 6-4 6-4 3-6 6-7 7-5; M. Bauer (USA) d. M. Vajda (CZ) 5-7 7-6 7-5 6-2; R. Seguso (USA) d. R. Harmon (USA) 6-4 6-3 6-0; S. B. Denton (USA) d. Tim Gullikson (USA) 6-4 6-3 3-6 6-3; D. Pate (USA) d. N. A. Fulwood 6-3 6-4 6-4; R. Acuna (CH) d. T. Benhabiles (F) 6-3 4-6 6-1 6-2; **P. Cash** (6) (A) d. T. Nelson (USA) 2-6 6-2 7-5 6-7 6-3; **A. Jarryd** (5) (SW) d. C. Panatta (IT) 4-6 3-6 6-4 6-4 6-3; S. E. Davis (USA) d. B. Moir (SA) 6-2 6-2 6-3; M. Mitchell (USA) d. T. Champion (F) 6-3 6-4 6-2; V. Van Patten (USA) d. P. Elter (G) 6-3 6-7 7-5 6-4; D. T. Visser (SA) d. D. Keretic (G) 7-6 6-4 6-7 6-3; J. Gunnarsson (SW) d. M. Davis (USA) 6-3 6-2 3-6 6-3; G. Holmes (USA) d. H. Sundstrom (SW) 6-3 4-6 6-7 6-4 6-2; B. Schultz (USA) d. **A. Krickstein** (10) (USA) 6-4 3-6 7-6 6-4; **Y. Noah** (11) (F) d. B. Gilbert (USA) 6-4 3-6 7-6 6-7 6-3; E. Edwards (SA) d. C. Dowdeswell 6-3 6-3 6-3; V. Amritraj (IN) d. J. Canter (USA) 6-3 6-4 6-4; B. D. Drewett (A) d. S. McCain (USA) 7-6 7-5 6-4; V. Gerulaitis (USA) d. P. Fleming (USA) 6-2 5-7 6-4 3-6 6-3; J. Sadri (USA) d. C. Motta (BR) 6-3 6-2 6-3; H. P. Gunthardt (SWZ) d. B. Teacher (USA) 6-4 7-5 6-7 6-2; S. Zivojinovic (YU) d. **M. Wilander** (4) (SW) 6-2 5-7 7-5 6-0; **J. Nystrom** (7) (SW) d. J. M. Goodall 6-3 6-3 3-6 6-0; P. Annacone (USA) d. D. Goldie (USA) 5-7 7-5 6-1 1-6 9-7; M. W. Anger (USA) d. Z. Kuharszky (HU) 5-7 6-2 6-2 3-6 6-1; B. Becker (G) d. H. Pfister (USA) 4-6 6-3 6-2 6-4; P. McNamee (A) d. S. Meister (USA) 6-2 6-4 7-6; R. Saad (ARG) d. R. B. Green (USA) 6-3 6-2 6-4; K. Flach (USA) d. P. Slozil (CZ) 6-3 6-7 6-1 7-6; **T. S. Mayotte** (16) (USA) d. T. Allan (A) 7-5 6-4 6-2; **E. Teltscher** (13) (USA) d. G. Ocleppo (IT) 5-7 7-6 7-6 6-0; J. M. Lloyd d. W. Popp (G) 6-2 6-4 7-6; H. Leconte (F) d. C. M. Dunk (USA) 6-3 7-6 7-6; W. Masur (A) d. D. Cassidy (USA) 7-6 7-6 6-1; S. Glickstein (IS) d. J. Lopez-Maeso (SP) 7-6 6-3 6-1; F. Gonzales (PA) d. M. R. Edmondson (A) 6-3 6-2 7-6; M. Leach (USA) d. W. Fibak (POL) 7-6 6-4 6-1; **I. Lendl** (2) (CZ) d. M. Purcell (USA) 6-4 7-6 7-6.

SECOND ROUND: McEnroe (1) d. Odizor 7-6 6-1 7-6; Steyn d. Lewis 3-6 7-6 6-4 6-4; Maurer d. Schwaier 6-3 7-5 7-5; **Kriek** (9) d. Fitzgerald 3-6 7-6 7-5 6-1; **Edberg** (14) d. Wilkison 6-1 7-5 3-6 6-7 9-7; Hooper d. Moor 6-4 6-4 7-5; Mustard d. Flur 7-6 6-4 2-6 6-4; **Curren** (8) d. Depalmer 7-5 5-7 6-4 6-4; **Connors** (3) d. Evernden 6-3 6-2 6-1; Krishnan d. Bourne 6-4 7-5 6-2; Testerman d. Shiras 6-4 6-7 4-6 6-1 7-5; Giammalva d. **Smid** (15) 6-3 6-1 6-2; Tom Gullikson d. Lapidus 6-7 6-7 6-4 6-2 6-3; Seguso d. Bauer 6-3 6-4 6-4; Pate d. Denton 7-6 6-4 6-4; Acuna d. **Cash** (6) 7-6 6-3 3-6 6-7 6-4; **Jarryd** (5) d. S. E. Davis 5-7 7-6 7-5 6-4; Van Patten d. Mitchell 7-5 6-3 6-2; Visser d. Gunnarsson 6-7 6-4 6-4 7-6; Holmes d. Schultz 6-4 6-7 6-2 6-3; **Noah** (11) d. Edwards 4-6 6-4 7-6 6-2; Amritraj d. Drewett 7-6 6-7 7-6 7-5; Gerulaitis d. Sadri 5-7 6-4 3-6 7-6 6-4; Gunthardt d. Zivojinovic 6-4 4-6 4-6 6-3 6-4; **Nystrom** (7) d. Annacone 7-5 7-5 6-3; Becker d. Anger 6-0 6-1 6-3; McNamee d. Saad 6-3 7-6 7-6; **Mayotte** (16) d. Flach 6-4 6-4 6-4; Lloyd d. **Teitscher** (13) 6-3 6-4 4-6 3-6 7-5; Leconte d. Masur 4-6 6-4 7-6 6-3; Glickstein d. Gonzales 6-3 6-4 3-6 7-5; **Lendl** (2) d. Leach 6-3 1-6 6-2 6-7 6-4.

THIRD ROUND: McEnroe (1) d. Steyn 6-3 7-5 6-4; Maurer d. **Kriek** (9) 6-1 6-4 3-6 6-3; **Edberg** (14) d. Hooper 6-3 6-4 6-4; **Curren** (8) d. Mustard 6-3 6-3 7-5; **Connors** (3) d. Krishnan 7-5 5-7 7-5 6-2; Giammalva d. Testerman 4-6 6-3 7-5 7-6; Seguso d. Tom Gullikson 4-6 6-3 7-5 6-2; Acuna d. Pate 7-5 6-4 6-2; **Jarryd** (5) d. Van Patten 6-3 6-3 6-1; Visser d. Holmes 6-3 4-6 6-7 6-0 10-8; Amritraj d. **Noah** (11) 4-6 7-6 6-3 7-6; Gunthardt d. Gerulaitis 6-3 6-7 6-1 3-6 7-5; Becker d. **Nystrom** (7) 3-6 7-6 6-1 4-6 9-7; **Mayotte** (16) d. McNamee 3-6 4-6 7-6 6-2 6-0; Leconte d. Lloyd 5-7 6-3 6-4 6-4; **Lendl** (2) d. Glickstein 7-6 4-6 6-3 6-2.

FOURTH ROUND	QUARTER-FINALS	SEMI-FINALS	FINAL	CHAMPION
McEnroe (1)	**McEnroe** (1)			
Maurer	6-0 6-4 6-2	**Curren** (8)		
Edberg (14)	**Curren** (8)	6-2 6-2 6-4		
Curren (8)	7-6 6-3 7-6		**Curren** (8)	
Connors (3)	**Connors** (3)		6-2 6-2 6-1	
Giammalva	6-3 6-4 6-3	**Connors** (3)		
Seguso	Acuna	6-1 7-6 6-2		
Acuna	6-4 7-6 6-2			Becker
Jarryd (5)	**Jarryd** (5)			6-3 6-7 7-6 6-4
Visser	6-1 6-4 6-1	**Jarryd** (5)		
Amritraj	Gunthardt	6-4 6-3 6-2		
Gunthardt	6-4 6-4 6-1		Becker	
Becker	Becker		2-6 7-6 6-3 6-3	
Mayotte (16)	6-3 4-6 6-7 7-6 6-2	Becker		
Leconte	Leconte	7-6 3-6 6-3 6-4		
Lendl (2)	3-6 6-4 6-3 6-1			

PRIZE MONEY

Champion	£130,000
Runner-up	65,000
Semi-finals	32,500
Quarter-finals	16,500
Fourth round	8,680
Third round	4,860
Second round	2,865
First round	1,750

LADIES' SINGLES

FIRST ROUND: Mrs J. M. Lloyd (1) (USA) d. M. L. Piatek (USA) 6-1 6-0; S. E. Mascarin (USA) d. T. Scheuer-Larsen (D) 7-6 3-6 6-3; J. Byrne (A) d. S. Amiach (F) 6-2 6-3; Y. Vermaak (SA) d. M. Jausovec (YU) 6-3 6-4; L. E. Drescher (SWZ) d. M. Skuherska (CZ) 6-1 6-2; I. Demongeot (F) d. B. K. Jordan (USA) 6-1 6-4; A. E. Smith (USA) d. V. L. Nelson (USA) 6-0 6-2; **B. Gadusek** (9) (USA) d. H. A. Ludloff (USA) 6-1 6-1; B. C. Potter (USA) d. **C. Lindqvist** (12) (SW) 6-0 7-5; S. L. Gomer d. B. A. Mould (SA) 6-7 7-6 6-3; P. A. Fendick (USA) d. M. L. Brown (USA) 6-4 6-1; K. B. Cummings (USA) d. K. J. Brasher 6-3 6-4; E. M. Burgin (USA) d. P. S. Medrado (BR) 7-6 6-2; A. C. Villagran (ARG) d. J. L. Klitch (USA) 6-7 6-4 6-3; J. M. Durie d. Mrs L. A. Shaefer (USA) 6-3 6-2; **C. Kohde-Kilsch** (6) (G) d. B. Nagelsen (USA) 7-5 6-1; **H. Mandlikova** (3) (CZ) d. I. Budarova (CZ) 6-0 6-1; Mrs C. M. Balestrat (A) d. N. P. Dias (BR) 6-0 6-2; J. C. Russell (USA) d. P. Keppeler (G) 5-7 6-2 6-1; Mrs P. D. Smylie (A) d. A. C. Leand (USA) 6-1 6-2; A. A. Moulton (USA) d. E. A. Herr (USA) 6-3 6-4; S. E. Reeves d. R. L. Einy 6-3 5-7 6-4; R. D. Fairbank (SA) d. M. Schropp (G) 7-5 6-4; **K. Rinaldi** (16) (USA) d. A. Betzner (G) 6-3 7-5; **W. M. Turnbull** (14) (A) d. G. A. Rush (USA) 7-5 6-3; E. A. Minter (A) d. M. Yanagi (J) 6-3 6-3; S. M. Hanika (G) d. C. Suire (F) 6-4 6-2; P. Paradis (F) d. E. Okagawa (J) 6-2 6-1; A. B. Henricksson (USA) d. C. J. Wood 6-1 7-5; W. E. White (USA) d. K. Kinney (USA) 6-3 2-6 6-4; V. Ruzici (RU) d. A. E. Holton (USA) 4-6 6-4 7-5; **H. Sukova** (7) (CZ) d. C. Jexell (SW) 6-3 6-3; **Z. L. Garrison** (8) (USA) d. E. Reinach (SA) 6-2 6-1; T. Phelps (USA) d. K. Skronska (CZ) 6-3 6-3; A. Holikova (CZ) d. P. Casale (USA) 5-7 6-1 6-3; M. A. Mesker (NTH) d. K. Gompert (USA) 6-3 4-6 6-4; M. E. Gurney (USA) d. S. J. Leo (A) 7-5 6-4; C. Tanvier (F) d. M. M. Groat (C) 6-3 6-2; C. Benjamin (USA) d. E. Eliseenko (USSR) 6-4 6-0; **G. Sabatini** (15) (ARG) d. A. J. Brown 3-6 6-3 6-3; **K. Jordan** (10) (USA) d. J. M. Tacon 6-0 6-2; L. Savchenko (USSR) d. S. Goles (YU) 6-1 4-6 6-3; M. Van Nostrand (USA) d. Mrs M. H. Walsh Pete (USA) 7-5 6-3; P. Louie (USA) d. H. Kelesi (C) 6-2 6-4; E. S. Pfaff (G) d. S. P. Foltz (USA) 6-3 6-3; R. M. White (USA) d. S. L. Collins (USA) 6-2 6-2; T. A. Holladay (USA) d. J. Thompson (A) 6-1 6-3; **M. Maleeva** (4) (BUL) d. M. B. Washington (USA) 6-0 6-1; **P. H. Shriver** (5) (USA) d. A. H. White (USA) 6-3 6-7 6-3; A. E. Hobbs d. G. M. Kim (USA) 6-4 6-2; B. Gerken (USA) d. C. Vanier (F) 6-3 6-2; S. V. Wade d. L. Antonoplis (USA) 6-4 7-5; E. Inoue (J) d. E. Ekblom (SW) 6-2 6-1; S. C. Rehe (USA) d. C. Jolissaint (SWZ) 6-4 6-3; A. Temesvari (HU) d. K. Maleeva (BUL) 3-6 7-6 6-4; **S. Graf** (11) (G) d. Mrs L. Spain-Short (USA) 6-7 6-4 6-2; **C. K. Bassett** (13) (C) d. M. Paz (ARG) 6-0 3-6 6-3; R. Uys (SA) d. J. Louis 7-6 4-6 6-2; Hu Na (CHI) d. A. N. Croft 6-3 7-5; L. Pichova (CZ) d. C. Karlsson (SW) 2-6 6-4 6-3; A. M. Cecchini (IT) d. J. A. Salmon 7-6 6-1; B. Bunge (G) d. L. M. McNeil (USA) 6-3 6-3; A. L. Minter (A) d. P. Vasquez (PE) 6-0 6-2; **Navratilova** (1) (USA) d. L. Bonder (USA) 6-0 6-2.

SECOND ROUND: Lloyd (1) d. Mascarin 6-3 6-0; Byrne d. Vermaak 6-2 6-3; Demongeot d. Drescher 6-4 6-3; Smith d. **Gadusek** (9) 2-6 6-4 6-2; Potter d. Gomer 6-4 7-5; Fendick d. Cummings 6-1 6-3; Burgin d. Villagran 6-0 6-3; Durie d. **Kohde-Kilsch** (6) 4-6 6-1 6-2; **Mandlikova** (3) d. Balestrat 4-6 6-2 7-5; Smylie d. Russell 6-4 6-4; Moulton d. Reeves 6-2 6-4; **Rinaldi** (16) d. Fairbank 7-5 6-4; **Turnbull** (14) d. E. A. Minter 7-5 7-5; Paradis d. Hanika 7-6 6-7 6-3; W. E. White d. Henricksson 6-4 2-6 6-4; **Sukova** (7) d. Ruzici 6-1 6-4; **Garrison** (8) d. Phelps 6-3 6-1; Mesker d. Holikova 6-2 6-7 6-3; Tanvier d. Gurney 6-3 6-4; **Sabatini** (15) d. Benjamin 6-3 6-4; Savchenko d. **K. Jordan** (10) 7-5 3-6 6-3; Van Nostrand d. Louie 6-2 6-3; R. M. White d. Pfaff 6-3 6-2; **Maleeva** (4) d. Holladay 6-7 6-1 6-4; **Shriver** (5) d. Hobbs 6-3 6-2; Wade d. Gerken 6-3 6-7 7-5; Rehe d. Inoue 6-1 6-3; **Graf** (11) d. Temesvari 6-3 7-6; Uys d. **Bassett** (13) 0-6 7-6 6-3; Hu Na d. Pichova 7-5 6-4; Bunge d. Cecchini 6-3 6-2; **Navratilova** (1) d. A. L. Minter 6-4 6-1.

THIRD ROUND: Lloyd (1) d. Byrne 6-2 6-1; Smith d. Demongeot 6-2 6-4; Potter d. Fendick 7-6 6-1; Durie d. Burgin 7-5 7-5; Smylie d. **Mandlikova** (3) 6-1 7-6; **Rinaldi** (16) d. Moulton 7-6 6-4; Paradis d. **Turnbull** (14) 2-6 7-5 6-1; **Sukova** (7) d. W. E. White 6-1 6-4; **Garrison** (8) d. Mesker 6-3 6-1; Tanvier d. **Sabatini** (15) 6-7 6-4 6-1; Van Nostrand d. Savchenko 7-6 3-6 7-5; **Maleeva** (4) d. R. M. White 6-3 6-3; **Shriver** (5) d. Wade 6-2 5-7 6-2; **Graf** (11) d. Rehe 6-3 6-2; Uys d. Hu Na 6-2 4-6 6-0; **Navratilova** (1) d. Bunge 7-6 6-3.

FOURTH ROUND	QUARTER-FINALS	SEMI-FINALS	FINAL	CHAMPION
Lloyd (1)	**Lloyd** (1)			
Smith	6-0 6-4	**Lloyd** (1)		
Potter	Potter	6-2 6-1		
Durie	7-6 6-7 6-1		**Lloyd** (1)	
Smylie	**Rinaldi** (16)		6-2 6-0	
Rinaldi (16)	6-2 6-1	**Rinaldi** (16)		
Paradis	**Sukova** (7)	6-1 1-6 6-1		
Sukova (7)	6-4 7-6			**Navratilova** (1)
Garrison (8)	**Garrison** (8)			4-6 6-3 6-2
Tanvier	6-1 6-3	**Garrison** (8)		
Van Nostrand	Van Nostrand	2-6 6-3 6-0		
Maleeva (4)	7-5 6-2		**Navratilova** (1)	
Shriver (5)	**Shriver** (5)		6-4 7-6	
Graf (11)	3-6 6-2 6-4	**Navratilova** (1)		
Uys	**Navratilova** (1)	7-6 6-3		
Navratilova (1)	6-2 6-2			

PRIZE MONEY

Champion	£117,000
Runner-up	58,500
Semi-finals	28,500
Quarter-finals	13,950
Fourth round	6,950
Third round	3,750
Second round	2,210
First round	1,350

OTHER FINALS

GENTLEMEN'S DOUBLES: Final — H. P. Gunthardt (SWZ)/B. Taroczy (HU) d. P. Cash (A)/J. B. Fitzgerald (A) 6-4 6-3 4-6 6-3.
LADIES' DOUBLES: Final — K. Jordan (USA)/Mrs P. D. Smylie (A) d. M. Navratilova (USA)/P. H. Shriver (USA) 5-7 6-3 6-4.
MIXED DOUBLES: Final — P. McNamee (A)/M. Navratilova (USA) d. J. B. Fitzgerald (A)/Mrs P. D. Smylie (A) 7-5 4-6 6-2.
LADIES' SINGLES PLATE: Final — E. Reinach (SA) d. T. A. Holladay (USA) 6-4 6-2.
BOYS' SINGLES: Final — L. Lavalle (M) d. E. Velez (M) 6-4 6-4.
GIRLS' SINGLES: Final — A. Holikova (CZ) d. J. Byrne (A) 7-5 6-1.
BOYS' DOUBLES: Final — A. Moreno (M)/J. Yzaga (PE) d. P. Korda (CZ)/C. Suk (CZ) 7-6 6-4.
GIRLS' DOUBLES: Final — L. Field (A)/J. Thompson (A) d. E. Reinach (SA)/J. Richardson (NZ) 6-1 6-2.
35 AND OVER GENTLEMEN'S INVITATION SINGLES: Final — S. R. Smith (USA) d. J. Fillol (CH) 4-6 7-6 7-6.
35 AND OVER GENTLEMEN'S INVITATION DOUBLES: Final — C. S. Dibley (A)/J. Fillol (CH) d. M. C. Riessen (USA)/S. E. Stewart (USA) 6-3 7-5.

GENTLEMEN'S SINGLES

1986

FIRST ROUND: I. Lendl (1) (CZ) d. L. Lavalle (M) 7-6 6-3 6-4; M. Freeman (USA) d. N. Aerts (BR) 6-4 6-4 7-6; A. Mansdorf (IS) d. G. Michibata (C) 3-6 6-2 6-3 6-4; P. Lundgren (SW) d. R. B. Green (USA) 6-2 6-2 7-6; N. A. Fulwood d. B. Pearce (USA) 7-6 6-7 6-2 7-6; M. W. Anger (USA) d. S. Casal (SP) 6-3 7-6 7-5; J. Sadri (USA) d. D. De Miguel (SP) 7-5 6-1 6-4; **J. C. Kriek** (16) (USA) d. B. Custer (A) 7-6 6-2 6-3; **T. S. Mayotte** (10) (USA) d. A. Zverev (USSR) 6-4 6-4 6-4; J. Canter (USA) d. H. Solomon (USA) 6-3 6-2 6-2; J. Gunnarsson (SW) d. H. Gildemeister (CH) 6-3 6-4 6-4; T. Smid (CZ) d. D. J. Cahill (A) 6-4 6-3 7-5; J. Hlasek (SWZ) d. P. Doohan (A) 6-1 6-2 6-3; C. Mezzadri (IT) d. M. T. Walker 7-6 4-6 1-6 6-2 6-1; E. Edwards (SA) d. K. Novacek (CZ) 7-5 7-6 3-6 6-2; **A. Jarryd** (8) (SW) d. W. Scanlon (USA) 6-4 3-6 6-3 5-7 6-4; R. Seguso (USA) d. **J. S. Connors** (3) (USA) 6-3 3-6 7-6 7-6; B. Teacher (USA) d. D. Keretic (G) 2-6 6-4 6-3 7-5; C. J. Van Rensburg (SA) d. C. Hooper (USA) 6-3 7-5 6-4; T. Wilkison (USA) d. S. M. Shaw 7-5 6-7 6-4 6-4; M. Wostenholme (C) d. T. Champion (F) 6-3 1-6 6-7 7-5 6-3; S. Zivojinovic (YU) d. S. Youl (A) 6-4 6-7 4-6 7-6 6-4; K. Flach (USA) d. J. Windahl (SA) 5-7 7-6 6-3 6-0; **M. Jaite** (14) (ARG) d. G. Forget (F) 7-6 6-3 3-6 3-6 6-2; E. Jelen (G) d. **K. Curren** (11) (USA) 6-4 6-7 2-6 6-4 12-10; M. Davis (USA) d. M. Flur (USA) 6-2 6-2 7-6; T. Witsken (USA) d. M. J. Bates 3-6 6-1 6-4 7-5; D. Pate (USA) d. T. Nelson (USA) 7-6 6-4 4-6 7-6; M. Bauer (USA) d. C. Saceanu (G) 7-6 6-4 3-6 6-3; R. Krishnan (IN) d. F. Maciel (M) 7-5 6-3 6-3; W. Fibak (POL) d. V. Amritraj (IN) 6-1 3-6 6-4 6-3; **J. Nystrom** (6) (SW) d. K. Evernden (NZ) 7-5 6-3 3-6 4-6 6-3; **S. Edberg** (5) (SW) d. V. Wilder (USA) 6-4 6-3 6-1; P. Annacone (USA) d. S. M. Bale 6-3 7-5 6-3; U. Stenlund (SW) d. P. Slozil (CZ) 6-4 1-6 1-6 6-4 7-5; M. Mecir (CZ) d. M. Schapers (NTH) 6-2 1-0 ret'd; M. Srejber (CZ) d. E. Teltscher (USA) 7-6 6-4 6-4; H. P. Gunthardt (SWZ) d. G. Layendecker (USA) 7-5 6-2 3-6 6-1; M. Leach (USA) d. R. Osterthun (G) 6-3 7-6 7-6; **B. Gilbert** (12) (USA) d. M. Woodforde (A) 6-3 6-4 6-4; **M. Pernfors** (13) (SW) d. M. Depalmer (USA) 2-6 6-4 6-4 7-5; A. Maurer (G) d. S. Glickstein (IS) 6-4 6-2 6-4; J. B. Svensson (SW) d. B. J. Levine (SA) 6-1 7-6 6-3; S. Giammalva (USA) d. M. R. Edmondson (A) 6-4 6-1 6-3; C. Steyn (SA) d. J. M. Lloyd 3-6 2-6 6-3 6-3 6-1; P. McNamee (A) d. P. Chamberlin (USA) 6-3 6-4 7-6; T. R. Gullikson (USA) d. B. Schultz (USA) 6-2 4-6 7-6 6-1; **B. Becker** (4) (G) d. E. Bengoechea (ARG) 6-4 6-2 6-1; **H. Leconte** (7) (F) d. R. Agenor (HAI) 7-5 6-2 6-3; C. Dowdeswell d. A. Chesnokov (USSR) 6-2 2-6 6-4 6-4; G. Holmes (USA) d. R. Acuna (CH) 6-3 7-6 6-4; M. Westphal (G) d. F. Segarceanu (RU) 7-5 6-4 6-7 7-6; S. Botfield d. E. Sanchez (SP) 6-3 3-6 6-2 2-6 6-3; W. Masur (A) d. B. Testerman (USA) 6-7 7-6 6-3 6-3; D. T. Visser (SA) d. M. Robertson (SA) 5-7 6-7 6-3 6-3 6-4; J. B. Fitzgerald (A) d. **A. Gomez** (9) (EC) 6-1 3-6 7-6 6-4; P. Cash (A) d. **G. Vilas** (15) (ARG) 6-4 6-2 6-3; R. J. Simpson (NZ) d. B. N. Moir (SA) 7-6 4-6 6-4 6-2; H. Schwaier (G) d. M. Ingaramo (ARG) 4-6 6-3 6-4 5-7 8-6; J. Lapidus (USA) d. K. Moir (SA) 6-2 6-4 6-3; M. Kratzmann (A) d. N. Odizor (NI) 4-6 6-3 7-6 4-6 8-6; C. Kirmayr (BR) d. H. Sundstrom (SW) 6-4 6-2 6-4; A. N. Castle d. B. Dyke (A) 7-6 7-6 6-3; **M. Wilander** (2) (SW) d. S. E. Davis (USA) 7-6 6-4 6-4.

SECOND ROUND: Lendl (1) d. Freeman 6-3 6-2 6-2; Mansdorf d. Lundgren 7-6 6-2 6-2; Anger d. Fulwood 6-2 6-4 6-2; Sadri d. **Kriek** (16) 2-6 6-3 7-6 6-3; **Mayotte** (10) d. Canter 7-5 6-4 7-6; Smid d. Gunnarsson 6-7 6-4 6-3 6-4; Hlasek d. Mezzadri 3-6 6-4 7-5 6-1; Edwards d. **Jarryd** (8) 3-6 6-4 7-6 6-2; Seguso d. Teacher 6-2 3-6 6-3 6-4; Van Rensburg d. Wilkison 6-4 6-2 6-1; Zivojinovic d. Wostenholme 7-5 6-2 6-4; Flach d. **Jaite** (14) 6-4 6-3 6-3; Jelen d. M. Davis 6-2 6-3 6-4; Pate d. Witsken 6-3 6-1 7-5; Krishnan d. Bauer 4-6 6-2 6-3 5-7 7-5; **Nystrom** (6) d. Fibak 4-6 6-0 6-1 6-2; **Edberg** (5) d. Annacone 6-4 6-7 4-6 7-5 6-0; Mecir d. Stenlund 6-2 6-1 4-6 6-0; Srejber d. Gunthardt 6-3 4-6 4-6 7-6 6-3; **Gilbert** (12) d. Leach 7-6 7-6 6-2; **Pernfors** (13) d. Maurer 7-5 6-2 4-6 6-2; Giammalva d. Svensson 2-6 6-2 6-1 6-4; McNamee d. Steyn 7-5 6-1 3-6 6-3; **Becker** (4) d. Gullikson 6-4 6-3 6-2; **Leconte** (7) d. Dowdeswell 6-1 6-4 6-4; Holmes d. Westphal 3-6 7-6 7-5 4-6 6-2; Masur d. Botfield 6-4 6-2 6-2; Fitzgerald d. Visser 6-3 3-6 4-6 7-6 6-2; Cash d. Simpson 6-7 6-3 6-2 7-5; Lapidus d. Schwaier 6-2 6-7 5-7 6-3 6-3; Kratzmann d. Kirmayr 7-5 6-2 4-6 6-1; **Wilander** (2) d. Castle 4-6 7-6 6-7 6-4 6-0.

THIRD ROUND: Lendl (1) d. Mansdorf 6-2 6-4 6-4; Anger d. Sadri 6-7 7-6 7-6 6-4; **Mayotte** (10) d. Smid 6-4 6-2 2-6 6-2; Edwards d. Hlasek 3-6 4-6 6-2 6-3 6-1; Van Rensburg d. Seguso 5-7 6-4 6-0 6-2; Zivojinovic d. Flach 4-6 6-4 7-5 6-3; Jelen d. Pate 7-6 6-3 6-4; Krishnan d. **Nystrom** (6) 6-7 6-2 7-6 6-4; Mecir d. **Edberg** (5) 6-4 6-4 6-4; **Gilbert** (12) d. Srejber 7-5 6-7 6-3 6-3; **Pernfors** (13) d. Giammalva 2-6 6-4 6-3 6-1; **Becker** (4) d. McNamee 6-4 6-4 4-6 6-4; **Leconte** (7) d. Holmes 6-4 6-2 7-6; Fitzgerald d. Masur 7-6 7-6 5-7 6-4; Cash d. Lapidus 6-1 6-4 6-7 7-5; **Wilander** (2) d. Kratzmann 6-4 6-4 2-6 6-1.

FOURTH ROUND	QUARTER-FINALS	SEMI-FINALS	FINAL	CHAMPION
Lendl (1)	**Lendl** (1)			
Anger	6-7 7-6 6-4 7-6	**Lendl** (1)		
Mayotte (10)	**Mayotte** (10)	6-4 4-6 6-4 3-6 9-7		
Edwards	6-3 6-4 7-6		**Lendl** (1)	
Van Rensburg	Zivojinovic		6-2 6-7 6-3 6-7 6-4	
Zivojinovic	7-6 7-5 4-6 7-5	Zivojinovic		
Jelen	Krishnan	6-2 7-6 4-6 6-3		
Krishnan	6-4 7-6 6-2			**Becker** (4)
Mecir	Mecir			6-4 6-3 7-5
Gilbert (12)	3-6 7-6 6-1 6-2	**Becker** (4)		
Pernfors (13)	**Becker** (4)	6-4 6-2 7-6		
Becker (4)	6-3 7-6 6-2		**Becker** (4)	
Leconte (7)	**Leconte** (7)		6-2 6-4 6-7 6-3	
Fitzgerald	7-6 6-7 6-2 6-3	**Leconte** (7)		
Cash	Cash	4-6 7-6 7-6 6-3		
Wilander (2)	4-6 7-5 6-4 6-3			

PRIZE MONEY

Champion	£140,000
Runner-up	70,000
Semi-finals	35,000
Quarter-finals	17,725
Fourth round	9,330
Third round	5,225
Second round	3,080
First round	1,880

LADIES' SINGLES

FIRST ROUND: M. Navratilova (1) (USA) d. Mrs G. R. Dingwall (A) 6-3 6-2; J. V. Forman (USA) d. E. S. Pfaff (G) 7-5 6-4; K. Kinney (USA) d. S. E. Reeves 3-6 6-4 6-2; S. L. Gomer d. A. H. White (USA) 4-6 7-5 6-4; S. P. Sloane (USA) d. M. Torres (USA) 6-3 6-4; T. Phelps (USA) d. A. L. Grunfeld 6-2 6-0; I. Demongeot (F) d. J. G. Thompson (A) 6-1 6-2; J. M. Byrne (A) d. **W. M. Turnbull** (14) (A) 7-6 6-2; L. Savchenko (USSR) d. **S. C. Rehe** (12) (USA) 1-6 6-4 8-6; B. Bunge (G) d. G. Fernandez (PR) 4-6 6-4 6-1; P. A. Fendick (USA) d. E. A. Herr (USA) 6-3 6-1; M. L. Piatek (USA) d. P. Barg (USA) 6-0 6-1; Mrs P. D. Smylie (A) d. D. S. Van Rensburg (SA) 6-3 6-2; W. E. White (USA) d. E. Reinach (SA) 6-4 6-1; S. E. Mascarin (USA) d. J. Novotna (CZ) 3-6 7-6 6-2; **M. Maleeva** (8) (BUL) d. K. A. Gompert (USA) 6-2 1-0 ret'd; **C. Kohde-Kilsch** (4) (G) d. E. Inoue (J) 0-6 6-1 6-2; A. A. Moulton (USA) d. Mrs K. Skronska-Bohm (CZ) 7-6 6-4; Hu Na (USA) d. J. Louis 6-0 6-2; R. Reggi (IT) d. C. Karlsson (SW) 5-7 6-0 6-1; A. M. Fernandez (USA) d. A. M. Cecchini (IT) 6-1 6-2; B. S. Gerken (USA) d. D. Spence (USA) 6-3 6-2; C. Suire (F) d. P. S. Medrado (BR) 6-4 3-6 6-4; **G. Sabatini** (10) (ARG) d. C. Jolissaint (SWZ) 6-2 1-6 6-4; **C. Lindqvist** (15) (SW) d. G. Rush (USA) 3-6 7-5 6-3; H. Kelesi (C) d. A. E. Smith (USA) 4-6 6-3 6-3; J. A. Mundel (SA) d. M. Van Nostrand (USA) 6-3 6-2; E. A. Minter (A) d. D. L. Farrell (USA) 6-1 3-6 6-1; Mrs C. M. Balestrat (A) d. Y. Vermaak (SA) 6-4 6-3; C. S. Reynolds (USA) d. N. Sodupe (USA) 6-3 6-4; J. M. Durie d. R. Marsikova (CZ) 6-3 1-6 8-6; N. Herreman (F) d. **K. Rinaldi** (6) (USA) 7-6 6-4; B. Nagelsen (USA) d. **P. H. Shriver** (5) (USA) 4-6 6-3 6-4; Mrs H. J. Short (USA) d. S. Hanika (G) 3-6 6-2 6-4; K. Maleeva (BUL) d. M. Paz (ARG) 6-3 6-2; N. Tauziat (F) d. Mrs V. Nelson-Dunbar (USA) 6-1 6-2; L. M. McNeil (USA) d. R. Bryant (A) 6-4 6-3; M. A. Mesker (NTH) d. L. Gildemeister (PE) 6-3 6-1; E. Burgin (USA) d. Mrs S. Parkhomenko (USSR) 6-0 6-2; R. Reis (USA) d. A. J. Brown 6-1 3-6 7-5; **C. K. Bassett** (11) (C) d. G. L. Coles 1-6 7-5 6-1; R. D. Fairbank (SA) d. Mrs T. A. Louie Harper (USA) 6-4 6-2; N. P. Dias (BR) d. A. N. Croft 1-6 6-2 6-4; M. C. Calleja (F) d. L. Garrone (IT) 6-4 3-6 6-0; C. Benjamin (USA) d. P. Paradis (F) 1-6 6-3 6-2; I. Budarova (CZ) d. S. Goles (YU) 6-1 6-2; C. Tanvier (F) d. C. E. Kuhlman (USA) 2-6 6-4 8-6; **H. Mandlikova** (3) (CZ) d. J. M. Tacon 6-1 6-1; **H. Sukova** (7) (CZ) d. D. Parnell 6-1 6-1; A. Betzner (G) d. J. A. Salmon 6-0 7-6; A. L. Minter (A) d. A. Kanellopoulou (GR) 6-2 6-0; L. J. Bonder (USA) d. M. Jausovec (YU) 3-6 6-4 6-4; A. Holikova (CZ) d. G. M. Kim (USA) 6-3 6-2; R. M. White (USA) d. K. Y. Sands (USA) 6-3 6-4; A. E. Hobbs d. B. A. Borneo 6-0 2-6 6-4; **Z. L. Garrison** (9) (USA) d. B. A. Bowes (USA) 6-1 6-4; **K. Jordan** (16) (USA) d. Mrs H. A. Mochizuki (USA) 6-1 6-3; A. B. Henricksson (USA) d. J. A. Richardson (NZ) 7-6 6-1; M. Gurney (USA) d. B. J. Cordwell (NZ) 6-0 6-7 6-0; T. Scheuer-Larsen (D) d. L. Antonoplis (USA) 6-2 6-4; E. K. Horvath (USA) d. K. A. Steinmetz (USA) 6-1 7-5; A. C. Villagran (ARG) d. K. D. McDaniel (USA) 6-4 2-6 6-4; P. Casale (USA) d. P. Huber (AU) 6-0 6-0; **Mrs J. M. Lloyd** (2) (USA) d. M. J. Fernandez (USA) 6-4 6-1.

SECOND ROUND: Navratilova (1) d. Forman 6-0 6-4; Kinney d. Gomer 2-6 7-6 6-3; Phelps d. Sloane 6-4 6-2; Demongeot d. Byrne 6-4 6-1; Bunge d. Savchenko 6-7 6-0 7-5; Fendick d. Piatek 6-0 6-3; Smylie d. W. E. White 6-1 1-6 12-10; **M. Maleeva** (8) d. Mascarin 6-4 7-6; **Kohde-Kilsch** (4) d. Moulton 6-2 6-2; Reggi d. Hu Na 6-2 6-4; Gerken d. Fernandez 5-7 7-6 6-4; **Sabatini** (10) d. Suire 6-3 6-3; **Lindqvist** (15) d. Kelesi 6-3 3-6 6-1; E. A. Minter d. Mundel 6-4 6-1; Balestrat d. Reynolds 6-2 6-3; Durie d. Herreman 6-3 7-5; Nagelsen d. Short 6-1 7-6; K. Maleeva d. Tauziat 6-4 6-2; McNeil d. Mesker 4-5 ret'd; Burgin d. Reis 6-1 7-5; **Bassett** (11) d. Fairbank 6-1 7-6; Calleja d. Dias 6-2 6-4; Budarova d. Benjamin 7-6 7-6; **Mandlikova** (3) d. Tanvier 7-5 6-2; **Sukova** (7) d. Betzner 6-2 6-1; A. L. Minter d. Bonder 3-6 6-2 6-2; R. M. White d. Holikova 6-1 6-3; Hobbs d. **Garrison** (9) 6-4 0-6 6-4; **Jordan** (16) d. Henricksson 6-1 6-1; Gurney d. Scheuer-Larsen 6-4 6-2; Horvath d. Villagran 6-4 6-4; **Lloyd** (2) d. Casale 6-0 5-7 6-1.

THIRD ROUND: Navratilova (1) d. Kinney 6-0 6-2; Demongeot d. Phelps 6-3 6-2; Bunge d. Fendick 6-2 6-3; **M. Maleeva** (8) d. Smylie 7-6 6-1; Reggi d. **Kohde-Kilsch** (4) 6-4 6-1; **Sabatini** (10) d. Gerken 6-2 6-1; **Lindqvist** (15) d. E. A. Minter 3-6 7-6 6-3; Balestrat d. Durie 5-7 6-3 6-2; Nagelsen d. K. Maleeva 6-4 6-1; McNeil d. Burgin 6-3 6-2; **Bassett** (11) d. Calleja 6-4 6-2; **Mandlikova** (3) d. Budarova 6-2 6-0; **Sukova** (7) d. A. L. Minter 6-1 6-4; R. M. White d. Hobbs 6-4 6-2; **Jordan** (16) d. Gurney 6-4 6-1; **Lloyd** (2) d. Horvath 6-4 6-1.

FOURTH ROUND	QUARTER-FINALS	SEMI-FINALS	FINAL	CHAMPION
Navratilova (1)	**Navratilova** (1)			
Demongeot	6-3 6-3	**Navratilova** (1)		
Bunge	Bunge	6-1 6-3		
M. Maleeva (8)	3-6 6-2 6-3		**Navratilova** (1)	
Reggi	**Sabatini** (10)		6-2 6-2	
Sabatini (10)	6-4 1-6 6-3	**Sabatini** (10)		
Lindqvist (15)	**Lindqvist** (15)	6-2 6-3		
Balestrat	7-6 7-5			**Navratilova** (1)
Nagelsen	McNeil			7-6 6-3
McNeil	7-5 6-1	**Mandlikova** (3)		
Bassett (11)	**Mandlikova** (3)	6-7 6-0 6-2		
Mandlikova (3)	6-4 7-6		**Mandlikova** (3)	
Sukova (7)	**Sukova** (7)		7-6 7-5	
White	6-3 6-0	**Lloyd** (2)		
Jordan (16)	**Lloyd** (2)	7-6 4-6 6-4		
Lloyd (2)	7-5 6-2			

PRIZE MONEY

Champion	£126,000
Runner-up	63,000
Semi-finals	30,700
Quarter-finals	15,025
Fourth round	7,485
Third round	4,040
Second round	2,380
First round	1,450

OTHER FINALS

GENTLEMEN'S DOUBLES: Final – J. Nystrom (SW)/M. Wilander (SW) d. G. Donnelly (USA)/P. Fleming (USA) 7-6 6-3 6-3.
LADIES' DOUBLES: Final – M. Navratilova (USA)/P. H. Shriver (USA) d. H. Mandlikova (CZ)/W. M. Turnbull (A) 6-1 6-3.
MIXED DOUBLES: Final – K. Flach (USA)/K. Jordan (USA) d. H. P. Gunthardt (SWZ)/M. Navratilova (USA) 6-3 7-6.
LADIES' SINGLES PLATE: Final – P. H. Shriver (USA) d. S. G. Rehe (USA) 4-6 7-6 6-0.
35 AND OVER GENTLEMEN'S INVITATION SINGLES: Final – J. Fillol (CH) d. A. D. Roche (A) 6-3 6-2.
35 AND OVER GENTLEMEN'S INVITATION DOUBLES: Final – M. C. Riessen (USA)/S. E. Stewart (USA) d. C. S. Dibley (A)/J. Fillol (CH) 6-3 6-4.
BOYS' SINGLES: Final – E. Velez (M) d. J. Sanchez (G) 6-3 7-5.
BOYS' DOUBLES: Final – T, Carbonnell and P. Korda d. S. Barnard and H. Karrasch 6-1 6-1.
GIRLS' SINGLES: Final – N. Zvereva (USSR) d. L. Meski (USSR) 2-6 6-2 9-7.
GIRLS' DOUBLES: Final – M. Jaggard (A)/L. O'Neill (A) d. L. Meski (USSR)/N. Zvereva (USSR) 7-5 6-7 6-4.

SELECT
BIBLIOGRAPHY

During the writing of this book frequent reference has been made to the following publications whose authors and publishers are duly acknowledged:

Tennis

Barrett, John (ed), *BP Yearbook of World Tennis 1969*. Ward Lock.
Barrett, John (ed), *BP Yearbook of World Tennis 1970*. Clipper Press.
Barrett, John (ed), *World of Tennis 1971–83*. Queen Anne Press.
Barrett, John (ed), *World of Tennis 1984–86*. Collins Willow.
Burrow, F. R., *Lawn Tennis, The World Game of Today*. Hodder and Stoughton, 1922.
Collins, Bud and Hollander, Zander, *Modern Encyclopedia of Tennis*. Doubleday, 1980.
Hillyard, G. W., *Forty Years of First-Class Lawn Tennis*. Williams and Norgate, 1924.
Little, Alan, *Portraits of the Lady Champions*. Wimbledon Lawn Tennis Museum.
Macaulay, Duncan and Smyth, John, *Behind the Scenes at Wimbledon*. Collins, 1965.
Perry, Fred, *An Autobiography*. Arrow Books, 1985.
Potter, E. C., *Kings of the Court*. A. S. Barnes and Company, 1963.
Robertson, Max (ed), *The Encyclopedia of Tennis*. George Allen and Unwin, 1974.
Robertson, Max, *Wimbledon, Centre Court of the Game*. BBC Publications, 1981.
Tingay, Lance, *100 Years of Wimbledon*. Guinness Superlatives, 1977.
Tinling, Ted, *Sixty Years in Tennis*. London: Sidgwick and Jackson, 1983.
Tinling, Teddy, *White Ladies*. Stanley Paul, 1963.
Todd, Tom, *The Tennis Players*. Vallency Press, 1979.
Wallis Myers, A. (ed), *Ayres Lawn Tennis Almanacs (1908–39)*. F. H. Ayres Ltd.
Wallis Myers, A., *Fifty Years of Wimbledon*. The Field, 1926.
Wallis Myers, A., *Twenty Years of Lawn Tennis*. Methuen, 1921.
Wilberforce, H. W. W., *Lawn Tennis*. George Bell and Sons, 1891.

General Background

Blake, Robert, *The Conservative Party from Peel to Thatcher*. Fontana, 1985.
Briggs, Asa, *A Social History of England*. Weidenfeld and Nicolson, 1983.
Elliot, Alan, *Wimbledon's Railways*. The Wimbledon Society, 1982.
Encyclopaedia Britannica (fifteenth edition). Encyclopaedia Britannica International Ltd, 1985.
Fawcett, Patrick, *Memories of a Wimbledon Childhood*. John Evelyn Society, 1981.
Fraser, Antonia (ed), *Kings and Queens of England*. Weidenfeld and Nicolson, 1975.
Gowing, Lawrence, Sir, *The Encyclopaedia of Modern Art*. Encyclopaedia Britannica International Ltd, 1984.
Judd Dennis, *George V*. Weidenfeld and Nicolson, 1973.
McLennan, G., Held, D., and Hall, S. (eds), *State and Society in Contemporary Britain*. Polity Press, 1984.
Marwick, Arthur, *British Society Since 1945*. Penguin Books, 1986.
Middlemas, Keith, *George VI*. Weidenfeld and Nicolson, 1973.
Milward, R. J., *Portrait of Wimbledon* (unpublished).
Milward, R. J., *Wimbledon's Manor Houses*. John Evelyn Society, 1982.
Plastow, Norman, *Safe as Houses*. John Evelyn Society, 1972.
Whitehead, Winifred, *Wimbledon 1885–1965*. Shamrock Press.

Magazines and Periodicals

The Field
Lawn Tennis and Badminton
Pastime